TM 9-230-289-20
CUCV
Commercial Utility Cargo Vehicle
Unit Maintenance Manual
January 1988

The CUCV or Commercial Utility Cargo Vehicle is a US Military vehicle based on readily available commercial trucks. Originally intended to augment the purpose-built, but expensive GAMA Goat 6x6 and older Jeeps. The first generation was based on Dodge / Chrysler trucks.

This book is focused on the M1008 series second generation CUCV which was General Motor's first major light-truck military vehicle production since World War II. They began production in 1984 and ended production in 1996 with most units being produced as 1984 model year units. Later production was focused on replacements for existing CUCV's. The majority of units were built from existing heavy duty light truck commercial parts. The M1009 was an upgraded/up-rated Chevy K5 Blazer with a 3/4 ton capacity. The M1008 series trucks were a 1-1/4 ton or 5/4 ton rated truck. In all 70,000 units were produced with three power trains.

This manual is the Unit Maintenance Manual for these vehicles. Including the 6.5 liter and other models. It is published as a convenience to enthusiasts who may wish to have a quality professionally printed copy of the manual.

This publisher has also printed other manuals for this series of vehicles. Should you have suggestions or feedback on ways to improve this book please send email to Books@OcotilloPress.com

---

Edited 2021 Ocotillo Press
ISBN 978-1-954285-82-8

Ocotillo Press
Houston, TX 77017
Books@OcotilloPress.com

Disclaimer: The user of this book is responsible for following safe and lawful practices at all times. The publisher assumes no responsibility for the use of the content of this book. The publisher has made an effort to ensure that the text is complete and properly typeset, however omissions, errors, and other issues may exist that the publisher is unaware of.

TM 9-2320-289-20

ARMY TM 9-2320-289-2 0
AIR FORCE TO 36A12-1A-2082-1
MARINE CORPS TM 2320-20/ 2

Supersedes Copy Dated April 1983
See Page i For Details

UNIT MAINTENANCE MANUA L
FOR

TRUCK, CARGO, TACTICAL, 1-1/4 TON, 4x4, M100   8
(2320-01-1 23-6827)

TRUCK, CARGO, TACTICAL, 1-1/4 TON, 4x4, M1008A   1
(2320-01-123-2671)

TRUCK, UTILITY, TACTICAL, 3/4 TON, 4x4, M100   9
(2320-01-1 23-2665)

TRUCK, AMBULANCE, TACTICAL, 1-1 /4 TON, 4x4, M101   0
(2310-01-1 23-2666)

TRUCK, SHELTER CARRIER, TACTICAL, 1-1/4 TON, 4x4, M102   8
(2320-01-1 27-5077)

TRUCK, SHELTER CARRIER W/PTO, TACTICAL, 1-1/4 TON, 4x4, MI 028A   1
(2320-01-158-082Q)

TRUCK, CHASSIS, TACTICAL, 1-1/4 TON, 4x4, M103   1
(2320-01-1 33-5368)

PMCS	2-3
Troubleshooting	2-25
Engine System	3-1
Electrical System	4-1
Transmission & Transfer Case	5-1
Special Purpose Kits	11-1
MAC	B-1

Approved for public release; distribution is unlimited.

**DEPARTMENTS OF THE ARMY, THE AIR FORCE, AND
HEADQUARTERS, MARINE CORP   S**   20 JANUARY 198 8

CHANGE

NO. 4

DEPARTMENT OF THE ARMY, THE AIR FORCE,
AND HEADQUARTERS, MARINE CORPS
Washington D.C., *1 November 1995*

UNIT MAINTENANCE MANUAL
FOR

TRUCK, CARGO, TACTICAL, 1-1/4 TON, 4X4, M1008
(2320-01-123-6827)
TRUCK, CARGO, TACTICAL, 1-1/4 TON, 4X4, M1008A1
(2320-01-123-2671)
TRUCK, UTILITY, TACTICAL, 3/4 TON, 4X4, M1009
(2320-01-123-2665)
TRUCK, AMBULANCE, TACTICAL, 1-1/4 TON, 4X4, M1010
(2310-01-123-2666)
TRUCK, SHELTER CARRIER, TACTICAL, 1-1/4 TON, 4X4, M1028
(2320-01-127-5077)
TRUCK, SHELTER CARRIER W/PTO, TACTICAL, 1-1/4 TON, 4X4, M1028A1
(2320-01-158-0820)
TRUCK, SHELTER CARRIER W/PTO, TACTICAL 1-1/4 TON, 4X4, M1028A2
(2320-01-295-0822)
TRUCK, CHASSIS, TACTICAL, 1-1/4 TON, 4X4, M1031
(2320-01-133-5368)

TM 9-2320-289-20, 20 January 1988, is changed as follows:

1. Remove old pages and insert new pages as indicated below.
2. New or changed material is indicated by a vertical bar in the margin of the page.

Remove Pages	Insert Pages
2-15 and 2-16	2-15 and 2-16
10-69 and 10-70	10-69 and 10-70
10-89/(10-90 blank)	10-89 thru 10-90.1/(10-90.2 blank)
Index 25 and Index 26	Index 25 and Index 26

File this change sheet in front of the publication for reference purposes.
Approved for public release; distribution is unlimited.

By Order of the Secretary of the Army:

DENNIS J. REIMER
General, United States Army
Chief of Staff

Official:

Yvonne M. Harrison

YVONNE M. HARRISON
Administrative Assistant to the
Secretary of the Army
01227

By Order of the Secretary of the Air Force:

RONALD R. FOGLEMAN
General, United States Air Force
Chief of Staff

Official:

HENRY VICCELLIO, JR.
General, United States Air Force
Commander, Air Force Materiel Command

DISTRIBUTION:
To be distributed in accordance with DA Form 12-38-E, block 0370, requirements for TM 9-2320-289-20.

CHANGE

DEPARTMENT OF THE ARMY, THE   AIR FORCE,
AND HEADQUARTERS, MARINE CORPS

NO. 3

WASHINGTON, D. C.,   *20 April 1993*

UNIT MAINTENANCE MANUAL
FOR

TRUCK, CARGO, TACTICAL, 1-1/4 TON, 4X4, M1008
(2320-01-123-6827)
TRUCK, CARGO, TACTICAL, 1-1/4 TON, 4X4, M1008A1
(2320-01-123-2671)
TRUCK, UTILITY, TACTICAL, 3/4 TON, 4X4, M1009
(2320-01-123-2665)
TRUCK, AMBULANCE, TACTICAL, 1-1/4 TON, 4X4, M1010
(2310-01-123-2666)
TRUCK, SHELTER CARRIER, TACTICAL, 1-1/4 TON, 4X4, M1028
(2320-01-127-5077)
TRUCK, SHELTER CARRIER W/PTO, TACTICAL, 1-1/4 TON, 4X4, M1028A1
(2320-01-158-0820)
TRUCK, SHELTER CARRIER W/PTO, TACTICAL 1-1/4 TON, 4X4, M1028A2
(2320-01-295-0822)
TRUCK, CHASSIS, TACTICAL, 1-1/4 TON, 4X4, M1031
(2320-01-133-5368)

TM 9-2320-289-20, 20 January 1988, is changed as follows:

1. Remove old pages and insert new pages as indicated below.
2. The Preventive Maintenance Checks and Services have been completely replaced; no change bars or
    pointing hands will appear on pages 2-3 through 2-24.8.

Remove Pages	**Insert Pages**
2-3 thru 2-24.	*2-3 thru 2-24.8*

3. File this change sheet in the front of the publication for information purposes.

By Order of the Secretary of the Army:

GORDON R. SULLIVAN
General, United States Army
Chief of Staff

Official:

MILTON H. HAMILTON
Administrative Assistant to the
Secretary of the Army
04027

By Order of the Secretary of the Air Force:

MERRILL A. McPEAK
General, United States Air Force
Chief of Staff

Official:

RONALD W. YATES
General, United States Air Force
Commander, Air Force Logistics Command

By Order of the Marine Corps:

RONALD D. ELLIOT
Executive Director
Marine Corps Systems Command

Distribution:
To be distributedin accordance with DA Form 12–38–E (Block 0370) requirements for TM9–2320–289–20.

CHANGE

NO. 2

DEPARTMENT OF THE ARMY, THE AIR FORCE,
AND HEADQUARTERS, MARINE CORPS
Washington, D.C. *1 May 1992*

UNIT MAINTENANCE MANUAL
FOR

TRUCK, CARGO, TACTICAL, 1-1/4 TON, 4X4, M1008
(2320-01-123-6827)

TRUCK, CARGO, TACTICAL, 1-1/4 TON, 4X4, M1008A1
(2320-01-123-2671)

TRUCK, UTILITY, TACTICAL, 3/4 TON, 4X4, M1009
(2320-01-123-2665)

TRUCK, AMBULANCE, TACTICAL, 1-1/4 TON, 4X4, M1010
(2310-01-123-2666)

TRUCK, SHELTER CARRIER, TACTICAL, 1-1/4 TON, 4X4, M1028
(2320-01-127-5077)

TRUCK, SHELTER CARRIER W/PTO, TACTICAL, 1-1/4 TON, 4X4, M1028A1
(2320-01-158-0820)

TRUCK, SHELTER CARRIER W/PTO, TACTICAL 1-1/4 TON, 4X4, M1028A2
(2320-01-295-0822)

TRUCK, SHELTER CARRIER, TACTICAL, 1-1/4 TON, 4X4, M1028A3
(2320-01-325-1937)

TRUCK, CHASSIS, TACTICAL, 1-1/4 TON, 4X4, M1031
(2320-01-133-5368)

TM 9-2320-289-20, 20 January 1988, is changed as follows:

1. The manual title is changed to read as shown above.

2. Remove old pages and insert new pages.

3. New or changed material is indicated by a vertical bar in the margin.

Remove Pages	Insert Pages
i and ii	*i and ii*
1-1 through 1-4	*1-1 through 1-4*
1-9 through 1-10.1/(10.2 blank)	*1-9 through 1-10.1/(1-10.2 blank)*
1-19/(1-20 blank)	*1-19/(1-20 blank)*
2-3 and 2-4	*2-3 and 2-4*
2-9 through 2-12	*2-9 through 2-12*
2-15 through 2-18	*2-15 through 2-18*
2-21 through 2-24	*2-21 through 2-24.1/(2-24.2 blank)*
2-29 and 2-30	*2-29 and 2-30*
2-33 and 2-34	*2-33 and 2-34*
2-37 and 2-38	*2-37 and 2-38*

Approved for public release; distribution is unlimited.

4. File this change sheet in front of the publication for reference purposes.

By Order of the Secretary of the Army:

GORDON R. SULLIVAN
General, United States Army
Chief of Staff

Official:

MILTON H. HAMILTON
Administrative Assistant to the
Secretary of the Army
02708

By Order of the Secretary of the Air Force;

MERRILL A. McPEAK
General, United States Air Force
Chief of Staff

Official;
CHARLES C. McDONALD
General, United States Air Force
Commander, Air Force Logistics Command

By Order of the Marine Corps:

H. E. REESE
Deputy for Support
Marine Corps Research, Development and
Acquisition Command

Distribution:
To be distributed in accordance with DA Form 12–38–E, Block   0370, Unit maintenance require–
ments for TM 9–2320–289–20.

TM 9-2320-289-20
TO 36A12-1A-2082-1
TM 2320-20/2
C 1

CHANGE

NO. 1

DEPARTMENT OF THE ARMY, THE AIR FORCE,
AND HEADQUARTERS, MARINE CORPS
Washington D.C., 7 July 1991

UNIT MAINTENANCE MANUAL
FOR

TRUCK, CARGO, TACTICAL, 1-1/4 TON, 4X4, M1008
(2320-01-123-6827)

TRUCK, CARGO, TACTICAL, 1-1/4 TON, 4X4, M1008A1
(2320-01-123-2671)

TRUCK, UTILITY, TACTICAL, 3/4 TON, 4X4, M1009
(2320-01-123-2665)

TRUCK, AMBULANCE, TACTICAL, 1-1/4 TON, 4X4, M1010
(2310-01-123-2666)

TRUCK, SHELTER CARRIER, TACTICAL, 1-1/4 TON, 4X4, M1028
(2320-01-127-5077)

TRUCK, SHELTER CARRIER W/PTO, TACTICAL, 1-1/4 TON, 4X4, M1028A1
(2320-01-158-0820)

TRUCK, SHELTER CARRIER W/PTO, TACTICAL 1-1/4 TON, 4X4, M1028A2
(2320-01-295-0822)

TRUCK, CHASSIS, TACTICAL, 1-1/4 TON, 4X4, M1031
(2320-01-133-5368)

TM 9-2320-289-20, 20 January 1988, is changed as follows:

1. The manual title is changed to read as shown above.

2. Remove old pages and insert new pages.

3. New or changed material is indicated by a vertical bar in the margin.

Remove Pages	Insert Pages
I and II	*I and II*
1-1 through 1-4	*1-1 through 1-4*
1-9 through 1-12	*1-9 through 1-12*
1-19/(1-20 blank)	*1-19/(1-20 blank)*
2-9 through 2-12	*2-9 through 2-12*
2-23 and 2-24	*2-23 and 2-24*
5-1 and 5-2	*5-1 and 5-2*
6-17 and 6-18	*6-17 and 6-18*
None	*6-23 through 6-25/(6-26 blank)*
8-1 through 8-4	*8-1 through 8-4*
10-29 and 10-30	*10-29 and 10-30*
A-1 through A-4	*A-1 through A-4*

Remove Pages (Con't)	Insert Pages (Con't)
B-3 through B-38	B-3 through B-40
F-1 and F-2	F-1 and F-2
None	F-16.1/(F-16.2 blank)
Index 3 through Index 12	Index 3 through Index 12
Index 19 and Index 20	Index 19 and Index 20
Index 23 through Index 28	Index 23 through Index 28.1/(Index 28.2 blank)
Index 31 and Index 32	Index 31 and Index 32

4. File this change sheet in front of the publication for reference purposes.

By Order of the Secretary of the Army:

GORDON R. SULLIVAN
General, United States Army
Chief of Staff

Official:

PATRICIA P. HICKERSON
Brigadier General, United States Army
The Adjutant General

By Order of the Secretary of the Air Force;

MERRILL A. McPEAK
General, United States Air Force
Chief of Staff

Official;

CHARLES C. McDONALD
General, United States Air Force
Commander, Air Force Logistics Command

Distribution:

By Order of the Marine Corps:

H. E. REESE
Deputy for Support
Marine Corps Research, Development and
Acquisition Command

Distribution:

To be distributed in accordance with DA Form 12-38-E (Block 0370) Unit maintenance requirements for TM9-2320-289-20.

WARNING

CARBON MONOXIDE (EXHAUST GASES) CAN KILL

Carbon monoxide is without color or smell, but can kill you. Breathing air with carbon monoxide produces symptoms of headache, dizziness, loss of muscular control, a sleepy feeling, and coma. Brain damage or death can result from heavy exposure. Carbon monoxide occurs in the exhaust fumes of fuel-burning heaters and internal combustion engines. Carbon monoxide can become dangerously concentrated under conditions of no air movement. Precautions must be followed to ensure crew safety when personnel heater or main or auxiliary engines of any truck are operated for any purpose.

1. **DO NOT** operate personnel heater or engine of truck in enclosed areas.

2. **DO NOT** idle truck engine without ventilator blower operating and truck windows open.

3. **BE ALERT** at all times for exhaust odors.

4. **BE ALERT** for exhaust poisoning symptoms. They are:
    - Headache
    - Dizziness
    - Sleepiness
    - Loss of muscular control

5. If you see another person with exhaust poisoning symptoms:
    - Remove person from area.
    - Expose to fresh air.
    - Keep person warm.
    - Do not permit physical exercise.
    - Administer artificial respiration, if necessary.
    - Notify a medic.

6. **BE AWARE:** The field protective mask for chemical-biological-radiological (CBR) protection will not protect you from carbon monoxide poisoning.

The Best Defense Against Carbon Monoxide Poisoning Is Good Ventilation

* For First Aid, refer to FM 21-11.

WARNING

ACCELERATOR SYSTEM

Use extreme caution to ensure that clothing or tools **DO NOT** get caught in truck's operating drivebelts. Failure to follow this warning may result in serious injury to personnel or equipment damage.

WARNING

BATTERY SYSTEM

● Battery acid (electrolyte) is extremely dangerous. Always wear goggles and rubber gloves when performing battery checks or inspections. Serious injury to personnel will result if battery acid contacts skin or eyes.

● DO NOT perform battery system checks or inspections while smoking or near fire, flames, or sparks. Batteries may explode, causing serious injury or death to personnel.

● Rotate cover to underside of clamp as each cable is disconnected. Remove all jewelry such as dog tags, rings, bracelets, etc. If jewelry or disconnected battery ground cable contacts battery terminal, a direct short will result. Failure to follow proper disconnection procedures will result in serious injury or death to personnel or equipment damage.

● Both negative battery cables must be disconnected before removing any electrical system components. Failure to follow this warning may result in serious injury or death to personnel.

● **DO NOT** charge, test, or slave start battery when built-in hydrometer shows clear or light yellow. An explosion may occur causing serious injury or death to personnel.

WARNING

BODY AND ACCESSORIES

● Radiator grille guard is heavy. Failure to use an assistant during removal or installation may cause serious injury to personnel.

● Support bumper during removal or installation. If dropped, it may cause serious injury to personnel.

Warning b

WARNING

BODY AND ACCESSORIES (Continued)

● Use extreme caution when removing rear door assembly (M1010). Rear door assembly is heavy and if dropped will cause equipment damage and serious injury to personnel.

● Wear heavy gloves when handling glass to avoid risk of injury. If glass is cracked but still intact, crisscross it with masking tape to reduce risk of injury to personnel.

● Ambulance attendant's seat stem assembly is spring loaded. Carefully raise and lower attendant's seat to avoid risk of injury to personnel.

● Only authorized and trained personnel are to remove and service gas-particulate filters that have been used in an NBC environment. See local SOP for disposing of contaminated filters. Failure to follow this warning may result in serious illness or death to personnel.

● Special protective clothing (see TM 10-277) must be used and special safety measures and decontamination procedures (see FM 3-5) must be followed when replacing contaminated filters. Failure to follow this warning may result in serious illness or death to personnel.

WARNING

BRAKE SYSTEM

● **DO NOT** use a dry brush or compressed air to clean brake shoes, brake pads, or brake components. There may be asbestos dust on brake shoes, brake pads or brake components which can be dangerous to you if you breathe it. Brake shoes, brake pads, and brake components must be wet, and a soft brush must be used. Failure to follow this warning may result in serious illness or death to personnel.

● Always wear goggles when bleeding brakes. Failure to follow this warning may result in serious eye injury.

● Always wear goggles during removal and installation of brake shoe springs. Failure to follow this warning may result in serious eye injury.

● Cautiously feel each wheel hub and brake drum. Wheel hub or brake drum may be hot. Failure to follow this warning may result in burns.

WARNING

CLEANING AGENTS

● Dry cleaning solvent P-D-680 is toxic and flammable. Always wear protective goggles and gloves and use only in a well-ventilated area. Avoid contact with skin, eyes, and clothes and DO NOT breathe vapors. DO NOT use near open flame or excessive heat. The solvent's flash point is 100°F-138°F (38°C-59°C). If you become dizzy while using cleaning solvent, immediately get fresh air and medical help. If solvent contacts eyes, immediately wash your eyes with water and get medical aid.

● Compressed air used when checking for restrictions or cleaning purposes should never exceed 30 psi (207 kPa). Use only effective chip guarding and personnel protective equipment (goggles/shield, gloves, etc.). Failure to follow this warning may result in serious injury to personnel.

WARNING

COOLING SYSTEM

● Servicing of engine cooling system should only be performed on a cool engine. Never remove a clamp or hose when engine is hot. Pressurized steam or hot water will cause serious burns.

● Wait for pressure release before removing radiator cap, Pressurized steam or hot water will cause serious burns.

● Never remove radiator cap when engine is hot. Pressurized steam or hot water will cause serious burns.

● DO NOT repair and reuse a fan with a bent or damaged blade. Replace fan as an assembly. A damaged fan is out of balance and may fall apart during use causing serious injury or death to personnel.

WARNING

EXHAUST SYSTEM

● Before attempting to inspect or service any part of exhaust system, allow exhaust system to cool. Failure to follow this warning will result in serious burns.

WARNING

FUEL SYSTEM

•Diesel fuel is flammable. When disconnecting fuel lines to test fuel flow, direct fuel spray away from source of ignition. A fire extinguisher must be on hand in work area. Failure to follow this warning may result in serious injury or death to personnel,

•Allow engine to cool before replacing drainback hose or pipe assembly. Failure to follow this warning may result in serious burns.

•Diesel fuel is flammable, **DO NOT** perform procedures near fire, flames, or sparks. A fire extinguisher must be on hand in work area. Failure to follow this warning may result in serious injury or death.

•Always wear goggles when working on underside of truck. Fuel and hydraulic fluid spillage can occur. Failure to follow this warning may result in serious eye injury.

WARNING

STARTER SYSTEM

•Support starter during removal and installation. Failure to support starter may cause it to fall, resulting in injury to personnel.

WARNING

TRANSMISSION

•Always wear goggles when working on underside of truck. Hydraulic fluid spillage can occur when removing transmission oil pan. Failure to follow this warning may result in serious eye injury.

WARNING

WHEELS

- Position wheel chocks at front and rear of tires opposite axle to be raised. Truck must be on level surface before attempting to remove wheel. Failure to follow this warning may result in serious injury or death to personnel.

- All air must be removed from tire before removing tire from wheel rim. Failure to follow this warning may result in serious injury to personnel.

- The tapered end of inner bearing assembly must be facing toward the outboard (cap end) of the axle shaft. The tapered end of the outer wheel bearing assembly must be facing toward the inboard (splined end) of the axle shaft. Failure to follow this warning may force wheel off truck during operation, causing serious injury or death to personnel.

- Splash shield and caliper bracket are factory-installed with 6 locknuts and washers. Refer to TM 9-2320-289-20P for proper replacement parts. Using improper replacement parts may cause caliper to fall off during operation, resulting in serious injury or death to personnel.

- Use extreme caution when lowering or raising spare tire and carrier. Spare tire is heavy. Dropping it may result in serious injury to personnel.

TECHNICAL MANUAL
TM 9-2320-289-20

DEPARTMENTS (OF THE ARMY, THE AIR FORCE,
AND HEADQUARTERS, MARINE CORPS
Washington, D.C.   *20 January 1988*

UNIT MAINTENANCE MANUA   L
FO R

TRUCK, CARGO, TACTICAL, 1-1/4 TON, 4x4, M1008
(2320-01-123-6827)

TRUCK, CARGO, TACTICAL, 1-1/4 TON, 4x4, M1008A1
(2320-01-123-2671)

TRUCK, UTILITY, TACTICAL, 3/4 TON, 4x4, M1009
(2320-01-123-2665)

TRUCK, AMBULANCE, TACTICAL, 1-1/4 TON, 4x4, M1010
(2310-01-123-2666]

TRUCK, SHELTER CARRIER, TACTICAL, 1-1/4 TON, 4x4, M1028
(2320-01-127-5077)

TRUCK, SHELTER CARRIER W/PTO, TACTICAL, 1-1/4 TON, 4x4, M1028A1
(2320-01-158-0820)

TRUCK, SHELTER CARRIER W/PTO, TACTICAL 1-1/4 TON, 4X4, M1028A2
(2320-01-295-0822)

TRUCK, SHELTER CARRIER, TACTICAL, 1-1/4 TON, 4X4, M1028A3
(2320-01-325-1937)

TRUCK, CHASSIS, TACTICAL, 1-1/4 TON, 4x4, M1031
(2320-01-133-5368)

REPORTING ERRORS AND RECOMMENDING IMPROVEMENTS

(Army) You can help improve this manual. If you find any mistakes or if you know of a way to improve the procedures, please let us know. Mail your letter, DA Form 2028 *(Recommended Changes to Publications and Blank Forms),* or DA Form 2028-2, located in the back of this manual, direct to: Commander, U.S. Army Tank-Automotive Command, ATTN: AMSTA-MB, Warren, MI 48397-5000. *(Marine Corps)* Submit NAVMC 10772 to the Commanding General, Marine Corps Logistic Base (Code 850), Albany, GA 31704, A reply will be furnished to y   o u.

Approved for public release; distribution is unlimited.

TABLE OF CONTENT   S

* This publication supersedes TM 9-2320-289-20 dated April 1983.

TABLE OF CONTENTS - Continue   d

TABLE OF CONTENTS - Continued

HOW TO USE THIS MANUAL

This manual is designed to help operate and maintain the CUCV Series trucks. This manual describes in detail the Unit Maintenance prescribed by the *Maintenance Allocation Chart* (Appendix B) and Source, Maintenance, and Recoverability (SMR) Codes (TM 9-2320-289-20P).

FEATURES OF THIS MANUAL:

- Bleed-to-edge indicators on the cover and on the edge of applicable manual pages provide quick access to chapters and sections most often used.

- A table of contents is provided for all chapters, sections, and appendices.

- WARNING s, CAUTION s, NOTE s, subject headings, and other important information are highlighted in **BOLD** print as a visual aid.

- Statements and words of particular importance are printed in capital letters to create emphasis.

- Instructions are located together with figures that illustrate the specific task you are working on. In many cases, the task steps and illustrations are located side-by-side, making identification and procedure sequence easier to follow.

- An alphabetical index is provided at the end of the manual to assist in locating information not readily found in the table of contents.

- Technical instructions include metric in addition to standard units. A metric conversion chart is provided on the inside back cover.

FOLLOW THESE GUIDELINES WHEN YOU USE THIS MANUAL:

- Quickly read through this manual and become familiar with its contents before proceeding to specific maintenance tasks.

- A warning summary is provided at the beginning of this manual and should be read before performing any maintenance tasks.

- In the actual maintenance tasks, follow all WARNING s, CAUTION s, and NOTE s. These are given immediately preceding the procedural steps to which they apply. If these instructions are not followed, or care is not taken, you may injure yourself or cause equipment damage.

- Within a chapter, section, or paragraph, headings are used to help mount the material and assist you in quickly finding tasks. Read all preliminary information found at the beginning of each task. After completing a task, ALWAYS perform the follow-on maintenance at the end of the task.

USING YOUR MANUAL: AN EXAMPLE

The operator of a CUCV truck complains that the truck engine cranks but will not start. The truck has been assigned to you for repair. To correct the problem you will need to follow these steps:

- Turn to the cover of your manual. On the right margin, find the listing for *Troubleshooting* and turn to the page listing given. When you reach the troubleshooting section, locate the paragraph entitled *Troubleshooting Symptom Index* (paragraph 2-11).

- Both mechanical and electrical troubleshooting symptoms are listed in the *Troubleshooting Symptom Index* and are organized according to equipment category.

Read through the index until you find a symptom listing which most closely matches the problem. The symptom "Cranks But Will Not Start" is found under the "ENGINE" category of mechanical troubleshooting. Turn to the page for the troubleshooting procedure that will help solve your problem.

- Follow the instructions for each "Step"   listed in the troubleshooting procedure. Start with Step 1 and proceed in order until you reach the step where a problem is actually found. In this case, let's assume that steps 1-5 are performed without difficulty, Step 6 reveals that the problem is with the fuel pump. The Corrective Action for Step 6 tells you where in the manual to go to correct the problem: *"If fuel flow is insufficient, replace fuel pump. (See paragraph 3-10)."*

- Paragraph 3-10 is located in Chapter 3. Using the Tab/e of Contents, find the listings for Chapter 3. Because the fuel pump is part of the fuel system, you would proceed to Section II, Fuel System Maintenance. The index at the beginning of Section II will tell you on which page paragraph 3-10 is located,

- Paragraph 3-10 is the maintenance procedure for replacing the fuel pump. Carefully read through the procedure, follow all instructions, and perform all steps in the proper sequence. When you have finished the last step, you will have replaced the fuel pump,

USE OF RTV SEALANT:

When maintenance instructions in this manual instruct you to use RTV sealant (Item 41, Appendix C), wait a minimum of 15 minutes before installing the part or assembly to allow the RTV sealant to cure.

TRUCKS EQUIPPED WITH SWINGFIRE HEATERS:

Maintenance tasks in this manual do not allow for trucks which may have swingfire heaters installed. If the truck you are working on has a swingfire heater, you may have to disconnect the heater's components to obtain access to other components if interference exists.

CHAPTER 1
INTRODUCTION

Section I. GENERAL INFORMATIO   N

1-1.   SCOPE.

a. This manual contains instructions for the performance of maintenance of CUCV Series trucks at the unit level. Models included are:

(1) M1008, Truck, Cargo, Tactical, 1¼ Ton, 4x4
(2) M1008A1 , Truck, Cargo, Tactical, 1¼ Ton, 4x4
(3) M1009, Truck, Utility, Tactical, ¾ Ton, 4x4
(4) M1010, Truck, Ambulance, Tactical, 1¼ Ton, 4x4
(5) M1028, Truck, Shelter Carrier, Tactical, 1¼ Ton, 4x4
(6) M1028A1, Truck, Shelter Carrier w/PTO, Tactical, 1¼ Ton, 4x4
(7) M1028A2, Truck, Shelter Carrier w/PTO, Tactical, 1¼ Ton, 4x4
(8) M1028A3, Truck, Sheller Carrier, Tactical, 1¼ Ton, 4x4
(9) M1031, Truck, Chassis, Tactical, 1¼ Ton, 4x4

b. Other manuals which may be referred to should be considered a part of this manual.

1-2   MAINTENANCE FORMS AND RECORDS

Department of the Army forms and procedures used for equipment maintenance will be those prescribed by DA Pam 738-750,   *The Army Maintenance Management System (TAMMS).*

1-3.   DESTRUCTION OF ARMY MATERIEL TO PREVENT ENEMY USE.

Procedures outlined in TM 750-244-6   *(Procedures for Destruction of Tank-Automotive Equipment to Prevent Enemy Use)*   are applicable to these trucks.

1-4.   PREPARATION FOR STORAGE OR SHIPMENT.

For information on storage or shipment of these trucks, see Chapter 12.

1-5.   OFFICIAL NOMENCLATURE, NAMES, AND DESIGNATIONS.

The nomenclature, names, and designations used in this manual are consistent with official usage. All hardware, assemblies, and subassemblies are named according to the nomenclature used in TM 9-2320-289-20P.

1-6.   REPORTING EQUIPMENT IMPROVEMENT RECOMMENDATIONS (EIRs).

If your CUCV Series truck needs improvement, let us know. Send us an EIR. You, the user, are the only one who can tell us what you don't like about your equipment. Let us know why you don't like the design or performance. Put it on an SF 368   *(Quality Deficiency Report).*   Mail it to us at: Commander, U.S. Army Tank-Automotive   Command, ATTN: AMSTA-QRD, Warren, MI 48397-5000. We'll send you a reply.

1-7.   WARRANTY INFORMATION.

To determine if your CUCV Series truck is under warranty, see TB 9-2300-295-15/24.

1-8.   METRIC SYSTEM.

The equipment described herein contains metric components and requires the use of metric tools; therefore, metric units, in addition to standard units, will be used throughout this manual. Standard units will be given first with the equivalent metric unit in parentheses,   for instance: 7000 lb. (3178 kg). A   metric conversion chart is located on the inside back cover of this manual.

1-9.   COMMON TOOLS, SPECIAL TOOLS, AND REPAIR PARTS.

a. For authorized common tools, refer to the Common Table of Allowance (CTA) and the Modified Table of Organization and Equipment (MTOE) applicable to   your unit.

b. For special tools, and Test, Measurement, and Diagnostic Equipment (TMDE), refer to the *Repair Parts and Special Took List (RPSTL)*   manual, TM 9-2320-289-20P, and the   *Maintenance Allocation Chart (MAC)*   in Appendix B of this manual.

c. Repair parts are listed and illustrated in the   *Repair Parts and Special Tools List (RPSTL)* manual, TM 9-2320-289-20P.

d. Torque wrenches are normally marked with a measurement term   *ft. -lb.* or *in. -lb.* The terms used within this manual are   *lb. -ft.* or *lb. -in.,*   unless otherwise noted in the text.

Section II. EQUIPMENT DESCRIPTION AND DATA

1-10. EQUIPMENT CHARACTERISTICS, CAPABILITIES, AND FEATURES.

---

a, These trucks are commercial vehicles suitable for use on all types of roads and limited off-road operations.

b. They are capable of occasional hardbottom fording to a depth of 16 in. (41 cm) at 5 mi/h (8 km/h) for not more than 3 minutes, without stalling the engine, causing permanent damage to components, or requiring immediate maintenance.

c. Commercial Utility Cargo Vehicle features include:

(1) 379 cu in. (6.2 l) diesel V-8 engine
(2) automatic transmission (Hydra-matic 400) with 3 forward and 1 reverse speeds
(3) manually activated transfer case for four-wheel drive operations
(4) hydraulically activated, power-assisted front disc and rear drum service brakes
(5) 12/24 volt electrical system
(6) NATO slave cable receptacle
(7) winterization kit available for each model
(8) multi-purpose tow hooks on front and rear bumpers and swivel-type pintles on rear bumper to permit tie-down of vehicle or towing

d. Cargo Truck. The M1008, M1008A1, M10028, M1028A1, M1028A2, and M1028A3 1¼ ton, 4x4, cargo trucks are light commercial trucks designed to provide standard tactical mobility and to carry cargo or passengers. The M1008 and M1008A1 can be equipped with troop seats to accommodate eight personnel. The M1008A1 includes a 100 amp/24 v communications kit. The M1028 has a 100 amp/24 v electrical system, and will accept an S250 communications shelter and a communications kit. The M1028A1 is equipped with a New Process Model 205 transfer case which allows for the addition of a power take-off (PTO) unit. Some M1028s have been equipped with heavy-duty electrical systems that incorporate the M1010 200 amp/24 v electrical system and air conditioner fixtures. These M1028s have not been provided with a different designation. The M1028A2 is an M1028A1 which has been converted to rear dual wheel configuration. The M1028A3 is an M1028 which has been converted to a rear dual wheel shelter carrier configuration and is equipped with a New Process 208 Transfer Case.

M1008

M1028

TA49617

e. Utility Truck. The M1009 is a ¾ ton truck that has an enclosed body and can be used for command and control purposes.

f. Ambulance. The M1010 is designed to carry a maximum of four litter or eight ambulatory patients with both upper litters in place. It is equipped with a 200 amp/24 v electrical system, which supports a gas-particulate filter unit (GPFU) system, a patient compartment air conditioner, and a fuel-fired compartment heater. It has mounting provisions inside the cab for the AN-GRC-60 radio. The AS-1729/GRC antenna is mounted outside on the front of the patient compartment.

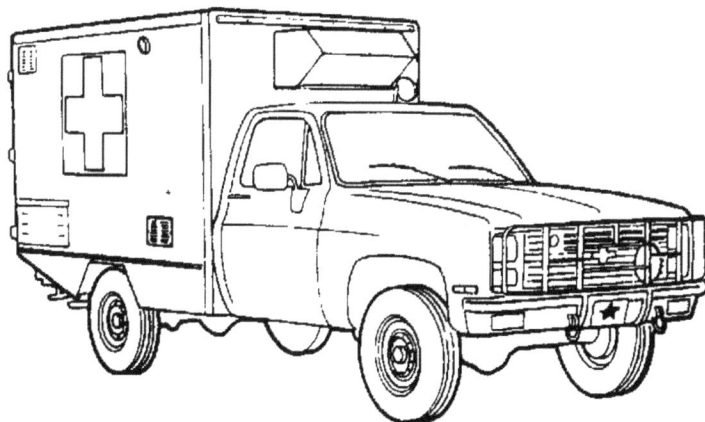

TA49618

g. **Chassis Truck.** The M1031 is a chassis and cab combination, which is designed for the mounting of special bodies as required. It is equipped with a New Process Model 205 transfer case, which allows for the addition of a power take-off (PTO) unit.

M1031

TA49619

1-11. LOCATION AND DESCRIPTION OF MAJOR COMPONENTS.

For information on the operation of the major components outlined below, see the *Operator's Manual,* TM 9-2320-289-10.

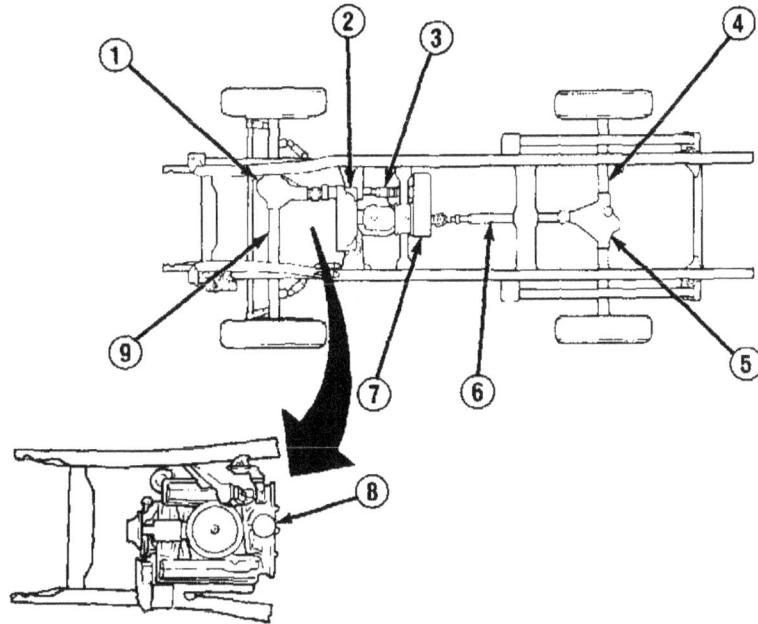

1. Front Differential
2. Transmission
3. Front Propeller Shaft
4. Rear Axle
5. Rear Differential
6. Rear Propeller Shaft
7. Transfer Case
8. Engine
9. Front Axle

TA49620

1-12. DIFFERENCES BETWEEN MODELS.

	M1008	M1008A1	M1009	M1010	M1028	M1028A1	M1031
a. Model 208 Transfer Case	x	x	x	x	x		
b. Model 205 Transfer Case						x	x
e. 100 amp, 12/24 volt Electrical System	x	x	x		x	x	x
d. 200 amp, 12/24 voft Electrical System				x	X		
e. Troop Seat Kit*	x	x					
f. Communicatlons Kit		x			x	x	
ɡ. Radio Mounting			x	x			
h. Weapon Brackets	x	x	x		x	x	x
l. Cargo Tie-downs	x	x					
j. Shelter Tie-downs					x	x	
k. Air Conditioner				x			
i. Gas-Particulate Filter Unit (GPFU) System				x			
m. Cargo Cover Kit*	x	x					
n. Rear Passenger Seating			x				
o. Spotlight				x			
p. Floodlights				x			
q. 10. 00R-15C Tires			x				
r. LT23W135R-16E Tires	x	x		x	x	x	x
e. Looking Differential			x				
t. No-spln Differential	x	x		x	x	x	x

* These items are not standard equipment, but the Indicated trucks may be equipped as shown.
* * Selected M1028 trucks only.

1-13. LOCATION AND CONTENTS OF WARNING, CAUTION, AND DATA PLATES.

See TM 9-2320-289-10 for the location and contents of warning, caution, and data plates.

1-14. EQUIPMENT DATA.

Vehicle performance data for the CUCV Series trucks is listed in the table below.

Table 1-1. Tabulated Data

DATA	MODEL				
	M1008 M1008A1	MI 009	M100	M1028 M1028A1	M1031
Weights:					
Curb	5900 lb (2679 kg)	5200 lb (2361 kg)	7370 lb (3346 kg)	5800 lb (2633 kg)	5250 lb (2384 kg)
Payload/ Passengers	2900 lb (1317 kg)	1200 lb (545 kg)	2080 lb (944 kg)	3600 lb (1634 kg)	3950 lb (1793 kg)
GVWR	8800 lb (3995 kg)	6400 lb (2906 kg)	9450 lb (4290 kg)	9400 lb (4268 kg)	9200 lb max (4177 kg)
GAWR (front)	4500 lb (2043 kg)	3600 lb (1634 kg)	4500 lb (2043 kg)	4500 lb (2043 kg)	4500 lb (2043 kg)
GAWR (rear)	7500 lb (3405 kg)	3750 lb (1703 kg)	7500 lb (3405 kg)	7500 lb (3405 kg)	7500 lb (3405 kg)
Wheelbase	131.5 in (334 cm)	106.5 in (271 cm)	131.5 in (334 cm)	131.5 in (334 cm)	131.5 in (334 cm)
Track (front)	67.8 in (172 cm)	57,4 in (146 cm)	67.8 ln (172 cm)	67.8 in (172 cm)	67,8 in (172 cm)
Track (rear)	65.8 in (167 cm)	54.4 iln (138 cm)	65.8 ln (167 cm)	65.8 in (167 cm)	65.8 in (167 cm)
Ground Clearance (to T/C skid plate @ GVWR)	10.7 in (27.2 cm)	9.8 ln (24.4 cm)	10.5 in (26.7 cm)	10,5 in (26.7 cm)	10,5 in (26.7 cm)
Rear Axle @ GVWR	7.8 in (19.8 cm)	8.6 ln (21.6 cm)	7.8 ln (19.8 cm)	7.8 in (19.8 cm)	7.8 in (19.8 cm)
Front Axle @ GVWR	8.6 in (21.8 cm)	8.4 in (21.3 cm)	6.6 ln (21.8 cm)	8.6 in (21.8 cm)	8.6 in (21.6 cm)
Height (overall) @ Curb	75.4 in (191.5 cm)	75.0 in (190.5 cm)	101.6 ln (258 cm)	107.1 ln' (272 cm)	76.3 in (193.8 cm)
Length (overall)	220.7 in (560.6 cm)	191.8 in (487. 1 cm)	227.7 ln (578.4 cm)	220.7 ln (560.6 cm)	212.9 in (504.8 cm)
Width (overall)	81.2 in (206.2 cm)	79.6 in (202 cm)	61.2 ln (206.2 cm)	81.2 in (206.2 cm)	81.2 in (206.2 cm)
Engine:					
Type	90-degree V8 Diesel	90-degree V8 Diesel	90-degree V8 Diesel	90-degree V8 Diesel	90-degree V8 Diesel
Piston Displacement	379 cu in (6.2 l)	379 cu in (6.2 l)	379 cu ln (6.2 l)	379 cu in (6.2 l)	379 cu in (6.2 l)
SAE Net Horsepower	135 hp @ 3600 rpm	135 hp @ 3600 rpm	135 hp @ 3600 rpm	135 hp @ 3600 rpm	135 hp @ 3600 rpm

I Height will vary with different shelters and loading.

Table 1-1. Tabulated Data (Continued)

DATA	MODEL				
	M1008 M1008A1	M1009	M1010	M1028 M1028A1	M1031
Fuel System:					
Low-pressure	Mechanical Lift Pump	Mechanical Lift Pump	Mechianical Lift Pump	Mechanical Lift Pump	Mechanical Lift Pump
High-pressure	Stanadyne Model DB2	Stanadyne Model DB2	Stanadyne Model DB2	Stanadyne Model DB2	Stanadyne Model DB2
Injection Nozzle	Bosch	Bosch	Bosch	Bosch	Bosch
Fuel Tank Capacity	20 gal (75.7 l)	27 gal (102.2 l)	20 gal (75.7 l)	20 gal (75.7 l)	20 gal (75.7 l)
Electrical System	12/24 volt	12/24 volt	1 2/24 volt	12/24 Volt	12/24 volt
Charging System	100 amp/ 28 volt	100 amp/ 28 volt	200 amp/ 28 volt	100 amp/ 28 volt	100 amp/ 28 volt
Transmission:					
Type	Automatic GM THM 400	Automatic GM THM 400	Automatic GM THM 400	Automatic GM THM 400	Automatic GM THM 400
Lubrication Capacity	19 pt (9 l)	19 pt (9 l)	19 pt (9 l)	19 pt (9 l)	19 pt (9 l)
Transfer Case:					
Model	New Process Model 208	New Process Model 208	New Process Model 208	New Process Model 208 or Model 205	New Process Model 205
Speed	2-speed	2-speed	2-speed	2-speed	2-speed
Ratios	2.61 & 1.00	2.61 & 1.00	2.61 & 1.00	2.61 & 1.00 or 1.96 & 1.00	1.96 & 1.00
Lubrication Capacity	5 qt (4.8 l)	5 qt (4.8 l)	5 qt (4.8 l)	5 qt (4.8 l) or 2 qt (2.5 l)	2 qt (2.5 l)
Front Axle:					
Type	Full-floating	Semi-floating	Full-floatlng	Full-floating	Full-floating
Differential Type	Two-pinion	Two-pinion	Two-pinion	Two-pinlon	Two-pinion
Lubrication Capacity	4.5 pt (2.13 l)	4.5 pt (2.13 l)	4.5 pt (2.13 l)	4.5 pt (2.13 l)	4.5 pt (2.13 l)
Rear Axle:					
Type	Full-floating	Semi-floatlng	Full-floating	Full-floatlng	Full-floating
Differential Type	Four-pinlon No-spin	Two-pinion Locking	Four-pinion No-spin	Four-pinion No-spin	Four-pinion No-spin
Lubrication Capacity	5.4 pt (2.1 l)	5.4 pt (2.1 l)	5.4 pt (2.1 l)	5.4 pt (2.1 l)	5.4 pt (2.1 l)
Service Brake:					
Front	Disc	Disc	Disc	Disc	Disc
Rear	Drum	Drum	Drum	Drum	Drum

1-14.1 DIFFERENCES BETWEEN MODELS.

	M1028A2	M1028A3		M1028A2	M1028A3
a. Model 208 Transfer Case		x	k. Air Conditioner		
b. Model 205 Transfer Case	x		l. Gas-Particulate Filter Unit (GPFU) System		
c. 100 amp, 12/24 volt Electrical System	x	x	m. Cargo Cover Kit		
d. 200 amp, 12/24 volt Electrical System			n. Rear Passenger Seating		
e. Troop Seat Kit'			o. Spotlight		
f. Communications Kit	x	x	p. Floodlights		
g. Radio Mounting			q. 10.00R-15C Tires		
h. Weapons Bracket	x	x	r. LT235/85R-16E Tires	x	x
i. Cargo Tie-downs	x	x	s. Locking Differential		
j. Shelter Tie-downs	x	x	t. No-spin Differential	x	x
			u. Dual Rear Wheels	x	x

1-14.2 EQUIPMENT DATA.

Table 1-1.1. Tabulated Data

DATA	M1028A2	M1028A3	DATA	M1028A2	M1028A3
Weights:			Rear Axle @ GVWR	7.7 in (19.6 cm)	7.7 in (19,6 cm)
Curb	6120 lb (2778 kg)	6120 lb (2778 kg)	Front Axle @ GVWR	8.6 in (21,8 cm)	8.6 in (21.8 cm)
Payload/ Passengers	3940 lb (1789 kg)	3940 lb (1789 kg)	Height (overall) @ Curb	107,1 in * (272 cm)	107.1 in * (272 cm)
GVWR	10,120 lb max (4594 kg)	10,120 lb rmax (4594 kg)	Length (overall)	220.7 in (560.6 cm)	220.7 in (560.6 cm)
GAWR (front)	3900 lb (1770 kg)	3900 lb (1770 kg)	Width (overall)	95.8 in (243.3 cm)	95,8 in (243.3 cm)
GAWR (rear)	6220 lb (2824 kg)	6220 lb (2824 kg)	Engine:		
Wheelbase	131,5 in (334 cm)	131.5 in (334 cm)	Type	90-degree V8 Diesel	90-degree V8 Diesel
Track (front)	67.8 in (172 cm)	67.8 in (172 cm)	Piston Displacement	379 cu in (6.2 l)	379 cu in (6.2 l)
Track (rear)	75,8 in (193 cm)	75,8 in (193 cm)	SAE Net Horsepower	135 bhp @ 3600 rpm	135 bhp @ 3600 rpm
Ground Clearance (to T/C skid plate @ GVWR)	10.7 in (27.2 cm)	10.7 in (27.2 cm)			

* Height will vary with different shelters and loading.

Table 1-1.1. Tabulated Data (Continued)

DATA	M1028A2	M1028A3	DATA	M1028A2	M1028A3
Fuel System:			Transfer Case (Con't):		
Low-pressure	Mechanical Lift Pump	Mechanical Lift Pump	Ratios	1.96 & 1.00	2.61 & 1.00
High-pressure	Stanadyne Model DB2	Stanadyne Model DB2	Lubrication Capacity	2 qt (2.5 1)	5 qt (4.6 l)
Injection Nozzle	Bosch	Bosch	Front Axle:		
Fuel Tank Capacity	20 gal (75.7 l)	20 gal (75.7 l)	Type	Full Floating	Full Floating
Electrical System	12124 volt	12124 volt	Differential Type	Two-pinion	Two-pinion
Charging System	100 amp/ 28 volt	100 amp/ 28 volt	Lubrication Capacity	4.5 pt (2.1 l)	4,5 pt (2.1 l)
Transmission:			Rear Axle:		
Type	Automatic GM THM 400	Automatic GM THM 400	Type	Full Floating	Full Floating
Lubrication Capacity	19 pt (9l)	19 pt (9 l)	Differential Type	Four-pinion No-spin	Four-pinion No-spin
Transfer Case:			Lubrication Capacity	5.4 pt (2.1 1)	5.4 pt (2.1 l)
Model	New Process Model 205	New Process Model 208	Service Brake:		
			Front	Disc	Disc
Speed	2-speed	2-speed	Rear	Drum	Drum

Section III. PRINCIPLES OF OPERATION

1-15. PRINCIPLES OF OPERATION INDEX.

1-16. DRIVETRAIN SYSTEM.

a. Functions to convert horsepower frorn engine into mechanical force needed to move truck.

b. Major components of drivetrain are:

   (1) **Engine:**

      (a) 6.2 liter diesel fueled V-8.

      (b) There is no carburetor on a diesel engine. Instead, fuel is injected under high pressure through nozzles into the combustion chamber at correct timing intervals.

      (c) ignition of fuel occours because of heat developed in combustion prechamber. As a result, no spark plugs or high-voltage ignition system is required. For cold starts, glow plugs heat up combustion prechamber,

      (d) Vacuum pump driven by engine supplies shift signals to transmission.

   (2) **Transmission:**

      (a) GM Hydra-matic 400 automatic with neutral, reverse, and 3 forward gears.

      (b) Provides operator with a selection of gear ranges while holding engine speeds within effective torque range.

      (c) Includes a 3-element torque converter and a compound planetary gear set with clutches and bands controlled by hydraulic system.

   (3) **Transfer Case:**

      (a) All trucks, except M1028A1 , M1028A2, and Ml 031, are equipped with a New Process Model 238 transfer case.

      (b) M1028A1 , M1028A2, and M1031 are equipped with a New Process Model 205 transfer case, which is designed to accommodate installation of a power take-off (PTO) unit (uses engine power to run auxiliary equipment).

      (c) Directs engine-to-transmission power to rear wheels for two-wheel drive or to front and rear wheels for four-wheel drive.

      (d) Manually locking hubs must be set by hand to "LOCK" position before shifting from two-wheel to four-wheel drive operation.

      (e) Bolted directly to an adapter plate behind transmission. No intermediate propeller shaft needed.

   (4) **Propeller Shafts:**

      (a) Transmit driving force from transer case to front and rear axle differentials.

      (b) Slip joints are installed to compensate for varying lengths of propeller shafts.

      (c) Universal joints compensate for changes in drive angle of propeller shafts.

1-17.   FUEL SYSTEM.

a. Combines a low-pressure and a high-pressure fuel delivery system.

(1) Low-pressure fuel delivery system consists of:

(a) **Fuel Tank.**

(b) **Fuel (Lift) Pump.**   Driven by camshaft. Pulls fuel from fuel tank and sends it through fuel filter to injector pump.

(c) **Fuel Filter.**   Mounted on bulkhead. Removes sediments and water from fuel before it reaches injector pump.

(d) **Fuel Lines.**   Connects fuel tank to injector pump.

(2) High-pressure fuel delivery system consists of:

(a) **Stanadyne Model DB2**   Fuel Injector Pump. Delivers high-pressure fuel from injector pump to nozzles.

(b) **Nozzles.**   Provide high-pressure fuel to each cylinder.

b. Fuel return system delivers excess fuel from the injector pump and injector nozzles back to the truck's fuel tank. Fuel lines provide fuel to and from the fuel tank and injector pump.

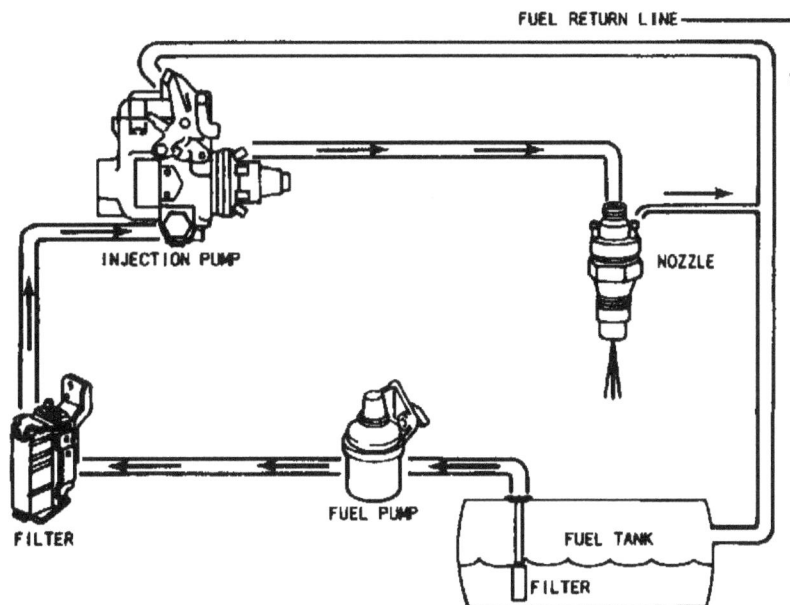

FUEL RETURN LINE

INJECTION PUMP

NOZZLE

FILTER

FUEL PUMP

FUEL TANK

FILTER

TA49521

1-18. COOLING SYSTEM.

a. **Cooling System.**   Engine is liquid-cooled by means of coolant flow through radiator and hoses.

b. **Thermostat.**   Located in coolant crossover pipe.   Designed to open and close at predetermined temperatures to supply correct engine operating temperature.

c. **Engine and Transmission Lubricating Oils.**   Temperature-controlled in separate coolers of radiator.

d. **Coolant Flow.**   The following illustration shows flow of coolant from radiator to engine.

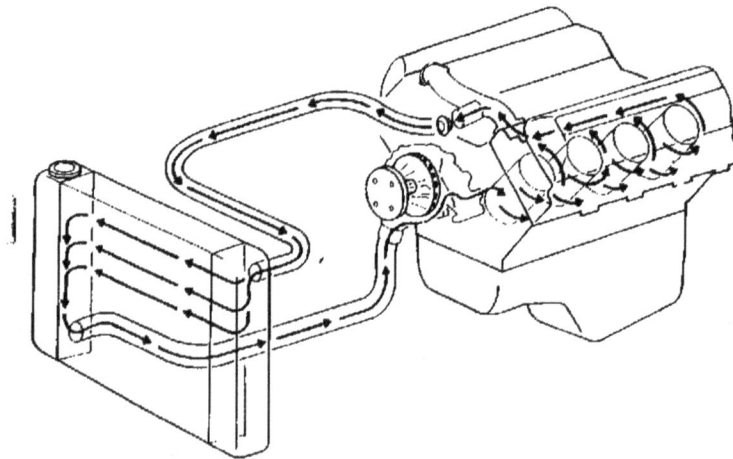

1-19. ELECTRICAL SYSTEM.

a. **28 v Charging System.**   Includes alternators and regulators to maintain a proper state of charge on both batteries.

b. **Standard System.**   100 amp, 12/24 v electrical system. includes two 12 v batteries (Delco 1200 or military-type 6TN) in series and two 100 amp alternators (Delco 27-S1).

c. **M1010 Ambulance and Selected M1028 System.**   200 amp, 12/24 v system, using 2 batteries (Delco 1200 or military-type 6TN) and 2 Leece/Neville alternators,

d. **Starting Motor.**   Heavy-duty 24 v 27MT starting motor, with increased strength pinion and ring gear teeth.

TA49622

e. Glow Plugs. Operate as part of electrical system and assist in engine starting in cold weather. Temperature self-regulating AC 13G glow plugs preheat air in precombustion chambers prior to combustion. Glow plugs are energized prior to engine cranking for a "pre-glow" period and remain on shortly after engine startup for an "after glow" period.

f. **L i g h t and Control Systems. Operate from 12 volts.**

(1) **Service Lights.** Standard vehicle lights, including headlights, taillights, turn indicators, and hazard warning.

(2) **Blackout Lights.** A military adaptation of the CUCV truck provides for driving during hours of limited visibility when service lights are not appropriate.

(3) **Toggle Switch.** Lights are controlled by 2 toggle switches on the instrument panel. When switches are in blackout mode, all exterior service lights, horn, taillights, stoplights, seat belt buzzer, and hazard warning flashers are inoperable while instrument panel warning signals remain functional.

(4) **M1010 Ambulance Lighting.** In addition to standard service and blackout lights:

(a) **Spotlight.** Mounted on top of operator's compartment; can be operated and directed from inside cab by a handle.

(b) **Floodlights.** Located on each side of ambulance body; can be adjusted to meet mission requirements.

(c) **Surgical Light.** Inside patient compartment provides overhead light.

(d) **Interior Focus Lights.** Provide direct light for specific medical applications.

(e) **Blackout Domelight.** Behind surgical light; provides overhead light in blackout situations.

1-20. CAB HEATING SYSTEM.

Standard Heater/Defroster System. Consists of blower and air inlet assembly, heater and defroster distributor assembly, and heater control assembly. Used to clear windshield of fog or ice and maintain a comfortable temperature level inside cab of truck. The system will maintain a temperature of 60°F (15°C) at floor level, at a -10°F (-23°C) ambient.

1-21. BRAKE SYSTEM.

a. Consists of parking brake and service brakes.

(1) **Parking Brake.** Able to hold truck, loaded to specified Gross Vehicle Weight Rating (GVWR), motionless on a 30% grade that is dry, hard, and free of loose material.

(2) **Service Brakes.** Hydraulically activated, power-assisted front disc and rear drum brakes.

b. The following schematic shows the major components of the system.

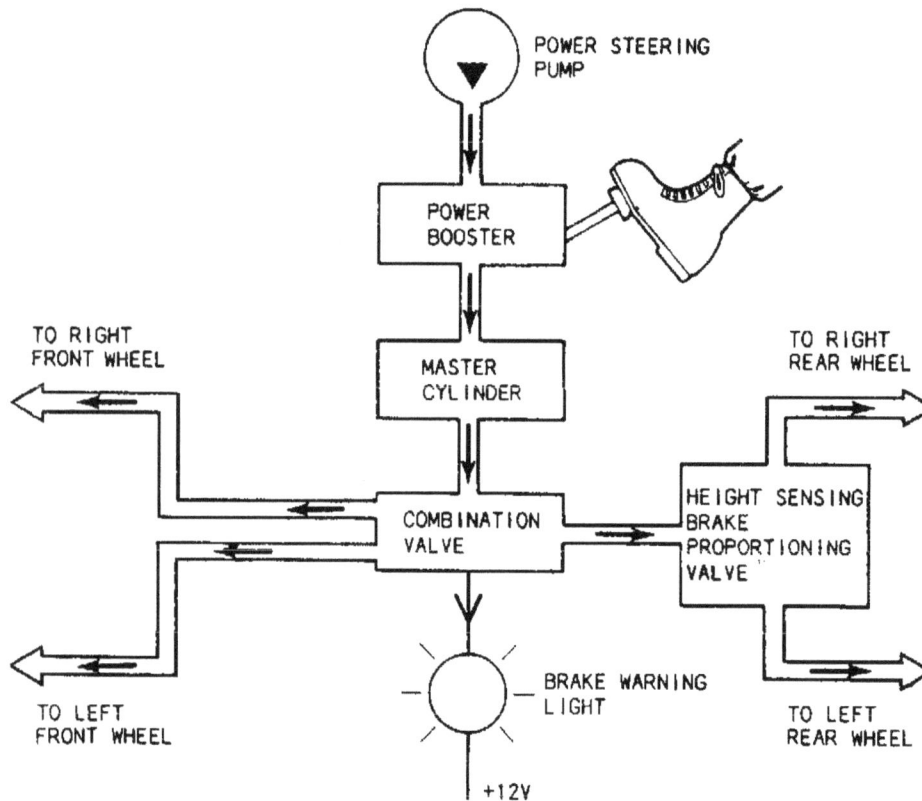

(1) **Power Steering Pump.** Supplies hydraulic power to the power booster.

(2) **Power Booster.** Transmits hydraulic power to the brake master cylinder.

(3) **Master Cylinder.** Sends hydraulic power to both front and rear brakes, from 1 of 2 chambers.

(4) **Brake Lines.** Carry hydraulic fluid from master cylinder to brake mechanisms at wheels.

TA49623

(5) **Combination Valve.** Performs 3 distinct functions:

    (a) Limits pressure to front disc brakes until a predetermined front input pressure is reached, which allows for the overcoming of the rear shoe retractor spring pressure.

    (b) Proportions outlet pressure to rear brakes after a predetermined rear input pressure has been reached.

    (c) A bypass feature assuring full system pressure to rear brakes in the event of front brake malfunction.

(6) **Height Sensing, Brake Proportioning Valve (All Except M1009).** Provides optimum brake balance and efficiency by distributing braking force to front and rear wheels as determined by payload.

1-22. STEERING SYSTEM.

a. Consists of the following major assemblies:

(1) **Steering Wheel, Column, Intermediate Shaft, and Coupling.** Mechanically activated by operator.

(2) **Power Steering Pump.** Runs continuously, supplying hydraulic power to power steering gear.

(3) **Power Stearing Gear.** Receives hydraulic power from power steering pump and mechanical force from driver through steering wheel, column, intermediate shaft, and coupling. Power steering gear can operate mechanically if hydraulic system failure occurs.

(4) **Steering Linkage.** Mechanical linkage between power steering gear and axle-mounted steering components.

(5) **Axle-mounted Steering Components.** Receive mechanical force from steering linkage to actually turn wheels.

b. The following illustration shows, in simplified form, how the steering system works.

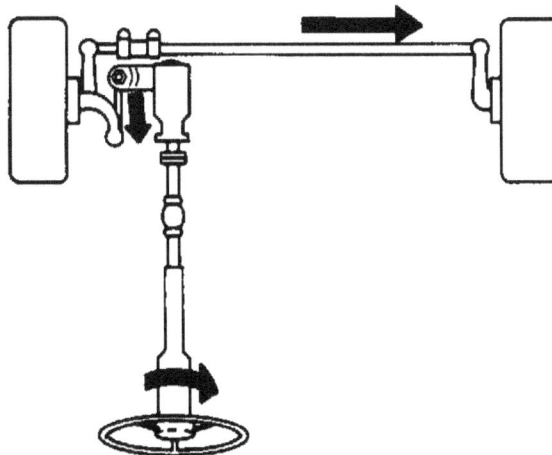

TA49624

1-23. SUSPENSION SYSTEM .

a. **Suspension System.**   Composed of springs, torsion bars, shock absorbers, axles, and wheels.

b. **Front Suspension.**   Features:

    (1) **Tapered-leaf Springs.**

    (2) **Front Stabilizer Bar.**

    (3) **Heavy-duty Shock Absorbers.**

c. **Rear Suspension.**   Features:

    (1) **3-stage Multileaf and Auxiliary Spring.**   M1028, M1028A1, and M1031 trucks.

    (2)   **2-stage Multileaf Springs.**   All other models.

    (3) **Heavy-duty Shock Absorbers.**

d. **Differentials.**   Provide equal traction to each wheel and, at the same time, permit each of them to run ahead or lag behind the other, as may be required, in rounding curves or riding over obstructions.

e. **Wheels and Tires.**

    (1) **All Except M1009.**   One-piece design, 16 in. x 6.50 in. wheels and LT235/85R-16E steel-belted radial blackwall tires.

    (2) **M1009.** One-piece design, 15 in. x 8 in. wheels and 10.00R-15C steel-belted radial blackwall tires.

1-24. WINTERIZATION KIT HEATERS.

a. **Winterization Kit Heaters.**   Available for CUCV Series trucks for severe cold weather areas. Three heaters are available for installation:

    (1) **Cab Heater (underhood).**   Heats batteries and cab.

    (2) **Engine Coolant Heater (underhood).**   Heats engine coolant. Exhaust from this heater heats engine and transmission oil.

    (3) **Cargo Compartment Heater (M1008 and M008A1 only).**   Heats insulated cargo enclosure of pickup box.

b. **Heater Control Panel.**   Located on right side of instrument panel and controls both underhood heaters.

c. **Cargo Compartment Heater Control Panel.**   Bracket-mounted to heater itself and controls only the cargo compartment heater.

1-25. AMBULANCE COMPONENTS.

a. **Air Conditioner.**   Provides cooling for the patient compartment allowing for a temperature of 77°F (25°C) to be maintained with full patient load plus attendant [at 30 mi/h and 125°F (52°C) outside ambient temperature after 1 hour).

b. **Air Conditioner Blower.** Provides ventilation using outside air when conditions do not warrant the use of the air conditioner.

c. **Air Conditioner Control Panel.** Located inside patient compartment above patient compartment front door. Allows attendant to vary the temperature and function of the air conditioner.

d. **Personnel Heater.** Provides heated air to patient compartment during periods of cold temperatures. Basic heater is the same heater used for warm air function in a winterized truck. After 1 hour of operation, 70°F can be maintained in ambient temperatures down to -50 °F (-46°C).

e. **Personnel Heater Control Panel.** Located under lower right side litter berth and controls the functioning of the heater,

f. **Gas-Particulate Filter Unit (GPFU) System.** In an NBC environment, provides each crew and patient station with clean, filtered, breathable air that is heated (if needed) to a comfortable temperature and free of toxic agents. The protective mask and filter will NOT protect against carbon monoxide.

1-26. DUAL WHEEL CONFIGURATION.

a. M1028A2 and M1028A3 are shelter carriers converted to dual rear wheels. This provides greater load carrying capability and increased stability,

b. Axles are heavier and dual wheels spread loads more evenly.

CHAPTER 2
SERVICE AND TROUBLESHOOTING INSTRUCTIONS

Section I. SERVICE UPON RECEIPT OF MATERIAL

2-1.   GENERAL.

Upon receipt of a new truck, it must be determined whether the truck has been properly prepared for service. Follow the inspection instructions found in paragraph 2-2. Read the servicing instructions found in paragraph 2-3 and follow any that apply to the truck to be serviced. See TM 9-2320-289-10 when checking equipment for proper operation. Before conducting the inspections and services listed below, perform the following preliminary servicing:

WARNING

Dry cleaning solvent P-D-680 is toxic and flammable. Always wear protective goggles and gloves and use only in a well-ventilated area. Avoid contact with skin, eyes, and clothes and DO NOT breathe vapors. DO NOT use near open flame or excessive heat. The solvent's flash point is 100°F-138°F (38°C-59°C). If you become dizzy while using cleaning solvent, immediately get fresh air and medical help. If solvent contacts eyes, immediately wash your eyes with water and get medical aid.

a. Use dry cleaning solvent (Item 15, Appendix C) to clean all exterior surfaces coated with rust-preventive compounds. Remove all protective materials used on the   truck during shipment,

b. Remove all tape and wrappings from the engine, crankcase   breathers, intake and exhaust openings, transmission, alternator, and brakes.

c. Remove wrappings from all machined surfaces.

2-2.   INSPECTION INSTRUCTIONS.

a. Perform the semiannual preventive maintenance checks and services listed in Section II of this chapter.

b. Make a complete visual inspection of the truck to see that the required publications, Basic Issue Items (BII), and accessories are present.

2-3.   SERVICING INSTRUCTIONS UPON RECEIPT.

a. If any truck system does not operate properly, refer to the troubleshooting instructions found in Section III of this chapter.

b. Schedule semiannual service on DD Form 314,   *Preventive Maintenance Schedule and Report Card.*

      c. Replace any missing or damaged components if authorized by the *Maintenance Allocation* Chart *(MAC)* in Appendix B. If not authorized to replace a damaged or missing component, notify your supervisor.

      d. Lubricate the truck and change/adjust fluids in accordance with LO 9-2320-289-12 and PMCS in Section II of this chapter .

      e. Make a final, complete inspection of the entire truck.

CHAPTER 2
SERVICE AND TROUBLESHOOTING INSTRUCTIONS

Section I. REPAIR PARTS, SPECIAL TOOLS, TEST, MEASUREMENT, AND DIAGNOSTIC EQUIPMENT (TMDE), AND SUPPORT EQUIPMENT

2-1. COMMON TOOLS AND EQUIPMENT

For authorized common tools and equipment, refer to the Modified Table of Organization and Equipment (MTOE) applicable to your unit.

2-2. SPECIAL TOOLS, TMDE, AND SUPPORT EQUIPMENT

Special Tools, Test, Measurement, and Diagnostic Equipment (TMDE), and Support Equipment used to maintain the vehicles covered in this manual can be found in TM 9-2320-289-20P.

2-3. REPAIR PARTS

Repair parts are listed and illustrated in TM 9-2320-289-20P.

Section II. SERVICE UPON   RECEIPT

2-4. GENERAL

a. Upon receipt of a new, used, or reconditioned vehicle, you must determine if the vehicle has been properly prepared for service. The following steps should be followed:

(1) Inspect all assemblies, subassemblies, and accessories to be sure they are in proper working order.

(2) Secure, clean, lubricate, or adjust as needed.

(3) Check all Basic Issue Items (TM 9-2320 -289-10) to be sure every item is present, in good condition, and properly mounted, or stowed.

(4) Follow general procedures for all services and inspections given in TM 9-2320-289-10.

b. The operator will assist when performing service upon receipt inspections.

c. See TM 9-2320-289-10 when checking equipment for proper operation.

d. Refer to TM 9-2320-289-10 for information concerning brake-in procedures.

2-5. GENERAL INSPECTION AND SERVICING INSTRUCTIONS

The following steps should be taken while performing general inspection and services:

(1) Use TM 9-2320-289-10 as well as other sections of this manual, when servicing and inspecting equipment.

WARNING

Drycleaning solvent is flammable and will not be used near an open flame. A fire extinguisher will be kept nearby when the solvent is used. Use only in well-ventilated places. Failure to do this may result in injury to personnel and/or damage to equipment.

(2) Clean all exterior surfaces coated with rust-preventive compounds. Use drycleaning solvent (Appendix C, Item 15).

(3) Clean fittings before lubrication. Clean parts with drycleaning solvent (SD), Type II, or equivalent. Dry before lubricating. Dotted arrow points indicate lubrication on both sides of equipment. A dotted circle indicates a drain below. Relubricate all items found contaminated after fording.

(4) Read "Processing and Reprocessing Record of Shipping, Storage, and Issue of Vehicles and Spare Engines," tag (DD Form 1397) and follow all precautions listed. This tag should be attached to steering wheel, steering column, or rotary switch.

2-6. SPECIFIC INSPECTION AND SERVICING INSTRUCTIONS

The following steps should be taken while performing specific inspections and services:

(1) Do the Semiannual (S) preventive maintenance checks and services listed in Section III in this chapter.

(2) Lubricate the vehicle. Do not lubricate gear cases and engine unless processing tab states that the oil is unsuitable for 500 miles (805 km) operation. If oil is suitable, just check level.

(3) Schedule semiannual service on DD Form 314 (Preventive Maintenance Schedule and Record Card).

(4) If vehicle is delivered with a dry charged battery, activate it according to TM 9-6140-200-14.

(5) Check vehicle coolant level and determine if solution is proper for climate (refer to TB 750-651 for preparation of antifreeze solutions).

Section III. PREVENTIVE MAINTENANCE CHECKS AND SERVICES

2-7. GENERAL

The best way to maintain vehicles covered by this manual is to inspect them on a regular basis so minor faults can be discovered and corrected before they result in serious damage, failure, or injury. All intervals are based on normal operation. Hard time intervals maybe shortened if your lubricants are contaminated or if you are operating the equipment under adverse conditions, including longer-than-usual operating hours. Hard time intervals may be extended during periods of low activity, though adequate preservation precautions must be taken. This section contains systematic instructions of inspection, adjustment, lubrication, and correction of vehicle components to avoid costly repairs or major breakdowns. This is Preventive Maintenance Checks and Services (PMCS).

2-8. INTERVALS

a. Unit maintenance, assisted by operator/crew, will perform checks and services contained in Table 2-1 at the following intervals:

(1) Semiannually (S). Every 6 months or 6,000 miles (9,654 km), whichever comes first.

(2) Annually (A). Every 12 months or 12,000 miles (19,308 km), whichever comes first.

(3) Biennially (B). Every 24 months or 24,000 miles (38,615 km), whichever comes first.

b. Refer to the following steps when performing lubrication checks and services:

(1) Intervals. Lubrication services coincide with the vehicle's Semiannual (S) Preventive Maintenance Service. For this purpose, a 10% tolerance (variation) in specified lubrication point mileage is permissible. Those vehicles not accumulating 1,000 miles (1,609 km) in a 6-month period will be lubricated at the time of (S) Preventive Maintenance Service.

(2) Army Oil Analysis Program (AOAP). AOAP does not apply to CUCV series vehicles.

(3) For Operation of Equipment in Protracted Cold Temperatures Below -15 °F. (-26 °C). Remove lubricants prescribed in lubrication table for temperatures above -15°F(-26°C). Relubricate with lubricants specified in lubrication table for temperatures below -15°F (-26°C). If OEA lubricant is required to meet the temperature ranges prescribed in the lubrication table. OEA lubricant is to be used in place of OE/HDO 10 lubricant for all temperature ranges where OE/HDO 10 is specified in the lubrication table.

c. Perform all (S) inspections in addition to(A) inspections at the time of the annual inspection. Perform all (A) and (S) inspections in addition to (B) inspections at the time of the biennial inspection.

2-9. REPORTING REPAIRS

All vehicle shortcomings will be reported on DA form 2404 (DA Pam 738-750), Equipment Inspection and Maintenance Worksheet, immediately after the PMCS, and before taking corrective action. All vehicle deficiencies will be reported in the equipment record.

2-10. GENERAL SERVICE AND INSPECTION PROCEDURES

a. While performing specific PMCS procedures, make sure items are correctly assembled, secure, not worn, serviceable, not leaking, and adequately lubricated as defined below.

(1) An item is CORRECTLY ASSEMBLED when it is in proper position and all parts are present.

(2) When wires, nuts, washers, hoses, or attaching hardware cannot be moved by hand, or wrench, they are SECURE.

(3) An item is WORN if there is too much play between joining parts or when marking data, warning, and caution plates are not readable.

(4) An item is UNSERVICEABLE if it is worn beyond repair and is likely to fail before the next scheduled inspection.

(5) LEAKS. TM 9-2320-289-10 contains definitions of Class I, II, and III leaks and their effect on vehicle operation.

(6) If an item meets the specified lubrication requirements, then it is ADEQUATELY LUBRICATED.

b. Where the instruction "lighten" appears in a procedure, you must tighten with a wrench to the given torque value even when the item appears to be secure.

WARNING

Drycleaning solvent is inflammable and will not be used near an open flame. A fire extinguisher will be kept nearby when the solvent is used. Use only in well-ventilated places. Failure to do this may result in injury to personnel, and/or damage to equipment.

c. Where the instruction "clean" appears in a procedure, you must use drycleaning solvent (Appendix C, Item 15) to clean grease or oil from metal parts. After the item is cleaned, rinsed, and dried, apply a light grade of oil to unprotected surfaces to prevent rusting.

d. Clean rubber and plastic materials with soap and water. Refer to TM 9-2320-289-10 for general vehicle cleaning instructions.

2-11. SPECIFIC PMCS PROCEDURES

a. The preventive maintenance for which you are responsible is provided in Table 2-1. The checks and services listed are arranged in logical order requiring minimal time and effort on your part.

b. The following columns read across on the PMCS schedule:

(1) Item Number. Provides logical order of PMCS performance and is used as a source number for DA Form 2404, on which your PMCS results will be recorded.

(2) Intervals. Shows the interval next to each item number to indicate when that check is to be performed. The interval will be repeated when consecutive item numbers are to be inspected during the same interval. Interval columns include:

(a) Semiannual (six month) checks;
(b) Annual (yearly) checks; and
(c) Biennial (every two years) checks.

(3) Item To Be Inspected. Lists the system, common name, or location of the item to be inspected.

(4) Procedures. Provides instructions for servicing, inspection, lubrication, replacement, or adjustment, and in some cases, having item repaired at a higher level.

NOTE

Always do your preventive maintenance checks and services in the order prepared. Once it gets to be a habit, you will be able to spot anything wrong in a hurry.

(5) Not Fully Mission Capable. If vehicle meets criteria in this column, vehicle is not mission capable (NMC).

Table 2-1. Unit Level Preventive Maintenance Checks and Services for CUCV

Item No.	Interval	Item To Be Inspected	Procedure	Not Mission Capable If:
1	Semi-Annual	PreService Checks	**BEFORE ROAD TEST** Ensure Operator/Crew has performed -10 PMCS listed in TM 9-2320-289-10. **NOTE** Fuse box is located on driver's side of cab under instrument panel. a. Check fuses, flashers, and switches for looseness and damage. If loose or damaged, tighten or replace as required. b. Check fire extinguisher (on trucks authorized to contain fire extinguishers) for serviceability in accordance with label on fire extinguisher. **ROAD TEST** Maintenance personnel will be with vehicle operator to verify pre-service checks. For road test, vehicle will be driven at least five miles over different ground to give enough time to detect any malfunctions. c. For M1009 and M1010, check seat locking mechanism for proper operation. d. Notice if starter engages smoothly and turns the engine at normal cranking speed. e. Listen for unusual engine noise at idle, at operating speeds, and under acceleration. Be alert for excessive vibration, the smell of oil, fuel, or any exhaust noises.	 b. Fire extinguisher damaged, seal broken or missing, gage in recharge area. c. Seat locking mechanism does not operate properly. d. Starter inoperative or makes excessive grinding sound. e. Engine knocks, rattles, smokes excessively, or any exhaust noise.

Table 2-1. Unit Level Preventive Maintenance Checks And Services for CUCV

Item No.	Interval	Item To Be Inspected	Procedure	Not Mission Capable If:
1	Semi-Annual	PreService Checks Continued	f. Check for transmission response to shifting and for smoothness of operation in all speed ranges. Be alert for unusual noises and difficulty in shifting in any speed range.	f. Transmission shifts improperly, does not shift or makes excessive noise.
			NOTE Lock front wheel hubs before checking transfer (see TM 9-2320-289-10).	
			g. Check for transfer response to shifting and for smoothness of operation in all gear ranges. Be alert for unusual noises and difficulty in shifting in any gear range.	g. Transfer jumps out of gear or makes excessive noise.
			h. Test for response to accelerator feed. Observe for sticking pedal.	h. Pedal sticking or binding.
			i. With vehicle speed approximately 5 mph (8 kph) turn steering wheel to left, then right, to detect hard steering, binding or excessive play. Play should not exceed 1 inch (25.4 mm) in either direction. With vehicle on straight, level terrain, lightly hold steering wheel to detect pull or wander.	i. Steering binds, grabs, wanders, or has excessive play.
			j. Apply brake pedal with steady force. Vehicle should slow and stop without pulling to one side or jerking. Release brake pedal. The brakes should release immediately and without difficulty.	j. Brakes chatter, pull to one side, or inoperative. Brakes will not release.
			k. Bring vehicle to a full stop. Engage parking brake while transmission is still in "D" (DRIVE). Vehicle should remain stationary.	k. Parking brake does not hold vehicle stationary.
			l. Observe vehicle response to road shock. Side sway, or continuous bouncing indicates a malfunction.	l. Handling is unstable.

Table 2-1. Unit Level Preventive Maintenance Checks and Services for CUCV

Item No.	Interval	Item To Be inspected	Procedure	Not Mission Capable If:
1	Semi-Annual	Cooling System	**AFTER ROAD TEST** a. Make sure the vehicle has been cleaned of mud, gravel, etc, from the underbody, outside and crew compartment area. **ENGINE COMPARTMENT** a. Inspect all hoses and fittings for deterioration. Inspect radiator probe and draincock for security of mounting. b. Inspect engine oil cooler lines and fittings, and transmission oil cooler lines and fittings for leaks and damage. Tighten any loose fittings. Pay special attention to areas where hoses or lines contact or may come close to contacting other components. These areas may be prone to damage. Notify your supervisor if any transmission or engine oil cooler lines are damaged or are leaking.	a. Any Class III water leak. Hoses cracked or dry rotted. b. Any damage that will prevent operation.

TRANSMISSION OIL COOLER LINES AND FITTINGS

ENGINE OIL COOLER LINES AND FITTINGS

Table 2-1. Unit Level Preventive Maintenance Checks And Services for CUCV

Item No.	Interval	Item To Be Inspected	Procedure	Not Mission Capable If:
1	Semi-Annual	Cooling System Continued	**WARNING** **If vehicle has been operating, use extreme care to avoid being burned when removing cooling system radiator cap. Use heavy rags or gloves to protect hands. Turn radiator cap only one-half turn counter-clockwise and allow pressure to be relieved before fully removing cap.** c. Test coolant (see TB 750-651).	
2	Semi-Annual	Drive Belts	a. Check for missing, broken, cracked, and frayed drivebelts. b. Check drive belts for proper adjustment using belt tensioning gage. If loose, adjust tension as required. ALT P.S. A/C NEW 146 lb. 146 lb. 169 lb. OLD 67 lb. 67 lb. 67 lb. If replacing belt, adjust to new specification and run engine for 15 minutes and readjust to old specifications (see Appendix E).	a. Any drivebelt is missing or broken. Belt fiber has more than one crack 1/8 inch in depth or 50% of belt thickness or has frays more than 2 inches long.

Table 2-1. Unit Level Preventive Maintenance Checks and Services for CUCV

Item No.	Interval	Item To Be Inspected	Procedure	Not Mission Capable If:
3	Semi-Annual	Batteries	**WARNING** Battery acid (electrolyte) is extremely dangerous. Always wear goggles and rubber gloves when performing battery checks or inspections. Serious injury to personnel will result if battery acid contacts skin or eyes. DO NOT perform battery system checks or inspections while smoking or near fire, flame, or sparks. Batteries may explode, causing serious injury or death to personnel. Rotate cover to underside of clamp as each cable is disconnected. Remove all jewelry such as dog tags, rings, bracelets, etc. If jewelry or disconnected battery ground cable contacts battery terminal, a direct short will result in serious injury or death to personnel or equipment damage. a. Check battery charge indicators on maintenance free batteries or specific gravity on non-maintenance free batteries (see TM 9-6140-200-14). Notify your supervisor if non-maintenance free batteries require servicing. b. Inspect battery cables for frays, splits, and tightness. c. Clean battery terminals and lightly coat with grease (Item 26, Appendix C).	b. Any damage that will prevent operation.

BATTERY CHARGER INDICATORS

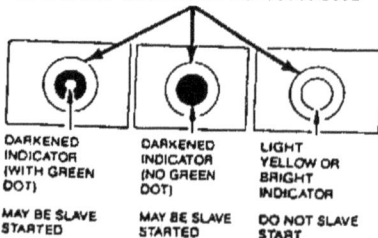

DARKENED INDICATOR (WITH GREEN DOT)

MAY BE SLAVE STARTED

DARKENED INDICATOR (NO GREEN DOT)

MAY BE SLAVE STARTED

LIGHT YELLOW OR BRIGHT INDICATOR

DO NOT SLAVE START

BATTERY TERMINALS

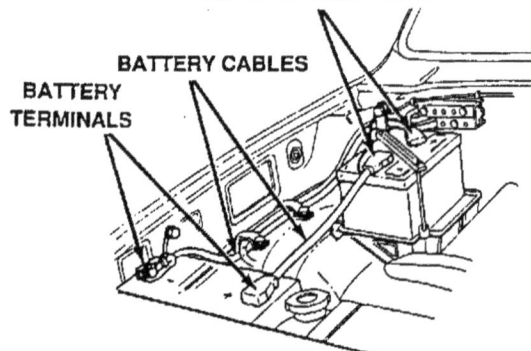

BATTERY CABLES

BATTERY TERMINALS

Table 2-1. Unit Level Preventive Maintenance Checks And Services for CUCV

tern No.	Interval	Item To Be Inspected	Procedure	Not Mission Capable If:
4	Semi-Annual	Steering System	**NOTE** If there is Loctite on bolts, DO NOT tighten without reapplying Loctite (Item 30, Appendix C). a. Inspect power steering pump and power steering gear for dents, cracks, leaks, and mounting security. Check fluid level. Fill as needed with Dexron II. If loose, tighten power steering pump bolts to 30 ft lbs, and/or steering gear to frame bolts to 75 ft lbs. b. Check power steering hoses for leakage and loose clamps and brackets.	a. Any mount bolt missing or unserviceable. Any Class III leak. b. Any Class III leak or loose clamp.
5	Semi-Annual	Alternator	Inspect alternators for security for security of mounting.	Mounting bolts loose or missing.
6	Semi-Annual	Fuel System	a. Inspect fuel pump and fittings for leaks. b. Inspect injector pump, injectors, and fittings for leaks. c. Inspect inlet and outlet lines for leaks, connections, cracks, splits, or wear. d. Inspect accelerator linkage for looseness, kinks, or damage.	a. Any Class III fuel leak. b. Rubber cap missing or damaged. Any Class III fuel leak. c. Any Class III fuel leak.

INJECTOR PUMP

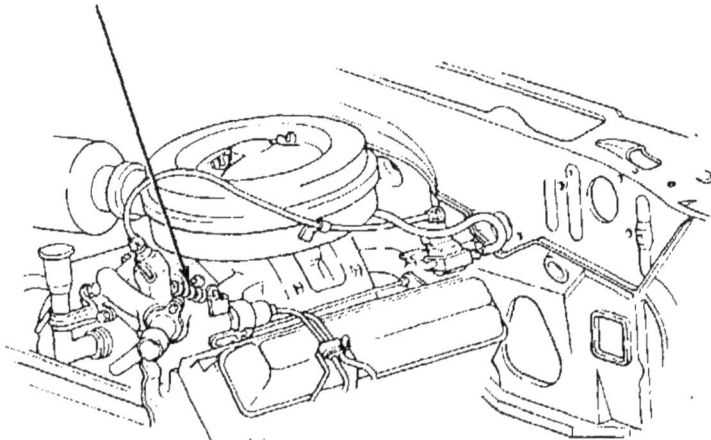

Table 2-1. Unit Level Preventive Maintenance Checks and Services for CUCV

Item No.	Interval	Item To Be Inspected	Procedure	Not Mission Capable If:
7	Semi-Annual	Air Intake System	a. Inspect air cleaner, hoses, and tubing for improper installation, cracks, breaks, and connections that could allow unfiltered air to enter engine. Inspect air filter element for restrictions. b. If vehicle is operating under unusual dust/dirt conditions, change element more frequently. Air filter element is normally changed annually or 12,000 miles.	a. Any damage that would allow unfiltered air to enter engine.
8	Semi-Annual	Electrical Wiring	a. Disconnect each glow plug lead and check for resistance between glow plug terminal and ground. Resistance should be 1-3 ohms. Check glow plugs for looseness or damage. Tighten glow plugs to 10 ft-lbs (14 N.m). b. Inspect all engine compartment wiring for frays, splits, missing insulation, or poor connections.	a. Replace any failed glow plug. b. Wiring frayed, broken, or loose connections.

Table 2-1. Unit Level Preventive Maintenance Checks And Services for CUCV

	Interval	Item To Be Inspected	Procedure	Not Mission Capable If:
9	Semi-Annual	Master Cylinder	a. Check brake fluid level in master cylinder. Maintain fluid level at 1/4 inch below lowest edge of each chamber. Fill with BFS (Brake Fluid Silicone) only. b. Inspect master cylinder, Hydrobooster lines, and fittings for leaks and damage. Tighten loose fittings or replace damaged components. MASTER CYLINDER 	b. Brake fluid low. Any brake fluid leakage.
10	Semi-Annual	Windshield Wiper System	a. Inspect wiper motor, hoses, nozzles, and bottle for security of mounting, restrictions, and damage. b. Check windshield wiper arms and linkage for excessive play, binding or damage.	
11	Semi-Annual	Cab Heater	Inspect heater case for wear, cracks, and security of mounting.	
12	Semi-Annual	Engine Lubrication System	**NOTE** Foamy or milky oil or rust on engine oil dipstick are evidence of contamination. a. Inspect engine dipstick for evidence of contamination.	

Table 2-1. Unit Level Preventive Maintenance Checks and Services for CUCV

Item No.	Interval	Item To Be Inspected	Procedure	Not Mission Capable If:
12	Semi-Annual	Engine Lubrication System Continued	b. Change engine oil and filter semi-annually or at 6,000 miles. When operating under unusual conditions, change the oil and filter at 3 months or 3,000 miles. Refer to paragraph 3-1 for oil and filter change instructions. Crankcase capacity is 7 quarts with filter. c. Inspect oil filter for leaks. d. Inspect valve covers for evidence of leaks. If there are any leaks, notify your supervisor. e. Inspect engine front covers for evidence of leaks. If there are any leaks, notify your supervisor. f. Inspect oil filler cap vent for build-up of sand, dirt, and other foreign material that may keep oil filler cap vent valve in an open position. If condition exists, remove oil filler cap, clean and shake to listen for rattling sound. if cap rattles, install. If cap does not rattle, replace.	
13	Semi-Annual	Transmission Fluid and Fill Tube	**CAUTION** **DO NOT remove transmission dipstick before cleaning dirt away from fill tube and transmission dipstick. Dirt could enter and damage transmission.** **NOTE** Foamy or milky oil or rust on transmission dipstick are evidence of contamination. a. Inspect transmission dipstick and fluid for evidence of contamination. If there is contamination, notify your supervisor and service transmission (see paragraph 5-2). b. Inspect fill tube for security of mounting and damage.	

Table 2-1. Unit Level Preventive Maintenance Checks and Services for CUCV

Item No.	Interval	Item To Be Inspected	Procedure	Not Mission Capable If:
14	Semi-Annual	Tow Pintle	**EXTERIOR OF TRUCK** Check operation and lubricate fitting and moving parts with GAA.	
14.1	Semi-Annual	Seatbelts	**INTERIOR OF CAB** Inspect lower left (driver's) side and lower right (passenger's) side mounting post pillars where seatbelt is attached for rusted conditions.	Any indication of rust. (See paragraph 10-23A.)
15	Semi-Annual	Body Exterior	**AMBULANCE BODY** Check for presence and security of Red Cross decals and clips.	
16	Semi-Annual	Relay Panel	Check for proper installation of and damage to fuses, relays, and cables. Inspect mounting screws, rivets for looseness or damage.	
17	Semi-Annual	Air Conditioner	a. Inspect air conditioner assembly and evaporator blower for proper installation and damage. **NOTE** Water condensation is normal on condenser coils. b. Inspect air conditioning lines and condenser coils for looseness, refrigerant leaks, or damage.	
18	Semi-Annual	Troop Seat Kit	**SPECIAL PURPOSE KITS** Inspect for operation of, and damage to all components. Check for proper installation of hinge pins and clamps. Check for proper installation of troop seat slats and stakes in cargo body sockets.	

Table 2-1. Unit Level Preventive Maintenance Checks and Services for CUCV

Item No.	Interval	Item To Be Inspected	Procedure	Not Mission Capable If:
19	Semi-Annual	Winterization Kits	Check hood, cab, and cargo body insulation for proper installation. Check heaters for proper operation, security of mounting, and damage.	
20	Semi-Annual	Tires	**WARNING** **Use extreme caution when lowering or raisng spare tire and carrier during 5 tire rotation for all except M1009. Dropping It may result In serious injury to personnel.** **NOTE** In case of unusual tire wear, the tire manufacturer recommends 2 optional methods for all except M1028A2 and M1028A3: 5 tire rotation and cross rotation. Before performing either of the optional methods, notify your supervisor. a. Rotate tires as follows for all except M1028A2 and M1028A3:	

(front)   (front)   (front)

Table 2-1. Unit Level Preventive Maintenance Checks And Services for CUCV

tern No.	Interval	Item To Be Inspected	Procedure	Not Mission Capable If:
20	Semi-Annual	Tires Continued	(1) Loosen lugnuts on left side wheels. Raise truck and remove left side tires (see paragraph 8-2). Position front tire on rear wheel hub and rear tire on front wheel hub, and finger tighten lugnuts. Lower truck and fully tighten lugnuts (see paragraph 8-2). (2) Repeat previous steps for right side tires. b. Rotate tires as follows for M1028A2 and M1028A3 only: (front) (front) NORMAL ROTATION OPTIONAL ROTATION M1028A2 (1) Loosen lugnuts on left side wheels. Raise truck and remove left side tires (see paragraph 8-2). Position rear outer tire on rear inner hub, front tire on rear outer hub, and rear inner tire on front hub and finger tighten lugnuts. Lower truck and fully tighten lugnuts (see paragraph 8-2). (2) Repeat previous steps for right side tires. c. Ensure all wheel lugnuts are present and tightened to 90 lbs. for M1009 and 140 lbs. for all except M1009.	 c. Any broken stud or missing lugnut.

Table 2-1. Unit Level Preventive Maintenance Checks and Services for CUCV

tern No.	Interval	Item To Be Inspected	Procedure	Not Mission Capable If:
21	Semi-Annual	Brakes	**UNDER SIDE OF TRUCK** Check brake lines, calipers, and hydraulic fittings for looseness, damage, or leakage. Check backing plates for indication of leakage from wheel cylinders or inner hub seals.	Any leak. Broken or damaged lines and fittings.
22	Semi-Annual	Park Brake Cable Guides and Pedal Spring	a. Lubricate the hook shaped park brake cable guide (located on the inside of the frame, driver's side, forward of the parking brake equalizer). Lubricate with GAA. b. Check cables, clips, and guide for adjustment and damage. c. Lubricate the service brake pedal spring located at the upper end of the foot pedal assembly. Lubricate with GAA.	b. Cable frayed or broken. Guide or clip missing.
23	Semi-Annual	Engine Underside	a. Inspect underside of engine for leaks. b. Inspect oil pan and pan drainplug for leaks and security. If oil pan mounting screws are loose tighten to 5 ft lbs. If drainplug is loose, tighten to 15-20 lb ft. c. Inspect attaching components for leaks, breaks, dents, and completeness of assembly.	c. Any damage that may prevent operation.

Table 2-1. Unit Level Preventive Maintenance Checks And Services for CUCV

Item No.	Interval	Item To Be Inspected	Procedure	Not Mission Capable If:
24	Semi-Annual	Steering System	a. Inspect tie-rod shock absorber for worn bushings, loose nuts, or leaks. b. Inspect pitman arm connecting rod, steering knuckles, and tie rod assemblies for cracks, breaks, mounting security, and deterioration of dust covers. If tie-rod socket moves on ball stud .015" (0.4m) replace tie rod end. c. Check for presence of steering stops, Check for presence of cotter pins on all mounting nuts. If cotter pins are missing, tighten pitman arm nut to 95 ft-lb, connecting rod nuts to 75 ft-lb, or tie rod mounting nuts to 40 ft-lbs as required, Install new cotter pins as required. d. If vehicle is being driven off road, in dust or mud, lubricate tie rod ends, connecting rods, and kingpins at fittings with GAA.	a. Any damage that will prevent operation. b. Tie rods, pitman arm, connecting rod worn or damaged.
25	Semi-Annual	Transmission	a. Inspect transmission case for loose bolts and leaks. If mounting bolts are loose, tighten to 80 ft-lb (108 N.m). b. Inspect transmission shift linkage for bends, excessive play and wear. Notify supervisor if any of these conditions exist. c. Check transmission oil pan bolts for looseness. If loose, tighten to 125-160 in.lb (14-18 N.m).	b. Shift linkage unserviceable.
26	Semi-Annual	Transfer	a. Inspect transfer case for loose bolts and leaks. If mounting bolts are loose, tighten to 30 ft-lb (41 N.m). b. Inspect shift linkage for cracks, bends, wear, and play. c. Ensure that fillplug and drainplug are secure. If drainplug is loose, tighten to 30-40 ft-lb (41-54 N.m).	a. Class III leak. Loose bolts. b. Shift linkage unserviceable. c. Class III leak.

Table 2-1. Unit Level Preventive Maintenance Checks and Services for CUCV

Item No.	Interval	Item To Be Inspected	Procedure	Not Mission Capable If:
27	Semi-Annual	Propeller Shafts	a. Inspect all propeller shafts for bends and cracks. b. inspect universal joints for wear and play. There should be no play at universal joints. c. Ensure that all companion flange mounting screws and universal joint mounting screws are tight. If loose, tighten to 15 ft-lb (20 N.m). If straps are retained with 6 lobe bolts, tighten to 25 ft-lb (34 N.m).	b. "U-joint is unserviceable. c. Missing or broken bolts.
28	Semi-Annual	Axles and Differentials	a. Inspect axle housings for security of mounting, cracks, and leaks. b. Ensure that axle breather vents are free of debris and are operative. Ensure that fill plugs are present and secure. c. Inspect differential covers for leaks.	a. Class III leak, Cracks and loose mounting bolts. b. Vent plugged. c. Class III leak.

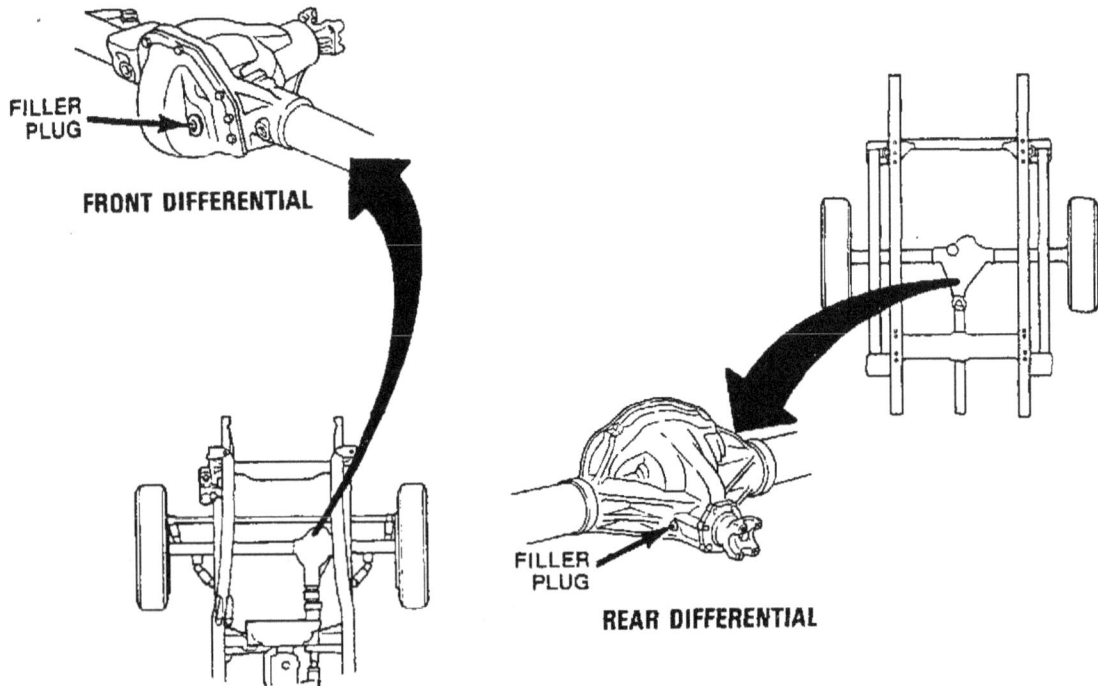

FILLER PLUG

FRONT DIFFERENTIAL

FILLER PLUG

REAR DIFFERENTIAL

Table 2-1. Unit Level Preventive Maintenance Checks And Services for CUCV

Item No.	Interval	Item To Be Inspected	Procedure	Not Mission Capable If:
29	Semi-Annual	Fuel System	a. Inspect fuel tank for leaks. Inspect all attaching hoses for wear, cracks, and splits. b. Inspect all fuel lines for leaks, loose connections, and crimps.	a. Any Class III fuel leak. b. Any Class III fuel leak.
30	Semi-Annual	Suspension	Inspect spring "U" bolts for mounting security. Tighten loose "U" bolt nuts to 40 ft-lb (54 N.m) in an "X" pattern. Tighten again in same pattern to 150 ft-lb (203 N.m) for front springs and to 145 ft-lbs for rear springs.	
31	Semi-Annual	Body, Frame, and Crossmembers	a. Inspect body, frame, and crossmembers for rust-through, discolored surface, blistered paint, surface separation, or other evidence of corrosion damage. If any corrosion damage exists, prepare corroded surfaces IAW TM 9-247, and treat surface IAW TB 43-0213. b. Inspect truck's main frame rails for cracks, breaks, and bends. c. Inspect crossmembers for breaks, bends, and loose or missing rivets or bolts d. Inspect body mounts and wheel housings for security and damage. e. For M1009 with additional engine mounting holes, inspect for cracks at additional engine mounting holes. f. For all except M1009, inspect cargo body mounting bolts for looseness. If loose, tighten to 50 ft-lbs (68 N.m).	b. Cracks, bends, breaks in frame. c. Any loose or missing fasteners.

Table 2-1. Unit Level Preventive Maintenance Checks and Services for CUCV

Item No.	Interval	Item To Be Inspected	Procedure	Not Mission Capable If:
1.	Annual	Cooling System	**NOTE** Perform all checks in Table 2-1 Preventive Maintenance Checks and Services, Semiannual Schedule, then perform the following inspections in the order given. **ENGINE COMPARTMENT** a. Check radiator for damage or leaks. b. Inspect radiator fan shroud for security of mounting and cracks. c, Inspect water pump, and water pump plug and nipple for leaks and security of mounting. Inspect fan clutch for security of mounting.	a. Any Class III fuel leaks. b. Fan blades or any pulley broken, cracked, or loose.
2	Annual	Engine	Inspect crankcase depression regulator valve (CDRV) and hoses for leaks, cracks, dirt, and clogs.	
3	Annual	Fuel System	Replace fuel filter (see paragraph 3-1 7).	
4	Annual	Air Filter	Replace filter element annually or 12,000 miles.	

Table 2-1. Unit Level Preventive Maintenance Checks And Services for CUCV

No.	Interval	Item To Be inspected	Procedure	Not Mission Capable If:
5	Annual	Brakes	**UNDERSIDE OF TRUCK** **WARNING** **DO NOT use a dry brush or compressed air to clean brake shoes, brake pads, or brake components. There may be asbestos dust on brake shoes, brake pads, and brake components which can be dangerous to you if you breathe it. Brake shoes, brake pads, and brake components must be wet, and a soft brush must be used. Failure to follow this warning may result in serious illness or death to personnel.** **NOTE** M1009 brake shoes are factory installed with bonded linings instead of riveted linings. Lining should not be less than 0.031" (0.80 mm) thick at any point. a. Check brake shoes and brake pads for damage or wear. Lining should not be less than 0.031" (0.80 mm) between rivets and lining. b. Check brake drums and rotors for damage or wear.	a. Worn or damaged drum or rotor.
6	Annual	Front Wheel Bearings and Hubs	If your records show that your vehicle has not accumulated 6,000 miles, the wheel bearing service may be deferred once until the next scheduled service, 12,000 miles is obtained, or until other services are required (i.e. brake replacement). No wheel bearing service will be extended beyond 24 months/2 years.	

Table 2-1. Unit Level Preventive Maintenance Checks and Services for CUCV'

tern No.	Interval	Item To Be Inspected	Procedure	Not Mission Capable If:
6	Annual	Front Wheel Bearings and Hubs Continued	a. Remove locking hubs (see paragraph 8-3). Clean and inspect for damage. b. Remove, clean, dry, and inspect front wheel bearings. c. Repack front wheel bearings with GAA and install. cl. Install locking hubs (see paragraph 8-3). **NOTE** The rear wheel bearings cm all except M1009 do not require routine repacking of the rear wheel bearings. They are lubricated by the rear differential fluid. They should only require repacting if the drum is turned during brake replacement or if contaminated after disassembly.	a. Any damage that will prevent operation.
7	Annual	Engine	Inspect for loose, cracked, or damaged engine mounts, expansion plugs, crankshaft pulley, and torsion damper. If engine mount retaining bolts are loose, tighten to 85 ft-lbs (115 N.m). If any of these components are cracked or damaged, notify your supervisor.	Engine mounts cracked, damaged. Any damage that will prevent operation. Class III leak.
8	Annual	Starter	a. Inspect starter mounting bolts to ensure that none are loose or missing. If loose, tighten to 33 ft-lbs (45 N.m). b. Inspect starter wiring connections for looseness.	a. Mounting bolt missing, broken or loose. b. Stud nut loose.

Table 2-1. Unit Level Preventive Maintenance Checks And Services for CUCV

Item No.	Interval	Item To Be Inspected	Procedure	Not Mission Capable If:
9	Annual	Steering Linkage	Lubricate annually or 12,000 miles. Lubricate tie-rod ends, connecting rods, and kingpins at fittings. Original M1009 ball joints do not have zirc fittings and do not require lubrication. If vehicle is being driven off-road, in dust or mud, lubricate every 3 months or 3,000 miles. Lubricate with GAA. STEERING LINKAGE (TYPICAL)	
10	Annual	Propeller Shaft Slip Joint	Annually or every 12,000 miles, lubricate shaft fittings with GAA.	
11	Annual	Propeller Shaft Universal Joints and C V Joint	Lubricate fittings annually or 12,000 miles with GAA. Use a needle point greaser with a flex hose to inject grease into CV joint fitting.	

Table 2-1. Unit Level Preventive Maintenance Checks and Services for CUCV

Item No.	Interval	Item To Be Inspected	Procedure	Not Mission Capable [f:
12	Annual	Trans mission	Normally, transmission filter and oil is changed biennially. However, if vehicle is primarily used for off-road or heavy duty operations, annually drain oil, change filter and refill with DEXRON II oil. **NOTE** Casting marks in torque converter cover have the appearance of small cracks and are considered normal. a. Inspect torque converter cover where transmission is connected to engine flywheel, for missing or loose mounting bolts. If bolts are loose, tighten 60 in-lb (27 N.m). b. Inspect vacuum modulator (right side of transmission near base of transmission fill tube) for cracks or leaks. If mounting bolt is loose, tighten to 20 ft-lbs (27 N.m). Notify your supervisor if damaged or leaking.	 b. Any damage that will prevent operation. Class III leak.
13	Annual	Transfer Case	a. Check fluid level in transfer case. Fluid should be approximately 1/4" (6.4 mm) below the edge of the filler plug hole. If low, fill with DEXRON II fluid. b. Inspect transfer case breather vent for looseness or damage.	 b. Vent plugged or damaged.

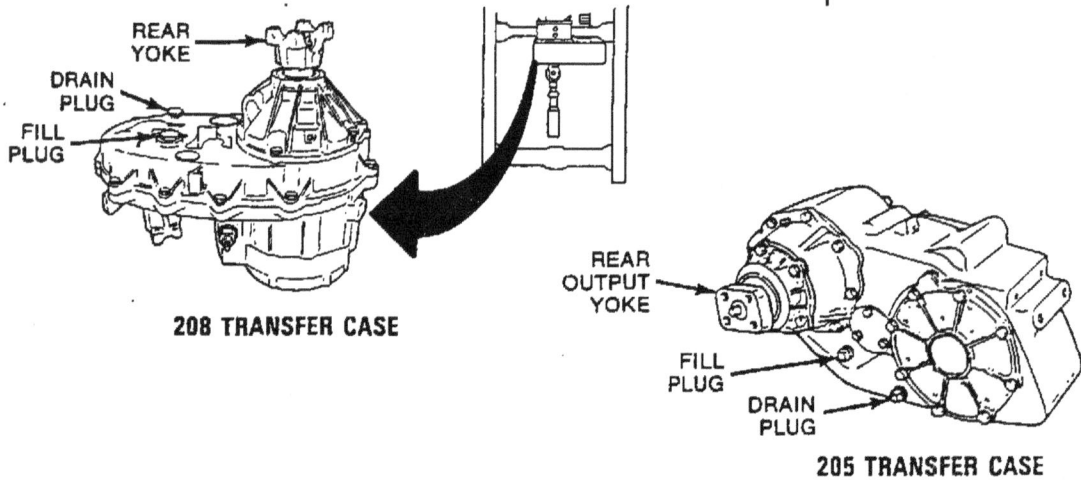

REAR YOKE

DRAIN PLUG

FILL PLUG

208 TRANSFER CASE

REAR OUTPUT YOKE

FILL PLUG

DRAIN PLUG

205 TRANSFER CASE

Table 2-1. Unit Level Preventive Maintenance Checks And Services for CUCV

Item No.	Interval	Item To Be Inspected	Procedure	Not Mission Capable If:
14	Annual	Axles and Dif-ferentials	Annually or every 12,000 miles, check and fill front and rear differentials with GO lubricating oil. Fill to level of filler plug hole. Ensure that differential cover bolts are tight and that none are missing. If bolts are loose, tighten to 35 ft-lbs (47 N.m).	Class III leaks. Missing bolts.
15	Annual	Exhaust System	**WARNING** **Before attempting to service any part of the exhaust system, allow exhaust system to COOL Failure to follow this warning will result in serious burns.** Inspect for damaged, cracked, or loose tailpipe, muffler, muffler supports, hangers, exhaust pipe, and exhaust manifold.	Any loose or damaged exhaust pipe, support, or any exhaust leak.
16	Annual	Suspension	a. Check front wheel toe alignment (see paragraph 8-6). **NOTE** Only M1028A2 and M1028A3 have rear stabilizer bars. b. Inspect front and rear stabilizer bars for loose mounting bolts or damage. Inspect bushings for wear. If bolts are loose, tighten to 55 ft-lbs (75 N.m).	a. Improper alignment. b. Any damage that will prevent damage.

Table 2-1. Unit Level Preventive Maintenance Checks and Services for CUCV

Item No.	Interval	Item To Be Inspected	Procedure	Not Mission Capable If:
1	Biennially	Differentials	Biennial or every 24,000 miles, drain and refill front and rear differentials with clean GO lubricating oil. For drain and refill of M1028, M1028A1, M1028A2, M1028A3, and M1031 front axles, four ounces of additive (NSN 9150-01-198-3829) must be added to lubricant (see paragraph 6-8.1, 6-8.2, or 6-8.3). Front differential capacity is 4.5 pt (2.1 L). Rear differential capacity is 5.4 pt (2.6 L).	
2	Biennially	Transmission	Remove oil pan, drain fluid, replace filter, install pan, and refill with new Dexron II fluid. DO NOT overfill (see paragraph 5-2). Transmission service capacity is 4.0 quarts (5.7 L).	
3	Biennially	Transfer	Change fluid by removing drain plug and allowing fluid to drain, then refill with new Dexron II fluid. Transfer service capacity is 5.0 quarts (5.7 L).	

REAR YOKE

DRAIN PLUG

FILL PLUG

208 TRANSFER CASE

REAR OUTPUT YOKE

FILL PLUG

DRAIN PLUG

205 TRANSFER CASE

| 4 | Biennially | Engine Coolant | Drain, flush, and refill system with a 50/50 mixture of new ethylene glycol and water. Cooling system capacity is 25 quarts (23.7 L). At temperatures below -10° F (-25° C), refill system with a mixture of 65% ethyene glycol and 35% water. | |

PARTS LIST

The following is a list of parts required when performing semi-annual, annual or biennial PMCS. The semi-annual parts list contains the mandatory replacement parts for one semi-annual PMCS. The annual parts list contains the mandatory replacement parts for one semi-annual PMCS and the peculiar replacement parts for one annual PMCS.

SEMIANNUAL (6,000 MILE) PMCS PARTS LIST

PART NUMBER	NSN	NOMENCLATURE	QTY
PF-35	2940-00-082-6034	Element, Engine Oil Filter	1

ANNUAL (1 2,000 MILE) PMCS PARTS LIST

PART NUMBER	NSN	NOMENCLATURE	QTY
PF-35	2940-00-082-6034	Element, Engine Oil Filter	1
14075347	2910-01-156-8361	Element, Fuel Filter	1
A644C	2940-01-155-3190	Element, Air Filter	1
27467	5330-01-106-7938	Seal, Plain, Front Hub (all except M1009) 2	
6273948	5330-01-086-3506	Seal, Plain, Front Hub (M1009 only)	2
469694	5330-01-085-0918	Seal Assy, Rear Hub (all except M1009)	2
327739	5330-01-076-3009	Gasket, Axle Shaft (all except M1009)	2
15528	2530-01-163-0800	Parts Kit, Four Wheel (all except M1009)	2
13446	5330-01-331-7230	Packing, Preformed, Locking Hub (M1009) 2	

BIENNIAL (24,000 MILE) PMCS PARTS LIST

PART NUMBER	NSN	NOMENCLATURE	QTY
6273951	5330-01-150-4022	Gasket, Front Diff Cover (all except MI 009) 1	
458860	5330-07-155-4399	Gasket, Front Diff Cover (MI 009 only)	1
3977387	5330-01-020-9319	Gasket, Rear Diff Cover (all except MI 009) 1	
26016662	5330-01-084-2410	Gasket, Rear Diff Cover (MI 009 only)	1
	9150-01-198-3829	Additive, Oil, Diff	1
8655625	5330-01-148-7492	Gasket, Trans Pan	1
6259423	2940-01-121-6350	Parts Kit, Fluid Pre	1

— KEY —

LUBRICANTS	CAPACITIES	EXPECTED TEMPERATURES				INTERVALS
		Above 32° F (Above 0° C)	+40°F to −10°F (4°C to −23°C)	0°F to -10°F (-18°C to -23° C)		
NSN 9150-00-698-2382 (Dexron® II) HYDRAULIC FLUID						
Transmission: Service Filter	4.0 qts. (3.8 l)	ALL TEMPERATURES				A: 12 Months or 12,000 Miles
Transfer Case	4.0 qts. (3.8 l)					
GO, HYDRAULIC FLUID, GEAR, (MIL-L-2105) MULTIPURPOSE						
Differential: Front	4.5 pts. (2.1 l)		GO 80/9	GO 75		B: 24 Months or 24,000 Miles
Rear	5.4 pts. (2.1 l)					
NSN 9150-01-198-3829 ADDITIVE, DIFFERENTIAL						
M1028, M1028A1 and M1031 Front Differential	4 oz. (113.4 g)	ALL TEMPERATURES				
BFS: BRAKE FLUID, SILICONE, AUTOMOTIVE, ALL WEATHER OPERATIONAL AND PRESERVATIVE MIL-B-46176						
Brake System and Master Cylinder	As Req.	ALL TEMPERATURES				
POWER STEERING FLUID NSN 9150-00-698-2382 (Dexron® II): OIL						
Power Steering System and Pump Reservoir	As Req.	ALL TEMPERATURES				
GAA: GREASE, AUTOMOTIVE, AND ARTILLERY MIL-G-10924						
Steering Linkage	As Req.					
Constant Velocity Joint	As Req.					
Front Propeller Shaft Slip Joint	As Req.					
Front Wheel Bearings	As Req.	ALL TEMPERATURES				
Parking Brake Cable Guide	As Req.					
Brake Pedal Springs	As Req.					
Tow Pintle	As Req.					

FOR ARCTIC OPERATION, REFER TO TM 9-207

— KEY —

LUBRICANTS	CAPACITIES	EXPECTED TEMPERATURES			
		+125°F to +60°F (52°C to 16°C)	+100°F to +5°F (38°C to −15°C)	+40°F to −25°F (4°C to −32°C)	+10°F to −50°F (−12°C to −46°C)
OE/HDO - LUBRICATING OIL, INTERNAL COMBUSTION ENGINE, TACTICAL SERVICE (MIL-L-2104D)		OE/HDO 30	OE/HDO 15W 40	OE/HDO 10	MIL-L-46167
OEA - LUBRICATING OIL, INTERNAL COMBUSTION ENGINE, TACTICAL SERVICE (MIL-L-46167)					
Oil Can Points					
Crankcase (w/filter)	7 qts. (6.6 l)				
ANTIFREEZE - ETHYLENE GLYCOL Cooling System (MIL-A-46153)	25 qts. (23.7 l)	ALL TEMPERATURES			
CLEANING COMPOUND - Windshield Washer (O-C-1901)	2 qts. (1.9 l)	To −20°F			

PIN: 053627-003

Section III. TROUBLESHOOTING

2-9. GENERAL.

a. This section provides information for identifying malfunctions which may develop in the CUCV. Because of the complexity of the CUCV, troubleshooting has been divided into two major areas: mechanical troubleshooting (Table 2-3) and electrical troubleshooting (Table 2-4). The troubleshooting symptom index (paragraph 2-11) provides a list of possible malfunctions, grouped alphabetically by major truck system, with the location of steps that can be taken to correct the malfunction.

b. For a better understanding of how a system operates, see *Principles of Operation* (Chapter 1, Section III). If you're unsure about the location of an item mentioned in troubleshooting, refer to the maintenance task where the item is replaced. DO NOT perform the maintenance task unless the troubleshooting table or your supervisor tell you to do so.

c. When troubleshooting a malfunction:

(1) Ensure that both batteries are fully charged.

(2) Question the operator to obtain any information that might help determine the cause of the problem. Also ensure that all applicable operator troubleshooting was performed before beginning troubleshooting procedures in this manual.

(3) Locate the symptom or symptoms in paragraph 2-11 that describe the malfunction. Check both mechanical and electrical symptoms. If a symptom of a truck malfunction is not listed, notify your supervisor.

(4) Turn to the page in the troubleshooting table where the troubleshooting procedures are listed. Headings at the top of each page show how each troubleshooting task is organized: **MALFUNCTION, TEST OR INSPECTION** (in step number order), and **CORRECTIVE ACTION.**

(5) Perform each step in the order listed until the malfunction is corrected.

d. If a malfunction cannot be corrected by the listed corrective actions, notify your supervisor.

2-10.   TROUBLESHOOTING ELECTRICAL MALFUNCTIONS.

WARNING

Both battery negative cables must be disconnected before removing any electrical system components. (See paragraph 4-38) Failure to follow this warning may result in seriuos injury or death to personnel.

CAUTION

Do not leave key in "RUN" position for more than 2 minutes for any electrical system test. Failure to follow this caution may result in damage to glow plugs.

a. **Introduction.** As a general rule,   when troubleshooting malfunctions of electrical systems, check for continuity through the component and any applicable switches and fuses. Use the wiring diagrams in Appendix F and the following instructions to determine the routing of the wiring. Replace any component, switch, or fuse that does not have continuity.

b. **Abbreviations, Lead Descriptions, and Symbols.**

(1) **Abbreviations.** The following abbreviations of wire colors are used throughout Appendix F:

BLK	Black
BLK/LT BLU	Black with one light blue stripe
BLK/WHT	Black with one white stripe
BLK/YEL	Black with one yellow stripe
BLU	Blue
BRN	Brown
BRN/RED	Brown with one red stripe
BRN/WHT	Brown with one white stripe
DK BLU	Dark blue
DKGRN	Dark green
DK GRN/WHT	Dark Greenwich one white stripe
LT BLU	Light blue
LT BLU/RED	Light blue with one red stripe
LT GRN	Light green
GRA	Gray
GRN	Green
ORN	Orange
ORN/BLK	Orange with one black stripe
PNK	Pink
PNK/BLK	Pink with one black stripe
PPL	Purple
PPL/WHT	Purple with one white stripe
RED/WHT	Red with one white stripe
TAN/WHT	Tan with one white stripe
WET	White
WHT/BLK	White with one black stripe
YEL	Yellow
YEL/BLK	Yellow with one black stripe

(2) Lead Descriptions. Each lead on a wiring diagram is designated according to wire size, wire color, and circuit. For example, lead 3 RED-2J (SXL) is designated as follows:

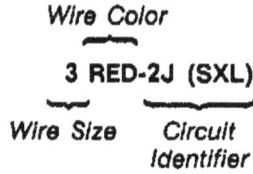

Wire Color

3 RED-2J (SXL)

Wire Size   Circuit
Identifier

(a)   *Wire size* is the diameter of the wire in millimeters. Use the following table to convert wire size into wire gage:

Wire size	Wire Gage
.5	20
.8	18
1	16
2	14
3	12
5	10
8	8
13	6
19	4
32	2

(b)   *Wire co/or* is as previously described.

(c)   The *circuit identifier* is only found on the wiring diagram and is used to help distinguish between leads of the same wire size and color. The following abbreviations may appear as part of the circuit identifier (temperature in parentheses is maximum temperature that the wire can withstand):

NOTE

● **A fusible link is connected to a lead by a splice and is always constructed of a wire   4 gages higher than the lead it connects to.**

● **Any wire that is not labeled will be poly-vinyl chloride wire.**

HDT	Heavy-walled, high-abrasion, poly-vinyl chloride wire (175°F or 97°C)
HW	Heavy-walled, high-abrasion, poly-vinyl chloride wire (275°F or 152°C)
SGT	Poly-vinyl chloride; negative battery cable
SGX	Cross-link polyethylene; positive battery cable
SXL	Heavy-walled, high-abrasion, cross-link polyethylene (275°F or 152°C)
THERMO HW	Fusible link; heavy-walled silicone over cross-link polyethylene.

(3) **Symbols.** Major items appearing in wiring diagrams and schematics are labeled. Other items that may require explanation are defined below:

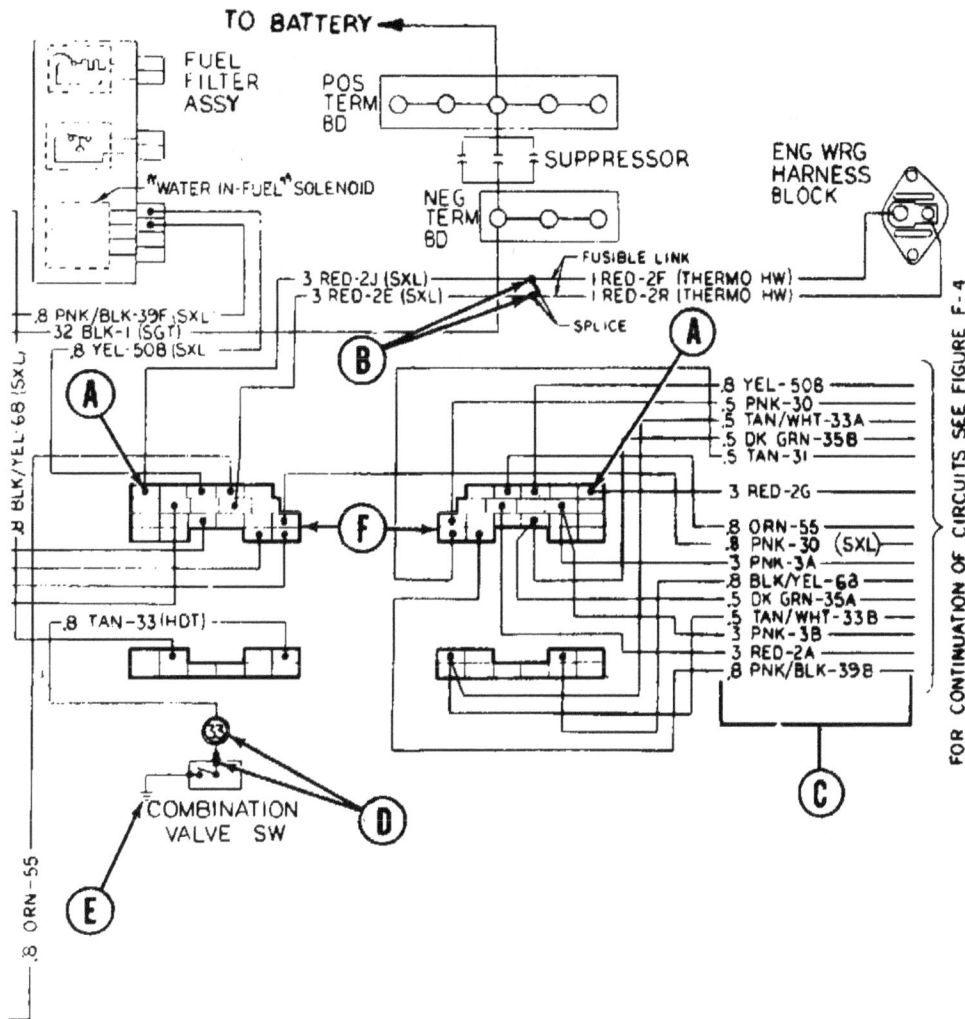

A. Wiring Harness Terminals, Will be found In "mirror image" locations on the wiring harness male/female connector (F), The circuit through lead 3 RED-2J (SXL) is shown at points marked "(A)." Note that only terminals for the applicable circuit will be shown on the wiring diagram. Terminals shown on other wiring diagrams will be represented by empty blocks on the wiring harness connectors.

B. Splice. Indicates where a lead Is soldered or otherwise connected to 1 or more other leads, Repair any broken soldered splice using soldering gun.

c. Wiring Harness, Can be Identified on a wiring diagram by a large number of leads going In the same direction. Wiring harnesses can be identified on the truck by a conduit (plastic sleeve) or a loom (string mesh) that wraps around the leads. The leads of each wiring harness are exposed at the base of the connectors.

D. Leads and Connectors, Transmit electricity to major components, When disconnecting more than one lead and connector from a major component, tag leads and connectors for installation.

E. Ground Lead. Connects to frame or body to complete electrical circuit, A disconnected or damaged ground lead can make a major component inoperative, or operative at lower efficiency.

F. Wiring Harness Male/Female Connectors, Are shown on the wiring diagram according to their actual shape. Anywhere that a female connector appears, the "mirror image" shown opposite It will be its male connector.

TA49631

c. **General Electrical Troubleshooting Instructions.**

(1) Any components that have been removed for testing must be installed again if they are not defective.

(2) Fuses are identified by amperage in the troubleshooting procedures, as well by as a number printed on the fuse itself. An easy way to identify fuses is by their color. The following is a list of fuses and their colors:

Amperage Fuse	_Color_
5 amps	Tan
10 amps	Red
15 amps	Light Blue
20 amps	Yellow
25 amps	White
30 amps	Light Green

(3) Many electrical troubleshooting tasks will require that you check for voltage or continuity through a lead or connector terminal. Leads will be identified by wire color if their location is unclear. Connector terminals will usually be identified by the leads that connect to the back of them.

2-11. TROUBLESHOOTING SYMPTOM INDEX.

MECHANICAL TROUBLESHOOTING

2-1 1   TROUBLESHOOTING SYMPTOM INDEX (Con't).

MECHANICAL TROUBLESHOOTING

2-11. TROUBLESHOOTING SYMPTOM INDEX (Con't).

MECHANICAL TROUBLESHOOTING

2-11.   TROUBLESHOOTING SYMPTOM INDEX (Con't).

ELECTRICAL TROUBLESHOOTING

2-11. TROUBLESHOOTING SYMPTOM INDEX (Con't).

ELECTRICAL TROUBLESHOOTING

Table 2-3. Mechanical Troubleshooting

MALFUNCTION
    TEST OR INSPECTION
        CORRECTIVE ACTION

BRAKE SYSTEM

1. **BRAKES DRAG**

    Step 1. Inspect brake lines and hoses. (See TB 9-2300-405-14)

        Clear restrictions or replace if damaged or crimped. (See paragraphs 7-9 and 7-10)

    Step 2. Check for incorrect parking brake adjustment on rear brakes.

        Adjust parking brake. (See paragraph 7-2)

    Step 3. Inspect brake shoes, brake pads, and all components for proper operation and installation. (See paragraphs 7-7 and 7-11)

2. **BRAKES PULL WHEN APPLIED**

    Step 1. Check for incorrect tire pressure.

        Inflate all tires to recommended pressure. (See TM 9-2320-289-10)

    Step 2. Inspect brake lines and hoses. (See TB 9-2300-405-14)

        Clear restrictions or replace if damaged or crimped. (See paragraphs 7-9 and 7-10)

    Step 3. Inspect for loose calipers.

        If calipers are loose, tighten bolts to specifications. (See paragraph 7-11)

    Step 4. Have assistant press brake pedal and check for movement of caliper piston.

        If pistons are stuck or sluggish, replace caliper. (See paragraph 7-11)

    Step 5. Check front wheel toe alinement. (See paragraph 8-6)

3. **SENSITIVE BRAKING ACTION (M1009)**

    Step 1. Check to ensure that the correct power booster has been installed (M1009 only). (See paragraph 7-8)

        If correct power booster is on truck and condition still exists, replace power booster. (See paragraph 7-8)

Table 2-3. Mechanical Troubleshooting (Con't)

MALFUNCTION
    TEST OR INSPECTION
        CORRECTIVE ACTION

---

4. GRABBING OR UNEVEN BRAKING ACTION BETWEEN FRONT AND REAR BRAKES

Step 1.   Inspect combination valve and lines for obvious damage.

        Replace valve and lines if damaged. (See paragraph 7-9)

Step 2.   Inspect proportioning valve (all except M1009) and lines for obvious damage.

        Replace proportioning valve and lines if damaged. (See paragraph 7-10)

        If proportioning valve is not damaged, adjust. (See paragraph 7-10)

5. HIGH-PITCHED SQUEAK

Step 1.   Inspect brake shoes and brake pads for incorrect installation, distortion, and excessive wear; thickness of lining or distance from rivet head must exceed 0.031 in. (0.80 mm).

        Repair if necessary. (See paragraphs 7-7 and 7-11)

6. PARKING BRAKE DOES NOT HOLD TRUCK

Step 1.   Check parking brake adjustment   and ensure that linkage operates properly.

        Adjust parking brake (see   paragraph 7-2) or replace damaged parts   (see paragraphs 7-3 and 7-4).

7. PEDAL EFFORT EXCESSIVE

Step 1.   Check for insufficient brake fluid   in master cylinder.

        Fill reservoir if low (see LO 9-2320-289-12) and check for leakage.

Step 2.   Check power steering pump fluid level. (See LO 9-2320-289-12)

Step 3.   Check to ensure that the correct power booster has been installed (all except M1009). (See paragraph 7-8)

        If condition still exists replace power booster. (See paragraph 7-8)

Step 4.   Inspect power steering belt.

        Tighten if loose or replace if worn. (See paragraph 8-15)

Step 5.   Inspect brake lines and hoses. (See TB 9-2300-405-14)

        Clear restrictions or replace if damaged or crimped. (See paragraphs 7-9 and 7-10)

Table 2-3. Mechanical Troubleshooting (Con't)

MALFUNCTION
    TEST OR INSPECTION
        CORRECTIVE ACTION

Step 6.   Inspect brake shoes and brake pads for incorrect installation, distortion, and excessive wear; thickness of lining or distance from rivet head must exceed 0.031 in. (0.80 mm).

Repair if required. (See paragraphs 7-7 and 7-11)

Step 7.   Have assistant press brake pedal; check for movement of caliper piston.

Replace calipers if required. (See paragraph 7-11)

Step 8.   Inspect for binding brake pedal mechanism.

Lubricate or replace bushing and spacer. (See paragraph 7-12)

8.   PEDAL RETURNS SLOWLY

NOTE

Pedal should travel 1-1½ in. (2.54-3.81 cm) before brakes take hold. After brakes take hold, pedal may exceed 1-1½ in. (2.54-3.81 cm) travel; this is normal.

Step 1.   Inspect power steering pump belt.

Tighten if loose or replace if worn. (See paragraph 8-15)

WARNING

Compressed air used to check for restrictions should never exceed 30 psi (207 kPa). Use only effective chip guarding and personnel protective equipment (goggles/shield, gloves, etc.). Failure to follow this warning may result in serious injury to personnel.

Step 2.   Check for restrictions in lines from power booster to power steering pump with low pressure air.

Clear restrictions or replace. (See paragraph 8-14)

Step 3.   Check power booster input rod end at brake pedal for wear or damage.

Replace if worn or damaged. (See paragraph 7-8)

9.   EXCESSIVE PEDAL TRAVEL

Step 1.   Check master cylinder reservoirs for low brake fluid. (See LO 9-2320-289-12)

Step 2.   Inspect master cylinder and brake lines for leakage.

Tighten or replace damaged parts. (See paragraphs 7-8, 7-9, and 7-10)

Fill reservoir if low. (See LO 9-2320-289-12)

Table 2-3. Mechanical Troubleshooting (Con't)

MALFUNCTION
    TEST OR INSPECTION
        CORRECTIVE ACTION

Step 3.   Check rear brake adjustment and inspect auto adjusters for damage,

        Adjust rear brakes and repair auto adjusters if damaged. (See paragraph 7-7)

Step 4.   Check power booster operation. Depress brake pedal several times to exhaust accumulator pressure. Start engine. Brake pedal should return to normal position.

        Replace power booster if not operating properly. (See paragraph 7-8)

Step 5.   Check wheel bearing adjustment. (See paragraphs 8-4 and 8-5)

10. SPONGY BRAKES

NOTE

Pedal should travel 1-1½ in. (2.54-3.81 cm) before brakes take hold. After brakes take hold, pedal may exceed 1-1½ in. (2.54-3.81 cm) travel; this is normal.

Step 1.   Bleed brakes. (See paragraph 7-6)

11. PEDAL VIBRATES (BOOSTER CHATTERS)

Step 1.   Inspect power steering pump belt.

        Tighten if loose or replace if worn. (See paragraph 8-15)

Step 2.   Check power steering pump reservoir for low power steering fluid. Inspect power steering pump and lines for leakage.

        Tighten hoses if leaking. If still leaking, replace pump and/or hoses. (See paragraphs 8-15 and 8-14)

        Fill reservoir if low. (See LO 9-2320-289-12)

12. ROUGHNESS FELT DURING NORMAL BRAKE APPLICATION

WARNING

DO NOT use a dry brush or compressed air to clean brake shoes, brake pads, or brake components. There may be asbestos dust on brake shoes, brake pads, or brake components which can be dangerous to you if you breathe it. Brake shoes, brake pads, and brake components must be wet, and a soft brush must be used. Failure to follow this warning may result in serious illness or death to personnel.

Step 1.   Inspect brake shoes and brake pads for incorrect installation, foreign material, distortion, and excessive wear; thickness of lining or distance from rivet head must exceed 0.031 in. (0.80 mm).

        Repair or replace if necessary. (See paragraphs 7-7 and 7-11)

Table 2-3. Mechanical Troubleshooting (Con't)

MALFUNCTION
    TEST OR INSPECTION
        CORRECTIVE ACTION

Step 2.   Check drums and rotors for heat spotting, glazing, or heavy scoring.

        Notify your supervisor if heat spotted, glazed, or scored.

Step 3.   Check tires for improper balancing. (See TM 9-2610-200-24)

Step 4.   Clean, inspect, and adjust wheel bearings.

        Replace if damaged. (See paragraph 8-4 or 8-5)

ENGINE

13. ENGINE WILL NOT CRANK

Step 1.   See Electrical Troubleshooting malfunction #42.

        If engine still will not crank, notify your supervisor.

14. SLOW CRANKING OR UNUSUAL NOISE DURING CRANKING

Step 1.   Check starter mounting bolts for looseness.

        Tighten any loose mounting bolts to 33 lb.-ft. (45 N•m).

Step 2.   Check clearance between starter pinion tooth and flywheel. (See paragraph 4-5, INSTALLATION)

Step 3.   Inspect flywheel ring gear for chipped or damaged teeth. (See paragraph 4-5, INSTALLATION)

        If chipped or damaged teeth are found, notify your supervisor.

15. CRANKS BUT WILL NOT START

Step 1.   Check to see if there is fuel in tank. Add fuel if empty.

Step 2.   Check fuel supply and return lines for restrictions, looseness, or damage.

        Tighten or replace if damaged. (See paragraph 3-13 or 3-14)

Step 3.   Inspect fuel filter, fuel pump, and injector pump for leakage.

        Notify your supervisor if injector pump is leaking. Replace other leaking components. (See paragraphs 3-10 and 3-17)

Step 4.   Check for inoperative glow plugs and glow plug system. (See *Electrical Troubleshooting malfunction #19*)

Table 2-3. Mechanical Troubleshooting (Con't)

MALFUNCTION
  TEST OR INSPECTION
    CORRECTIVE ACTION

Step 5.   Check for contaminated fuel by draining fuel from fuel filter draincock into suitable container. Check color of fuel to determine if the correct fuel is in fuel system.

Drain fuel and replace if contaminated or incorrect fuel is in fuel system.

WARNING

Diesel fuel is flammable. When disconnecting fuel lines to test fuel flow, direct fuel spray away from source of ignition. A fire extinguisher must be on hand in work area. Failure to follow this warning may result in serious injury or death to personnel.

Step 6.   Check fuel pump operation. Disconnect input fuel line at the fuel filter. Disconnect pink lead from fuel injector pump. Use a quart capacity container, and crank engine for 15 seconds. Container should be at least   ¼ full or contain ½ pt (0.231) of fuel. Install low pressure gage in fuel line. Crank engine for 15 more seconds. Fuel pressure should be 5.5-6.5 psi (38-45 kPa). Reconnect fuel inlet line to fuel filter, and reconnect pink lead to fuel injector pump.

If fuel flow is insufficient, replace fuel pump. (See paragraph 3-10)

Step 7.   Bleed fuel filter. (See paragraph 3-17)

16. HIGH-PITCHED WHINE FOLLOWING STARTUP

Step 1.   Check starter mounting bolts for looseness.

Tighten any loose mounting bolts to 33   lb.-ft. (45 N•m).

Step 2.   Check clearance between starter pinion tooth and flywheel. (See paragraph 4-5, INSTALLATION)

If condition still exists, replace starter. (See paragraph 4-5)

17. ACCELERATOR PEDAL STICKS OR FULL THROTTLE CANNOT BE OBTAINED

Step 1.   Inspect accelerator pedal components for binding or damage that would limit pedal travel.

Replace components if required. (See paragraph 3-24)

Step 2.   Inspect accelerator cable and control spring on left side of injection pump for damage that would restrict cable movement.

Replace cable or spring if damaged. (See paragraph 3-23)

Table 2-3. Mechanical Troubleshooting (Con't)

MALFUNCTION
    TEST OR INSPECTION
        CORRECTIVE ACTION

18. WILL NOT RETURN TO IDLE

Step 1.   Inspect accelerator cable for binding or damage,

        Replace cable if damaged. (See paragraph 3-23)

Step 2.   Check for missing or damaged control spring on left side of fuel injector pump.

        Install control spring if missing or replace if damaged. (See paragraph 3-23)

Step 3.   Check idle speed setting. (See paragraph 3-25)

19. IDLES ROUGH ON COLD-STARTS WITH BLACK SMOKE BUT CLEARS UP AFTER WARM-UP

Step 1.   Check for improper starting procedures. (See TM 9-2320-289-10)

Step 2.   Check for inoperative glow plugs and glow plug system. (See *Electrical Troubleshooting malfunction* #19)

20. STARTS BUT WILL NOT CONTINUE TO RUN, HARD RESTARTING

Step 1.   Inspect air cleaner filter and polywrap,

        Replace air cleaner filter if required.   Clean polywrap if required. (See paragraph 3-9)

Step 2.   Check idle speed setting. (See paragraph 3-25)

WARNING

Diesel fuel is flammable. When disconnecting fuel lines to test fuel flow, direct fuel spray away from source of ignition. A fire extinguisher must be on hand in work area. Failure to follow this warning may result in serious injury or death to personnel.

Step 3.   Check for leaking or restricted fuel lines.

        Tighten fittings or replace leaking or restricted lines. (See paragraph 3-13 or 3-14)

        If no leaks or crimps are obvious, bleed fuel filter. (See paragraph 3-17)

Step 4.   Check for contaminated fuel by draining fuel from fuel filter draincock into suitable container. Check color of fuel to determine if the correct fuel is in fuel system.

        Drain fuel and replace if contaminated or incorrect fuel is in fuel system.

Step 5.   Check seals on vent plug and draincock on fuel filter for damage. (See paragraph 3-17)

        Replace damaged seals. (See paragraph 3-17)

Table 2-3. Mechanical Troubleshooting (Con't)

MALFUNCTION
   TEST OR INSPECTION
      CORRECTIVE ACTION

___

WARNING
___

Diesel fuel is flammable. When disconnecting fuel lines to test fuel flow, direct fuel spray away from source of ignition. A fire extinguisher must be on hand in work area. Failure to follow this warning may result in serious injury or death to personnel.

Step 6.   Check fuel pump operation. Disconnect input fuel line at the fuel filter. Disconnect pink lead from fuel injector pump. Use a quart capacity container and crank engine for 15 seconds. Container should be at least   ¼ full or contain ½ pt (0.23 1) of fuel, Install low pressure gage in fuel line. Crank engine for 15 more seconds. Fuel pressure should be 5.5-6.5 psi (38-45 kPa). Connect fuel inlet line to fuel filter and connect pink lead to fuel injector pump.

   If fuel flow is insufficient, replace fuel pump. (See paragraph 3-10)

21. STARTS, IDLES ROUGH WHEN HOT

___

WARNING
___

Diesel fuel is flammable. When disconnecting fuel lines to test fuel flow, direct fuel spray away from source of ignition. A fire extinguisher must be on hand in work area. Failure to follow this warning may result in serious injury or death to personnel.

Step 1.   Check for leaking or restricted fuel lines.

   Tighten fittings or replace leaking or restricted lines as required, (See paragraph 3-13 or 3-14)

   If no leaks or crimps are obvious, bleed fuel filter. (See paragraph 3-17)

Step 2.   Check for contaminated fuel by draining fuel from fuel filter draincock into suitable container. Check color of fuel to determine if the correct fuel is in fuel system.

   Drain fuel and replace if contaminated or incorrect fuel is in fuel system.

22. KNOCKS AT IDLE WHEN HOT

Step 1.   Check oil level indicator for proper reading. (See TM 9-2320-289-10)

Step 2.   With engine cool, check level of coolant. (See TM 9-2320-289-10)

Table 2-3. Mechanical Troubleshooting (Con't)

MALFUNCTION
  TEST OR INSPECTION
    CORRECTIVE ACTION

WARNING

Before checking for improper positioning and damage, allow exhaust system to cool. Failure to follow this warning will result in serious burns.

Step 3.   Check tailpipe, muffler, and exhaust pipe for improper positioning and damage.

Reposition and tighten mounting hardware.

Replace any damaged components. (See paragraph 3-27)

Step 4.   Check. engine mounts and insulators for looseness and damage.

Tighten bolts securing mount to frame or engine if loose. If there is any damage, notify your supervisor.

Step 5.   Check alternator belts for improper tension or damage.

Adjust or replace if damaged. (See paragraph 4-2 or 4-3)

Step 6.   Check for contaminated fuel by draining fuel   from fuel filter draincock into suitable container. Check color of fuel to determine   if the correct fuel is in fuel system.

Drain fuel and replace if contaminated   or incorrect fuel is in fuel system.

WARNING

Diesel fuel is flammable. When disconnecting fuel lines to test fuel flow, direct fuel spray away from source of ignition. A fire extinguisher must be on hand in work area. Failure to follow this warning may result in serious injury or death to personnel.

Step 7.   Check fuel pump operation. Disconnect input fuel line at the fuel filter. Disconnect pink lead from fuel injector pump. Use a quart capacity container and crank engine for 15 seconds. Container should be at least   ¼ full or contain ½ pt (0.23 l) of fuel. Install low pressure gage in fuel line. Crank engine for 15 more seconds. Fuel pressure should be 5.5-6.5 psi (38-45 kPa). Connect fuel inlet line to fuel filter and connect pink lead to fuel injector pump.

If fuel flow is insufficient, replace fuel pump. (See paragraph 3-10)

23. EXCESSIVE VIBRATION

Step 1.   Check engine mounts, insulators, and components for looseness and damage.

Tighten any loose components. Tighten bolts securing mounts to frame or engine if loose. If there is any damage, notify your supervisor.

Table 2-3. Mechanical Troubleshooting (Con't)

MALFUNCTION
    TEST OR INSPECTION
        CORRECTIVE ACTION

24. EXCESSIVE OIL LOSS

Step 1.   Check oil level indicator for proper reading. (See TM 9-2320-289-10)

Step 2.   Inspect oil filler cap vent for buildup of sand, dirt, and other foreign material that may keep oil filler cap vent valve in an open position. If condition exists, remove oil filler cap, clean, and shake to listen for rattling sound.

    If cap rattles, install.

    If cap does not rattle, replace.

Step 3.   Remove crankcase depression regulator valve (CDRV) assembly and CDRV hoses. Clean with a rag and inspect for cracks. Test CDRV for proper operation.

    Clear foreign material and test or replace if necessary.

Step 4.   Clean excess oil from exterior of valve cover, oil level indicator tube, oil pan and plug, oil filter, fuel pump, engine oil cooler lines, and oil pressure sending unit; check for looseness, damage, and leakage.

    If leakage is evident, notify your supervisor.

25. OIL PRESSURE LIGHT ON AT IDLE

Step 1.   Check oil level indicator for proper reading. (See TM 9-2320-289-10)

Step 2.   Check engine idle speed. (See paragraph 3-25)

Step 3.   Check oil pressure sending unit for looseness, damage, or leakage.

    Repair as necessary.

Step 4.   If light remains on, replace oil pressure sending unit. (See paragraph 4-14)

26. COOLANT LOSS

Step 1.   Pressurize cooling system and check for leakage on all hoses and components. (See TM 750-254)

    Tighten loose clamps, fasteners, or fittings. Replace leaking hoses and components. (See paragraphs 3-32, 3-33, and 3-34)

Step 2.   Check radiator cap for proper relief pressure. (See TM 750-254) Relief pressure should be 15 psi (103 kPa).

    Replace if defective.

Table 2-3. Mechanical Troubleshooting   (con't)

MALFUNCTION
     TEST OR INSPECTION
          CORRECTIVE ACTION

27. OVERHEATS

Step 1.   Check for loose, damaged, or missing fan belts.

Adjust or replace if damaged. (See paragraph 4-2 or 4-3)

Step 2.   Pressurize cooling system and check for leakage on all hoses and components. (See TM 750-254)

Tighten loose clamps, fasteners, or fittings. Replace leaking hoses and components. (See paragraphs 3-6, 3-32, 3-33, and 3-34)

Step 3.   If engine continues to overheat, replace thermostat. (See paragraph 3-34)

Step 4.   Check fan clutch.

Replace fan clutch. (See paragraph 3-35)

28. NOTICEABLE LOSS OF POWER

Step 1.   Inspect air cleaner filter and polywrap.

Replace air cleaner filter if required. Clean polywrap if required. (See paragraph 3-9).

WARNING

Diesel fuel is flammable. When disconnecting fuel lines to test fuel flow, direct fuel spray away from source of ignition. A fire extinguisher must be on hand in work area. Failure to follow this warning may result in serious injury or death to personnel.

Step 2.   Check for restricted fuel filter. Bleed air from fuel system. (See paragraph 3-17)

If fuel flow is insufficient, replace fuel filter. (See paragraph 3-17)

Step 3.   Check for leaking or restricted fuel lines.

Tighten fittings or replace leaking or restricted lines. (See paragraph 3-13 or 3-14)

WARNING

Before checking for improper positioning and damage, allow exhaust system to cool. Failure to follow this warning will result in serious burns.

Step 4.   Check tailpipe, muffler, and exhaust pipe for improper positioning and damage.

Reposition and tighten mounting hardware.

Replace any damaged components. (See paragraph 3-27)

Table 2-3. Mechanical Troubleshooting   (Con't)

MALFUNCTION
    TEST OR INSPECTION
        CORRECTIVE ACTION

29. EXCESSIVE EXHAUST SMOKE DURING OPERATION

Step 1.   Inspect air cleaner filter and polywrap.

        Replace air cleaner filter if required. Clean polywrap if required. (See paragraph 3-9)

Step 2.   Check for contaminated fuel by draining fuel from fuel filter draincock into suitable container. Check color of fuel to determine if the correct fuel is in fuel system.

        Drain fuel and replace if contaminated or incorrect fuel is in fuel system.

WARNING

Diesel fuel is flammable. When disconnecting fuel lines to test fuel flow, direct fuel spray away from source of ignition. A fire extinguisher must be on hand in work area. Failure to follow this warning may result in serious injury or death to personnel.

Step 3.   Check fuel pump operation. Disconnect input fuel line at the fuel filter. Disconnect pink lead from fuel injector pump. Use a quart capacity container and crank engine for 15 seconds. Container should be at least ¼ full or contain ½ pt (0.23 l) of fuel. Install low pressure gage in fuel line. Crank engine for 15 more seconds. Fuel pressure should be 5.5-6.5 psi (38-45 kPa). Connect fuel inlet line to fuel filter and connect pink lead to fuel injector pump.

        If fuel flow is insufficient, replace fuel pump. (See paragraph 3-10)

Step 4.   Bleed fuel filter. (See paragraph 3-17)

Step 5.   Check crankcase depression regulator valve (CDRV) and hose for restrictions. Inspect hose and air intake manifold for evidence of oil.

        Clean off all traces of oil and clear restrictions or replace CDRV and hose as required. (See paragraph 3-5)

30. HEAVY KNOCK WITH ENGINE TORQUE APPLIED

WARNING

Before checking for improper positioning and damage, allow exhaust system to cool. Failure to follow this warning will result in serious burns.

Table 2-3. Mechanical Troubleshooting (Con't)

MALFUNCTION
    TEST OR INSPECTION
        CORRECTIVE ACTION

NOTE

Knocking and rattling will result if air cleaner wingnut is loose.

Step 1.   Check tailpipe, muffler, and exhaust pipe for improper positioning and damage.

        Reposition and tighten mounting hardware.

        Replace any damaged components. (See paragraph 3-27)

Step 2.   Check engine mounts and insulators for looseness and damage.

        Tighten bolts securing mounts to frame or engine if loose. If there is any damage, notify your supervisor.

Step 3.   Check alternator belts for improper tension or damage.

        Adjust or replace if damaged. (See paragraph 4-2 or 4-3)

Step 4.   If knock is still evident, notify your supervisor.

31. WILL NOT SHUT OFF USING KEY

NOTE

Ground wire for ignition switch goes to top of parking brake bracket. If ground wire is broke, engine will not shut off if light switch is on.

Step 1.   With engine at idle, pinch flexible part of the fuel return line at fuel injector pump to stop engine. Notify your supervisor.

EXHAUST SYSTEM

32. EXCESSIVE NOISE OR LEAKING EXHAUST GASES

WARNING

Before checking for looseness, damage, or restrictions, allow exhaust system to cool. Failure to follow this warning will result in serious burns.

Step 1.   Check tailpipe, muffler,   exhaust manifolds, and exhaust   pipe for looseness, damage, or restrictions.

        Tighten or replace   any damaged components. (See   paragraphs 3-27 and 3-28)

Table 2-3. Mechanical Troubleshooting (Con't)

MALFUNCTION
    TEST OR INSPECTION
        CORRECTIVE ACTION

AMBULANCE PERSONNEL HEATER

33. SMOKY HEATER EXHAUST AFTER 5 MINUTES CONTINUOUS OPERATION

WARNING

Before checking for restrictions, allow exhaust pipe to cool. Failure to follow this warning will result in serious burns.

Step 1.   Check air inlet or exhaust outlet for restrictions.

        Remove any restrictions.

        If there are no restrictions, replace heater, (See paragraph 10-36)

34. STARTS BUT SHUTS OFF COMPLETELY

Step 1.   Ensure that truck fuel tank is at least   ¼ full. Add fuel if low.

Step 2.   Inspect air passages for restrictions.

        Clear restrictions. Allow system   to cool before retesting.

WARNING

Diesel fuel is flammable. When disconnecting fuel lines to test fuel flow, direct fuel spray away from source of ignition. A fire extinguisher must be on hand in work area. Failure to follow this warning may result in serious injury or death to personnel.

Step 3.   Remove side panel from heater compartment. Disconnect fuel line from inlet side of heater. Place suitable container under inlet line. Check for fuel flow to heater while holding run-start switch in the "START" position.

        If fuel flow is evident, replace heater (See   paragraph 10-36)

        If fuel flow is not evident, perform step 4.

Step 4.   Check for restrictions in heater inlet fuel line.

        If line is restricted, clear restriction.

Table 2-3. Mechanical Troubleshooting (Con't)

MALFUNCTION
  TEST OR INSPECTION
    CORRECTIVE ACTION

WINTERIZATION KIT HEATERS

35. WITERIZATION KIT HEATERS WILL NOT START

Step 1. Perform *Electrical Troubleshooting* malfunction #22.

36. SMOKY HEATER EXHAUST AFTER 5 MINUTES CONTINUOUS OPERATION

WARNING

Before checking for restrictions, allow exhaust pipe to cool. Failure to follow this warning may result in serious burns.

Step 1. Check air inlet or exhaust outlet for restrictions.

Remove any restrictions.

If there are no restrictions, replace heater. (See paragraph 11-8, 11-16, or 11-21)

37. STARTS BUT SHUTS OFF COMPLETELY

Step 1. Ensure that truck fuel tank is at least ¼ full.

Add fuel if low.

Step 2. Inspect air passages for restrictions.

Clear restrictions. Allow system to cool before retesting.

Table 2-3. Mechanical Troubleshooting (Con't)

MALFUNCTION
   TEST OR INSPECTION
      CORRECTIVE ACTION

WARNING

Diesel fuel is flammable. When disconnecting fuel lines to test fuel flow, direct fuel spray away from source of ignition. A fire extinguisher must be on hand in work area. Failure to follow this warning may result in serious injury or death to personnel.

Step 3.   If troubleshooting cargo compartment heater malfunction, remove heater cover. Disconnect fuel line from inlet side of heater. Place a suitable container under inlet line. Check for fuel flow to heater while holding run-start switch in "START" position (all except engine coolant heater) or on-off switch in "ON" position (engine coolant heater only).

   If fuel flow is evident, replace heater, (See paragraph 11-8 or 11-21)

   If fuel flow is not evident, perform step 4.

Step 4.   Check for restrictions in heater inlet fuel line.

   If line is restricted, clear restrictions.

Step 5.   Perform *Electrical Troubleshooting* malfunction #22.

HEATER (ENGINE COOLANT ONLY)

38. FAN RUNS CONTINUALLY WITH SWITCH OFF; RUN LAMP STAYS ON; NO HEAT PRODUCED

   Step 1.   Replace heater. (See paragraph 11-16)

39. HEATER OPERATES; ENGINE REMAINS COLD

   Step 1.   Check to see if coolant shutoff valves are open.

   Step 2.   Replace heater. (See paragraph 11-16)

40. WILL NOT START

   Step 1.   Perform *Electrical Troubleshooting* malfunction #22.

Table 2-3. Mechanical Troubleshooting (Con't)

MALFUNCTION
  TEST OR INSPECTION
    CORRECTIVE ACTION

WARNING

Diesel fuel is flammable, When disconnecting fuel lines to test fuel flow, direct fuel spray away from source of ignition. A fire extinguisher must be on hand in work area. Failure to follow this warning may result in serious injury or death to personnel.

Step 2. Disconnect fuel line from inlet side of heater. Place a suitable container under inlet line. Check for fuel flow to heater while holding cm-off switch in "ON" position.

   If fuel flow is evident, replace heater. (See paragraph 11-16)

   If fuel flow is not evident, perform step 3.

Step 3. Check for restrictions in heater inlet fuel line.

   If line is restricted, clear restrictions.

PROPELLER SHAFT

41. MAKES "KLUNKING" SOUND WHEN SHIFTING

Step 1. Inspect propeller shaft universal joints for play. Attempt to move propeller shaft forward and back to detect play on yoke.

   Replace if there is play. (See paragraph 6-3 or 6-5)

Step 2. If "klunking" persists, notify your supervisor.

42. VIBRATES

Step 1. Check propeller shaft mounting bolts for looseness.

   Tighten if loose. (See paragraphs 6-2 and 6-4)

Step 2. Inspect propeller shaft for damage, buildup of foreign material, and missing weights.

   Remove foreign material or replace propeller shaft if damaged or weights are missing. (See paragraphs 6-2, 6-3, 6-4, and 6-5)

Step 3. Inspect propeller shaft universal joints for play and binding. Attempt to move propeller shaft ends forward and back to detect play or binding on yoke.

   Replace universal joint if there is play or binding. (See paragraphs 6-3 and 6-5)

Table 2-3. Mechanical Troubleshooting (Con't)

MALFUNCTION
    TEST OR INSPECTION
        CORRECTIVE ACTION

Step 4.   Check wheels for improper balancing. (See TM 9-2610-200-24)

STEERING

43. EXCESSIVE PLAY IN STEERING

Step 1.   Check for incorrect tire pressure. (See TM 9-2320-289-10)

Step 2.   Inspect connecting rod, pitman arm, and tie-rod ends for looseness or wear.

        Tighten or replace as required. (See paragraph 8-10, 8-11, or 8-13)

Step 3.   Inspect power steering pump reservoir for air in power steering fluid. Power steering fluid will have milky appearance if it contains air. If there is air in system, inspect pump and hoses for leakage.

        Tighten hoses if leaking. If still leaking, replace pump and/or hoses (see paragraphs 8-15 and 8-14) and bleed power steering system (see paragraph 8-8).

NOTE

If there is Loctite on bolts, DO NOT tighten without reapplying Loctite (Item 30, Appendix C).

Step 4.   Inspect steering gear.

        If loose, tighten mounting bolts 75 lb.-ft. (102 N-m).

Step 5.   Clean, inspect, and adjust wheel bearings. (See paragraphs 8-4 and 8-5)

        Replace if required.

44. HARD STEERING OR LACK OF ASSIST

Step 1.   Check for incorrect tire pressure. (See TM 9-2320-289-10)

Step 2.   Inspect power steering pump belt for looseness or wear. (See paragraph 8-15)

Step 3.   Inspect power steering pump reservoir for contamination and insufficient fluid; inspect power steering pump and hoses for leakage.

        If fluid is contaminated, flush with clean fluid. (See paragraph 8-8) Tighten hoses if leaking, If still leaking, replace pump and/or hoses. (See paragraphs 8-15 and 8-14)

Step 4.   Check for binding in steering linkage at tie-rod ends, connecting rod, and kingpins.

        Lubricate (see LO 9-2320-289-12) or redate tie-rod ends (see paragraph 8-13) or connecting rod (see paragraph 8-10) as required. If kingpins need to be replaced, notify your supervisor.

Table 2-3. Mechanical Troubleshooting (Con't)

MALFUNCTION
    TEST OR INSPECTION
        CORRECTIVE ACTION

45. NOISY STEERING

Step 1.   Inspect power steering belt and pump pulley for looseness or damage.

        Tighten if loose and replace if damaged. (See paragraph 8-15)

Step 2.   Check power steering pump fluid level (see LO 9-2320-289-12)

Step 3.   Inspect power steering pump reservoir for air in power steering fluid. Power steering fluid will have milky appearance if it contains air. If there is air in system, inspect pump and hoses for leakage.

        Tighten hoses if leaking.   If still leaking, replace pump and/or hoses (see paragraphs 8-15 and 8-14) and bleed steering system (see paragraph 8-8).

NOTE

If there is Loctite on bolts, DO NOT tighten without reapplying Loctite (Item 30, Appendix C).

Step 4.   Inspect steering gear.

        If loose, tighten mounting bolts   to 75 lb.-ft. (102 N·m).

Step 5.   Inspect power steering hoses for restrictions and to see if they are touching other parts of the truck.

        Clear restrictions or reposition hoses as required. (See paragraph 8-14)

Step 6.   Inspect connecting rod, pitman arm, and tie-rod ends for looseness or wear.

        Adjust or replace as required. (See paragraphs 8-10, 8-11, and 8-13)

43. SLOW RETURN OF STEERING

Step 1.   Check for incorrect tire pressure. (see   TM 9-2320-289-10)

Step 2.   Check for binding in steering linkage at tie-rod ends, connecting rod, and kingpins.

        Lubricate (see LO 9-2320-289-12) or replace tie-rod ends (see paragraph 8-13) or connecting rod (see paragraph 8-10) as required. If kingpins need to be replaced, notify your supervisor.

Step 3.   Check front wheel toe alinement (see paragraph 8-6)

SUSPENSION

47. EXCESSIVE NOISE DURING OPERATION

Step 1.   Inspect shock absorber and components mounting for looseness or damage.

        Tighten or replace as required. (see paragraphs 6-10 and 6-11)

Table 2-3. Mechanical Troubleshooting (Con't)

MALFUNCTION
> **TEST OR INSPECTION**
>> **CORRECTIVE ACTION**

Step 2.   Inspect shock absorber for leakage. A slight trace of fluid is normal.

Replace if required. (See paragraphs 6-10 and 6-11)

Step 3.   Inspect front and rear springs for loose or damaged "U" bolts and mounting bolts where it mounts to axle and frame.   Inspect springs for damaged mounting brackets.

Tighten any loose "U" bolt nuts to 40 lb.-ft. (54 N•m) in an "X" pattern; tighten again in same pattern to 150 lb.-ft. (203 NŽm) for front springs and to 145 lb.-ft. (197 N•m) for rear springs. Tighten front spring forward mounting bolts to 90 lb.-ft. (122 N•m) and rearward mounting bolts to 50 lb.-ft. (68 N•m). Tighten all rear spring mounting bolts to 110 lb.-ft. (149 N•m). Notify your supervisor if any components are damaged.

Step 4.   Inspect front and rear spring bumpers for damage.

Replace if required. (See paragraph 6-10 or 6-11)

TRANSFER CASE

48. DIFFICULT TO SHIFT AND/OR NOISY

Step 1.   Check transfer case fluid   level. (See LO 9-2320-289-12)

Step 2.   Check transfer case shift   linkage for improper adjustment or damage which would interfere with operation.

Adjust or replace damaged components. (See paragraph 5-5 or 5-6)

TRANSMISSION

49. EXCESSIVE OIL LOSS

Step 1.   Check transmission fluid indicator for proper reading. (See TM 9-2320-289-10)

Step 2.   Inspect vacuum modulator (right side of transmission near base of transmission fill tube) for leakage and damage.

Tighten mounting bolt to 20 lb.-ft. (27 N•m). Notify your supervisor if damaged or still leaking.

Table 2-3. Mechanical Troubleshooting (Con't)

MALFUNCTION
   TEST OR INSPECTION
      CORRECTIVE ACTION

Step 3.   Inspect transmission oil pan for leakage and damage.

      Tighten mounting bolts to 144 lb.-in. (16 N•m). If leaking, replace transmission oil pan gasket or RTV sealant. (See paragraph 5-2). If damaged, replace.

Step 4.   Inspect transmission oil cooler lines for leakage and damage.

      Tighten lines if required. Notify your supervisor if damaged or still leaking.

Step 5.   Inspect speedometer cable adapter and seal for oil leakage   from transfer case.

      Tighten or replace as required. (See paragraph 4-10)

50. NOISY (WHINES OR "KLUNKS")

Step 1.   Check transmission fluid indicator for proper reading. (See TM 9-2320-289-10)

Step 2.   Check transmission mounting for looseness or damage.

      Tighten any loose retaining screws to 80 lb.-ft. (108 N•m). Notify your supervisor if there is any damage.

51. WILL NOT SHIFT PROPERLY

Step 1.   Check transmission fluid indicator for proper reading. (See TM 9-2320-289-10)

Step 2.   Inspect vacuum hoses, vacuum pump, and vacuum regulator valve for improper connection, leakage, or damage.

      Connect or replace vacuum hoses and vacuum pump as required. (See paragraphs 3-21 and 3-7) Adjust vacuum regulator valve. (See paragraph 3-21.1)

Step 3.   Inspect vacuum modulator (right side of transmission near base of transmission fill tube) for leakage and damage.

      Tighten mounting bolt to 20 lb.-ft. (27 N•m). Notify your supervisor if damaged or still leaking.

WHEELS AND TIRES

52. UNEVEN TIRE WEAR

Step 1.   Check for incorrect tire pressure (See TM 9-2320-289-10)

Table 2-3. Mechanical Troubleshooting (Con't)

MALFUNCTION
    TEST OR INSPECTION
        CORRECTIVE ACTION

Step 2.   Check front wheel toe alinement. (See paragraph 8-6)

Step 3.   Inspect shock absorber for leakage. A slight trace of fluid is normal.

        Replace if required. (See paragraphs 6-10 and 6-11)

Step 4.   Inspect connecting rod and pitman arm for looseness.

        Tighten or replace as required. (See paragraphs 8-10 and 8-11)

53. TRUCK WANDERS   TO ONE SIDE

Step 1.   Check for incorrect tire pressure. (See TM 9-2320-289-10)

Step 2.   Check front wheel toe alinement. (See paragraph 8-6)

Step 3.   Check for binding in steering linkage at tie-rod ends, connecting rod, and kingpins.

        Lubricate (see LO 9-2320-289-12) or replace tie-rod ends (see paragraph 8-13) or connecting rod (see paragraph 8-10) as required.

54. WHEEL VIBRATION

Step 1.   Check for loose lugnuts.

        Tighten lugnuts on M1009 wheels to 90 lb. -ft. (122 NŽm); tighten lugnuts on all other truck wheels to 140 lb. -ft. (190 NŽm).

Step 2.   Check for incorrect tire pressure. (See TM 9-2320-289-10)

Step 3.   Inspect tires for cuts, gouges, cracks, and sidewall damage. Inspect wheels for bends and other damage.

        Replace damaged tires and wheels if required. (See paragraph 8-2)

Step 4.   Inspect connecting rod and pitman arm for looseness.

        Tighten or replace as required. (See paragraphs 8-10 and 8-11)

Step 5.   Check for front axle spindle end play. Raise and support truck on jack stands. Grasp tire at outer edges and attempt to move up and down.

        Clean, inspect,   and adjust wheel bearings if excessive movement is apparent. (See paragraph 8-4) Replace if required.

Step 6.   Check tires for improper balancing. (See TM 9-2610-200-24)

Step 7.   Inspect tie-rod shock absorber for leakage. A slight trace of fluid is normal.

        Replace if required. (See paragraph 8-12)

Table 2-4. Electrical Troubleshooting

MALFUNCTION
    TEST OR INSPECTION
        CORRECTIVE ACTION

AIR CONDITIONER

1.   **COOLING INSUFFICIENT; AIR FLOW NORMAL**

    Step 1.   Check setting of air conditioner controls. (See TM 9-2320-289-10)

    Step 2.   Check compressor belt tension. (See Appendix E)

        Adjust if loose.

    Step 3.   Check air conditioner compressor clutch/pulley assembly to ensure it is operating. If clutch/pulley assembly is not operating, check 30 amp flasher, back-up lights, and accessories fuse. (See paragraph 4-12)

        Replace fuse if burned out.

    Step 4.   Unplug connector from 24 volt air conditioner relay. (See paragraph 4-13) Check to see that there are 12.0 volts at orange lead terminal and 24.0 volts at light blue lead terminal,

        If voltage is correct at both leads, replace relay.

        If voltage is not correct at both leads, perform step 5.

    Step 5.   Unplug Connector from 12 volt air conditioner relay. (See paragraph 4-13) Check for 12.0 volts at tan lead terminal and 24.0 volts at gray lead terminal.

        If voltage is correct at both leads, replace relay.

        If voltage is not correct at both leads, check 25 amp air conditioner fuse. (See paragraph 4-13) Replace fuse if burned out.

2. LOW OR NO AIR   **FLOW**

    Step 1.   Check 20 amp in-line air conditioner blower fuse. (See paragraph 4-13)

        Replace fuse if burned out.

    Step 2.   Remove air conditioner condenser cover assembly. (See paragraph 10-33) Check for voltage through each lead from fan switch to resistor. Voltage should be 24.0.

        If voltage is not correct through any lead, trace circuit through lead back to 20 amp in-line air conditioner fuse. (See wiring diagram F-26)

        If voltage is correct through each lead, perform step 3.

Table 2-4. Electrical Troubleshooting (Con't)

MALFUNCTION
** TEST OR INSPECTION**
**   CORRECTIVE ACTION**

Step 3.   Check resistance through lead from resistor to evaporator motor. Resistance should be 0 ohms with switch in high position, 1.4 ohms with switch in medium position, and 4.5 ohms with switch in low position.

If resistance is correct, check security and condition of ground. If ground is good, replace evaporator motor. (See paragraph 10-34)

If resistance is not correct in all positions, replace blower resistor (see paragraph 10-34) and retest.

AMBULANCE BODY SERVICE OUTLETS

3.   15 amp OUTLETS (ONE OR MORE) INOPERATIVE (ACCESSORIES WORK AT OTHER OUTLETS)

Step 1.   Remove access cover from ambulance body fuse panel. (See paragraph 4-13) Check applicable 15 amp fuse.

Replace fuse if burned out.

If fuse is good, trace circuit.   (See wiring diagram F-25)

4.   60 amp SERVICE   OUTLET INOPERATIVE

NOTE

Circuit breaker cannot be manually reset. After 2-3 minutes cool down time, it will reset itself.

Step 1.   Remove access cover from ambulance body fuse panel. (See paragraph 4-13) Allow circuit breaker to reset, Check for voltage from circuit breaker.

If there is no voltage, check for voltage from circuit breaker back to positive terminal board.

If there is voltage, replace circuit breaker. (See paragraph 4-13)

Table 2-4. Electrical Troubleshooting (Con't)

MALFUNCTION
    TEST OR INSPECTION
        CORRECTIVE ACTION

BATTERIES/CHARGING/SYSTEM

5. **ALL TRUCK ELECTRICAL SYSTEMS INOPERATAVE**

    Step 1.   Check batteries for proper charge and electrolyte level. (See paragraph 4-39) Voltage between ground and positive (+) terminal of rear battery should be 24.0.

        Service replace. Notify your supervisior if non-maintenace free batteries require service.

    Step 2.   Check 12 volt bus bar for loose connections.

        Tighten loose connections.

    Step 3.   Check alternator belt tension. (See Appendix E)

    Step 4.   Remove and clean all battery cable and clamp connections.

        Replace worn or damaged battery cables and clamps. (See paragraph 4-38)

    Step 5   Check voltage between positive and negative terminal boards where battery cables connect. Voltage should be 24.0.

        If voltage is not correct, trace circuit to batteries. (See wiring diagram F-1 or F-2)

5.1. **GENERATOR LIGHT DOES NOT COME ON WITH KEY IN "ON" POSITION BEFORE ENGINE IS STARTED (ALL MODELS EXCEPT M1010)**

    Step 1.   Trace all circits from generator to generator light in instrument panel (including fuse, bulb, arm relay}. (See wiring diagram F-11)

        If circuits are good, replace alternator. (See paragraph 4-2)

6. **GENERATOR LIGHT REMAINS ON OR TURNS ON DURING OPERATION (ALL EXCEPT M1010)**

    Step 1.   Check engine idle speed. (See paragraph 3-25)

    Step 2.   Disconnect connector from left alternator (if "GEN 1" light is on) or right alternator (if "GEN 2" light is on). Turn key to "RUN" position.

        If generator light is not on, trace circuit from alternator connector to generator light in instrument panel. (See wiring diagram F-11) If circuit is good, replace alternator. (See paragraph 4-2)

        If generator light is on, trace circuit from alternator connector to generator light if instrument panel. (See wiring diagram F-9)

Table 2-4. Electrical Troubleshooting (Con't)

MALFUNCTION
    TEST OR INSPECTION
        CORRECTIVE ACTION

---

7. "GEN 2" LIGHT REMAINS ON WITH KEY IN "OFF" POSITION (ALL EXCEPT M1010)

    Step 1.   Remove generator 2 relay. (See paragraph 4-9)

               If light goes out, replace relay.

               If light remains on, trace circuit through brown/red lead to "GEN 2" light in instrument panel. (See wiring diagram F-9)

8. VOLTMETER INOPERATIVE OR IN YELLOW (UNDERCHARGE) ZONE; GENERATOR LIGHTS OPERATING PROPERLY (ALL EXCEPT M1010)

    Step 1.   Check alternator belts for looseness or damage. (See paragraph 4-2)

    Step 2.   Check 20 amp ignition fuse and 10 amp/28 v (voltmeter) fuse. (See paragraph 4-1 2)

               Replace fuse if burned out.

    Step 3.   Remove voltmeter relay. (See paragraph 4-9) Start engine. Using jumper wire, connect white lead terminal and black lead terminal.

               If voltmeter reads in green zone, replace relay.

               If voltmeter does not read in green zone, trace circuit from bus bar ground to fuse block. (See wiring diagram F-4) If circuit is good, replace voltmeter, (See paragraph 4-9)

9. VOLTMETER IN RED (OVERCHARGE) ZONE (ALL EXCEPT M1010)

    Step 1.   Start engine. Check voltage at left and right alternators at positive (+) terminals. Voltage should not exceed 16.0 at left alternator or 31.8 at right alternator.

               If voltage is over 16,0 at left alternator or 31.8 at right alternator, replace alternator. (See paragraph 4-2)

               If voltage is correct, replace voltmeter. (See paragraph 4-9)

10. VOLTMETER REMAINS OPERATIVE WITH KEY IN "OFF" POSITION

    Step 1.   Remove voltmeter relay. (See paragraph 4-9)

               If voltmeter becomes inoperative, replace relay.

               (All except M1010) If voltmeter still operates, trace   circuit from white lead at relay connector to voltmeter. (See wiring diagram   F-4)

               (M1000) If voltmeter still operares, trace circuit between pink blacK lead and brown/red lead. (See wiring diagram F-6)

Table 2-4. Electrical Troubleshooting (Con't)

MALFUNCTION
    TEST OR INSPECTION
        CORRECTIVE ACTION

---

11. VOLTMETER INOPERATIVE (MI 010 AND M1028 WITH 200 amp SYSTEM)

Step 1.   Check 20 amp ignition fuse and 10 amp/28 v (voltmeter) fuse. (See paragraph 4-12)

        Replace fuse if burned out.

Step 2.   Remove voltmeter relay. (See paragraph 4-9) Start engine. Using jumper wire, connect brown lead terminal and brown/red lead terminal.

        If voltmeter reads in green zone, replace relay.

        If voltmeter does not read in green zone, trace circuit from bus bar ground to fuse block. (See wiring diagram F-6) If circuit is good, replace voltmeter. (See paragraph 4-9)

12. VOLTMETER IN RED (OVERCHARGE) ZONE AT ALL TIMES (M1010 AND M1028 WITH 200 amp SYSTEM)

Step 1.   Start engine, bring to full operating temperature, then shut off. Remove 20 amp engine control fuse. (See paragraph 4-12) Start engine and check voltage at lower alternator positive (+) terminal.

        If voltage is over 29.1, replace lower alternator voltage regulator. (See paragraph 4-4)

        If voltage is between 28.5 and 29.1, replace voltmeter. (See paragraph 4-9)

13. VOLTMETER IN YELLOW (UNDERCHARGE) ZONE (MI 010 AND MI 028 WITH 200 amp SYSTEM)

Step 1.   Check alternator belts for looseness or damage. (See paragraph 4-3)

Step 2.   Start engine, bring to full operating temperature, then shut off. Remove 20 amp engine control fuse. (See paragraph 4-12) Start engine and check voltage at lower alternator positive (+) terminal.

        If voltage is below 28.5, trace circuit from lower alternator "IGN" terminal to bulkhead connector. (See wiring diagram F-10) If voltage is still below 28.5, perform step 3.

        If voltage is between 28.5 and 29.1, replace voltmeter. (See paragraph 4-9)

Step 3.   Install 20 amp engine control fuse. Check voltage at lower alternator positive (+) terminal.

        If voltage is below 28.5, remove lower alternator voltage regulator (see paragraph 4-4) and ensure that adjustment screw is in "HI" position. If adjustment screw is in "HI" position and voltage is still below 28.5, replace lower alternator voltage regulator. If voltage is still below 28.5, replace lower alternator. (See paragraph 4-3) If voltage is still below 28.5, notify your supervisor.

Table 2-4. Electrical Troubleshooting (Con't)

MALFUNCTION
  TEST OR INSPECTION
    CORRECTIVE ACTION

14. SLAVE RECEPTACLE INOPERATIVE

Step 1.   Check battery and cables. (See *Electrical Troubleshooting* malfunction #5)

Step 2.   Inspect slave receptacle and cables for corrosion or damage. Check for loose connections at positive terminal board terminal, negative terminal board terminal, and at receptacle. Check for continuity through   receptacle and receptacle cables.

CAUTION

DO NOT use solvents or cleaners of any kind   when cleaning slave receptacle. Only use water. Failure to follow this   caution may result in damage to slave receptacle.

If slave receptacle is corroded, remove   (see paragraph 4-40),   clean, and rinse with water. Dry thoroughly and check again for continuity.

If there is no continuity, replace. (See paragraph 4-40)

If there is continuity, install; replace any cables that do not have   continuity. (See paragraph 4-40)

GLOW PLUG SYSTEM

NOTE

Glow plug system cycling can be detected by listening for clicking at glow plug relay or by observing voltmeter. Indicator should be to the left of the normal range during cycling and return to normal range after cycling.

15. GLOW PLUG MODULE INOPERATIVE

NOTE

The only way to determine if your glow plug module is operating properly is through testing. The glow plug module should not be replaced until the following tests are performed.

Step 1.   Disconnect pink wire from fuel injector pump.   Remove printed circuit board from glow plug module. Check each circuit to the glow plug module as described. Trace any circuit that does not operate properly. (See wiring diagram F-7 or F-8) If all circuits operate properly, replace glow plug module. (See paragraph 4-8)

Table 2-4. Electrical Troubleshooting (Con't)

MALFUNCTION
    TEST OR INSPECTION
        CORRECTIVE ACTION

Wire Color	*Key Position*	*Instructions and Normal Results*
Purple/white	"START"	Approximately 12.0 volts at wire. If voltage is not correct, trace circuit.
Light blue	" RUN "	Jump wire to ground; glow plug relay energizes. If relay does not energize, trace circuit. If circuit is good, replace relay. (See paragraph 4-8)
Dark blue	"RUN"	Jump wire to ground; "WAIT" light turns on. If "WAIT" light does not turn on, replace bulb. (See paragraph 4-7) If "WAIT" light still does not turn on, trace circuit.
Pink/black	"RUN"	Approximately 12.0 volts at wire. If voltage is not correct, trace circuit.
Orange	"RUN"	Jump light blue wire to ground; Approximately 12.0 volts at orange wire. If voltage is not correct, trace circuit.
Yellow	"OFF"	800 ohms (minimum) at wire (engine cold). If resistance is not correct, trace circuit. If resistance is still not correct, replace glow plug switch. (See paragraph 3-20)
Black	"OFF"	0 ohms at wire. Clean connection and tighten if not correct.
Pink/black and light blue at glow plug relay	"OFF"	6-10 ohms between wires. If resistance is not correct, replace glow plug relay. (See paragraph 4-8)

16. "WAIT" LIGHT INOPERATIVE (ENGINE COLD)

Step 1.   Check 20 amp   engine control fuse and 20 amp ignition fuse   . (See paragraph 4-12)

        Replace fuse if burned out.

Table 2-4. Electrical Troubleshooting (Con't)

MALFUNCTIO N
    TEST OR INSPECTION
        CORRECTIVE ACTION

CAUTION

Do not leave key in "RUN" position for more than 2 minutes. Failure to follow this caution may resuit in damage to glow plugs.

Step 2.   Remove glow plug module. (See paragraph 4-8) Turn key to "RUN" position. Using jumper wire, ground dark blue lead.

        If "WAIT" light turns on, turn key to "OFF" position, reinstall glow plug module, and perform step 3.

        If "WAIl " light does not turn on, replace bulb. If "WAIT" light still does not turn cm, trace circuit. (See wiring diagram F-7 or F-8)

Step 3.   Turn key to "RUN" position. Disconnect connector from glow plug switch on upper left rear of cylinder head.

        If "WAIT" light turns on, replace glow plug switch. (See paragraph 3-20)

        If "WAIT" light does not turn on, perform *Electrical Troubleshooting* malfunction #15

17. "WAIT" LIGHT ON CONTINUOUSLY WITH KEY IN "RUN" POSITION

Step 1.   Remove glow plug module

        If "WAIT" light stays on, trace circuit through dark blue lead to "WAIT" light. (See wiring diagram F-7 or F-8)

        If "WAIT" light goes out, perform *Electrical Troubleshooting* malfunction #15.

18. "WAIT" LIGHT OPERATES UPON RESTARTING (ENGINE HOT)

Step 1.   Check connections at glow plug switch on upper left rear of cylinder head and glow plug module.

        If connections are not good, clean and secure all connectors.

        If connections are good, perform *Electrical Troubleshooting* malfunction #15.

19. ENGINE CRANKS BUT WILL NOT START; ENGINE COLD; "WAIT" LIGHT OPERATES

Step 1.   Ensure that key is in "OFF" position. Check for voltage between glow plug relay terminal where orange lead connects and ground.

        If there is voltage, replace glow plug relay (see paragraph 4-8) and perform step 3.

        If there is no voltage, perform step 3.

Table 2-4. Electrical Troubleshooting (Con't)

MALFUNCTION
    TEST OR INSPECTION
        CORRECTIVE ACTION

CAUTION

DO NOT leave key in "RUN" position for more than 2 minutes. Failure to follow this caution may result in damage to glow plugs.

Step 2.   Turn key to "RUN" position. Check for voltage between glow plug relay terminal where orange lead connects and ground.

NOTE

Glow plugs will cycle to 0 volts in approximately 20 seconds after first operation. Time will shorten as glow plugs become hotter.

        If there are 10.0-15.0 volts, ensure that engine is mechanically sound and fuel system is operating properly,

        If there are 22.0-28.0 volts, perform step 3.

        If there is no voltage, perform step 4.

Step 3.   Disconnect each glow plug lead and check for resistance between glow plug terminal and ground. Resistance should be 1-3 ohms. Check glow plugs for looseness or damage.

        If any glow plug does not have correct resistance or is damaged, replace, (See paragraph 3-20) Tighten any loose glow plugs.

Step 4.   Tag and disconnect all glow plug leads from glow plugs. Check for voltage between glow plug relay terminal where red lead connects and ground.

        If voltage is 10.0-15.0 volts, connect glow plug leads and start engine.

        If voltage is 22,0-28.0 volts, perform step 5.

        If there is no voltage, trace circuit back to positive terminal board. (See wiring diagram F-7 or F-8)

Table 2-4. Electrical Troubleshooting (Con't)

MALFUNCTION
    TEST OR INSPECTION
        CORRECTIVE ACTION

WARNING

Resistor may be hot. Use care when performing this step or injury to personnel may occur.

Step 5.   Disconnect batteries, pull out bracket and resistor assembly (see paragraph 4-44, REMOVAL, step 4), disconnect output (red wire) from relay, disconnect input (blue wire) from input to resistors. Connect positive lead of multimeter to blue wire; connect negative lead to red wire. Check resistance between resistors and ground. Resistance should be 0.28 ohms.

        If resistance is not correct, replace resistor, connect glow plug leads and perform step 6.

        If resistance is correct, connect glow plug leads and perform step 6.

Step 6.   Check for voltage between glow plug relay terminal where pink/black lead connects and ground.

        If there is voltage, perform step 7.

        If there is no voltage, trace circuit. (See wiring diagram F-7 or F-8)

Step 7.   Check for voltage between glow plug relay terminal where light blue lead connects and ground.

        If there is voltage, perform step 8.

        If there is no voltage, replace glow plug relay. (See paragraph 4-8)

Step 8.   Check for voltage at light blue lead on glow plug module.

        If there is no voltage, trace circuit (See wiring diagram F-7 or F-8)

        If there is voltage, perform *Electrical Troubleshooting* malfunction #15.

Table 2-4. Electrical Troubleshooting (Con't)

MALFUNCTION
    TEST OR INSPECTION
        CORRECTIVE ACTION

HEATER (GAS-PARTICULATE FILTER UNIT)

20. WILL NOT START

    Step 1.   Trace circuit. (See wiring diagram F-23)

HEATER (AMBULANCE AND WINTERIZATION KIT)

21. WILL NOT SHUT OFF

    Step 1.   Set run-start or on-off switch to "OFF" position.

                If heater runs for less than 5 minutes, heater is good.

                If heater runs for more than 5 minutes, perform step 2.

NOTE

Disconnecting wiring harness will shut off heater.

    Step 2.   Set all controls for normal starting of heater. (See TM 9-2320-289-10) Disconnect wiring harness from heater control box. Check for voltage at terminal "A" of heater control box.

                If there is voltage, replace switch (cab heater or engine coolant heater) (see paragraph 11-3) or heater control box (ambulance heater or cargo compartment heater) (see paragraph 10-35 or 11-20).

                If there is no voltage, replace heater. (See paragraph 10-36, 11-8, 11-16, or 11-21)

22. WILL NOT START

    Step 1.   Check fuel shutoff petcock on fuel inlet line.

                Open if closed.

Table 2-4. Electrical Troubleshooting (Con't)

MALFUNCTION
  TEST OR INSPECTION
    CORRECTIVE ACTION

NOTE

Step 2 applies to M1010 personnel heater only.

Step 2. Remove access cover from ambulance body fuse panel. (See paragraph 4-13) Check 30 amp heater fuses.

Replace fuse if burned out.

If fuse is good, perform step 3.

Step 3. Ensure that truck fuel tank is at least ¼ full. Add fuel if low.

Step 4. Hold run-start switch in "START" position.

If heater fuel pump runs, perform step 5.

If heater fuel pump does not run, trace circuit. (See wiring diagram F-22 or F-28)

Step 5. Bleed heater. (See paragraph 10-36, 11-7, 11-14, or 11-21)

Step 6. Set run-start switch to "OFF" position. Remove side panel from heater compartment (ambulance heater only). Disconnect wiring harness from heater and heater control box. Check continuity through all wiring harness terminals.

If there is continuity, perform step 7.

If there is no continuity, repair if possible or replace. (See paragraph 10-35, 11-10, 11-17, or 11-23)

Step 7. Connect wiring harness to heater. Check voltage between terminal "D" of heater control box connector and ground. Voltage should be 24.0.

If voltage is correct, perform step 8.

If voltage is not correct, check voltage at gray lead into heater control box (ambulance heater) or red lead into heater control box (all except ambulance heater). If there is still no voltage, trace circuit. (See wiring diagram F-22, F-29, or F-30) If there is voltage, replace heater control box. (See paragraph 10-35, 11-3, or 11-20)

Step 8. Hold run-start switch in "START" position or on-off switch in "ON" position. Check voltage between terminal "C" of heater control box connector and ground. Voltage should be 24.0.

If voltage is correct, perform step 9.

If voltage is not correct, replace heater control box. (See paragraph 10-35, 11-3, or 11-20)

Table 2-4. Electrical Troubleshooting (Con't)

MALFUNCTION
    TEST OR INSPECTION
        CORRECTIVE ACTION

Step 9.   Hold run-start switch in "START" position or on-off switch in "ON" position. Check voltage between terminal "D" of heater wiring harness connector and ground. Voltage should be 24.0.

        If voltage is correct, perform step 10.

        If voltage is not correct, replace heater control box. (See paragraph 10-35, 11-3, or 11-20)

Step 10. Hold run-start switch in "START" position or on-off switch in "ON" position. Check voltage between terminal "B" of heater wiring harness connector and ground. Voltage should be 24.0.

        If voltage is correct, replace heater. (See paragraph 10-36, 11-8, 11-16, or 11-21)

        If voltage is not correct, replace heater control box, (See paragraph 10-35, 11-3, or 11-20)

HORN

23. INOPERATIVE

Step 1.   Check 15 amp horn fuse. (See paragraph 4-12)

        Replace if burned out.

Step 2.   Disconnect lead from horn. Check for voltage while pressing horn button,

        If there is voltage, check security and condition of horn ground. If ground is good, replace horn. (See paragraph 4-22)

        If there is no voltage, perform step 3.

Step 3.   Remove horn relay. (See paragraph 4-22) Turn key to "RUN" position. Using jumper wire, connect lead terminals. Depress horn button.

        If horn sounds, replace relay.

        If horn does not sound, trace circuit back to fuse box. (See wiring diagram F-20 or F-21)

Table 2-4. Electrical Troubleshooting (Con't)

MALFUNCTION
    TEST OR INSPECTION
        CORRECTIVE ACTION

---

24. WILL NOT SHUT OFF

Step 1.   Remove horn relay. (See paragraph 4-22)

        If horn shuts off, replace relay.

        If horn does not shut off, trace circuit. (See wiring diagram F-20 or F-21)

INSTRUMENT PANEL

25. BRAKE WARNING LIGHT FLICKERING OR WILL NOT TURN OFF

NOTE

Brake warning light operation is considered normal if brake warning light turns on when brake pedal is rapidly applied or released and turns off with next brake application.

Step 1.   Check that parking brake is fully released. If light stays on, disconnect lead from parking brake switch. (See paragraph 4-17, REMOVAL, step 1)

        If brake warning light goes out,   replace parking brake switch. (See paragraph 4-17)

        If brake warning light does not go out, perform step 2.

Step 2.   Disconnect lead at combination valve. (See paragraph 7-9, REMOVAL, step 5)

        If brake warning light stays on, trace circuit. (See wiring diagram F-4 or F-5)

        If brake warning light goes out, bleed brakes. (See paragraph 7-6) If brake warning light still does not go out,   replace combination valve. (See paragraph 7-9)

26. COOLANT LIGHT FLICKERING OR WILL NOT TURN OFF

Step 1.   Check coolant for proper level. (See TM 9-2320-289-10)

Step 2.   Turn key to "RUN" position. Disconnect black/yellow lead from low coolant sensor on radiator and touch to any ground.

        If light goes out, replace low engine coolant sensor. (See paragraph 3-31)

        If light does not go out, perform step 3.

Table 2-4. Electrical Troubleshooting (Con't)

MALFUNCTION
   TEST OR INSPECTION
      CORRECTIVE ACTION

Step 3.   Remove low coolant module (located near fuse box).

   If light goes out, replace low coolant module.

   If light does not go out, trace circuit. (See wiring diagram F-4 or F-6)

27. FOUR-WHEEL DRIVE LIGHT INOPERATIVE (TRANSFER CASE IN FOUR-WHEEL DRIVE)

Step 1.   Check 20 amp ignition fuse.

   Replace fuse if burned out.

Step 2.   Turn key to "RUN" position. Disconnect lead from four-wheel drive switch on transfer case and touch lead to any ground.

   If four-wheel drive light turns on, replace switch.

   If four-wheel drive light does not turn on, replace bulb. (See paragraph 4-7) If light still does not turn on, trace circuit. (See wiring diagram F-4 or F-6)

28. FOUR-WHEEL DRIVE LIGHT TURNS ON (TRANSFER CASE NOT IN FOUR-WHEEL DRIVE)

Step 1.   Turn key to "RUN" position. Disconnect lead from four-wheel drive switch on transfer case.

   If four-wheel   drive light goes out,   replace switch.

   If four-wheel   drive light stays on,   trace circuit. (See wiring diagram F-4 or F-6)

29. FUEL GAGE INACCURATE

Step 1.   Check 20 amp ignition fuse.

   Replace if burned out.

CAUTION
————

**DO NOT leave key   in "RUN" position for more than 2 minutes. Failure to
follow this caution   may result in damage to glow plugs.**

Step 2.   Disconnect fuel tank sending unit ground from frame. Turn key to "RUN" position.

   If fuel gage reads "F" (Full), perform step 3.

   If fuel gage does not read "F" (Full), replace fuel gage. (See paragraph 4-7)

Table 2-4. Electrical Troubleshooting   (Con't)

MALFUNCTION
    TEST OR INSPECTION
        CORRECTIVE ACTION

Step 3.   Disconnect pink fuel tank sending unit lead and touch lead to any ground.

If fuel gage reads   "E" (Empty), replace fuel tank sending unit,   (See paragraph 3-11 or 3-12)

If fuel gage does not read   "E" (Empty), replace fuel gage.   (See paragraph 4-7)

30. OIL PRESSURE LIGHT INOPERATIVE

Step 1.   Turn key to "RUN" position. Disconnect lead from oil pressure sending unit and touch lead to any ground.

If light goes on, replace oil pressure sending unit. (See paragraph 4-14)

If light does not go on, replace bulb. (See paragraph 4-7) If light still does not go on, trace circuit. (See wiring diagram F-4 or F-6)

LIGHTING SYSTEM

31. BACK-UP LIGHT (ONE OR BOTH) WILL NOT TURN OFF

Step 1.   Disconnect lead from back-up light switch.

If lights go out, replace switch. (See paragraph 4-19)

If lights do not go out, trace circuit. (See wiring diagram   F-14, F-15, or F-17)

32. BACK-UP LIGHTS (BOTH) INOPERATIVE

Step 1.   Check 30 amp back-up light fuse. (See paragraph 4-12)

Replace fuse if burned out.

Step 2.   Ensure that all lead connectors are secure at back-up light switch and at back-up lights. Inspect connections for corrosion or damage.

Clean any corroded connections if possible. If connections are damaged, replace.

If all connections are secure and there is no damage, check bulbs. (See paragraph 4-28 or 4-29)

Table 2-4. Electrical Troubleshooting (Con't)

MALFUNCTION
    TEST OR INSPECTION
        CORRECTIVE ACTION

Step 3.   Disconnect lead from back-up light switch. Using jumper wire, connect terminals of wiring harness lead.

        If lights turn on, replace switch. (See paragraph 4-19)

        If lights do not turn on, trace circuit. (See wiring diagram F-14, F-15, or F-17)

33. HEADLIGHTS INOPERATIVE IN HIGH AND LOW BEAM (ALL OTHER LIGHTS OPERATE)

NOTE

It may be necessary to remove headlights to perform this step.

Step 1.   Check for voltage at headlight connectors.

        If there is voltage, replace headlights. (See paragraph 4-24)

        If there is no voltage, trace circuit from headlight connectors to blackout toggle switch. (See wiring diagram F-1 3 or F-16)

34. ALL PARKING/MARKER LIGHTS INOPERATIVE (HEADLIGHTS OPERATE)

Step 1.   Check 20 amp parking/marker light fuse. (See paragraph 4-12)

        Replace fuse if burned out.

Step 2.   Trace circuit from marker light connectors. (See wiring diagram F-13 or F-16)

35. BLACKOUT LIGHTS INOPERATIVE

Step 1.   Ensure that blackout toggle switch is in   "ON" position and blackout drive light switch is in "ON" position.

Step 2.   Check 5 amp blackout marker   fuse and 10 amp stoplight fuse. (See paragraph 4-12)

        Replace fuse if burned out.

Step 3.   Turn key to "RUN" position. Check for voltage at orange lead on blackout toggle switch connector.

        If there is voltage, replace switch. (See paragraph 4-18)

        If there is no voltage, trace circuit. (See wiring diagram F-18 or F-19)

Table 2-4. Electrical Troubleshooting (Con't)

MALFUNCTION
    TEST OR INSPECTION
        CORRECTIVE ACTION

---

36. BLACKOUT DRIVE LIGHT INOPERATIVE (OTHER BLACKOUT LIGHTS OPERATE)

Step 1.   Ensure that blackout drive light switch is in "ON" position.

Step 2.   Remove and check blackout drive light bulb. (See paragraph 4-25)

        If bulb is good, trace circuit to switch. (See wiring diagram F-18 or F-19)

        Replace bulb if burned out.

Step 3.   Check for voltage at white lead on switch connector.

        If there is voltage, replace switch. (See paragraph 4-18)

        If there is no voltage, trace circuit. (See wiring diagram F-18 or F-19)

37. HAZARD WARNING LIGHTS INOPERATIVE (TURN SIGNALS OPERATE)

Step 1.   Remove hazard warning flasher. (See paragraph 4-12) Using jumper wire, connect fuse box terminals where flasher was installed. Lights should turn on, but not flash.

        If lights turn on, replace flasher.

        If lights do not turn on, trace circuit. (See wiring diagram F-13 or F-16)

38. STOPLIGHTS (BOTH) INOPERATIVE (HEADLIGHTS OPERATE)

Step 1.   Check 10 amp stoplight fuse. (See paragraph 4-12)

        Replace fuse if burned out.

Step 2.   Remove and check stoplight bulbs. (See paragraph 4-28 or 4-29)

        Replace bulbs if burned out.

Step 3.   Check for voltage at orange lead on stoplight switch.

        If there is voltage, perform step 4.

        If there is no voltage, trace circuit. (See wiring diagram F-14, F-15, or F-17)

Step 4.   With brake pedal depressed, check for voltage at white/black lead on stoplight switch.

        Adjust switch for proper contact. (See paragraph 4-16, INSTALLATION) If there is still no voltage, trace circuit. (See wiring diagram F-14, F-15 or F-17)

        If there is voltage, replace switch. (See paragraph 4-19)

Table 2-4. Electrical Troubleshooting (Con't)

MALFUNCTION
  TEST OR INSPECTION
    CORRECTIVE ACTION

---

39. STOPLIGHTS WILL NOT TURN OFF

Step 1.   Disconnect connector from stoplight switch,

If lights go out, reconnect connector and adjust stoplight switch for proper contact with brake pedal. (See paragraph 4-16, INSTALLATION) If lights remain on, replace switch (See paragraph 4-16)

If lights remain on after disconnecting connector, trace circuit. (See wiring diagram F-14, F-15, or F-17)

40. TURN SIGNALS INOPERATIVE (HAZARD WARNING LIGHTS OPERATE)

Step 1.   Remove turn signal flasher. (See paragraph 4-12) Using jumper wire, connect fuse box terminals where flasher was installed. Lights should turn on, but not flash.

If lights turn on, replace flasher.

If lights do not turn on, trace circuit. (See wiring diagram F-13 or F-16)

41. TURN SIGNALS LIGHT BUT DO NOT FLASH

Step 1.   Check appropriate marker light or parking light bulb. (See paragraph 4-26 or 4-27)

Replace bulb if burned out.

Step 2.   Remove turn signal flasher. (See paragraph 4-12) Using jumper wire, connect fuse box terminals where flasher was installed. Lights should turn on, but not flash.

If lights turn on, replace flasher.

If lights do not turn on, trace circuit. (See wiring diagram F-13 or F-16)

STARTING SYSTEM

42. ENGINE WILL NOT CRANK (NO AUDIBLE CLICK FROM   STARTER SOLENOID)

Step 1.   Check 20 amp ignition fuse. (See paragraph 4-12)

Replace fuse if burned out.

Step 2.   Perform *Electrical Troubleshooting*   malfunction #5.

Table 2-4. Electrical Troubleshooting (Con't)

MALFUNCTION
    TEST OR INSPECTION
        CORRECTIVE ACTION

Step 3.   Inspect lead connections at starter solenoid for corrosion and damage. Check starter mounting bolts for looseness.

        Clean any corroded connections. Tighten any loose connections. Replace any damaged connections. Tighten starter mounting bolts to 33 lb.-ft. (45 N•m).

Step 4.   Have assistant hold key in "START" position. Check for voltage at purple lead on starter solenoid.

        If there is voltage, replace starter. (See paragraph 4-5)

        If there is no voltage, perform step 5.

Step 5.   Remove starter relay. (See paragraph 4-13) Turn key to "START" position. Check for voltage at purple/white lead terminal on starter relay connector.

        If there is voltage, perform step 6.

        If there is no voltage, trace circuit. (See wiring diagram F-1 or F-2)

Step 6.   Check for voltage at purple/white lead terminal on starter relay connector.

        If there is voltage, replace relay.

        If there is no voltage, trace circuit, (See wiring diagram F-1 or F-2)

Step 7.   Check for voltage at red lead terminal or starter relay connector.

        If there is voltage, replace relay.

        If there is no voltage, trace circuit. (See wiring diagram F-1 or F-2)

42.1. STARTER STAYS ENGAGED

NOTE

Original starter relays on vehicles prior to July 1985 production were defective. The point gap inside was too small causing starter to stay engaged. Vehicles produced after July 1985 and the current starter relay in supply system have a wider point gap to correct this problem.

    Perform *Electrical Troubleshooting* malfunction #42. (See wiring diagram F-1 or F-2)

    Replace relay.

Table 2-4. Electrical Troubleshooting (Con't)

MALFUNCTION
> **TEST OR INSPECTION**
>> **CORRECTIVE ACTION**

---

43. SLOW OR NO CRANKING, SOLENOID CLICKS

Step 1.   Perform *Electrical Troubleshooting*   malfunction #5.

Step 2.   Disconnect pink lead from fuel injector pump. Have assistant hold key in "START" position. Check voltage between front battery negative terminal and rear battery positive terminal.

> If voltage is not between 18.0 and 22.0, replace starter.

> If voltage is between 18.0 and 22.0, perform   *Mechanical Troubleshooting* malfunction #14.

WINDSHIELD WIPER/WASHER SYSTEM

44. WIPER MOTOR INOPERATIVE (ONE OR ALL SPEEDS)

Step 1.   Check 25 amp windshield wiper fuse, (See paragraph 4-12)

> Replace if burned out.

Step 2.   Turn key to "RUN" position. Turn wiper switch on. Check for voltage at windshield wiper motor.

> If there is voltage, replace windshield wiper motor, (See paragraph 10-11)

> If there is no voltage, trace circuit. (See wiring diagram F-20 or F-21)

45. WIPER MOTOR WILL NOT TURN OFF

Step 1.   Trace circuit. (See wiring diagram F-20 or F-21)

> If switch is good, replace windshield wiper motor. (See paragraph 10-11)

> If switch is not good, notify your supervisor.

Table 2-4. Electrical Troubleshooting (Con't)

MALFUNCTION
    TEST OR INSPECTION
        CORRECTIVE ACTION

---

46. WASHER INOPERATIVE; WIPER OPERATIVE

Step 1.   Check washer fluid reservoir for proper level.

Step 2.   Check washer nozzles and hoses for restrictions or damage.

Clear restrictions or replace if damaged. (See paragraph 10-11)

Step 3.   Turn key to "RUN" position. Have assistant hold control lever in "WASHER" position. Check for voltage to windshield washer solenoid.

If there is voltage, replace windshield wiper motor. (See paragraph 10-11)

If there is no voltage, trace circuit. (See wiring diagram F-20 or F-21)

2-12.   STE/ICE TROUBLESHOOTING

Simplified Test Equipment for Internal Combustion Engines (STE/ICE) for use with the CUCV Series trucks is in the process of being developed. When development is complete, STE/ICE troubleshooting procedures will be added to this manual.

CHAPTER 3
ENGINE SYSTEMS MAINTENANCE

Section I. LUBRICATION SYSTEM MAINTENANCE

3-1. LUBRICATION SYSTEM MAINTENANCE INDEX.

3-2. CRANKSHAFT PULLEY ASSEMBLY REPLACEMENT.

This task covers: a. Removal   b. Installation

INITIAL SETUP:

Equipment Condition

  Alternator belts removed. (See paragraph 4-2 or 4-3)
  Power steering belt removed. (See paragraph 8-15)
  Air conditioner belt removed (M1010) See paragraph 3-35)

---

a. REMOVAL

1.   Remove 4 bolts (1) and crankshaft pulley assembly (2) from torsional damper assembly (3).

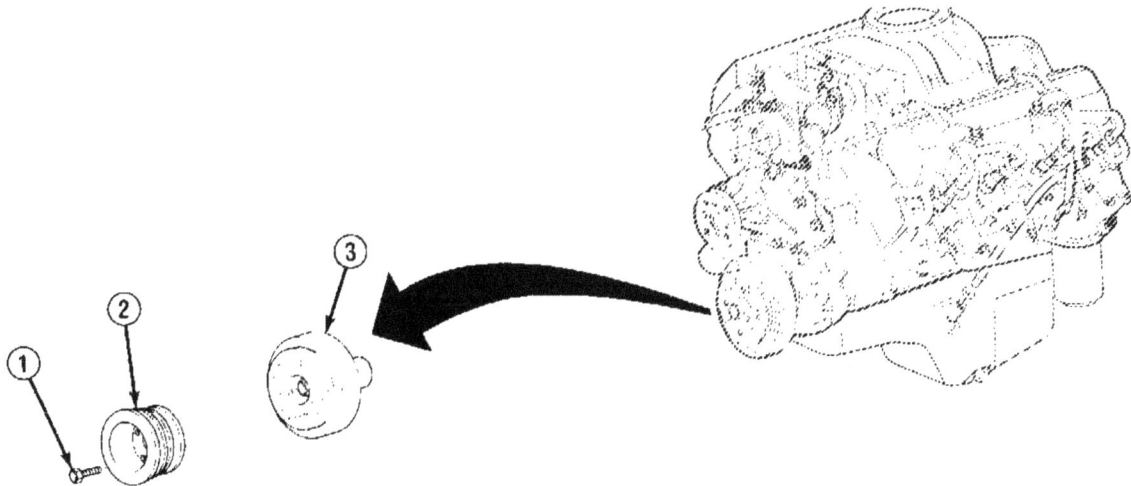

b. INSTALLATION

1.   Position crankshaft pulley assembly (2) against torsional damper assembly (3).

2.   Install 4 bolts (1) and tighten.

FOLLOW-ON TASKS:

  Install air conditioner belt (M1010). (See paragraph 3-35)
  Install power steering belt. (See paragraph 8-15)
  Install alternator belts. (See paragraph 4-2 or 4-3)

TA49770

3-3. ENGINE OIL LEVEL INDICATOR TUBE SEAL REPLACEMENT.

This task covers: a. Removal   b. Installation

INITIAL SETUP:

Equipment Condition   *Materials/Parts*
 Engine oil level indicator removed.   One seal

| a. | REMOVAL |

1. Remove nut (3) and washer (4) from mounting bracket (2).

2. Remove engine oil level indicator tube (1).

3. Remove and discard engine oil level indicator tube seal (5).

| b. | INSTALLATION |

1. Lubricate new engine oil level indicator tube seal (5) with engine oil, and install and seat against collar of engine oil level indicator tube (1).

2. Install engine oil level indicator tube (1).

3. Install and tighten nut (3) and washer (4) on mounting bracket (2).

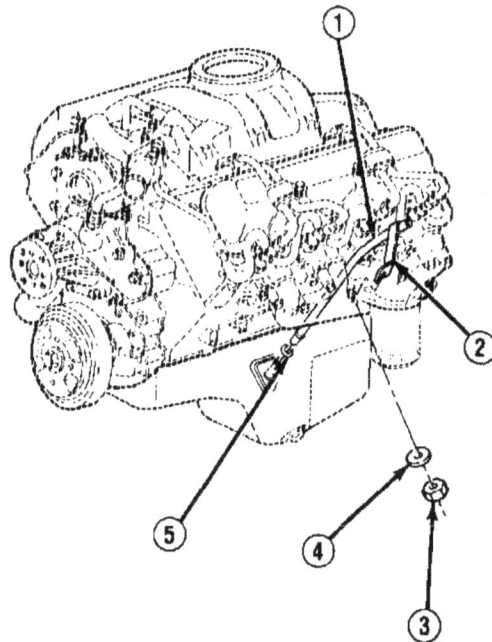

FOLLOW-ON TASKS:

 Install engine oil level indicator.

TA49771

3-4. ENGINE OIL AND OIL FILTER REPLACEMENT.

This task covers: a. Removal   b. Installation

INITIAL SETUP:

Materials/Parts
 • Engine oil filter

Manual References
 • LO 9-2320-289-12

Tools/Test Equipment
 • Torque wrench

| a. | **REMOVAL** |

1. Remove drainplug (3) and drain engine oil into a suitable container.

2. Remove engine oil filter (2) from engine oil filter connector (1). Discard engine oil filter.

| **b. INSTALLATION** |

1. Apply small amount of engine oil to sealing surface of new engine oil filter (2).

2. Install new engine oil filter (2) to engine oil filter connector (1).

3. Tighten engine oil filter (2) one full turn after sealing surface contacts engine block. DO NOT overtighten.

4. Install drainplug (3) and tighten to 20 lb.-ft. (27 N•m).

5. Refill engine oil. (See LO 9-2320-289-12)

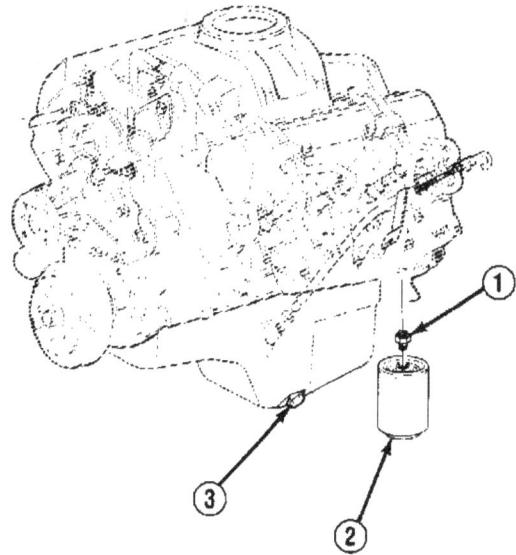

FOLLOW-ON TASKS:

 • Run engine and check for leaks.

TA49772

3-5. CRANKCASE DEPRESSION REGULATOR VALVE (CDRV) ASSEMBLY AND HOSES REPLACEMENT.

This task covers:	a. Removal	c. Installation
	b. Inspection	

INITIAL SETUP:

Equipment Condition

• Air cleaner removed. (See paragraph 3-9)

a. REMOVAL

NOTE

If removing crankcase depression regulator valve (CDRV) assembly (2), perform steps 1-4.

1. Loosen clamp (3) and disconnect crankcase depression hose (5).

2. Remove 2 bolts (1) attaching CDRV assembly (2) to bracket (17).

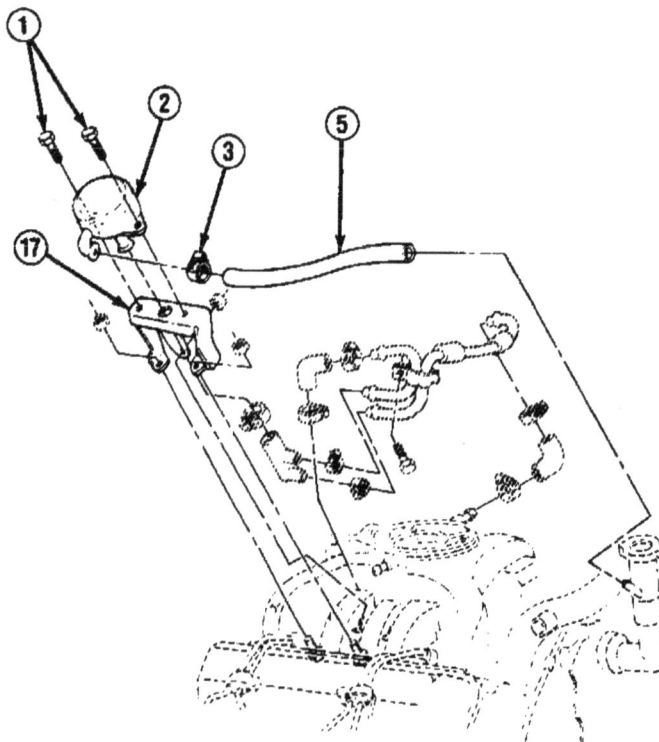

TA49773

3-5. CRANKCASE DEPRESSION REGULATOR VALVE (CDRV) ASSEMBLY AND HOSES REPLACEMENT (Con't).

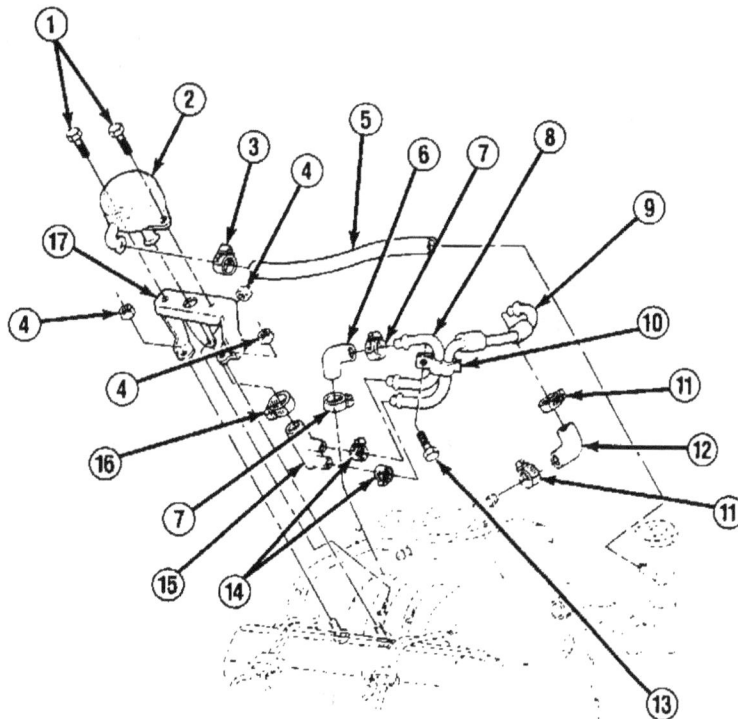

3. Loosen clamp (16) and disconnect crankcase depression connector (15).

4. Remove CDRV assembly (2).

5. Remove 3 nuts (4) and bracket (17).

6. Loosen 2 clamps (14) and disconnect 2 tubes (8 and 9) from crankcase depression connector (15).

7, Loosen 2 clamps (11) and remove left crankcase depression connector elbow (12).

TA49774

3-5.   CRANKCASE DEPRESSION REGULATOR VALVE (CDRV) ASSEMBLY AND HOSES REPLACEMENT (Con't).

8.   Loosen 2 clamps   (7) and remove right crankcase depression connector elbow (6).

9.   Separate 2 tubes   (8 and 9) by removing screw (13) and clamp (10).

b.   INSPECTION

1.   Inspect tubes (8 and 9) and hose (5) for cracks, splits, or breaks. Replace as required.

2.   Inspect bracket (17) and all clamps (3, 7, 10, 11, 14, and 16) to ensure that they are not bent or broken. Replace as required.

c.   INSTALLATION

NOTE

If installing CDRV assembly (2), perform steps 5-8.

1.   Secure 2 tubes (8 and 9) with clamp (10) and screw (13).

2.   Install longer tube (9) and clamp (11) to left crankcase depression connector elbow (12). Install left crankcase depression connector elbow at left side of intake manifold with clamp.

3.   Install shorter tube (8) and clamp (7) to right crankcase depression connector elbow (6). Install right crankcase depression connector elbow at right side of intake manifold with clamp.

4.   Install 2 clamps (14) and other ends of 2 tubes (8 and 9) to crankcase depression connector (15).

5.   Install CDRV assembly (2) through bracket (17) and connect to crankcase depression connector (15) with clamp (16).

6.   Connect crankcase depression hose (5) to CDRV assembly (2) with clamp (3).

7.   Install CDRV assembly (2) to bracket (17) with 2 bolts (1).

8.   Secure bracket (17) to engine block with   3 nuts (4).

FOLLOW-ON TASKS:

  •Install air cleaner. (See paragraph 3-9)

3-6. ENGINE OIL COOLER SUPPLY AND RETURN PIPES AND HOSES REPLACEMENT.

This task covers: a. Removal   c. Installation
                         b. Inspection

INITIAL SETUP:

Equipment Condition   *Materials/Parts*
  Fan shroud removed. (See paragraph 3-31)   ●One lockwasher

---

a.	REMOVAL

NOTE

- All connection points have seals (9). DO NOT lose these seals. If not damaged, they can be reused for installation of replacement pipes (14 and 15) and hoses (2 and 11).

- If removing engine   oil cooler pipes (14 and 15), perform steps 1-3.

- If removing engine   oil cooler hoses (2 and 11), perform steps 2 and 4 through 6.

1.   Disconnect engine oil cooler pipes (14 and 15) from   right side of radiator (1).

NOTE

Some trucks have an engine oil sampling   valve (13) which taps into engine oil cooler system at connection between hose (2) and pipe (14).

Tag pipes (14 and 15) and hoses (2 and 11) for installation.

2.   Disconnect engine oil cooler pipes (14 and 15) from engine oil cooler hoses (2 and 11) at left side of radiator (1). If present, disconnect engine oil sampling valve (13) at square connector (16).

3.   Remove engine oil cooler pipes (14 and 15).

4.   Disconnect engine oil cooler hoses (2 and 11) at connectors (4).

5.   At engine block, remove bolt (8), insulation washer   (6), lockwasher (7), and clip (10) from bracket (5). Discard lockwasher.

NOTE

On trucks with winterization kits, engine oil cooler hoses (2 and 11) run under engine coolant heater. To remove hoses, pull them out from under this heater.

6.   Remove nut (3), hose clamp (12), and engine oil cooler hoses (2 and 11).

3-6. ENGINE OIL COOLER SUPPLY AND RETURN PIPES AND HOSES REPLACEMENT (Con't).

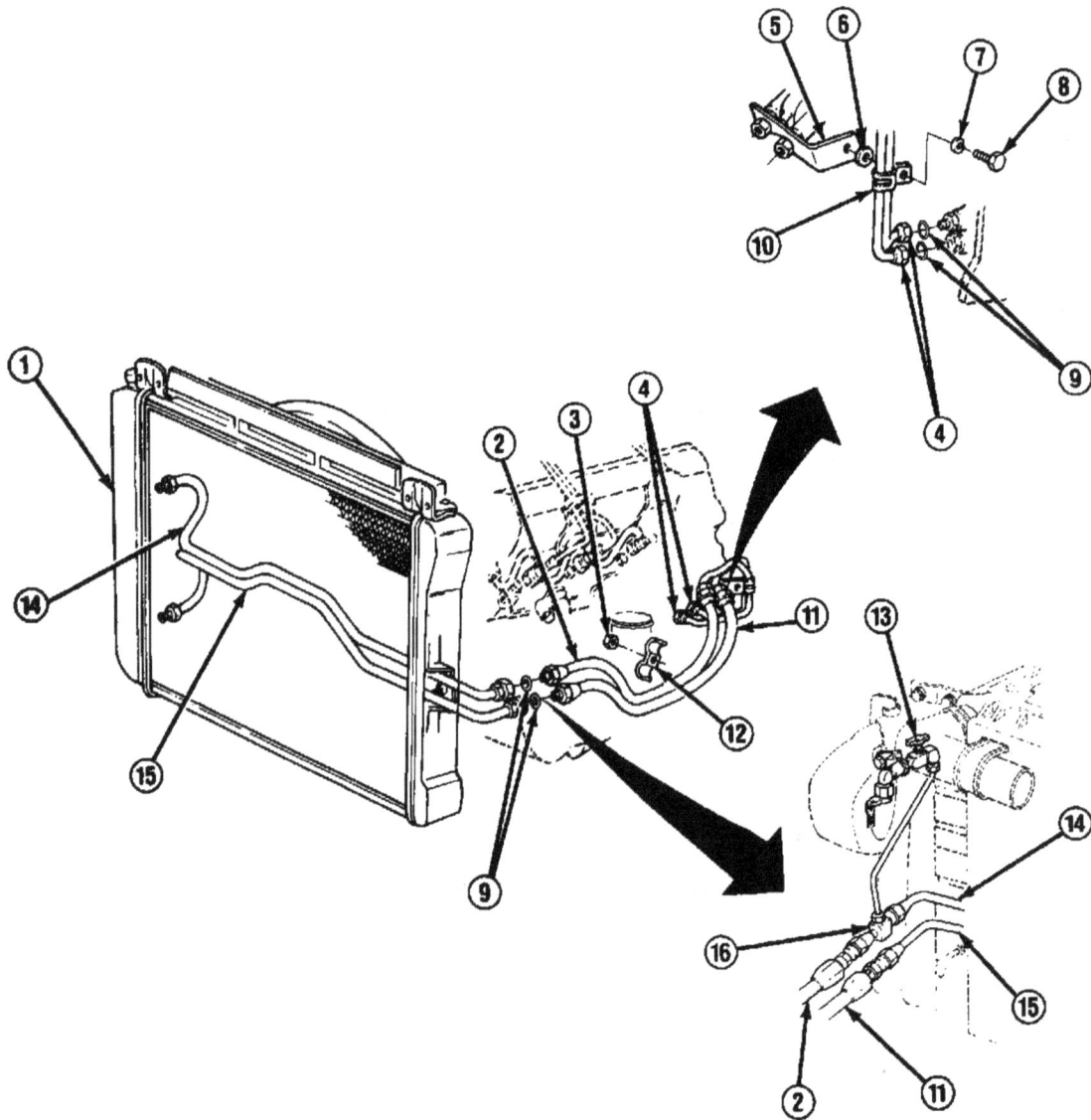

| b. | INSPECTION |

1. Inspect all hoses (2 and 11) and pipes (14 and 15) for signs of cracks, splits, and punctures. Replace as required.

2. Replace any damaged seals (9).

TA49775

3-6. ENGINE OIL COOLER SUPPLY AND RETURN PIPES AND HOSES REPLACEMENT (Con't).

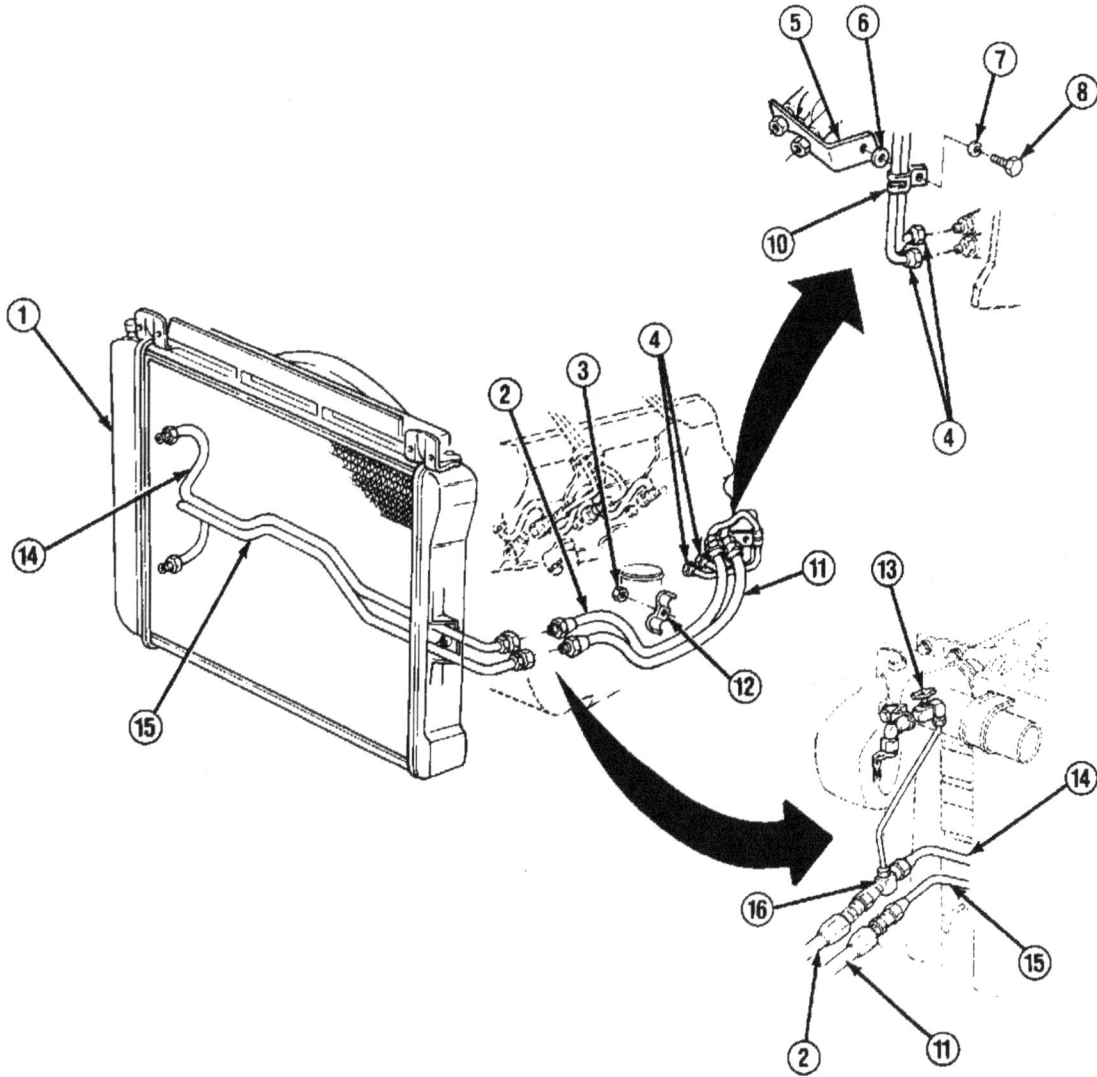

c. INSTALLATION

NOTE

◀f installing engine oil cooler hoses (2 and 11), perform steps 1-5.

◀f installing engine oil cooler pipes (14 and 15), perform steps 5-8.

1. Connect engine oil cooler hoses (2 and 11) at connectors (4).

TA49776

3-6. ENGINE OIL COOLER SUPPLY AND RETURN PIPES AND HOSES REPLACEMENT (Con't).

2.   Secure engine oil cooler hoses (2 and 11) to bracket (5) at engine block with clip (10), new lockwasher (7), insulation washer (6), and bolt (8).

NOTE

Step 3 only applies to trucks equipped with winterization kits.

3.   Feed engine oil cooler hoses (2 and 11) under engine coolant heater brackets.

4.   Secure engine oil cooler hoses (2 and 11) to wheelwell with hose clamp (12) and nut (3).

5.   Connect engine oil cooler hose   11) to engine oil cooler pipe (15) at left side of radiator (1).

NOTE

Step 6   only applies to   trucks equipped with engine oil sampling valve.

If truck is equipped with engine oil sampling valve (13), perform steps 6 and 8.

6.   Connect engine oil cooler hose (2) to engine oil sampling valve (13) at square connector (16). Connect square connector to engine oil cooler pipe (14).

7.   Connect engine oil cooler hose (2) to engine oil cooler pipe (14).

8.   Connect engine oil cooler pipes (14 and 15) to radiator (1) at right side.

FOLLOW-ON TASKS:

Install fan shroud.   (See paragraph 3-31)
Check for leaks.

3-7. VACUUM PUMP REPLACEMENT.

This task covers: a. Removal b. Installation

INITIAL SETUP:

Equipment Condition
  ● Both battery negative cables disconnected. (See paragraph 4-38)
  ● Air cleaner removed. (See paragraph 3-9)

Tools/Test Equipment
  ● Torque wrench

Materials/Parts
  ● One gasket

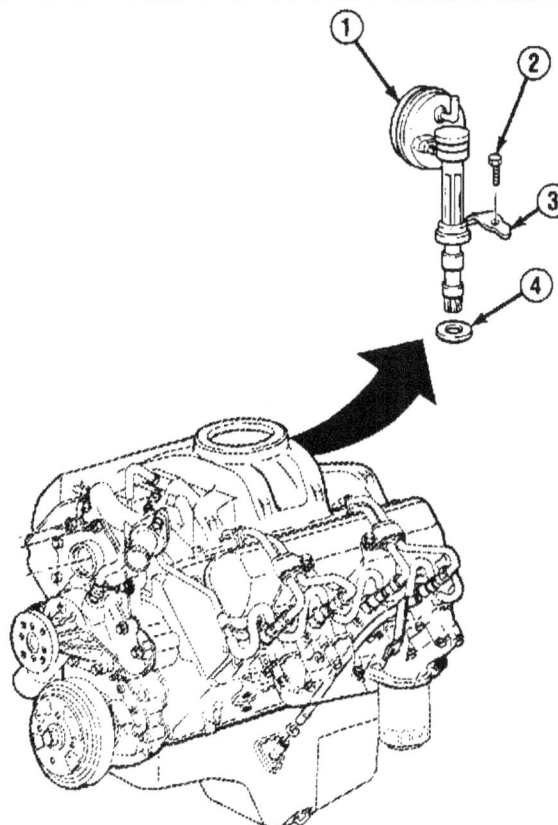

| a. | **REMOVAL** |

1. Remove vacuum line from vacuum pump (1). Remove bolt (2) and lift clamp (3) away from vacuum pump.

2. Remove vacuum pump (1).

3. Inspect gasket (4). Remove and discard if damaged.

| b. | **INSTALLATION** |

1. Install new gasket (4) if removed.

2. Install vacuum pump (1) into engine.

3. Position clamp (3) on vacuum pump (1).

4. Install bolt (2) in clamp (3) and tighten to 20 lb.-ft. (27 N•m).

5. Install vacuum line on vacuum pump (1).

FOLLOW-ON TASKS:

  ● Install air cleaner. (See paragraph 3-9)
  ● Connect both battery negative cables. (See paragraph 4-38)

TA49777

3-7.1. ENGINE OIL PAN REPLACEMENT.

This task covers: a. Removal   c. Installation
                           b. Cleaning and Inspection

INITIAL SETUP:

Equipment Condition

Front of truck raised and supported by jack
stands with front axle hanging free.
Starter removed. (See paragraph 4-5)
Engine oil level indicator tube and seal
removed. (See paragraph 3-3)
Engine oil drained. (See paragraph 3-4)
Engine oil filter removed.
(See paragraph 3-4)

Materials/Parts

• One engine oil pan gasket
• One engine oil pan seal
• Dry cleaning solvent
    (Item 15, Appendix C)
• RTV sealant (Item 41, Appendix C)

General Safety Instructions
Dry cleaning solvent is flammable and
    must not be used near open flame.
    Use only in a well-ventilated area.

| a. | REMOVAL |

NOTE

Step 1 only applies to trucks equipped with winterization kits.

1. Loosen clamp (4) and disconnect
front exhaust pipe (3) from engine oil
pan (5). Remove 4 screws (1) and
heat exchange pipe (2).

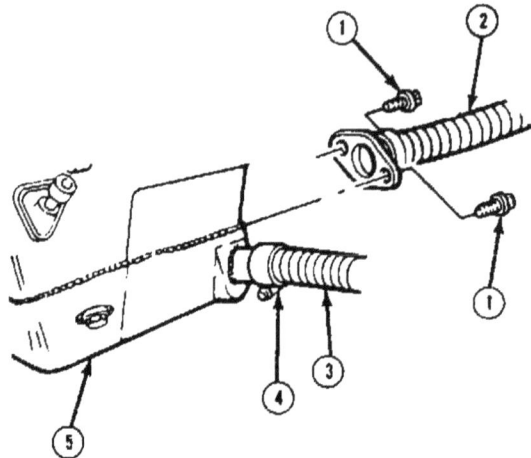

TA701823

3-7.1. ENGINE OIL PAN REPLACEMENT (Con't).

2. Remove 6 bolts (6) and torque converter cover (8) from transmission assembly (7).

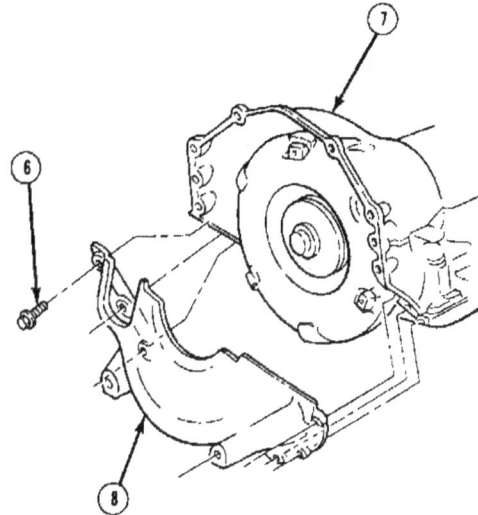

NOTE

Ensure that location of transmission oil cooler line clip is noted for installation.

3. Remove 2 1 bolts (12) and transmission oil cooler line clip. Remove 2 rear bolts (11).

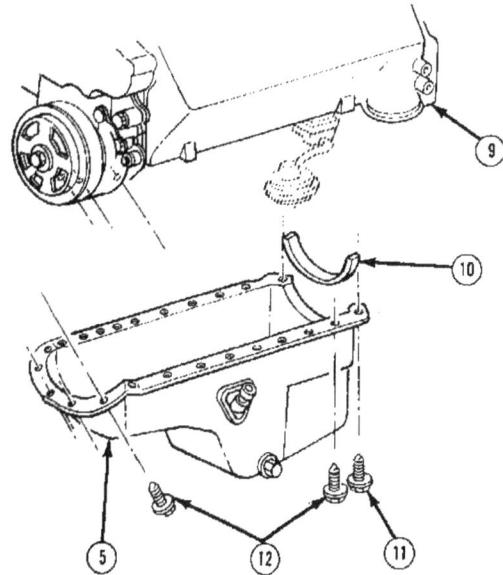

TA701824

3-7.1. ENGINE OIL PAN REPLACEMENT (Con't).

NOTE

Ensure that location of engine oil pan stud (13) is noted for installation.

4. Remove nut (15) and starter lead clip (14) from engine oil pan stud (13). Remove engine oil pan stud.

NOTE

Early 1984 model trucks have engine oil pan (5) with a ridged lip which requires an engine oil pan gasket. Late 1984-87 model truck engine oil pans and replacement engine oil pans have a flat lip which requires RTV sealant.

5. Remove engine oil pan (5) and engine oil pan seal (10). Remove and discard engine oil pan gasket if present. Discard engine oil pan seal.

b. CLEANING AND INSPECTION

WARNING

Dry cleaning solvent P-D-680 is toxic and flammable. Always wear protective goggles and gloves and use only in a well-ventilated area. Avoid contact with skin, eyes, and clothes and DO NOT breathe vapors. DO NOT use near open flame or excessive heat. The solvent's flash point is 100°F-138°F (38°C-59°C). If you become dizzy while using cleaning solvent, immediately get fresh air and medical help. If solvent contacts eyes, immediately wash your eyes with water and get medical aid.

1. Clean oil and all RTV sealant or gasket material from mating surfaces of engine oil pan (5) and engine (9) block with dry cleaning solvent.

TA701825

3-7.1. ENGINE OIL PAN REPLACEMENT (Con't).

2. Inspect engine oil pan (5) for damage.
Discard engine oil pan if damaged.

c. INSTALLATION

1. Install new engine oil pan seal (10) in
groove at rear of engine (9) block.
Apply RTV sealant to each end of
engine oil pan seal.

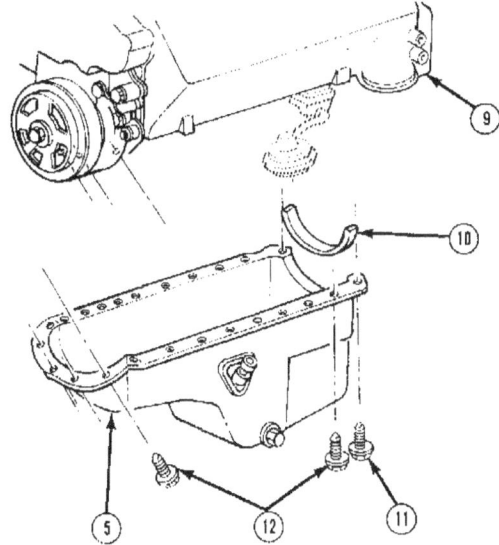

NOTE

◀f installing new engine oil pan gasket with engine oil pan (5), perform
step 2.

◀f applying RTV sealant or installing new engine oil pan (5). Perform step
3.

2. Install new engine oil pan gasket on lip
of engine oil pan (5) and aline with bolt
holes.

3. Apply a 0.19 in. (5 mm) bead of RTV
sealant (16) along engine oil pan (5)
sealing surface as shown.

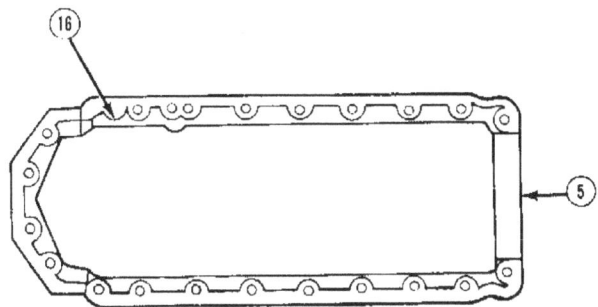

TA701826

3-7.1. ENGINE OIL PAN REPLACEMENT (Con't).

4. Position engine oil pan (5) under engine (9) block and install engine oil pan stud (13). Install starter lead clip (14) on engine oil pan stud with nut (15).

5. Install 2 rear bolts (11). Install transmission oil cooler line clip and 21 bolts (12) .

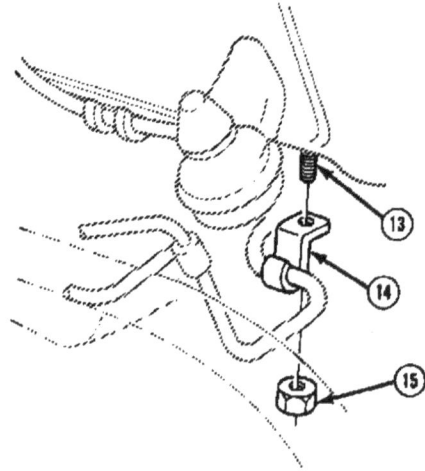

6. Install torque converter cover (8) on transmission assembly (7) with 6 bolts (6) .

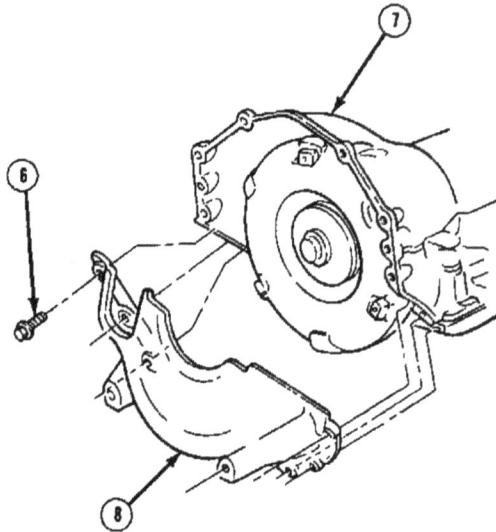

TA701827

3-32. ENGINE OIL PAN REPLACEMENT (Con't).

NOTE

Step 7 only applies to trucks equipped with winterization kits.

7. Install heat exchange pipe (2) with 4 screws (1). Connect front exhaust pipe (3) to engine oil pan (5) and tighten clamp (4).

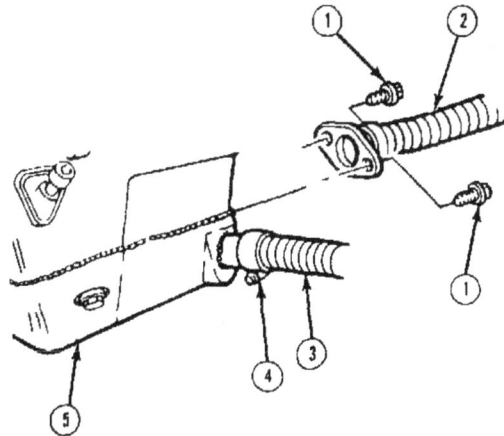

FOLLOW-ON TASKS:

- Install engine oil filter. (See paragraph 3-4)
- Install engine oil level indicator tube and seal. (See paragraph 3-3)
- Fill engine oil. (See paragraph 3-4)
- Install starter. (See paragraph 4-5)
- Remove jack stands and lower truck, if raised.

TA701828

Section II.   FUEL SYSTEM MAINTENANCE

3-8.   FUEL SYSTEM MAINTENANCE INDEX.

3-9. AIR CLEANER AND SEAL REPLACEMENT.

This task covers: a.   Removal   b. Installation

a.   REMOVAL

CAUTION

When servicing air cleaner assembly (6), place a screen or a clean rag over air intake opening to guard against objects falling   inside. Failure to follow this caution may result in equipment damage.

1.   Remove 2 nuts (2), 2 washers (1), and lid (3) of air cleaner assembly (6).

2.   Remove filter element (4), polywrap band (5), and air cleaner assembly (6).

3.   Remove air cleaner seal (7) and discard if damaged.

4.   Clean polywrap band (5) if required. (See TM 9-2320-289-10)

b.   INSTALLATION

NOTE

Remove screen or   rag from air intake opening.

1.   If removed, install air cleaner seal (7) over intake manifold inlet (9).

2.   Install air cleaner assembly (6) on air cleaner seal (7).

3.   Install filter element (4) and polywrap band (5) inside air cleaner assembly (6).

4.   Install lid (3) of air cleaner assembly (6) with studs (8) on intake manifold (9) fitted through holes in lid.

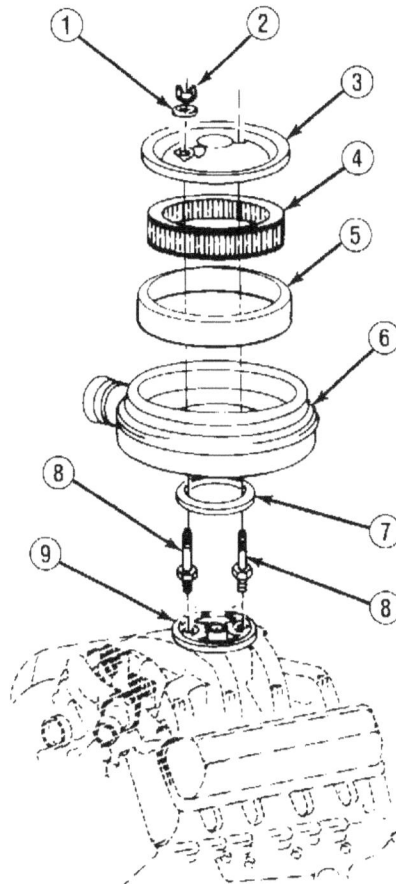

TA49778

3-9. AIR CLEANER AND SEAL REPLACEMENT (Con't).

CAUTION

DO NOT install nuts (2) without a washer (1) under each   nut. Washers
prevent dust and dirt from entering intake manifold (9)   and causing
premature engine failure.

5.   Install 2 washers (1) and nuts (2) finger tight.

3-10. FUEL PUMP AND PUSHROD REPLACEMENT.

This task covers:	a. Removal	b. Installation

INITIAL SETUP:

Equipment Condition

- Both battery negative cables disconnected. (See paragraph 4-38)
- Alternators, alternator brackets, and mounting hardware removed (M1010). (See paragraph 4-3)

Too/s/Test Equipment

- 10 mm socket

Materials/Parts

- One fuel pump gasket
- One mounting plate gasket
- Grease (Item 26, Appendix C)
- Tie-down strap (Item 44, Appendix C)

General Safety Instructions

- DO NOT perform this procedure near fire, flames, or sparks.

---

a. REMOVAL

WARNING

Diesel fuel is flammable. DO NOT perform this procedure near fire, flames, or sparks. A fire extinguisher must be on hand in work area. Failure to follow this warning may result in serious injury or death.

NOTE

Place suitable container under fuel pump (3) to catch any escaping fuel.

1. Disconnect fuel inlet hose (9) and fuel injector pump pipe assembly line (1) from fuel pump (3).

2. Remove 2 bolts (2), fuel pump (3), and gasket (4). Discard gasket.

NOTE

Perform step 3 only if removing pushrod (7).

3. Use metric socket to remove 2 bolts (8), mounting plate (5), gasket (6), and pushrod (7). Discard gasket.

3-10. FUEL PUMP AND PUSHROD REPLACEMENT (Con't).

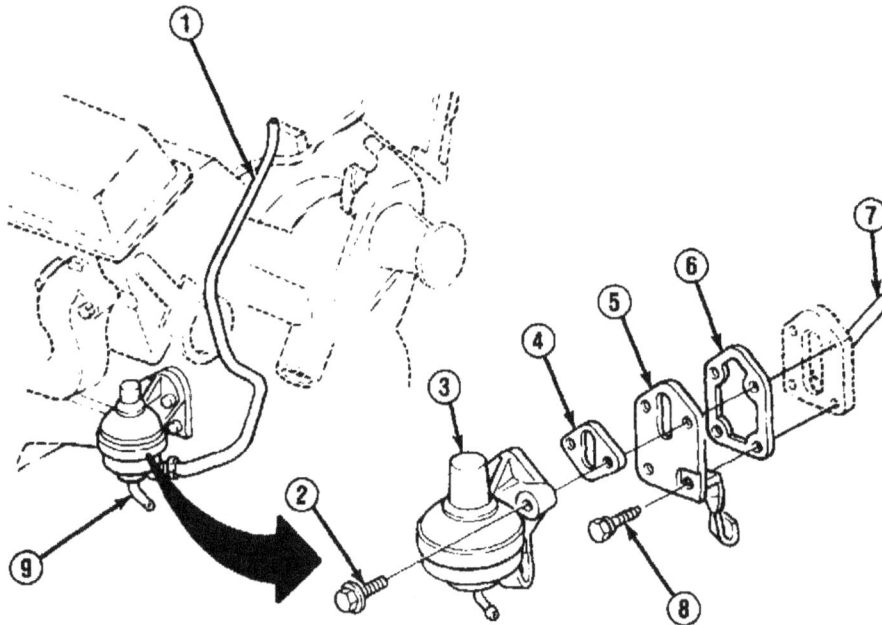

---

b. INSTALLATION

NOTE

- Alternately and evenly tighten bolts (8) to guarantee a tight fit and to avoid a possible oil leak.

- Ensure that all gasket material   has been removed from surfaces and that surfaces are clean.

- Perform steps 1 and 2 only if installing pushrod (7).

1. Apply a coat of grease on pushrod (7) to hold it up against camshaft as required.

2. If removed, install push rod (7), new gasket (6), and mounting plate (5). Use metric socket to install 2 bolts (8).

3. Install new gasket (4), fuel pump (3), and 2 bolts (2).

4. Install fuel injection pump pipe assembly line (1) and fuel inlet hose (9) to fuel pump (3).

FOLLOW-ON TASKS:

Install alternators, alternator brackets, and mounting hardware (M1010). (See paragraph 4-3)
Connect both battery negative cables. (See paragraph 4-38)
Check for leaks. If engine fails to start, bleed air from fuel system. (See paragraph 3-17)

TA49779

3-11.   FUEL TANK AND SHIELD MAINTENANCE (ALL EXCEPT M1009).

This task covers: a. Removal   c. Installation
                            b. Inspection

INITIAL SETUP:

Equipment Condition

●Both battery negative cables disconnected.
   (See paragraph 4-38)
●Fuel tank drained.

Too/s/Test Equipment

Fuel remover/installer, J-24187

Materials/Parts

●One gasket
●Seven lockwashers
●One starwasher

Personnel Required

●MOS 63B (2)

General Safety Instructions

●DO NOT perform this procedure near fire, flames, or sparks.
●Always wear goggles when working on underside of truck.

---

a.   REMOVAL

WARNING

● Diesel fuel is flammable.   DO NOT perform this procedure near fire,
  flames, or sparks. A fire extinguisher must be on hand in work area.
  Failure to follow this warning may result in serious injury or death.

● Always wear goggles when working on underside of truck. Fuel spillage
  can occur when disconnecting fuel lines. Failure to follow this warning
  may result in serious eye injury.

NOTE

● If removing fuel tank shield assembly (25), perform step 1.

● When removing fuel tank shield assembly (25), 2 bolts (23) remain in
  support assemblies (4) as a guide when installing fuel tank shield
  assembly.

1.   Remove 5 nuts (11), lockwashers (10), and 3 bolts (7), and remove fuel tank shield assembly
      (25). Discard lockwashers.

2.   Remove 2 bolts (5), nuts (9), lockwashers (8), and brackets (6). Discard lockwashers.

3.   Remove 2 bolts (24), nuts (27), and bracket (26).

4.   Loosen clamp (13) and remove fuel tank fill vent hose (12) from fuel tank (19).

5.   Loosen clamp (15) and remove fuel tank fill hose (14) from fuel tank (19).

3-11. FUEL TANK AND SHIELD MAINTENANCE (ALL EXCEPT M1009) (Con't).

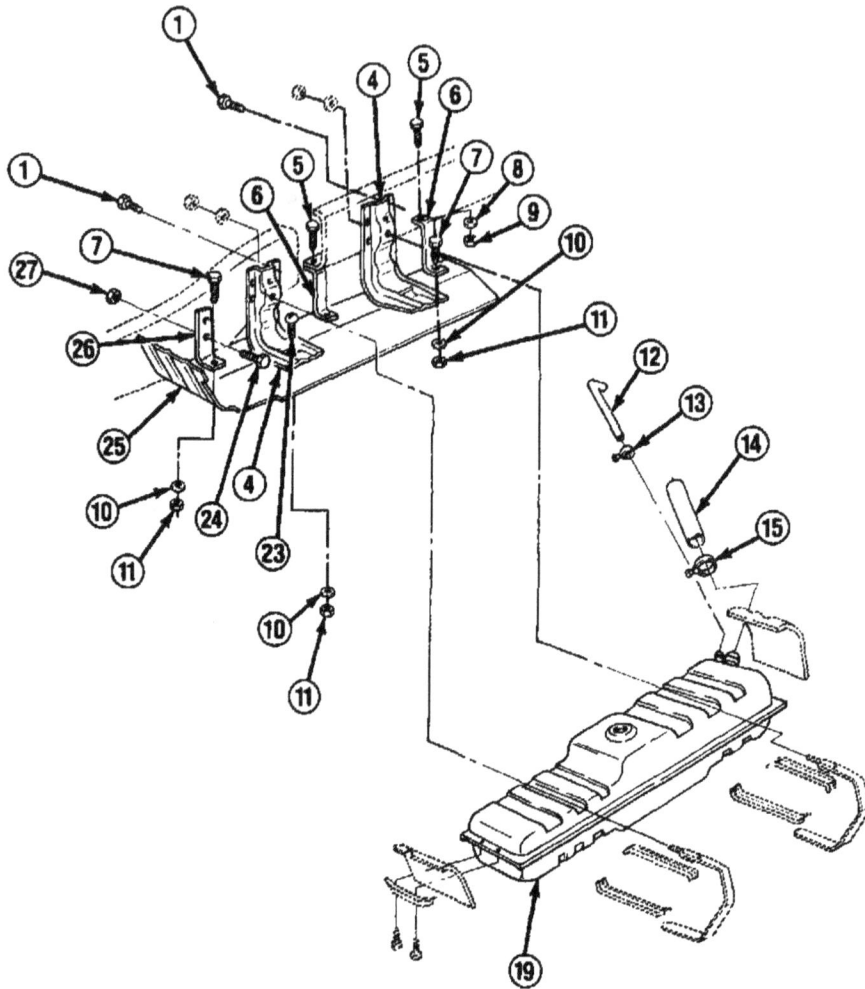

6. Disconnect ground wire (34) from truck frame (28). Discard starwasher.

NOTE

Use an assistant and suitable support when performing steps 7-9.

7. Remove 8 bolts (1) from 2 support assemblies (4).

8. Lower fuel tank (19) and 2 support assemblies (4) enough to remove drain (30), feed (33), 2 return (29) hoses and sending unit wire (32) from fuel tank sending unit (31).

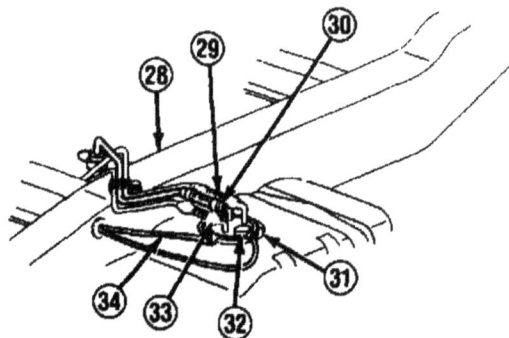

TA49780

3-11.   FUEL TANK AND SHIELD MAINTENANCE (ALL EXCEPT M1009) (Con't).

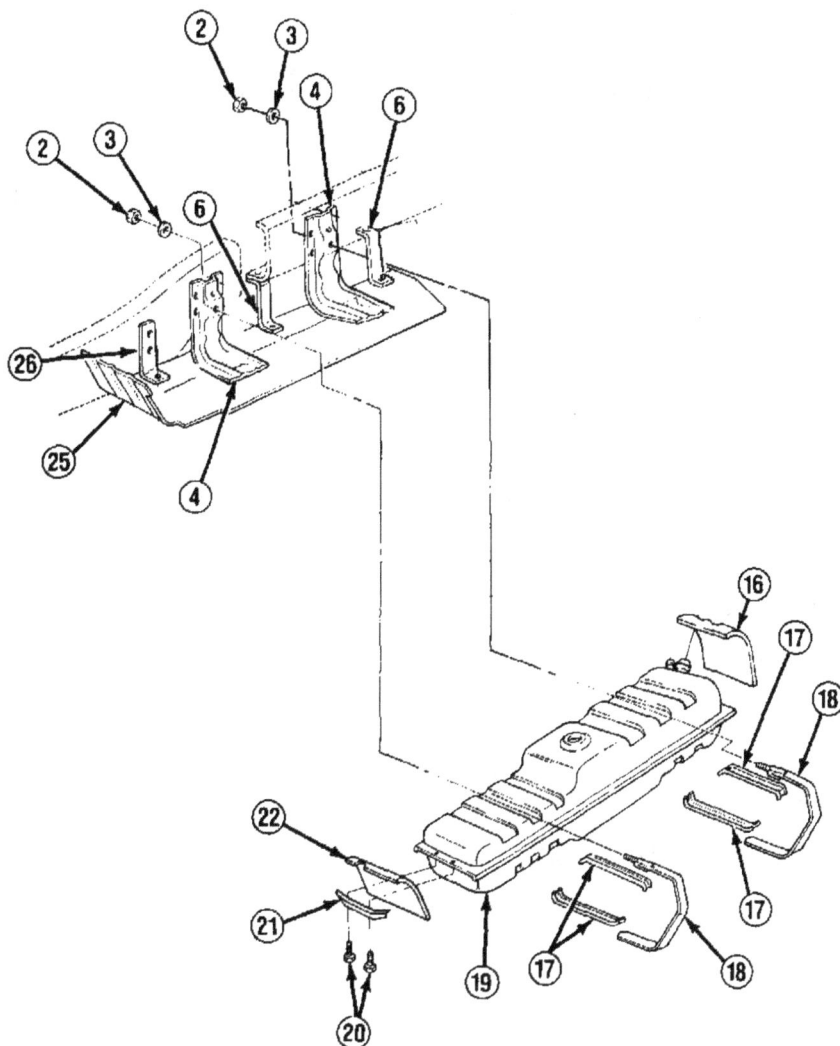

9.   Lower fuel tank (19) to floor.

10.   Remove 2 nuts (2) and lockwashers (3), and pull back 2 flexible strap assemblies (18) from fuel tank (19).

11.   Remove 2 strap insulators (17) and remove fuel tank (19).

12.   Remove 2 screws (20), support (21), and front shield (22).

13.   Remove rear shield (16) from fuel tank (19).

TA49781

3-11. FUEL TANK AND SHIELD MAINTENANCE (ALL EXCEPT M1009) (Con't).

CAUTION

Thoroughly clean area before removing fuel tank sending unit (31) from fuel tank (19). Failure to follow this caution may result in dirt falling into fuel tank.

14. Remove fuel tank sending unit cam (35).

15. Remove fuel tank sending unit (31) and gasket (36). Discard gasket.

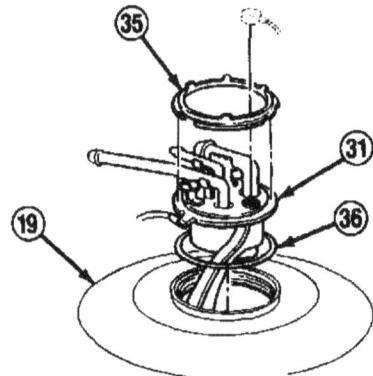

| b. | INSPECTION |

1. Inspect fuel tank shields (16 and 22) for tears or holes.

2. Inspect fuel tank (19) for corrosion, splits, cracks, or punctures.

3. Inspect 2 strap assemblies (18), 2 support assemblies (4), and 3 brackets (6 and 26) for dents, cracks, or corrosion.

4. Inspect fuel tank insulators (17) for signs of wear.

5. Replace any corroded, damaged, or worn components as required.

| c. | INSTALLATION |

NOTE

If installing fuel tank shield assembly (25), perform steps 18 and 19.

1. Install new gasket (36) over fuel tank (19) opening. Install fuel tank sending unit (31) and fuel sending unit cam (35).

2. Install 2 strap insulators (17) inside 2 strap assemblies (18).

3. Position 2 strap assemblies (18) with 2 attached support assemblies (4) around fuel tank (19).

4. Install 2 new lockwashers (3) and nuts (2) to ends of 2 strap assemblies (18). DO NOT fully tighten nuts.

5. Install rear shield (16) over fuel tank (19).

6. Install front shield (22), brace (21), and 2 bolts (20).

TA49782

3-11. FUEL TANK AND SHIELD MAINTENANCE (ALL EXCEPT M1009) (Con't).

NOTE

Use an assistant and suitable support when performing steps 7-11.

7. Raise fuel tank (19) to within approximately 5 in. (12.7 cm) of fully installed position and install feed (33), return (29), and drain (30) hoses to sending unit (31).

8. Install sending unit wire (32) on fuel tank sending unit (31).

9. Feed ground wire (34) through access hole in truck frame (28), but DO NOT connect.

10. Raise fuel tank (19) to fully raised position.

11. Partially install 8 bolts (1) through truck frame (28) and suppor t assemblies (4).

12. Tighten 8 bolts (1) and remove support from fuel tank (19).

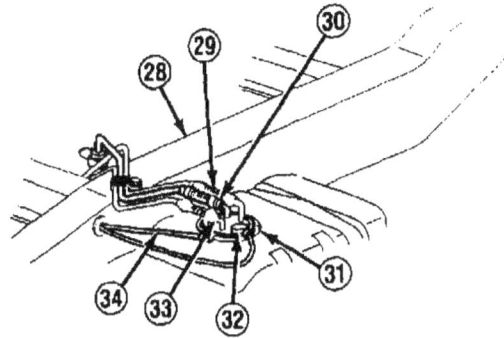

NOTE

Ensure that starwasher is installed between ground wire (34) terminal and truck frame (28).

13. Install ground wire (34) to truck frame (28) using new starwasher.

14. Install fuel tank fill hose (14) and clamp (15) at fuel tank (19).

15. Install fuel tank fill vent hose (12) and clamp (13) at fuel tank (19).

16. Install bracket (26) with 2 bolts (24) and nuts (27).

17. Install 2 brackets (6) with 2 bolts (5), new lockwashers (8), and nuts (9). DO NOT fully tighten.

18. Guide shield (25) onto 2 guide bolts (23) and install 2 new lockwashers (10) and nuts (11). DO NOT fully tighten.

19. Install 3 bolts (7) through 2 brackets (6) and bracket (26) using 3 new lockwashers (10) and nuts (11). DO NOT fully tighten.

20. Tighten 2 nuts (2) which secure 2 strap assemblies (18) to 2 support assemblies (4).

21. Tighten 2 nuts (9) and 5 nuts (11).

TA49783

3-11. FUEL TANK AND SHIELD MAINTENANCE (ALL EXCEPT M1009) (Con't).

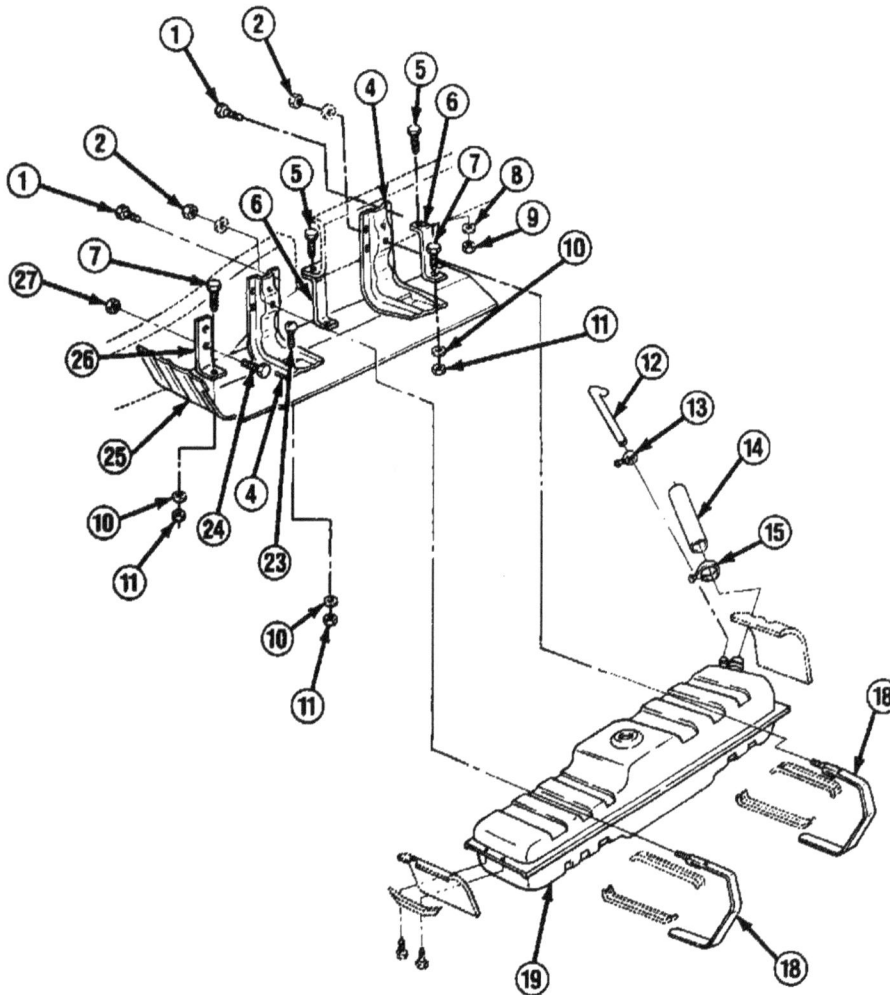

FOLLOW-ON TASKS:

● Refill fuel tank,
● Connect both battery negative cables. (See paragraph 4-38)
● Bleed air from fuel system. (See paragraph 3-17)
● Check for leaks.

TA49784

3-12. FUEL TANK AND SHIELD MAINTENANCE (M1009).

This task covers: a. Removal   b. Installation

INITIAL SETUP:

Equipment Condition

● Both battery negative cables disconnected.
   (See paragraph 4-38)
● Fuel tank drained.

Tools/Test Equipment

● Fuel remover/installer,   J-24187
● Torque wrench

Materials/Parts

● One gasket
● Four lockwashers
● One starwasher

Personnel Required

● MOS 63B (2)

General Safety Instructions

● DO NOT perform this procedure near fire, flames, or sparks.
● Always wear goggles when working on underside of truck.

---

a.	REMOVAL

WARNING

Diesel fuel is flammable. DO NOT perform this procedure near fire,
   flames, or sparks. A fire extinguisher must be on hand in work area.
   Failure to follow this warning may result in serious injury or death.

Always wear goggles when working on underside of truck. Fuel spillage
   can occur when disconnecting fuel lines. Failure to follow this warning
   may result in serious eye injury.

NOTE

If removing fuel tank shield (25), perform steps 1-5.

Access to bolts (12) and washers (11) in step 1, bolts in step 5, and
   nuts and washers in step 7, is easier with endgate   **down**.

1.   Remove 2 bolts (12) and washers (11) at tow hook bracket (10).

NOTE

At center of rear bumper brace (1), 2 bolts (5) are installed into
   weldnuts (2).

2.   Remove 6 bolts (5), 10 washers (4), and 4 nuts (3), and remove rear bumper brace (1).

3.   Remove 4 bolts (9), nuts (6), lockwashers (7), and washers (8) which secure tow hook
     bracket (10) to rear bumper. Discard lockwashers.

3-12.   FUEL TANK AND SHIELD MAINTENANCE (M1009) (Con't).

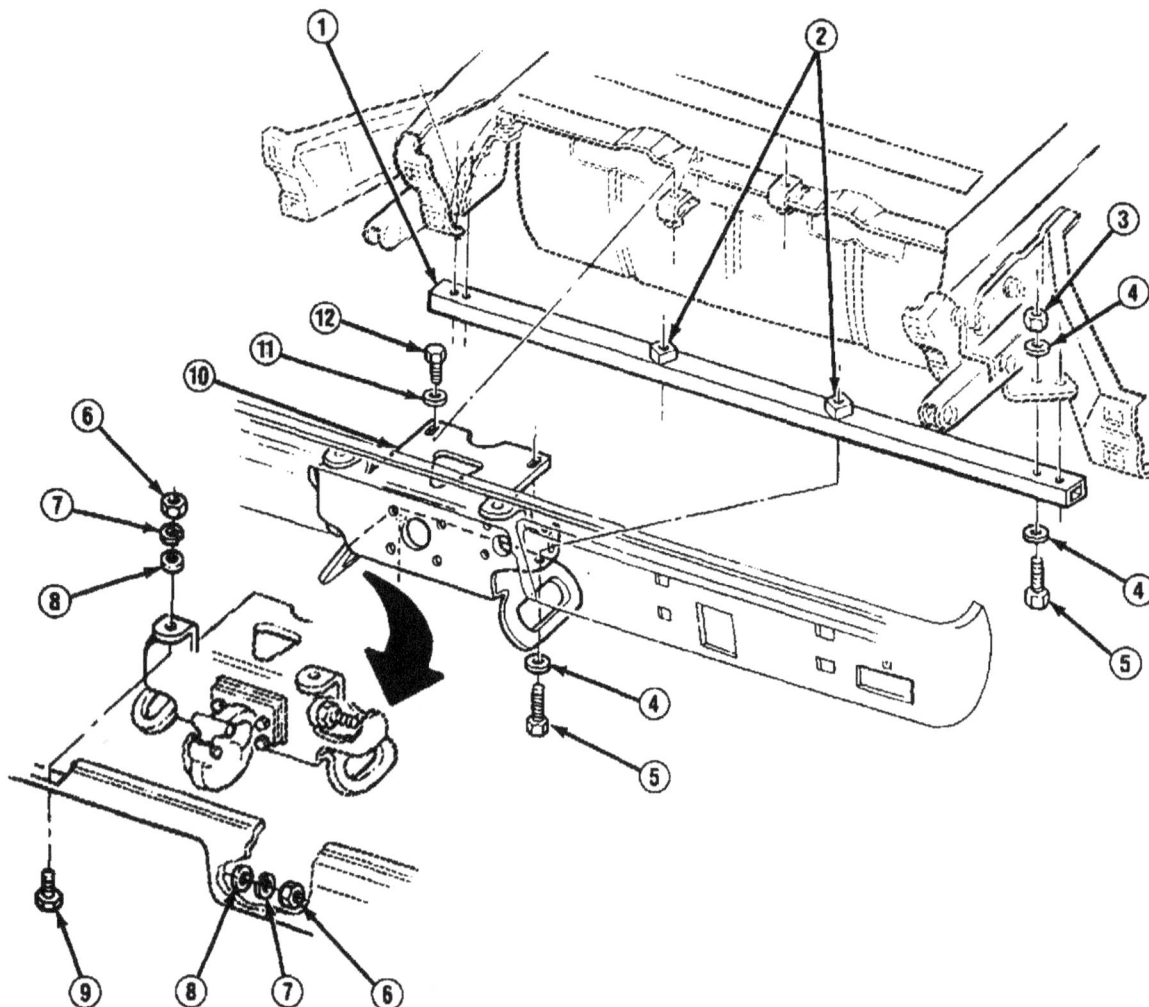

4.   Move tow hook bracket (10) to rear
2-3 in. (5.1-7.6 cm) to clear fuel
tank shield (25).

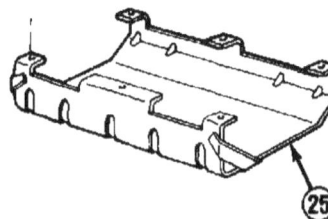

TA49785

3-12. FUEL TANK AND SHIELD MAINTENANCE (M1009) (Con't).

5. Remove 6 bolts (28) from fuel tank shield (25). Remove fuel tank shield.

6. Disconnect ground wire (17) from top of frame on left of truck. Discard starwasher.

NOTE

2 nuts (20) function as spacers for 2 strap assemblies (24) and should not be removed from strap assemblies.

Use an assistant and provide suitable support when performing steps 7-15.

7. Remove 2 nuts (18), wiring harness tabs, and washers (19) from 2 strap assemblies (24). Remove strap assemblies through frame.

8. Remove 2 insulators (23).

9. Loosen clamp (48) and disconnect fill hose (47) from fill pipe assembly (30).

10. Loosen clamp (31) and remove vent hose (32) from fill pipe assembly (30).

11. Remove screw (39) and clip (41).

12. Lower fuel tank (26) approximately 6 in. (15.2 cm) to gain access to 2 sending unit hoses (37) and sending unit drain hose (45).

13. Remove sending unit wire (29) from sending unit (15).

14. Loosen 2 clamps (38) and remove 2 sending unit hoses (37) from pipes leading to front of truck.

NOTE

When fuel tank (26) is removed, the following hoses and pipes are removed with it: sending unit drain hose (45) and drain pipe (40), 2 sending unit hoses (37), fuel tank fill hose (47), fuel tank vent pipe (33), and vent hoses (32 and 35).

15. Remove fuel tank (26).

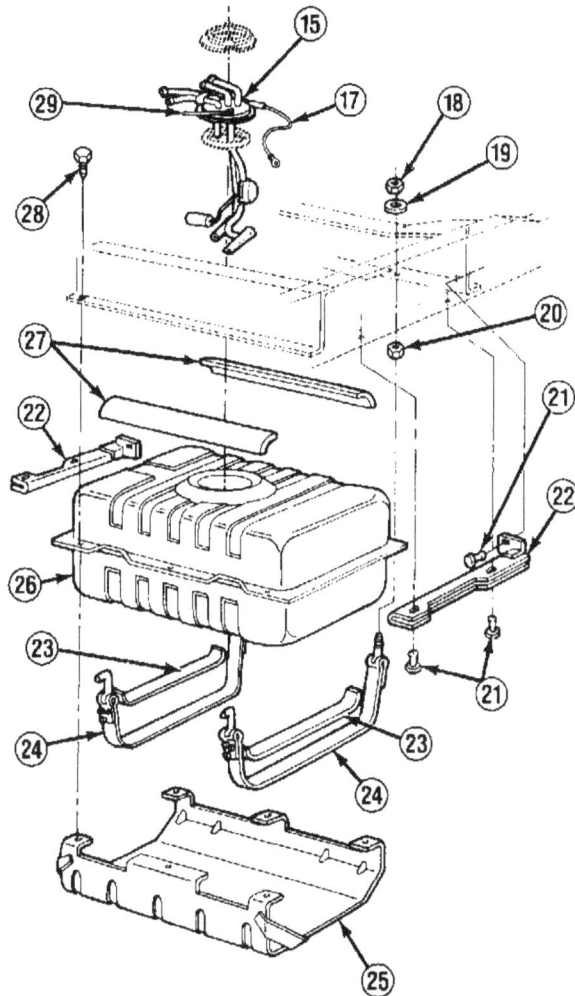

TA49786

3-12. FUEL TANK AND SHIELD MAINTENANCE (M1009) (Con't).

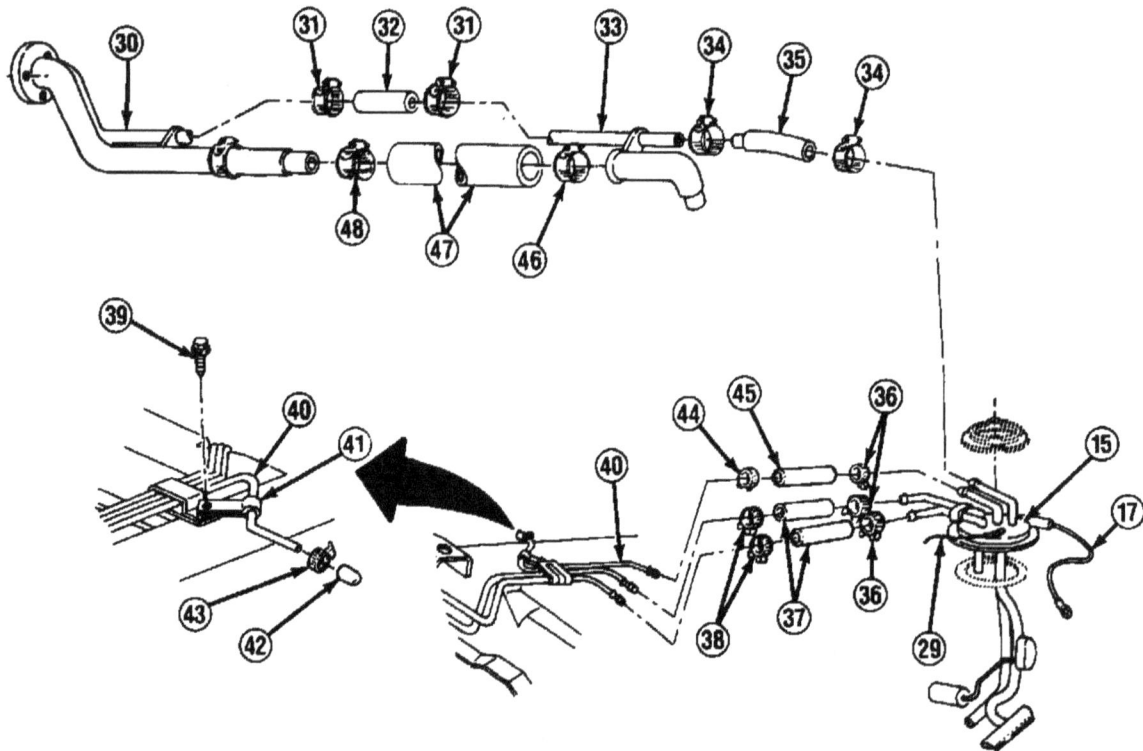

16. Unhook 2 strap assemblies (24) from crossmember.

17. Remove 2 insulators (27) from fuel tank (26).

18. Remove 6 plugs (21) and 2 protector assemblies (22).

19. Loosen 3 clamps (36) and remove 2 sending unit hoses (37) and sending unit drain hose (45) from sending unit (15).

20. Loosen 2 clamps (34) and remove vent hose (35).

21. Loosen clamp (31) and remove vent hose (32).

22. Loosen clamp (46) at fuel tank elbow and remove fill hose (47).

23. Loosen clamp (44) and remove drain pipe (40) from sending unit   drain hose (45).

24. Remove clamp (43) and cap (42) from end of drain pipe (40).

TA49787

3-12. FUEL TANK AND SHIELD MAINTENANCE (M1009) (Con't).

CAUTION

Before removing sending unit (15) from fuel tank (26), thoroughly clean area. Failure to follow this caution may result in dirt falling into fuel tank.

25. Remove sending unit cam (14), sending unit (15), and gasket (16). Discard gasket.

b. INSTALLATION

NOTE

If installing fuel tank shield (25),   perform steps 26-30.

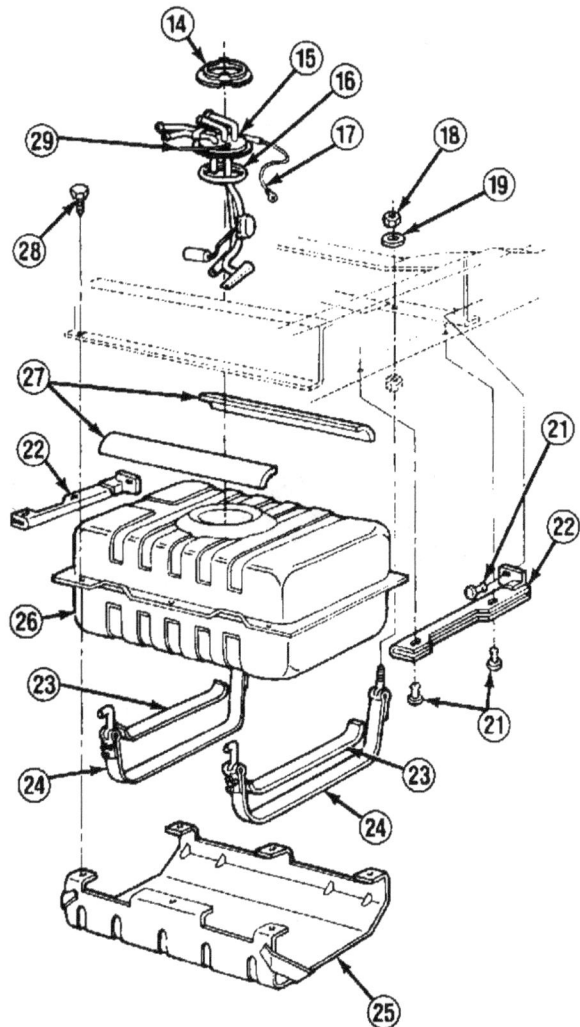

1. Install new gasket (16) at fuel tank opening.

2. Install sending unit (15) and sending unit cam (14).

3. Install vent hose (35) to vent pipe (33) and sending unit (15) with 2 clamps (34).

4. Install vent hose (32) to vent pipe (33) with clamp (31).

5. Install fill hose (47) to fuel tank elbow with clamp (46).

6. Install cap (42) to drain pipe (40) with clamp (43).

7. Install drain pipe (40) to sending unit drain hose (45) with clamp (44).

8. Install 2 sending unit hoses (37) to sending unit (15) with 2 clamps (36).

9. Install sending unit drain hose (45) to sending unit (15) with clamp (36).

10. Install 2 protector assemblies (22) with 6 plugs (21).

11. Install 2 insulators (27) to top of fuel tank (26) and 2 insulators (23) inside strap assemblies (24).

12. Hook front of each strap assembly (24) through crossmember.

13. Position fuel tank (26) inside 2 strap assemblies (24).

NOTE

Use an assistant and provide suitable support when performing steps 14-23.

14. Lift fuel tank (26) to within 6 in. (15.2 cm) of fully raised position, ensuring that all hoses clear frame and chassis.

TA49788

3-12. FUEL TANK AND SHIELD MAINTENANCE (M1009) (Con't).

15. Install fill hose (47) to fill pipe assembly (30) with clamp (48).

16. Install vent hose (32) to fill pipe assembly (30) with clamp (31).

17. Position sending unit drain hose (45) and drain pipe (40) along frame. DO NOT install at this time.

18. Connect 2 sending unit hoses (37) to ends of pipes and secure with 2 clamps (38).

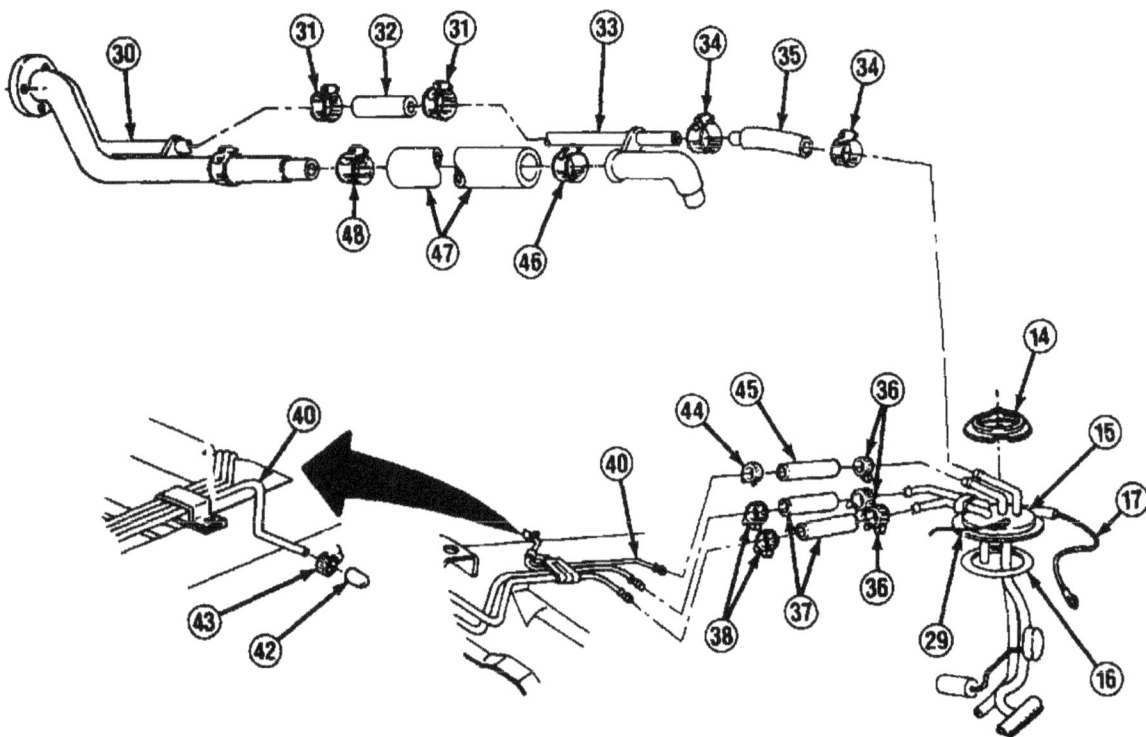

19. Install sending unit wire (29) to sending unit (15).

20. Position ground wire (17) over top of frame. DO NOT connect at this time.

21. Raise fuel tank (26) into position.

22. Insert 2 strap assemblies (24) through holes in rear crossmember.

NOTE

Steps 23, 27, and 28 are easier to perform with endgate down.

23. Secure 2 strap assemblies (24) and 2 wiring harness tabs with washers (19) and nuts (18).

TA49789

3-12. FUEL TANK AND SHIELD MAINTENANCE (M1009) (Con't).

24. Install clip (41) with screw (39).

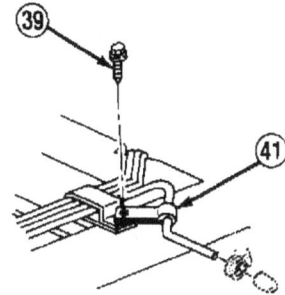

25. Connect ground wire (17) to frame using a new starwasher between ground wire terminal and frame.

26. Move tow hook bracket (10) to rear as needed.

NOTE

An assistant is needed to perform step 27.

27. Position fuel tank shield (25). Install 6 bolts (28) through crossmember, fuel tank (26), and fuel tank shield. Tighten bolts to 20-30 lb.-ft. (27-41 N•m).

28. Push tow hook bracket (10) forward into position. Install 2 washers (11) and bolts (12).

29. Install tow hook bracket (10) to rear bumper with 4 bolts (9), washers (8), new lockwashers (7), and nuts (6).

30 Install rear bumper brace (1) with 6 bolts (5), 10 washers (4), and 4 nuts (3).

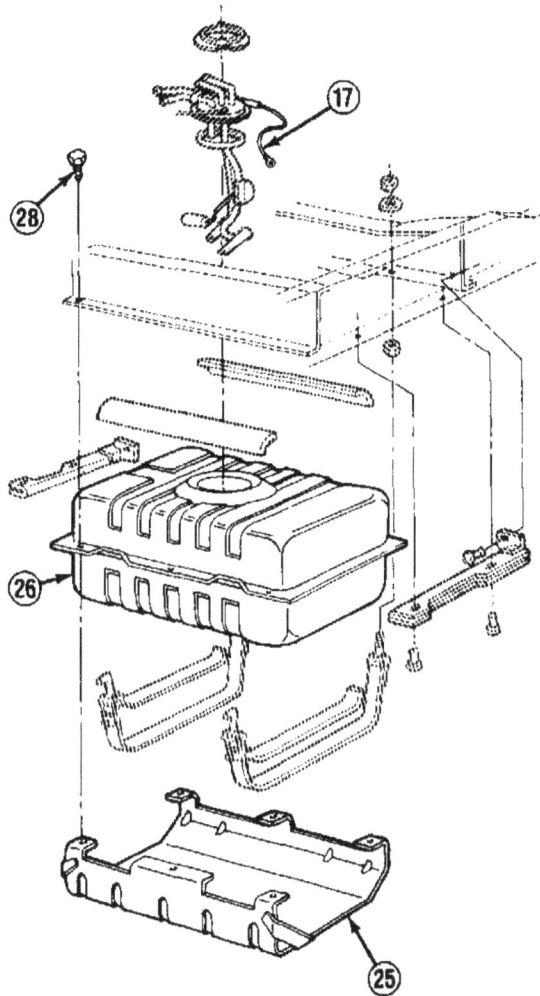

TA49790

3-12.   FUEL TANK AND SHIELD MAINTENANCE (M1009) (Con't).

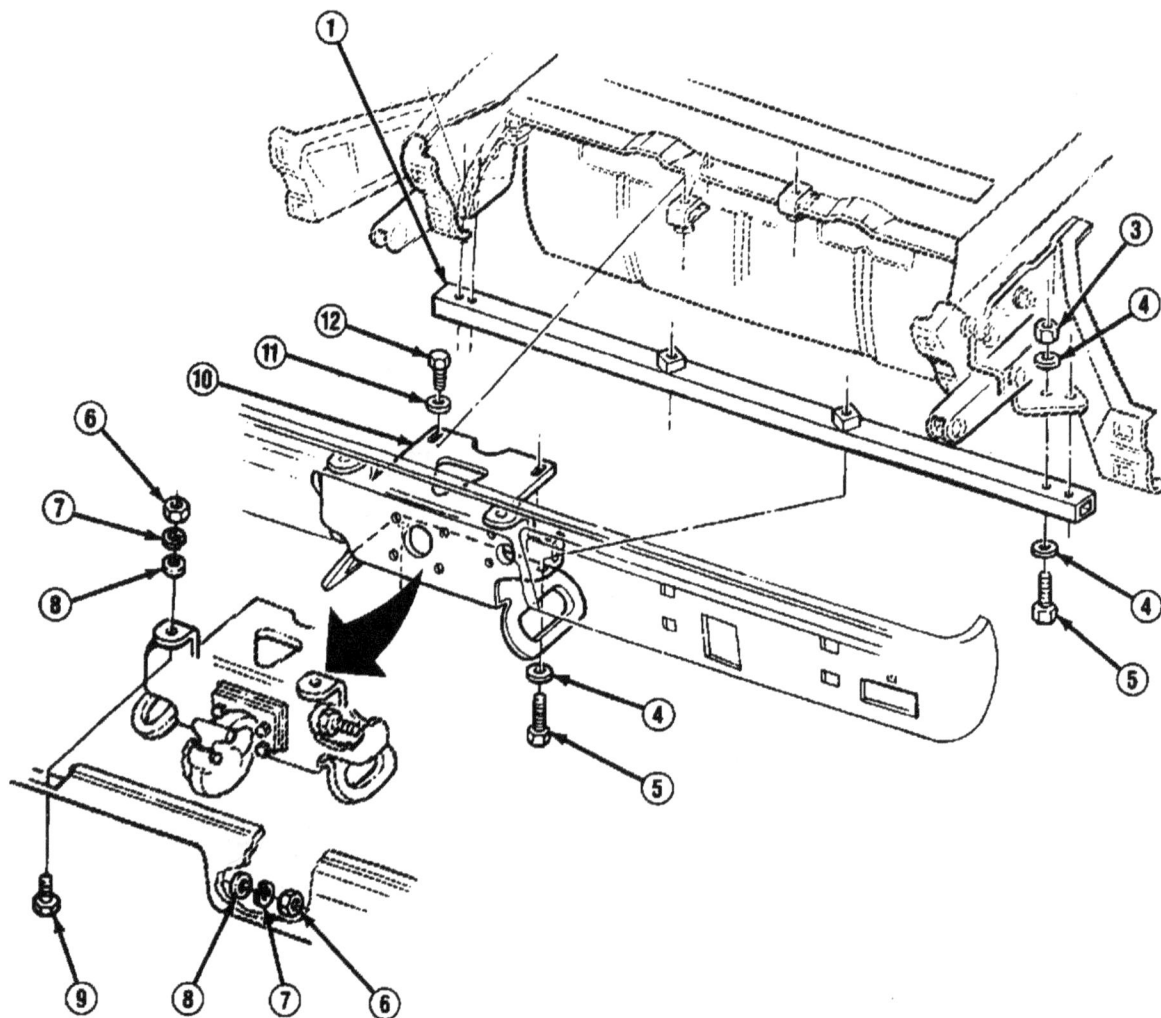

FOLLOW-ON TASKS:

- Refill fuel tank.
- Connect both battery negative cables. (See paragraph 4-38)
- Bleed air from fuel system. (See paragraph 3-17)
- Check for leaks.

TA49791

3-13. FUEL TANK SUPPLY AND RETURN HOSES AND PIPES REPLACEMENT (ALL EXCEPT M1009).

| This task covers: | a. Removal | b. Installation |

INITIAL SETUP:

Equipment Condition

• Both battery negative cables disconnected. (See paragraph 4-38)

General Safety Instructions

• DO NOT perform this procedure near fire, flames, or sparks.
• Always wear goggles when working on underside of truck.

---

a. REMOVAL

WARNING

• Diesel fuel is flammable. Do NOT perform this procedure near fire, flames, or sparks. A fire extinguisher must be on hand in work area. Failure to follow this warning may result in serious injury or death.

• Always wear goggles when working on underside of truck. Fuel spillage can occur when disconnecting fuel lines. Failure to follow this warning may result in serious eye injury.

NOTE

• Fuel tank must be removed to perform steps 1-7. (See paragraph 3-11)

• Tag all hoses and pipes for installation.

• If removing feed pipe (12), perform steps 8 and 10 through 12.

• If removing front feed pipe (5), perform steps 14-17.

• If removing front feed hose (4), perform step 15.

• If removing return pipe (38), perform steps 9, 18, and 19.

• If removing front return hose (40), perform step 18.

1. Remove 3 clamps (21) and remove 3 sending unit hoses (22) from drain pipe (17), feed pipe (23), and return pipe (20).

2. Loosen clamp (32) and remove cap (24).

3. Remove bolt (30), nut (35), washer (34), and clip (33).

4. Remove screw (18), clip (19), and drain pipe (17).

5. Remove nut (26), bolt (29), and washer (28). Remove 2 screws (27) and remove shield (25).

6. Loosen clamp (13) and disconnect feed hose (14) from feed pipe (23). Remove feed pipe.

3-13. FUEL TANK SUPPLY AND RETURN HOSES AND PIPES REPLACEMENT (ALL EXCEPT M1009) (Con't).

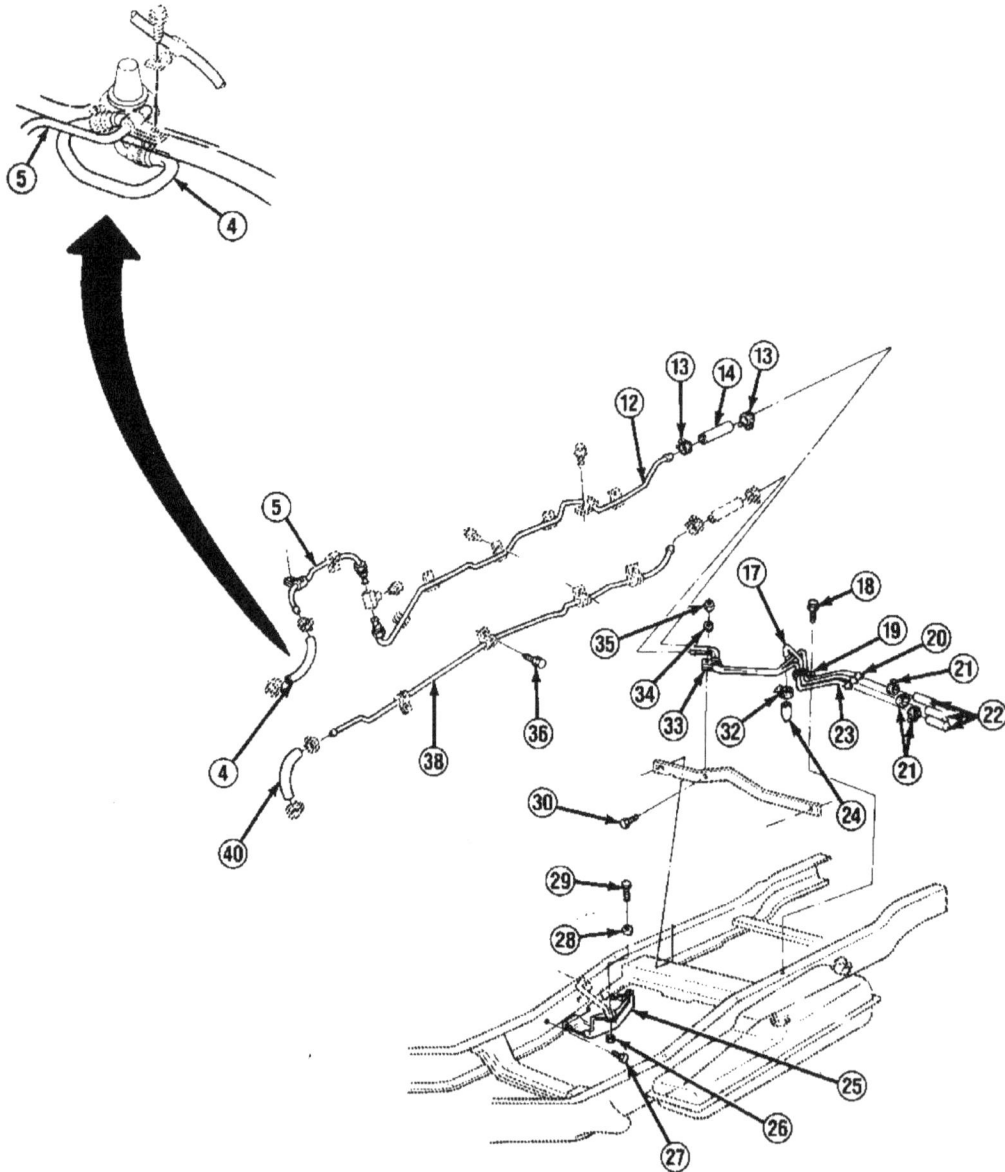

TA49792

3-13. FUEL TANK SUPPLY AND RETURN HOSES AND PIPES REPLACEMENT (ALL EXCEPT M1009) (Con't).

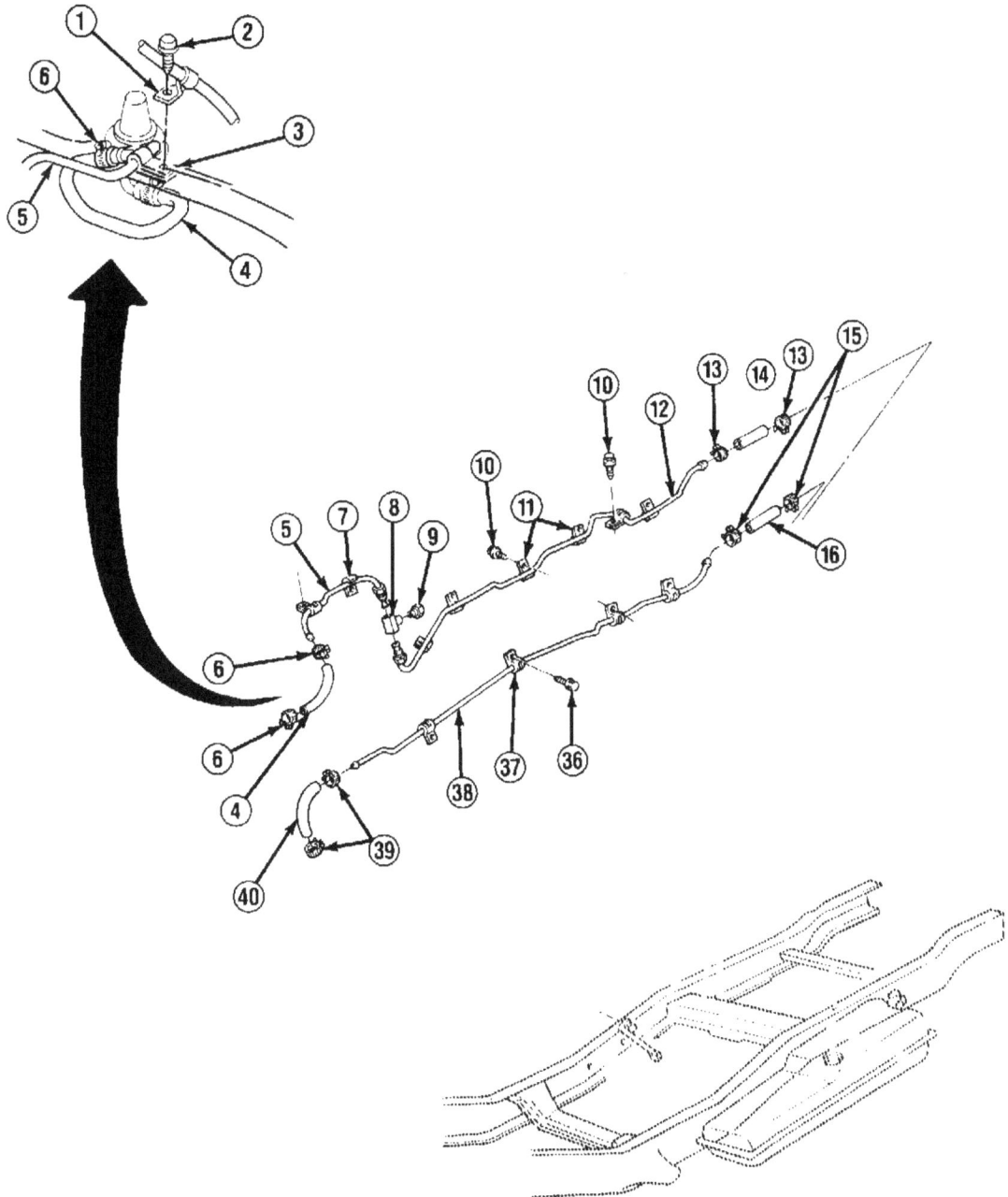

TA49793

3-13. FUEL TANK SUPPLY AND RETURN HOSES AND PIPES REPLACEMENT (ALL EXCEPT M1009) (Con't).

7. Loosen clamp (15) and disconnect return hose (16) from return pipe (38). Remove return pipe.

8. Remove clamp (13) and feed hose (14) from feed pipe (12).

9. Remove clamp (15) and return hose (16) from return pipe (38).

10. Remove 6 screws (10) and clips (11) securing feed pipe (12) to frame.

NOTE

- **If truck is not equipped with winterization kits, perform steps 11 and 13 through 19.**

- **If truck is equipped with winterization kits, perform steps 12-19.**

11. Remove feed pipe (12) from fitting (8).

12. Disconnect feed pipe (12) and auxiliary heater fuel inlet hose (41) from fitting (8). Remove screw (43) and clip (42) which hold feed pipe and auxiliary heater fuel inlet hose together.

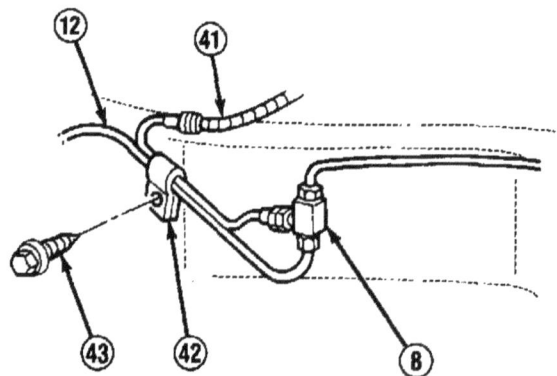

NOTE

M1010 and trucks equipped with winterization kits DO NOT have a plug (9) in fitting (8).

13. Remove plug (9) from fitting (8).

14. Remove fitting (8) from feed pipe (5).

15. Remove 2 clamps (6) and front feed hose (4).

16. Remove clip (7) securing front feed pipe (5) to frame.

17. Remove bolt (2), clip (3), battery cable bracket (1), and front feed pipe (5).

18. Remove 2 clamps (39), and remove front return hose (40).

19. Remove 4 screws (36) and clips (37), and remove return pipe (38).

TA49794

3-13. FUEL TANK SUPPLY AND RETURN HOSES AND PIPES REPLACEMENT (ALL EXCEPT M1009) (Con't).

<u>b. INSTALLATION</u>

NOTE

◀f installing feed pipe (12), perform steps 7-10.

◀f installing front feed pipe (5), perform steps 3-6.

◀f installing front feed hose (4), perform step 5.

◀f installing return pipe (38), perform steps 1, 2, and 11.

◀f installing front return hose (40), perform step 2.

1.   Install front return pipe (38) with 4 clips (37) and screws (36).

2.   Install front return hose (40) with 2 clamps (39).

3.   Install front feed pipe (5) with clip (7).

4.   Install bolt (2), clip (3), and battery cable bracket (1).

5.   Install front feed hose (4) with 2 clamps (6).

NOTE

M1010 and trucks equipped with winterization kits DO NOT have a plug (9) in fitting (8).

6.   Install plug (9) into fitting (8) and install fitting to feed pipe (5).

7.   Install feed pipe (12) to fitting (8).

NOTE

Step 8 only applies to trucks equipped with winterization kits.

8.   Install auxiliary heater fuel inlet hose (41) to fitting (8), and install auxiliary heater fuel inlet hose to frame and feed pipe (12) with clip (42) and screw (43).

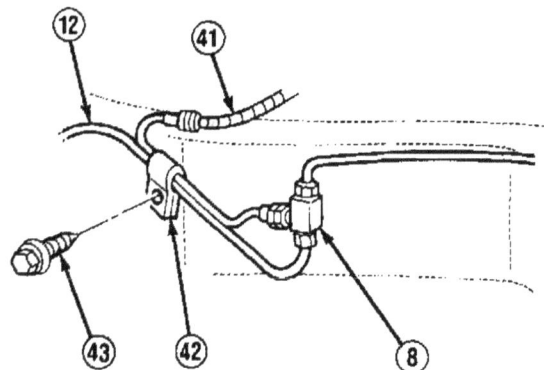

9.   Install feed pipe (12) to frame with 6 clips (11) and bolts (10).

10. Install feed hose (14) to feed pipe (12) with clamp (13).

11. Install return hose (16) to return pipe (38) with clamp (15).

12. Install shield (25) with 2 screws (27).

TA49795

3-13.   FUEL TANK SUPPLY AND RETURN HOSES AND PIPES REPLACEMENT (ALL EXCEPT M1009) (Con't).

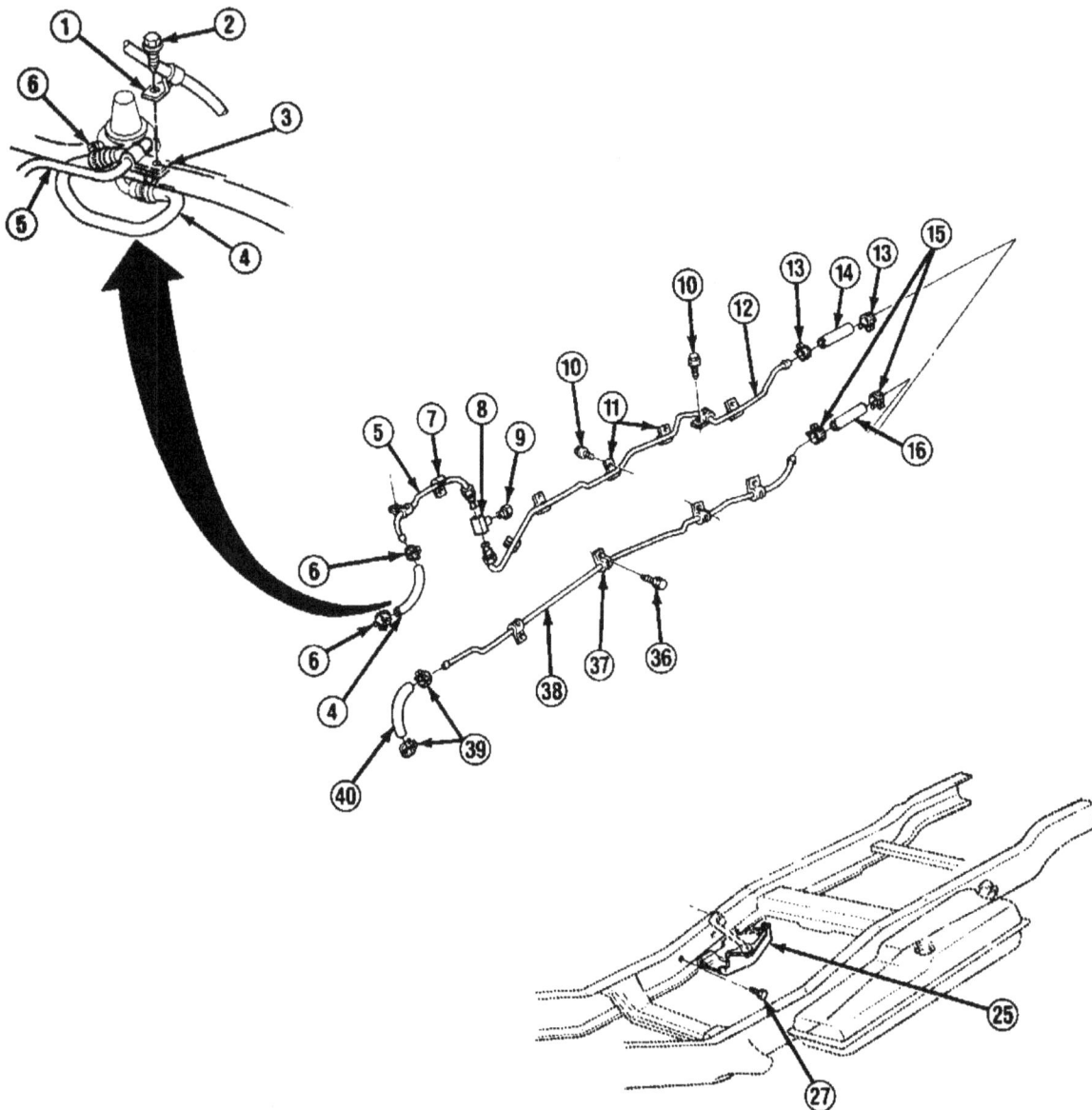

TA49796

3-13. FUEL TANK SUPPLY AND RETURN HOSES AND PIPES REPLACEMENT (ALL EXCEPT M1009) (Con't).

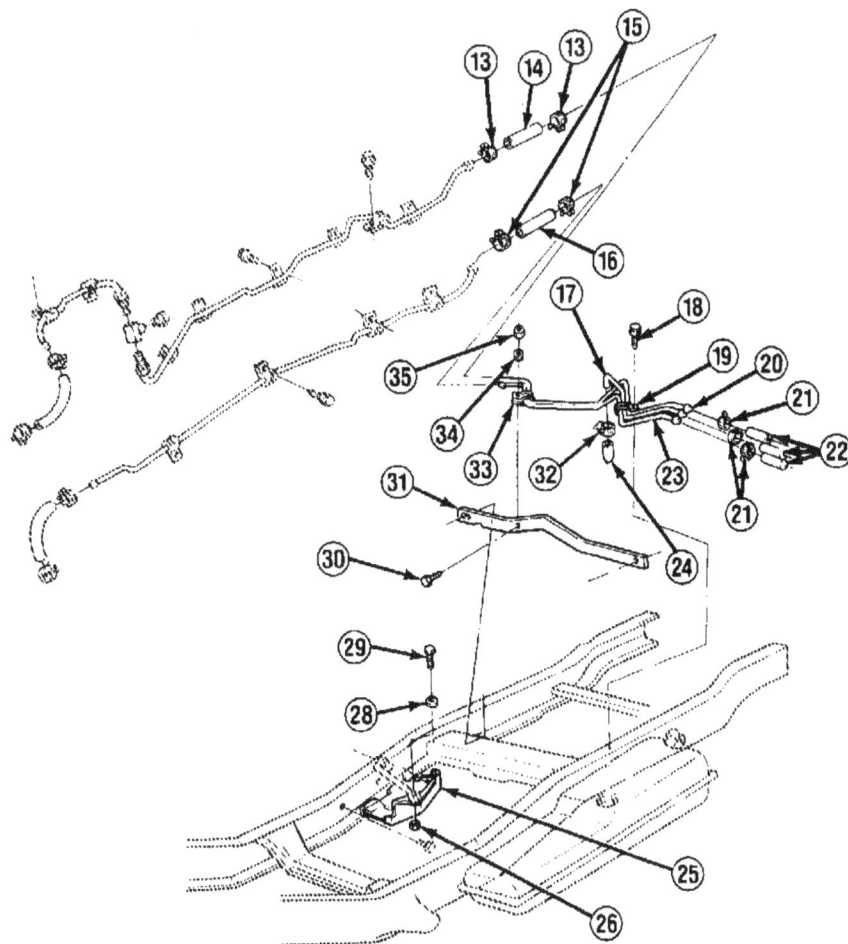

TA49797

3-13. FUEL TANK SUPPLY AND RETURN HOSES AND PIPES REPLACEMENT (ALL EXCEPT M1009) (Con't).

13. Install bolt (29), washer (28), and nut (26) to shield (25).

14. Install ends of feed pipe (23) and return pipe (20) over support (31) and over left side of frame.

15. Connect feed hose (14) to feed pipe (23) and secure with clamp (13).

16. Connect return hose (16) to return pipe (20) with clamp (15).

17. Install pipes with clip (19) and screw (18) so that feed pipe (23) is to front, drain pipe (17) is in middle, and return pipe (20) is to back.

18. Install cap (24) and clamp (32) to drain pipe (17).

19. Install feed pipe (23) and return pipe (20) to support (31) with clip (33), bolt (30), washer (34), and nut (35).

20. Install 3 hoses (22) to pipes (17, 20 and 23) with clamps (21).

FOLLOW-ON TASKS:

- Install fuel tank if removed. (See paragraph 3-11)
- Connect both battery negative cables. (See paragraph 4-38)
- Bleed air from fuel system if required. (See paragraph 3-17)
- Check for leaks.

3-14. FUEL TANK SUPPLY AND RETURN HOSES AND PIPES REPLACEMENT (M1009).

This task covers: a. Removal   b. Installation

INITIAL SETUP:

Equipment Condition

Both battery negative cables disconnected.
(See paragraph 4-38)

Personnel Required

• MOS 63B (2)

Materials/Parts

One feed pipe
One return pipe

General Safety Instructions

• DO NOT perform this procedure near fire, flames, or sparks.
• Always wear goggles when working on underside of truck.

---

a. REMOVAL

WARNING

●Diesel fuel is flammable. DO NOT perform this procedure near fire, flames, or sparks. A fire extinguisher must be on hand in work area. Failure to follow this warning may result in serious injury or death.

●Always wear goggles when working on underside of truck. Fuel spillage can occur when disconnecting fuel lines. Failure to follow this warning may result in serious eye injury.

NOTE

Access to feed hose (8) and clamp (7) is difficult. It may be necessary to lower fuel tank to make step 1 easier to perform. (See paragraph 3-12)

1.   Remove clamp (7) and feed hose (8) from feed pipe (11).

2.   Remove screw (6) and 2 clips (5).

3.   Loosen clamp (22) and remove feed hose (23) from feed pipe (11).

NOTE

Rear feed pipe (11) must be cut before it can be removed.

4.   Remove 3 screws (2) and clips (1). Remove feed pipe (11). Discard feed pipe.

5.   Loosen clamp (24) and remove feed hose (23).

6.   Remove 3 screws (19), 3 clips (20), and remove feed pipe (21) from fitting (25).

3-14. FUEL TANK SUPPLY AND RETURN HOSES AND PIPES REPLACEMENT (M1009) (Con't).

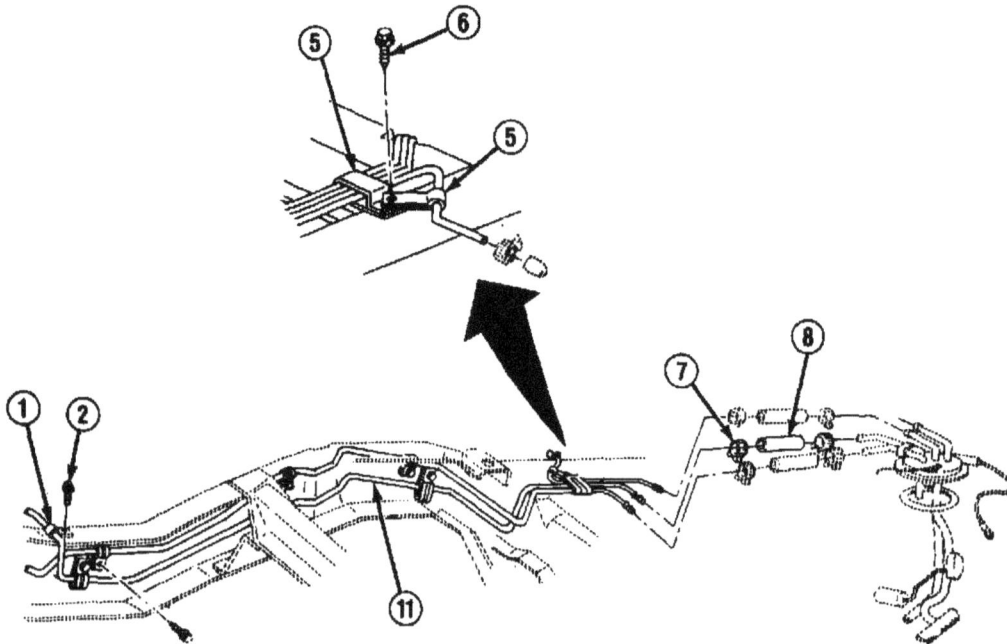

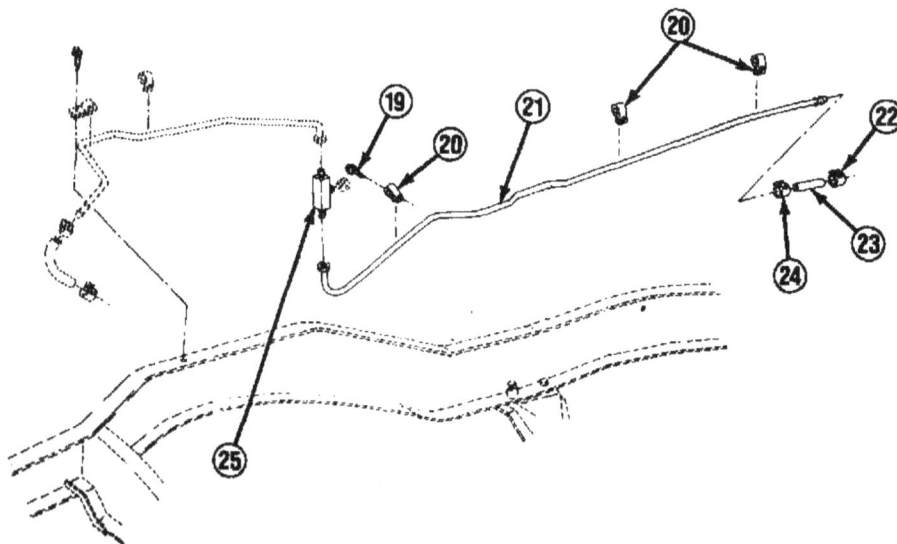

TA49798

3-14. FUEL TANK SUPPLY AND RETURN HOSES AND PIPES REPLACEMENT (M1009) (Con't).

NOTE

Step 7 only applies to trucks equipped with winterization kits.

7. Remove screw (28) and clip (27), and remove auxiliary heater fuel inlet hose (26) from fitting (25).

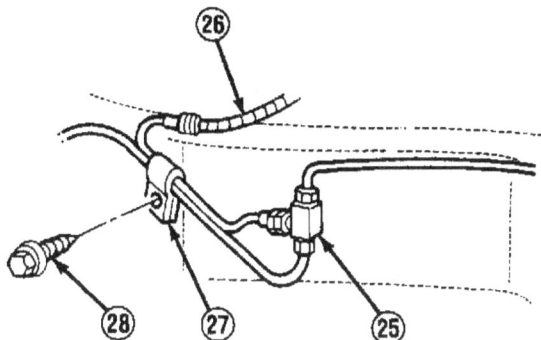

NOTE

Trucks equipped with winterization kits DO NOT have a plug (18) in fitting (25).

8. Remove plug (18) and fitting (25) from feed pipe (13).

9. Loosen 2 clamps (14) and remove feed hose (15).

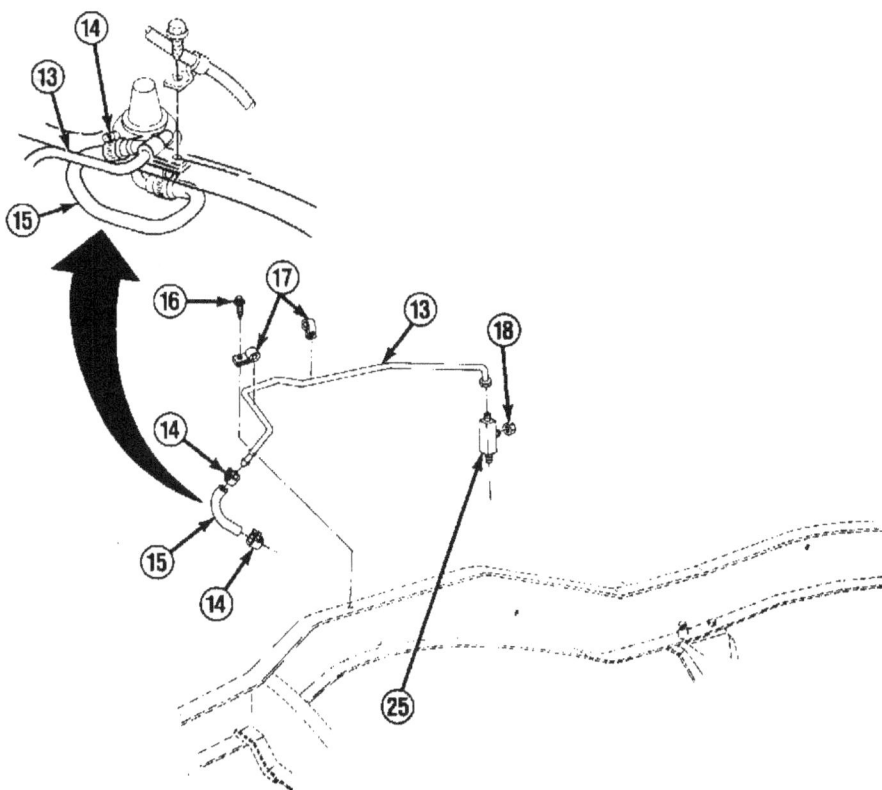

TA49799

3-14. FUEL TANK SUPPLY AND RETURN HOSES AND PIPES REPLACEMENT (M1009) (Con't).

10. Remove 3 screws (16) and clips (17), and remove feed pipe (13).

11. Remove clamp (10) and return hose (9) from return pipe (4).

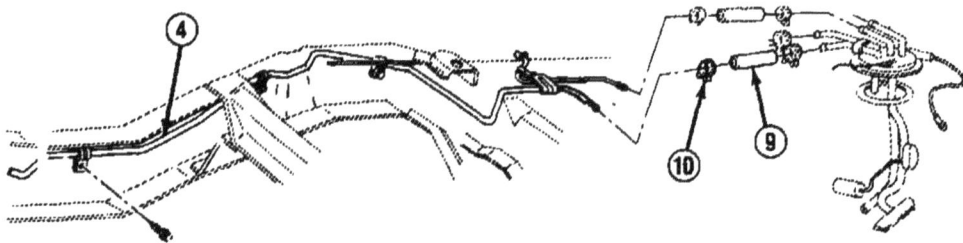

12. Remove clamp (32) and return hose (33) from return pipe (4).

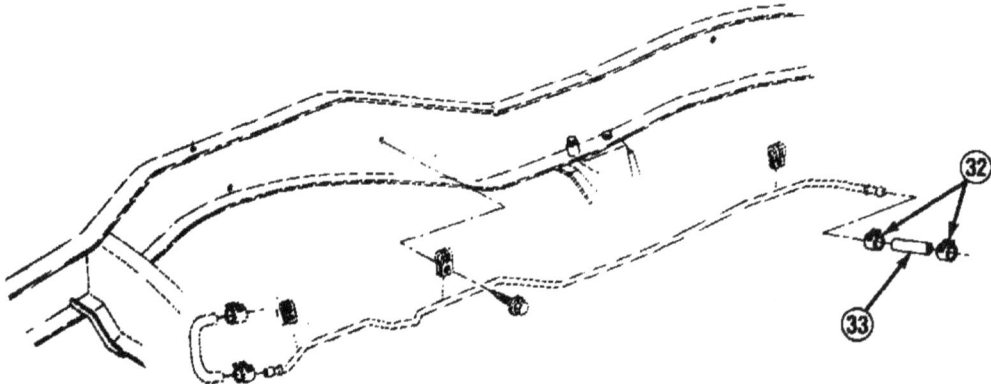

TA49800

3-14. FUEL TANK SUPPLY AND RETURN HOSES AND PIPES REPLACEMENT (M1009) (Con't).

NOTE

Rear return pipe (4) must be cut before it can be removed.

13.   Remove 3 screws (12) and clips (3), and remove return pipe (4). Discard return pipe.

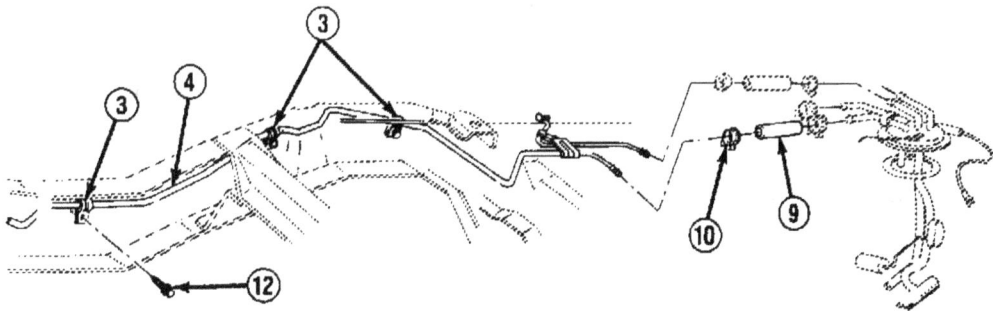

14.   Remove clamp (32) and remove return hose (33).

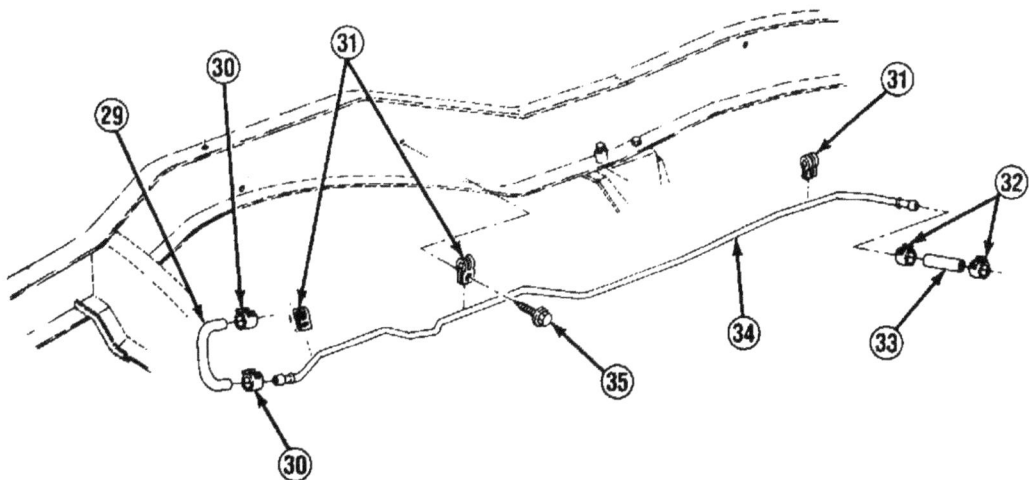

TA49801

3-14. FUEL TANK SUPPLY AND RETURN HOSES AND PIPES REPLACEMENT (M1009) (Con't).

15. Remove 2 clamps (30) and remove return hose (29).

16. Remove 3 screws (35) and clips (31), and remove return pipe (34).

b. INSTALLATION

1. Install return pipe (34) with 3 clips (31) and screws (35).

2. Install return hose (29) with 2 clamps (30).

3. Install return hose (33) to return pipe (34) with clamp (32).

4. Install new return pipe (4), bending it into position, to return hose (33) with clamp (32).

5. Install return pipe (4) to frame with 3 clips (3) and screws (12).

6. Install new return hose (9) to return pipe (4) with clamp (10).

7. If fuel tank was lowered, raise at this time. (See paragraph 3-12)

8. Install feed pipe (13) to frame with 3 clips (17) and screws (16).

9. Install feed hose (15) to fuel pump and feed pipe (13) with 2 clamps (14).

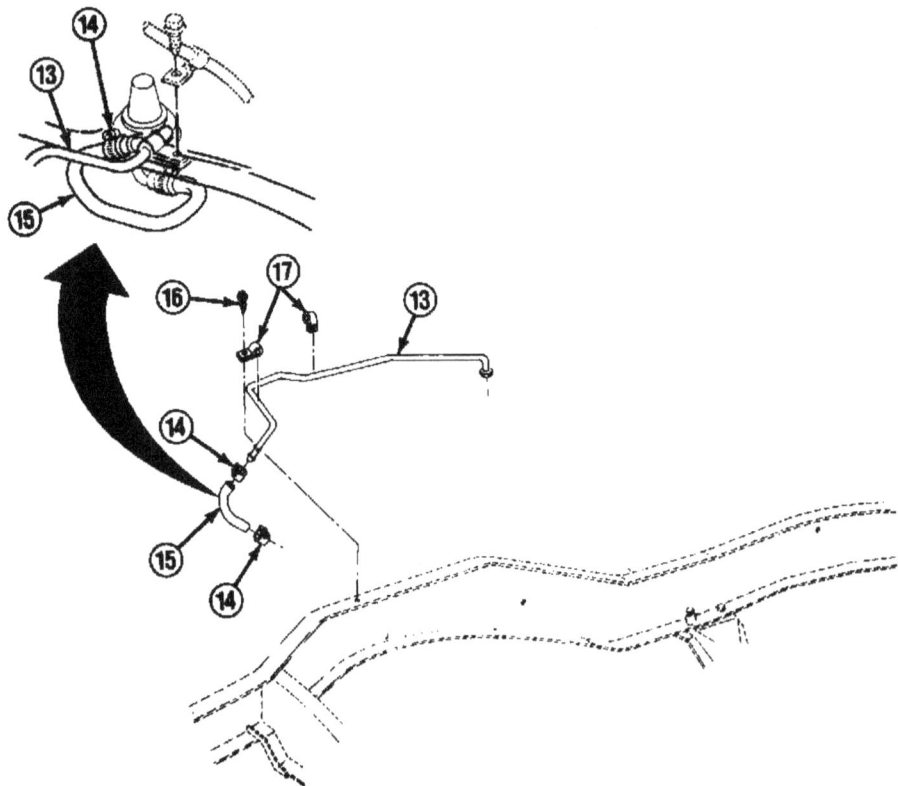

TA49802

3-14. FUEL TANK SUPPLY AND RETURN HOSES AND PIPES REPLACEMENT (M1009) (Con't).

NOTE

Trucks equipped with winterization kits DO NOT have a plug (18) in fitting (25).

10. Install plug (18) into fitting (25) and install fitting to feed pipe (13).

11. Install feed pipe (21) to fitting (25) and to frame with 3 clips (20) and screws (19).

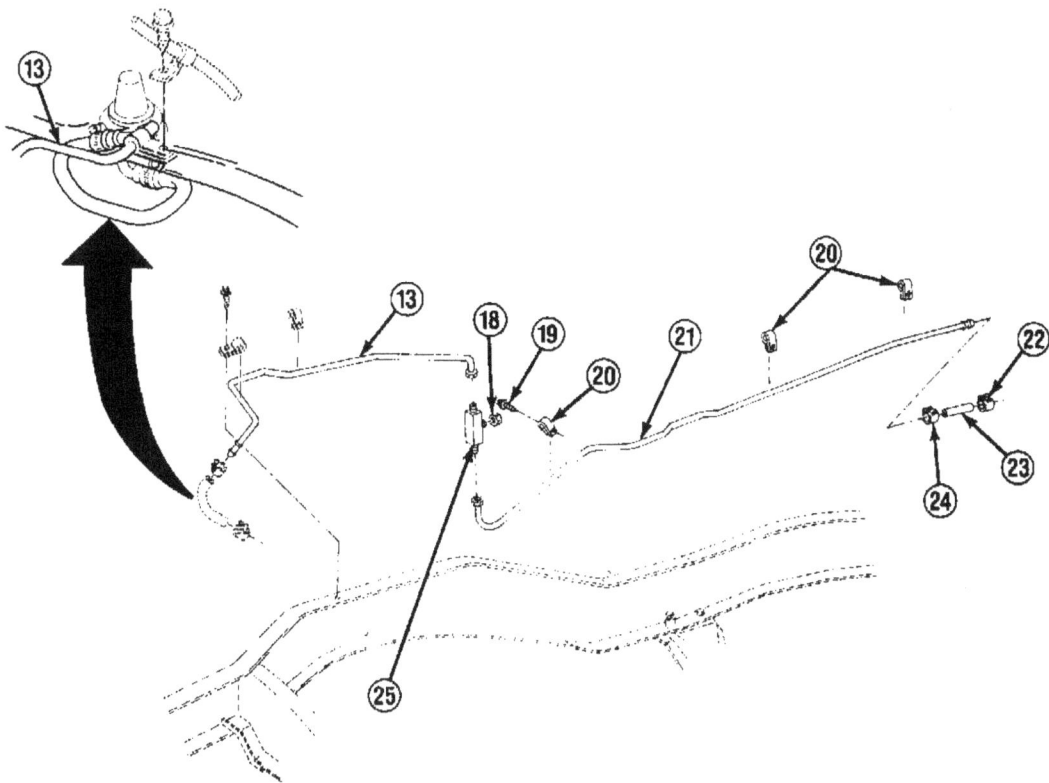

NOTE

Step 12 only applies to trucks equipped with winterization kits.

12. Install auxiliary heater fuel inlet hose (26) to fitting (25), and install clip (27) and screw (28).

13. Install feed hose (23) to feed pipe (21) with clamp (24).

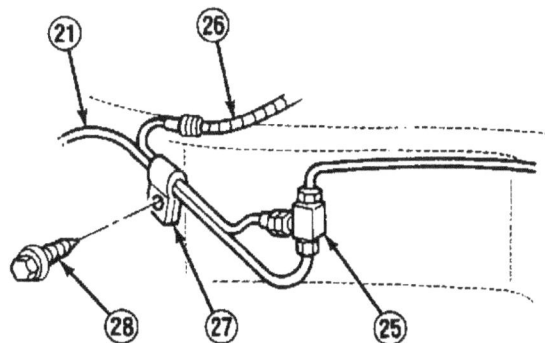

TA49803

3-14. FUEL TANK SUPPLY AND RETURN HOSES AND PIPES REPLACEMENT (M1009) (Con't).

14. Install new feed pipe (11), bending it into position. Install 3 clips (1) and screws (2). Install feed pipe to feed hose (23)   with camp (22).

15. Install feed hose (8) to feed   pipe (11) with clamp   (7) .

16. Install 2 clips (5) with screw   (6) .

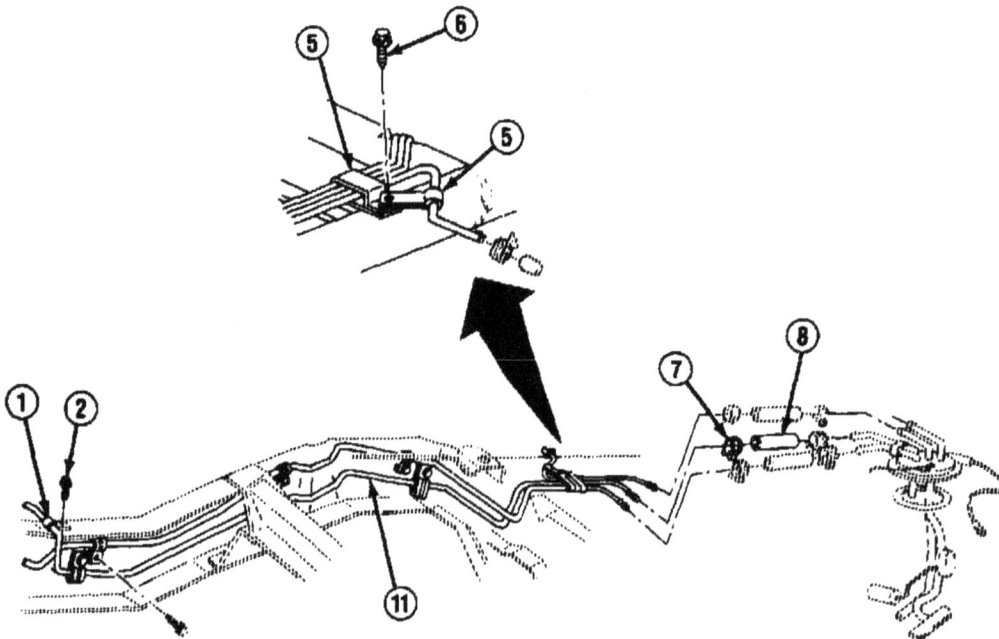

FOLLOW-ON TASKS:

- Refill fuel tank if required.
- Connect both battery negative cables. (See paragraph 4-38)
- Bleed air from fuel system if required. (See paragraph 3-17)
- Check for leaks.

TA49804

3-15. FUEL TANK FILLER DOOR, FILL PIPE ASSEMBLY, AND FILL/VENT HOSES REPLACEMENT (ALL EXCEPT M1009 AND M1010).

This task covers: a. Removal   c. Installation
                      b. Inspection

INITIAL SETUP:

Equipment Condition

- Both battery negative cables disconnected. (See paragraph 4-38)
- Fuel tank drained halfway.

Tools/Test Equipment

- Screwdriver bit set, J-29843

General Safety Instructions

- DO NOT perform this procedure near fire, flames, or sparks.
- Always wear goggles when working on underside of truck.

| a. | **REMOVAL** |

WARNING

- **Diesel fuel is flammable. DO NOT perform this procedure near fire, flames, or sparks. A fire extinguisher must be on hand in work area. Failure to follow this warning may result in serious injury or death.**

- **Always wear goggles when working on underside of truck. Fuel spillage can occur when disconnecting fuel lines. Failure to follow this warning may result in serious eye injury.**

1. Loosen clamps (10 and 11), and disconnect fill hose (9) and vent hose (12) from fuel tank.

2. Remove 3 screws (4), and remove housing (6), fill pipe assembly (7),   and attached fill hose (9) and vent hose (12).

3. Remove 2 bolts (2) and remove door assembly (3).

4. Remove any door bumpers (1) if damaged.

| b. | **INSPECTION** |

1. Inspect fill pipe assembly (7) for cracks or punctures.

2. Inspect fill hose (9) and vent hose (12) for cracks, punctures, or soft   spots .

3. Remove 2 clamps (8 and 13) and 3 screws (5), and disassemble   housing (6), fill pipe assembly (7), fill hose (9), and vent hose (12) only as required   to replace damaged components. Note position of hoses for assembly.

| c. | **INSTALLATION** |

1. Install new door bumpers (1) if removed.

3-15. FUEL TANK FILLER DOOR, FILL PIPE ASSEMBLY, AND FILL/VENT HOSES REPLACEMENT (ALL EXCEPT M1009 AND M1010) (Con't).

2. Install door assembly (3) with 2 bolts (2).

3. Assemble fill pipe assembly (7), housing (6), fill hose (9), and vent hose (12), as required, with 3 screws (5) and 2 clamps (8 and 13). DO NOT fully tighten clamps.

4. Install assembled unit to body panel with 3 screws (4).

5. Install vent hose (12) and fill hose (9) at fuel tank with clamps (11 and 10). Tighten clamps (8, 10, 11, and 13).

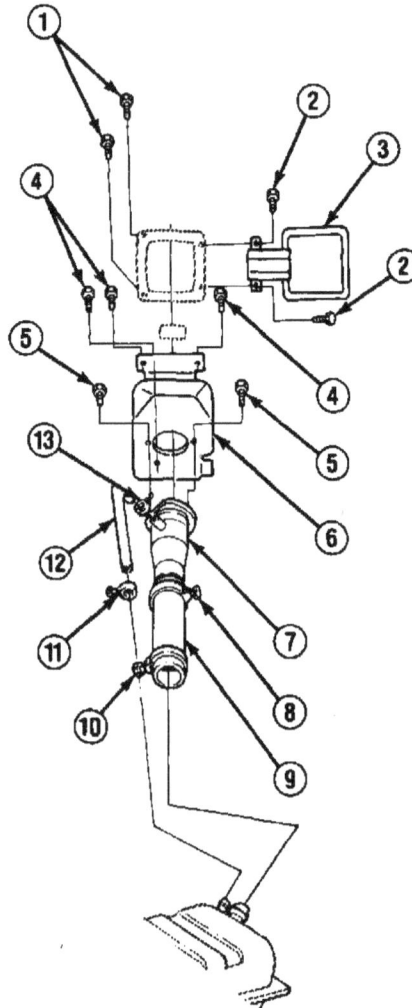

FOLLOW-ON TASKS:

*   Refill fuel tank.
*   Connect both battery negative cables. (See paragraph 4-38)
*   Bleed air from fuel system if required. (See paragraph 3-17)
*   Check for leaks.

TA49805

3-16. FUEL TANK FILLER DOOR, CAP, AND FILL PIPE ASSEMBLY REPLACEMENT (M1009).

This task covers: a. Removal   b. Installation

INITIAL SETUP:

Equipment Condition

●Both battery negative cables disconnected.
   (See paragraph 4-38)

Tools/Test Equipment

●Screwdriver bit set, J-29843

General Safety Instructions

●DO NOT perform this procedure near fire, flames, or sparks.
●Always wear goggles when working on underside of truck.

| a. | REMOVAL |

WARNING

- Diesel fuel is flammable. DO NOT perform this procedure near fire, flames, or sparks. A fire extinguisher must be on hand in work area. Failure to follow this warning may result in serious injury or death.

- Always wear goggles when working on underside of truck. Fuel spillage can occur when disconnecting fuel lines. Failure to follow this warning may result in serious eye injury.

1. Unscrew fuel cap assembly (7).

2. Remove clamp (9) and remove vent hose (10) from fill pipe assembly (8).

3. Remove clamp (12) and remove fill hose (11) from fill pipe assembly (8).

4. Remove 3 screws (2) and screws (14). Remove clamp (13), fill pipe assembly (8), and housing (1).

5. Remove fuel cap chain clip (6) and fuel cap assembly (7) from housing (1).

6. Remove 2 bolts (4) and door assembly (3).

7. Remove any door bumpers (5) if damaged.

| b. | INSTALLATION |

1. Install door assembly (3) with 2 bolts (4).

2. Install new door bumpers (5) if removed.

3. Install chain clip (11) with attached fuel cap assembly (7) to housing (1).

4. Install housing (1) with 3 screws (2).

3-16. FUEL TANK FILLER DOOR, CAP, AND FILL PIPE ASSEMBLY REPLACEMENT (M1009) (Con't).

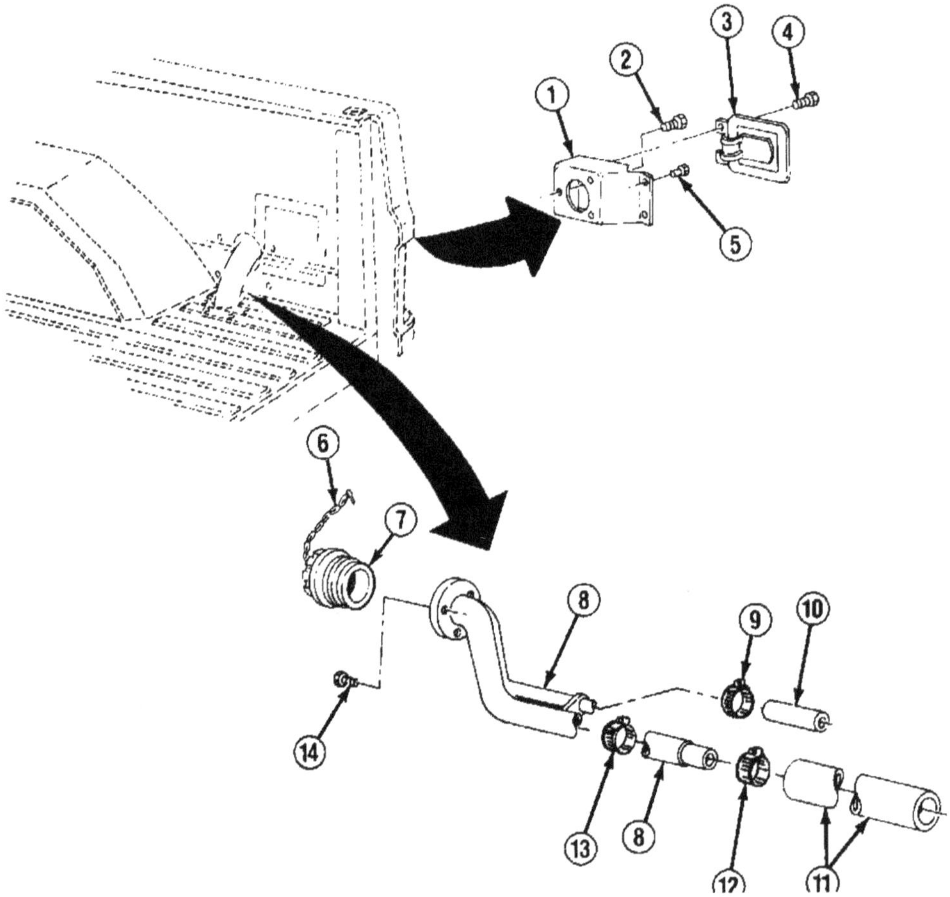

5. Screw fuel cap assembly (7) into place.

6. Install fill pipe assembly (8) with 3 screws (14).

7. Install clamp (13) to fill pipe assembly (8).

8. Install vent hose (10) to fill pipe assembly (8) with clamp (9).

9. Install fill hose (11) to fill pipe assembly (8) with clamp (12).

FOLLOW-ON TASKS:

Connect both battery negative cables. (See paragraph 4-38)
Check for leaks.

TA49806

3-17. FUEL FILTER MAINTENANCE.

This task covers:

a. Removal
b. Installation

c. Bleeding
d. Drain Water From Fuel Filter

INITIAL SETUP:

Materials/Parts

● Two seals
● Plastic tube (Item 49, Appendix C)

Personnel Required

● MOS 63B (2)

General Safety Instructions

● DO NOT perform this procedure near fire, flames, or sparks.

---

a.   REMOVAL

WARNING

Diesel fuel is flammable. DO NOT perform this procedure near fire, flames, or sparks. A fire extinguisher must be on hand in work area. Failure to follow this warning may result in serious injury or death.

1. Disconnect both battery negative cables. (See paragraph 4-38)

2. Place suitable container under fuel filter drain hose (16).

3. Remove fuel tank cap to release pressure in fuel tank.

4. Remove vent plug (5), loosen drainplug (17), and allow all fuel to drain from fuel filter assembly (1). Remove drainplug, and 2 seals (4). Discard seals.

5. Disengage 2 filter clamps (7) and remove fuel filter assembly (1).

6. Remove clamp (13), fuel filter inlet hose (12), clamp (15), and fuel filter outlet hose (14).

7. Remove 3 bolts (10), washers (9), and filter mounting bracket (8).

8. Remove 4 screws (11) and base assembly (2) from filter mounting bracket (8).

9. Remove 3 switches (6) from base assembly (2), as required.

b. INSTALLATION

1. Install 3 switches (6) in base assembly (2) if removed.

2. Install filter base assembly (2) to filter mounting bracket (8) with 4 screws (11).

3. Install filter mounting bracket (8) with 3 washers (9) and bolts (10).

4. Install fuel filter inlet hose (12) at point marked "IN" on base assembly (2) with clamp (13).

5. Install fuel filter outlet hose (14) at point marked "OUT" on base assembly (2) with clamp (15).

3-17. FUEL FILTER MAINTENANCE (Con't).

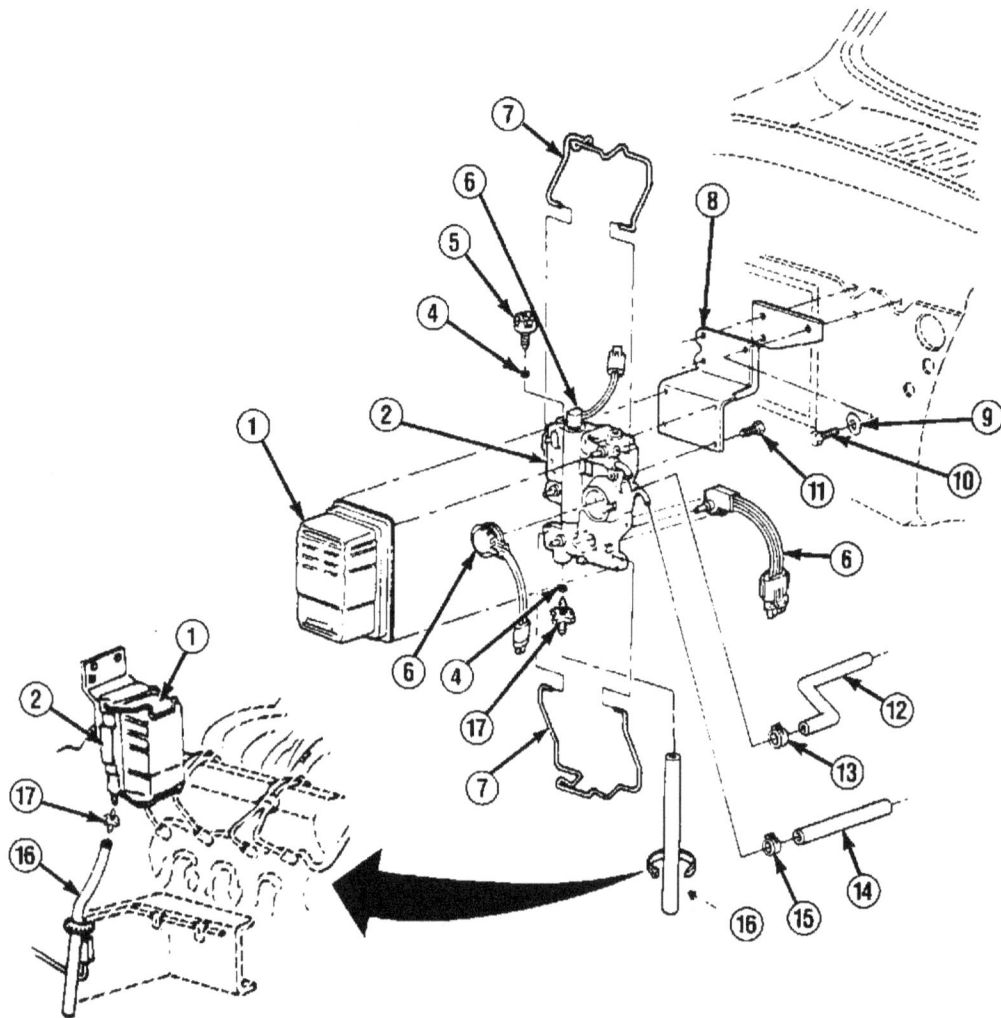

6. Install fuel filter assembly (1) with 2 filter clamps (7).

7. Install 2 new seals (4), vent plug (5), and drainplug (17).

8. Install fuel tank cap.

TA49807

3-17.   FUEL FILTER MAINTENANCE (Con't).

c. BLEEDING

WARNING

Diesel fuel is flammable. DO NOT perform this procedure near fire, flames, or sparks. A fire extinguisher must be on hand in work area. Failure to follow this warning may result in serious injury or death.

1.   Connect both battery negative cables if disconnected. (See paragraph 4-38)

2.   Remove fuel tank cap.

NOTE

An assistant is needed to perform steps 3-6.

3.   Connect a plastic tube to vent plug port (3) in base assembly (2) with free end of tube in a suitable container.

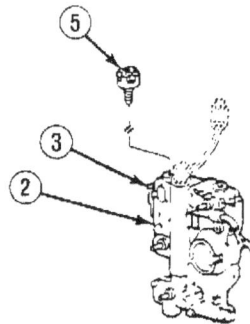

4.   Disconnect pink fuel injection pump shutoff solenoid wire (18).

5.   Open vent plug (5) at top of base assembly (2). Crank engine for 10–15 seconds,   then wait 1 minute for starter motor to cool. Repeat until clear fuel is observed coming from tube connected to vent plug port (3).

6.   Close vent plug (5) at top of base assembly (2). Remove plastic tube from vent plug port (3).

7.   Connect pink fuel injection pump shutoff solenoid wire (18).

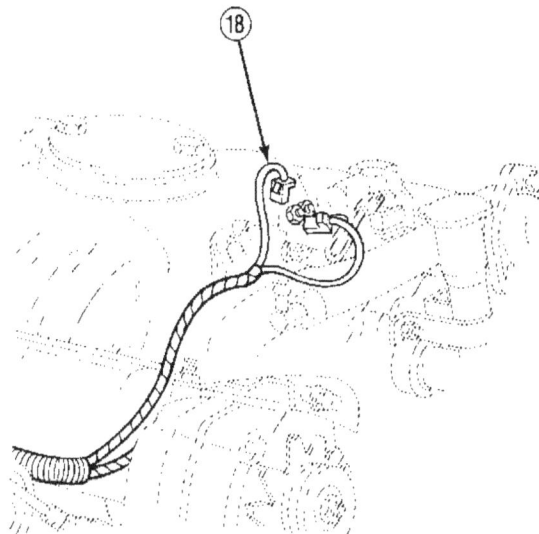

TA49808

3-17. FUEL FILTER MAINTENANCE (Con't).

8. Install fuel tank cap.

9. Start engine and allow to idle for 5 minutes.

10. Check fuel filter for leaks.

d. DRAIN WATER FROM FUEL FILTER

WARNING

Diesel fuel is flammable. DO NOT perform this procedure near fire, flames, or sparks. A fire extinguisher must be on hand in work area. Failure to follow this warning may result In serious injury or death.

NOTE

Engine should not be running at this time.

1. Remove fuel tank cap.

2. Place a suitable container under fuel filter drain hose (16) and open drainplug (17) 2-3 turns.

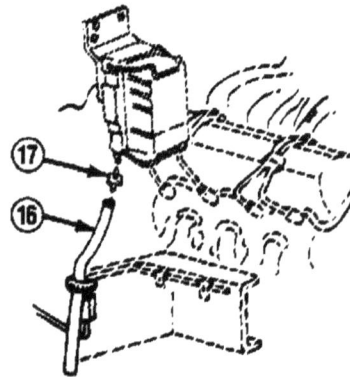

3. Start engine and allow it to idle 1-2 minutes or until clear fuel is observed.

4. Turn off engine and close drainplug (17).

5. Install fuel tank cap.

TA49809

3-18. FUEL DRAINBACK HOSES REPLACEMENT.

This task covers: a. Removal   b. Installation

INITIAL SETUP:

Equipment Condition
  ●Both battery negative cables disconnected.
    (See paragraph 4-38)
  ●Rear battery removed (M1010).
    (See paragraph 4-39)

General Safety Instructions
  ●DO NOT perform this procedure near
    fire, flames, or sparks.
  ●Allow engine to cool before replacing
    drainback hoses.

a.   REMOVAL

WARNING

●Diesel fuel is flammable. DO NOT perform this procedure near fire,
  flames, or sparks. A fire extinguisher must be on hand in work area.
  Failure to follow this warning may result   in serious injury or death.

●Allow engine to   cool before replacing   drainback hoses (3 and 5).
  Failure to follow this warning may result   in serious burns.

NOTE

Perform step 1 only if visual inspection shows fuel leaking from either rear
injector nozzle (4).

1.   Remove 2 clamps (2) and caps (1) from 2 rear injector nozzles (4).

2.   Remove 12 clamps (7) and 6 drainback hoses (3).

NOTE

When working on M1010, the right drainback hose (5) in step 3 cannot be
removed unless alternators, alternator brackets, and mounting hardware
are removed. (See paragraph 4-3)

3.   Remove 4 clamps (6) and 2 drainback hoses (5).

b .   INSTALLATION

1.   Install 2 caps (1) and clamps (2) at 2 rear injector nozzles (4) if removed.

2.   Install 6 drainback hoses (3) with 12 clamps (7).

3.   Install 2 drainback hoses (5) with 4 clamps (6).

3-18.   FUEL DRAINBACK HOSES REPLACEMENT (Con't).

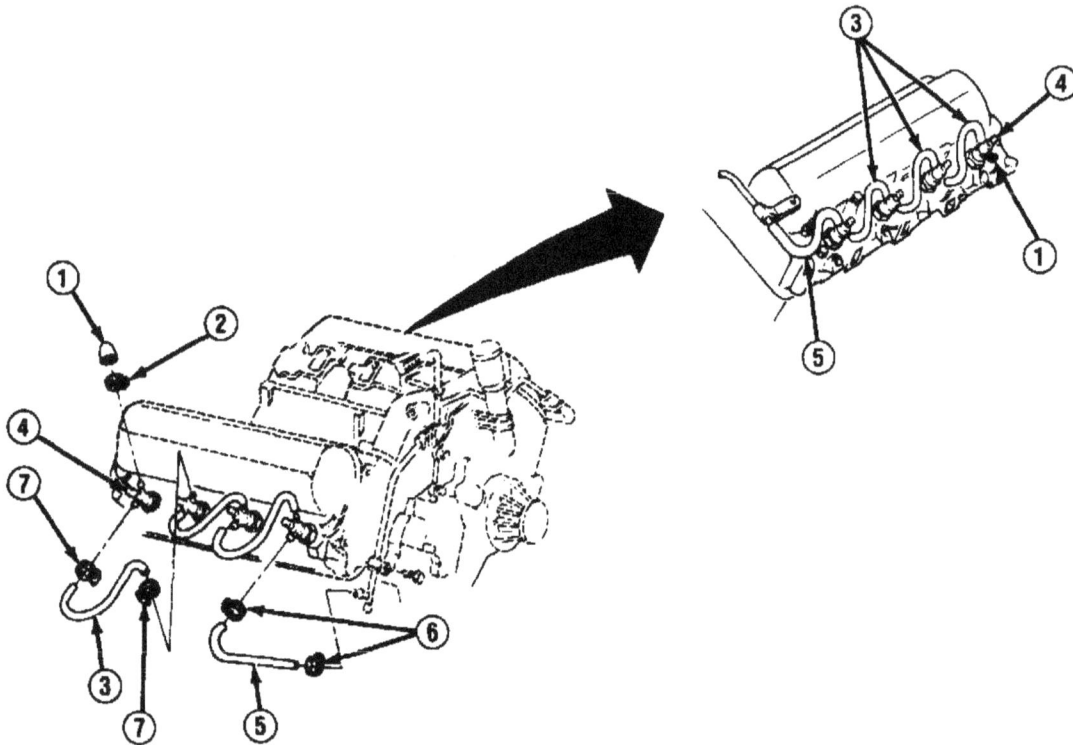

NOTE

Step 4 only applies to M1010.

4.   Install alternator, alternator brackets, and mounting hardware. (See paragraph 4-3)

FOLLOW-ON TASKS:

- Install rear battery if removed (M1010). (See paragraph 4-39)
- Connect both battery negative cables. (See paragraph 4-38)
- Check for leaks.

TA49800

3-19. FUEL DRAINBACK PIPE ASSEMBLY REPLACEMENT.

This task covers:	a. Removal	b. Installation

INITIAL SETUP:

Equipment Condition

- Alternators, alternator brackets, and mounting hardware removed (M1010). (See paragraph 4-3)

General Safety Instructions

- DO NOT perform this procedure near fire, flames, or sparks.
- Allow engine to cool before replacing drainback pipe assembly and drainback hose.

---

a.	**REMOVAL**

WARNING

- **Diesel fuel is flammable. DO NOT perform this procedure near fire, flames, or sparks. A fire extinguisher must be on hand in work area. Failure to follow this warning may result in serious injury or death.**

- **Allow engine to cool before replacing drainback pipe assembly (5) and drainback hose (1). Failure to follow-this warning may result in serious burns.**

1. Remove 2 clamps (9) and disconnect 2 drainback hoses (8).

2. Remove clamp (2) and disconnect fuel injector pump drainback hose (1).

3. Remove nut (7) and clip (6). Remove bolt (10) and clip (11). Remove bolt (4), clip (3), and drainback pipe assembly (5).

b.	**INSTALLATION**

1. Install drainback pipe assembly (5) with bolt (4) and clip (3), bolt (10) and clip (11), and nut (7) and clip (6).

2. Install 2 drainback hoses (8) with 2 clamps (9).

3. Install fuel injector pump drainback hose (1) with clamp (2).

3-19. FUEL DRAINBACK PIPE ASSEMBLY REPLACEMENT (Con't).

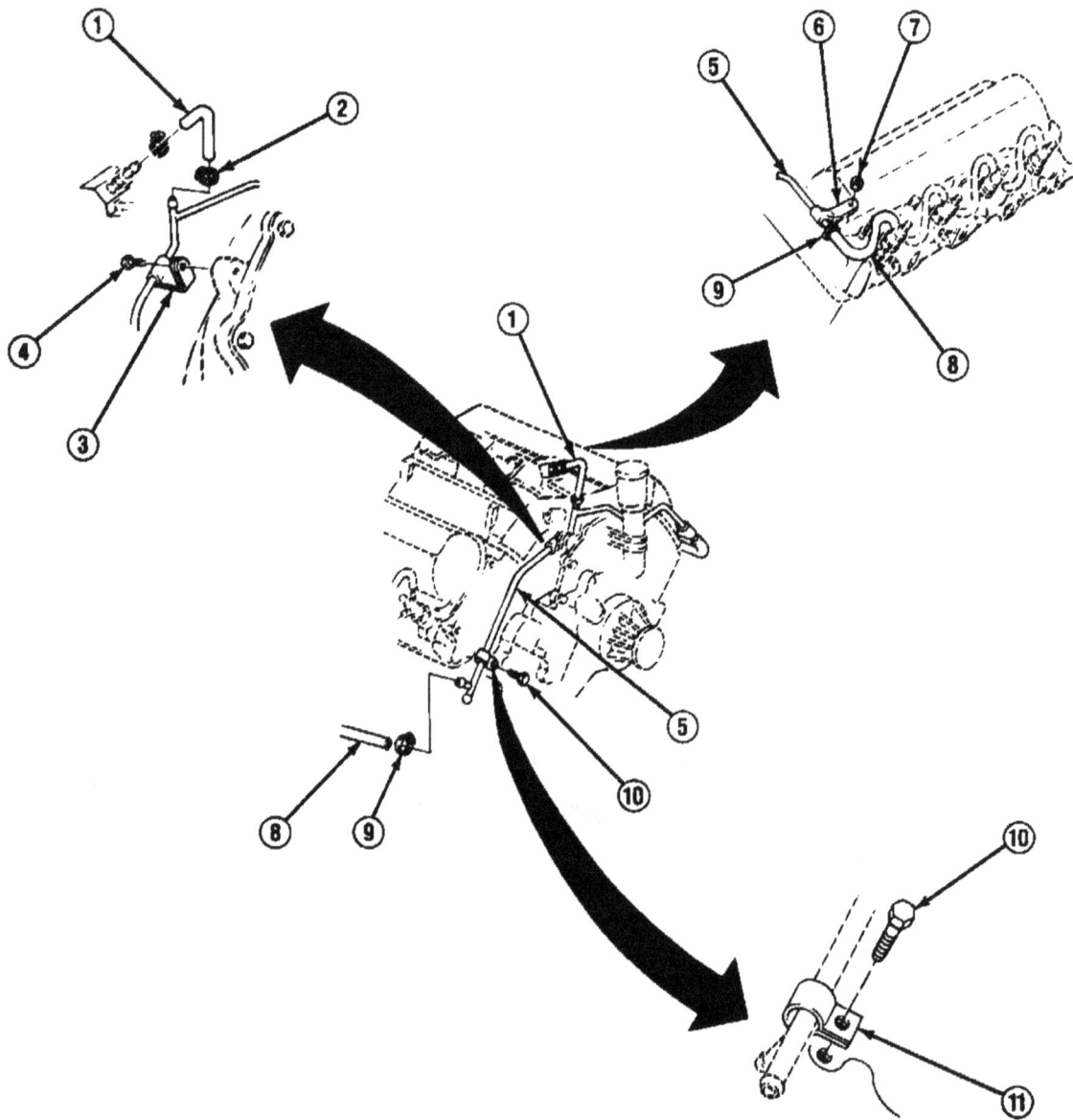

TA49811

FOLLOW-ON TASKS:

•Install alternators, alternator brackets, and mounting hardware (M1010). (See paragraph 4-3)
•Check for leaks.

3-20.   GLOW PLUG AND GLOW PLUG SWITCH REPLACEMENT.

This task covers: a. Removal   c. Installation
                           b. Inspection

INITIAL SETUP:

Equipment Condition   *Tools/Test Equipment*

•Both battery negative cables disconnected.   •Torque wrench
   (See paragraph 4-38)

| a.   REMOVAL |

NOTE

If removing glow plug switch (4), perform steps 1 and 2.

If removing glow plug (1), perform step 3.

1.   At top rear of left cylinder head,   disconnect connector wire (3) from glow plug switch (4).

2.   Remove glow plug switch (4).   Remove bushing (5). Discard bushing if threads appear damaged.

NOTE

Notify supervisor if glow   plug (1) does not come out in one piece. Removal of glow plug fragments is not authorized at this maintenance level.

3.   Disconnect glow plug connector wire (2) from each glow plug (1) to be removed. Remove glow plug.

| b.   INSPECTION |

1.   Inspect glow plug (1) threads to ensure that they are not stripped. If glow plug threads are stripped, notify your supervisor.

| c.   INSTALLATION |

NOTE

● If installing glow plug (1), perform steps 1 and 2.

● If installing glow plug switch (4), perform steps 3 and 4.

1.   Install each removed glow plug (1). Tighten to 10 lb.-ft. (14 N•m).

2.   Install glow plug connector wire (2) to each glow plug (1).

3.   Install new bushing (5) if required.

3-20. GLOW PLUG AND GLOW PLUG SWITCH REPLACEMENT (Con't).

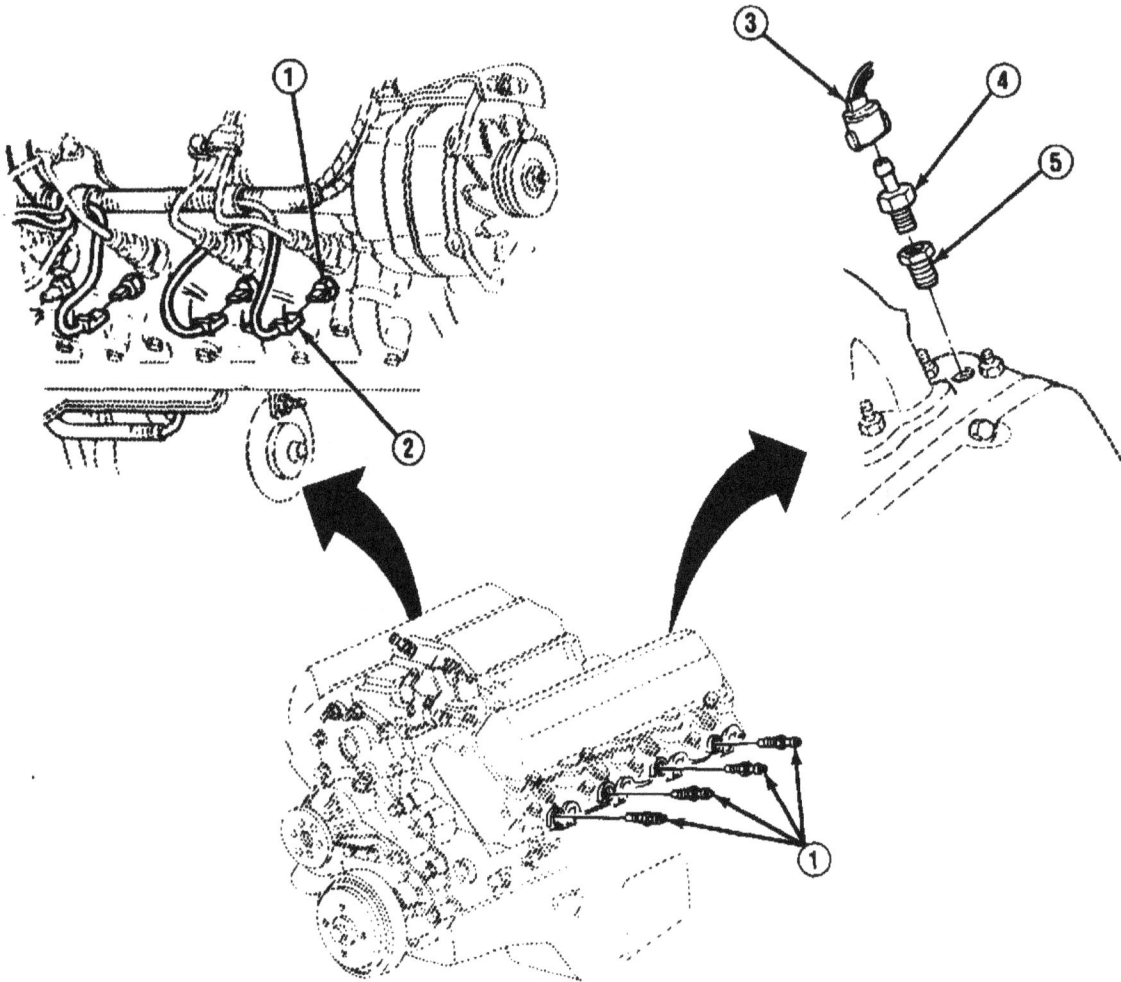

4.   Install glow plug switch (4) and connector wire (3).

FOLLOW-ON TASKS:

Connect both battery negative cables. (See paragraph 4-38)

TA49812

3-21.   TRANSMISSION VACUUM HOSES REPLACEMENT.

This task covers: a. Removal   b. Installation

INITIAL SETUP:

Equipment Condition

 ●Air cleaner removed. (See paragraph 3-9)

---

a.   REMOVAL

1.   Remove connector (8) from transmission vacuum valve assembly (9).

2.   Remove vacuum pump hose assembly (5) from connector (4) and   remove connector   (6).

3.   Remove connector (4) and hose (3) from vacuum pump (2).

4.   Remove 2 connectors (7) from vacuum pump hose assembly (5) and vacuum hose (1).

5.   Remove vacuum hose (1) from pipe assembly (10).

b.   INSTALLATION

1.   Install connector (8) to transmission vacuum valve assembly (9).

2.   Install connector (4) and hose (3) at vacuum pump (2).

3.   Install vacuum pump hose assembly (5) to connector (6).

4.   Install vacuum pump hose assembly (5) to connector (4).

5.   Install vacuum hose (1) to pipe assembly (10).

6.   Install 2 connectors (7) to vacuum pump hose assembly (5) and vacuum hose (1).

NOTE

Ensure that vacuum pump hose assembly (5) is   connected to bottom of connector (8).

7.   Install 2 connectors (7) with attached vacuum hoses (1   and 5) to connector (8).

3-21. TRANSMISSION VACUUM HOSES REPLACEMENT (Con't),

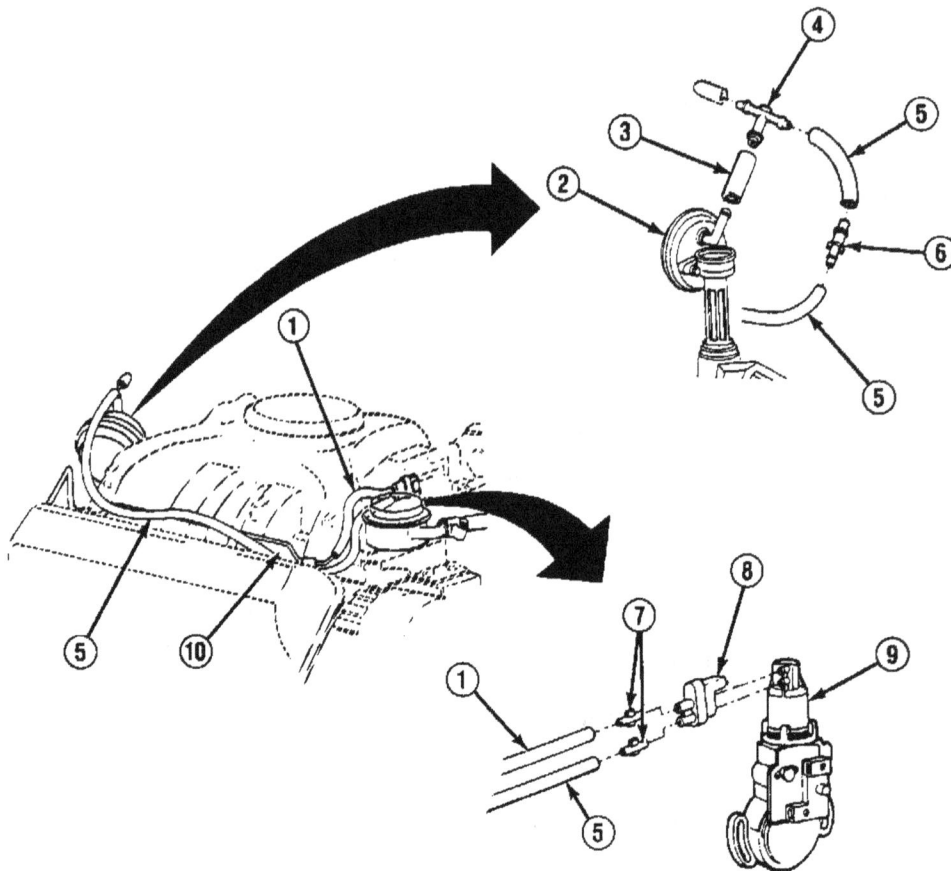

FOLLOW-ON TASKS:

- Install air cleaner. (See paragraph 3-9)

TA49813

3-21.1. TRANSMISSION VACUUM VALVE REPLACEMENT.

This task covers:	a. Removal	b. Installation

INITIAL SETUP:

Equipment Condition

● Air cleaner removed.
   (See paragraph 3-9)

Tools/Test Equipment

● Valve gage block, J-33043
● Vacuum gage
● Vacuum pump

---

a.	**REMOVAL**

NOTE

If only adjusting transmission vacuum valve (5), perform REMOVAL, step 1 and INSTALLATION, steps 2-7.

1. Disconnect vacuum hose connector (2) from transmission vacuum valve (5).

2. Remove 2 screws (6) and transmission vacuum valve from fuel injector pump (1).

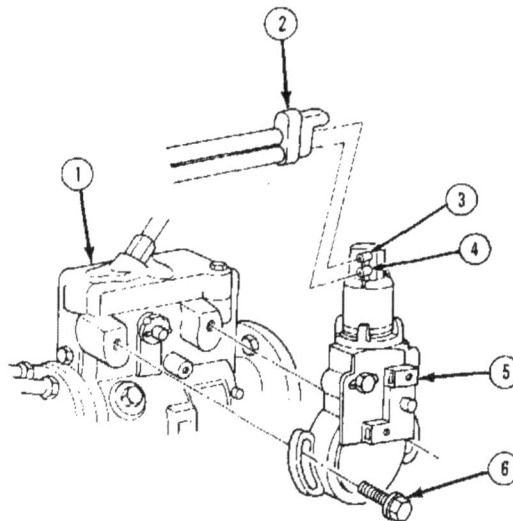

TA701829

3-21.1. TRANSMISSION VACUUM VALVE REPLACEMENT (Con't).

| b. | INSTALLATION |

NOTE

Transmission vacuum valve (5) must always be adjusted when it is installed.

1. Install transmission vacuum valve (5) on fuel injector pump (1) with 2 screws (6). DO NOT fully tighten screws. Transmission vacuum valve must be free to rotate on fuel injector pump.

2. Attach vacuum source to lower vacuum nipple (4). Attach vacuum gage to upper vacuum nipple (3). Bring vacuum down to 20 in. Hg.

3. Insert valve gage block (9) between gage boss (10) and wide-open stop screw (8) on throttle lever (7). Rotate and hold throttle lever against valve gage block.

4. Loosen 2 screws (6), if not already loose. Slowly rotate transmission vacuum valve (5) clockwise (toward front of truck) until vacuum gage reads 8 in. Hg. Hold transmission vacuum valve in this position, and tighten 2 screws.

5. Check adjustment by releasing throttle lever (7) then rotating throttle lever against valve gage block (9). If vacuum gage does not read 8 in. Hg, loosen 2 screws (6) and repeat steps 2-5.

6. Disconnect vacuum source and vacuum gage.

7. Connect vacuum hose connector (2) to transmission vacuum valve (5).

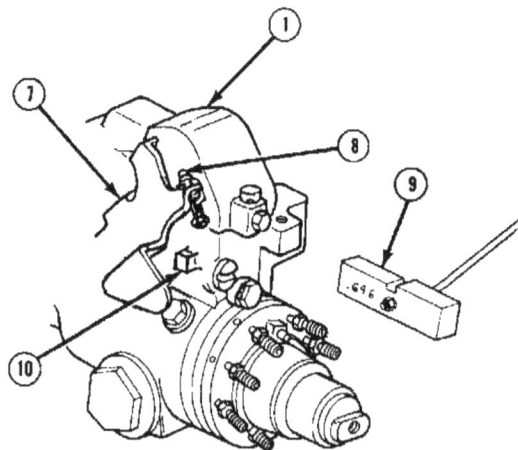

FOLLOW-ON TASKS:

● Install air cleaner. (See paragraph 3-9)

TA701830

Section III. ACCELERATOR SYSTEM MAINTENANCE

3-22. ACCELERATOR SYSTEM MAINTENANCE INDEX.

3-23. ACCELERATOR CABLE AND FAST IDLE SOLENOID ASSEMBLY REPLACEMENT.

This task covers: a. Removal   b. Installation

INITIAL SETUP:

Equipment Condition
 Both battery negative cables disconnected. (See paragraph 4-38)

| a. | REMOVAL |

NOTE

 If removing accelerator cable assembly (1), perform steps 1-5.

 If removing support (6) and fast idle   solenoid assembly (5), perform steps 1 and 6 through 9.

1. In engine compartment, remove accelerator   cable retainer (9) and accelerator cable assembly (1) from support (6).

2. Remove accelerator cable assembly (1) from clip (2).

3. In driver's compartment, remove retainer (3) securing accelerator cable assembly (1) to accelerator pedal lever assembly (4).

4. In driver's compartment, depress tangs on accelerator cable assembly (1) and push accelerator cable assembly through bulkhead into engine compartment.

5. From engine compartment, pull accelerator cable assembly (1) through bulkhead. Remove accelerator cable assembly.

6. Disconnect connector from fast idle solenoid assembly (5).

7. Remove 2 screws (10) and fast idle solenoid assembly (5) from support (6).

8. Remove spring assembly (7) from support (6).

9. Remove 2 screws (8) and support (6).

| b. | INSTALLATION |

CAUTION

Use extreme caution when installing accelerator cable assembly (1) to ensure that it is not kinked. Damage to accelerator cable assembly may result in uneven acceleration.

NOTE

 If installing support (6) and fast idle solenoid assembly (5), perform steps 1-4.

 If installing accelerator cable assembly (1), perform steps 3 and 5 through 7.

1. Install support (6) with 2 screws (8).

3-23. ACCELERATOR CABLE AND FAST IDLE SOLENOID ASSEMBLY REPLACEMENT (Con't).

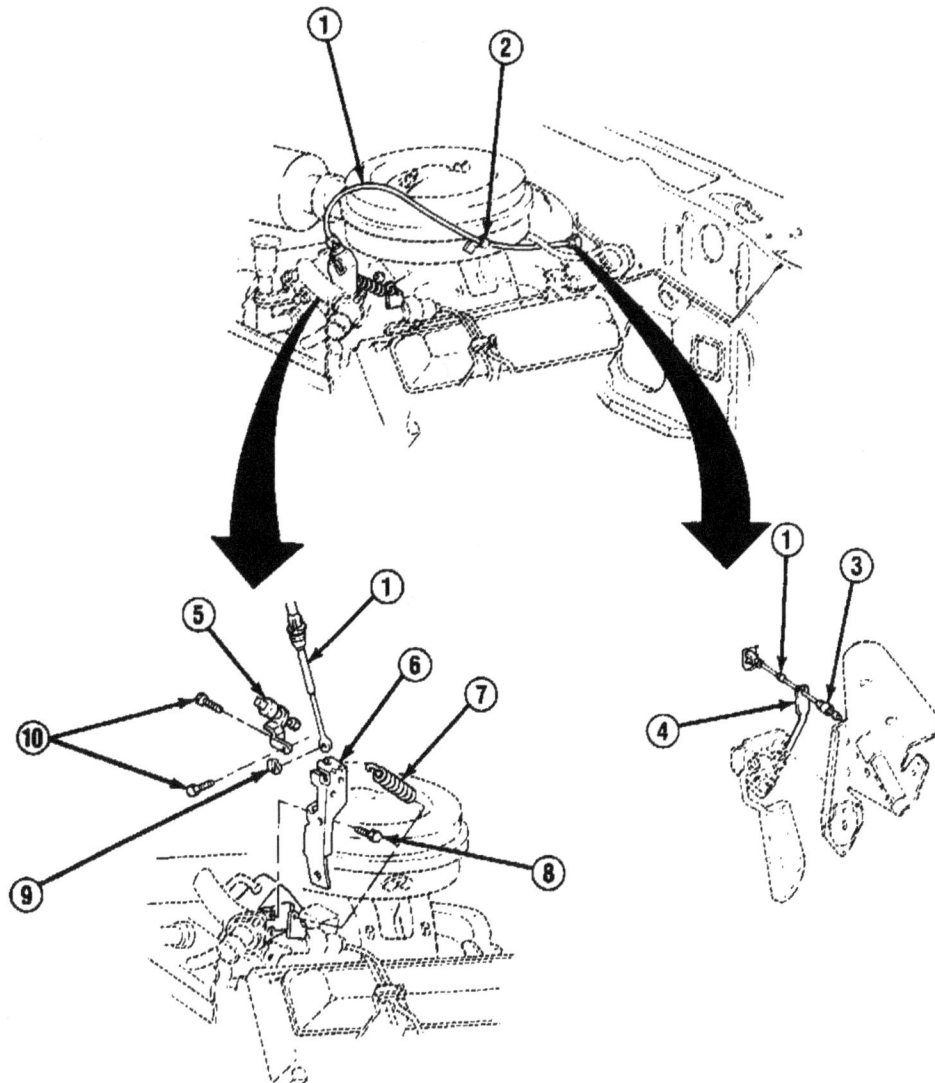

2. Install spring assembly (7) to support (6).

3. Install accelerator cable assembly (1) to support (6) with accelerator cable retainer (9).

4. Install fast idle solenoid assembly (5) to support (6) with 2 screws (10). Install connector to fast idle solenoid assembly.

5. Install accelerator cable assembly (1) into clip (2) on air cleaner.

TA49814

3-23. ACCELERATOR CABLE AND FAST IDLE SOLENOID ASSEMBLY REPLACEMENT (Con't).

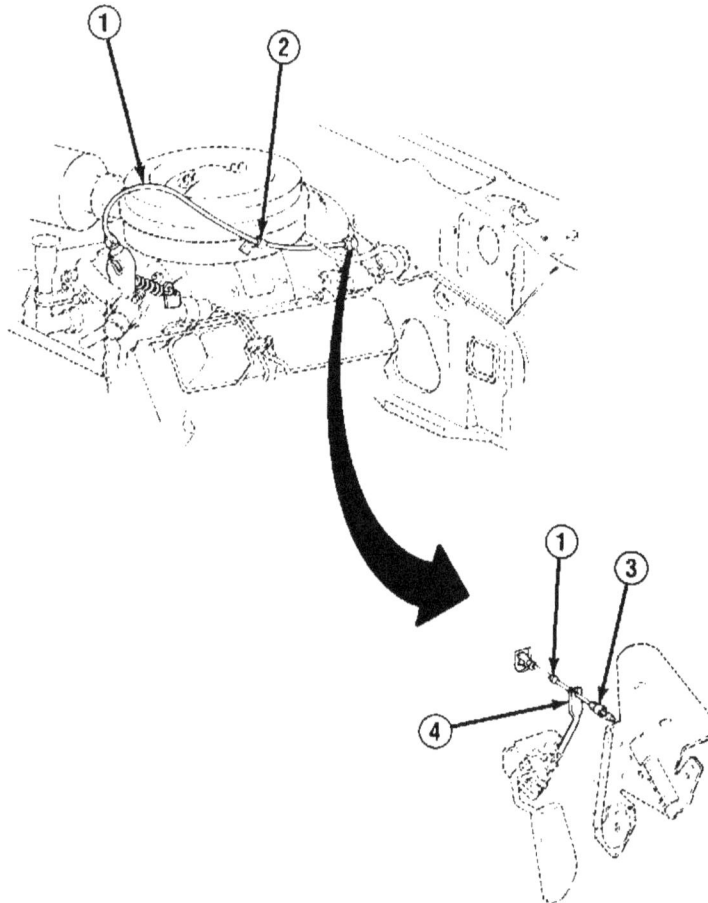

6. Carefully push accelerator cable assembly (1) through bulkhead into driver's compartment.

7. In driver's compartment, install accelerator cable assembly (1) into forked end of accelerator pedal lever assembly (4). Install retainer (3) to end of accelerator cable assembly until it is seated.

FOLLOW-ON TASKS:

Connect both battery negative cables. (See paragraph 4-38)
If fast idle solenoid was replaced, adjust as required. (See paragraph 3-25)

TA49815

3-24. ACCELERATOR PEDAL AND LEVER ASSEMBLY REPLACEMENT.

This task covers: a. Removal   b. Installation

INITIAL SETUP:

Equipment Condition   *Materials/Parts*
  ●Both battery negative cables disconnected.   ●One retainer
    (See paragraph 4-38)

---

a.   REMOVAL

NOTE

If removing accelerator pedal (1), perform steps 1 and 2.

1.   Remove accelerator cable assembly (5) from lever assembly (2).

2.   Remove spring (3) from lever assembly (2). Remove retainer (8), accelerator pedal (1), and spring. Remove spring from accelerator pedal. Discard retainer.

3.   Remove electrical plug from left side of plate (6).

4.   Remove 3 screws (7) and plate (6).

5.   Remove lever assembly (2) and support (4).

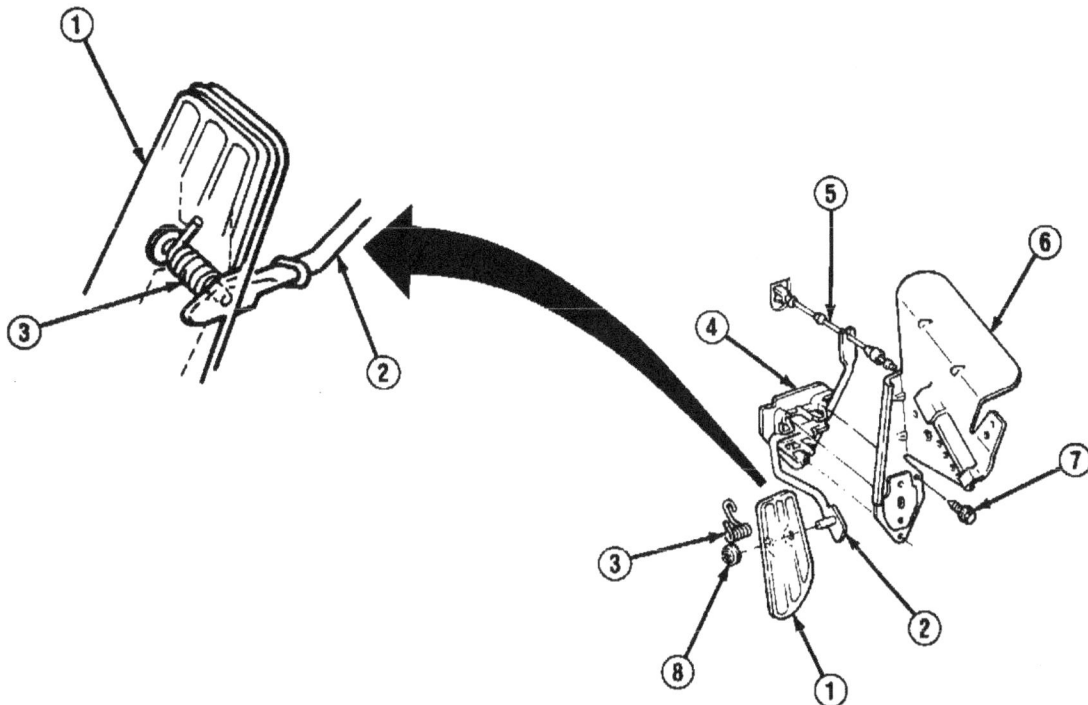

TA49816

3-24. ACCELERATOR PEDAL AND LEVER ASSEMBLY REPLACEMENT (Con't).

b. INSTALLATION

NOTE

If installing accelerator pedal (1), perform steps 4 and 5.

1. Install support (4) and lever assembly (2) into grooves of support.

2. Install plate (6) with 3 screws (7).

3. Install electrical plug on left side of plate (6).

4. Install spring (3) to accelerator pedal (1). Install spring and accelerator pedal to lever assembly (2).

NOTE

Retainer (8) must be tight against pedal (1) rib.

5. Install new retainer (8) to secure accelerator pedal (1) to lever assembly (2).

6. Install accelerator cable assembly (5) to lever assembly (2).

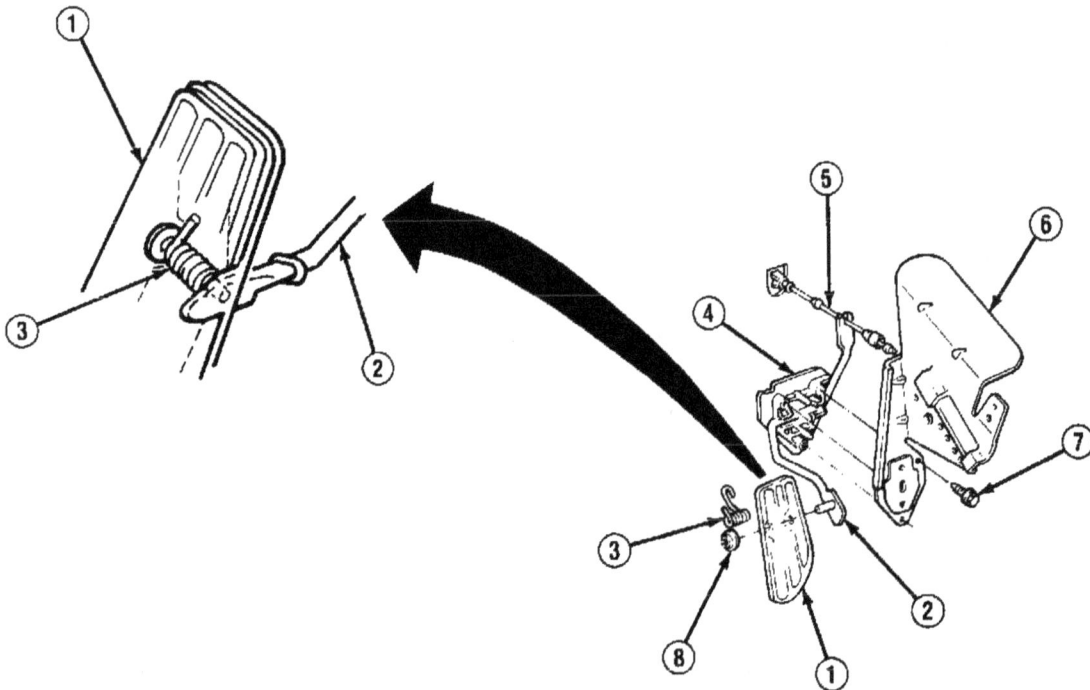

FOLLOW-ON TASKS:

•Connect both battery negative cables. (See paragraph 4-38)

TA49817

3-25. ENGINE IDLE SPEED ADJUSTMENT.

This task covers: a. Adjustment

INITIAL SETUP:

Equipment Condition

- Parking brake set.
- Transmission in "P" (Park).

Manual References

- TM 9-4910-571-12&P

Tools/Test Equipment

- STE/IC E

General Safety Instructions

- Use extreme caution to ensure that clothing or tools DO NOT get caught in truck's operating drivebelts.

WARNING

Use extreme caution to ensure that clothing, tools, and insulated jumper wires DO NOT get caught in truck's operating drivebelts. Failure to follow this warning may result in serious injury to personnel and equipment damage.

---

a. ADJUSTMENT

1. Start engine and allow it to reach normal operating temperature.

2. Connect STE/ICE tester to STE/ICE DCA connector under dash. (See TM 9-4910-571-12&P)

3. Adjust low idle speed screw (6) on fuel injector pump (5) to 625 rpm for all except M1010 and 725 rpm for M1010.

4. Remove connector (1) from fast idle solenoid (4).

CAUTION

Connecting insulated jumper wire to any terminal other than front positive (+) terminal will result in equipment damage.

5. Use an insulated jumper wire from front battery positive (+) terminal to adenoid terminal (3) to energize fast idle solenoid (4).

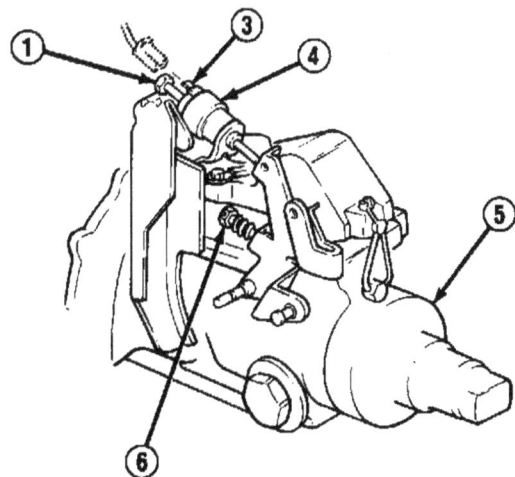

TA49818

3-25.   ENGINE IDLE SPEED ADJUSTMENT (Con't).

6.   Momentarily open throttle to ensure that fast idle solenoid plunger (2) is energized and fully extended.

7.   Adjust extended fast idle solenoid plunger (2) by turning hex head of fast idle solenoid plunger to an engine fast idle speed of 800 rpm.

8.   Turn off engine.

9.   Remove jumper wire and install connector (1) to fast idle solenoid (4).

10.   Remove STE/ICE tester from STE/ICE DCA connector. (See TM 9-4910-571-12&P)

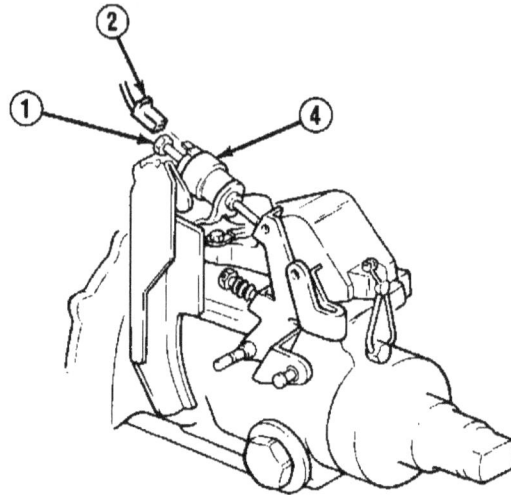

TA49819

Section IV. EXHAUST SYSTEM MAINTENANCE

3-26.   EXHAUST SYSTEM MAINTENANCE INDEX.

3-27. EXHAUST PIPE, MUFFLER, AND TAILPIPE REPLACEMENT.

This task covers: a. Removal   b. Installation

INITIAL SETUP:

Materials/Parts

  • Seven lockwashers (M1009)
  • Nine lockwashers (all except M1009)
  • Four locknuts (M1009 with winterization kits)
  • Eight locknuts (all except M1009 and M1010
     with winterization kits)
  • Twenty locknuts (M1010 with winterization kits)
  • One seal

Tools/ Test Equipment

  Torque wrench

General Safety Instructions

  • Allow exhaust system to cool before attempting to service.

---

a. REMOVAL

WARNING

Before attempting to service any part of exhaust system, allow exhaust
system to cool. Failure to follow this warning will result in serious burns.

NOTE

• Removal of left side exhaust system for all except M1009 is described
in this paragraph.

• Right side exhaust system for all except M1009 and both sides of M1009
exhaust system are removed the same way except for minor
differences which will be described as they occur.

1. Remove 2 bolts (1), nuts (2), lockwashers (3), and 2 clamps (4) from tailpipe (5). Discard
lockwashers.

NOTE

Factory-installed muffler (7) and tailpipe (5) are welded to form a 1-piece
assembly. If original muffler or tailpipe require replacement, both muffler
and tailpipe must be replaced. Clamp kits will be required for installation.

2. Remove clamp kit (6) and tailpipe (5). Discard 2 lockwashers.

3-27. EXHAUST PIPE, MUFFLER, AND TAILPIPE REPLACEMENT (Con't).

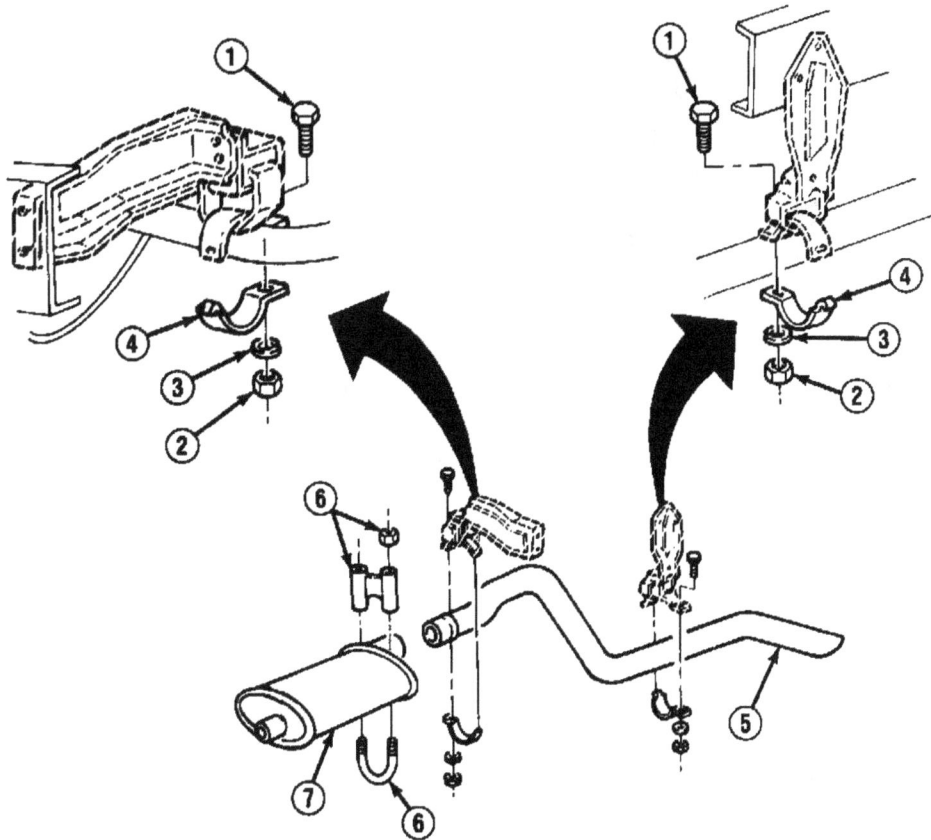

NOTE

- Both sides of M1009 exhaust have hangers (11) bolted to mufflers (7).

- Perform step 3 only if working on M1009 exhaust system.

3. Remove bolt (9), lockwasher (10), and hanger (11) from muffler (7). Remove hanger from support assembly (8) only if damaged . Discard lockwasher.

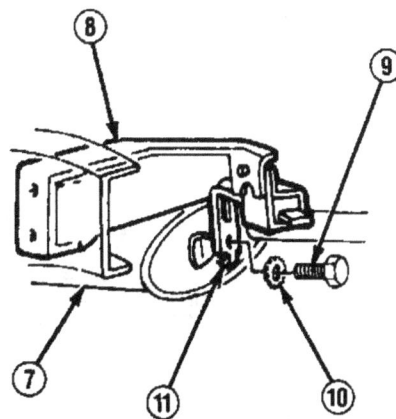

TA49820

3-27. EXHAUST PIPE, MUFFLER, AND TAILPIPE REPLACEMENT (Con't).

4. Remove clamp kit (16) and muffler (7). Discard 2 lockwashers.

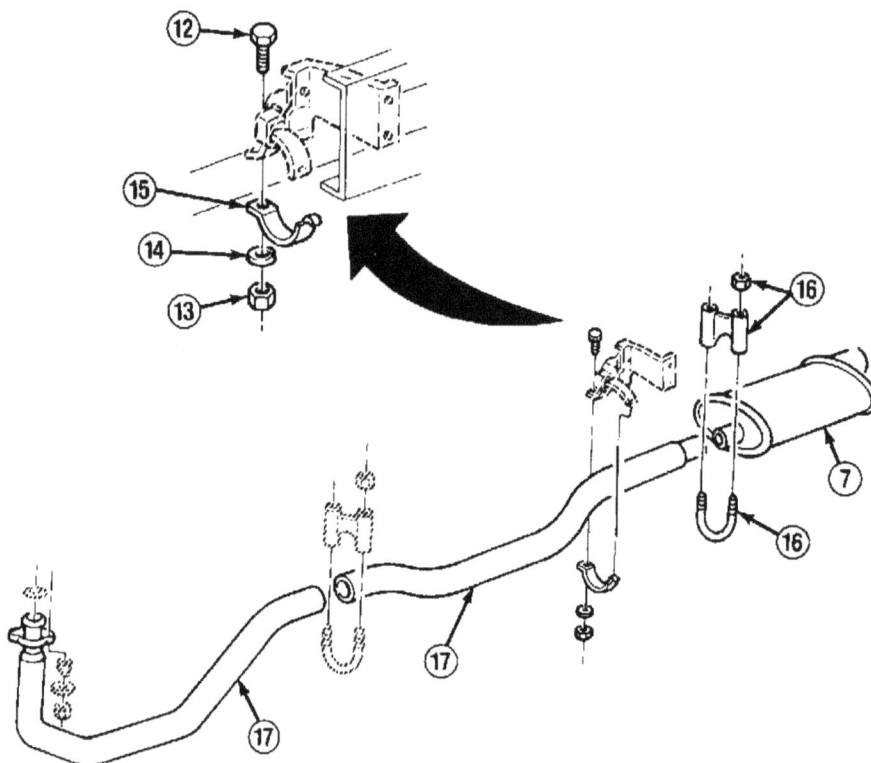

NOTE

Perform step 5 only if working on truck equipped with winterization kits.

5. Remove clamp kits (18) and separate exhaust pipe (17) and winterization kit exhaust flex pipe (19). Discard clamp kit locknuts.

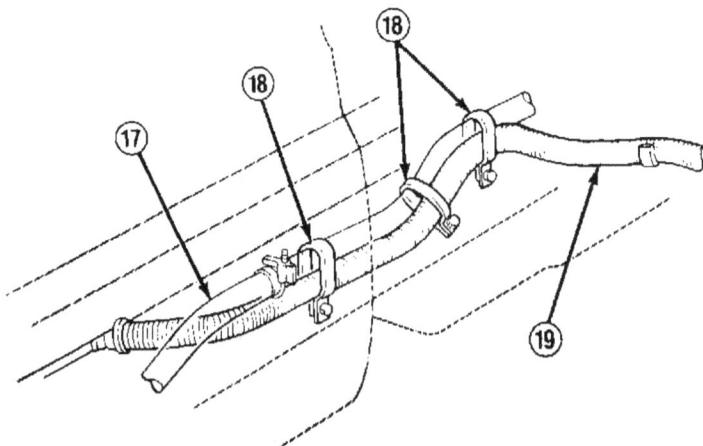

TA49821

3-27. EXHAUST PIPE, MUFFLER, AND TAILPIPE REPLACEMENT (Con't).

NOTE

Perform step 6 for all except M1009.

6. Remove bolt (12), nut (13), lockwasher (14), and clamp (15) from exhaust pipe (17). Discard lockwasher.

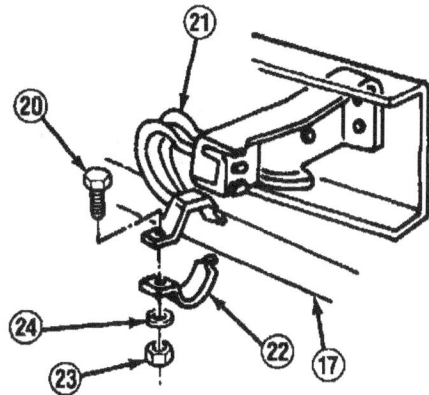

NOTE

Perform step 7 only if working on right side of M1009.

7. Remove bolt (20), nut (23), lockwasher (24), and clamp (22) from exhaust pipe (17). Remove hanger (21) only if damaged. Discard damaged hanger and lockwasher.

NOTE

Perform step 8 for left side exhaust systems for all except M1009.

8. Remove clamp kit (29) and exhaust pipe (17). Discard 2 lockwashers.

9. Remove 3 nuts (28), washers (27), springs (26), and exhaust pipe (17) from exhaust manifold. Remove seal (25) and discard.

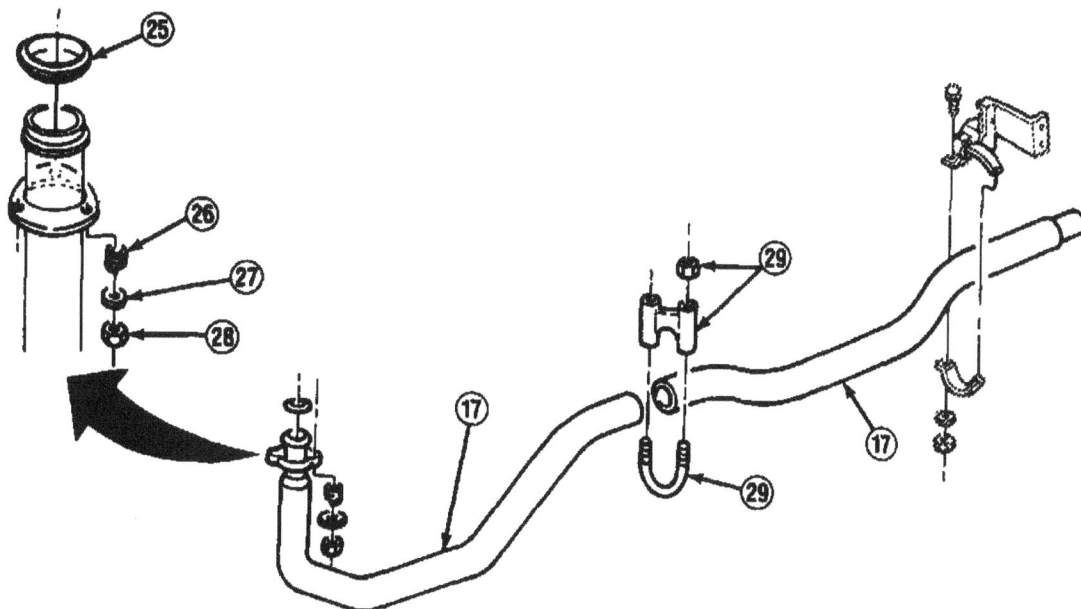

TA49822

3-27. EXHAUST PIPE, MUFFLER, AND TAILPIPE REPLACEMENT (Con't).

NOTE

- M1009 exhaust system has a support assembly in frame at rear of both mufflers and a hanger assembly in frame at rear of exhaust pipe on right side only.

- Factory-installed support or hanger assemblies are riveted to frame. Replacement support or hanger assemblies are installed with bolts, lockwashers, and nuts.

- Perform step 10 only if working on M1009.

10. Remove and discard hanger or support assemblies only if damaged.

b. INSTALLATION

NOTE

- Installation   of left side exhaust systems   for all except M1009 is described in this paragraph.

- Right side exhaust systems for all except   M1009 and both sides of M1009 exhaust system are installed the same way except for minor differences which will be described as they occur.

- M1009 exhaust system has a support assembly in frame at rear of both mufflers and a hanger assembly in frame at rear of exhaust pipe on right side only.

- Perform step 1 only if working on M1009.

1. Install new hanger or support assemblies if required.

2. Install new seal (25) at exhaust manifold. Install exhaust pipe (17) with 3 springs (26), washers (27), and nuts (28). Tighten nuts to 180 lb.-in. (20 N•m).

NOTE

Perform step 3 for all except M1009 left side exhaust systems.

3. Install rear portion   of exhaust pipe (17) to front portion with clamp kit (29)   using 2 new lockwashers.

3-27. EXHAUST PIPE, MUFFLER, AND TAILPIPE REPLACEMENT (Con't).

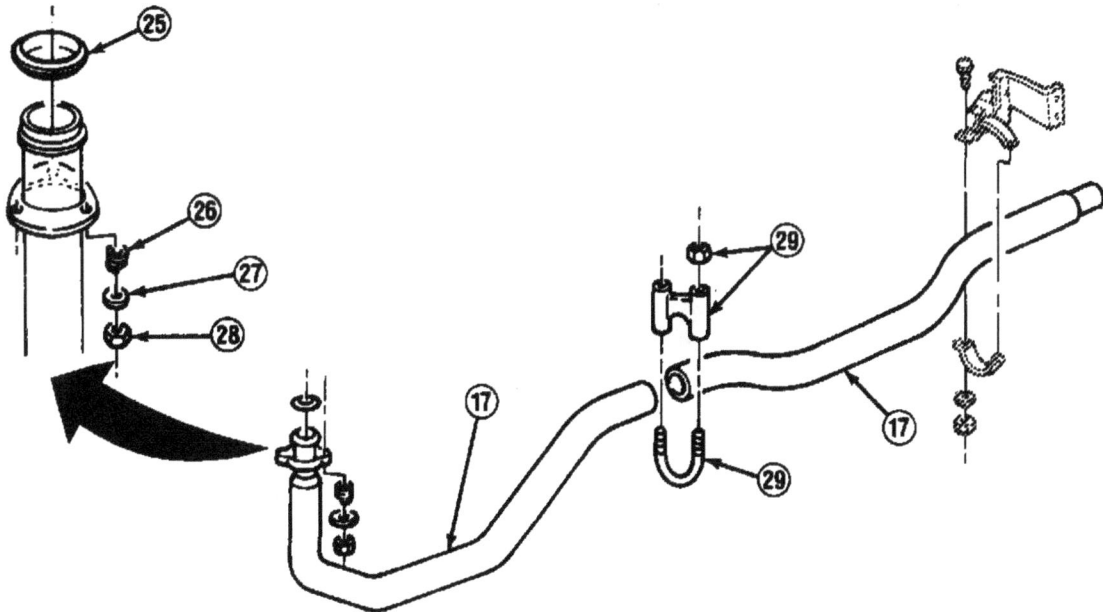

NOTE

Perform step 4 only if working on M1009 right side exhaust system.

4.   If removed, install new hanger (21) to hanger assembly. Install exhaust pipe (17) to hanger with clamp (22), bolt (20), new lockwasher (24), and nut (23).

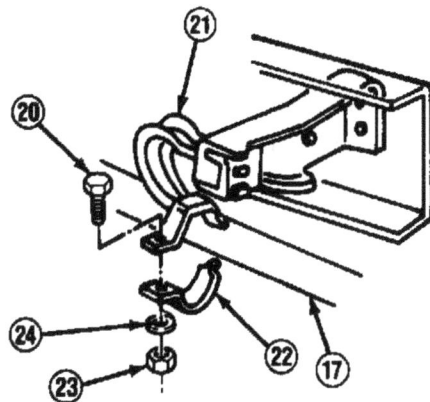

TA49823

3-27.   EXHAUST PIPE, MUFFLER, AND TAILPIPE REPLACEMENT (Con't).

NOTE

Perform step 5 for all except M1009.

5.   Install exhaust pipe (17) to frame with clamp (15), bolt (12), new lockwasher (14), and nut (13).

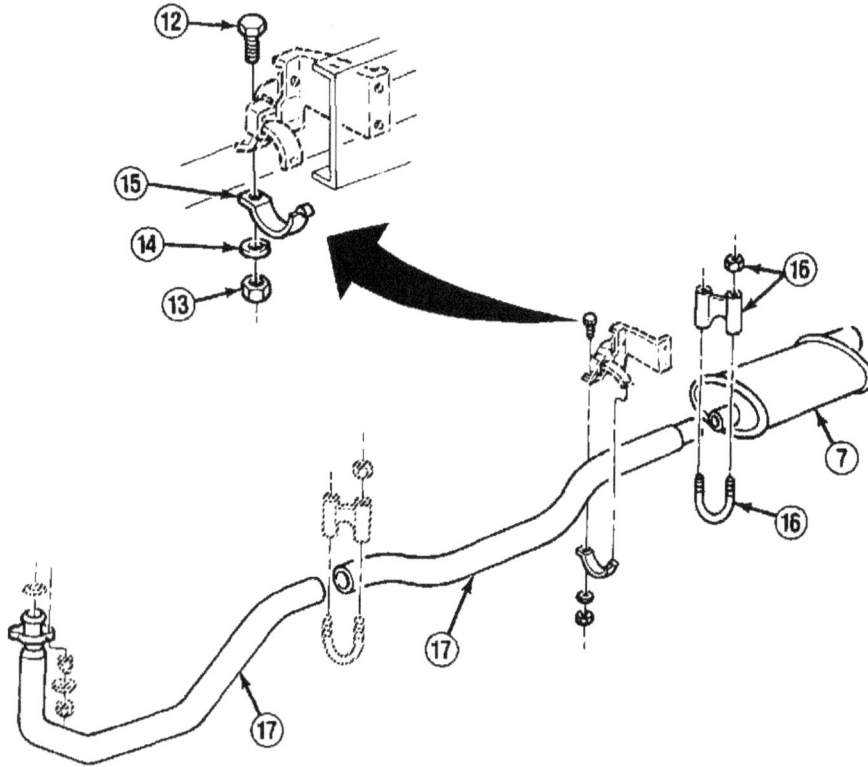

NOTE

Perform step 6 only if working on truck equipped with winterization kits.

6.   Install winterization kit exhaust flex pipe (19) to exhaust pipe (17) with clamp kits (18) using new locknuts.

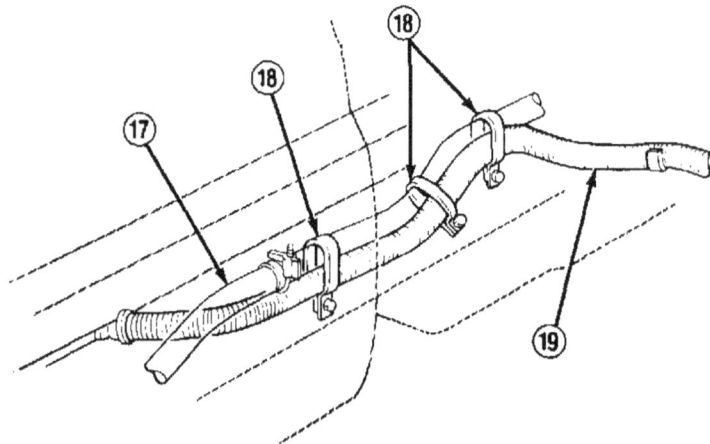

TA49824

3-27.   EXHAUST PIPE, MUFFLER, AND TAILPIPE REPLACEMENT (Con't).

7.   Install muffler (7) to exhaust pipe (17) with clamp kit (16) using 2 new lockwashers.

NOTE

Perform step 8   only if working on M1009.

8.   If removed, install new hanger (11) to support assembly (8). Install hanger to muffler (7) with new lockwasher (10) and bolt (9).

9.   Install tailpipe (5) to muffler (7). Install tailpipe to 2 hangers at frame with 2 clamps (4), bolts (1), new lockwashers (3), and nuts (2).

10.   Install clamp kit (6) at rear of muffler (7) using 2 new lockwashers.

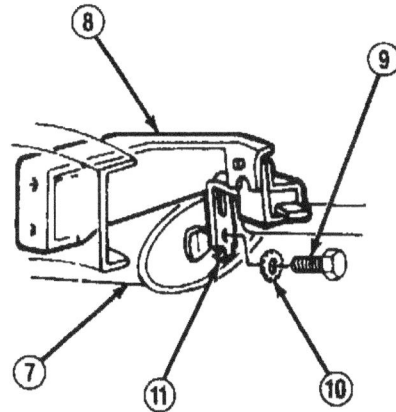

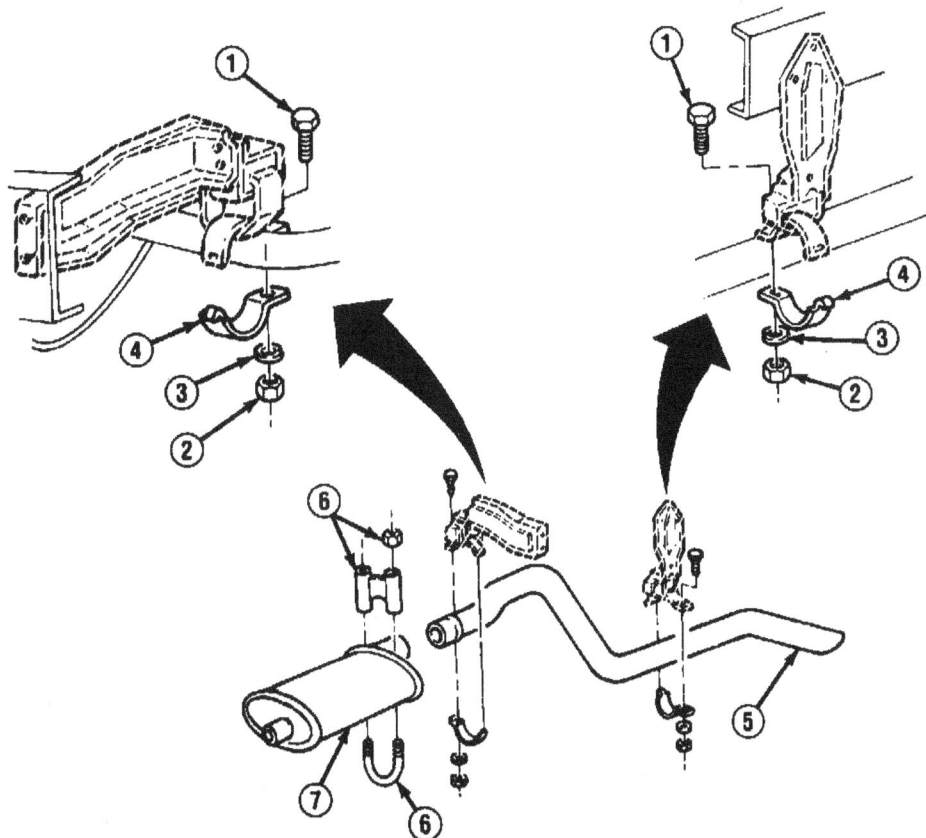

TA49825

3-28. EXHAUST MANIFOLD REPLACEMENT.

This task covers: a. Removal   b. Installation

INITIAL SETUP:

Equipment Condition

- Both battery negative cables disconnected. (See paragraph 4-38)
- Rear battery removed (if removing right side exhaust manifold, M1010). (See paragraph 4-39)
- Alternators and alternator brackets removed (if removing right side exhaust manifold, M1010). (See paragraph 4-3)

Tools/Test Equipment

- Torque wrench

Materials/Parts

- One exhaust pipe seal
- Three lockwashers (right side)
- Four lockwashers (left side)

General Safety Instructions

- Allow exhaust system to cool before attempting to service.

---

a.	REMOVAL

WARNING

Before attempting to service any part of exhaust system, allow exhaust system to cool. Failure to follow this warning will result in serious burns.

NOTE

- If removing right   side exhaust manifold (16), perform steps 1-3.

- If removing left   side exhaust manifold (6), perform steps 1 and 4 through 9.

- Tag glow plug leads for installation.

1. Disconnect glow plug leads.

2. Remove 3 nuts (5), lockwashers (4), and springs (3), and disconnect exhaust pipe (2) from right or left side exhaust manifold (6 or 16). Remove exhaust pipe seal (1) and discard.

3. Remove 8 bolts (13) and remove right side exhaust manifold (16). Remove 3 studs (15) from right side exhaust manifold as required.

4. At oil cooler hose bracket (11) remove 3 nuts (7), bolt (9), lockwasher (8), and insulator (10). Remove oil cooler hose bracket from left side exhaust manifold (6).

5. Remove nut and washer securing engine oil level indicator tube mounting bracket to stud (14).

3-28. EXHAUST MANIFOLD REPLACEMENT (Con't).

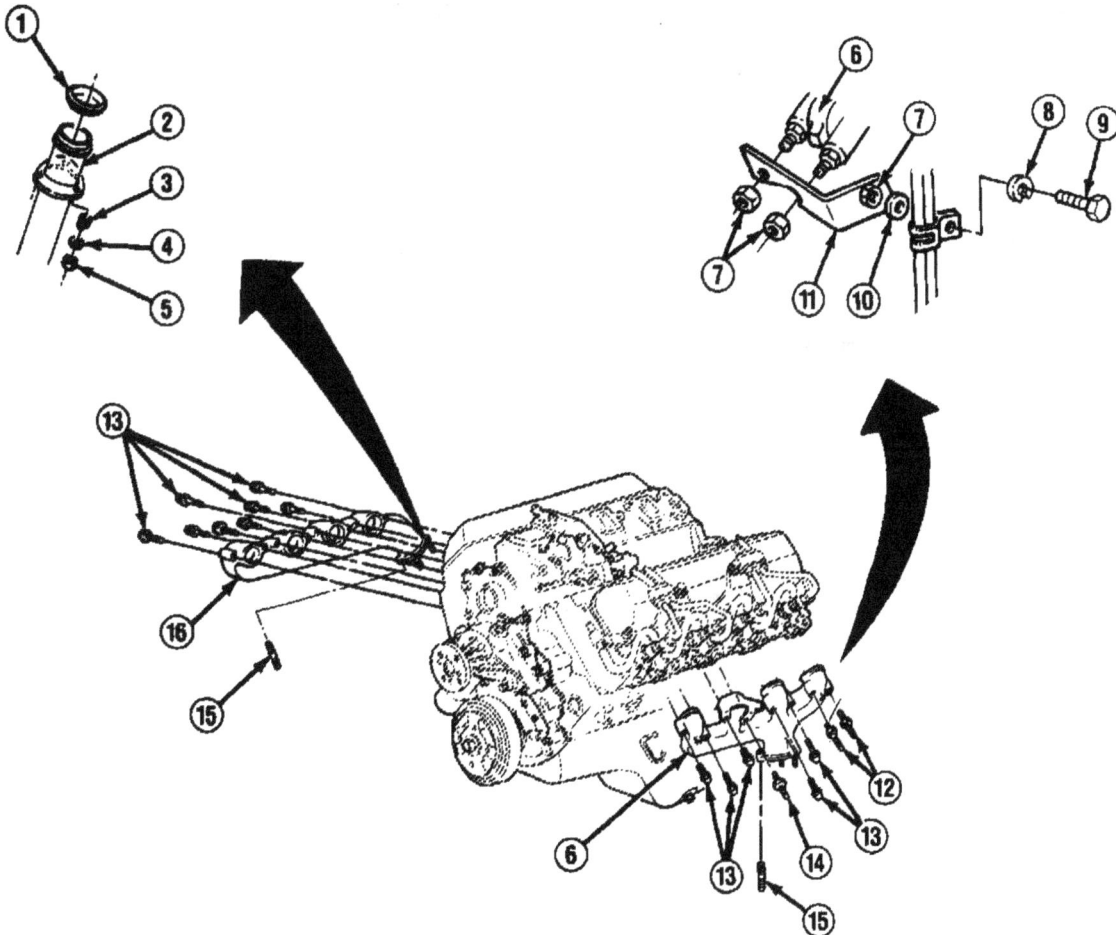

TA49826

NOTE

Perform step 6 only if working on left side of M1010.

6. Remove bolt (19) securing air conditioner compressor (18) to bracket (17) at left side exhaust manifold (6).

7. Remove 2 studs (12), stud (14), and 5 bolts (13) at left side exhaust manifold (6).

NOTE

Perform step 8 only if working on left side of M1010.

8. Remove bracket (17).

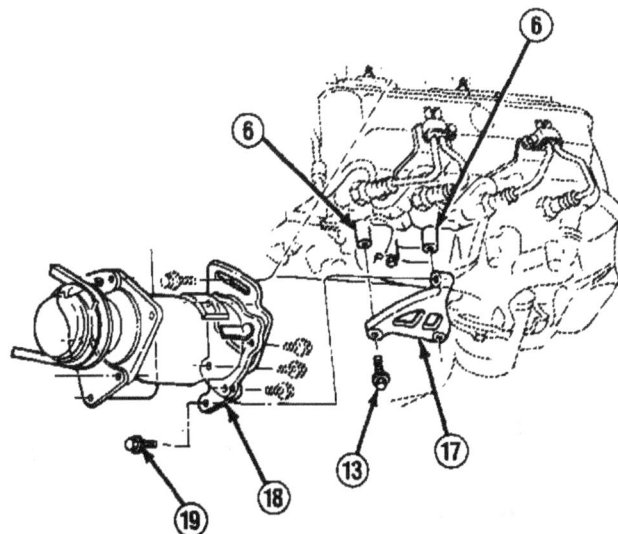

3-28.   EXHAUST MANIFOLD REPLACEMENT (Con't).

9.   Remove left side exhaust manifold (6). Remove 3 studs (15) as required.

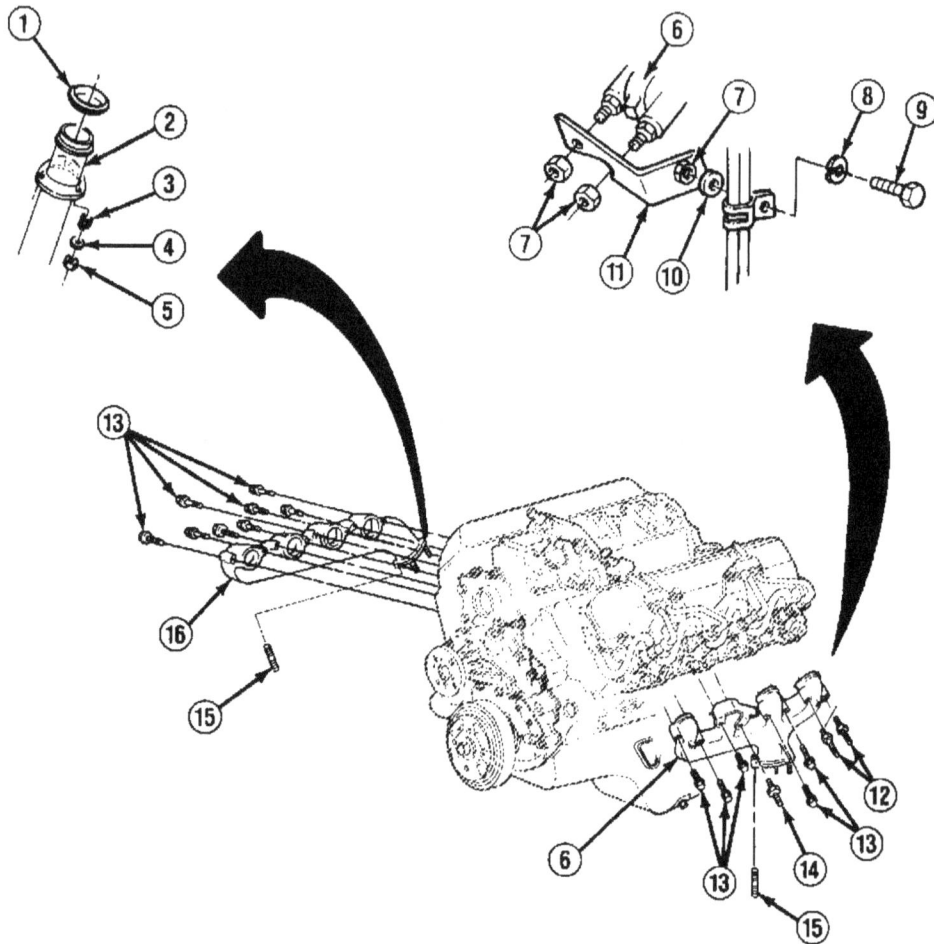

b. INSTALLATION

NOTE

◄If installing left side exhaust manifold (6), perform steps 1-6, 8, and 9.

◄If installing right side exhaust manifold (16), perform steps 7-9.

1.   Position left side exhaust manifold (6) over bolt holes in engine cylinder block and install 2 studs (12) and stud (14). DO NOT fully tighten studs.

2.   Install nut and washer securing oil level indicator tube mounting bracket to stud (14).

TA49827

3-28. EXHAUST MANIFOLD REPLACEMENT (Con't).

NOTE

Perform step 3 only if working on left side of M1010.

3. Position bracket (17), alining 2 bottom holes in bracket with bolt holes in engine cylinder block.

4. Install 5 bolts (13) securing left side exhaust manifold (6) to engine cylinder block. Tighten bolts, 2 studs (12), and stud (14) to 25 lb.-ft. (34 N•m).

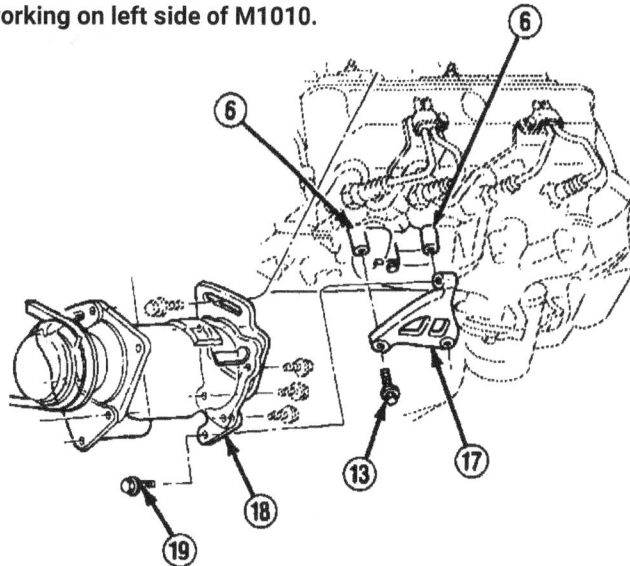

NOTE

Perform step 5 only if working on left side of M1010.

5. Install air conditioner compressor (18) to bracket (17) with bolt (19).

6. Install oil cooler hose bracket (11) to left side exhaust manifold (6) with insulator (10), new lockwasher (8), bolt (9), and 3 nuts (7).

NOTE

Perform step 7 only if working on right side exhaust manifold (16).

7. Install right side exhaust manifold (16) with 8 bolts (13). Tighten bolts to 25 lb.-ft. (34 N•m).

8. Install new exhaust pipe seal (1) and secure exhaust pipe (2) to right or left side exhaust manifold (6 or 16) with 3 studs (15), springs (3), 3 new lockwashers (4), and nuts (5). Tighten nuts to 15 lb.-ft. (20 N•m).

9. Connect glow plug leads as tagged.

FOLLOW-ON TASKS:

  Install alternators and alternator brackets if removed (M1010). (See paragraph 4-3)
  Install rear battery if removed (M1010). (See paragraph 4-39)
  Connect both battery negative cables. (See paragraph 4-38)

TA49828

Section V. COOLING SYSTEM MAINTENANCE

3-29. COOLING SYSTEM MAINTENANCE INDEX.

3-30.   COOLING SYSTEM SERVICING.

This task covers:	a. Draining	c. Filling
	b. Cleaning	

INITIAL SETUP:

Manual References

  LO 9-2320-289-12
  TB 750-651

General Safety Instructions

  Servicing of engine cooling system
    should only be performed on a cool
    engine.
  DO NOT remove radiator cap without
    first releasing internal pressure.

---

a.	DRAINING

WARNING

Never remove radiator cap when engine is hot. Pressurized steam or hot water will cause serious burns.

1.   Remove radiator cap (2).

2.   Open radiator petcock (3) and drain coolant into a suitable container placed under radiator (1).

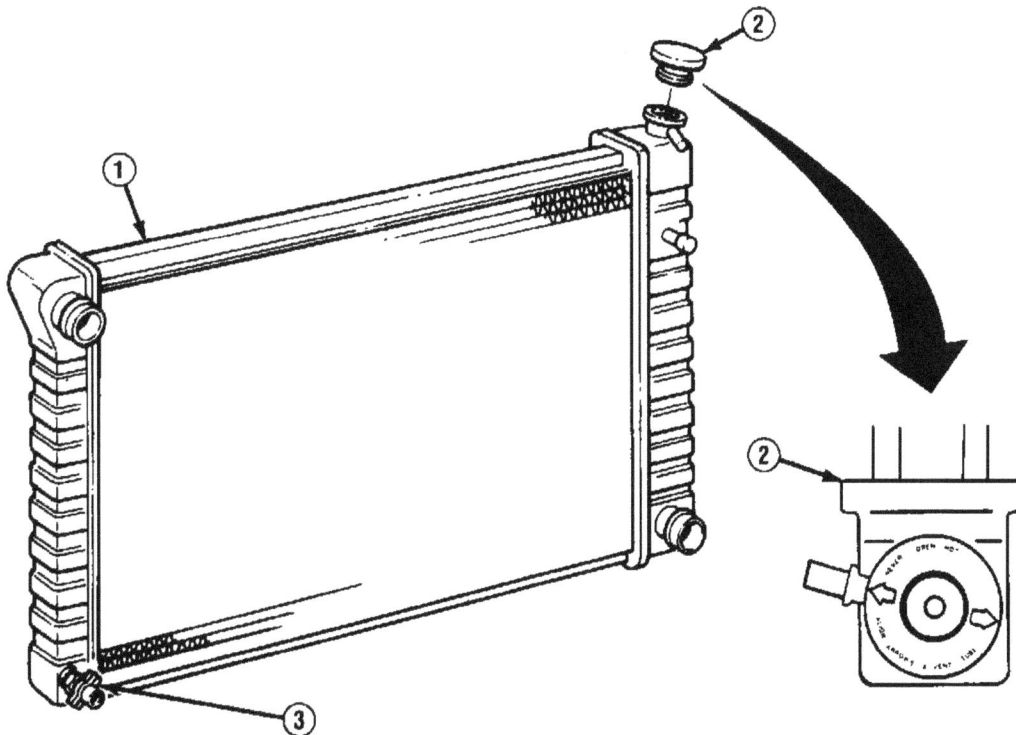

TA49829

3-30.   COOLING SYSTEM SERVICING (Con't).

b. CLEANING

1.   For cleaning,   refer to TB 750-651

c. FILLING

1.   Close radiator   petcock (3) and refill cooling system. (See L0 9-2320-289-12 and TB 750-651)

NOTE

Ensure that arrows on radiator cap (2) line up with coolant overflow hose nipple.

2.   Install radiator cap (2).

3-31.   RADIATOR AND FAN SHROUD REPLACEMENT.

This task covers: a. Removal   c. Installation
                         b. Cleaning and Inspection

INITIAL SETUP:

Equipment Condition

•Fan and clutch assembly removed.
  (See paragraph 3-35)
•Cooling system drained (if removing
  radiator). (See paragraph 3-30)

Materials/Parts

•Antiseize tape (Item 46, Appendix C)

General Safety Instructions

•Servicing of engine cooling system should only be performed on a cool engine.
•Compressed air used for cleaning purposes should never exceed 30 psi (207 kPa).

| a.   **REMOVAL** |

NOTE

•**Removal of top left screw (3) releases radiator overflow vent tube (5)
  from its attachment to fan shroud (2).**

•If removing fan shroud (2), perform steps 1-7.

1.   Remove 2 bolts (4) and 4 screws (3) securing fan shroud   (2) to radiator   (1).

2.   If installed, remove bolt (7) and clip (6) at left side of fan   shroud (2).

TA49830

3-31. RADIATOR AND FAN SHROUD REPLACEMENT (Con't).

3. Unsnap radiator overflow vent tube (5) from top middle of fan shroud (2).

4. At top left of fan shroud (2), remove bolt from hose support and front axle vent hose.

NOTE

Perform step 5 only if fan shroud (2) is being replaced.

5. Remove hose support from fan shroud (2).

NOTE

Step 6 only applies to trucks equipped with winterization kits.

6. Remove engine coolant heater hose (9) from attachment at top middle of fan shroud (2).

7. Remove fan shroud (2).

8. Disconnect upper and lower radiator hoses from radiator (1).

9. Disconnect transmission oil cooler lines (8) from left side of radiator (1).

10. Disconnect engine oil cooler lines from right side of radiator (1).

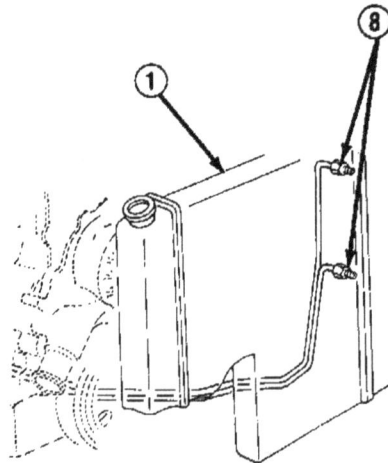

NOTE

Step 11 only applies to trucks equipped with winterization kits.

11. At upper right rear corner of radiator (1), loosen clamp (11) and disconnect engine coolant heater hose (9) from heater assembly hose (10).

12. Remove heater assembly hose (10) from attachment at upper right rear corner of radiator (1).

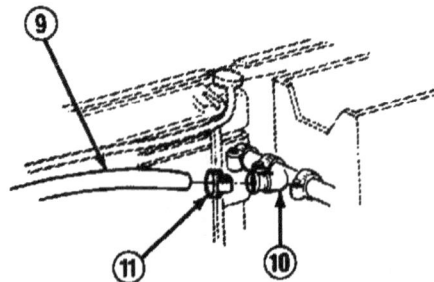

Winterization Kits Only

TA49831

3-31.   RADIATOR AND FAN SHROUD REPLACEMENT (Con't).

13.   Remove terminal wire and low engine coolant sensor assembly (16).

14.   Remove 4 bolts (12)   from top and front of upper mounting panel (13).

15.   Remove 4 bolts (18)   and upper radiator mounting brackets (15 and 17) from frame.

16.   Remove radiator (1)   and upper and lower radiator insulators (14).

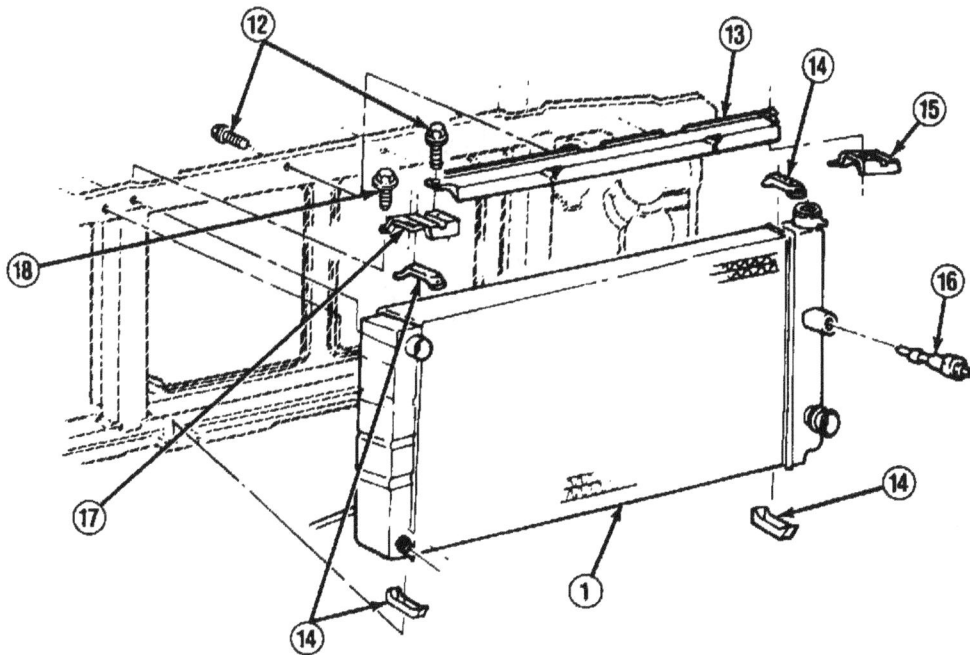

| b.   CLEANING AND INSPECTION |

WARNING

Compressed air used for cleaning purposes should never exceed 30 psi (207 kPa). Use only effective chip guarding and personnel protective equipment (goggles/shield, gloves, etc.). Failure to follow this warning may result in serious injury to personnel.

NOTE

If inspecting fan shroud (2), perform step 3.

1.   Use compressed air and water to remove dirt and debris embedded in radiator (1).

TA49832

3-31. RADIATOR AND FAN SHROUD REPLACEMENT (Con't).

2. Inspect radiator (1) and soldered seams for breaks, punctures, and splits. Notify your supervisor if any of these conditions exist.

3. Inspect fan shroud (2) for cracks, splits, or breaks. Notify your supervisor if any of these conditions exist.

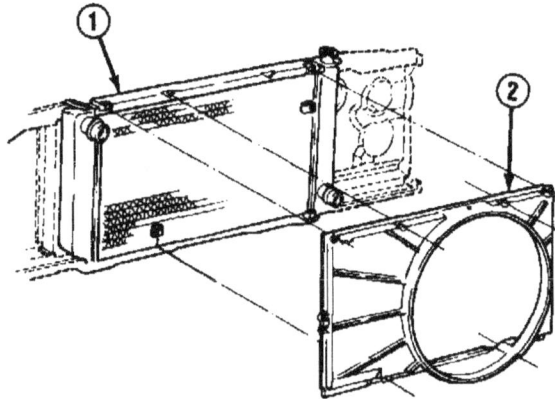

| c. INSTALLATION |

NOTE

If installing fan shroud (2), perform steps 10-15.

1. install 2 lower radiator mounting insulators (14), radiator (1), and 2 upper radiator mounting insulators (14).

2. Install 2 upper radiator mounting brackets (15 and 17) with 4 bolts (18).

3. Install upper mounting panel (13) with 4 bolts (12).

4. Apply antiseize tape to low engine coolant sensor assembly (16) threads. Install low engine coolant sensor assembly and install terminal wire to sensor assembly.

TA49833

3-31. RADIATOR AND FAN SHROUD REPLACEMENT (Con't).

5. Install engine oil cooler lines to right side of radiator (1).

6. Install transmission oil cooler lines (8) to left side of radiator (1).

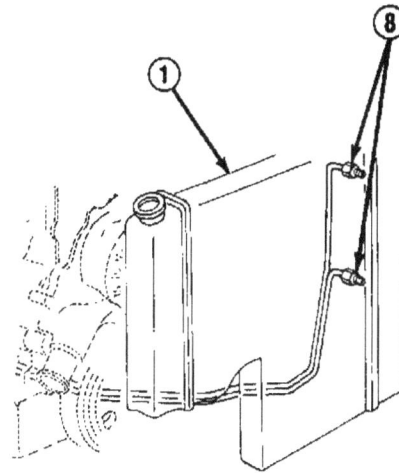

7. Install heater assembly hose (10) to upper right rear of radiator (1).

NOTE

Step 8 only applies to trucks equipped with winterization kits.

8. Install engine coolant heater hose (9) to connector at heater assembly hose (10) and tighten clamp (11).

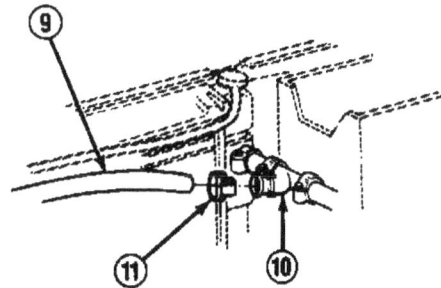

Winterization Kits Only

9. Install upper and lower radiator hoses to radiator (1).

10. Install hose support to fan shroud (2), if removed.

11. Install fan shroud (2) with 2 bolts (4) and 4 screws (3).

12. If removed, install clip (6) and bolt (7) at left side of fan shroud (2).

13. Install radiator overflow vent tube (5) to top middle of fan shroud (2).

NOTE

Step 14 only applies to trucks equipped with winterization kits.

14. Connect engine coolant heater hose (9) to top middle of fan shroud (2).

15. Install front axle vent tube and hose support to top left of fan shroud (2) with bolt.

TA49834

3-31. RADIATOR AND FAN SHROUD REPLACEMENT (Con't).

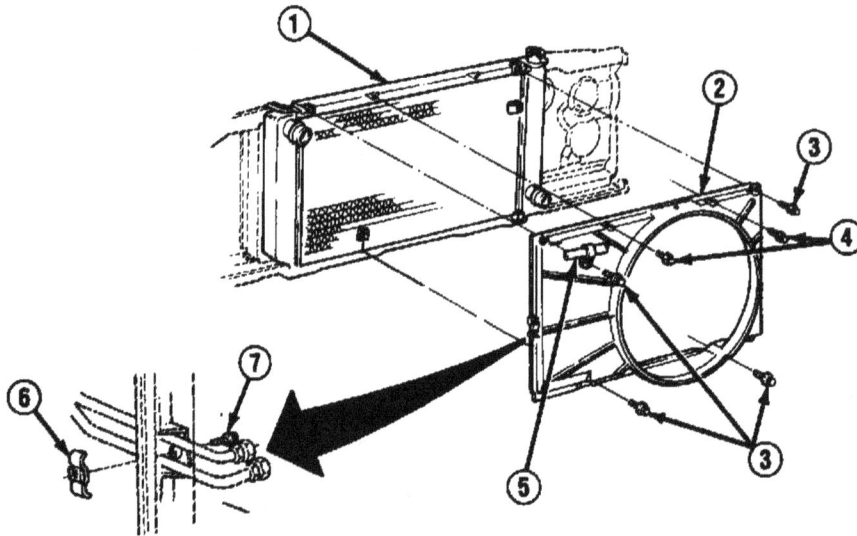

FOLLOW-ON TASKS:

• Install fan and clutch assembly. (See paragraph 3-35)
• Refill cooling system as required. (See paragraph 3-30)
• Check for leaks.

TA49835

3-32. COOLANT RECOVERY RESERVOIR REPLACEMENT.

This task covers:

a. Removal
b. Cleaning and Inspection

c. Installation

INITIAL SETUP:

Materials/Parts

● One starwasher

General Safety Instructions

● Servicing of engine cooling system should only be performed on a cool engine.

| a. | **REMOVAL** |

WARNING

Servicing of engine cooling system should only be performed on a cool engine.   Never remove clamp (7) or hose (6) when engine is hot. Pressurized steam or hot water will cause serious burns.

1. Position drain pan under coolant reservoir (5). Remove coolant reservoir hose (6) and clamp (7) from coolant reservoir. Allow coolant to drain from coolant reservoir and coolant reservoir hose.

2. Remove drain pan and dispose of coolant.

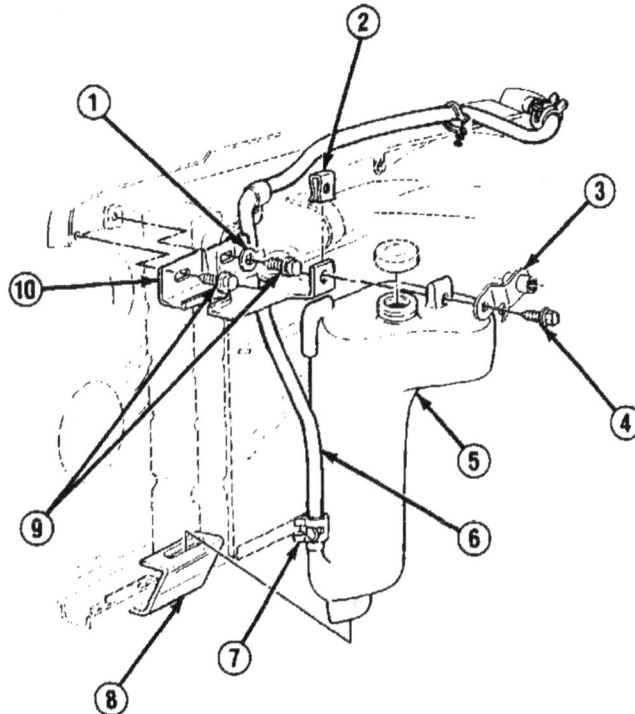

TA49836

3-32.   COOLANT RECOVERY RESERVOIR REPLACEMENT (Con't).

NOTE

When bolt (4) securing coolant reservoir (5) to mounting bracket (10) is removed, engine oil sampling valve bracket (3) is also removed. Save it for installation.

3.   Remove bolt (4), engine oil sampling valve bracket (3), and nut (2).

4.   Remove 2 bolts (9) from mounting bracket (10).

5.   Remove forward lamp harness ground wire (1), starwasher, mounting bracket (10), and coolant reservoir (5). Discard starwasher.

| b. CLEANING AND INSPECTION |

1.   Empty coolant reservoir (5) and ensure that it is clean and free of contamination. If required, wash with soap and water. Rinse thoroughly.

2.   Inspect coolant reservoir (5) for cracks, punctures, or splits. If any of these conditions exist, install new coolant reservoir.

3.   Inspect all coolant reservoir (5) mounting hardware. Replace if bent or broken.

| c.   INSTALLATION |

1.   Install bottom lip of coolant reservoir (5) into bracket (8).

2.   Install mounting bracket (10), new starwasher, forward lamp harness ground wire (1), and 2 bolts (9) .

3.   Install engine oil sampling valve bracket (3) with bolt (4) and nut (2) through mounting bracket (10).

4.   Install coolant reservoir hose (6) with clamp (7).

5.   Refill coolant reservoir (5). (See LO 9-2320-289-12)

3-33. RADIATOR HOSES AND CLAMPS REPLACEMENT.

This task covers:
a. Removal
b. Cleaning and Inspection
c. Installation

INITIAL SETUP:

Equipment Condition

● Cooling system drained.
(See paragraph 3-30)

General Safety Instructions

● Servicing of engine cooling system should only be performed on a cool engine.

---

a. REMOVAL

WARNING

Servicing of engine cooling system should only be performed on a cool engine. Never remove clamps (2 and 5) or hoses (4 and 6) when engine is hot. Pressurized steam or hot water will cause serious burns.

NOTE

Hose support (1) secures both radiator inlet hose (4) and front axle vent hose (7) to fan shroud.

1. Remove bolt (3), front axle vent hose (7), and hose support (1).

2. Remove 2 clamps (2 and 5) and radiator inlet hose (4).

3. Remove 2 clamps (2) and radiator outlet hose (6).

b. CLEANING AND INSPECTION

1. Clean all hose connection areas.

2. Inspect radiator inlet hose (4) and radiator outlet hose (6) for cracks, punctures, or splits. Replace if any of these conditions exist.

3. Inspect all clamps (2 and 5) and hose support (1) for signs of damage, wear, or corrosion. Replace if any of these conditions exist.

c. INSTALLATION

CAUTION

Ensure that extra large tab (hose protector) on clamp (5) is positioned at bottom when clamp is fully installed to prevent radiator hose damage from air conditioner or alternator belt.

1. Install radiator inlet hose (4) with 2 clamps (2 and 5).

3-33.   RADIATOR HOSES AND CLAMPS REPLACEMENT (Con't).

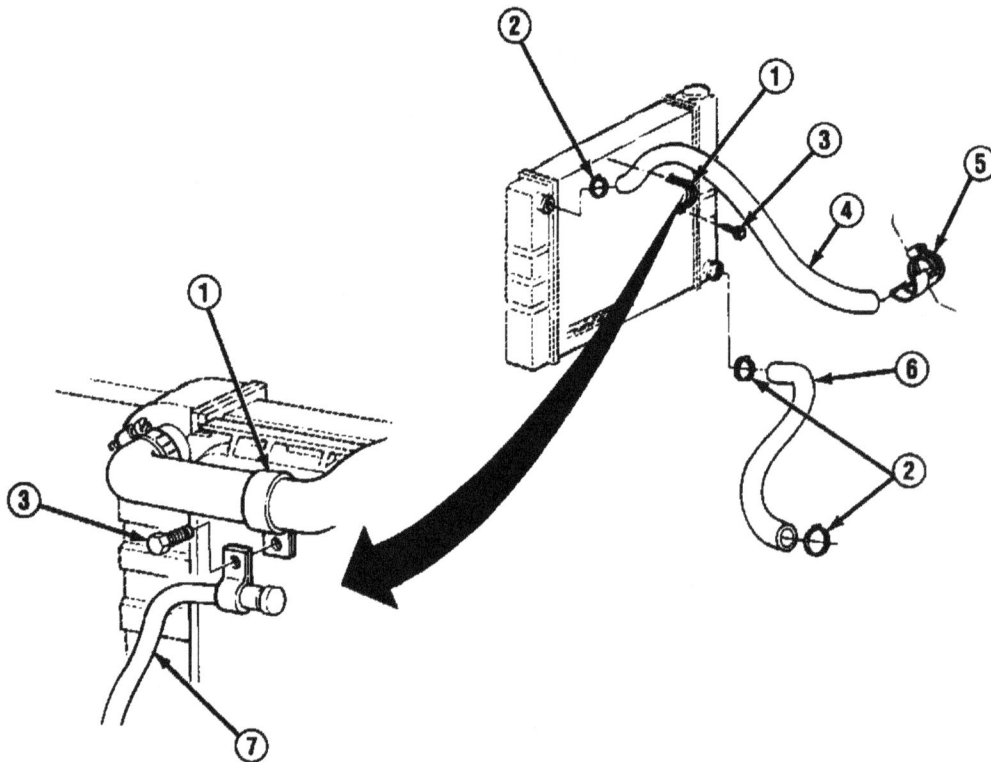

2.   Install radiator outlet hose (6) with 2 clamps (2).

3.   Install front axle vent hose (7) and hose support (1) at fan shroud with bolt (3).

FOLLOW-ON TASKS:

Refill cooling system. (See paragraph 3-30)
Check for leaks.

TA49837

3-34. THERMOSTAT, WATER OUTLET, AND CROSSOVER PIPE HOUSIN G REPLACEMENT.

This task covers:	a. Removal	b. Installation

INITIAL SETUP:

Equipment Condition
- Both battery negative cables disconnected.
  (See paragraph 4-38)
- Cooling system drained.
  (See paragraph 3-30)

Materials/Parts
- One thermostat gasket
- Two crossover pipe gaskets
- One tie-down strap
  (Item 44, Appendix C)
- Antiseize tape (Item 46, Appendix C)

---

a. REMOVAL

NOTE

- There are 2 types of crossover pipes: standard crossover pipe (15) which has seatings for 2 nipples (5 and 7) and crossover pipe (6) on trucks equipped with winterization kits which has a third nipple (12) seated at a 90° angle.

- If removing thermostat assembly (11) and water outlet (10), perform steps 1 and 2.

1. Remove clamp (20) and radiator inlet hose (19) from water outlet (10).

2. Remove 2 bolts (9) at water outlet (10). Remove water outlet and gasket (8). Remove thermostat assembly (11). Discard gasket.

3. Loosen right alternator belt (see paragraph 4-2 or 4-3) and move alternator to side.

4. Remove 2 bolts (4), nut (2), and alternator bracket (3).

5. Remove 2 clamps (17) and thermal bypass hose (18).

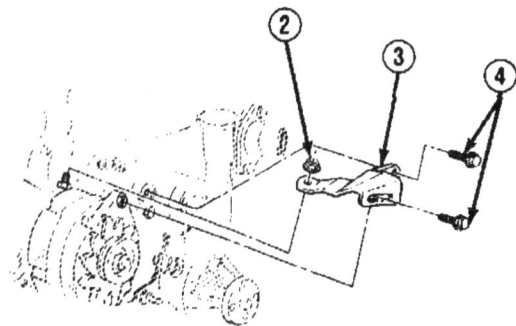

TA49838

3-34. THERMOSTAT, WATER OUTLET, AND CROSSOVER PIPE HOUSIN G REPLACEMENT (Con't).

6. Remove nipple (7) from crossover pipe (6 or 15). Save nipple for later installation if not damaged.

7. Disconnect heater hose from nipple (5) at crossover pipe (6 or 15). Remove nipple and save for later installation if not damaged.

NOTE

Step 8 only applies to trucks equipped with winterization kits.

8. Disconnect heater hose at nipple (12). Remove nipple and save for later installation if not damaged.

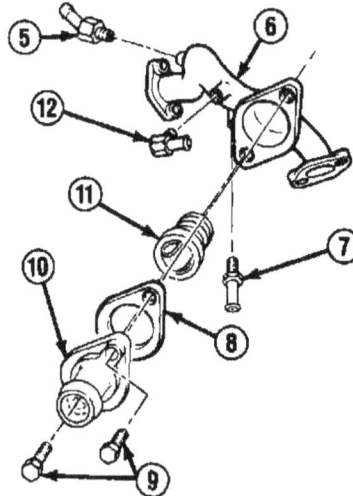

Winterization Kits Only

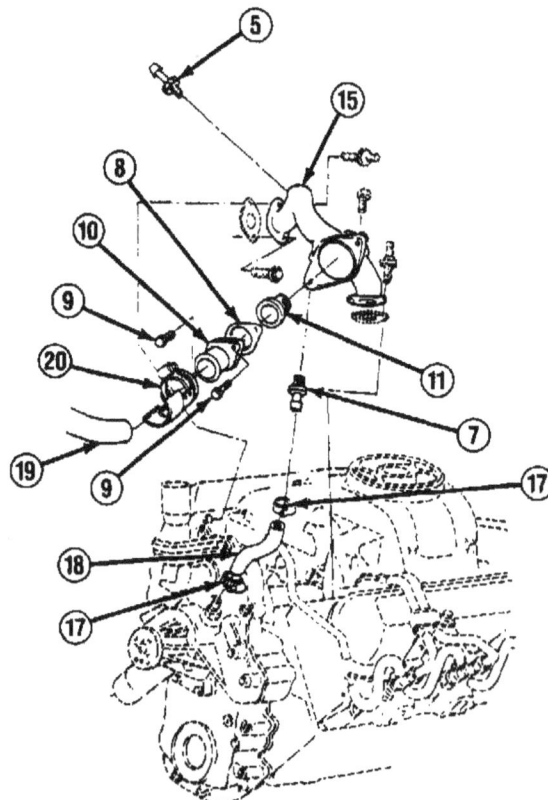

TA49839

3-34. THERMOSTAT, WATER OUTLET, AND CROSSOVER PIPE HOUSIN G REPLACEMENT (Con't).

9. Remove clamp (22) and crankcase depression regulator valve hose (21) from oil filler neck (23).

NOTE

- **In order to perform step 10, it may be necessary to remove air cleaner. (See paragraph 3-9)**

- **Nut described in step 10 is located on right side of cylinder block in M1010.**

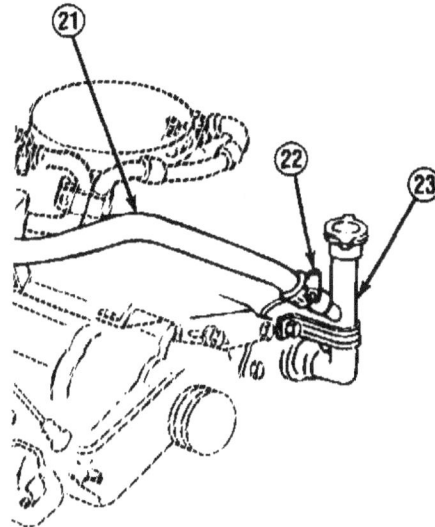

10. On left side, remove nut from alternator ground wires from point where crossover pipe (6 or 15) attaches to cylinder block.

11. Remove 2 studs (16) and 2 bolts (13) from crossover pipe (6 or 15) at attachments to left and right cylinder head. Remove crossover pipe and 2 gaskets (14). Discard gaskets.

| b. INSTALLATION |

NOTE

- **Ensure that all gaskets and mating surfaces are clean.**

- **If installing thermostat assembly (11) and water outlet (10), perform steps 11-14.**

1. Install 2 new gaskets (14) and crossover pipe (6 or 15) with 2 studs (16) and bolts (13).

NOTE

Nut described in step 2 is located on right side of cylinder block in M1010.

2. On left side, install nut securing alternator ground wires at point where crossover pipe (6 or 15) attaches to cylinder block.

3. Install crankcase depression regulator valve hose (21) to oil filler neck (23) with clamp (22).

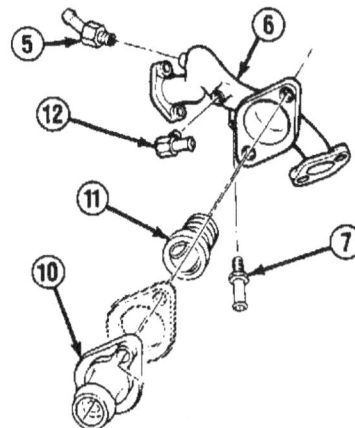

TA49840

3-34. THERMOSTAT, WATER OUTLET, AND CROSSOVER PIPE HOUSIN G REPLACEMENT (Con't).

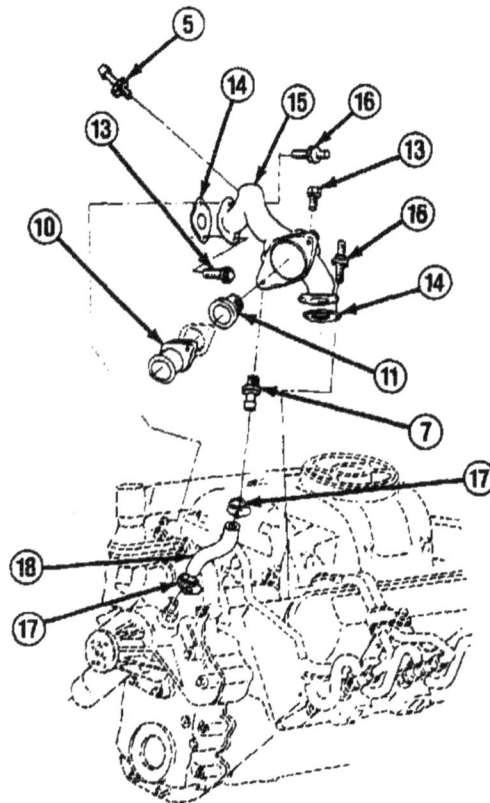

NOTE

Step 4 only applies to trucks equipped with winterization kits.

4. Apply antiseize tape to threads of nipple (12). Install nipple to crossover pipe (6). Connect heater hose to nipple.

5. Apply antiseize tape to threads of nipple (5). Install nipple to crossover pipe (6 or 15) and connect nipple to heater hose.

6. Apply antiseize tape to threads of nipple (7). Install nipple to crossover pipe (6 or 15).

7. Install thermal bypass hose (18) to nipple (7) and to water pump with 2 clamps (17).

TA49841

3-34. THERMOSTAT, WATER OUTLET, AND CROSSOVER PIPE HOUSIN G REPLACEMENT (Con't).

8. Install alternator bracket (3) with 2 bolts (4). Install nut (2) onto stud (1).

9. Install alternator and tighten alternator belt. (See paragraph 4-2 or 4-3)

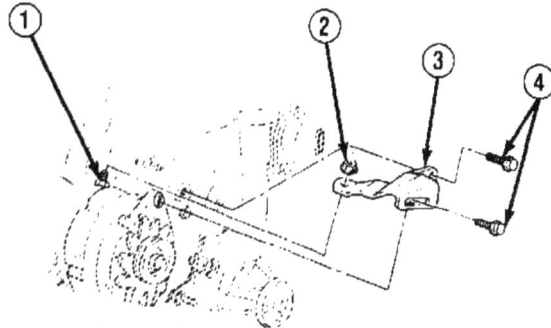

10. Position thermostat assembly (11) inside crossover pipe (6 or 15).

11. Install new gasket (8) and water outlet (10) at crossover pipe (6 or 15) with 2 bolts (9).

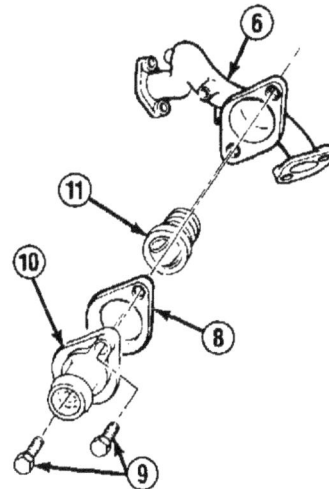

Winterization Kits Only

CAUTION

Ensure that clamp (20) is installed with hose protector tab at bottom. This tab prevents damage to radiator inlet hose (19) from alternator belt.

12. Install radiator inlet hose (19) at water outlet (10) with clamp (20).

13. Install air cleaner assembly if removed. (See paragraph 3-9)

TA49842

3-34. THERMOSTAT, WATER OUTLET, AND CROSSOVER PIPE HOUSIN G REPLACEMENT (Con't).

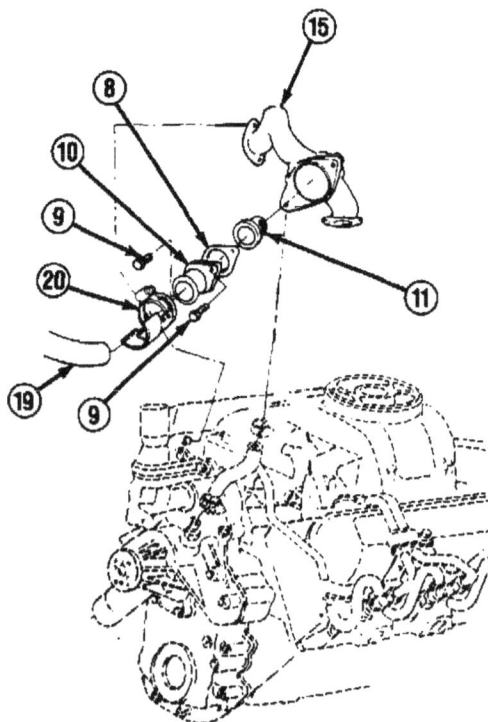

FOLLOW-ON TASKS:

- Refill cooling system. (See paragraph 3-30)
- Connect both battery negative cables. (See paragraph 4-38)
- Check for leaks.

TA49843

3-35.   FAN, CLUTCH ASSEMBLY, PULLEY, AND AIR CONDITIONER BEL   T REPLACEMENT.

This task covers:	a. Removal	c. Installation
	b. Inspection	

INITIAL SETUP:

Equipment Conditions

   Both battery negative cables   disconnected.
     (See paragraph 4-38)

Tools/Test Equipment

   Belt tensioning gage

---

a.   REMOVAL

NOTE

If removing air conditioner belt (4), perform steps 1 and 2.

1.   Loosen 3 adjusting bolts (1) and pivot nut (3), and move compressor (2) to right.

2.   Remove air conditioner belt (4).

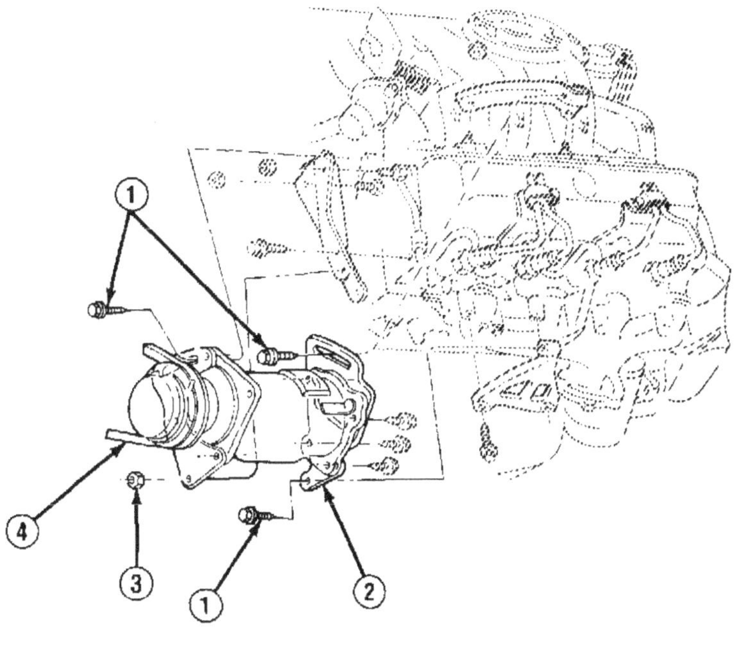

3.   Loosen 4 nuts (9) securing fan (7) and clutch assembly (8) to studs (10).

4.   Remove alternator belts (see paragraph 4-2 or 4-3) and power steering pump belt (see paragraph 8-15).

TA49844

3-35.   FAN, CLUTCH ASSEMBLY, PULLEY, AND AIR CONDITIONER BEL   T
         REPLACEMENT (Con't).

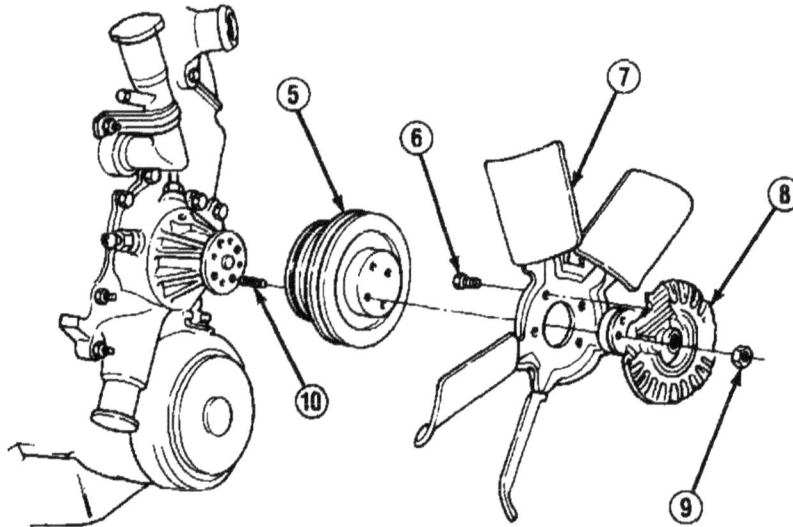

5.   Remove 4 nuts (9), fan (7), and clutch assembly (8).

6.   Remove 4 screws (6) and remove fan (7) from clutch assembly (8).

7.   Remove pulley assembly (5) and 4 studs (10).

| b.   INSPECTION |

1.   Inspect air conditioner belt (4) for cracks, splits, or frayed surfaces.

2.   Inspect fan (7) and clutch assembly (8) to ensure that they are not cracked or bent.

3.   Inspect pulley assembly (5)   to ensure that it is not cracked or bent.

4.   Inspect all mounting nuts (3   and 9), bolts (1), studs (10), and screws (6)   for signs of wear.

5.   Inspect all mating surfaces   on pulley assembly (5), fan (7), and clutch   assembly (8) for
      smoothness.

8.   Replace any cracked, bent,   worn, split, or frayed component as required.

TA49845

3-35. FAN, CLUTCH ASSEMBLY, PULLEY, AND AIR CONDITIONER BEL   T REPLACEMENT (Con't).

| c. | **INSTALLATION** |

NOTE

If installing air conditioner belt (4), perform steps 9-13.

1.   Install 4 studs (10) and pulley assembly (5).

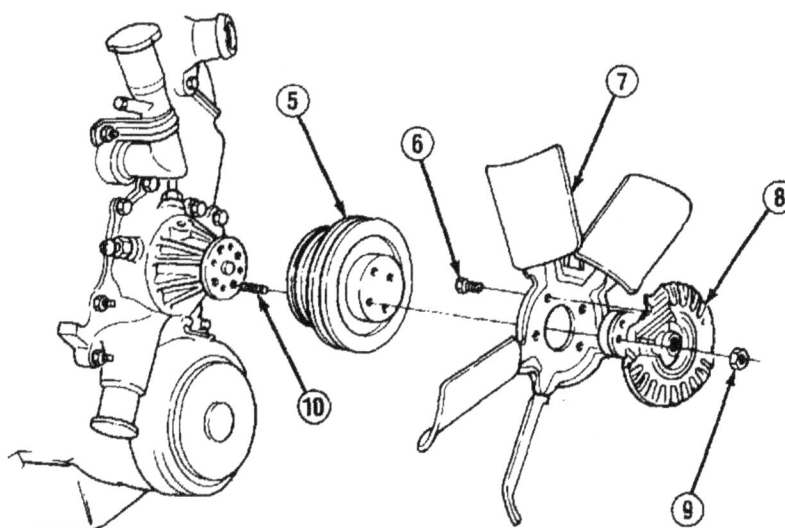

2.   Install power steering belt (see paragraph 8-15) and alternator belts (see paragraph 4-2 or 4-3). DO NOT tighten belts at this time.

WARNING

DO NOT repair and reuse a fan (7) with a bent or damaged blade. Replace fan as an assembly. A damaged fan is out of balance and may fall apart during use causing serious injury or death to personnel.

3.   Install fan (7) to clutch assembly (8) with 4 screws (6).

TA49846

3-35. FAN, CLUTCH ASSEMBLY, PULLEY, AND AIR CONDITIONER BEL T REPLACEMENT (Con't).

---

4. Install fan (7) and clutch assembly (8) to studs (10).

5. Install 4 nuts (9). DO NOT fully tighten.

6. Snug right alternator belt.

7. Fully tighten 4 nuts (9).

8. Using a belt tensioning gage, check alternator belts and power steering belt tension. (See Appendix E)

9. Install air conditioner belt (4).

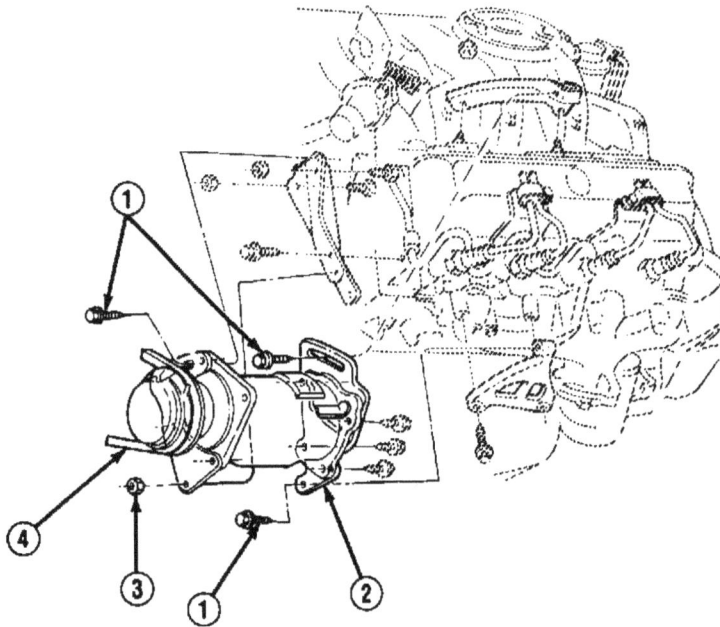

10. Move compressor (2) to left until air conditioner belt (4) appears tight.

11. Tighten 3 adjusting bolts (1) and pivot nut (3).

12. Connect both battery negative cables. (See paragraph 4-38)

13. Using a belt tensioning gage, check air conditioner belt (4) tension. (See Appendix E)

TA49847

CHAPTER 4
ELECTRICAL SYSTEMS MAINTENANCE

Section I. GENERATING SYSTEM MAINTENANCE

4-1. GENERATING SYSTEM MAINTENANCE INDEX.

4-2.   ALTERNATOR AND BELT REPLACEMENT (ALL EXCEPT M1010).

This task covers: a. Removal   b. Installation

INITIAL SETUP:

Equipment Condition   *Tools/Test Equipment*
   Both battery negative cables disconnected.   Belt tensioning gage
      (See paragraph 4-38)

| a.   REMOVAL |

NOTE

- **If removing belt (11 or 20), perform step 1.**

- **If removing left side alternator (9), perform steps 1, 2, and 4.**

- **If removing right side alternator (15), perform steps 1, 3, and 4.**

- **If removing left side alternator brackets (1 or 13), perform steps 1, 2, 4, and 6.**

- **If removing right side alternator brackets (17 or 25), perform steps 1 and 3 through 5.**

1.   Loosen pivot bolt (22) or bolts (10) and adjusting bolt (5 or 19). Rotate alternator (9 or 15) to loosen belt (11 or 20), then remove belt. Discard belt if worn or damaged.

2.   Remove 2 pivot bolts (10), adjusting bolt (5), and washer (4).

3.   Remove pivot bolt (22), spacer (26), and adjusting bolt (19).

NOTE

Tag plugs and leads for installation.

4.   Disconnect terminal plugs and alternator electrical leads. Remove alternator (9 or 15).

5.   Remove 2 nuts (23), washers (24), and support bracket (25). Remove bolt (18), nut (16), and adjusting bracket (17).

6.   Remove bolt (3), nut (7), and brace (6). Remove 3 bolts (2) and adjusting bracket (1). Remove 2 nuts (14) and bolt (12). Move power steering pump as necessary, and remove support bracket (13).

4-2. ALTERNATOR AND BELT REPLACEMENT (ALL EXCEPT M1010) (Con't).

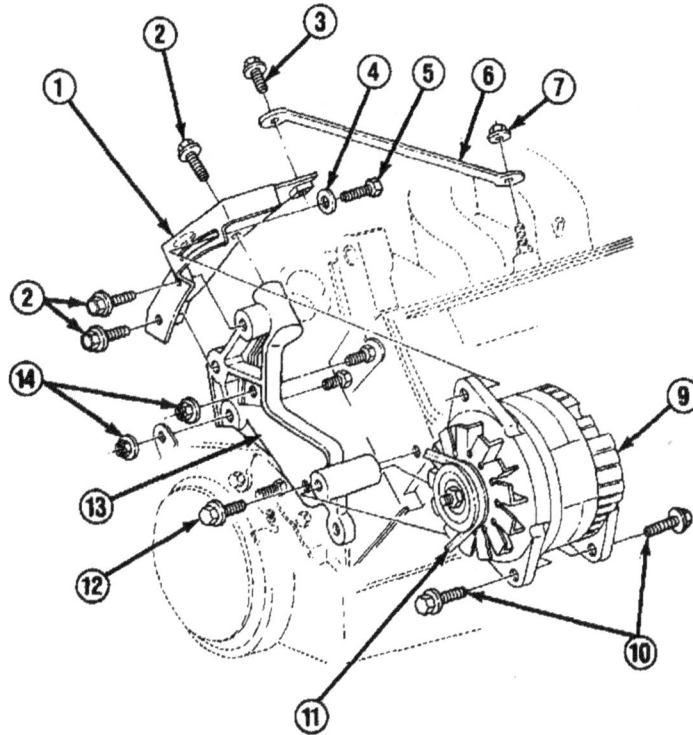

Left Side

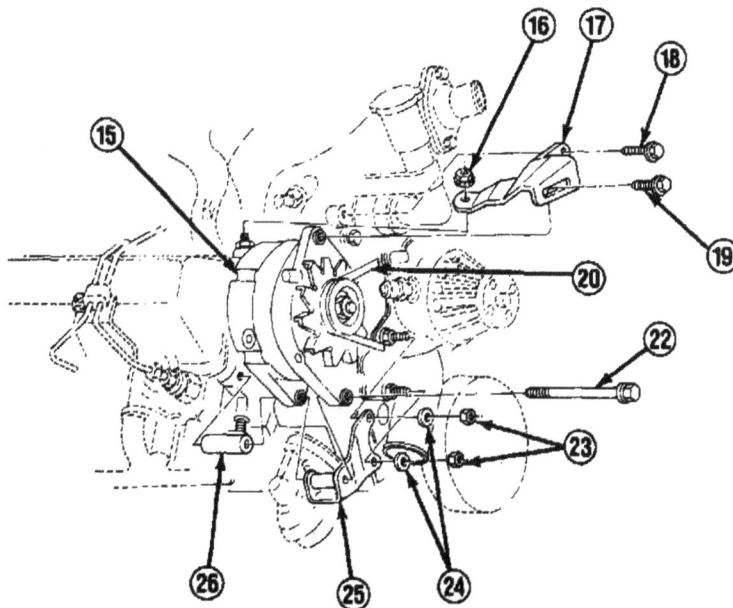

Right Side

TA49848

4-2.   ALTERNATOR AND BELT REPLACEMENT (ALL EXCEPT M1010) (Con't).

| b. INSTALLATION |

NOTE

- **If installing belt (11 or 20), perform steps   6-8.**

- **If installing left side alternator brackets (1   or 13), perform steps 1, 3, and 6 through 9.**

- **If installing right side alternator brackets (17 or 25), perform steps 2, 4, and 5 through 9.**

- **If installing left side alternator (9), perform steps 3 and 5 through 9.**

- **If installing right side alternator (15), perform steps 4 and 5 through 9.**

1.   Position support bracket (13) on studs (8). Move power steering pump as required and install support bracket with 2 nuts (14) and bolt (12). Install adjusting bracket (1) with 3 bolts (2). Install brace (6) with nut (7) and bolt (3).

2.   Install adjusting bracket (17) with nut (16) and bolt (18). Position support bracket (25) on studs (21) and install with 2 washers (24) and nuts (23).

3.   Position alternator (9) on brackets (1 and 13) and install with washer (4), adjusting bolt (5), and 2 pivot bolts (10). DO NOT fully tighten bolts.

4.   Position alternator (15) on brackets (17 and 25) and install with spacer (26), pivot bolt (22), and adjusting bolt (19). DO NOT fully tighten bolts.

5.   Connect alternator electrical leads and terminal plugs.

6.   Position belt (11 or 20) on pulleys.

CAUTION

Ensure that belt (11 or 20) tension is correct. A belt too loose or too tight can cause damage to alternator (9 or 15) and belt.

7.   Rotate alternator (9 or 15) until belt (11 or 20) appears tight. Tighten adjusting bolt (5 or 19) and pivot bolt (22) or pivot bolts (10).

8.   Connect both battery negative cables. (See paragraph 4-38)

9.   Using belt tensioning gage, check belt (11 or 20) tension. (See Appendix E)

4-2.   ALTERNATOR AND BELT REPLACEMENT (ALL EXCEPT M1010) (Con't).

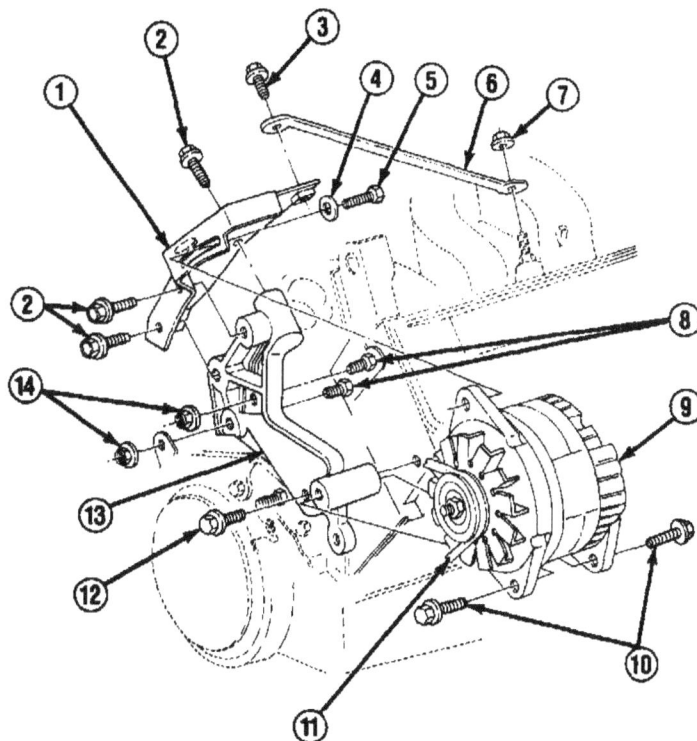

Left Side

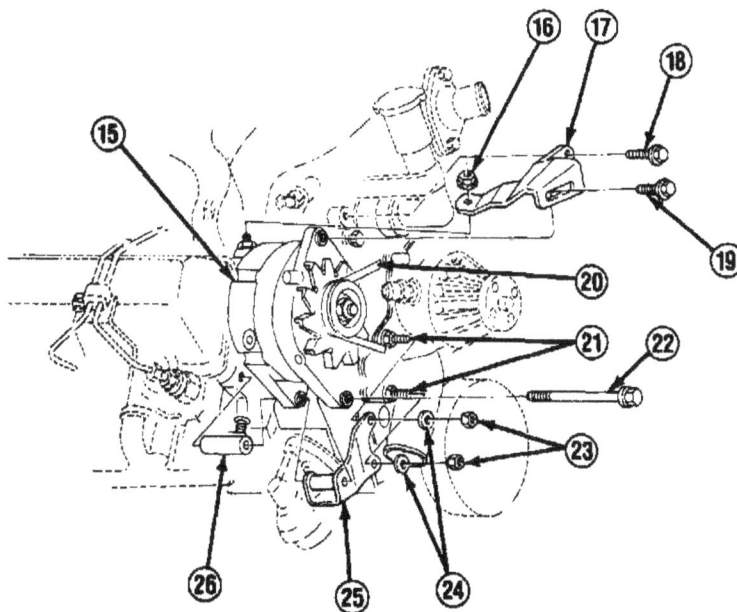

Right Side

TA49849

4-3.   ALTERNATOR, BELT, AND PULLEY REPLACEMENT (M1010).

This task covers:	a. Removal	b. Installation

INITIAL SETUP:

Equipment Condition

• Both battery negative cables disconnected.
 (See paragraph 4-38)
• Heater hose disconnected from crossover
 pipe. (See paragraph 3-34)

Tools/Test Equipment

• Belt tensioning gage
• 15 mm socket
• Torque wrench

Materials/Parts

• One tie-down strap
 (Item 44, Appendix C)

---

a.	**REMOVAL**

NOTE

• If removing   belt (4 or 14), perform step 1.

• If removing   upper alternator (2), perform steps 1, 2, and 4.

• If removing   lower alternator (17), perform steps 1, 3, find 4.

• If removing   upper alternator pulley (3), perform steps 1, 2, 4, and 5.

If removing lower alternator   pulley (13), perform steps 1 and
 3 through 5.

1.   Loosen pivot bolts (1 or 16) and adjusting   bolt (6 or 11). Rotate alternator (2 or 17) to loosen
  belt (4 or 14). Remove belt. Discard belt   if worn or damaged.

2.   Remove 2 pivot bolts (1), adjusting bolt (6), and washer (7).

3.   Remove adjusting bracket mounting nuts (9), adjusting bolt (11), washer (10), and adjusting
  bracket (8). Remove two pivot bolts (16).

NOTE

Tag plugs and leads for installation.

4.   Disconnect terminal plugs and battery leads. Remove alternator (2 or 17).

5.   Place alternator (2 or 17) in soft-jawed vise. Remove pulley retaining nut (5 or 15) and remove
  alternator pulley (3 or 13).

6.   With metric socket, remove studs (12), nut (18), mounting bracket (19), and stud (20) as
  required.

4-3. ALTERNATOR, BELT, AND PULLEY REPLACEMENT (M1010) (Con't).

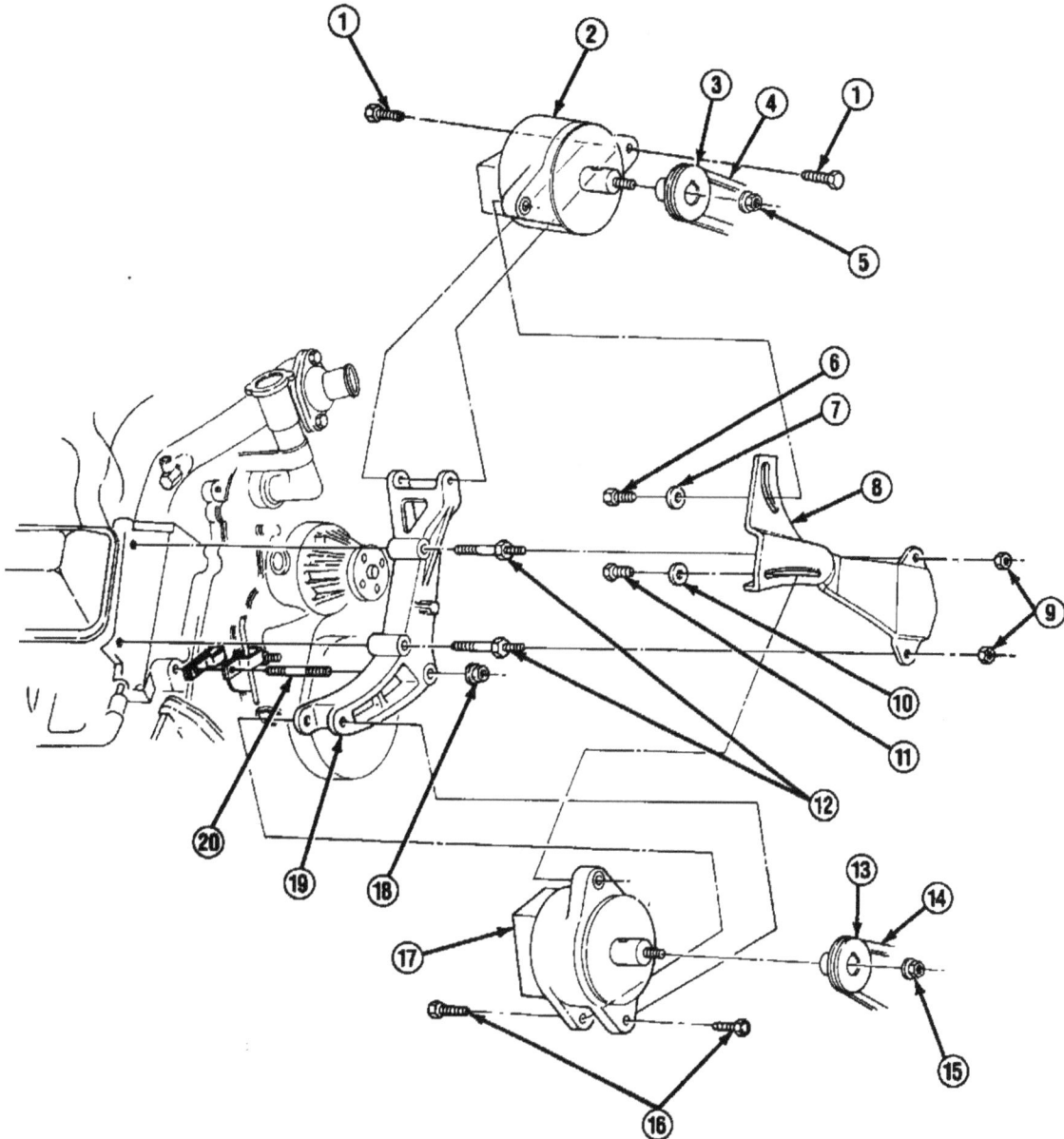

TA49850

4-3. ALTERNATOR, BELT, AND PULLEY REPLACEMENT (M1010) (Con't).

| b. INSTALLATION |

NOTE

◀f installing belt (4 or 14), perform steps 6-9.

◀f installing alternator pulley (3 or 13), perform step 2.

◀f installing lower alternator (17), perform steps 3 and 5 through 9.

◀f installing upper alternator (2), perform steps 4-9.

1. Using metric socket, install stud (20) on engine block through fuel line clamps (21). Position mounting bracket (19) on stud and install with nut (18) and two studs (12) if removed.

2. Place alternator (2 or 17) in soft-jawed vise. Install alternator pulley (3 or 13) with retaining nut (5 or 15). Tighten retaining nut to 25-30 lb.-ft. (34-41 N•m), and remove alternator from vise.

3. Position lower alternator (17) on mounting bracket (19) and install with two pivot bolts (16). DO NOT tighten bolts. Position adjusting bracket (8) on studs (12) and install with two adjusting bracket mounting nuts (9). Place washer (10) and adjusting bolt (11) through adjusting bracket, and install on lower alternator. DO NOT tighten bolt.

4. Install upper alternator (2) on mounting bracket (19) with two pivot bolts (1). DO NOT tighten bolts. Install upper alternator on adjusting bracket (8) with washer (7) and adjusting bolt (6). DO NOT tighten bolt.

5. Connect battery leads and terminal plugs.

6. Position belt (4 or 14) on alternator pulley (3 or 13).

CAUTION

Ensure that belt (4 or 14) tension is correct. A belt too loose or too tight can cause damage to alternator (2 or 17) and belt.

7. Rotate alternator (2 or 17) until belt (4 or 14) appears tight. Tighten adjusting bolt (6 or 11) and pivot bolts (1 or 16).

8. Connect both battery negative cables. (See   paragraph 4-38)   Connect heater hose to crossover pipe. (See paragraph 3-34)

9. Using belt tensioning gage, check belt tension.   (See Appendix E)

4-3. ALTERNATOR, BELT, AND PULLEY REPLACEMENT (M1010) (Con't).

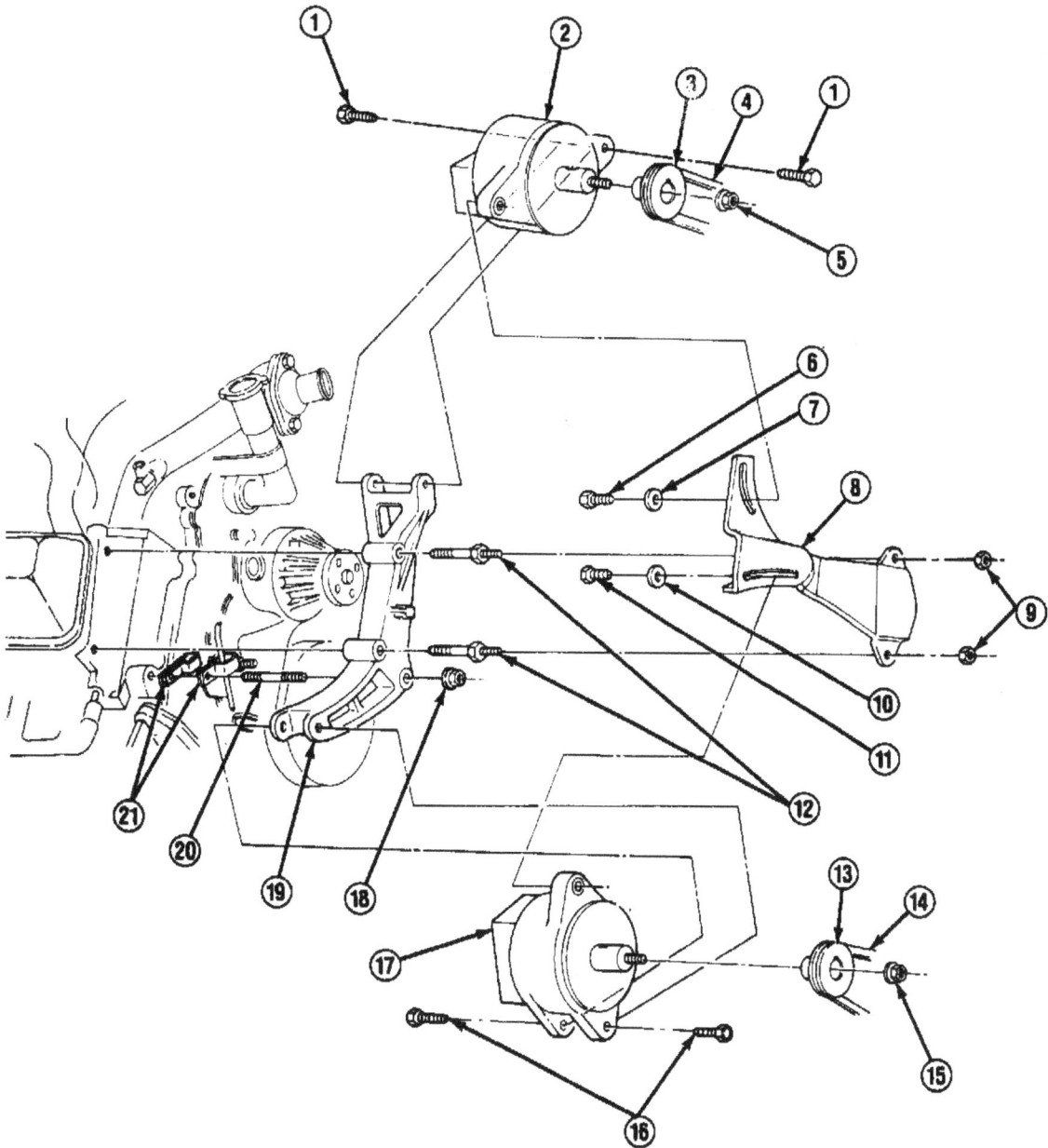

TA49851

4-4. ALTERNATOR REGULATOR REPLACEMENT AND ADJUSTMENT (M1010).

This task covers: a. Removal   b. Installation

INITIAL SETUP:

Equipment Condition   *Materials/Parts*

Both battery negative cables disconnected.   Five lockwashers
   (See paragraph 4-38)

---

a.	**REMOVAL**

1. Remove nut (1) and lockwasher (2), and disconnect lead (3) from regulator (6). Discard lockwasher.

CAUTION

DO NOT pry on regulator (6) to remove.   Failure to follow this caution may result in damage to regulator.

2. Remove 4 screws (4) and lockwashers (5), and remove regulator (6). Discard lockwashers.

b.	**INSTALLATION**

1. Ensure that adjustment screw (7) is in "HI" position.

2. Install regulator (6) on alternator (8) with 4 new lockwashers (5) and screws (4).

3. Connect lead (3) to regulator (6) and install new lockwasher (2) and nut (1).

FOLLOW-ON TASKS:

Connect both battery negative cables. (See paragraph 4-38)

TA49852

Section II. STARTER SYSTEM MAINTENANC   E

4-5.   STARTER AND STARTER RELAY REPLACEMENT.

This task covers:	a. Removal	b. Installation

INITIAL SETUP:

Equipment Condition
● Both battery negative cables disconnected.
   (See paragraph 4-38)

Tools/Test Equipment
● Torque wrench

Materials/Parts
● One locknut
● One lockwasher

General Safety Instructions
● Support starter during removal and
   installation.

---

a.   REMOVAL

NOTE

● If removing starter (7), perform steps 1-3.

● If removing starter relay, perform step 4.

1.   Remove locknut (5), washer (6), bolt
      (3), and bracket (4). Discard locknut.

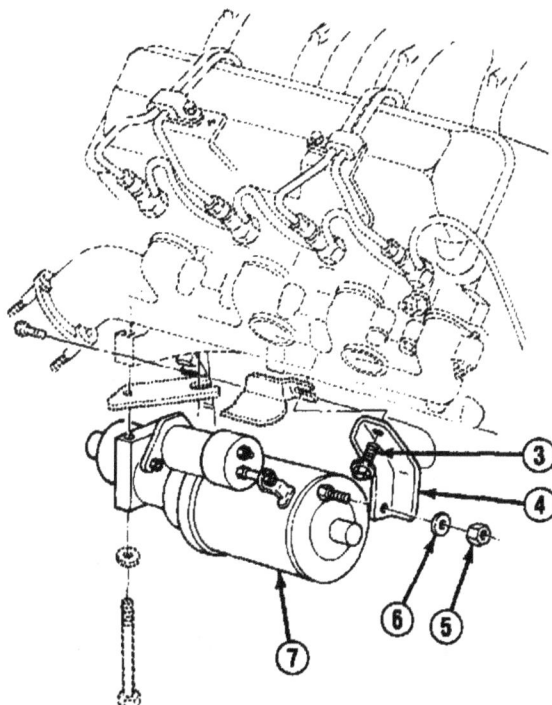

TA49853

4-5.   STARTER AND STARTER RELAY REPLACEMENT (Con't).

NOTE

Note position of battery terminal and solenoid terminal leads (12 and 14) before removing from solenoid (11).

2.   Remove 2 nuts (15), battery terminal lead (12),   solenoid terminal lead (14),   and lockwasher (13) from solenoid (11). Discard lockwasher.

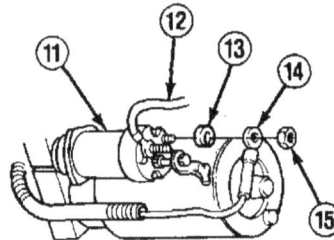

WARNING

Support   starter   (7)   during removal. Failure to support starter may cause it to fall, resulting in injury to personnel.

NOTE

1985-87 model starters (7) may not have shims (10).

3.   Remove 2 screws (9) and washers (8), and carefully lower starter (7). Remove starter and shims (10). Remove screw (1) and starter shield (2) as required.

4.   Remove   2 screws (18) from diagnostic connector bracket (19), dash panel (17), and wiring harness accessory bracket   (16).   Remove screw (20). Unplug   lead (22) and remove starter relay   (21).

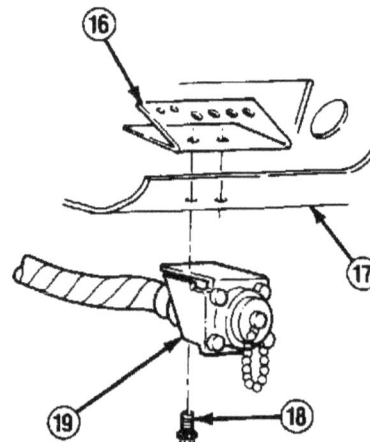

b.   INSTALLATION

NOTE

◆f installing starter   relay (21), perform step 1.

◆f installing starter (7), perform steps 2-5.

1.   Plug lead (22) into starter relay (21). Install starter relay on wiring harness accessory bracket (16) with screw (20). Install diagnostic connector bracket (19) and wiring harness accessory bracket on dash panel (17) with 2 screws (18).

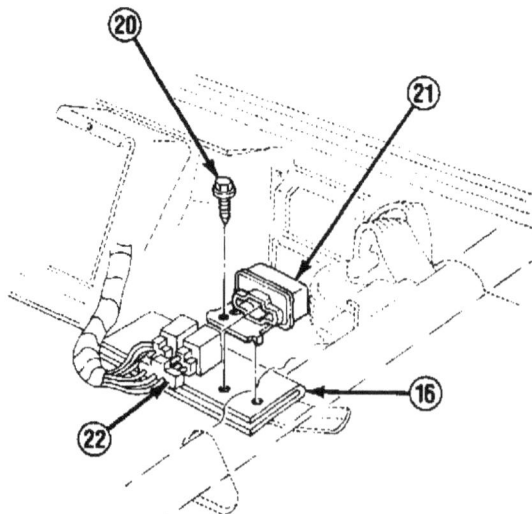

TA49854

4-5.   STARTER AND STARTER RELAY REPLACEMENT (Con't).

WARNING

Support starter (7) during installation. Failure to support starter may cause it to fall, resulting in injury to personnel.

2.   Install starter shield (2) with screw (1) if removed. Support starter (7) and install with inner screw (9). DO NOT tighten screw (9). Install outer screw (9) through starter. Tighten screws to 33 lb.-ft. (45 N•m).

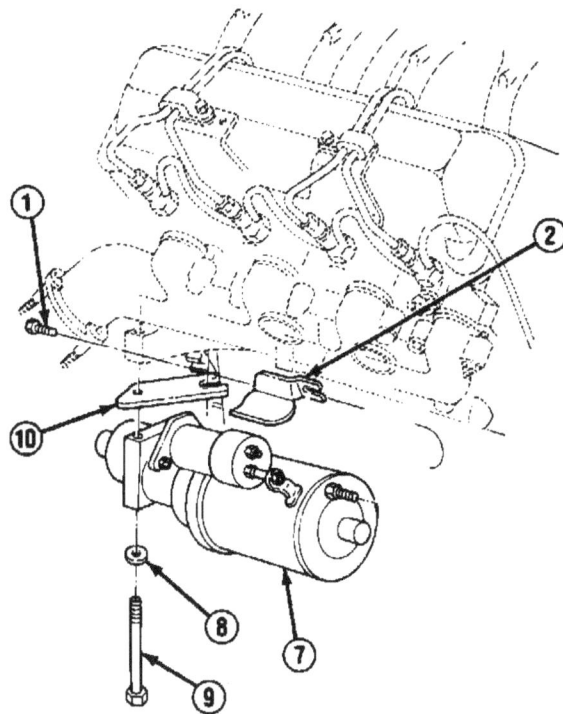

NOTE

Ensure that battery terminal lead (12) tab is positioned in slot on solenoid (11).

3.   Install new lockwasher (13), solenoid terminal lead (14), and battery terminal lead (12) with 2 nuts (15) on solenoid (11).

TA49855

4-5.   STARTER AND STARTER RELAY REPLACEMENT (Con't).

NOTE

Starter pinion tooth-to-flywheel clearance may be measured using a wire gage.

4.   Remove 6 bolts (25) and access cover (27) from transmission housing (26). Measure clearance between starter pinion (24) tooth and flywheel (23). Clearance should be 0.02 in. to 0.06 in. (0.50 mm to 1.50 mm). Add shims (10) as required. Install access cover (27) with 6 bolts.

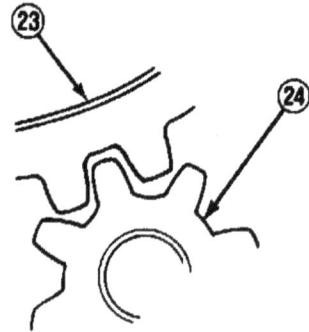

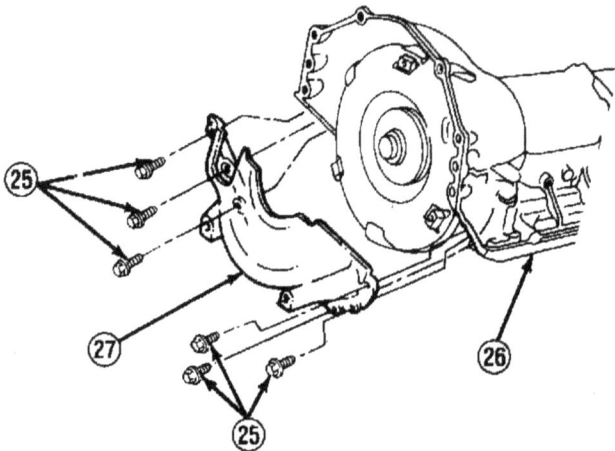

5.   Install bracket (4) on starter (7) and starter shield (2) with bolt (3), washer (6), and new locknut (5). Tighten bolt to 33 lb.-ft. (45 N•m).

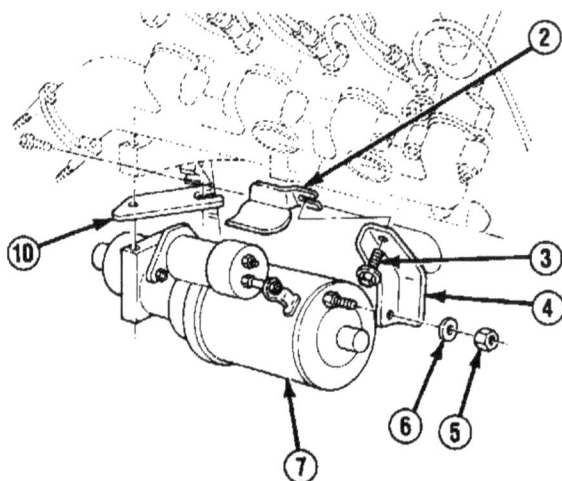

FOLLOW-ON TASKS:

Connect both battery negative cables. (See paragraph 4-38)

TA49856

Section III. INSTRUMENTS, SENDING UNITS, SWITCHES , AND HORN MAINTENANC E

4-6. INSTRUMENTS, SENDING UNITS, SWITCHES, AND HORN MAINTENANCE INDEX.

4-7.   INSTRUMENT CLUSTER MAINTENANCE.

| This task covers: | a. Removal | c. Assembly |
| | b. Disassembly | d. Installation |

INITIAL SETUP:

Equipment Condition   *Materials/Parts*

  ◄Both battery negative cables disconnected.   ◄Chalk (Item 9, Appendix C)
   (See paragraph 4-38)

a. REMOVAL

NOTE

◄If removing instrument cluster
plate (10), perform steps 1 and
3.

◄If removing gages, filters, or
gaskets, perform steps 1 and 3,
and DISASSEMBLY steps as
required.

◄If removing instrument cluster
bulbs and sockets, perform
DISASSEMBLY steps 9 and 10.

1.   Remove 4 screws (3) and steering
column filler (2) from dash panel (1).
Remove 2 screws (5) and steering
column filler (4).

2.   Depress clip on back of speedometer
(13) and disconnect speedometer
cable (6).

NOTE

Tag plugs for installation.

3.   Remove 5 screws (11) and 3 screws
(12). Disconnect plugs from back of
instrument cluster plate (10).
Remove instrument cluster plate.

4.   Mark cable clip (21) location on
steering column for installation.
Disconnect cable clip. Remove 2
screws (18) and transmission position
indicator (17).

TA49857

4-7.   INSTRUMENT CLUSTER MAINTENANCE (Con't).

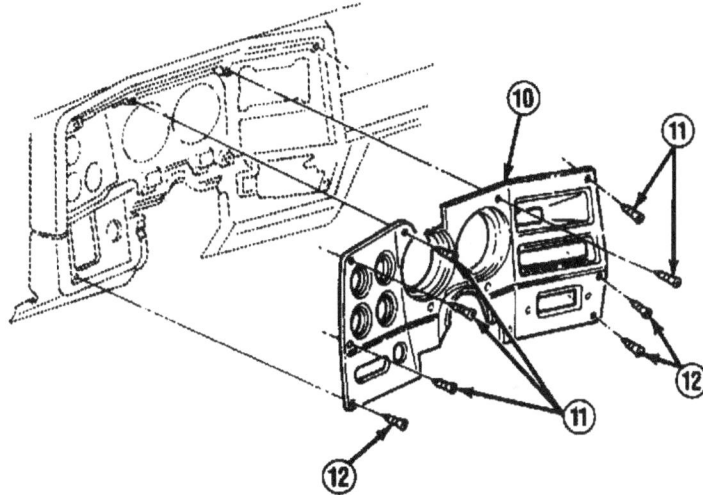

5.   Remove 4 screws   (8) from white instrument cluster (7) bezel and pull out instrument cluster.

6.   Disconnect wiring   harness (9) and remove instrument cluster (7).

b.   DISASSEMBLY

NOTE

• If removing any gages, filters, or gaskets, perform steps 1-8 as required.

• If removing instrument cluster bulbs and sockets, perform steps 9 and 10.

• If removing printed circuit   , perform steps 9-11.

1.   Remove 6 screws (20), instrument cluster lens (19), and retainer (25).

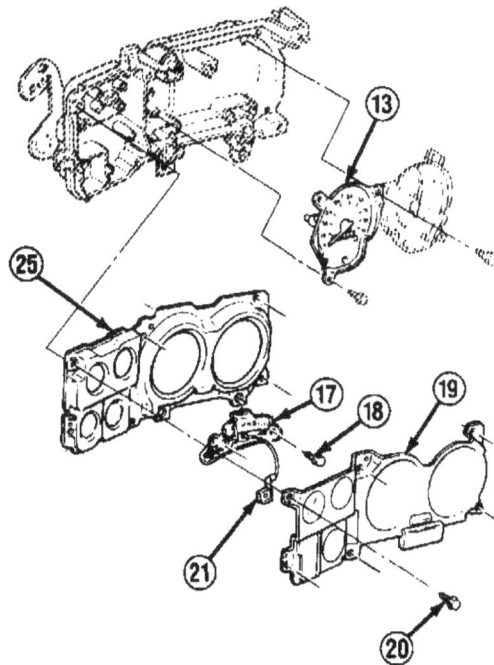

TA49858

4-7. INSTRUMENT CLUSTER MAINTENANCE (Con't).

2. Remove generator 1 filter (23), generator 2 filter (22), and 4-wheel drive and oil pressure filter (24) from retainer (25) as required.

3. Remove screw (15) and fuel gage (14).

4. Remove mounting screw (16) and speedometer (13). Retain gasket on back of speedometer for installation.

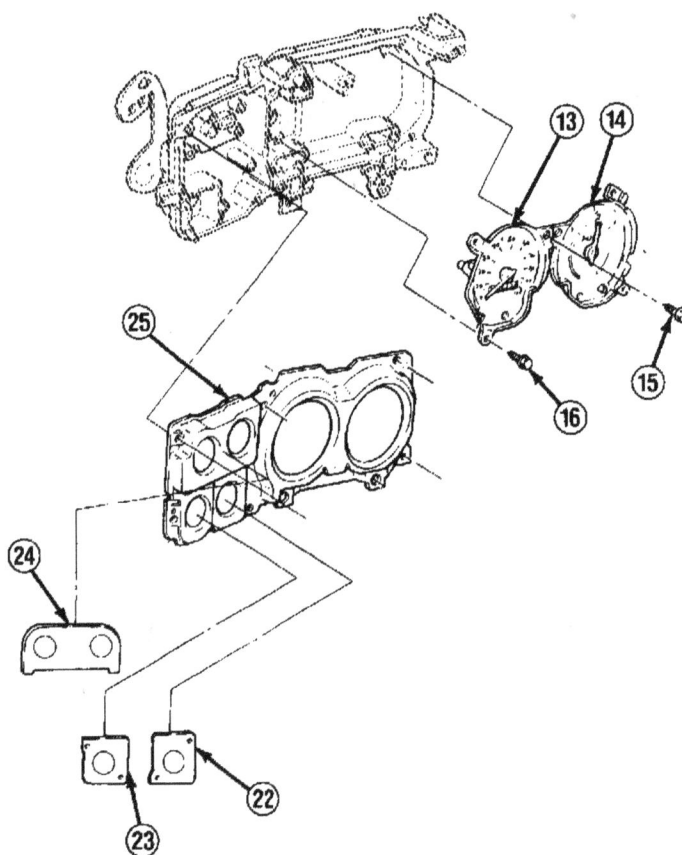

5. Remove seatbelt and brake light filter (27), and remove gasket (26).

6. Remove coolant indicator filter (32) and gasket (31).

7. Remove high beam filter (30) and gasket (29).

8. Remove 2 turn signal filters (28).

TA49859

4-7. INSTRUMENT CLUSTER MAINTENANCE (Con't).

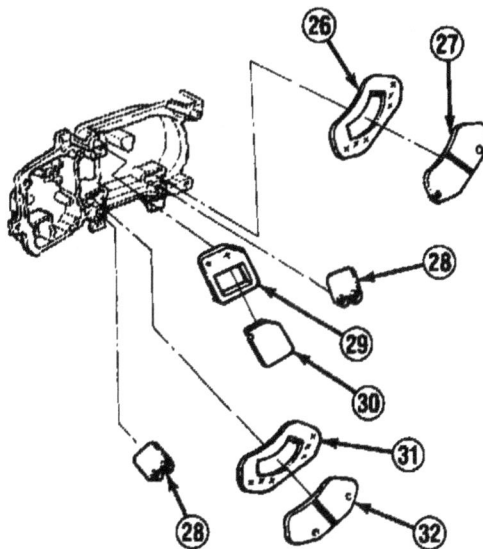

NOTE

◆Remove all socket (35) assemblies only if removing printed circuit (33).

◆If removing socket (35) assemblies without removing instrument cluster, reach under instrument panel to gain access to socket assemblies.

9. Remove 14 socket (35) assemblies as required by turning.

10. Remove bulbs (34) from sockets (35) as required.

11. Press tangs on back of 3 clips (36) and push out to remove. Remove printed circuit (33).

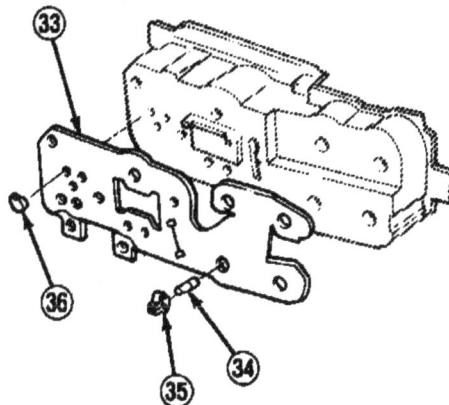

| c. | **ASSEMBLY** |

NOTE

◆If installing printed circuit (33), perform steps 1-3.

◆If installing bulbs (34), perform steps 2 and 3.

◆If installing any gages, filters, and gaskets perform steps 4-10 as required and step 11.

1. Install printed circuit (33) with 3 clips (36).

TA49860

4-7.   INSTRUMENT CLUSTER MAINTENANCE (Con't).

2.   Press bulbs (34) into sockets (35) so
they lock into place.

NOTE

**If installing socket (35) assemblies
without   instrument cluster (7)
removed, reach under instrument
panel to gain access to printed
circuit (33) holes.**

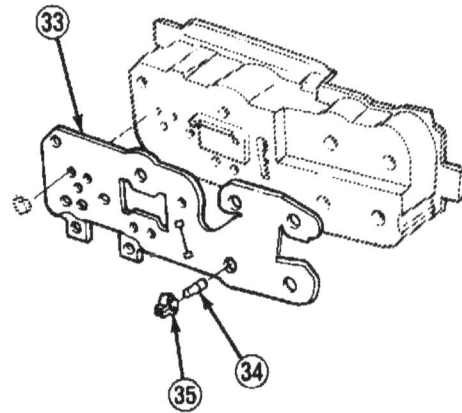

3.   Install   socket (35) assemblies
through holes in printed circuit (33)
and instrument cluster (7), and turn.

4.   Install 2 turn signal filters (28).

5.   Install gasket (29) and high beam filter (30).

6.   Install gasket (31) and coolant indicator filter (32).

7.   Install gasket (26) and seatbelt and brake light filter (27).

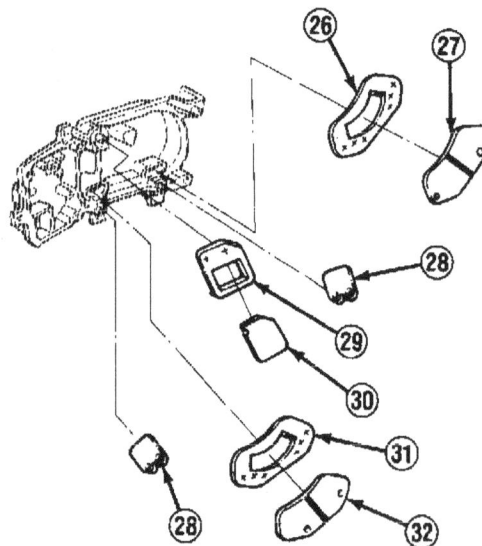

8.   Position gasket on back of speedometer (13) if removed. Install speedometer with mounting
screw (16).

9.   Install fuel gage (14) with screw (15).

10.   Install generator 1 filter (23), generator 2 filter (22), and 4-wheel drive and oil pressure filter
(24) by pressing into locking tabs on retainer (25).

11.   Install retainer (25) and instrument cluster lens (19) with 6 screws (20).

TA49861

4-7. INSTRUMENT CLUSTER MAINTENANCE (Con't).

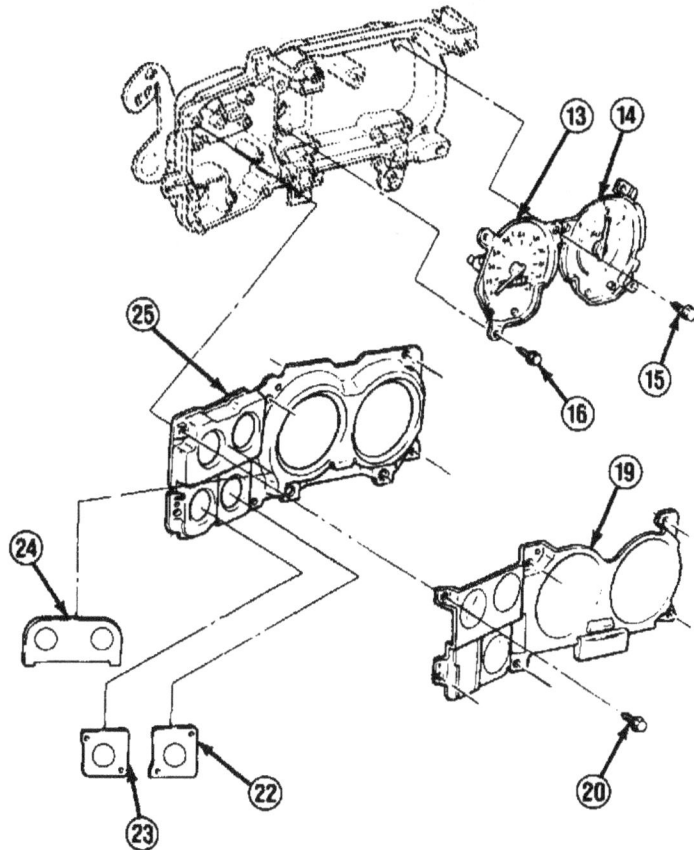

d. INSTALLATION

NOTE

- **If installing instrument cluster plate, perform steps 4 and 6.**

- **Ensure that "WAIT" and "WATER-IN-FUEL" leads are placed over top of instrument cluster (7) before installation.**

1. Connect wiring harness (9) to instrument cluster (7).

2. Install instrument cluster (7) with 4 screws (8).

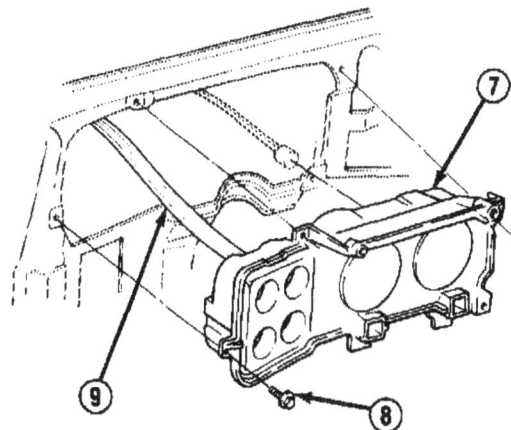

TA49862

4-7. INSTRUMENT CLUSTER MAINTENANCE (Con't).

3.   Install transmission position indicator (17) with 2 screws (18). Connect cable clip (21) to steering column. Check indicator needle for proper position and adjust as required.

4.   Connect plugs to back of instrument cluster plate (10). Position instrument cluster plate and loosely install with 5 screws (11) and 3 screws (12). Tighten screws.

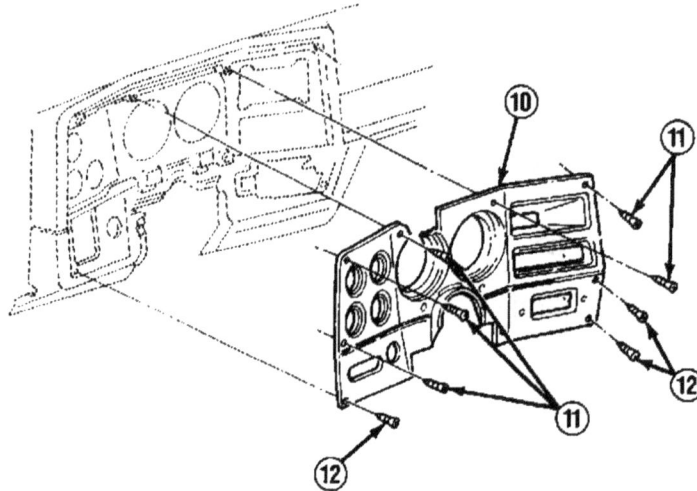

5.   Connect speedometer cable (6) to back of speedometer (13) by pressing   into retaining clip.

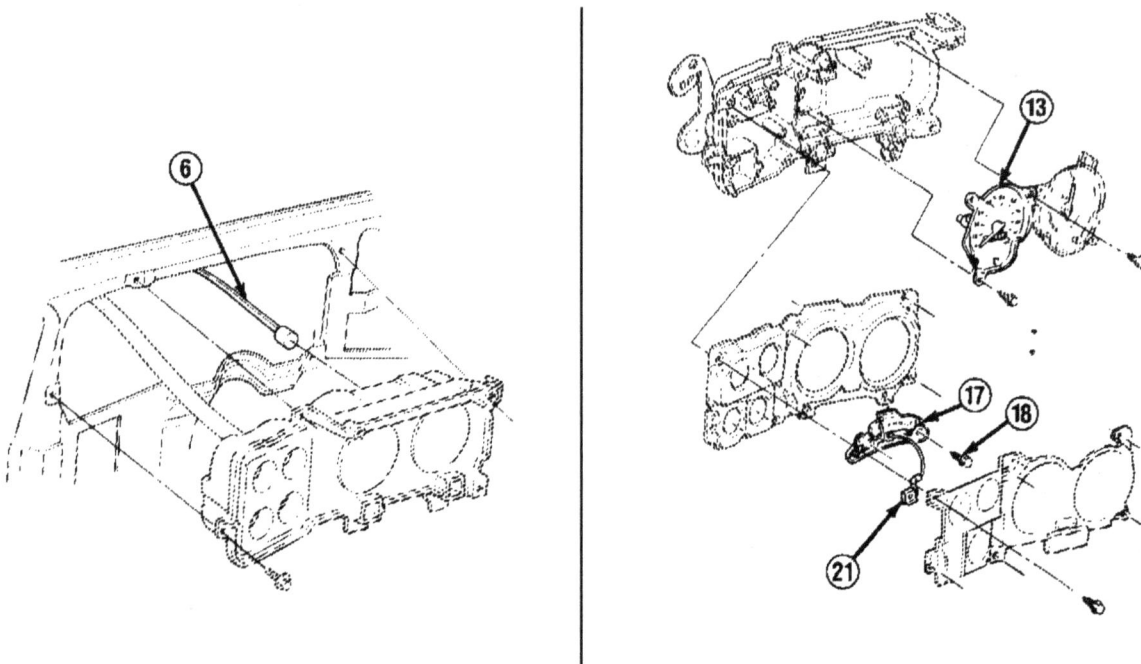

TA49863

4-7. INSTRUMENT CLUSTER MAINTENANCE (Con't).

6. Install steering column filler (4) with 2 screws (5). Install steering column filler (2) on dash panel (1) with 4 screws (3).

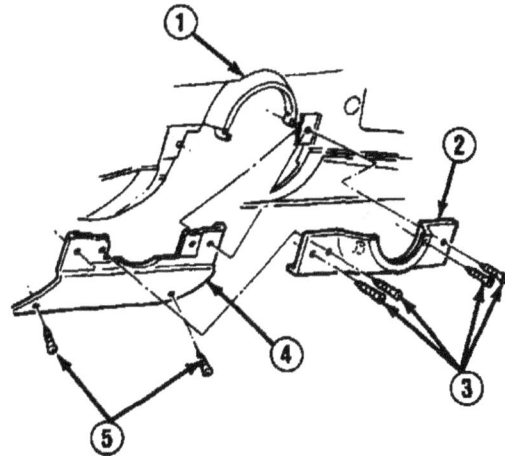

FOLLOW-ON TASKS:

●Connect both battery negative cables. (See paragraph 4-38)
●Check operation of instrument cluster components.

TA49864

4-8. GLOW PLUG RELAY AND MODULE REPLACEMENT.

This task covers: a. Removal   b. Installation

INITIAL SETUP:

Equipment Condition
  •Both battery negative cables disconnected
    (if replacing relay). (See paragraph 4-38)

Materials/Parts
  •Two lockwashers

| a. | REMOVAL |

NOTE

•If removing module (2), perform steps 1 and   2.

•If removing relay (7), perform steps 3-5.

1.   Remove glow plug module housing (1) from bracket under instrument panel to left of steering column.

2.   Remove end cap (3) and remove glow plug module (2).

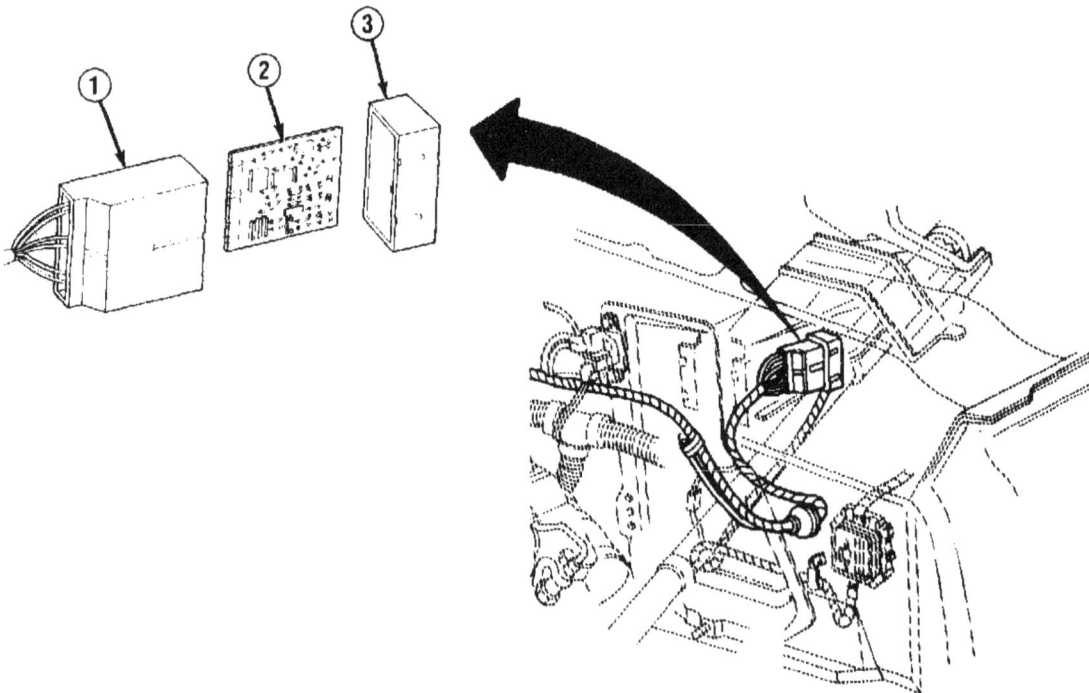

NOTE

Tag leads for installation.

3.   Remove 2 nuts (12), lead (11), 2 washers (10), and 2 leads (9).

TA49865

4-8. GLOW PLUG RELAY AND MODULE REPLACEMENT (Con't).

4.   Remove 2 nuts (4) and leads (8).

5.   Remove 2 bolts (5) and lockwashers (6). Remove glow plug relay (7). Discard lockwashers.

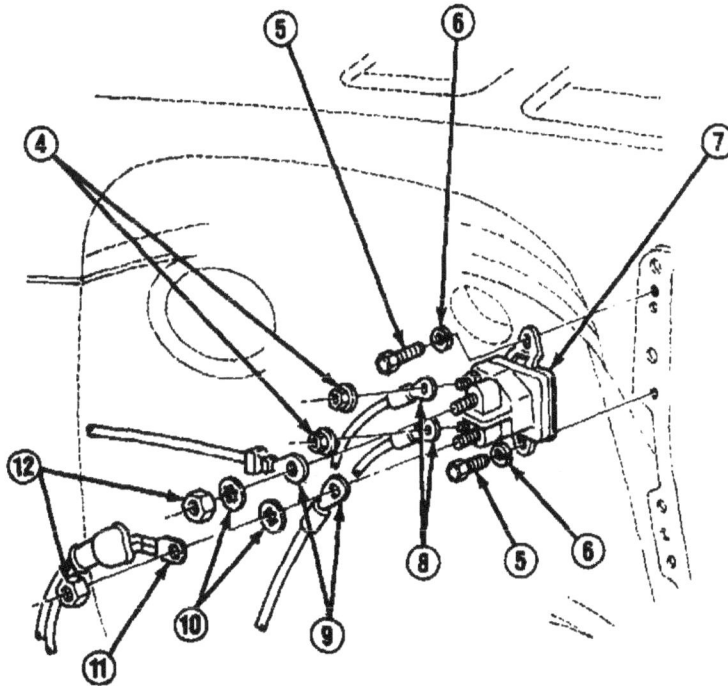

b. INSTALLATION

NOTE

◄f installing relay (7), perform steps 1-3.

◄f installing module (2), perform steps 4 and 5.

1.   Install glow plug relay (7) with 2 new lockwashers (6) and bolts (5).

2.   Install leads (8) with 2 nuts (4).

3.   Install 2 leads (9), 2 washers (10), lead (11), and 2 nuts (12).

4.   Install glow plug module (2) inside glow plug module housing (1) and install end cap (3).

5.   Install glow plug module housing (1) to bracket under instrument panel to left of steering column.

FOLLOW-ON TASKS:

◄Connect both battery negative cables if disconnected. (See paragraph 4-38)
◄Check operation of glow plugs.

TA49866

4-9. VOLTMETER, VOLTMETER RELAY , AND GENERATOR 2 RELAY REPLACEMENT.

This task covers: a. Removal   b. Installation

INITIAL SETUP:

Equipment Condition

   Instrument cluster plate removed (if removing voltmeter or door ajar housing). (See paragraph 4-7)

---

a. REMOVAL

NOTE

   If removing voltmeter (6), perform step 1.

   If removing door ajar housing (3) on M1010 only, perform step 2.

   Generator 2 relay (7) is on all except M1010. If removing generator 2 relay or voltmeter relay (8), perform step 3.

1. Remove 2 nuts (5) and washers (4), and retaining bracket (1). Remove voltmeter (6) from instrument cluster plate (2).

2. Remove door ajar housing (3) from instrument cluster plate (2).

3. Reach up under bracket (10) beside steering column (9) and disconnect lead (12) from generator 2 relay (7) or lead (11) from voltmeter relay (8). Remove generator 2 relay or voltmeter relay.

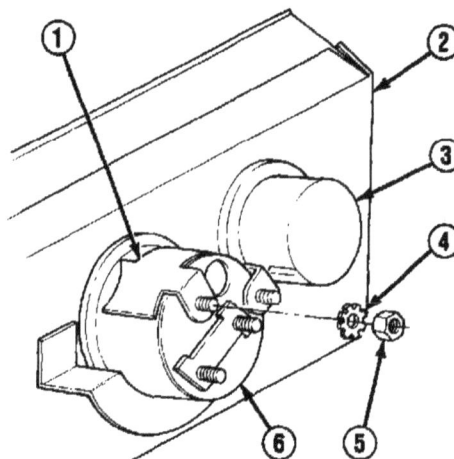

b. INSTALLATION

NOTE

   If installing generator 2 relay (7) or voltmeter relay (8) for all except M1010, perform step 1.

   If installing door ajar housing (3) on M1010 only, perform step 1.

   If installing voltmeter (6), perform step 2.

1. Install generator 2 relay (7) or voltmeter relay (8) on bracket (10) beside steering column (9). Connect lead (12) to generator 2 relay or lead (11) to voltmeter relay.

2. Install door ajar housing (3) on instrument cluster plate (2).

TA49867

4-9. VOLTMETER, VOLTMETER RELAY , AND GENERATOR 2 RELA Y REPLACEMENT (Con't).

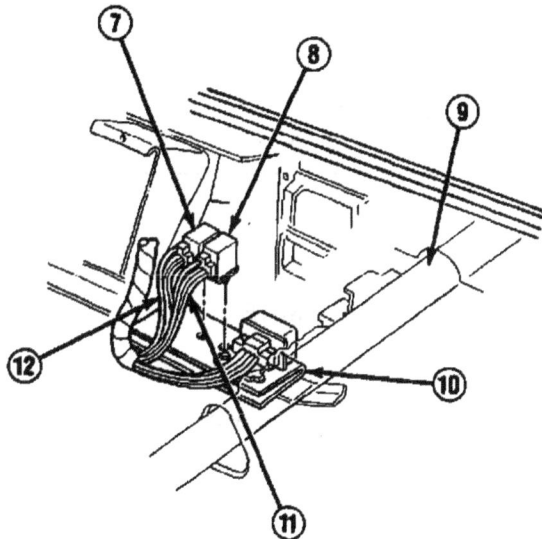

3.   Install voltmeter (6) on instrument cluster plate (2). Install retaining bracket (1) with 2 washers (4) and nuts (5).

FOLLOW-ON TASKS:

•Install instrument cluster plate   if removed. (See paragraph 4-7)
•Check operation of voltmeter,   door ajar light, or generator 2.

TA49868

4-10.   SPEEDOMETER CABLE AND ADAPTER REPLACEMENT.

This task covers: a. Removal   b. Installation

INITIAL SETUP:

Equipment Condition   *Materials/Parts*
  Both battery negative cables disconnected.   One seal
      (See paragraph 4-38)

---

a.   REMOVAL

NOTE

If removing speedometer cable (2), perform steps 1-5.

If removing M1009 speedometer adapter assembly (6), perform steps 4-6.

1.   Depress lock (3) and disconnect speedometer cable (2) from back of speedometer (4).

2.   Pull speedometer cable (2) through engine compartment bulkhead (1). Remove grommet (11) from engine compartment bulkhead if damaged.

3.   Remove nut (9) and clip (10).

4.   Loosen nut (8) and disconnect speedometer cable (2) from speedometer adapter assembly (6) or transfer case.

5.   Remove seal (7) from speedometer cable (2). Discard seal.

6.   Loosen nut (5) and remove speedometer adapter   assembly (6).

b.   INSTALLATION

NOTE

● **If installing   M1009 speedometer adapter   assembly (6), perform steps 1-3.**

● **If installing   speedometer cable (2), perform steps 2-8.**

● **M1009 uses a ring-shaped plastic seal (6) inside speedometer adapter nut (5) instead of a seal inside speedometer cable nut (8).**

1.   Install speedometer adapter assembly (6) by tightening nut (5).

2.   Install new seal (7) in speedometer cable (2).

3.   Connect speedometer cable (2) to speedometer adapter assembly (6) or transfer case by tightening nut (8).

4.   Place clip (10) on speedometer cable (2) and install with nut (9).

4-10. SPEEDOMETER CABLE AND ADAPTER REPLACEMENT (Con't).

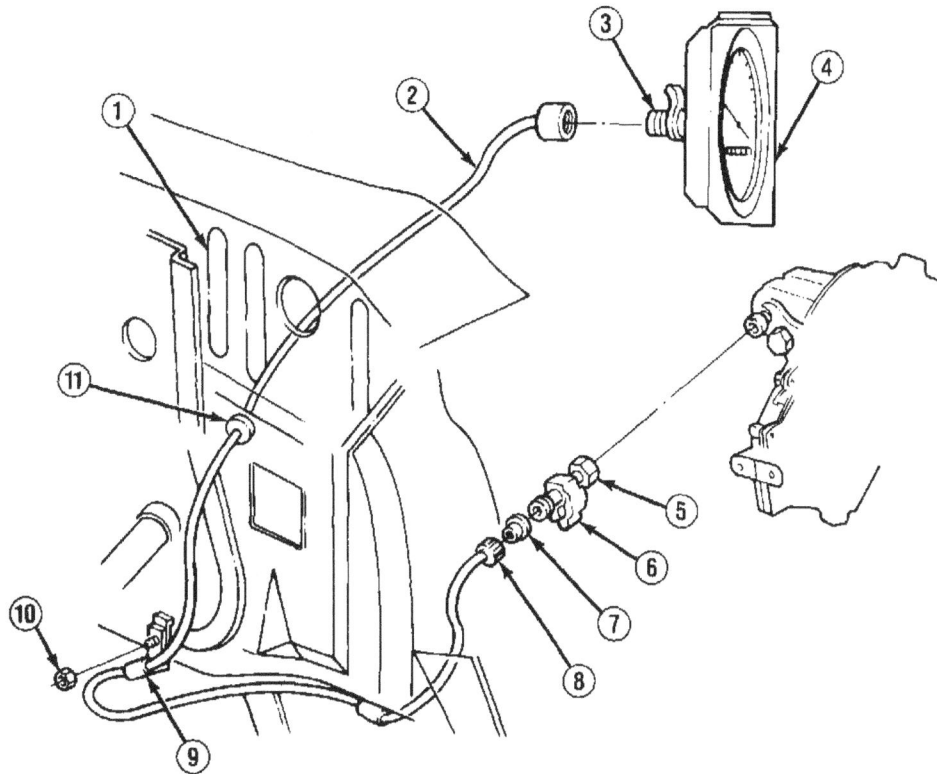

5. Install grommet (11) if removed.

CAUTION

Use extreme caution when pushing speedometer cable (2) through engine compartment bulkhead (1) to prevent damage to speedometer cable.

6. Carefully push speedometer cable (2) through engine compartment bulkhead (1).

7. Install speedometer cable (2) on back of speedometer (4) by pushing until it engages on lock (3).

FOLLOW-ON TASKS:

• Connect both battery negative cables. (See paragraph 4-38)
• Check operation of speedometer.

TA49869

4-10.1. SPEEDOMETER GEAR REPLACEMENT (ALL EXCEPT M1028A1, M1028A2, AND M1031).

| This task covers: | a. Removal | b. Installation |

INITIAL SETUP:

Equipment Condition
- Speedometer cable and adapter removed. (See paragraph 4-10)

Materials/Parts
- One seal

---

a. REMOVAL

1. Remove bolt (1) and retainer (2) from transfer case housing (6).

2. Remove sleeve (4) and speedometer gear (5).

3. Remove seal (3) from sleeve (4) and discard.

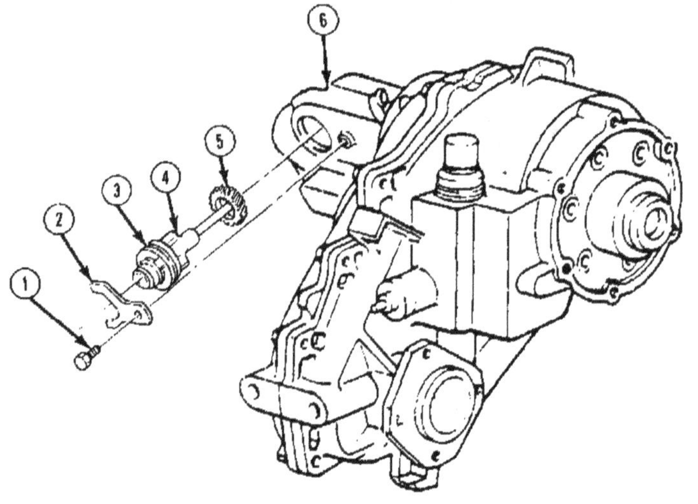

b. INSTALLATION

1. Install new seal (3) on sleeve (4).

2. Install speedometer gear (5) in sleeve (4) and install assembly into transfer case housing (6).

3. Install retainer (2) on transfer case housing (6) with bolt (1), indexing retainer with slot in sleeve (4).

FOLLOW-ON TASKS:

- Install speedometer cable and adapter. (See paragraph 4-10)

TA701831

4-10.2. SPEEDOMETER GEAR REPLACEMENT (M1028A1, M1028A2, AND M1031).

This task covers:	a. Removal	b. Installation

INITIAL SETUP:

Equipment Condition

   Speedometer cable and adapter removed. (See paragraph 4-10)

---

a.	REMOVAL

1. Remove sleeve (3) and speedometer gear (2) from transfer case retainer (1).

2. Remove speedometer gear (2) from sleeve (3).

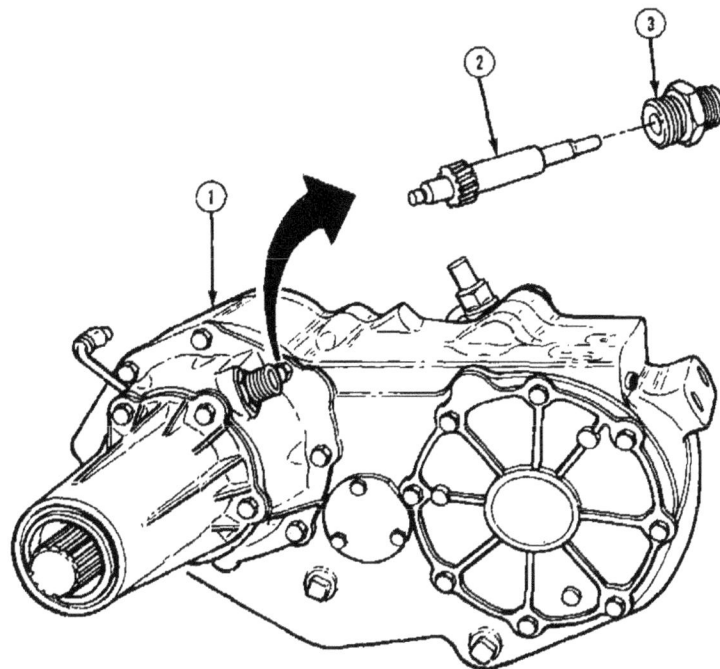

b.	INSTALLATION

1. Install speedometer gear (2) into sleeve (3).

2. Install speedometer gear (2) and sleeve (3) into transfer case retainer (1).

FOLLOW-ON TASKS:

   Install adapter and speedometer cable. (See paragraph 4-10)

TA701832

4-11. OPEN DOOR BUZZER AND SEATBELT BUZZER REPLACEMENT.

This task covers: a. Removal   b. Installation

INITIAL SETUP:

Equipment Condition

●Both battery negative cables disconnected. (See paragraph 4-38)

| a. **REMOVAL** |

NOTE

Tag wiring harness connectors for installation.

Step 1 only applies to M1010.

1. Unplug open door buzzer (2) from wiring harness (1).

2. Unplug seatbelt buzzer (3) from wiring harness (1).

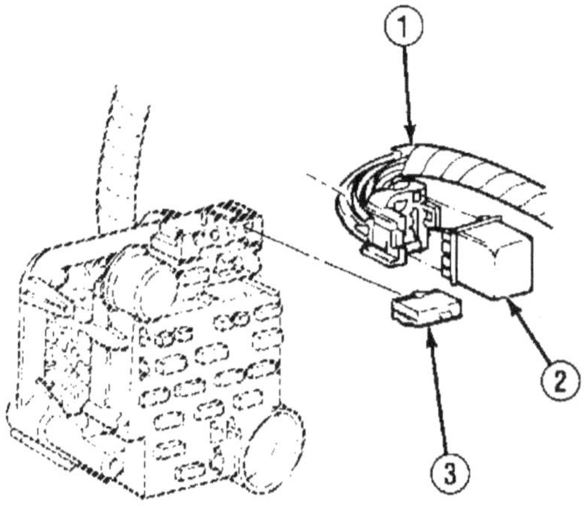

| b. **INSTALLATION** |

1. Plug seatbelt buzzer (3) into wiring harness (1).

NOTE

Step 2 only applies to M1010.

2. Plug open door   buzzer (2) into wiring harness (1).

FOLLOW-ON TASKS:

●Connect both battery negative cables. (See paragraph 4-38)
●Check operation of open door buzzer and seatbelt buzzer.

TA49870

4-12. CAB FLASHERS AND FUSES REPLACEMENT.

This task covers: a. Replacement

INITIAL SETUP:

Materials/Parts

Fuses (as required) (Items 19-24, Appendix C)

---

a.   REPLACEMENT

CAUTION

Ensure that fuses of correct amperage rating are installed as indicated. Failure to follow this caution may result in damage to fuse, fuse box, and wiring.

NOTE

Fuse box is located on driver's side of cab under instrument panel. All fuses and flashers are removed and installed in same way.

1.   Replace fuses and flashers. Check operation of circuit after replacement.

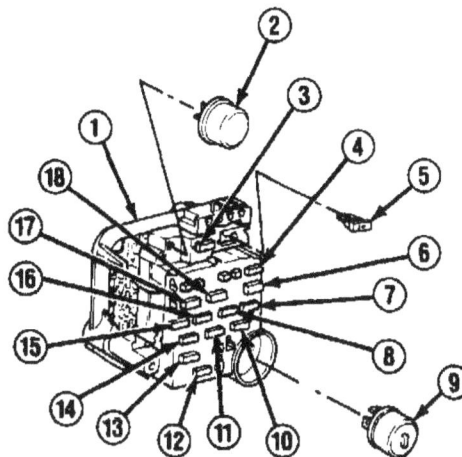

1. Fuse Box
2. Hazard Warning Flasher
3. 20 amp Ambulance Accessories Fuse
4. 20 amp Parking/Marker Light Fuse
5. 20 amp Heater Fuee
6. 10 amp Stoplight Fuse
7. 30 amp Unmarked (Headlight) Fuse
8. 25 amp Windshield Wiper Fuse
9. Turn Signal Flasher
10. 30 amp Gas-Particulate Filter Unit (GPFU) and Air Conditioner Fuse
11. 15 amp Horn Fuse
12. 10 amp/28 v (Voltmeter) Fuse
13. 5 amp Instrument Panel Lights Fuse
14. 30 amp Flasher, Back-up Lights, and Accessories Fuse
15. 20 amp Ignition Fuse
16. 5 amp Courtesy Light Fuse
17. 20 amp Engine Control Fuse
18. 5 amp Blackout Marker Fuse

TA49871

4-13. BODY FUSES AND RELAYS REPLACEMENT (M1010).

This task covers: a. Removal   b. Installation

INITIAL SETUP:

Equipment Condition   *Materials/Parts*

  Both battery negative cables disconnected.   Fuses (as required)
    (See paragraph 4-38)   (Items 21, 23, or 24, Appendix C)

---

a. REMOVAL

NOTE

- **If removing fuses (19 and 25-28), relays (3, 4, 6, 7, and 17), electrical studs (15 and 22), circuit breaker (10), and jumper cable (8), perform step 1 and 2-9 as required.**

- **Relay panel (5) is located in M1010 body left side stowage box.**

- **Tag all leads and relay plugs for installation.**

1. Remove 4 screws (2) and cover (1).

NOTE

There are four 15 amp receptacle fuses. All are in upper fuse block (23).

2. Remove 15 amp receptacle fuses (28) from upper fuse block (23) if burned out.

3. Remove 25 amp air conditioner fuse (26), 30 amp heater and blackout light fuse (25), and 30 amp heater fuse (27) from lower fuse block (24) if burned out.

4. Remove 20 amp in-line air conditioner fuse (19) if burned out.

5. Disconnect relay plug (18) from 24 v air conditioner relay (17). Remove 2 screws (16) and remove 24 v air conditioner relay. Repeat as required for gas-particulate filter unit relays (3 and 4), 12 v air conditioner relay (6), and blackout light relay (7).

6. Remove 2 nuts (9). Disconnect service outlet positive lead (20). Remove jumper cable (8) from circuit breaker (10) and positive electrical stud (22).

7. Remove nut (14) and disconnect service outlet negative lead (13).

8. Disconnect remaining leads from positive electrical stud (22). Remove 2 screws (21) and positive electrical stud. Repeat as required for negative electrical stud (15).

9. Remove nut (11) and disconnect accessory wiring terminal board lead (12). Disconnect remaining leads from circuit breaker (10). Remove 2 nuts (11) and circuit breaker.

4-13. BODY FUSES AND RELAYS REPLACEMENT (M1010) (Con't).

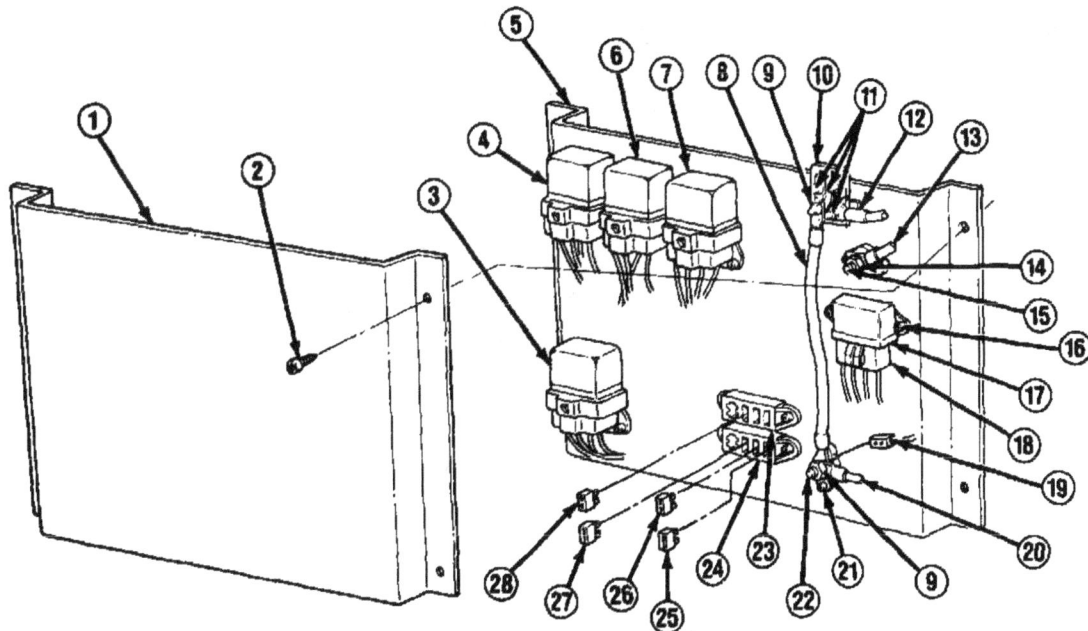

| b. | INSTALLATION |

CAUTION

Ensure that fuses of correct amperage rating are installed as indicated. Failure to follow this caution may result in damage to fuse, fuse box, and wiring.

NOTE

Perform steps 1-8 as required and step 9 to install fuses (19 and 25-28), relays (3, 4, 6, 7, and 17), electrical studs (15 and 22), circuit breaker (10), and jumper cable (8).

1. Install circuit breaker (10) with 2 nuts (11). Connect disconnected leads. Install accessory wiring terminal board lead (12) with nut (11).

2. Install positive electrical stud (22) with 2 screws (21). Connect disconnected leads. Repeat as required for negative electrical stud (15).

TA49872

4-13.   BODY FUSES AND RELAYS REPLACEMENT (M1010) (Con't).

3.   Connect service outlet negative lead (13) with nut (14).

4.   Install jumper cable (8) on positive electrical stud (22) and circuit breaker (10). Connect outlet positive lead (20). Install 2 nuts (9).

5.   Install 24 v air conditioner relay (17) with 2 screws (16). Connect relay plug (18) to 24 v air conditioner relay. Repeat as required for gas-particulate filter unit relays (3 and 4), 12 v air conditioner relay (6), and blackout light relay (7).

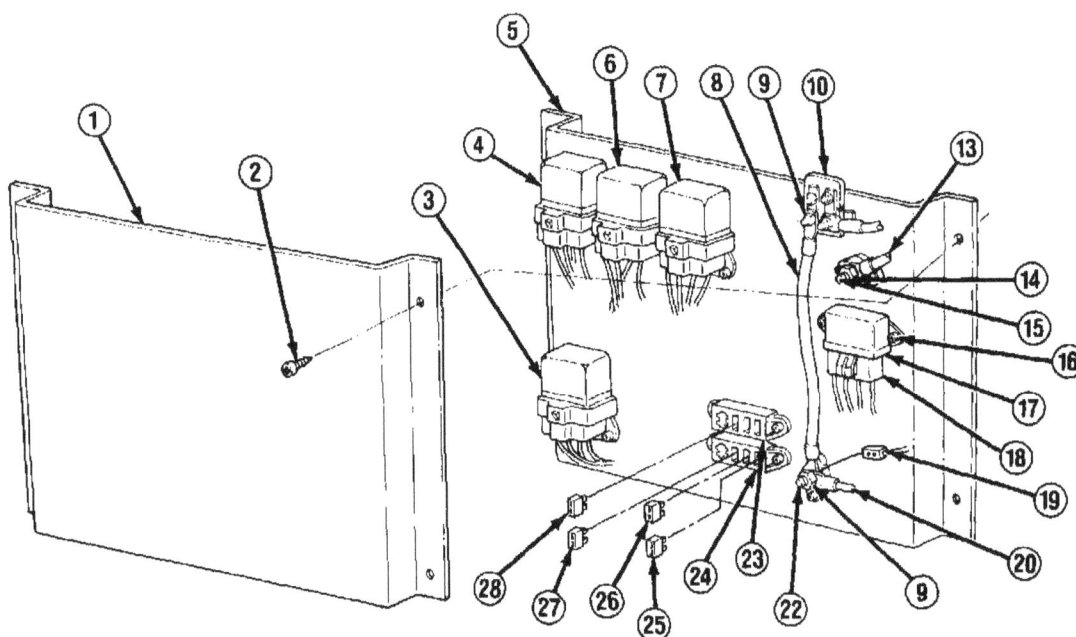

6.   Install 25 amp air conditioner fuse (26), 30 amp heater and blackout light fuse (25), and 30 amp heater fuse (27) on lower fuse block (24) if removed.

7.   Install 20 amp in-line air conditioner fuse (19) if removed.

8.   Install 15 amp receptacle fuses (28) on upper fuse block (23) if removed.

9.   Install cover (1) on relay panel (5) with 4 screws (2).

FOLLOW-ON TASKS:

•Connect both battery negative cables. (See paragraph 4-38)
•Check operation of applicable circuit.

TA49873

4-14. OIL PRESSURE AND COOLANT TEMPERATURE SENDING UNIT REPLACEMENT.   S

This task covers:	a. Removal	b. Installation

INITIAL SETUP:

Equipment Condition

● Both battery negative cables disconnected. (See paragraph 4-38)

Materials/Parts

● Pipe sealant (Item 43, Appendix C)

---

a. REMOVAL

NOTE

● If removing oil pressure sending unit (2), perform step 1.

● If removing coolant temperature sending unit (4), perform step 2.

● Tag all leads for installation.

1. Remove air cleaner. (See paragraph 3-9) Disconnect lead from oil pressure sending unit (2). Remove oil pressure sending unit from fitting (3). Remove fitting from engine block (1).

2. Drain cooling system. (See paragraph 3-30) Disconnect lead from coolant temperature sending unit (4). Remove coolant temperature sending unit from engine block (1). Clean old pipe sealant from engine block.

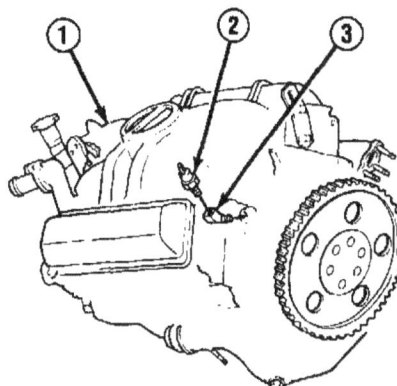

b. INSTALLATION

NOTE

● If installing coolant temperature sending unit (4), perform step 1.

● If installing oil pressure sending unit (2), perform step 2.

1. Coat coolant temperature sending unit (4) threads with pipe sealant and install on engine block (1). Connect lead to coolant temperature sending unit. Fill cooling system. (See paragraph 3-30)

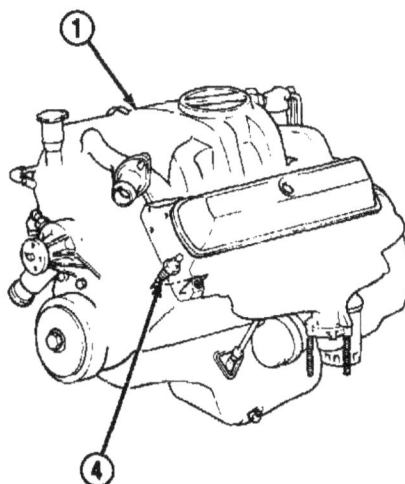

TA49874

4-14. **OIL PRESSURE AND COOLANT TEMPERATURE SENDING UNIT**   S
       REPLACEMENT (Con't).

2.   Install fitting (3) on engine block (1). Install oil pressure sending unit (2) on fitting. Connect lead to oil pressure sending unit. Install air cleaner. (See paragraph 3-9)

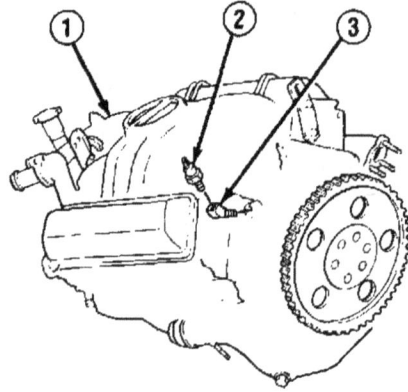

FOLLOW-ON TASKS:

   •Connect both battery negative cables. (See paragraph 4-38)
   •Check operation of oil pressure light and coolant temperature light.

TA49875

4-15. HEADLIGHT CONTROL SWITCH REPLACEMENT.

This task covers: a. Removal   b. Installation

| a. REMOVAL |

NOTE

If removing headlight control (3), perform step 1.

1. Pull out headlight control (3) and depress release button (4) on side of switch assembly (1) to remove headlight control.

NOTE

Tag leads for installation.

2. Unscrew bezel (2) to disengage switch assembly (1). Disconnect leads at switch assembly and remove.

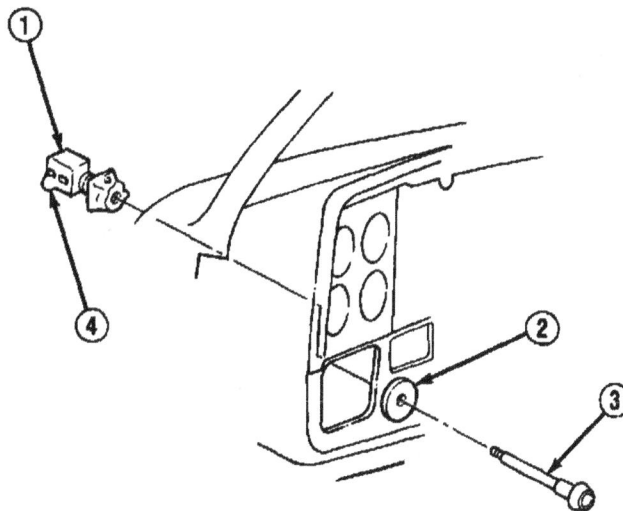

| b. INSTALLATION |

NOTE

If installing headlight control (3), perform step 2.

1. Connect leads to switch assembly (1). Hold switch assembly in place and screw on bezel (2) to install.

2. Push headlight control (3) through bezel (2) to engage switch assembly (1).

FOLLOW-ON TASKS:

 Check operation of headlight.

TA49876

4-16. STOPLIGHT SWITCH REPLACEMENT AND ADJUSTMENT.

This task covers:	a. Removal	b. Installation

INITIAL SETUP:

Equipment Condition
●Both battery negative cables disconnected.
  (See paragraph 4-38)

Materials/Parts
●One lockwasher

---

a.	**REMOVAL**

NOTE

●If removing stoplight switch (2), perform step 1.

●Tag lead for installation.

1. Depress brake pedal (4). Pull out stoplight switch (2) and disconnect lead.

2. Remove nut (6) and lockwasher (5) from screw (3) on brake pedal (4). Discard lockwasher.

3. Remove actuator (7) and retainer (8) from bracket (1).

b.	**INSTALLATION**

NOTE

If installing stoplight switch (2), perform steps 3 and 4.

1. Position retainer (8) on bracket (1).

2. Position actuator (7) on brake pedal (4) and install new lockwasher (5) and nut (6) on screw (3) .

3. Depress brake pedal (4). Pull lead through retainer (8) and bracket (1), and install on stoplight switch (2).

NOTE

Clicking sound   will be heard as stoplight switch (2) is installed in
retainer (8).

4. Install stoplight switch (2) in retainer (8). Pull brake pedal (4) back until pedal stops making clicking sound.

FOLLOW-ON TASKS:

●Connect both battery negative cables. (See paragraph 4-38)
●Check operation of stoplight.

TA49877

4-17. PARKING BRAKE SWITCH REPLACEMENT.

This task covers: a. Removal   b. Installation

INITIAL SETUP:

Equipment Condition

Both battery negative cables disconnected. (See paragraph 4-38)
Hazard flasher removed from fuse box. (See paragraph 4-12)

| a. | REMOVAL |

1. Disconnect lead (4) from parking brake switch (2).

2. Remove screw (3) and parking brake switch (2) from bracket (1).

| b. | INSTALLATION |

1. Install parking brake switch (2) on bracket (1) with screw (3).

2. Connect lead (4) to parking brake switch (2).

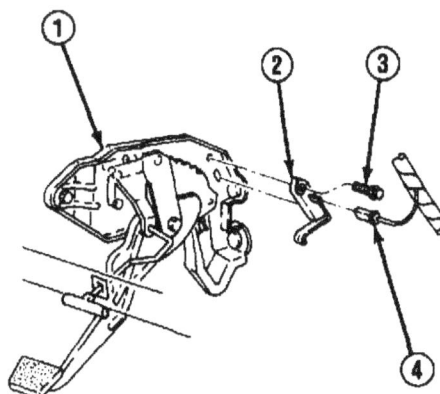

FOLLOW-ON TASKS:

Install hazard flasher on fuse box. (See paragraph 4-12)
Connect both battery negative cables. (See paragraph 4-38)
Check operation of parking brake indicator light.

TA49878

4-18. BLACKOUT LIGHT SWITCHES REPLACEMENT.

This task covers: a. Removal   b. Installation

INITIAL SETUP:

Equipment Condition

- Both battery negative cables disconnected. (See paragraph 4-38)
- Instrument cluster plate removed. (See paragraph 4-7)

| a. | REMOVAL |

1. Remove nut (3) and washer (4). Remove switch (2) and washer (5). Disconnect lead (1) from switch.

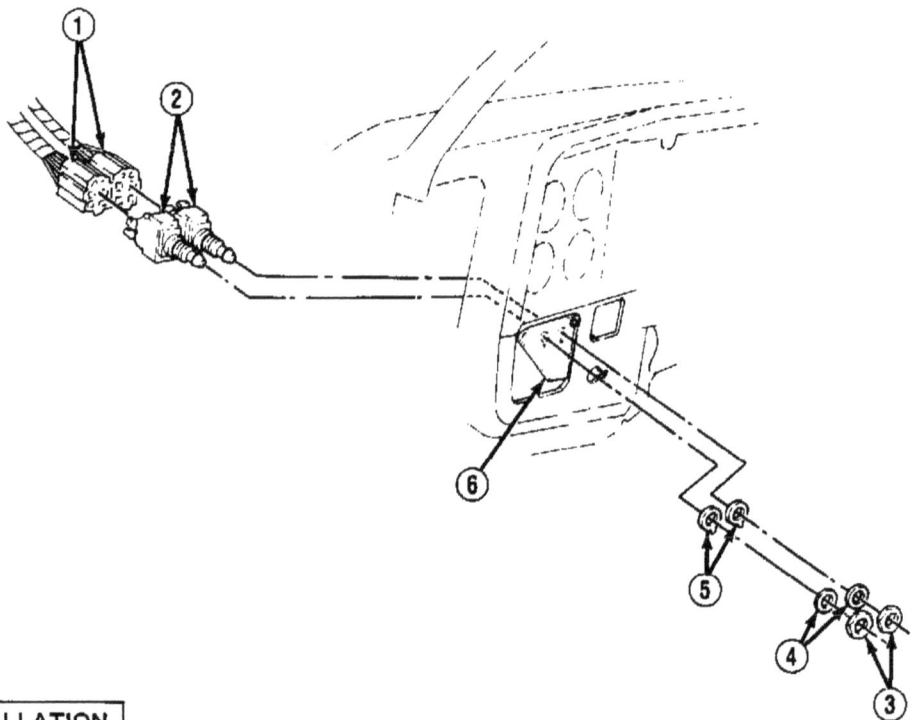

| b. | INSTALLATION |

1. Connect lead (1) to switch (2). Install washer (5) on switch and place switch through mounting plate (6). Install washer (4) and nut (3) on switch.

FOLLOW-ON TASKS:

- Check operation of blackout light.

TA49879

4-19. BACK-UP LIGHT SWITCH REPLACEMENT.

This task covers:	a. Removal	b. Installation

INITIAL SETUP:

Equipment Condition

Both battery negative cables disconnected. (See paragraph 4-38)

---

a. REMOVAL

1. Set parking brake and place transmission gearshift lever in "N" (Neutral).

2. Unsnap back-up light switch (2) at tangs (5) to remove from steering column jacket (1).

3. Disconnect lead from back-up light switch (2). Remove back-up light switch.

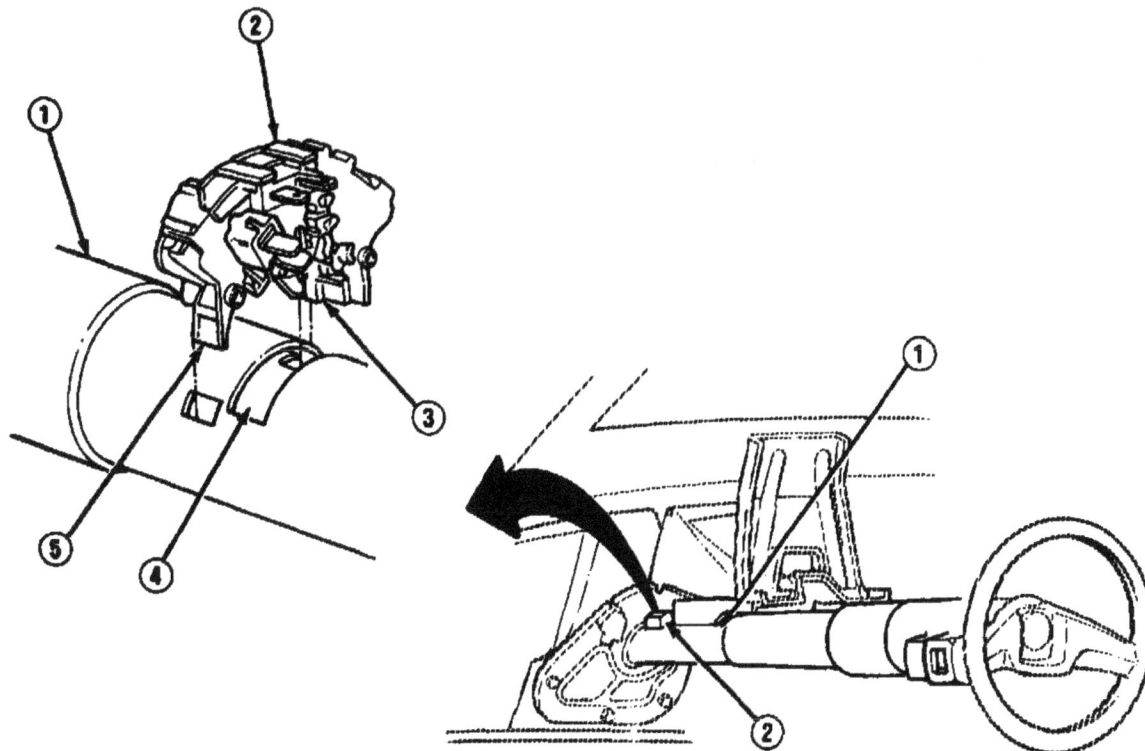

b. INSTALLATION

1. Connect lead to back-up light switch (2).

2. Aline actuator (3) on back-up light switch (2) with hole in shift tube (4).

3. Position back-up light switch (2) on cutout in lower part of steering column jacket (1).

TA49880

4-19.   BACK-UP LIGHT SWITCH REPLACEMENT (Con't).

4.   Push down on front of back-up light switch (2). Snap 2 tangs (5) on back-up light switch into place on steering column jacket (1).

5.   Adjust back-up light switch (2) by moving transmission gearshift lever to "P" (Park). Main back-up light switch housing and back-up light switch housing back should make a clicking noise, providing proper adjustment.

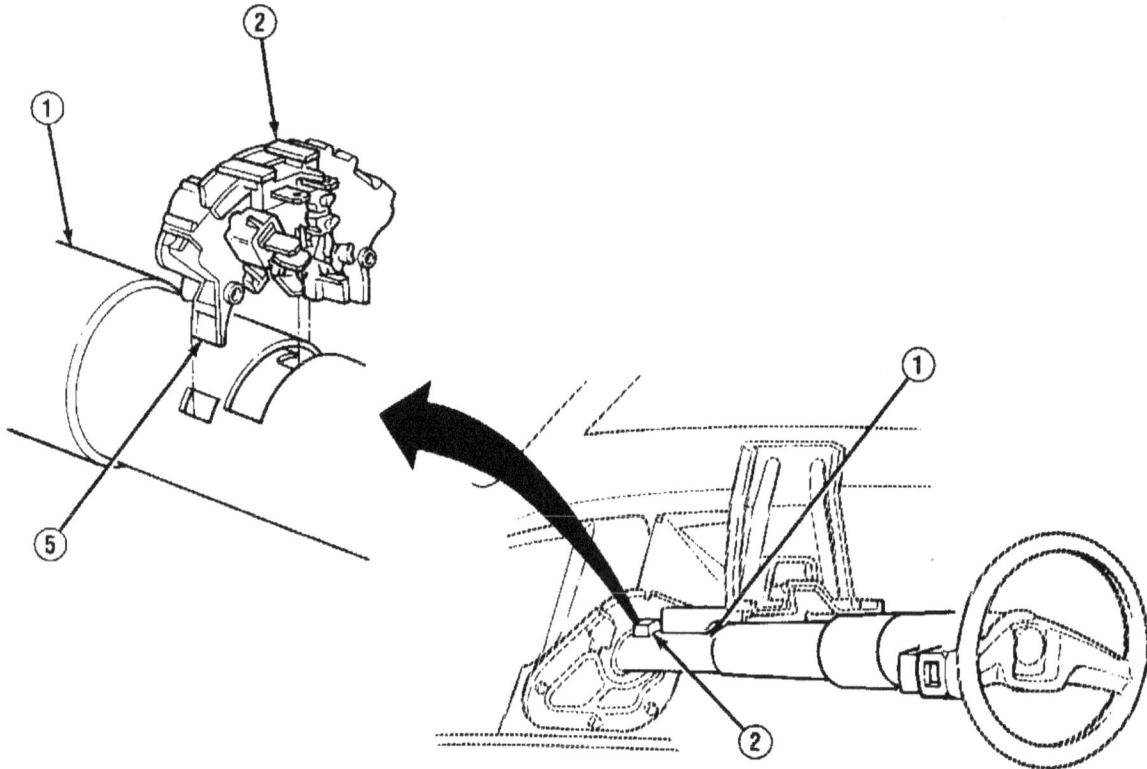

FOLLOW-ON TASKS:

●Connect both battery negative cables. (See paragraph 4-38)
●Check operation of back-up light.

TA49881

4-20. HAZARD WARNING CONTROL REPLACEMENT.

This task covers: a. Removal   b. Installation

INITIAL SETUP:

Equipment Condition

Both battery negative cables disconnected. (See paragraph 4-38)

---

a.   REMOVAL

1. Loosen screw (5) and remove hazard warning button (4), spring (3), and knob (2) assembly.

2. Remove screw (5), button (4), and spring (3) from knob (2).

b.   INSTALLATION

1. Install spring (3), hazard warning button (4), and screw (5) in knob (2).

2. Install hazard warning button (4), spring (3), and knob (2) assembly on steering column (1) by tightening screw (5).

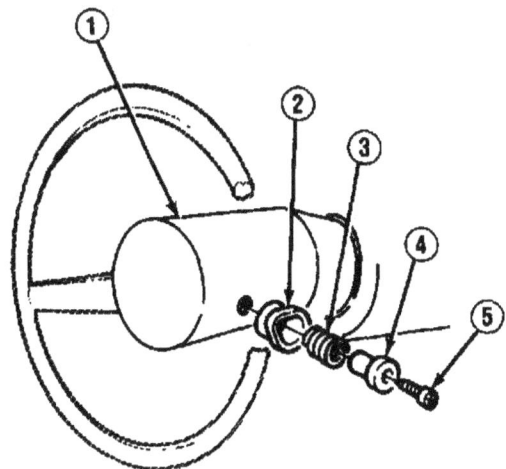

FOLLOW-ON TASKS:

Connect both battery negative cables. (See paragraph 4-38)
Check operation of hazard warning system.

TA49882

4-21. FLOODLIGHT AND GAS-PARTICULATE FILTER UNIT (GPFU) SWITCHE   S
REPLACEMENT (M1010).

This task covers: a. Removal   b. Installation

INITIAL SETUP:

Equipment Condition

◄Instrument cluster plate removed. (See paragraph 4-7)

| a. | REMOVAL |

1.   Remove screw (7) and retainer (6) from back of instrument panel (1). Remove switch cover plate (2). Remove 1 or both floodlight switches (5) and GPFU switch (4) as required.

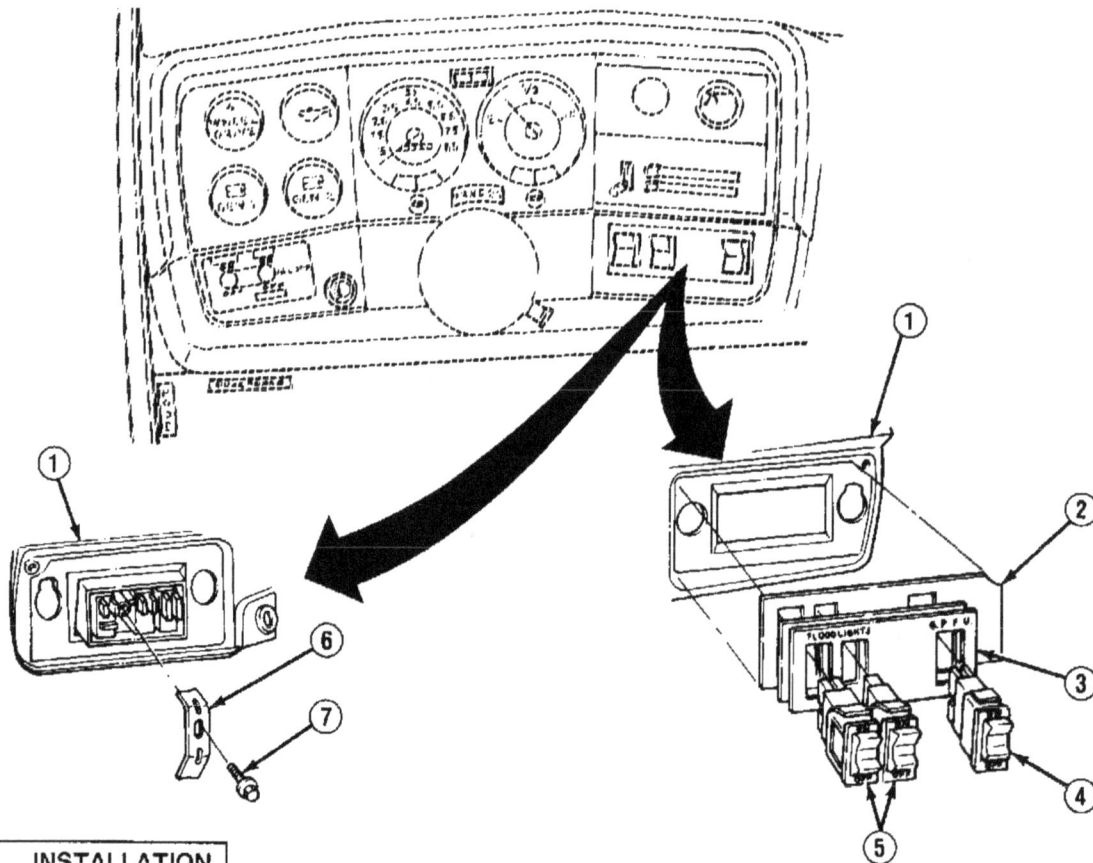

| b. | INSTALLATION |

1.   Install 1 or both floodlight switches (5) and GPFU switch (4) on switch cover (3) if removed. Position switch plate (2) and switch cover on instrument panel (1). Install retainer (6) on back of instrument panel and on back of switch plate with screw (7).

FOLLOW-ON TASKS:

◄Install instrument cluster plate. (See paragraph 4-7)
◄Check operation of floodlight and gas-particulate filter unit.

TA49883

4-22. HORN AND HORN RELAY REPLACEMENT.

This task covers: a. Removal   b.   Installation

INITIAL SETUP:

Equipment Condition
Both battery negative cables disconnected. (See paragraph 4-38)
Radiator grille removed. (See paragraph 10-2)

---

a.   REMOVAL

NOTE

If removing **horn (8), perform steps 1 and 2.**
If removing **capacitor (6), perform steps 1 and 3.**
If removing **horn relay (2), perform step 4.**

1.   Disconnect capacitor (6) lead from horn (8).

2.   Remove bolt (3) and horn (8).

3.   Remove screw (7) and capacitor (6). Remove nut (5) from radiator support (4) if damaged.

NOTE

Tag wiring harness (1) connector for installation.

4.   Unplug horn   relay (2) from wiring harness (1).

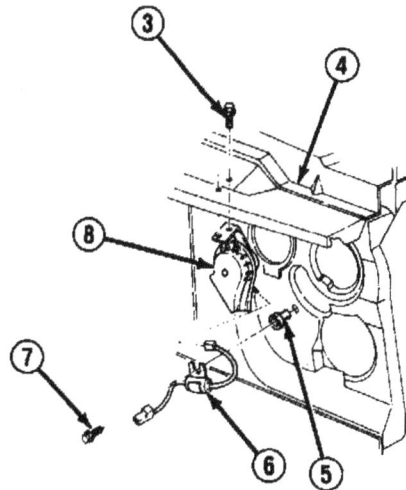

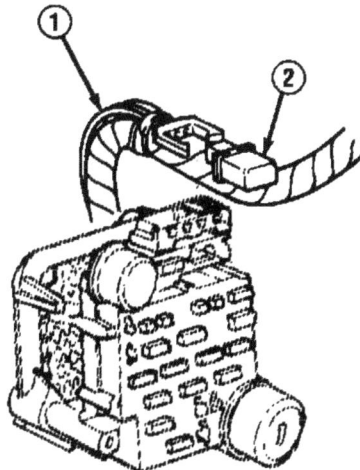

TA49884

4-22. HORN AND HORN RELAY REPLACEMENT (Con't).

| b. | INSTALLATION |

NOTE

◄If installing horn relay (2), perform step 1.

◄If installing capacitor (6), perform steps 2 and 4.

◄If installing horn (8), perform steps 3 and 4.

1. Plug horn relay (2) into wiring harness (1).

2. Install nut (5) in radiator support (4) if removed. Install capacitor (6) with screw (7).

3. Install horn (8) on radiator support (4) with bolt (3).

4. Connect capacitor (6) lead to horn (8).

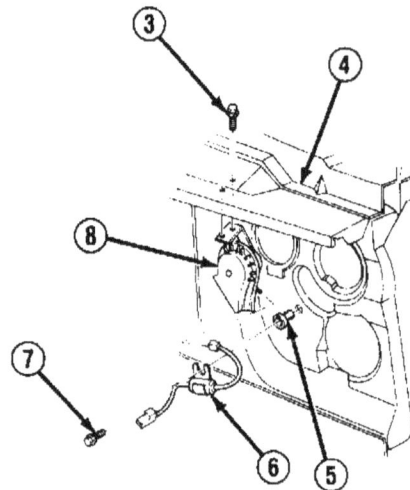

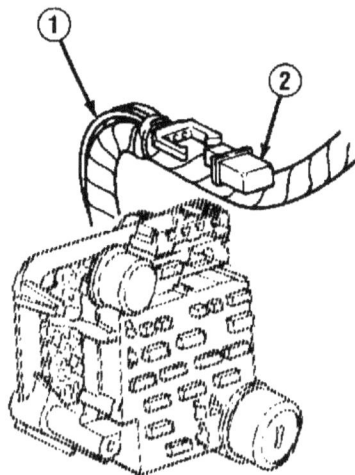

FOLLOW-ON TASKS:

- Install radiator grille. (See paragraph 10-2)
- Connect both battery negative cables. (See paragraph 4-38)
- Check operation of horn.

TA49885

4-22.1. BRAKE INDICATOR LIGHT WIRE REPLACEMENT.

This task covers: a. Removal   b. Installation

INITIAL SETUP:

Equipment Condition

●Both battery negative cables disconnected. (See paragraph 4-38)

| a. | REMOVAL |

1. Disconnect combination valve connector (3) from brake indicator light bracket (1).

2. Disconnect brake indicator light wire (4) from combination valve (5) and brake indicator light bracket (1).

3. If damaged, remove screw (2) and brake indicator light bracket (1).

| b. INSTALLATION |

1. If removed, install brake indicator light bracket (1) with screw (2).

2. Connect brake indicator light wire (4) to combination valve (5) and brake indicator light bracket (1).

3. Connect combination valve connector (3) to brake indicator light   bracket (1).

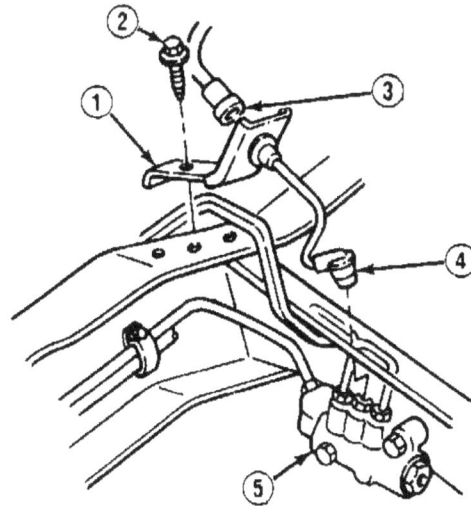

FOLLOW-ON   TASKS:

●Connec t both battery negative cables. (See paragraph 4-38)

TA702217

Section IV. LIGHTING SYSTEM MAINTENANCE

4-23. LIGHTING SYSTEM MAINTENANCE INDEX.

4 - 2 .   SERVICE HEADLIGHT MAINTENANCE.

| This task covers: | a. Removal | c. Adjustment |
| | b. Installation | |

INITIAL SETUP:

Equipment Condition
  •Both battery negative cables disconnected.
   (See paragraph 4-38)

Tools/Test Equipment
  •Screwdriver bit set, J-29843

| a. | **REMOVAL** |

NOTE

DO NOT tamper with headlight adjusting screws (6).

1.   Remove 2 screws (10), screws (5), and bezel (9).

2.   Unhook spring (4) from radiator support (3) and remove mounting ring   (2).

3.   Pull out headlight (1) and disconnect from wiring harness connector.

4.   Remove 4 screws (8) and retaining ring (7). Remove headlight (1).

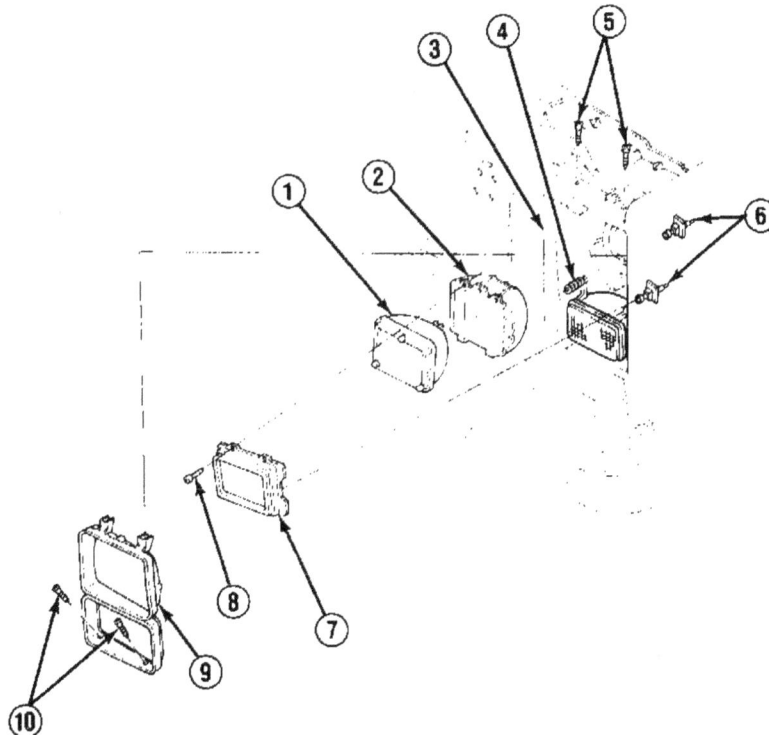

TA49886

4-24.   SERVICE HEADLIGHT MAINTENANCE (Con't).

| b. INSTALLATION |

1.   Position headlight (1) in mounting ring (2). Install retaining ring (7) on mounting ring with 4 screws (8).

2.   Connect wiring harness connector to headlight (1).

3.   Hook spring (4) to radiator support (3).

4.   Install bezel (9) with 2 screws (5) and screws (10).

| c. ADJUSTMENT |

1.   Connect both battery negative cables. (See paragraph 4-38)

2.   Measure distance from centerline of headlights to level surface.

3.   Subtract 3 in. from measurement obtained in step 1 and mark it on a vertical surface.

4.   Mark centerline of vehicle on vertical surface and intersect it with line obtained in step 2.

5.   Measure distance between centers of headlights. Divide that distance equally on both sides of centerline of vehicle line and mark along line in step 2.

6.   Turn on headlights and use high beam.

NOTE

Adjust 1 headlight   at a time while covering the other.

7.   Turn adjusting screws (6) in or out   until center of beam intersects with crossed line in step 4.

8.   Repeat step 7 for other headlight.

4-25. BLACKOUT DRIVE LIGHT AND LAMP REPLACEMENT.

This task covers: a.   Removal   b. Installation

INITIAL SETUP:

Equipment Condition

• Both battery negative cables disconnected.
  (See paragraph 4-38)
• Radiator grille removed (if removing blackout
  light housing). (See paragraph 10-2)

Materials/Parts

• One lockwasher
• One "O" ring

---

a.   REMOVAL

NOTE

- **If removing lamp (3), perform step 1.**

- **If removing blackout light assembly, perform step 2.**

- **If removing mounting bracket (6), perform steps 2 and 3.**

1.   Remove cover (1), "O" ring (2), and   gasket (13). Remove lamp (3).

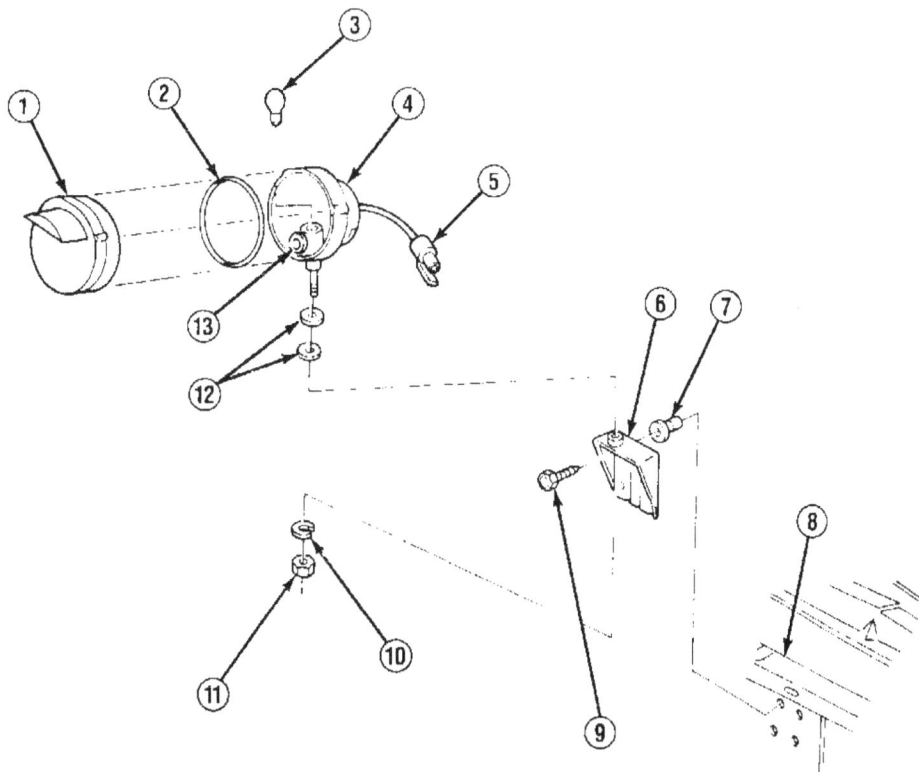

TA49887

4-25. BLACKOUT DRIVE LIGHT AND LAMP REPLACEMENT (Con't).

2. Remove nut (11) and lockwasher (10). Pull out blackout light housing (4) from mounting bracket (6) and remove 2 washers (12). Disconnect lead (5) and remove housing. Discard lockwasher.

3. Remove 4 bolts (9), mounting bracket (6), and 4 retaining nuts (7) from radiator support (8).

b. INSTALLATION

NOTE

● If installing mounting bracket (6), perform steps 1 and 2.

● If installing blackout light assembly, perform step 2.

● If installing lamp (3), perform step 3.

1. Install 4 retaining nuts (7) on radiator support (8). Install mounting bracket (6) with 4 bolts (9).

2. Connect lead (5). Install 2 washers (12) on blackout light housing (4). Install blackout light housing on mounting bracket (6) with new lockwasher (10) and nut (11).

3. Install lamp (3). Install gasket (13), "O" ring (2), and cover (1).

FOLLOW-ON TASKS:

● Install radiator grille. (See paragraph 10-2)
● Connect both battery negative cables (See paragraph 4-38)
● Check operation of blackout light.

4-26.   PARKING LIGHT AND LAMP REPLACEMENT.

This task covers: a. Removal   b. Installation

| a.   REMOVAL |

1.   Remove headlight bezel. (See paragraph 4-24, REMOVAL, step 1)

2.   Remove 3 screws (1) and parking light housing (2) from radiator support (3).

3.   Remove lamp (5) from wiring harness connector (4).

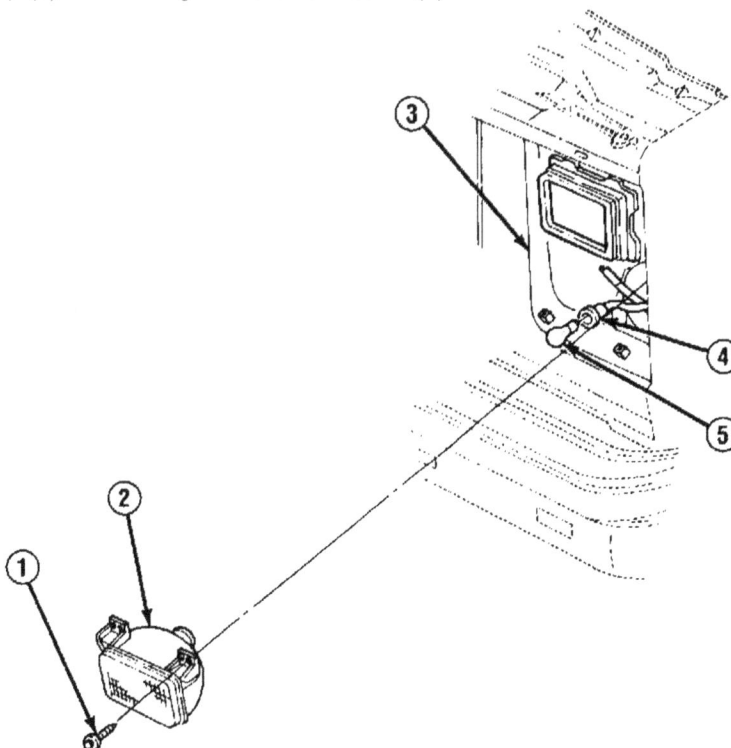

| b.   INSTALLATION |

1.   Install lamp (5) on wiring harness connector (4).

2.   Install parking light housing (2) on radiator support (3) with 3 screws   (1).

3.   Install headlight bezel. (See paragraph 4-24, INSTALLATION, step 4)

FOLLOW-ON TASKS:

  •Check operation of parking light.

TA49888

4-27. MARKER LIGHT AND LAMP REPLACEMENT.

This task covers:	a. Removal	b. Installation

INITIAL SETUP:

Equipment Condition
◆Both battery negative cables disconnected.
(See paragraph 4-38)

Tools/Test Equipment
◆Screwdriver bit set, J-29843

---

a. REMOVAL

NOTE

◆**If removing side marker light and** lamp (3), perform step 1.

◆**If removing blackout marker light** (8), perform step 2.

◆**If removing blackout marker light** bracket (9), perform steps 2 and 3.

1. Remove 2 screws (5), side marker light housing (4), and 2 retaining nuts (1). Remove lamp (3) from wiring harness connector (6).

2. Remove nut (11) and wiring harness (10) ground. Remove two nuts (13). Disconnect blackout marker light (8) from wiring harness connector.

3. Remove bolt (7), nut (12), and mounting bracket (9) from bumper (14).

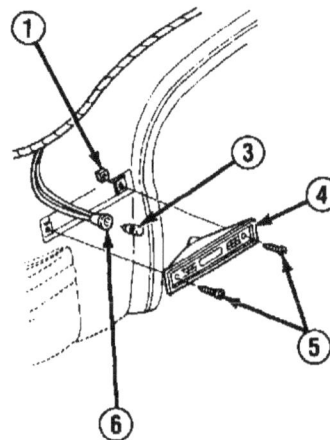

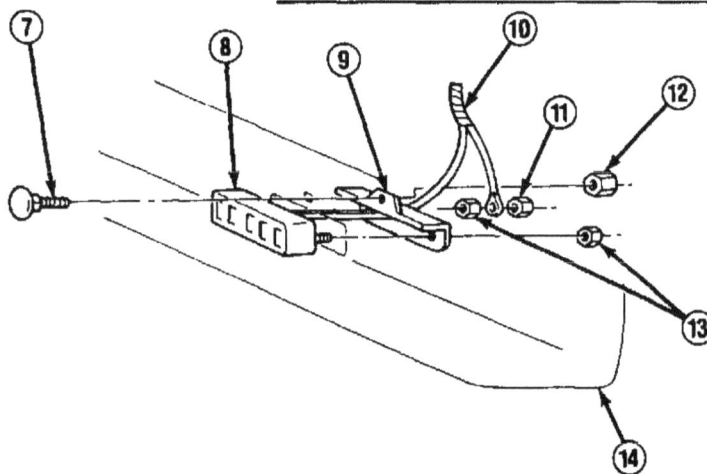

TA49889

4-27.   MARKER LIGHT AND LAMP REPLACEMENT (Con't).

| b. INSTALLATION |

NOTE

◀If installing blackout marker light bracket (9), perform steps 1 and 2.

◀If installing blackout marker light (8), perform step 2.

◀If installing side marker light and lamp (3), perform step 3.

1.   Install mounting bracket (9) on bumper (14) with bolt (7) and nut (12).

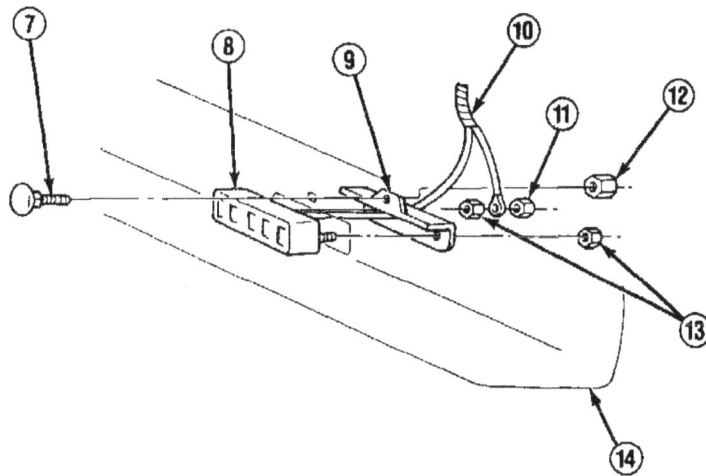

2.   Position blackout marker light (8) on mounting bracket (9) and connect wiring harness (10) connector. Install blackout marker light with 2 nuts (13). Install wiring harness ground with nut (11).

3.   Install lamp (3) on wiring harness connector (6).   Install side marker light housing (4) on fender (2) with 2 screws (5) and retaining nuts (1).

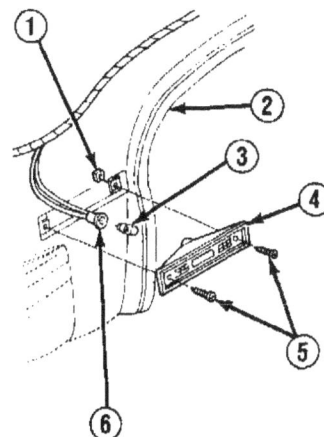

FOLLOW-ON TASKS:

◀Connect both battery negative cables. (See paragraph 4-38)
◀Check operation of marker light.

TA49890

4-28. TAILLIGHT AND LAMP REPLACEMENT (ALL EXCEPT M1010 AND M1031).

This task covers:	a. Removal	b. Installation

INITIAL SETUP:

Equipment Condition
- Both battery negative cables disconnected. (See paragraph 4-38)

Tools/Test Equipment
- Screwdriver bit set, J-29843

a. REMOVAL

1. Remove 4 screws (11), taillight lens (1), and gasket (3). Remove turn signal lamp (5), back-up lamp (8), and stop lamp (10) as required.

2. Remove 4 screws (2) and taillight housing (4).

NOTE

Tag wiring harness leads for installation.

3. Remove turn signal lamp socket (6), back-up lamp socket (7), and stop lamp socket (9) as required.

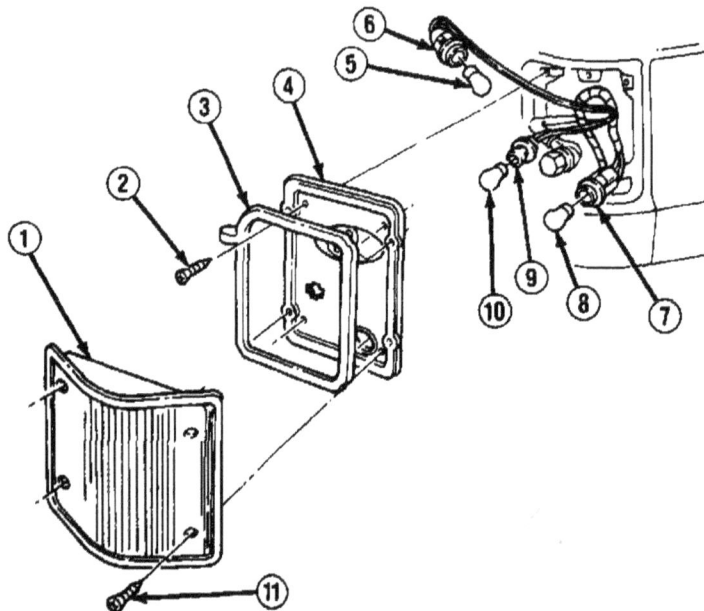

b. INSTALLATION

1. Install turn signal lamp socket (6), back-up lamp socket (7), and stop lamp socket (9) on wiring harness if removed.

TA49891

4-28. TAILLIGHT AND LAMP REPLACEMENT (ALL EXCEPT M1010 AND M1031) (Con't).

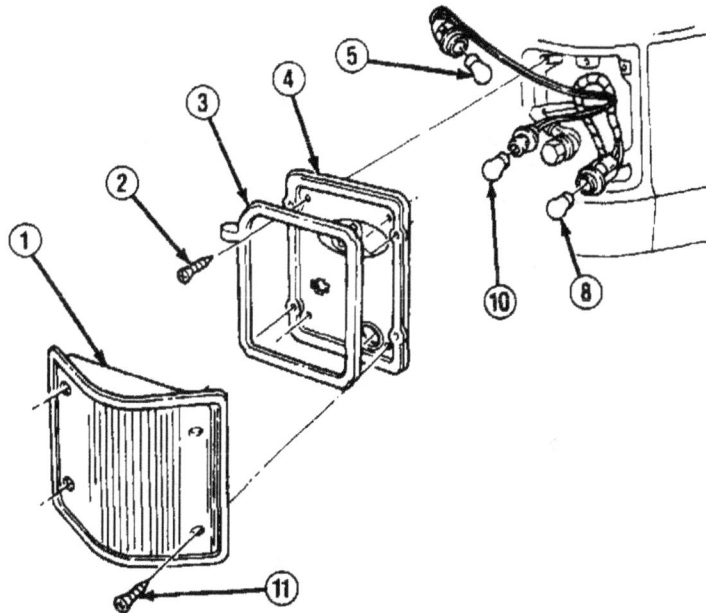

2.   Install taillight housing (4) with 4 screws (2).

3.   Install turn signal lamp (5), back-up lamp (8), and stop lamp (10) as required. Install gasket (3) and taillight lens (1) with 4 screws (11).

FOLLOW-ON TASKS:

   • Connect both battery negative cables. (See paragraph 4-38)
   • Check operation of taillight.

TA49892

4-29.   TAILLIGHT AND LAMP REPLACEMENT (M1010 AND M1031).

This task covers:	a. Removal	b. Installation

INITIAL SETUP:

Equipment Condition
 ●Both battery negative cables disconnected.
  (See paragraph 4-38)

Materials/Parts
 ●Five lockwashers
 ●Plastic ties (as required)

| a.   **REMOVAL** |

NOTE

●If removing taillight lens (9), perform step 1.

●If removing taillight lamps (11 or 12), perform steps 1 and 2.

●If removing taillight housing (8), perform steps 1-4. Remove both lamps (11 and 12) in step 2.

1.   Remove 4 screws (10) and taillight lens (9). Retain taillight lens gasket for installation.

NOTE

Tag sockets for installation.

2.   Remove stoplight lamp (12) and back-up light lamp (11) as required.

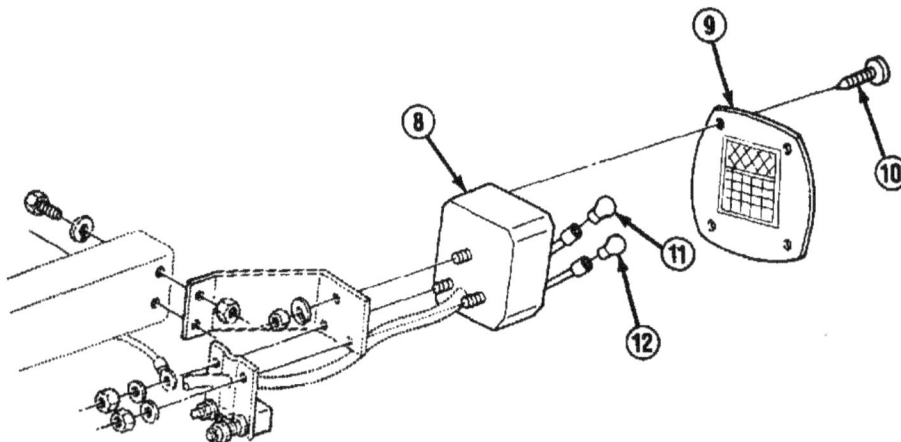

TA49893

4-29.   TAILLIGHT AND LAMP REPLACEMENT (M1010 AND M1031) (Con't).

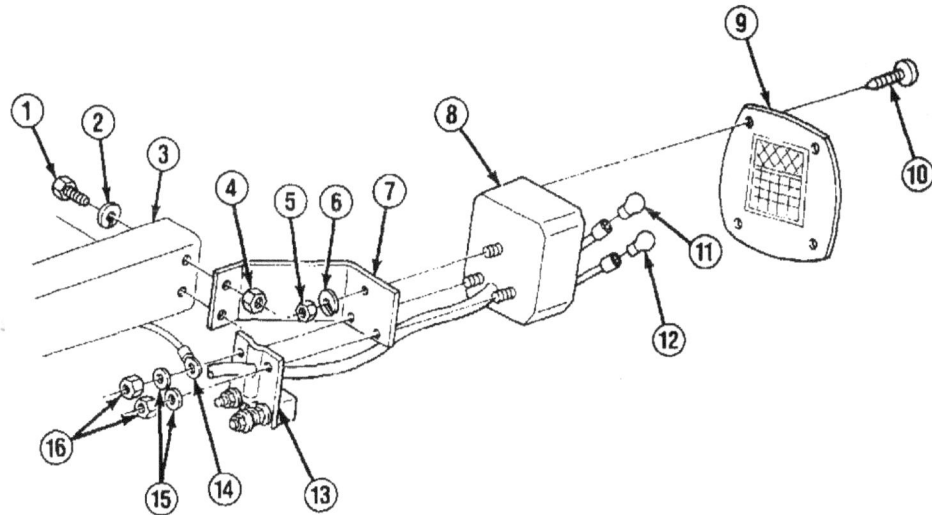

NOTE

On 1984   model trucks, ground (14)   is connected to blackout light
mounting   bolt and does not need to be   disconnected for this task.

3.   Remove 2 nuts   (16), lockwashers (15), and ground (14). Discard lockwashers.

NOTE

◆On 1984 model trucks, blackout light mounting bracket (13) is not
    attached to taillight mounting bracket (7).

◆Tag wiring harness leads for installation.

4.   Remove nut (5) and lockwasher (6). Remove and discard plastic ties if present. Unplug wiring
    harness leads from wiring harness connector. Remove taillight housing (8) from taillight
    mounting bracket (7) and blackout light mounting bracket (13). Discard lockwasher.

5.   Remove 2 nuts (4), screws (1), and lockwashers (2). Remove taillight mounting bracket (7).
    Discard lockwashers.

TA49894

4-29.   TAILLIGHT AND LAMP REPLACEMENT (M1010 AND M1031) (Con't).

| b.   INSTALLATION |

NOTE

•If installing taillight housing (8), perform steps 2-6. Install both lamps
    (11 and 12) in step 5.

•If installing taillight lamps (11 or 12), perform steps 5 and 6.

•If installing taillight lens (9), perform step 6.

1.   Install taillight mounting bracket (7) on frame rail (3) with 2 new lockwashers (2), screws (1),
      and nuts (4).

2.   Plug wiring harness leads into wiring harness connector and install taillight housing (8) on
      taillight mounting bracket (7) with new lockwasher (6) and nut (5). Install plastic ties as
      required.

NOTE

On 1984 model trucks, blackout light mounting bracket (13) is not
attached to taillight mounting bracket (7).

3.   Position blackout light mounting bracket (13) on taillight housing (8) studs.

NOTE

On 1984 model trucks, ground (14) is connected to blackout light
mounting bolt.

4.   Install ground (14), 2 new lockwashers (15), and nuts (16).

5.   Install stoplight lamp (12) and back-up light lamp (11) as required.

6.   Install taillight lens (9) gasket and taillight lens with 4 screws (10).

FOLLOW-ON TASKS:

•Connect both battery negative cables. (See paragraph 4-38)
•Check operation of taillight.

4-30. REAR BLACKOUT LIGHT REPLACEMENT (ALL EXCEPT M1010 AND M1031).

This task covers: a.   Removal   b. Installation

INITIAL SETUP:

Equipment Condition   *Materials/Parts*
  Both battery negative cables disconnected.   Plastic ties (as required)
    (See paragraph 4-38)

---

a.   REMOVAL

NOTE

If removing rear blackout light (6) only, perform steps 1-3.

1.   Remove plastic tie if installed .
     Disconnect rear blackout light (6)
     plug from wiring harness plug (3).

2.   Remove nut (1) and ground (4).

3.   Remove 2 nuts (9) and rear blackout
     light (6).

4.   Remove nut (2), screw (8), and
     mounting bracket (5).

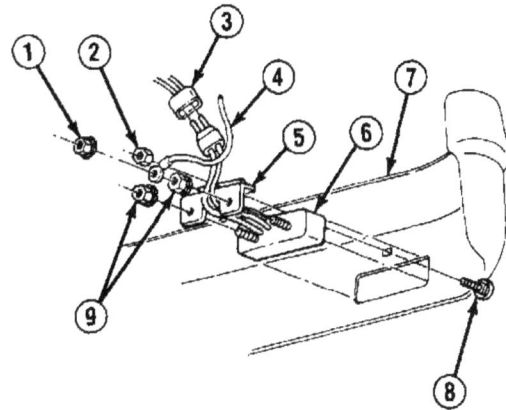

b.   INSTALLATION

1.   Install mounting bracket (5) on rear
     bumper (7) with screw (8) and nut
     (2) .

2.   Install rear blackout light (6) on
     mounting bracket (5) with 2 nuts (9).

3.   Install ground (4) with nut (1).

4.   Connect rear blackout light (6) plug
     to wiring harness plug (3). Install
     plastic tie as required.

FOLLOW-ON TASKS:

  Connect both battery negative cables. (See paragraph 4-38)
  Check operation of rear blackout light.

TA49895

4-31.   REAR BLACKOUT LIGHT REPLACEMENT (M1010 AND M1031).

This task covers: a. Removal   b. Installation

INITIAL SETUP:

Equipment Condition

Both battery negative cables disconnected.(See paragraph 4-38)

a.   REMOVAL

NOTE

On 1984 model trucks, blackout   light (2) is installed on bracket welded to
bumper.

1.   Disconnect blackout light (2) lead
      from wiring harness.

2.   Remove nut (5) and ground (4).

3.   Remove 2 nuts (1) and blackout light
      (2) .

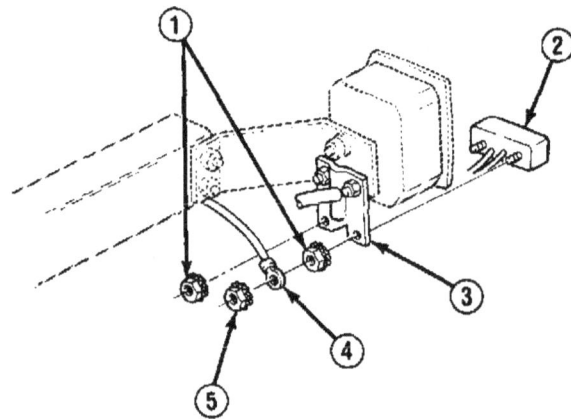

b.   INSTALLATION

NOTE

On 1984 model trucks, blackout light (2) is installed on bracket welded to
bumper.

1.   Install blackout light (2) on mounting bracket (3) with 2 nuts (1).

2.   Install ground (4) with nut (5).

3.   Connect blackout light (2) lead to wiring harness.

FOLLOW-ON TASKS:

Connect both battery negative cables. (See paragraph 4-38)
Check operation of blackout light.

TA49896

4-32.   SURGICAL LAMP REPLACEMENT (M1010).

This task covers: a. Removal   b. Installation

INITIAL SETUP:

Equipment Condition

Both battery negative cables disconnected. (See paragraph 4-38)

| a.   REMOVAL |

1.   Remove lens cover (4) by carefully pulling retaining flanges out of fixture (1) tracks, 1 side at a time.

NOTE

Fluorescent tube (2) is spring-loaded at rear socket (3).

2.   Push fluorescent tube (2) against rear socket (3) to free fluorescent tube from front fixture socket, and remove fluorescent tube.

| b.   INSTALLATION |

1.   Insert 1 end of fluorescent tube (2) into rear socket (3). While pushing fluorescent tube against rear socket, guide fluorescent tube contacts into front fixture socket. Ensure that fluorescent tube is securely in place before releasing.

2.   Install lens cover (4) by carefully pushing retaining flanges into fixture (1) tracks, 1 side at a time.

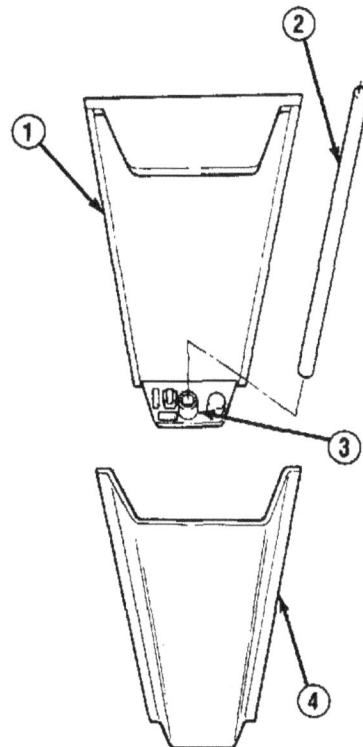

FOLLOW-ON TASKS:

Connect both battery negative cables. (See paragraph 4-38)
Check operation of surgical light.

TA49897

4-33.   BLACKOUT DOMELIGHT LAMP REPLACEMENT (M1010).

This task covers: a. Removal   b. Installation

INITIAL SETUP:

Equipment Condition

   ●Both battery negative cables disconnected, (See paragraph 4-38)

| a.   REMOVAL. |

1.   Remove retaining ring (4) and lens
      (3).

2.   Remove lamp (2)   from housing (1).

| b.   INSTALLATION |

1.   Install lamp (2) in housing (1).

2.   Position lens (3) in housing (1) and
      install with retaining ring (4).

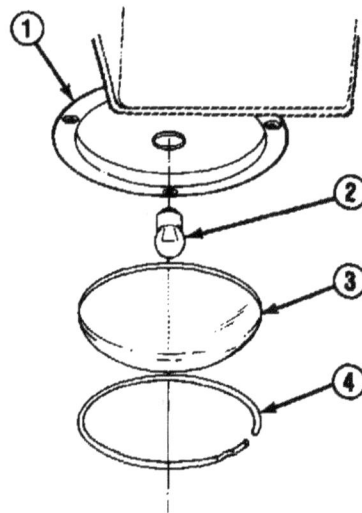

FOLLOW-ON TASKS:

   ●Connect both battery negative cables. (See paragraph 4-38)
   ●Check operation of blackout domelight.

TA49898

4-34. FLOODLIGHT AND LAMP REPLACEMENT (M1010).

This task covers: a. Removal   b. Installation

INITIAL SETUP:

Equipment Condition

● Both battery negative cables disconnected.
   (See paragraph 4-38)

Materials/Parts

● One lockwasher

| a. | **REMOVAL** |

NOTE

● On 1984 model trucks, leads are attached to floodlight housing (3) by rivets, and to floodlight lamp (1) by screws.

● If removing floodlight lamp (1), perform step 1.

● If removing floodlight assembly, perform steps 2 and 3.

● Tag leads for installation.

1. Pry floodlight lamp (1) away from floodlight housing (3). Disconnect leads (2) from floodlight lamp and remove floodlight lamp.

2. Remove nut (8), lockwasher (6), and bolt (4).   Disconnect electrical plug from ambulance
    body connector. Remove floodlight housing (3).

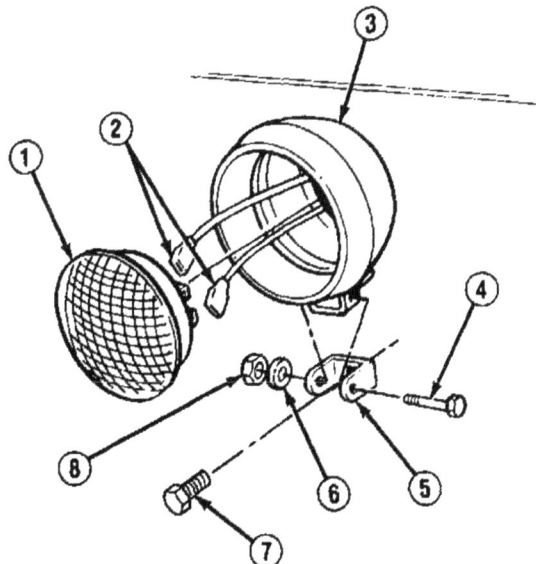

TA49899

4-34. FLOODLIGHT AND LAMP REPLACEMENT (M1010) (Con't).

NOTE

Tag leads for installation.

3. From back of floodlight housing (3), press retainer clip together and remove 2 leads (2) as required. Remove bolt (7) and mounting bracket (5) as required.

| b. INSTALLATION |

NOTE

If installing floodlight lamp (1), perform step 3.

If installing floodlight assembly, perform steps 1 and 2.

1. Install mounting bracket (5) with bolt (7) if removed. From back of floodlight housing (3), press retainer clip together and install 2 leads (2) if removed.

2. Position floodlight housing (3) on mounting bracket (5). Connect electrical plug to ambulance body connector. Install floodlight housing with bolt (4), new lockwasher (6), and nut (8).

3. Connect leads (2) to floodlight lamp (1). Install floodlight lamp in floodlight housing (3).

FOLLOW-ON TASKS:

Connect both battery negative cables. (See paragraph 4-38)
Check operation of floodlight.

4-35. INTERIOR FOCUS LIGHT, LAMP, AND SWITCH REPLACEMENT (M1010).

This task covers: a. Removal b. Installation

INITIAL SETUP:

Equipment Condition
• Both battery negative cables disconnected.
(See paragraph 4-38)

Materials/Parts
• Two rivets

---

a.   REMOVAL

NOTE

• If removing focus light lamp (3), perform step 1.

• If removing focus light assembly, perform step 2.

• If removing switch (4.1), perform steps 1, 3, and 4.

1. Remove 4 screws (7) on switch plate (2) and remove focus light housing (4). Remove focus light lamp (3).

2. Disconnect lead (1) from ambulance body connector. Loosen setscrew (6) and remove switch plate (2) from mounting base (5).

3. Disconnect orange and white terminal wires from switch (4.1).

4. Drill out 2 rivets (8) and remove switch (4.1). Discard rivets.

b.   INSTALLATION

NOTE

• If installing   switch, perform steps 1, 2, and 4.

• If installing   focus light assembly, perform step 3.

• If installing   focus light lamp (3), perform step 4.

1. Install switch (4.1) with 2 new   rivets (8).

2. Connect white wire to center terminal and orange wire to right terminal of switch (4.1).

3. Install switch plate (2) onto mounting base (5) and tighten setscrew (6). Connect lead (1) to ambulance body connector.

4. Install focus light lamp (3). Install focus light housing (4) on switch plate (2) with 4 screws (7).

FOLLOW-ON TASKS:

• Connect both battery negative cables. (See paragraph 4-38)
• Check operation of focus light.

TA701833

4-36. SPOTLIGHT AND LAMP REPLACEMENT (M1010).

This task covers: a. Removal   b.   Installation

INITIAL SETUP:

Equipment Condition

Both battery negative cables disconnected. (See paragraph 4-38)

| a.   **REMOVAL** |

NOTE

If removing spotlight lamp (1),   perform step 1.

If removing spotlight assembly,   perform steps 2-4.

Tag leads for installation.

1.   Remove screw (8). Pull spotlight lamp (1) and bracket (9) assembly out and disconnect spotlight housing (3) leads. Remove 4 clips (2) holding spotlight lamp to bracket. Remove spotlight lamp.

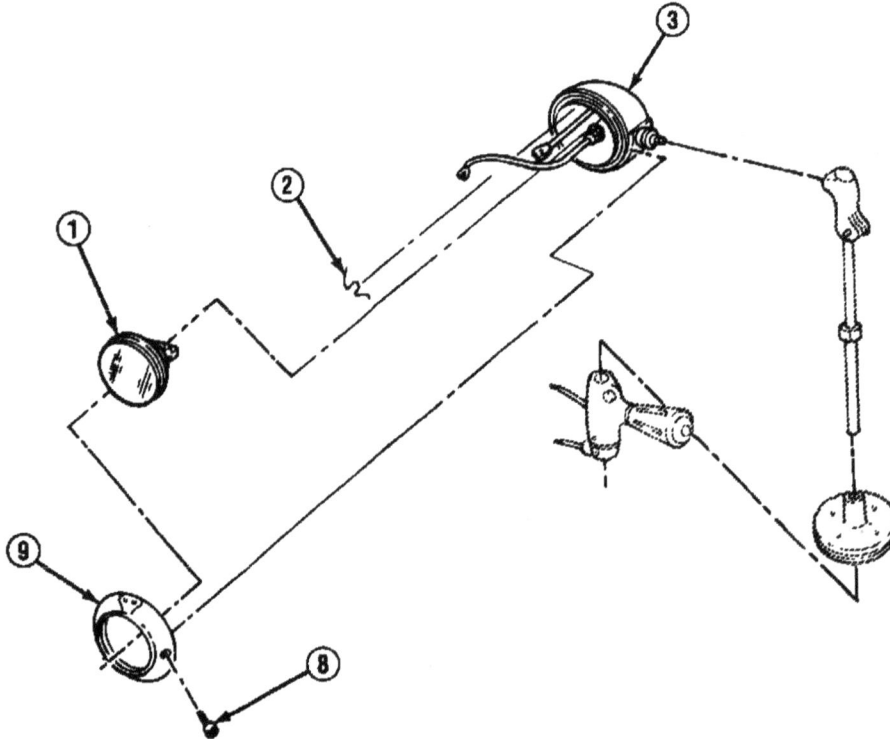

TA49901

4-36. SPOTLIGHT AND LAMP REPLACEMENT (M1010) (Con't).

NOTE

Tag lead for installation.

2. Disconnect lead from handle (6) to roof.

3. Loosen bolt (7) and remove handle (6).

NOTE

Retain mounting hardware for installation.

4. Remove spotlight assembly (11) and spacer (15). Unscrew spotlight housing (3) from shaft (4) as required. Remove 4 nuts (14) , washers (13), and bolts (10) to remove spotlight bracket (5) and gasket (12) as required.

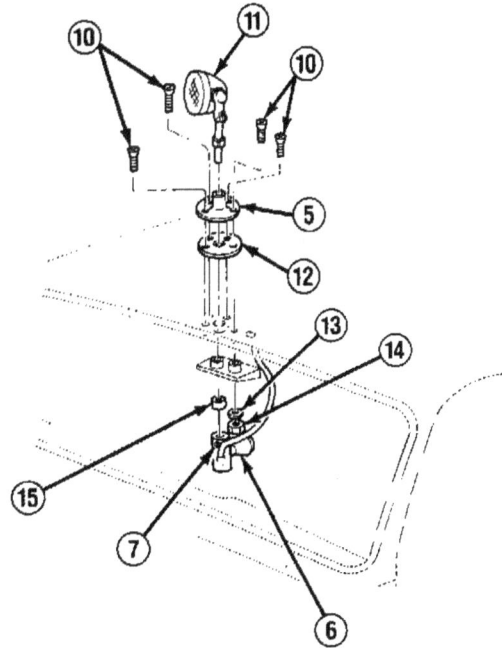

---

b. INSTALLATION

NOTE

◄f installing spotlight assembly (11), perform steps 1-3.

◄f installing spotlight lamp (1), perform step 4.

1. Install gasket (12) and spotlight bracket (5) on roof with 4 bolts (10), washers (13), and nuts (14). Screw spotlight housing (3) onto shaft (4). Place spotlight assembly (11) through spotlight bracket and gasket.

2. Position spacer (15) and handle (6) on shaft (4). Tighten bolt (7) to install handle.

3. Connect lead from handle (6) to roof.

4. Install spotlight lamp (1) on bracket (9), with 4 clips (2). Connect spotlight housing (3) leads to spotlight lamp. Install spotlight lamp and bracket assembly in spotlight housing with screw (8).

TA49902

4-36. SPOTLIGHT AND LAMP REPLACEMENT (M1010) (Con't).

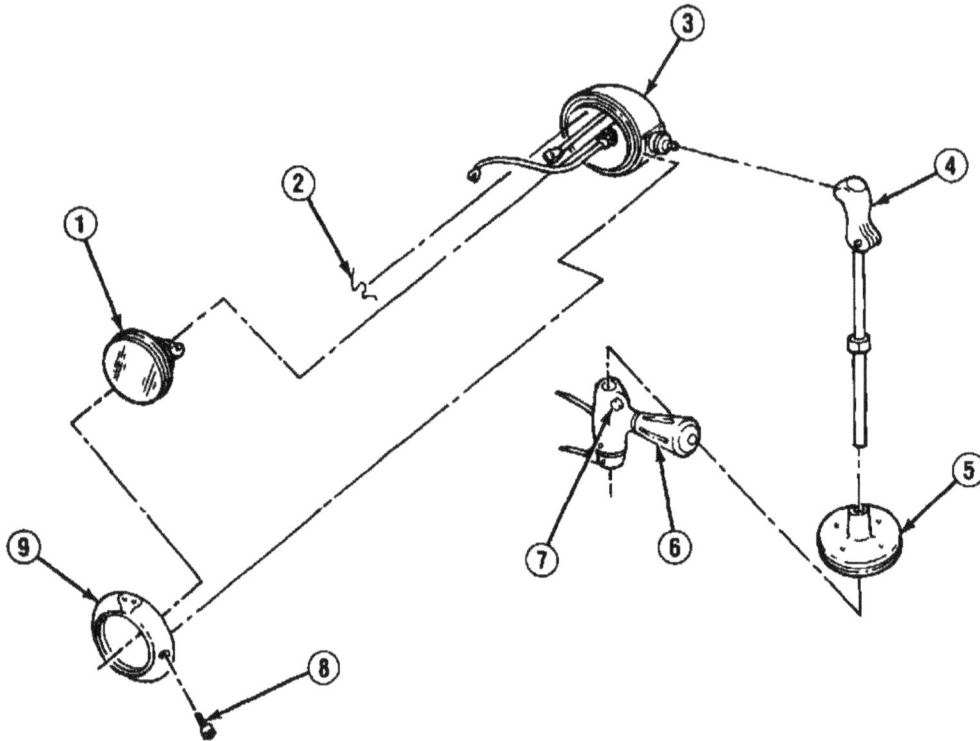

FOLLOW-ON TASKS:

Connect both battery negative cables. (See paragraph 4-38)
Check operation of spotlight.

TA49903

Section V. BATTERY SYSTEM MAINTENANCE

4-37.   BATTERY SYSTEM MAINTENANCE INDEX.

4-38.   BATTERY CABLE MAINTENANCE.

This task covers:

a. Cable Disconnection   d. Cable Installation
b. Inspection and Cleaning   e. Cable Connection
c. Cable Removal

INITIAL SETUP:

Equipment Condition

• Accessory wiring terminal board covers removed. (See paragraph 4-46)

Manual References

• TM 9-6140-200-14

Materials/Parts

• Two locknuts
• Two lockwashers

General Safety Instructions

• Always wear goggles and rubber gloves.
• DO NOT perform battery system maintenance while smoking or near fire, flames, or sparks.
• Remove all jewelry.
• Rotate covers to underside of clamp as each cable is disconnected.

WARNING

- Battery acid (electrolyte) is extremely dangerous. Always wear goggles and rubber gloves when performing battery checks or inspections. Serious injury to personnel will result if battery acid contacts skin or eyes.

- DO NOT perform battery system checks or inspections while smoking or near fire, flames, or sparks. Batteries may explode, causing serious injury or death to personnel.

- Rotate covers to underside of clamps as each cable is disconnected. Remove all jewelry such as dog tags, rings, bracelets, etc. If jewelry or disconnected battery ground cable contacts battery terminal, a direct short will result. Failure to follow proper disconnection procedures will result in serious injury or   death to personnel,   or equipment damage.

| a.   CABLE DISCONNECTION |

NOTE

- If   truck is not equipped with winterization kits, perform steps 2-5.

- If   disconnecting negative cables, perform steps 2 and 3.

- If   disconnecting positive cables, perform steps 2-5.

1.   Loosen stud (27) and remove battery box cover (26).

2.   Slide back cover (23) from clamp (22) of negative cable (3). Loosen nut (21) and disconnect negative cable from front battery (4) negative (-) terminal. Rotate cover to underside of clamp.

4-38. BATTERY CABLE MAINTENANCE (Con't).

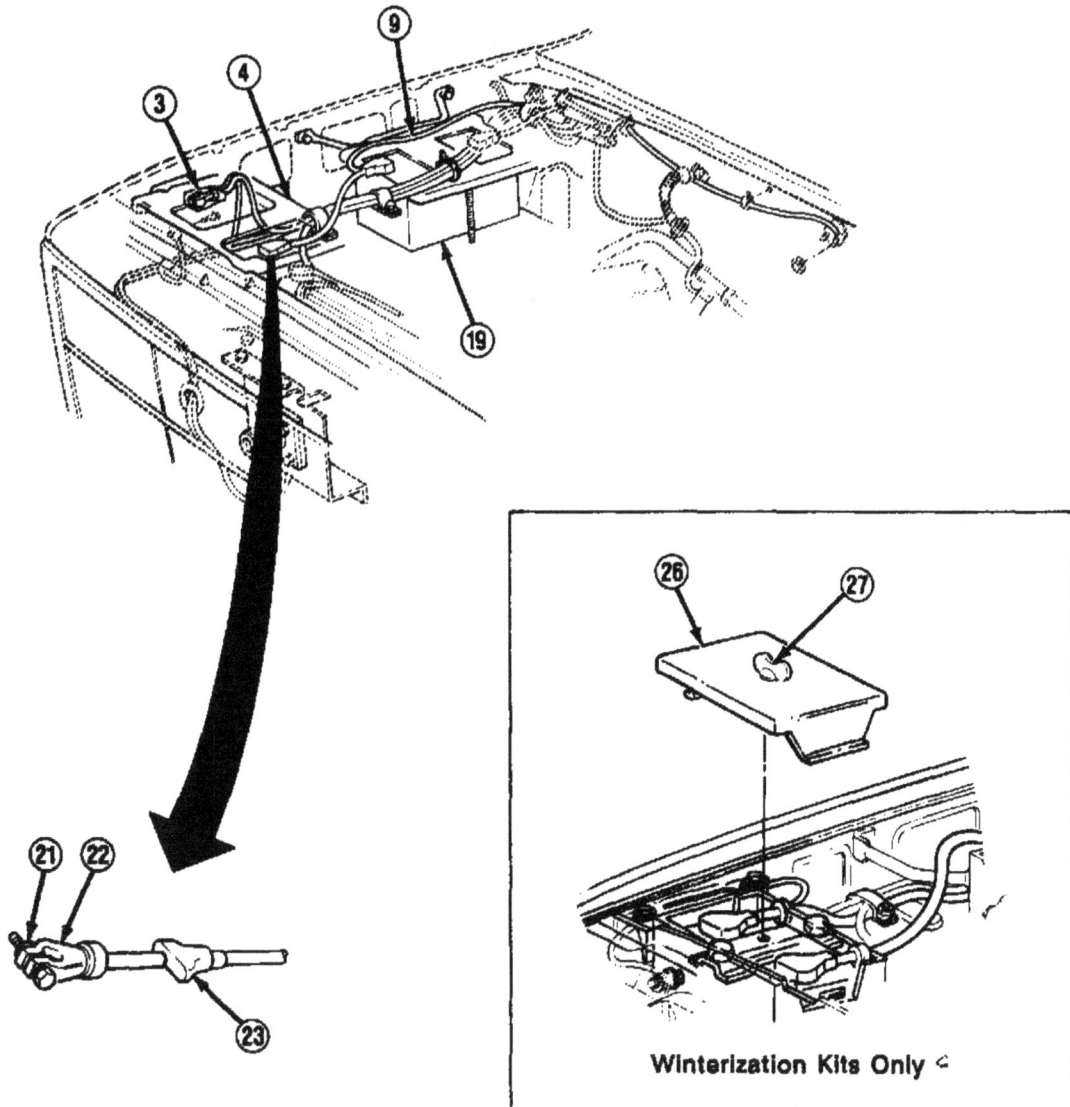

Winterization Kits Only

3. Slide back cover (23) from clamp (22) of connector cable (9) at rear battery (19) negative (-) terminal. Loosen nut (21) and disconnect connector cable. Rotate cover to underside of clamp.

4. Slide back cover (23) from clamp (22) of connector cable (9). Loosen nut (21) and disconnect connector cable from front battery (4) positive (+) terminal. Rotate cover to underside of clamp.

TA49904

4-38. BATTERY CABLE MAINTENANCE (Con't).

---

5. Slide back cover (23) from clamp (22) of positive cable (11). Loosen nut (21) and disconnect positive cable from rear battery (19) positive (+) terminal. Rotate cover to underside of clamp.

6. Remove grommets (28) from any disconnected battery cable.

b.	INSPECTION AND CLEANING

1. See TM 9-6140-200-14.

c.	CABLE REMOVAL

NOTE

• If removing negative cable (3), perform steps 1-5.

• If removing connector cable (9), perform steps 3, 6, and 7.

• If removing positive cable (11), perform step 9.

• Battery cables may be pulled through clips (5 and 13) and retainers (10 and 16), without removing clips or retainers. Remove as required.

1. Remove front battery hold-down bracket. (See paragraph 4-39)

2. Remove bolt (2), starwasher, and washer (1). Remove battery ground (25) and frame ground lead, and position clear of battery terminals.

3. Remove bolt (12) and clip (13) from negative cable (3), connector cable (9), and 2 slave receptacle cables (24). Remove retaining nut (14) as required.

NOTE

Tag terminal stud for installation.

4. Remove nut and lockwasher from lower accessory wiring terminal board (15) stud and disconnect negative cable (3). Discard lockwasher.

5. Remove retainer (10) from negative cable (3), starter lead (20), and 2 slave receptacle cables (24). Remove 2 locknuts (6), clips (5), screws (8), and washers (7) from negative cable, starter lead, and slave receptacle cables. Remove negative cable. Discard locknuts.

NOTE

Tag leads for installation.

6. Remove nuts (18), leads, and connector cable (9) from engine   wiring harness block (17).

7. Remove 3 retainers (16) from connector cable (9) as required.   Remove connector cable.

8. Remove nut and lockwasher from upper accessory wiring terminal board (15) stud and disconnect positive cable (11). Remove positive cable. Discard lockwasher.

4-38. BATTERY CABLE MAINTENANCE (Con't).

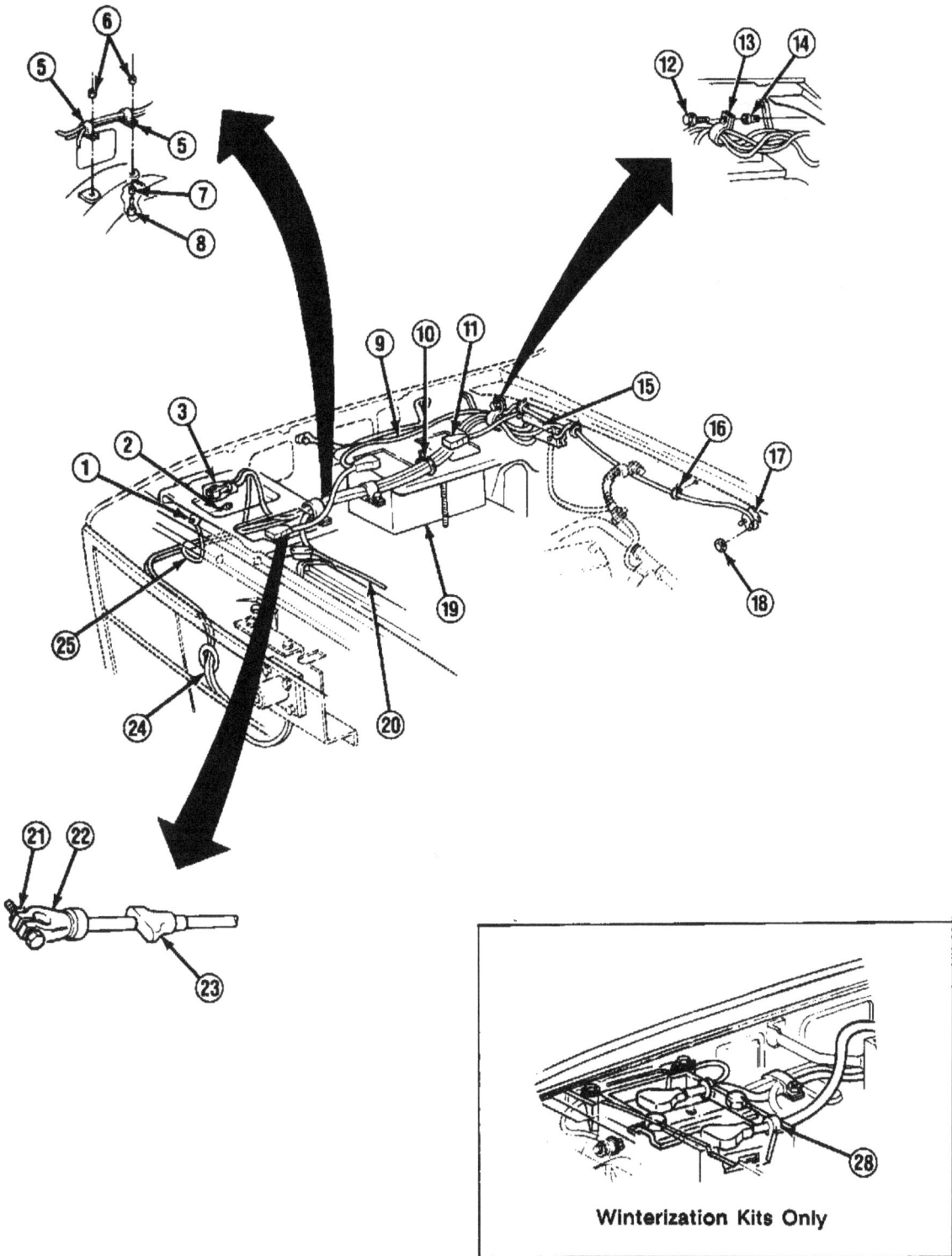

Winterization Kits Only

TA49905

4-38.   BATTERY CABLE MAINTENANCE (Con't).

---

d.   CABLE INSTALLATION

NOTE

◀f installing   positive cable (11), perform step 1.

◀f installing   connector cable (9), perform steps 2 and 3.

◀f installing   negative cable (3), perform steps 4-8.

1.   Install positive cable (11) on upper accessory wiring terminal board (15) stud with new lockwasher and nut.

2.   Install 3 retainers (16) on connector cable (9) if removed.

NOTE

DO NOT connect connector cable (9) to front battery (4)   terminal if hold-down bracket was removed.

3.   Install connector cable (9) and leads on engine wiring harness block   (17) with nuts (18).

4.   Install 2 clips (5) on negative cable (3), starter lead (20), and slave   receptacle cables (24) with two screws (8), washers (7), and new locknuts (6) if removed.   Install retainer (10) on negative cable, starter lead, and slave receptacle cables if removed.

5.   Install negative cable (3) on lower accessory wiring terminal board (15) stud with new lockwasher and nut.

6.   Install retaining nut (14) if removed. Install clip (13) on connector cable (9), negative cable (3), and slave receptacle cables (24). Install clip with bolt (12) if removed.

7.   Install starwasher, frame ground lead, and battery ground (25) with washer (1) and bolt (2).

8.   Install front battery hold-down bracket. (See paragraph 4-39)

e.   CABLE CONNECTION

NOTE

◀f truck is not equipped with winterization kits, perform steps 2-5.

◀f installing positive cables, perform steps 2-5.

◀f installing negative cables, perform steps 4 and 5.

1.   Install grommets (28) on any disconnected battery cable. Fit grommets into battery box notches as required.

2.   Install positive cable (11) clamp (22) on rear battery (19) positive (+) terminal. Tighten nut (21) and slide cover (23) over clamp.

3.   Install connector cable (9) clamp (22) on front battery (4) positive (+) terminal. Tighten nut (21) and slide cover (23) over clamp.

4-38.   BATTERY CABLE MAINTENANCE (Con't).

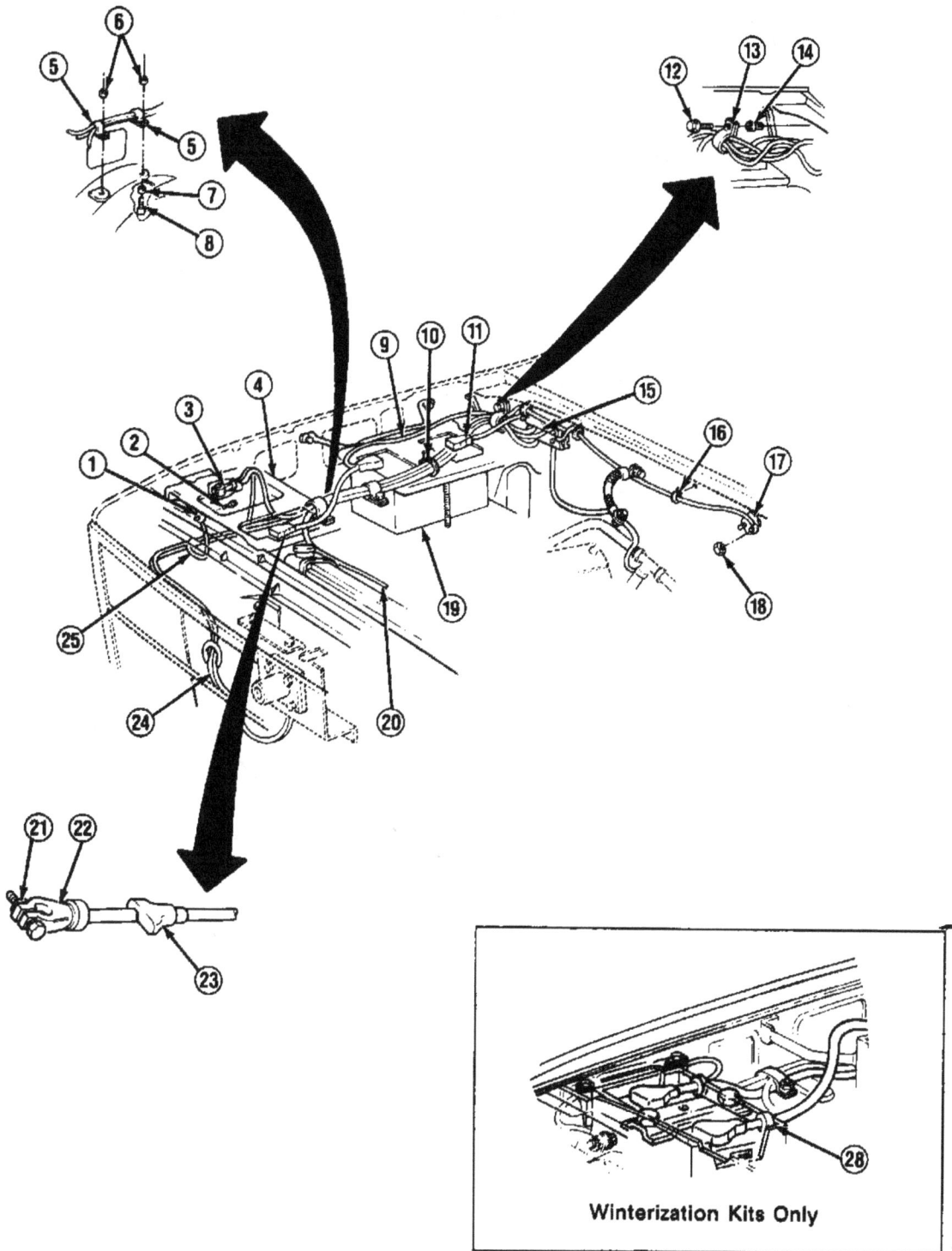

TA49906

Winterization Kits Only

4-38. BATTERY CABLE MAINTENANCE (Con't).

4. Install connector cable (9) clamp (22) on rear battery (19) negative (-) terminal. Tighten nut (21) and slide cover (23) over clamp.

5. Install negative cable (3) clamp (22) on front battery (4) negative (-) terminal. Tighten nut (21) and slide cover (23) over clamp.

6. Install battery box cover (26) and tighten stud (27).

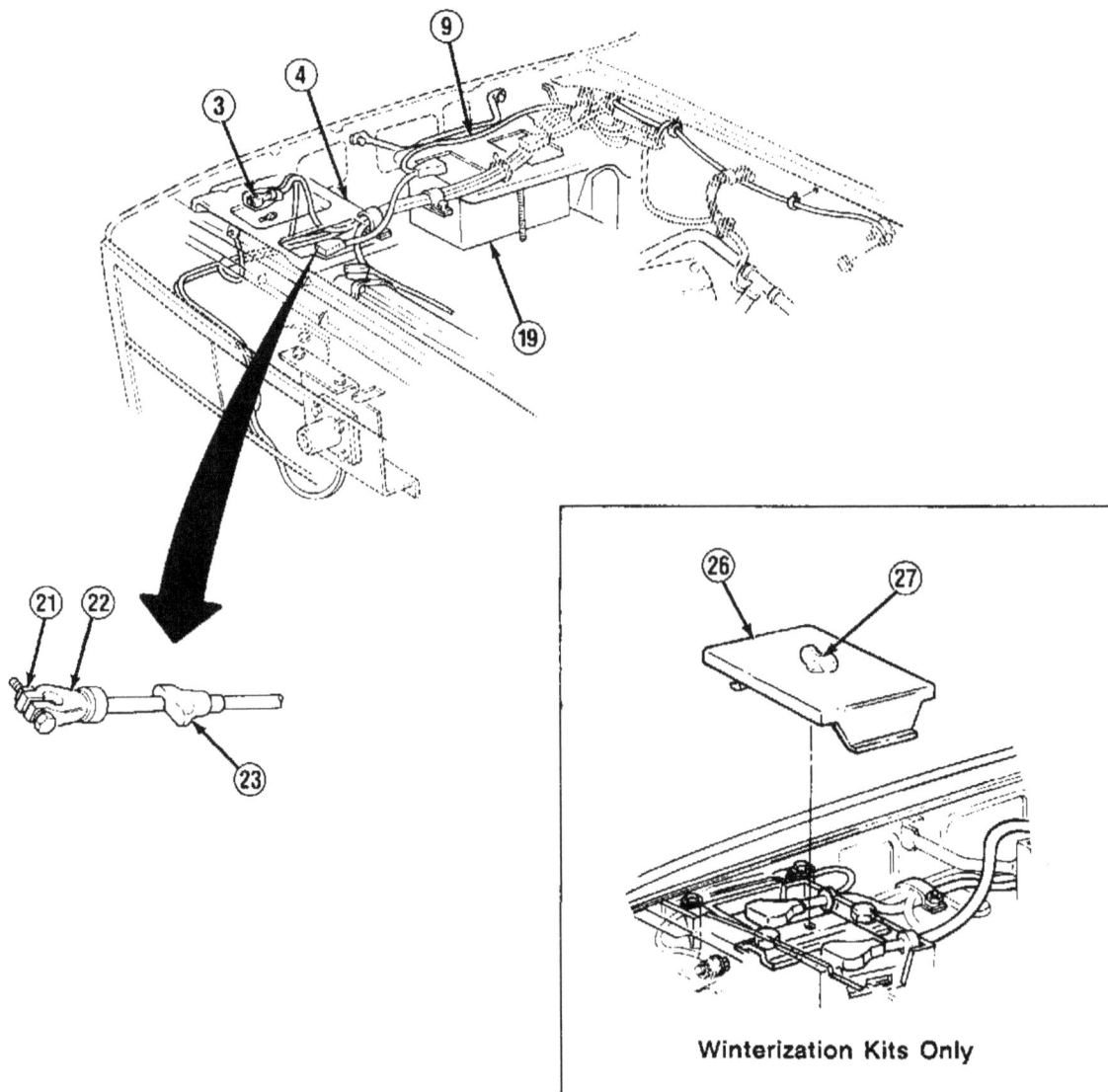

Winterization Kits Only

FOLLOW-ON TASKS:

Install accessory wiring terminal board covers. (See paragraph 4-46)

TA49907

4-39. BATTERY AND RELATED COMPONENTS MAINTENANCE.

This task covers:

a. Inspection and Servicing   c. Installation
b. Removal

INITIAL SETUP:

Equipment Condition

●Battery cables disconnected.
(See paragraph 4-38)

Tools/Test Equipment

●Torque wrench

General Safety Instructions

●Always wear goggles and rubber gloves.
●DO NOT perform battery system maintenance while smoking or near fire, flames, or sparks.
●Remove all jewelry.

Materials/Parts

●Grease (Item 26, Appendix C)
●Chalk (Item 9, Appendix C)

Manual References

●TM 9-6140-200-14

WARNING

- Battery acid (electrolyte) is extremely dangerous. Always wear goggles and rubber gloves when performing battery checks or inspections. Serious injury to personnel will result if battery acid contacts skin or eyes.

- DO NOT perform battery system checks or inspections while smoking or near fire, flames, or sparks. Batteries may explode, causing serious injury or death to personnel.

- Remove all jewelry such as dog tags, rings, bracelets, etc. If jewelry or disconnected battery ground cable contacts battery terminal, a direct short will result, causing serious injury or death to personnel.

---

a. INSPECTION AND SERVICING

NOTE

●If truck is not equipped   with winterization kits, perform steps 2-9.

●If truck is equipped with   maintenance free batteries, perform steps 1-4
  and steps 6-9.

●If truck is equipped with   military-type 6TN batteries, perform steps 6-9.

4-39.   BATTERY AND RELATED COMPONENTS MAINTENANCE (Con't).

1.   Remove 2 nuts (2) and battery
     retainer (1) from hook bolts (4).

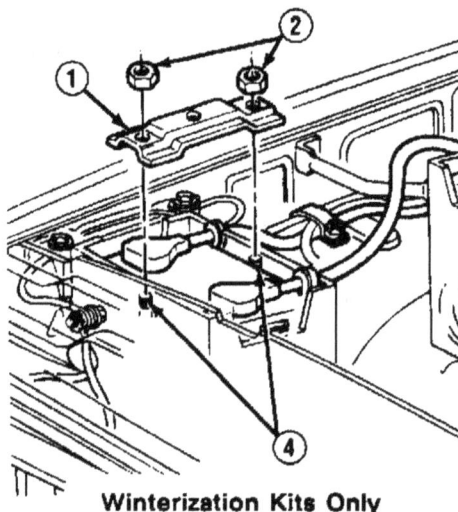

Winterization Kits Only

2.   Check charge indicators (5) on top of
     batteries.

3.   if indicator (5) shows a green dot,
     battery is okay.

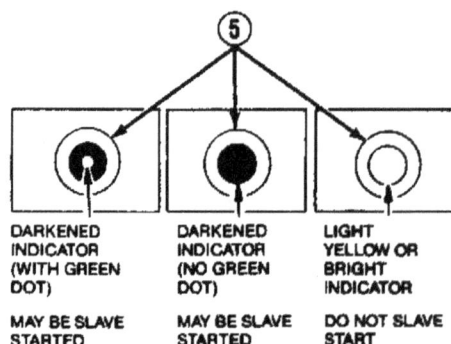

WARNING

DO NOT charge, test, or slave start battery when built-in hydrometer
shows clear or light yellow. An explosion may occur causing serious injury
or death to personnel.

4.   If indicator (5) appears dark with no green dot, recharge and test battery.   (See
     TM 9-6140-200-14)

5.   If indicator (5) shows a clear or light yellow dot, replace battery.

6.   Remove battery caps and check electrolyte level. If level is low, notify your supervisor.

7.   Check specific gravity. (See TM 9-6140-200-14)

8.   Visually check for corrosion and damage.

9.   If corroded, clean battery posts and cable connections with wire brush and soda solution, and
     lightly coat battery posts with grease. If damaged, replace as required.

TA49908

4-39. BATTERY AND RELATED COMPONENTS MAINTENANCE (Con't).

b. REMOVAL

NOTE

- Batteries in trucks with winterization kits are removed from battery box instead of battery tray.

- Battery supports and trays are factory-installed with hex nuts and body studs instead of bolts (7) and mounting nuts (8). Replace hex nuts and body studs with bolts and mounting nuts if damaged.

- If removing front battery, perform step 1.

- If removing front battery tray and supports, perform steps 1-3.

- If removing rear battery, perform step 4.

- If removing rear battery tray and supports, perform steps 4-6.

- If replacing maintenance-free battery with 6TN battery, support rods must be repositioned to outboard threaded holes.

1. Remove 2 bolts (7) and nuts (8). Remove front battery hold-down bracket (9). Remove front battery.

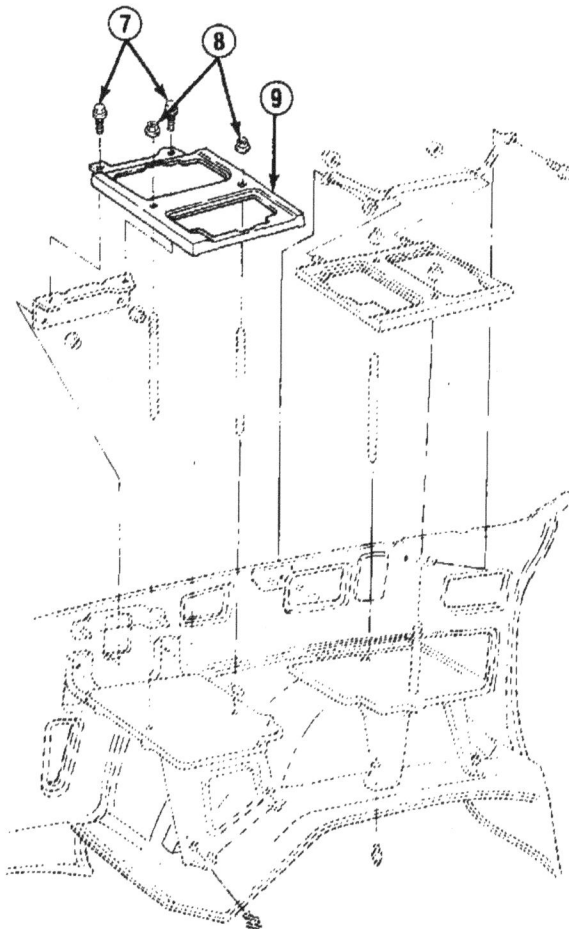

TA49909

4-39. BATTERY AND RELATED COMPONENTS MAINTENANCE (Con't).

2. Remove 2 support rods (24). Remove 2 nuts (25), support (6), and reinforcement bracket (23) as required.

3. Remove 2 nuts (21), 4 bolts (20), and front battery tray and support (22).

4. Remove 3 nuts (13), bolt (12), and rear battery hold-down bracket (14) and support (11) assembly. Remove 2 nuts (10), and separate rear battery hold-down bracket and support.

5. Remove rear battery. Remove 2 support rods (15). Remove mounting nut (16) as required.

6. Remove 2 nuts (18), 4 bolts (19), and rear battery tray and support (17).

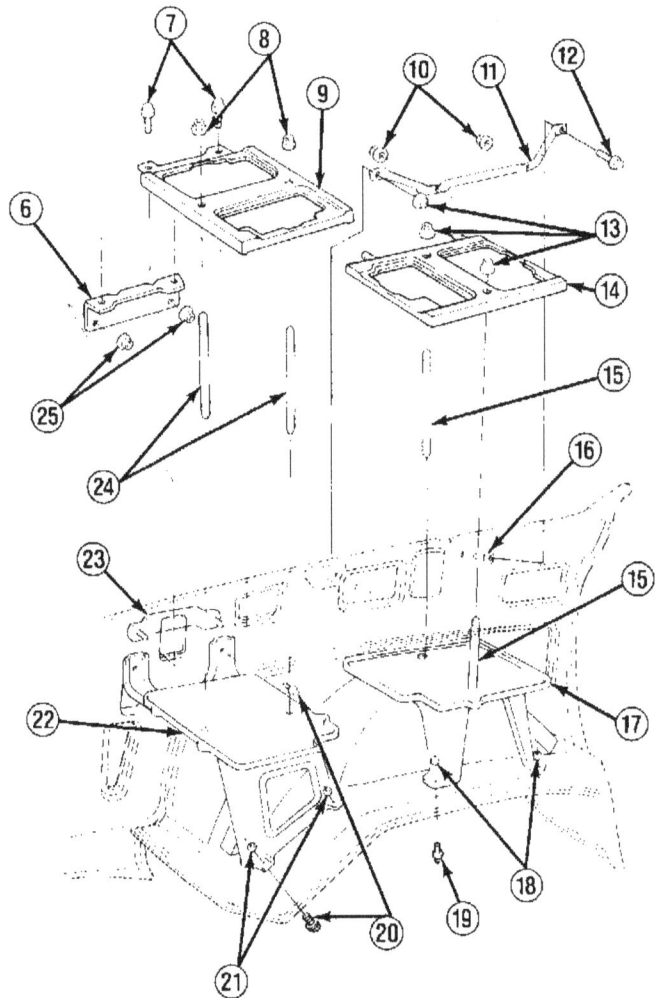

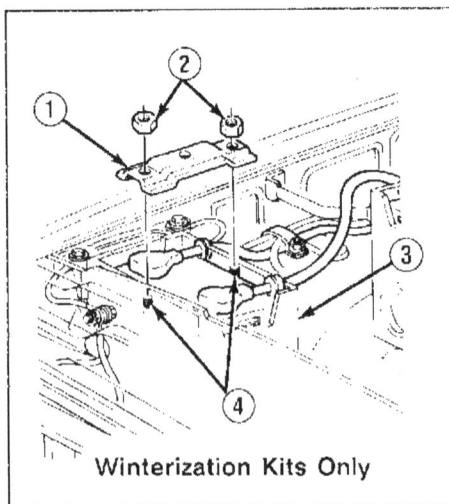

Winterization Kits Only

TA49910

4-39. BATTERY AND RELATED COMPONENTS MAINTENANCE (Con't).

| c. | INSTALLATION |

NOTE

- Batteries in trucks with winterization kits are installed in battery box (3) instead of battery tray. If truck is not equipped with winterization kits, perform steps 1-6.

- If installing rear battery tray and supports (11 and 17), perform steps 1 and 2.

- If installing rear battery, perform steps 1-3.

- If installing front battery tray and supports (6 and 22), perform steps 4-6.

- If installing front battery, perform step 6.

1. Install rear battery tray and support (17) with 4 bolts (19) and 2 nuts (18).

NOTE

If replacing maintenance-free battery with   6TN battery, support rods must
be installed in outboard threaded holes.

2. Install mounting nut (16) if removed. Install short   threaded end of 2 support rods (15) on rear
battery tray and support (17).

NOTE

Negative (-) terminal should face toward front of truck.

3. Position rear battery on rear battery tray and support (17) on battery box (3). Install support (11) on rear battery hold-down bracket (14) with 2 nuts (10). Install rear battery hold-down bracket and support (11) assembly with 3 nuts (13) and bolt (12).

4. Install front battery tray and support (22) with 4 bolts (20) and 2 nuts (21).

NOTE

If replacing maintenance-free battery with 6TN battery, support rods must
be installed in outboard threaded holes.

5. Mount reinforcement bracket (23) in fender, if removed. Install support (6) on reinforcement bracket with 2 nuts (25), if removed. Install short threaded end of 2 support rods (24) on front battery tray and support (22).

NOTE

Negative (-) terminal should face toward right side of truck.

6. Position front battery on front battery tray and support (22) or battery box (3). Install front battery hold-down bracket (9) with 2 nuts (8) and bolts (7).

7. Install battery retainer (1) on hook bolts (4) with 2 nuts (2). Tighten nuts to 40-60 lb.-in. (5-7 N•m).

FOLLOW-ON TASKS:

Connect battery cables. (See paragraph 4-38)

4-40. SLAVE RECEPTACLE REPLACEMENT.

This task covers: a. Removal   b. Installation

INITIAL SETUP:

Equipment Condition
- Both battery negative cables disconnected.
  (See paragraph 4-38)
- Radiator grille removed. (See paragraph 10-2)
- Retainers and clips removed from cables,
  as required, if replacing cables.
  (See paragraph 4-38)

Materials/Parts
- Two lockwashers

NOTE

- **If removing slave receptacle cables (6 and 20), perform steps 1 and 2.**

- **If removing slave receptacle (17), perform steps 2 and 4-8.**

- **Tag terminal studs and both ends of slave receptacle cables (6 and 20) for installation.**

1. Loosen nuts (4) and remove accessory wiring terminal board covers (1). Remove 2 nuts and lockwashers from accessory wiring terminal board studs (2 and 3). Disconnect positive cable (6) from stud (2). Disconnect negative cable (20) from stud (3). Discard lockwashers.

2. Remove 2 screws (13) and washers (12), and disconnect cables (6 and 20).

3. Pull slave receptacle cables (6 and 20) through slave receptacle bracket (8) and grommet (5). Replace grommet if damaged.

4. Remove 4 nuts (11) and bolts (19). Remove cover (18) from slave receptacle (17) as required.

5. Remove slave receptacle (17) and 2 spacers (10).

6. Remove 2 screws (16), screws (9), and "U" nuts (7).

7. Remove slave receptacle bracket (8). Replace grommet (15) if damaged.

8. Remove 2 mounting nuts (14) if damaged.

TA49911

4-40.   SLAVE RECEPTACLE REPLACEMENT (Con't).

b.   **INSTALLATION**

NOTE

•f installing slave receptacle (17), perform steps 1-7.

•f installing slave receptacle cables (6 and 20), perform steps 6-8.

1.   Install 2 mounting nuts (14) if removed.

2.   Install grommet (15) in slave receptacle bracket (8) if removed.

3.   Install slave receptacle bracket (8) with 2 "U" nuts (7), screws (9), and screws (16).

4.   Install cover (18) on slave receptacle (17) if removed.

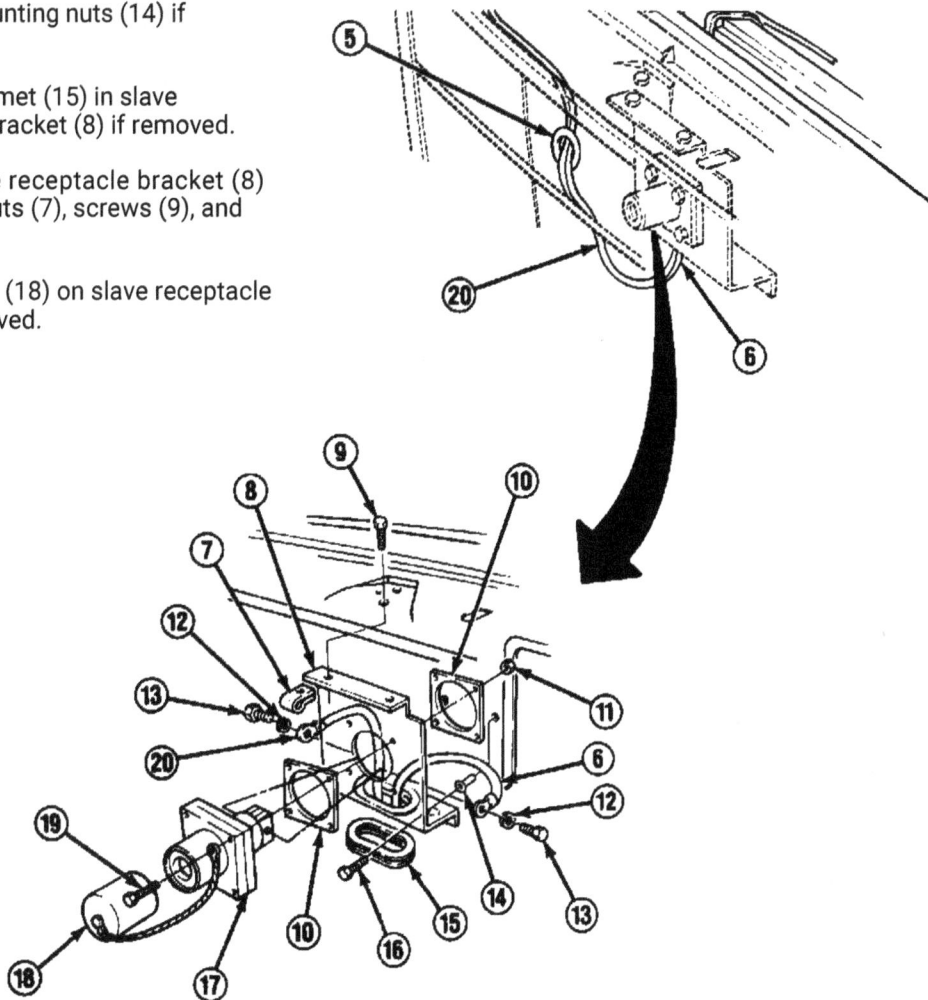

NOTE

Ensure that 1 bolt (19) is installed through slave receptacle cover (18) retainer cord.

5.   Install slave receptacle (17) and 2 spacers (10) with 4 bolts (19) and nuts (11).

TA49912

4-40. SLAVE RECEPTACLE REPLACEMENT (Con't).

6. Install grommet (5) if removed.

7. Push cables (6 and 20) through grommet (5) and slave receptacle bracket (8), and install on slave receptacle (17) with 2 washers (12) and screws (13).

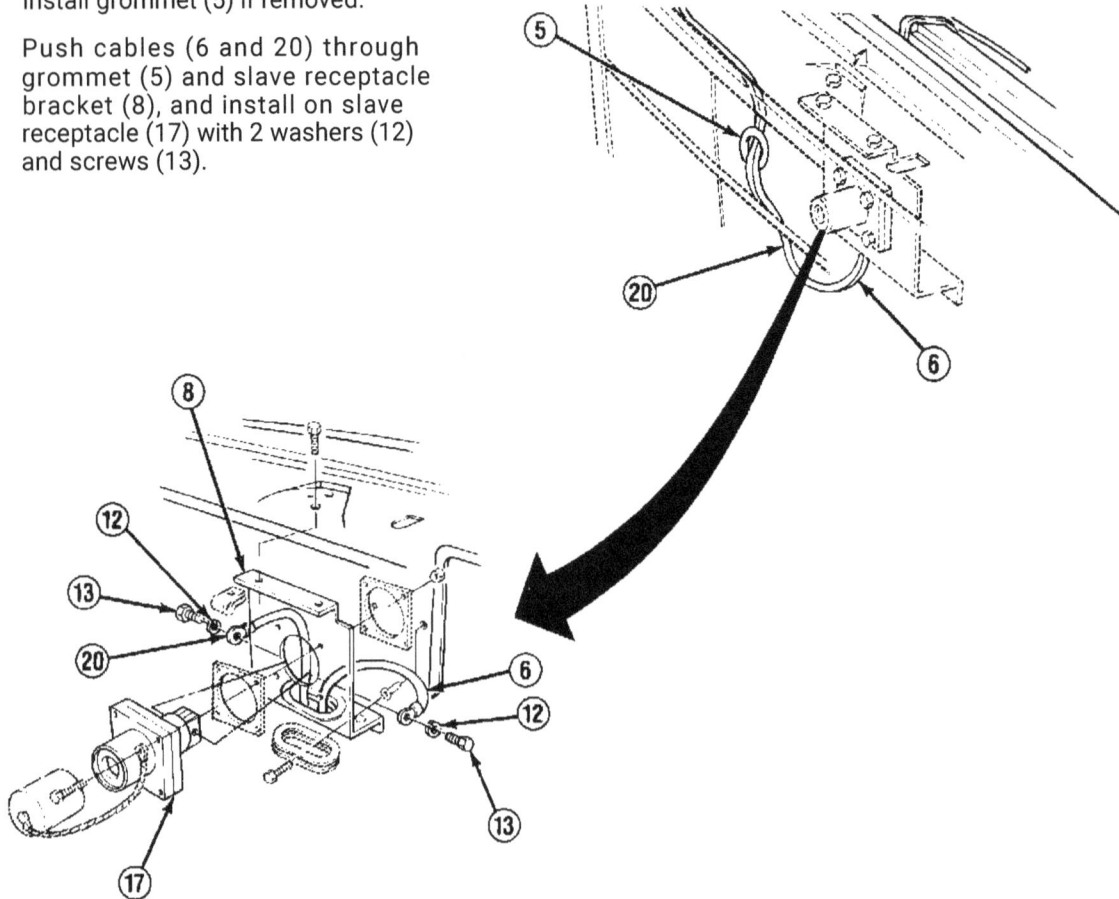

8. Connect negative cable (20) to stud (3). Connect positive cable (6) to stud (2). Install 2 new lockwashers and nuts. Install accessory wiring terminal board covers (1) and tighten nuts (4).

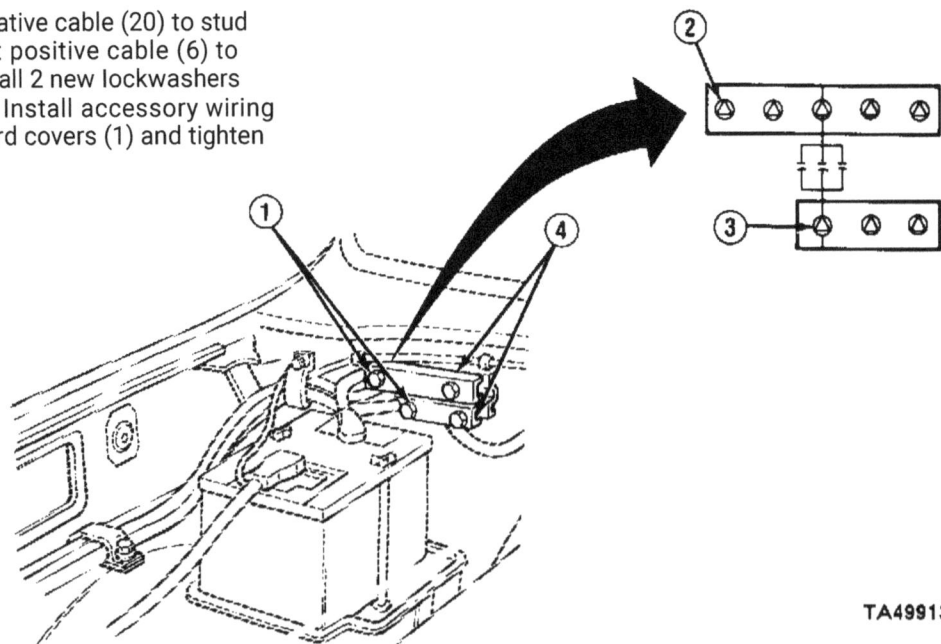

TA49913

4-40.   SLAVE RECEPTACLE REPLACEMENT (Con't).

FOLLOW-ON TASKS:

- Install retainers and clips on cables if removed. (See paragraph   4-38)
- Install radiator grille. (See paragraph 10-2)
- Connect both battery negative cables. (See paragraph 4-38)

4-41. TRAILER ELECTRICAL RECEPTACLE REPLACEMENT.

This task covers: a.   Removal   b. Installation

INITIAL SETUP:

Equipment Condition

  •Both battery negative cables disconnected. (See paragraph 4-38)

---

a.   REMOVAL

1.   Remove 4 nuts (7), washers (6), and bolts (5), and remove trailer electrical receptacle door (4). Unplug trailer electrical receptacle (1) from wiring harness (2) and remove.

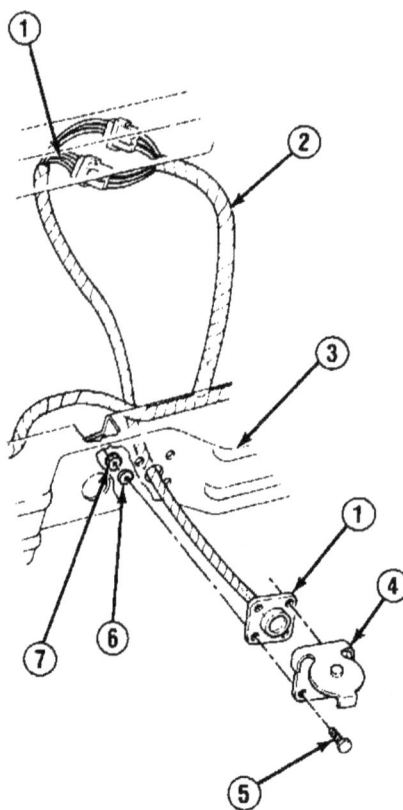

b.   INSTALLATION

1.   Place trailer electrical receptacle (1) through bumper (3) and connect to wiring harness (2). Aline trailer electrical receptacle holes with holes in bumper. Install trailer electrical receptacle door (4) and trailer electrical receptacle with 4 bolts (5), washers (6), and nuts (7).

FOLLOW-ON TASKS:

  •Connect both battery negative cables. (See paragraph 4-38)

TA49914

4-42. ENGINE WIRING HARNESS BLOCK REPLACEMENT.

This task covers: a. Removal   b. Installation

INITIAL SETUP:

Equipment Condition

Both battery negative cables disconnected. (See paragraph 4-38)

---

a. REMOVAL

NOTE

Tag leads for installation.

1. Remove nut (1), nut (2), and 4 leads
    (3). Remove 2 bolts (4
    wiring harness block (5)

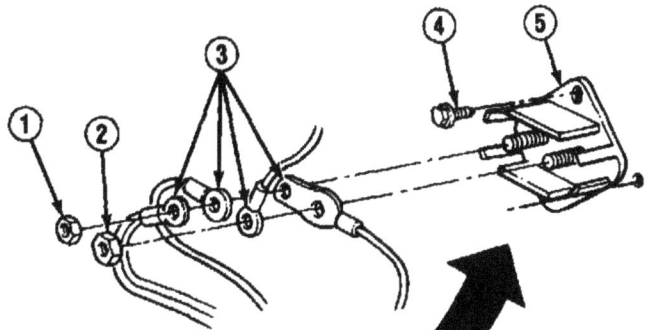

b. INSTALLATION

1. Install engine wiring barn
    with 2 bolts (4). Install
    with nut (2) and nut (1)

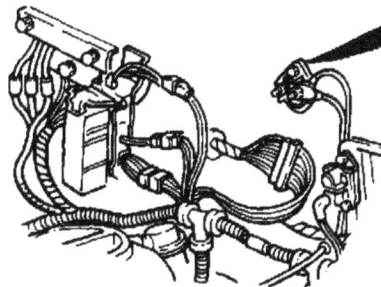

FOLLOW-ON TASKS:

Connec t both battery negative cables. (See paragraph   4-38)

Section VI. COMMUNICATIONS SYSTEM MAINTENANCE

4-43.   COMMUNICATIONS SYSTEM MAINTENANCE INDEX.

4-44.   RESISTOR AND BRACKET REPLACEMENT.

This task covers: a. Removal   b. Installation

INITIAL SETUP:

Equipment Condition   *Materials/Parts*
   ●Both battery negative cables disconnected.   ●Three lockwashers
      (See paragraph 4-38)
   ●Air cleaner removed. (See paragraph 3-9)

| a.   REMOVAL |

NOTE

If removing resistors (7), perform steps 4-6.

1.   Loosen 2 nuts (16) and remove accessory wiring terminal board cover (1).

NOTE

Tag both ends of leads (5 and 9) and terminal for installation.

2.   Remove nut (2) and starwasher (3), and disconnect lead (5) from accessory wiring terminal board (4).

3.   Remove nut and washer, and disconnect lead (9) from glow plug relay (13).

4.   Remove 3 bolts (15) and lockwashers (14), and remove bracket and resistor assembly (6).

5.   Remove 4 nuts (10) and bolts (12), and separate resistor (7) assembly from bracket (6).

6.   Remove 2 nuts (8) and screws (11), and separate 2 resistors (7) from lead (5) and lead (9).

| b.   INSTALLATION |

1.   Assemble 2 resistors (7), lead (5), and lead (9) with 2 screws (11) and nuts (8).

2.   Attach resistor (7) assembly to bracket (6) with 4 bolts (12) and nuts (10).

3.   Install bracket and resistor assembly (6) with 3 new lockwashers (14) and bolts (15).

4.   Connect lead (9) to glow plug relay (13) with nut and washer.

5.   Connect lead (5) to accessory wiring terminal board (4) with starwasher (3) and nut (2).

6.   Position accessory wiring terminal board cover (1) and tighten 2 nuts (16).

4-44. RESISTOR AND BRACKET REPLACEMENT (Con't).

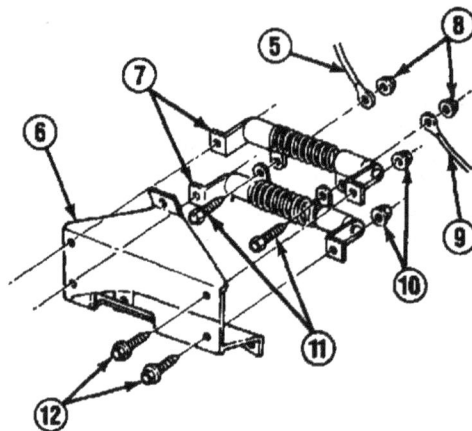

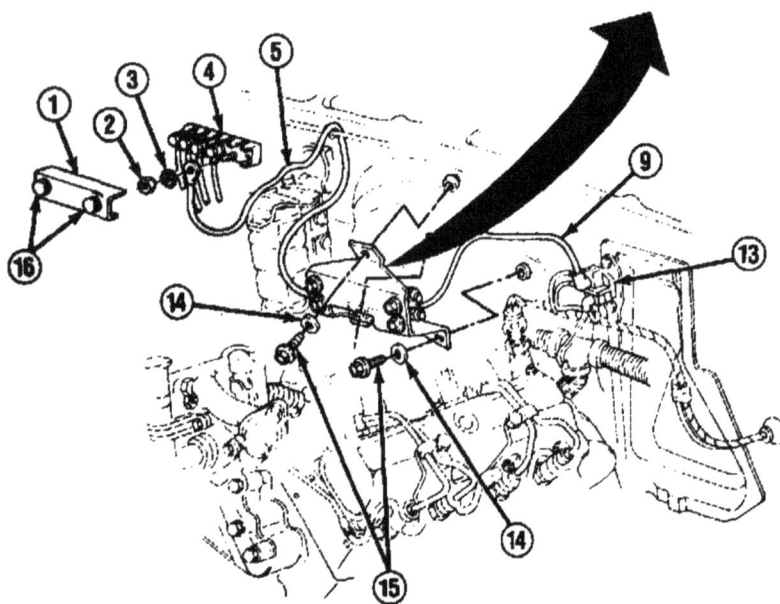

FOLLOW-ON TASKS:

- Install air cleaner. (See paragraph 3-9)
- Connect both battery negative cables. (See paragraph 4-38)

TA49916

4-45.   RADIO FEED HARNESS REPLACEMENT (ALL EXCEPT M1010).

This task covers: a. Removal   b. Installation

INITIAL SETUP:

Equipment Condition   *Materials/Parts*

   •Radio feed leads disconnected from accessory   •Two rivets
      wiring terminal board and radio terminal board   •Eleven straps
      (M1009). (See paragraph 4-46)   (winterization kit heaters only)
   •Cargo compartment floor panel insulators
      removed if equipped with winterization kits.
      (See paragraph 11-28 or 11-31)

| a. | **REMOVAL** |

NOTE

   **•If removing radio feed harness (2) from all except M1009, perform
     steps 1-5 and steps 7-11.**

   **•If removing radio feed harness (2) from M1009, perform   steps 2,
     5 through 8, 10, and 11.**

   **•Step 1 only applies to M1008A1 equipped with winterization   kit cargo
     compartment heater.**

   •Tag all leads and terminals for installation.

1.   Remove 11 straps from radio feed harness (2) and winterization kit cargo compartment heater
     wiring harness. Discard straps.

NOTE

M1009 clip (7) is attached to stud with nut.

2.   Remove screw (14) or nut and clip (7) from radio feed harness (2).

3.   Remove screw (12) and clip (13) from wiring harness (2).

4.   Remove nut (11), washer (10), screw (16), and clip (15).

5.   Remove screws (6) and clips (8).

6.   Pull floor mat and pad away from passenger compartment floor.

7.   Remove screw (4) and clip (3).

NOTE

Only M1009 radio feed harness grommet   (5) uses rivets (1).

8.   Remove 2 rivets (1) from grommet (5). Discard rivets.

4-45. RADIO FEED HARNESS REPLACEMENT (ALL EXCEPT M1010) (Con't).

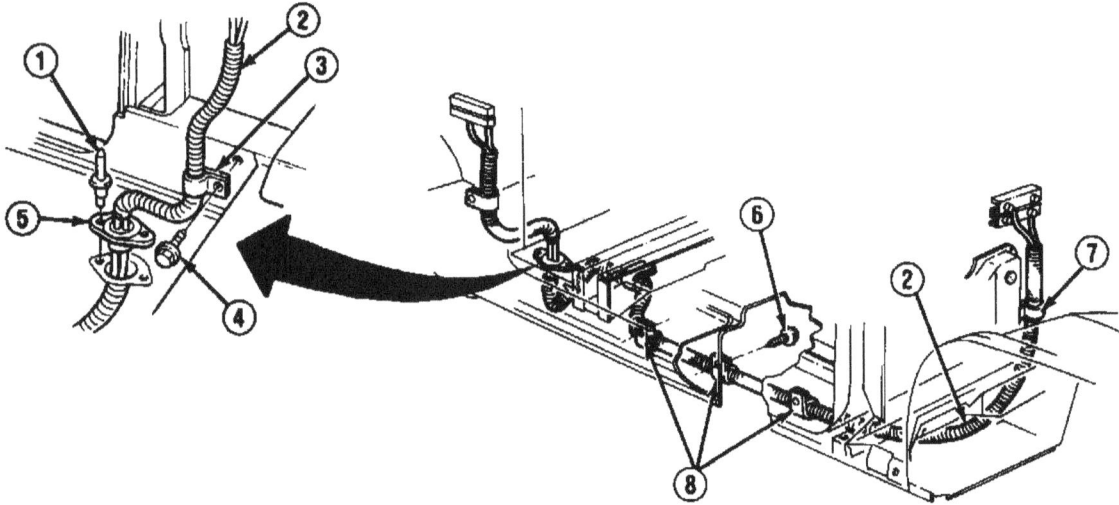

M1009

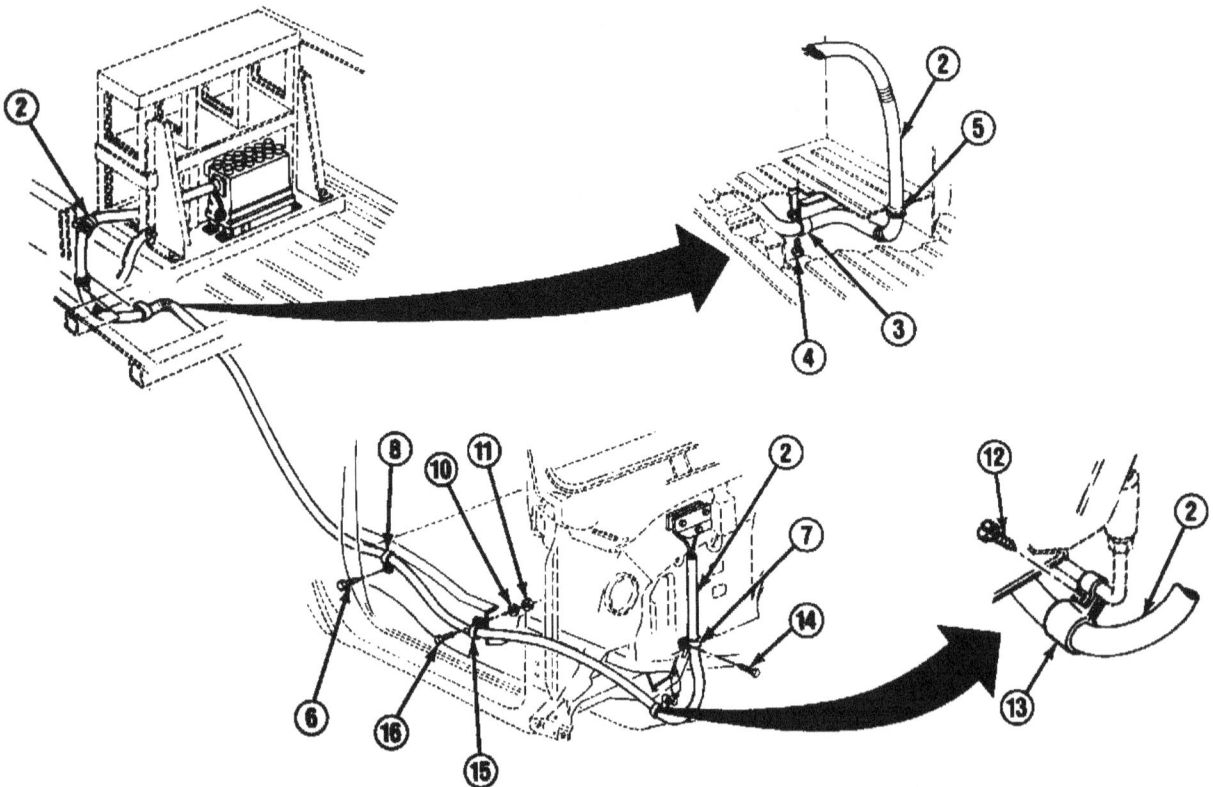

All Except M1009

TA49917

4-45.   RADIO FEED HARNESS REPLACEMENT (ALL EXCEPT M1010) (Con't).

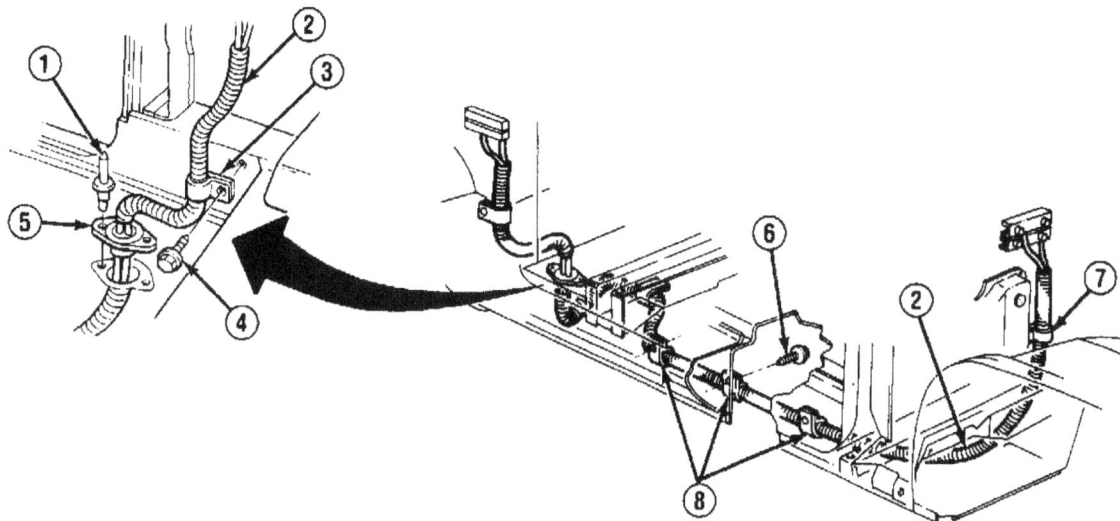

M1009

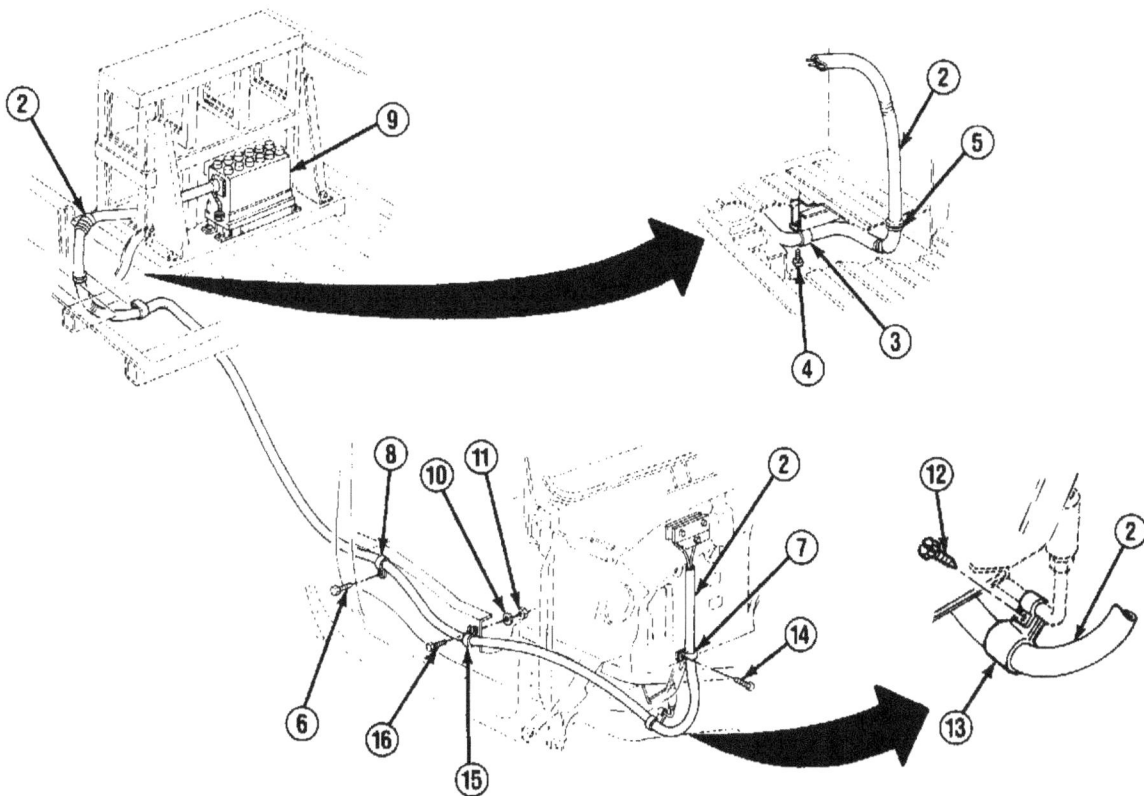

All Except M1009

TA49918

4-45.   RADIO FEED HARNESS REPLACEMENT (ALL EXCEPT M1010) (Con't).

9.   Disconnect radio feed harness (2) from junction box (9).

10.   Remove radio feed harness (2) through cargo body floor.

11.   Remove grommet (5) from radio feed harness (2).

b.   INSTALLATION

NOTE

◆f installing radio feed harness (2) on M1009, perform steps 1, 2, 4 through 7, 10, and 11.

◆f installing radio feed harness (2) on all except M1009, perform steps 1-5 and steps 7-11.

1.   Install grommet (5) on radio feed harness (2).

2.   Push radio feed harness (2) through cargo body floor.

3.   Connect radio feed harness (2) to junction box (9).

NOTE

Only M1009 radio feed harness grommet   (5) uses rivets (1).

4.   Install grommet (5) with 2 new rivets (1).

5.   Install clip (3) with screw (4).

6.   Install floor mat and pad into place on passenger compartment floor.

7.   Install clips (8) with screws (6).

8.   Install clip (15) with screw (16), washer (10), and nut (11).

9.   Install clip (13) with screw (12).

NOTE

M1009 clip (7) is attached to stud with nut.

10.   Install clip (7) with nut or screw (14).

NOTE

Step 11 only applies to M1008A1 equipped   with winterization kit cargo compartment heater.

11.   Install 11 new straps around winterization kit cargo   compartment heater wiring harness and radio feed harness (2).

FOLLOW-ON TASKS:

◆nstall cargo compartment floor panel insulators if removed. (See paragraph 11-28 or 11-31)
◆nstall radio feed leads. (See paragraph 4-46)
◆Check operation of radio.

4-46.   ACCESSORY WIRING TERMINAL BOARD AND RADIO TERMINAL BOARD
         REPLACEMENT.

This task covers: a. Removal   b. Installation

INITIAL SETUP:

Equipment Condition   *Materials/Parts*
  Both battery negative cables disconnected.   Ten lockwashers
    (See paragraph 4-38)

| a. | REMOVAL |

NOTE

● Procedures for removing accessory wiring terminal board and radio
  terminal board are similar.

● If removing accessory wiring terminal board (5 or 19), perform steps
  1-4 and steps 6-8.

● If removing radio terminal board (5 or 19), perform steps 1-3, 5, 6,   9,
  and 10.

1.   Loosen nuts (11) and remove terminal board covers (10 or 12) as required.

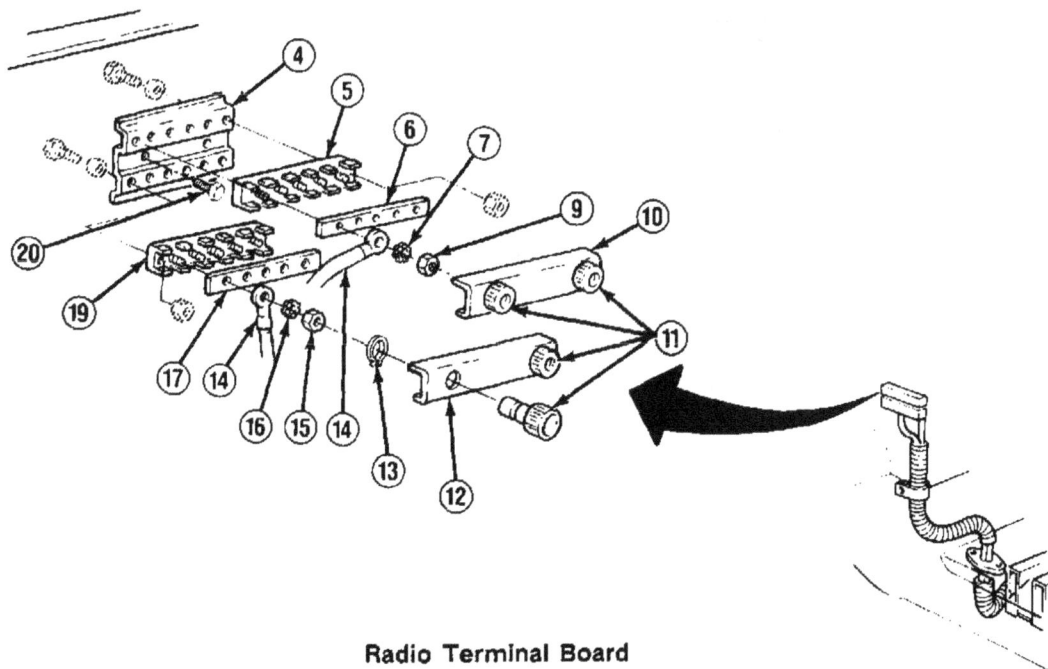

Radio Terminal Board

TA49919

4-46. ACCESSORY WIRING TERMINAL BOARD AND RADIO TERMINAL BOARD REPLACEMENT (Con't).

2. Remove snaprings (13) holding nuts (11) in place and remove nuts if damaged.

3. Remove nuts (9 or 15) and lockwashers (7 or 16) as required. Discard lockwashers.

NOTE

Tag leads and terminals for installation.

4. Disconnect leads from positive terminal board (5) and negative terminal board (19) as required. Remove connectors (6 and 17) and capacitor (22) as required.

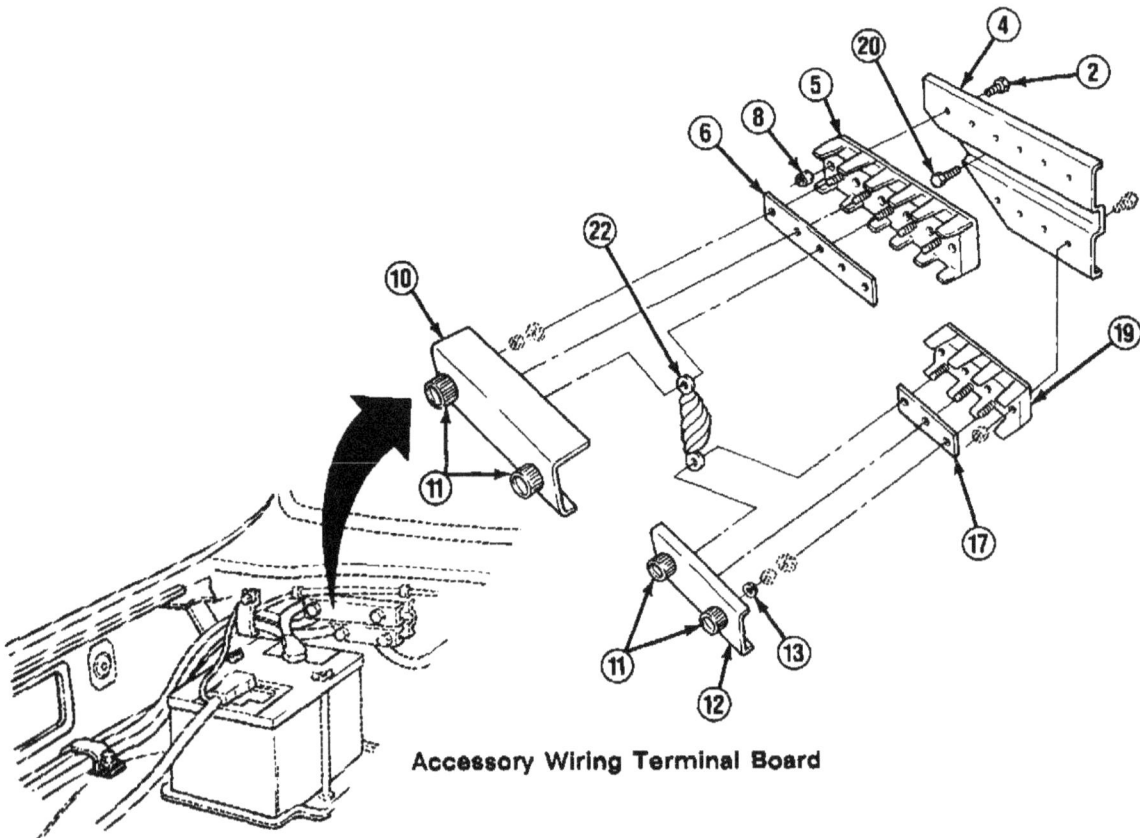

Accessory Wiring Terminal Board

NOTE

Tag leads and terminals   for installation.

5. Disconnect radio feed wiring harness (14) leads from upper terminal board (5) and lower terminal board (19). Remove connectors (6 and 17) as required.

6. Remove 2 bolts (20) and remove bracket (4) assembly.

7. Remove 6 bolts (2) and nuts (8), and remove positive accessory wiring terminal board (5).

TA49920

4-46. ACCESSORY WIRING TERMINAL BOARD AND RADIO TERMINAL BOARD REPLACEMENT (Con't).

8. Remove 4 bolts (21) and nuts (18), and remove negative accessory wiring terminal board (19).

9. Remove 2 bolts (2), washers (3), and nuts (8), and remove upper radio terminal board (5).

10, Remove 2 bolts (21), washers (1), and nuts (18), and remove lower radio terminal board (19).

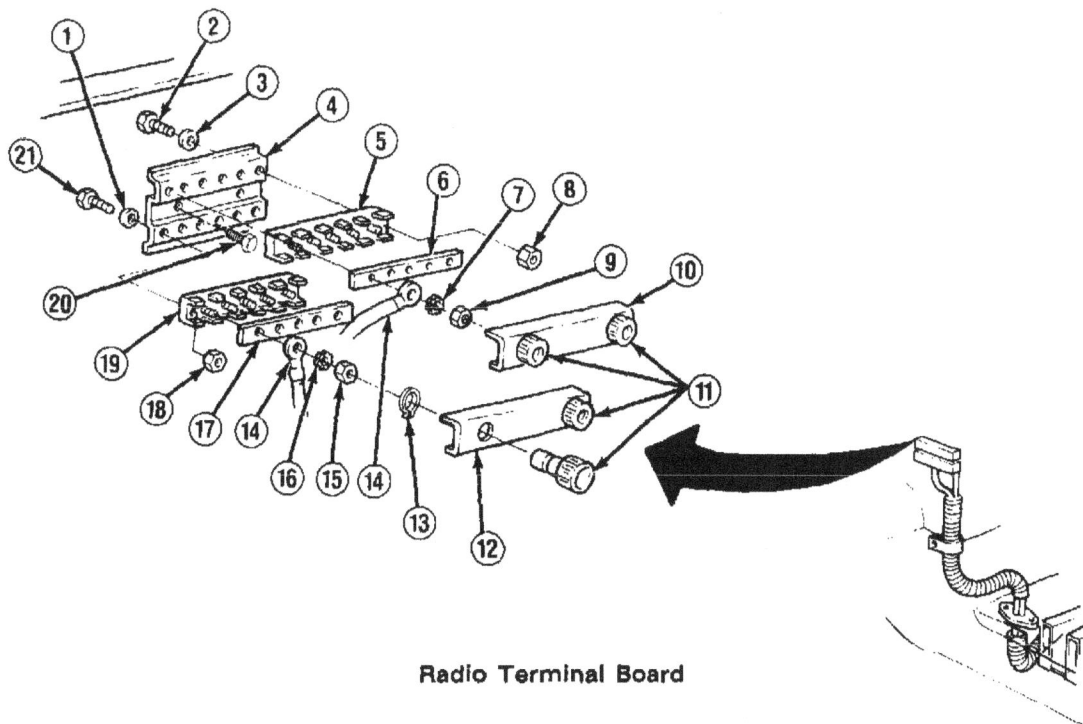

Radio Terminal Board

| b. INSTALLATION |

NOTE

•Procedures for installing accessory wiring terminal board and radio terminal board are similar.

•If installing radio terminal board (5 or 19), perform steps 1, 2, 5 through 7, and 10 through 12.

•If installing accessory wiring terminal board (5 or 19), perform steps 3-5 and steps 8-12.

1. Install lower radio terminal board (19) with 2 nuts (18), bolts (21), and washers (1).

2. Install upper radio terminal board (5) with 2 nuts (8), bolts (2), and washers (3).

TA49921

4-46. ACCESSORY WIRING TERMINAL BOARD AND RADIO TERMINAL BOARD REPLACEMENT (Con't).

3. Install negative accessory wiring terminal board (19) with 4 nuts (18) and bolts (21).

4. Install positive accessory wiring terminal board (5) with 6 nuts (8) and bolts (2).

5. Install bracket (4) assembly with 2 bolts (20).

6. Position connectors (6 and 17) if removed.

7. Connect radio feed wiring harness (14) leads to upper terminal board (5) and lower terminal board (19).

8. Position 2 connectors (6 and 17) and capacitor (22) if removed.

9. Connect leads to positive terminal board (5) and negative terminal board (19) if removed.

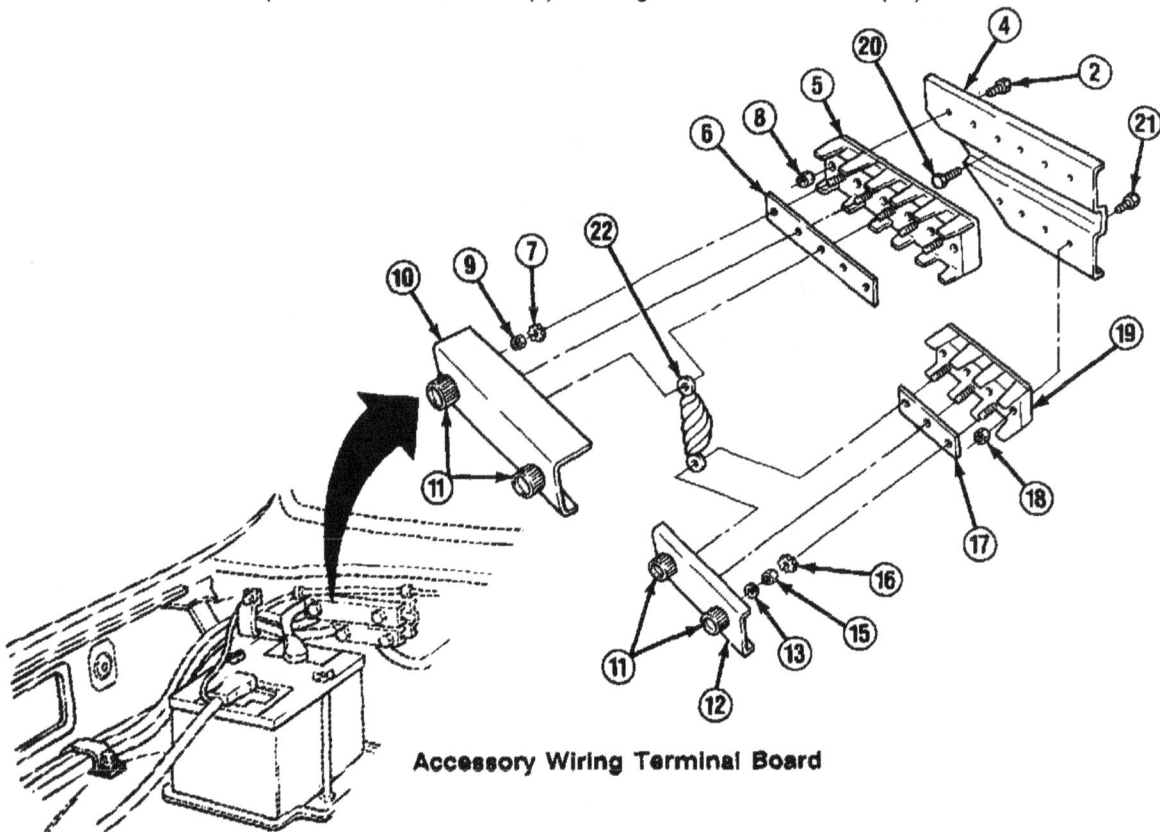

Accessory Wiring Terminal Board

10. Install new lockwashers (7 or 16) and nuts (9 or 15) if removed.

11. Install nuts (11) on terminal board covers (10 or 12) with snaprings (13) if removed.

12. Install terminal board covers (10 or 12) by tightening nuts (11).

FOLLOW-ON TASKS:

Connect both battery negative cables. (See paragraph 4-38)
Check operation of radio if radio terminal board was replaced.

TA49922

4-47.   RADIO MOUNTING BRACKET REPLACEMENT (M1009).

This task covers: a.   Removal   b. Installation

INITIAL SETUP:

Equipment Condition   *Materials/Parts*

Communications equipment removed.   Six lockwashers
   (See appropriate TM)

---

a.   **REMOVAL**

NOTE

If removing   braces (6), perform steps 1 and 2.

If removing   radio mounting bracket (1), perform steps 2 and 3.

1.   Remove 3 bolts (7) and   lockwashers (8). Discard lockwashers.

2.   Remove 3 bolts (3), lockwashers (2), and braces (6) as required. Discard lockwashers.

3.   Remove 3 bolts (5) and washers (4), and remove radio mounting bracket (1).

b. INSTALLATION

CAUTION

Ensure that rear passenger seat is pushed to its most rearward position before installing radio mounting bracket (1). Rack corner and edge of platform could damage seatback.

NOTE

If installing radio mounting bracket (1), perform steps 1 and 2.

If installing braces (6), perform steps 2 and 3.

1.   Install radio mounting bracket (1) with 3 washers (4) and bolts (5).

NOTE

Ensure that longest brace (6) is installed toward front of truck and shortest brace is installed toward rear of truck.

2.   Install 3 braces (6) on radio mounting bracket (1) with 3 new lockwashers   (2) and bolts (3).

3.   Install 3 new lockwashers (8) and bolts (7) on 3 braces (6) and mounting   brackets (9).

4-47.   RADIO MOUNTING BRACKET REPLACEMENT (M1009) (Con't).

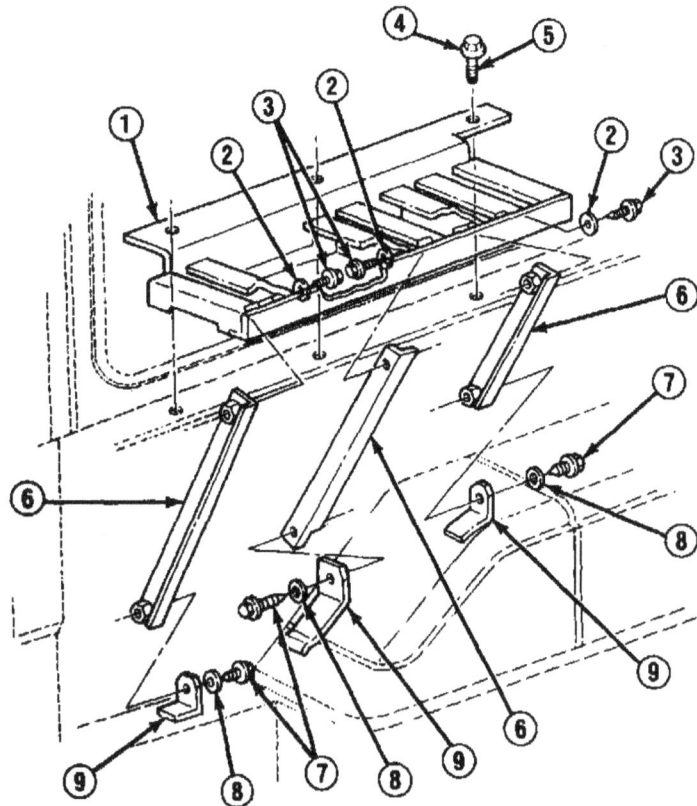

FOLLOW-ON TASKS:

● Install communications equipment. (See appropriate TM)

TA49923

4-48. JUNCTION BOX AND COMMUNICATIONS RACK REPLACEMENT.

This task covers:	a. Removal	b. Installation

INITIAL SETUP:

Equipment Condition

◄Both battery negative cables   disconnected.
   (See paragraph 4-38)

Personnel Required

◄MOS 63B (2)

Materials/Parts

◄Nine lockwashers

---

a	REMOVAL

NOTE

◄Only M1008A1 trucks have   communications racks (14).

◄If removing junction box (4), perform steps 1 and 2.

◄If removin g   communications rack (14), perform steps 1 and 3 through 6.

1.   Disconnect radio feed harness (2) from junction box (4).

2.   Remove 4 screws (3), strap (5), and 4 lockwashers (1). Discard   lockwashers. Remove junction box (4).

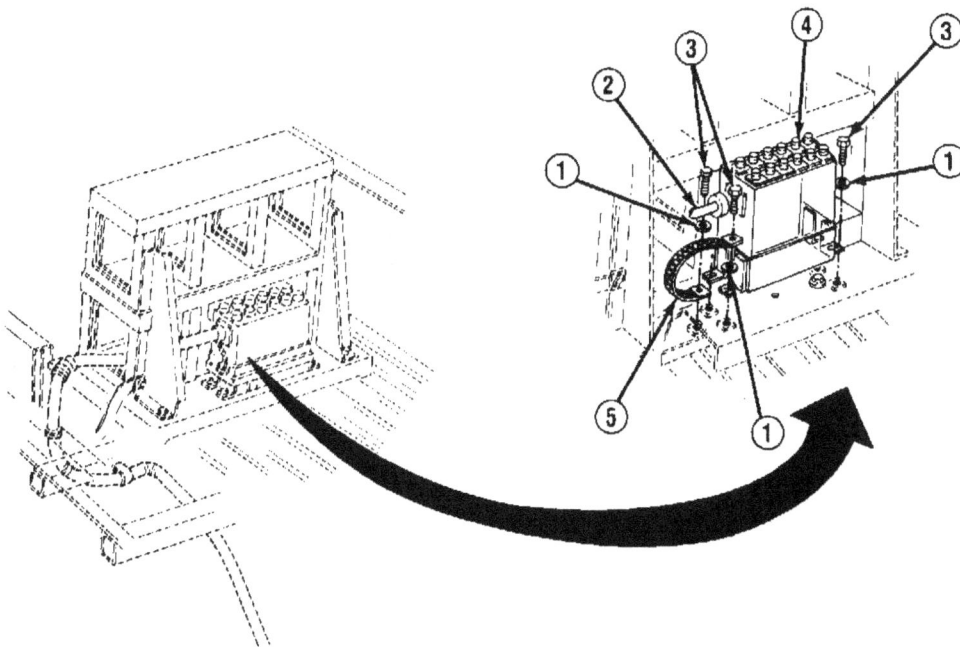

TA49924

4-48. JUNCTION BOX AND COMMUNICATIONS RACK REPLACEMENT (Con't).

3.   Remove nut (6), 2 lockwashers (7), lockwashers (8), and screw (9). Remove nut (17), screw (13), lockwasher (12), and strap (10). Discard lockwashers.

NOTE

Support reinforcement brackets (16) under cargo bed during removal.

4.   Remove 12 bolts (11) and 2 reinforcement brackets (16).

NOTE

Step 5 only applies to trucks equipped with winterization kit cargo compartment heater.

5.   Remove cargo compartment heater. (See paragraph 11-21)

6.   Remove communications rack (14) and bracket (15).

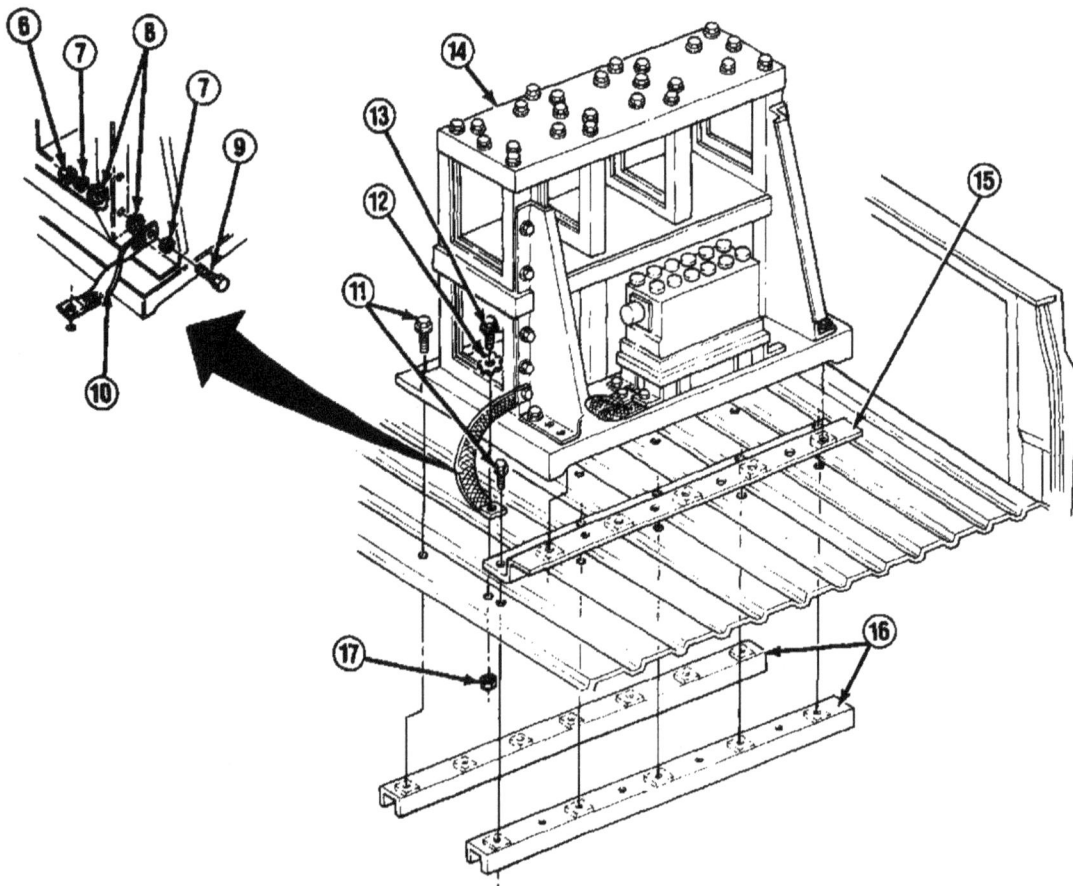

TA49925

4-48.   JUNCTION BOX AND COMMUNICATIONS RACK REPLACEMENT (Con't).

| b.   INSTALLATION |

NOTE

◀f installing communications rack (14), perform steps 1-4, and 6.

◀f installing junction box (4), perform steps 5 and 6.

1.   Position bracket (15) and communications rack (14).

NOTE

Step 2 only applies to trucks equipped with winterization kit cargo compartment heater.

2.   Install cargo compartment heater. (See paragraph 11-21)

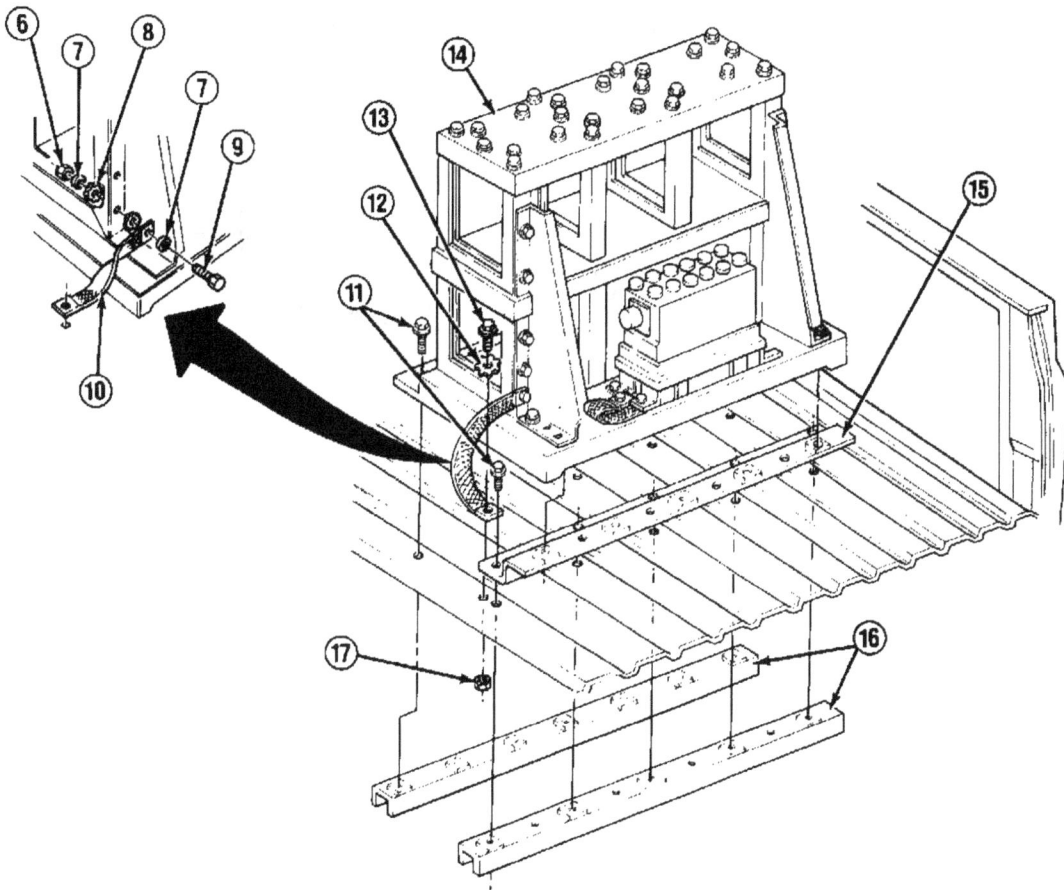

TA49926

4-48. JUNCTION BOX AND COMMUNICATIONS RACK REPLACEMENT (Con't).

NOTE

Support reinforcement brackets (16) under cargo bed during installation.

3. Install 2 reinforcement brackets (16) with 12 bolts (11).

4. Install strap (10) on cargo bed with new lockwasher (12), screw (13), and nut (17). Install strap on communications rack (14) with 2 new lockwashers (8), new lockwashers (7), screw (9), and nut (6).

5. Install junction box (4) and strap (5) with 4 new lockwashers (1) and screws (3).

6. Connect radio feed harness (2) to junction box (4).

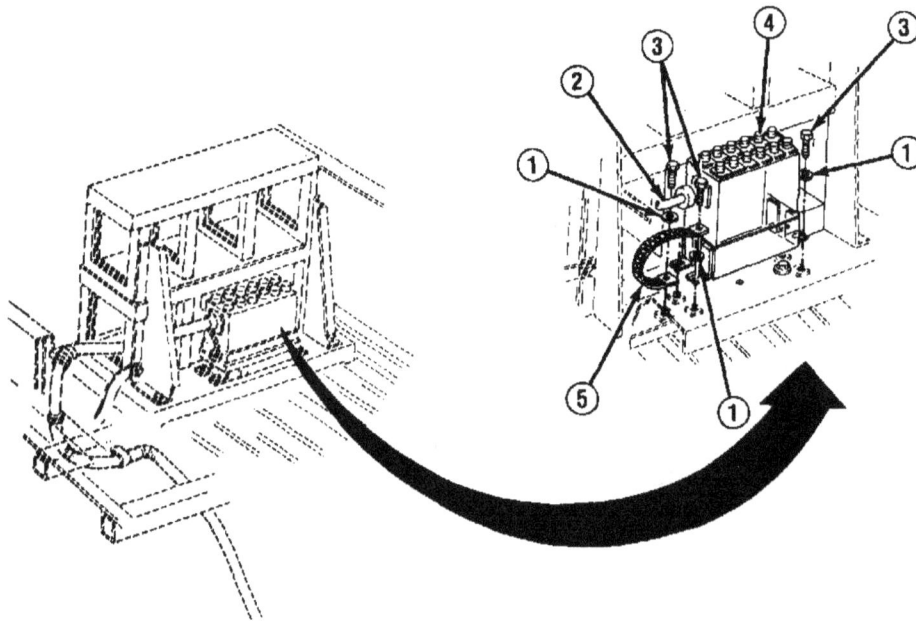

FOLLOW-ON TASKS:

Connect both battery negative cables. (See paragraph 4-38)

TA49927

CHAPTER 5
TRANSMISSION AND TRANSFER CASE MAINTENANCE

5-1. TRANSMISSION AND TRANSFER CASE MAINTENANCE INDEX.

5-2.   TRANSMISSION FILTER ASSEMBLY MAINTENANCE.

This task covers:
a. Removal
b. Cleaning
c. Installation

INITIAL SETUP:

Materials/Parts

- One seal
- One transmission filter assembly with screen grommet
- One transmission oil pan gasket
- Dry cleaning solvent (Item 15, Appendix C)
- Hydraulic fluid (Item 28, Appendix C)
- RTV sealant (Item 41, Appendix C)

Tools/Test Equipment

- Torque wrench

Manual References

- LO 9-2320-289-12

General Safety Instructions

- Always wear goggles when working on underside of truck.
- Compressed air used for cleaning purposes will not exceed 30 psi (207 kPa).
- Dry cleaning solvent is flammable and must not be used near open flame. Use only in a well-ventilated area.

| a.   REMOVAL |

WARNING

Always wear goggles when working on underside of truck. Hydraulic fluid spillage can occur when removing transmission oil pan. Failure to follow this warning may result in serious eye injury.

1.   Place drain pan under transmission oil pan (2).

NOTE

Steps 2 and 3 only apply to trucks equipped with winterization kits.

2.   Remove 2 bolts (1) and disconnect heat exchange pipe (6) from front of transmission oil pan (2).

3.   Loosen clamp (3) and disconnect rear exhaust pipe (4) from transmission oil pan (2).

4.   Remove 1 0 front and side transmission oil pan screws (5). Loosen 3 rear transmission oil pan screws (5) about 4 turns.

TA49632

5-2.   TRANSMISSION FILTER ASSEMBLY MAINTENANCE (Con't).

5.   Carefully pry front of transmission oil pan (2) loose and allow hydraulic fluid to drain into drain pan.

NOTE

- **Transmission oil pans (2) with a ridged lip will have a transmission oil pan gasket (11).**

- **Transmission oil pans (2) with a flat lip will have RTV sealant.**

6.   Remove 3 rear transmission oil pan screws (5), transmission oil pan (2), magnet (12), and transmission oil pan gasket (11) if present. Discard gasket if present.

7.   Remove bolt (10) and remove transmission oil filter assembly (9), spacer (8), and screen grommet (13). Discard filter assembly and screen grommet.

8.   Remove intake pipe (14) and seal (7). Discard seal.

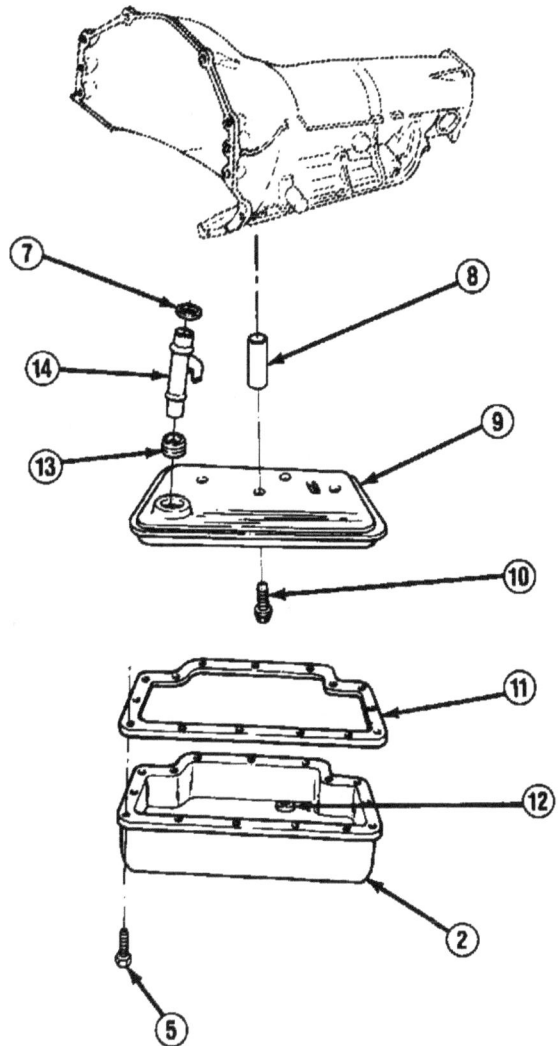

TA49633

5-2. TRANSMISSION FILTER ASSEMBLY MAINTENANCE (Con't).

b. CLEANING

WARNING

Dry cleaning solvent P-D-680 is toxic and flammable. Always wear protective goggles and gloves and use only in a well-ventilated area. Avoid contact with skin, eyes, and clothes and DO NOT breathe vapors. DO NOT use near open flame or excessive heat. The solvent's flash point is 100°F-138°F (38°C-59°C). If you become dizzy while using cleaning solvent, immediately get fresh air and medical help. If solvent contacts eyes, immediately wash your eyes with water and get medical aid.

Compressed air used for cleaning purposes will not exceed 30 psi (207 kPa). Use only effective chip guarding and personnel protective equipment (goggles/shield, gloves). Failure to follow this warning may result in serious injury to personnel.

1. Clean old RTV sealant or old transmission oil pan gasket (11) from lip of transmission oil pan (2) and from transmission housing with dry cleaning solvent. Thoroughly dry with compressed air.

NOTE

When cleaning magnet (12), ensure that all metal filings are removed.

2. Clean transmission oil pan (2) and magnet (12) with dry cleaning solvent. Thoroughly dry with compressed air.

c. INSTALLATION

1. Install screen grommet (13) into neck of transmission oil filter assembly (8).

NOTE

Note markings on intake pipe (14) and ensure that it is installed properly. One end is marked "FILTER" and other end is marked "CASE."

2. Install new seal (7) and intake pipe (14) into transmission oil filter assembly (9).

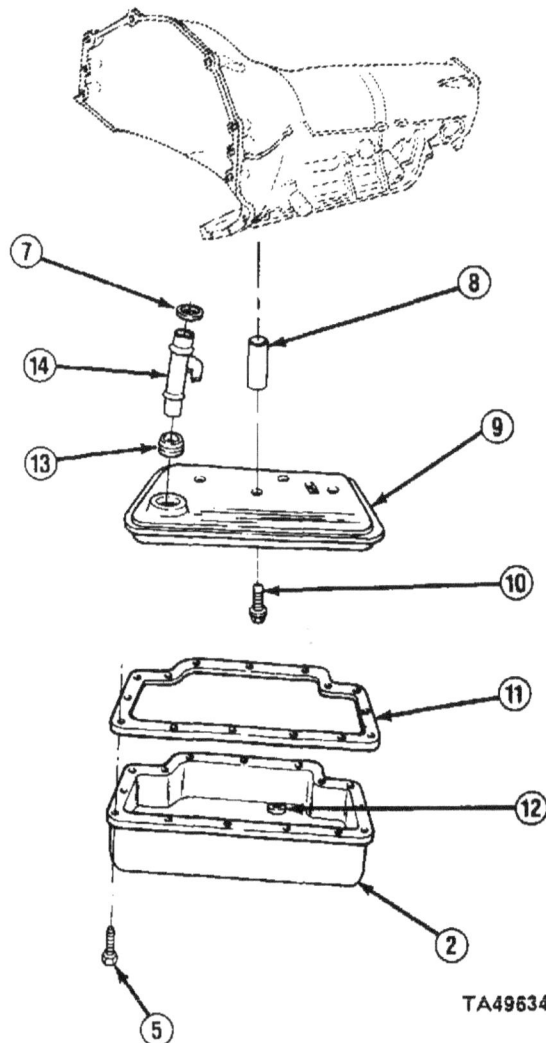

TA49634

5-2.   TRANSMISSION FILTER ASSEMBLY MAINTENANCE (Con't).

3.   Install new transmission oil filter assembly (9), spacer (8), new screen grommet (13), intake pipe (14), and seal (7) into transmission housing with bolt (10), ensuring that locating tab is alined. Tighten bolt to 125-160 lb.-in. (14–18 N•m).

NOTE

◀If installing a new transmission oil pan gasket (11) with transmission oil pan (2), perform steps 4 and 6 through 12.

●If applying RTV   sealant or installing a new transmission oit pan, perform steps 5-12.

4.   Install new transmission   oil pan gasket (11) on lip of transmission oil pan (2) and aline with screw holes.

NOTE

Transmission oil pan (1) must be clean and dry before applying   RTV sealant.

5.   Apply a 3/16 in. (4.7 mm) bead of RTV sealant around lip of transmission oil   pan (2).

6.   Install magnet (12) into transmission oil pan (2).

7.   Install transmission oil pan (2) with 13 transmission oil pan screws (5). Evenly tighten screws to 125-160 lb.-in. (14-18 N•m).

NOTE

Steps 8 and 9 only apply to trucks equipped with winterization kits.

8.   Install rear exhaust pipe (4) and clamp (3) to rear of transmission oil pan   (2).   Tighten   clamp to 75-95 lb.-in. (9-11 N•m).

9.   Install heat exchange pipe (6) to front of transmission oil pan (2) using 2 bolts   (1).   Tighten   bolts to 25-30 lb.-in. (2-3 N•m).

10. Fill transmission with hydraulic fluid. (See LO 9-2320-289-12)

11. With engine idling, and with parking brake   set,   move   transmission gearshift lever through all gear positions, then return it to "P" (Park). Check hydraulic fluid level and add as required.

12. Check transmission oil pan (2) for leaks.

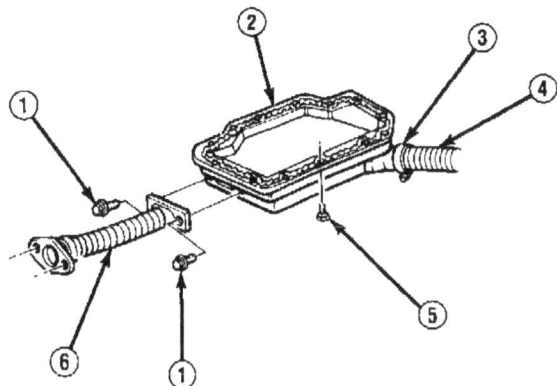

TA49635

5-2.1. TRANSMISSION VACUUM LINES REPLACEMENT.

This task covers:	a. Removal	b. Installation

INITIAL SETUP:

Equipment Conditions

Both battery negative cables disconnected. (See paragraph 4-38)
Air cleaner removed. (See paragraph 3-9)

1. Disconnect hose (8) from vacuum modulator assembly (7).

2. Remove clip (10) from fill tube assembly (9) and vacuum pipe (5).

3. Remove 2 nuts (1) from valve cover studs (3).

4. Remove 3 nuts securing crankcase depression regulator valve (CDRV) assembly (4) mounting bracket to valve cover and intake manifold. Move CDRV assembly free of vacuum pipe (5).

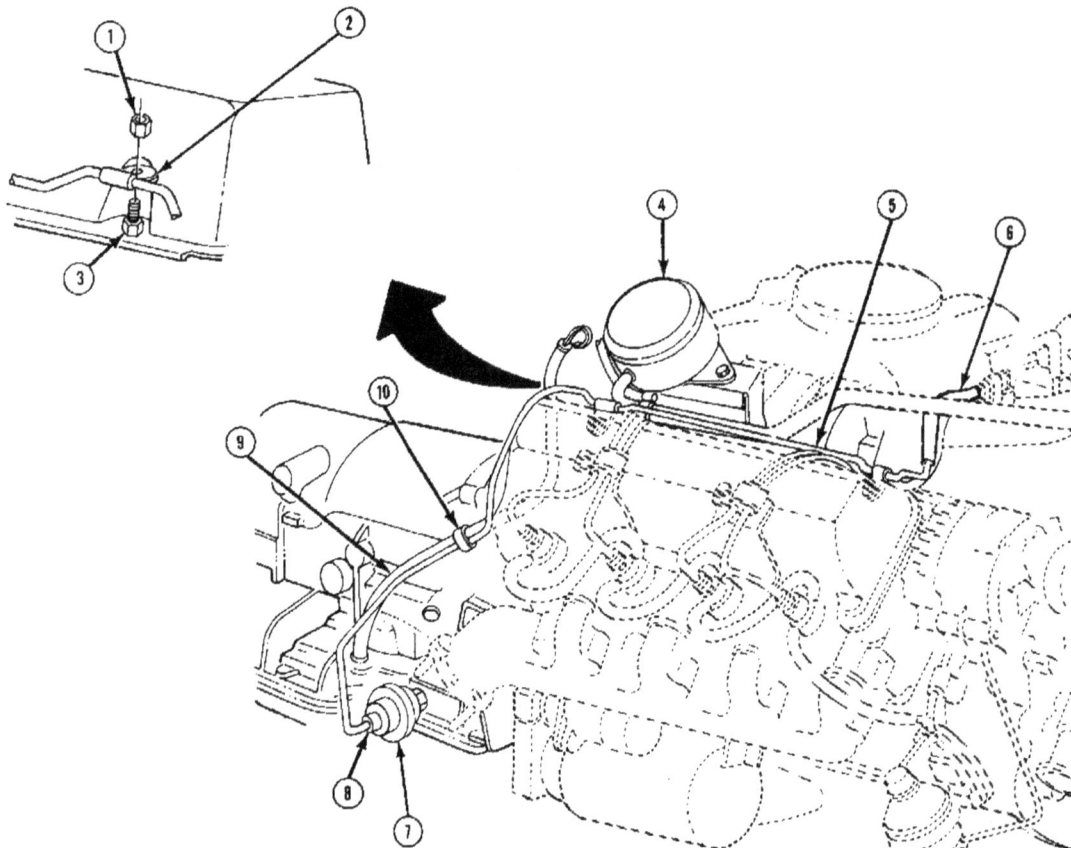

TA701834

5-2.1. TRANSMISSION VACUUM LINES REPLACEMENT (Con't).

5. Remove 3 bolts (11) and fuel filter assembly (12) mounting bracket from bulkhead.

6. Remove drain pipe (13) from fuel filter assembly (12).

7. Place fuel filter assembly (12) on engine free of vacuum pipe (5).

8. Disconnect vacuum pipe (5) from 2 hoses (6 and 8) and remove vacuum pipe. Remove 2 clips (2) from vacuum pipe.

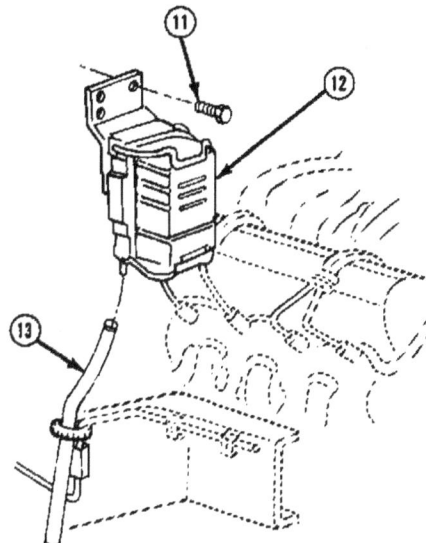

b. INSTALLATION

1. From engine compartment, install vacuum pipe (5).

2. Install 2 hoses (6 and 8) to vacuum pipe (5).

3. Install 2 clips (2) to vacuum pipe (5). Install 2 clips to valve cover studs (3) with 2 nuts (1).

4. Install CDRV assembly (4) mounting bracket to valve cover and intake manifold with 3 nuts.

5. Install drain pipe (13) to fuel filter assembly (12).

6. Install fuel filter assembly (12) to bulkhead with 3 bolts (11).

7. Install clip (10) to fill tube assembly (9) and vacuum pipe (5).

8. Connect hose (8) to vacuum modulator assembly (7).

FOLLOW-ON TASKS:

Install air cleaner if removed. (See paragraph 3-9)
Connect both battery negative cables. (See paragraph 4-38)
Check hydraulic fluid level. (See LO 9-2320-289-12)

TA701835

5-3.   **TRANSFER CASE PLATE AND BOOT REPLACEMENT (M1028A1 AND M1031).**

This task covers: a.   Removal   b. Installation

| a.   REMOVAL |

1.   Loosen locknut (3) and   remove knob
      (2) leaving locknut   installed on
      control lever (5).

2.   Remove 4 screws (1)   and remove
      plate (4).

3.   Remove 4 screws (8),   and remove
      retainer (6) and boot (7).

| b. INSTALLATION |

1.   Install boot (7) and retainer (6) over
      control lever (5) with 4 screws (8).

2.   Install plate (4) over retainer (6) with
      4 screws (1).

3.   Install knob (2) onto control lever (5)
      and tighten locknut (3).

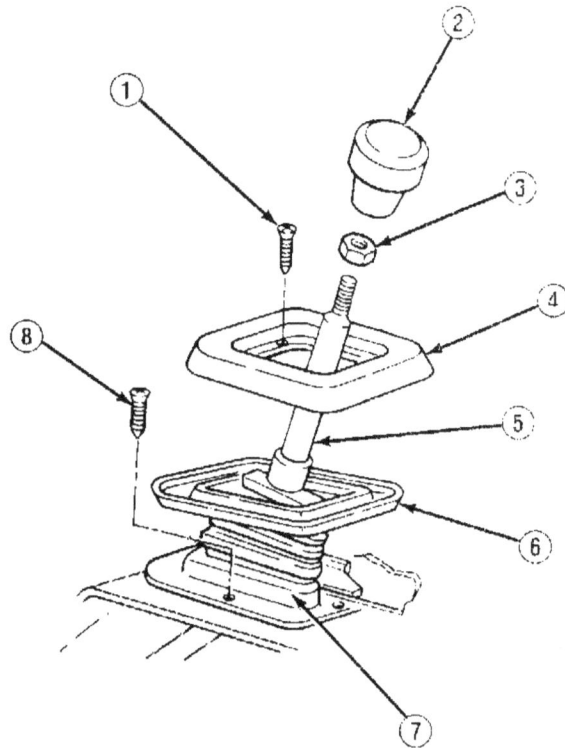

TA49636

5-4. TRANSFER CASE BEZEL AND BOOT REPLACEMENT (ALL EXCEPT M1028A1 AND M1031).

This task covers: a. Removal b. Installation

a. REMOVAL

1. Remove knob (1).

2. Pry off and remove (2).

3. Slide boot assembly lever assembly (8).

4. Remove 4 screws (5) and bezel assembly (7).

b. INSTALLATION

NOTE

When installing bezel assembly (7), lever assembly (8) must pass through bezel's central slot (4).

1. Install bezel assembly (7) onto housing (6) with 4 screws (5).

2. Install boot assembly (3) over control lever assembly (8).

3. Snap retaining plate (2) over boot assembly (3) and bezel assembly (7).

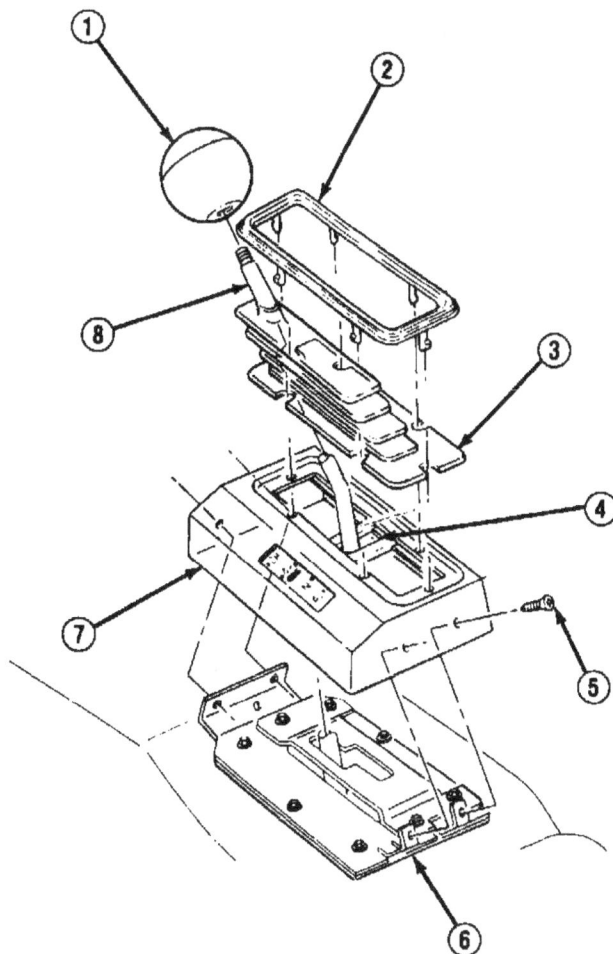

4. Install knob (1).

TA49637

5-5. TRANSFER CASE LINKAGE AND CONTROL LEVER REPLACEMENT (M1028A1 AND M1031).

This task covers: a. Removal c. Installation
b. Inspection

INITIAL SETUP:

Equipment Condition

•Transfer case plate and boot removed
(if removing control lever).
(See paragraph 5-3)

Materials/Parts

•Two spring washers
•Two cotter pins

---

a. REMOVAL

NOTE

If removing transfer case linkage, perform steps 1 and 2.

1. Remove 2 cotter pins (4), washers (9), and spring washers (10) from selector rod (1). Discard cotter pins and spring washers.

2. Remove selector rod (1) from link (11) and control lever (2). Remove grommet (12) and discard if damaged.

3. Remove fitting (7), pivot bolt (8), and 3 washers (5) from control lever (2).

4. Remove control lever (2) from transfer case (6).

5. Count threads where jam nut (3) rests on threaded end of control lever (2) and tag for installation. Remove jam nut and retain for later use.

b. INSPECTION

1. Inspect selector rod (1) for breaks, bends, corrosion, or other signs of wear. Replace as required.

2. Inspect all other components for cracks, corrosion, or other signs of wear. Replace as required.

c. INSTALLATION

NOTE

If installing transfer case linkage, perform steps 3 and 4.

1. Install jam nut (3) on threaded end of control lever (2), leaving same number of threads showing as when removed.

2. Install control lever (2), 3 washers (5), pivot bolt (8) and fitting (7).

5-5. TRANSFER CASE LINKAGE AND CONTROL LEVER REPLACEMENT (M1028A1 AND M1031) (Con't).

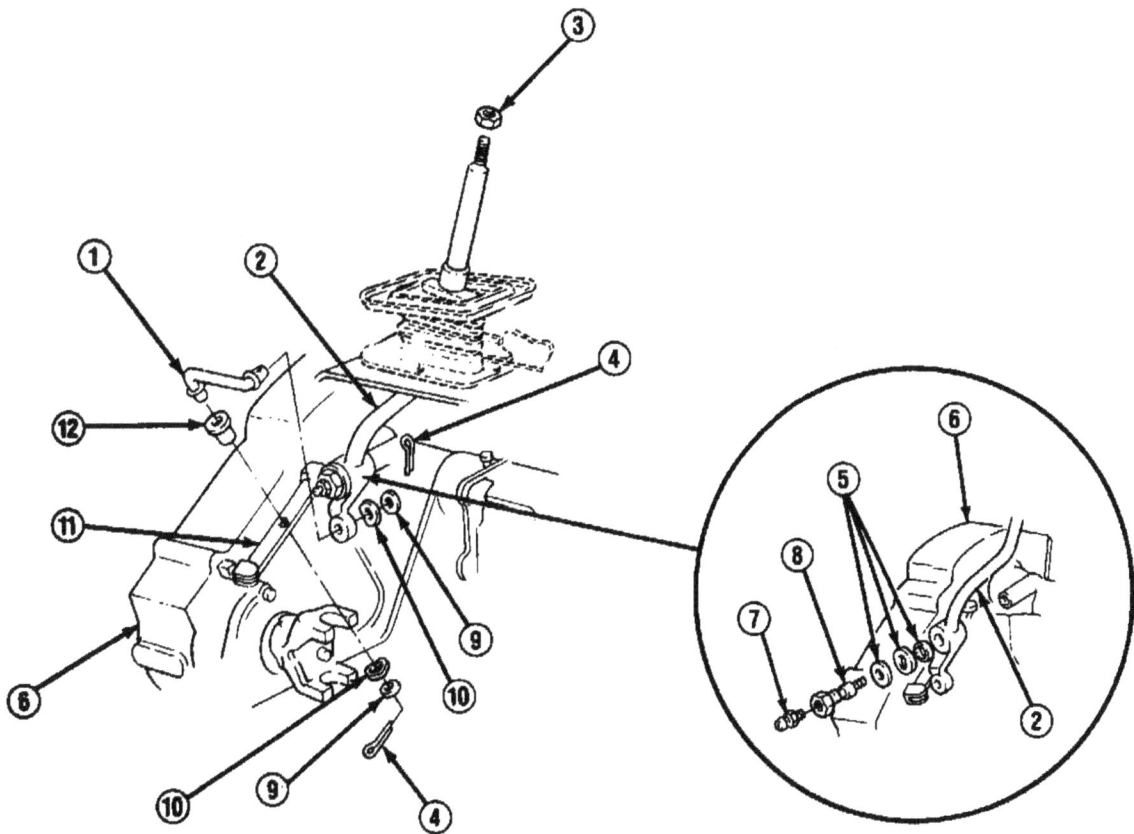

3.   If removed, install new grommet (12) into link (11).

4.   Install selector rod (1) into link (11) and control lever (2), with 2 new spring washers (10), washers (9), and new cotter pins (4).

FOLLOW-ON TASKS:

   If control lever was replaced, install transfer case plate and boot. (See paragraph 5-3)

TA49638

5-6. TRANSFER CASE LINKAGE AND CONTROL LEVER ASSEMBLY MAINTENANCE (ALL EXCEPT M1028A1 AND M1031).

This task covers:
a. Removal
b. Installation
c. Adjustment

INITIAL SETUP:

Equipment Condition

● Transfer case bezel and boot removed
  (if removing control lever).
  (See paragraph 5-4)

General Safety Instructions

● Always wear goggles when working on underside of truck.

Materials/Parts

• Two locknuts
• One lockwasher
• Three cotter pins

| a. | REMOVAL |

WARNING

Always wear goggles when working on underside of truck, Failure to follow this warning may result in serious eye injury.

NOTE

● If removing control lever assembly, perform steps 1-5.

● If removing transfer case linkage, perform steps 1 and 6 through 8.

1. Remove cotter pin (13) and washer (12) at actuator lever (9). Discard cotter pin.

2. Remove 8 bolts (4) and washers (5) at guide (3) and housing (11). Remove guide and housing with assembled control lever assembly from truck. Remove seal (19).

3. Remove nut (14), washer (15), and bushing (16) securing actuator lever (9) to housing (11),

4. Remove 2 bolts (10) and locknuts (17), and remove actuator lever (9) from fork (7) and housing (11). Discard locknuts.

5. Remove cotter pin (18), washer (1), and pin (8) and remove control lever (2), spring (6), and fork (7). Discard cotter pin,

6. Place operating lever (20) into "4L" position. Remove cotter pin (22), washer (21), and rod (29) from operating lever. Remove grommet (31) and discard if damaged. Discard cotter pin.

7. Remove nut (25), swivel (26), and nut (27) from rod (29). Remove grommet (24) if worn or damaged.

8. Remove nut (30), lockwasher (28), and operating lever (20) from transfer case (23) as required. Discard lockwasher.

5-6. TRANSFER CASE LINKAGE AND CONTROL LEVER ASSEMBLY MAINTENANCE (ALL EXCEPT M1028A1 AND M1031) (Con't).

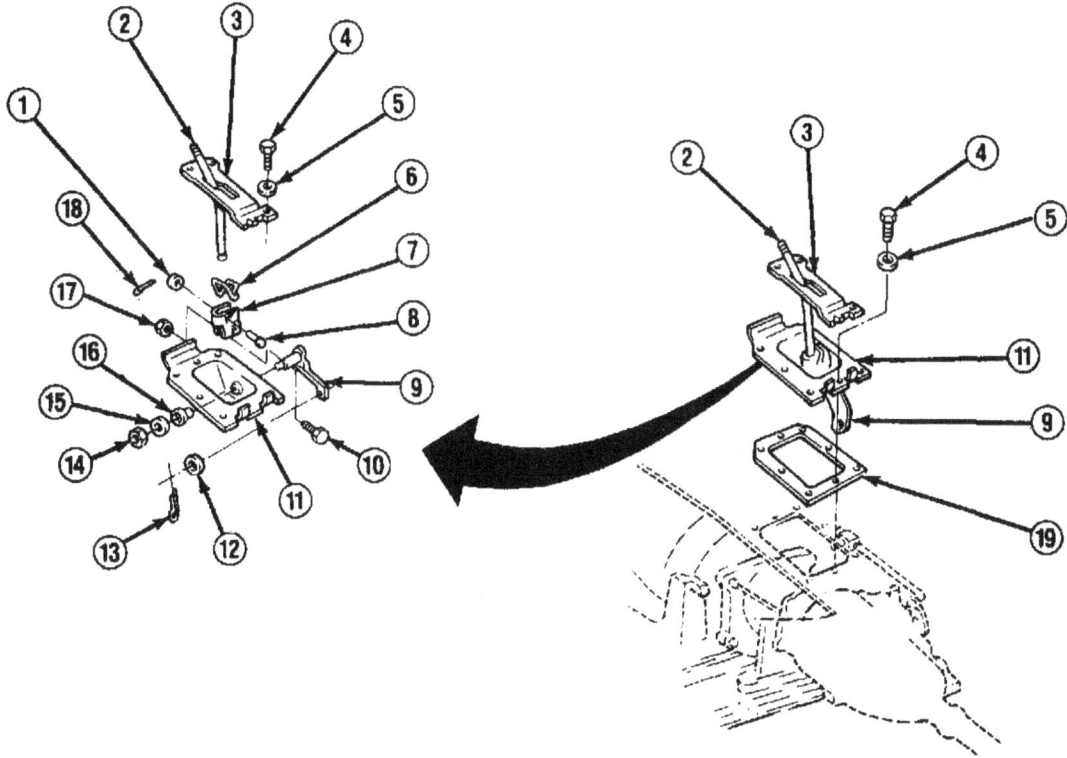

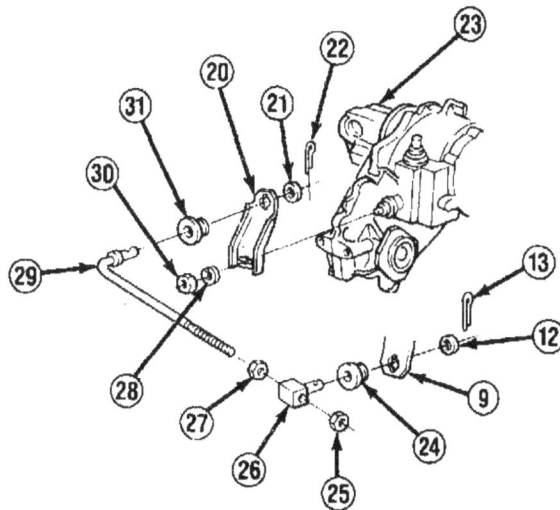

TA49639

5-6. TRANSFER CASE LINKAGE AND CONTROL LEVER ASSEMBLY MAINTENANCE (ALL EXCEPT M1028A1 AND M1031) (Con't).

| b. INSTALLATION |

WARNING

Always wear goggles when working on underside of truck. Failure to follow this warning may result in serious eye injury.

NOTE

• If installing control lever assembly, perform steps 1-4 and 8.

• If installing transfer case linkage, perform steps 5-8.

1.   Install control lever (2) and spring (6) to fork (7) with pin (8), washer (1), and new cotter pin (18).

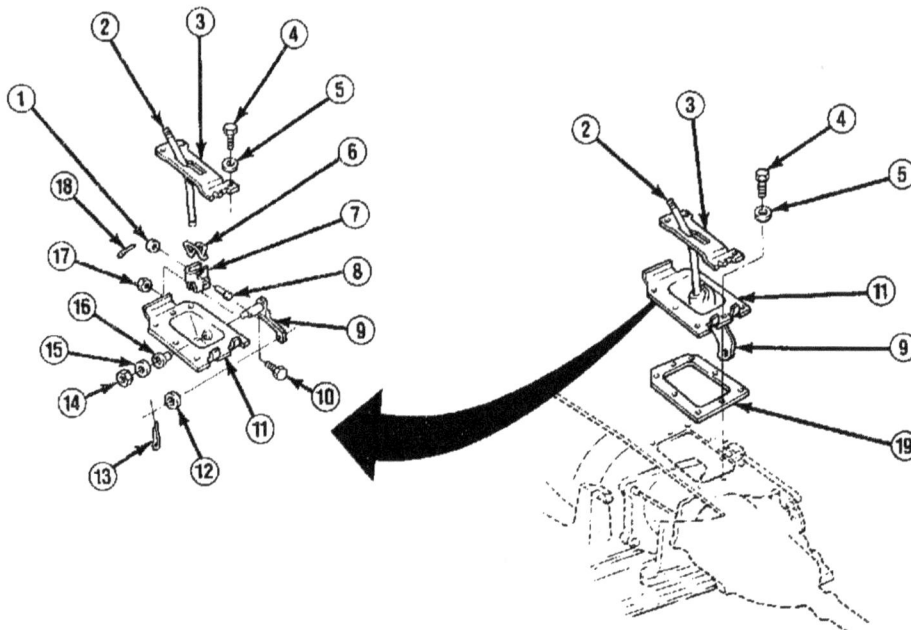

TA49640

5-6. TRANSFER CASE LINKAGE AND CONTROL LEVER ASSEMBLY MAINTENANCE (ALL EXCEPT M1028A1 AND M1031) (Con't).

2. Position actuator lever (9) through housing (11) and install to fork (7) with 2 bolts (10) and new locknuts (17).

3. Install actuator lever (9) to housing (11) with bushing (16), washer (15), and nut (14).

4. Place guide (3) through control lever (2). Install seal (19) and housing (11) with assembled control lever assembly to floor of truck with 8 bolts (4) and washers (5).

5. If removed, install operating lever (20) to transfer case (23) with new lockwasher (28) and nut (30).

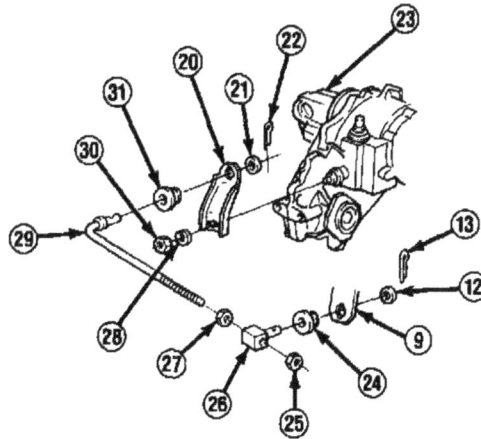

6. Install grommet (31) to transfer case end of rod (29). Install rod to operating lever (20) with washer (21) and new cotter pin (22).

7. Install nut (27), swivel (26), and nut (25) to threaded end of rod (29). Install grommet (24) to swivel.

8. Install swivel (26) to actuator lever (9) with washer (12) and new cotter pin (13).

TA49641

5-6. TRANSFER CASE LINKAGE AND CONTROL LEVER ASSEMBLY MAINTENANCE (ALL EXCEPT M1028A1 AND M1031) (Con't).

| c. | ADJUSTMENT |

1. At transfer case (23), place operating lever (20) into "4H" position.

2. Inside truck, place transfer case control lever into "4H" position.

NOTE

A 0.200 in. (0.51 cm) gage (32) must be made for use in steps 3 and 4. It may be made from any material and shaped as illustrated.

3. Hang gage (32) over rod (29) behind swivel (26). Run nut (27) against gage with shifter against "4H" stop.

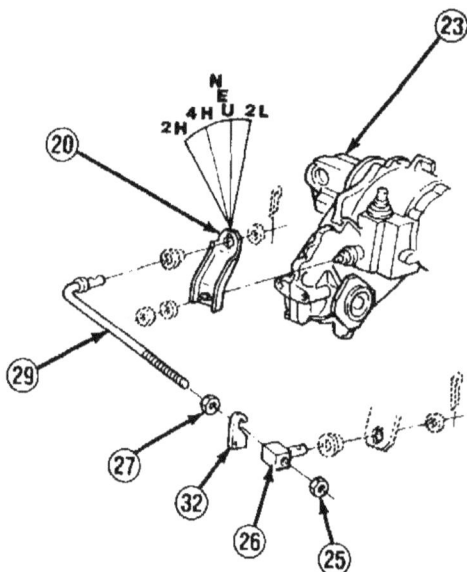

4. Remove gage (32) and push swivel (26) rearward against nut (27).

5. Run nut (25) against swivel (26) and tighten.

FOLLOW-ON TASKS:

• If removed, install transfer case bezel and boot. (See paragraph 5-4)
• Check operation of control lever and linkage.

TA49642

CHAPTER 6
PROPELLER SHAFTS, AXLES, AND SUSPENSION   MAINTENANCE

Section I. PROPELLER SHAFTS MAINTENANCE

6-1.   PROPELLER SHAFTS MAINTENANCE INDEX.

6-2. FRONT PROPELLER SHAFT ASSEMBLY REPLACEMENT.

This task covers: a. Removal   b. Installation

INITIAL SETUP:

Materials/Parts
* Four lockwashers

Tools/Test Equipment
* Torque wrench

| a. | REMOVAL |

NOTE

* Second design propeller shafts have a boot while first design propeller shafts do not. This does not affect propeller shaft maintenance. The first design propeller shaft is shown in this procedure.

* If removing front propeller shaft (1) from all except M1009, perform steps 1, 3, and 4.

* If removing front propeller shaft from M1009, perform steps 2-4.

1. Remove 4 nuts (12), lockwashers (11), and 2 "U" bolts (9) at axle flange (10). Discard lockwashers.

2. Remove 4 bolts (6) and 2 straps (7) at axle flange (8).

3. Push shaft (1) toward rear, Lower and support loose end.

4. Remove 4 bolts (2) from transfer case flange yoke (3).

| b. | INSTALLATION |

NOTE

· If installing front propeller shaft (1) on M1009, perform steps 1 and 2.

· If installing front propeller shaft (1) on all except M1009, perform steps 2 and 3.

1. Install front propeller shaft (1) on transfer case flange yoke (3) with 4 bolts (2). Tighten bolts to 70-80 lb.-ft, (95-108 N·m).

2. Position 2 strain (7) on universal joint (4) and install at axle flange (8) with 4 bolts (6). Tighten bolts to 15 lb-ft. (20 N·m).

3. Position 2 "U" bolts (9) on universal joint (4) and install at axle flange (10) with 4 new lockwashers (11) and nuts (12). Tighten nuts to 15 lb.-ft. (20 N·m).

6-2. FRONT PROPELLER SHAFT ASSEMBLY REPLACEMENT (Con't).

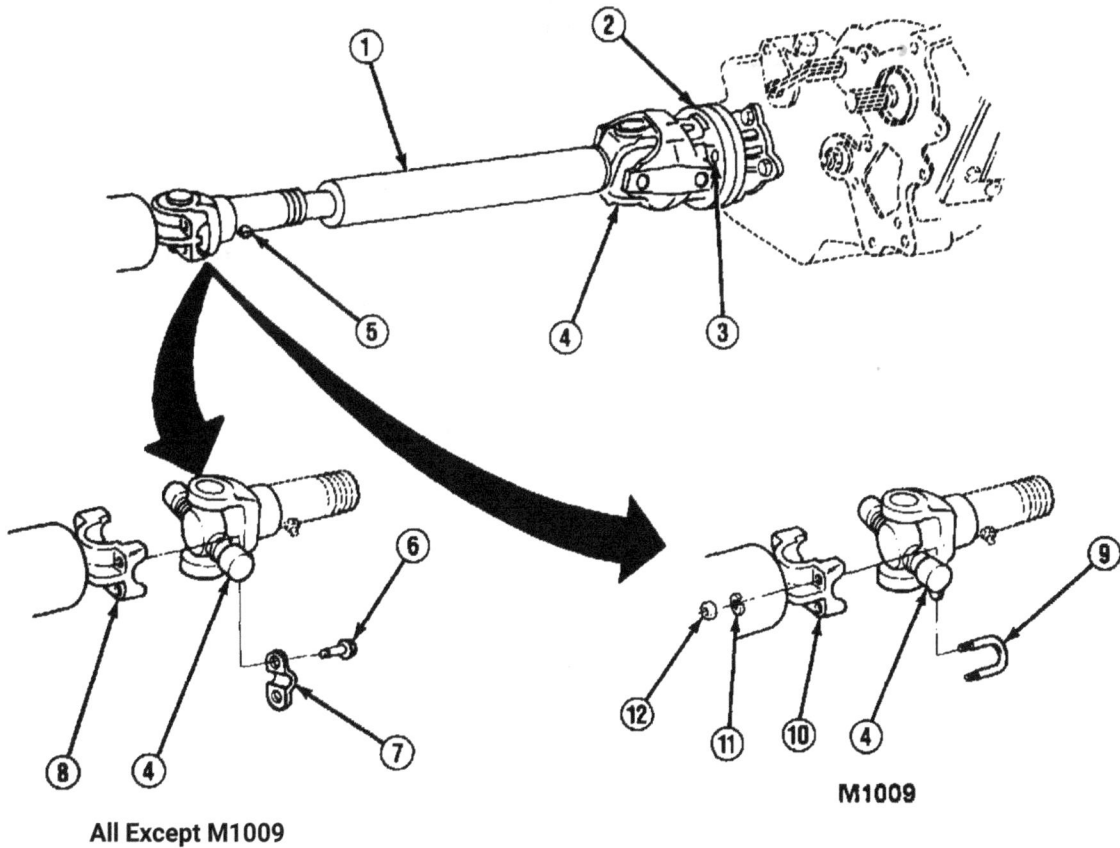

All Except M1009

M1009

FOLLOW-ON TASKS:

• Lubricate propeller shaft. (See LO 9-2320-289-12)

TA49643

6-3. FRONT PROPELLER SHAFT REPAIR.

This task covers: a. Disassembly   c. Assembly
                      b. Cleaning and Inspection

INITIAL SETUP:

Equipment Condition

- Front propeller shaft assembly removed.
  (See paragraph 6-2)

Materials/Parts

- Two boot clamps
- One seal
- Universal joint kits (as required)
- Dry cleaning solvent
  (Item 15, Appendix C)

General Safety Instructions

- Dry cleaning solvent is flammable and must   not be used near open flame. Use only in a
  well-ventilated area.

---

a. DISASSEMBLY

NOTE

- **If disassembling first design front propeller shaft, perform steps 1-3, 5, and 6.**

- **If disassembling second**   **design front propeller shaft, perform**   **steps 1-4 and 6.**

- **Universal joints (7, 14, or 16) on constant velocity joint**   **(12) and driveshaft (6) are factory-installed using plastic injection**   **retainers instead of bearing rings.**

1.   Remove 2 bearing rings (2), 4 bearing rings (10), or 4 bearing rings (13) as required.

2.   Position universal joint (7, 14, or 16) over wood blocks. Using brass drift, drive out bearing cup (1, 8, or 12). Drive out each bearing cup as required and remove universal joint. Discard universal joints and bearing cups.

NOTE

Retain constant velocity joint assembly (9) for installation. If damaged, notify your supervisor.

3.   Remove rear yoke (11) and constant velocity joint assembly (9).

4.   Remove 2 clamps (17) from boot (18). Separate front yoke (3) from driveshaft (6), and remove boot. Discard clamps.

6-3.   FRONT PROPELLER SHAFT REPAIR (Con't).

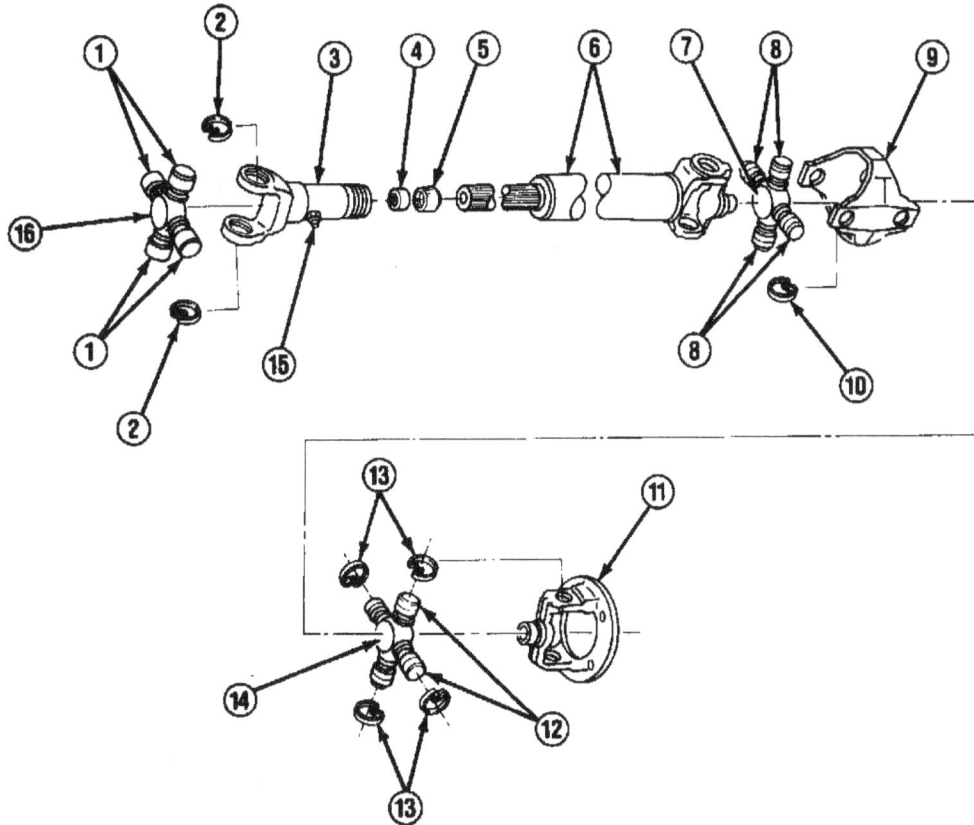

5.   Unscrew seal cap (5) and separate front yoke (3) from driveshaft (6). Remove seal cap and seal (4). Discard seal.

NOTE

Second design propeller shafts DO NOT have a grease fitting (15).

6.   Remove grease fitting (15) if damaged.

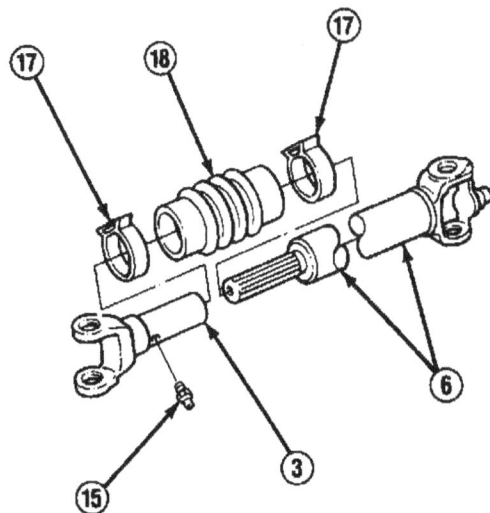

TA49644

6-3.   FRONT PROPELLER SHAFT REPAIR (Con't).

b. CLEANING AND INSPECTION

WARNING

Dry cleaning solvent P-D-680 is toxic and flammable. Always wear
protective goggles and gloves and use only in a well-ventilated area. Avoid
contact with skin, eyes, and clothes and DO NOT breathe vapors. DO NOT
use near open flame or excessive heat. The solvent's flash point is
100°F-138°F (38°C-59°C). If you become dizzy while using cleaning
solvent, immediately get fresh air and medical help. If solvent contacts
eyes, immediately wash your eyes with water and get medical aid.

CAUTION

DO NOT allow rubber parts to soak in dry cleaning solvent for extended
periods of time. Dry cleaning solvent may damage rubber parts.

1.   Clean all metallic parts with dry cleaning solvent.

2.   inspect all components for cracks, dents, burrs, or darnage. Remove burrs and install new
components as required.

c.   ASSEMBLY

NOTE

• If assembling   first design front propeller shaft, perform steps 1, 2, and
4 through 6.

• If assembling   second design front propeller shaft, perform steps 1-3,
5, and 6.

• Second design propeller shafts DO NOT   have a grease fitting (15).

1.   Install grease fitting (15) if removed.

NOTE

Ensure that flanged end of front yoke (3) and flanged end of driveshaft (6)
are alined when performing step 2.

2.   Install new seal (4) and seal cap (5) on front yoke (3). Install driveshaft 6) in front yoke and
tighten seal cap.

6-3.   FRONT PROPELLER SHAFT REPAIR (Con't).

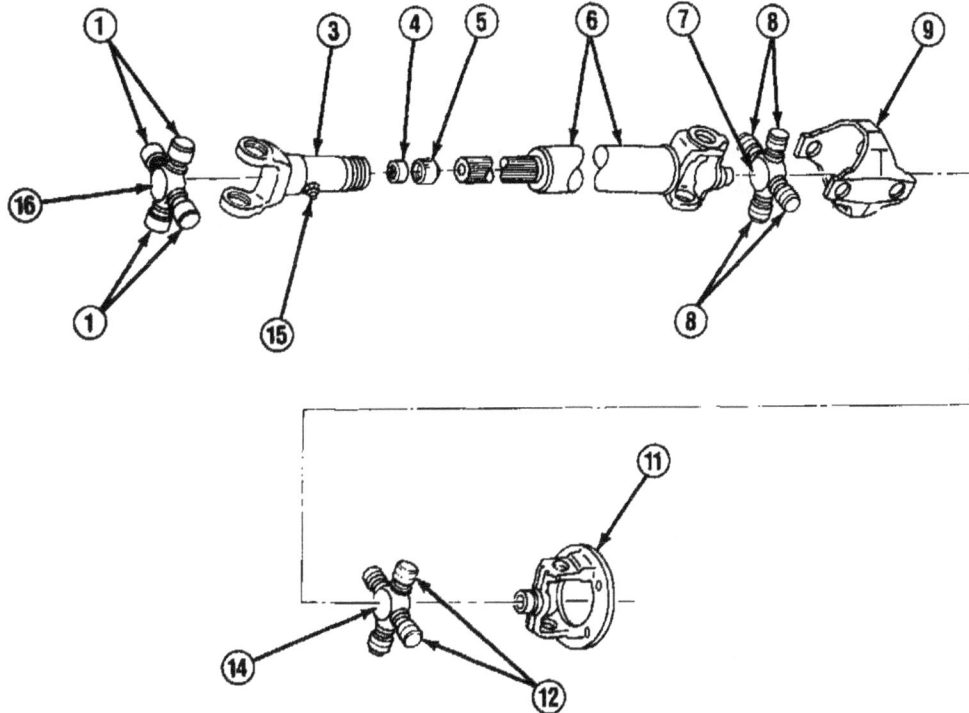

3.   Slide 1 new clamp (17) onto front yoke (3) and 1 new clamp onto driveshaft (6). Position boot (18) between front yoke and driveshaft, and install driveshaft in front yoke. Slide clamps over ends of boot and tighten.

NOTE

Perform step 4 as require   d depending on which universal joint (7 or 14) was removed.

4.   Position new universal joint (16) in front yoke (3). Position new universal joint (7) in driveshaft (6) and constant velocity joint assembly (9). Position new universal joint (14) in constant velocity joint assembly and rear yoke (11). Position new bearing   CUP (1, 8, or 12) on universal joint (7, 14, or 16).

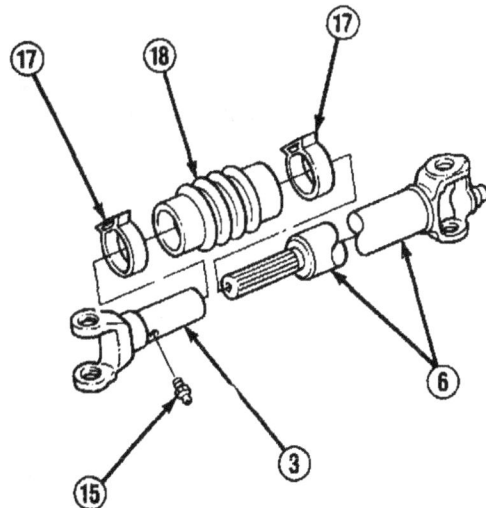

TA49645

6-3. FRONT PROPELLER SHAFT REPAIR (Con't).

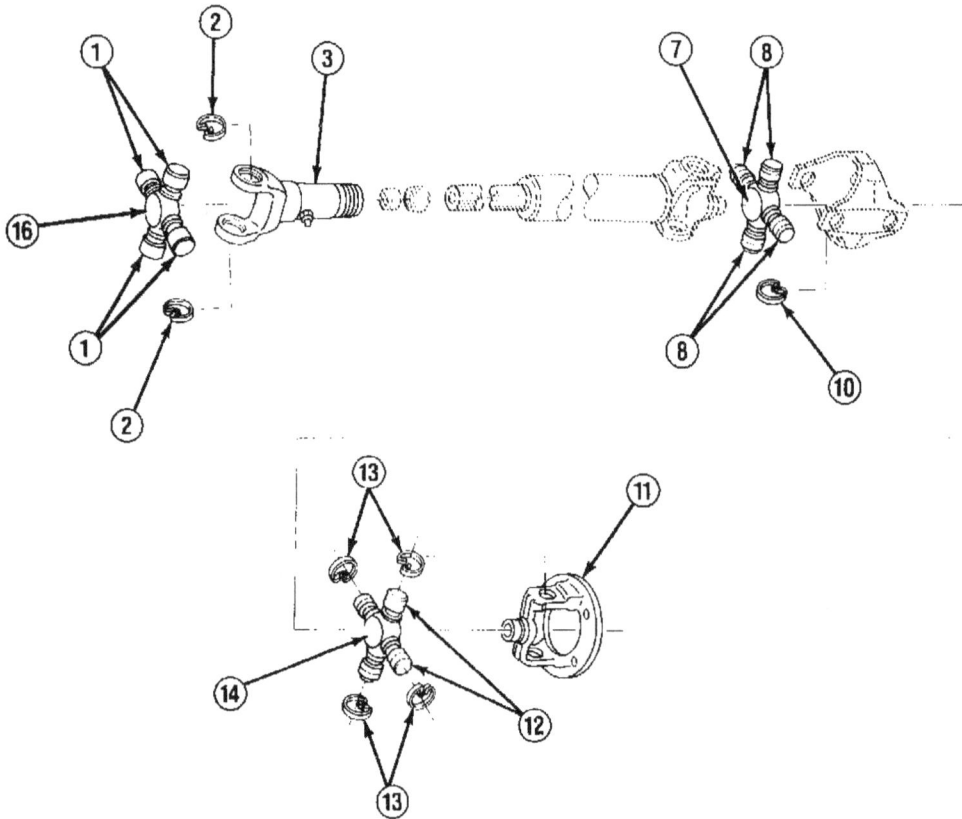

CAUTION

Ensure that bearing cup (1, 8, or 12) is alined with yoke (3 or 11) before pressing in with vise. Damage to universal joint and bearing cup may result if forced into yoke.

5.   Position universal joint (7, 14, or 16) in vise with a socket between vise jaw and bearing cup (1, 8, or 12) to be installed. Press bearing cup in far enough to install bearing ring (2, 10, or 13).

NOTE

Rear universal joints (7 and 14) each use 4 bearing rings (10 or 13). Front universal joint (16) uses 2 bearing rings (2).

6.   Install bearing ring (2, 10, or 13) and bearing cup (1 , 8, or 12) completely in place. Repeat steps 5 and 6 for each bearing cup and bearing ring.

FOLLOW-ON TASKS:

●Install front propeller   shaft assembly. (See paragraph 6-2)

TA49646

6-4. REAR PROPELLER SHAFT ASSEMBLY REPLACEMENT.

| This task covers: | a. Removal | b. Installation |

INITIAL SETUP:

Tools/Test Equipment
  • Torque wrench

---

a. REMOVAL

1. Remove 4 bolts (7) and 2 straps (6).

2. Slide rear propeller shaft (3) forward to disengage from axle flange (5).

3. Slide rear propeller shaft (3) rearward to disengage from transfer case propeller shaft.   (1). Remove rear

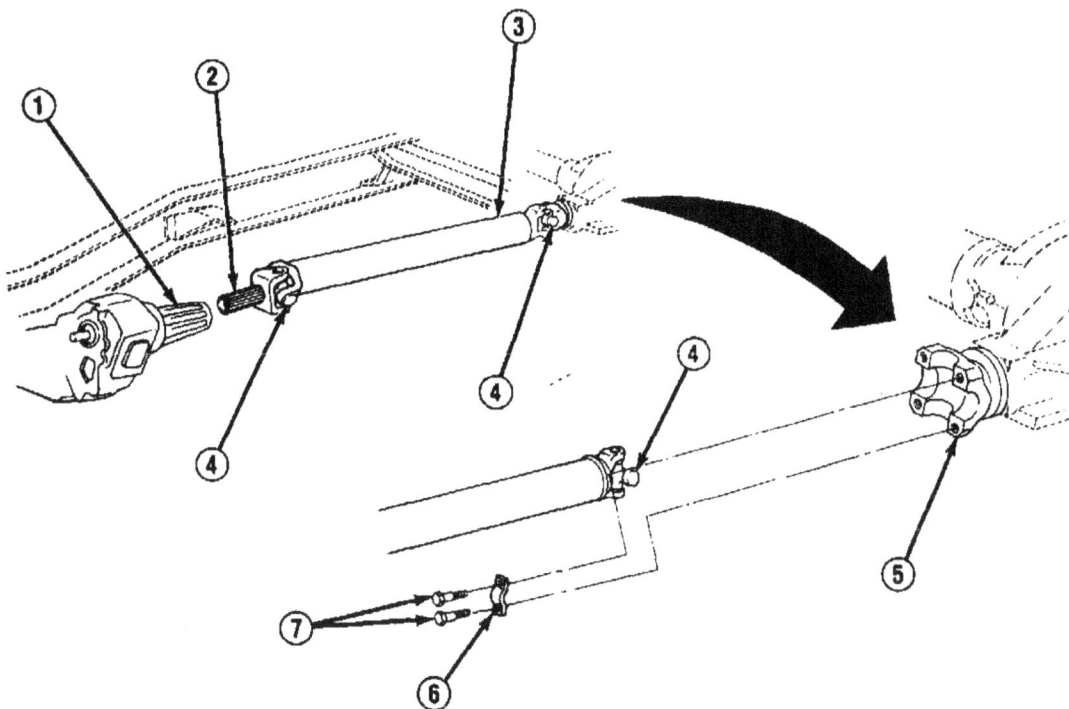

b. INSTALLATION

1. Slide rear propeller shaft yoke (2) into transfer case (1).

2. Position 2 clamps (6) on universal joint (4) and install rear propeller shaft (3) on axle flange (5) with 4 bolts (7). Tighten bolts to 25-30 lb.-ft. (34-41 Nom).

TA49647

6-5. REAR PROPELLER SHAFT REPAIR.

This task covers: a. Disassembly   c. Assembly
                                    b. Cleaning and Inspection

---

INITIAL SETUP:

Equipment Condition   *Materials/Parts*

  • Rear propeller shaft assembly removed.   • Universal joint kits (as required)
     (See paragraph 6-4)   • Dry cleaning solvent
                                               (Item 15, Appendix C)

General Safety Instructions

  • Dry cleaning solvent is   flammable and must not be used near open flame.   Use only in a
     well-ventilated area.

---

a.	DISASSEMBLY

1.   Remove 4 bearing rings (2) or 2 bearing rings   (5) as required.

2.   Position universal joint (7 or 8) over wood blocks, Using brass drift, drive out bearing cup   (3
       or *6)* as required, and remove universal joint (8) and yoke (1) or universal joint (7) from
       driveshaft (4). Discard universal joint and bearing cups.

b.	CLEANING AND INSPECTION

WARNING

    **Dry cleaning solvent P-D-680 is toxic and flammable. Always wear
protective goggles and gloves and use only in a well-ventilated area, Avoid
contact with skin, eyes, and clothes and DO NOT breathe vapors, DO NOT
use near open flame or excessive heat. The solvent's flash point is
100°F-138°F (38°C-59°C). If you become dizzy while using cleaning
solvent, immediately get fresh air and medical help. If solvent contacts
eyes, immediately wash your eyes with water and get medical aid.**

CAUTION

    **DO NOT allow rubber parts to soak in dry cleaning solvent for extended
periods of time, Dry cleaning solvent may damage rubber parts.**

1.   Clean all metallic parts with dry cleaning solvent.

2.   Inspect all components for cracks, dents, burrs, or damage, Remove burrs and install new
       components as required.

6-5.   REAR PROPELLER SHAFT REPAIR (Con't).

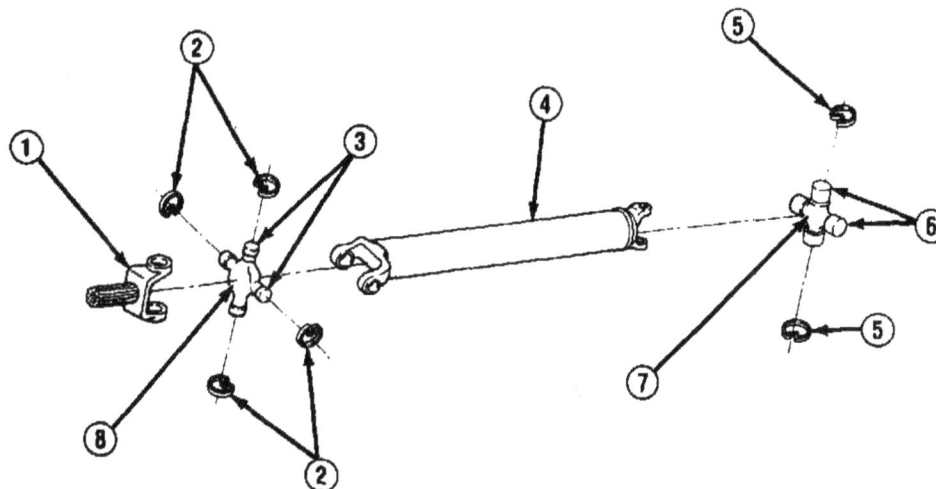

| c. | ASSEMBLY |

1.   Position new universal joint (8) in yoke (1) or driveshaft (4) and new universal joint (7) in driveshaft. Position new bearing cup (3 or 6) on universal joint (7 or 8).

CAUTION

Ensure that bearing cup (3 or 6) is alined with yoke (1) before pressing in with vise. Damage to universal joint (7 or 8) and bearing cup may result if forced into yoke.

2.   Position universal joint (7 or 6) in vise with a socket between vise jaw and bearing cup (3 or 6) to be installed. Press bearing cup in far enough to install bearing ring (2 or 5).

NOTE

Rear universal joint (7) uses 2 bearing rings (5). Front universal joint (8) uses 4 bearing rings (2).

3.   Install bearing ring (2 or 5) and bearing cup (3 or 6) completely in place. Repeat steps 2 and 3 for each bearing cup and ring.

FOLLOW-ON TASKS:

· Install rear propeller shaft assembly. (See paragraph 6-4)

TA49648

Section II. FRONT AND REAR AXLES MAINTENANCE

6-6. FRONT AND REAR AXLES MAINTENANCE INDEX.

6-7. FRONT AXLE SPINDLE AND WHEEL BEARINGS REPLACEMENT.

This task covers: a. Removal   b. Installation

INITIAL SETUP:

Equipment Condition

• Rotor and caliper mounting bracket
  removed. (See paragraph 8-4)

Tools/Test Equipment

• Puller Kit

Materials/Parts

• Axle shaft seal
• Spindle seal
• Grease (Item 26, Appendix C)

```
a.   REMOVAL
```

NOTE

✸ **1985-87 M1009 trucks have a spindle (6) that is 0.25 in. (6.3 mm) longer than 1984 trucks.**

✸ **To remove spindle (6), it may be necessary to tap end with plastic or rubber mallet.**

1. Remove spindle (6).

2. Remove axle shaft seal (2) and spacer (3) from axle shaft (1). Remove spindle seal (4) and wheel bearing assembly (5) from spindle (6). Discard seals.

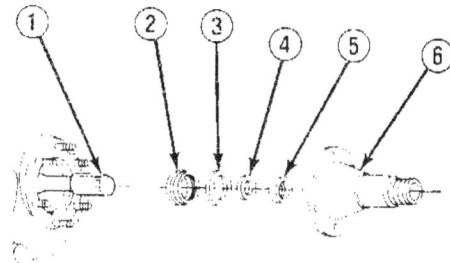

All Except M1009

```
b.   INSTALLATION
```

1. Grease wheel bearing assembly (5) and install in spindle (6). Install new spindle seal (4) into spindle with sealing lips facing outward, Install spacer (3) onto axle shaft (1) with chamfer toward axle housing. Install new axle shaft seal (2) with lip facing outward.

2. Install spindle (6).

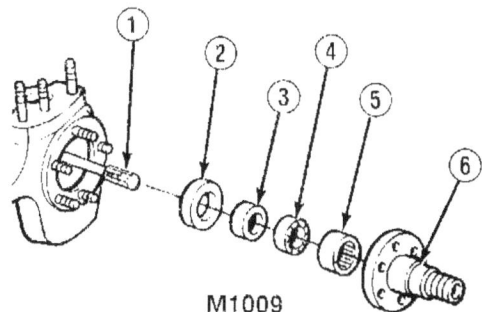

M1009

FOLLOW-ON TASKS:

• Install caliper mounting bracket and rotor. (See paragraph 8-4)

TA49649

6-8. REAR AXLE SHAFT REPLACEMENT (ALL EXCEPT M1009).

This task covers: a. Removal   b. Installation

INITIAL SETUP:

Equipment Condition
 • Wheel to be serviced, raised and supported by jack stand.

Materials/Parts
 • One gasket

Tools/Test Equipment
 • Torque wrench

---

a.	REMOVAL

NOTE

Rear axle shafts (3) are factory-installed with RTV sealant instead of gasket (4). Use gasket instead of RTV sealant for installation.

1. Remove 8 bolts (1). Remove rear axle shaft (3) and gasket (4), if present, from wheel hub (5). Discard gasket.

2. Clean any sealant from bolts (1) and mating surfaces of rear axle shaft flange (2) and exterior of wheel hub (5).

b.	INSTALLATION

1. Position rear axle shaft (3) through new gasket (4) and wheel hub (5), and install with 8 bolts (1). Tighten bolts to 115 lb.-ft. (156 N•m).

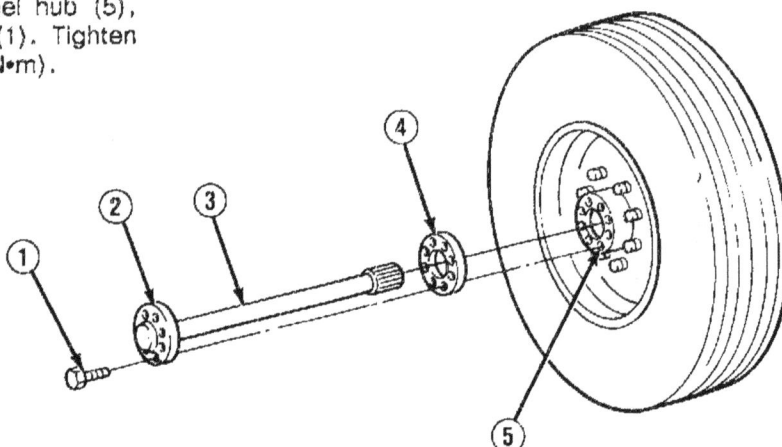

FOLLOW-ON TASKS:

 • Remove jack stand and lower truck.

TA49650

6-8.1. SERVICE FRONT DIFFERENTIAL.

This task covers: a. Service

INITIAL SETUP:

Materials/Parts
 • One differential cover gasket

Tools/Test Equipment
 • Torque wrench

---

a.	SERVICE

1. **Place a suitable container under differential housing.**

2. **Remove 10 bolts (1) and differential cover (3) and allow all lubricating oil to drain.**

3. **Remove differential cover gasket (2) and discard.**

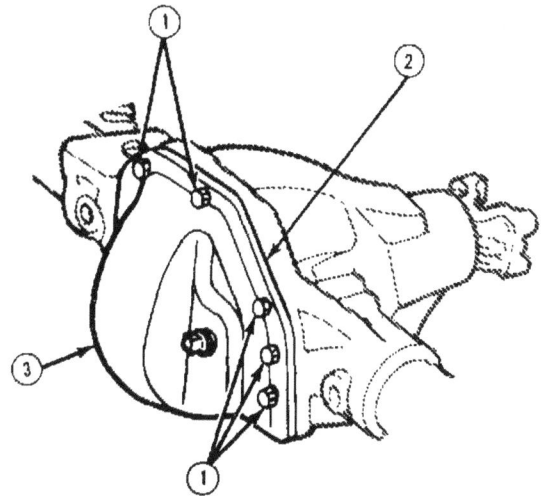

NOTE

Ensure that differential cover and magnet are clean.

4. **Install new differential cover gasket (2) and differential cover (3) with 10 bolts (1).**

5. **Tighten 10 bolts (1) to 35 lb.-ft. (47 N•m).**

6. **Fill differential with lubricating oil. (See LO 9-2320-289-12)**

TA701836 ■

6-8.2. SERVICE REAR DIFFERENTIAL (ALL EXCEPT M1009, M1028A2, AND M1028A3).

This task covers: a. Service

INITIAL SETUP:

Materials/Parts
- One differential cover gasket
- Sealant (Item 41, Appendix C)

Tools/Test Equipment
- Torque wrench

---

a.	SERVICE

NOTE

When removing differential cover bolts, location of clips should be noted.

1. Place a suitable container under housing.

2. Remove 14 bolts (1) at differential cover (3) .

3. Move vent tube bracket, brake line and bracket, and proportioning valve lever out of the way.

4. Remove differential cover (3) and allow all lubricating oil to drain.

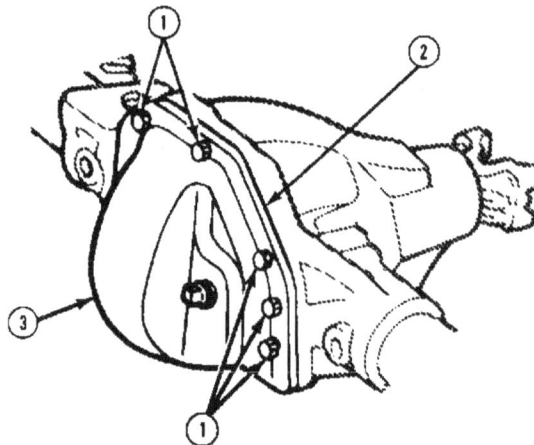

NOTE

Some differentials will use a gasket (2), and some will use RTV sealant.

5. Remove gasket (2), if present, and discard.

6. If RTV sealant was utilized, remove all old RTV sealant from differential housing.

NOTE

Ensure that differential cover (3) is clean.

7. Apply a bead of RTV sealant to differential housing or install new gasket (2) and differential cover (3) with 14 bolts (1).

8. Tighten 14 bolts (1) to 35 lb.-ft (47 N•m).

9. Fill differential with lubricating oil. (See LO 9-2320-289-12)

TA701837

6-8.3. SERVICE REAR DIFFERENTIAL (M1009, M1028A2, AND M1028A3).

This task covers: a. Service

INITIAL SETUP:

Materials/Parts
· Sealant (Item 41, Appendix C)

Tools/Test Equipment
· Torque wrench

a.	SERVICE

1.   Place a suitable container under differential housing.

2.   Remove 10 bolts (1) and differential cover (3) and allow all lubricating oil to drain.

3.   Remove old RTV sealant from differential housing (2).

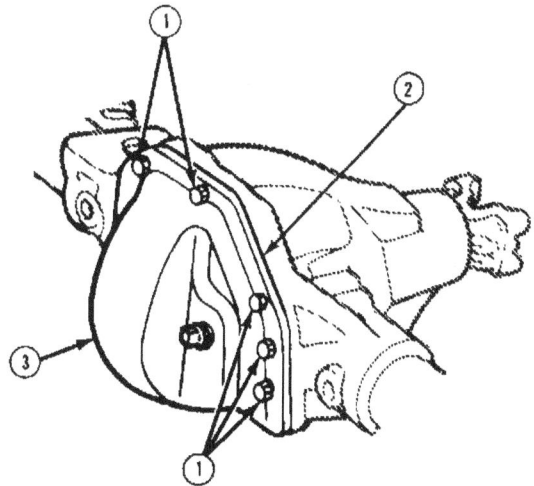

NOTE

Ensure that differential cover and magnet are clean.

4.   Apply bead of RTV sealant to differential housing (2).

5.   Install differential cover (3) with 10 bolts (1).

6.   Tighten 10 bolts (1) to 35 lb.-ft. (47 N·m).

7.   Fill differential with lubricating oil. (See LO 9-2320-289-12)

TA701838

Section III. SUSPENSION MAINTENANCE

6-9. SUSPENSION MAINTENANCE INDEX.

6-10. FRONT SHOCK ABSORBER, AXLE BUMPER, AND SPRING BUMPER REPLACEMENT.

This task covers: a. Removal b. Installation

INITIAL SETUP:

Materials/Parts

• Nine lockwashers

Tools/Test Equipment

• Torque wrench

---

a. REMOVAL

NOTE

● If removing shock absorber (5), perform step 1.

● I f removing right o r left bumpers, perform step 2.

1. Remove 2 nuts (1), lockwashers (2), and bolts (4), and remove shock absorber (5). Discard lockwashers.

2. Remove nut (7 or 10), lockwasher (6 or 11), and axle bumper (14 or 12). Remove 2 nuts (8), lockwashers (9), and spring bumpers (13) as required. Discard lockwashers.

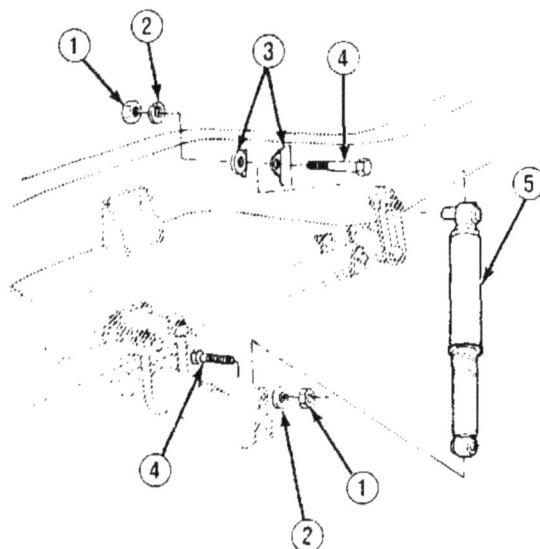

b. INSTALLATION

NOTE

● I f installing right o r left bumpers, perform step 1.

● If installing shock absorber (5), perform step 2.

1. Install 2 spring bumpers (13) with 2 new lockwashers (9) and nuts (8). Install axle bumper (14 or 12) with new lockwasher (6 or 11) and nut (7 or 10) if removed.

2. Install shock absorber (5) on frame bracket (3) and front axle bracket with 2 bolts (4), new lockwashers (2), and nuts (1). Tighten nuts to 65 lb.-ft. (88 N•m).

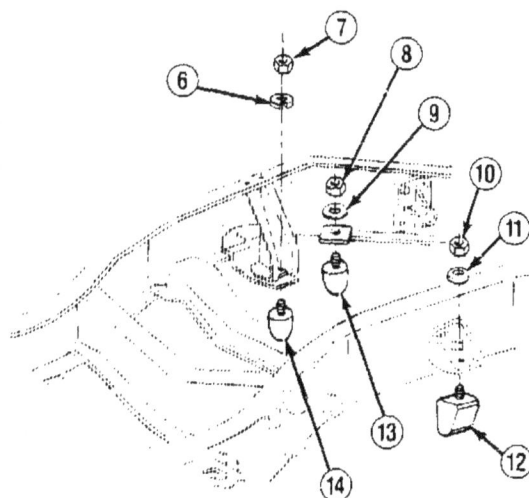

TA49651

6-11. REAR SHOCK ABSORBER AND AXLE BUMPER REPLACEMENT.

| This task covers: | a. Removal | b. Installation |

INITIAL SETUP:

Materials/Parts
• Three lockwashers

Tools/Test Equipment
• Torque wrench

a. REMOVAL

NOTE

● If removing shock absorber (3), perform step 1.

● If removing spring bumper (10), perform step 2.

1. Remove nut (7), lockwasher (6), and washer (5) or nut (2) and lockwasher (1). Remove nut (11), lockwasher (12), and bolt (13), and remove shock absorber (3). Discard lockwashers (1 or 6, and 12).

2. Remove nut (8), lockwasher (9), and spring bumper (10). Discard lockwasher.

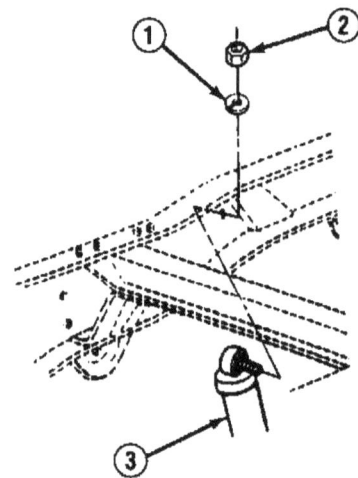

M1009

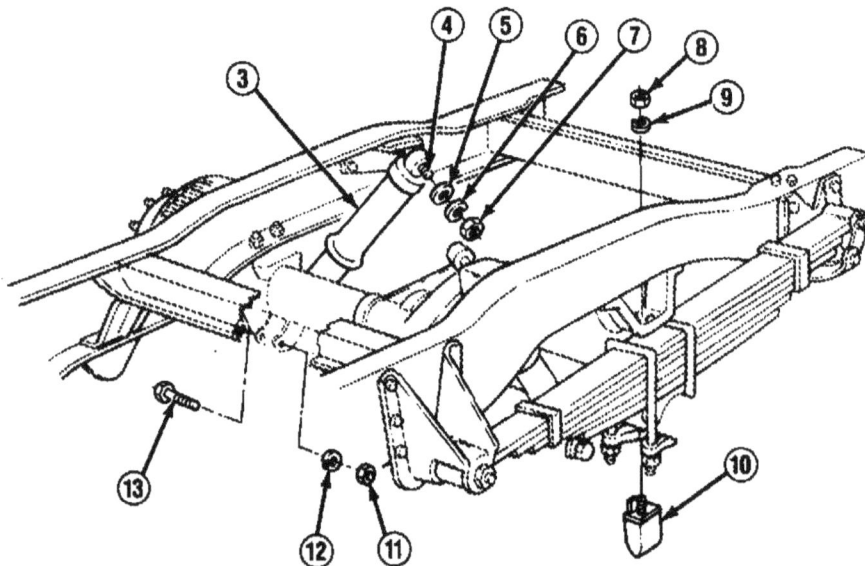

TA49652

6-11.   REAR SHOCK ABSORBER AND AXLE BUMPER REPLACEMENT (Con't).

b. INSTALLATION

NOTE

· If installing spring   bumper (10),
   perform step 1.

· If installing   shock absorber (3),
   perform step 2.

1.   Install spring bumper (10) with new
     lockwasher (9) and nut (8).

2.   Position shock absorber (3) and
     install bolt (13), new lockwasher
     (12), and nut (11). Install washer (5),
     new lockwasher (6), and nut (7) on
     stud (4) or install new lockwasher (1)
     and nut (2). Tighten nuts to 65 lb.-ft.
     (88 N·m).

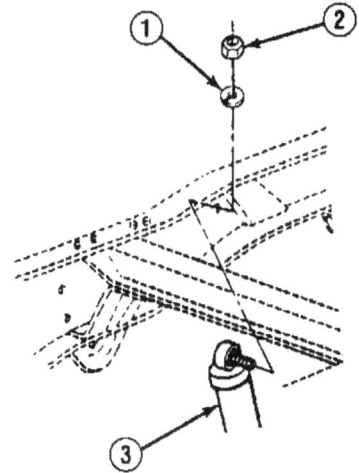

M1009

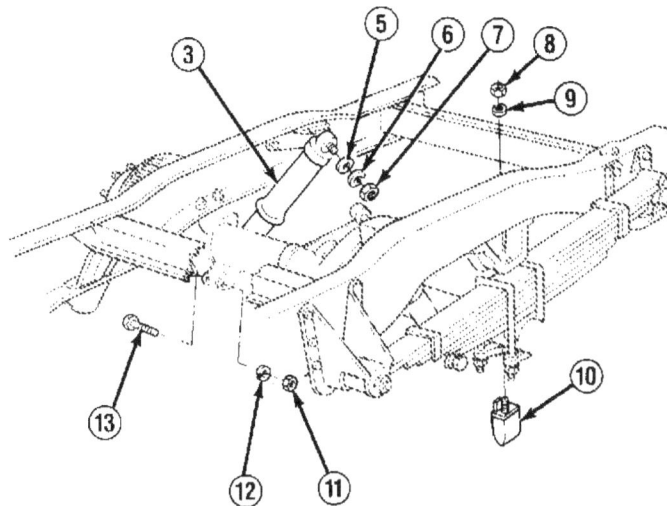

TA49653

6-12.   FRONT STABILIZER BAR AND BUSHINGS REPLACEMENT.

This task covers:	a. Removal	b. Installation

INITIAL SETUP:

Materiais/Parts
 • Four locknuts

Tools/Test Equipment
 • Torque wrench

---

a.	**REMOVAL**

1.   Remove 4 locknuts (8), 8 washers (7), 2 clamps (9), and 4 bolts (8). Discard locknuts.

2.   Remove 2 bushings (10) from stabilizer bar (3). Inspect bushings for wear and discard if damaged.

3.   Remove 2 bolts (1) and 4 washers (2). Remove stabilizer bar (3). Inspect bushings (5) for damage. If damaged, notify your supervisor.

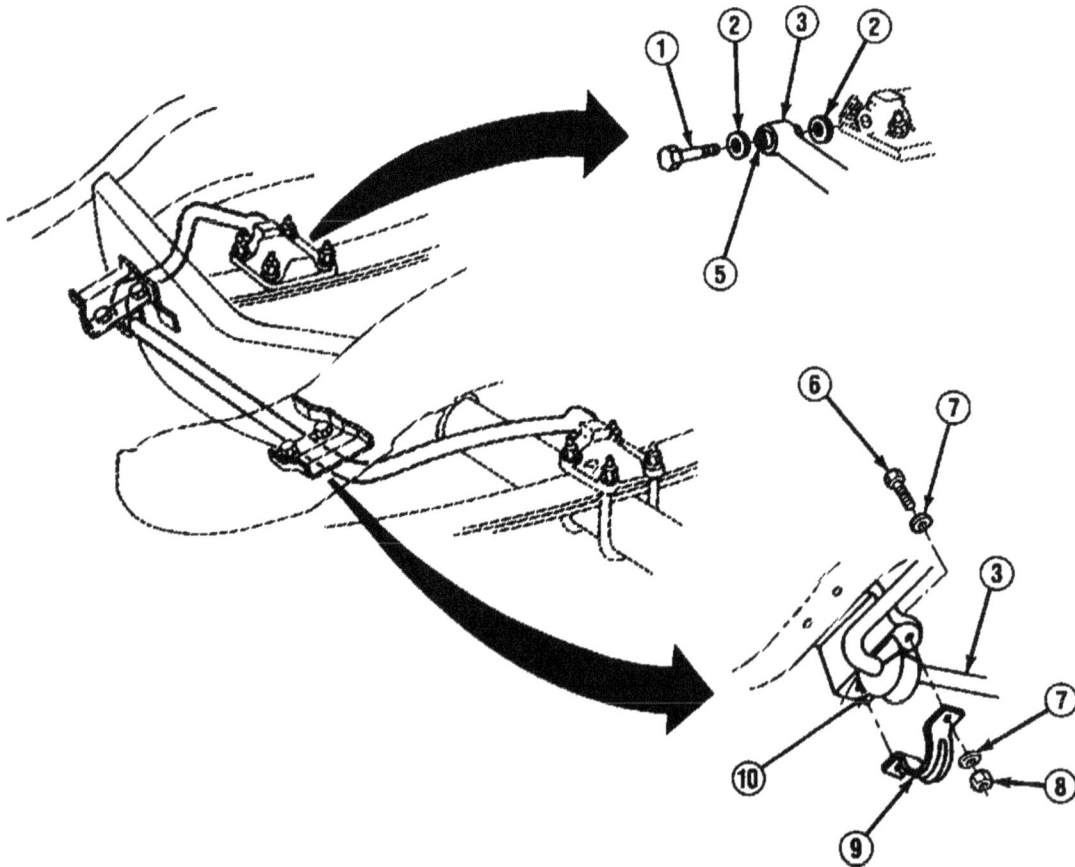

TA49654

6-12. FRONT STABILIZER BAR AND BUSHINGS REPLACEMENT (Con't).

b.	INSTALLATION

1. Position stabilizer bar (3) and install on lower spring anchor plates (4) with   4 washers (2) and 2 bolts (1). Tighten bolts to 230 lb.-ft. (312 N•m).

NOTE

Ensure that bushings (10) are installed with slit facing backward   and are alined under frame bracket. Install new bushings if removed.

2. Install 2 bushings (10) on stabilizer bar (3). Position 2 clamps (9) over bushings and install with 4 bolts (6), 8 washers (7), and 4 new locknuts (8). Tighten locknuts to 55 lb.-ft. (75 N•m).

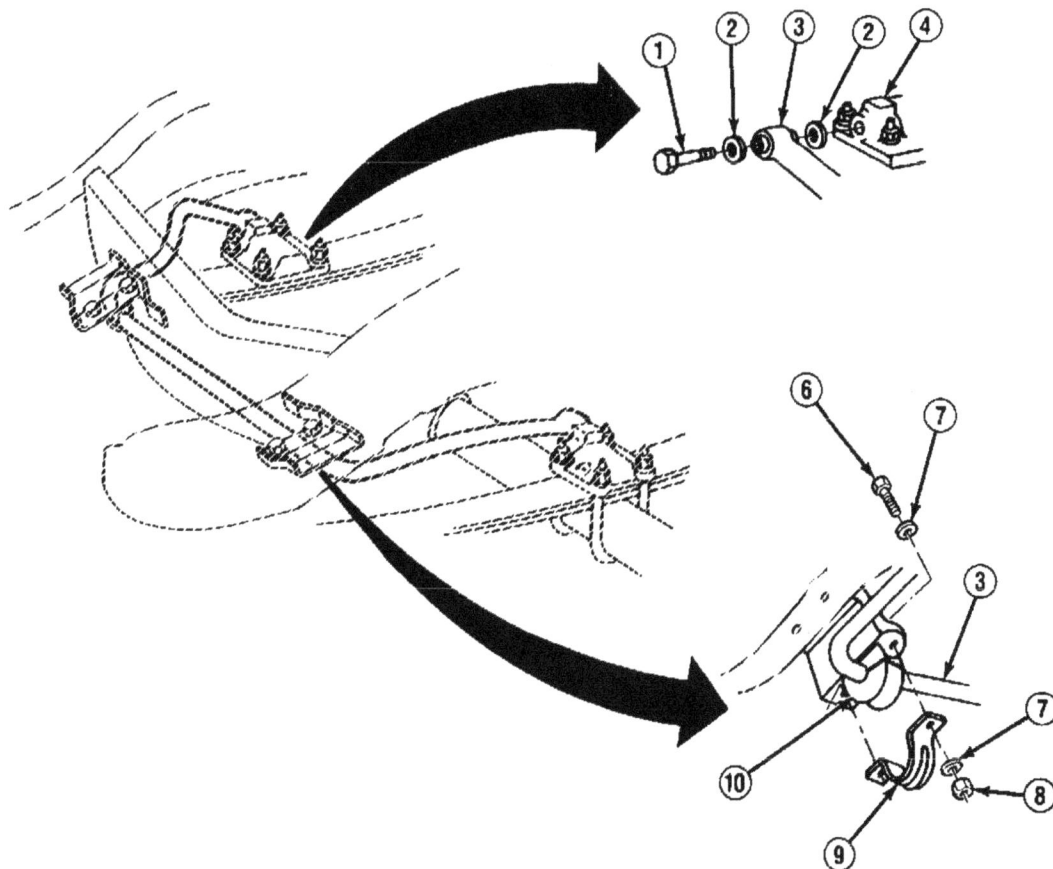

TA49655

6-13. REAR STABILIZER BAR, BUSHINGS, AND REINFORCEMENT BRACKET REPLACEMENT.

This task covers:	a. Removal	b. Installation

INITIAL SETUP:

Materials/Parts
• Nine locknuts

Tools/Test Equipment
• Torque wrench

---

a. REMOVAL

1. Remove 4 locknuts (4), washers (5), 2 clamps (7), and 4 bolts (8). Discard locknuts.

2. Remove 2 bushings (6) from stabilizer bar (9). Inspect bushings for wear and discard if damaged.

3. Remove 2 locknuts (3), 8 washers (2), 8 grommets (1), 2 spacers (11), 2 bolts (10), and rear stabilizer bar (9). Discard locknuts.

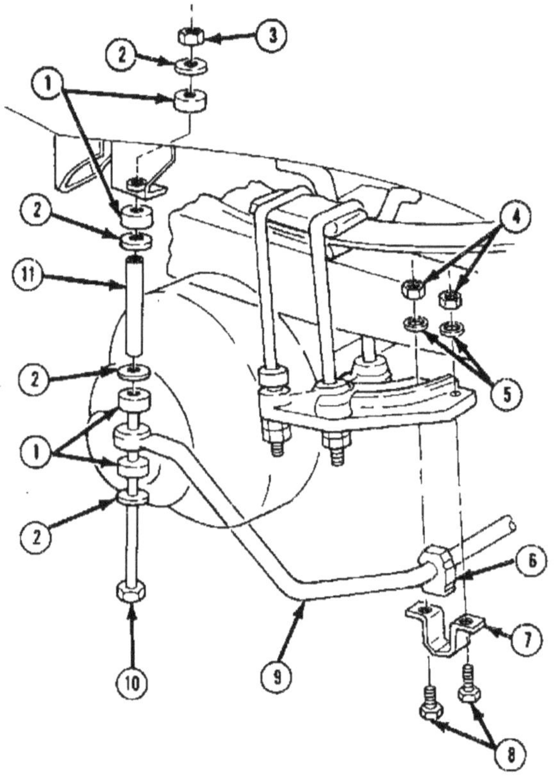

6-13. REAR STABILIZER BAR, BUSHINGS, AND REINFORCEMENT BRACKET REPLACEMENT (Con't).

NOTE

Perform step 4 only if bracket is damaged.

4. Remove 3 bolts (14), washers (13), locknuts (12), and reinforcemen t bracket (15) . Discard locknuts.

b. INSTALLATION

NOTE

Perform step 1 only if bracket was removed.

1. Install reinforcement bracket (15) to frame (16) with 3 new locknuts (12), washers   (13), and bolts (14).

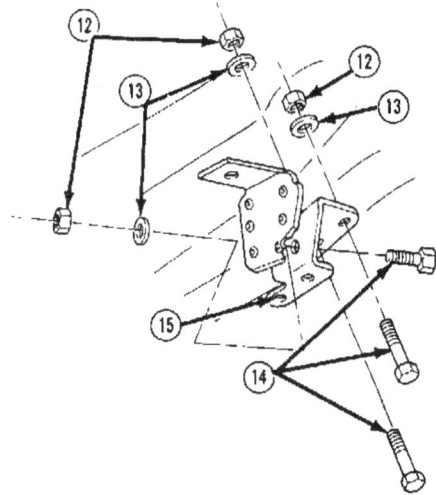

2. Position rear stabilizer bar (9) and install on 2 reinforcement brackets (15) with 2 bolts (10), 2 spacers (11), 8 grommets (1), 8 washers (2), and 2 new locknuts (3). Tighten locknuts to the nonthreaded portion of bolts.

3. Install 2 bushings (6) on rear stabilizer bar (9).

6-13. REAR STABILIZER BAR, BUSHINGS, AND REINFORCEMENT BRACKET REPLACEMENT (Con't).

4. Install 2 clamps (7), 4 bolts (8), washers (5), and new locknuts (4). Tighten bolts to 35 lb.-ft. (50 N•m).

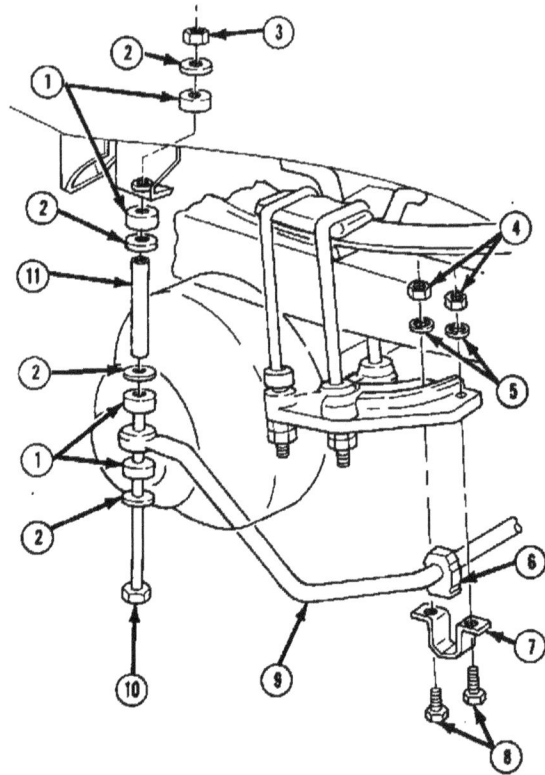

CHAPTER 7
BRAKE   SYSTEM MAINTENANCE

Section I. PARKING BRAKE SYSTEM MAINTENANCE

7-1.   PARKING BRAKE SYSTEM MAINTENANCE INDEX.

7-2. PARKING BRAKE CABLE ADJUSTMENT.

This task covers: a. Adjustmen t

INITIAL SETUP:

Equipment Condition
- Front wheels chocked.
- Rear of truck supported by jack stands under axle housing.

---

a. ADJUSTMENT

NOTE

Ensure that adjuster assembly (2) is clean.

1. Depress parking brake pedal   4 notches from fully-released position.

2. Rotate rear wheels forward.

3. Loosen or tighten equalizer nut (1) as required until a moderate drag is felt.

4. Fully release parking brake pedal.

5. Rotate rear wheels. No drag should be present. If drag is present , depress and release parking brake pedal 3 times and repeat steps 1-4.

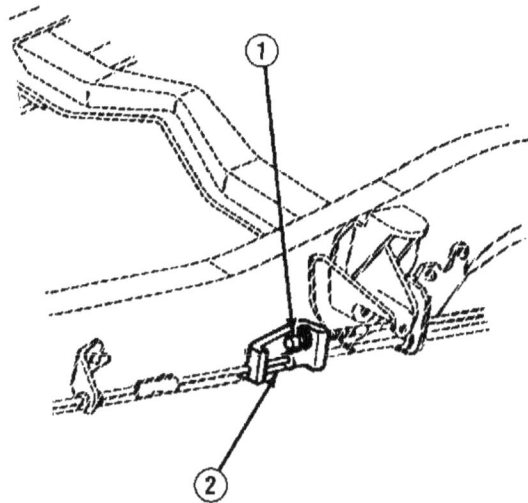

FOLLOW-ON TASKS:

- Remove jack stands and lower truck.
- Remove wheel chocks from front wheels.
- Check parking brake operation.

TA49656

7-3. PARKING BRAKE PEDAL REPLACEMENT.

This task covers: a. Removal b. Installation

INITIAL SETUP:

Equipment Condition
- Wheels chocked.
- Parking brake cable loosened.
  (See paragraph 7-2)
- Parking brake switch removed.
  (See paragraph 4-17)
- Parking brake pedal in released position.

Materials/Parts
- Bolt and lockwasher
- Two nuts and washers

---

a. REMOVAL

1. Disconnect release handle rod (10) from parking brake retainer (9). Remove parking brake retainer if damaged. Remove release handle (13) and release handle rod, Remove pedal cover (14) and grommet (12) if damaged.

    NOTE

    Parking brake assembly (1) is factory-installed with washer-assembled bolt. DO NOT use washer-assembied boit for installation.

2. Remove bolt (11) and lockwasher (7). Discard lockwasher.

    NOTE

    Parking brake assembly (1) is factory-installed with flanged nuts. DO NOT use flanged nuts for installation.

3. Remove 2 nuts (6) and washers (5) from engine compartment wall.

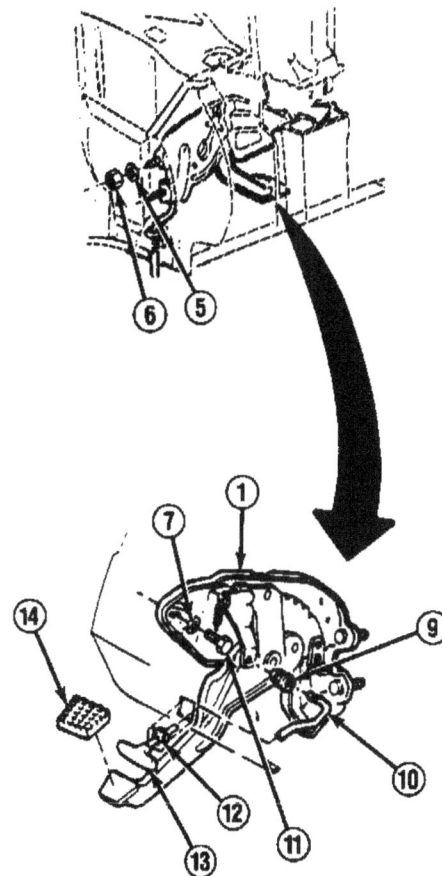

TA49657

7-3.   PARKING BRAKE PEDAL REPLACEMENT (Con't).

4.   Depress tabs on finger clip (3) and disconnect parking brake cable (4) from parking brake assembly clip (2). Remove parking brake assembly (1).

b.   INSTALLATION

1.   Push finger clip (3) through parking brake assembly (1). Connect parking brake cable (4) to parking brake assembly clip (2).

2.   Install parking brake assembly (1) with studs through engine compartment wall using 2 washers (5) and nuts (6).

3.   Install new lockwasher (7) and bolt (11).

4.   Install grommet (12) on instrument panel and pedal cover (14) on pedal if removed. Push release handle rod (10) through grommet. Install parking brake retainer (9) on parking brake lever (8) if removed and connect release handle rod to parking brake retainer.

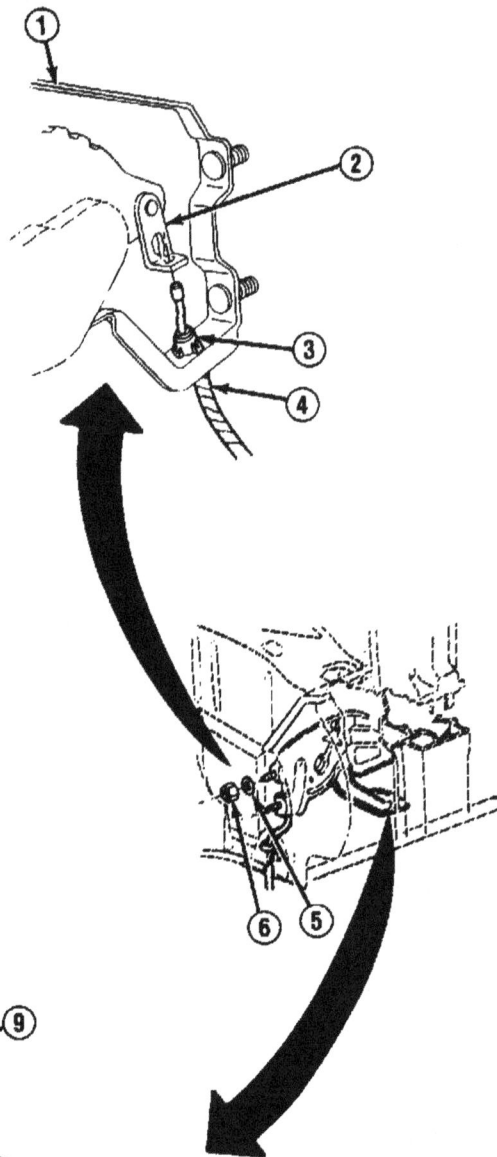

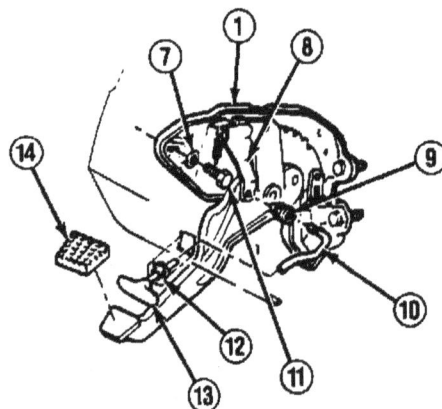

FOLLOW-ON TASKS:

• Adjust parking brake cable. (See paragraph 7-2)
• Install parking brake switch. (See paragraph 4-17)
• Remove wheel chocks.

TA49658

7-4. PARKING BRAKE CABLE REPLACEMENT.

This task covers:	a. Removal	b. Installation

INITIAL SETUP:

Equipment Condition
- Wheels chocked.
- Parking brake cable disconnected at parking brake pedal assembly, if removing front cable, (See paragraph 7-3)
- Brake drum removed, if removing rear cable. (See paragraph 8-5)

---

a.	REMOVAL

NOTE

- **If removing front parking brake cable (16), perform steps 1 and 2.**

- **If removing right rear parking brake cable (2), perform steps 3-5.**

- **If removing left rear parking brake cable (6), perform steps 3, 4, and 6.**

1. Disconnect front parking brake cable (16) at connector (15), Remove connector as required, Retain parking brake cable grommet (20) for installation.

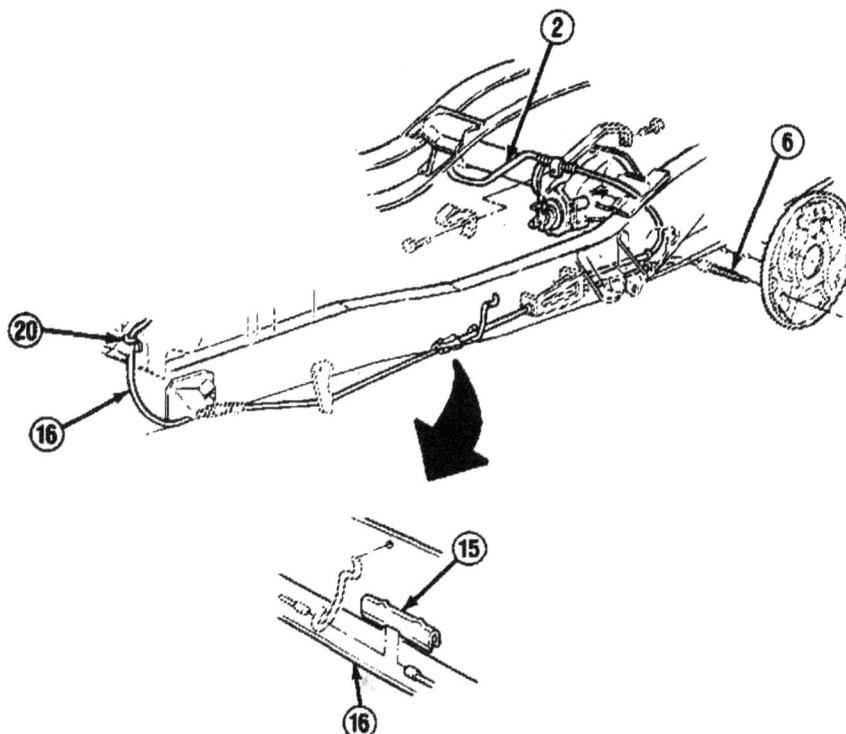

TA49659

7-4.   PARKING BRAKE CABLE REPLACEMENT (Con't).

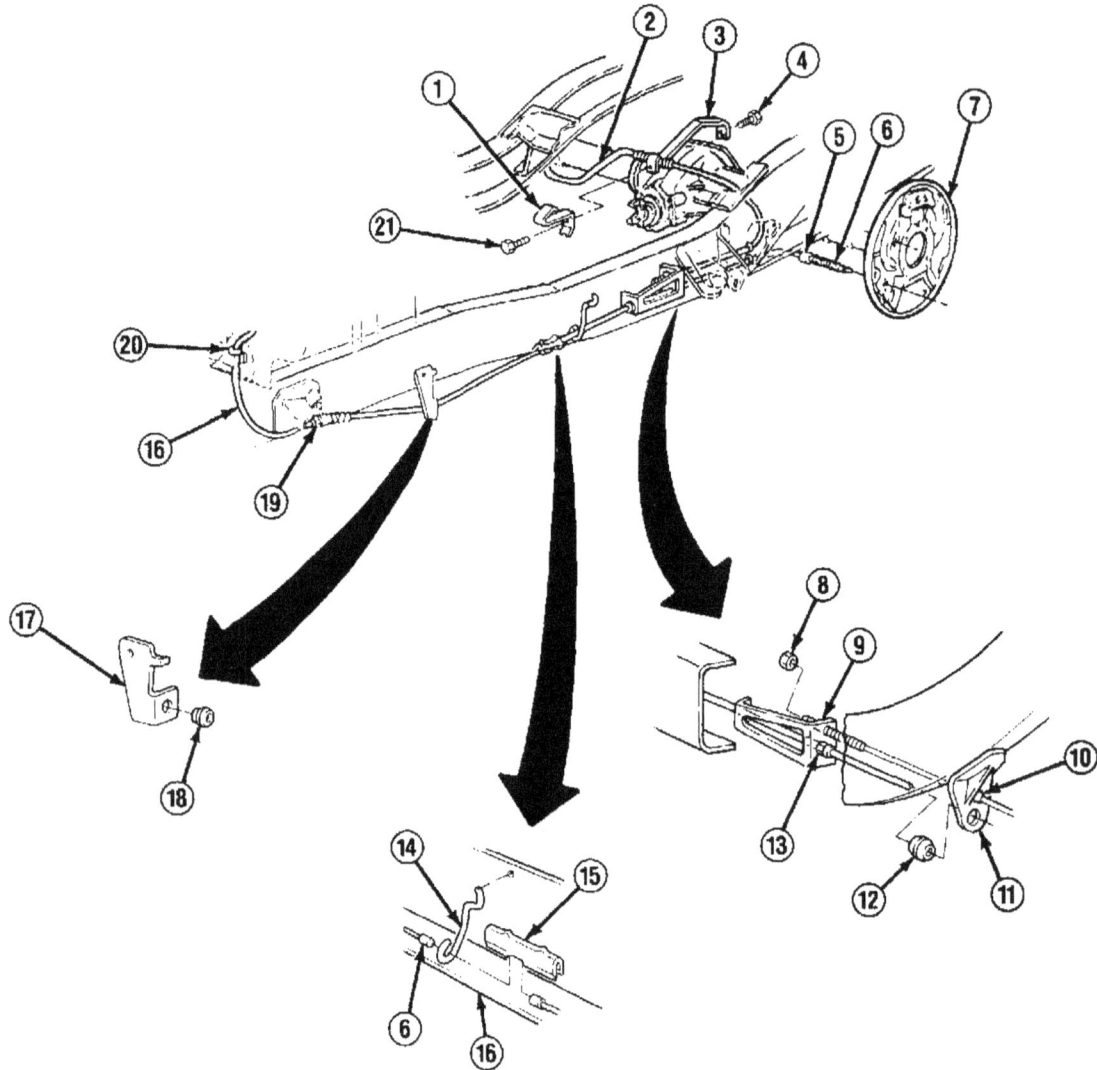

2.   Depress tabs on finger clip (19) and pull front parking brake cable (16) through bracket (17) and into cab to remove. Remove grommet (18) as required.

3.   If removing right rear parking brake cable (2), remove equalizer nut (8). If removing left rear parking brake cable (6), loosen equalizer nut.

4.   Disconnect rear parking brake cable (2 or 6) from parking brake lever. Depress tabs on finger clip (5) and remove rear parking brake cable from backing plate (7).

5.   Remove bolt (21) and clip (1), or bolt (4) and clip (3), and remove right rear parking brake cable (2).

TA49660

7-4. PARKING BRAKE CABLE REPLACEMENT (Con't).

NOTE

Only M1009 has a cable guide (14).

6. Depress finger clip (13) and disconnect left rear parking cable (6) from connector (15). Depress tabs on finger clip (10) and pull cable through bracket (11) to remove. Remove equalizer (9) and grommet (12) from left rear parking brake cable as required. Remove cable guide (14) as required.

b. INSTALLATION

NOTE

- **If installing   left rear parking brake cable (6), perform steps 1 and 3.**
- **If installing   right rear parking brake cable (2), perform steps 2-4.**
- **If installing   front parking brake cable (16), perform steps 5-7.**
- **Only M1009 has a cable guide (14).**

1. Install cable guide (14) if removed. Push left rear parking brake cable (6) through cable guide and bracket (11) with grommet (12) installed in bracket. Install left rear parking brake cable through equalizer (9) until finger clip (13) snaps in place. Connect left rear parking brake cable to connector (15).

2. Install clip (1) with bolt (21) or clip (3) with bolt (4), Position right rear parking brake cable (2).

3. Push rear parking brake cable (2 or 6) through backing plate (7) until finger clip (5) snaps in place and connect to parking brake lever.

4. Install equalizer nut (8).

5. Install grommet (18) on bracket (17) if removed. Push front parking brake cable (16) through bracket. Push front parking brake cable through hole in cab. Pull through from underneath truck until finger clip (19) snaps in place.

6. Position front parking brake cable (16) with left rear parking brake cable (6). Install connector (15) if removed.

7. Press parking brake cable grommet (20) into place on cab floor.

FOLLOW-ON TASKS:

- Install brake drum if removed. (See paragraph 8-5)
- Connect parking brake cable at parking brake pedal assembly if disconnected. (See paragraph 7-3)
- Adjust parking brake cable. (See   paragraph 7-2)
- Remove wheel chocks.
- Check parking brake operation.

Section II. SERVICE BRAKE SYSTEM MAINTENANCE

7-5.   SERVICE BRAKE SYSTEM MAINTENANCE INDEX.

7-6.   SERVICE BRAKE SYSTEM BLEEDING INSTRUCTIONS.

This task covers:	a. Pressure Bleeding	b. Manual Bleeding

INITIAL SETUP:

Equipment Condition
 • Master cylinder filled to proper level,
   (See LO 9-2320-289-12)

Tools/Test Equipment
 • Combination valve depressor, J-23709

General Safety Instructions
 • Always wear goggles when bleeding brakes.

Materials/Parts
 • Brake fluid (Item   6, Appendix C)

Personnel Required
 • MOS 63B (2)
   (During MANUAL   BLEEDING only.)

---

a.   **PRESSURE BLEEDING**

WARNING

**Always wear goggles when bleeding brakes.   Failure to follow this warning
may result in serious eye injury.**

CAUTION

**When using a pressure bleeding tank, follow manufacturer's instructions
for use. Fill pressure bleeding tank at least 1/3 full of brake fluid. Failure to
follow this caution may result in damage to pressure bleeding tank or
brake system.**

NOTE

**PRESSURE BLEEDING procedures should be used   whenever possible. If
pressure bleeding equipment is not available,   bleed brake system
manually.**

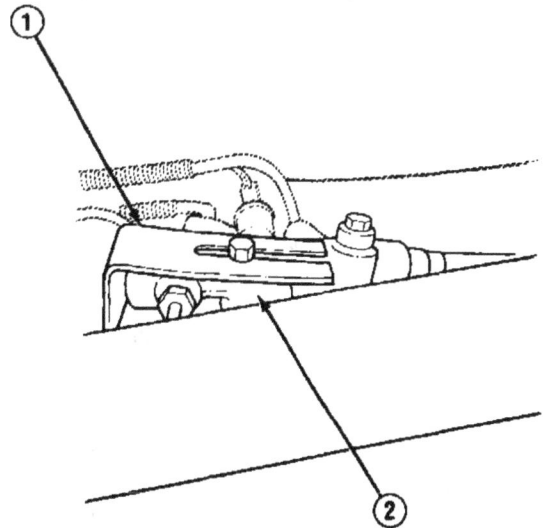

1.   Loosen mounting bolt and install
       combination valve depressor (1) on
       combination   valve (2). Tighte n
       mounting bolt and combination valve
       depressor in place.

2.   Build up tank pressure to 20-25 psi
       (138-172 kPa).

TA49661

7-6.   SERVICE BRAKE SYSTEM BLEEDING INSTRUCTIONS (Con't).

NOTE

- If only front or rear half of system has been serviced, it is usually necessary to bleed only that half of system; however, if firm braking action cannot be obtained after bleeding, it will be necessary to bleed entire system.

- PRESSURE BLEEDING procedures cover bleeding at one wheel, Repeat steps for each wheel 'and bleed brakes in the following order: right rear, left rear, right front, left front.

3.   Remove master cylinder cover (3). install pressure bleeding adapter on master cylinder, and connect hose to adapter and pressure bleeding tank. Open pressure bleeding tank valve.

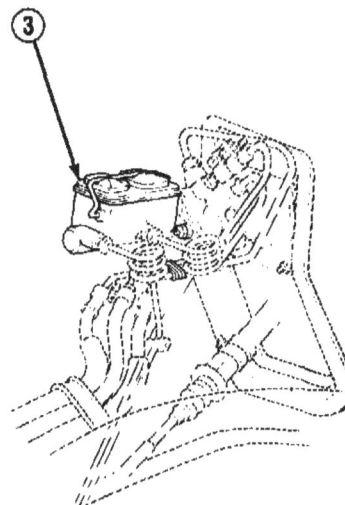

4.   If bleeding rear brake line, remove cap (10) from wheel cylinder bleeder valve (9) on backing piate (8). if bleeding front brake line, remove cap (7) from bleeder valve (6) on caliper (5) .

5.   Connect a short piece of hose to bleeder valve (6 or 9) and immerse other end of hose in container partially full of clean brake fluid.

6.   Open bleeder valve (6 or 9) ¾ turn and observe brake fluid. Close valve when brake fluid flows free o   f hubbies.

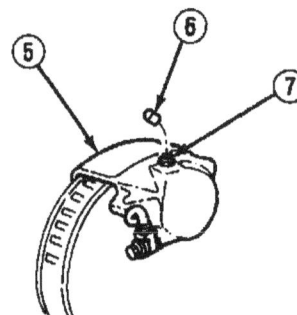

7.   Tighten bleeder valve (6 or 9), remove hose ,   and   install   cap (7 or 10).

NOTE

DO NOT continue with step 8 until all bleeding has been completed.

8.   Close bleeding tank valve, disconnect hose, and remove pressure bleeding adapter. Install master cylinder cover (3). Repressurize pressure bleeding tank.

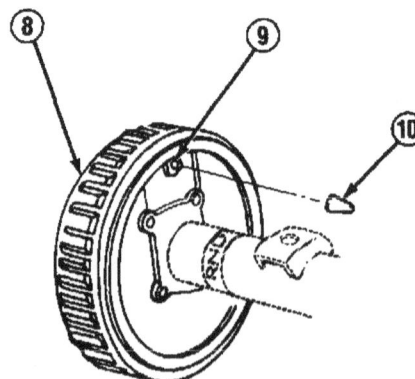

9.   Loosen mounting bolt and remove combination valve depressor (1) from combination   valve (2). Tighte n mounting bolt.

TA49662

7-6. SERVICE BRAKE SYSTEM BLEEDING INSTRUCTIONS (Con't).

10. Fill master cylinder reservoir to proper level. (See   LO 9-2320-289-12)

---

b.	MANUAL BLEEDING

WARNING

Always wear **goggles when** bleeding brakes. **Failure** to follow this warning may result in serious eye injury.

CAUTION

DO NOT allow master cylinder to run out of brake fluid during bleeding procedures. Frequently **check** master cylinder fluid level and refill as required. Ensure that master cylinder cover is securely installed. Failure to follow this caution will allow air into brake system.

NOTE

- If only front or rear half of system has been   serviced, it is usually necessary to bleed only that half of system; however, if firm braking action cannot be obtained after bleeding, it will be necessary to   bleed entire system.

- MANUAL BLEEDING procedures cover bleeding at one wheel. Repeat steps for each wheel and bleed brakes in the following order: right rear, left rear, right front, left front.

- If master cylinder is suspected to have air in its bore, perform steps 1-3.

1. Disconnect front brake pipe fitting (4) and drain fluid into a suitable container. Connect front brake pipe fitting, but DO NOT tighten.

2. Have an assistant slowly depress brake pedal to bleed air from loose front brake pipe fitting (4). Tighten front brake pipe fitting, then slowly release brake pedal.

3. Wait 15 seconds, then repeat steps 1 and 2 until all air is purged from front connection. Repeat steps 1-3 for rear brake pipe fitting (4).

4. Perform steps 4 and 5 in PRESSURE BLEEDING.

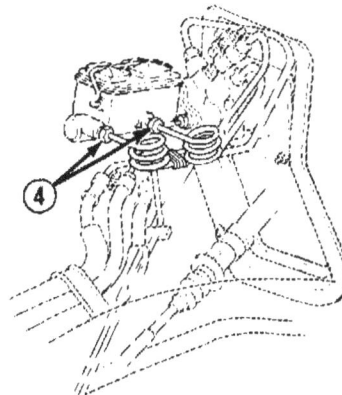

TA49663

7-6.   SERVICE BRAKE SYSTEM BLEEDING INSTRUCTIONS (Con't).

NOTE

If bleeding rear brakes, it may be necessary to depress brake pedal 8-10 times before seeing first sign of bubbles.

5.   Have an assistant depress brake pedal. Loosen bleeder valve (6 or 9) to bleed air from caliper (5) or wheel cylinder. Open bleeder valve and observe brake fluid for bubbles. Tighten bleeder valve, then slowly release brake pedal.

6.   Wait 15 seconds, then repeat step 5 until brake fluid flows free of bubbles.

7.   Remove hose and install cap (7 or 10).

8.   Fill master cylinder reservoir to proper level, (See LO 9-2320-289-12)

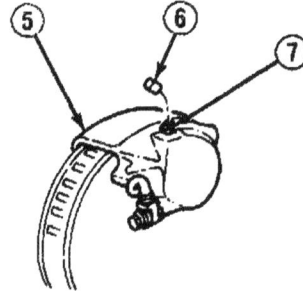

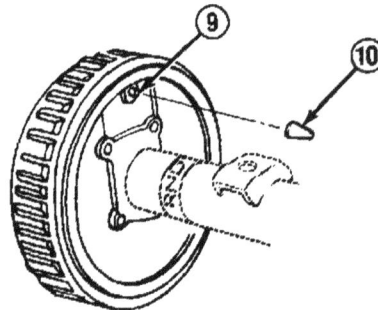

FOLLOW-ON TASKS:

• Check brake pedal for "sponginess" and brake system warning light for indication of unbalanced pressure.
• Check operation of brakes,
• Check for leaks.

TA49664

7-7.   BRAKE SHOE AND WHEEL CYLINDER REPLACEMENT.

This task covers: a. Removal   c. Adjustment
                           b. Installation

INITIAL SETUP:

Equipment Condition
  • Brake drum removed. (See paragraph 8-5)
  • Rear brake line disconnected (if removing
    wheel cylinder). (See paragraph 7-10)

Tools/Test Equipment
  • Brake spring pliers
  • Torque wrench (0–600 lb.-ft.)

Materials/Parts
  • One adjusting hole cover
  • Five lockwashers
  • Grease (Item 26, Appendix C)

General Safety Instructions
  • DO NOT use a dry brush or
    compressed air to clean brake shoes
    or brake components.
  • Always wear goggles during removal
    and installation of brake shoe springs,

| a. REMOVAL. |

WARNING

• DO NOT use a dry brush or compressed air to clean brake shoes or brake
  components. There may be asbestos dust on brake shoes or brake
  components which can be dangerous to you if you breathe it. Brake
  shoes and brake components must be wet, and a soft brush must be
  used. Failure to follow this warning may result in serious illness or death
  to personnel.

• Always wear goggles during removal of brake shoe springs. Failure to
  follow this warning may result in serious eye injury.

CAUTION

When brake shoes (5 and 17) are replaced, grooved, scored, tapered, or
out-of-round brake drums should be repaired to prevent damage to new
brake shoes. Notify your supervisor.

NOTE

• If removing brake shoes (5 and 17) and mounting hardware, perform
  steps 1-12.

• If removing wheel cylinder, perform steps 1-13.

1.   Back off adjusting screw (11).

NOTE

Adjusting assembly is factory-installed without washer (10). Use washer for
installation.

2.   Pull forward on bottom of primary brake shoe (17). Remove socket (9), washer (10), adjusting
      screw (11), and nut (12).

3.   Unhook primary return spring (26) and secondary return spring (19).

7-7. BRAKE SHOE AND WHEEL CYLINDER REPLACEMENT (Con't).

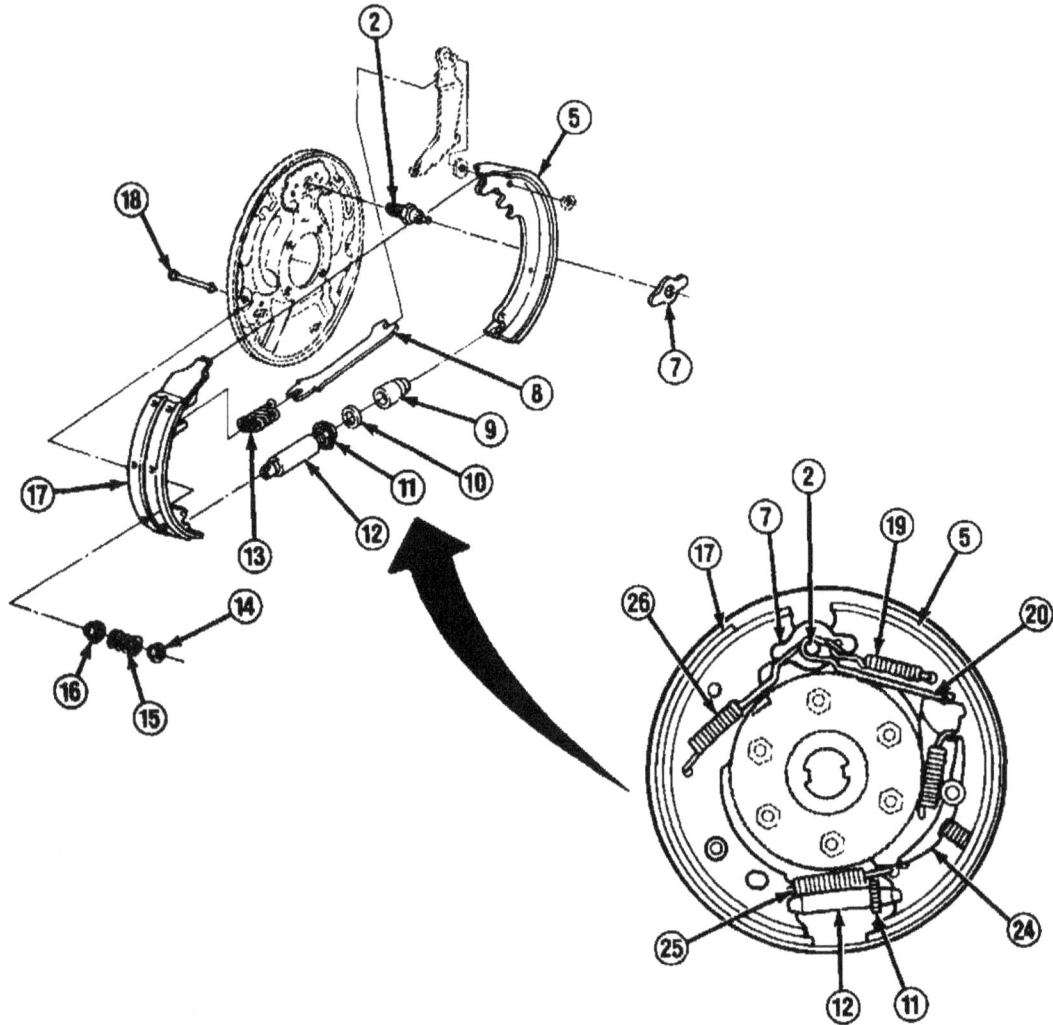

4. Remove parking brake strut (8) and strut spring (13). Remove adjusting spring (25).

NOTE

Brake shoe assembly is factory-installed without pivot (16).

5. Remove hold-down washer (14), spring (15), pivot (16), and pin (18) on primary brake shoe (17) side. Remove primary brake shoe.

6. Remove brake shoe guide (7).

7. Depress bottom of adjusting lever (24). Unhook actuating link (20) from anchor pin (2) and adjusting lever.

TA49665

7-7. BRAKE SHOE AND WHEEL CYLINDER REPLACEMENT (Con't).

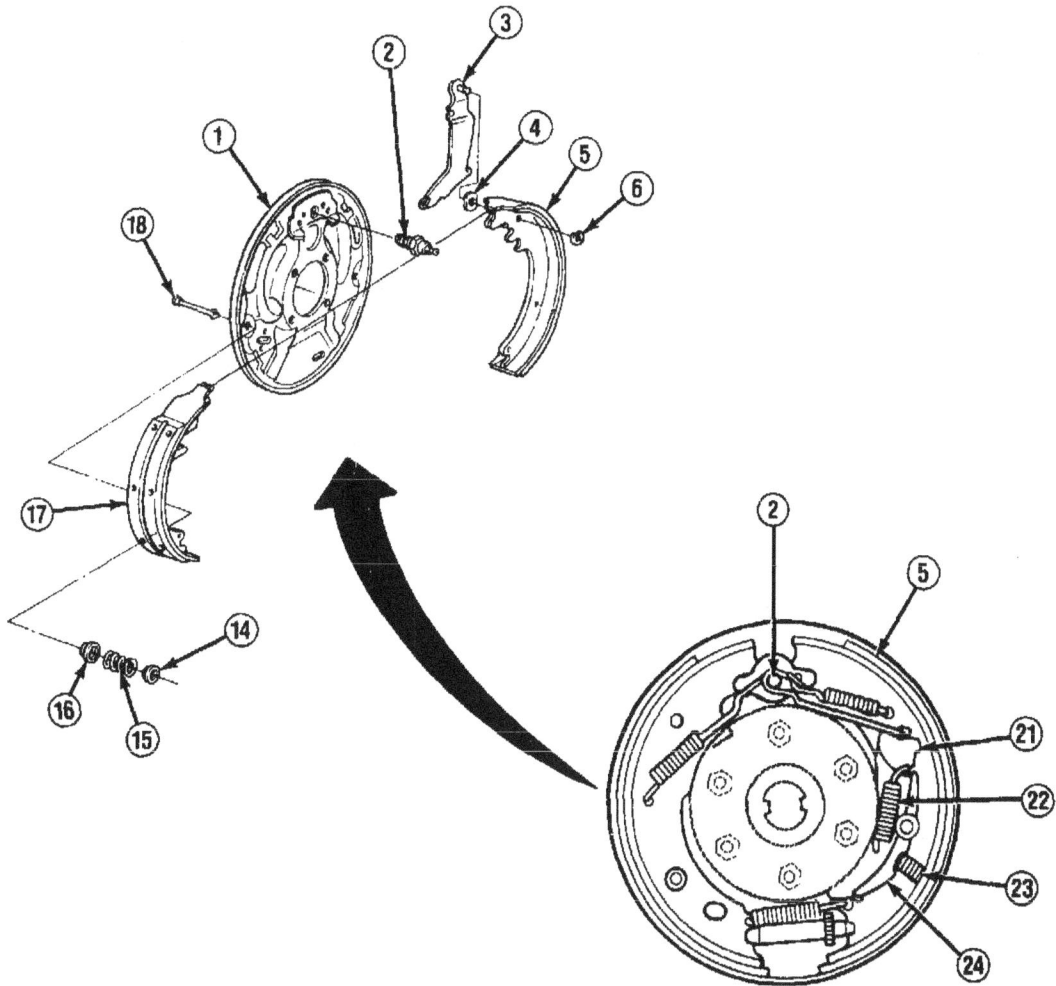

NOTE

Brake shoe assembly is factory-installed without pivot (16).

8. Remove hold-down washer (14), spring (15), pivot (16), and pin (18) on secondary brake shoe (5) side.

9. Remove adjusting lever (24), adjusting spring (22), and pivot (21) assembly. Disassemble as required.

10. Remove adjusting spring (23). Remove clip (6), secondary brake shoe (5), and washer (4) from parking brake lever (3).

11. Depress tabs on parking brake cable finger nut, and disconnect parking brake cable from parking brake lever (3) as required.

TA49666

7-7. BRAKE SHOE AND WHEEL CYLINDER REPLACEMENT (Con't).

NOTE

M1009 DOES NOT use a lock-washer (31) with anchor pin (2).

12. Remove nut (30), lockwasher (31), and anchor pin (2) as required. Discard lockwasher.

13. Remove cap (28), bleeder valve (29), and 2 link rods (35) as required. Remove 2 bolts (27) and wheel cylinder (34) from backing plate (1).

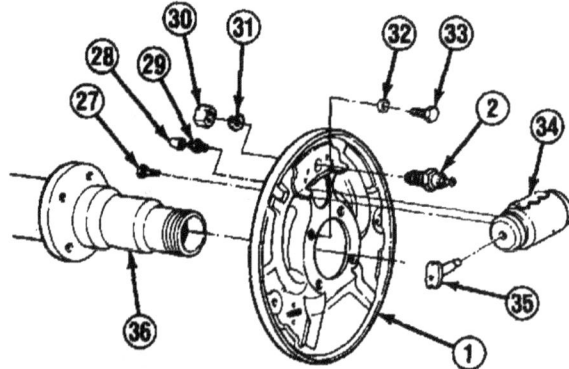

NOTE

Step 14 applies to all except M1009.

14. Remove 4 bolts (33) and lockwashers (32), and remove backing plate (1) from axle (36). Discard lockwashers.

b. INSTALLATION

WARNING

- DO NOT use a dry brush or compressed air to clean brake shoes or brake components. There may be asbestos dust on brake shoes or brake components which can be dangerous to you if you breathe it, Brake shoes and brake components must be wet, and a soft brush must be used. Failure to follow this warning may result in serious illness or death to personnel.

- Always wear goggles during installation of brake shoe springs. Failure to follow this warning may result in serious eye injury.

NOTE

- If installing wheel cylinder (34), perform steps 2-16.

- If Installing brake shoes (5 and 17) and mounting hardware, perform steps 3-16.

- Step 1 applies to all except M1009.

1. Install backing plate (1) on axle (36) with 4 new lockwashers (32) and bolts (33). Tighten bolts to 105 lb.-ft. (142 N•m).

TA49667

7-7. BRAKE SHOE AND WHEEL CYLINDER REPLACEMENT (Con't).

2. Install wheel cylinder (34) on backing plate (1) with 2 bolts (27). Tighten bolts to 15 lb.-ft. (20 N·m). Install 2 link rods (35), bleeder valve (29), and cap (28) if removed.

NOTE

M1009 DOES NOT use a lockwasher (31) with anchor pin (2).

3. Install anchor pin (2) with new lockwasher (31) and nut (30) i f removed. Tighten nut to 230 lb.-ft. (312 N·m).

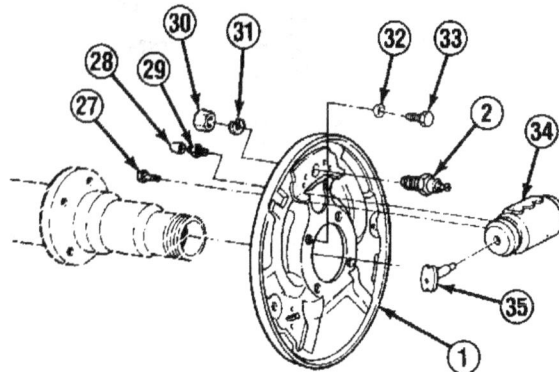

NOTE

Primary brake shoe (17) has a shorter lining than the secondary brake shoe (5), and is always installed toward front of truck.

4. Connect parking brake cable t o parking brake lever (3) if disconnected.

5. Install washer (4) on parking brake lever (3) pin. Install secondary brake shoe (5) on parking brake lever pin. Install clip (6) on secondary brake shoe.

6. Install pin (18) in backing plate (1) on secondary brake shoe (5) side. Position adjusting lever (24), adjusting spring (22), and pivot (21) assembly, ensuring that pin (18) is through secondary brake shoe and adjusting lever hole.

7. Install pivot (16), spring (15), and hold-down washer (14), turning hold-down washer to lock in place on pin (18).

8. Position primary brake shoe (17) and install pin (18), pivot (16), spring (15), and hold-down washer (14), turning hold-down washer to lock in place.

9. Install brake shoe guide (7) on anchor pin (2). Install actuating link (20) on pivot (21) and anchor pin.

10. Hook adjusting spring (25) on secondary brake shoe (5) and primary brake shoe (17).

11. With primary brake shoe (17) moved forward, install strut spring (13) and parking brake strut (8). Ensure that link rods (35) are engaged in secondary brake shoe (5) and primary brake shoe notches.

TA49668

7-7.   BRAKE SHOE AND WHEEL CYLINDER REPLACEMENT (Con't).

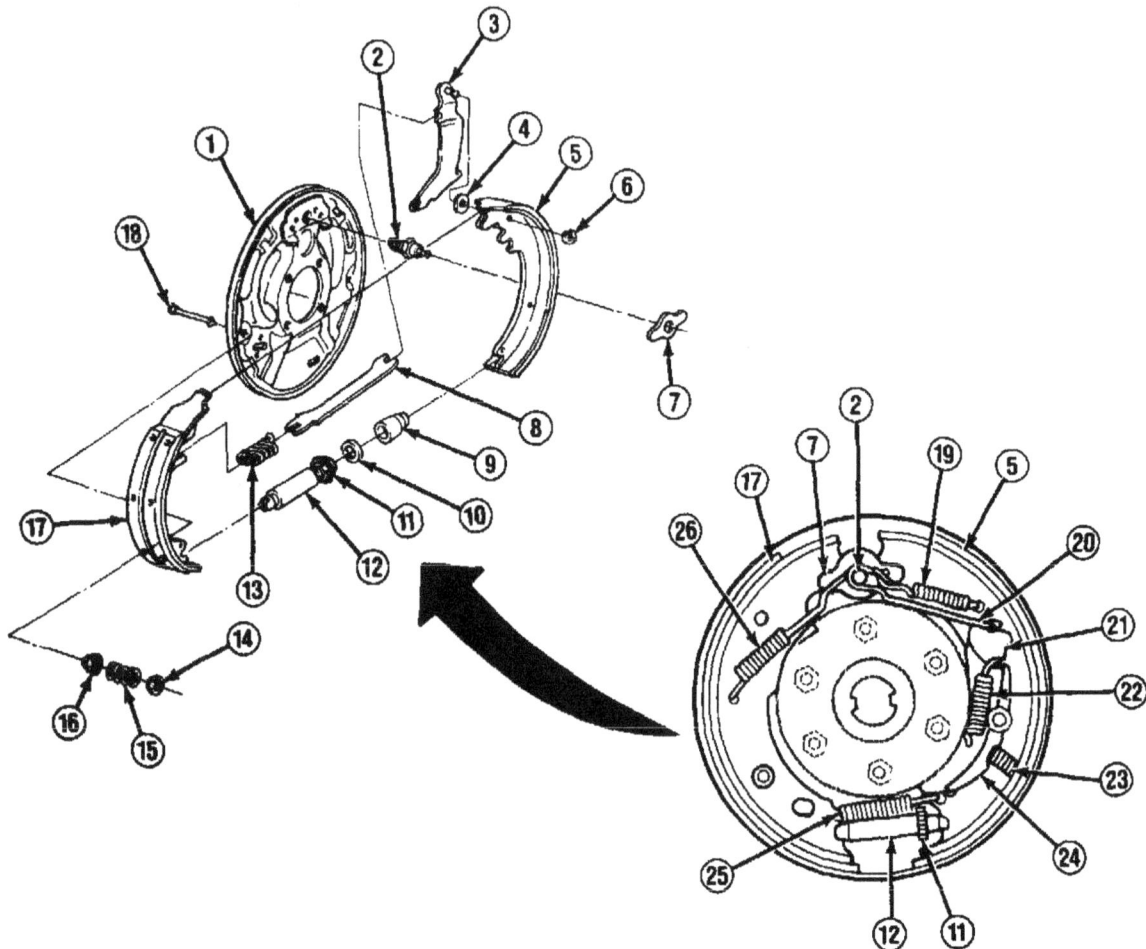

NOTE

Primary return spring (26) is longer than secondary return spring (19).

12.   Hook primary return spring (26) on primary brake shoe (17) and anchor pin (2). Hook secondary return spring (19) on secondary brake shoe (15) and actuator link (20).

13.   Assemble nut (12), adjusting screw (11), washer (10), and socket (9). Grease adjusting screw (11). Install adjusting assembly between secondary brake shoe (5) and primary brake shoe (17).

14.   Install adjusting spring (23) between adjusting lever (24) and inside of secondary brake shoe (5). Ensure that adjusting spring (25) DOES NOT touch adjusting screw (11).

15.   Check security of hold-down washers (14), link rods (35), and all springs. Ensure that parking brake strut (8) and strut spring (13) are correctly seated. Carefully pull forward on adjusting lever (24). Ensure that adjusting lever returns to position after releasing.

16.   Firmly tap top of secondary brake shoe (5) and primary brake shoe (17) to seat in place.

TA49669

7-7.   BRAKE SHOE AND WHEEL CYLINDER REPLACEMENT (Con't).

c.	ADJUSTMENT

NOTE

To gain access to adjusting screw (11), it may be necessary to knock out lanced area in backing plate (1) or brake drum or remove cover.

1.   Install brake drum. (See paragraph 8-5)

2.   Working through slot in backing plate (1) or brake drum, turn adjusting screw (11) until wheel cannot be turned by hand.

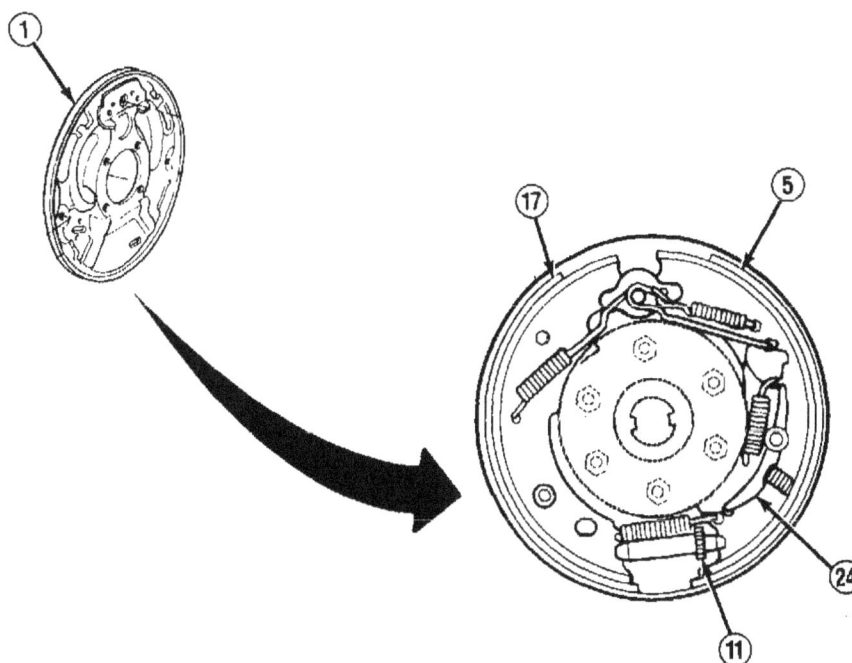

3.   Hold adjusting lever (24) away from adjusting screw (11). Back off adjusting screw 30 notches. If brake shoes (5 and 17) still drag lightly on drum, back off adjusting screw by 1 or 2 notches. Install cover on backing plate (1) or brake drum access hole.

4.   If drag is still evident, adjust parking brake cable. (See paragraph 7-2)

FOLLOW-ON TASKS:

   • Connect rear brake line if disconnected. (See paragraph 7-10)
   • Bleed brakes if wheel cylinder was removed. (See paragraph 7-6)
   • Check operation of brakes.

TA49670

7-8.   MASTER CYLINDER AND POWER BOOSTER REPLACEMENT.

This task covers: a. Removal   b. Installation

INITIAL SETUP:

Equipment Condition

- Front brake lines disconnected from master cylinder. (See paragraph 7-9)
- Power booster rod disconnected from service brake pedal (if removing power booster). (See paragraph 7-12)
- Power steering lines disconnected from power booster (if removing power booster). (See paragraph 8-14)

Materials/Parts
- Eight locknuts

Tools/Test Equipment
- Torque wrench

a. REMOVAL

NOTE

If removing   master cylinder (4), perform steps 1 and 2.

1.   Remove master cylinder cover bail (2), cover (1), and gasket (3). Inspect cover and gasket for damage and discard as required.

2.   Remove 2 locknuts (12), power brake bracket (11), and master cylinder (4). Discard locknuts.

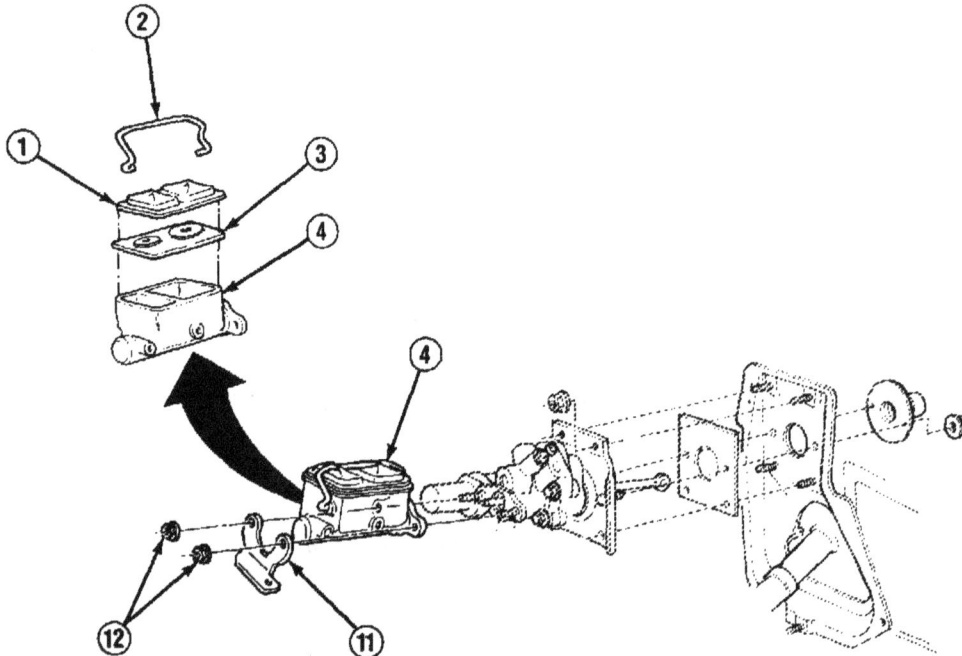

TA49671

7-8.   MASTER CYLINDER AND POWER BOOSTER REPLACEMENT (Con't).

NOTE

Only M1009 uses pedal rod boot (8), retain for installation.

3.   Remove 2 locknuts (9) and pedal rod boot (8), Remove 4 locknuts (6), and remove power booster (5) and seal (10). Inspect seal for damage and discard as required, Discard locknuts.

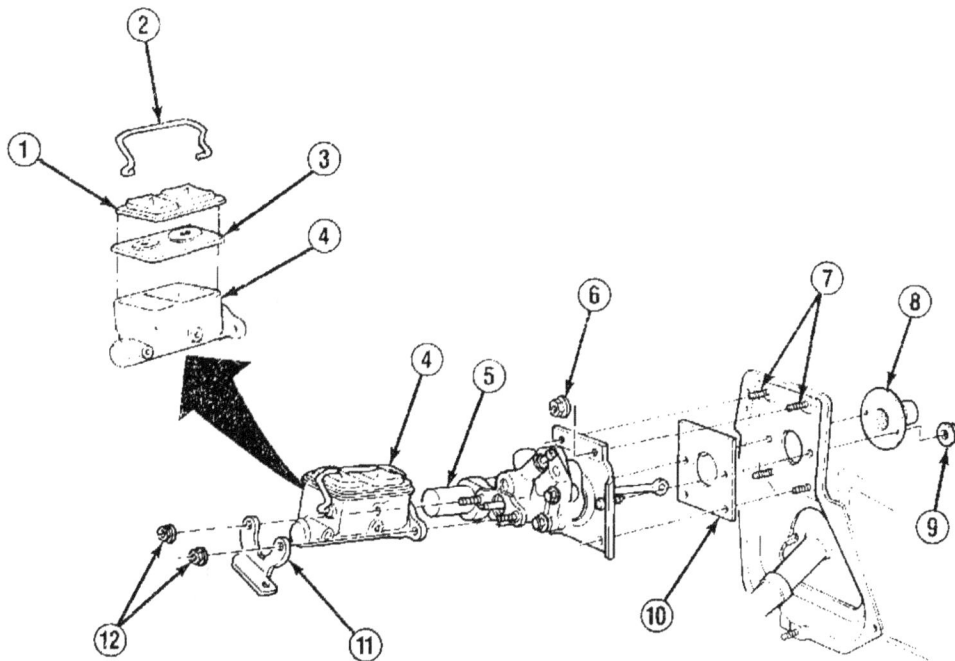

| b. | INSTALLATION |

NOTE

- When replacing power booster (5) assembly, ensure that proper power booster is used. M1009 housing is machined flat or has 40°-50° bevel at pushrod end and has a broadcast code sticker with "FY" or "KA" on it, All other models are 20°-30° beveled and have a broadcast code sticker with "CM" on it.

- If installing master cylinder (4), perform steps 2 and 3.

- Only M1009 uses pedal rod boot (8).

1.   Install seal (10) on power booster (5) studs. Install power booster on engine compartment studs (7). Install 4 new locknuts (6) on engine compartment studs. Install pedal rod boot (8) and 2 new locknuts (9) on power booster studs. Tighten locknuts to 25 lb.-ft. (34 N·m).

TA49672

7-8.   MASTER CYLINDER AND POWER BOOSTER REPLACEMENT (Con't).

NOTE

An Installed M1009 master cylinder (4) will have larger reservoir facing forward. On all other models, larger reservoir will be facing rearward when installed. If incorrect master cylinder is installed, erratic braking action may be experienced.

2.   Position master cylinder (4) and power brake bracket (11) on power booster (5)   studs, and install with 2 new locknuts (12), Tighten locknuts to 35 lb.-ft. (47 N•m).

3.   Install gasket (3), cover (1), and cover bail (2) on master cylinder (4).

FOLLOW-ON TASKS:

   - Connect front brake lines to master cylinder. (See paragraph 7-9)
   - Connect power booster rod to service brake pedal if disconnected. (See paragraph 7-12)
   - Connect power steering lines to power booster if disconnected. (See paragraph 8-14)
   - Bleed brake system. (See paragraph 7-6)
   - Bleed power steering system if hoses were disconnected. (See paragraph 8-8)

7-9.   FRONT BRAKE LINES AND COMBINATION VALVE REPLACEMENT.

This task covers: a. Removal   b. Installation

INITIAL SETUP:

Materials/Parts
- Four copper washers
- Two locknuts

General Safety Instructions
- Always wear goggles when working on underside of truck and disconnecting brake lines.

| a.   REMOVAL |

WARNING

Always wear goggles when bleeding brakes. may result   **in serious eye injury.**   **Failure to follow this warning**

CAUTION

Plug all openings and connections immediately after disconnection to prevent contamination of brake system.

NOTE

- **Use suitable container to catch brake fluid.**

- **If removing combination valve   (20), perform steps 3-6.**

1.   Disconnect brake pipes (2 and 3) from master cylinder (1).

2.   Remove screw (15) and clip (26) from brake pipes (2 and 3). Remove retainer (4) as required.

3.   Loosen brake pipes (2 and 3) at combination valve (20). Remove 2 locknuts (21) and bolts (23), and pull combination valve away from crossmember. Discard locknuts.

4.   Disconnect brake pipes (2 and 3) from combination valve (20), Inspect fittings for damage and replace as required.

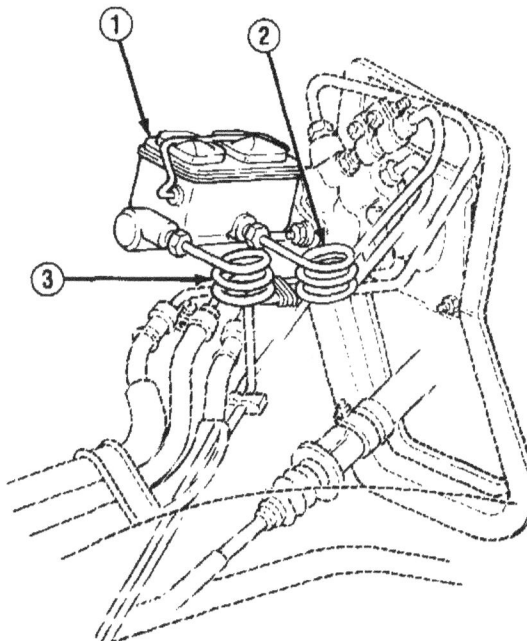

TA49673

7-9. FRONT BRAKE LINES AND COMBINATION VALVE REPLACEMENT (Con't).

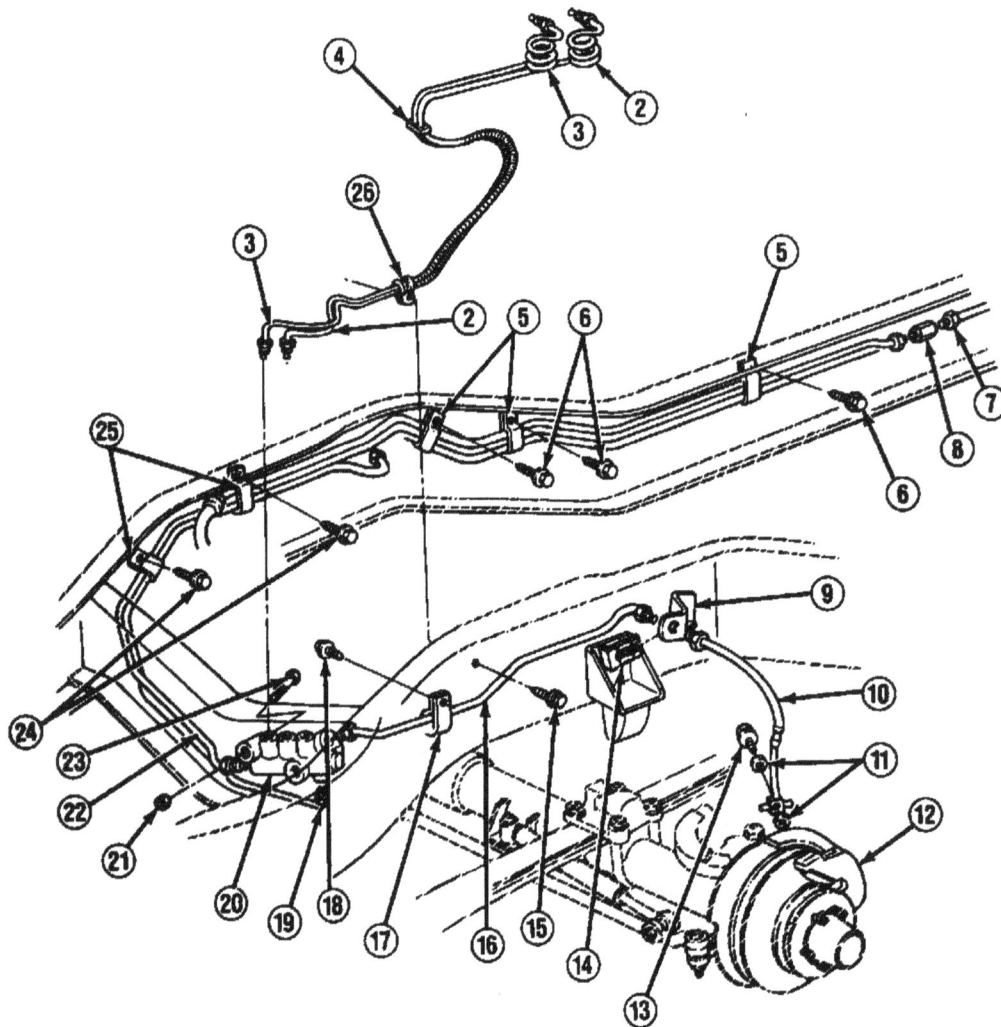

5. Disconnect electrical lead from combination valve (20).

6. Disconnect brake pipes (22, 16, and 19) from combination valve (20), and remove combination valve.

7. Remove screw (18) and clip (17). Disconnect brake pipe (16) from caliper flex hose (10) and remove. Remove bolt (13) and 2 copper washers (11), and disconnect caliper flex hose from caliper (12). Remove clip (14) to disconnect hose from bracket (9) and remove. Inspect fittings for damage and replace as required. Discard copper washers.

8. Remove 2 screws (24) and clips (25). Repeat step 7, as required, to disconnect brake pipe (19) from right caliper flex hose (10). Inspect fittings for damage and replace as required.

9. Disconnect rear brake pipe (7) from fitting (8). Remove fitting. Remove 3 screws (6) and clips (5) and remove brake pipe (22). Inspect fittings for damage and replace as required.

TA49674

7-9. FRONT BRAKE LINES AND COMBINATION VALVE REPLACEMENT (Con't).

| b. | INSTALLATION |

NOTE

• Remove   all plugs   before connection.

• If installing combination valve (20), perform steps 4-7.

1. Position brake pipe (22) along frame. Install 3 clips (5) on brake pipe and install screws (6), Install fitting (8) on brake pipe. Connect rear brake pipe (7) to fitting.

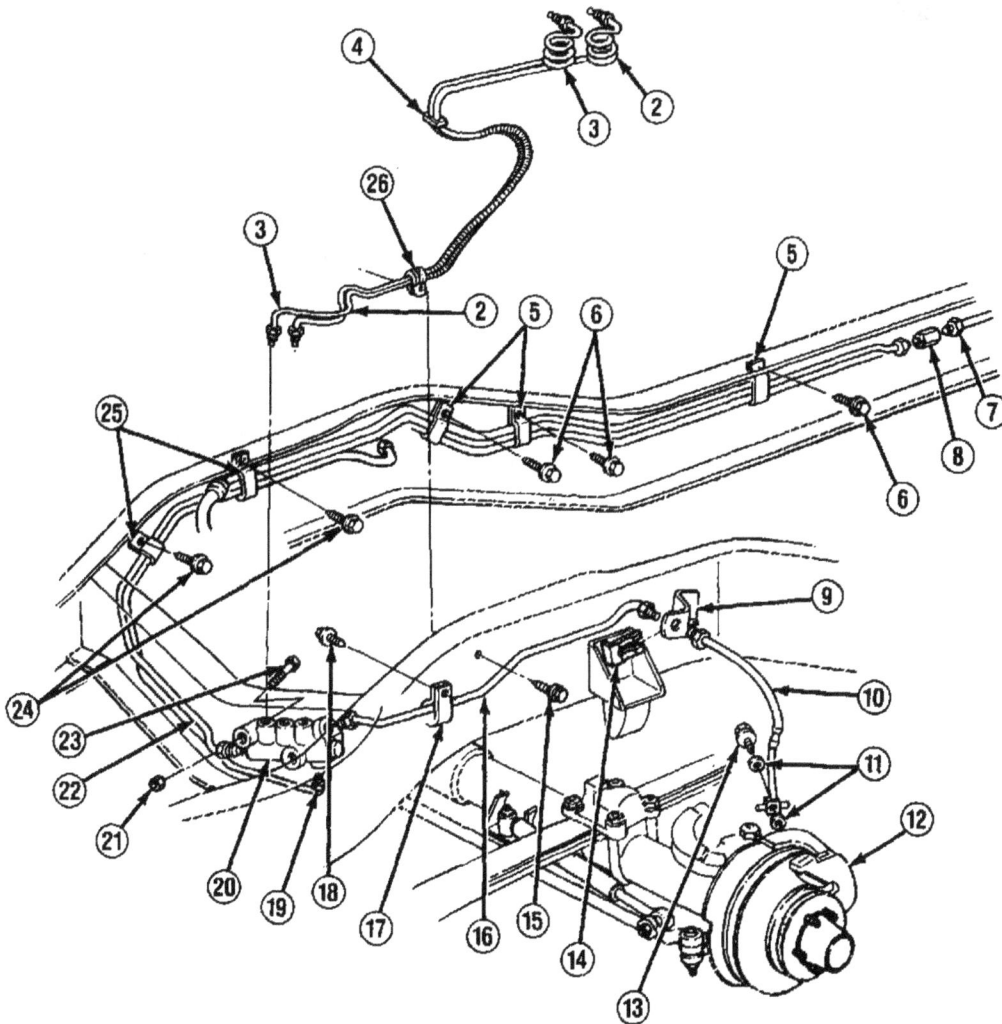

TA49675

7-9. FRONT BRAKE LINES AND COMBINATION VALVE REPLACEMENT (Con't).

2. Connect caliper flex hose (10) to caliper (12) with 2 new copper washers (11) and bolt (13). Connect caliper flex hose to brake pipe (16) through bracket (9) and install clip (14). Install clip (17) on brake pipe and install screw (18).

3. Position brake pipe (19) on frame and frame crossmember. Install 2 clips (25) on brake pipe and install 2 screws (24). Repeat step 2, as required, to connect brake pipe to right side caliper flex hose (10).

4. From underneath truck, connect brake pipes (22, 16, and 19) to combination valve (20),

5. Connect electrical lead to combination valve (20).

6. Connect brake pipes (2 and 3) to combination valve (20). DO NOT fully tighten pipes at this time.

7. Install combination valve (20) on frame crossmember with 2 bolts (23) and new locknuts (21). Tighten brake pipes (2 and 3) at combination valve.

8. Install retainer (4) on brake pipes (2 and 3) if removed. Install clip (26) on brake pipes and install screw (15).

9. Connect brake pipes (2 and 3) to master cylinder (1).

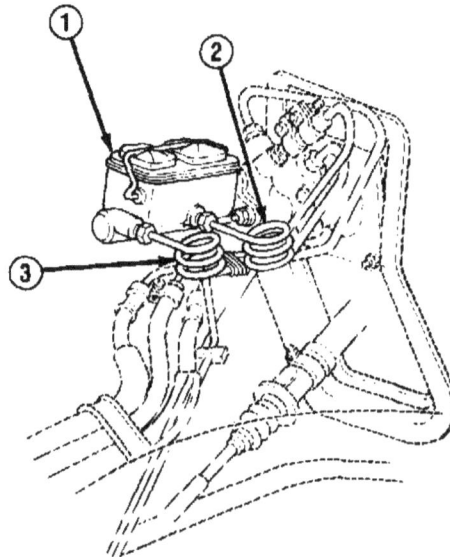

FOLLOW-ON TASKS:

• Bleed brake system. (See paragraph 7-6)
• Check operation of brakes.

TA49676

7-10. REAR BRAKE LINES AND PROPORTIONING VALVE REPLACEMENT AND ADJUSTMENT.

This task covers:
a. Removal
b. Installation
c. Valve Adjustment

INITIAL SETUP:

Equipment Condition

• Rear of truck raised, frame supported by jack stands (if removing or adjusting proportioning valve, all except M1009).

Tools/Test Equipment

• Torque wrench

Materials/Parts

• Four lockwashers
• One proportioning valve adjustment gage

---

a. REMOVAL

CAUTION

Plug all openings and connections immediately after disconnection to prevent contamination of brake system.

NOTE

• Use suitable container to catch brake fluid.

• If removing brake lines from M1009, perform steps 1 and 3 through 6.

• If removing brake lines from all except M1009, perform steps 1, 2, 4, 5, 7, and 8.

• If removing proportioning valve (7), perform steps 2 and 8 through 10.

• If removing proportioning valve lever (8), perform steps 9 and 11.

1. Disconnect fitting (1) from brake pipe (2). Remove 3 screws (4) and clips (3).

2. Remove screw (11) and clip (10). Disconnect brake pipe (2) from proportioning valve (7) and remove. Inspect fittings for damage and replace as required.

3. Remove retainer (31). Disconnect brake pipe (2) from hose (30) and remove. Inspect fittings for damage and replace as required.

4. Bend clip (24) and remove right brake pipe (25) from hose (9 or 30) fitting. Disconnect right brake pipe from wheel cylinder fitting (23) and remove. Inspect fittings for damage and replace as required.

5. Repeat step 4 for left brake pipe as required.

6. Remove screw (29) and hose (30). Remove bolt (33) and bracket (32) from differential (22) as required.

7. Remove screw (26) and disconnect hose (9) from proportioning valve lever (8).

8. Disconnect hose (9) from pipe (5) and remove. Loosen pipe fitting, remove retainer (6), and disconnect pipe from proportioning valve   (7).

7-10. REAR BRAKE LINES AND PROPORTIONING VALVE REPLACEMENT AND ADJUSTMENT (Con't).

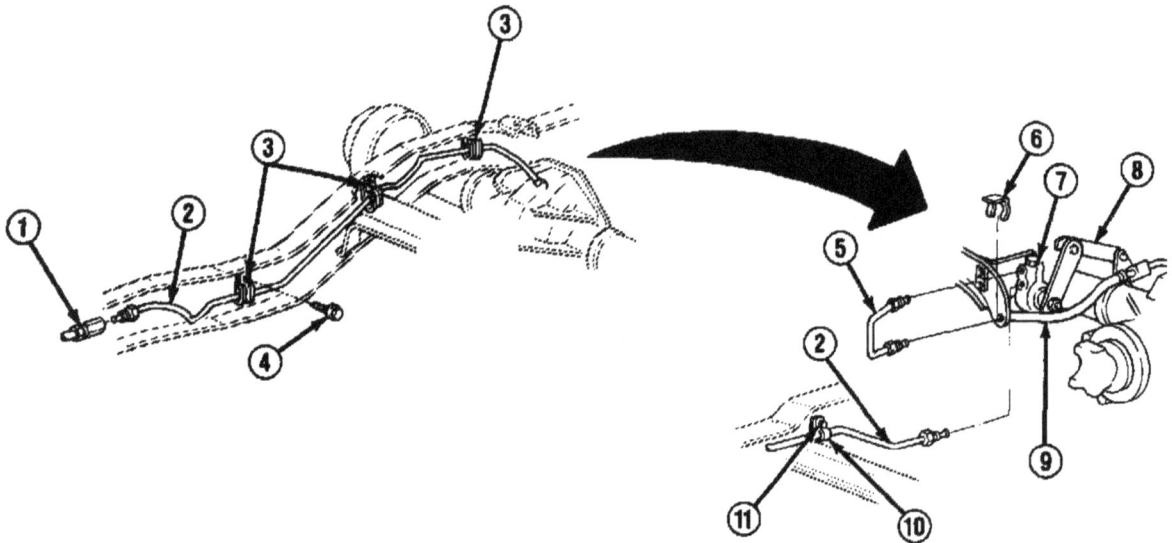

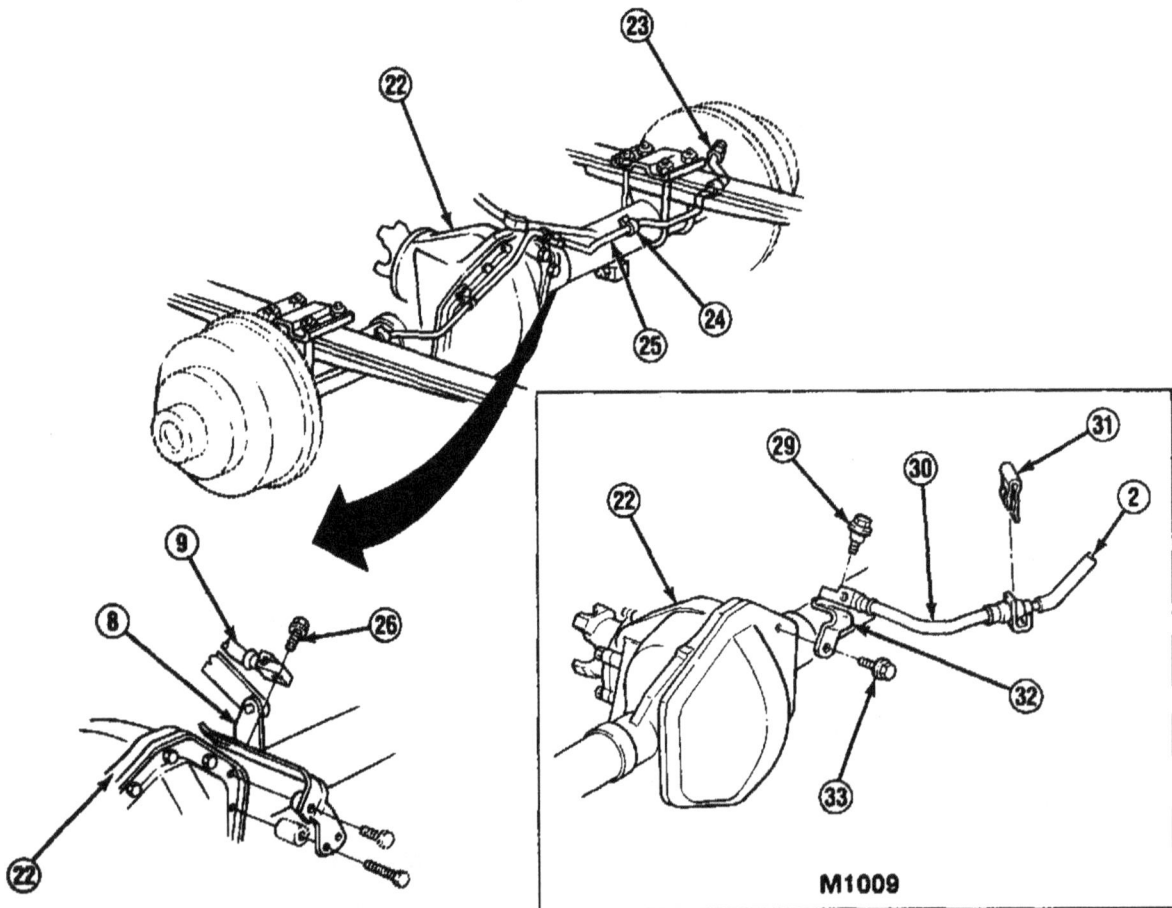

M1009

TA49677

7-10. REAR BRAKE LINES AND PROPORTIONING VALVE REPLACEMENT AND ADJUSTMENT (Con't).

NOTE

If proportioning valve (7) was previously replaced, proportioning valve adjustment gage (19) located between proportioning valve lever (8) and proportioning valve must be discarded.

9. Remove nut (16) and bushing (17), Pull proportioning valve lever (8) away from proportioning valve (7) and remove retainer (18) as required.

10. Remove 2 bolts (12) and lockwashers (13) and remove proportioning valve (7), Remove 2 bolts (20) and lockwashers (21), and remove bracket (14) as required, Discard lockwashers.

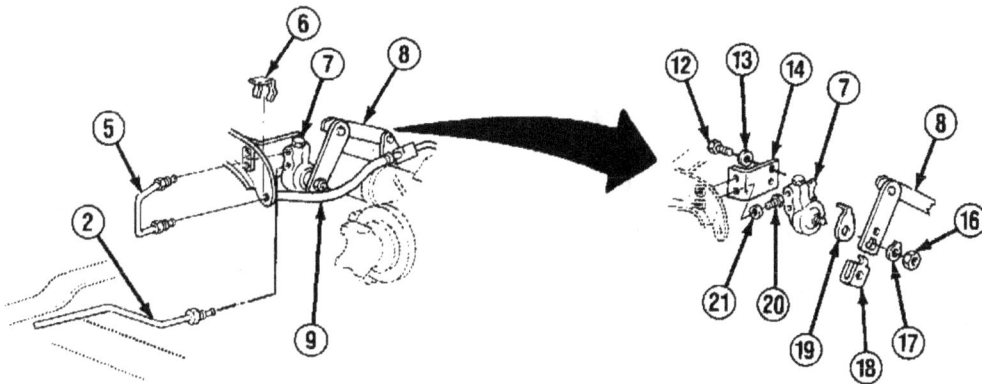

11. Remove 2 bolts (27), spacer (28), and proportioning valve lever (8) from differential (22).

| b. | INSTALLATION |

NOTE

· Remove all plugs before connection.

· If installing proportioning valve lever (8), perform steps 1 and 4.

· If installing proportioning valve (7), perform steps 2-5, and 11.

· If installing brake lines on all except M1009, perform steps 5, 6, 8, 9, 11, and 12.

· If installing brake lines on M1009, perform steps 7-10 and 12.

1. Install proportioning valve lever (8) on differential (22) with spacer (28) and 2 bolts (27). Tighten bolts to 35 lb.-ft. (47 N•m).

2. Install bracket (14) with 2 new lockwashers (21) and bolts (20) if removed. Install proportioning valve (7) with 2 new lockwashers (13) and bolts (1 2). Tighten all bolts to 35 lb.-ft. (47 N•m).

TA49678

7-10. REAR BRAKE LINES AND PROPORTIONING VALVE REPLACEMENT AND ADJUSTMENT (Con't).

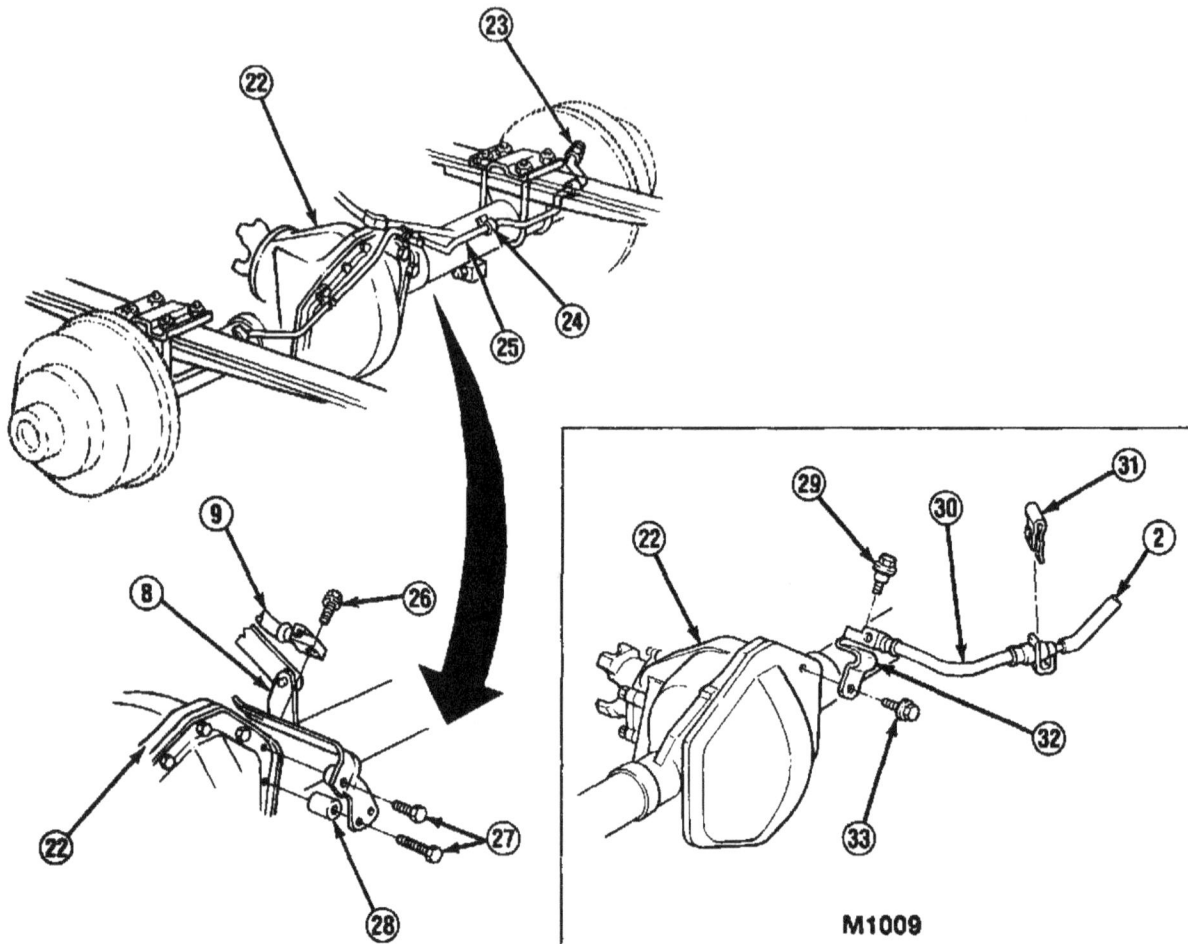

M1009

3.   Adjust proportioning valve (7). (See VALVE ADJUSTMENT steps.)

4.   Install retainer (18) on proportioning valve lever (8) if removed, Install proportioning valve lever on proportioning valve (7) with bushing (17) and nut (16). Tighten nut to 10-15 lb.-ft. (14-20 N•m).

5.   Connect pipe (5) to proportioning valve (7). Connect hose (9) to pipe and install retainer (6).

6.   Connect hose (9) to proportioning valve lever (8) with screw (26).

7.   Install bracket (32) on differential (22) with bolt (33) if removed. Install hose (30) on bracket (32) with screw (29). Tighten bolt to 35 lb.-ft. (47 N•m).

8.   Connect right brake pipe (25) to wheel cylinder fitting (23). Connect right brake pipe to hose (9 or 30) fitting and secure with clip (24).

9.   Repeat step 8 for left brake pipe (25) as required.

10.   Connect brake pipe (2) to brake hose (30) and install retainer (31).

TA49679

7-10. REAR BRAKE LINES AND PROPORTIONING VALVE REPLACEMENT AND ADJUSTMENT (Con't).

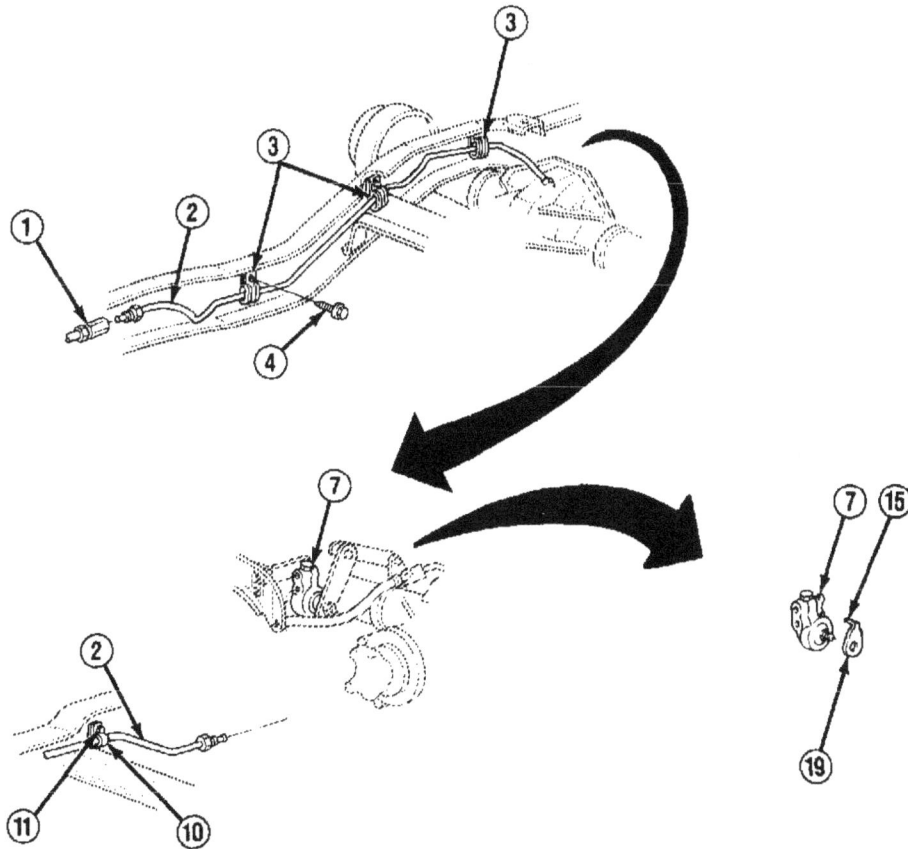

11. Connect brake pipe (2) to proportioning valve (7). Install clip (10) on brake pipe and install with screw (11).

12. Position brake pipe (2) along frame. Install 3 clips (3) on brake pipe and install with 3 screws (4). Connect fitting (1) to brake pipe.

c. VALVE ADJUSTMENT

1. Perform step 9 of REMOVAL as required.

2. Position "D"-shaped hole of proportioning valve adjustment gage (19) over "D"-shape of proportioning valve (7) shaft, Rotate shaft until tang (15) can be positioned in proportioning valve lower mounting hole.

3. Perform step 4 of INSTALLATION.

4. Cut tang (15) off of proportioning valve adjustment gage (19).

FOLLOW-ON TASKS:

- Remove jack stands and lower truck as required.
- Bleed brake system. (See paragraph 7-6)
- Check operation of brakes.

TA49680

7-11. BRAKE PAD AND CALIPER REPLACEMENT.

This task covers: a. Removal   b. Installation

INITIAL SETUP:

Equipment Condition
• Front wheel removed. (See paragraph 8-2)

Materials/Parts
• Two copper washers
• Brake fluid (Item 6, Appendix C)
• Grease (Item 26, Appendix C)

General Safety Instructions
• DO NOT use a dry brush or compressed air to clean brake pads or brake components.

| a. | **REMOVAL** |

NOTE

● **If removing caliper (2) from all except M1009, perform steps 1-4 and 8.**

● **If removing caliper (2) from M1009, perform steps 1-3, 5, and 8.**

● **If removing brake pads from all except M1009, perform steps 3, 4, and 6 through 8.**

● **If removing brake pads from M1009, perform steps 3 and 5 through 8.**

● **Use a suitable container to catch brake fluid from disconnected caliper fiex hose.**

1. Remove bolt and 2 copper washers and disconnect caliper flex hose from caliper (2). Discard copper washers.

2. Remove dust cap (10) and bleeder valve (9) if damaged.

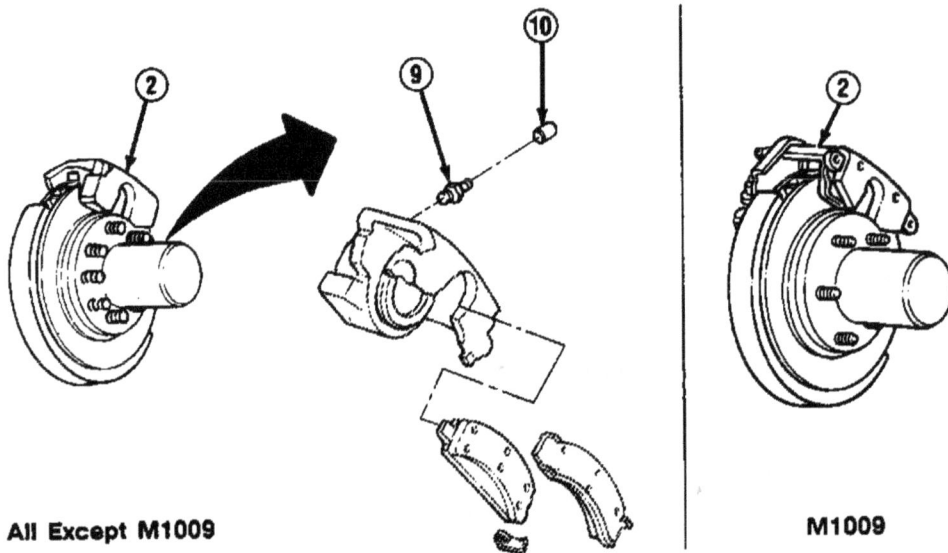

All Except M1009   **M1009**

TA49581

7-11.   BRAKE PAD AND CALIPER REPLACEMENT (Con't).

3.   Position "C" clamp around caliper (2) so that foot of clamp on shaft rests through access hole (3) against outer brake pad (11 or 22) and stationary foot of clamp rests on piston (14), Tighten "C" clamp until piston reaches bottom of piston bore. Remove "C" clamp.

NOTE

- Use soft-faced hammer and drift to remove key (5) and spring (7).

- Note position of spring (7) for installation.

4.   Remove screw (6), Tap key (5) and spring (7) from bracket (4). Remove caliper bracket and rotor (1).

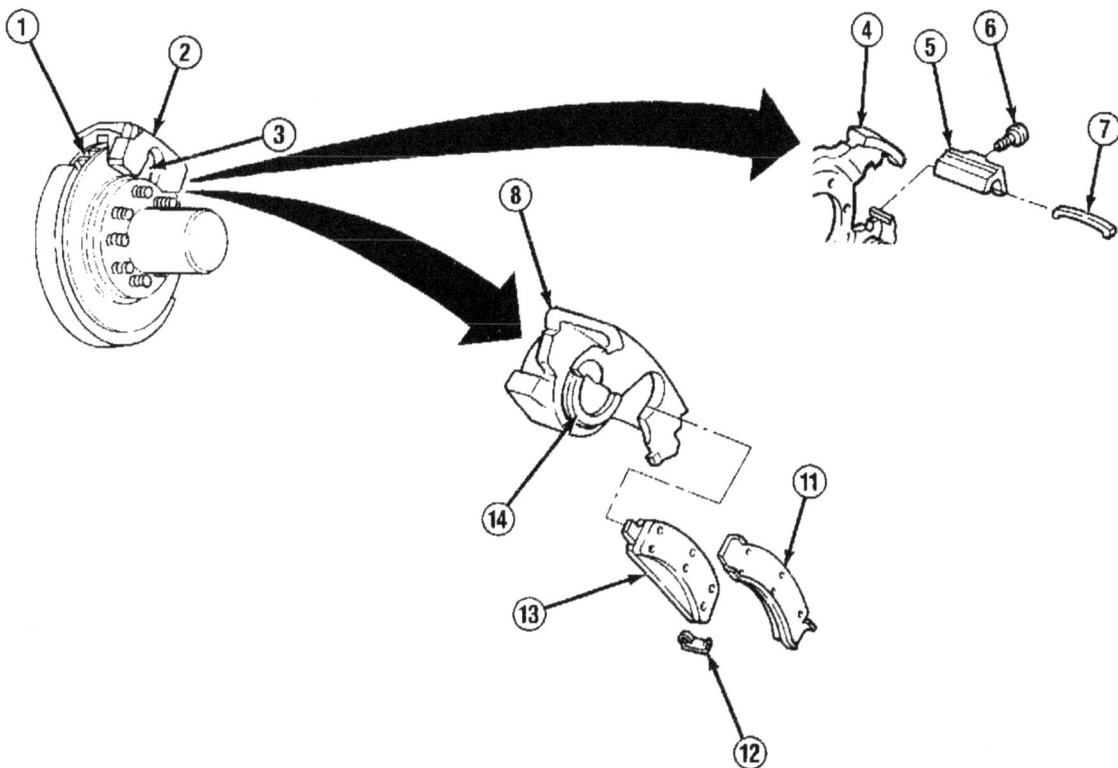

All Except M1009

5.   Remove 2 mounting bolts (15). Remove caliper (2) from bracket (18) and rotor (1).

CAUTION

DO NOT allow caliper (2) to hang from brake hoses. Damage to hoses may result.

6.   Position caliper (2) on axle and secure with supporting wire.

TA49682

7-11.   BRAKE PAD AND CALIPER REPLACEMENT   (Con't).

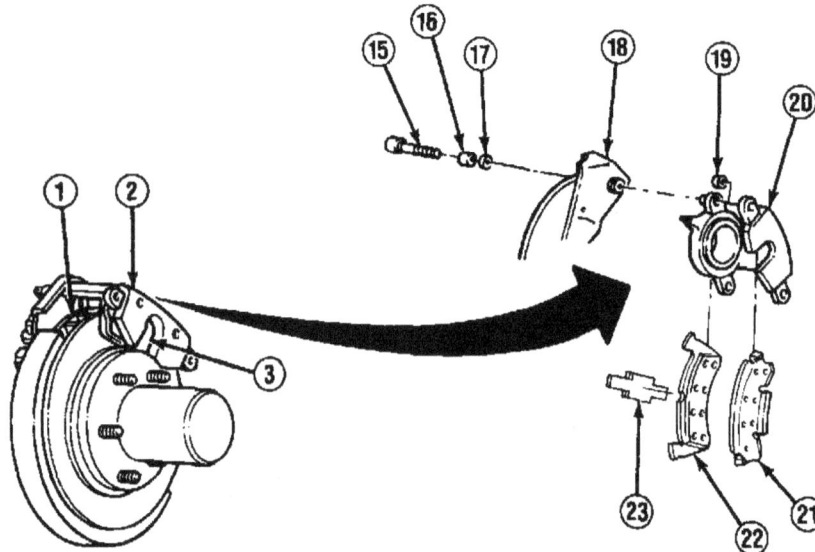

M1009

NOTE

Note location of anti-rattle clip (12) or spring (23) for installation.

7.   Remove brake pads (11 and 13) or (21 and 22) from caliper housing (8 or 20). Remove anti-rattle clip (12) or spring (23). Remove 2 sleeves (16), inner bushings (17), and outer bushings (19) as required.

WARNING

DO NOT use a dry brush or compressed air to clean brake pads or brake components, There may be asbestos dust on brake pads or brake components which can be dangerous to you if you breathe it. Brake pads and brake components must be wet, and a soft brush must be used. Failure to follow this warning may result in serious illness or death to personnel.

NOTE

Always replace brake pads (11, 13, 21, and 22) in sets, If 1 brake pad is replaced, ensure that all brake pads are replaced.

8.   Clean off dirt from brake pads (11 and 13) or (21 and 22). Inspect for glazing, oil saturation, or excessive wear. Replace brake pads if glazed or oil saturated, or if brake pad lining is worn to within 0.031 in. (0.80 mm) of a rivet head or pad itself.

TA49683

F-2.   WIRING DIAGRAMS AND SCHEMATICS INDEX (Con't).

7-11.   BRAKE PAD AND CALIPER REPLACEMENT (Con't).

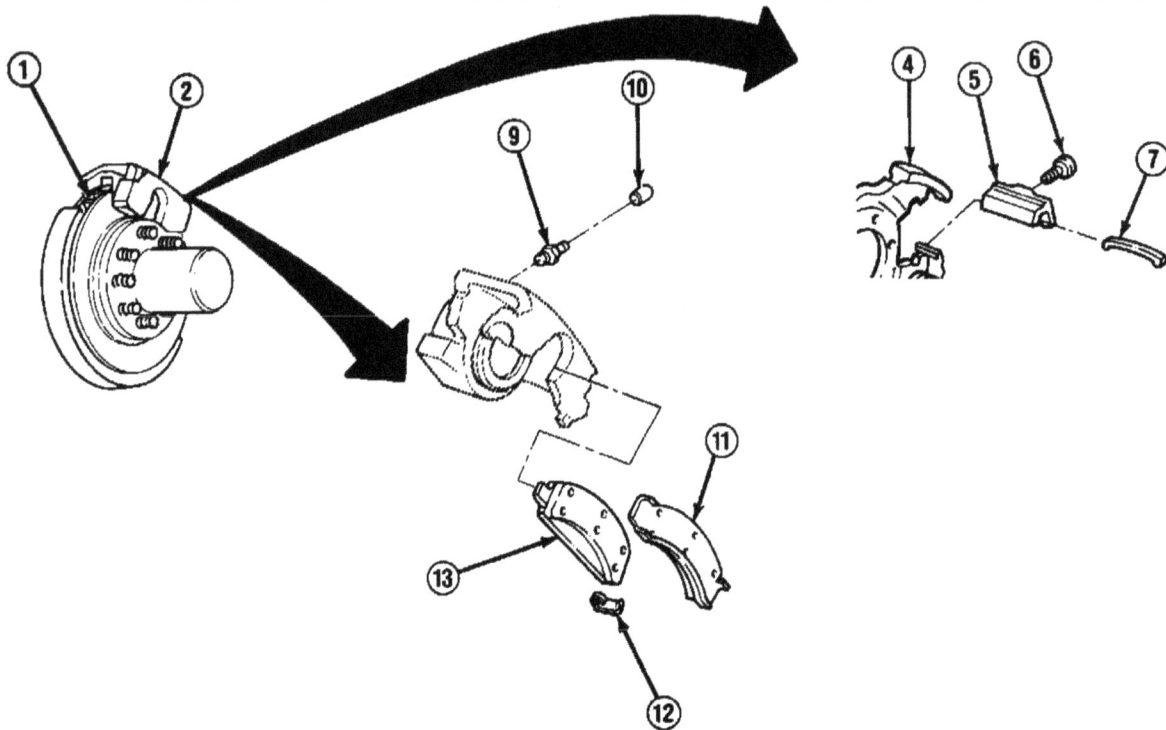

All Except M1009

NOTE

• Spring (7) must be installed on top of key (5).

• Use soft-faced hammer and punch to install key (5) and spring (7).

4.   Position caliper (2) on bracket (4) and rotor (1). Install spring (7) and key (5) on bracket with screw (6). Securely tighten screw.

5.   Install bleeder valve (9) and dust cap (10) if removed.

NOTE

One copper washer must be installed between caliper flex hose and caliper (2).

6.   Connect caliper flex hose to caliper (2) with bolt and 2 new copper washers.

FOLLOW-ON TASKS:

- Fill master cylinder to proper level. (See LO 9-2320-289-12)
- Install front wheel. (See paragraph 8-2)
- Pump brake pedal several times to adjust caliper, then check operation of brakes.
- Bleed system if caliper was replaced. (See paragraph 7-6)

TA49685

7-12. SERVICE BRAKE PEDAL REPLACEMENT.

This task covers: a. Removal   b. Installation

INITIAL SETUP:

Equipment Condition

• Stoplight switch and actuator removed.
  (See paragraph 4-16)

Materials/Parts

• One locknut
• One retaine r

| a. | **REMOVAL** |

1. Remove 2 screws (5) and wiring harness shield (4) from brake pedal bracket (2),

NOTE

Brake pedal is factory-installed without washer (14). Ensure that a washer
is used for installation.

2. Remove retainer (15) and washer (14) and disconnect power booster rod (13). Remove return spring retainer (12) and return spring (3). Discard retainer (15).

3. Remove locknut (1), Remove brake pedal (11) assembly. Remove 2 bushings (8) and spacer (7) from brake pedal pivot bolt (6). Remove screw (9) and brake pedal pad (10) if damaged, Discard locknut.

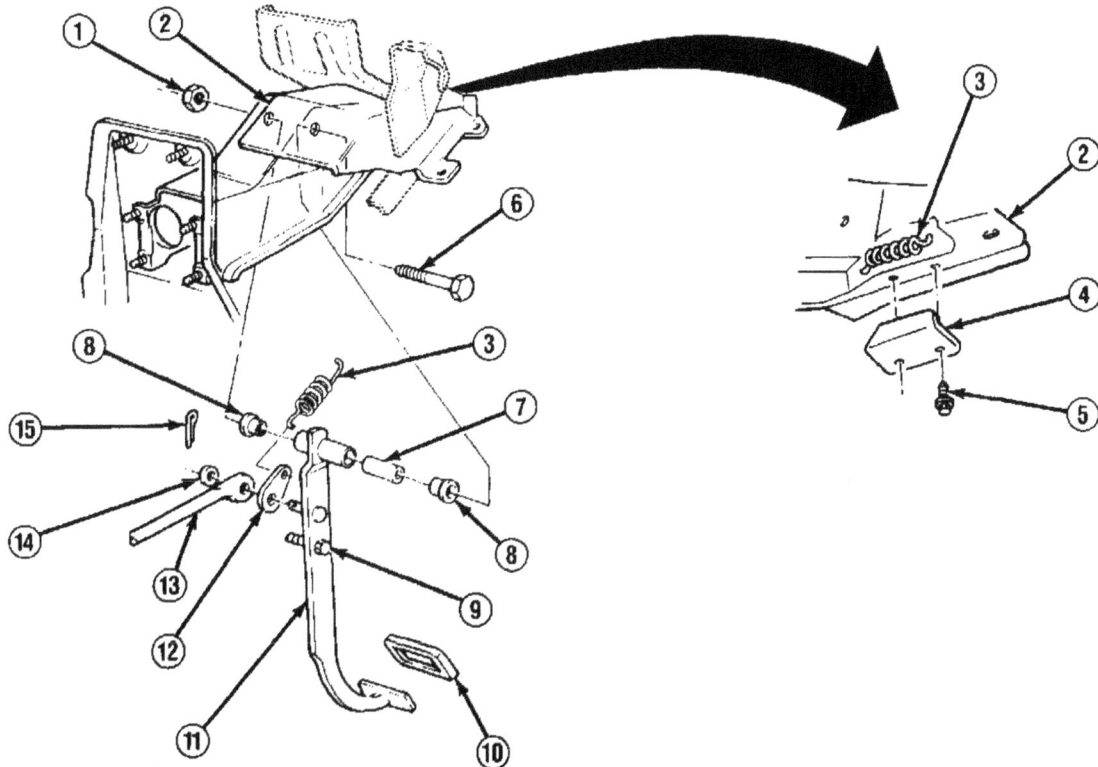

TA49686

7-12.   SERVICE BRAKE PEDAL REPLACEMENT (Con't).

| b.   INSTALLATION |

1.   Install brake pedal pad (10) and screw (9) if removed. Install spacer (7) and 2 bushings (8) on brake pedal (11). Install brake pedal assembly with pivot bolt (6) and new locknut (1).

2.   Install return spring (3) and return spring retainer (12). Install power booster rod (13) on brake pedal (11) pin with washer (14) and new retainer (15).

3.   Install wiring harness shield (4) on   brake pedal bracket (2) with 2 screws (5).

FOLLOW-ON TASKS:

• Install actuator and stoplight switch.   (See paragraph 4-16)
• Check operation of brakes.

CHAPTER 8
WHEELS AND STEERING SYSTEM MAINTENANCE

Section I. WHEEL AND TIRE MAINTENANCE

8-1. WHEEL AND TIRE MAINTENANCE INDEX.

8-2. WHEEL AND TIRE MAINTENANCE.

This task covers:

a. Removal   c. Installation
b. Inspection

INITIAL SETUP:

Tools/Test Equipment   *Manual References*

• Torque wrench   • TM 9-2320-289-10
                                              • TM 9-2610-200-14

General Safety Instructions

• Position wheel chocks at front and rear of tires opposite axle to be raised.

---

a.	REMOVAL

WARNING

Position wheel chocks at front and rear of tires opposite axle to be raised.
Truck must be on level surface before attempting to remove wheel   *(3).*
Failure to follow this warning may result in injury or death to personnel.

NOTE

Perform step 1.1   for M1028A2 and M1028A3.

1.   Position wheel chocks. Loosen lugnuts
      (1), but DO NOT remove. Raise truck
      and support on jack stand (2)   .
      Remove lugnuts and wheel (3).

NOTE

Only rear dual wheel has spacer ring (3.1).

1.1.   Position wheel chocks. Loosen lugnuts (1), but DO NOT remove. Raise truck and support on jack
       stand (2). Remove lugnuts, clamping ring (3.2), outer rear wheel (3) or front wheel, spacer ring
       (3.1), and inner rear wheel.

8-2. WHEEL AND TIRE MAINTENANCE (Con't).

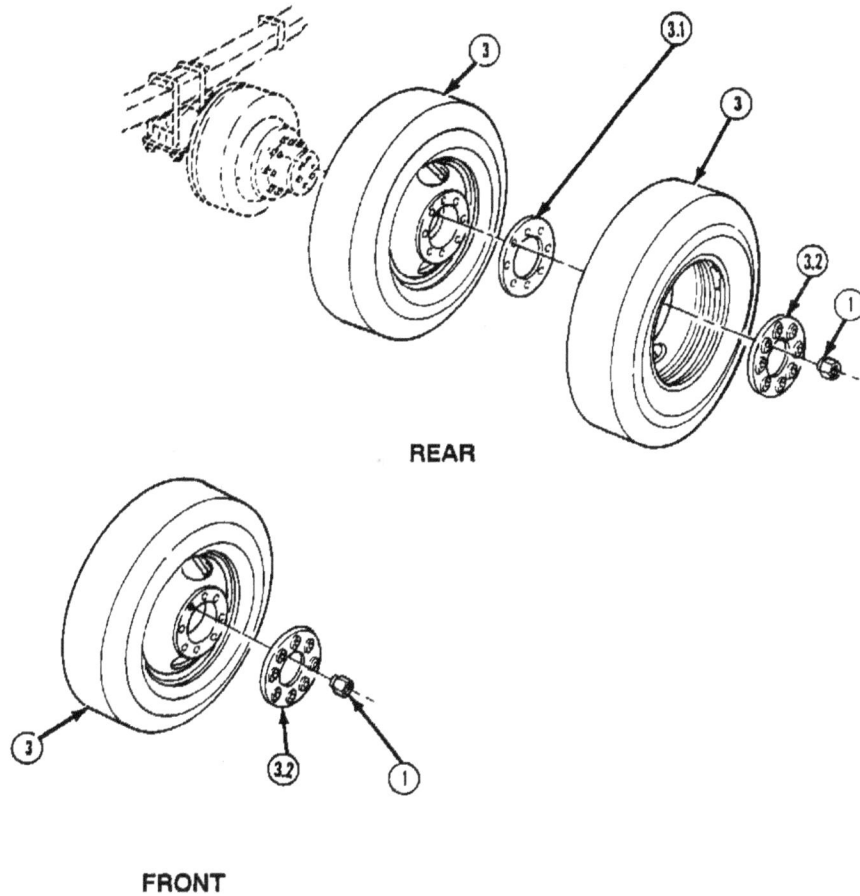

REAR

FRONT

WARNING

All air must be removed from tire before removing tire from wheel rim (4). Failure to follow this warning may result in serious injury to personnel.

2. Remove valve cap (5) and valve core (6) from valve stem (7), and allow tire to completely deflate. Remove tire from wheel rim (4), (See TM 9-2610-200-14)

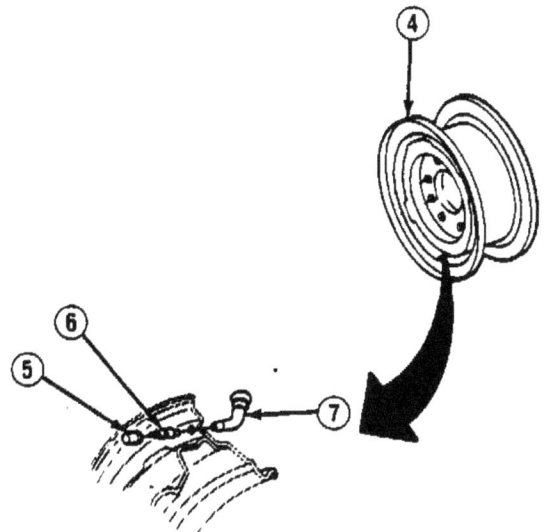

8-2. WHEEL AND TIRE MAINTENANCE (Con't).

b. INSPECTION

1. Inspect tire for cuts, gouges, cracks, and sidewall damage. (See TM 9-2610-200-14) Check for protruding objects inside tire which may not be visible from outside . Repair tire as required. (See TM 9-2610-200-14)

2. Inspect valve stem (7) and valve core (6) for cracks. Replace if cracked.

3. Inspect wheel rim (4) for bends and other damage. Replace if bent or damaged.

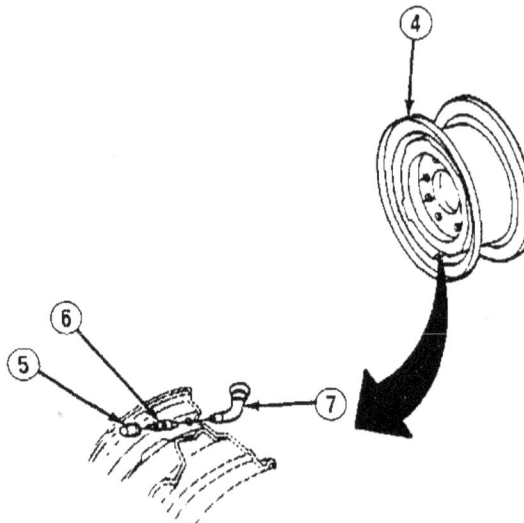

c. INSTALLATION

1. Install valve core (6) in valve stem (7) and install tire on wheel rim (4), (See TM 9-2610-200-14) Inflate tire as required. (See TM 9-2320-289-10) Check for leaks in valve stem, valve core, and around edge of wheel rim. Install valve cap (5). Balance tire and wheel assembly. (See TM 9-4910-743-14&P)

NOTE

* **Perform step 1.1 for M1028A2 and M1028A3 only.**

* **Only rear   dual wheel has spacer ring   (3.1).**

* **When installing   outer rear wheel   (3), ensure that valve stems are positioned 180°   apart and that inner valve stems are accessible through hole in outer rim.**

1.1. Position inner rear wheel (3), spacer ring (3.1), outer rear wheel or front wheel, and clamping ring (3.2) on wheel hub. Install lugnuts (1) finger tight. Remove jack stand (2) and lower truck.

8-2. WHEEL AND TIRE MAINTENANCE (Con't).

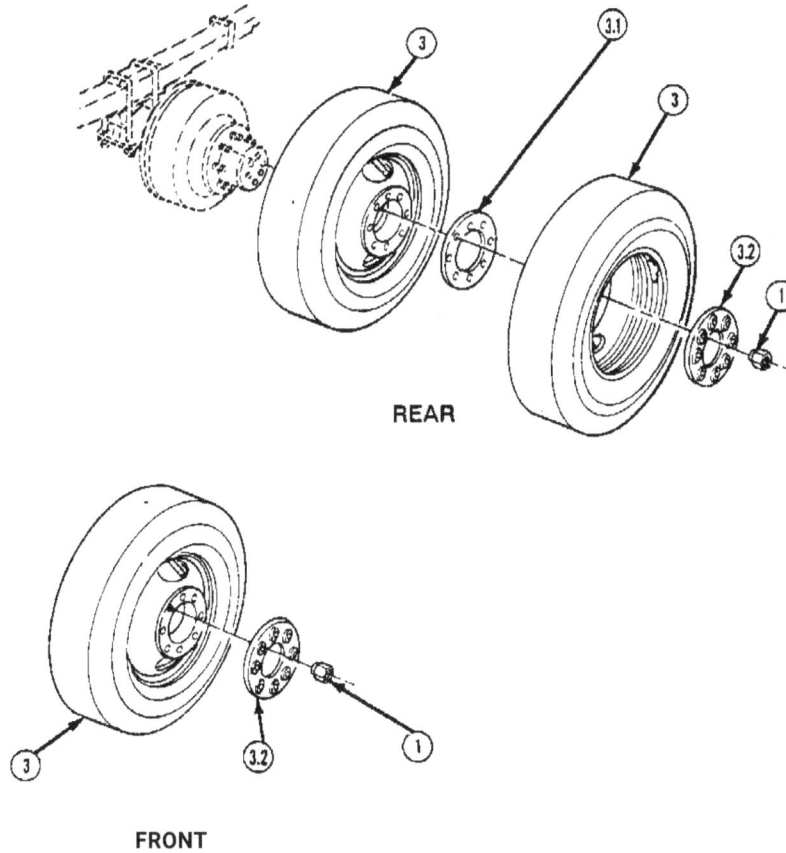

REAR

FRONT

2. Position wheel (3) on wheel hub. Install lugnuts (1) finger tight. Remove jack stand (2) and lower truck.

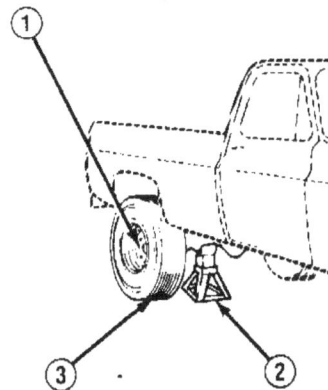

8-2.   WHEEL AND TIRE MAINTENANCE (Con't).

3.   For M1009, tighten lugnuts (1) to 90 lb.-ft. (122 N·m) in sequence shown. For all except M1009, tighten lugnuts to 140 lb.-ft. (190 N·m) in sequence   shown. Continue tightening sequence as required to obtain required torque. Remove wheel   chocks.

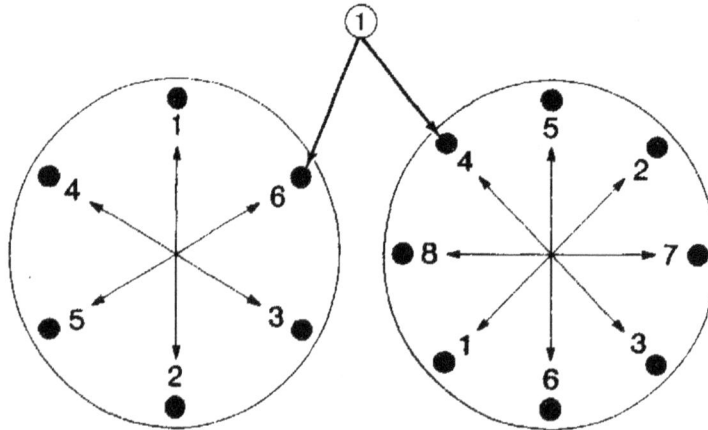

4.   Stow spare tire in tire carrier. For M1028A2 and M1028A3, stow tire in tire carrier with wheel offset up.

8-3. FRONT LOCKING HUB REPLACEMENT.

This task covers: a. Removal   b. Installation

INITIAL SETUP:

Materials/Parts
 • One "O" ring seal
 • Grease (Item 26, Appendix C)

Too/s/Test Equipment
 • Snapring pliers
 • Torque wrench
 • Screwdriver bit set, J-29843

| a.   REMOVAL |

1.   Remove 6 screws   (1) and locking hubcap unit (2).

NOTE

Snapring (3)   may not be on truck. Snapring is not necessary for operation, but may be installed if desired.

2.   Remove "O" ring seal (4) and lockring (5). Remove snapring (3) from axle shaft (7), Remove locking hub body unit (6) from wheel hub (8). Discard "O" ring seal.

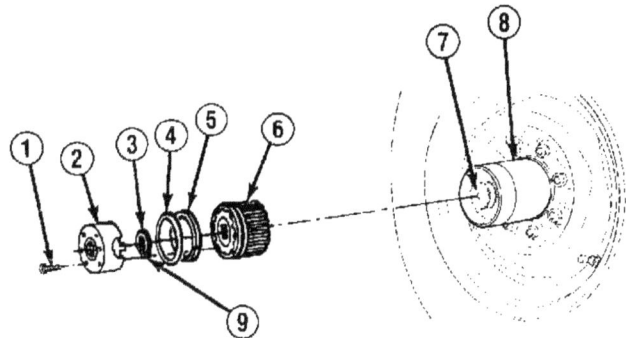

| b.   INSTALLATION |

NOTE

 • **Clean all components   and axle shaft (7), and lubricate with grease before installation.**

 • **Flat side of snapring (3) must face inward.**

1.   Position locking hub body unit (6) in wheel hub (8). Install snapring (3) on axle shaft (7) groove. Install lockring (5) and new "O" ring seal (4) on inside of locking hubcap unit (2).

2.   Aline tabs (9) with locking hub body unit (6) slots and install locking hubcap unit (2) with 6 screws (1). Tighten screws to 45 lb.-in. (5 N•m).

FOLLOW-ON TASKS:

 • Check operation of locking hub.

TA49720

8-4. ROTOR AND WHEEL BEARINGS MAINTENANCE .

This task cowers:
a. Removal
b. Cleaning and Inspection
c. Installation

INITIAL SETUP:

Equipment Condition

- Caliper removed. (See paragraph 7-11)
- Front locking hub removed.
  (See paragraph 8-3)

Materials/Parts

- #4-40 Screw
- One seal
- Six lockwashers (all except M1009)
- Six locknuts (MI 009)
- Dry cleaning solvent
  (Item 15, Appendix C)
- Grease (Item 26, Appendix C)

Tools/Test Equipment

- Annular bearing inserter, J-23445-A
- Nut wrench, J-26878-A (all except M1009)
- Nut wrench, J-34616 (1984, M1009 trucks)
- Hub nut wrench, J-6893-D
  (1985-87, M1009 trucks)
- Snapring pliers
- Torque wrench

Manual References

- TM 9-2320-289-20P

General/Safety Instructions

- Dry cleaning solvent is flammable and must not be used near an open flame. Use only in a well-ventilated area.
- DO NOT use a dry brush or compressed air to clean brake pads or brake components.

---

a. REMOVAL

NOTE

- If removing rotor, wheel bearings, and caliper bracket from all except RA1009, perform steps 1, 4, and 5.

- If removing rotor, wheel bearings, and caliper bracket from M1009, perform steps 2-4, and 6.

8-4. ROTOR AND WHEEL BEARINGS MAINTENANCE (Con't).

1. Remove outer adjusting nut   (5), adjusting lock (6), and inner adjusting nut (5).

NOTE

· A #4-40 screw should be used in step 2.

• Step 2 only applies to 1984, M1009 trucks.

2. Remove snapring (1) and washer (2). Insert screw into end of key (3), and pull out screw and key. Remove screw from key. Remove adjusting nut (4).

NOTE

Step 3 only applies to 1985-87, M1009 trucks.

3. Remove snapring (1) and washer (2). Remove locking nut (21), ring (22), and adjusting nut (23) .

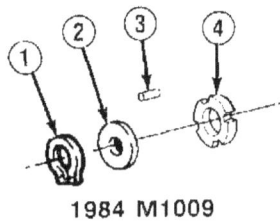

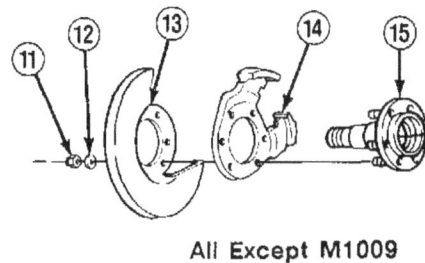

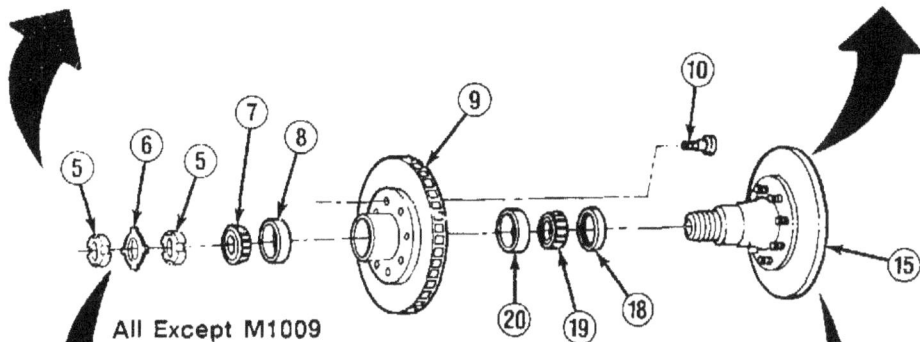

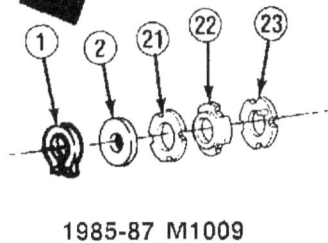

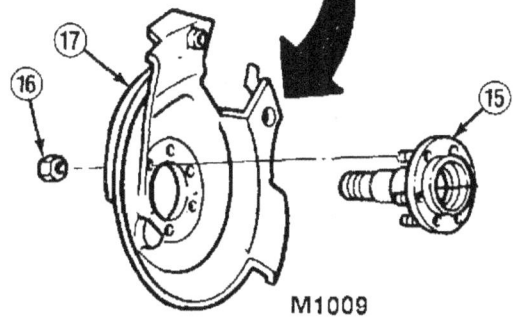

1984 M1009

All Except M1009

All Except M1009

1985-87 M1009

M1009

TA49721

8-4.   ROTOR AND WHEEL BEARINGS MAINTENANCE (Con't).

4.   Remove outer wheel bearing (7). Remove rotor (9), Remove seal (18) and inner wheel bearing (19) from rotor. Drive out outer race (8) and inner race (20) by evenly tapping around inner edges with soft-faced drift. Press out 6 or 8 wheel studs (10) as required. Discard seal.

WARNING

Splash shield (13) and caliper bracket (17) are factory-installed with 6 locknuts and washers. Refer to TM 9-2320-289-20P for proper replacement parts. Using improper replacement parts may cause caliper to fall off during operation, resulting in injury or death to personnel.

NOTE

Note position of caliper bracket (14) for Installation.

5.   Remove 6 nuts (11) and lockwashers (12). Remove splash shield (13) and caliper bracket (14) from spindle (15). Discard lockwashers.

NOTE

Note position of caliper bracket (17) for Installation.

6.   Remove 6 locknuts (16) and caliper bracket (17) from spindle (15). Discard locknuts.

b.   CLEANING AND INSPECTION

WARNING

- **Dry cleaning solvent P-D-680 is toxic and flammable. Always wear protective goggles and gloves and use only in a well-ventilated area. Avoid contact with skin, eyes, and clothes and DO NOT breathe vapors. DO NOT use near open flame or excessive heat. The solvent's flash point is 100°F-138°F (38°C-59°C). If you become dizzy while using cleaning solvent, immediately get fresh air and medical help. If solvent contacts eyes, immediately wash your eyes with water and get medical aid.**

- **DO NOT use a dry brush or compressed air to clean brake pads or brake components. There may be asbestos dust on brake pads or brake components which can be dangerous to you if you breathe it. Brake pads and brake components must be wet, and a soft brush must be used. Failure to follow this warning may result in serious illness or death to personnel.**

1.   Clean wheel bearings (7 and 19) and races (8 and 20). Inspect wheel bearings and races for scratches, discoloration, wear, bends, and cracks. Replace if rough or noisy after cleaning, or if worn, bent, or cracked.

2.   Clean cooling fins of rotor (9). Inspect rotor for scoring, pitting, or cracks. Notify your supervisor if scored, pitted, or cracked.

8-4.   ROTOR AND WHEEL BEARINGS MAINTENANCE (Con't).

c.   INSTALLATION

NOTE

- If installing rotor (9), wheel bearings (19), and caliper bracket (14) on all except M1009, perform steps 1, 3, and 4.

- If installing rotor (9), wheel bearings (19), and caliper bracket (17) on M1009, perform steps 2, 3, 5, and 6.

1.   Install caliper bracket (14) and splash shield (13) on spindle (15) with 6 new lockwashers (12) and nuts (11). Tighten nuts to 65 lb.-ft. (88 N·m).

2.   Install caliper bracket (17) on spindle (15) studs with 6 new locknuts (16). Tighten locknuts to 65 lb.-ft. (88 N·m).

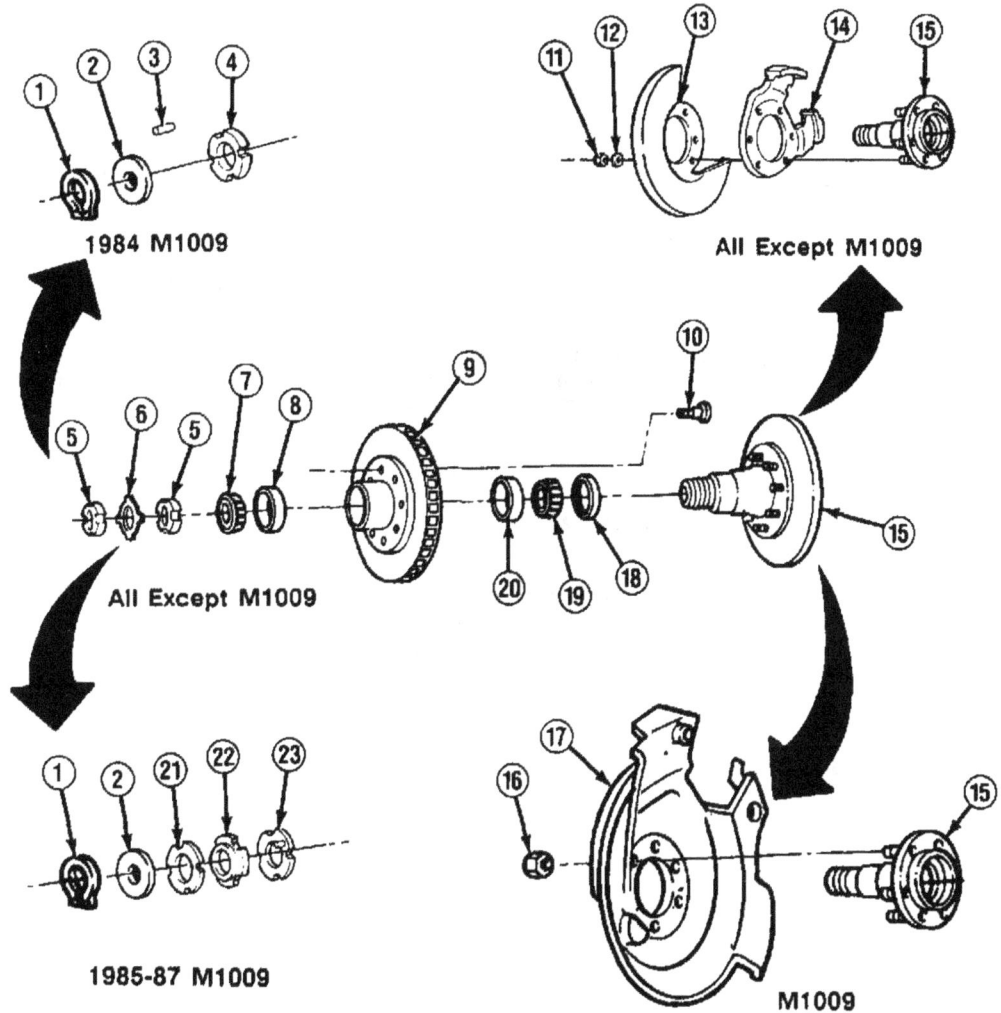

1984 M1009

All Except M1009

All Except M1009

1985-87 M1009

M1009

TA49722

8-4. ROTOR AND WHEEL BEARINGS MAINTENANCE (Con't).

WARNING

The tapered end of inner wheel bearing assembly must be facing toward the outboard (cap end) of axle shaft. The tapered end of the outer wheel bearing assembly must be facing toward the inboard (splined end) of the axle shaft. Failure to follow this warning may force wheel off truck during operation, causing serious injury or death to personnel.

NOTE

Apply grease to wheel bearing assemblies before installation.

3.   Press 6 or 8 wheel studs (10) into rotor (9) if removed. Drive inner race (20) and outer race (8) into rotor with soft-faced drift until fully seated. Install inner wheel bearing (19) and new seal (18) on rotor. Install rotor on spindle (15). Install outer wheel bearing (7).

4.   Position inner adjusting nut (5) with pin facing outward and tighten to 50 lb.-ft. (68 N•m) while turning rotor (9) to seat wheel bearing assemblies. Loosen inner adjusting nut and tighten to 50 lb.-ft. (68 N•m). Back off inner adjusting nut far enough to install adjusting lock (6). Position adjusting lock with hole on inner adjusting nut pin. Install outer adjusting nut (5) and tighten to 160 lb.-ft. (217 N•m).

NOTE

• **Step 5 only applies to 1984, M1009 trucks.**

• **Ensure that end of key (3) with threaded hole faces outward.**

5.   Position adjusting nut (4) and tighten to 50 lb.-ft. (68 N•m) while turning rotor (9) to seat wheel bearing assemblies. Loosen adjusting nut and tighten to 25 lb.-ft. (34 N•m). Back off adjusting nut to nearest slot and install key (3), Install snapring (1) and washer (2).

NOTE

Step 6 only applies to 1985-87, M1009 trucks.

6.   Position adjusting nut (23) and tighten to 50 lb.-ft. (68 N•m) while turning rotor (9) to seat wheel bearing assemblies. Loosen adjusting nut and tighten to 35 lb.-ft. (47 N•m). Back off adjusting nut 3/8 turn. Install ring (22) with tang alined to slot on spindle (15) and hole alined to pin on adjusting nut. Install locking nut (21). Tighten locking nut to 160 lb.-ft. (217 N•m). Install snapring (1) and washer (2).

FOLLOW-ON TASKS:

• Install front locking hub. (See paragraph 8-3)
• Install caliper. (See paragraph 7-11)

8-5. DRUM, HUB, AND WHEEL BEARINGS MAINTENANCE.

This task covers:	a. Removal	c. Installation
	b. Cleaning and Inspection	

INITIAL SETUP:

Equipment Condition

- Rear   axle shaft removed (all except M1009). (See paragraph 6-8)
- Wheel removed. (See paragraph 8-2)
- Transmission in "N" (Neutral).
- Parking brake released.

Tools/Test Equipment

- Wheel bearing remover, J-24426
- Driver handle, J-8092
- Wheel bearing wrench, J-2222-C
- Snapring pliers
- Torque wrenc h

Materials/Parts

- One adjusting hole cover
- One sea l
- Dry cleaning solvent (Item 15, Appendix C)
- Grease (Item   26, Appendix C)

Manual References

- TM 9-214

General Safety   Instructions

- Dry cleaning solvent is flammable and must not be used near open flame. Use only in a well-ventilated area.
- DO NOT use a dry brush or compressed air to clean brake shoes or brake components.

---

a. REMOVAL

NOTE

- If removing hub   (8),   drum (9), and wheel bearings (15 or 17) from all except M1009, perform steps 1 and   2 as required.

- If removing drum (1) from M1009, perform steps 1 and 3.

- It may be necessary to knock out lanced area (5) in backing plate (12) or drum (1), or remove covers to gain access to adjusting screw (3 or 13).

1. Insert a screwdriver through access hole (5) in backing plate (12) or drum (1). Loosen adjusting screw (3 or 13) until no drag is felt on drum.

2. Remove retainer (6), key (7),   and adjusting nut (18) from spindle   (11). Remove hub (8) and dru m   (9) assembly from spindle (11). Rem   ove inner wheel bearing assembly   (15) and seal (14) from hub. Remove snapring (16) and outer whee l bearing assembly (17) from hub . Remove 8 wheel stud s (10) to separate hub from drum. Discard seal.

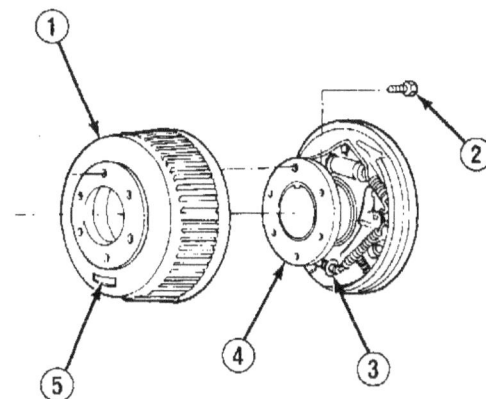

M1009

TA49723

8-5. DRUM, HUB, AND WHEEL BEARINGS MAINTENANCE (Con't).

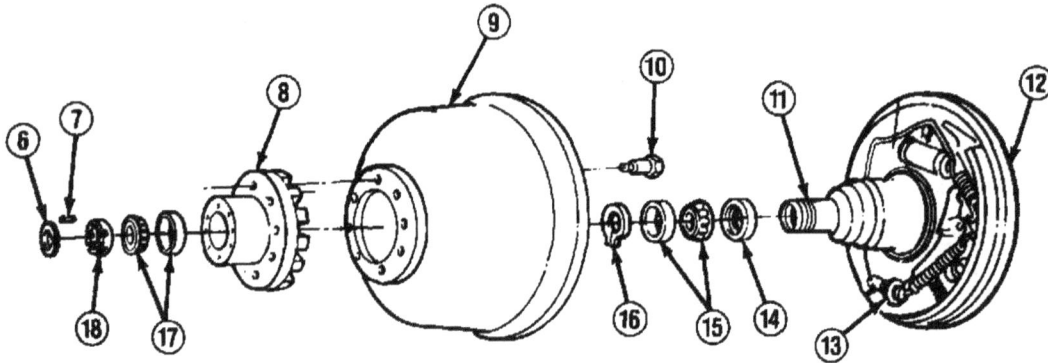

All Except M1009

3. Remove 2 retainers, if present, from 2 wheel studs (2), Evenly tap around edge of drum (1) and remove drum. Press 6 wheel studs from axle shaft (4) as required. Discard retainers.

b.	CLEANING AND INSPECTION

WARNING

- Dry cleaning solvent P-D-680 is toxic and flammable. Always wear protective goggles and gloves and use only in   a well-ventilated area. Avoid contact with skin, eyes, and clothes and DO NOT breathe vapors. DO NOT use near open flame or excessive heat, The solvent's flash point is 100°F-138°F (38°C-59°C). If you become dizzy while using cleaning solvent, immediately get fresh air and medical help. If solvent contacts eyes, immediately wash your eyes with water and get medical aid.

- DO NOT use a dry brush or compressed air to clean brake shoes or brake components. There may be asbestos dust on brake shoes or brake components which can be dangerous to you if you breathe it. Brake shoes and brake components must be wet, and a soft brush must be used. Failure to follow this warning may result in serious illness or death to personnel.

1. Clean and inspect wheel bearing assemblies (15 and 17). (See TM 9-214)

2. Clean hub (8) and drum (1 or 9). Inspect for scoring, pitting, or cracks. Notify your supervisor if scored, pitted, or cracked.

TA49724

8-5.   DRUM, HUB, AND WHEEL BEARINGS MAINTENANCE (Con't).

c.   INSTALLATION

WARNING

The tapered end of inner wheel bearing assembly (15) must be facing toward the outboard (cap end) of axle shaft (4 or 11). The tapered end of the outer wheel bearing assembly (17) must be facing toward the inboard (splined end) of the axle shaft. Failure to follow this warning may force wheel off truck during operation, causing serious injury or death to personnel.

NOTE

• If installing drum (1) on M1009, perform step 4.

• If installing hub (8), drum (9), and wheel bearings (15 or 17) on all except M1009, perform steps 1-3 as required.

• Apply grease to wheel bearing assemblies (15 or 17) before installation. (See TM 9-214)

. Before adjusting bearings (15 or 17), ensure that brakes are fully released and do not drag.

1.   Aline hub (8) and drum (9) stud holes. Press 8 wheel studs (10) into hub and drum with arbor press. Hub must seat tightly against drum.

2.   Install outer wheel bearing assembly (17) in hub (8) past snapring slot, Install snapring (16) in slot. Tap outer wheel bearing assembly to seat on ring. Install inner wheel bearing assembly (15) and new seal (14) in hub. Position hub and drum assembly on spindle (11).

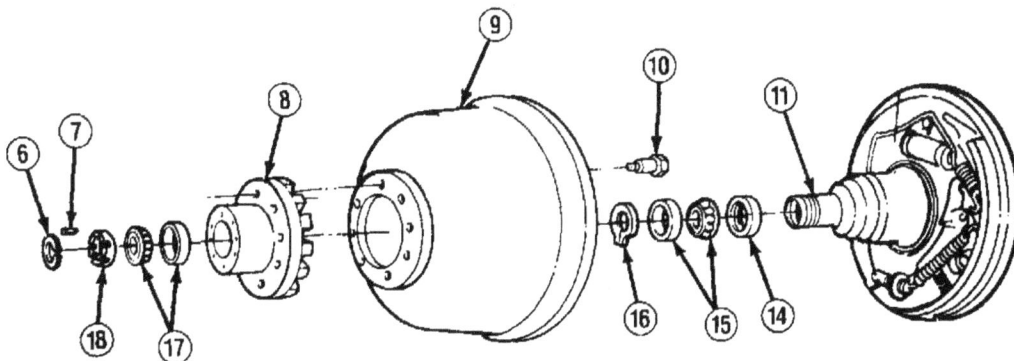

All Except M1009

TA49725

8-5. DRUM, HUB, AND WHEEL BEARINGS MAINTENANCE (Con't).

3. Install adjusting nut (18). Tighten adjusting nut to 50 lb.-ft. (68 N•m) while rotating hub (8) and drum (9) assembly to seat bearings (15 and 17). Loosen adjusting nut slightly to aline for installation of key (7). Install key in adjusting nut, Install retainer (6) on spindle (11). Ensure that retainer is properly seated.

4. Install 6 wheel studs (2) to axle shaft (4), if removed. Install drum (1) on axle shaft studs.

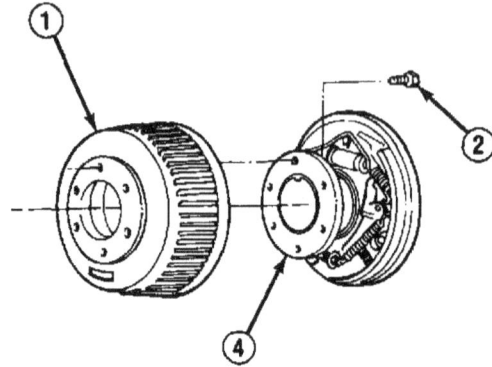

M1009

FOLLOW-ON TASKS:

- Adjust brake shoes. (See paragraph 7-7)
- Install wheel. (See paragraph 8-2)
- Install rear axle shaft if removed. (See paragraph 6-8)
- Check operation of brakes.

TA49726

8-6. FRONT WHEEL TOE ALINEMENT.

This task covers: a. Toe Check   b. Toe Adjustment

INITIAL SETUP:

Equipment Condition
- Tires inflated to proper pressure.
  (See TM 9-2320-289-10)
- Truck on level ground with wheels
  straight ahead.

Personnel Required
- MOS 63B (2)

Tools/Test Equipment
- Toe-in bar gage
- Torque wrench

---

a. TOE CHECK

1. Inspect all axle components fo r
   obvious looseness or damage that
   might affect toe measurement.
   Tighten or replace as required.

2. Measure toe using toe-in bar gage.
   Place gage at largest point on inside
   of front tires and toward front so that
   chains are just touching ground. Roll
   truck forward until chains are just
   touching ground toward rear.
   Maximum toe-in and toe-out
   measurement should be no more
   than 0.375 in. (0.953 cm).

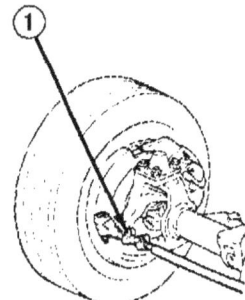

All Except M1009

b. TOE ADJUSTMENT

NOTE

- **If adjusting toe on all except
  M1009, perform step 1.**

- **If adjusting toe on M1009 ,
  perform step 2.**

1. Loosen nuts on adjusting sleeve (1).
   Rotate adjusting sleeve as required to
   bring toe within range. Check toe
   (see TOE CHECK, step 2). Tighten
   nuts on adjusting sleeve to 40 lb.-ft.
   (54 N·m).

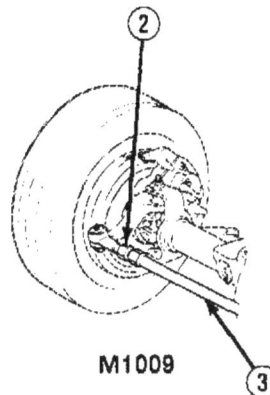

M1009

2. Check toe (see TOE CHECK, step 2). If alinement is off, loosen adjusting nuts (2) at both ends
   of tie-rod (3) and adjust as required to bring toe within range. Check toe (see TOE CHECK,
   step 2). Tighten adjusting nuts.

FOLLOW-ON TASKS:

- Operate truck and check for pull or wander.

TA49727

Section II. STEERING SYSTEM MAINTENANCE

8-7. STEERING SYSTEM MAINTENANCE INDEX.

8-8.   POWER STEERING SYSTEM BLEEDING INSTRUCTIONS.

This task covers: a.   Bleeding

INITIAL SETUP:

Equipment Condition
• Front of truck raised and supported
  by jack stands.

Manual References
• LO 9-2320-289-12

Materials/Parts
• Hydraulic fluid (Item 28, Appendix C)

General Safety Instructions
• Always wear goggles when bleeding
  power steering system.

| a. BLEEDING |

WARNING

Always wear goggles when bleeding power steering system. Hydraulic fluid
spillage can occur. Failure to follow this warning may result in serious eye
injury.

CAUTION

Hydraulic fluid and brake fluid cannot be mixed. Damage to seals will
result if hydraulic fluid contacts brake seals or brake fluid contacts
steering seals.

NOTE

Ensure that power steering hoses
are not touching any other parts of
truck,   particularly sheet metal.
This will prevent noise from power
steering hoses during operation.

1.   Check belt (1) tightness and inspect
      pulley (3) for looseness or damage.
      Tighten or replace belt and pulley as
      required. (See paragraph 8-15)

2.   Remove cap (2) and fill hydraulic fluid
      reservoir to prope r level. (Se e
      LO 9-2320-289-12)

3.   Start engine and run momentarily,
      Turn off engine. Check hydraulic fluid
      level and add as required. Repeat
      until hydraulic   fluid level remains
      constant after running engine.

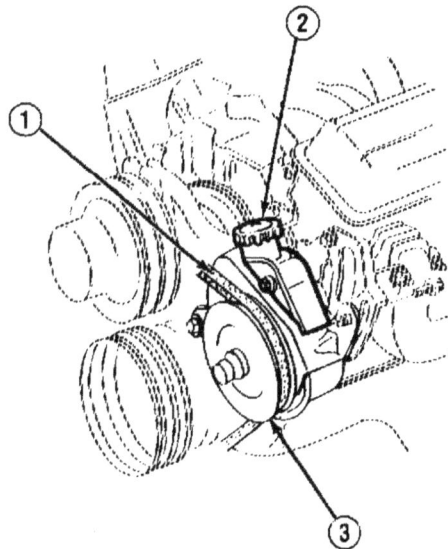

TA49728

8-8.   POWER STEERING SYSTEM BLEEDING INSTRUCTIONS (Con't).

4.   Start engine and depress brake pedal several times while rotating steering wheel right and left, lightly contacting wheel stops. Turn off engine. Check hydraulic fluid level and add as required.

5.   Check for air in hydraulic fluid. Hydraulic fluid will appear foamy or milky if it contains air. If air is present, allow truck to stand a few minutes with engine off, then repeat steps 2 through 4 as required. If hydraulic fluid still appears foamy or milky after a few attempts, notify your supervisor.

FOLLOW-ON TASKS:

• Remove jack stands and lower truck.
• Check operation of power steering.
• Check for leaks.

8-9. STEERING WHEEL AND DIRECTIONAL SIGNAL LEVER REPLACEMENT.

This task covers: a. Removal   b. Installation

INITIAL SETUP:

Equipment Condition
• Both battery negative cables disconnected,
   (See paragraph 4-38)

Tools/Test Equipment
• Steering wheel puller
• Torque wrench

| a. | REMOVAL |

NOTE

If removing directional signal lever (12), perform step 3.

1. Remove horn button cover (5), Remove 3 screws inside cup (4) and remove cup, horn bushing (3), and horn contact spring (2) from steering   wheel (1). Remove clip (10) and nut (9), Remove insulator (8), eyelet (7), and spring (6).

NOTE

Using alinement mark (11) on steering column shaft, mark position of steering wheel for installation.

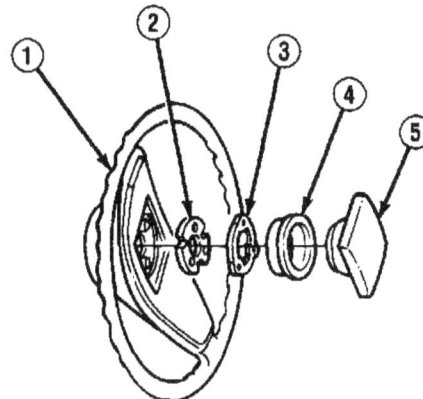

2. Remove steering wheel (1) using steering wheel puller.

3. Push in directional signal lever (12) while rotating counterclockwise, then rotate clockwise while pulling out to remove from steering column.

| b. | INSTALLATION |

NOTE

If installing directional signal lever (12), perform step 1.

1. Aline pin on directional signal lever (12) with notch in steering column, and install directional signal lever while turning counterclockwise.

NOTE

Ensure that directional signal lever (12) is in "OFF" position while installing steering wheel (1).

2. Position steering wheel (1) using alinement mark (11).

TA49729

8-9. STEERING WHEEL AND DIRECTIONAL SIGNAL LEVER REPLACEMENT (Con't).

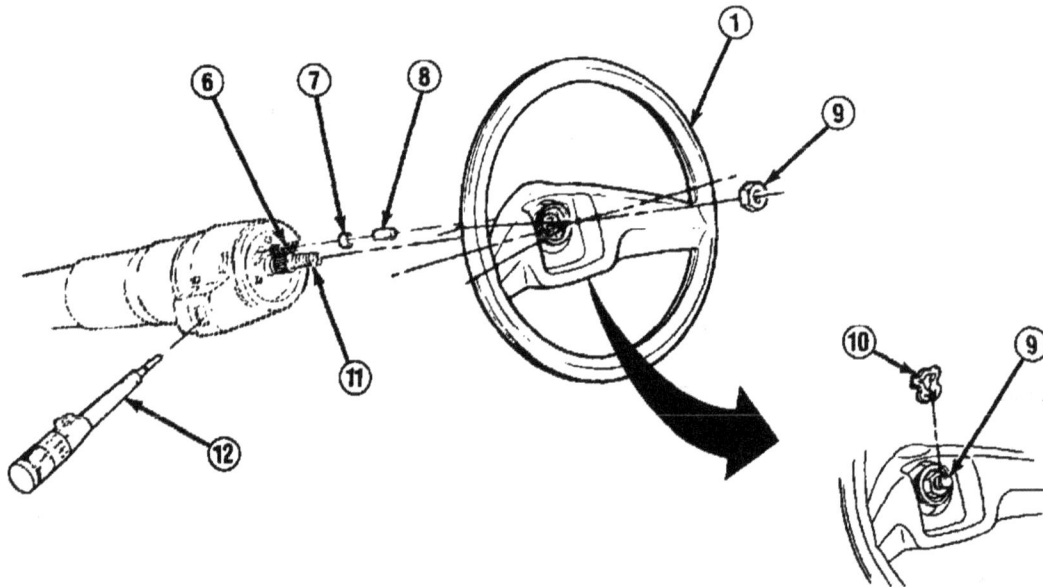

3.   Install spring (6), eyelet (7), and insulator (8). Install nut (9) and tighten to 30 lb.-ft. (41 N•m). Install clip (10). Position horn contact spring (2) with bowed part facing outward, and install horn bushing (3) and cup (4), Install 3 screws inside cup. Install horn button cover (5).

FOLLOW-ON TASKS:

• Connect both battery negative cables. (See paragraph 4-38)
• Check horn operation.

TA49730

8-10. CONNECTING ROD REPLACEMENT.

This task covers:	a. Removal	b. Installation

INITIAL SETUP:

Materials/Parts
- Two cotter pins

Tools/Test Equipment
- Puller
- Torque wrench

---

a.	**REMOVAL**

1. Remove 2 cotter pins (2) and nuts (1). Using puller, remove connecting rod sockets (5 and 8) from steering arm (6) and pitman arm (9). Remove 2 grease fittings (4) if damaged. Discard cotter pins.

2. Inspect connecting rod sockets (5 and 8) for damage. If damaged perform step 3. If not damaged, clean threads on connecting rod sockets.

NOTE

Note position of sleeve (7) and number of exposed threads on connecting rod sockets (5 and 8) for installation.

3. Loosen 2 nuts (3) and unscrew connecting rod sockets (5 and 8) from sleeve (7).

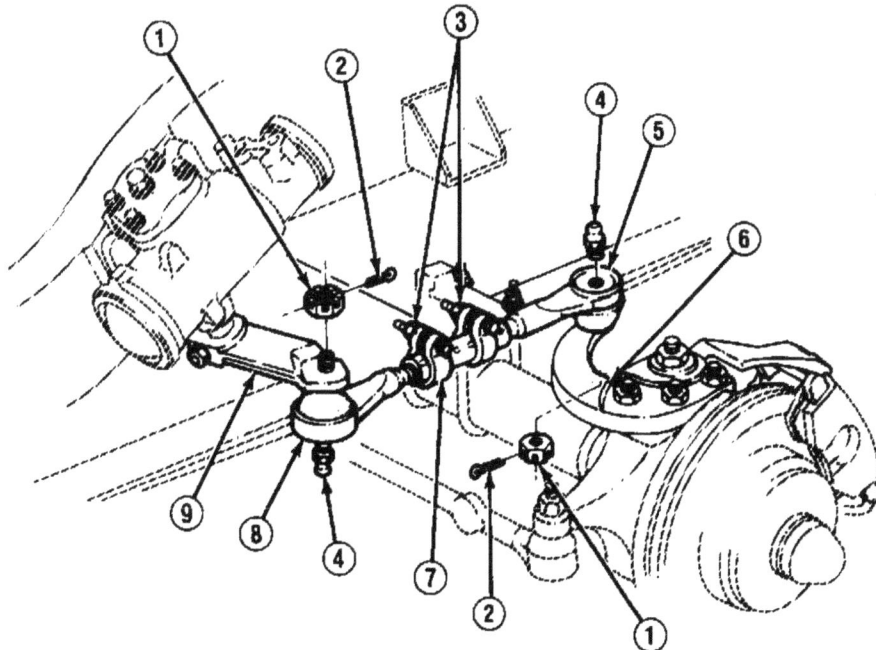

TA49731

8-10. CONNECTING ROD REPLACEMENT (Con't).

| b. | INSTALLATION |

1. Screw connecting rod sockets (5 and 8) onto sleeve (7) if removed. Tighten 2 nuts (3) to 40 lb.-ft. (54 N•m).

NOTE

Ensure that shorter connecting rod socket (8) is installed on pitman arm (9).

2 Install 2 grease fittings (4) if removed. Position connecting rod socket (8) on pitman arm (9) and connecting rod socket (5) on steering arm (6), and install 2 nuts (1). Tighten nuts to 70 lb.-ft. (95 N•m). Advance nuts as required to aline cotter pin (2) holes. Install 2 new cotter pins.

FOLLOW-ON TASKS:

• Lubricate connecting rod sockets. (See LO 9-2320-289-12)

8-11. PITMAN ARM REPLACEMENT.

This task covers: a. Removal   b. Installation

INITIAL SETUP:

Equipment Condition

- Truck raised and supported by frame on jack stands.
- Connecting rod socket disconnected from pitman arm. (See paragraph 8-10)

Tools/Test Equipment

- Mechanical puller, J-6632-01
- Torque wrench

Materials/Parts

- One locknut

---

a. REMOVAL

NOTE

Mark position of pitman arm (3) on steering gear shaft (1) for installation.

1. Remove locknut (5), washer (4), and bolt (2). Remove pitman arm (3) from steering gear shaft (1). Discard locknut.

b. INSTALLATION

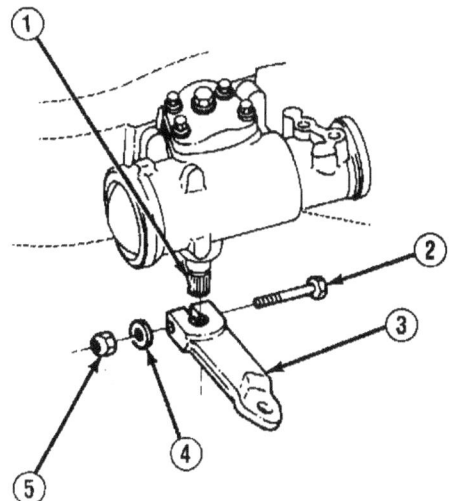

CAUTION

If a clamp-type pitman arm (3) is used, spread pitman arm with a wedge just enough to slip pitman arm onto steering gear shaft (I). DO NOT spread pitman arm more than required to slip over steering gear shaft with hand pressure. DO NOT use a hammer to install pitman arm.

NOTE

Before tightening locknut (5), ensure that position of pitman arm (3) is alined with marks made during removal.

1. Position pitman arm (3) on steering gear shaft (1). Install bolt (2), washer (4), and new locknut (5). Tighten locknut to 95 lb.-ft. (129 N·m).

FOLLOW-ON TASKS:

- Connect connecting rod socket to pitman arm. (See paragraph 8-10)
- Remove jack stands and lower truck.

TA49732

8-12. TIE-ROD SHOCK ABSORBER REPLACEMENT.

This task covers:	a. Removal	b. Installation

INITIAL SETUP:

Materials/Parts

• One cotter pin
• One lockwasher

Tools/Test Equipment

• Torque wrench

---

a. REMOVAL

1. Remove nut (7) and lockwasher (8). Remove cotter pin (4) and nut (5). Remove tie-rod shock absorber (2). Discard lockwasher and cotter pin.

2. Inspect tie-rod shock absorber (2) for leaks and damage. Inspect tie-rod shock absorber bushings (1) for wear and damage. Replace if damaged.

b. INSTALLATION

1. Position tie-rod shock absorber (2) on axle (3) and tie-rod (6). Install new lockwasher (8) and nut (7). Install nut (5). Tighten nut (7) to 80 lb.-ft (108 N·m). Tighten nut (5) to 45 lb.-ft. (61 N·m). Advance nut (5) as required to aline cotter pin (4) holes. Install new cotter pin.

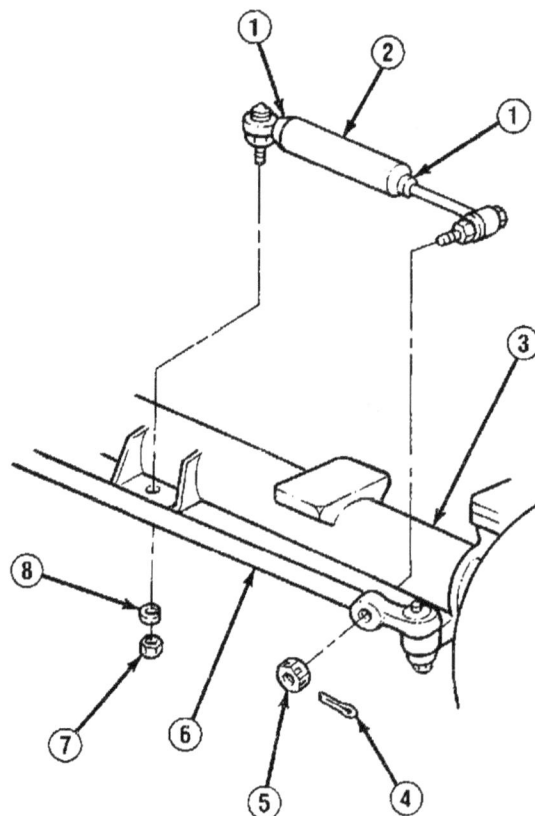

TA49733

8-13. TIE-ROD MAINTENANCE.

This task covers: a. Removal c. Assembly
b. Disassembly d. Installation

INITIAL SETUP:

Equipment Condition
 • Tie-rod shock absorber removed.
  (See paragraph 8-12)

Materials/Parts
 • Two cotter pins
 • Two tie-rod socket seals
 • Lubricating oil (Item 36, Appendix C)

Too/s/Test Equipment
 • Puller
 • Torque wrench

| a. | **REMOVAL** |

NOTE

 • M1009 tie-rod assembly is mounted from below steering arms (3).

 • All other tie-rod assemblies are mounted from above steering arms (3).

1. Attempt to move tie-rod end. If socket moves 0.015 in. (0.4 mm) on stud, tie-rod end must be replaced.

2. Remove 2 grease fittings (6). Remove 2 cotter pins (2) and nuts (1) . Discard cotter pins.

NOTE

Note number of exposed threads on tie-rod ends (5 and 9) or (10 and 13) for installation.

3. Use puller until tie-rod end (5 or 10) unseats. Repeat for other tie-rod end (9 or 10). Remove tie-rod assembly. Remove 2 tie-rod socket seals (4) from steering arms (3). Discard seals.

| b. DISASSEMBLY |

NOTE

 • If disassembling tie-rod assembly for all except M1009, perform step 1.

 • If disassembling tie-rod assembly for M1009, perform step 2.

 • Note position of sleeve (11) and number of exposed threads for installation.

1. Loosen 2 nuts (14) and remove tie-rod end (10) from sleeve (11). Remove sleeve from tie-rod tube (12). Inspect all components for damage and replace as required.

NOTE

Note number of exposed threads on adjusting nut (7) for installation.

2. Remove tie-rod ends (5 and 9) and adjusting nut (7) from tie-rod tube (8) as required. Inspect all components for damage and replace as required.

8-13. TIE-ROD MAINTENANCE (Con't).

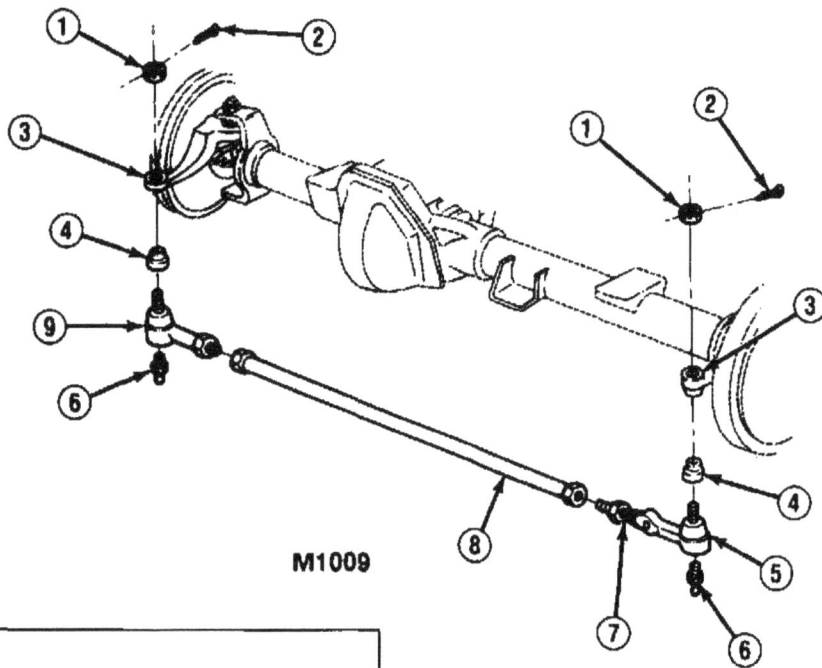

M1009

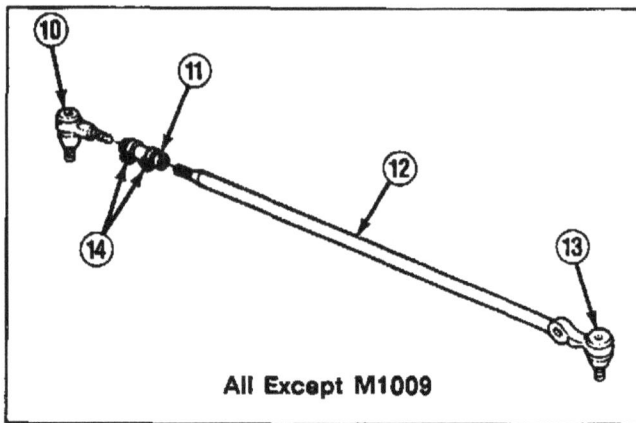

All Except M1009

---

c. ASSEMBLY

NOTE

- If assembling tie-rod assembly on M1009, perform step 1.

- If assembling tie-rod assembly on all except M1009, perform step 2.

- Ensure that tie-rod end (5 and 9) or (10 and 13) threads are clean and lubricated.

1. Install tie-rod end (9) on tie-rod tube (8). Install adjusting nut (7) on tie-rod tube, Install tie-rod end (5) on adjusting nut.

2. Install sleeve (11) on tie-rod tube (12). Install tie-rod end (10) on sleeve. Tighten nuts (14) to 40 lb.-ft. (54 N•m).

TA49734

8-13. TIE-ROD MAINTENANCE (Con't).

d. INSTALLATION

NOTE

♦M1009 tie-rod assembly is mounted from below steering arms (3).

●All other tie-rod assemblies are mounted from above steering arms (3).

1. Position 2 new tie-rod socket seals (4) and tie-rod ends (5 and 9) or (10 and 13) on 2 steering arms (3). Install 2 nuts (1), Tighten nuts to 40 lb.-ft. (54 N•m). Advance nuts as required to aline cotter pin (2) holes. Install 2 new cotter pins. Install 2 grease fittings (6).

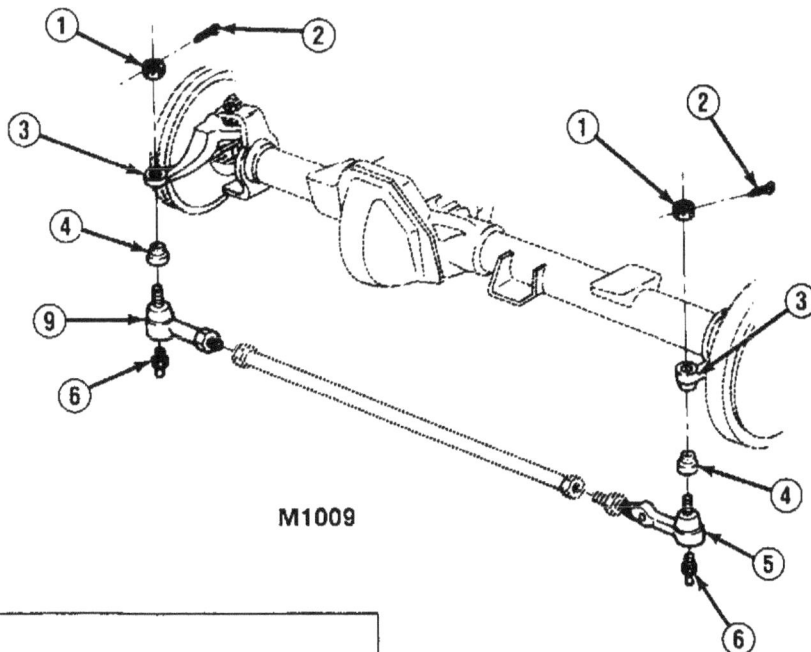

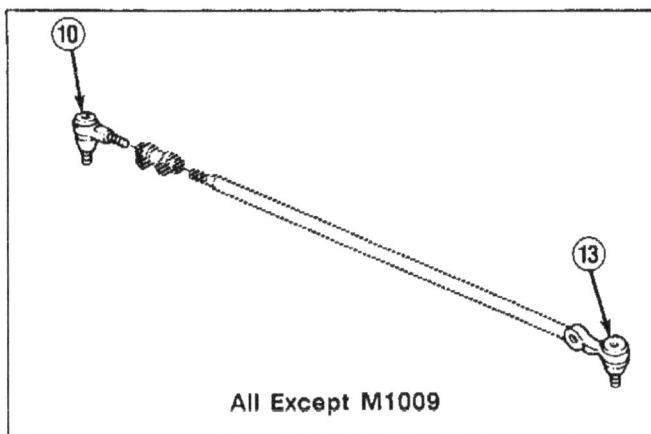

M1009

All Except M1009

FOLLOW-ON TASKS:

- Install tie-rod shock absorber. (See paragraph 8-12)
- Adjust toe alinement. (See paragraph 8-6)
- Lubricate tie-rod ends. (See LO 9-2320-289-12)

TA49735

8-14.   POWER STEERING LINES REPLACEMENT.

This task covers: a. Removal   b. Installation

INITIAL SETUP:

Equipment Condition   *Materials/Parts*

• Both battery negative cables disconnected.   • One lockwasher
   (See paragraph 4-38)   • One power steering   gear outlet seal

Too/s/Test Equipment

• Open end wrench
   (16 mm and 18 mm), J-33124

---

a.   REMOVAL

CAUTION
<u></u>

Immediately after disconnection, plug all lines and ports to prevent
contamination.

NOTE

• Note location of hoses and pipes for installation.

• Use suitable container to catch power steering fluid.

8-14. POWER STEERING LINES REPLACEMENT (Con't).

NOTE

- Perform the following steps as required to remove or disconnect desired power steering line   (9 or 18).

- Remove clamps (3, 5, 8, 14, or 17) from hoses (4, 10, or 15) as required after disconnection.

1. Remove nut (19), lockwasher (20), and bolt (1). Remove clip (7).

2. Loosen 2 clamps (14) and disconnect hose (15) from power steering pump (16) and power steering gear (13). Remove hose. Remove outlet pipe (11) and seal (12) as required, Discard seal if removed.

3. Disconnect line (18) and line (9) at power booster (2). Loosen clamp (3) and disconnect hose (4) from power booster.

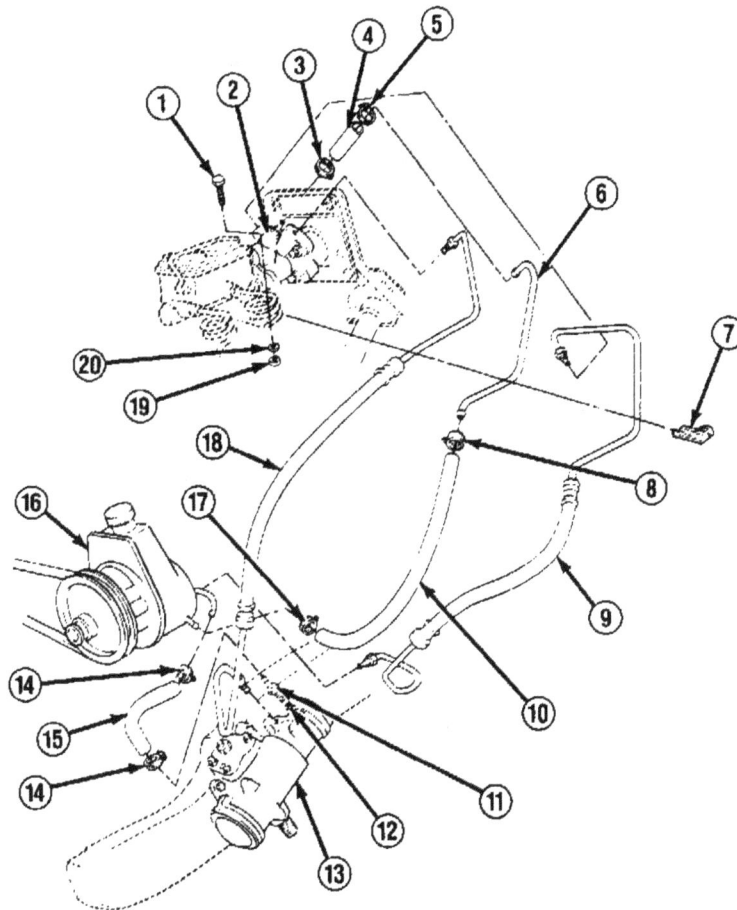

TA49736

8-14.   POWER STEERING LINES REPLACEMENT (Con't).

NOTE

If disconnecting line (9) from rear of power steering pump (16), it may be necessary to remove power steering pump mounting hardware and pull out power steering pump.

4.   Disconnect line (18) from power steering gear (13). Disconnect line (9) from power steering pump (16). Loosen clamp (17) and disconnect hose (10) from power steering pump. Remove hoses and lines as required. Loosen clamps (5 and 8), and disconnect hose (4) and pipe (6) as required.

5.   Inspect all hoses (4, 10, and 15), pipes (6 and 11), lines (9 and 18), and fittings for damage. Replace as required.

| b.   INSTALLATION |

CAUTION

Remove all plugs before connection.

NOTE

Install clamps (3, 5, 8, 14, or 17) on disconnected hoses (4, 10, or 15) if removed.

1.   Connect hose (4) to pipe (6) and pipe to hose (10), Tighten clamps (5 and 8) if disconnected. Connect hose (10) to power steering pump (16) and tighten clamp (17). Connect line (9) to power steering pump. Connect line (18) to power steering gear (13), install power steering pump if removed.

2.   Connect hose (4) to power booster (2) and tighten clamp (3). Connect lines (9 and 18) to power booster.

3.   Install new seal (12) and outlet pipe (11) if removed. Connect hose (15) to power steering gear (13) and power steering pump (16), and tighten clamps (14).

4.   Install clip (7) on line (9), pipe (6), and line (18), and install with bolt (1), new lockwasher (20), and nut (19).

FOLLOW-ON TASKS:

• Connect both battery negative cables. (See paragraph 4-38)
• Bleed power steering system. (See paragraph 8-8)

8-15. POWER STEERING PUMP, BELT, AND PULLEY REPLACEMENT.

This task covers: a. Removal   b. Installation

INITIAL SETUP:

Equipment Condition
- Alternator belts removed (if   removing
  power steering pump belt).
  (See paragraph 4-2 or 4-3)
- Air conditioner belt removed (M1010 only).
  (See paragraph 3-35)

Too/s/Test Equipment
- Power steering pump pulley remover,
  J-25034-B
- Steering pulley installer, J-25033-B
- Open end wrench
  (16 mm and 18 mm), J-33124

---

a.   REMOVAL

CAUTION

DO NOT pry on power steering pump (5) reservoir or pull on filler neck when
rotating power steering pump, Failure to follow this caution may result in
damage to power steering pump.

NOTE

• If removing belt (1), perform step 1.

• If removing power steering pump (5), perform steps 1-3.

1.   Loosen adjusting nut (2) and adjusting bolts (7 and 12). Rotate power steering pump (5) to
loosen belt (1). Remove belt from pulley (14), Discard belt if worn or damaged.

NOTE

On all except M1010, bolt (12) is removed from behind power steering
pump (5).

2.   Remove bolt (8), adjusting bolt (7), and bracket (9). Remove nut (10) and brace (11).
Disconnect power steering lines at power steering pump (5). (See paragraph 8-14)

3.   Remove adjusting nut (2), nut (3), and adjusting bolt (12). Remove power steering pump (5) and
bracket (4) assembly.

4.   Remove power steering pump pulley (14).

5.   Remove 3 bolts (13) and bracket from power steering pump (5).

8-15. POWER STEERING PUMP, BELT, AND PULLEY REPLACEMENT (Con't).

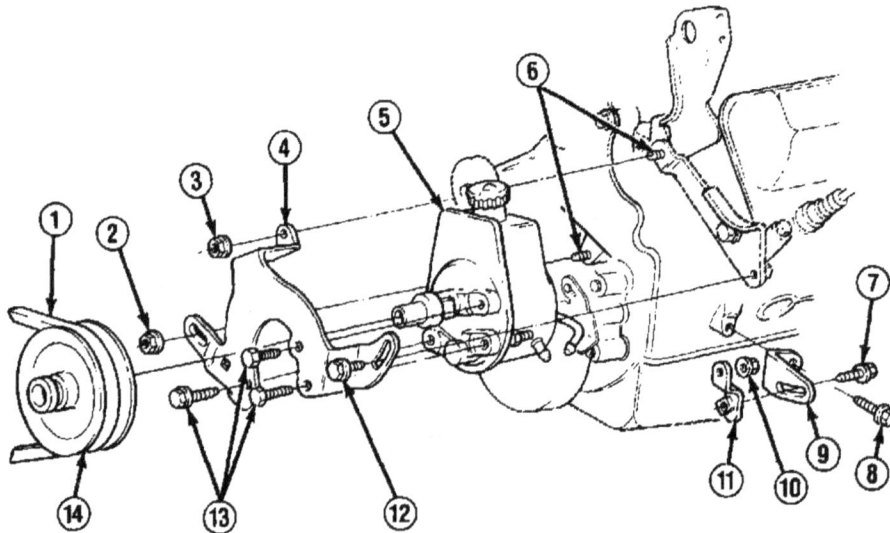

---

b. INSTALLATION

NOTE

- If installing   power steering pump (5), perform steps 2-5.
- If installing   belt (1), perform steps 6 and 7.

1. Install bracket (4) on power steering pump (5) with 3 bolts (13).

2. Install power steering pump pulley (14).

NOTE

On all except M1010, bolt (12) is installed from behind power steering pump (5).

3. Position power steering pump (5) and bracket (4) assembly on studs (6) and install with adjusting bolt (12), adjusting nut (2), and nut (3). DO NOT fully tighten adjusting bolt or nut.

4. Connect power steering lines   at power steering pump   (5). (See paragraph 8-14)

5. Install nut (10) and brace (11) on power steering pump (5). Install bracket (9) with bolt (8) and adjusting bolt (7). DO NOT fully tighten adjusting bolt.

TA49737

8-15.   POWER STEERING PUMP, BELT, AND PULLEY REPLACEMENT (Con't).

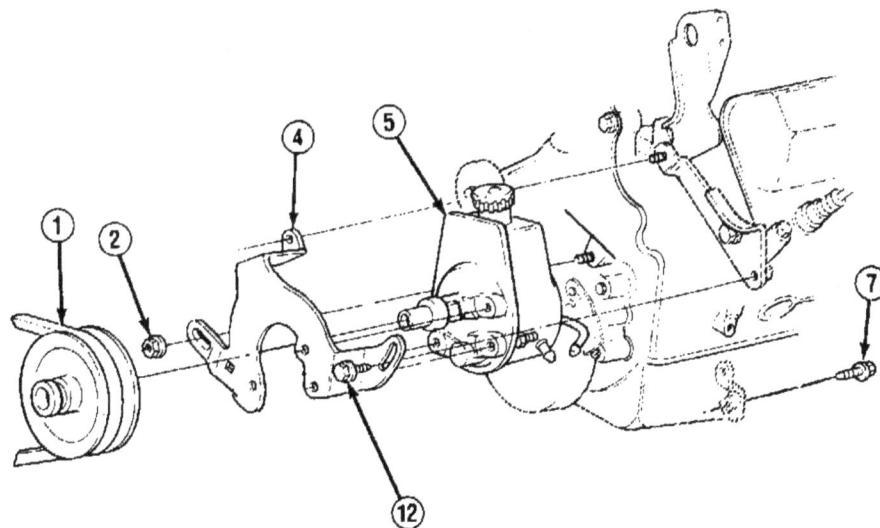

CAUTION

Ensure that belt (1) tension is correct. A belt too loose or too tight can cause damage to power steering pump (5) or belt.

6.   Position belt (1) on pulleys. Rotate power steering pump (5) by placing a pry bar between engine and bracket (4), and pulling pry bar toward power steering pump until belt appears tight. Tighten adjusting nut (2) and adjusting bolts (7 and 12).

7.   Using belt tensioning gage, check belt (1) tension. (See Appendix E)

FOLLOW-ON TASKS:

- Install air conditioner belt if removed. (See paragraph 3-35)
- Install alternator belts if removed. (See paragraph 4-2 or 4-3)
- Bleed power steering system. (See paragraph 8-8)

8-16.   POWER STEERING GEAR REPLACEMENT.

| This task covers: | a. Removal | b. Installation |

INITIAL SETUP:

Equipment Condition
  • Pitman arm removed. (See paragraph 8-11)

Tools/Test Equipment
  • Torque wrench

Materials/Parts
  • Two lockwashers

---

a.   REMOVAL

1.   Disconnect power   steering lines from power steering gear (10).

2.   Remove nut (7)   and lockwasher (6). Remove nut (8) and lockwasher (9). Discard lockwashers.

NOTE

It may be necessary to lightly tap on coupling (4) to separate it from steering shaft flange (5).

3.   Remove 4 bolts (1) and spacers (2) while supporting steering gear (10). Remove steering gear from frame (3).

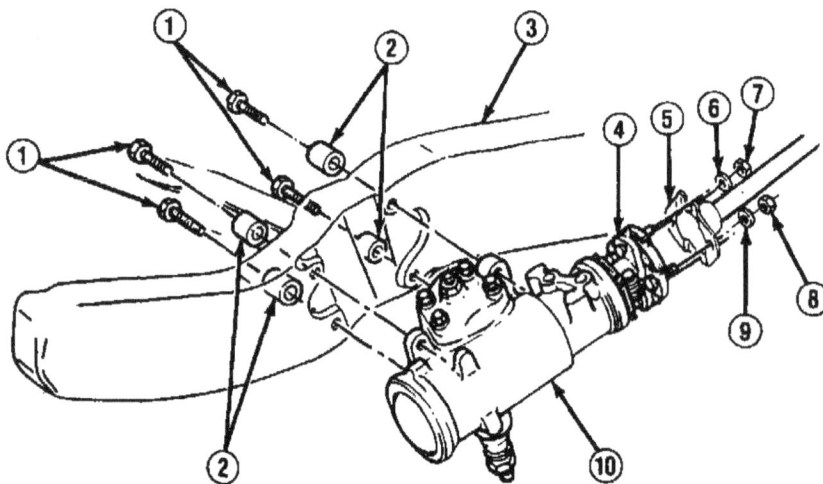

TA49739

8-16.   POWER STEERING GEAR REPLACEMENT (Con't).

| b. | INSTALLATION |

1. Position steering gear (10) so coupling (4) studs aline with holes in steering shaft flange (5). Install steering gear on frame (3) with 4 spacers (2) and bolts (1). Tighten bolts to 75 lb.-ft. (102 N•m).

2. Install coupling (4) on steering shaft flange (5) with new lockwasher (6) and nut (7), and new lockwasher (9) and nut (8). Tighten nuts to 20 lb.-ft. (27 N•m).

3. Install power steering lines to power steering gear (10).

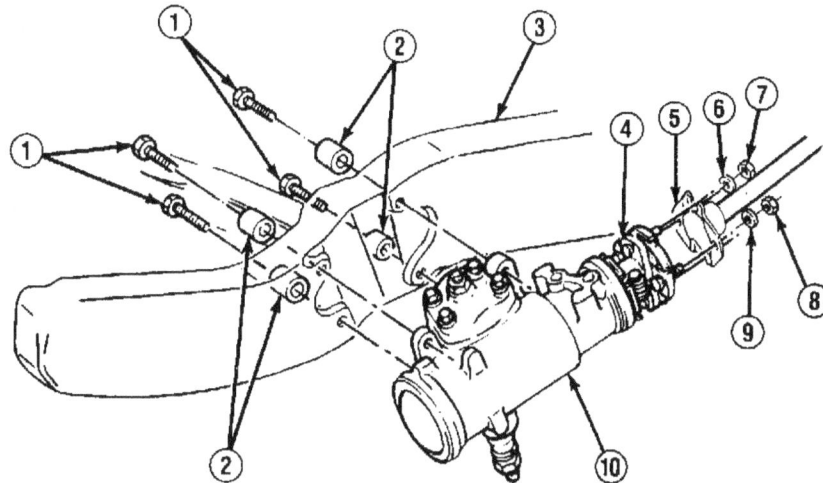

TA49740

FOLLOW-ON TASKS:

• Install pitman arm. (See paragraph 8-11)

8-17.   STEERING SHAFT REPLACEMENT.

This task covers: a. Removal   b. Installation

INITIAL SETUP:

Materials/Parts   *Tools/Test Equipment*
  • Grease (Item 26, Appendix C)   • Torque wrench

| a. | **REMOVAL** |

NOTE

Ensure that position of flanged end of lower steering shaft (6) and steering shaft are marked for assembly.

1.   Remove 2 nuts (4 and 7) and washers (3 and 8) from flexible coupling (2) at steering gear (1). Remove flanged end of lower steering shaft (6) from steering gear.

2.   Remove nut securing upper shaft (5) to lower steering shaft (6) and tap out bolt. Tap steering shaft off at upper end and remove.

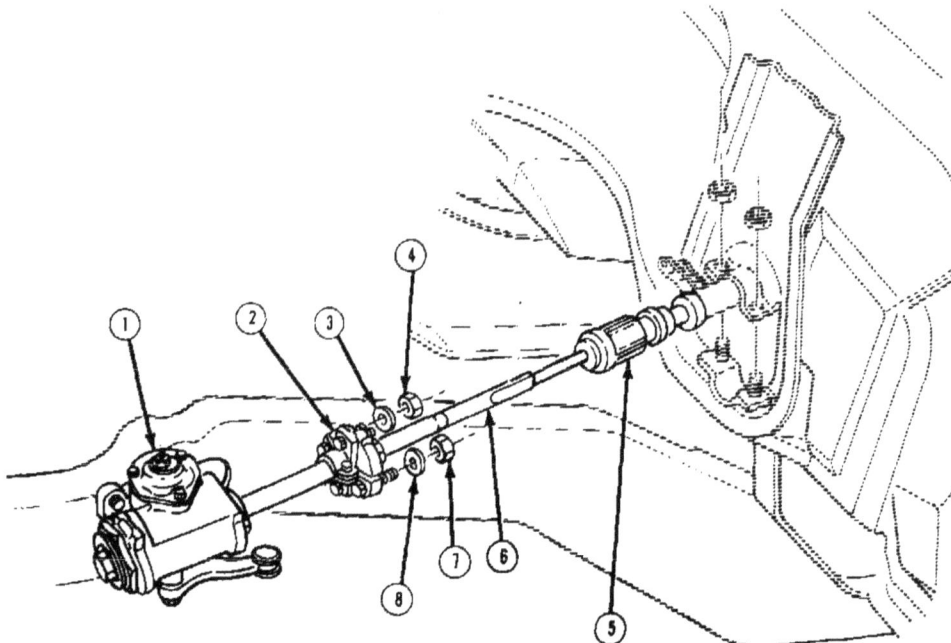

TA701839

8-17.   STEERING SHAFT REPLACEMENT (Con't).

| b. | INSTALLATION |

1.   Lubricate end of upper shaft (5) with grease. Install lower steering shaft (6) onto upper shaft with notch in cover toward flat side of spline on upper shaft. Tap into place.

2.   Tap bolt into upper and lower steering shafts (5 and 6) and install nut.

3.   Install 2 nuts (4 and 7), washers (3 and 8), and flanged end of lower steering shaft (6) to flexible coupling (2) at steering gear (1). Tighten nuts to 20 lb.-ft. (27 N•m).

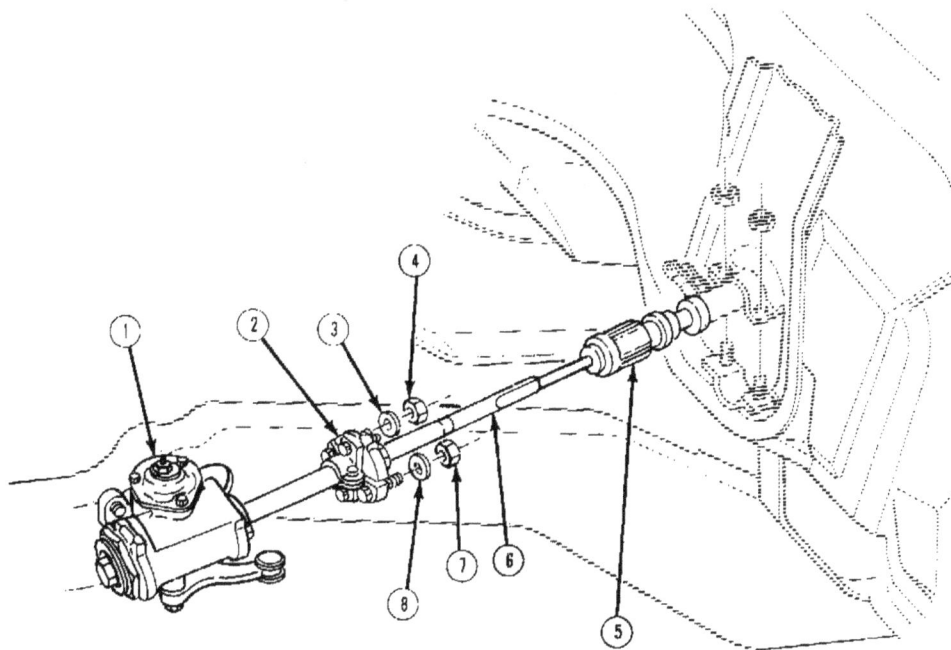

TA701840

CHAPTER 9
FRAME MAINTENANCE

9-1. FRAME MAINTENANCE INDEX.

9-2. FRONT BUMPER, RADIATOR GRILLE GUARD, AND TIE-DOWN CLEVISES REPLACEMENT.

This task covers: a.   Removal   b. Installation

INITIAL SETUP:

Materials/Parts

• Two cotter pins

Personnel Required

• MOS 63B (2)

Tools/Test Equipment

• Torque wrench

General Safety Instructions

• Use an assistant during removal and installation of radiator grille guard.

a.	REMOVAL

WARNING

Radiator grille guard is heavy. Failure to use an assistant during removal may cause serious injury to personnel.

NOTE

If removing radiator grille guard (10), perform step 1.

1.   Remove 6 nuts (4), washers (3), bolts (11), and radiator grille guard (10).

2.   Remove cotter pin (7) from pin (8) and remove tie-down clevis (9). Repeat step to remove other tie-down clevis.

3.   Remove 2 blackout light brackets from bumper (1). (See paragraph 4-25)

4.   Remove 2 nuts (5), washers (3), bolts (1   2), and bumper (1).

5.   Remove weight classification marker (2).

b.	INSTALLATION

WARNING

Radiator grille guard is heavy, Failure to use an assistant during installation may cause serious injury to personnel.

NOTE

If installing radiator grille guard (10), perform step 5.

1.   Install weight classification marker (2) to bumper (1).

9-2. FRONT BUMPER, RADIATOR GRILLE GUARD, AND TIE-DOWN CLEVISES REPLACEMENT (Con't).

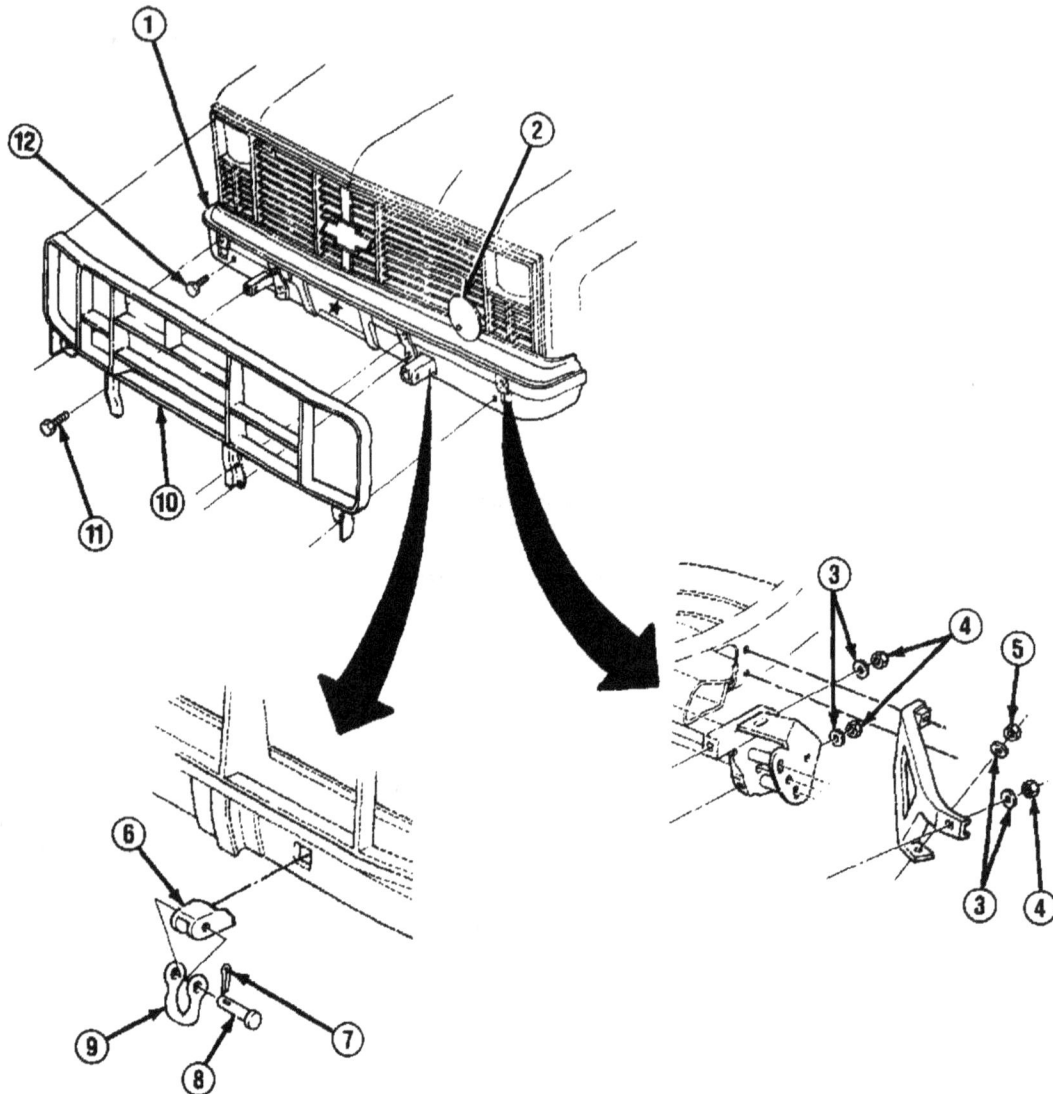

2. Install bumper (1) with 2 bolts (12), washers (3), and   nuts (5), DO NOT fully tighten nuts.

3. Install 2 blackout light brackets to bumper (1). (See paragraph 4-25)

4. Install each tie-down clevis (9) to each tie-down extension (6) with pin (8) and new cotter pin (7).

5. Install radiator grille guard (10) with 6 bolts (11), washers (3), and nuts (4). Tighten nuts to 35 lb.-ft. (47 N•m).

6. Tighten 2 nuts (5) to 35 lb.-ft. (47 N•m).

TA49703

9-3. FRONT BUMPER SUPPORTS REPLACEMENT.

This task covers: a. Removal   b. installation

INITIAL SETUP:

Equipment Condition
• Radiator   grille guard and front bumper
  removed, (See paragraph 9-2)

Materials/Parts
• One plastic tie
• Four lockwashers

Tools/Test Equipment
• Torque wrench

| a. | REMOVAL |

NOTE

• **If removing bumper braces (6), perform steps 1 and 2.**

• **If removing bumper brackets (5), tie-down extensions (11), and shims
   (10), perform steps 3 and 4.**

1,   Remove plastic tie securing wiring harness to bumper brace (6). Discard plastic tie.

2.   Remove 2 bolts (1), washers (2), and bumper brace (6).

3.   Remove 4 nuts (13), lockwashers (12), washers (8), and bolts (7). Discard lockwashers.

4.   Remove nut (9),   2 washers (4), bolt (3), bumper bracket (5), shim (10), and tie-down
      extension (11).

| b. | INSTALLATION |

NOTE

• **If installing bumper brackets (5), shims (10), and tie-down extensions
   (11), perform steps 1-3.**

• **If installing bumper braces (6), perform steps 4 and 5.**

1.   Install tie-down extension (11) inside bumper bracket (5) and secure with bolt (3), 2 washers
      (4), and nut (9). DO NOT fully tighten nut.

2.   Install bumper bracket (5), shim (10), and tie-down extension (11) with 4 bolts (7), washers
      (8), new lockwashers (12), and nuts (13).

3.   Tighten 4 nuts (13) and nut (9) to 70 lb.-ft. (95 N•m).

4.   Install bumper brace (6) with 2 washers (2) and bolts (1). Tighten bolts to 40 lb.-ft. (54 N•m).

5.   Install wiring harness to bumper brace (6) with plastic tie.

9-3. FRONT BUMPER SUPPORTS REPLACEMENT (Con't).

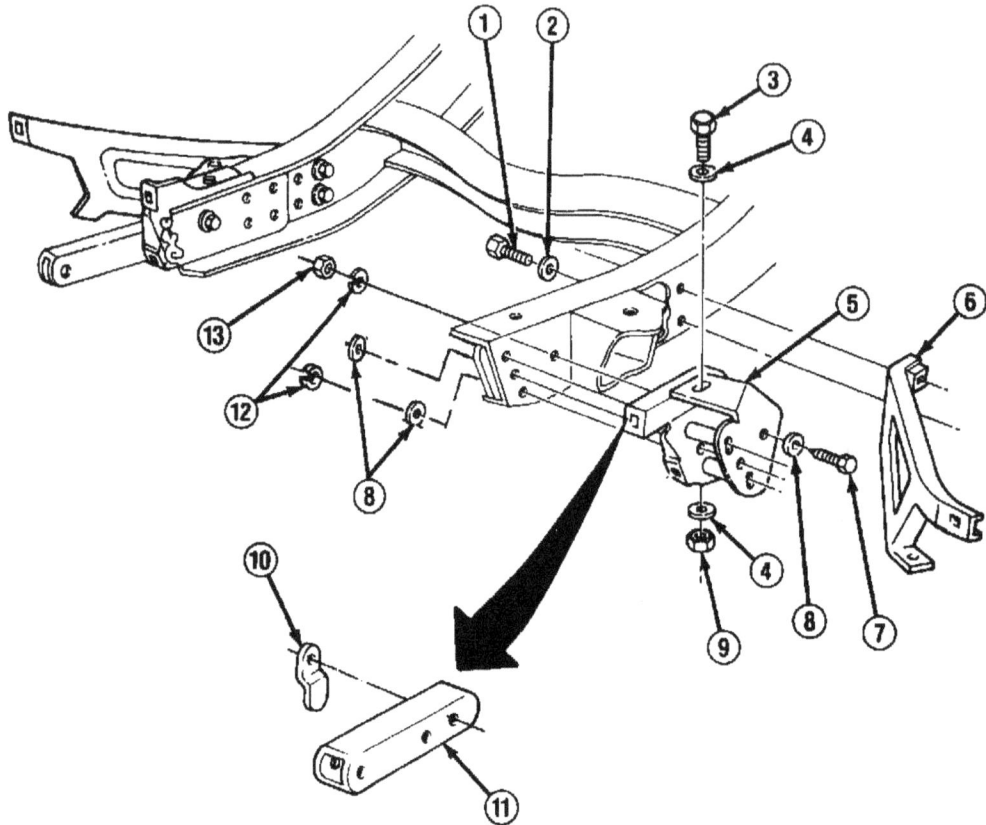

FOLLOW-ON TASKS:

• Install front bumper and radiator grille guard. (See paragraph 9-2)

TA49704

9-4. PINTLE ASSEMBLY REPLACEMENT (ALL EXCEPT M1009 AND M1010).

This task covers:	a. Removal	b. Installation

INITIAL SETUP:

Equipment Condition

• Spare tire removed. (See paragraph 9-10)

Tools/Test Equipment

• Torque wrench

Materials/Parts

• One cotter pin
• Four lockwashers
• Grease (Item 26, Appendix C)

Manual References

• LO 9-2320-289-12

---

a. REMOVAL

1. Remove cotter pin (4), nut (3), and washer (2). Remove pintle hook (10). Discard cotter pin.

2. Remove 4 nuts (5), lockwashers (6), bolts (9), and 2 brackets (1 and 8). Discard lockwashers.

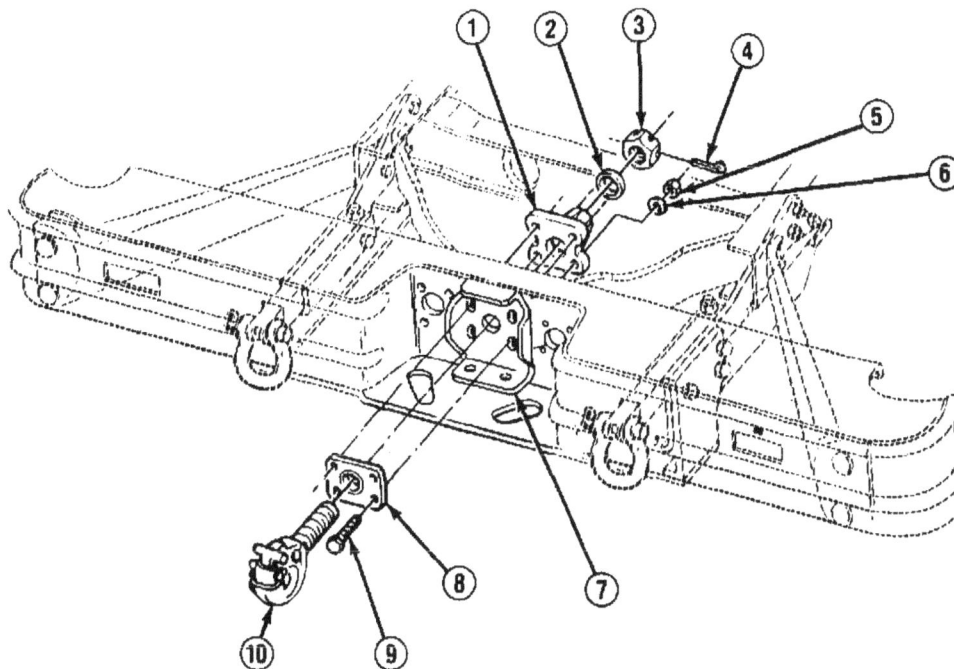

TA49705

9-4. PINTLE ASSEMBLY REPLACEMENT (ALL EXCEPT M1009 AND M1010) (Con't).

b. INSTALLATION

NOTE

During installation, check that pintle hook (10) swivels freely.

1. Assemble bracket (8) and pintle hook (10) with flat side of bracket facing reinforcement (7).

2. Install pintle hook (10) and bracket (8).

3. Install bracket (1) with grease fitting toward bottom.

4. Install 4 bolts (9), new lockwashers (6), and nuts (5), Tighten nuts to 70-80 Ib.-ft. (95-108 N•m).

5. Install washer (2) and nut (3).

6. Loosen nut (3) until it alines with hole in pintle hook (10). Install new cotter pin (4).

7. Lubricate pintle   assembly. (See LO 9-2320-289-12)

FOLLOW-ON TASKS:

• Install spare tire.   (See paragraph 9-10)

9-5.   PINTLE ASSEMBLY REPLACEMENT (M1009).

This task covers: a. Removal   b. Installation

INITIAL SETUP:

Materials/Parts

• One cotter pin
• Four lockwashers
• Grease (Item 26, Appendix C)

Manual References

• LO 9-2320-289-12

Tools/Test Equipment

• Torque wrench

| a. | **REMOVAL** |

1.   Remove cotter pin (4), nut (3), and washer   (2). Remove pintle hook (10). Discard cotter pin.

2.   Remove 4 nuts (5), lockwashers (6), and   bolts (9). Remove 2 brackets (1 and 8) and 2
       spacers (7). Discard lockwashers.

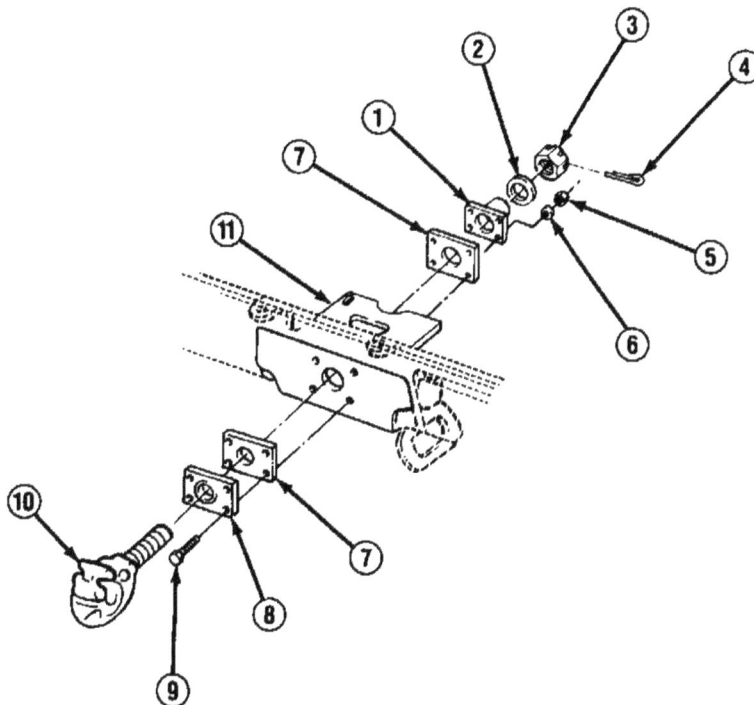

TA49706

9-5.   PINTLE ASSEMBLY REPLACEMENT (M1009) (Con't).

| b. INSTALLATION |

NOTE

During installation check that pintle hook (10) swivels freely.

1.   Install bracket (8) and spacer (7) to pintle hook (10) and install pintle hook   through tow hook
      bracket (11).

2.   Install spacer (7) and bracket (1) with grease fitting toward bottom.

3.   Install 4 bolts (9), new lockwashers (6), and nuts (5). Tighten nuts to 70-80 lb.-ft.
      (95-108 N•m).

4.   Install washer (2) and nut (3).

5.   Loosen nut (3) until it alines with hole in pintle hook (10). Install new cotter pin (4).

6.   Lubricate pintle assembly. (See LO 9-2320-289-12)

9-6. REAR BUMPER AND TIE-DOWN CLEVISES REPLACEMENT (ALL EXCEPT M1009).

This task covers: a.   Removal   b. Installation

INITIAL SETUP:

Equipment Condition

- Trailer electrical receptacle disconnected. (See paragraph 4-41)
- Pintle assembly and related brackets removed. (See paragraph 9-4)
- Blackout marker brackets removed from bumper, (See paragraph 4-27)

Materials/Parts

- Two cotter pins
- Six lockwashers
- Ten locknuts

Tools/Test Equipment

- Torque wrench

Personnel Required

- MOS 63B (2)

| a. | REMOVAL |

1. Remove cotter pin (19). Support tie-down clevis. Repeat step to remove other side tie-down (21), and remove pin (20) and tie-down clevis. Discard cotter pins.

NOTE

Reinforcement (18) is factory-installed with locknuts and washers instead of nuts (17) and lockwashers (16). Use nuts and lockwashers for installation.

2. Remove 2 nuts (17), lockwashers (16), washers (15), bolts (14), and reinforcement (18), Discard lockwashers.

3. Remove 8 locknuts (1), 4 bolts (10), and 4 bolts (11) on left or right side. Discard locknuts.

4. Remove 2 locknuts (3), bolts (5), and washers (4), and remove left and right tie-down extensions (2) through holes in bumper (12). Discard locknuts.

5. Remove clips securing wiring harness to bumper (12). Clear wiring harness from underneath bumper.

NOTE

- Bumper (12) is factory-installed with locknuts and washers instead of nuts (6) and lockwashers (7), Use nuts and lockwashers for installation.

- Use an assistant to perform step 6.

6. Remove 4 nuts (6), lockwashers (7), washers (8), and bolts (13) on left and right side. Remove bumper (12). Discard lockwashers.

9-6. REAR BUMPER AND TIE-DOWN CLEVISES REPLACEMENT (ALL EXCEPT M1009) (Con't).

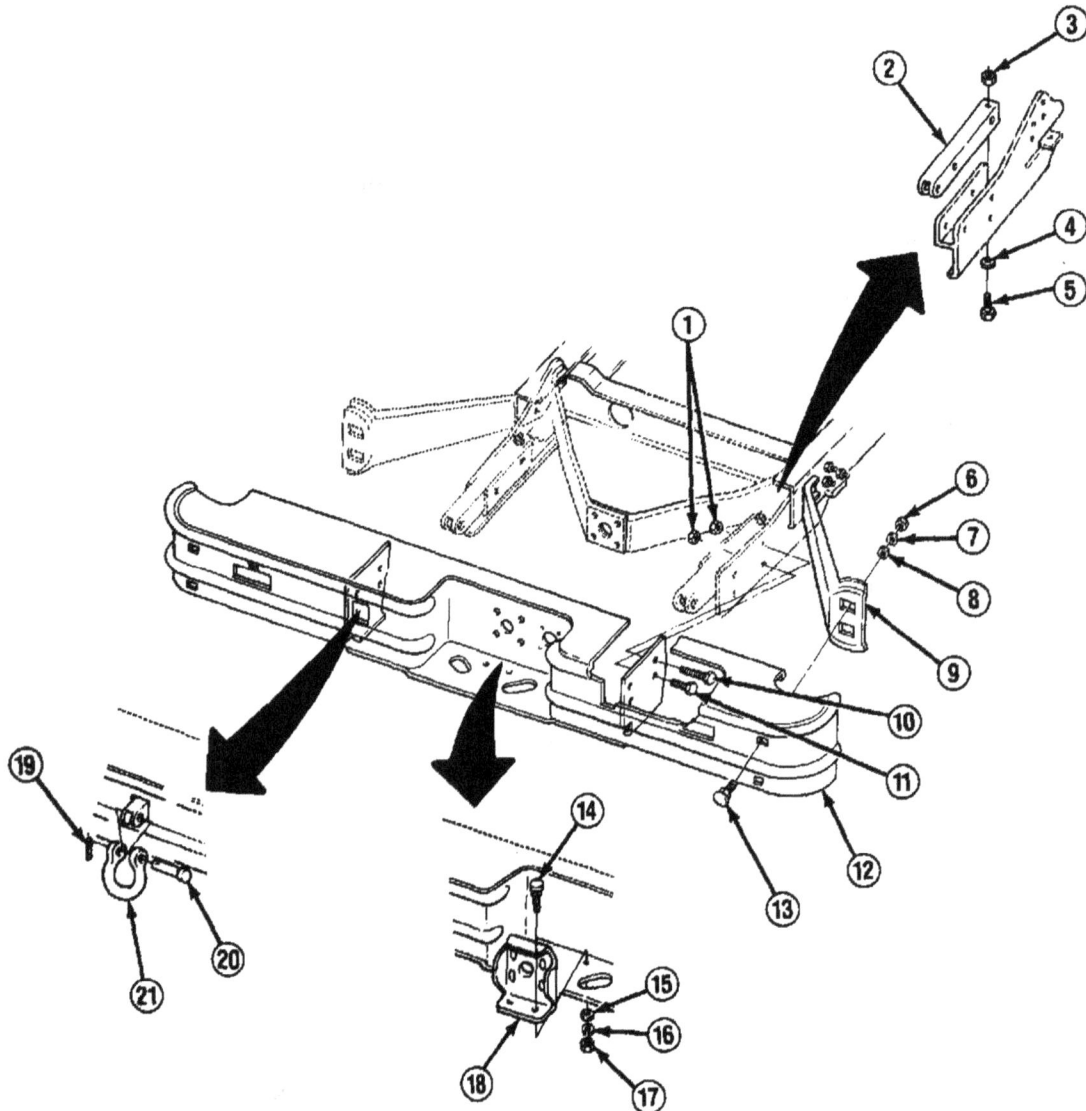

b. INSTALLATION

NOTE

Use an assistant to perform step 1.
harness when positioning bumper (12).

Be careful to not damage wiring

1. Install bumper (12) by hooking 2 bumper braces (9) inside bumper.

2. Install reinforcement (18) with 2 bolts (14), washers (15), new lockwashers (16), and nuts (17).

TA49707

9-6.   REAR BUMPER AND TIE-DOWN CLEVISES REPLACEMENT (ALL EXCEPT M1009) (Con't).

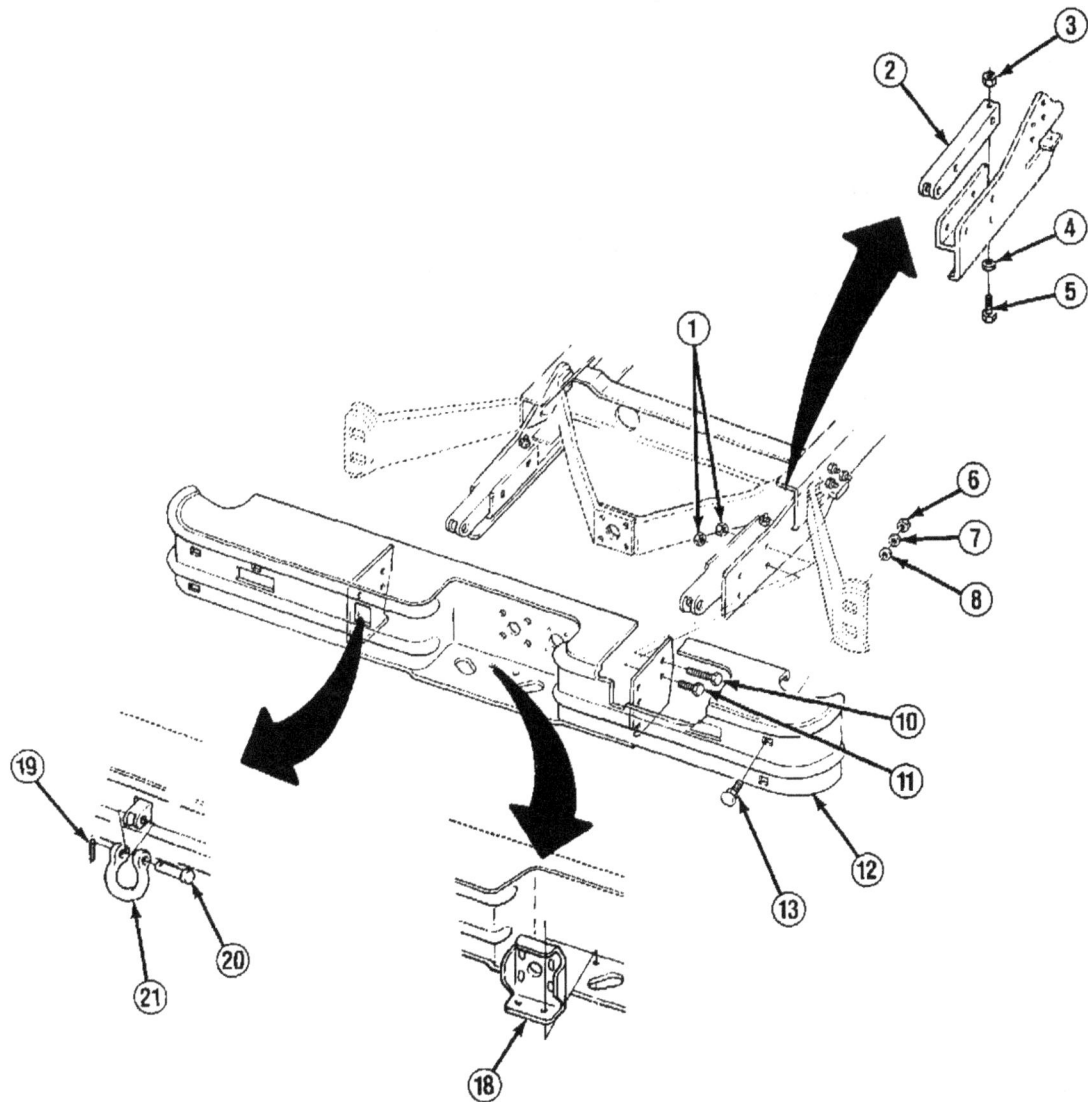

3.   Install 4 bolts (13), washers (8), new lockwashers (7), and nuts (6) on left and right sides. DO NOT fully tighten nuts.

4.   Install 2 tie-down extensions (2) with 2 bolts (5), washers (4), and new locknuts (3). DO NOT fully tighten locknuts.

5.   Install 4 bolts (10), 4 bolts (11), and 8 new locknuts (1). DO   NOT fully tighten locknuts.

TA49708

9-6. REAR BUMPER AND TIE-DOWN CLEVISES REPLACEMENT (ALL EXCEPT M1009) (Con't).

NOTE

Ensure that holes in bumper (12) and reinforcement (18) are alined before tightening nuts (3 and 6) and locknuts (1) in steps 6 and 7.

6.   Tighten 4 nuts (6) and 8 locknuts (1) to 60-75 lb.-ft. (81-102 N•m).

7.   Tighten 2 locknuts (3) to 45-60 lb.-ft. (61-81 N•m).

8.   Install clips securing wiring harness to bumper (12).

9.   Install each tie-down clevis (21) with pin (20) and new   cotter pin (19).

FOLLOW-ON TASKS:

• Install pintle assembly and related brackets. (See paragraph 9-4)
• Install blackout marker brackets to bumper. (See paragraph 4-27)
• Connect trailer electrical receptacle. (See paragraph 4-41)

9-7. REAR BUMPER SUPPORTS REPLACEMENT (ALL EXCEPT M1009).

This task covers: a. Remova l   b. Installation

INITIAL SETUP:

Equipment Condition
* Rear bumper removed. (See paragraph 9-6)

Materials/Parts
* Six locknuts

Tools/Test Equipment
* Torque wrench

| a. | **REMOVAL** |

NOTE
Rear bumper supports are removed the same way on both sides.

1. Remove 2 locknuts (6), washers (2), bolts (1), and tow hook reinforcement (3). Discard locknuts.

2. Remove 2 locknuts (8), 2 bolts (4), and bumper brace (9). Discard locknuts.

3. Remove locknut (11), washer (10), and bolt (5). Remove locknut (7), bolt (13), and tie-down clevis bracket (12). Discard locknuts.

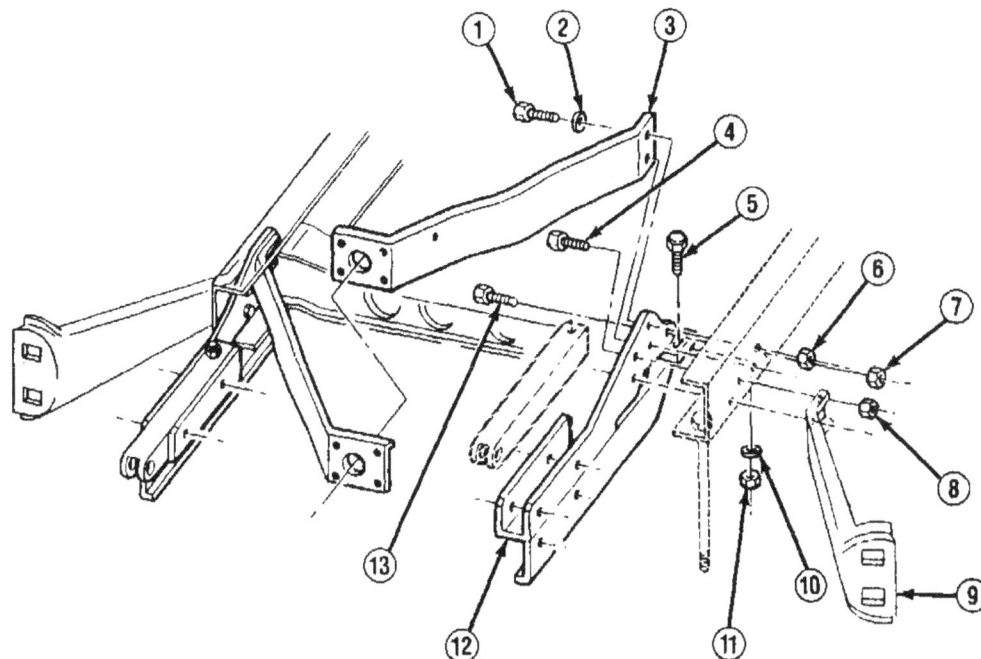

TA49709

9-7. REAR BUMPER SUPPORTS REPLACEMENT (ALL EXCEPT M1009) (Con't).

| b. INSTALLATION |

NOTE

- **Rear bumper supports are installed the same way on both sides.**

- **Ensure that rear wiring harness is positioned above tow hook reinforcements (3), bumper braces (9), and tie-down clevis brackets (12) before installing them.**

1. Install tie-down clevis (12) to bottom of frame with bolt (5), washer (10), and new locknut (11). DO NOT fully tighten locknut.

2. Install bolt (13) and new locknut (7) through side of frame. DO NOT fully tighten locknut.

3. Install bumper brace (9) with 2 bolts (4) and new locknuts (8). DO NOT fully tighten locknuts.

4. Install tow hook reinforcement (3) with 2 bolts (1), new washers (2), and new locknuts (6). DO NOT fully tighten locknuts.

5. Install rear bumper, (See paragraph 9-6)

6. Tighten locknuts (6, 7, 8, and 11) to 45-60 lb.-ft. (61-81 N•m).

9-8. REAR BUMPER, TOW HOOK BRACKET, AND TIE-DOWN CLEVISES REPLACEMENT (M1009).

| This task covers: | a. Removal | b. Installation |

INITIAL SETUP:

Materials/Parts
- Two cotter pins
- Twelve lockwashers
- Two tie-clown straps (Item 44, Appendix C)

Tools/Test Equipment
- Torque wrench

Personnel Required
- MOS 636 (2)

General Safety Instructions
- Provide support when removing or installing bumper.

| a. REMOVAL |

1. Remove 2 rear blackout marker brackets from bumper (2).

2. Disconnect trailer electrical receptacle.

3. Remove 2 wiring harness tie-down straps   from bumper braces (19). Discard tie-down straps,

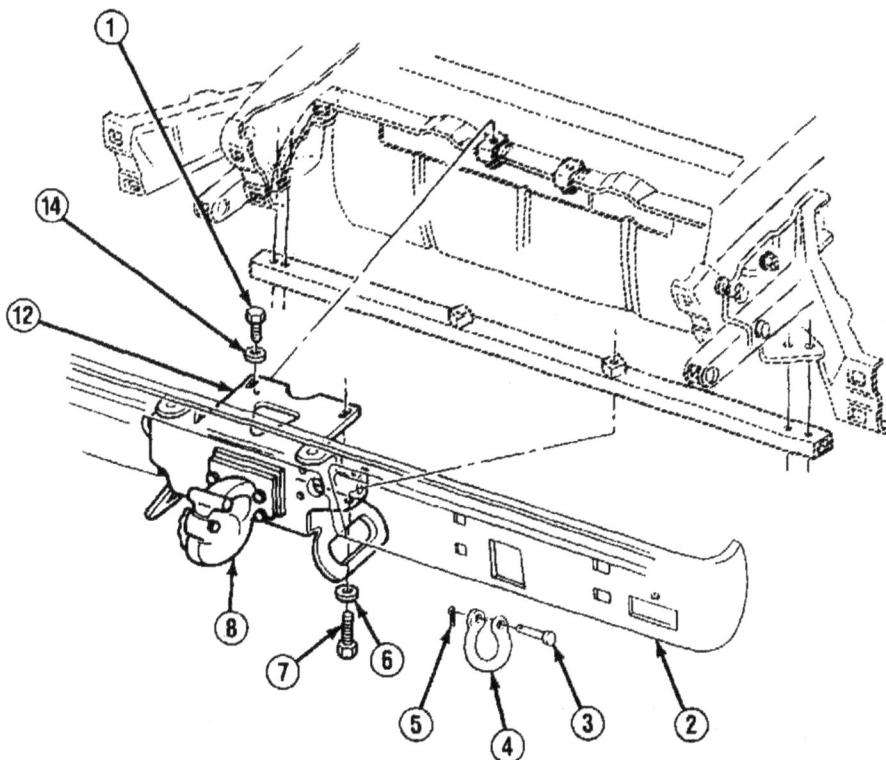

TA49710

9-8. REAR BUMPER, TOW HOOK BRACKET, AND TIE-DOWN CLEVISES REPLACEMENT (M1009) (Con't).

4. Remove cotter pin (5) from pin (3). Remove pin and tie-down clevis (4). Discard cotter pin. Repeat step to remove other tie-down clevis.

5. Remove 2 bolts (1) and washers (14) securing tow hook bracket (12) to crossmember. Remove 2 bolts (7) and washers (6).

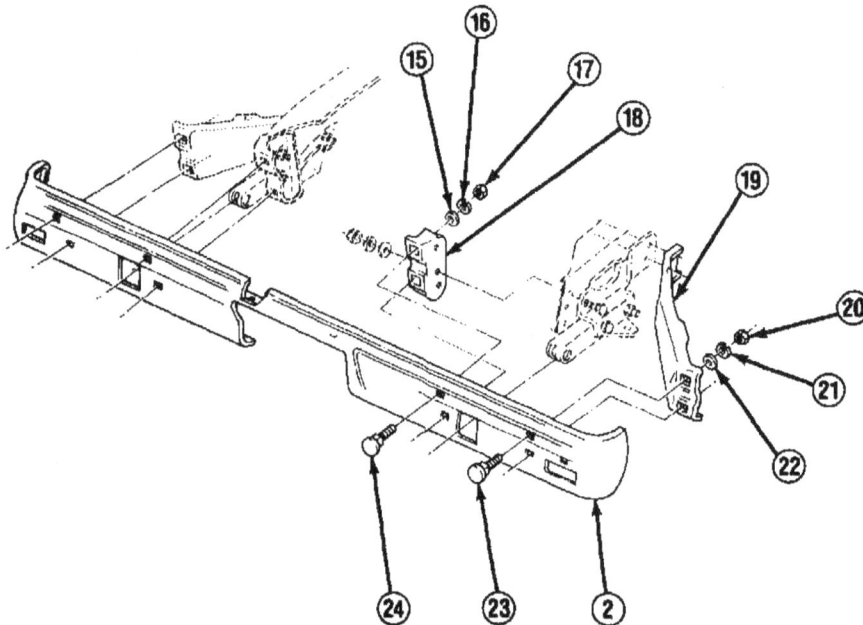

NOTE

Bumper (2) is factory-installed with locknuts and washers instead of nuts (17) and lockwashers (16). Use nuts and lockwashers for installation.

6. Remove 4 nuts (17), lockwashers (16), washers (15), and bolts (24) securing bumper (2) to 2 bumper braces (18). Discard lockwashers.

WARNING

Support bumper (2) during removal, If dropped, it may cause serious injury to personnel.

7. Remove 4 nuts (20), lockwashers (21), washers (22), and bolts (23) securing bumper (2) to 2 bumper braces (19), Remove bumper with tow hook bracket (12) and pintle hook (8) attached. Discard lockwashers.

8. Remove pintle hook (8). (See paragraph 9-5)

TA49711

9-8. REAR BUMPER, TOW HOOK BRACKET, AND TIE-DOWN CLEVISES REPLACEMENT (M1009) (Con't).

9.   Remove 4 nuts (10), lockwashers (11), washers (9), and bolts (13). Remove tow hook bracket (12) from bumper (2). Discard lockwashers.

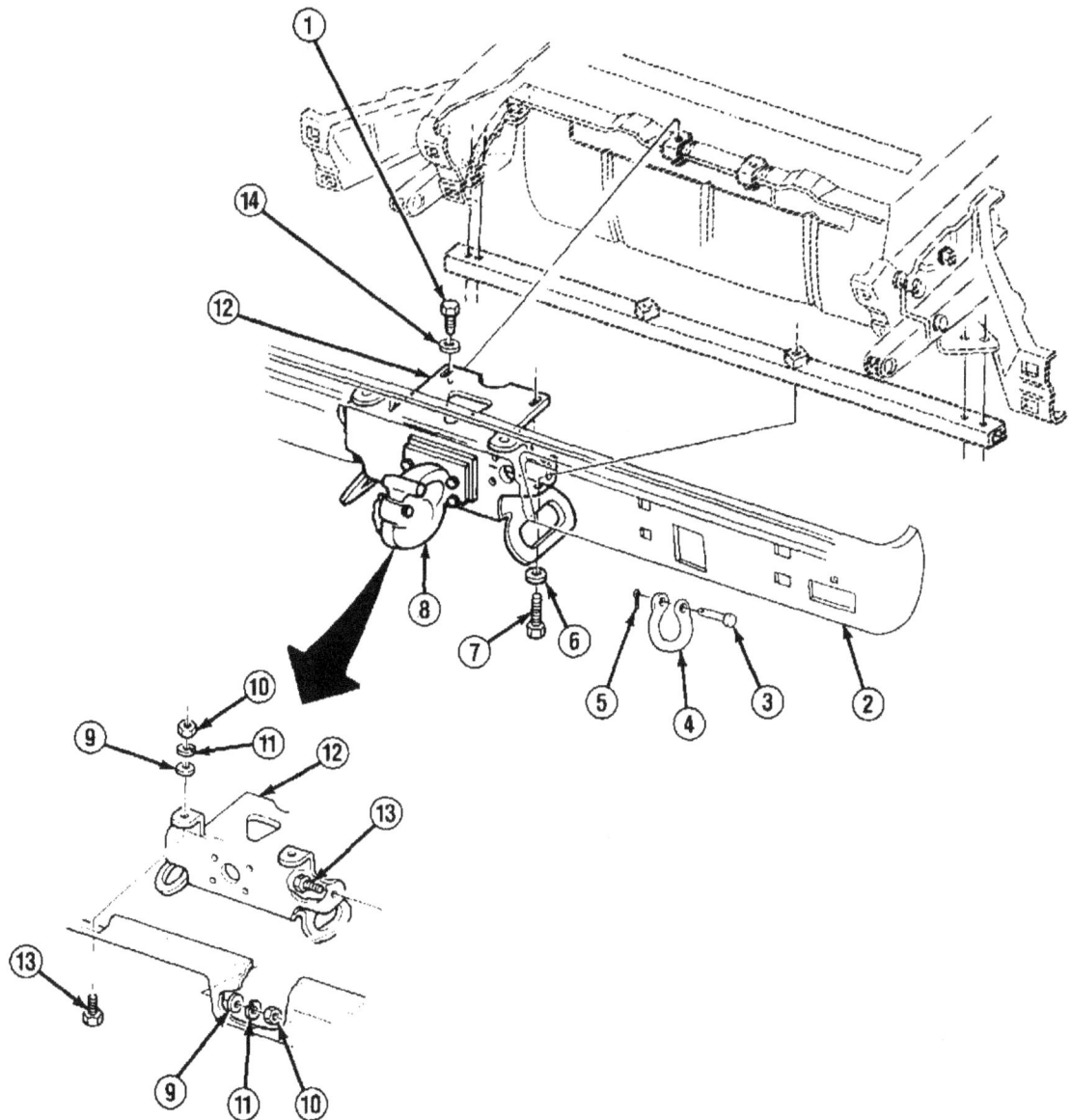

TA49712

---

b.	INSTALLATION

1.   Install tow hook bracket (12) to bumper (2) with 4 bolts (13), washers (9), new lockwashers (11), and nuts (10). DO NOT fully tighten nuts.

2.   Install pintle hook (8), (See paragraph 9-5)

9-8. REAR BUMPER, TOW HOOK BRACKET, AND TIE-DOWN CLEVISES REPLACEMENT (M1009) (Con't).

WARNING

Support bumper (2) during removal. If dropped, it may cause serious injury to personnel.

NOTE

Use an assistant to perform step 3.

3. Position bumper (2) with tow hook bracket (12) and pintle hook (8) attached, and install 4 bolts (24), washers (15), new lockwashers (16), and nuts (17). DO NOT fully tighten nuts.

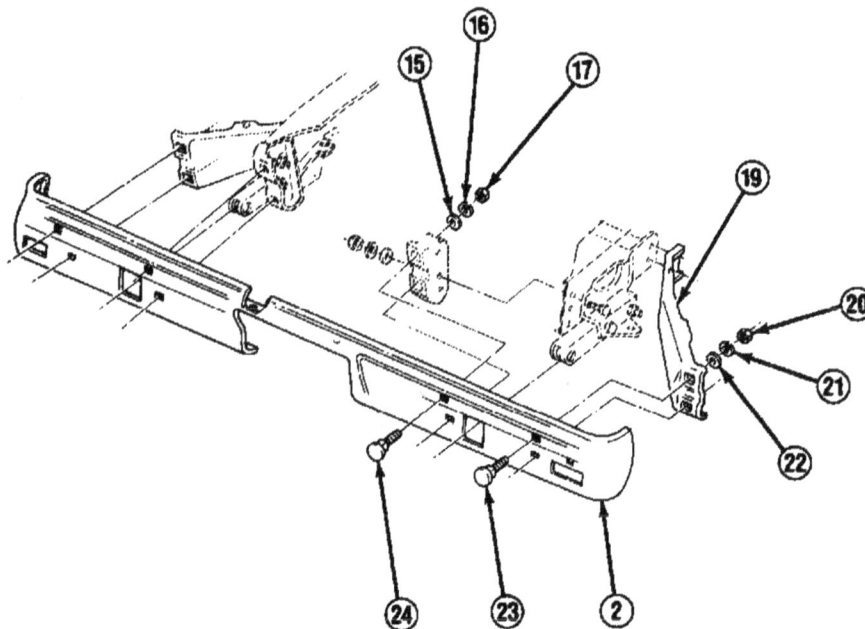

4. Install 4 bolts (23), washers (22), new lockwashers (21), and nuts (20). Tighten nuts (17 and 20) to 45-60 lb.-ft. (61-81 N•m).

5. Install tow hook bracket (12) to crossmember with 2 bolts (1) and washers (14).

6. Install 2 bolts (7) and washers (6). Tighten 4 nuts (10).

7. Install each tie-down clevis (4) with pin (3) and new cotter pin (5).

8. Secure wiring harness to 2 bumper braces (19) with 2 new tie-down straps.

9. Connect trailer electrical receptacle.

10. Install 2 rear blackout marker brackets to bumper (2).

TA49713

9-9. REAR BUMPER SUPPORTS REPLACEMENT (M1009).

This task covers: a. Remova l   b. Installation

INITIAL SETUP:

Equipment Condition

* Rear bumper, tow hook bracket, and
  tie-down clevises removed.
  (See paragraph 9-8)

Too/s/Test Equipment

●Torque wrenc h
●Screwdriver bit set, J-29843

Materials/Parts

● One locknut
● Seven lockwashers
● One plastic tie

| a. REMOVAL |

NOTE

**Rear bumper supports are removed the same way on both sides. Right
side removal is shown.**

1.   Remove 4 nuts (8), 8 washers (9), 4 bolts (25), and reinforcement (24).

2.   Remove plastic tie securing wiring harness to bumper brace (16). Discard plastic tie.

3.   Remove 2 nuts (3), lockwashers (4), and bolts (15), and remove bumper brace (16). Discard
     lockwashers.

4.   Remove nut (30), lockwasher (1), and stud (7).   Discard lockwasher.

5.   Remove 2 nuts (27 and 29), lockwashers (26   and 28), and bolts (18 and 19). Discard
     lockwashers.

6.   Remove nut (14), lockwasher (13), and bolt (2)   Discard lockwasher.

7.   Remove nut (23), lockwasher (22), washer (21), and bolt (5) securing tow hook reinforcement
     bracket (11) to frame. Discard lockwasher.

8.   Remove locknut (17), bolt (10), and tow hook reinforcement bracket (11). Remove tie-down
     clevis bracket (12), tie-down extension (20), and bumper brace (6). Discard locknut.

9.   Remove tie-down extension (20) from tie-down clevis bracket (12).

| b.   INSTALLATION |

NOTE

**Rear bumper supports are installed the same way on both sides. Right side
installation is shown.**

1.   Install tie-down clevis bracket (12) to frame with bolt (2), new lockwasher (13), and nut (14).
     DO NOT fully tighten nut.

9-9. REAR BUMPER SUPPORTS REPLACEMENT (M1009) (Con't).

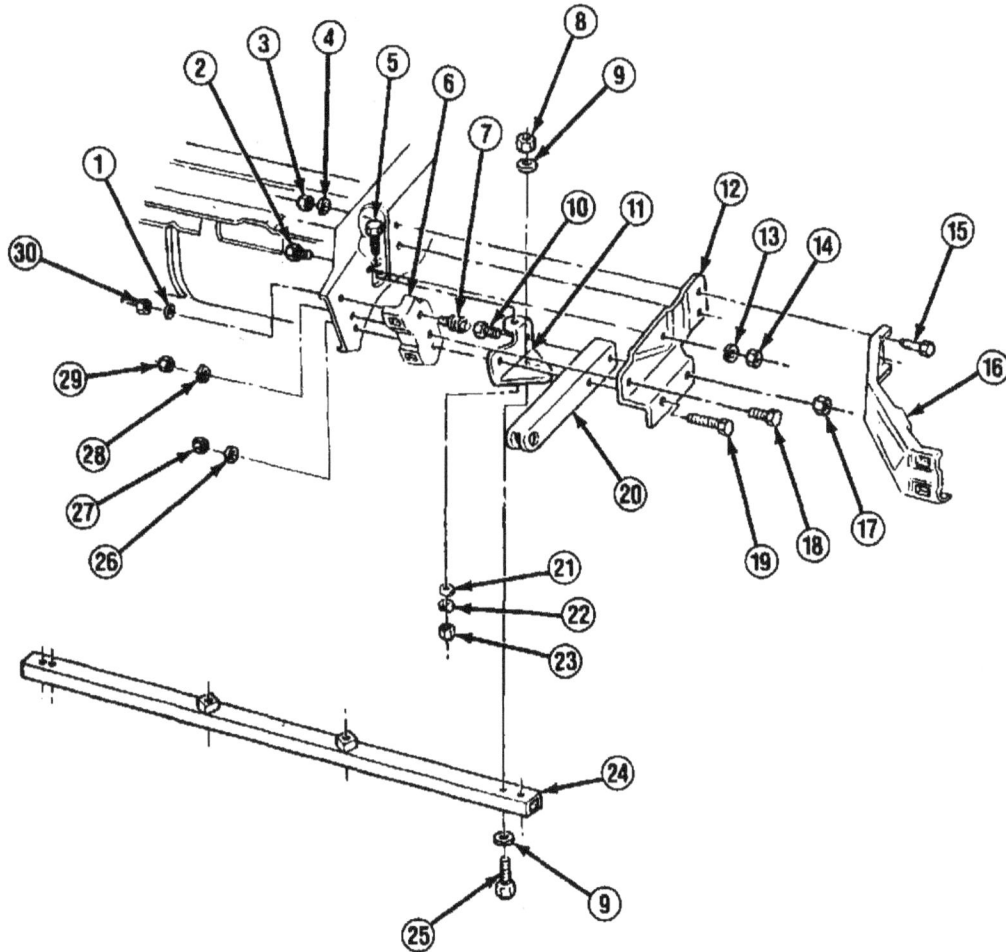

2. Install tow hook reinforcement bracket (11) and tie-down extension (20) at tie-down clevis bracket (12) with bolt (10) and new locknut (17). DO NOT fully tighten locknut.

3. Position bumper brace (6) between frame and tow hook reinforcement bracket (11) and install bolt (19), new lockwasher (26), and nut (27). DO NOT fully tighten nut.

4. Install bolt (18), new lockwasher (28), and nut (29), DO NOT fully tighten nut.

5. Install bolt (5), washer (21), new lockwasher (22), and nut (23). DO NOT fully tighten nut.

6. Install stud (7), engage torque rod on stud, and install new lockwasher (1) and nut (30). DO NOT fully tighten nut.

TA49714

9-9.   REAR BUMPER SUPPORTS REPLACEMENT (M1009) (Con't).

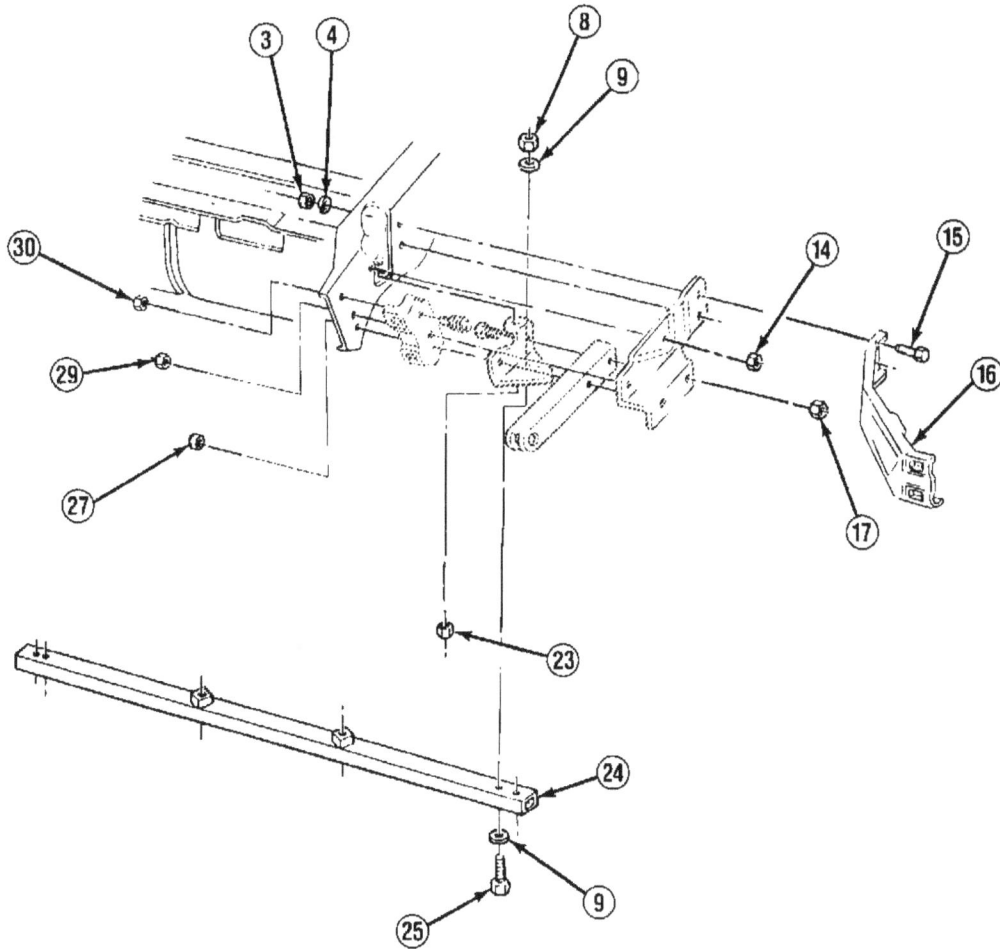

7.   Install bumper brace (16) with   2 bolts (15), new lockwashers (4), and nuts (3), Install wiring harness to bumper brace with new plastic tie. DO NOT fully tighten nuts.

8.   Install reinforcement (24) with 4 bolts (25), 8 washers (9), and 4 nuts (8). DO NOT fully tighten nuts.

9.   Tighten nuts (3, 8, 14, 23, 27, 29, and 30) and locknut (17) to 55 lb.-ft. (75 N·m).

FOLLOW-ON TASKS:

• Install rear bumper, tow hook bracket, and tie-down clevises. (See paragraph 9-8)

TA49715

9-10. SPARE TIRE CARRIER REPLACEMENT (ALL EXCEPT M1009).

This task covers:	a. Removal	b. Installation

INITIAL SETUP:

Materials/Parts
• Four rivets

Personnel Required
• MOS 63B (2)

General Safety Instructions
• Use extreme caution when lowering or raising spare tire and carrier.

---

a.   REMOVAL

WARNING

Use extreme caution when lowering spare tire (9) and carrier (4). Spare tke is heavy. Dropping   It may result in serious injury to personnel.

NOTE

If removing spare tire (9), perform steps 1 and 2.

1.   Remove nut (5) from bolt (2), Lower spare tire (9) and carrier (4) to ground. Remove locking bracket (3) from bolt.

2.   Remove spare tire (9) from carrier (4).

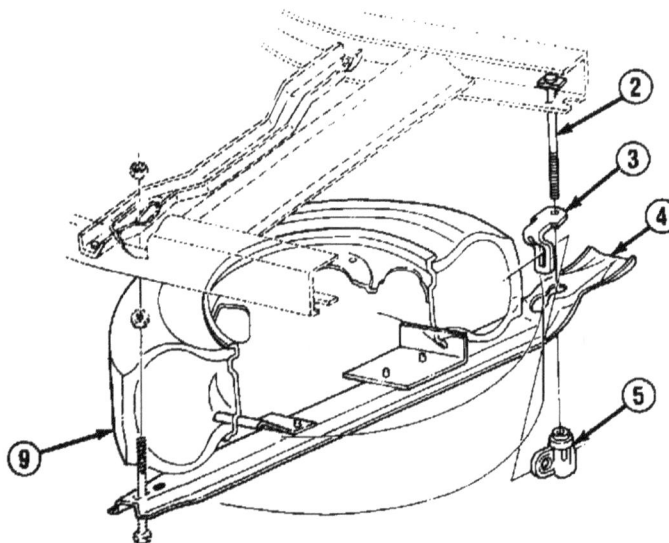

TA49716

9-10. SPARE TIRE CARRIER REPLACEMENT (ALL EXCEPT M1009) (Con't).

NOTE

Perform steps 3 and 4 as required to remove carrier (4) from attachment to frame.

3. Remove nut (1) from above frame. Remove carrier (4) with attached bolt (8) and nut (10).

4. Remove nut (10) from bolt (8) and remove bolt from carrier (4).

5. Remove 4 rivets (7) and 2 guides (6) from carrier (4) if damaged. Discard rivets.

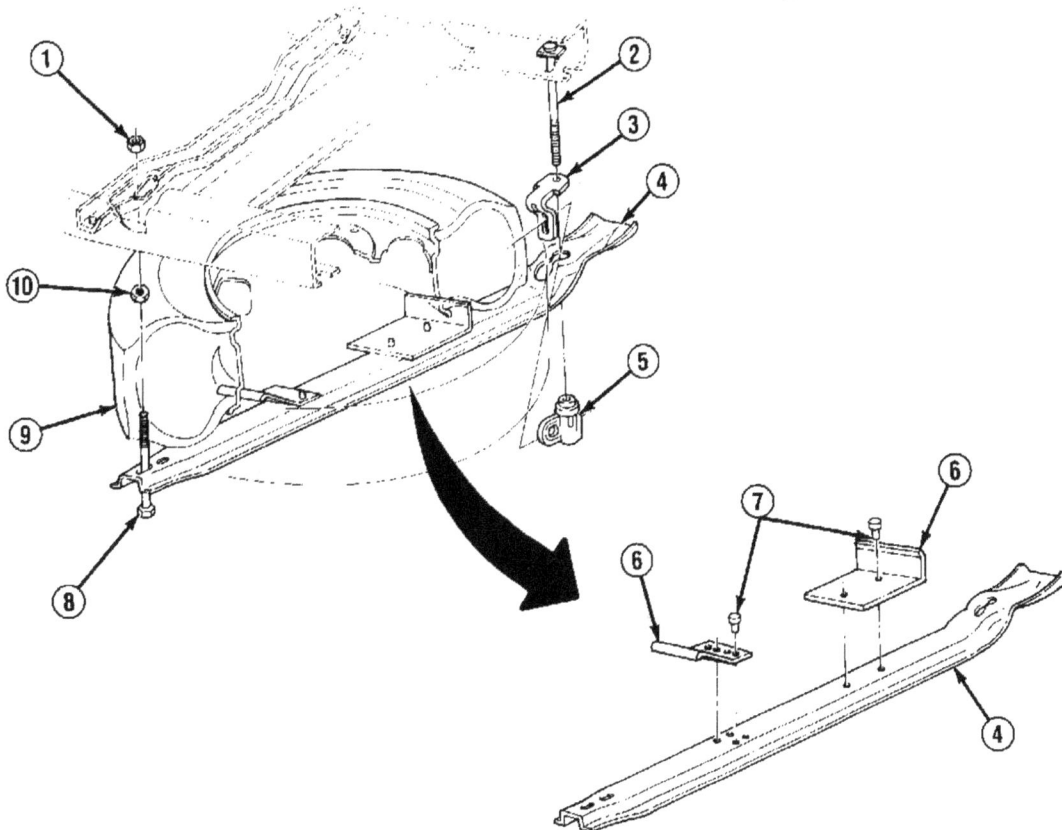

NOTE

Removal of bolt (2) is difficult. Remove only cannot be removed except by bending it. On removed only after pintle assembly and right removed. (See paragraphs 9-4 and 9-7)

if damaged. On M1010, bolt all other trucks, bolt can be tow hook reinforcement are

6. Remove bolt (2).

9-10. SPARE TIRE CARRIER REPLACEMENT (ALL EXCEPT M1009) (Con't).

| b. | INSTALLATION |

NOTE

If installing spare tire (9), perform steps 6-9.

1. If removed, install 2 guides (6) to carrier (4) with 4 new rivets (7).

2. Install carrier (4) and nut (10) to bolt (8).

3. Install carrier (4), bolt (8), and nut (10) assembly through left frame.

4. Install nut (1) to bolt (8) above frame.

5. Install bolt (2) if removed.

6. Install spare tire (9) on carrier (4) so that guides (6) catch on spare tire rim.

WARNING

Use extreme caution when raising spare tire (9) and carrier. Spare tire is heavy. Dropping it may result in serious injury to personnel.

7. Install locking bracket (3) to bolt (2). Lift spare tire (9) on carrier (4) until bolt passes through slot in carrier.

8. Install nut (5) to boit (2) and turn nut at least 8 turns. Tighten nut until spare tire (9) and carrier (4) are securely installed.

9. Tighten nut (10) on bolt (8) until nut jams against frame.

CHAPTER 10
BODY AND ACCESSORIES MAINTENANCE

Section I. STANDARD BODY MAINTENANCE

10-1. STANDARD BODY MAINTENANCE INDEX.

10-2. RADIATOR GRILLE AND FRONT END PANEL MOLDING REPLACEMENT.

This task covers:	a. Removal	b. Installation

INITIAL SETUP:

Equipment Condition

* Headlight bezels removed. (See paragraph 4-24)

---

a.	REMOVAL

NOTE

* If removing radiator grille (1), perform steps 1 and 2.

* Center screw (3) is removed from behind front bumper.

1.   Remove 5 screws (5) and 3 screws (3). Remove radiator grille (1) from behind radiator grille guard (6).

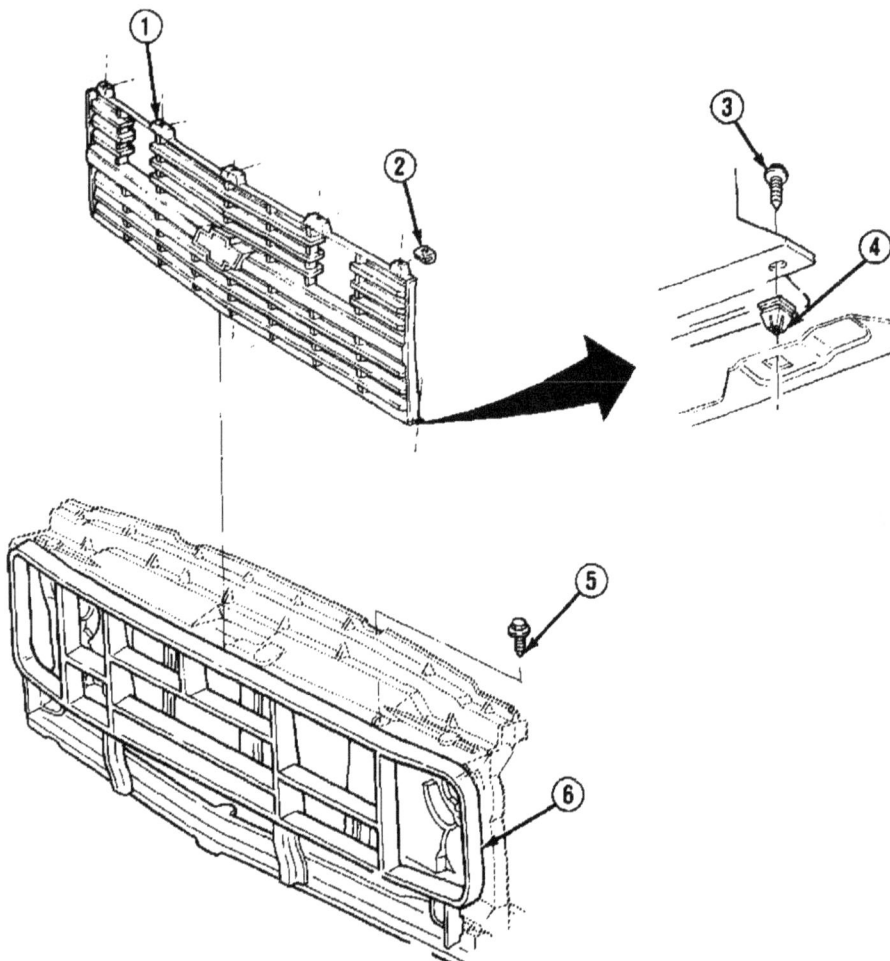

TA49928

10-2. RADIATOR GRILLE AND FRONT END PANEL MOLDING REPLACEMENT (Con't).

2.   Remove 5 retaining nuts (2) and 3 retaining nuts (4) if damaged.

3.   Remove 18 nuts (8) and molding assembly. Remove 2 side moldings (9) and 4 clips (10) from upper molding (7)   and lower molding (11) if damaged.

| b. | INSTALLATION |

NOTE

If installing radiator grille (1), perform steps 2 and 3.

1.   Install 2 side moldings (9) and 4 clips (10) on upper molding (7), and install lower molding (11) if removed. Install molding assembly with 18 nuts (8).

2.   Install 5 retaining nuts (2) and 3 retaining nuts (4) if removed.

3.   Install radiator grille (1) behind radiator grille guard (6) with 5 screws (5) and 3 screws (3).

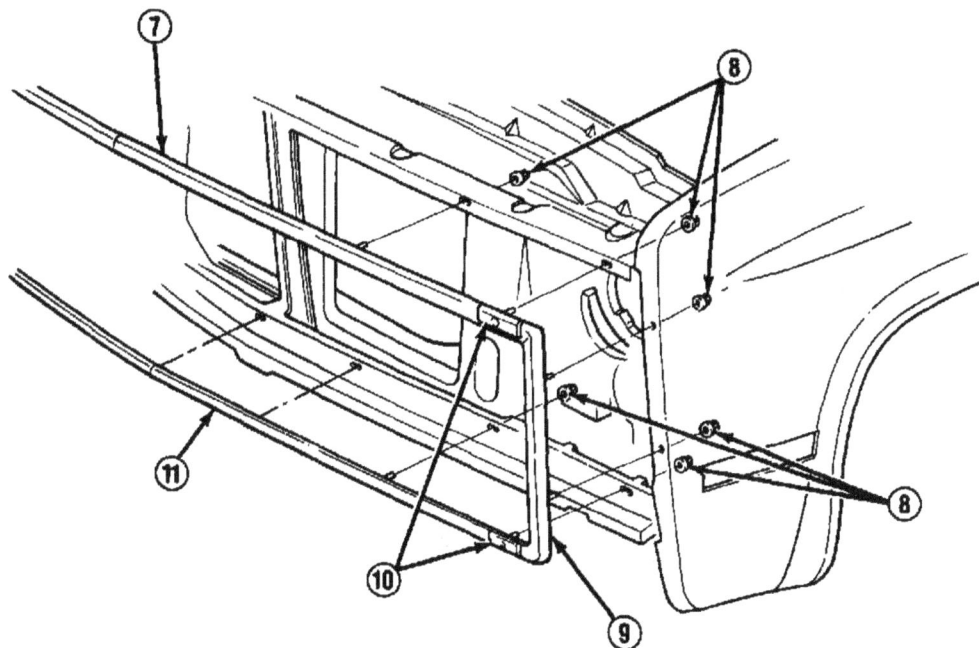

FOLLOW-ON TASKS:

• Install headlight bezels. (See paragraph 4-24)

TA49929

10-3. VENTILATOR PANEL REPLACEMENT.

This task covers: a. Removal   b. Installation

INITIAL SETUP:

Equipment Condition
• Windshield wiper arms removed. (See paragraph 10-11)

---

a.   REMOVAL

NOTE

If removing washer   nozzle (2) only, perform step 1.

1.   Remove 4 bolts (11). Remove 1 screw (3) from each washer nozzle (2), Remove retainer (4) from each washer hose (5), and remove each washer nozzle from ventilator panel (1).

2.   Remove ventilator panel (1). Remove 2 retainers (6), 3 retainers (7), and 2 retainer nuts (10) as required.

3.   Inspect air inlet screen (12) for dust, dirt buildup, and damage. If there is dust,   dirt buildup, or damage , perform step 4.

4.   Remove 2 bolts (8) and screen retainers (9). Carefully depress 2 tangs (13) with a flat-bladed tool and remove air inlet screen (12). Clean dust or dirt from air inlet screen, or replace if damaged.

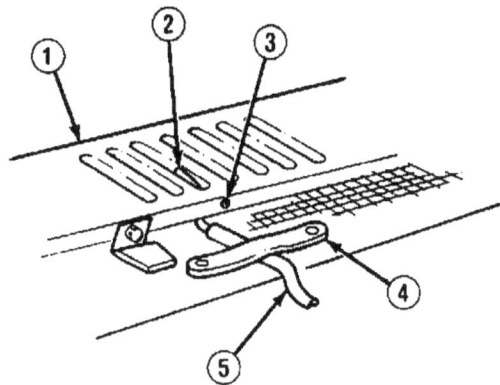

b. INSTALLATION

NOTE

If installing washer nozzle (2) only, perform step 3.

1.   Position air inlet screen (12) and snap 2 tangs (13) into place.   Install 2 screen retainers (9) with 2 bolts (8).

2.   Install 2 retainer nuts (10), 3 retainers (7), and 2 retainers (6)   if removed. Install ventilator panel (1).

3.   Install each washer hose (5) with retainer (4). Install each washer nozzle (2) with 1 screw (3), Install 4 bolts (11).

TA49930

10-3.   VENTILATOR PANEL REPLACEMENT (Con't).

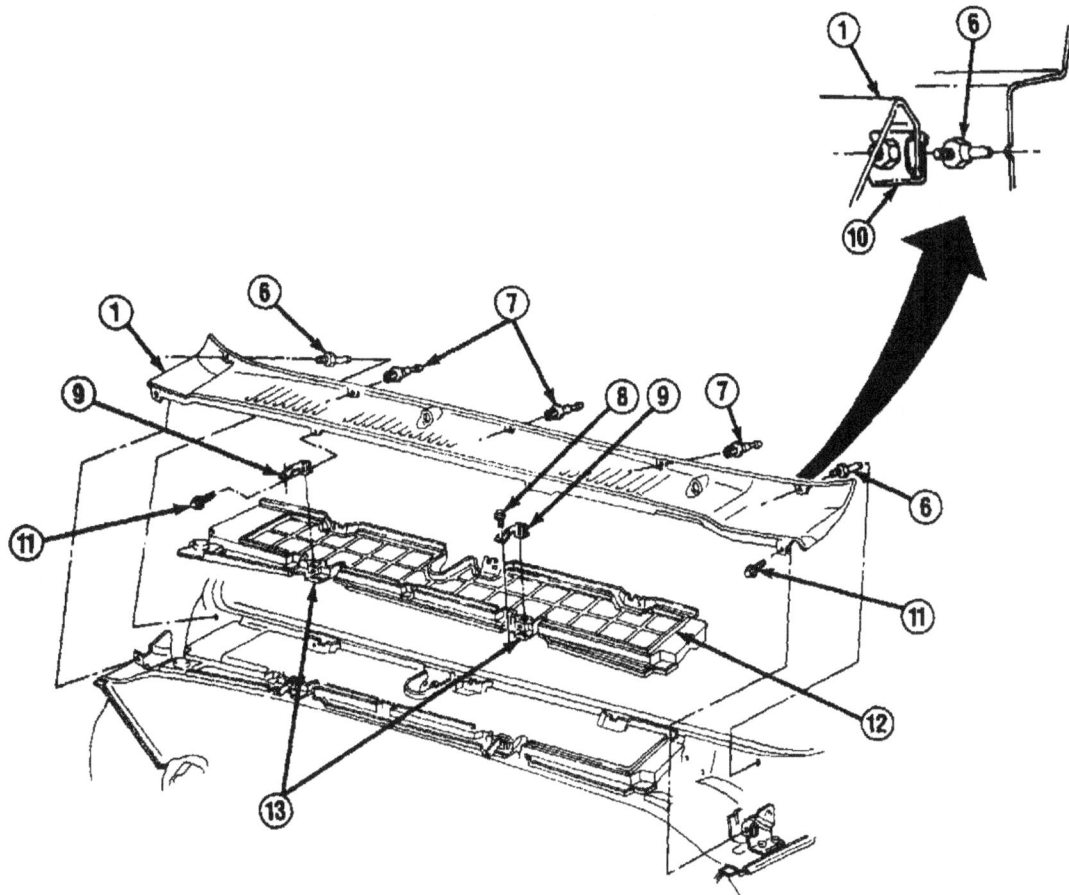

FOLLOW-ON TASKS:

• Install windshield wiper arms.   (See paragraph 10-11)

TA49931

10-4. HOOD, HINGE, AND LATCH REPLACEMENT.

This task covers:	a. Removal	c. Hood Alinement
	b. Installation	

INITIAL SETUP:

Equipment Condition

• Ventilator panel removed (if removing hinge).
  (See paragraph 10-3)

Personnel Required

• MOS 63B (2)

---

a. REMOVAL

NOTE

● if removing primary latch (2), perform steps 1 and 2.

● If removing hood (8), perform steps 3 and 4,

● If removing hinge (11) or hinge spring (14), perform steps 3 and 5 as
   required.

1. Open cable clip (4), remove grommet (6) from primary latch (2), and remove hood latch cable (5) from primary latch.

2. Remove 2 bolts (7) and primary latch (2). Remove 2 bolts (3) and support (1) if damaged.

NOTE

• If removing hinge (11) or hinge spring (14), only remove 4 bolts (9) from one side.

• Mark position of hinges (11) on hood for installation.

• If hood seal (15) is not damaged, save for installation on new hood.

3. Remove 4 bolts (9) from each side of hood (8). Remove hood. Inspect hood seal (15) for damage. Remove hood seal and discard if damaged.

4. Remove 2 bolts (18), secondary latch (17), and spring (16) if damaged.

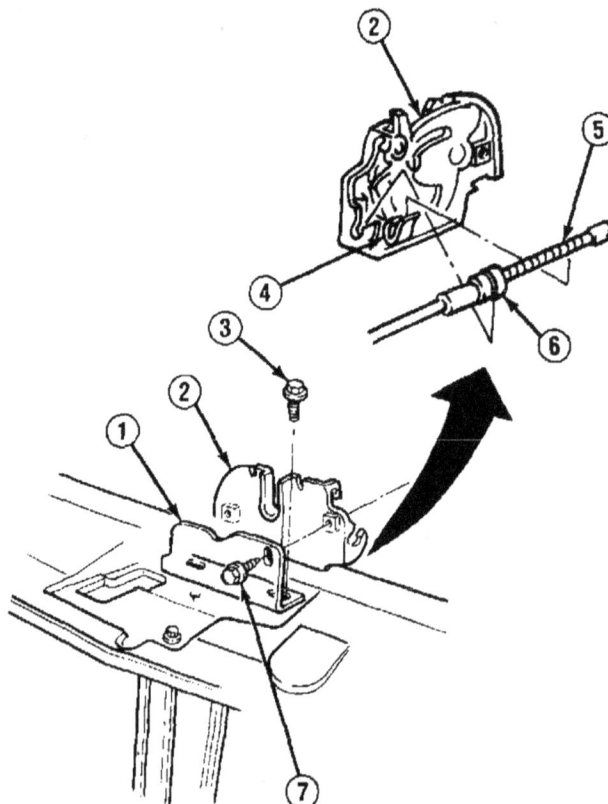

TA49932

10-4. HOOD, HINGE, AND LATCH REPLACEMENT (Con't).

5. Remove 2 bolts (10) and hinge (11) as required. Remove 2 bolts (13) and hinge spring (14) from fender (12) as required.

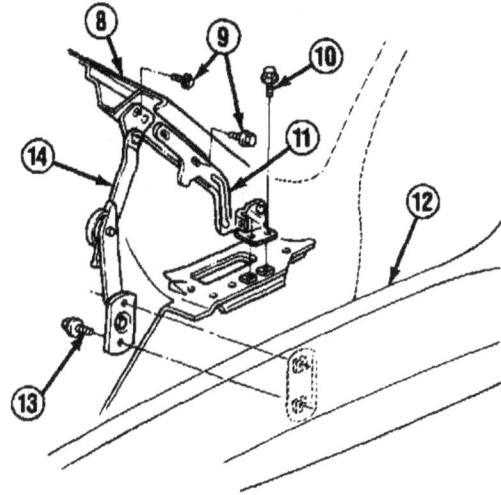

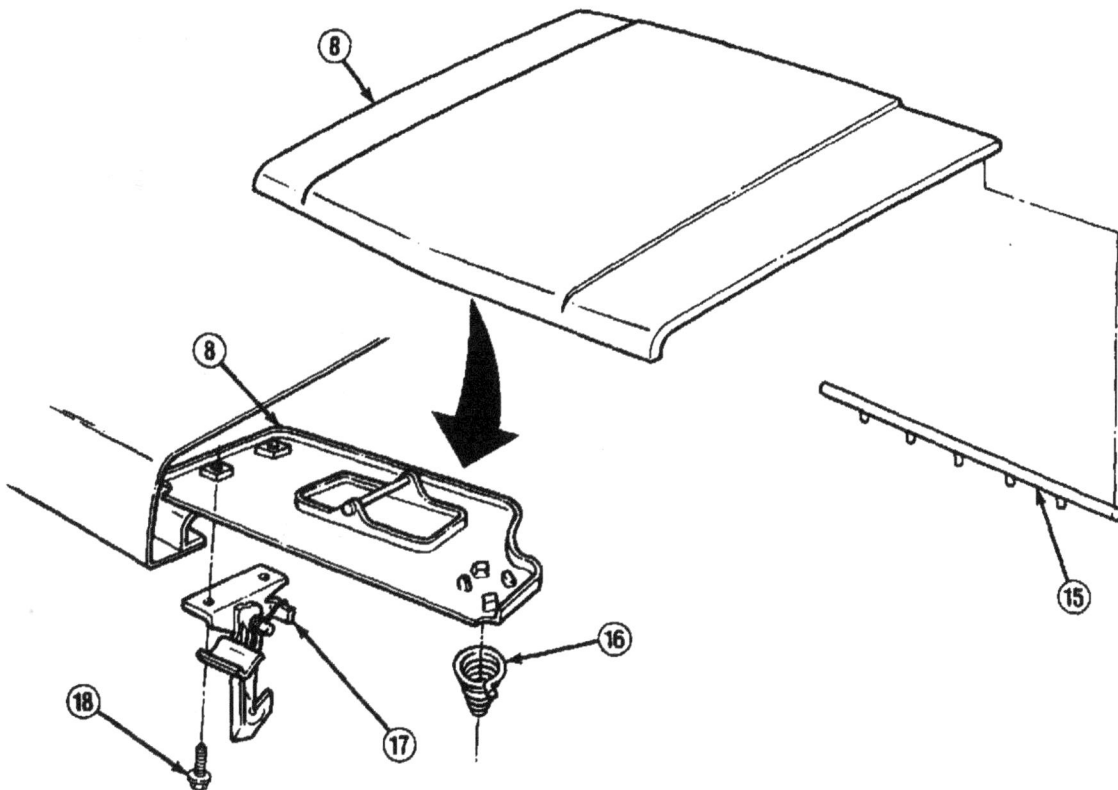

TA49933

10-4.   HOOD, HINGE, AND LATCH REPLACEMENT (Con't).

| b. INSTALLATION |

NOTE

- If installing primary latch (2), perform steps 5-7,

- If installing hinge (11) or hinge spring (14), perform steps 1, 2, and 4, as required.

- If installing hood (8), perform steps 3 and 4.

1.   Install hinge spring (14) on fender (12) with 2 bolts (13).

2.   Install hinge (11) with 2 bolts (10). DO NOT fully tighten bolts.

3.   Install spring (16) if removed. Install secondary latch (17) with 2 bolts (18) if removed.

4.   Install hood seal (15) on hood (8) if removed. Install hood with 4 bolts (9) on each side of hood.

5.   Install support (1) with 2 bolts (3) if removed.

6.   Install primary latch (2) with 2 bolts (7). DO NOT fully tighten bolts.

7.   Install hood latch cable (5) on cable clip (4) and grommet (6) on primary latch (2).

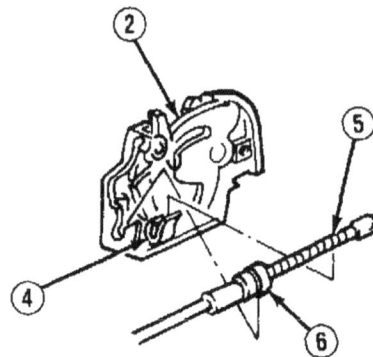

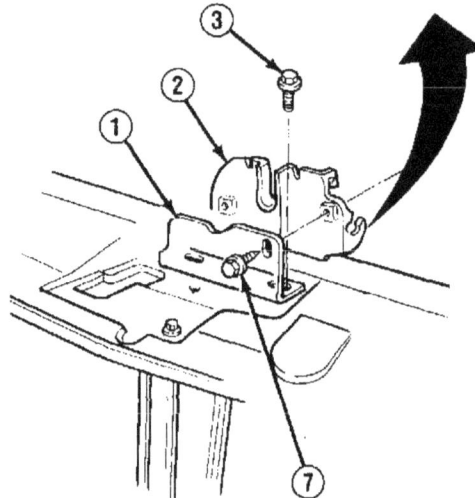

TA49934

10-4. HOOD, HINGE, AND LATCH REPLACEMENT (Con't).

c. HOOD ALINEMENT

1. Check hood (8) operation to ensure that secondary latch (17) assembly engages easily in primary latch (2), and that top of hood is flush with fenders (12).

2. Adjust hood bumpers. Loosen bolts (7 and 10) and adjust positioning of hinges (11) and primary latch (2) as required. Tighten bolts.

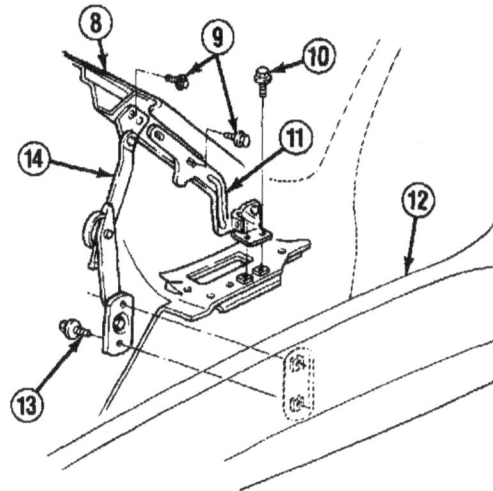

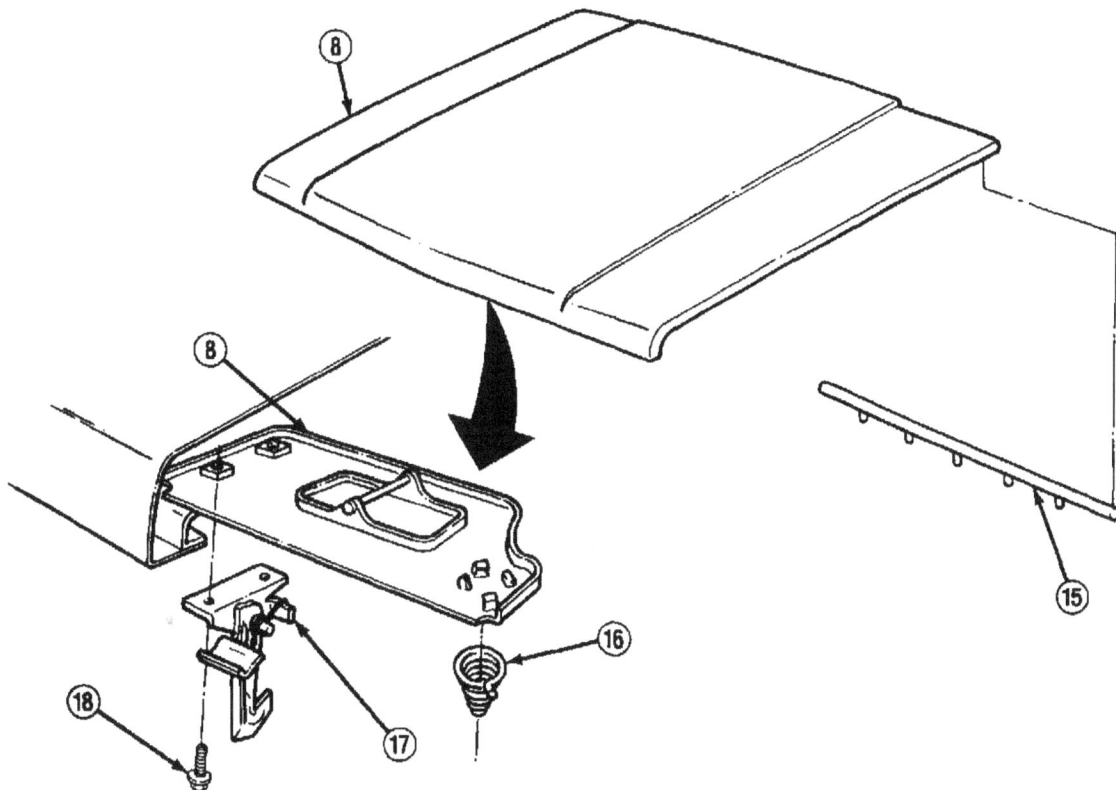

FOLLOW-ON TASKS:

◆Install ventilator panel if removed. (See paragraph 10-3)

TA49935

10-5. DOOR AND HINGE ASSEMBLY MAINTENANCE.

This task covers:
                      a. Remova l   d. Installation
                                      b. Hinge Disassembly   e. Adjustmen t
                                      c. Hinge Assembly

INITIAL SETUP

Equipment Condition   *Tools/Test Equipment*

  • Window glass completely raised.   • Screwdriver bit set, J-29843

Personnel Required

  • MOS 63B (2)

---

a.	REMOVAL

NOTE

  • **If removing door   (4) only, perform step 1.**

  • **Provide support for door (4) while removing it.**

1.   Mark position of hinge assemblies (3 and 9) on body side pillar and door (4), Remove 3 bolts (12) at lower hinge assembly (9) and 3 bolts (2) at upper hinge assembly (3), Remove door (4) .

2.   Reach up under instrument panel and remove plug from hidden bolt (1). Remove hidden bolt and 5 bolts (8), and upper and lower hinge assemblies (3 and 9) from body side pillar.

b.	HINGE DISASSEMBLY

1.   If worn or damaged, remove torque rod (5) from upper hinge assembly (3). Remove pin (6) and 2 bushings (7) from upper hinge assembly if worn or damaged.

2.   Remove pin (10) and 2 bushings (11) from lower hinge assembly (9) if worn or damaged.

c.	HINGE ASSEMBLY

1.   Install pin (10) and 2 bushings (11) to lower hinge assembly (9) as required.

2.   Install torque rod (5), pin (6), and 2 bushings (7) to upper hinge assembly (3)   as required.

d.	INSTALLATION

NOTE

If installing door (4) only, perform step 2.

1.   Reach up under instrument panel and install upper hinge assembly (3) to body side pillar with hidden bolt (1). Install 2 bolts (8) on upper hinge assembly. Install lower hinge assembly (9) with 3 bolts (8), Ensure that upper and lower hinge assemblies are alined with marks on body side pillar.

10-5. DOOR AND HINGE ASSEMBLY MAINTENANCE (Con't).

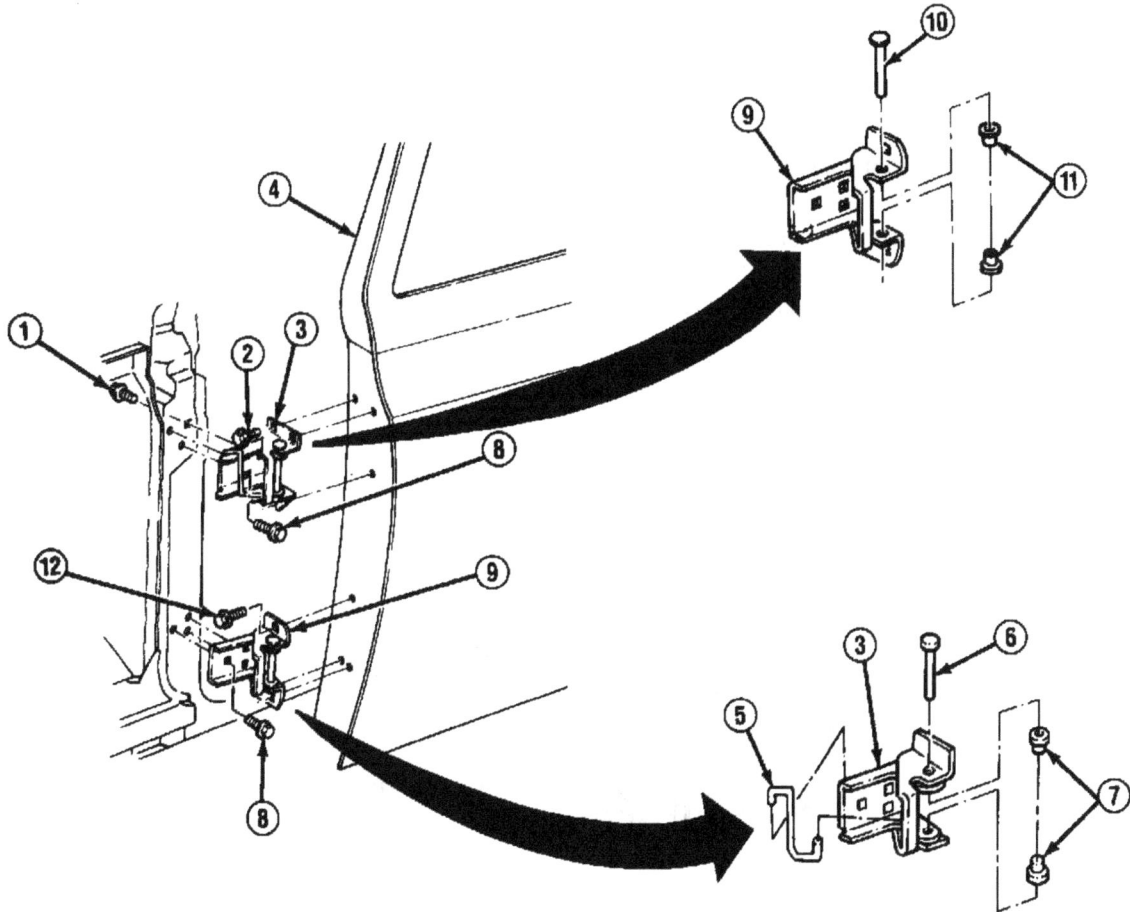

2. Position door (4) at upper and lower hinge assemblies (3 and 9). Aline upper and lower hinge assemblies to marks made on door. Install 3 bolts (2) at upper hinge assembly (3) and 3 bolts (12) at lower hinge assembly (9).

TA49936

10-5.   DOOR AND HINGE ASSEMBLY MAINTENANCE (Con't).

| e.   ADJUSTMENT |

1.   Check measurements as follows:

- Gap between windshield pillar (14) and door (4) should be 0.02 in. to 0.14 in. (0.5 mm to 3.5 mm).

- Gap between roof panel (13) and door (4) should be 0.1 in. to 0.28 in. (3 mm to 7 mm).

- Gap between rear pillar (15) and door (4) should be 0.1 in. to 0.28 in. (3 mm to 7 mm).

- Gap between rocker panel (16) and door (4) should be 0.15 in. to 0.33 in. (4 mm to 8 mm).

If these measurements require adjustment, perform ADJUSTMENT steps 2-4.

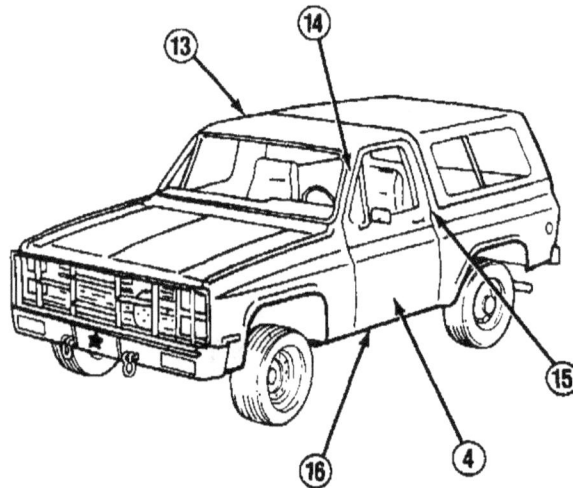

2.   Remove door lock striker (17) and washer (18) from striker plate (19).

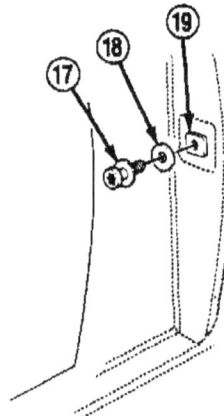

TA49937

10-5. DOOR AND HINGE ASSEMBLY MAINTENANCE (Con't).

3.   Loosen 5 bolts (8) and hidden bolt (1). Adjust door (4) on upper and lower hinge assemblies
(3 and 9) until all measurements in step 1 are obtained. Tighten bolts and install plug on hidden
bolt.

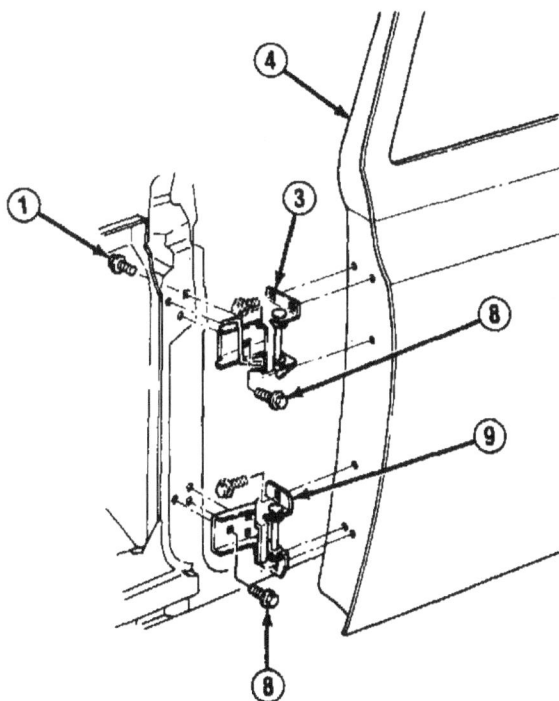

4.   Install washer (18) and door lock striker (17) on striker plate (19). Adjust door lock striker as
required to engage door (4) lock. Tighten door lock striker.

TA49938

10-6   DOOR HANDLE, LOCK, AND CYLINDER REPLACEMENT.

This task covers: a. Removal   b. Installation

INITIAL SETUP:

Equipment Condition   *Materials/Parts*
  • Door panel removed. (See paragraph 10-7)   • Three gaskets

| a. REMOVAL |

CAUTION

When removing clips (11, 14, and 16), carefully push at top of   clip where
it is connected to connecting links (4, 12, or 17) to pivot clip away from
link. Failure to follow this   caution will result in damage to clips,

NOTE

• If removing handle (6)   and lock cylinder unit (7), perform steps 1-3.

• If removing lock assembly (10) and   control assembly   (18), perform
  steps 1, 4, and 5.

1.   Remove clip (11) and disconnect outside door   connecting link (4) from lock assembly (10).

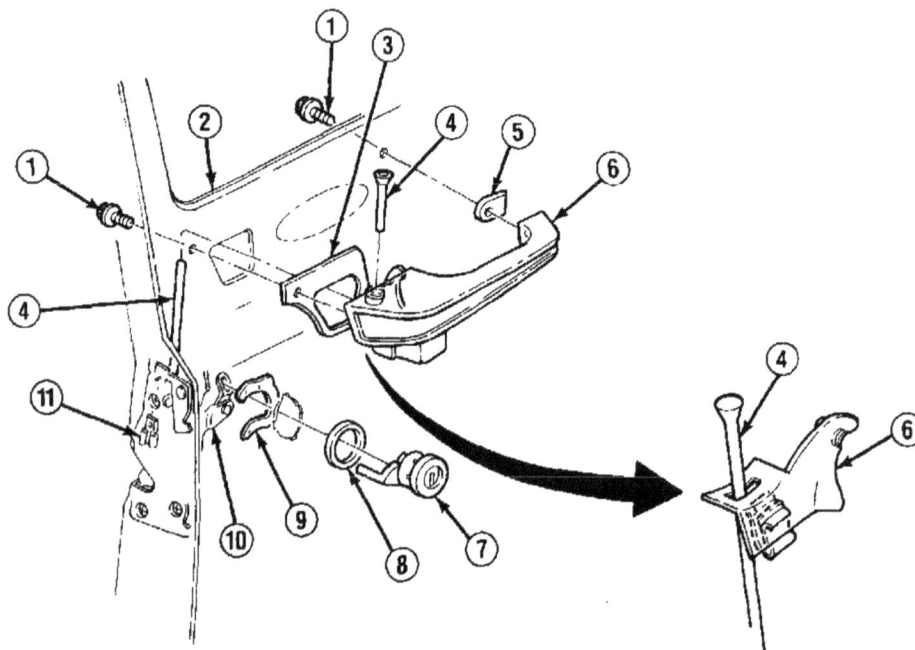

TA49939

10-6 DOOR HANDLE, LOCK, AND CYLINDER REPLACEMENT (Con't).

2. Remove 2 bolts (1), handle (6), and outside door connecting link (4) from door (2). Remove outside door connecting link from handle. Remove large gasket (3) and small gasket (5). Discard gaskets.

3. Remove retainer (9), lock cylinder unit (7), and gasket (8), Discard gasket.

4. Remove clips (14 and 16) and disconnect inside handle connecting link (17) and inside door connecting link (12). Remove lock knob (13). Remove 3 screws (15) and lock assembly (10).

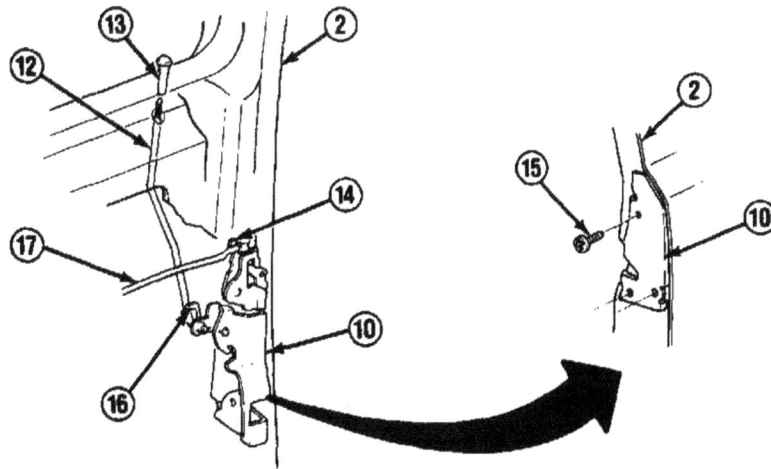

5. Remove seal (20). Remove 3 screws (19). Slide clip (21) until large slot alines with inside handle connecting link (17). Disconnect inside handle connecting link and remove control assembly (18).

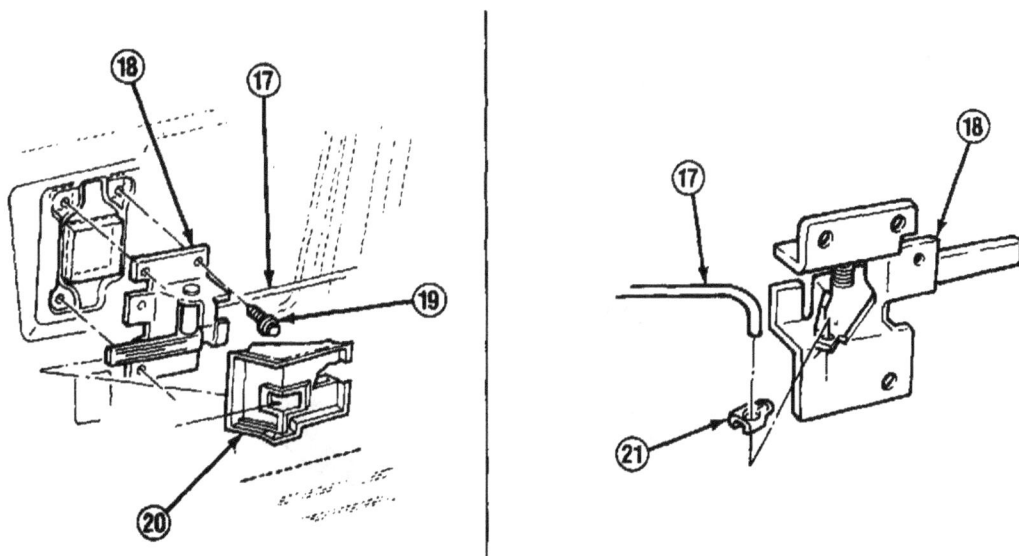

TA49940

10-6   DOOR HANDLE, LOCK, AND CYLINDER REPLACEMENT (Con't).

b.   INSTALLATION

NOTE

- If installing lock assembly (10) and control assembly (18), perform steps 1, 2, and 5.
- If installing handle (6) and lock cylinder unit (7), perform steps 3-5.

1.   Connect inside handle connecting link (17) to control assembly (18). Slide clip (21) until small slot alines with inside handle connecting link. Install control assembly with 3 screws (19), Install seal (20).

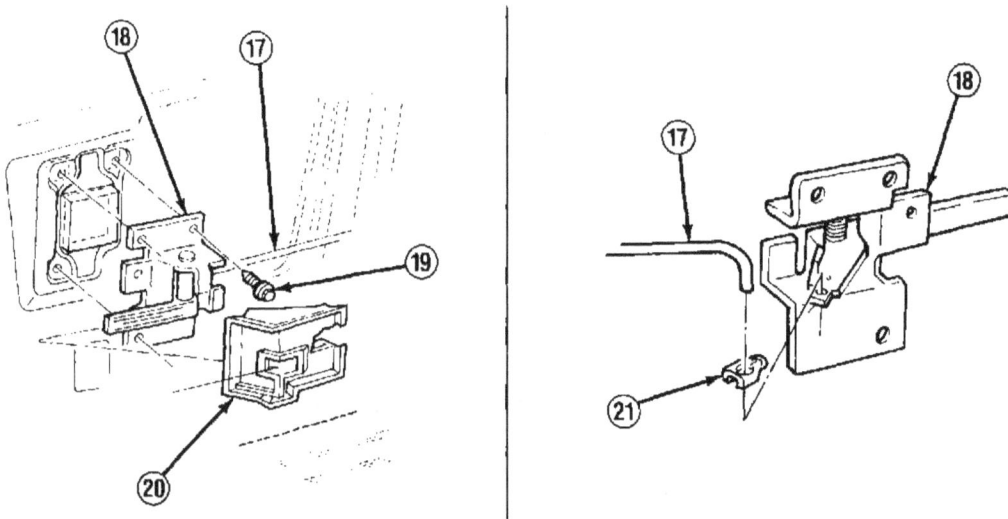

2.   Install lock assembly (10) in door (2) with 3 screws (15). Install lock knob (13). Connect inside handle connecting link (12) and inside door connecting link (17) to lock assembly and install clips (14 and 16).

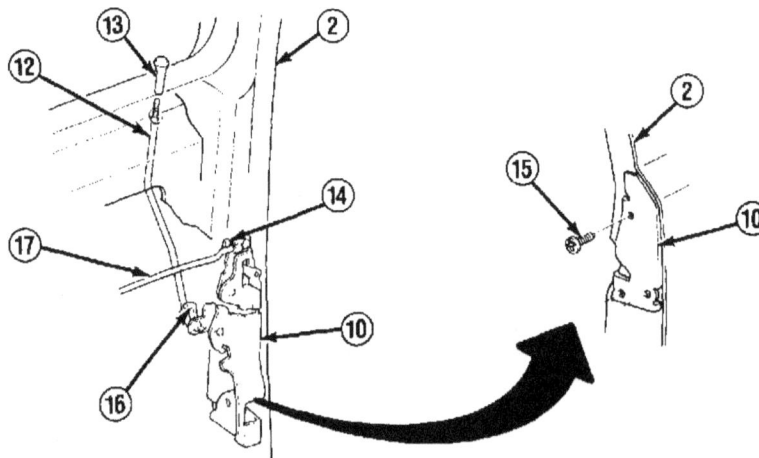

TA49941

10-6 DOOR HANDLE, LOCK, AND CYLINDER REPLACEMENT (Con't).

3. Install new gasket (8) and lock cylinder unit (7) on door (2). Install retainer (9).

4. Install new large gasket (3) on handle (6). Install outside door connecting link (4) on handle. Install outside door connecting link and handle in door (2). Loosely install 1 bolt (1) on large gasket side. Install new small gasket (5) between door and handle. Install other bolt (1) and tighten both bolts.

5. Connect outside door connecting link (4) to lock assembly (10) and install clip (11).

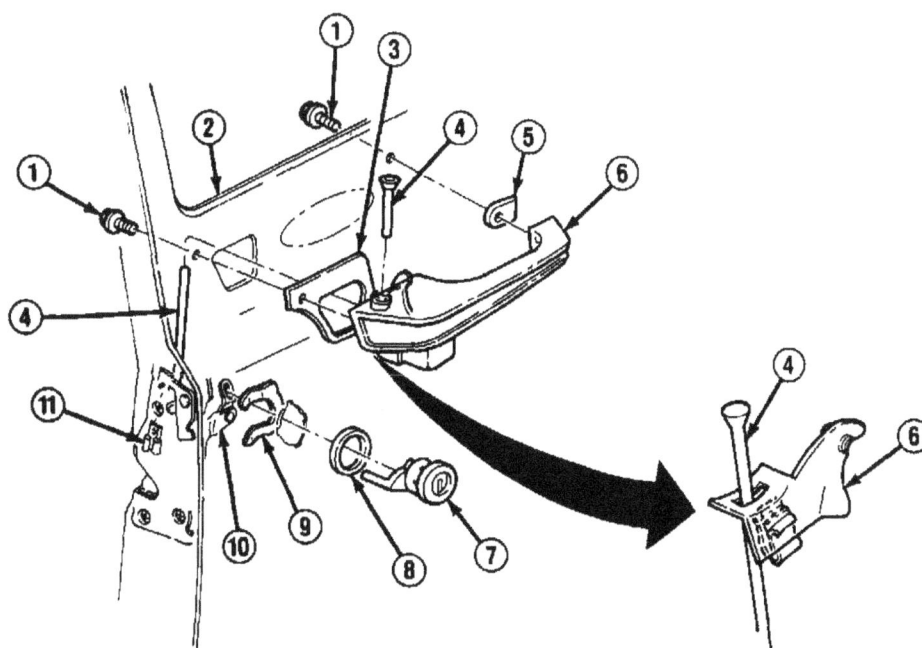

FOLLOW-ON TASKS:

• Install door panel. (See paragraph 10-7)

TA49942

10-7.   **DOOR PANEL, ARMREST, AND WINDOW REGULATOR REPLACEMENT.**

This task covers: a.   Removal   b. Installation

INITIAL SETUP:

Equipment Condition

• Window glass raised and taped in full up
   position (if removing window regulator).

Materials/Parts

• One door panel seal
• Grease (Item 27, Appendix C)
• Duct tape (Item 47, Appendix C)

Tools/Test Equipment

• Retaining clip remover, J-24595-B

---

a.	REMOVAL

NOTE

If removing door panel (4), perform steps 1-5.

1.   Remove door lock knob. Remove grommet (6) if damaged.

2.   Remove handle (1 2), retainer (11), and handle plate (10).

3.   Remove 2 screws (5) and 6 screws (8). Pry door panel (4) away from door (1) and remove.
      Remove spacer (3) and handle plate (2) from window regulator assembly (14) pin as required.

NOTE

**Perform step   4 only if armrest (7) is damaged or door panel (4) is being
replaced.**

4.   Remove nut (9) and armrest (7) if required.

5.   Inspect door panel seal (13) for damage, and replace if required. Clean all seal material from
      door panel (4) if removed.

6.   Remove 4 screws (20). install handle (12), without retainer (11), on window regulator
      assembly (14). Crank window regulator to disengage front roller (15) from sash channel (16).
      While holding front roller clear of sash channel, crank window regulator in opposite direction to
      disengage lower roller (18) from regulator rail (19), Remove handle and move window
      regulator assembly rearward to disengage rear roller (17) from sash channel. Remove window
      regulator assembly through access hole in door.

10-7. DOOR PANEL, ARMREST, AND WINDOW REGULATOR REPLACEMENT (Con't).

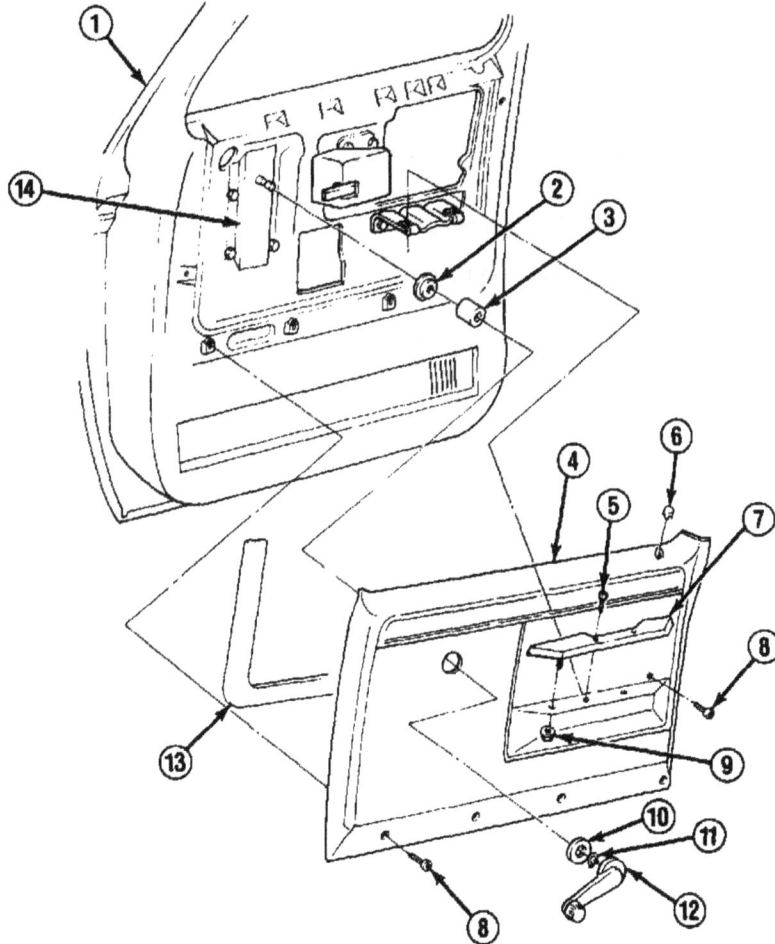

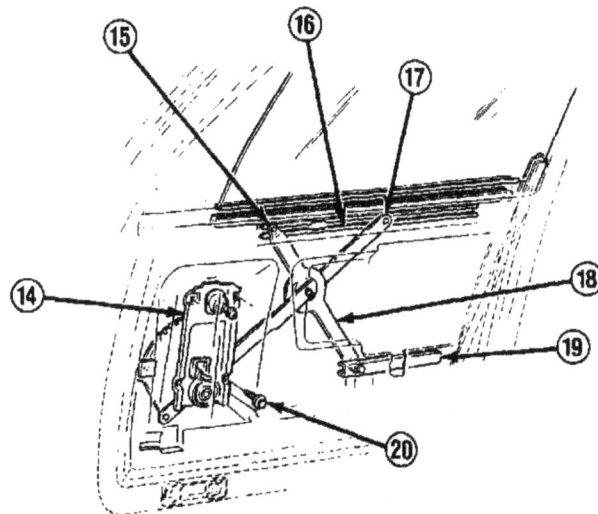

TA49943

10-7. DOOR PANEL, ARMREST, AND WINDOW REGULATOR REPLACEMENT (Con't).

| b.   INSTALLATION |

NOTE
If installing door panel (4), perform steps 3-8.

1. Lubricate rollers (15, 17, and 18), sash channel (16), and regulator rail (19).

2. Insert window regulator assembly (14) through access hole in door and engage rear roller (17) in sash channel (16). Install handle (12), without retainer (11), and crank window regulator until lower roller (18) engages on regulator rail (19). Continue cranking window regulator until forward roller (15) engages through notch in sash channel. Aline screw holes, then remove handle. Install window regulator assembly with 4 screws (20).

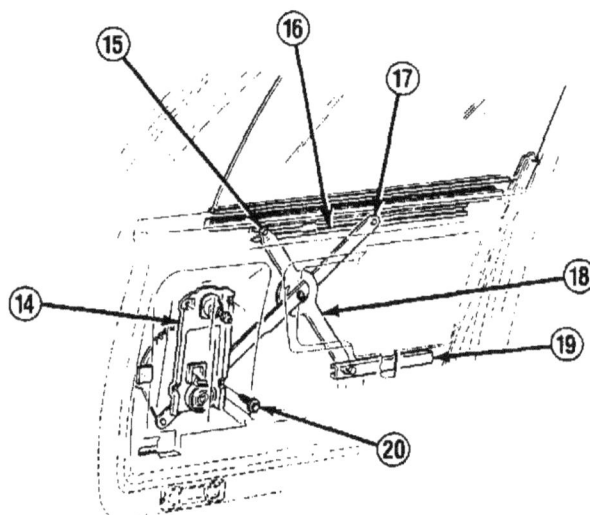

3. Peel backing from new door panel seal (13) and install on door panel (4) if removed.

4. Install handle plate (2) and spacer (3) on window regulator assembly (14) pin if removed.

5. If removed, install armrest (7) on door panel (4) with nut (9).

6. Snap door panel (4) into place on door (1), Install 6 screws (8) and 2 screws (5).

7. Position handle plate (10) on handle (12), and install retainer (11) on notch in handle. Snap handle assembly into place on door panel (4) and window regulator assembly (14) pin.

8. Install grommet (6) if removed. Install door lock knob.

TA49944

10-7. DOOR PANEL, ARMREST, AND WINDOW REGULATOR REPLACEMENT (Con't).

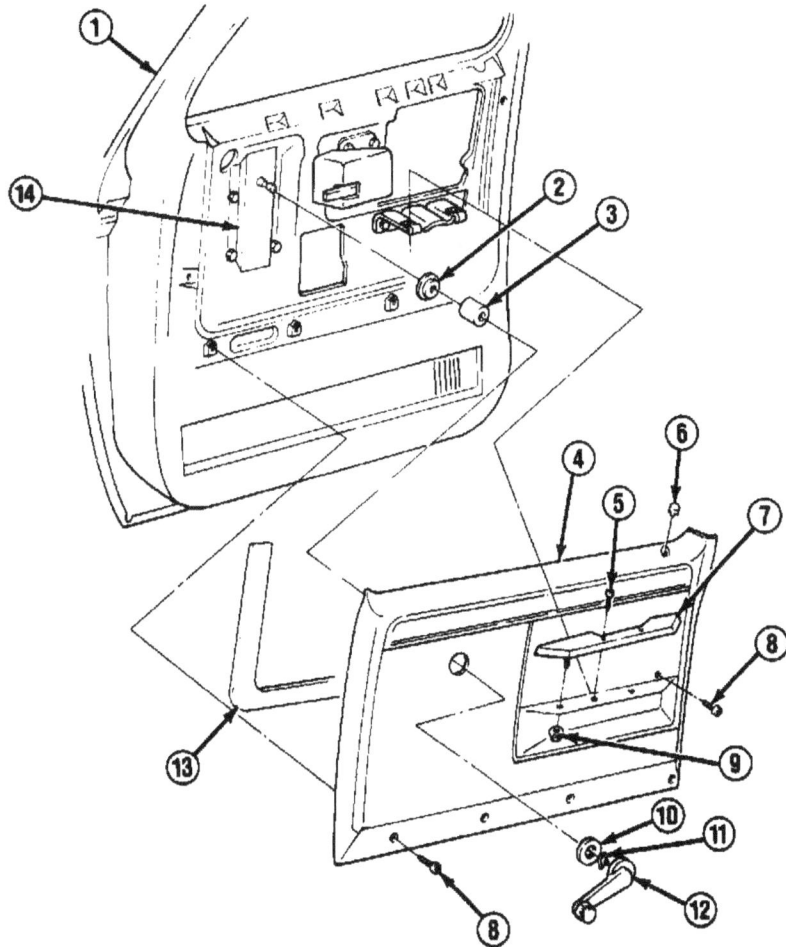

FOLLOW-ON TASKS:

• Remove tape from window if used.
• Check operation of handle and window regulator.

TA49945

10-8. DOOR AND VENT WINDOW MAINTENANCE.

This task covers:

a. Removal	c. Assembly
b. Disassembly	d. Installation

INITIAL SETUP:

Equipment Condition

- Window glass lowered to full down position.
- Door panel removed.
  (See paragraph 10-7)
- Sharp edges of door frame covered.

Materials/Parts

- One rivet
- One vent window filler or one door window filler
- Adhesive (Item 2, Appendix C)
- Dry cleaning solvent (Item 15, Appendix C)
- Tape (Item 48, Appendix C)

Too/s/Test Equipment

- Screwdriver bit set, J-29843

General Safety Instructions

- Dry cleaning solvent is flammable and must not be used near open flame. Use only in a well-ventilated area.

---

a. REMOVAL

NOTE

- If replacing vent window, perform **DISASSEMBLY** steps **2** and **3**.

- If removing vent window assembly (17), perform steps 1-4.

1. Remove screw (5) and slide up cover (3). Remove bolt (4), From inside of door, remove bolt (1) and reinforcement (6). Remove spacer (2).

2. Remove 2 screws (10) and spacers (11). Remove screw (12).

3. Remove screw (16). Loosen screw (9). Peel top of window glass run (14) from door (13), Peel edge of window glass run from vent window assembly (17). Pull vent window assembly and window glass run from door, and remove vent window assembly from window glass run.

4. Remove screw (9), retaining nut (7), and bumper (8) if damaged.

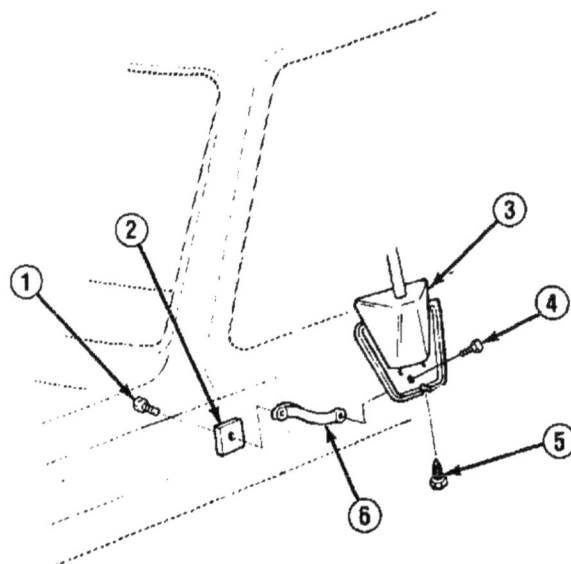

TA49946

10-8. DOOR AND VENT WINDOW MAINTENANCE (Con't).

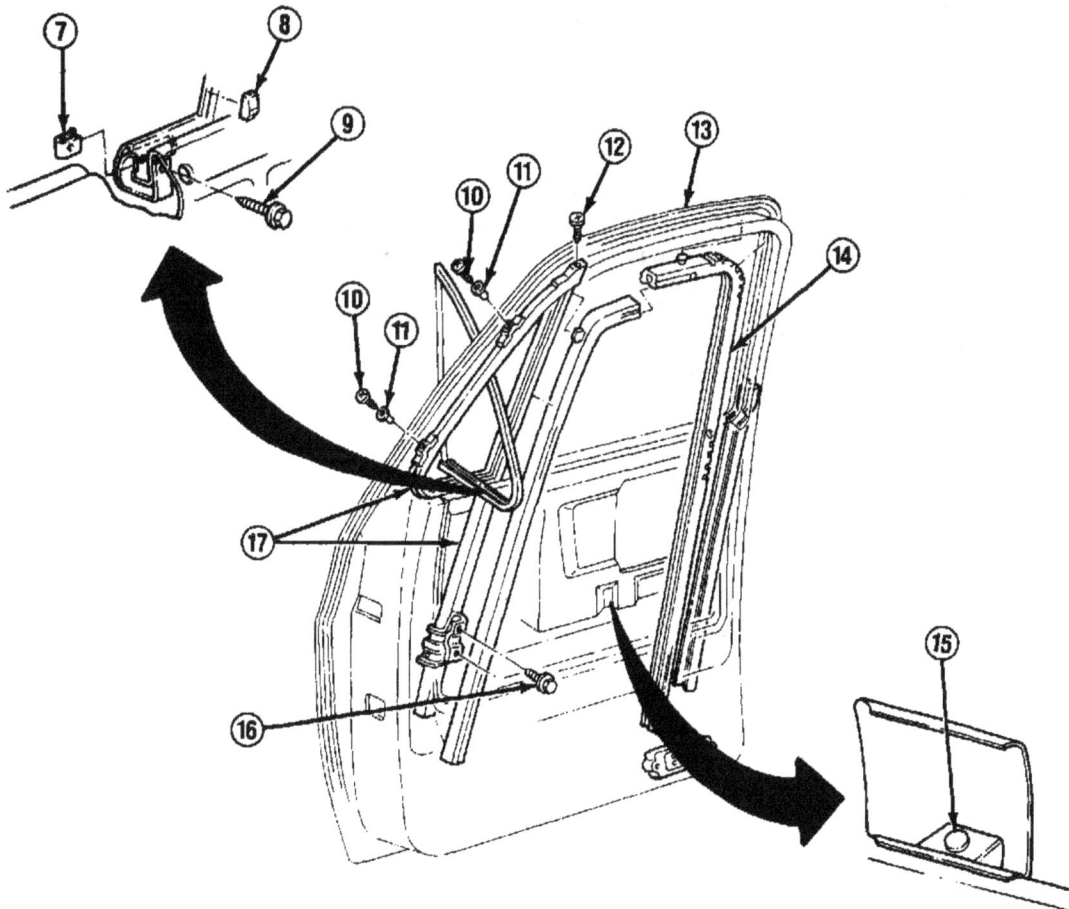

NOTE

If window will not disengage using the procedure in step 5, raise window slightly, remove bumper (15), lower window, and repeat step 5.

5. Slide window glass (18) forward to disengage forward window regulator assembly roller (21) from notch in sash channel (20). Push window glass forward, then tilt up until rear window regulator assembly roller is disengaged. Place window glass and sash channel assembly in level position and pull straight up and out of door (13).

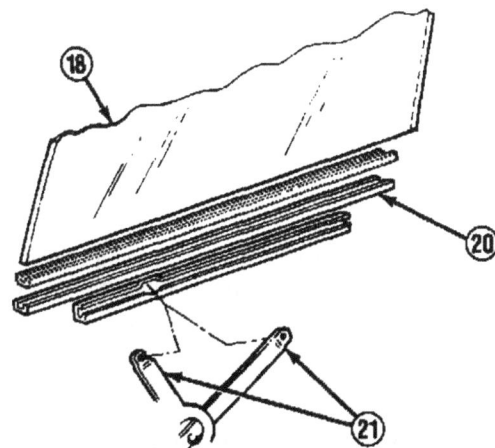

TA49947

10-8.   DOOR AND VENT WINDOW MAINTENANCE (Con't).

| b. DISASSEMBLY |

WARNING

Dry cleaning   solvent P-D-680 is toxic and flammable. Always wear protective goggles and gloves and use only in a well-ventilated area. Avoid contact with skin, eyes, and clothes and DO NOT breathe vapors. DO NOT use near open flame or excessive heat. The solvent's flash point is 100°F-138°F (38°C-59°C). If you become dizzy while using cleaning solvent, immediately get fresh air and medical help. If solvent contacts eyes, immediately wash your eyes with water and get medical aid.

NOTE

* If disassembling door window, perform step 1.

* If disassembling vent window assembly, perform steps 2-6.

1.   Separate window glass (18) fro   m sash channel (20), Apply dry cleaning solvent to filler (19) and remove filler from window glass.

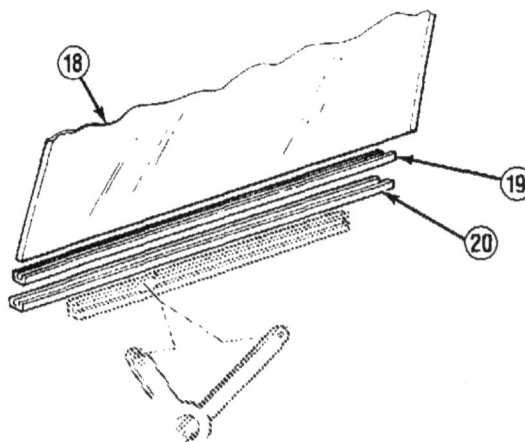

2.   Remove pin (32) and pull off handle (22), plunger (23), and spring (24). Remove screw (31) and stud (30). Remove washer (29), plastic washer (25), plate (27), and spacer (26) from vent window glass (28).

CAUTION

Immediately wipe off dry cleaning solvent if it drips onto truck. Failure to follow this caution may result in damage to truck interior or exterior paint.

3.   Open vent window and apply dry cleaning solvent to filler (44) around vent window glass (28). When filler softens, pull vent window glass and old filler from sash (45). Discard filler.

4.   Straighten tabs on back of weatherstrip (43) and remove if damaged.

TA49948

10-8. DOOR AND VENT WINDOW MAINTENANCE (Con't).

5. Remove rivet (35) and sash hinge (34) from frame hinge (36), Straighten tab on tab washer (41), remove nut (42), tab washer, spring (40), spring retainer washer (39), 2 washers (38), and stop (37). Discard rivet.

6. Remove sash (45) from frame   (33). Remove weatherstrip (46) from frame.

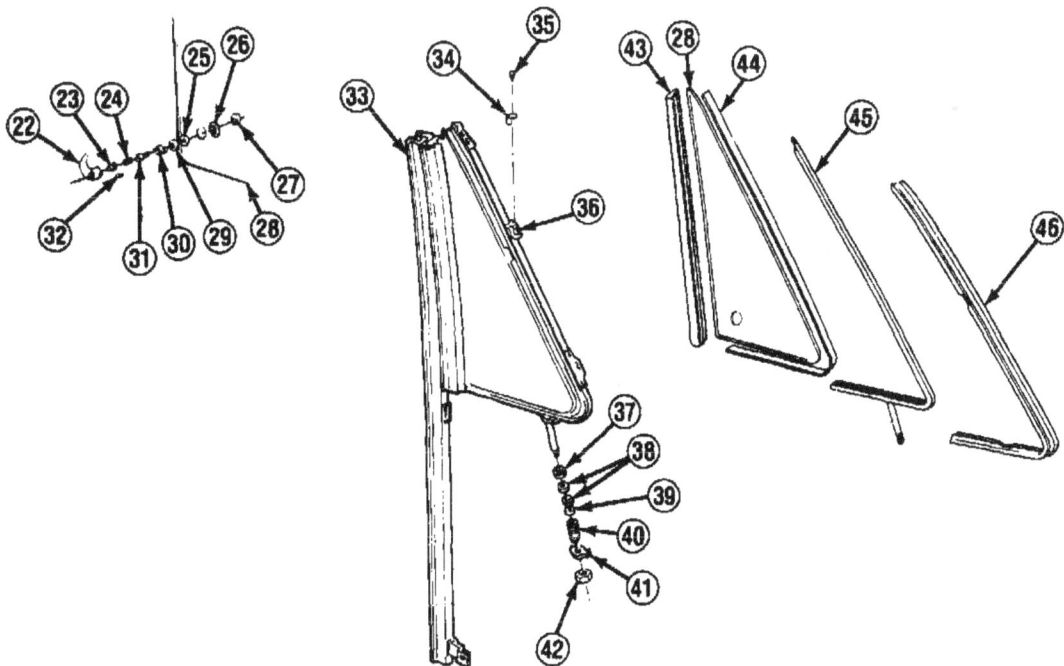

c. **ASSEMBLY**

NOTE

• If replacing door window, perform step 8.

• If replacing vent window, perform steps 4-7.

1. Position weatherstrip (46) on frame (33). Position sash (45) on frame.

2. Install stop (37), 2 washers (38), spring retainer washer (39), spring (40), tab washer (41), and nut (42) on sash (45). Bend tab on tab washer back to   lock nut into position. Install sash hinge (34) on frame hinge (36) with new rivet (35).

3. Apply adhesive to weatherstrip (43) as required. Install weatherstrip on frame (33) and bend tabs on back of weatherstrip.

TA49949

10-8.   DOOR AND VENT WINDOW MAINTENANCE (Con't).

4.   Thoroughly clean inside of sash (45), Install new filler (44) on vent window glass (28).

5.   Brush inside of sash (45) with soap solution. Firmly press new filler (44) and vent window glass (28) into sash,

6.   Install spacer (26) and plastic washer (25) on vent window glass (28) with flanged side facing glass. Install plate (27) with small end toward top of glass. Install stud (30) with screw (31).

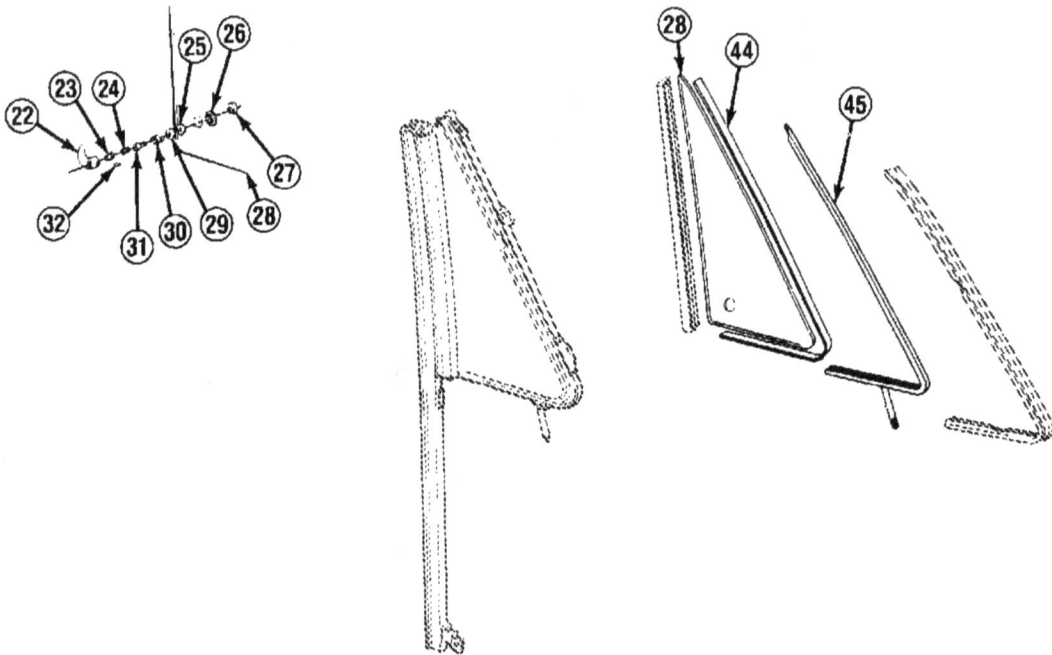

7,   Install spring (24) and plunger (23) with fins alined to notches in stud (30). Position handle (22) and aline handle hole with hole in stud. Install pin (32).

8.   Firmly press new filler (19) an   d window glass (18) into sash channel (20) .

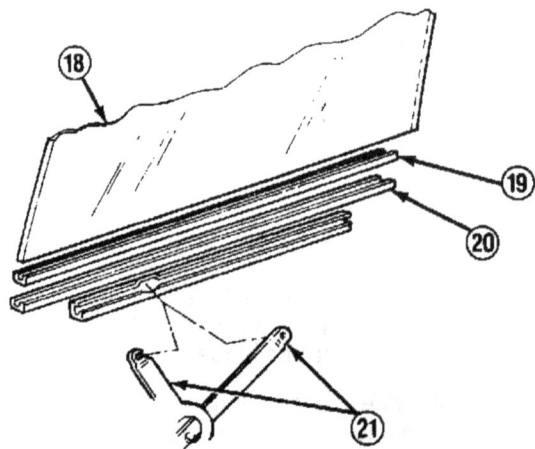

TA49950

10-8. DOOR AND VENT WINDOW MAINTENANCE (Con't).

| d. | INSTALLATION |

NOTE
If installing vent window assembly (17), perform steps 2-6.

1. Install bumper (15) if removed. Position window glass (18) and sash channel (20) assembly in door. Push window glass forward, then tilt up and slide rear window regulator assembly roller (21) into sash channel. Slide window glass backward until forward window regulator assembly roller is alined with notch in sash channel, then engage. Slide window glass assembly backward into window glass run (14) channel.

2. Install bumper (8), retaining nut (7), and screw (9) if removed. DO NOT tighten screw.

3. Position window glass run (14) along vent window assembly (17). Position vent window assembly in door (13), and seat edge of vent window assembly and window glass run along inside of door.

4. Tighten screw (9), Install window regulator handle and operate window. Loosen or tighten screw as required for smooth operation, then remove window regulator handle. Install screw (16).

5. Install screw (12). Install 2 spacers (11) and screws (10).

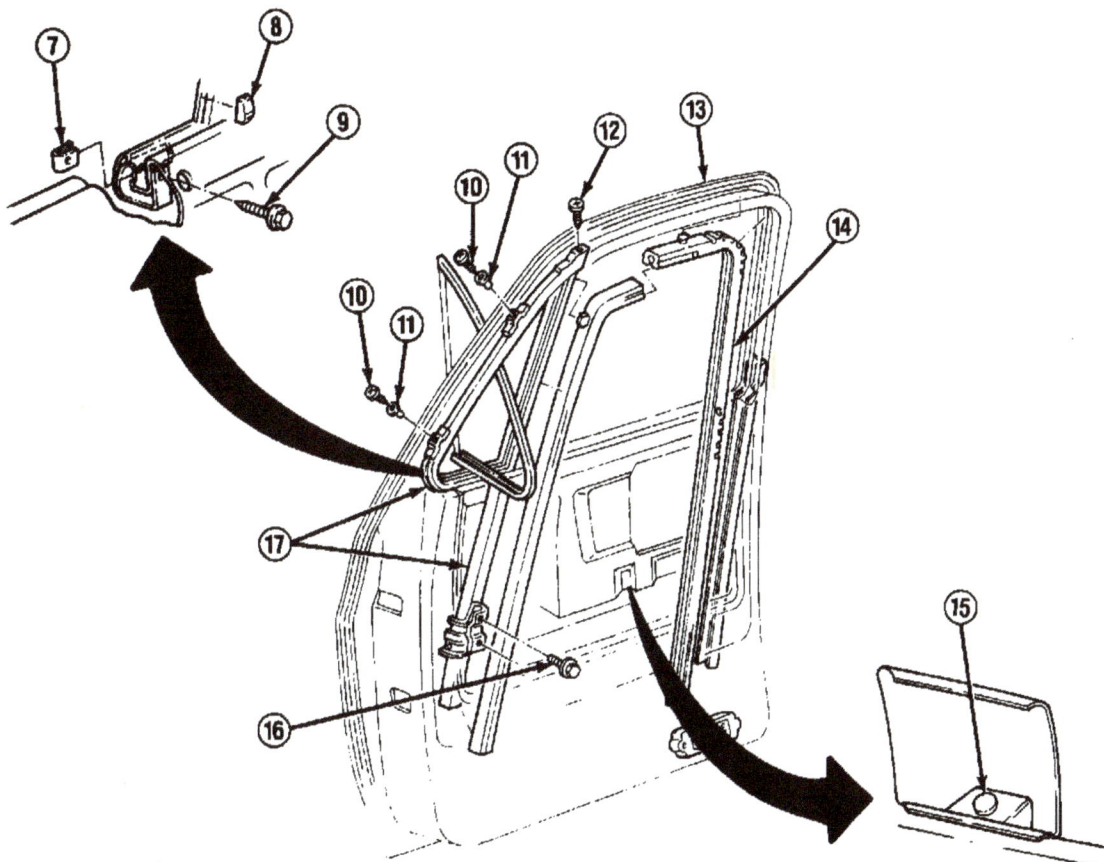

TA49951

10-8.   DOOR AND VENT WINDOW MAINTENANCE (Con't).

6.   Install spacer (2) if removed. From
      inside of door, install reinforcement
      (6) with bolt (1). Install bolt (4). Slide
      cover (3) down and install screw (5).

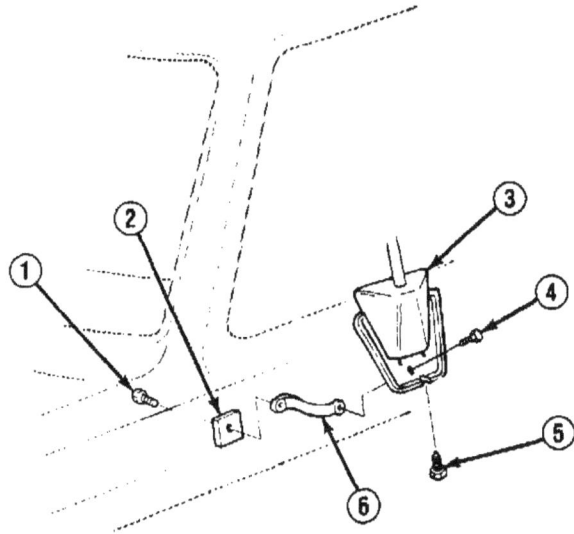

FOLLOW-ON TASKS:

• Remove any masking.
• Install door panel. (See paragraph 10-7)

TA49952

Section II. STANDARD BODY ACCESSORIES MAINTENANCE

10-9.   STANDARD BODY ACCESSORIES MAINTENANCE INDEX.

10-10. REARVIEW MIRROR REPLACEMENT.

This task covers: a.   Removal   b. Installation

a. REMOVAL

1.   Remove bolt (10) and slide up cover (9) while turning outside rearview mirror (7) toward window. Remove 3 bolts (11), and remove outside rearview mirror assembly and gasket (2).

2.   Remove 2 bolts (1) and separate clamp (4) from bracket (3). Remove retainer (5) and sleeve (6), and separate cover (9) from outside rearview mirror (7). Remove 2 grommets (8) and retaining nut (12) as required.

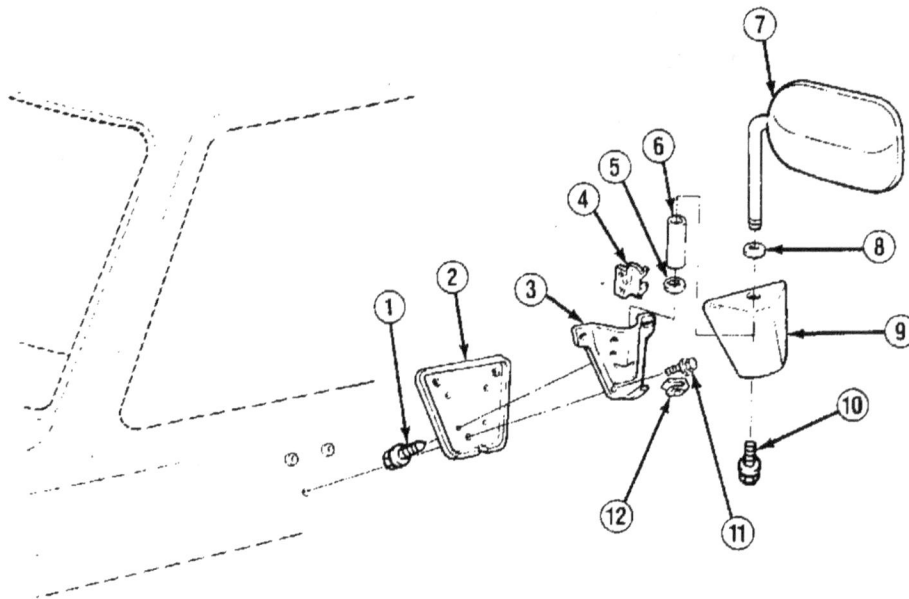

b.   INSTALLATION

NOTE

M1028A2 and M1028A3 driver's side mirrors have a longer shaft than do other models.

1.   Install retaining nut (12) on bracket (3) and 2 grommets (8) on outside rearview mirror (7) arm if removed. Position outside rearview mirror arm through hole in cover (9) with lower grommet against cover.

2.   Install sleeve (6) and retainer (5) on outside rearview mirror (7) arm. Install bracket (3) and clamp (4) around sleeve with 2 bolts (1).

3.   Install gasket (2) and outside rearview mirror (7) assembly with 3 bolts (11), Slide down cover (9) and install bolt (10).

10-11. WINDSHIELD WIPER AND WASHER REPLACEMENT.

This task covers: a. Removal   b. Installation

INITIAL SETUP:

Equipment Condition
  • Both battery negative cables disconnected
    (if removing windshield wiper motor).
    (See paragraph 4-38)

Tools/Test Equipment
  • 10 mm socket

Materials/Parts
  • Six lockwashers
  • One windshield wiper motor gasket
  • Grease (Item 26, Appendix C)

| a. | **REMOVAL** |

NOTE

  ● **If removing wiper arms (1), perform step 1.**

  ● **If removing wiper transmissions, perform steps 1-3.**

  ● **If removing windshield wiper motor, perform steps 4-6.**

  ● **If removing hoses and washer solvent container, perform   steps 7 and 8
    as required.**

1.   Remove wiper blade (2) from wiper arm (1), Remove wiper arm from wiper transmission (4
      or 7). Remove insert (3) from wiper blade if damaged.

2.   Remove ventilator panel. (See paragraph 10-3)

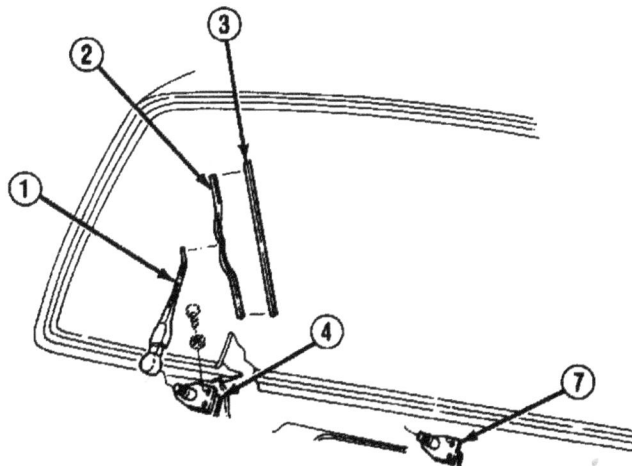

TA49954

10-11. WINDSHIELD WIPER AND WASHER REPLACEMENT (Con't).

3. Remove 6 bolts (23) and lockwashers (22). Using 10 mm socket, loosen nuts (8) and disconnect right wiper transmission (4) rod from windshield wiper motor pin (11). Remove wiper transmission assembly.   Separate left wiper transmission (7) from right wiper transmission (4) if damaged. Discard lockwashers.

4. Disconnect leads from windshield wiper motor (14). Disconnect pump hose (12) and 2 nozzle hoses (6) from windshield wiper motor.

5. If ventilator panel was not removed, loosen nuts (8) using 10 mm socket through access hole in top of bulkhead (9), and disconnect right wiper transmission (4)   rod from windshield wiper motor pin (11).

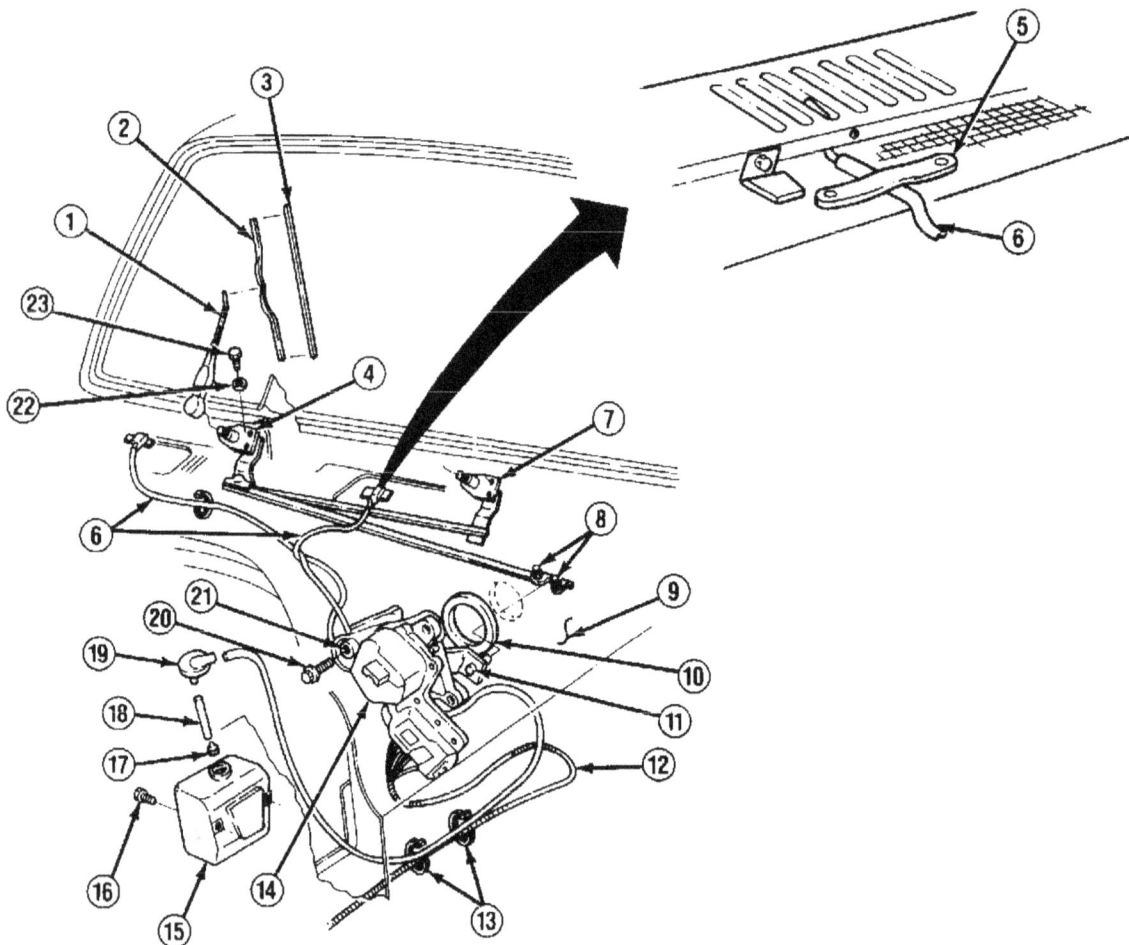

TA49955

10-11. WINDSHIELD WIPER AND WASHER REPLACEMENT (Con't).

6. Remove 3 bolts (20) and grommets (21). Remove windshield wiper motor (14) and gasket (10). Discard gasket.

7. If ventilator panel was not removed, remove retainer (5) and disconnect nozzle hose (6) if damaged.

8. Remove 2 retainers (13) and disconnect and remove pump hose (12) if damaged. Remove and disassemble cap (19), hose (18), and filter (17). Clean filter if clogged. Remove 2 screws (16) and washer solvent container (15).

b. INSTALLATION

NOTE

- **If installing hoses (6, 12, and 18) and washer solvent container (15), perform steps 1 and 2 as required.**

- **If installing windshield wiper motor (14), perform steps 3-5.**

- **If installing wiper transmissions (4 or 7), performs steps 6-8.**

- **If installing wiper arms (1), perform step 8.**

1. Install washer solvent container (15) with 2 screws (16). Assemble and install filter (17), hose (18), and cap (19). Connect pump hose (12) to washer solvent container and install retainers (13) if removed.

2. Connect nozzle hose (6) if disconnected and install retainer (5).

3. Position new gasket (10) and windshield wiper motor (14) on bulkhead (9) and install with 3 grommets (21) and bolts (20).

4. Grease windshield wiper motor pin (11). If ventilator panel was not removed, connect right wiper transmission (4) rod to windshield wiper motor pin. Tighten nuts (8) using 10 mm socket through access hole in top of bulkhead (9).

5. Connect 2 nozzle hoses (6) and pump hose (12) to windshield wiper motor (14). Connect leads to windshield wiper motor.

6. Install left wiper transmission (7) on right wiper transmission (4) if separated, Position wiper transmission assembly. Grease windshield wiper motor pin (11). Connect right wiper transmission rod to windshield wiper motor pin. Using 10 mm socket tighten nuts (8). Install 6 new lockwashers (22) and bolts (23).

7. Install ventilator panel. (See paragraph 10-3)

8. Install insert (3) on wiper blade (2) if removed. install wiper arm (1) on wiper transmission (4 or 7) until wiper arms are parallel. Install wiper blade on wiper arm.

FOLLOW-ON TASKS:

- Connect both battery negative cables if disconnected. (See paragraph 4-38)

10-12. HEATER BLOWER MOTOR, FAN, RESISTOR, AND CAPACITOR REPLACEMENT.

This task covers: a. Remova l   b. Installation

INITIAL SETUP:

Equipment Condition

• Rear battery removed (if removing blower motor and fan). (See paragraph 4-39)

Too/s/Test Equipment

• ½ in. drive metric socket set

Materials/Parts

• One blower motor seal
• One locknut

---

a.   REMOVAL

NOTE

● **If removing   resistor (7), perform step 1.**

● **If removing   capacitor (3), perform step 2.**

● **If removing   heater blower motor (2) and fan (13), perform steps 2-4.**

1.   Disconnect leads (8) from resistor (7). Remove 2 screws (6) and remove resistor.

2.   Disconnect leads (5) from capacitor (3). Remove screw (4) and capacitor.

3.   Disconnect vent hose (9) from heater blower motor (2). Remove 5 screws (10), heater blower motor and fan (13) assembly, and   seal (14). Discard seal.

4.   Remove locknut (11), washer (12),   and fan (13). Replace heater blower motor (2) and/or fan if damaged. Discard locknut.

b.   INSTALLATION

NOTE

◀f installing heater blower   motor (2) and fan   (13), perform steps 1-3.

◀f in tailing capacitor (3),   perform step 3.

◀f installing resistor (7), perform step 4.

1.   Install fan (13) on heater blower motor (2) with washer (12) and new locknut (11).

2.   Install new seal (14) on heater blower motor (2) assembly and position on blower motor case (1). Install 5 screws (10). DO NOT install upper right-hand screw (4) at this time. Connect vent hose (9) to heater blower motor.

3.   Install capacitor (3) with screw (4). Connect capacitor leads (5).

4.   Install resistor (7) with 2 screws (6). Connect resistor leads (8).

10-12. HEATER BLOWER MOTOR, FAN, RESISTOR, AND CAPACITOR REPLACEMENT (Con't).

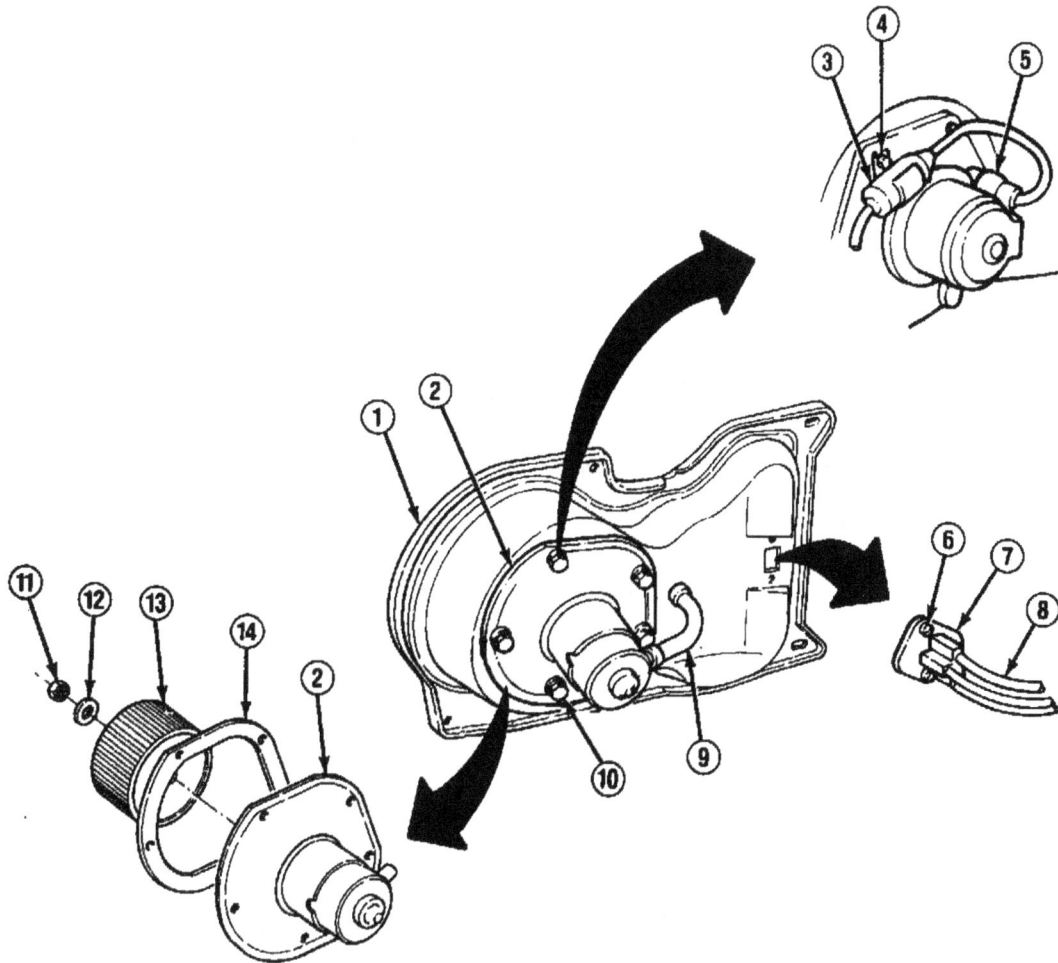

FOLLOW-ON TASKS:

• Install rear battery if removed. (See paragraph 4-39)

TA49956

10-13. HEATER ASSEMBLY, HEATER CORE, AND HEATER HOSES REPLACEMENT.

This task covers:	a. Removal	b. Installation

INITIAL SETUP:

Equipment Condition
  • Rear battery removed, (See paragraph 4-39)

Materials/Parts
  • One heater core seal
  • One strap

| a. | **REMOVAL** |

NOTE

  • Drain coolant from hoses (3 and 9) and heater core (28) into a suitable container.

  • If removing heater hoses (3 and 9), perform steps 1-3.

  • If removing heater core (28), perform steps 1 and 4 through 10.

1. Loosen clamps (2) and disconnect outlet hose (3) and inlet hose (9) from heater core tubes (1).

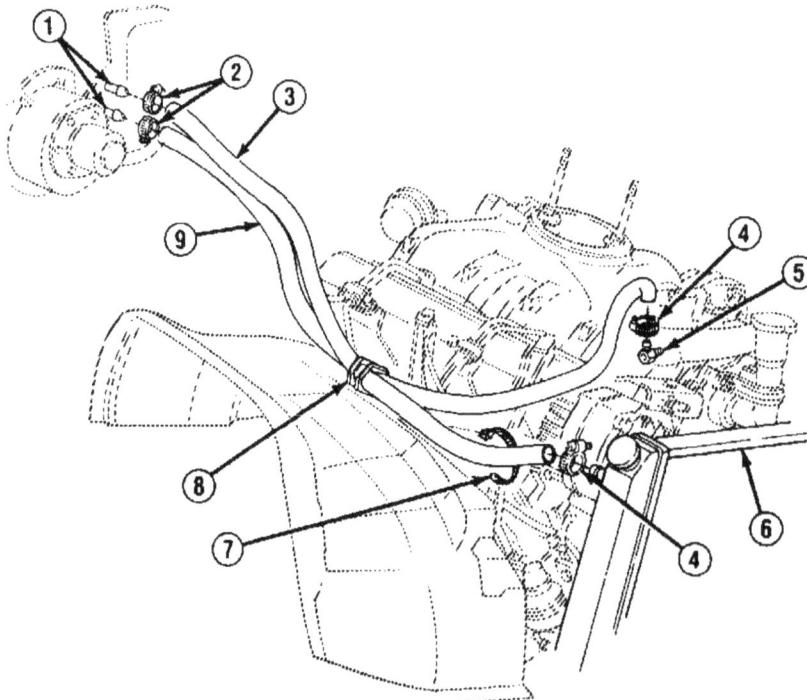

TA49957

10-13. HEATER ASSEMBLY, HEATER CORE, AND HEATER HOSES REPLACEMENT (Con't).

2. Loosen clamps (4) and disconnect outlet hose (3) from radiator (6) and inlet hose (9) from crossover pipe (5).

3. Remove and discard strap (7). Remove hose clip (8) from inner fender and   remove inlet and outlet hoses (3 and 9). Remove hose clip from hoses.

4. Remove 4 screws and remove instrument panel compartment.

5. Remove 2 screws (13) and spring retainers (12). Disconnect temperature cable (14) from temperature shaft (15) and defroster cable (10) from defroster shaft (11).

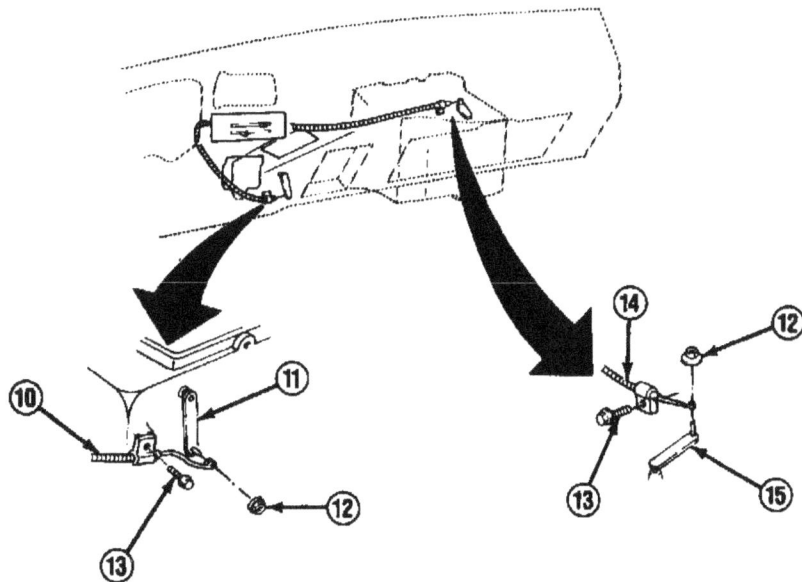

6. Remove screw (19) and air outlet (18) from heater assembly (16) if damaged.   Remove defroster duct screw (17) from heater assembly.

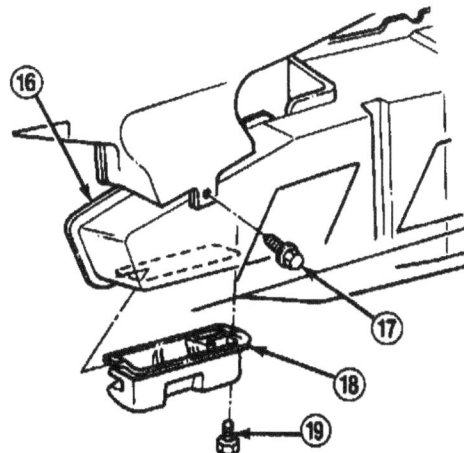

TA49958

10-13. HEATER ASSEMBLY, HEATER CORE, AND HEATER HOSES REPLACEMENT (Con't).

NOTE

Step 7 only applies to trucks equipped with winterization kits.

7. Tag leads and disconnect from safety switch (20). Remove 2 bolts (21), safety switch, and gasket (22).

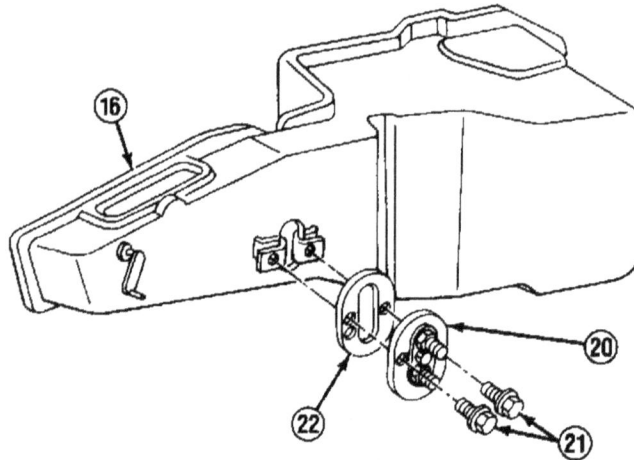

8. Remove 3 nuts (25) and harness retainer (23) from heater assembly studs (24) on bulkhead.

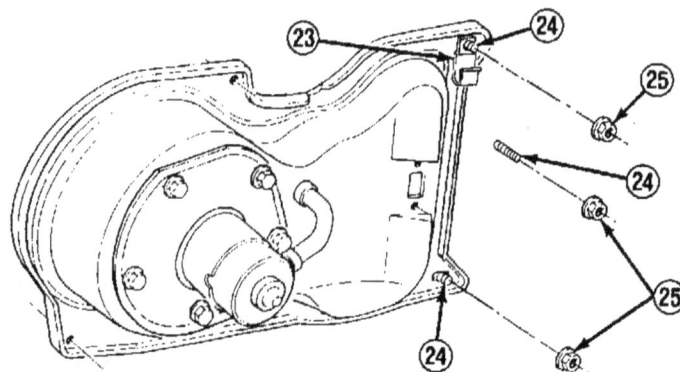

TA49959

10-13. HEATER ASSEMBLY, HEATER CORE, AND HEATER HOSES REPLACEMENT (Con't).

9.   Remove screw (27). Remove heater assembly (16) and heater core seal (26). Discard heater core seal.

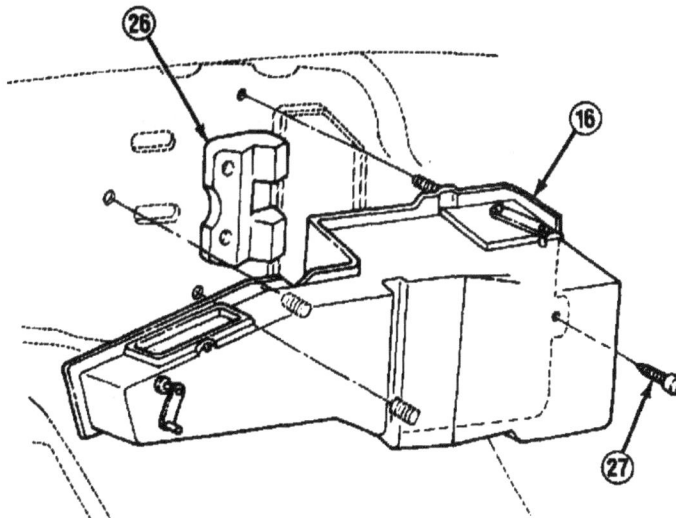

10.   Remove 4 screws (30), clamps (29 and 31), and heater core (28).

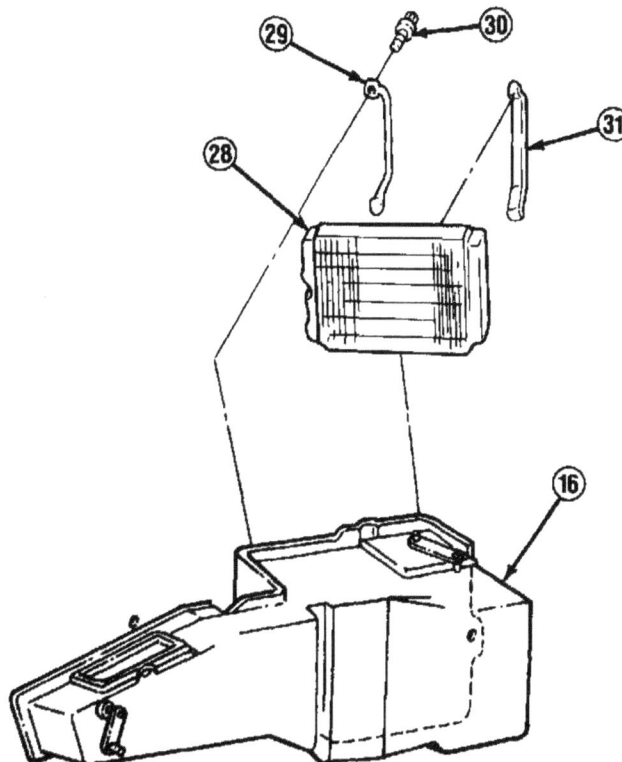

TA49960

10-13. HEATER ASSEMBLY, HEATER CORE, AND HEATER HOSES REPLACEMENT (Con't).

| b. | INSTALLATION |

NOTE

- If installing heater core (28), perform steps 1-7, and 9.

- If installing heater hoses, perform steps 8-10.

1. Install heater core (28) on heater assembly (16) with clamps (29 and 31) and 4 screws (30).

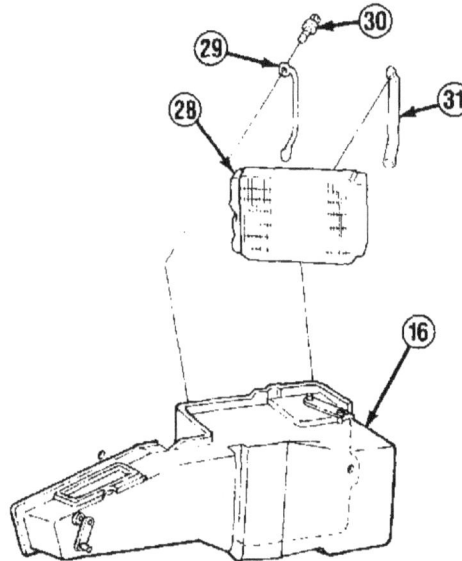

NOTE

Ensure that control cables are not behind heater assembly (16) when installing heater assembly.

2. Position new heater core seal (26) with holes over heater core tubes. Position heater assembly (16) with studs and heater core tubes through bulkhead. Install screw (27).

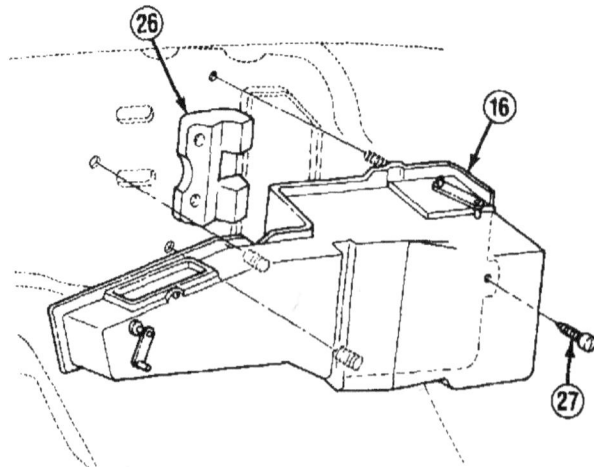

TA49961

10-13. HEATER ASSEMBLY, HEATER CORE, AND HEATER HOSES REPLACEMENT (Con't).

NOTE

Step 3 only applies to trucks equipped with winterization kits,

3. Install gasket (22) and safety switch (20) on heater assembly (16) with 2 bolts (21). Connect leads.

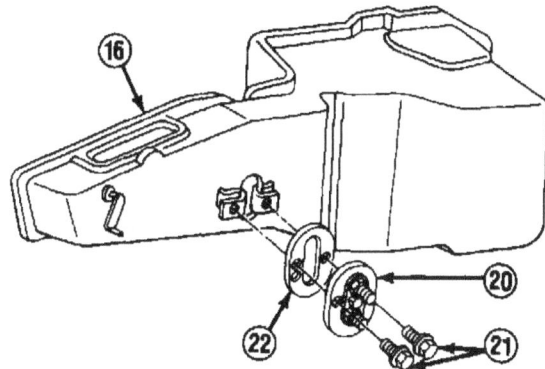

4. Install harness retainer (23) on upper right stud (24), and install 3 nuts (25).

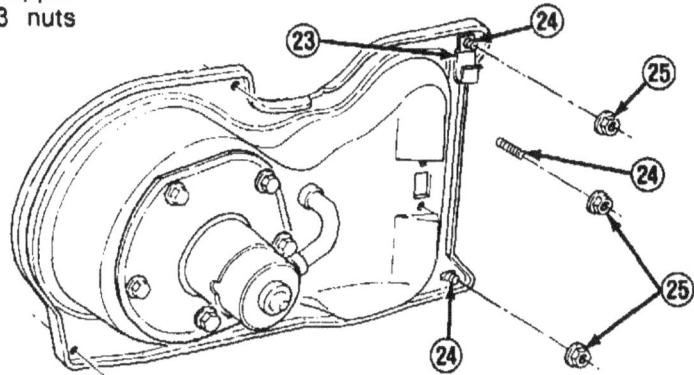

5. Install defroster duct screw (17). If removed, position air outlet (18) in heater assembly (16), and install with screw (19).

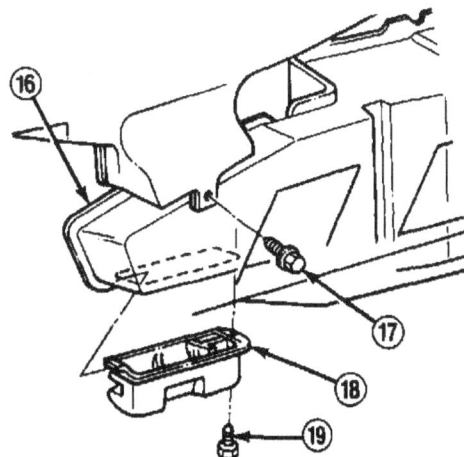

TA49962

10-13. HEATER ASSEMBLY, HEATER CORE, AND HEATER HOSES REPLACEMENT (Con't).

6. Connect defroster cable (10) to defroster shaft (11) with spring retainer (12) and install screw (13). Connect temperature cable (14) to temperature shaft (15) with spring retainer and install screw.

7. Install instrument panel compartment with 4 screws.

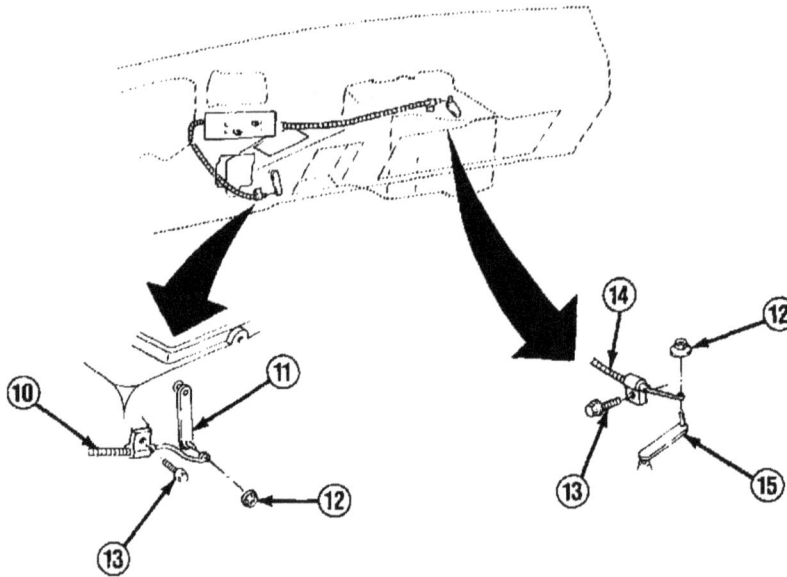

8. Install hose clip (8) to inner fender. Connect outlet hose (3) to radiator (6) and inlet hose (9) to crossover pipe (5).

9. Connect outlet hose (3) to upper heater core tube (1) and inlet hose (9) to lower heater core tube. Tighten 2 clamps (2) and clamps (4).

10. Install hose clip (8) to hoses (3 and 9), and install a new strap (7) around hoses.

TA49963

10-13. HEATER ASSEMBLY, HEATER CORE, AND HEATER HOSES REPLACEMENT (Con't).

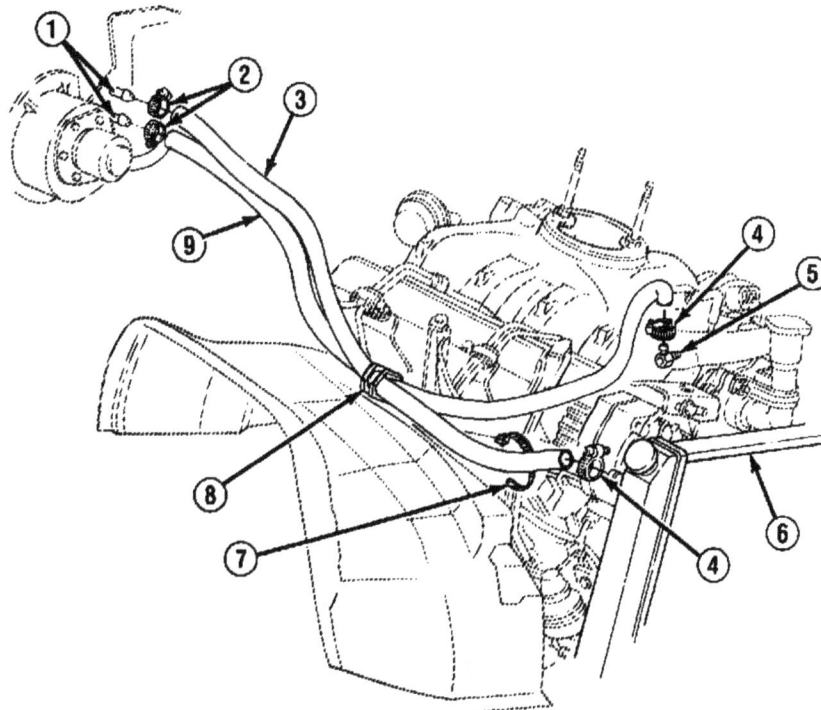

FOLLOW-ON TASKS:

- Refill cooling system. (See paragraph 3-30)
- Install rear battery. (See paragraph 4-39)
- Check operation of heater.

TA49964

10-14. HEATER CONTROL REPLACEMENT.

This task covers: a.   Removal   b. Installation

INITIAL SETUP:

Equipment Condition

• Instrument cluster plate removed. (See paragraph 4-7)

| a. REMOVAL |

1.   Remove 4 screws (7) and pull out heater control assembly (6).

2.   Remove nut (4) and disconnect defroster cable (3) from upper control arm (5) and heater control base (2). Remove nut (10) and disconnect temperature cable (9) from lower control arm (8) and heater control base.

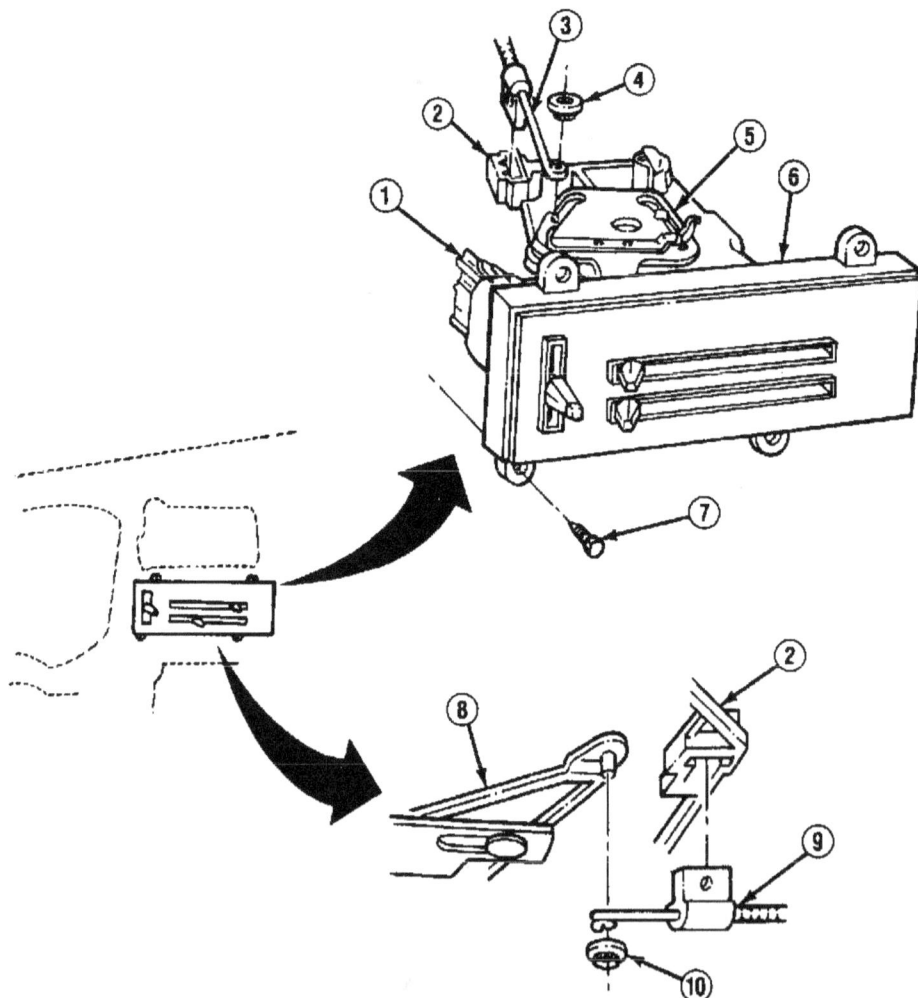

TA49965

10-14. HEATER CONTROL REPLACEMENT (Con't).

3.   Disconnect wiring harness (11) from blower switch (1). Disconnect wiring harness lead (12) and indicator bulb (13) from heater control assembly (6). Remove heater control assembly.

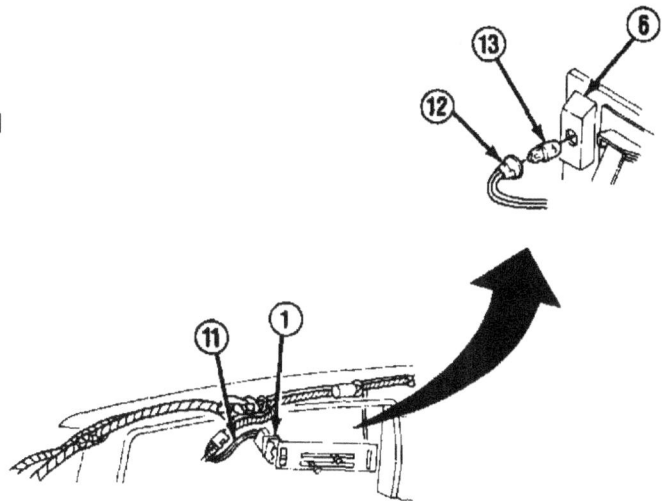

---

b.   INSTALLATION

1.   Connect indicator bulb (13) and wiring harness lead (12) to heater control assembly (6). Connect wiring harness (11) to blower switch (1).

2.   Connect temperature cable (9) to lower control arm (8) and heater control base (2), and install nut (10). Connect defroster cable (3) to upper control arm (5) and heater control base, and install nut (4).

3.   Install heater control assembly (6) with 4 screws (7).

FOLLOW-ON TASKS:

• Install instrument cluster plate, (See paragraph 4-7)

TA49966

Section III. CARGO BODY MAINTENANCE

10-15. CARGO BODY MAINTENANCE INDEX.

10-16. ENDGATE REPLACEMENT (M1008 AND M1008A1).

This task covers: a. Removal b. Installation

INITIAL SETUP:

Personnel Required
 • MOS   63B (2)

---

    a.   REMOVAL

NOTE

- • If removing endgate (10), perform steps 1 and 2.
- • If removing plates (1), perform steps 1 and 4.
- • If removing latch assemblies (9) and handle assembly (13), perform steps 1 and 7 through 14.

1.   Lower endgate (10) and pull up on 2 plates (1). Raise endgate partway and disconnect plates from latch assemblies (9).

2.   Lift right bushing (11) out of right trunnion (16). Lift left bushing (11) out of left trunnion (16) and remove endgate (10).

3.   Remove 4 bolts (17) and remove 2 trunnions (16).

4.   Remove 4 bolts (2) and remove 2 plates (1).

5.   Remove 4 screws (4) and 4 bumpers (3 and 5).

6.   Remove 4 bolts (15) and remove 2 bushings (11).

7.   Remove 3 bolts (6) and loosen handle assembly (13).

8.   Disconnect right rod (7) from clip (12) at handle assembly (13).

9.   Remove 2 bolts (14) at left latch assembly (9). Disconnect rod (7) and remove left latch assembly.

10.   Remove handle assembly (13) and left rod (7).

11.   Disconnect left rod (7) from clip (12) at handle assembly (13).

12.   Remove 2 bolts (14) and remove right latch assembly (9) and rod (7).

13.   Remove rod (7) from right latch assembly (9).

14.   Remove 2 insulators (8) from 2 rods (7).

10-16. ENDGATE REPLACEMENT (M1008 AND M1008A1) (Con't).

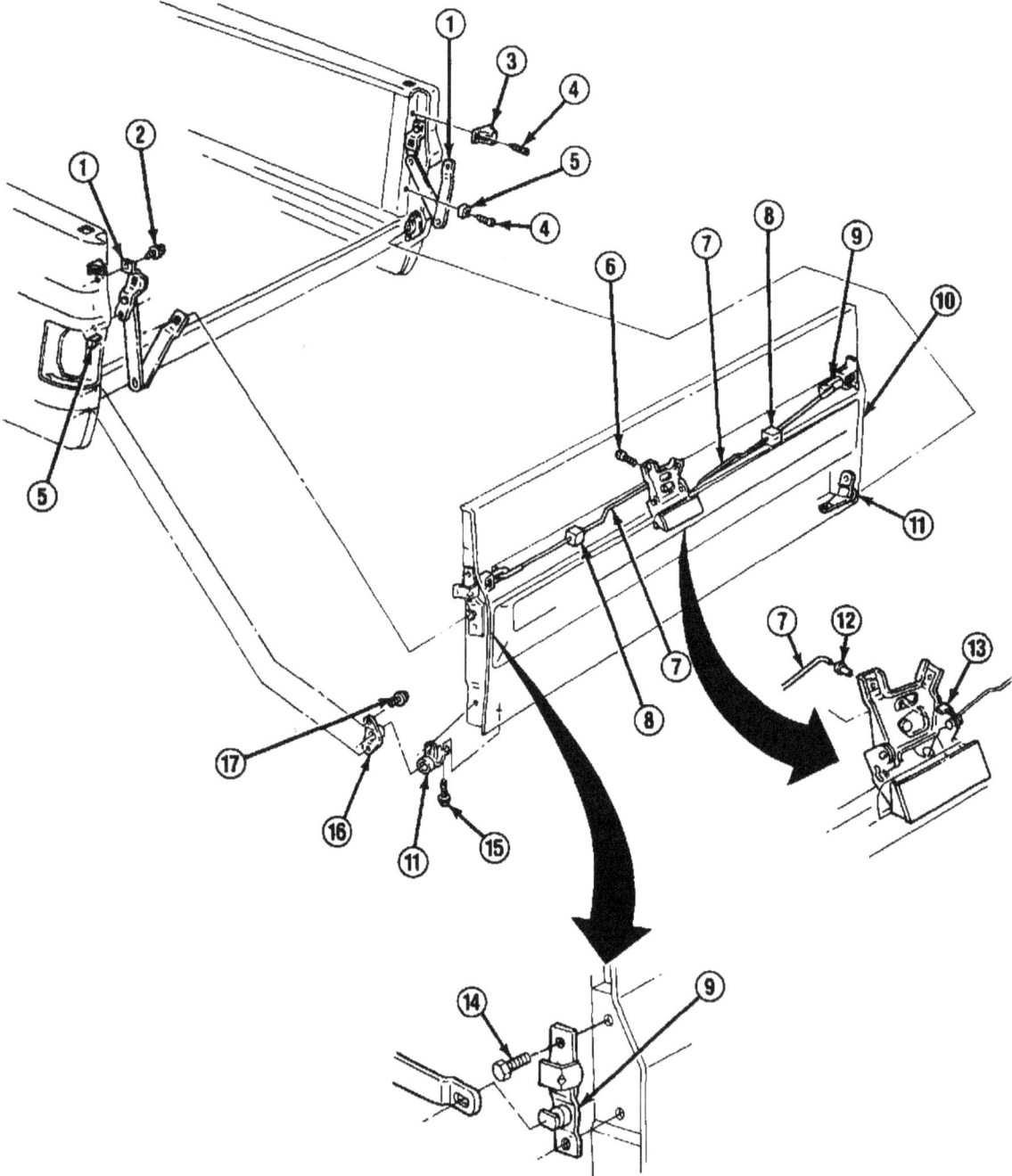

TA49967

10-16. ENDGATE REPLACEMENT (M1008 AND M1008A1) (Con't).

| b. | INSTALLATION |

NOTE

- **If installing   plates (1), perform steps 10 and 14.**
- **If installing   endgate (10), perform steps 13 and 14.**
- **If installing   latch assemblies (9) and handle assembly (13), perform steps 1-8.**

1.   Install 2 insulators (8)   to rods (7).

2.   Install right rod (7) to   right latch assembly (9).

3.   Install right latch assembly (9) and attached right rod (7) with 2 bolts (14).

4.   Install left rod (7) to handle assembly (13) at clip (12).

5.   Install left rod (7) and handle assembly (13) through handle assembly hole in endgate (10).

6.   Position left latch assembly (9) and connect to left rod (7). Install left latch assembly with 2 bolts (14) .

7.   Connect right rod (7) to handle assembly (13) at clip (12).

8.   Install handle assembly (13) with 3 bolts (6).

9.   Install 4 bumpers (3 and 5) with 4 screws (4).

10.   Install 2 plates (1) with 4 bolts (2).

11.   Install 2 trunnions (16) with 4 bolts (17).

12.   Install 2 bushings (11) with 4 bolts (15).

13.   Position left bushing (11) onto left trunnion (16) and right bushing (11) onto right trunnion (16).

14.   Raise endgate (10) partway and install 2 plates (1) at latch assemblies (9).

10-16. ENDGATE REPLACEMENT (M1008 AND M1008A1) (Con't).

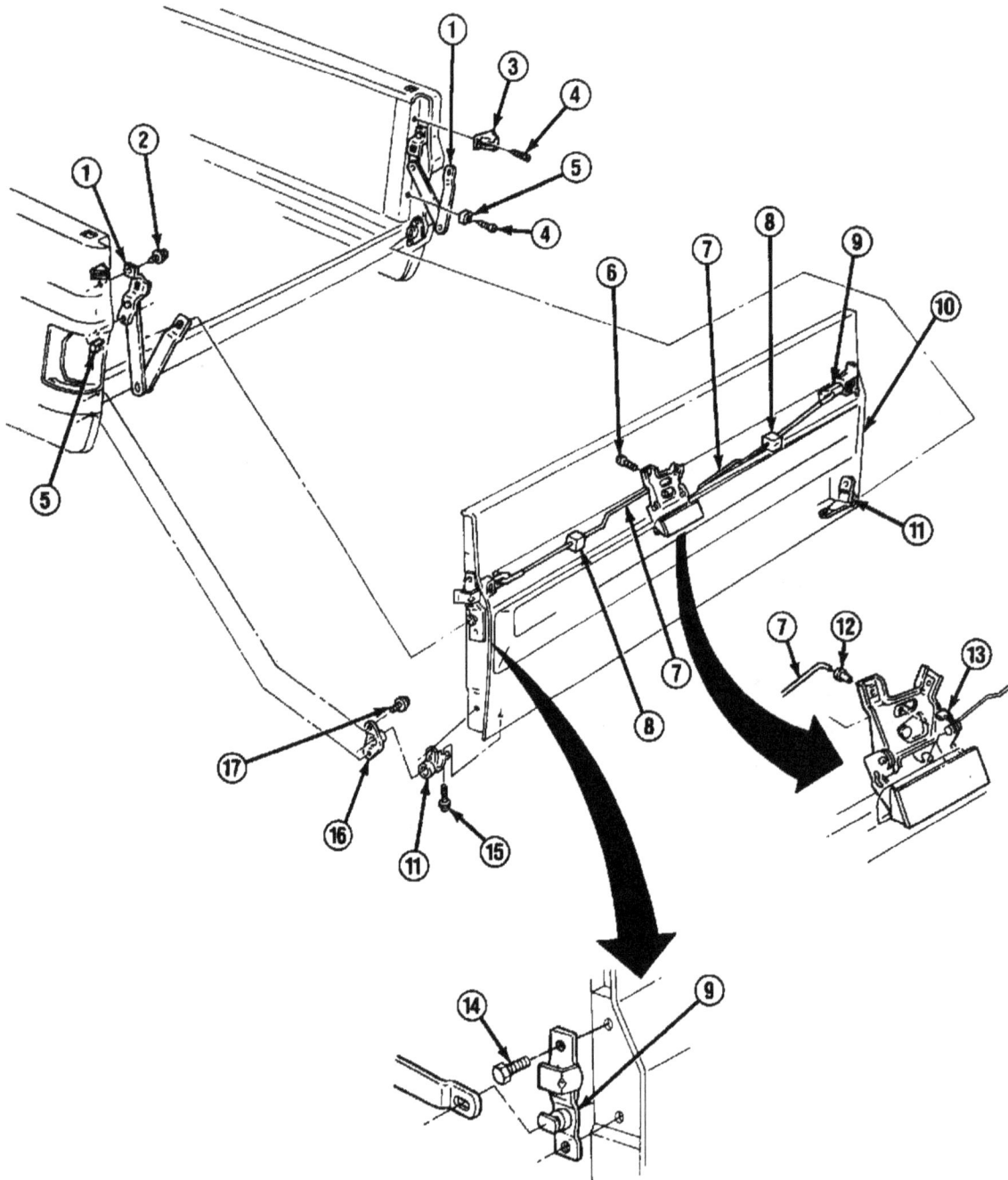

TA49968

10-17. SHELTER TIE-DOWN REPLACEMENT (M1028).

This task covers:
a. Removal
b. Installation

INITIAL SETUP:

Too/s/Test Equipment

• Torque wrench

| a. | **REMOVAL** |

NOTE

• Left and right shelter tie-downs are removed the same way.

• If removing rear shelter tie-downs, perform steps 1-4.

• If removing front shelter tie-downs, perform step 5.

• Nut (13) is tack welded. Remove nut only if threads appear damaged.

1. Remove nut (2) and bolt (7) securing brace (3), bracket (5), and support (6). Remove bolt (1) and brace.

NOTE

Hold bolt (4) while loosening nut (10) to keep bolt from turning.

2. While supporting reinforcement (8), remove 2 nuts (9), nut (10), and reinforcement.

3. Remove bolt (4), bracket (5), and support (6).

4. Remove pad (14) and save for installation. Remove spacer (11) from rear stake pocket (12).

NOTE

Hold bolt (15) while loosening nut (19) to keep bolt from turning.

5. Remove nut (19), bolt (15), and reinforcement (20) from both front stake pockets (12). Remove front bracket (16) and 2 pads (17). Remove spacer (18) from each stake pocket.

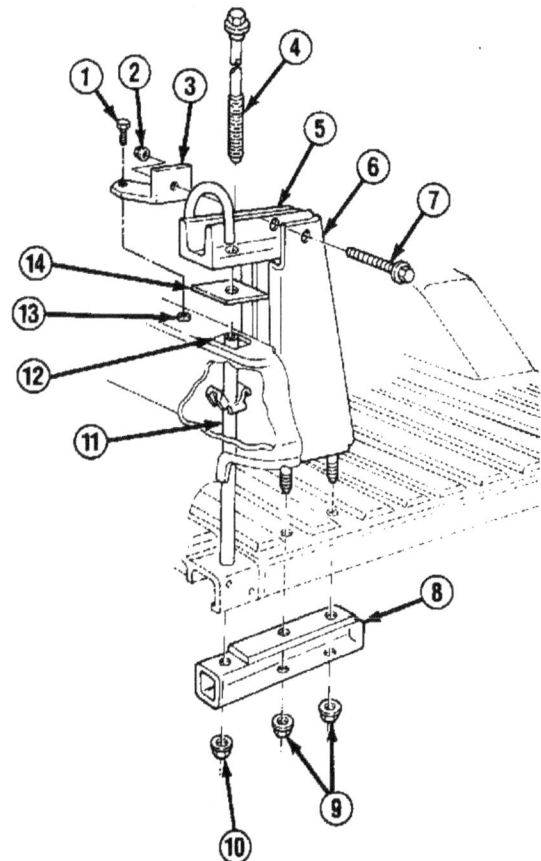

TA49969

10-17. SHELTER TIE-DOWN REPLACEMENT (M1028) (Con't).

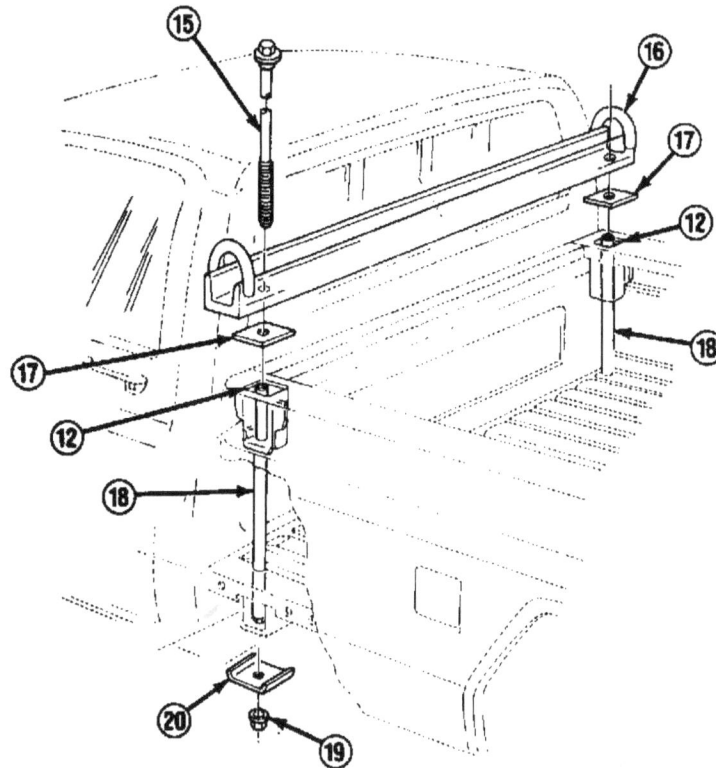

| b. | INSTALLATION |

NOTE

• Left and right shelter tie-downs are installed the same way.

• If installing front shelter tie-downs, perform steps 1 and 2.

• If installing rear shelter tie-downs, perform steps 3-8.

1. Install spacer (18) into each front stake pocket (12). Position 2 pads (17) and front bracket (16).

2. Install 2 bolts (15), 2 reinforcements (20), and 2 nuts (19). Tighten nuts to 50-65 lb.-ft. (68-88 N•m).

3. Install spacer (11) into rear stake pocket (12).

4. Position pad (14) at rear stake pocket (12) and install support (6) into cargo bed of truck.

5. Position bracket (5) at pad (14) and support (6). Thread bolt (4) through hole in pad into rear stake pocket (12).

TA49970

10-17. SHELTER TIE-DOWN REPLACEMENT (M1028) (Con't).

6. Install new nut (13) if removed. Install brace (3) with bolt (1). DO NOT fully tighten bolt.

7. Install bolt (7) and nut (2). Tighten nut to 30-45 lb.-ft. (41-61 N•m). Tighten bolt (1).

NOTE

Hold bolt (4) while tightening nut (10) to keep bolt from turning.

8. Install reinforcement (8), 2 nuts (9), and nut (10). Tighten nuts to 50-65 lb.-ft. (68-88 N•m).

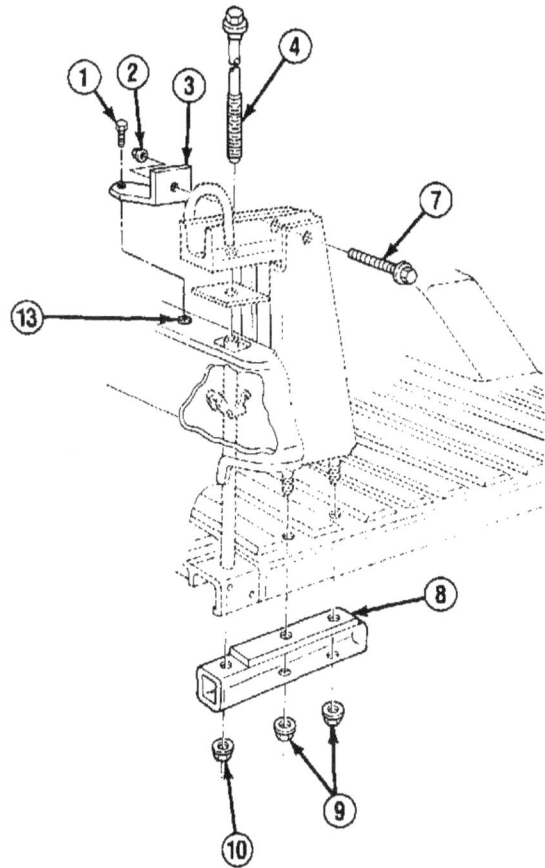

TA49971

10-17.1. INSTRUMENT PAD REPLACEMENT,

This task covers: a. Removal   b. Installation

INITIAL SETUP:

Equipment Condition

• Heater control panel housing removed (if truck is equipped with winterization kits). (See paragraph 11-4)

---

a.	**REMOVAL**

1. If present, remove 4 screws (3), washers (2), and reinforcement (4) from instrument pad assembly (1).

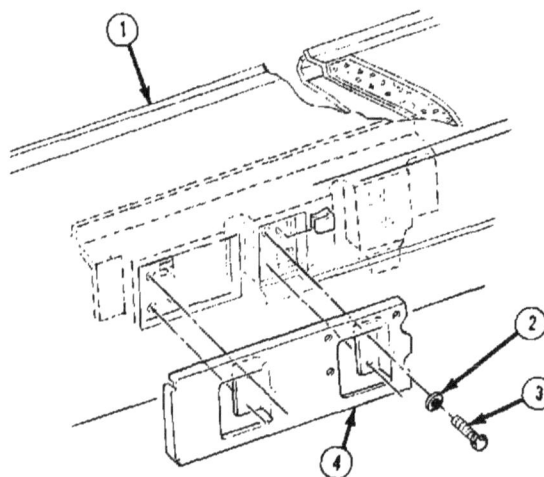

10-17.1. INSTRUMENT PAD REPLACEMENT (Con't).

2. Remove 4 screws (8) and screw (6), Lift up on instrument pad assembly (1) and remove. If damaged, or if replacing instrument pad assembly, remove 6 retainers (5). Remove any damaged push nuts (7) from instrument panel assembly (9).

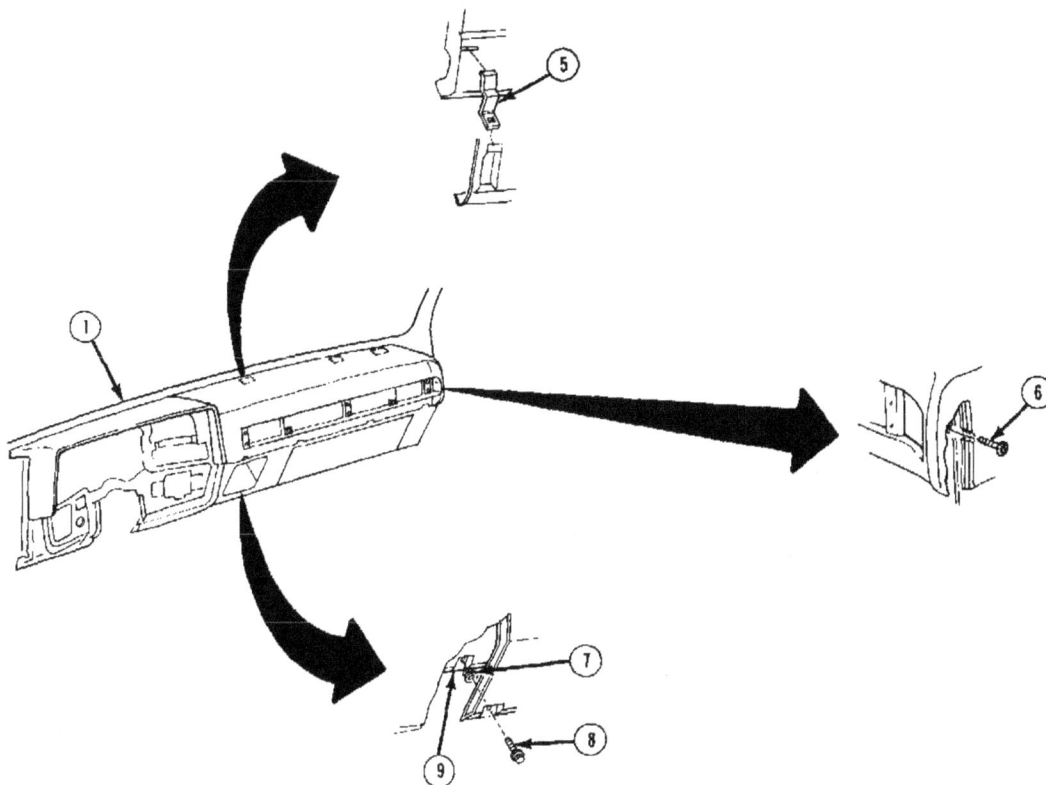

| **b.** | **INSTALLATION** |

1. Replace any removed push nuts (7) at instrument panel assembly (9).

2. If removed, install 6 retainers (5) to instrument pad assembly (1). Position instrument pad assembly and snap into place, Install 4 screws (8) and screw (6).

TA701842

10-17.1. INSTRUMENT PAD REPLACEMENT (Con't).

3.   If removed, install reinforcement (4) to instrument pad assembly (1) with 4 washers (2) and screws (3).

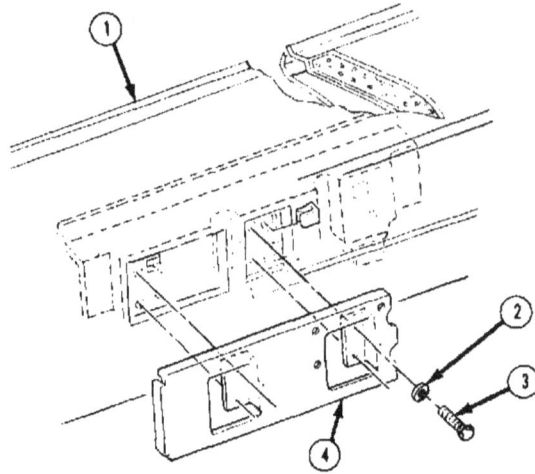

FOLLOW-ON TASKS:

• Install heater control panel housing if removed, (See paragraph 11-4)

TA701843

10-18. CARGO BENCH SEAT AND SEATBELT REPLACEMENT (ALL EXCEPT M1009).

This task covers:	a. Removal	b. Installation

INITIAL SETUP:

Tools/Test Equipment
 • Torque wrench

---

a. **REMOVAL**

NOTE

 • **If removing**   **seatbelt assemblies (1 and 7), perform steps 1-4.**

 • **If removing**   **bench seat (2), perform steps 4-7.**

 • **If removing**   **seat adjustment assemblies, perform steps 5-8.**

 • **Bolts (4 and 6) may have plugs covering them. Save for installation.**

1.   Pry cover down to expose bolt (3) and remove bolt. Remove bolt (4) at seatbelt assembly (1) retractor.

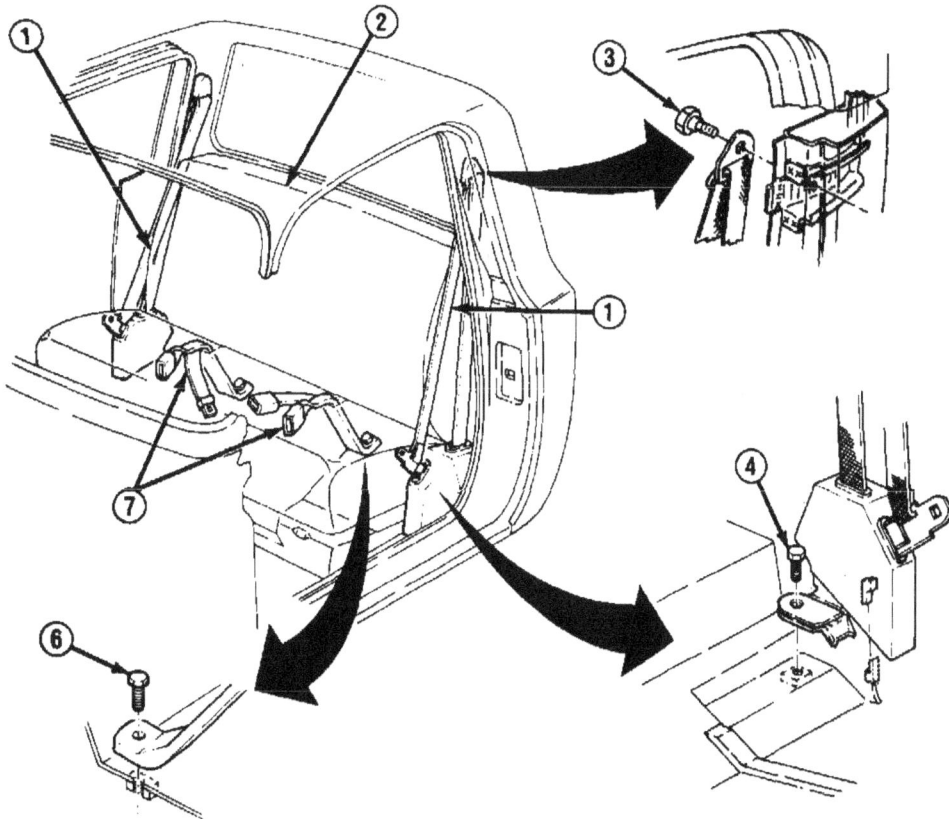

TA49972

10-18. CARGO BENCH SEAT AND SEATBELT REPLACEMENT (ALL EXCEPT M1009) (Con't).

NOTE

Step 2 only applies to left side.

2. Disconnect wire assembly (5) from retractor.

3. Remove seatbelt assembly (1).

4. Move bench seat (2) forward to gain access to bolt (6). Remove bolt and remove seatbelt assembly (7) through bench seat.

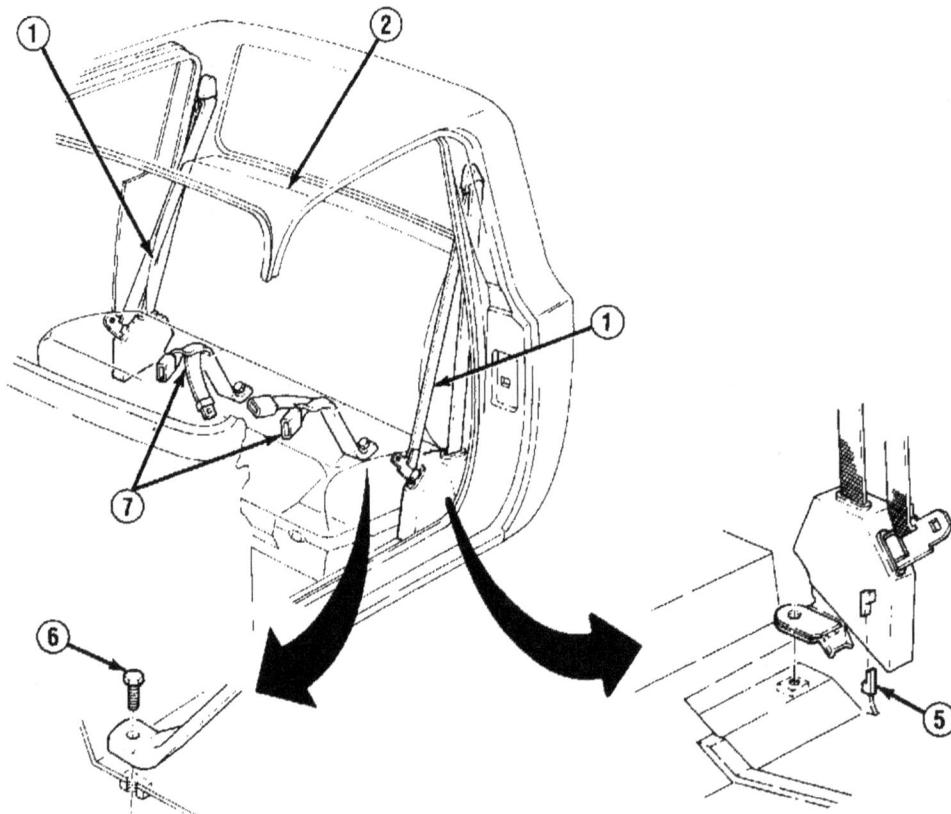

TA49973

10-18. CARGO BENCH SEAT AND SEATBELT REPLACEMENT (ALL EXCEPT MI 009) (Con't).

NOTE

- Both seatbelt assemblies (7) must be removed to remove bench seat (2).

- Ž Bolts (8) may have covers. Remove these as required and save for installation.

5. Remove 4 bolts (8) at 2 seat adjustment assemblies (12). Remove bench seat (2) and seat adjustment assemblies from truck.

6. Remove wire assembly (11) from bench seat (2) and from 2 seat adjustment assemblies (12).

7. Remove 6 bolts (9) and 2 seat adjustment assemblies (12) from bench seat (2).

8. Remove 2 springs (10) from each seat adjustment assembly (12). Note position of springs for installation.

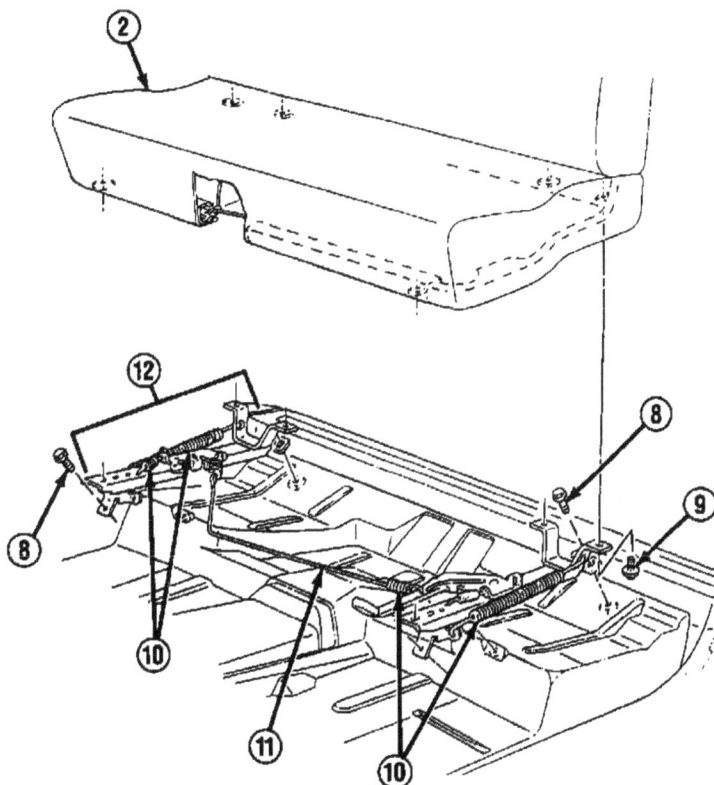

TA49974

10-18. CARGO BENCH SEAT AND SEATBELT REPLACEMENT (ALL EXCEPT M1009) (Con't).

b. INSTALLATION

NOTE

• If installing   bench seat (2) and seat adjustment assemblies (12), perform steps 1-5.

• If installing seatbelt assemblies (1 and 7), perform steps 5-8.

1.   Install 2 springs (10) at each seat adjustment assembly (12).

2.   Install 2 seat adjustment assemblies (12) to bench seat (2) with 6 bolts (9).

3.   Install wire assembly (11) to bench seat (2) and to 2 seat adjustment assemblies (12).

4.   Install bench seat (2) and attached seat adjustment assemblies (12) to truck with 4 bolts (8). Install bolt covers as required.

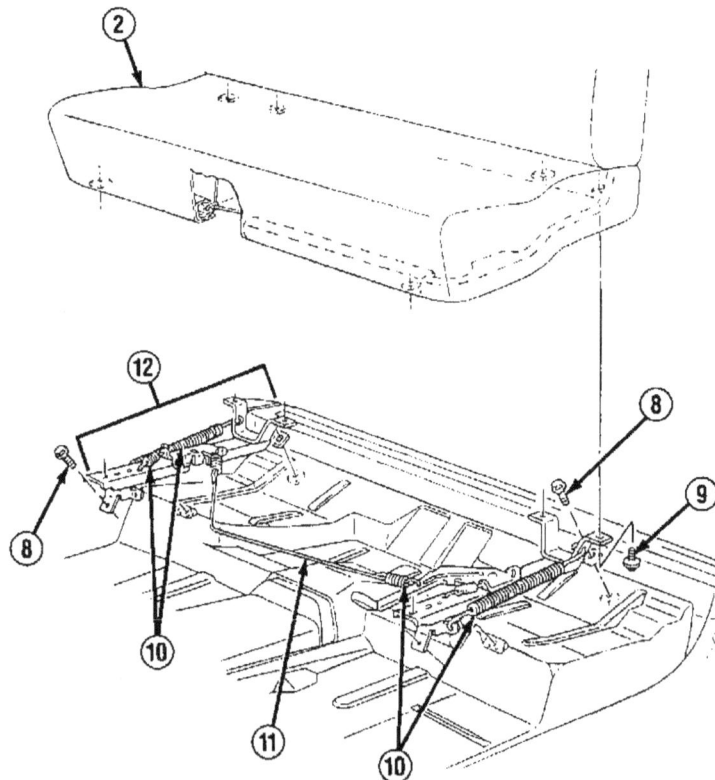

5.   Move bench seat (2) forward. Position seatbelt assembly (7) through bench seat and install to cab floor with bolt (6). Tighten bolt to 40 lb.-ft. (54 N•m). Install plug as required.

TA49975

10-18. CARGO BENCH SEAT AND SEATBELT REPLACEMENT (ALL EXCEPT M1009) (Con't).

6. Install seatbelt assembly (1) to door pillar with bolt (3). Tighten bolt to 40 lb.-ft. (54 N•m). Install cover over bolt.

NOTE

Step 7 only applies to left side.

7. Position seatbelt assembly (1) retractor and connect wire assembly (5).

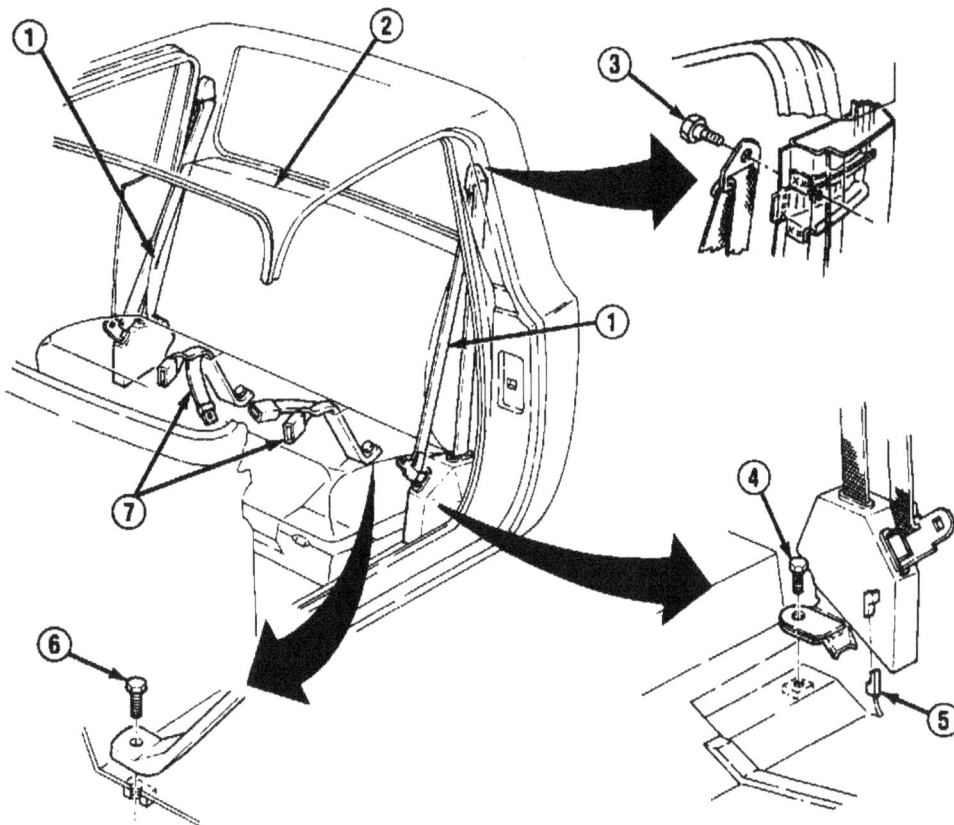

8. Install seatbelt assembly (1) retractor with bolt (4). Tighten bolt to 40 lb.-ft. (54 N•m). Install plug as required.

TA49976

10-19. CARGO COVER AND FRAME MAINTENANCE (M1008 AND M1008A1).

This task covers:	a. Remova l b. Repair	c. Installation

INITIAL SETUP:

Materials/Parts

● Locknuts (as required)
● RTV sealant (Item 41, Appendix C)

Personnel Required

• MOS 63B (2)

---

a.	**REMOVAL**

NOTE

- If removing   cargo cover (1), perform steps 1-5.

- If removing   cargo cover frame assembly components, perform steps 1-13.

- If removing   front rail assemblies (23), perform steps 1, 3, 14, and 15.

- If removing   rear rail assembly (12), perform steps 3, 4, and 16.

- If removing   side rail assemblies (10), perform steps 1-10, and 17.

1. Inside cargo area, detach cargo cover (1) from all turnbuttons (4).

2. Inside cargo area, remove 4 straps (2) along front and rear roof bows (3).

3. Remove 4 straps (5) from rail assemblies.

4. On outside, detach remaining edges from all turnbuttons (4).

5. Remove cargo cover (1).

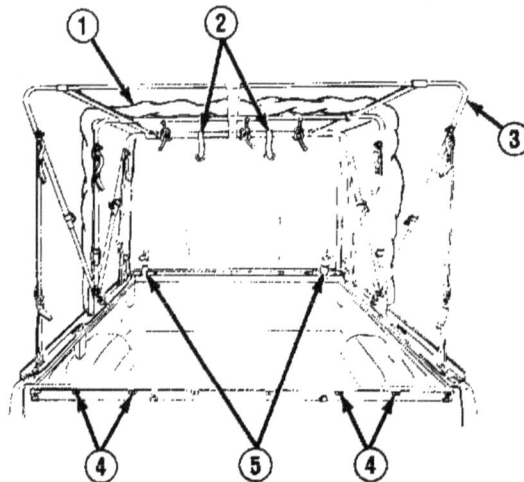

TA49977

10-19. CARGO COVER AND FRAME MAINTENANCE (M1008 AND M1008A1) (Con't).

6.   At each corner, remove bow strap (11) from side rail assembly (10).

7.   Fold 3 roof bows (3) forward until they rest on roof of truck cab.

8.   At bow hinge bracket (15), remove nut (18), 2 washers (14), and bolt (13). Remove strut (17) and 2 bushings (16) from bow hinge bracket.

9.   Remove 3 roof bows (3) with 6 attached struts (17).

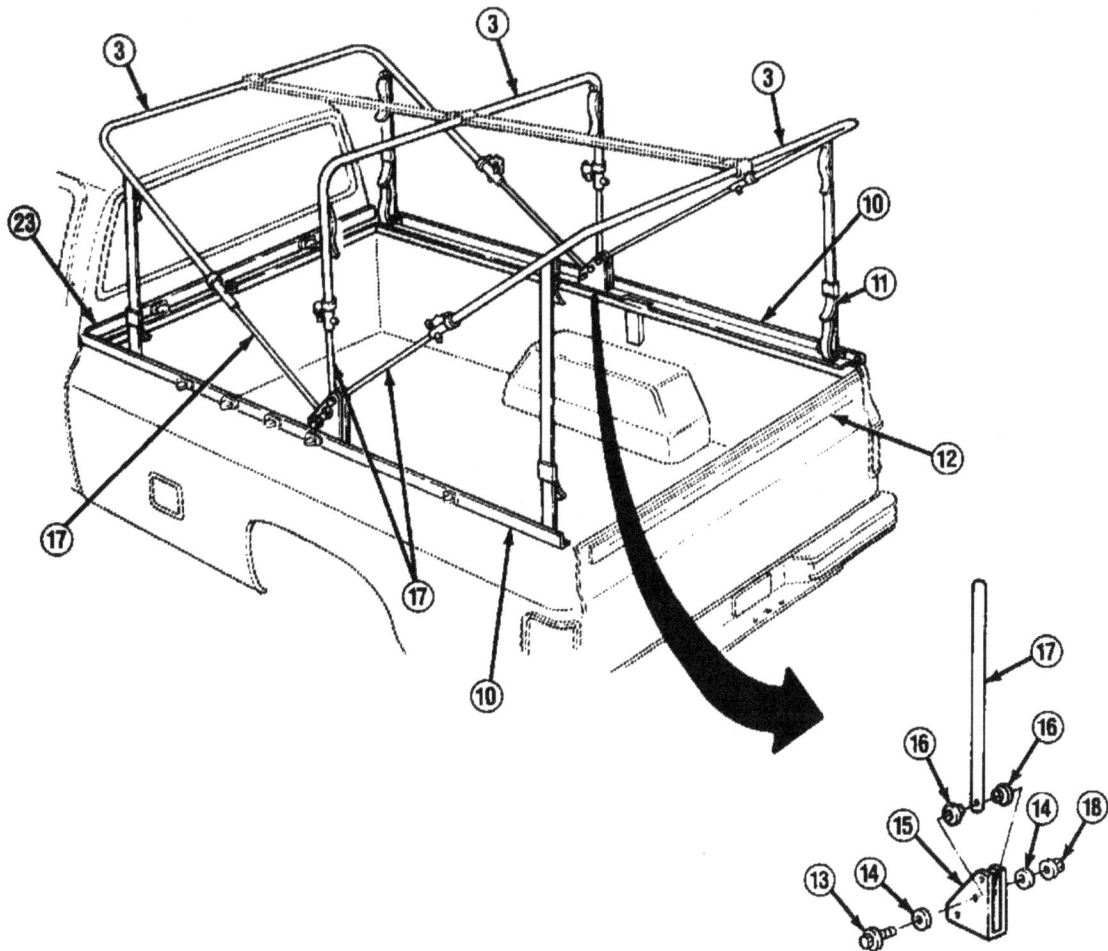

TA49978

10-19. CARGO COVER AND FRAME MAINTENANCE (M1008 AND M1008A1) (Con't).

10. Remove 2 nuts (26), washers (25), bolts (24), and bow hinge bracket (15).

11. Remove nut (8), bolt (7), and bow strap (11) or strap (9) from roof bow (3).

12. Pull out pin (21) and disconnect strut (17) from roof bow (3). Remove nut (20), screw (19), and retainer (22) from roof bow.

13. Remove roof strap (6) from roof bows (3).

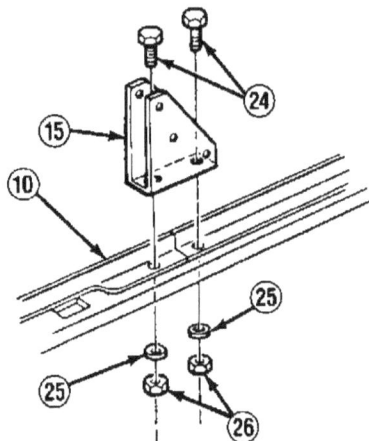

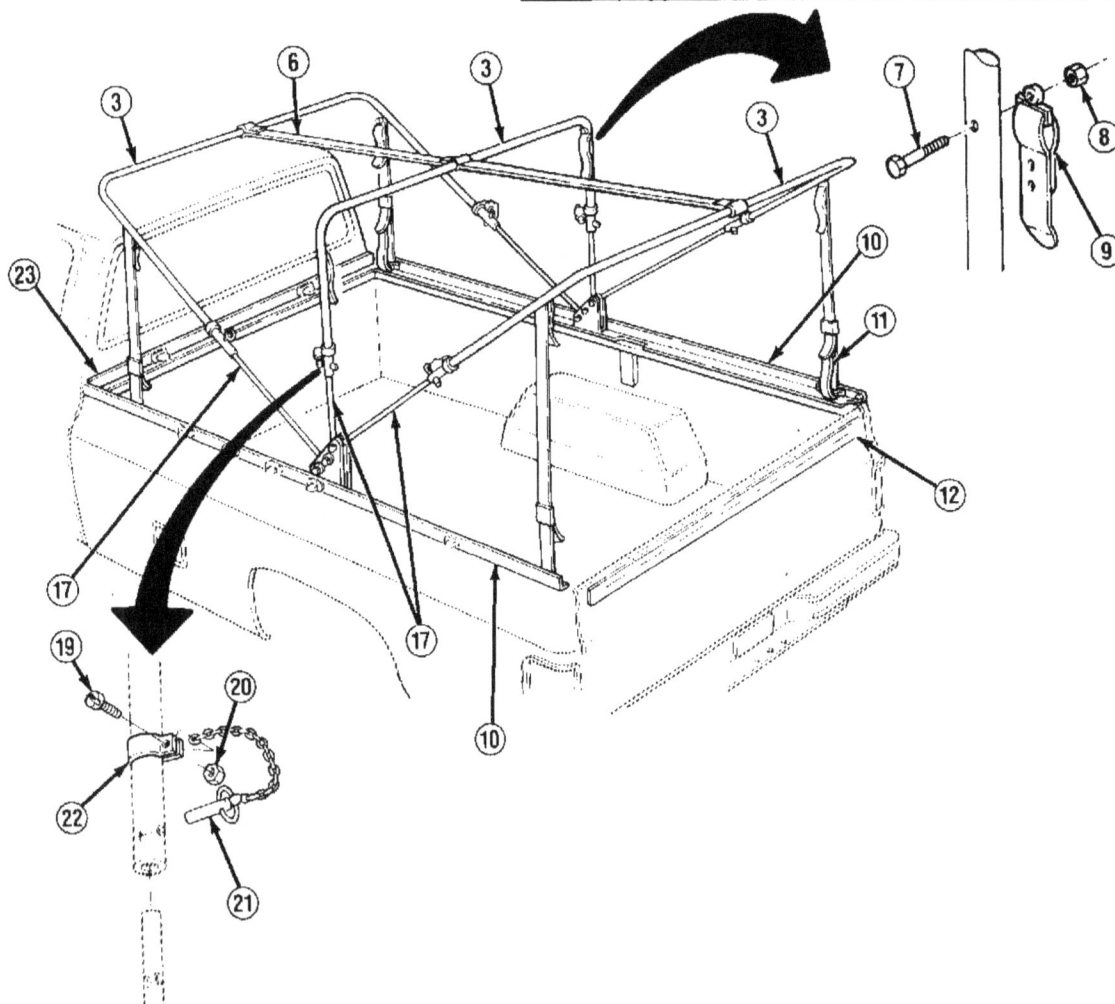

TA49979

10-19. CARGO COVER AND FRAME MAINTENANCE (M1008 AND M1008A1) (Con't).

14. Remove 2 bolts (27) and front rail assembly (23). Scrape off old RTV sealant from rail assembly and from truck.

15. Remove and discard 2 tube anchor nuts (28) if damaged.

16. Remove 4 bolts (27) and rear rail assembly (12). Scrape off old RTV sealant from rear rail assembly and from truck. Remove and discard 4 tube anchor nuts (28) if damaged.

17. Remove 2 nuts (26), washers (25), bolts (24), and side rail assembly (10). Scrape off old RTV sealant from side rail assembly and from truck.

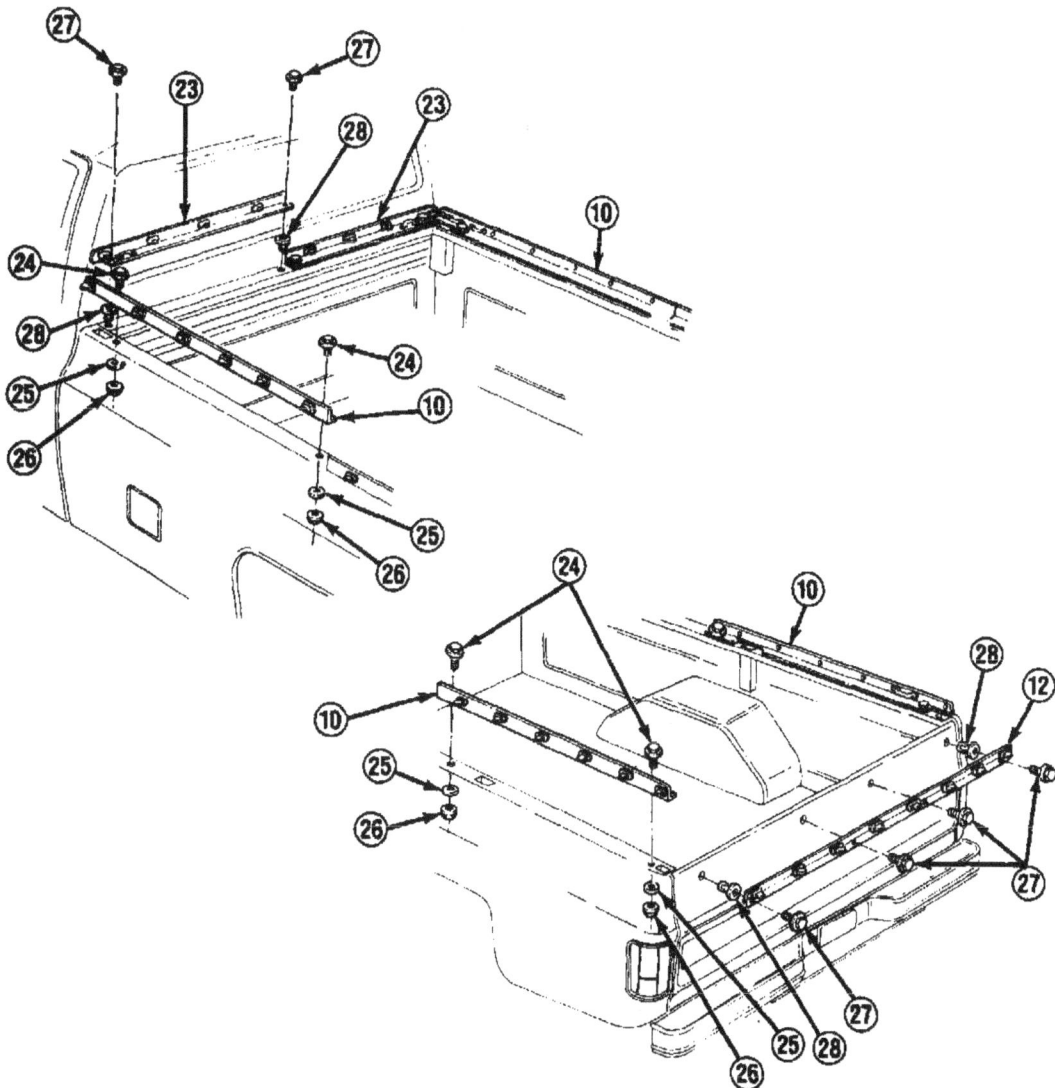

TA49980

10-19. CARGO COVER AND FRAME MAINTENANCE (M1008 AND M1008A1) (Con't),

b. REPAIR

NOTE
All rail assemblies (10, 12, and 23) are repaired in same way.

1. Position rail assembly (10, 12, or 23) in vise.

2. Grind back of broken turnbutton (4) until flush with surface of rail.

3. Using a punch, drive broken turnbutton (4) out of rail assembly (10, 12, or 23).

4. Install new turnbutton (4) and install new locknut on back of turnbutton.

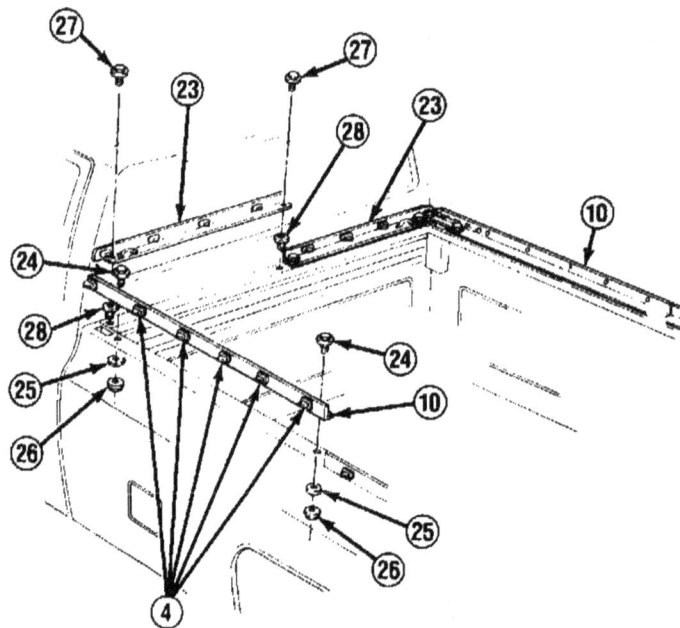

TA49981

10-19. CARGO COVER AND FRAME MAINTENANCE (M1008 AND M1008A1) (Con't).

| c. | INSTALLATION |

CAUTION

DO NOT overtighten bolts (24) in nuts (26) or nuts will break.

NOTE

- If installing side rail assemblies (10), perform steps 1 and 11.

- If installing rear rail assembly (12), perform steps 2, 3, and 13.

- If installing front rail assemblies (23), perform steps 4, 5, and 13.

- If installing cargo cover frame assembly components,   perform steps 5-15.

- If installing cargo cover, perform steps 12-15.

1. Apply RTV sealant and install side rail assembly (10) with 2 bolts (24), washers (25), and nuts (26). Be careful to install each side rail assembly so that built-in handles are at front and rear corners.

2. Install 4 new tube anchor nuts (28) in endgate as required.

3. Apply RTV sealant and install rear rail assembly (12) with 4 bolts (27).

4. Install 2 new tube anchor nuts (28) as required. Apply RTV sealant and install front rail assembly (23) with 2 bolts (27).

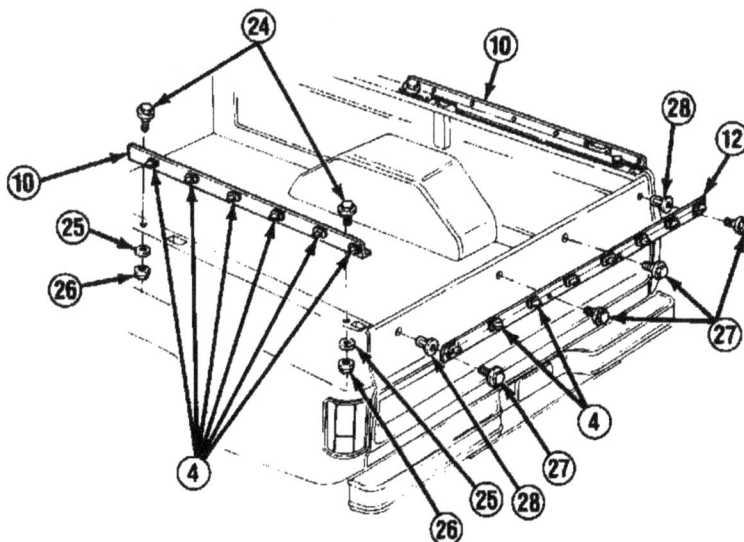

TA49982

10-19. CARGO COVER AND FRAME MAINTENANCE (M1008 AND M1008A1) (Con't).

5. Install roof strap (6) on roof bows (3) as required,

6. Install bow strap (11) or strap (9) to roof bow (3) with bolt (7) and nut (8).

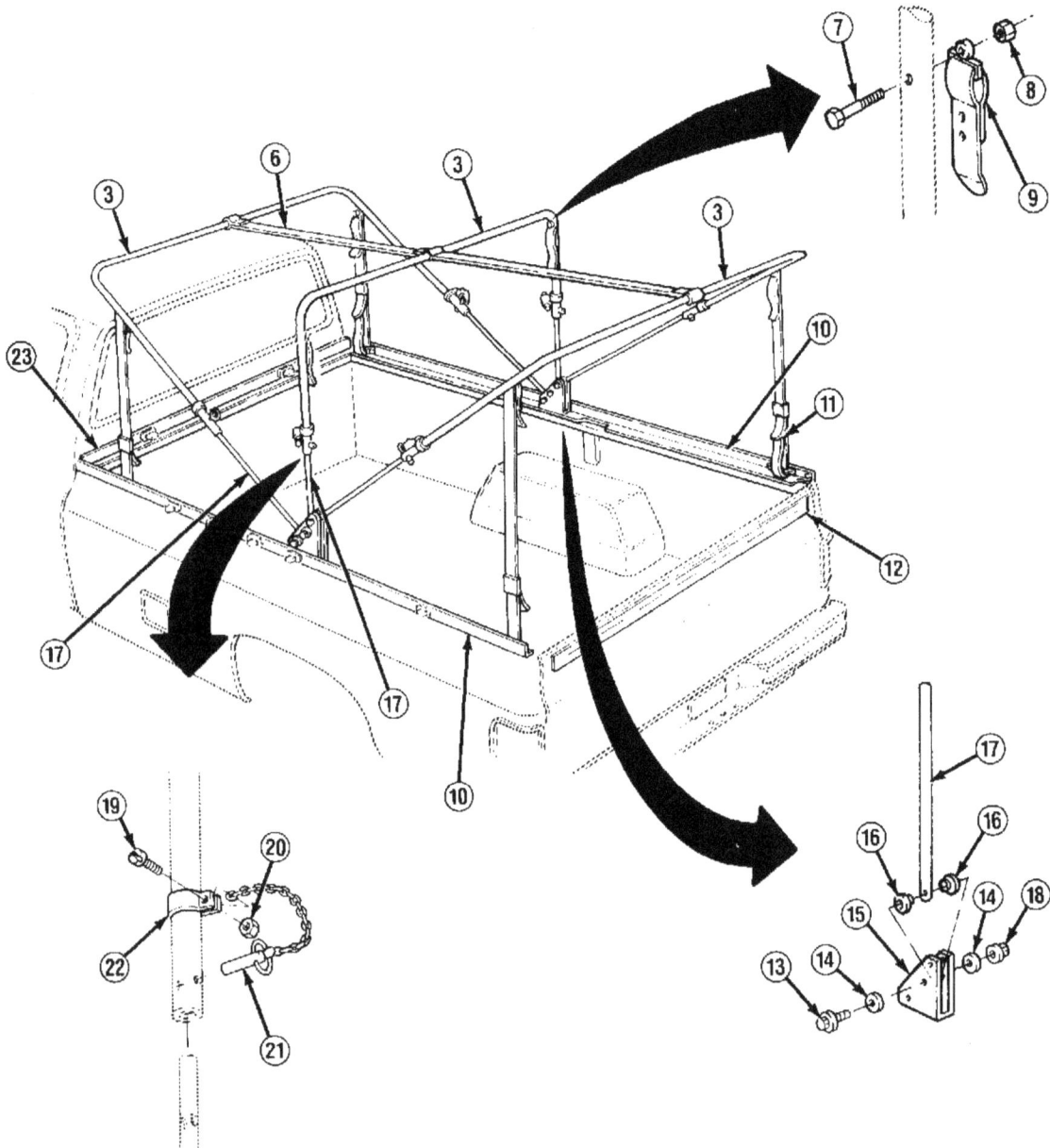

TA49983

10-19. CARGO COVER AND FRAME MAINTENANCE (M1008 AND M1008A1) (Con't).

7. Install bow hinge bracket (15) with 2 bolts (24), washers (25), and nuts (26), Install front bolt, washer, and nut through rearmost hole of front side rail assembly (10). Install rear bolt, washer, and nut through frontmost hole of rear side rai l assembly.

8. Install retainer (22) to end of roof bow (3) with screw (19) and nut (20).

9. Install strut (17) to roof bow (3) with pin (21) through holes in roof bow and strut.

10. Place 6 assembled struts (17) and 3 roof bows (3) folded forward over top of truck cab. Install each strut at bow hinge bracket (15) with bolt (13), 2 washers (14), nut (18), and 2 bushings (16). Unfold all 3 roof bows.

11. Install 4 bow straps (11) to corner handles of side rail assemblies (10).

12. Install cargo cover (1) over cargo cover frame assembly.

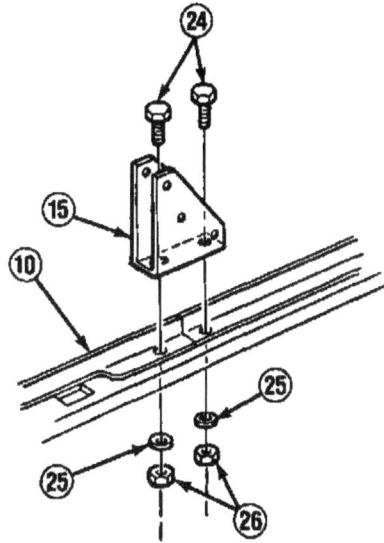

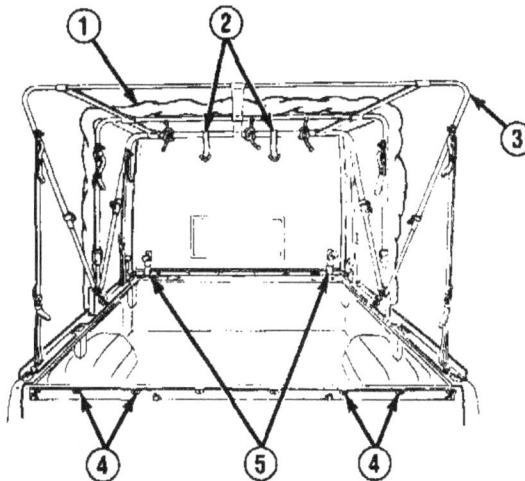

13. Secure 4 straps (5) to handles at front and rear rail assemblies (12 and 23).

14. Secure top of cargo cover (1) to front and rear roof bows (3) with 4 straps (2).

15. On inside and outside, secure bottom edges of cargo cover (1) to turnbuttons (4).

TA49984

Section IV. UTILITY TRUCK BODY MAINTENANCE

10-20. UTILITY TRUCK BODY MAINTENANCE INDEX.

10-21. ENDGATE MAINTENANCE (M1009).

This task covers:	a. Removal	c. Assembly
	b. Disassembly	d. Installation

INITIAL SETUP:

Equipment Condition

● **Endgate window removed.
(See paragraph 10-22)**

Tools/Test Equipment

● **Torque wrench**
● **Screwdriver bit set, J-29843**

Materials/Parts

● **Three lockwashers**

Personnel Required

● **MOS 63B (2) (if removing endgate)**

---

a. REMOVAL

NOTE

● **If removing endgate (8), perform steps   1-3.**

● **Support   endgate (8) on suitable   support   when performing
maintenance.**

● **If removing run channel, latch rods, handle, or control assembly,
perform DISASSEMBLY steps as required.**

1. **Remove   nut (12), lockwasher (11), and stud (9) from each frame extension (10). Discard
lockwashers.**

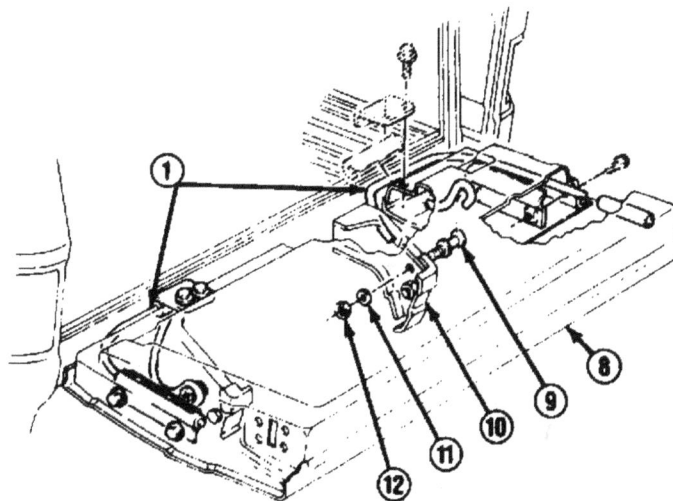

TA49985

10-21. ENDGATE MAINTENANCE (M1009) (Con't).

2.   Remove 2 bolts (1 6), disconnect 2 supports (15), and remove 2 spacers (14) and washers (13).

CAUTION

Carefully guide out torque rods   (1) when removing endgate (8). Failure to
follow this caution may result in   damage to torque rods.

3.   Remove 8 bolts   (19) attaching 2 hinge   assemblies (18) to floor panel. Remove endgate (8).

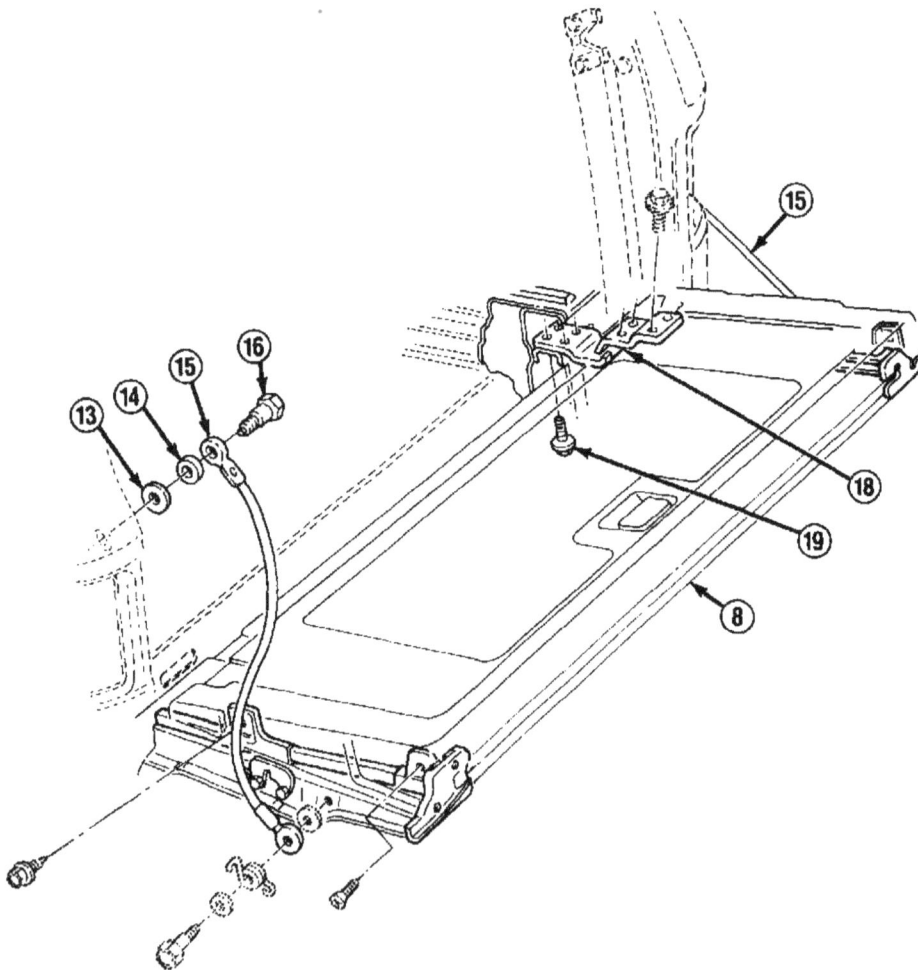

TA49986

10-21. ENDGATE MAINTENANCE (M1009) (Con't).

| b. DISASSEMBLY |

NOTE

• Opposite side is disassembled in same way.

• If removing run channel (25), perform step 1.

• If removing torque rod (1), perform steps 1 and 4.

• If removing latch rods (30) or latch assembly (27), perform steps 5 and 6.

• If removing handle, perform step 7.

• If removing control assembly, perform steps 5, 7, 8, and 9.

1.   Remove 2 screws (20). Twist run channel (25) to clear window opening and remove run channel.

2.   Remove bolt (24), washer (23), spring (22), support (15), and washer (21).

3.   Remove 4 bolts (17) and hinge assembly (18).

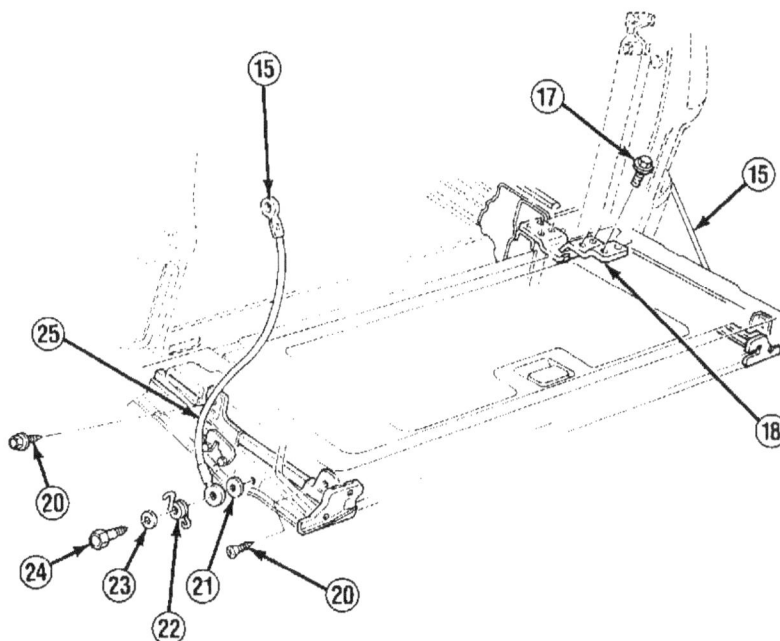

TA49987

10-21. ENDGATE MAINTENANCE (M1009) (Con't).

4. Remove 4 bolts (4) and 2 brackets (3), Remove 4 bolts (5). Remove 2 torque rods (1) with silencers (2 and 6). Remove 2 torque rod brackets (7).

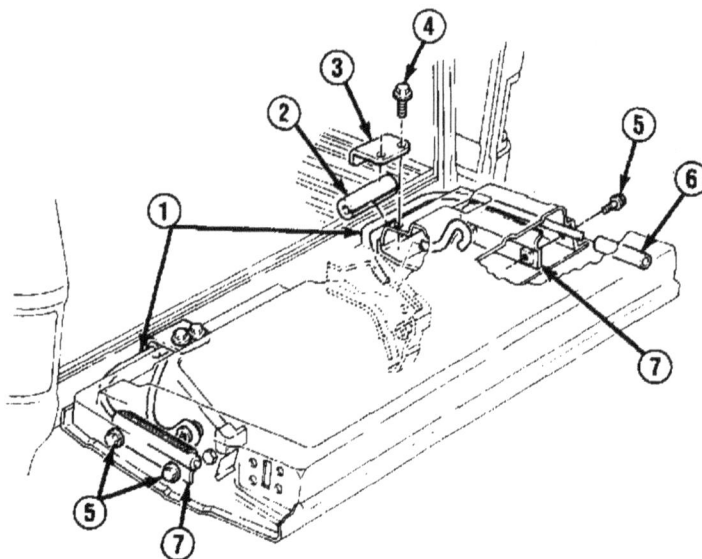

5. Remove clip (31) and disconnect latch rod (30) from control assembly (28).

6. Remove 4 screws (26) and pull out latch assembly (27) with latch rod (30). Remove clip (29) and disconnect latch rod from latch assembly.

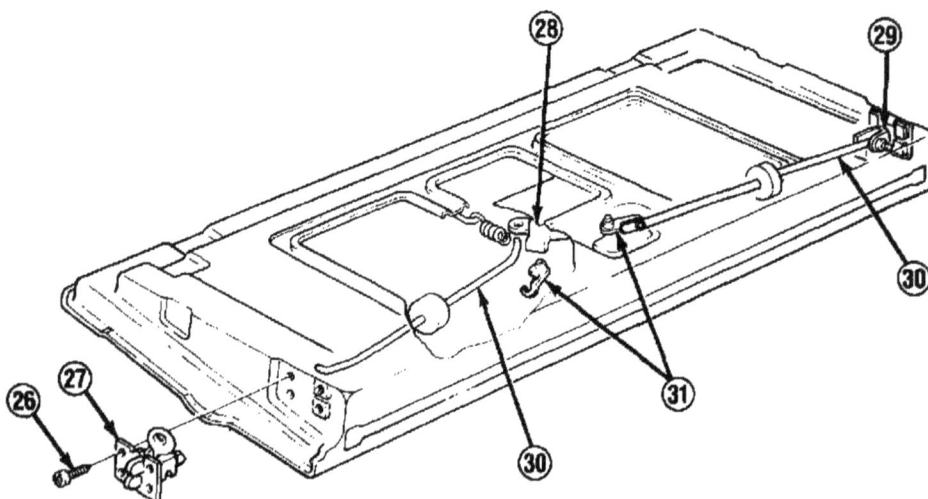

TA49988

10-21. ENDGATE MAINTENANCE (M1009) (Con't).

7. Remove clip (42) and disconnect handle rod (43) from handle (40). Remove 2 screws (41) and handle.

8. Remove 3 screws (39) and control assembly (28). Disconnect handle rod (43) from control assembly.

NOTE

Stop (34) is factory-installed with flanged nut and washer instead of nut (36) and lockwasher (35). Use nut and lockwasher for installation.

9. Remove spring (38). Remove 2 screws (33) and lockout rod (32). Remove nut (36), lockwasher (35), bolt (37), and stop (34). Discard lockwasher.

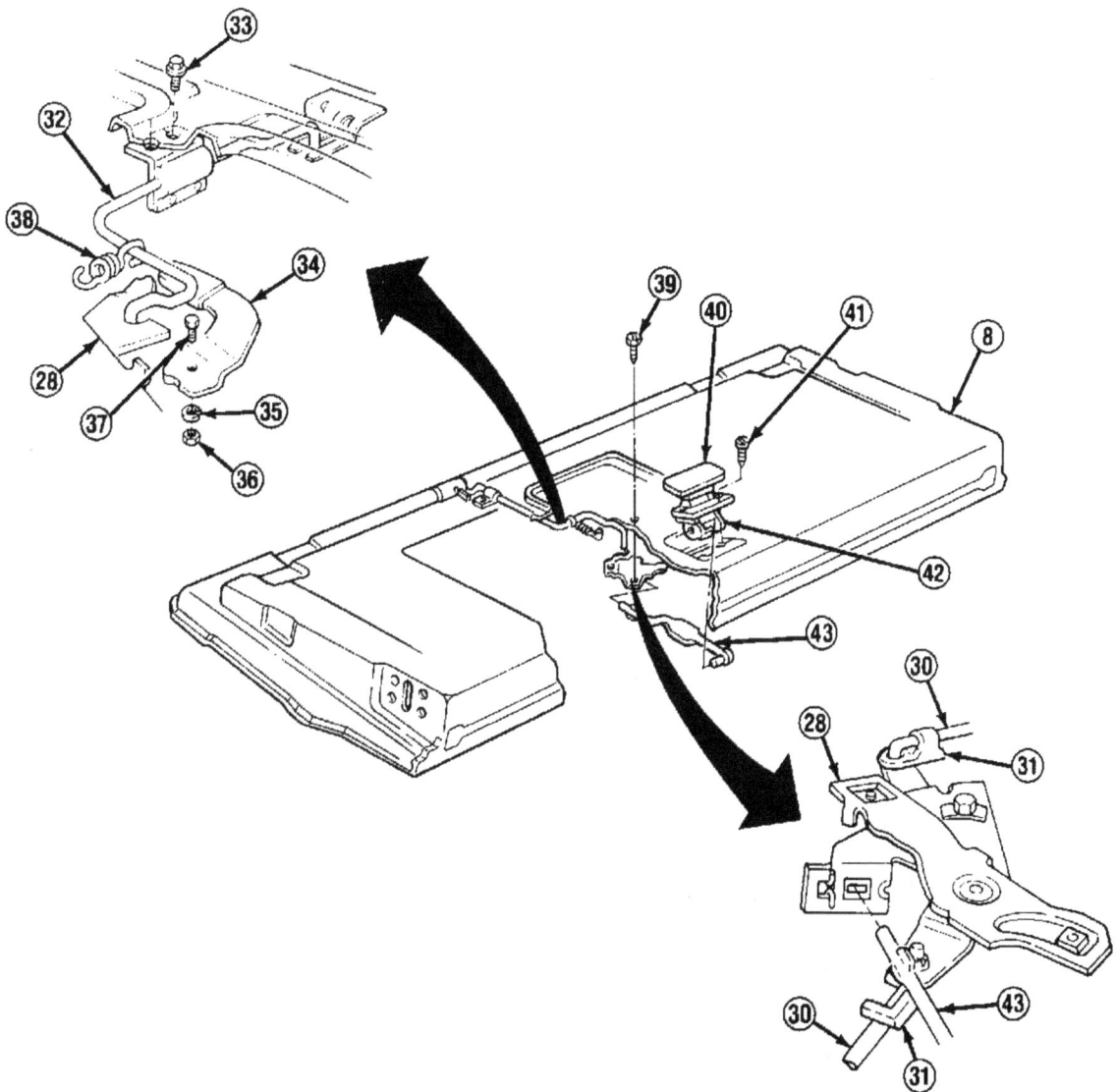

TA49989

10-21. ENDGATE MAINTENANCE (M1009) (Con't).

| c. ASSEMBLY |

NOTE

- If installing control assembly (28), perform steps 1-3, and 5.

- If installing handle (40), perform step 3.

- If installing latch rods (30) or latch assembly (27), perform steps 4 and 5.

- If installing support, perform step 8 and INSTALLATION, step 2 as required.

- If installing torque rod, perform steps 5, 6, and 9.

- If installing hinge assembly, perform step 7 and INSTALLATION, step 1.

- If installing run channel, perform step 9.

1. Install stop (34) on endgate (8) with bolt (37), new lockwasher (35), and nut (36). Install lockout rod (32) with 2 screws (33). Install spring (38).

2. Connect handle rod (43) to control assembly (28). Engage control assembly with lockout rod (32) and install with 3 screws (39).

3. install handie (40) with 2 screws (41). Connect handle rod (43) to handle and install clip (42).

4. Connect latch rod (30) to latch assembly (27) and install clip (29). Position latch rod with latch assembly in endgate (8) and install with 4 screws (26).

5. Connect latch rod (30) to control assembly (28) and install clip (31).

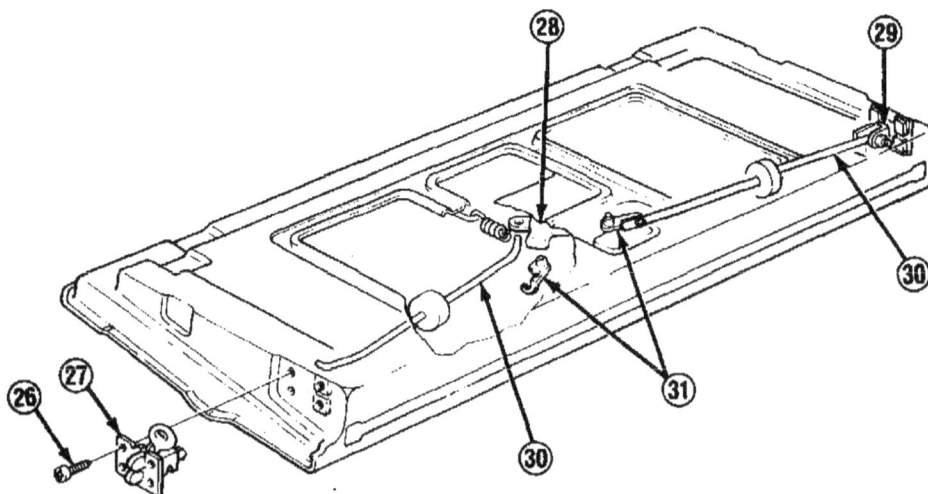

TA49990

10-21. ENDGATE MAINTENANCE (M1009) (Con't).

6.   Position 2 torque rod brackets (7) in endgate (8). Position 2 torque rods (1) with silencers (2 and 6) in endgate. Install 4 bolts (5). Position 2 brackets (3), ensure that they cover silencers (2), and install with 4 bolts (4).

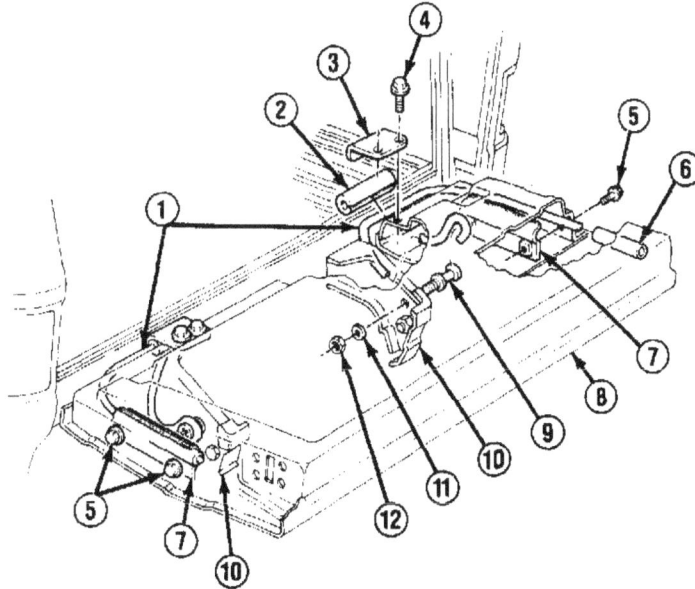

7.   Install hinge assembly (18) with 4 bolts (17).

8.   Install washer (21), support (15), spring (22), and washer (23) with bolt (24).

9.   Twist run channel (25) into window opening and position in endgate (8). Install 2 screws (20).

| d. | INSTALLATION |

CAUTION

Carefully guide in torque rods (1) when installing endgate   (8). Failure to follow this caution may result in damage to torque rods.

1.   Install 2 hinge assemblies (18) on floor panel with 8 bolts (19).

2.   Connect 2 washers (13), spacers (14), and supports (15) with 2 bolts (16).

3.   Position torque rods (1), and install each on frame extension (10) with stud (9), new lockwasher (11), and nut (12). Tighten nuts to 45-60 lb.-ft. (61-81 N•m).

TA49991

10-21. ENDGATE MAINTENANCE (M1009) (Con't).

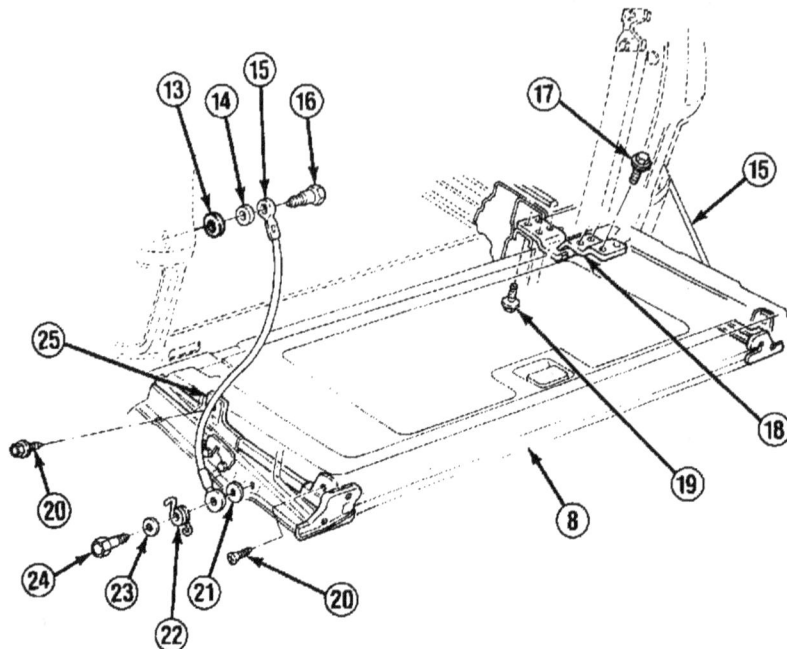

FOLLOW-ON TASKS:

* Install endgate window. (See paragraph 10-22)

TA49992

10-22. ENDGATE WINDOW AND WINDOW REGULATOR REPLACEMENT (M1009).

This task covers: a. Removal   b. Installation

INITIAL SETUP:

Equipment Condition

* Handle and control assembly removed
  (if removing window regulator or handle),
  (See paragraph 10-21)

Materials/Parts

* One window filler
* Three access cover seals
* Dry cleaning solvent
  (Item 15, Appendix C)
* Tape (Item 47.1, Appendix C)

General Safety Instructions

* Dry cleaning solvent is flammable and must not be used near open flame. Use in a well-ventilated
  area.

---

a.	**REMOVAL**

NOTE

* **If removing**   **access cover (3), perform step 1.**

* **If removing**   **window (17), perform steps 1-3, and 5.**

* **If removing**   **window regulator (12), perform steps 1-4.**

* **If removing handle assembly, perform steps 1 and 6 through 8 as
   required.**

1. Remove 16 screws (4) and access
   cover (3) from endgate (1). Remove
   seals (2 and 5) from access cover and
   discard if damaged.

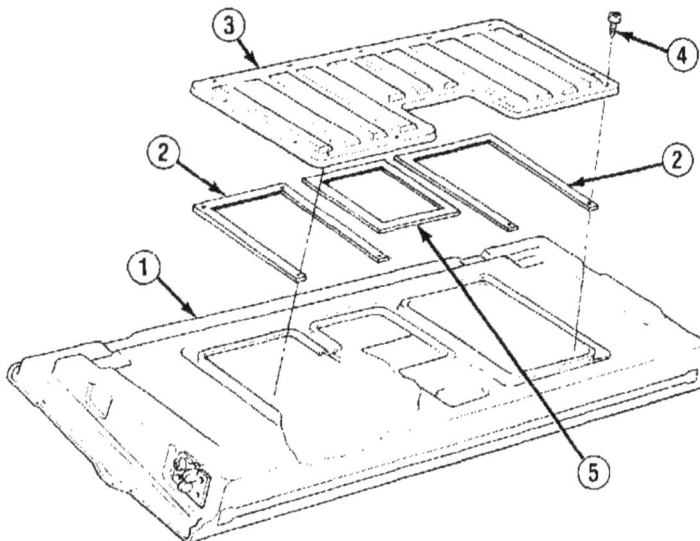

TA49993

10-22. ENDGATE WINDOW AND WINDOW REGULATOR REPLACEMENT (M1009) (Con't).

2. Remove 2 screws (7) and cap (6) from each side of endgate (1). Remove seal (8 or 9) by unsnapping clips (10).

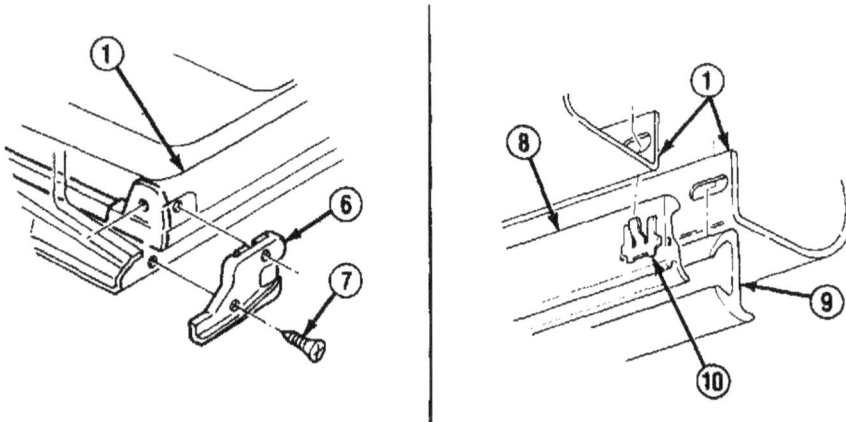

3. Regulate window (17) until screws (14) are accessible. Remove 4 screws and sash channels (13) from sash (15). Remove sash channels from window regulator (12) arms as required.

4. Remove 4 screws (11) and window regulator (12).

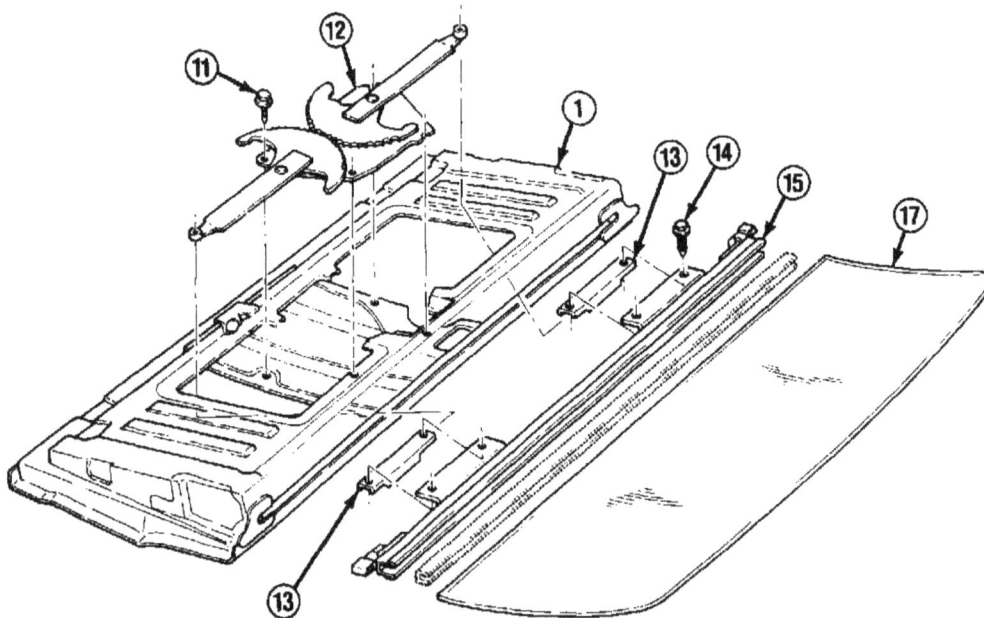

TA49994

10-22. ENDGATE WINDOW AND WINDOW REGULATOR REPLACEMENT (M1009) (Con't).

WARNING

Dry cleaning solvent P-D-680 is toxic and flammable. Always wear protective goggles and gloves and use only in a well-ventilated area. Avoid contact with skin, eyes, and clothes and DO NOT breathe vapors. DO NOT use near open flame or excessive heat, The solvent's flash point is 100°F-138°F (38°C-59°C). If you become dizzy while using cleaning solvent, immediately get fresh air and medical help. If solvent contacts eyes, immediately wash your eyes with water and get medical aid.

5. Carefully remove sash (15), filler (16), and window (17) assembly. Apply dry cleaning solvent to filler along sash on both sides of window glass. When filler softens, remove window and filler from sash. Remove old filler from sash and window. Discard filler.

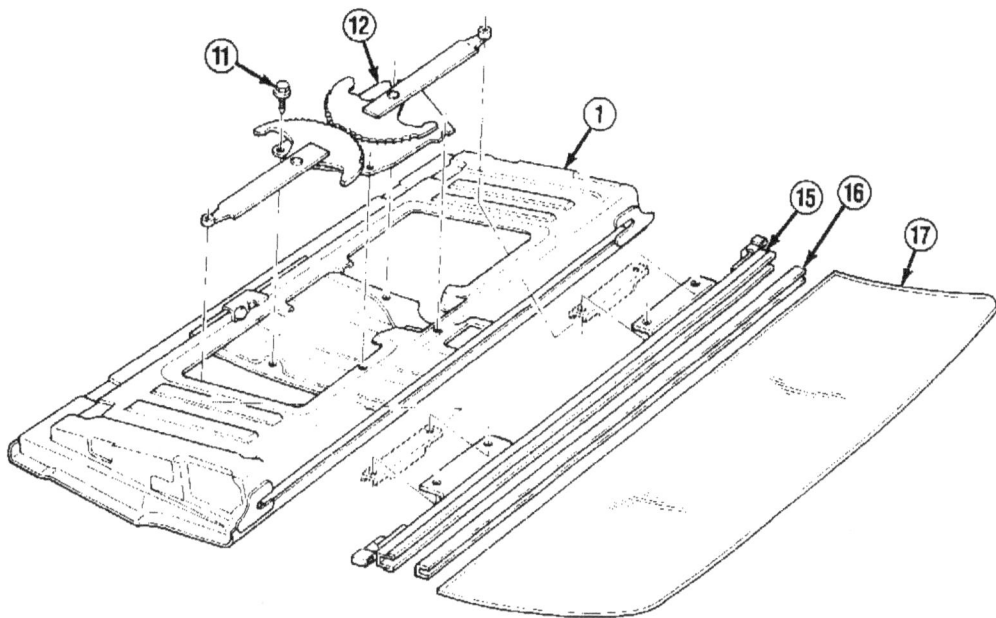

6. Remove 2 nuts (27), base (19), and handle assembly (28).

7. Remove bezel (26) and gasket (20) from base (19). Remove 2 screws (29), Separate arm of handle assembly (28) from base and remove pin (30).

8. Remove clip (25) and clutch (24). Remove retainer (23), spring washer (22), and ring (21), Remove pawl (32) and spring (31), and remove lock unit (18).

TA49995

10-22. ENDGATE WINDOW AND WINDOW REGULATOR REPLACEMENT (M1009) (Con't).

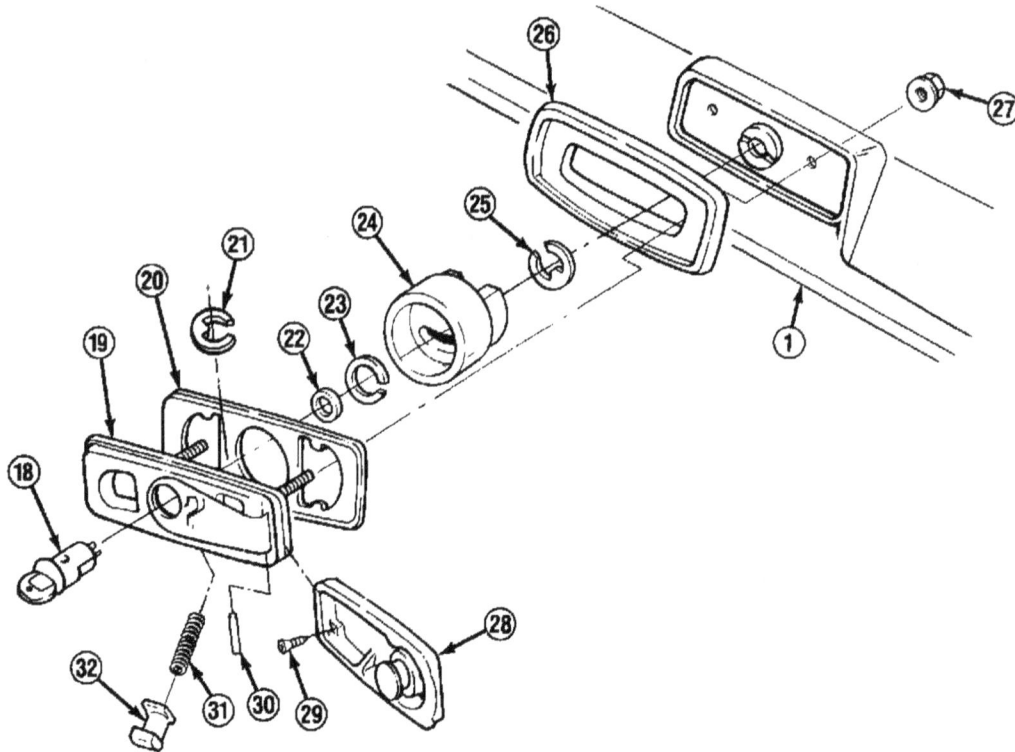

| b. INSTALLATION |

NOTE

● If installing handle assembly (28), perform steps 1-3, and 9 as required.

● If installing window regulator (12), perform steps 4, 5, and 7 through 9.

● If installing window (17), perform steps 4 and 6 through 9.

● If installing access cover, perform step 9.

1.   Install lock unit (18) on base (19) with spring (31) and pawl (32). Install spring washer (22) and retainer (23). Install clutch (24) with clip (25).

2.   Install pin (30) on arm of base (19). Position arm of handle assembly (28) on base and install 2 screws (29), Install gasket (20) and bezel (26) on base.

3.   Install base (19) and handle assembly (28) on endgate (1) with 2 nuts (27).

4.   Install window regulator (12) in endgate (1) with 4 screws (11).

TA49996

10-22. ENDGATE WINDOW AND WINDOW REGULATOR REPLACEMENT (M1009) (Con't).

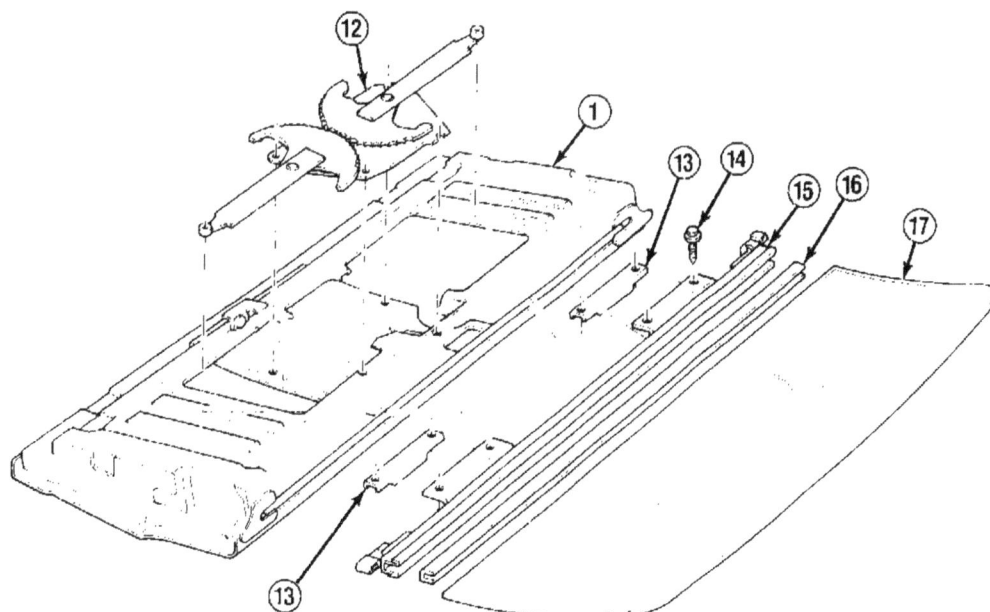

5. Install sash channels (13) on window regulator (12) arms if removed. Regulate window (17) until sash channels and screws (14) can be installed.

6. Install new filler (16) on window (17) if removed. Apply a ½ in. wide strip of red tape along top edge of rear tailgate window. Press filler and window assembly into sash (15) . Position sash, filler, and window assembly in endgate (1).

7. Install sash channels (13) on sash (15) with 4 screws (14).

TA49997

10-22. ENDGATE WINDOW AND WINDOW REGULATOR REPLACEMENT (M1009) (Con't).

8. Install seals (8 and 9) on endgate (1) by snapping clips (10) in place. Install cap (6) on each side of endgate with 2 screws (7).

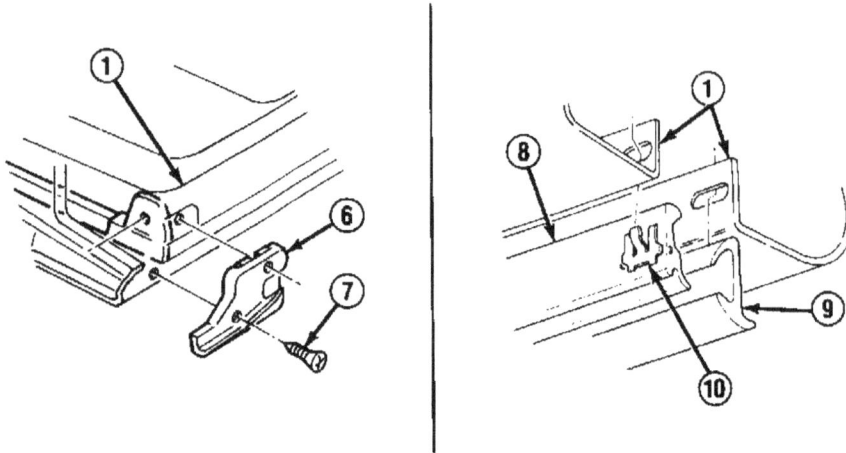

9. Install seals (2 and 5) on access cover (3) if removed. Install access cover on endgate (1) with 16 screws (4).

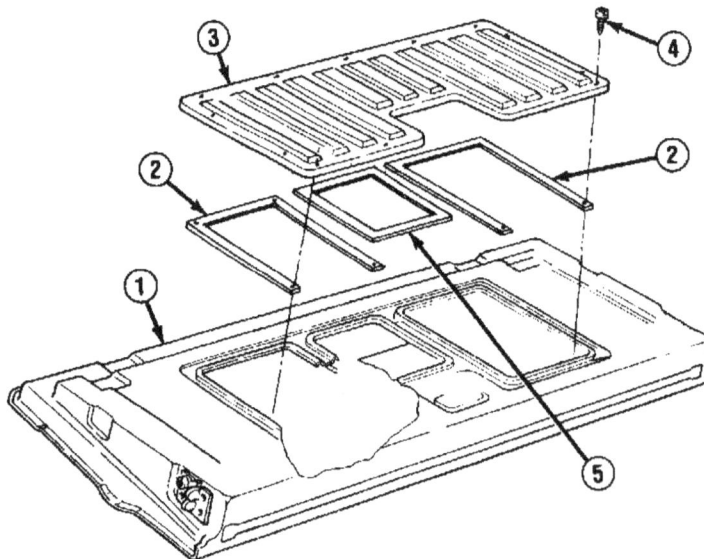

FOLLOW-ON TASKS:

• Install handle and control assembly if removed. (See paragraph 10-21)

TA49998

10-23. DRIVER'S, PASSENGER'S, REAR BENCH SEAT, AND SEATBELT REPLACEMENT (M1009).

This task covers: a.   Removal   b. Installation

INITIAL SETUP:

Equipment Condition

* Radio mounting bracket removed (if removing rear bench seat). (See paragraph 4-47)

Tools/Test Equipment

* Torque wrench
* Screwdriver bit set, J-29843

Materials/Parts

• T wo lockwashers

| a. | **REMOVAL** |

NOTE

* If removing seatbelts (1 and 2), perform step 1.

* If removing seats (9) and seat adjuster assemblies (4 or 8), perform steps 2-4.

* If removing rear bench seatbelts, perform step 5.

* If removing rear bench seat, perform step 6.

1.   Remove plug from retractor cove r (3). Pry back seatbelt (2) covers to expose mounting bolts at door pillar and floor. Remove 3 mounting bolts and seatbelt. Remove seatbelt buckle (1) mounting bolt plug. Remov e mounting bolt and seatbelt buckle.

2.   Remove 2 forward bolts (7), Adjust seat (9) forward and remove 2 rear bolts (11) at adjuster bracket (13). Remove seat and seat adjuste r assembly.

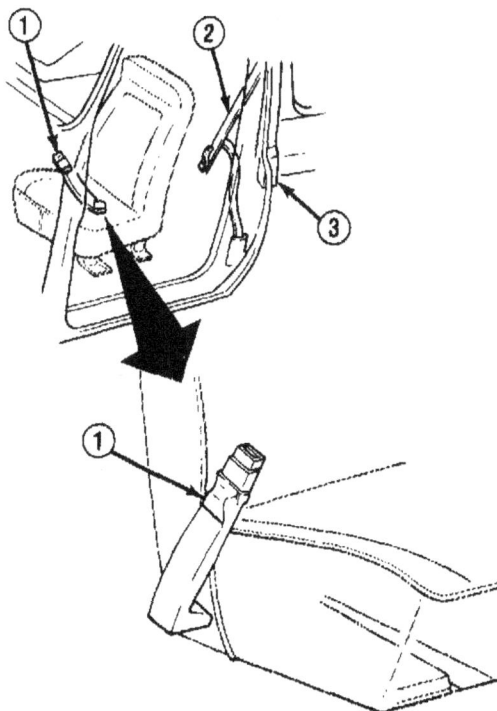

TA49999

10-23. DRIVER'S, PASSENGER'S, REAR BENCH SEAT, AND SEATBELT REPLACEMENT (M1009) (Con't).

NOTE

- Driver's and passenger's seat adjusters (4 and 8) are removed the same way but component locations are reversed. Driver's seat adjuster removal is described.

- Note position of springs (6, 10, and 12) for installation.

3. Remove outer springs (6 and 12) and inner spring (10) if damaged or broken.

4. Remove wire assembly (5). Remove 4 bolts (14) and remove inner seat adjuster (8) and outer seat adjuster (4) from seat (9).

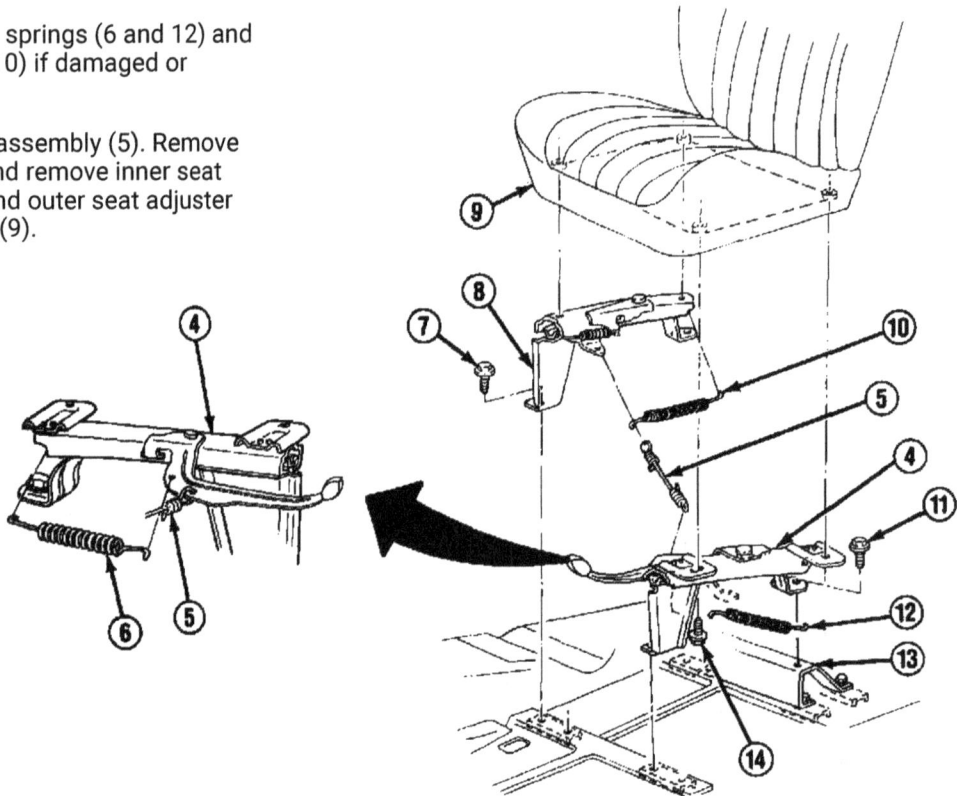

TA50000

10-23. DRIVER'S, PASSENGER'S, REAR BENCH SEAT, AND SEATBELT REPLACEMENT (M1009) (Con't).

5. Fold rear bench seat (16) forward. Remove 4 seatbelt mounting bolts (17) and pull rear seatbelts (15) through rear bench seat.

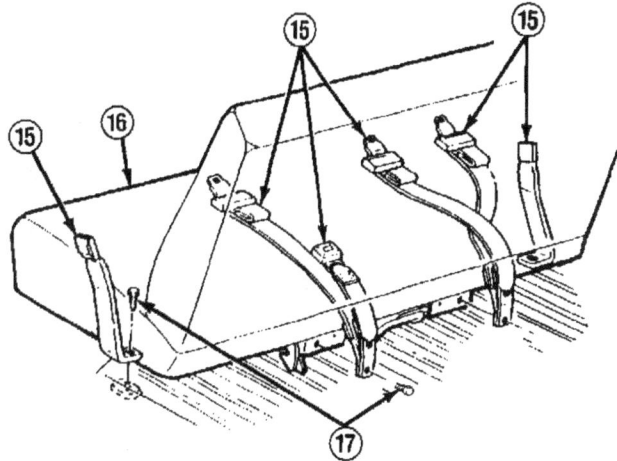

6. Remove 2 bolts (22) and disconnect strut and lockwashers (19) from hinges (20). (21) from rear bench seat (16). Remove 2 bolts (18) Remove rear bench seat. Discard lockwashers.

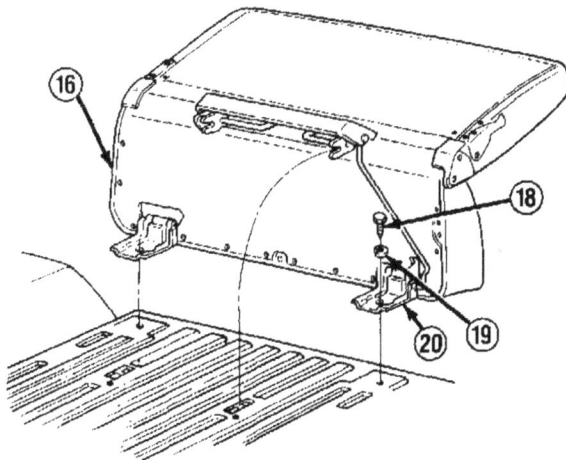

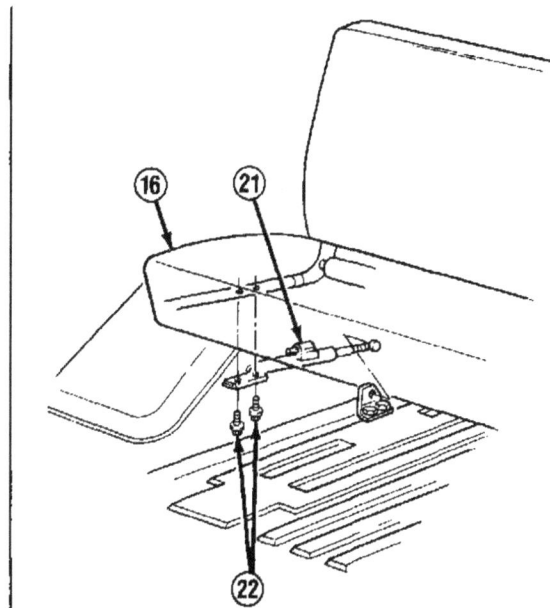

TA50001

10-23. DRIVER'S, PASSENGER'S, REAR BENCH SEAT, AND SEATBELT REPLACEMENT (M1009) (Con't).

| b. | INSTALLATION |

NOTE

- **If installing** rear bench seat (16), perform step 1.

- **If installing** rear bench seatbelts (15), perform step 2.

- **If installing** seats (9) and seat adjuster assemblies (4 and 8), perform steps 3-6.

- **If installing** seatbelts, perform step 7.

1. Position rear bench seat (16). Install hinges (20) with 2 new lockwashers (19) and bolts (18). Connect strut (21) to rear bench seat with 2 bolts (22). Fold rear bench seat back. Tighten bolts (18) to 30-45 lb.-ft. (41-61 N·m). Tighten bolts (22) to 10-15 lb.-ft. (14-20 N·m).

2. Position seatbelts (15) through rear bench seat (16) and install to floor with 4 seatbelt mounting bolts (17). Tighten bolts to 40 lb.-ft. (54 N·m).

3. If removed, install outer springs (6 and 12) and inner spring (10).

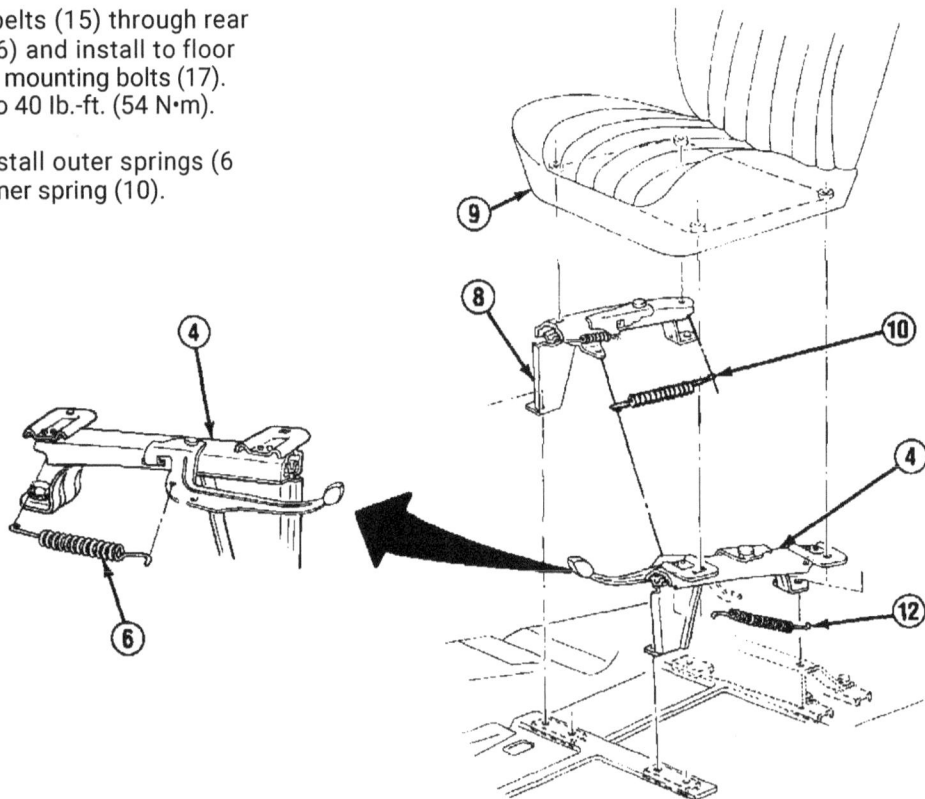

TA50002

10-23. DRIVER'S, PASSENGER'S, REAR BENCH SEAT, AND SEATBELT REPLACEMENT (M1009) (Con't).

NOTE

Driver's and passenger's seat adjusters (4 and 8) are installed the same way but component locations are reversed. Driver's seat adjuster installation is described.

4. Install outer seat adjuster (4) and inner seat adjuster (8) on seat (9) with 4 bolts (14). Lock outer seat adjuster and inner seat adjuster in place. Tighten bolts to 20-30 lb.-ft (27-41 N·m).

5. Install wire assembly (5). If wire assembly is too loose or too tight, disconnect from inner seat adjuster (8) adjustment hole and connect to a different inner seat adjuster adjustment hole as required.

6. Position seat (9) and seat adjuster (8) assembly in truck and install with 2 forward bolts (7) and 2 rear bolts (11). Tighten bolts to 20-25 lb.-ft. (27-34 N·m).

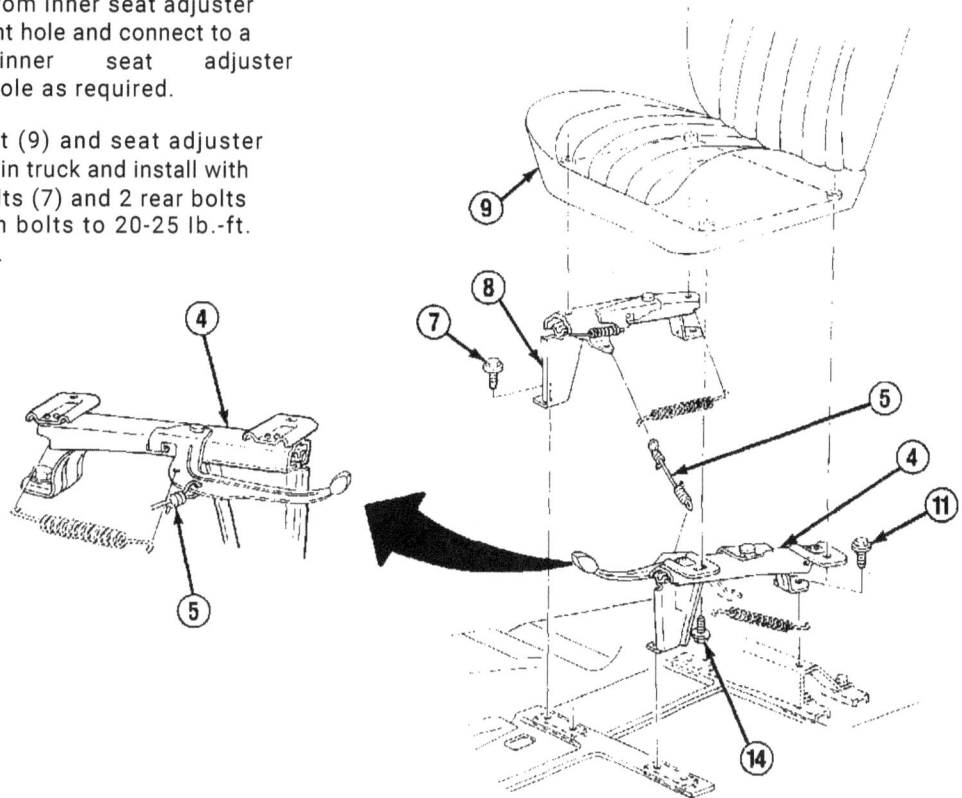

TA50003

10-23. DRIVER'S, PASSENGER'S, REAR BENCH SEAT, AND SEATBELT REPLACEMENT (M1009) (Con't).

7.   Install seatbelt buckle (1) with mounting bolt. Install bolt plug. Install seatbelt (2) with 3 mounting bolts, Tighten mounting bolts to 40 lb.-ft. (54 N•m). Snap seatbelt covers into place over mounting bolts at door pillar and floor. Install plug to retractor cover (3).

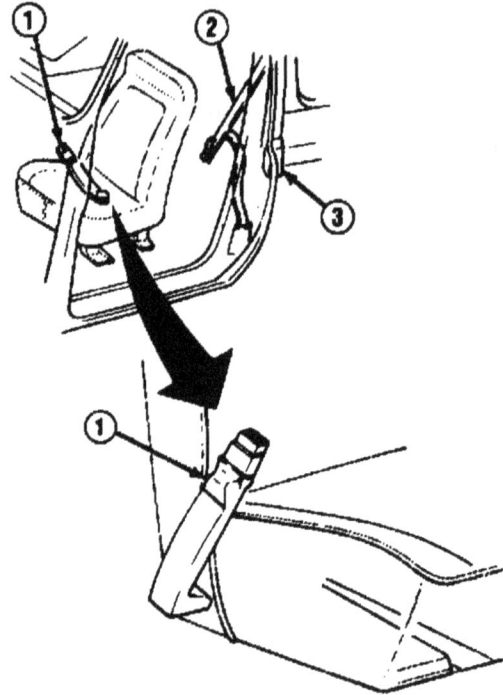

FOLLOW-ON TASKS:

● Install radio mounting bracket if removed, (See paragraph 4-47)

TA50004

10-23A. SEATBELT ANCHORPOINT REPAIR (M1009).

This task covers: a. Repair

INITIAL SETUP:

Too/s/Test Equipment

• General mechanic's tool kit
Ž Drill motor
• 1/2-inch drill

Materials/Parts

Ž Bolt, NSN 5305-00-071-2077 (1 ea)
• Flatwasher, NSN 5310-00-809-5997
  (2 ea)
• Locknut, NSN 5310-00-225-6993
Ž Primer, NSN 8010-01-193-0517

Personnel Required
• MOS 63B (2)

References
TM 9-2320-289-20P (Fig.
166 & 167)

| a. | REPAIR |

1. Inside of the vehicle (driver's side), remove the bolt that attaches the lower portion of the seatbelt to the mounting post/pillar and discard it.

2. Outside of the vehicle, use the rear edge of the cab door opening to find the reinforcement crossmember under the cab floor. Follow this crossmember inboard approximately 10 inches and locate an existing 5/8-inch hole approximately 2 inches from the cab body mount.

3. From underneath the vehicle, using the existing 5/8-hch hole as a guide, drill   a 1/2-inch diameter hole straight up through the cab floor and floormat. This new attaching hole should be approximately 6 inches straight back from the rear seat mounting bolt location.

4. If the floormat is still in the truck, cut and remove a 1 3/4-inch diameter section from the mat around the drilled hole.

NOTE

If the floormat and jute backing   are wet, go to step   5; if not, go to step 6.

5. Remove floormat. When floor is dry, remove any rust with a wire brush and paint bare spots with primer (NSN 8010-01-193-0517). Replace floormat.

6. From inside the vehicle cab, place one hex head grade 8 bolt (1/2-inch – 13 coarse thread x 3-1/2 inch long (NSN 5305-00-071-2077) through the mounting plate of the seatbelt. Plaoe two 1/2-inch flatwashers (NSN 5310-00-809-5997) onto the bolt and install the bolt into the drilled hole in the floor.

10-23A. SEATBELT ANCHORPOINT REPAIR (M1009) (Con't.)

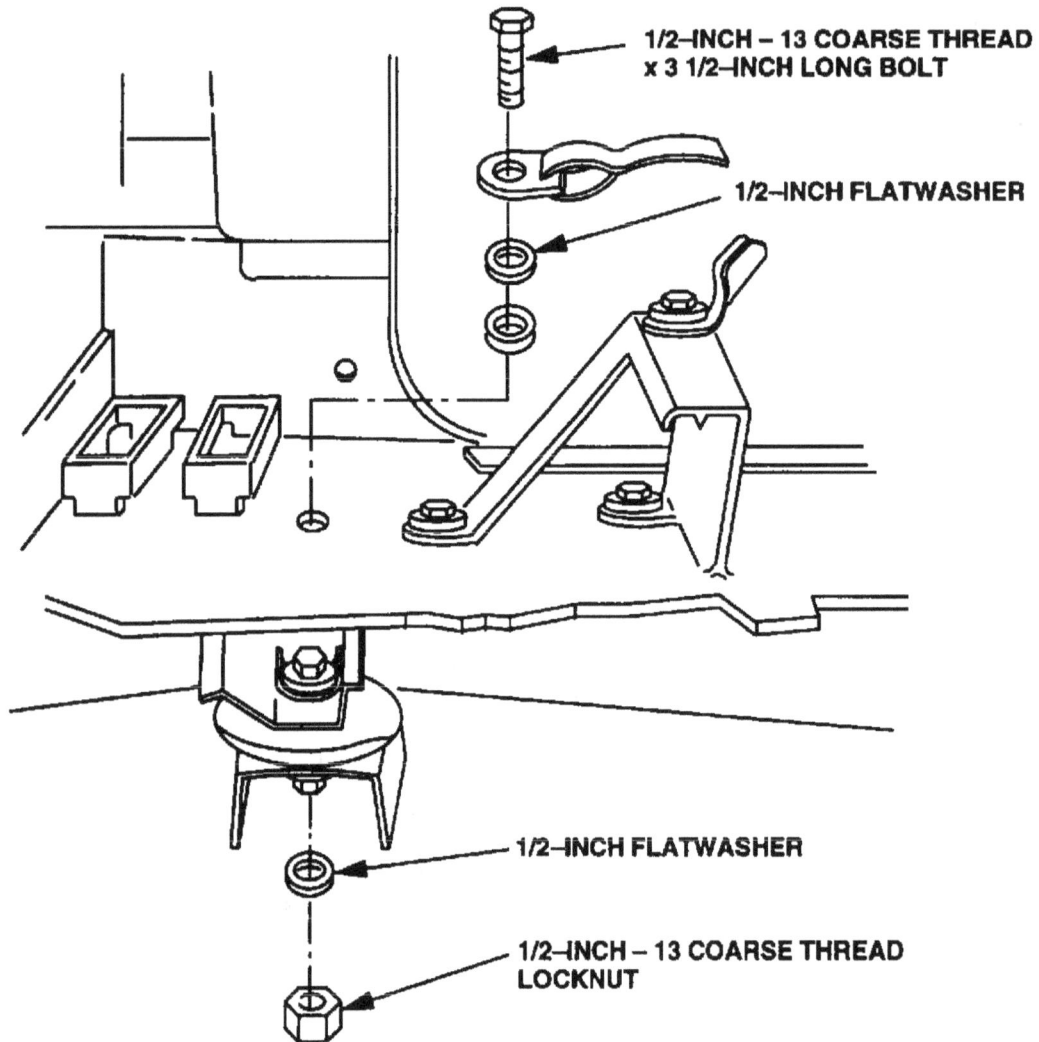

1/2–INCH – 13 COARSE THREAD x 3 1/2–INCH LONG BOLT

1/2–INCH FLATWASHER

1/2–INCH FLATWASHER

1/2–INCH – 13 COARSE THREAD LOCKNUT

7. From underneath the vehicle, have an assistant place one 1/2-inch flatwasher (NSN 5310-00-809-5997) and one UNC-2B locknut (1/2–inch – 13 coarse thread, NSN 5310-00-225-6993) onto the seatbelt mounting bolt. Tighten the nut until all clearance between the mounting plate, flatwasher, and cab floor is removed. Tighten the nut one additional turn; don't overtighten.

8. Repeat steps 1 through 7 for the passenger's side.

9. After relocating the seatbelt, ensure that the plastic covers are installed over the seat hinge. The sharp edge of the seat hinges may cause damage to the seatbelts. Refer to TM 9-2320-289-20P (May 92), driver's side, Figure 166, Item 7 and Item 8; passenger side, Figure 167, Item 7 and Item 11.

Section V. AMBULANCE BODY MAINTENANCE

10-24. AMBULANCE BODY MAINTENANCE INDEX.

10-25. DRIVER'S AND PASSENGER'S SEAT AND SEATBELT REPLACEMENT (M1010).

This task covers: a. Removal   b. Installation

INITIAL SETUP:

Tools/Test Equipment
* Torque wrench

| a. | REMOVAL |

NOTE

* If removing driver's seatbelt assembly (3), perform step 1.

* If removing passenger's seatbelt assembly (6), perform steps 2 and 9.

* If removing driver's seat (11) and seat adjuster assemblies (7), perform steps 3-7,

* If removing passenger's seat and supports, perform steps 9-11.

1.   Remove bolt covers and remove bolt (2) and 2 floor-mounted bolts (4). Disconnect electrical connector at seatbelt retractor (5). Remove driver's seatbelt assembly (3).

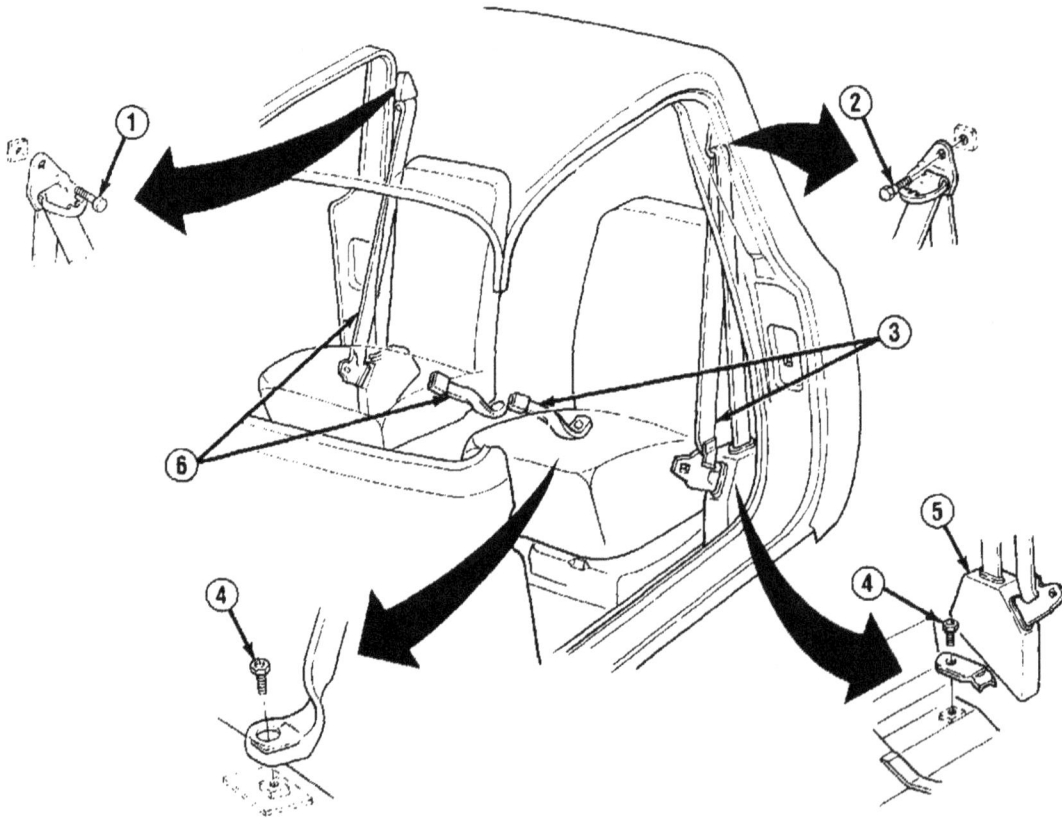

TA50005

10-25. DRIVER'S AND PASSENGER'S SEAT AND SEATBELT REPLACEMENT (M1010) (Con't).

2. Remove bolt cover and remove bolt (1).

3. Remove 2 front bolts (12) securing 2 seat adjuster assemblies (7) to floor-mounted weldnuts (15).

4. Adjust driver's seat (11) forward and remove 2 rear bolts (12). Remove seat and 2 seat adjuster assemblies (7).

NOTE

Note location of outer spring (13) and wire assembly (8) for installation.

5. Remove wire assembly (8).

6. Inspect 2 seat latch springs (16) at each seat adjuster assembly (7) and remove if damaged or broken,

7. Remove outer spring (13) from front of left seat adjuster assembly (7) and driver's seat (11). Remove 6 bolts (14) and 2 seat adjuster assemblies from driver's seat and brackets (10).

8. Remove 4 bolts (9) and 2 brackets (10) from driver's seat (11).

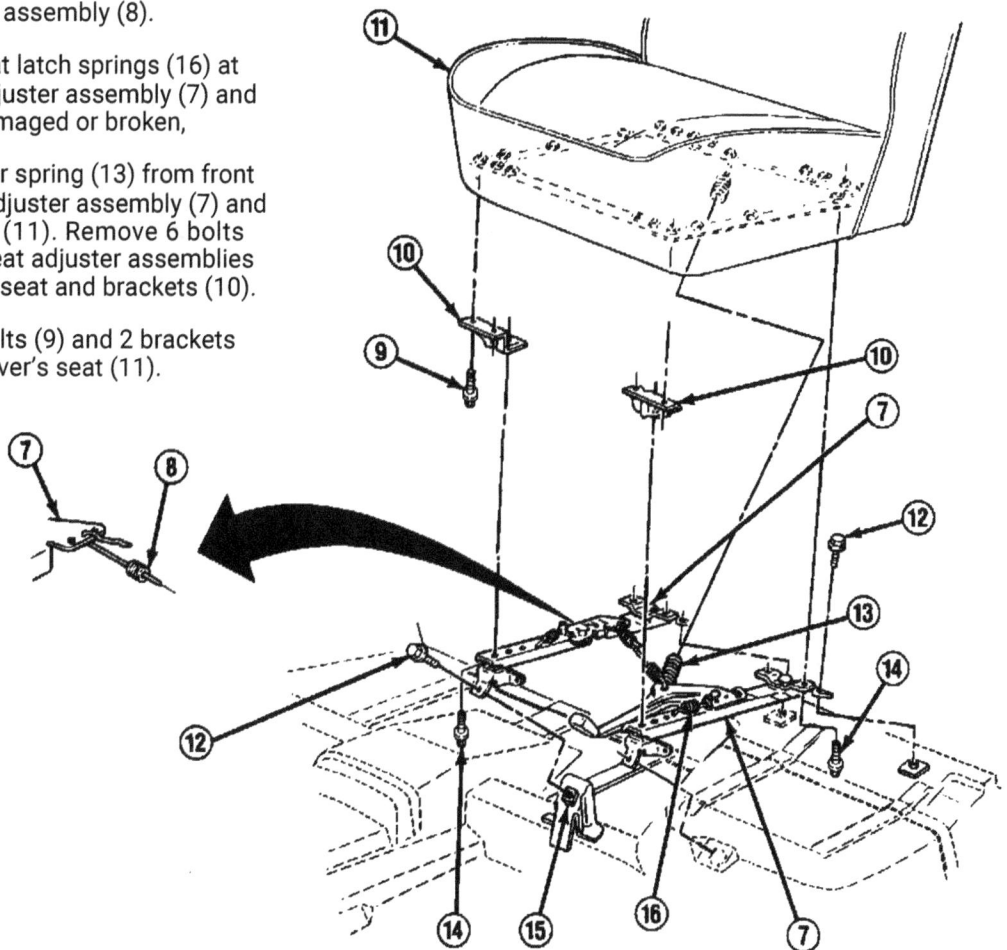

TA50006

10-25. DRIVER'S AND PASSENGER'S SEAT AND SEATBELT REPLACEMENT (M1010) (Con't).

9. Remove 2 bolts (18) and passenger's seatbelt assembly (6) from 2 rear supports (19).

10. Remove 2 bolts (23) at 2 front supports (22). Remove passenger's seat (17) with attached supports (19 and 22) from bracket assembly (21).

11. Remove 8 bolts (20), 2 front supports (22), and 2 rear supports (19) from passenger's seat (17).

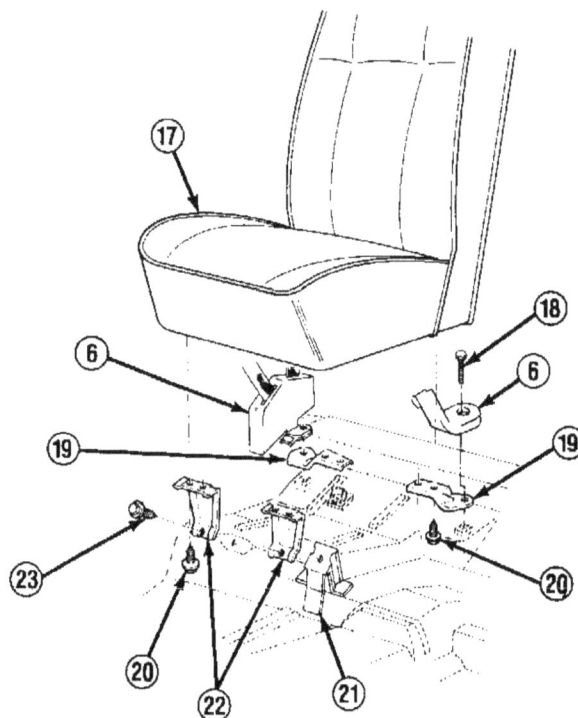

---

b.	INSTALLATION

NOTE

- If installing   passenger's seat (17) and supports (19 and 22), perform steps 1-4.

- If installing seat adjuster assemblies (7) and driver's seat (11), perform steps 5-9.

- If installing passenger's seatbelt assembly (6), perform steps 4 and 10.

- If installing driver's seatbelt assembly, perform step 11.

1. Install 2 front supports (22) and 2 rear supports (19) to passenger's seat (17) with 8 bolts (20). Tighten bolts to 15-25 lb.-ft. (20-34 N•m).

2. Position passenger's seat (17) with attached supports (19 and 22) at truck floor.

3. At right front corner, install bolt (23) through front support (22) into floor. At left front corner, install bolt through front support into bracket assembly (21).   DO NOT FULLY   tighten bolts.

4. Install passenger's seatbelt assembly (6) at 2 rear supports (19) with 2 bolts (18). Tighten bolts to 40 lb.-ft. (54 N•m). Tighten bolts (23) to 25 lb.-ft. (34 N•m).

TA50007

10-25. DRIVER'S AND PASSENGER'S SEAT AND SEATBELT REPLACEMENT (M1010) (Con't).

5.   Install 2 brackets (10) to driver's seat (11) with 4 bolts (9).

6.   If removed, install seat latch spring (16) to each seat adjuster assembly (7).

7.   Install 2 seat adjuster assemblies (7) to driver's seat (11) and to 2 brackets (10) with 6 bolts (14). Tighten bolts to 20-30 lb.-ft. (27-41 N•m). Install outer spring (13) between front of left adjuster assembly and back of driver's seat.

NOTE

A properly installed wire assembly (8) should not be in tension.

8.   Lock both seat adjuster assemblies (7). Install wire assembly (8) with wire in middle hole at right adjuster assembly. Move wire to forward or rearward hole as required to adjust for proper tension.

9.   Install driver's seat (11) and 2 seat adjuster assemblies (7) to floor-mounted weldnuts (15) with 4 bolts (12). Tighten bolts to 25 lb.-ft. (34 N•m).

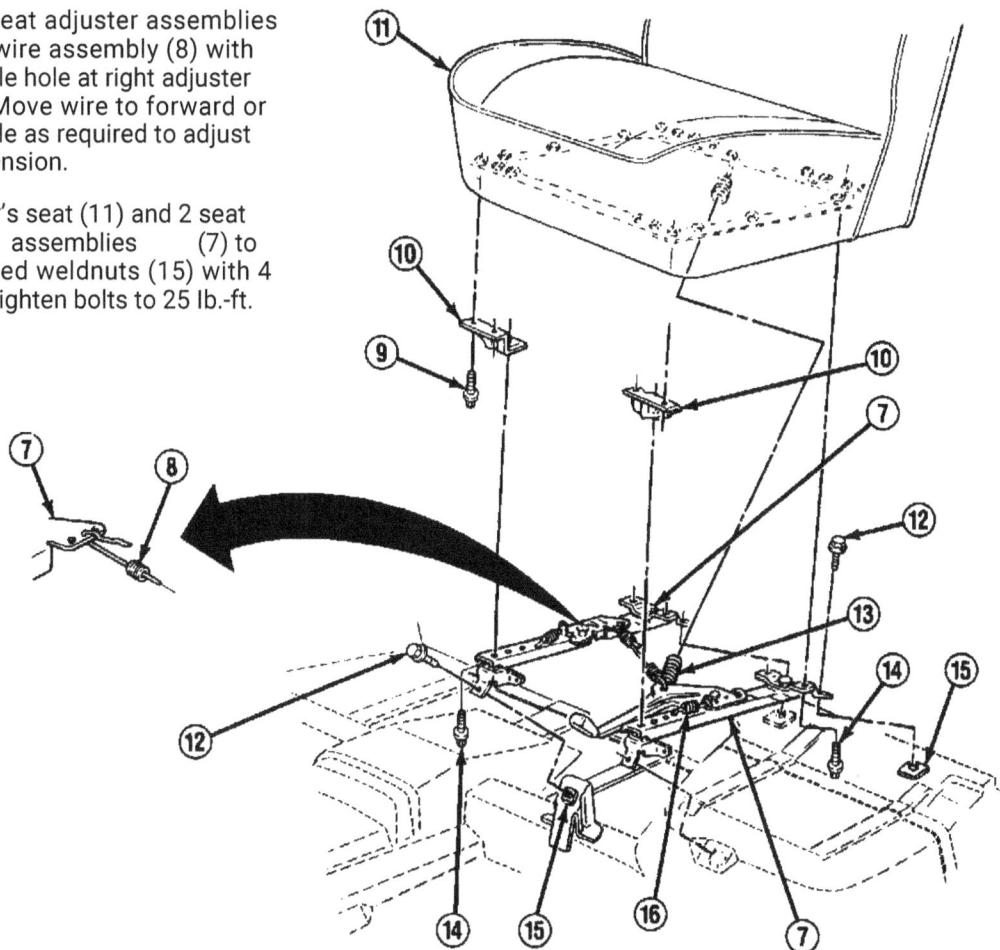

TA50008

10-25. DRIVER'S AND PASSENGER'S SEAT AND SEATBELT REPLACEMENT (M1010) (Con't).

10.   Install passenger's seatbelt assembly (6) to door pillar with bolt (1). Tighten bolt to 40 lb.-ft. (54 N•m). Install bolt cover.

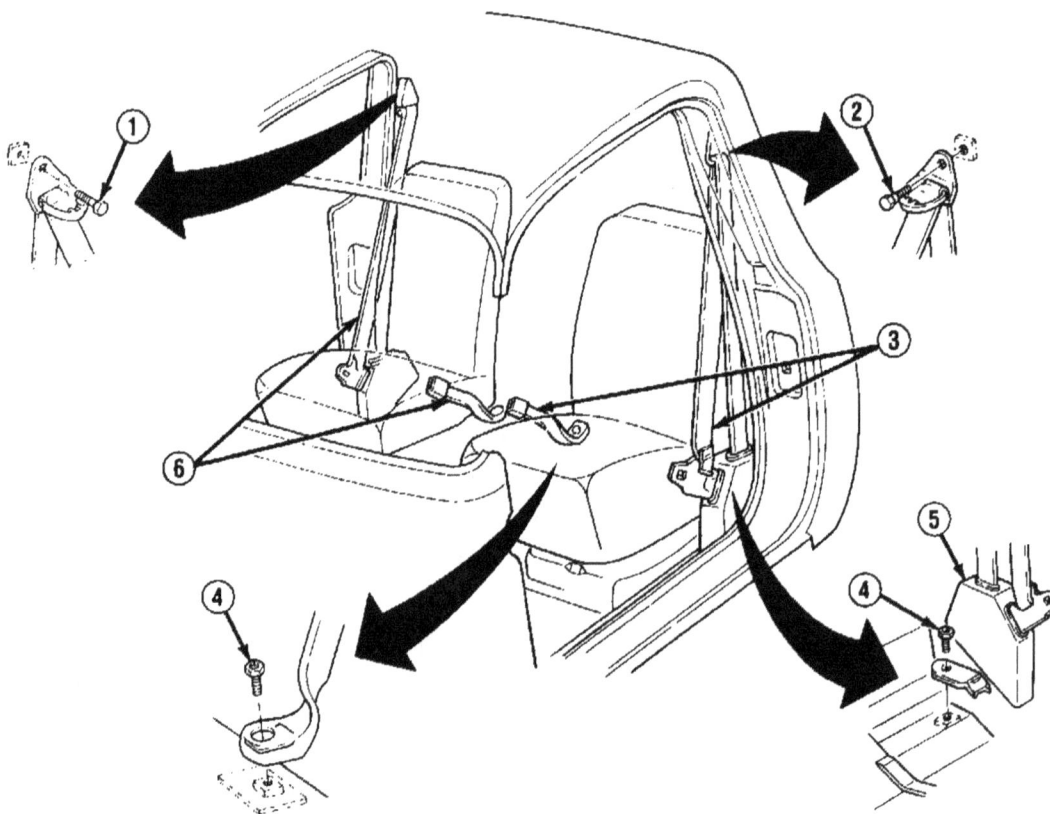

11.   Install driver's seatbelt assembly (3) to door pillar with bolt (2). Tighten bolt to 40 lb.-ft. (54 N•m).   Position seatbelt retractor (5) and install electrical connector. Install 2 floor-mounted bolts (4) and tighten to 40 lb.-ft. (54 N•m). Install bolt covers.

TA50009

10-26. REAR DOOR ASSEMBLY, HINGES, AND LOCK MECHANISM REPLACEMENT (M1010).

This task covers: a. Removal   b. Installation

INITIAL SETUP:

Materials/Parts
 * Two cotter pins
 * Four locknuts
 * Tape (Item 48, Appendix C)

Personnel Required
 * MOS 63B (2)

General Safety Instructions
 • Use extreme caution when removing or installing rear door assembly.

---

a.	**REMOVAL**

WARNING

Use extreme caution when removing rear door assembly. Rear door assembly is heavy and if dropped will cause equipment damage and serious injury to personnel.

10-26. REAR DOOR ASSEMBLY, HINGES, AND LOCK MECHANISM REPLACEMENT (M1010) (Con't).

NOTE

- If removing rear door assembly (6) and hinges (5), perform steps 1 and 2.

- If removing right door assembly handles (8 and 14) and lock assembly (7, 11, and 16), perform steps 3 and 5 through 12,

- If removing left door assembly inside handle and lock assembly (7, 11, and 16), perform steps 4, 5, and 7 through 12.

1. Open door assembly (6). Support door assembly and remove 6 bolts (3) and washers (4). Remove door assembly from truck.

2. Remove 6 bolts (2), washers (1), and 3 hinges (5) from truck if damaged.

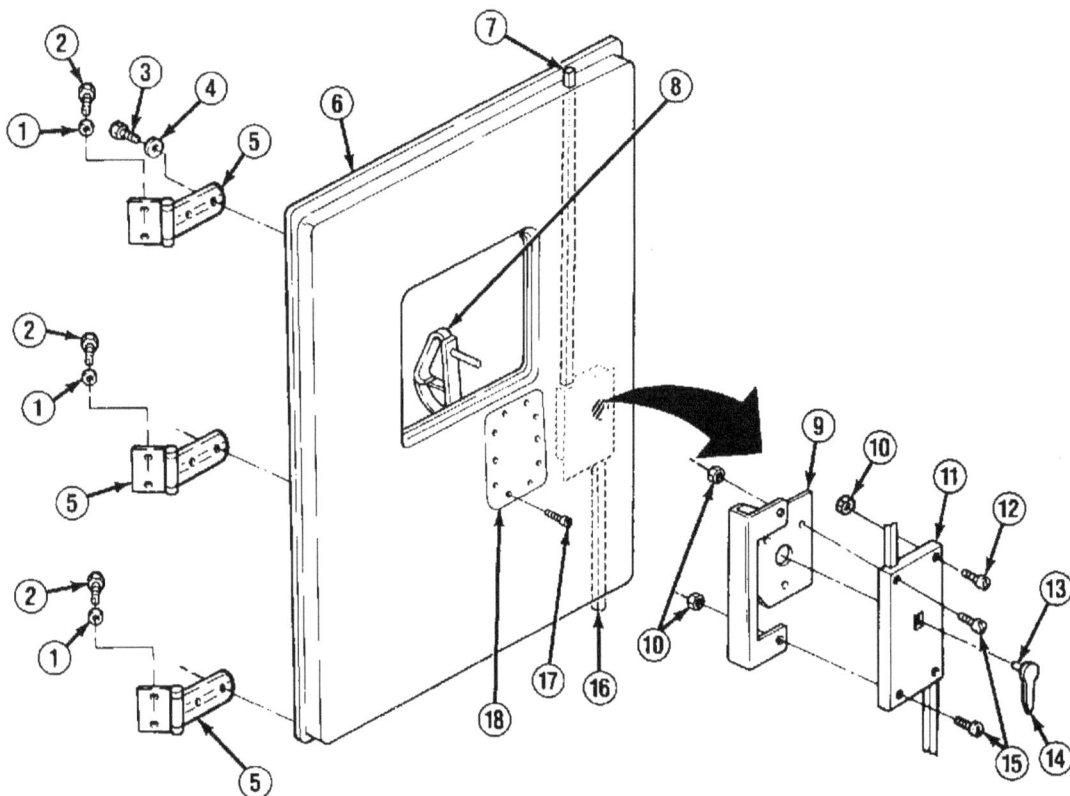

TA50010

10-26. REAR DOOR ASSEMBLY, HINGES, AND LOCK MECHANISM REPLACEMENT (M1010) (Con't).

3. Remove setscrew (13) and right inside handle (14).

4. Remove 2 screws and left inside handle.

5. Remove 10 screws (17) and access panel (18).

6. Remove 4 screws and outside handle (8).

NOTE

- When removing 4 bolts (12 and 15), position hand   to prevent 4 locknuts (10) from falling down between door panels.

- Left rear door assembly has no handle bracket (9).

7. Remove 2 bolts (15) and locknuts (10). Remove handle bracket (9). Discard locknuts.

8. Remove 2 bolts (12) and locknuts (10). Discard locknuts.

9. Pull lock mechanism (11) aside in door assembly (6) to gain working room at access panel (18) opening.

10. Remove cotter pin, steel washer, rubber washer, and bottom lock rod (16) through access panel (18) opening. Discard cotter pin.

11. Remove top lock rod (7) and attached lock mechanism (11) through access panel (18) opening.

12. Remove cotter pin, steel washer, rubber washer, and top lock rod (7) from lock mechanism (11). Discard cotter pin.

b. INSTALLATION

WARNING

Use extreme caution when installing rear door assembly. Rear door assembly is heavy and if dropped will cause equipment damage and serious injury to personnel.

NOTE

- If installing right door assembly handles (8 and 14) and lock assembly (7, 11, and 16), perform steps 1-11.

- If installing left door assembly inside handle and lock assembly (7, 11, and 16), perform steps 1-7, 9, and 12.

- If installing rear door assembly (6) and hinges (5), perform steps 13-16.

1. Apply tape to ends of top and bottom lock rods (7 and 16) to prevent them from pivoting as they are installed.

10-26. REAR DOOR ASSEMBLY, HINGES, AND LOCK MECHANISM REPLACEMENT (M1010) (Con't).

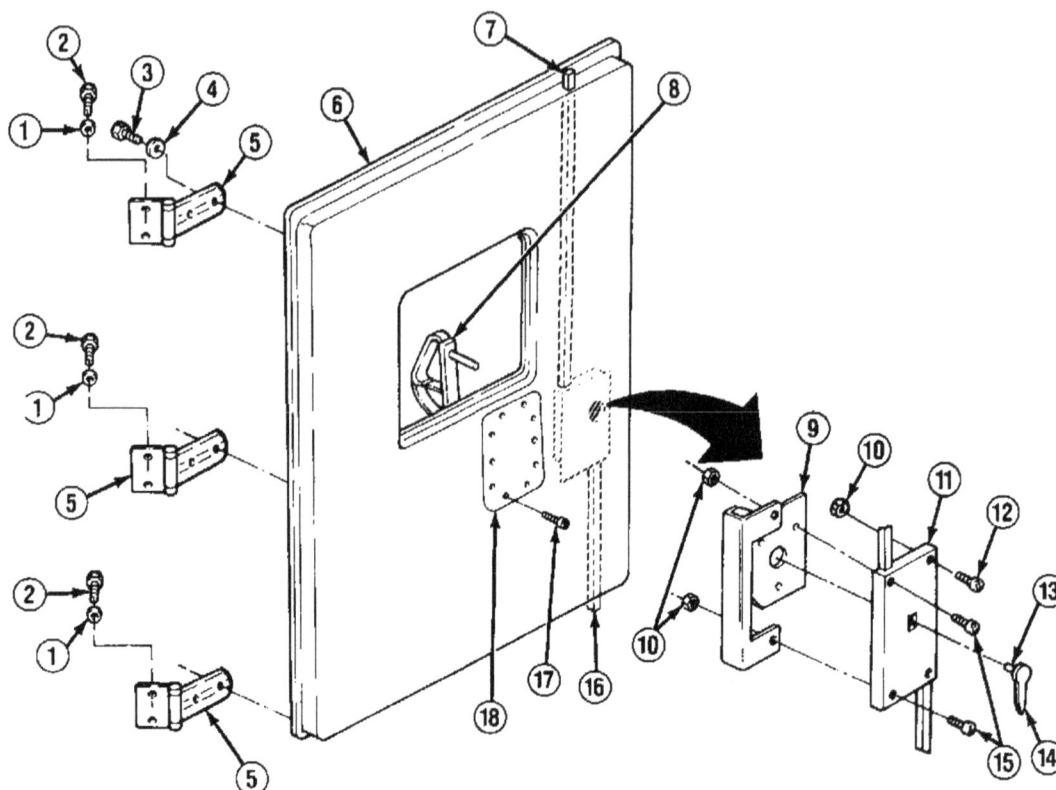

2. Install bottom lock rod (16) through access panel (18) opening and out bottom of door assembly (6).

3. Install top lock rod (7) to lock mechanism (11) with rubber washer, steel washer, and new cotter pin.

4. Install top lock rod (7) with attached lock mechanism (11) through access panel (18) opening and out top of door assembly (6), Once installed, have assistant secure top lock rod to keep it from falling out of position.

5. Install bottom lock rod (16) to lock mechanism (11) with rubber washer, steel washer, and new cotter pin.

6. Loosely install 2 bolts (12) and new locknuts (10) through door assembly (6) and lock mechanism (11).

TA50011

10-26. REAR DOOR ASSEMBLY, HINGES, AND LOCK MECHANISM REPLACEMENT (M1010) (Con't).

NOTE

Left rear door assembly has no handle bracket (9).

7. Position handle bracket (9) behind lock mechanism (11) and new locknuts (10).   loosely install 2 bolts (15) and

8. Install outside handle (8) with 4 screws.

9. Tighten 2 bolts (12) and bolts (15).

10. Install access panel (18) with 10 screws (17).

11. Install right inside handle (14) with setscrew (13).

12. Install left inside handle with 2 screws.

NOTE

Door-mounted portion of 3 hinges (5) has 6 slotted   holes to allow for adjustment and proper fit.

13. Install 3 hinges (5) to truck with 6 bolts (2) and washers   (1). Tighten bolts to 40 lb.-ft. (54 N•m).

14. While supporting door assembly (6), install 3 hinges (5) to door assembly with 6 bolts (3) and washers (4). DO NOT fully tighten bolts.

15. Close 2 door assemblies (6) and check for proper fit.

16. Adjust as required at 3 hinges (5). Tighten 6 bolts (3) to 40 lb.-ft. (54 N•m).

10-27. REAR DOOR ASSEMBLY FIXED GLASS REPLACEMENT (M1010).

This task covers:	a. Remova l	c. Installation
	b. Inspection	

INITIAL SETUP:

Materials/Parts

* Chalk (Item 9, Appendix C)
* Tape (Item 48, Appendix C)
* Twine (Item 50, Appendix C)

General Safety Instructions

* Wear heavy gloves when handling glass.

Personnel Required

* MOS 63B (2)

---

a.	REMOVAL

WARNING

* **Wear heavy gloves when handling glass to avoid risk of injury.**

* **If glass is cracked but still intact, crisscross glass with masking tape to reduce risk of injury to personnel.**

NOTE

Chalk mark in step 1 will be used during inspection of window flange (4).

1. If fixed glass (3) has a crack which extends to edge of glass glazing (2), mark door panel (1), with a piece of chalk, at that point.

2. Run a putty knife around window on inside and outside between glass glazing (2) and door panel (1).

3. Have an assistant stand outside next to window.

4. Use a blunt tool to force edge of glass glazing off window flange (4) o f window opening inside cab, while pushing out on fixed glass (3).

5. Continue around window opening until fixed glass (3) and glass glazing (2) are free.

6. Have assistant remove fixed glass (3) and glass glazing (2) from outside.

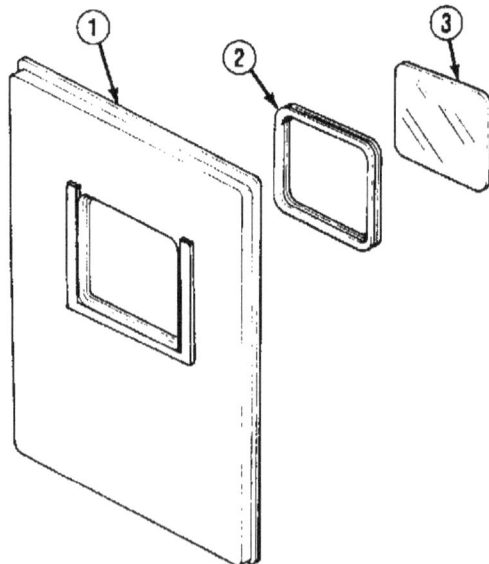

TA50012

10-27. REAR DOOR ASSEMBLY FIXED GLASS REPLACEMENT (M1010) (Con't).

7.   Remove fixed glass (3) from glass glazing (2).

| b. | **INSPECTION** |

1.   If a crack was found which extended to edge of fixed glass (3), inspect window flange (4) for damage where chalk mark was made.

2.   If a high point or any other irregularity is found in window flange (4) surface, notify your supervisor.

3.   Inspect glass glazing (2) for irregularities or obstructions.

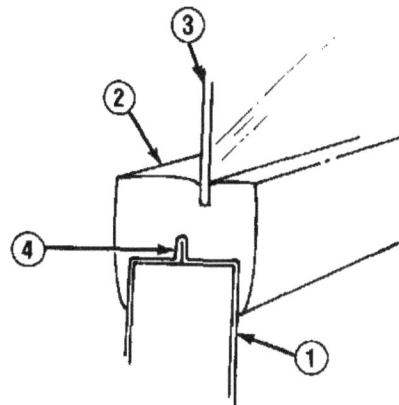

WARNING

Wear heavy gloves when handling glass to avoid risk of injury.

4.   Inspect replacement fixed glass (3) to ensure that there are no rough or chipped edges.

| c. | **INSTALLATION** |

WARNING

Wear heavy gloves when handling glass to avoid risk of injury.

NOTE

To ease installation, glass glazing (2) can be heated with a nonflame source.

1.   Install fixed glass (3) in glass glazing (2).

2.   Place a length of twine in glass glazing (2) groove where window flange (4) will fit. Overlap ends of twine about 6 in. (152 mm) and locate at bottom of glass glazing.

3.   Brush a soapy solution of water around outside window opening.

4.   Have an assistant hold glass glazing (2) with fixed glass (3) and twine up to outside window opening. Place ends of twine through window and let them hang loosely inside.

5.   While assistant holds fixed glass (3) in place, pull on one end of twine, forcing lip of glass glazing (2) up and over window flange (4).

6.   Pull all twine out from around glass glazing (2).

TA50013

10-28. REAR STEP ASSEMBLY REPLACEMENT (M1010).

This task covers: a. Removal   b. Installation

INITIAL SETUP:

Materials/Parts   *Manual References*
* Three lockwashers   • TM 9-2320-289-10

| a. REMOVAL |

NOTE

◀f **removing return spring (4), perform steps 1 and 5.**

◀f **removing step (11), perform steps 1 and 4.**

◀f **removing step frame (7), perform steps 1-3.**

1.   Unfold rear step assembly. (See TM 9-2320-289-10)

2.   Remove 2 nuts (6), washers (9), bolts (10), and hook assembly (8).

3.   Remove step frame (7) from truck.

4.   Remove 2 nuts (13), 6 washers (12), 2 bolts (5), and step (11). Remove   other step if
      required.

5.   Remove 2 nuts (3), washers (2), and bolts (1), and remove return spring (4).

| b.   INSTALLATION |

NOTE

● **If installing step frame (7), perform steps 3 and 4.**

● **If installing step (11), perform step 2.**

◀f **installing return spring (4), perform step 1.**

1.   Install return spring (4) with 2 bolts (1), washers (2), and nuts (3).

2.   Install step (11) with 2 bolts (5), 6 washers (12), and 2 nuts (13). Install other step if removed.

3.   Install step frame (7) to truck.

4.   Install hook assembly (8) to step frame (7) with 2 bolts (10), washers (9), and nuts (6).

5.   Fold rear step assembly. (See TM 9-2320-289-10)

10-28. REAR STEP ASSEMBLY REPLACEMENT (M1010) (Con't).

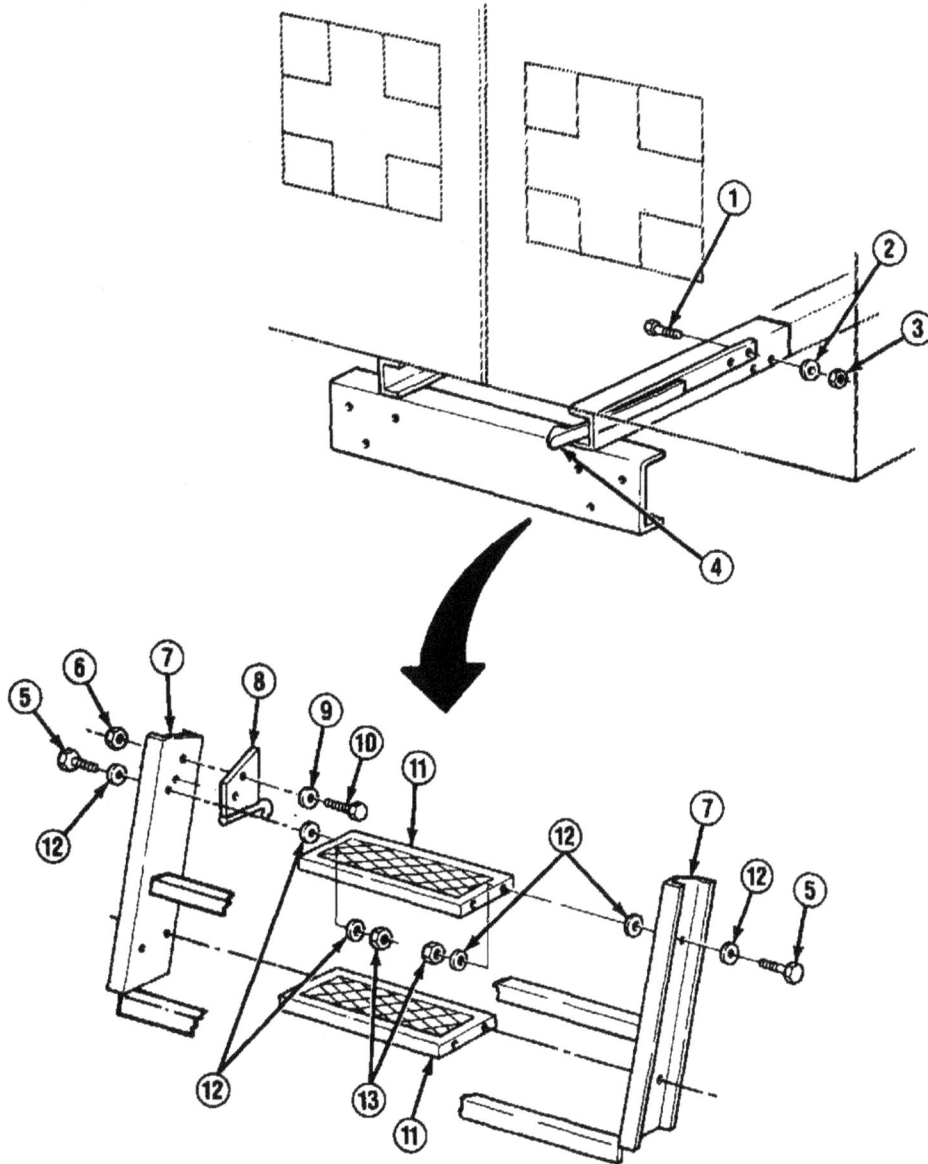

TA50014

10-29. ATTENDANT'S SEAT MAINTENANCE (M1010).

This task covers:
    a. Remova l   c. Assembly
    b. Disassembly   d. Installation

INITIAL SETUP:

Materials/Parts

• One cotter pin
• One locknu t
• Six lockwashers

Tools/Test Equipment

• Torque wrench

General Safety Instructions

• Use extreme caution when raising or lowering ambulance attendant's seat.

---

a.	REMOVAL

1. Depress pedal of travel adjustment arm (18) and slide attendant's seat assembly rearward to stop bolt. Remove stop bolt from track. Remove attendant's seat assembly from tracks.

b.	DISASSEMBLY

NOTE

Perform the following steps as required to remove the damaged component.

1. Remove 3 screws (7), lockwashers (6), and seatbelt bracket (5).

2. Remove 3 screws (27), lockwashers (1), and seat (2). Discard lockwashers.

3. Remove 2 nuts (8), washers (9), and bolts (3), and remove 2 seatbelts (4) from seatbelt bracket (5).

4. Remove cotter pin (11), support bracket pin (25), and support bracket (10). Discard cotter pin.

WARNING

Ambulance attendant's   **seat stem assembly (26) is spring loaded.**
Carefully raise and lower   **attendant's seat to avoid risk of injury.**

5. Depress pedal at height adjustment arm (21), pull back expansion pin (13) at travel adjustment arm (18), and remove stem assembly (26) and stem spring (12).

6. Remove locknut (20) and track lockpin (19). Discard locknut.

10-29. ATTENDANT'S SEAT MAINTENANCE (M1010) (Con't).

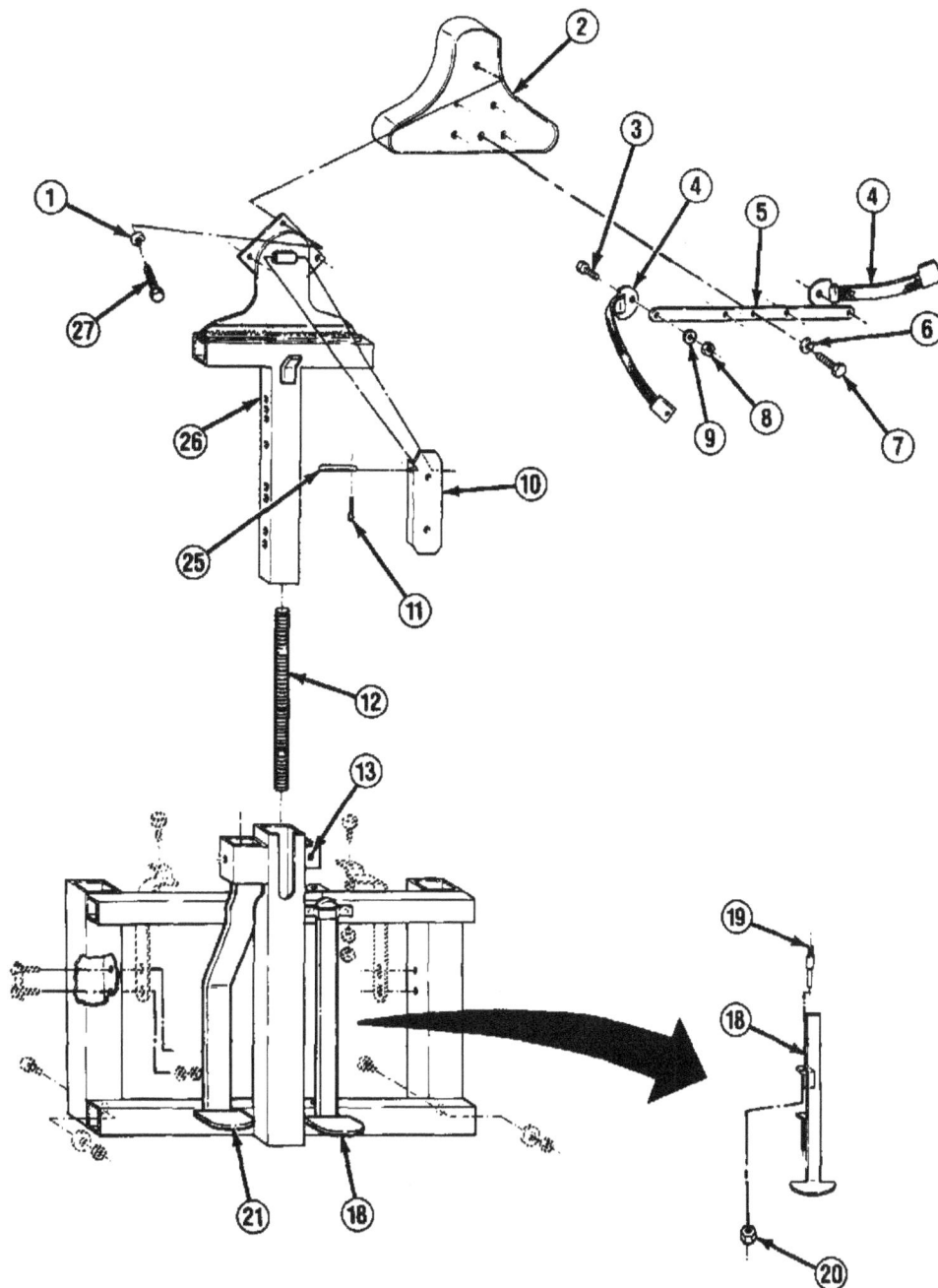

TA50015

10-29. ATTENDANT'S SEAT MAINTENANCE (M1010) (Con't).

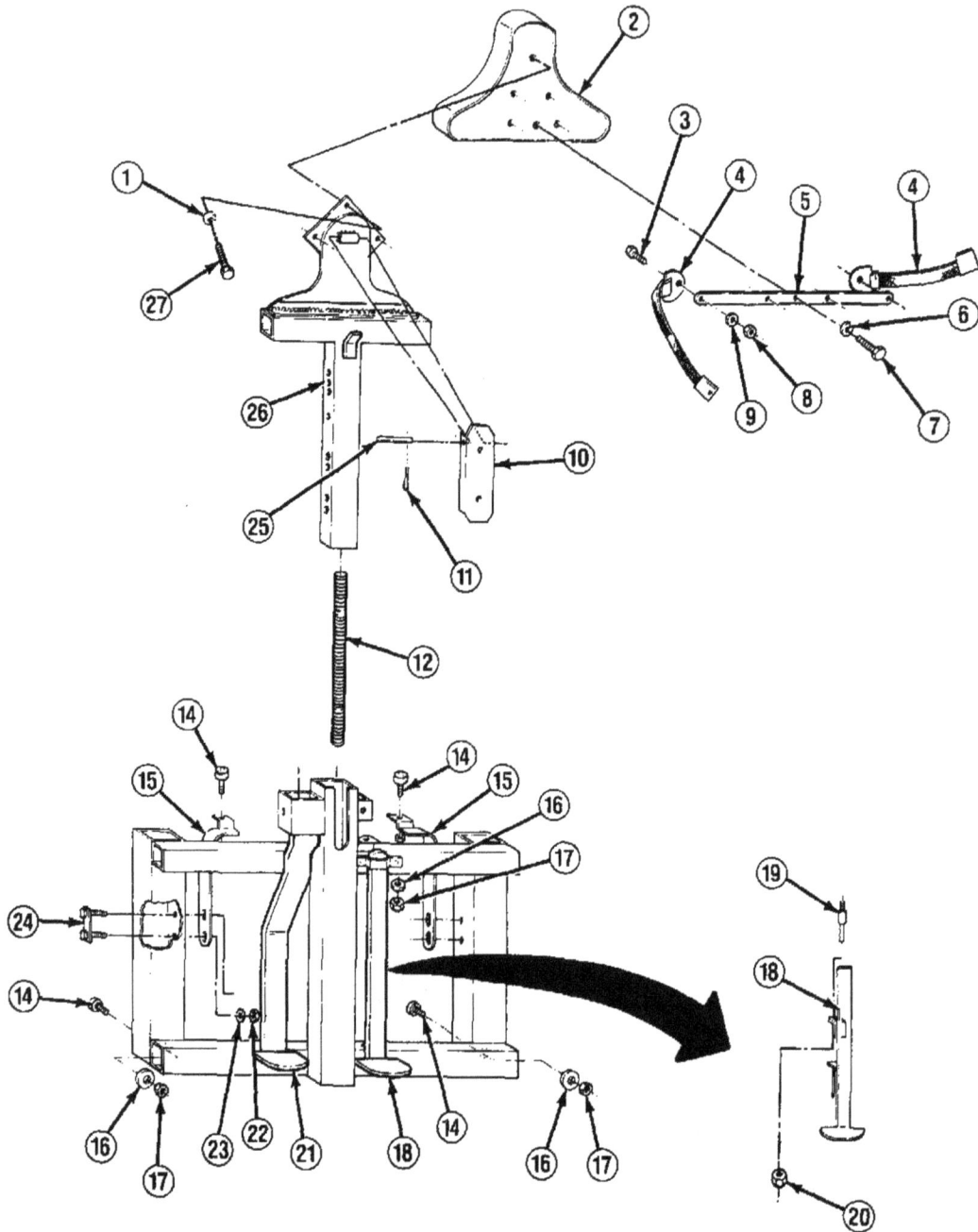

TA50016

10-29. ATTENDANT'S SEAT MAINTENANCE (M1010) (Con't).

NOTE

Some models use a locknut instead of a washer (16) and nut (17) at roller (14).

7.   Remove 4 nuts (17), washers (16), and rollers (14).

NOTE

Mark location of brackets (15) on attendant's seat frame for Installation.

8.   Remove 4 nuts (22), 4 washers (23), 2 brackets (24), and 2 brackets (15).

c.   ASSEMBLY

1.   Install 2 brackets (15) and 2 brackets (24) with 4 washers (23) and nuts (22).

2.   Install 4 rollers (14) with washers (16) and nuts (17).

3.   Install track lockpin (19) at travel adjustment arm (18) with new locknut (20).

WARNING

**Ambulance attendant's seat stem assembly (26) is spring loaded.
Carefully raise and lower attendant's seat to avoid risk of injury.**

4.   Depress pedal at height adjustment arm (21). Install stem spring (12) and stem assembly (26).,

5.   Install support bracket (10) with support bracket pin (25) and new cotter pin (11).

6.   Install 2 seatbelts (4) to seatbelt bracket (5) with 2 bolts (3), washers (9), and nuts (8). Tighten nuts to 40 lb.-ft. (54 N•m).

7.   Install seat (2) with 3 new lockwashers (1) and screws (27),

8.   Install seatbelt bracket (5) on seat (2) with 3 new lockwashers (6) and screws (7).

d.   INSTALLATION

1.   Aline rollers (14) on top and bottom tracks

2.   Depress pedal at travel adjustment arm (18) and slide attendant's seat assembly into first locking position.

3.   Install stop bolt on track.

4.   Check attendant's seat for free travel.

10-30. INTERIOR SLIDING DOOR REPLACEMENT (M1010).

This task covers: a.   Removal   b. Installation

INITIAL SETUP:

Materials/Parts
- Four rivets
- Two screws

| a. | **REMOVAL** |

NOTE

• If removing window glass, see paragraph 10-27.

• If removing sliding door (2), perform steps 1-5.

• If removing handles (8 and 16), slam lock (9), and hasp and shaft assembly (11), perform steps 6-9.

• If removing blackout curtain (5), perform step 10.

• Rivets (14) are not replaceable, use screws for installation.

1.   Remove 2 rivets (14) securing bracket (13) to side frame. Discard rivets.

2.   Remove 2 screws (12) and floor track (15) with attached bracket (13).

NOTE

Some models may have 2 washers and lockwashers in addition to 2 bolts (1) and nuts (4), DO NOT use washer and lockwasher for installation.

3.   Remove left nut (4) at roller track (3). Remove left bolt (1).

4.   Close sliding door (2) and remove right nut (4) at roller track (3). Remove right bolt (1).

5.   Open sliding door (2). Remove sliding door while holding roller track (3) stationary.

6.   Remove setscrew and handle (8).

7.   Remove 4 nuts (10), bolts (7), and slam lock (9).

8.   Turn handle (16) to gain access to 2 screws (17). Remove screws, handle, and hasp and shaft assembly (11).

9.   Remove pin and remove handle (16) from hasp and shaft assembly (11).

10.   Remove 4 rivets (6), snap fastener, and blackout curtain (5). Discard rivets.

10-30. INTERIOR SLIDING DOOR REPLACEMENT (M1010) (Con't).

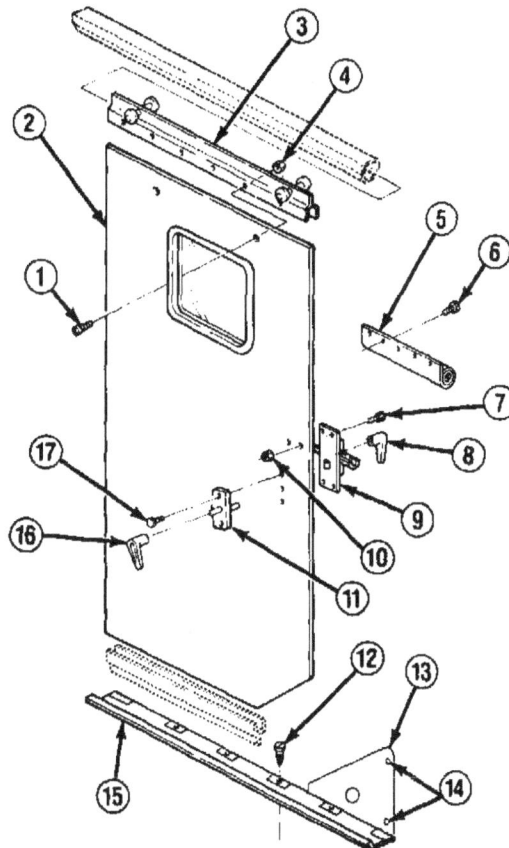

b. **INSTALLATION**

NOTE

- If installing   blackout curtain (5), perform step 1.

- If installing handles (8 and 16), slam lock (9), and hasp and shaft assembly (11), perform steps 2-5.

- If installing sliding door (2), perform steps 6-11.

1. Install blackout curtain (5) with 4 new rivets (6) and snap fastener.

2. Install handie (16) to hasp and shaft assembly (11) with pin.

3. Install handle (16) and hasp and shaft assembly (11) at sliding door (2) with 2 screws (17).

4. Install slam lock (9) with 4 bolts (7) and nuts (10).

TA50017

10-30. INTERIOR SLIDING DOOR REPLACEMENT (M1010) (Con't).

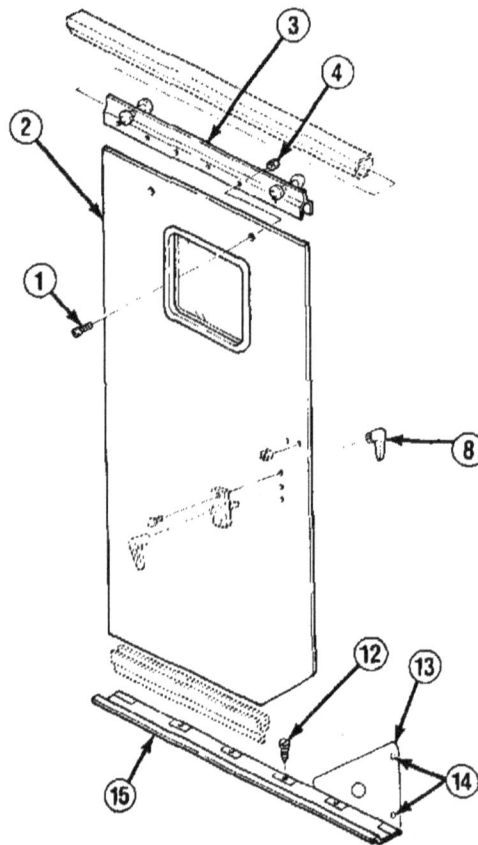

5. Install handle (8) with setscrew.

6. Fully open roller track (3). Hold roller track stationary and install sliding door (2).

NOTE

Ensure that bolts (1) are installed with heads facing toward rear of truck.

7. Close sliding door (2) and install right bolt (1) and nut (4).

8. Partially open sliding door (2) and install left bolt (1) and nut (4).

9. Clean area where floor track (15) is to be installed. Install   floor track with 2 screws (12).

10. Install 2 new screws (14) at bracket (13) into side frame.

11. Check operation of sliding door (2). Adjust sliding door   height by loosening 2 nuts (4), adjusting height, and tightening nuts.

TA50018

10-31. GAS-PARTICULATE FILTER MAINTENANCE (MI 010).

This task covers:	a. Removal	c. Installation
	b. Cleaning and Inspection	

INITIAL SETUP:

Equipment Condition

* Both battery negative cables disconnected.
  (See paragraph 4-38)

Materials/Parts

* Four lockwashers
* Dry cleaning solvent
  (Item 15, Appendix C)

Manual References

* FM 3-5
* TM 10-277
* TM 9-2320-289-10

General Safety Instructions

* If filter has been used in a Nuclear, Biological, or Chemical (NBC) environment special precautions must be taken.
* Dry cleaning solvent is flammable and must not be used near open flame. Use only in a well-ventilated area.

a. REMOVAL

WARNING

* Only authorized and trained personnel are to remove and service gas-particulate filters that have been used in an NBC environment. See local SOP for disposing contaminated filters. Failure to follow this warning may result in serious illness or death to personnel.

* Special protective clothing (See TM 10-277) must be used and special safety measures and decontamination procedures (See FM 3-5) must be followed when replacing contaminated filters. Failure to follow this warning may result in serious illness or death to personnel.

10-31. GAS-PARTICULATE FILTER MAINTENANCE (M1010) (Con't).

NOTE

If the following conditions exist,   replace gas canisters (12) and gas-particulate filter (9):   physical darnage or water immersion; filter becomes clogged, resulting in insufficient air flow. Replace ALL gas canisters and gas-particulate filters after operating in an NBC environment.

1. Loosen 2 clamps (3) and disconnect hoses (4) from filter manifold (5).

2. Disconnect ground wire from back of filter housing (10).

3. Lift clip (2) and remove filter assembly (1).

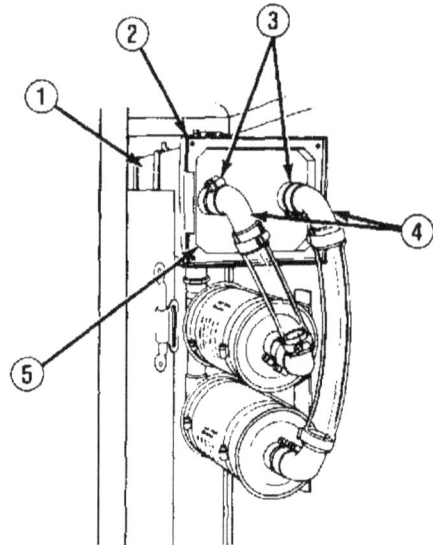

4. Remove 4 screws (6) and lockwashers (7), and remove manifold (5). Discard lockwashers.

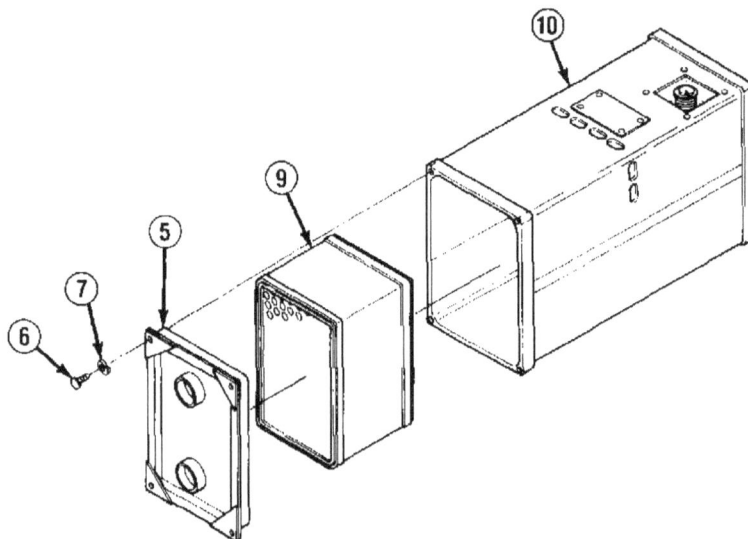

NOTE

If gas-particulate filter (9) is likely to be reused and no arrow is present, mark an arrow on its side showing direction of airflow.

5. Remove gas-particulate filter (9).

TA50019

10-31. GAS-PARTICULATE FILTER MAINTENANCE (M1010) (Con't).

NOTE

Both gas canisters (12) are replaced in same way.

6. Loosen 2 hose clamps (11) and remove hoses from both ends of gas canister (12).

7. Loosen 2 band clamps (13) and remove gas canister (12).

8. Dispose of gas canister (12) properly, as it cannot be reused.

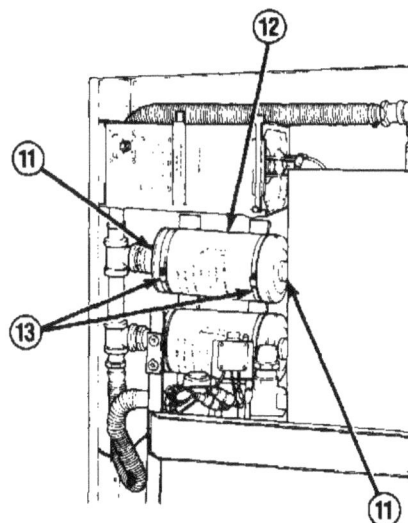

---

b.	CLEANING AND INSPECTION

WARNING

Dry cleaning solvent P-D-680 is toxic and flammable. Always wear protective goggles and gloves and use only in a well-ventilated area. Avoid contact with skin, eyes, and clothes and DO NOT breathe vapors. DO NOT use near open flame or excessive heat. The solvent's flash point is 100°F-138°F (38°C-59°C). If you become dizzy while using cleaning solvent, immediately get fresh air and medical help. If solvent contacts eyes, immediately wash your eyes with water and get medical aid.

CAUTION

DO NOT allow moisture to come in contact with filter material or filter will be damaged.

1. Clean gas-particulate filter (9) and manifold (5) with a cloth moistened with dry cleaning solvent.

2. Inspect manifold (5), gas-particulate filter (9), and all gaskets for damage. Ensure that gaskets will make an airtight seal. If gaskets are damaged, notify your supervisor.

TA50020

10-31. GAS-PARTICULATE FILTER MAINTENANCE (M1010) (Con't).

| c. INSTALLATION |

NOTE

- See TM 9-2320-289-10 for gas-particulate filter (9) and gas canister (12) part number information.

- Both gas   canisters (12) are installed in same way.

1. Install new gas canister (12) with 2 band clamps (13).

2. Install 2 hoses to ends of gas canister (12) with 2 hose clamps (11).

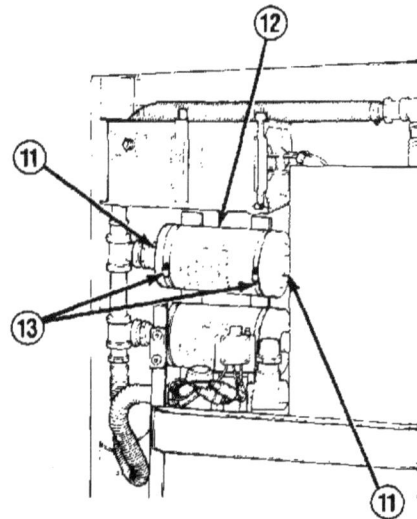

NOTE

If installing a used gas-particulate filter (9), ensure   that arrow marked on the side is in direction of airflow.

3. Install gas-particulate filter (9) into filter housing (10) and   ensure that felt gasket (8) will be against manifold (5).

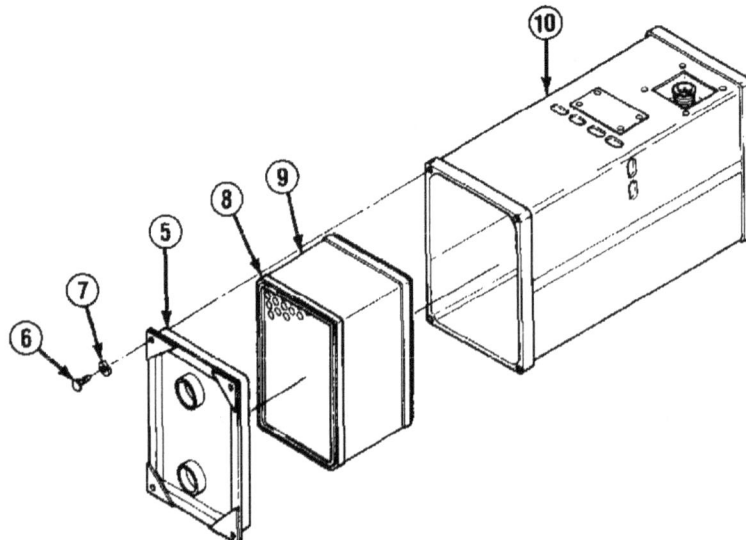

TA50021

10-31. GAS-PARTICULATE FILTER MAINTENANCE (M1010) (Con't).

4. Install manifold (5) with 4 screws (6) and new lockwashers (7).

5. Install filter assembly (1) to filter mount with clip (2).

6. Connect ground wire to back of filter housing (10).

7. Connect 2 hoses (4) to manifold (5) and tighten clamps (3).

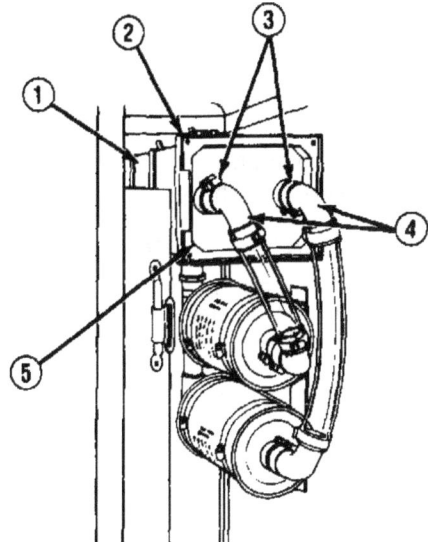

FOLLOW-ON TASKS:

- Connect both battery negative cables. (See paragraph 4-38)
- Check GPFU for proper operation. (See TM 9-2320-289-10)

TA50022

10-32. HEATER FUEL PUMP REPLACEMENT (M1010).

This task covers: a.   Removal   c. Installation
                                    b. Cleaning

INITIAL SETUP:

Equipment Condition

- Both battery negative cables disconnected, (See paragraph 4-38)

Materials/Parts

- One gasket

General Safety Instructions

- DO NOT perform this procedure near fire, flames, or sparks. A fire extinguisher must be on hand in work area.

a.	REMOVAL

WARNING

Diesel fuel is flammable. DO NOT perform procedures near fire, flames, or sparks. A fire extinguisher must be on hand in work area. Failure to follow this warning may result in serious injury or death.

NOTE

If removing cut-out switch (7), perform steps 3, 6, and 7.

1. **Loosen 2 nuts (4) and disconnect intake pipe (16) and output pipe (3) from 2 fittings (1 and 15).**

NOTE

Trucks equipped with winterization kits will have an engine coolant heater fuel line (2) at fitting (1) instead of cap (14) and gasket (13).

2. Remove 2 fittings (1 and 15) from heater fuel pump (5), and cap (14) and gasket (13) from fitting (1) if damaged. Discard gasket if removed.

3. Disconnect 2 electrical connectors (10).

4. Remove 2 bolts (12) and heater fuel pump (5). Remove 2 nuts (9) if damaged.

5. Remove filter (11) from heater fuel pump (5) and set aside for cleaning.

6. Remove cut-out switch (7) from clip (8) on inner fender.

7. Remove 2 screws (6) and clip (8).

10-32. HEATER FUEL PUMP REPLACEMENT (M1010) (Con't).

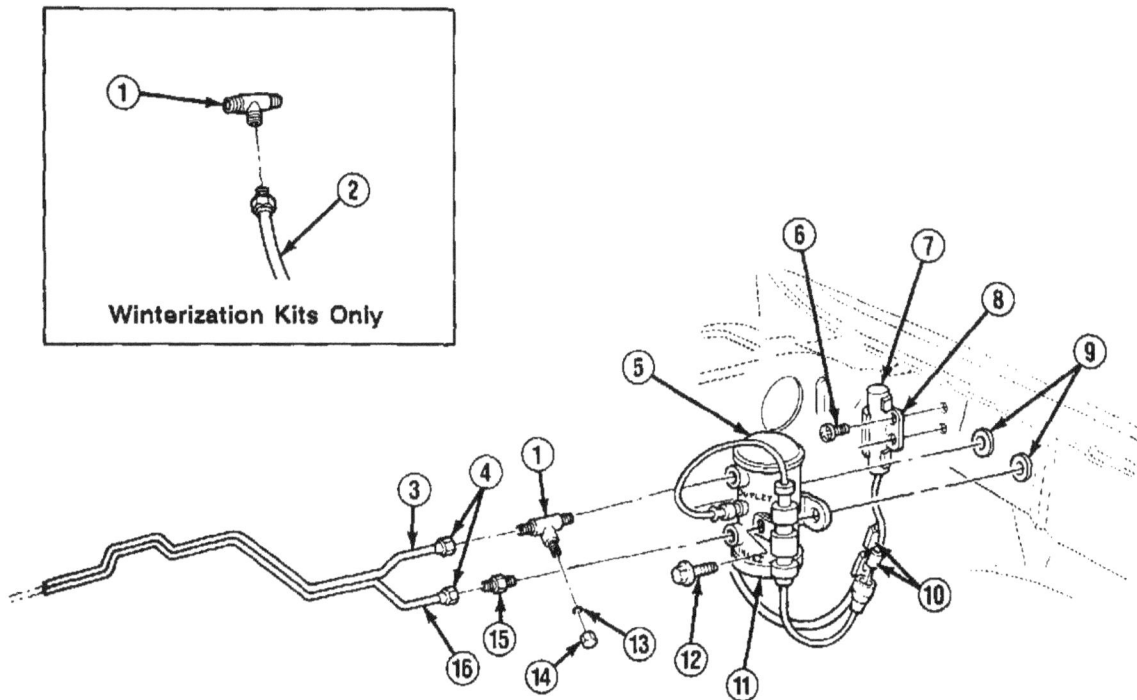

Winterization Kits Only

| b. | CLEANING |

WARNING

Diesel fuel is flammable. DO NOT perform procedures near fire, flames, or sparks. A fire extinguisher must be on hand in   work area. Failure to follow this warning may result in serious injury or death.

1. Disassemble filter (11) and drain.

2. Flush out filter (11) with clean fuel, removing any dirt and sediment.

3. Assemble filter (11).

TA50023

10-32. HEATER FUEL PUMP REPLACEMENT (M1010) (Con't).

| c. INSTALLATION |

NOTE

If installing cut-out switch (7), perform steps 1, 2, and 5.

1.   Install clip (8) on inner fender with 2 screws (6).

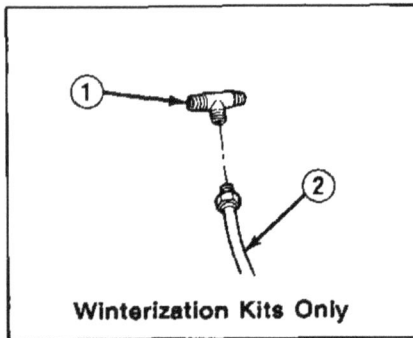

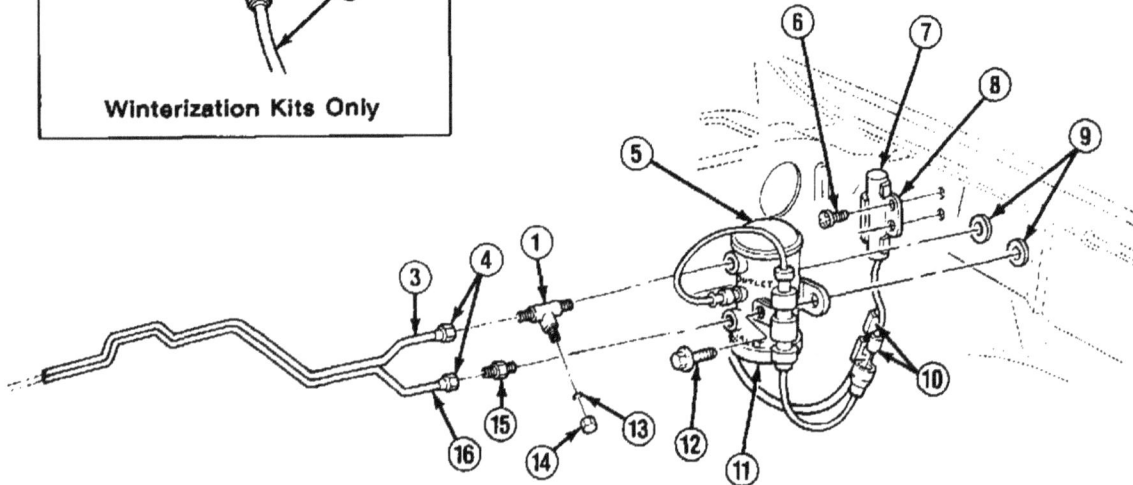

Winterization Kits Only

2.   Install cut-out switch (7) to clip (8).

3.   Install filter (11) to heater fuel pump (5).

4.   Install 2 nuts (9) if removed, Install heater fuel pump (5) with 2 bolts (12).

5.   Connect 2 electrical connectors (10).

TA50024

10-32. HEATER FUEL PUMP REPLACEMENT (M1010) (Con't).

NOTE

Trucks equipped with winterization kits will have an engine coolant heater fuel line (2) at fitting (1) instead of cap (14) and gasket (13).

6.   install new gasket (13) and cap (14) to fitting (1) if removed.

7.   Install 2 fittings (1 and 15) to heater fuel pump (5) if removed.

8.   Connect intake pipe (16) and output pipe (3) to 2 fittings (1 and 15) by tightening 2 nuts (4).

FOLLOW-ON TASKS:

- Connect both battery negative cables. (See paragraph 4-38)
- Check operation of heater fuel pump.
- Check for leaks.

10-33. AIR CONDITIONER COVER AND CONDENSER ASSEMBLY REPLACEMENT (M1010).

This task covers: a. Removal   b. Installation

INITIAL SETUP:

Equipment Condition

●Both battery negative cables disconnected. (See paragraph 4-38)

| a. | **REMOVAL** |

NOTE

If removing capacitor (7), perform steps 1-5.

1. Remove 20 screws (3).

2. Raise cover assembly (1) and disconnect 2 wires (8) at 2 condenser motors (11) and ground wire at left condenser motor. Remove cover assembly.

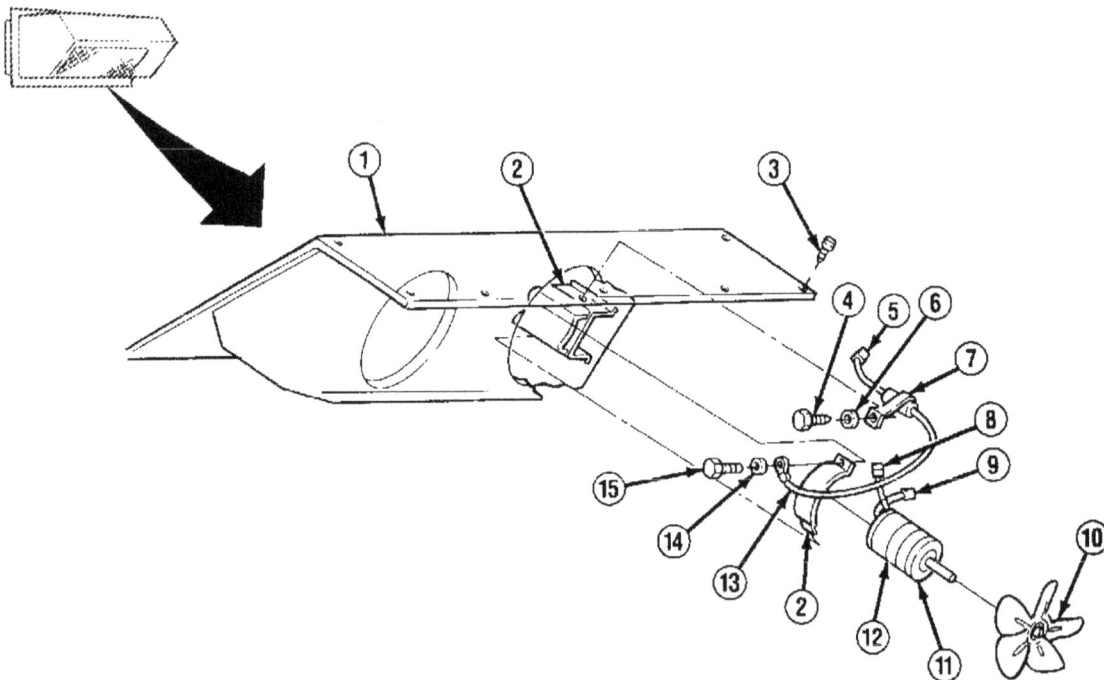

TA50025

10-33. AIR CONDITIONER COVER AND CONDENSER ASSEMBLY REPLACEMENT (M1010) (Con't).

3. Remove bolt (15), washer (14), and ground wire (13) at clamp (2).

4. Disconnect condenser motor connector (9) from capacitor connector (5).

5. Remove screw (4), washer (6), and capacitor (7).

6. Remove condenser motor (11) and fan (10) from clamp (2).

7. Remove setscrew on fan (10) and remove fan from condenser motor (11).

8. Remove insulator (12) from condenser motor (11).

b.   INSTALLATION

NOTE

If installing capacitor (7), perform steps 5-8.

1. Install insulator (12) on condenser motor (11).

2. Install fan (10) to condenser motor (11) with setscrew. Ensure that setscrew is indexed to flat side of condenser motor shaft.

3. Position condenser motor (11) and fan (10) inside clamp (2).

4. Install ground wire and tighten condenser motor (11) and fan (10) with washer (14) and bolt (15).

5. Install capacitor (7) with screw (4) and washer (6).

6. Connect condenser motor connector (9) to capacitor connector (5).

7. Position cover assembly (1) and connect 2 wires (8) at 2 condenser motors (11) and ground wire at left condenser motor.

8. Install cover assembly (1) with 20 screws (3).

FOLLOW-ON TASKS:

*   Connect both battery negative cables. (See paragraph 4-38)
*   Check operation of condenser motor.

10-34. AIR CONDITIONER BLOWER REPLACEMENT (M1010).

This task covers: a, Removal   b. Installation

INITIAL SETUP:

Equipment Condition

- Air conditioner cover assembly removed. (See paragraph 10-33)

---

a.	**REMOVAL**

1. Remove cover (8) from above evaporator.

2. Remove 12 screws (3) at insulated covers (2 and 4).

3. Disconnect plug at blower resistor (18).

4. Disconnect 2 wires at evaporator motor (6).

5. Remove screw and starwasher, and remove 2 ground wires and capacitor (12) from insulated cover (4).

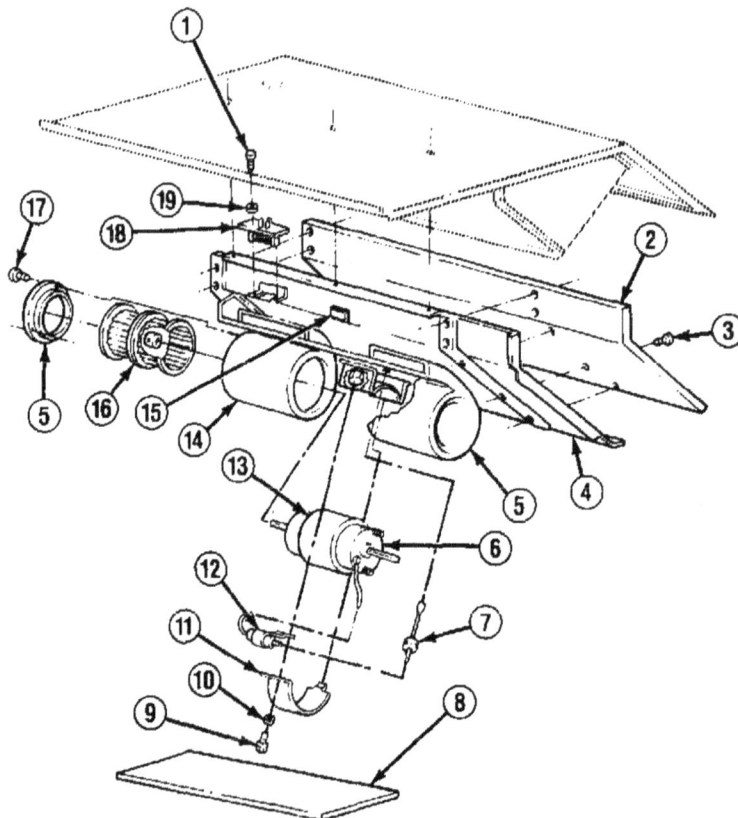

TA50026

10-34. AIR CONDITIONER BLOWER REPLACEMENT (M1010) (Con't).

6.   Remove insulated cover (4) with attached blower assembly.

7.   Remove 2 screws (1), washers (19), and blower resistor (18).

8.   Remove 6 screws (17) and 2 wheel guards (5).

9.   Remove bolt (9) and starwasher (10), and bend back clamp (11).

10. Aline setscrew at 1 wheel (16) with access hole in housing (14). Loosen setscrew.

11. Remove 1 wheel (16) with attached evaporator motor (6) from housing (14). Remove remaining wheel from housing.

12. Loosen setscrew and remove attached wheel (16) from evaporator motor (6).

13. Remove insulator (13) from evaporator motor (6).

| b. | INSTALLATION |

NOTE

**When installing 2   wheels (16) to evaporator motor (6), ensure that 2
setscrews and flat   side of evaporator motor shafts are alined.**

1.   Install insulator (13) to evaporator motor (6).

2.   Install 1 wheel (16) to evaporator motor (6) with setscrew.

3.   Position remaining wheel (16) inside housing (14).

4.   Position evaporator motor (6) with attached wheel (16) in housing (14) and install to other wheel with setscrew.

5.   Install 2 wheel guards (5) with 6 screws (17).

6.   Install evaporator motor (6) to clamp (11) with starwasher (10) and bolt (9). Ensure that 2 wires from evaporator motor are fed straight through grommet (7) in insulated cover (4).

7.   Check to see that 2 wheels (16) turn freely inside housing (14). If adjustment is needed, loosen bolt (9), adjust, and tighten.

8.   Install blower resistor (18) with 2 washers (19) and screws (1).

9.   Position blower assembly inside   air conditioner assembly.

10. Connect plug at blower resistor   (18).

NOTE

**When connecting wires, ensure that they are routed through side slot in
insulated cover (4) and installed to wiring harness clip (15).**

11. Install 2 ground wires and capacitor (12) to insulated cover (4) with screw and starwasher.

12. Install 2 wires to evaporator motor (6).

10-34. AIR CONDITIONER BLOWER REPLACEMENT (M1010) (Con't).

13.   Install insulated covers (2 and 4) with 12 screws (3). Ensure that wiring harness is not crimped.

14.   Install cover (8) above evaporator.

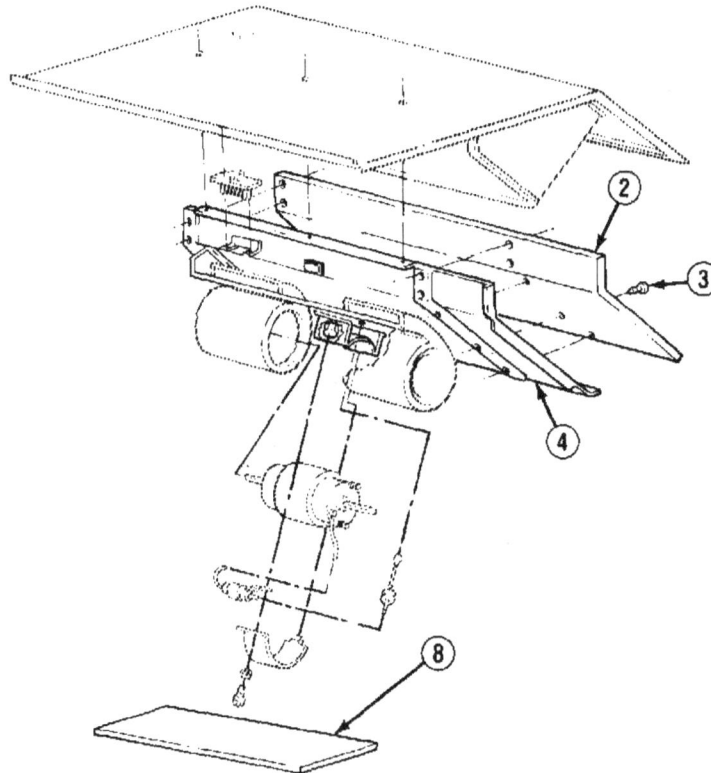

TA50027

FOLLOW-ON TASKS:

- Install air conditioner cover assembly. (See paragraph 10-33)
- Check operation of air conditioner blower.

10-35. PERSONNEL HEATER CONTROL BOX REPLACEMENT (M1010).

This task covers:	a. Removal	b. Installation

INITIAL SETUP:

Equipment Condition

- Both battery negative cables disconnected.
  (See paragraph 4-38)

Tools/Test Equipment

- 90 degree angle drill
- 3/16 in. drill bit

Materials/Parts

- Eight pop rivets
- RTV sealant (Item 41, Appendix C)

---

a. REMOVAL

1. Remove outside access panel from right rear ambulance body.

NOTE

Tag cables for installation.

2. Remove 2 pushnuts (4). Remove 2 screws (5) and clamps (3) from heater base (1). Disconnect 2 cables (2) from vent door control levers (6).

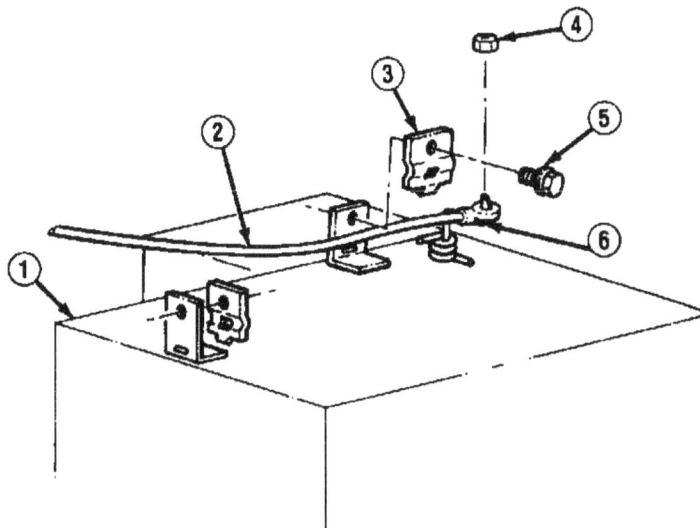

TA50028

10-35. PERSONNEL HEATER CONTROL BOX REPLACEMENT (M1010) (Con't).

3. Disconnect wiring harness (15) from control box (11). Disconnect control box wire assembly from blower motor lead.

4. Loosen clamp (8) and disconnect duct hose (9) from weldment (7). Loosen clamp (17) and disconnect flex hose (16) from weldment. Remove 4 screws (13) from adapter (14). Remove adapter and flex hose assembly from personnel heater (12).

5. Using 90 degree angle drill, remove 8 pop rivets (10). Remove control box (11) and clean old sealant from mating surfaces. Discard   pop rivets.

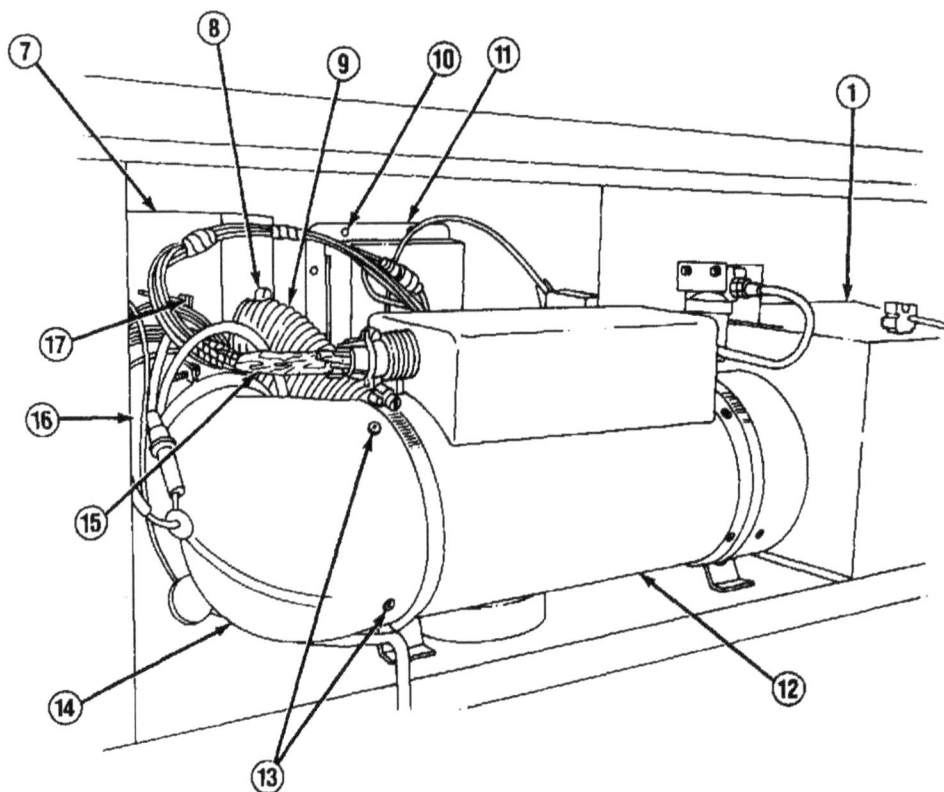

b. **INSTALLATION**

1. Apply RTV sealant to inside flange of control box (11). Install control box with 8 new pop rivets (10).

2. Install adapter (14) and flex hose (16) assembly on personnel heater (12) with 4 screws (13). Connect flex hose to weldment (7) and tighten clamp (17). Connect duct hose (9) to weldment and tighten clamp (8).

3. Connect control box (11) wire assembly to blower motor lead. Connect wiring harness (15) to control box.

TA50029

10-35. PERSONNEL HEATER CONTROL BOX REPLACEMENT (M1010) (Con't).

4, Connect 2 cables (2) to vent door
    control levers (6). Install 2 clamps (3)
    on cables and heater base (1) with 2
    screws (5). Install 2 pushnuts (4).

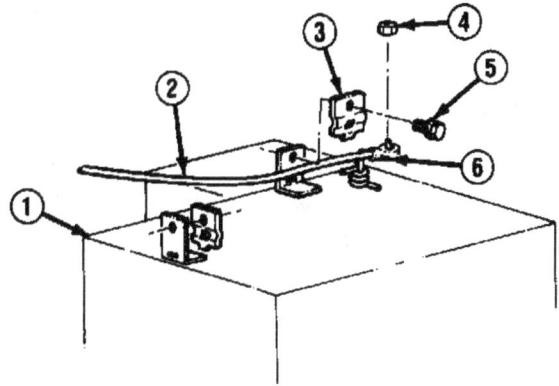

5. Install outside access panel on right rear ambulance body.

FOLLOW-ON TASKS:

• Connect both battery negative cables. (See paragraph 4-38)
• Check operation of heater and cables.

TA50030

10-36. PERSONNEL HEATER, FUEL FILTER, AND BLOWER REPLACEMENT (M1010).

This task covers: a. Removal   c. Heater Bleeding
     b. Installation

INITIAL SETUP:

Equipment Condition

* Both battery negative cables disconnected.
  (See paragraph 4-38)

Materials/Parts

* Cotter pin
* Exhaust gasket
* Filter element
* Filter seal
* Fuel oil (Item 17, Appendix C)
* Pipe sealant (Item 43, Appendix C)
* Plastic tube (Item 49, Appendix C)

Personnel Required

· MOS 63B (2)

General Safety Instructions

* DO NOT perform this procedure near
  fire, flames, or sparks.

---

a.   REMOVAL

WARNING

Diesel fuel is flammable, DO NOT perform this procedure near fire,
flames, or sparks. A fire extinguisher must be on hand in work area.
Failure to follow this warning   may result in serious injury or death to
personnel.

NOTE

* If removing personnel   heater (1), perform steps 1-6.

* If removing fuel filter assembly, perform steps   1, 2, and 7.

* If removing blower motor, perform steps 1-6,   and 8.

* Clean all old sealant from all pipe threads.

1. Remove outside access panel from right rear ambulance body.

NOTE

Use suitable container to catch fuel when disconnecting hose (5) and
disassembling fuel filter assembly.

2. Disconnect hose (5) from personnel heater. Loosen fitting   (3) and remove hose from fuel filter
   body (2).

3. Loosen clamp (10) and disconnect flex hose (11) from adapter (8). Remove 4 screws (7) and
   adapter.

10-36. PERSONNEL HEATER, FUEL FILTER, AND BLOWER REPLACEMENT (M1010) (Con't).

4. Disconnect wiring harness (9) from personnel heater (1). Unscrew 2 clamps (6) and open completely.

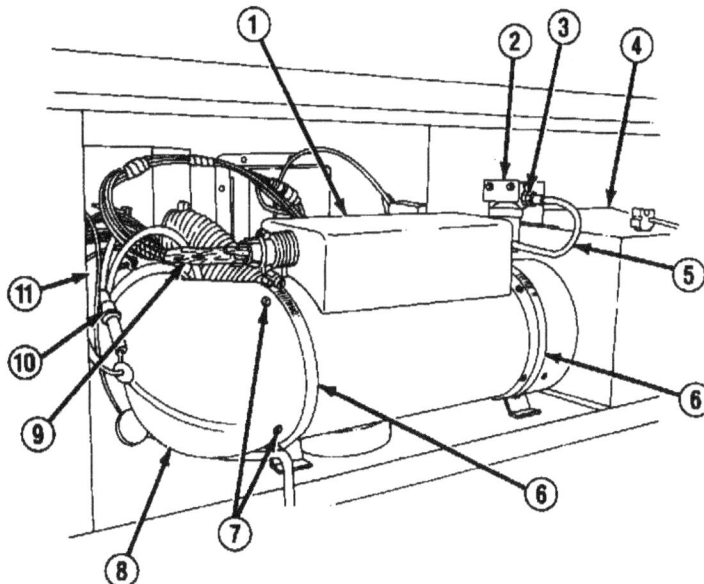

5. From under truck, remove exhaust pipe hanger from exhaust pipe (16), loosen clamp (15), and remove exhaust pipe from adapter (13). Raise personnel heater (1) and remove cotter pin (14) and adapter. Discard cotter pin.

6. Remove personnel heater (1) and exhaust gasket (17) from heater base (4). Discard exhaust gasket. Remove and discard seal (12) if damaged.

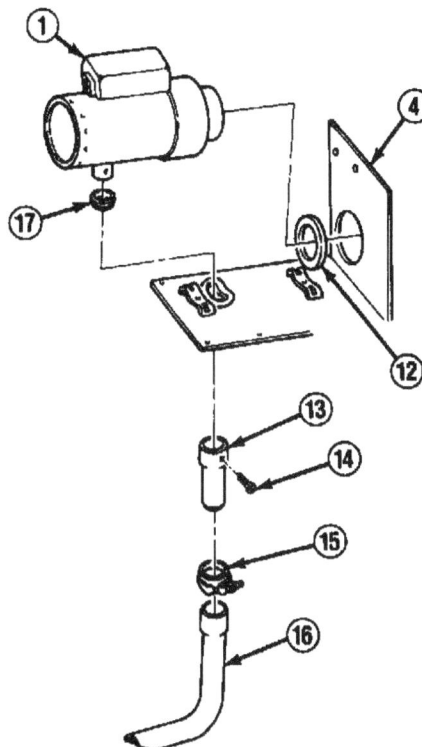

TA50031

10-36. PERSONNEL HEATER, FUEL FILTER, AND BLOWER REPLACEMENT (M1010) (Con't).

7, From under truck, close shutoff valve
on hose connected to "IN" side of
fuel filter body (2). Disconnect hose.
Remove 2 screws (18), washers
(19),   and fuel filter assembly .
Unscrew casing (22) and remove
filter seal (20) and filter element (21).
Discard filter seal and filter element.

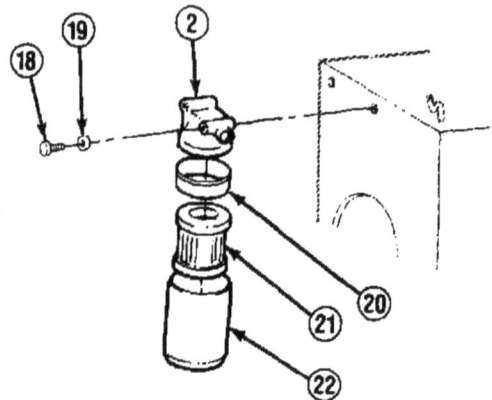

NOTE

**Tag   leads   (23   and 29) for
installation.**

8. Disconnect   ground   lead   (23).
Disconnect lead (29) from control box
wire assembly (30). Remove   3
screws (25) securing plate (26) to
heater base (4) and remove blower
motor (24) assembly. Remove nut
(28), blower wheel (27), and plate
from blower motor.

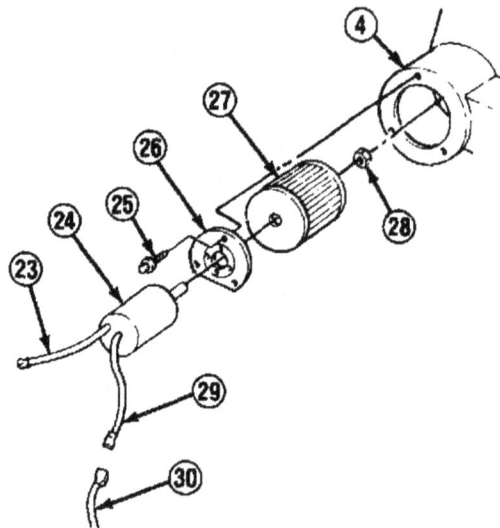

TA50032

10-36. PERSONNEL HEATER, FUEL FILTER, AND BLOWER REPLACEMENT (M1010) (Con't).

| b. | INSTALLATION |

NOTE

- If installing blower motor (24), perform steps 1, 3 through 8, and HEATER BLEEDING steps.

- If installing fuel filter assembly, perform steps 2, 7, and HEATER BLEEDING steps.

- If installing personnel heater (1), perform   steps 3 through 8 and HEATER BLEEDING steps.

- Apply pipe sealant to all pipe threads before   installation.

1. Install plate (26) and blower wheel (27) on blower motor (24) with nut (28). Install blower motor assembly by securing plate to heater base (4) with 3 screws (25). Connect lead (29) to control box wire assembly (30). Connect ground lead (23).

2. Fill casing (22) ¼ full of fuel oil. Install new filter element (21) in casing and new filter seal (20) on fuel filter body (2). Screw casing onto fuel filter body. Install fuel filter assembly with 2 washers (19) and screws (18). Connect hose to "IN" side of fuel filter body and open shutoff valve under truck.

3. Install new exhaust gasket (17) on personnel heater (1). Install seal (12) on personnel heater if removed. Install personnel heater on heater base (4).

4. Raise personnel heater (1) and install adapter (13) with new cotter pin (14), Install exhaust pipe (16) on adapter and tighten clamp (15). Instal   I exhaust pipe hanger to exhaust pipe.

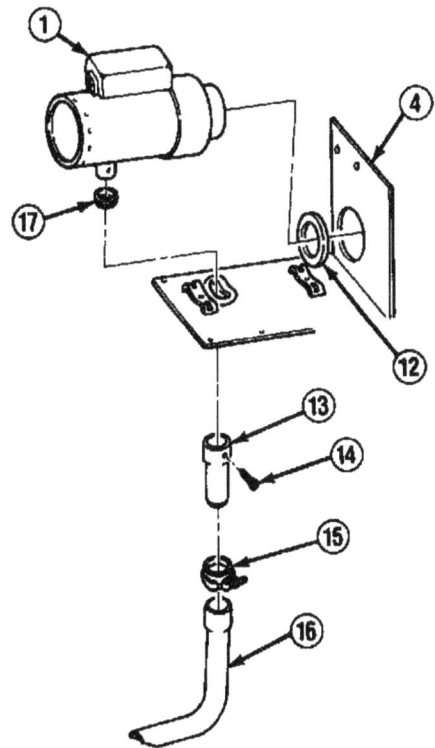

TA50033

10-36. PERSONNEL HEATER, FUEL FILTER, AND BLOWER REPLACEMENT (M1010) (Con't).

5. With personnel heater (1) securely in heater base (4) opening, compress seal (12) about 0.5 in. (1.2 cm) Loosely install 2 clamps (6) around personnel heater.

6. Install adapter (8) with 4 screws (7) if removed. Connect flex hose (11) to adapter and tighten clamp (10).

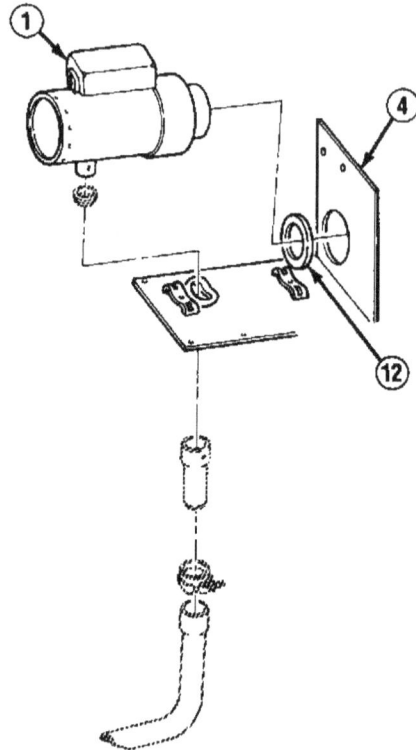

7. Connect hose (5) to fuel filter body (2) and tighten fitting (3).

8. Tighten clamps (6) securely.

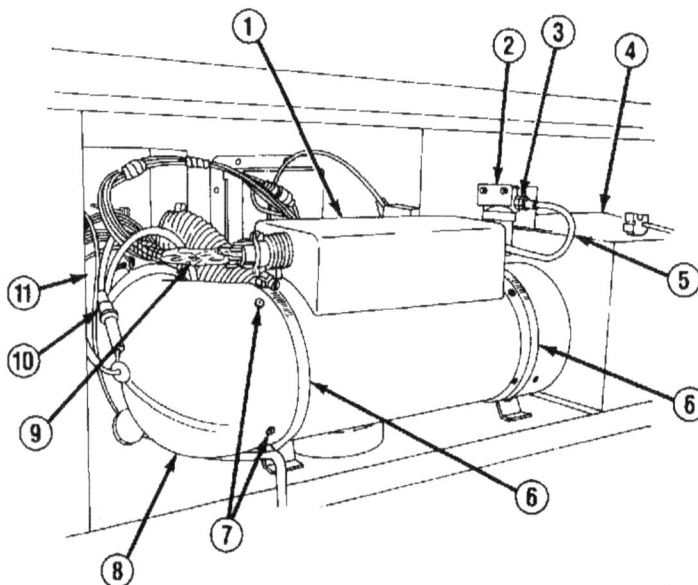

TA50034

10-36. PERSONNEL HEATER, FUEL FILTER, AND BLOWER REPLACEMENT (M1010) (Con't).

| c. | HEATER BLEEDING |

WARNING

Diesel fuel is flammable. DO NOT perform **this procedure near fire,**
flames, or sparks. A fire extinguisher must **be on hand in work area.**
Failure to follow this warning may result in **serious injury or death to**
personnel.

NOTE

Use suitable container to catch fuel from hose (5) and bleed port (31).

1. Connect both battery negative cables. (See paragraph 4-38)

2. Hold personnel heater switch in "START" position. Continue operation until a clean, steady flow of fuel is obtained, then shut off personnel heater. Connect hose (5) to personnel heater (1).

3. Connect wiring harness (9) to personnel heater (1).

4. Remove personnel heater (1) cover. Connect plastic tube to bleed port (31). Open bleed port. Hold cab heater switch in "START" position. Continue operation until a clean, steady flow of fuel is obtained, then shut off cab heater. Close bleed port and remove plastic tube.

5. Install personnel heater (1) cover.

6. Install outside access panel on right rear ambulance body.

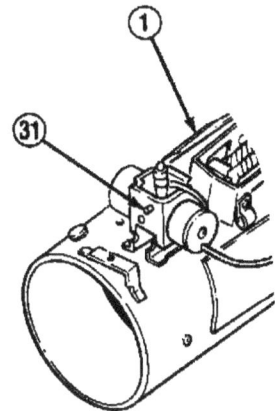

TA50035

CHAPTER 11
SPECIAL PURPOSE KITS MAINTENANCE

Section I. TROOP SEAT KIT REPAIR

11-1. TROOP SEAT KIT REPAIR.

This task covers:	a. Disassembly	b. Assembly

INITIAL SETUP:

Materials/Parts
· Sixteen locknuts
Ž Sixteen cotter pins

Personnel Required
· MOS 63B (2)

---

a.	DISASSEMBLY

NOTE

· DISASSEMBLY steps given are for one section of right side troop seat. All other sections are disassembled the same way.

Ž If removing support assembly from truck, perform steps 1 and 6 through 8.

1. Remove safety strap from eye bolt.

11-1.   TROOP SEAT KIT REPAIR (Con't).

2.   Remove 6 nuts (5) and bolts (6), and 3 seatback slats (7).

3.   Remove screw (10) and detent pin (11) from bottom of slat (13) closest to support assembly (8). Remove 8 nuts (15), washers (14), bolts (12), and 4 slats (13).

4.   Remove 2 locknuts (19), bolts (20), and 2 legs (17 or 18) from 2 troop seat frames (16). Discard locknuts.

5.   Remove 2 cotter pins (21), clevis pins (22), and 2 troop seat frames (16) from support assembly (8). Discard cotter pins.

6.   Remove 3 retaining pins (4) from pin holes of 2 clamps (1) and clamp (9). If damaged, remove 3 screws (2) and lanyards (3) from support assembly (8), Remove 3 retaining pins from lanyards if damaged.

7.   Remove 2 clamps (1) and clamp (9) from support assembly (8) and from 3 truck stake pockets.

8.   With the help of an assistant, remove support assembly (8) from truck.

| b.   ASSEMBLY |

NOTE

• ASSEMBLY steps given are for one section of right side troop seat. All other sections are assembled the same way.

• If installing support assembly (8) in truck, perform steps 1-4, and 10.

1.   With the help of an assistant, install support assembly (8) to top of side rail with supports in 3 truck stake pockets.

2.   Install front and middle clamps (1) in 2 stake pockets with clamps hooked over support assembly (8) and clamp plugs through holes provided in support assembly.

3.   Install rear clamp (9) in rear stake pocket with clamp hooked over support assembly (8) and clamp plug through hole in side of support assembly. Apply pressure as required to install clamp plug.

4.   If removed, install 3 lanyards (3) to support assembly (8) with 3 screws (2). If removed, install 3 retaining pins (4) to lanyards. Install retaining pins through pin holes of 2 clamps (1) and clamp (9).

5.   Install 2 troop seat frames (16) to support assembly (8) with 2 clevis pins (22) and 2 new cotter pins (21).

NOTE

Shorter legs (18) are installed at seats over wheel well.

6.   Install 2 legs (17 or 18) to 2 troop seat frames (16) with 2 bolts (20) and new locknuts (19).

7.   Install 4 slats (13) to 2 troop seat frames (16) with 8 bolts (12), washers (14), and nuts (15).

11-1. TROOP SEAT KIT REPAIR (Con't).

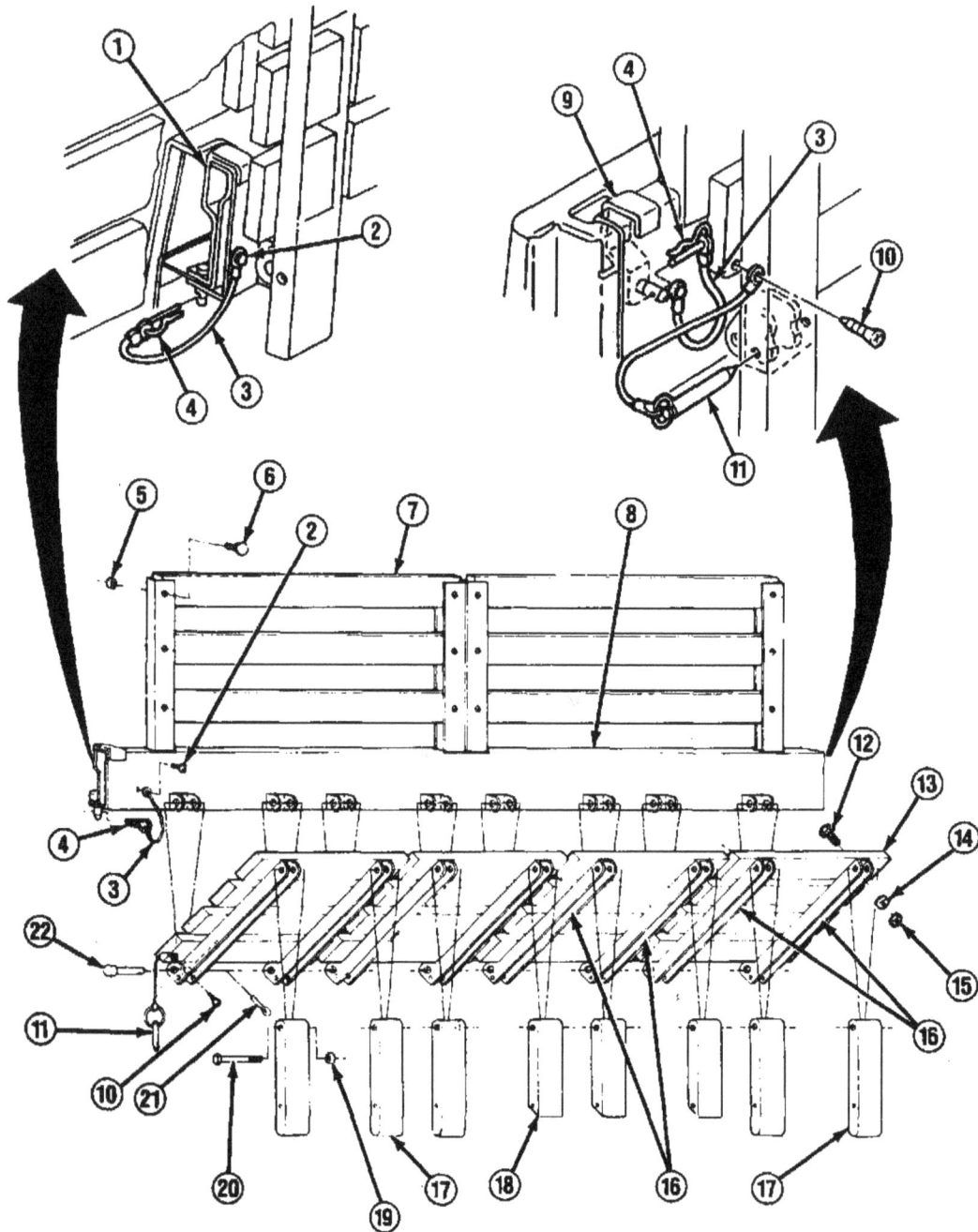

8.   Install detent pin (11) at underside of slat (13)   closest to   support assembly (8) with screw
     (10).

9.   Install 3 seatback slats (7) with 6 bolts (6) and nuts (5).

10.   Install safety strap at eye bolt.

TA50036

Section II. WINTERIZATION KIT CAB HEATER MAINTENANCE

11-2.   WINTERIZATION KIT CAB HEATER MAINTENANCE INDEX.

11-3. HEATER CONTROL PANEL MAINTENANCE.

This task covers:

a. Removal   c. Assembly
b. Disassembly   d. Installation

INITIAL SETUP:

Equipment Condition
• Both battery negative cables disconnected.
(See paragraph 4-38)

Materials/Parts
• Eight lockwashers

| a. REMOVAL |

NOTE

Tag leads for installation.

1. Disconnect 2 wiring harness cables (13) and disconnect plug (15).

NOTE

•If removing heater control panel (1) assembly, tag and disconnect all leads.

•If removing individual controls or indicators, perform DISASSEMBLY as required.

2. Remove 2 screws (10). Pull heater control panel (1) assembly away from housing.

| b. DISASSEMBLY |

NOTE

• Each DISASSEMBLY step can be performed separately from other DISASSEMBLY steps. Perform only as required.

• Tag all disconnected leads for installation if not already disconnected during REMOVAL.

1. Disconnect lead from back of indicator light (2). Remove nut from back of indicator light and remove indicator light.

2. Remove 2 screws (3). Disconnect leads and remove circuit breaker (4). Repeat for other circuit breaker as required.

3. Disconnect lead from back of indicator light (9). Remove nut and washer from back of indicator light, and remove indicator light.

4. Remove nut (6, 7, or 11). Disconnect leads and remove toggle switch (5, 8, or 12).

5. On underside of heater control panel (1), remove 4 nuts (17), lockwashers (16), and screws (19). Remove receptacle connector (14), Repeat for other receptacle connector as required. Remove grommet (18) as required. Discard lockwashers.

11-3. HEATER CONTROL PANEL MAINTENANCE (Con't).

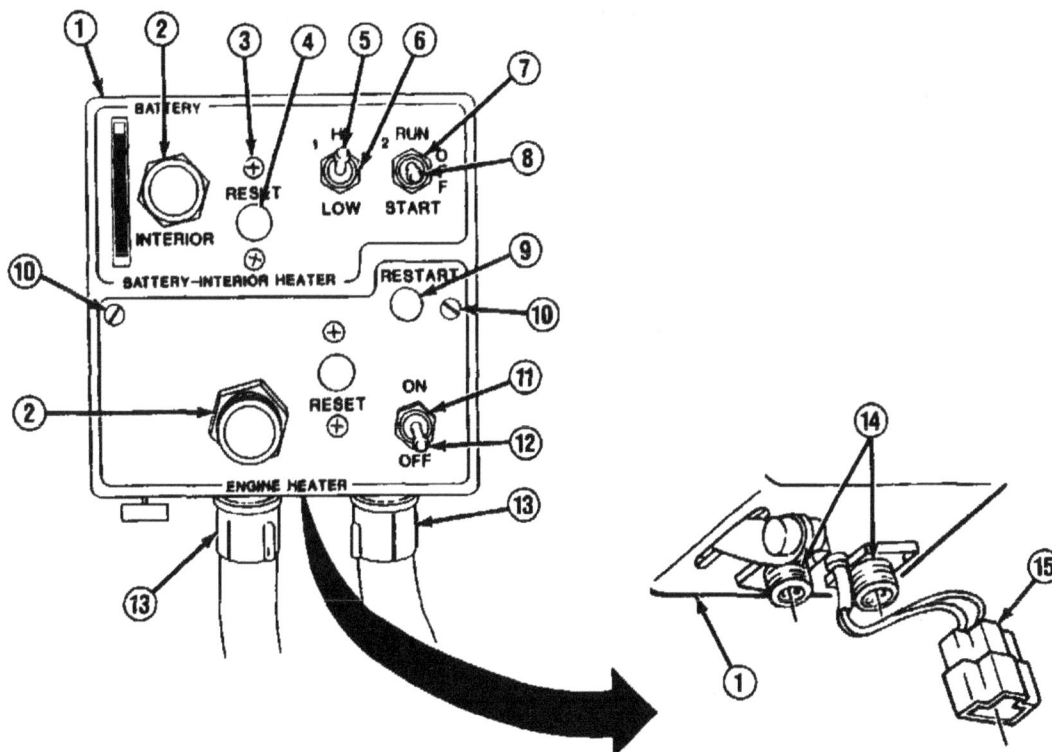

c. ASSEMBLY

NOTE

Each ASSEMBLY step can be performed separately from other ASSEMBLY steps. Perform only as required.

1. Install grommet (18) if removed. Install receptacle connector (14) on underside of heater control panel (1) with 4 screws (19), new lockwashers (16), and nuts (17). Repeat for other receptacle connector if removed.

2. Position toggle switch (5, 8, or 12) through heater control panel (1) hole and install with nut (6, 7, or 11). DO NOT fully tighten nut. Connect leads to toggle switch and tighten nut.

   Install indicator light (9) through heater control panel (1) hole with washer and nut. Connect lead to back of indicator light.

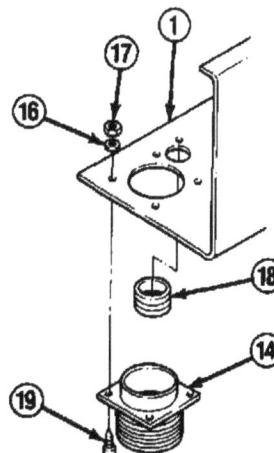

TA50037

11-3. HEATER CONTROL PANEL MAINTENANCE (Con't).

4. Install circuit breaker (4) through heater control panel (1) hole with 2 screws (3). Connect leads to back of circuit breaker. Repeat for other circuit breaker if removed.

5. Install indicator light (2) through heater control panel (1) hole with nut. Connect lead to back of indicator light.

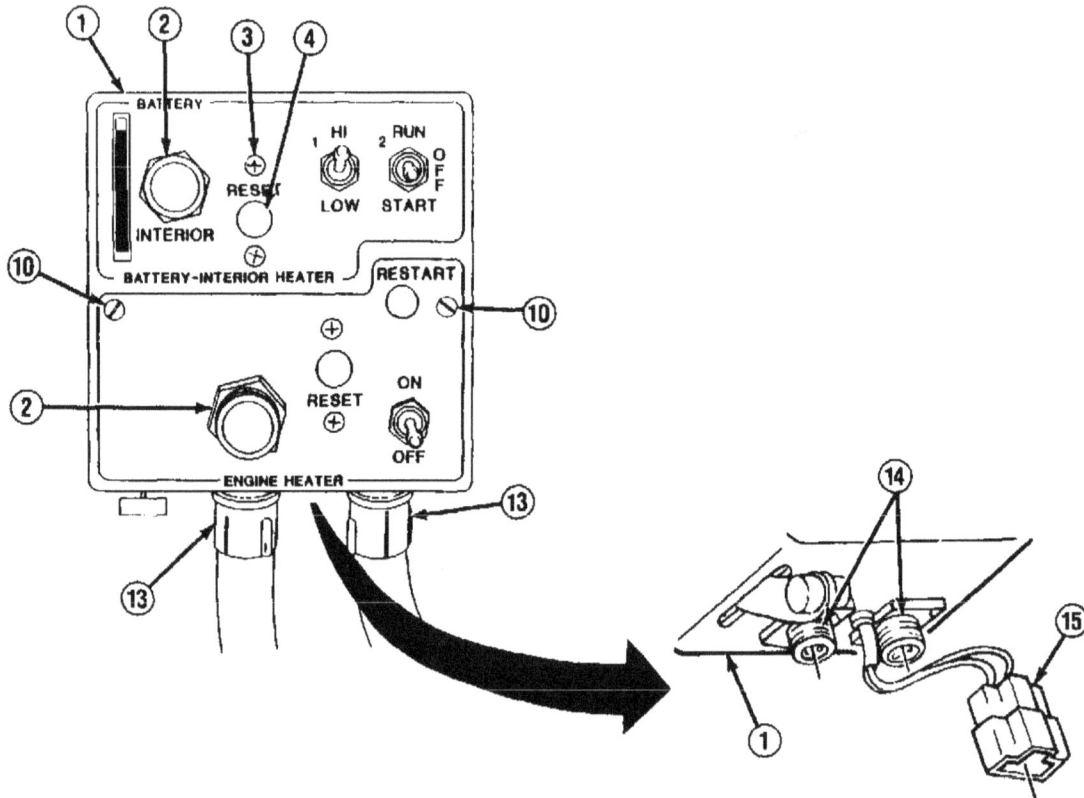

| d. | INSTALLATION |

1. Connect all leads if not connected during ASSEMBLY. Install heater control panel (1) assembly on housing with 2 screws (10).

2. Connect plug (15). Connect 2 wiring harness cables (13) to receptacle connectors (14).

FOLLOW-ON TASKS:

• Connect both battery negative cables. (See paragraph 4-38)
• Check operation of cab heater. (See TM 9-2320-289-10)

TA50038

11-4. HEATER CONTROL PANEL HOUSING REPLACEMENT.

This task covers: a. Removal   b. Installation

INITIAL SETUP:

Equipment Condition
  • Heater control panel removed.
    (See paragraph 11-3)

Tools/Test Equipment
  • Torque wrench

Materials/Parts
  • Three lockwashers

| a. REMOVAL |

NOTE

If removing heater control panel housing, perform steps 1-3.

1.   Loosen nut on clip (6). Remove push-on nut (5) and disconnect control cable (2) from diverter assembly (1). Pull control cable through clip.

2.   Loosen retaining strap (3) and pull control cable (2) through retaining strap. Connect guide wire to end of control cable to assist in installation.

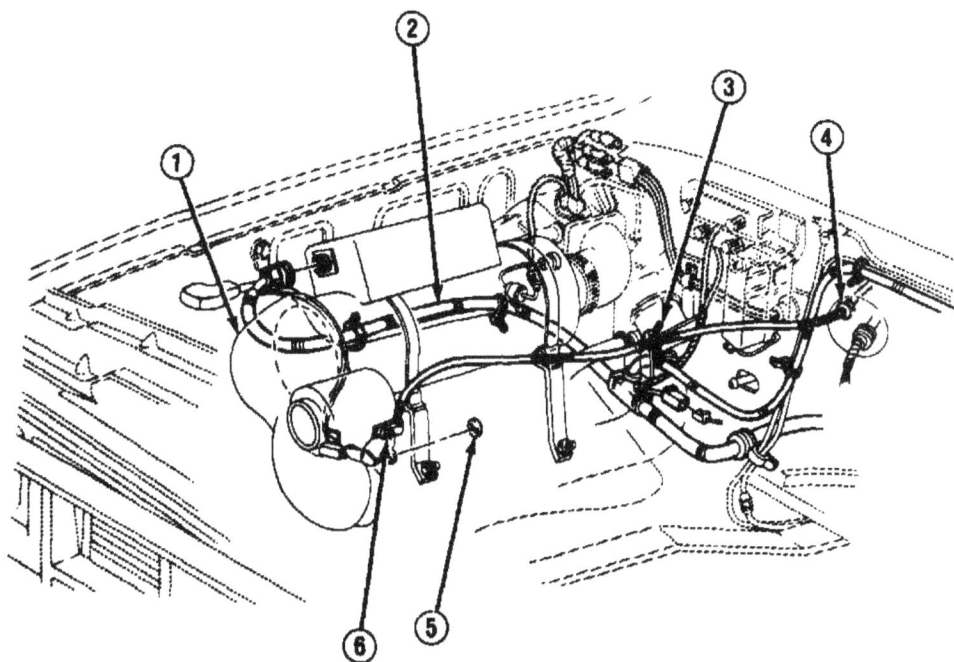

TA50039

11-4. HEATER CONTROL PANEL HOUSING REPLACEMENT (Con't).

3. Remove 3 nuts (11), lockwashers (10), and screws (7). Pull heater control panel housing (9) until control cable (2) and guide wire go through grommet (4). Disconnect guide wire and leave in place for installation. Discard lockwashers.

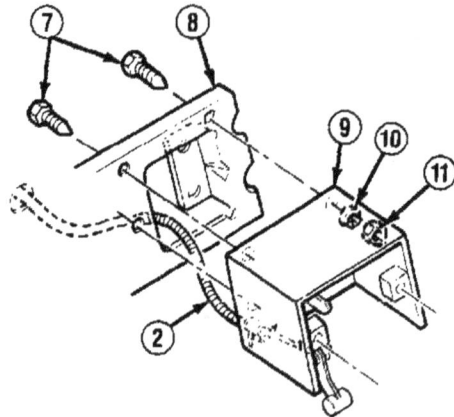

4. Remove 4 bolts (14) and washers (15). Remove mounting bracket (8) from instrument panel (12). Remove mounting nuts (13) as required.

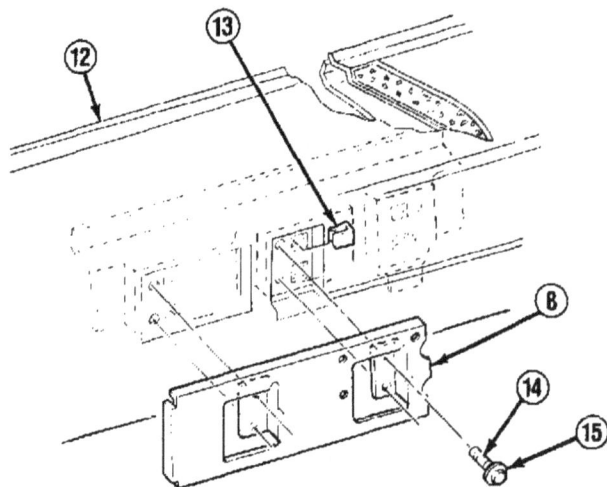

b. INSTALLATION

NOTE

• Some production models may have screw (7) installed behind mounting bracket (8).

• If installing heater control panel housing (9), perform steps 2-4.

1. Install mounting nuts (13) if removed. Install mounting bracket (8) on instrument panel (12) with 4 bolts (14) and washers (15). Tighten bolts to 50-65 lb.-in. (6–7 N•m).

2. Connect guide wire to end of control cable (2). Pull control cable through grommet (4) with guide wire, Install heater control panel housing (9) on mounting bracket (8) with 3 screws (7), new lockwashers (10), and nuts (11).

TA50040

11-4.   HEATER CONTROL PANEL HOUSING REPLACEMENT (Con't).

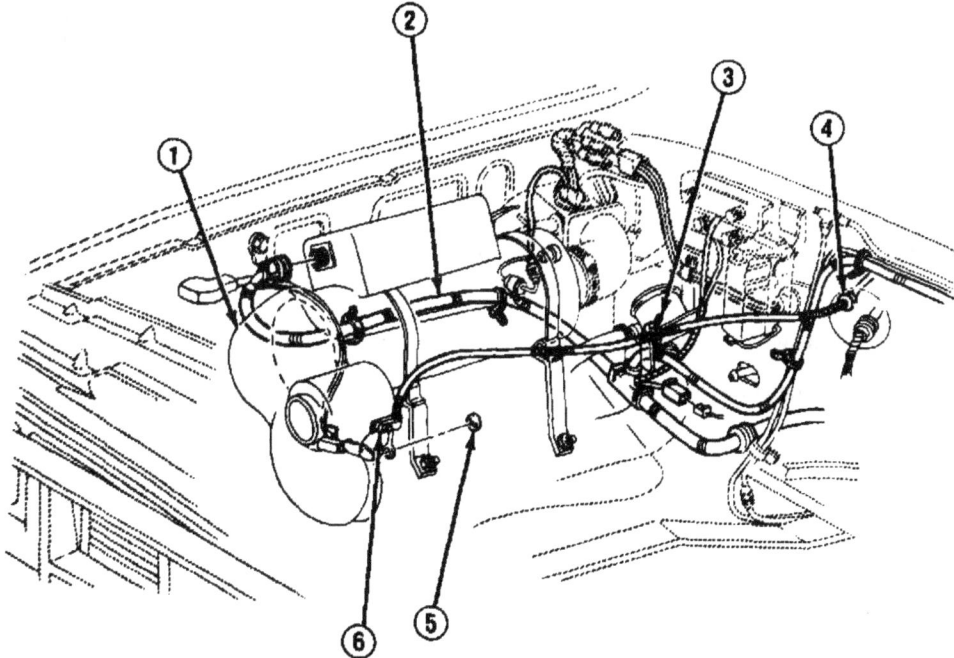

3.   Remove guide wire from end of control cable (2). Guide control cable through retaining strap (3) .

4.   Guide control cable (2) through clip (6). Connect control cable to diverter assembly (1) and install push-on nut (5). Tighten nut on clip. Tighten retaining strap (3).

FOLLOW-ON TASKS:

* Install heater control panel. (See paragraph 11-3)

TA50041

11-5. ENGINE COMPARTMENT AND CAB INSULATOR REPLACEMENT.

This task covers: a. Removal   b. Installation

INITIAL SETUP:

Tools/Test Equipment
  • Torque wrench

| a. | **REMOVAL** |

NOTE

  • **If removing hood or radiator insulators**   **(3 or 8), perform steps 1 or 2.**

  • **If removing cab floor insulators, perform steps**   **3-6.**

1.   Pry 24 retainers (2) from hood inner panel (4). Remove hood   insulator (3) from hood (1).

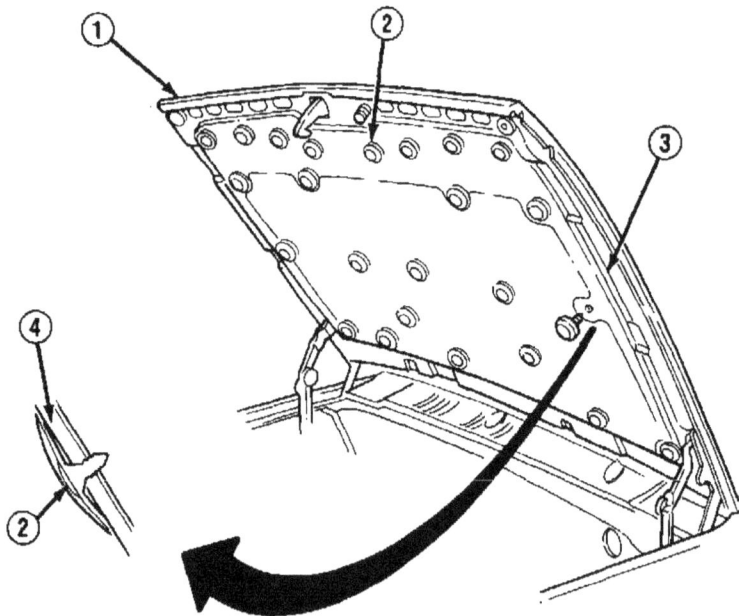

2.   From underneath bumper, disconnect and remove 3 springs (5) from insulator loops (7) and radiator support (6). Remove 2 turnbutton studs (9), Unsnap radiator insulator (8) from top of grille, and remove.

TA50042

11-5. ENGINE COMPARTMENT AND CAB INSULATOR REPLACEMENT (Con't).

NOTE

Remove jack, handle, and wheel wrench from all trucks except M1009.

3. Remove front seats and seatbelt floor mounting. (See paragraph 10-18, 10-23, or 10-25)
Remove transfer case bezel and boot (see paragraph 5-4) or transfer case plate and boot
(see paragraph 5-3).

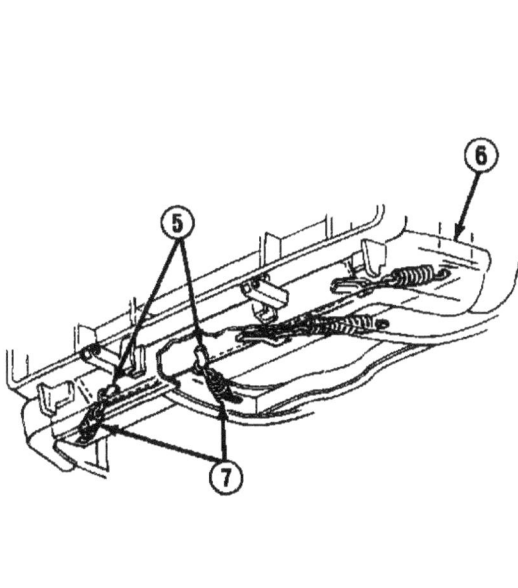

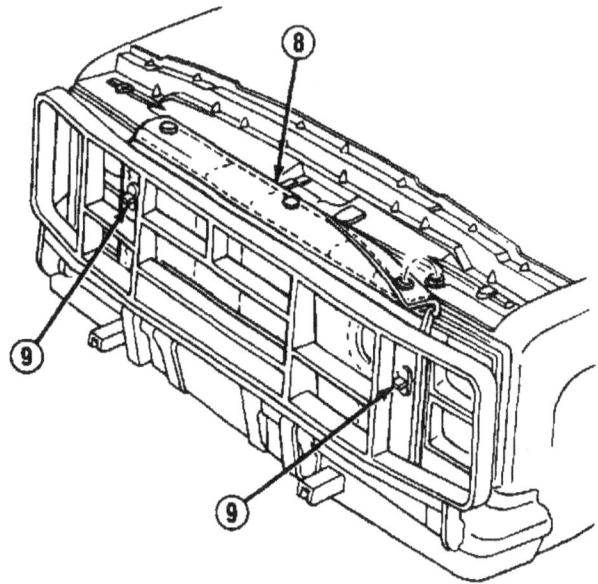

4. Remove chemical agent alarm unit.
Remove 4 bolts (11) and chemical
agent alarm bracket (10).

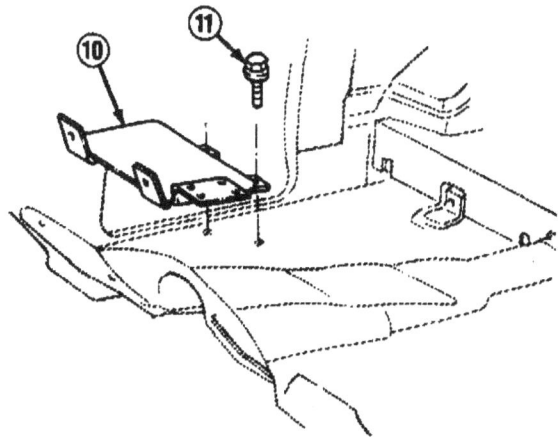

TA50043

11-5.   ENGINE COMPARTMENT AND CAB INSULATOR REPLACEMENT (Con't).

NOTE

M1009 sill plates (15) are fiat and use screws (13).   **6 vertically-removed mounting**

5.   Remove 6 screws (13) and 2 sill plates (15).

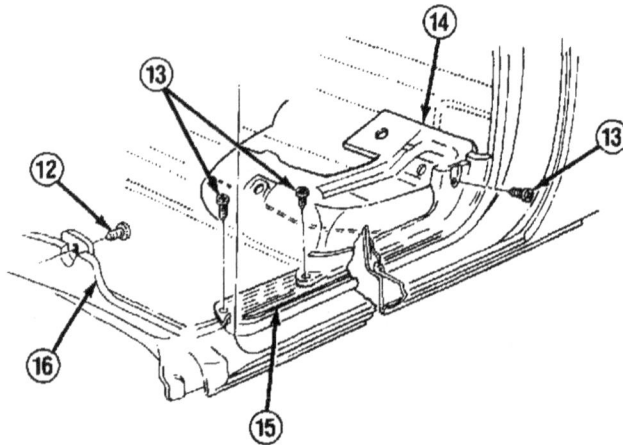

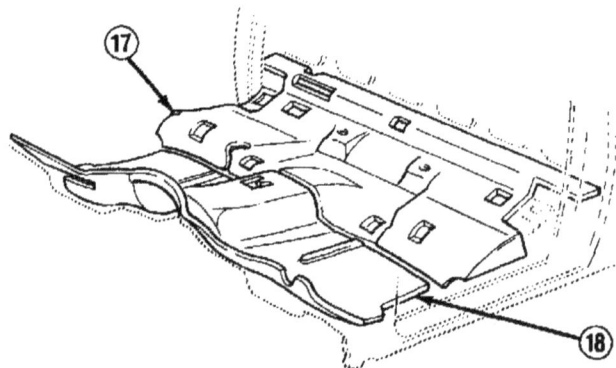

6.   Pry 2 retainers (12) from bulkhead (16). Remove floor mat (14). Remove front cab floor insulator (18) and rear cab floor insulator (17).

| b.   INSTALLATION |

NOTE

• If installing   radiator or hood insulators, perform steps 5 or 6.

• If installing   cab floor insulators (17 or 18), perform steps 1-4.

• Ensure that holes in insulators aline with holes in cab floor.

1.   Install rear cab floor insulator (17) and front cab floor insulator (18). Install floor mat (14) on bulkhead (16) with 2 retainers (12).

TA50044

11-5. ENGINE COMPARTMENT AND CAB INSULATOR REPLACEMENT (Con't).

NOTE

M1009 sill plates (15) are flat and use screws (13).

6 vertically-installed   mounting

2. Install 2 sill plates (15) with 6 screws (13).

3. Install chemical agent alarm bracket (10) with 4 bolts (11). Tighten bolts to 35-55 lb.-in .   (4-6 N•m). Install chemical agent alarm unit.

4. install transfer case bezel and boot (see paragraph 5-4) or transfer case plate and boot (see paragraph 5-3). Install front seats and seatbelt floor mounting. (See paragraph 10-18, 10-23, or 10-25) Install jack, handle, and wheel wrench if removed.

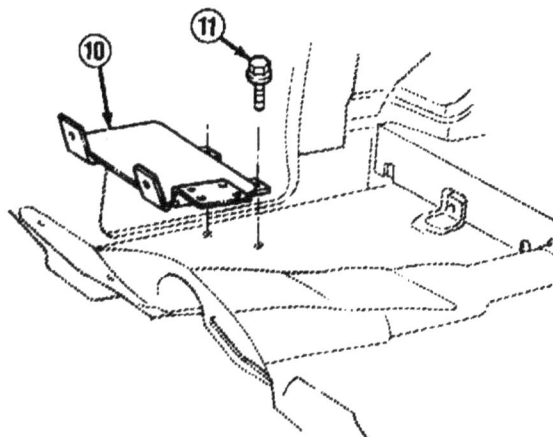

5. Snap radiator insulator (8) to top of grille. Install 2 turnbutton studs (9). From underneath bumper, connect 3 springs (5) to insulator loops (7) and radiator support (6).

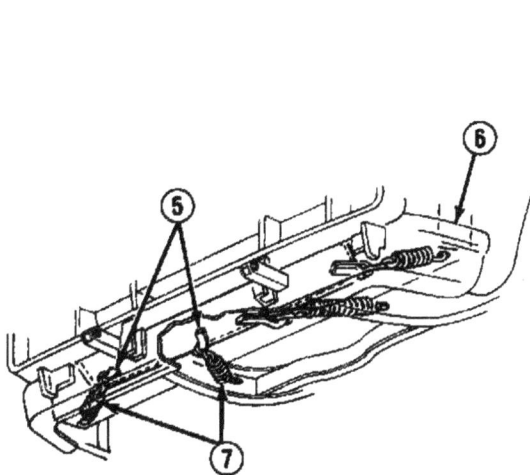

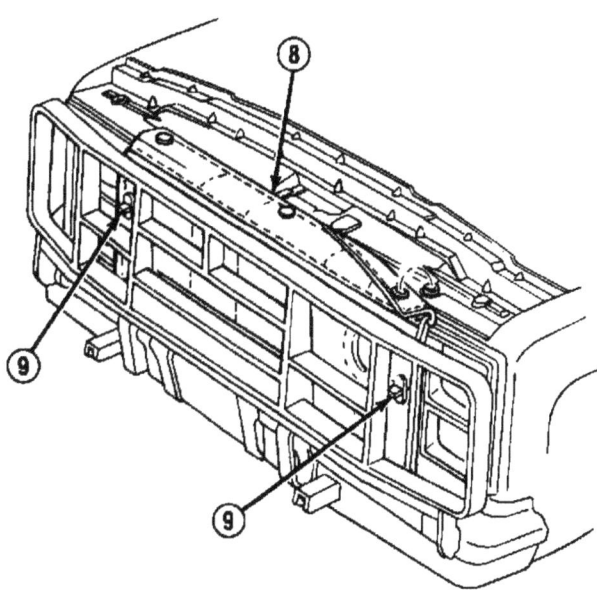

TA50045

11-5.   ENGINE COMPARTMENT AND CAB INSULATOR REPLACEMENT (Con't).

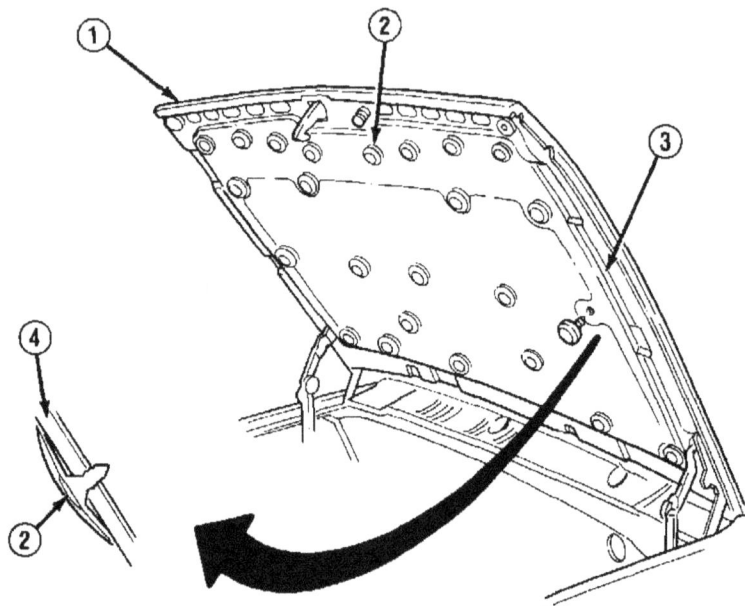

6.   Position hood insulator (3) on hood (1). Install 24 retainers (2) by pressing firmly into hood inner panel (4) holes.

TA50046

11-6.   FRONT AND REAR BATTERY BOX REPLACEMENT.

| This task covers: | a. Removal | b. Installation |

INITIAL SETUP:

Equipment Condition

• Front or rear battery removed.
  (See paragraph 4-39)

Materials/Parts

• One locknut (all except M1010)
• Two locknuts (M1010)
• Two lockwashers (all except M1010)
• Four lockwashers (M1010)

Personnel Required

• MOS 63B (2)

---

a.   REMOVAL

NOTE

• **If removing   front battery box (1), perform step   1.**

• **If removing   rear battery box (7), perform steps   2-6.**

1.   Remove 2 bolts (9). Remove 2 bolts (2) from bracket (3) and bolt (5) from fender nut (4).
      Remove front battery box (1).

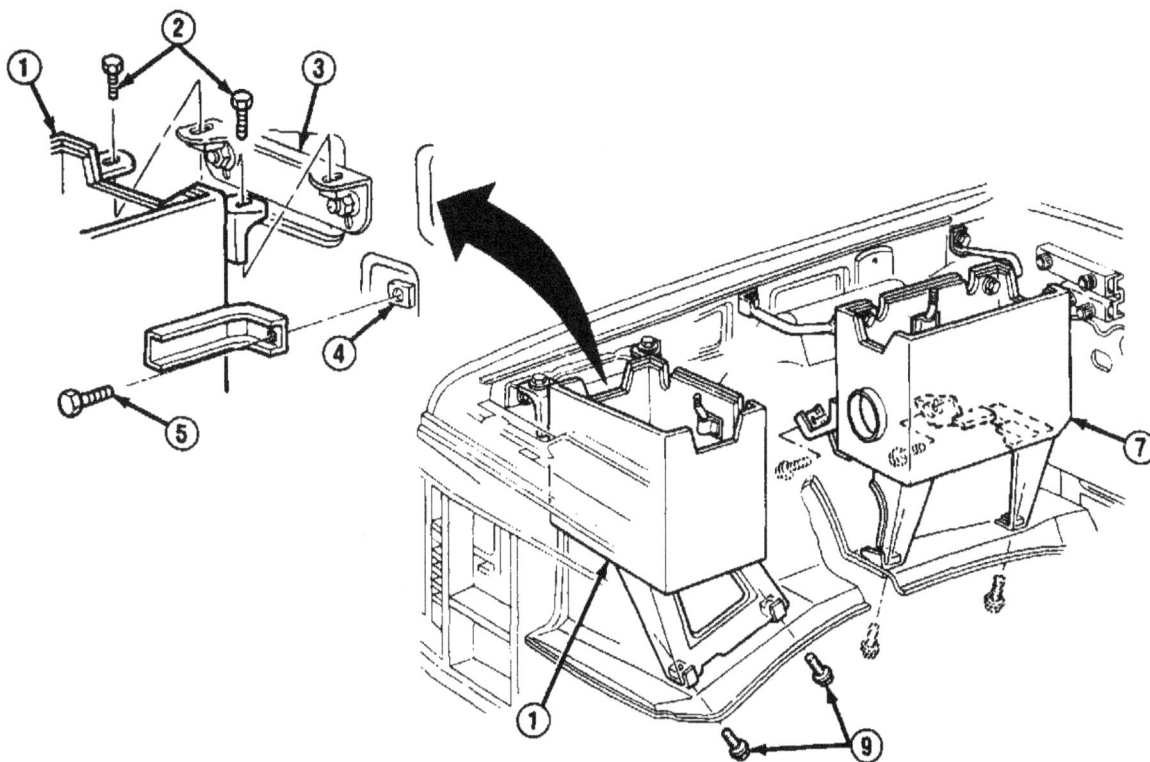

TA50047

11-6. FRONT AND REAR BATTERY BOX REPLACEMENT (Con't).

NOTE

All except M1010 use 1 locknut (13), lockwasher (14), bolt (10), washer
(11), and clip (21) each for inlet and outlet heater hoses (12). M1010 uses
2 each for inlet and outlet heater hoses,

2.   Remove locknut(s) (13), lockwasher(s) (14), bolt(s) (10), and washer(s) (11) from each
heater hose (12) clip. Discard locknuts and lockwashers.

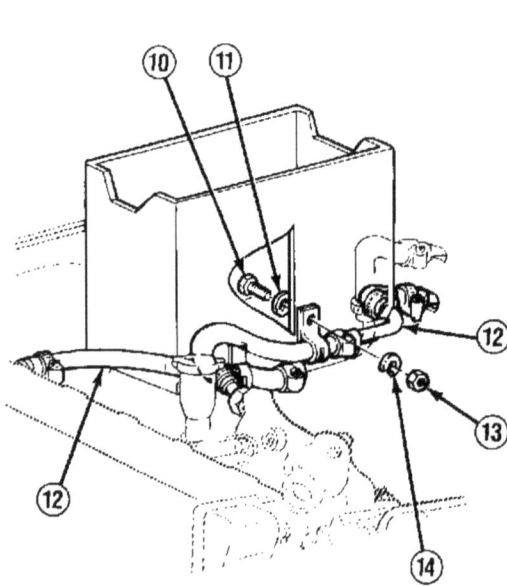

All Except M1010   M1010

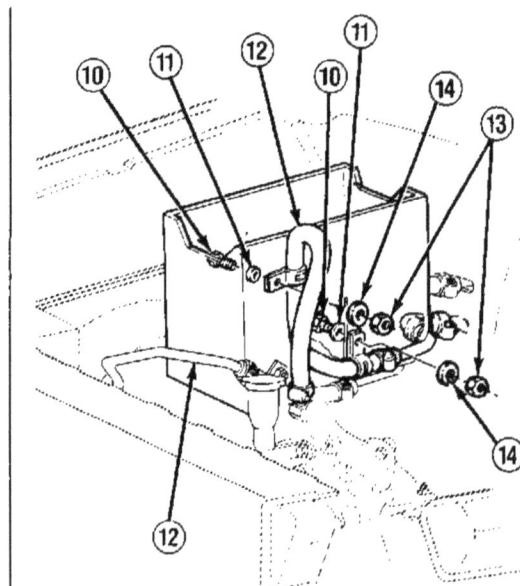

3.   Loosen clamp (15) and disconnect
diverter hose (16) from rear battery
box (7).

NOTE

Perform step 4, if necessary, to
prevent damage to engine fuel
filter.

4.   Remove engine fuel filter . (See
paragraph 3-17)

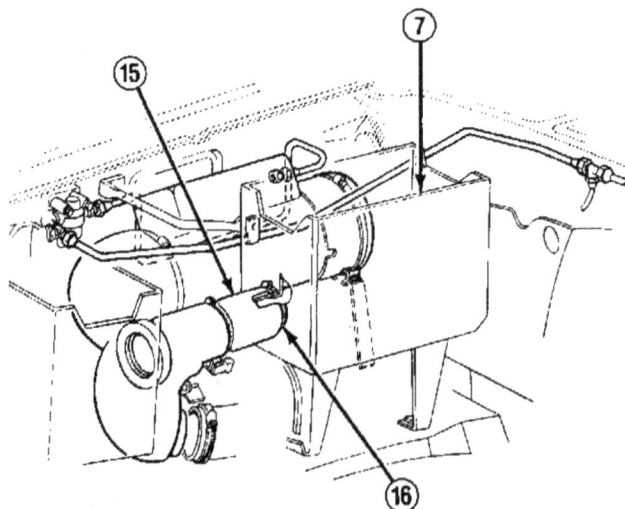

TA50048

11-6.   FRONT AND REAR BATTERY BOX REPLACEMENT (Con't).

5.   Remove 2 nuts (17) from heater exhaust pipe studs (18). Remove 2 bolts (8) and 2 bolts (6). Remove 2 nuts (20) and bolts (25) from supports (24) and fuel line clip (21).

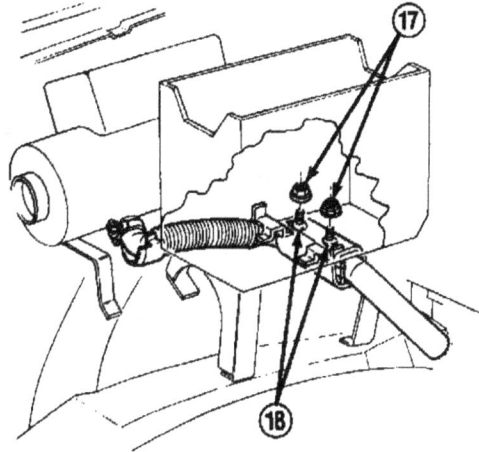

6.   Remove rear battery box (7). Remove nut (19), bolt (23), and 2 supports (24) from fender well (22) if damaged.

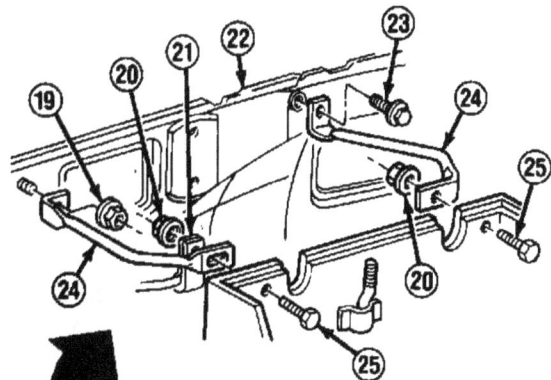

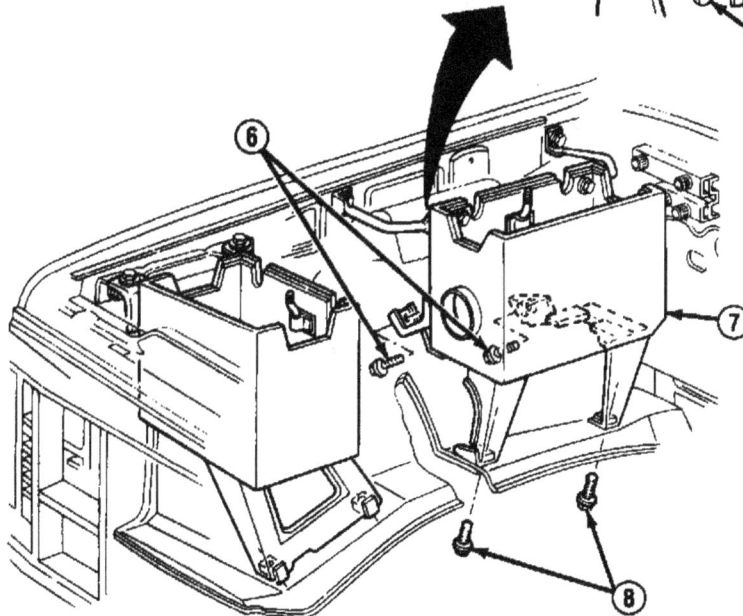

TA50049

11-6. FRONT AND REAR BATTERY BOX REPLACEMENT (Con't).

| b. INSTALLATION |

NOTE

- If installing rear battery box (7), perform steps 1-7.

- If installing front battery box (1), perform step 8.

1. Install 2 supports (24) on fender well (22) with nut (19) and bolt (23) if removed. Position rear battery box (7).

2. Install 2 supports (24) and fuel line clip (21) on rear battery box (7) with 2 bolts (25) and nuts (20).

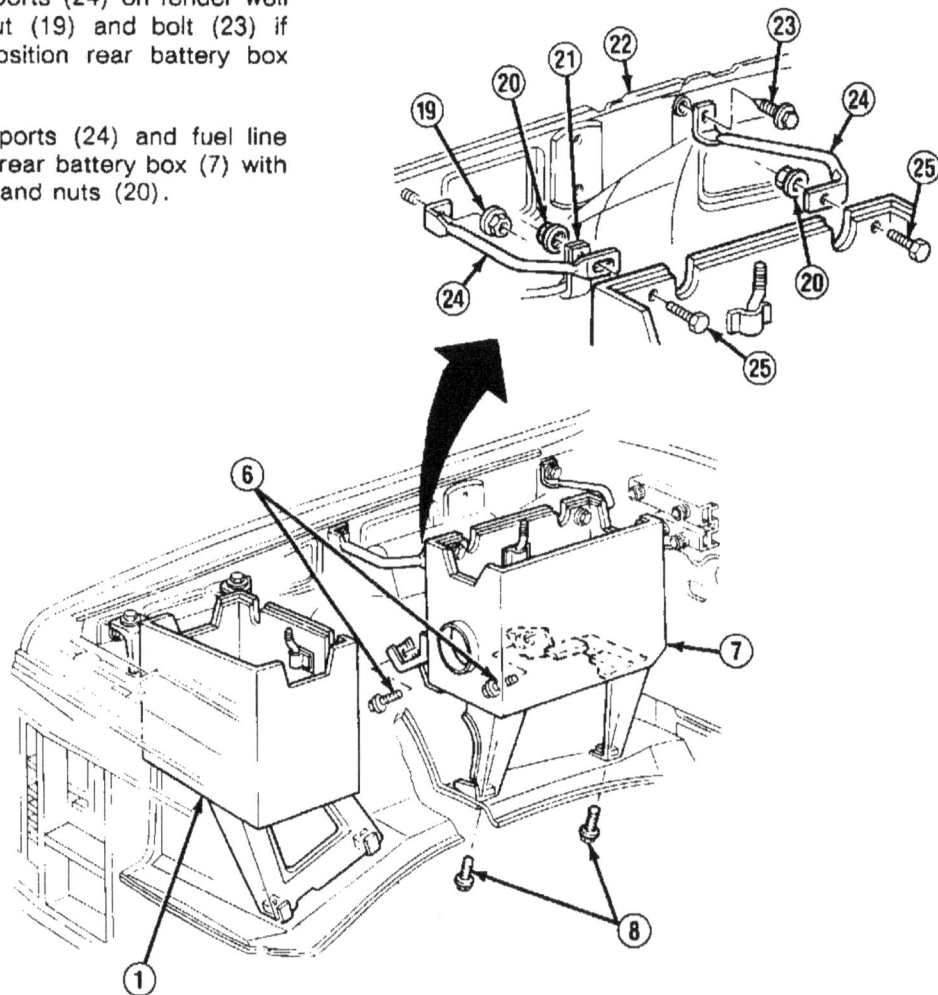

TA50050

11-6.   FRONT AND REAR BATTERY BOX REPLACEMENT (Con't).

3.   Position heater exhaust pipe studs
      (18) through rear battery box (7)
      holes and install 2 nuts (17).

4.   Loosely install 2 bolts (8) and 2 bolts
      (6). Tighten all bolts.

5.   Install engine fuel filter if removed.
      (See paragraph 3-17)

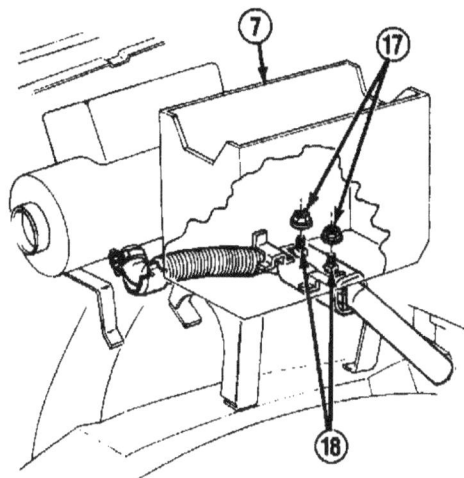

6.   Connect diverter hose (16) to rear
      battery box (7) and tighten clamp
      (15).

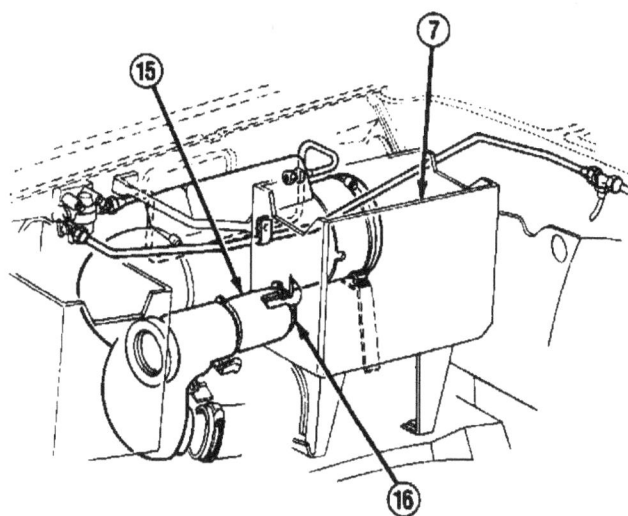

TA50051

11-6.   FRONT AND REAR BATTERY BOX REPLACEMENT (Con't).

NOTE

All except M1010 use 1 locknut (13), lockwasher (14), bolt (10), washer
(11), and clip each for inlet and outlet heater hoses (12). M1010 uses 2
each for inlet and outlet heater hoses.

7.   Position each   heater hose (12) clip and install with washer(s) (11), bolt(s) (10), new
lockwasher(s)   (14), and new locknut (s)   (13).

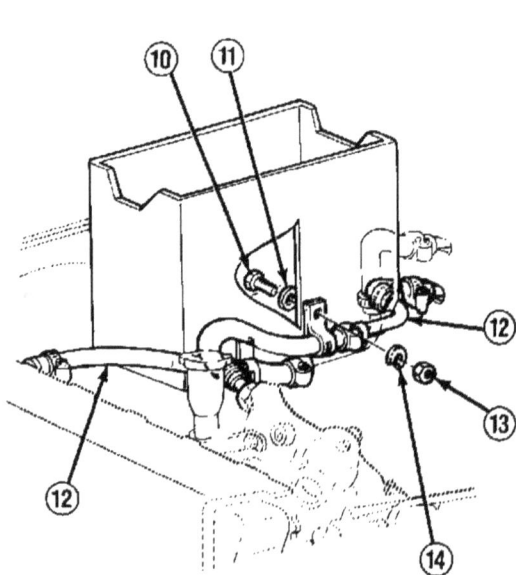

All Except M1010   **M1010**

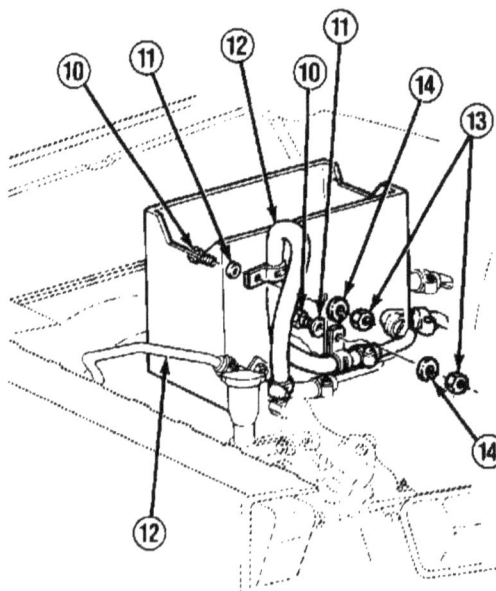

8.   Position front battery box (1). Loosely install 2 bolts (9). Install bolt   (5) on fender nut (4) and 2
bolts (2) on bracket (3). Tighten all bolts (9).

TA50052

11-6. FRONT AND REAR BATTERY BOX REPLACEMENT (Con't).

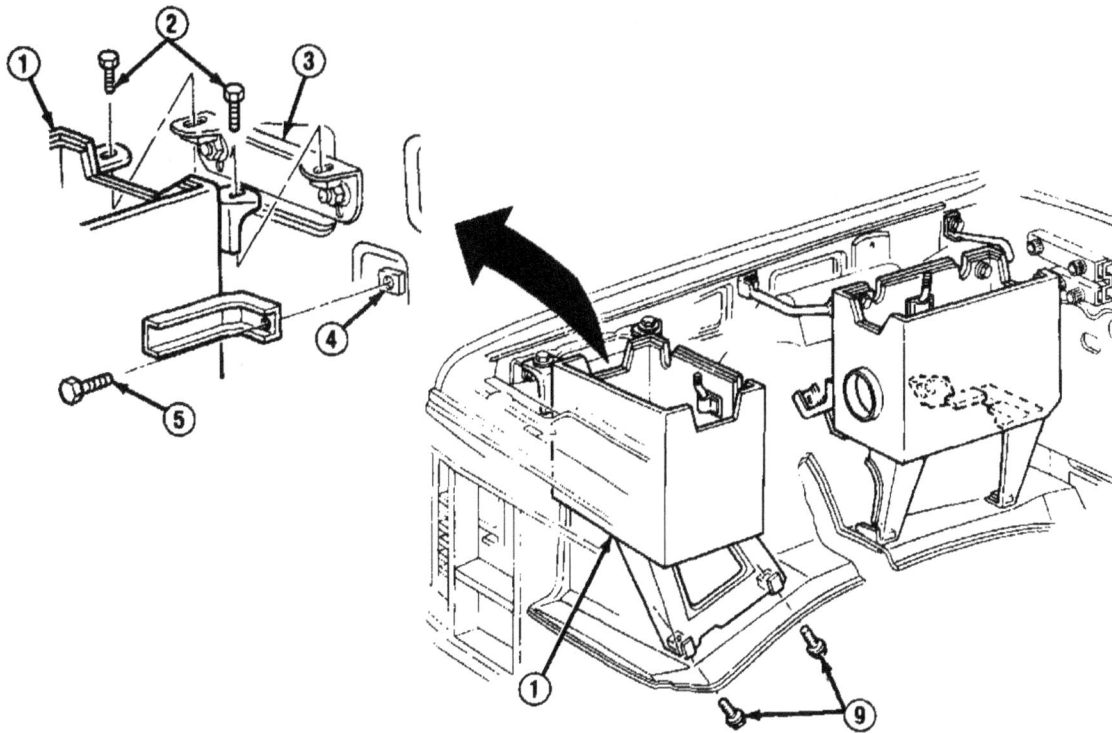

FOLLOW-ON TASKS:

• Install front or rear battery. (See paragraph 4-39)

TA50053

11-7. CAB HEATER FUEL FILTER AND LINES REPLACEMENT.

This task covers:	a. Remova l	c. Heater Bleeding
	b. Installation	

INITIAL SETUP:

Equipment Condition

* Both battery negative cables disconnected
   (if removing fuel filter). (See paragraph 4-38)

Personnel Required

* MOS 63B (2)

Materials/Parts

* Pipe sealant (Item 43, Appendix C)
* Plastic tube (Item   49, Appendix C)

General Safety Instructions

* DO NOT perform this procedure near
   fire, flames, or sparks.

---

a.	REMOVAL

WARNING

Diesel fuel is flammable. DO NOT perform this procedure near fire,
flames, or sparks. A fire extinguisher must be on hand in work area.
Failure to follow this warning may result in serious injury or death.

NOTE

* If removing fuel filter (2), perform steps 1 and 2.

* If removing fuel lines (11 or 12), perform steps 1, 3, and 4.

* Clean old sealant from all pipe threads.

* Use suitable container to catch fuel when disconnecting fuel lines.

1.   Close fuel shutoff valve (6). Loosen
     fitting (15) and disconnect fuel line
     (12) from fuel filter (2). Loosen fitting
     (8) and disconnect fuel line (11) from
     fuel filter.

2.   Remove 2 screws (5) and washers
     (4). Remove fuel filter (2) assembly
     and spacer (1). Remove fuel shutoff
     valve (6), elbow (7), and connector
     (3) from fuel filter.

3.   Remove nut (19), bolt (16), and fuel
     line clamp (18) from support (20) and
     rear battery box (17).

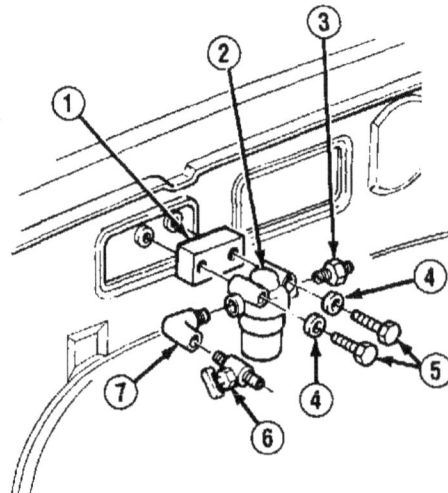

TA50054

11-7. CAB HEATER FUEL FILTER AND LINES REPLACEMENT (Con't).

4. Loosen fitting (13) and disconnect fuel line (12) from tee (14). Remove fuel line. Loosen fitting (10) and disconnect fuel line (11) from cab heater (9). Remove fuel line. Remove connector (21) as required.

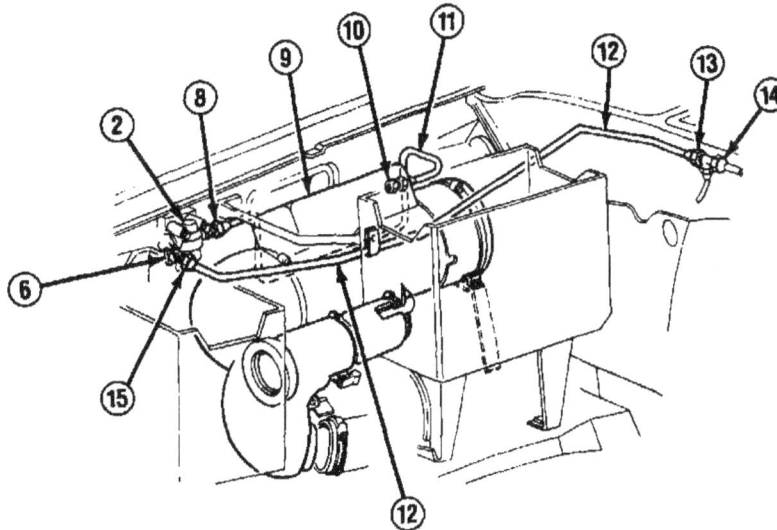

b. INSTALLATION

NOTE

• **If installing fuel lines (11 or 12), perform steps 1, 2, and 4.**

• **If installing fuel filter (2), perform steps 3 and 4.**

• **Apply pipe sealant to all pipe threads before installation.**

1. Install connector (21) if removed. Position fuel line (11) and connect to connector (21), but DO NOT tighten fitting (10). Position fuel line (12) and connect to tee (14) by tightening fitting (13).

2. Install fuel line clamp (18) on fuel line (12) and install on rear battery box (17) and support (20) with bolt (16) and nut (19).

3. Install connector (3), elbow (7), and shutoff valve (6) on fuel filter (2). Install spacer (1) and fuel filter assembly with 2 washers (4) and screws (5).

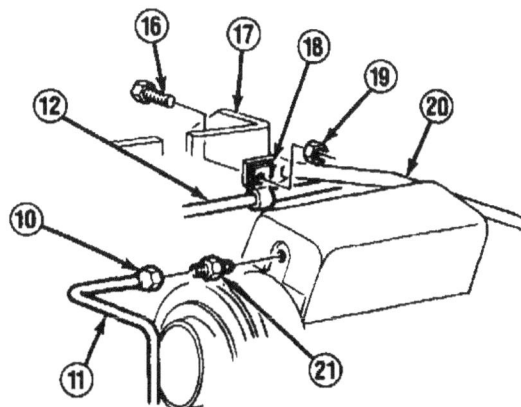

TA50055

11-7.   CAB HEATER FUEL FILTER AND LINES REPLACEMENT (Con't).

4.   Connect fuel line (11) to fuel filter (2) by tightening fitting (8). Connect fuel line (12) to fuel filter by tightening fitting (15).

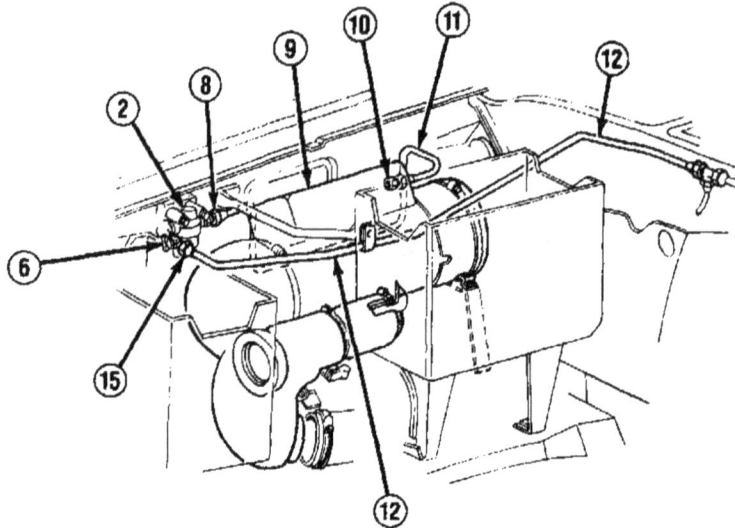

c.	**HEATER BLEEDING**

WARNING

Diesel fuel is flammable. DO NOT perform this procedure near fire, flames, or sparks. A fire extinguisher must be on hand in work area. Failure to follow this warning may result in serious injury or death.

NOTE

Use suitable container to catch fuel from fuel line (11) and bleed port (23).

1.   Connect both battery negative cables. (See paragraph 4-38)

2.   Loosen 2 screws (24) and remove cover (22), Open shutoff valve (6). Disconnect wiring harness assembly from cab heater (9).

TA50056

11-7.   CAB HEATER FUEL FILTER AND LINES REPLACEMENT (Con't).

3.   Move fitting (10) clear of connector (21). Hold cab heater switch in "START" position. Continue operation until a clean, steady flow of fuel is obtained, then shut off cab heater. Connect fitting to connector and tighten.

4.   Connect wiring harness assembly to cab heater (9).

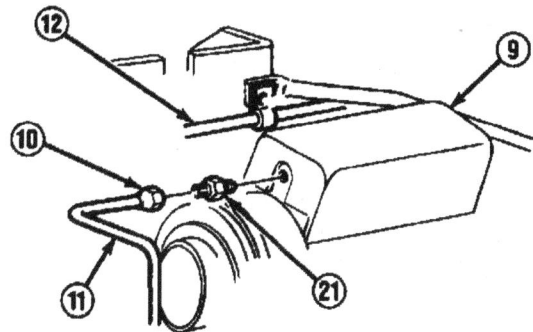

5.   Connect plastic tube to bleed port (23). Open bleed port. Hold cab heater switch in "START" position. Continue operation until a clean, steady flow of fuel is obtained, then shut off cab heater. Close bleed port and remove plastic tube.

6.   Install cover (22) and tighten 2 screws (24).

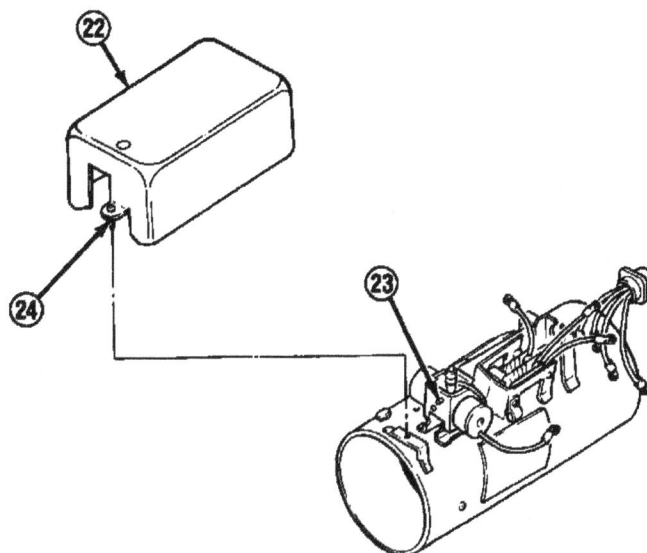

FOLLOW-ON TASKS:

• Check for leaks.

TA50057

11-8. CAB HEATER AND DIVERTER REPLACEMENT.

This task covers:	a. Removal	b. Installation

INITIAL SETUP:

Equipment Condition

- Cab heater control cable disconnected from diverter assembly. (See paragraph 11-4, REMOVAL, step 1)
- Rear battery box and supports removed. (See paragraph 11-6)
- Cab heater fuel lines disconnected. (See paragraph 11-7)

Materials/Parts

- Two lockwashers
- RTV sealant (Item 41, Appendix C)

Tools/Test Equipment

- Torque wrench

---

a.	REMOVAL

NOTE

- **If removing diverter (8), perform steps 1-3.**

- **If removing cab heater (2), perform steps 1-4.**

1. Remove cab heater (2) cover and disconnect wiring harness assembly (1). Loosen clamp (5) and disconnect blower inlet hose (4), Loosen clamp (7) and disconnect diverter hose (6). Unscrew clamps (3) and completely open. Loosen clamp (9) and disconnect exhaust pipe (10).

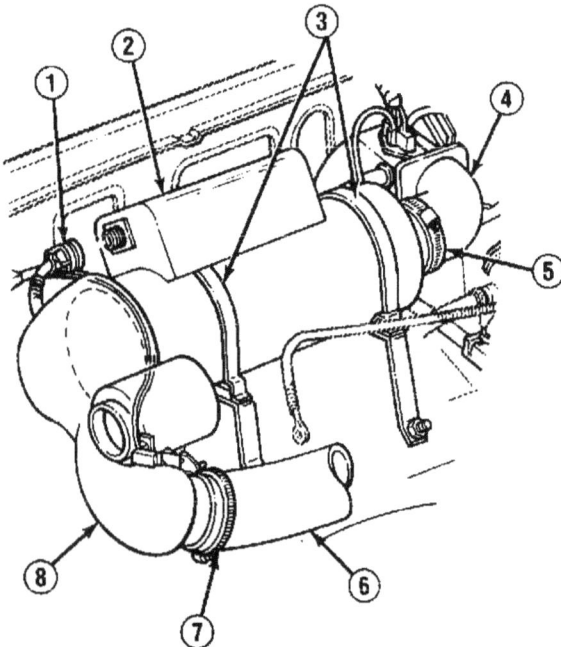

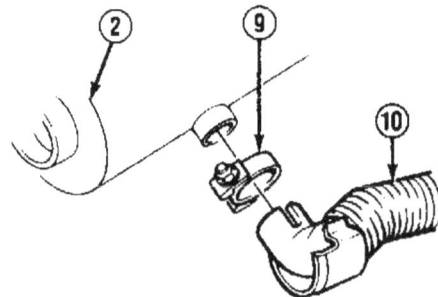

TA50058

11-8.   CAB HEATER AND DIVERTER REPLACEMENT (Con't).

2.   Disconnect lead from diverter switch
(12). Remove cab heater (2) and
diverter (8) assembly.

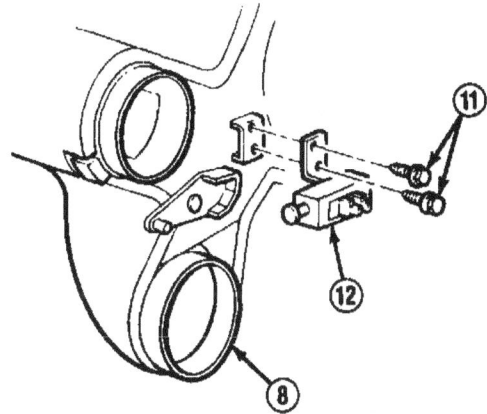

3.   Remove 2 screws (11) and diverter
switch (12). Remove 4 screws (13)
and remove diverter (8) from cab
heater (2). Remove and discard seal
(14) as required.

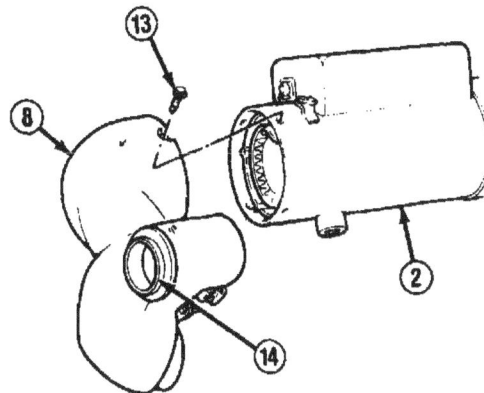

4.   Remove 3 screws (17) and washers
(16). Remove heater adapter (15).
Clean old sealant from mating
surfaces of cab heater (2) and heater
adapter.

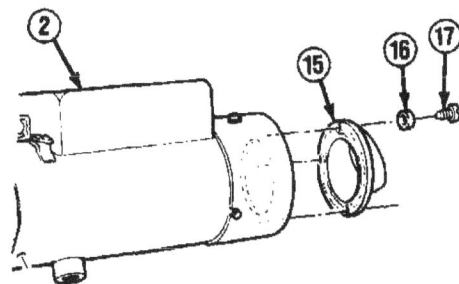

TA50059

11-29

11-8. CAB HEATER AND DIVERTER REPLACEMENT (Con't).

5. Remove heater clamp (21) from clamp bracket (20). Remove 2 bolts (19), washers (18), and clamp bracket. Remove 2 nuts (22), lockwashers (23), bolts (26), and washers (25). Remove heater bracket (24). Discard lockwashers.

| b. | INSTALLATION |

NOTE

- If installing cab heater (2), perform steps 2-7.

- If installing diverter (8), perform steps 3-7.

- Ensure that heater clamp (21) screws face toward outside of truck.

1. Install heater bracket (24) on fender with 2 washers (25), bolts (26), new lockwashers (23), and nuts (22). Install clamp bracket (20) with 2 washers (18) and bolts (19). Install heater clamp (21) through clamp bracket, Tighten nuts to 15-20 lb.-ft. (20-27 N•m). Tighten bolts to 75-95 lb.-in, (9-11 N•m).

2. Apply sealant to heater adapter (15). Install heater adapter to cab heater (2) with 3 washers (16) and screws (17).

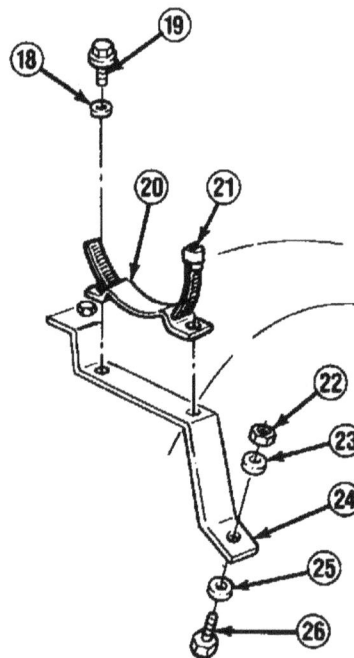

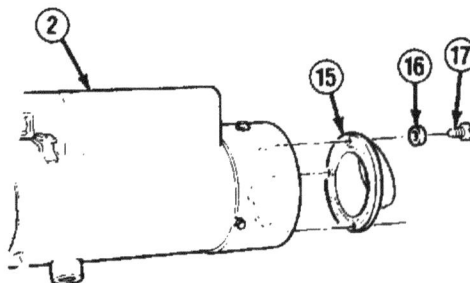

TA50060

11-8.   CAB HEATER AND DIVERTER REPLACEMENT (Con't).

3.   Install new seal (14) if removed.
Install diverter (8) to cab heater (2)
with 4 screws (13). Install diverter
switch (12) on diverter with 2 screws
(11).

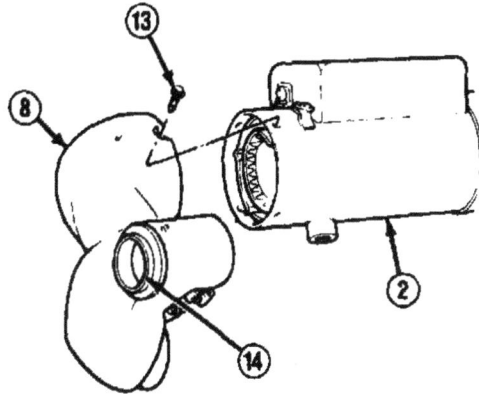

4.   Position cab heater (2) and diverter
(8) assembly. Ensure there is about 1
in. (2.5 cm) clearance between cab
heater and fender skirt. Connect lead
to diverter switch (12).

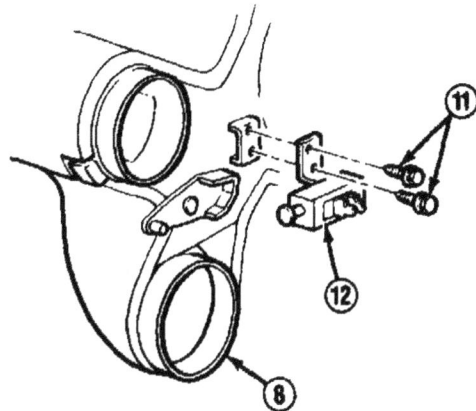

5.   Connect exhaust pipe (10) and
tighten clamp (9) to 75-95 lb.-in.
(9-11 N•m).

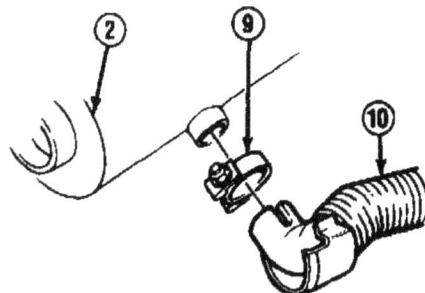

TA50061

11-8. CAB HEATER AND DIVERTER REPLACEMENT (Con't).

6. Rotate heater (2) to aline seal (14) with front battery box hole, and compress seal about 0.5 in. (1.2 cm). When all components are alined, loosely install 2 clamps (3) around cab heater.

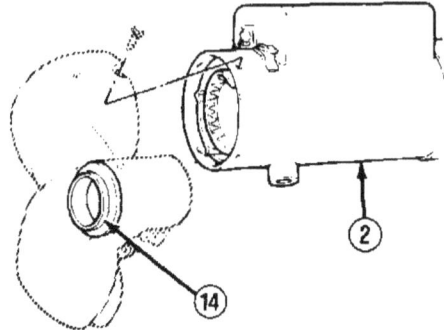

7. Connect diverter hose (6) and tighten clamp (7). Connect blower inlet hose (4) and tighten clamp (5). Connect wiring harness assembly (1) to cab heater (2). Tighten clamps (3) securely. Install cab heater cover.

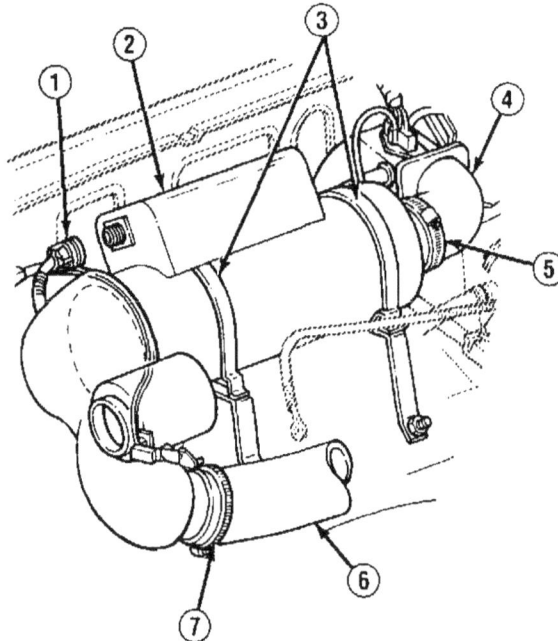

FOLLOW-ON TASKS:

- Connect cab heater fuel lines. (See paragraph 11-7)
- Install rear battery box and supports, (See paragraph 11-6)
- Connect cab heater control cable to diverter assembly. (See paragraph 11-4, INSTALLATION, step 4)
- Check operation of cab heater. (See TM 9-2320-289-10)

TA50062

11-9. CAB HEATER BLOWER AND HOSES REPLACEMENT.

This task covers:	a. Removal	b. Installation

INITIAL SETUP:

Equipment Condition
  • Cab heater removed. (See paragraph 11-8)

Materials/Parts
  • RTV sealant (Item 41, Appendix C)

---

a. REMOVAL

NOTE

  • **If removing hoses (1 or 5), perform step 1.**

  • **If removing blower motor, perform steps 2, 3, and 6 through 8.**

  • **If removing capacitor, perform step 4.**

1. Loosen clamps (2 and 4) and disconnect hoses (1 and 5) from blower motor assembly (3).

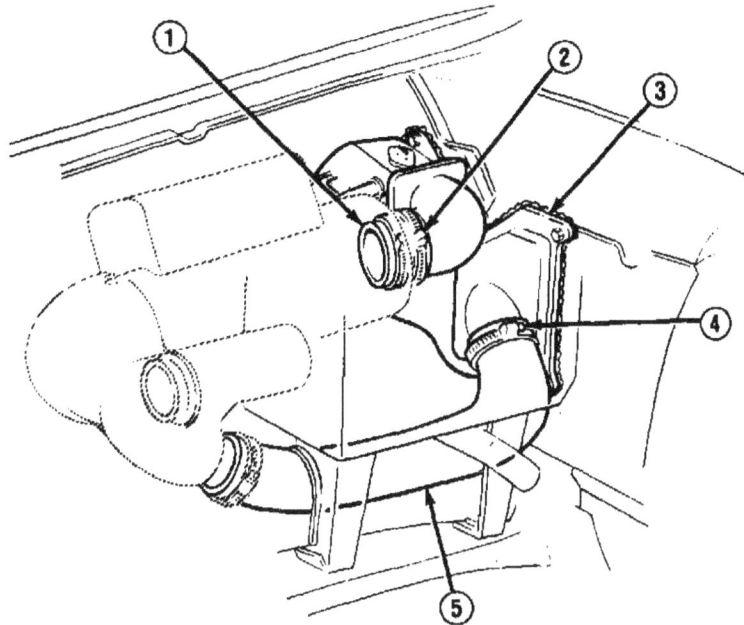

TA50063

11-9.   CAB HEATER BLOWER AND HOSES REPLACEMENT (Con't).

2.   Disconnect and remove lead (6) and lead assembly (8) from resistor (13) and harness plug (9) .

3.   Remove 2 screws (7) and resistor (13). Clean old sealant from resistor and blower motor assembly (3).

4,   Disconnect lead (6) from capacitor (14), Unplug capacitor from blower motor assembly (3). Remove screw and capacitor.

5.   Remove 3 screws (12). Remove 2 nuts (10) from studs (11) and remove blower motor assembly (3).

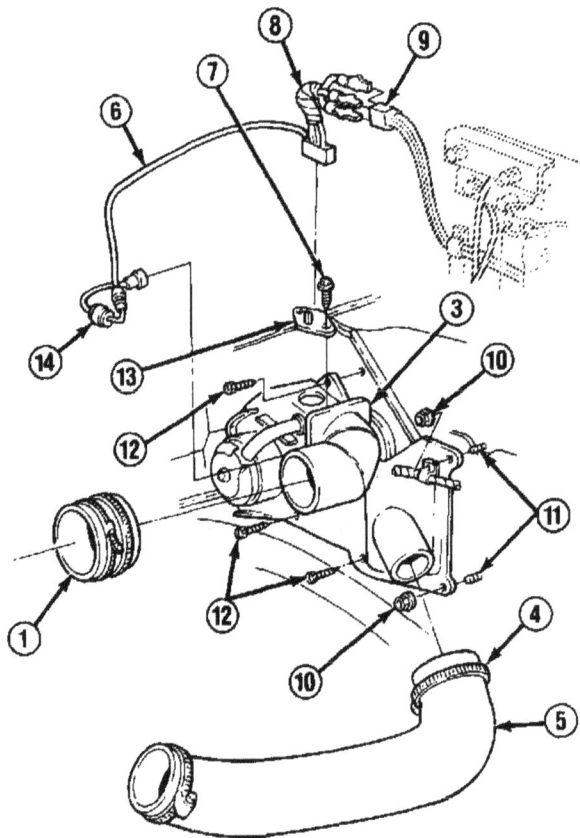

6.   Disconnect and remove pipe (21) from pipe (16) and blower motor (19). Remove screw (15) and pipe (16).

7.   Remove 5 screws (20) and blower motor (19) from blower motor case (17), Clean old sealant from blower motor and blower motor case.

8.   Remove nut holding fan (18) to blower motor (19), and remove fan as required.

TA50064

11-9. CAB HEATER BLOWER AND HOSES REPLACEMENT (Con't).

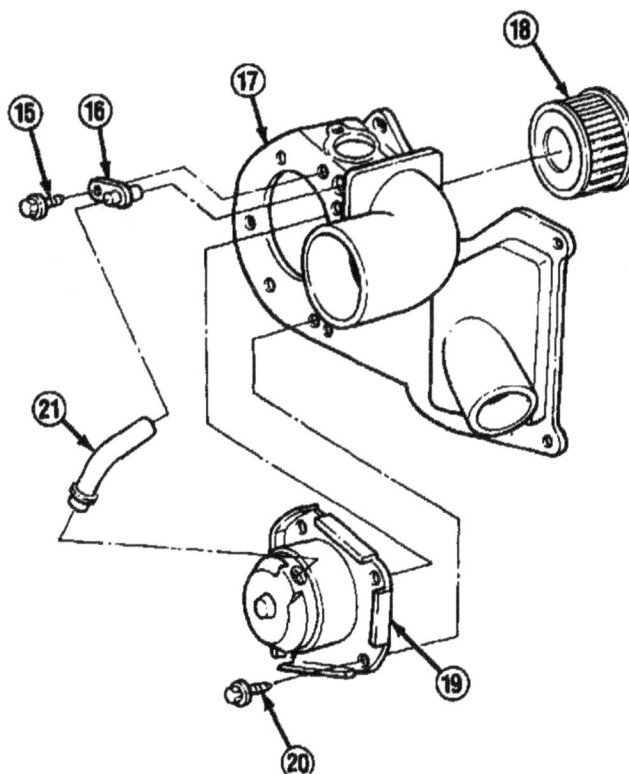

| b. | INSTALLATION |

NOTE

- **If installing blower motor (19), perform steps 1-3, 5, and 7.**

- **If installing hoses (1 or 5), perform step 8.**

- **If installing capacitor (14), perform step 6.**

1. Install fan (18) on blower motor (19) with nut if removed.

2. Apply sealant to mating surfaces of blower motor (19) and blower motor case (17). Install blower motor on blower motor case with 5 screws (20).

3. Install pipe (16) with screw (15). Connect pipe (21) to blower motor (19) and pipe (16).

4. Position blower motor assembly (3). Install 2 nuts (10) on studs (11). Install 3 screws (12).

5. Apply sealant to mating surfaces of blower motor assembly (3) and resistor (13). Install resistor with 2 screws (7).

6. Connect lead (6) to capacitor (14). Install capacitor to blower motor assembly (3) with screw, Plug capacitor into blower motor assembly.

7. Connect lead assembly (8) to resistor (13) and harness plug (9).

TA50065

11-9.   CAB HIEATER BLOWER AND HOSES REPLACEMENT (Con't).

8.   Connect hoses (1 and 5) to blower motor assembly (3), and tighten clamps (2 and 4).

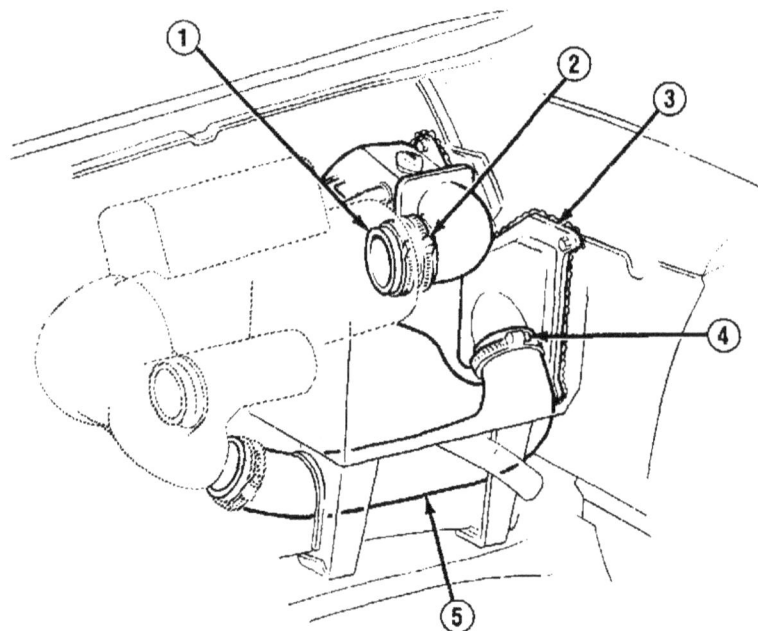

FOLLOW-ON TASKS:

* Install cab heater. (See paragraph 11-8)

TA50066

11-10. CAB HEATER WIRING HARNESS REPLACEMENT.

This task covers:	a. Removal	b. Installation

INITIAL SETUP:

Equipment Condition
- Rear battery box removed.
  (See paragraph 11-6)

Materials/Parts
- Two lockwashers
- Ten straps

---

a.	**REMOVAL**

NOTE

- **If removing relay (2), perform step 2.**
- **Tag all leads and connectors for installation.**

1. Disconnect wiring harness (1) cable from cab heater control panel assembly (6). Remove 2 nuts (8) and disconnect wiring harness leads from safety switch (9). Remove screw (3), washer (4), and clip (5). Loosen nut on strap (7) and disconnect wiring harness.

2. Unsnap relay (2) and wiring harness (1) connector from bracket (10). Unplug relay (2) from wiring harness connector.

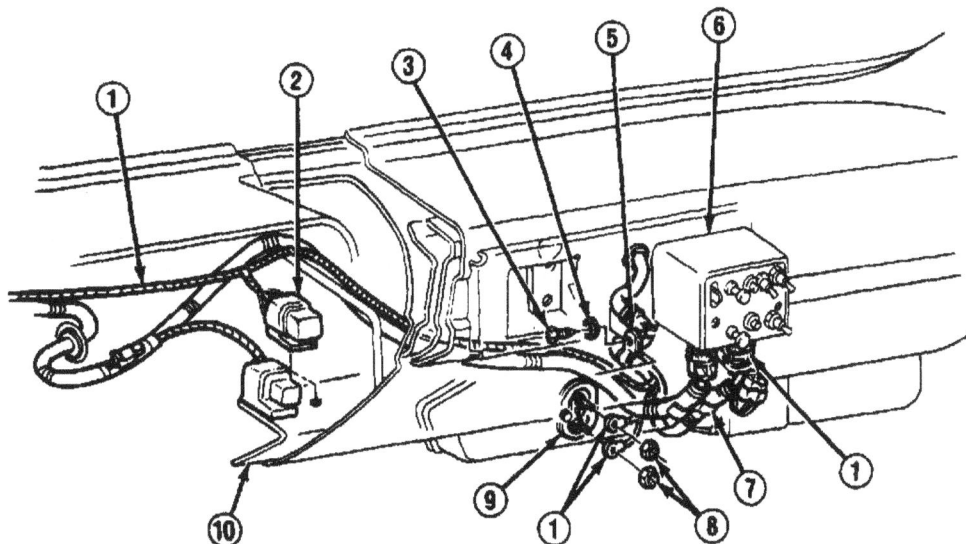

TA50067

11-10. CAB HEATER WIRING HARNESS REPLACEMENT (Con't).

3. Disconnect wiring harness (1) connectors from wiring harness terminal (11) and fuse panel (12) at " IGN" terminal.

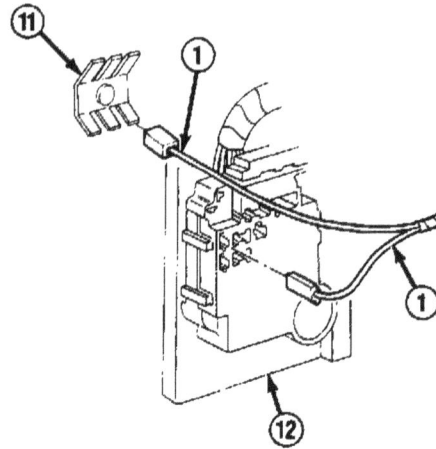

4. Disconnect wiring harness (1) from cab heater (13) and diverter switch (19). Cut and discard straps securing wiring harness.

5. Loosen 2 nuts (15) and remove positive accessory wiring terminal board (16) cover. Remove nut and lockwasher from positive accessory wiring terminal board stud, and disconnect wiring harness (1) lead. Repeat for negative accessory wiring terminal board (14). Discard lockwashers.

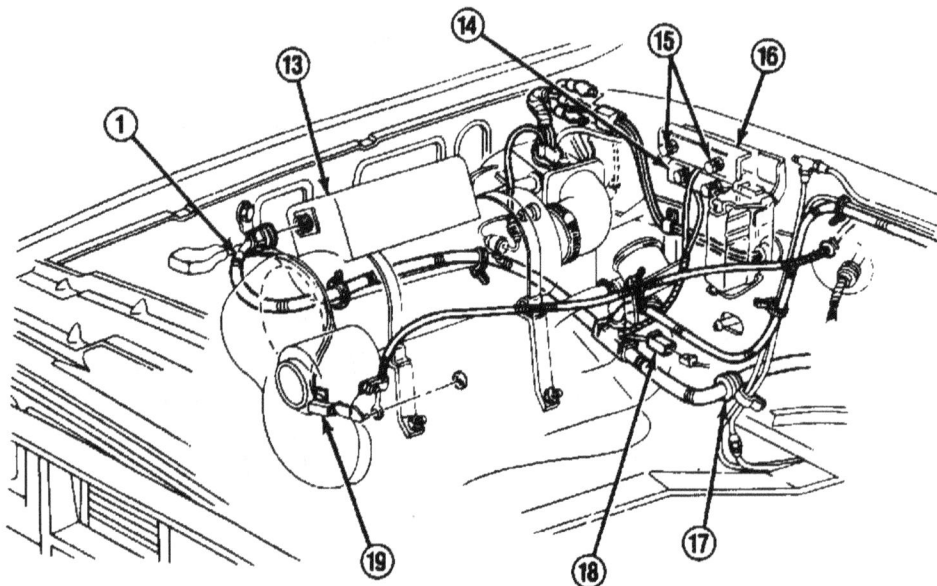

TA50068

11-10. CAB HEATER WIRING HARNESS REPLACEMENT (Con't).

NOTE

Step 6 only applies to trucks equipped a with cargo compartment heater.

6.   Disconnect harness connector (18) from cargo compartment heater connector.

7.   Disconnect wiring harness (1) at switch connector (21) and engine coolant heater connector (22). Cut and discard all straps securing wiring harness to fuel lines (20). Carefully pull wiring harness through grommet (17) into engine compartment and remove.

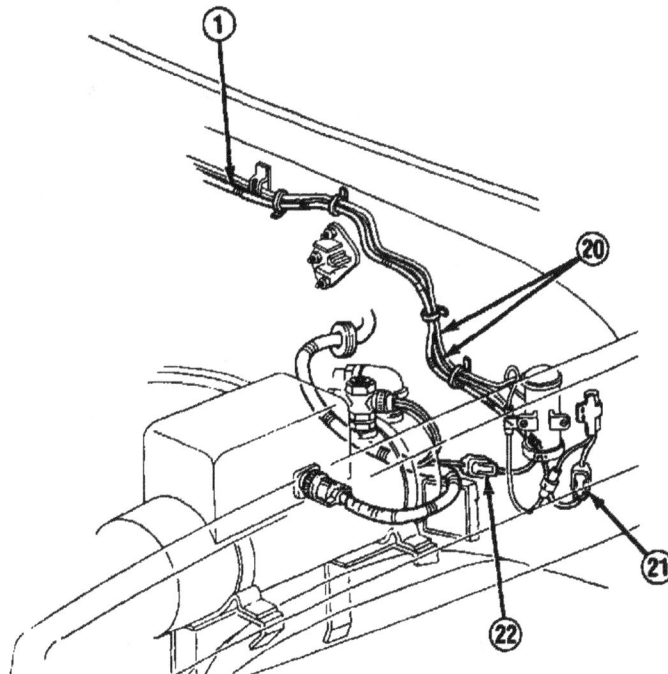

---

b. INSTALLATION

NOTE

If installing relay, perform step 6.

1.   Position wiring harness (1) in engine compartment. Carefully push wiring harness through grommet (17) up to white band on wiring harness. Connect wiring harness at switch connector (21) and engine coolant heater connector (22). Route wiring harness along fuel lines (20) and install new straps,

TA50069

11-10. CAB HEATER WIRING HARNESS REPLACEMENT (Con't).

NOTE

Step **2** only applies to trucks equipped with cargo compartment heater.

2. Connect harness connector (18) to cargo compartment heater connector.

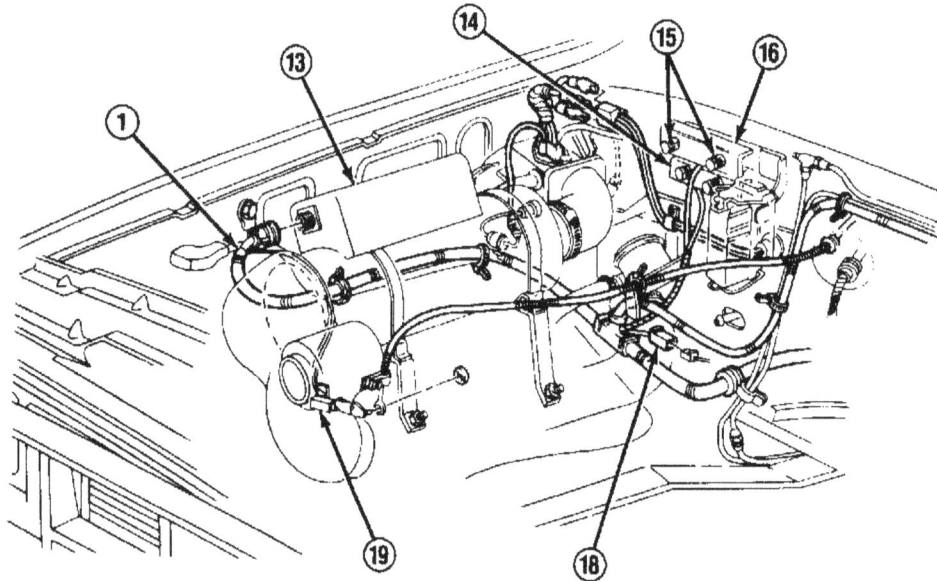

3. Connect wiring harness (1) lead to positive accessory wiring terminal board (16) stud and install new lockwasher and nut. Install positive accessory wiring terminal board cover and tighten 2 nuts (15). Repeat for negative accessory wiring terminal board (14).

4. Connect wiring harness (1) to cab heater (13) and diverter switch (19). Install new straps on wiring harness as required.

5. Connect wiring harness (1) connectors to wiring harness terminal (11) and fuse panel (12) at "IGN" terminal.

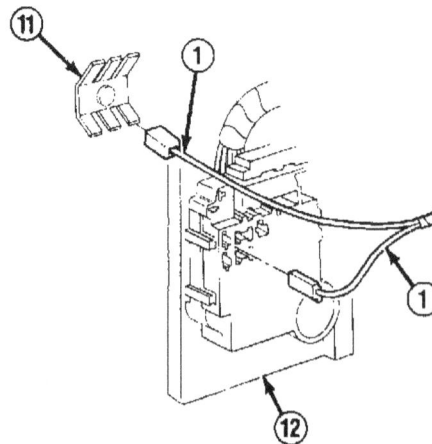

TA50070

11-10. CAB HEATER WIRING HARNESS REPLACEMENT (Con't).

6. Plug relay (2) into wiring harness (1) connector. Snap relay and wiring harness connector onto bracket (10).

7. Position wiring harness (1) in strap (7) and tighten nut. Install clip (5) on wiring harness and install with screw (3) and washer (4). Connect 2 wiring harness leads to safety switch (9) and install 2 nuts (8). Connect wiring harness cable to cab heater control panel assembly (6).

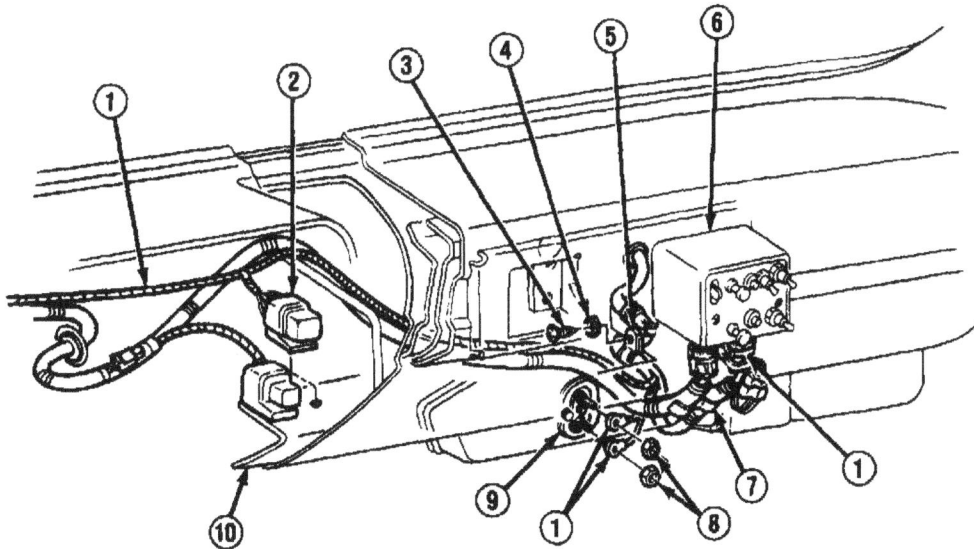

FOLLOW-ON TASKS:

• Install rear battery box, (See paragraph 11-6)
• Check operation of cab heater. (See TM 9-2320-289-10)

TA50071

11-11. CAB HEATER EXHAUST PIPE REPLACEMENT.

This task covers: a. Removal   b. Installation

INITIAL SETUP:

Equipment Condition

* Rear battery removed. (See paragraph 4-39)

Materials/Parts

* Five locknuts (all except M1009 and M1010)
* Three locknuts (M1009)
* Eleven locknuts (M1010)

General Safety Instructions

* Allow exhaust system to cool before attempting to service exhaust pipes.

---

a.   **REMOVAL**

WARNING

Before attempting to service any part of exhaust system, allow exhaust system to cool. Failure to follow this warning will result in serious burns.

NOTE

* If removing front exhaust pipe (4), perform steps 1 and 2.

* If removing rear exhaust pipe (6), perform steps 1, 3, and 4.

1. Loosen clamp (7) and disconnect front exhaust pipe (4) from cab heater (1). Remove 2 nuts (3) from rear battery box (2).

2. Loosen clamp (5) and disconnect front exhaust pipe (4) from rear exhaust pipe (6). Remove front exhaust pipe as required.

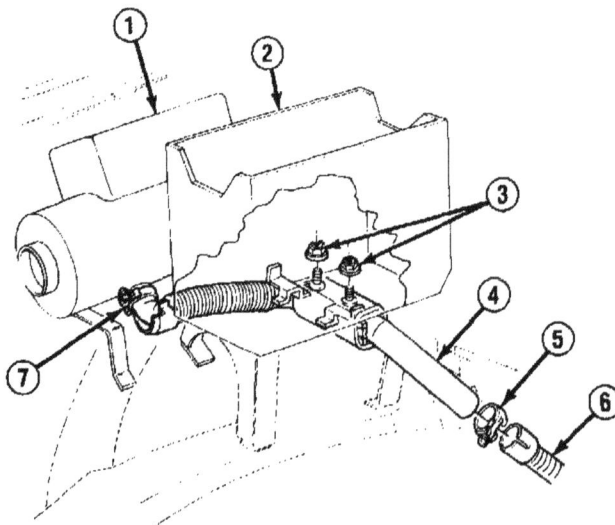

TA50072

11-11. CAB HEATER EXHAUST PIPE REPLACEMENT (Con't).

NOTE

M1009 uses 2 clamps (11) and M1010 uses 11 clamps, All other models use 4 clamps. Note position of clamps for installation.

3.　Remove locknut (10) and screw (12) from each clamp (11). Remove each clamp from rear exhaust pipe (6) and engine exhaust pipe (8). Remove rear exhaust pipe (M1010 only). Discard locknuts.

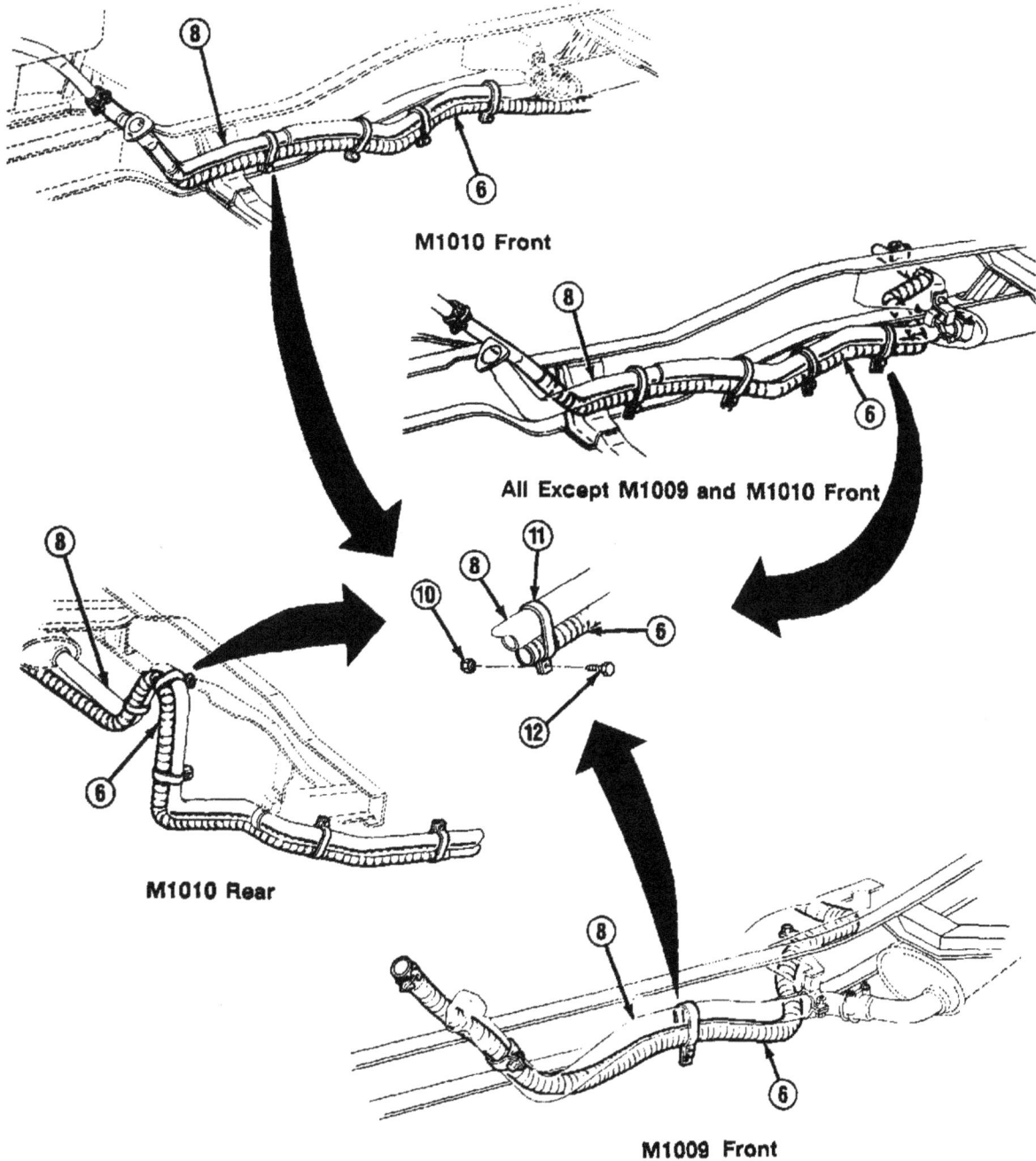

M1010 Front

All Except M1009 and M1010 Front

M1010 Rear

M1009 Front

TA50073

11-11. CAB HEATER EXHAUST PIPE REPLACEMENT (Con't).

NOTE

Perform step 4 for all except M1010.

4. Remove locknut (10), washer (16), clip (15), and screw (14) from frame (9) and rear exhaust pipe (6). Remove screw (7) from fender (13), and remove rear exhaust pipe. Discard locknut.

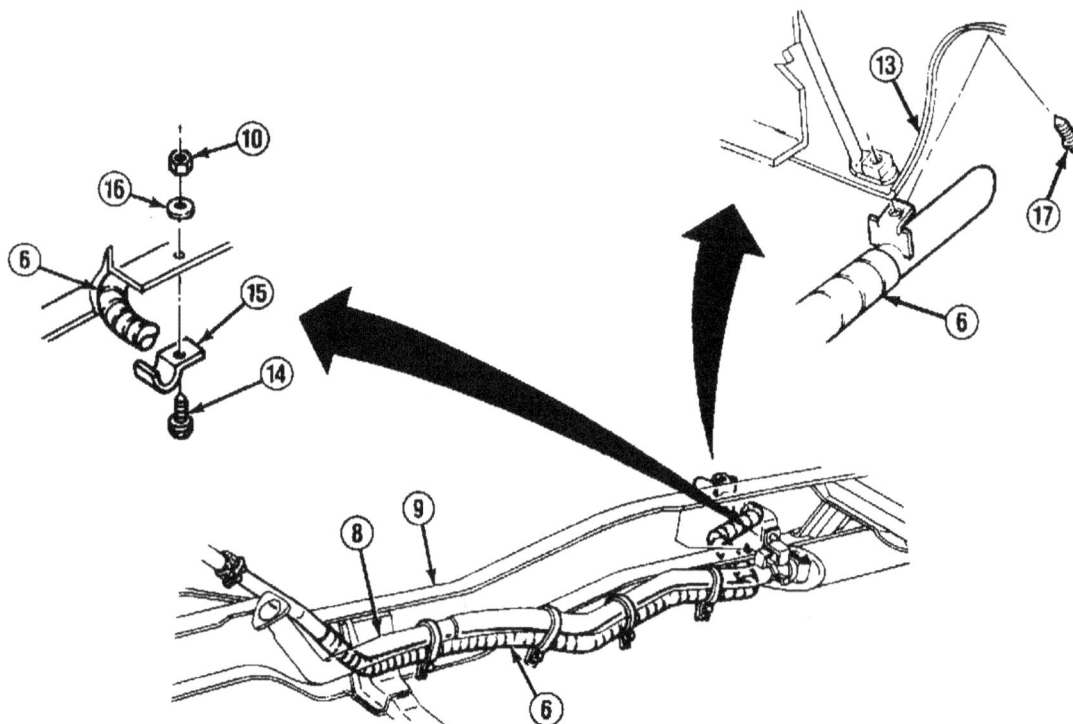

All Except M1009 and M1010

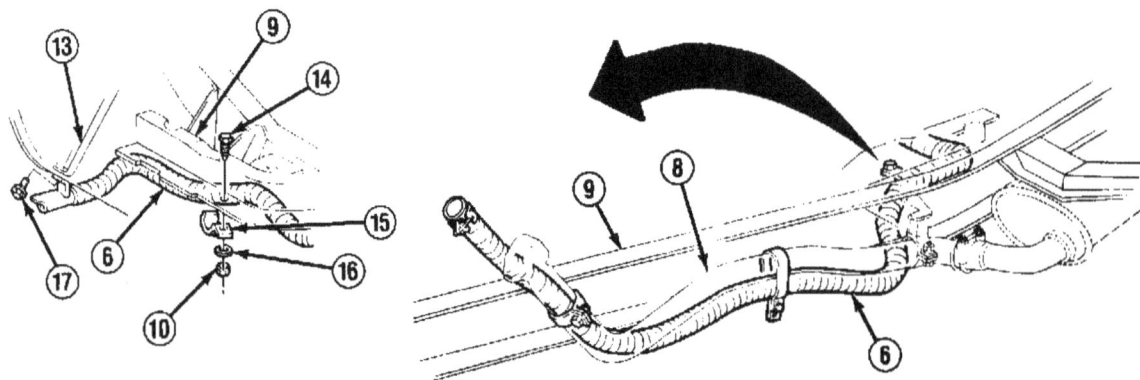

M1009

TA50074

11-11. CAB HEATER EXHAUST PIPE REPLACEMENT (Con't).

| b. INSTALLATION |

NOTE

- If installing rear exhaust pipe (6), perform steps 1, 2, and 4.

- If installing front exhaust pipe, perform steps 3 and 4.

Ž Perform step 1 for all except M1010.

1. Install rear exhaust pipe (6) on fender (13) with screw (17). Install on frame (9) with screw (14), clip (15), washer (16), and new locknut (10).

NOTE

- Install M1009 rear exhaust pipe (6) on top of engine exhaust pipe (8). install all others below engine exhaust pipe.

- M1009 uses 2 clamps (11) and M1010 uses 11 clamps, all others use 4 clamps.

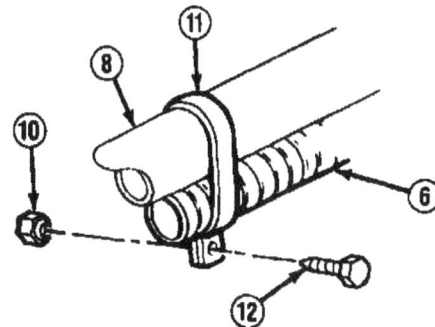

2. Position rear exhaust pipe (6), install each clamp (11) around rear exhaust pipe and engine exhaust pipe (8) with screw (12) and new locknut (10).

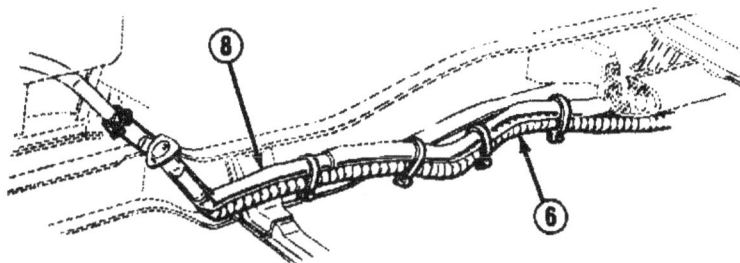

M1010 Front

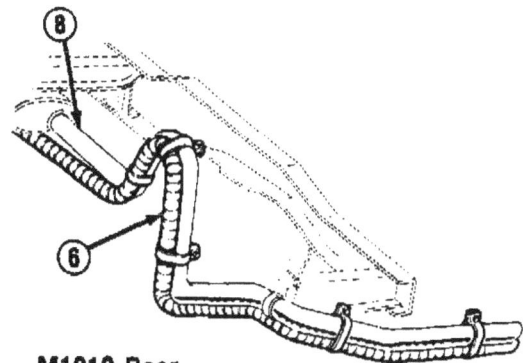

M1010 Rear

TA50075

11-11. CAB HEATER EXHAUST PIPE REPLACEMENT (Con't).

3. Connect front exhaust pipe (4) to rear exhaust pipe (6) and tighten clamp (5).

4. Position front exhaust pipe (4) studs through rear battery box (2) holes and install 2 nuts (3). Connect front exhaust pipe to cab heater (1) and tighten clamp (7).

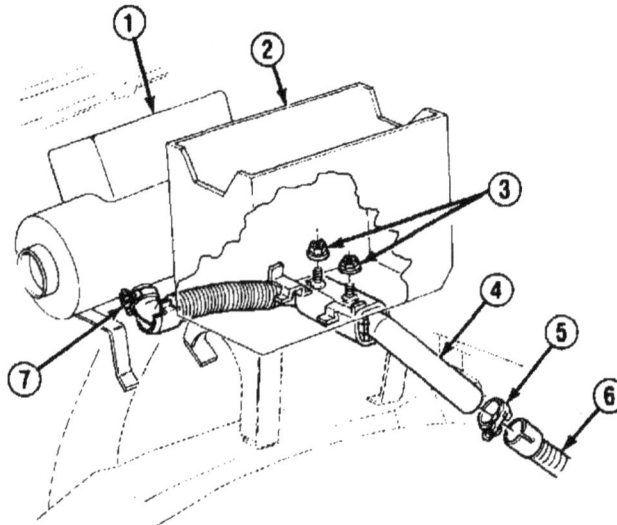

FOLLOW-ON TASKS:

• Install rear battery. (See paragraph 4-39)

TA50076

11-12. CAB HEATER COOLANT HOSES REPLACEMENT.

This task covers:	a. Removal	b. Installation

INITIAL SETUP:

Equipment Condition
- Rear battery box removed. (See paragraph 11-6)

---

a. **REMOVAL**

NOTE

- **If removing   outlet hose components, perform steps 1-3.**
- **If removing   inlet hose components, perform steps 4 and 5.**
- **Drain coolant from hoses into suitable container.**
- **Tag hoses for installation.**

1.   Loosen clamp (2) and disconnect engine coolant heater hose (3) from pipe assembly (6). Loosen clamps (8) and disconnect hose (1) from pipe assembly and radiator (7).

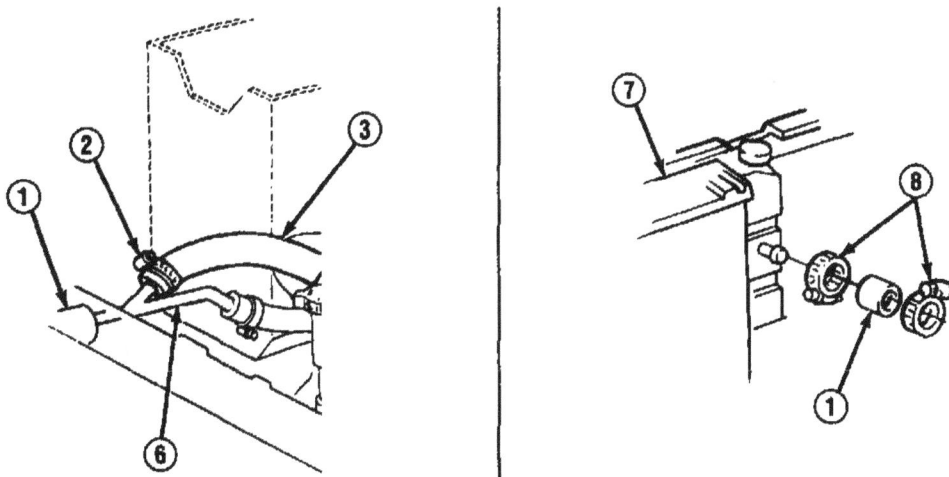

TA50077

11-12. CAB HEATER COOLANT HOSES REPLACEMENT (Con't).

2.　Loosen clamp (10) and disconnect outlet hose (11) from upper heater core tube (9), Remove outlet hose assembly.

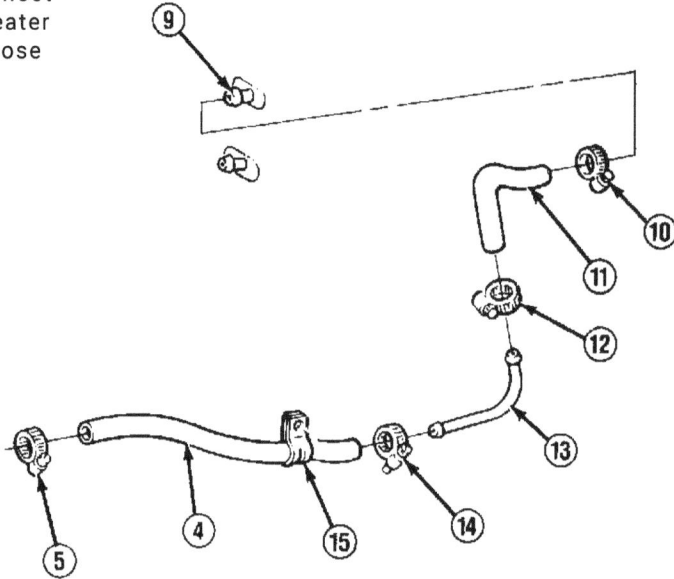

NOTE

M1010 uses 2 clamps (15), all others use 1 clamp.

3.　Loosen clamp (5) and disconnect pipe assembly (6) from outlet hose (4). Loosen clamp (14) and disconnect outlet hose from tube (13). Loosen clamp (12) and disconnect tube from outlet hose (11). Remove clamp(s) (15).

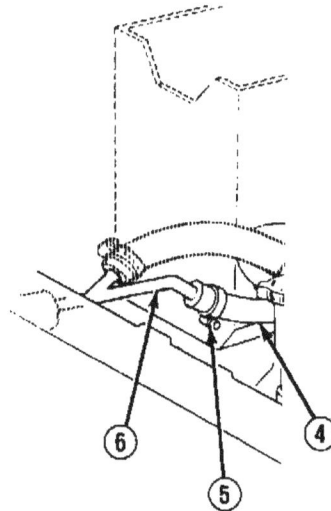

4.　Loosen clamp (22) and disconnect inlet hose (23) from crossover (18) and disconnect inlet hose (17) from lower heater core tube assembly. pipe (24). Loosen clamp (16). Remove inlet hose

5.　Loosen clamp (21) and disconnect inlet hose (23) from tube (20). Loosen clamp (19) and disconnect tube from inlet hose (17). Remove clamp(s) (15).

TA50078

11-12. CAB HEATER COOLANT HOSES REPLACEMENT (Con't).

| b. INSTALLATION |

NOTE

- **If installing outlet hose (11) components, perform steps 3-5.**

- **If installing inlet hose (17) components, perform steps 1 and 2.**

1.   Install clamp(s) (15) on inlet hose (23). Connect tube (20) to inlet hose (17) and tighten clamp (19). Connect inlet hose to tube and tighten clamp (21).

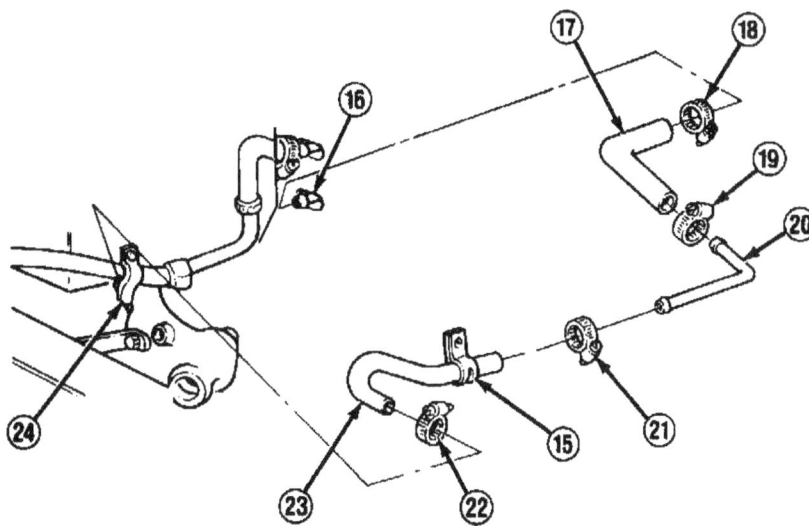

All Except M1010

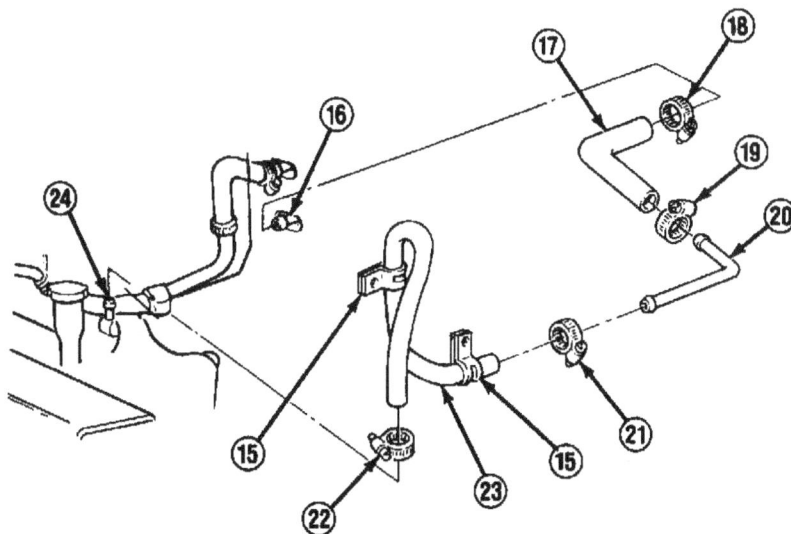

M1010

TA50079

11-49

11-12. CAB HEATER COOLANT HOSES REPLACEMENT (Con't).

2. Connect inlet hose (17) to lower heater core tube (16) and tighten clamp (18). Connect inlet hose (23) to crossover pipe (24) and tighten clamp (22).

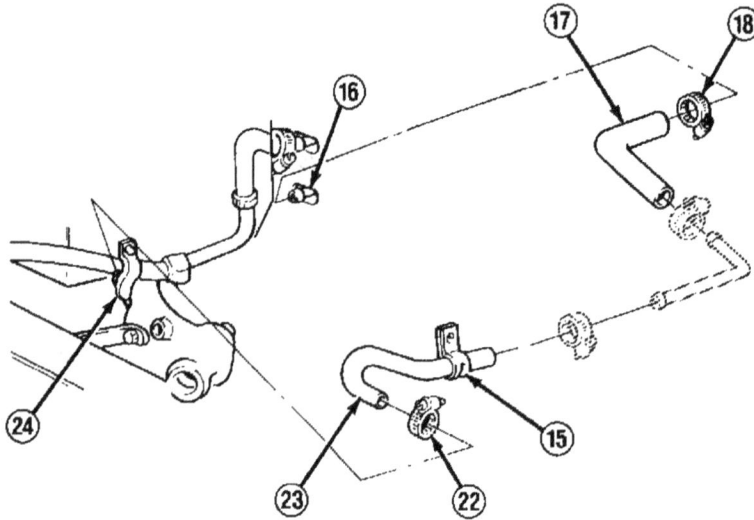

All Except M1010

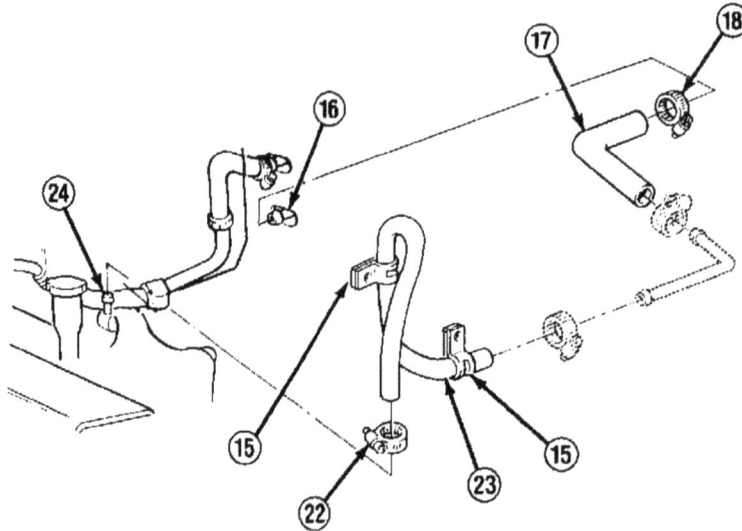

M1010

NOTE

M1010 uses 2 clamps (15), all others use 1 clamp.

3. Install clamp(s) (15) on outlet hose (4). Connect tube (13) to outlet hose (11) and tighten clamp (12). Connect outlet hose (4) to tube and tighten clamp (14). Connect pipe assembly (6) to outlet hose (4) and tighten clamp (5).

TA50080

11-12. CAB HEATER COOLANT HOSES REPLACEMENT (Con't).

4. Connect outlet hose (11) to upper heater core tube (9) and tighten clamp (10).

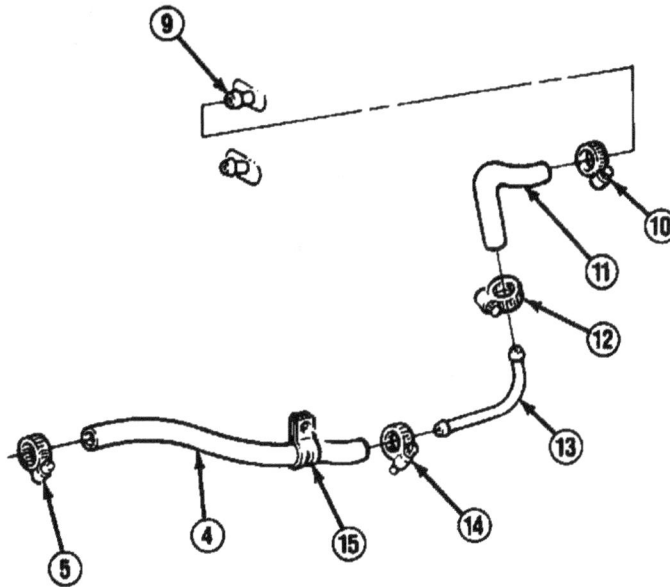

5. Connect hose (1) to radiator (7) and pipe assembly (6), and tighten clamps (8). Connect engine coolant heater hose (3) to pipe assembly and tighten clamp (2).

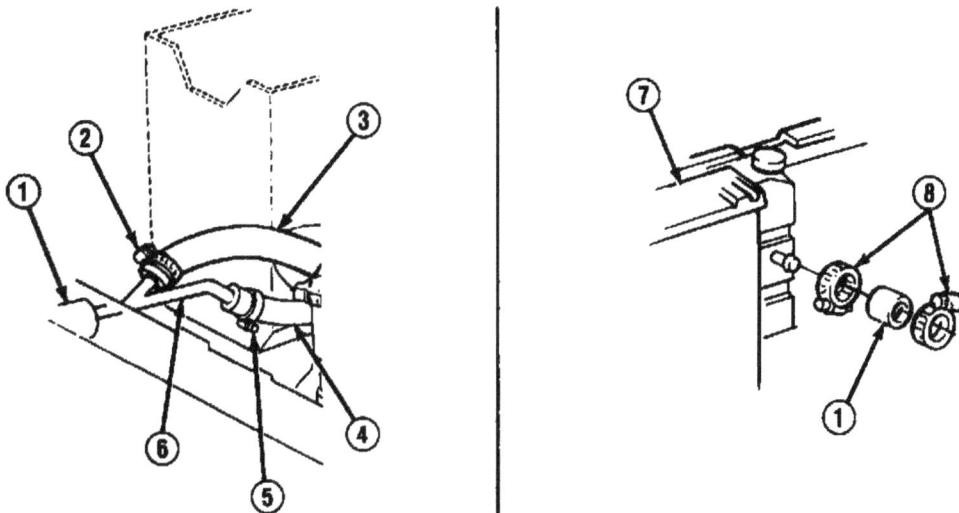

FOLLOW-ON TASKS:

- Install rear battery box. (See paragraph 11-6)
- Fill cooling system. (See paragraph 3-30)
- Check for leaks.

TA50081

Section III. WINTERIZATION KIT ENGINE HEATER MAINTENANCE

11-13. WINTERIZATION KIT ENGINE HEATER MAINTENANCE INDEX.

11-14. ENGINE COOLANT HEATER FUEL FILTER AND LINES REPLACEMENT.

This task covers:	a. Removal	c. Heater Bleeding
	b. Installation	

INITIAL SETUP:

Equipment Condition

* Both battery negative cables disconnected.
  (See paragraph 4-38)

General Safety Instructions

* DO NOT perform this procedure near fire, flames, or sparks.

Materials/Parts

* One lockwasher
* Pipe sealant (Item 43, Appendix C)
* plastic tube (Item 49, Appendix C)

---

a.	REMOVAL

WARNING

Diesel fuel is flammable. DO NOT perform this procedure near fire, flames, or sparks, A fire extinguisher must be on hand in work area. Failure to follow this warning may result in serious injury or death.

NOTE

* **Clean old sealant from all pipe threads.**

* **Use suitable container to catch fuel when disconnecting fuel lines.**

* **If removing fuel filter (3), perform steps 1 and 2.**

* **If removing fuel lines, perform steps 1, 3, and 4.**

1. Close fuel shutoff valve (1). Loosen fitting (15) and disconnect pipe (16) from fuel filter (3). Loosen fitting (14) and disconnect pipe (13) from fuel filter.

2. Remove 2 screws (7) and washers (6). Remove fuel filter (3) assembly and spacer (4), Remove fuel shutoff valve (1), coupling (2), and adapter (5) from fuel filter.

3. Remove nut (22), lockwasher (21), and clamp (19) from stud (17). Discard lockwasher.

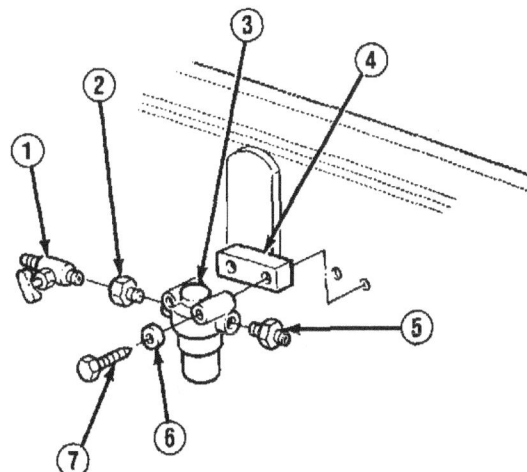

TA50082

11-14. ENGINE COOLANT HEATER FUEL FILTER AND LINES REPLACEMENT (Con't).

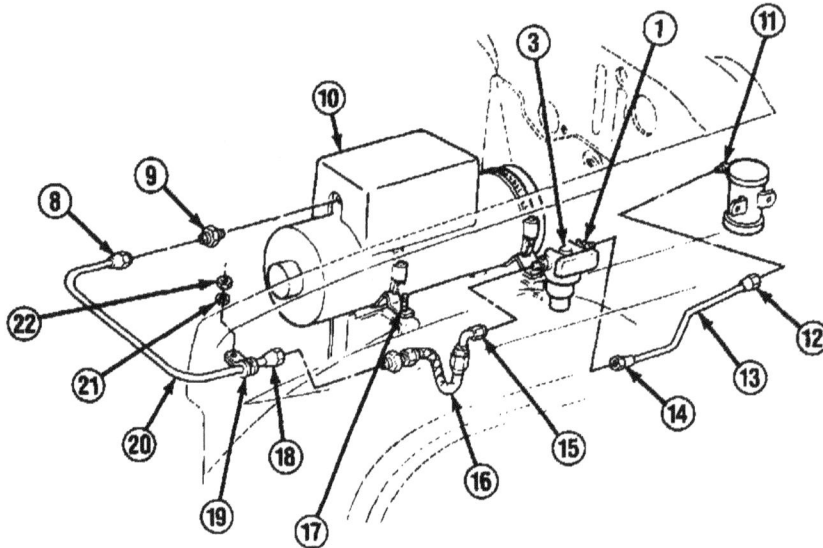

4. Loosen fitting (12) and disconnect pipe (13) from heater fuel pump tee (11). Remove pipe (13). Loosen fitting (18) and disconnect pipe (20) from pipe (16) as required. Loosen fitting (8) and disconnect pipe (20) from adapter (9). Remove adapter from engine coolant heater (10) as required.

b. INSTALLATION

NOTE

- If installing fuel lines, perform steps 1, 2, and 4.

- If installing fuel filter (3), perform steps 3 and 4.

- Apply pipe sealant to all pipe threads before installation.

1. Install adapter (9) on engine coolant heater (10) if removed. Connect pipe (20) to adapter, but DO NOT tighten fitting (8). Connect pipe (20) to pipe (16) and tighten fitting (18) if disconnected. Position pipe (13) and connect to heater fuel pump tee (11) by tightening fitting (12).

2. Install clamp (19) on pipe (20) and install on stud (17) with new lockwasher (21) and nut (22).

3. Install adapter (5), coupling (2), and fuel shutoff valve (1) on fuel filter (3). Install spacer (4) and fuel filter assembly with 2 washers (6) and screws (7).

4. Connect pipe (13) to fuel filter (3) and tighten fitting (14). Connect pipe (16) to fuel filter and tighten fitting (15).

TA50083

11-14. ENGINE COOLANT HEATER FUEL FILTER AND LINES REPLACEMENT (Con't).

c.   HEATER BLEEDING

WARNING

Diesel fuel is flammable.   DO NOT   perform this procedure near fire, flames, or sparks. A fire extinguisher must be on hand in work area. Failure to follow this warning may result in serious injury or death.

1.   Bleed engine coolant heater (10) the same way as cab heater, except that pipe plug must be removed to open bleed valve. (See paragraph 11-7)

2.   Ensure that fitting (8) is tightened on adapter (9) and pipe plug is installed after bleeding is completed.

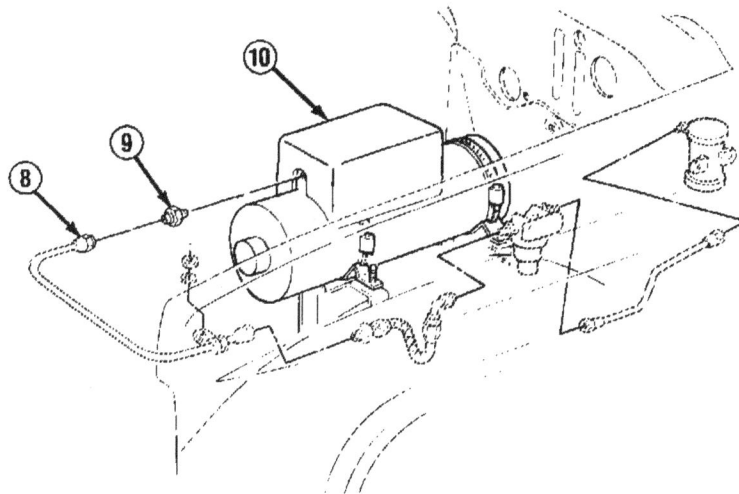

FOLLOW-ON TASKS:

* Check for leaks.

TA50084

11-15. ENGINE COOLANT HEATER HOSES AND FITTINGS REPLACEMENT.

This task covers:	a. Removal	b. Installation

INITIAL SETUP:

Materials/Parts
  • Pipe sealant (Item 43, Appendix C)

---

a.	**REMOVAL**

NOTE

  • **If removing hoses, perform steps 1-3.**

  • **If removing fittings, perform steps 2, 4, and 5.**

  • **Drain coolant from hoses into suitable container.**

  • **Tag hoses for installation.**

  • **Clean old pipe sealant from all pipe threads.**

  • **On M1010, clamp (5) is removed from compressor alternator bracket (20).** **bracket instead of**

1.   Remove bolt and clamp (5) from alternator bracket (20), inlet hose (7), and outlet hose (6). Remove nut (22), washer (21), bolt (1), and clamp (2) from outlet hose.

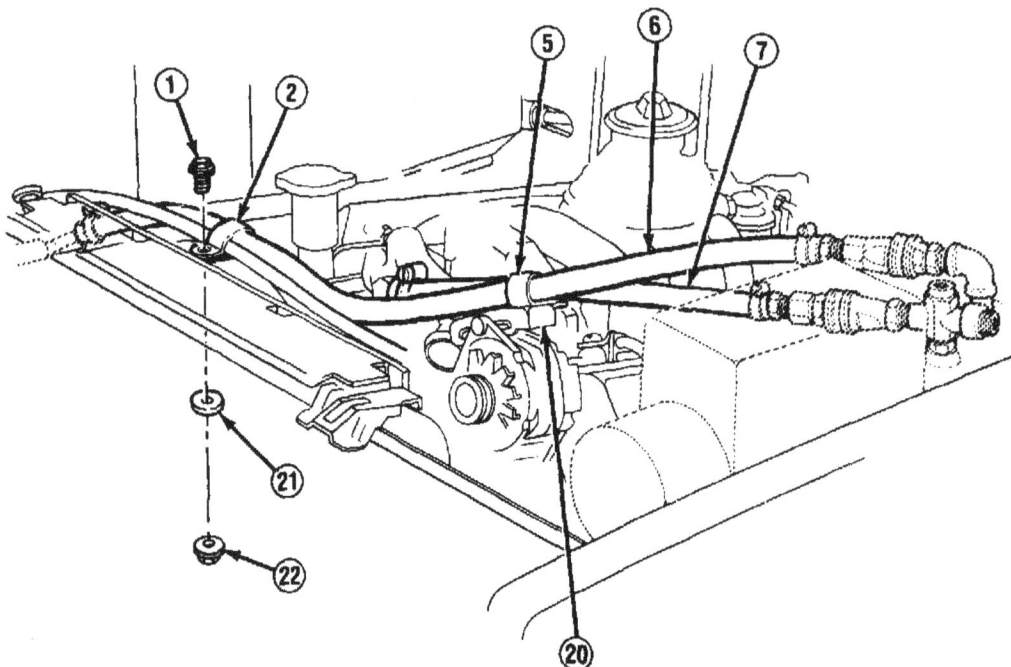

TA50085

11-15. ENGINE COOLANT HEATER HOSES AND FITTINGS REPLACEMENT (Con't).

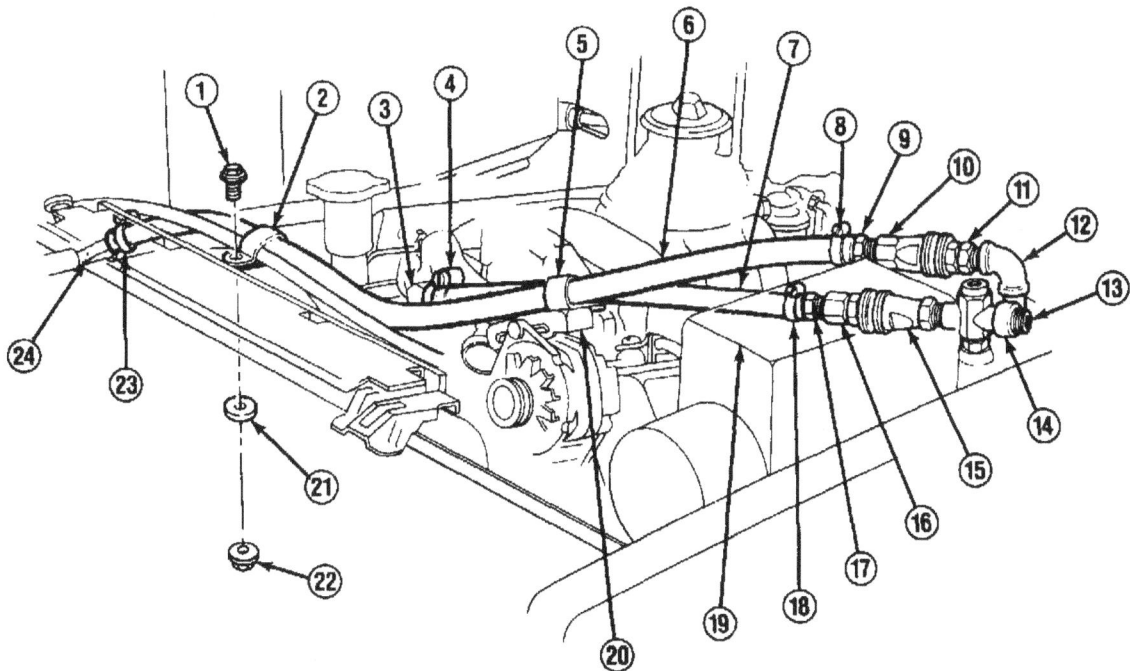

2. Disconnect coupling half (10) from coupling half (11). Disconnect coupling half (16) from coupling half (15).

3. Loosen clamp (4) and disconnect inlet hose (7) from crossover pipe (3). Loosen clamp (23) and disconnect outlet hose (6) from pipe assembly (24). Remove inlet hose and outlet hose.

4. Disconnect coupling half (10) from adapter (9). Loosen clamp (8) and disconnect adapter (9) from outlet hose (6). Disconnect coupling half (16) from adapter (17). Loosen clamp (18) and disconnect adapter (17) from inlet hose (7).

5. Disconnect electrical connector from heater thermostat (14). Remove coupling half (15). Remove heater thermostat from engine coolant heater (19). Remove coupling half (11) and elbow (12). Remove pipe nipple (13) from engine coolant heater.

TA50086

11-15. ENGINE COOLANT HEATER HOSES AND FITTINGS REPLACEMENT (Con't).

| b. INSTALLATION |

NOTE

• If installing fittings, perform steps 1, 2, and 4.

• If installing hoses, perform steps 3-5 as required.

1. Apply pipe sealant to pipe nipple (13) threads and install on engine coolant heater (19). Apply pipe sealant to elbow (12) and coupling half (11) threads and install. Install heater thermostat (14) on engine coolant heater. Apply pipe sealant to coupling half (15) threads and install. Connect electrical connector to heater thermostat.

2. Connect adapter (17) to inlet hose (7) and tighten clamp (18). Apply pipe sealant to coupling half (16) threads and connect to adapter (17). Connect adapter (9) to outlet hose (6) and tighten clamp (8), Apply pipe sealant to coupling half (10) threads and connect to adapter (9) .

3. Connect outlet hose (6) to pipe assembly (24) and tighten clamp (23). Connect inlet hose (7) to crossover pipe (3) and tighten clamp (4).

4. Apply pipe sealant to coupling half (16) threads and connect to coupling half (15). Apply pipe sealant to coupling half (10) threads and connect to coupling half (11).

NOTE

On M1010, clamp (5) is installed on compressor bracket instead of alternator bracket (20).

5. Install clamp (2) on outlet hose (6). Install clamp (2) with bolt (1), washer (21), and nut (22). Install clamp (5) on outlet hose and inlet hose (7). Install clamp (5) on alternator bracket (20) with bolt.

FOLLOW-ON TASKS:

• Fill cooling system. (See paragraph 3-30)
• Start engine and check for leaks.

11-16. ENGINE COOLANT HEATER REPLACEMENT.

This task covers:	a. Removal	b. Installation

INITIAL SETUP:

Equipment Condition
• Engine coolant heater fuel lines disconnected.
   (See paragraph 11-14)
• Engine coolant heater fittings removed.
   (See paragraph 11-15)

Materials/Parts
• Six lockwashers

---

a.	**REMOVAL**

NOTE

If removing engine   coolant heater (1), perform step 1.

1.   Remove engine coolant heater (1) cover and disconnect wiring harness assembly (5). Unscrew clamps (4) and open completely. Rotate engine coolant heater to gain access to exhaust pipe (3). Loosen clamp (2) and disconnect exhaust pipe. Remove engine coolant heater.

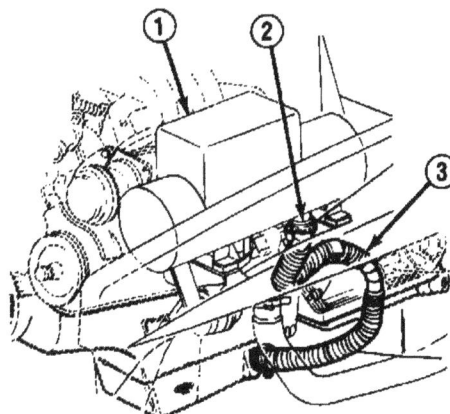

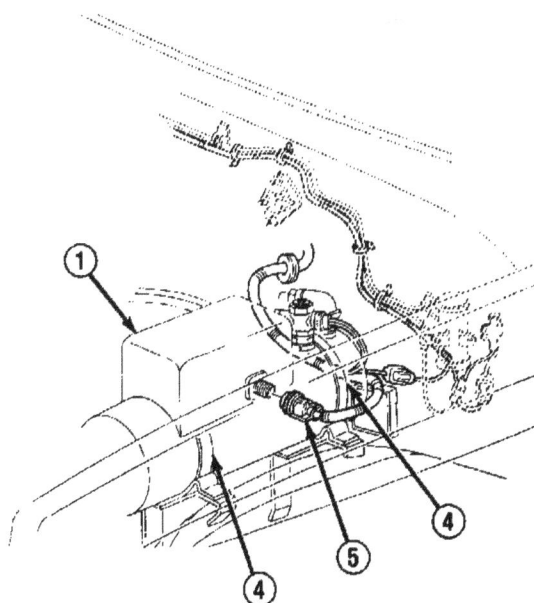

TA50087

11-16. ENGINE COOLANT HEATER REPLACEMENT (Con't).

2. Remove clamp (4) from clamp bracket (16). Remove 2 nuts (6) and lockwashers (7), Remove clamp bracket.   Remove 2 nuts (9), lockwashers (8), and mounts (15). Remove 2 nuts (13), lockwashers (12), bolts (10), and washers (11). Remove heater bracket (14). Discard lockwashers.

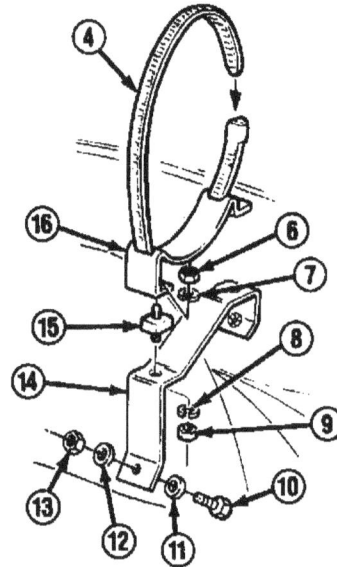

| b. | INSTALLATION |

NOTE

If installing engine coolant heater (1), perform step 2.

1. Install heater bracket (14) on fender with 2 washers (11), bolts (10), new lockwashers (12), and nuts (13). Install 2 mounts (15) on heater bracket with 2 new lockwashers (8) and nuts (9). Install clamp bracket (16) on mounts with 2 new lockwashers (7) and nuts (6). Install heater clamp (4) through clamp bracket.

2. Position engine coolant heater (1), Connect exhaust pipe (3) and tighten clamp (2). Install 2 clamps (4) around engine coolant heater and tighten securely. Connect wiring harness assembly (5). Install engine coolant heater cover.

FOLLOW-ON TASKS:

• Install engine coolant heater fittings, (See paragraph 11-15)
• Connect engine coolant heater fuel lines. (See paragraph 11-14)

TA50088

11-17. ENGINE COOLANT HEATER WIRING HARNESS REPLACEMENT.

This task covers: a. Remova l   b. Installation

INITIAL SETUP:

Equipment Condition

• Both battery negative cables disconnected.
  (See paragraph 4-38)

Materials/parts

• Tie-down straps (Item 44, Appendix C)

| a. | **REMOVAL** |

NOTE

• **If removing relay (10), perform step 3.**

Ž Tag all leads and connectors for installation.

1. Disconnect wiring harness connector
    (5) from engine coolant heate r
    thermostat (4). Remove engin e
    coolant heater (1) cover and
    disconnect wiring harness (2) from
    engine coolant heater, Disconnect
    wiring harness connector (6) from
    cab heater connector (7). Remove
    and discard tie-down straps fro m
    wiring harness.

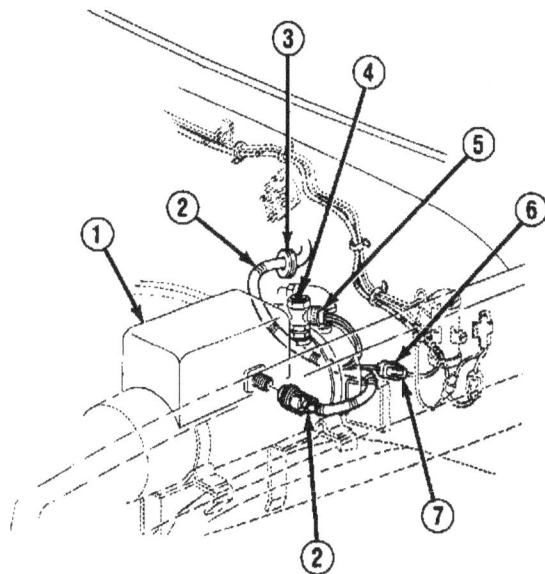

2. Disconnect wiring harness (2) from cab heater control panel assembly (8). Loosen nut on
    strap (9) and disconnect wiring harness.

3. Remove relay (10) and disconnect from wiring harness (2).

4. Remove wiring harness (2) and grommet   (3) from bulkhead. Retain grommet for installation if
    not damaged.

TA50089

11-17. ENGINE COOLANT HEATER WIRING HARNESS REPLACEMENT (Con't).

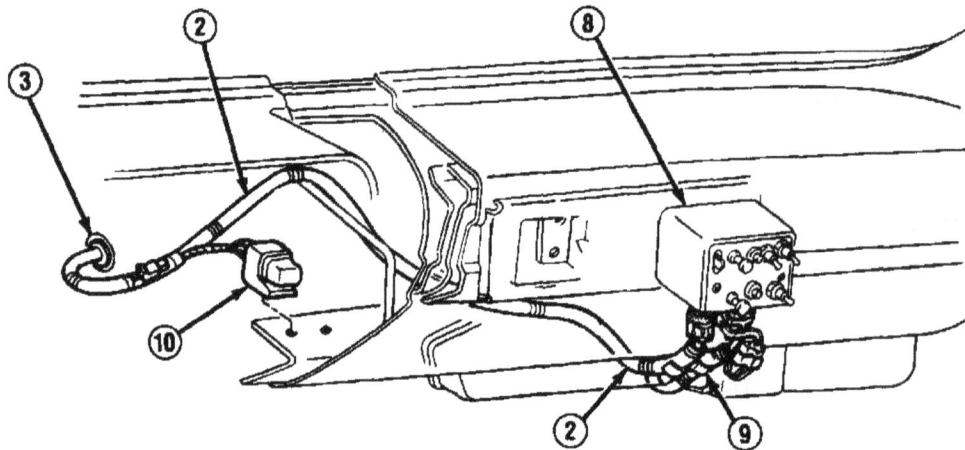

| **b.** | **INSTALLATION** |

NOTE

If installing relay (10), perform step 2.

1. Install grommet (3)   on wiring harness (2). Position wiring harness in cab. Push wiring harness through bulkhead.

2. Plug relay (10) into wiring harness (2) and connect to mount.

3. Position wiring harness (2) in strap (9) and tighten nut. Connect wiring harness to cab heater control panel assembly (8).

4. Connect wiring harness connector (6) to cab heater connector (7). Connect wiring harness (2) to engine coolant heater (1). Install engine coolant heater cover. Connect wiring harness connector (5) to engine coolant heater thermostat (4). Install new tie-down straps to wiring harness.

FOLLOW-ON TASKS:

   • Connect both battery negative cables. (See paragraph 4-38)
   • Check operation of engine coolant heater. (See TM 9-2320-289-10)

TA50090

11-18. ENGINE COOLANT HEATER EXHAUST PIPE REPLACEMENT.

This task covers: a. Removal   b. Installation

INITIAL SETUP:

Materials/Parts
  • Five locknuts (all except M1009)
  • Three locknuts (M1009)

General Safety Instructions
  • Allow exhaust system to cool before attempting to service.

---

a.	REMOVAL

WARNING

Before attempting to service any part of exhaust system, allow exhaust system to cool. Failure to follow this warning will result in serious burns.

NOTE

  • If removing front exhaust pipe (7), perform steps 1 and 2.

  • If removing heat exchange pipe (12), perform step 3.

  • If removing rear exhaust pipe (21), perform steps 4-7.

1.   Loosen clamp (2) and disconnect front exhaust pipe (7) from engine coolant heater (1). Remove nut (3) and clip (4) to free front exhaust pipe. Remove screw (6) and bracket (5) as required.

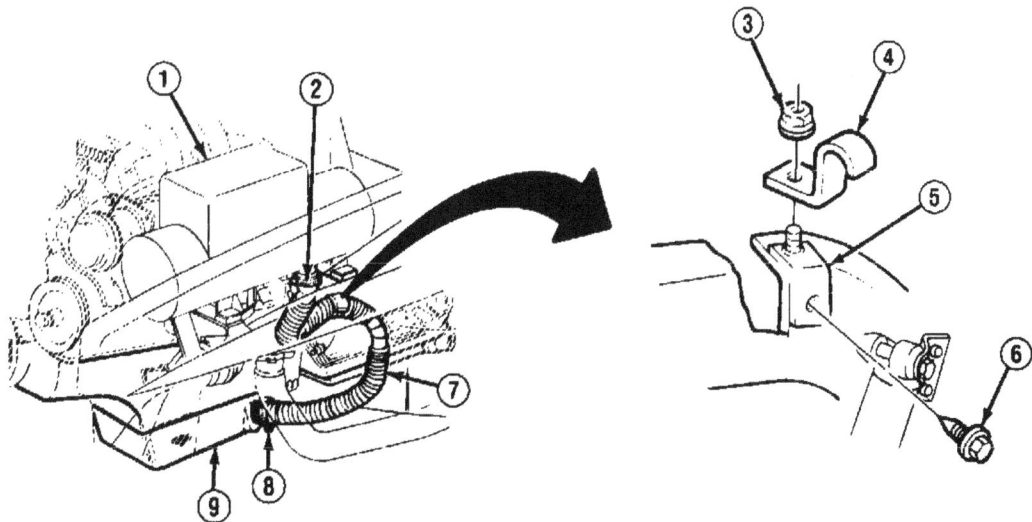

TA50091

11-18. ENGINE COOLANT HEATER EXHAUST PIPE REPLACEMENT (Con't).

2.   Loosen clamp (8) and remove front exhaust pipe (7) from engine oil pan (9).

3.   Remove 4 screws (10) and remove heat exchange pipe (12) from engine oil pan (9) and transmission oil pan (11).

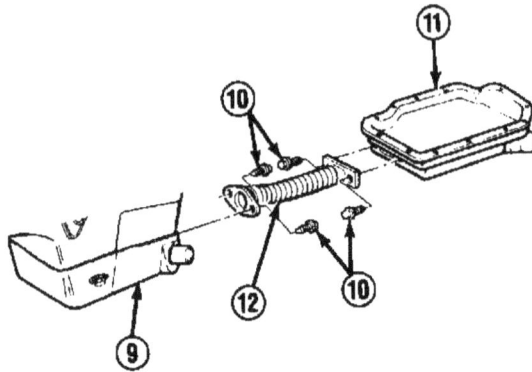

4.   Loosen clamp (22) and disconnect rear exhaust pipe (21) from transmission oil pan (11).

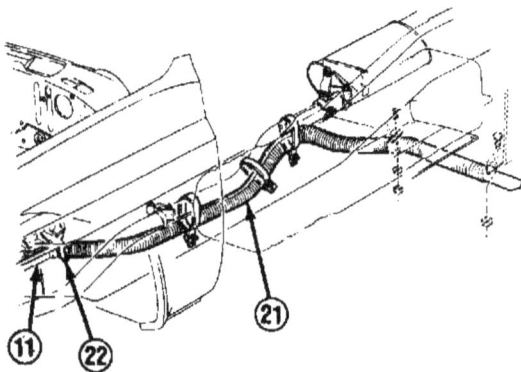

All Except M1009

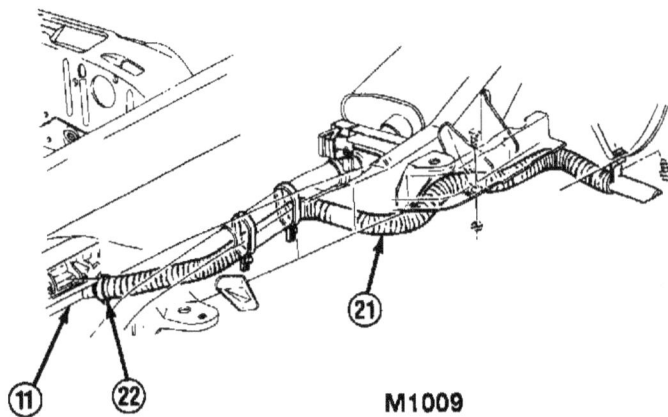

M1009

TA50092

11-18. ENGINE COOLANT HEATER EXHAUST PIPE REPLACEMENT (Con't).

NOTE

M1009 uses 2 clamps (29), al l others use 3 clamps.

5.   Remove locknut (31) and screw (30) from each clamp (29). Remove each clamp from rear exhaust pipe (21) and engin e exhaust pipe (28) . Discard locknuts.

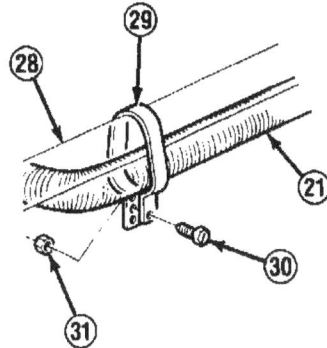

NOTE

Step 6 applies   to all except M1009.

6.   Remove locknut (18), washer (19), clip (16), and screw (14) from rear quarter locknuts.

(20), and screw (13). Remove locknut (17), washer panel (15). Remove rear exhaust pipe (21), Discard

NOTE

Step 7 only applies to M1009.

7.   Remove locknut (27), clip (23), and screw (24). Remove screw (26) from rear quarter panel (25). Remove rear exhaust pipe (21). Discard locknut.

b.	INSTALLATION

NOTE

• **If installing rear exhaust pipe (21), perform steps   1-3.**

• **If installing heat exchange pipe, perform step 4.**

• **If installing front exhaust pipe, perform steps 5 and 6.**

• **Step 1 only applies to M1009.**

1.   Install rear exhaust pipe (21) on rear quarter panel (25) with screw (26). Install clip (23) on rear exhaust pipe with screw (24) and new locknut (27).

NOTE

Step 2 applies to all except M1009.

2.   Install rear exhaust pipe (21) on rear quarter panel (15) with screw (14), washer (16), and new locknut (17), Install clip (20) on rear exhaust pipe with screw (13), washer (19), and new locknut (18).

TA50093

11-18. ENGINE COOLANT HEATER EXHAUST PIPE REPLACEMENT (Con't).

NOTE

M1009 uses 2 clamps (29), all others use 3 clamps.

3. Position rear exhaust pipe (21) along engine exhaust pipe (28). Install each clamp (29) around rear exhaust pipe and engine exhaust pipe with screw (30) and new locknut (31). Connect rear exhaust pipe to transmission oil pan (11) and tighten clamp (22).

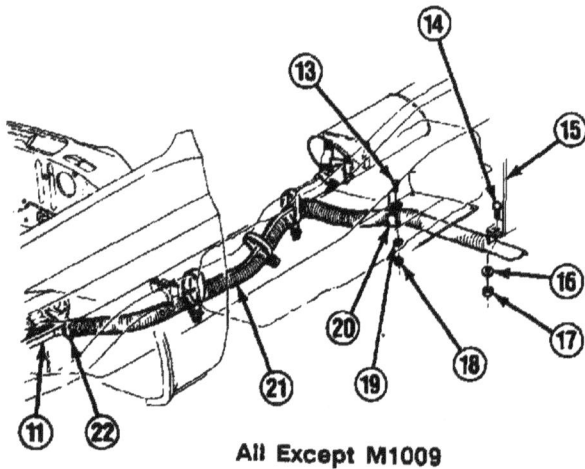

All Except M1009

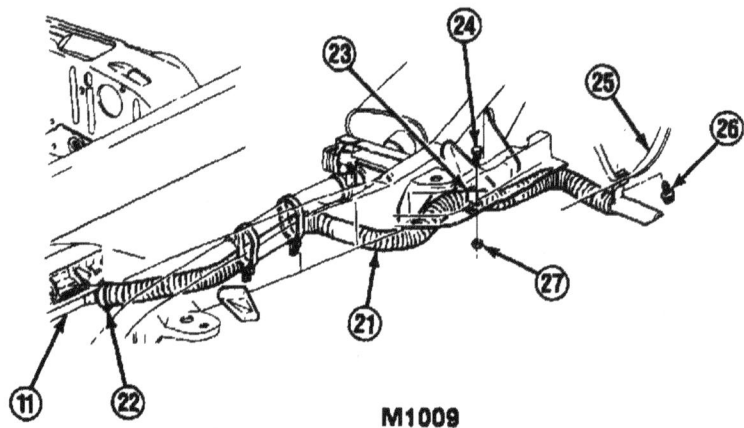

M1009

TA500i94

11-18. ENGINE COOLANT HEATER EXHAUST PIPE REPLACEMENT (Con't).

4. Install heat exchange pipe (12) to transmission oil pan (11) and engine oil pan (9) with 4 screws (10).

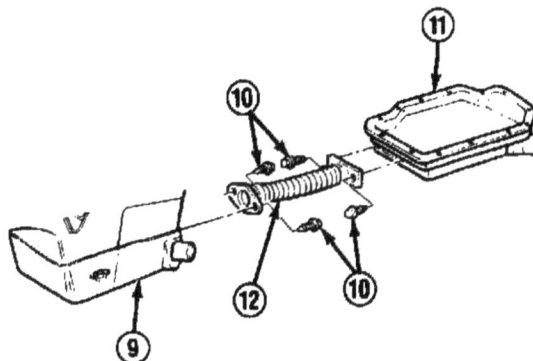

5. Connect front exhaust pipe (7) to engine oil pan (9) and tighten clamp (8).

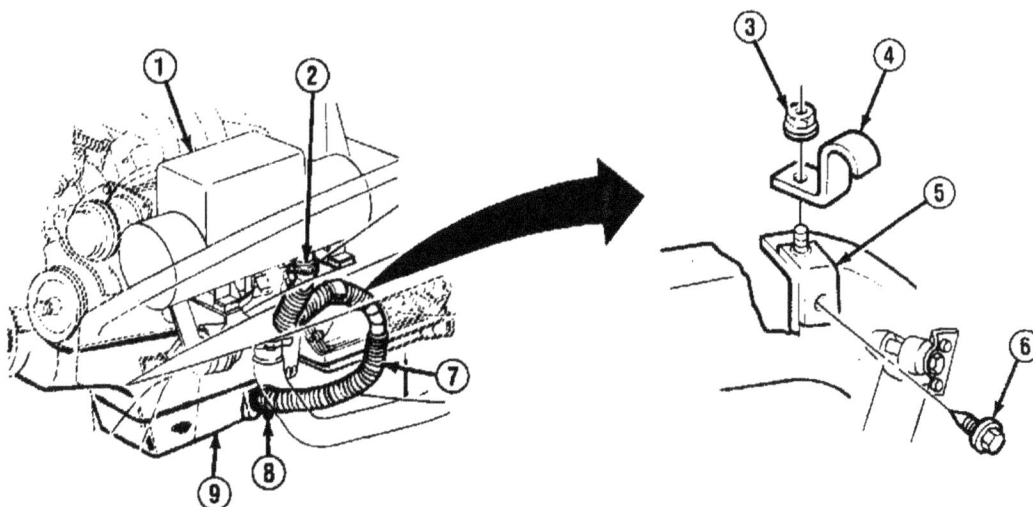

6. Install bracket (5) with screw (6) if removed, Install clip (3) on front exhaust pipe (7) with nut (3), Connect front exhaust pipe to engine coolant heater (1) and tighten clamp (2).

TA50095

Section IV. WINTERIZATION KIT CARGO COMPARTMENT HEATER MAINTENANCE

11-19. WINTERIZATION KIT CARGO COMPARTMENT HEATER MAINTENANCE INDEX.

11-20. CARGO COMPARTMENT HEATER CONTROL REPLACEMENT (M1008 AND M1008A1).

This task covers:	a. Removal	b. Installation

INITIAL SETUP:

Equipment Condition
- Both battery negative cables disconnected. (See paragraph 4-38)

Materials/Parts
- Four locknuts

---

a.	REMOVAL

NOTE

- **If removing control box   (7), perform steps 1 and 2.**

- **If removing lead (4), perform steps 1-3 as required.**

1. Open catches (2) and remove heater shield (1).

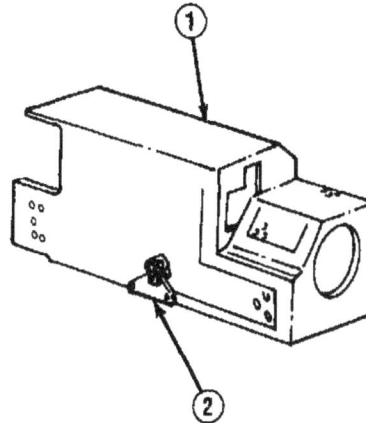

2. Disconnect lead (4) from control box (7). Disconnect control box plug from heater wiring harness. Remove 2 nuts (3) and control box.

NOTE

Note clamp locations for installation.

3. Remove 2 screws, washers, and clamps from lead (4), Disconnect lead from cargo compartment heater (6).

4. Remove 2 locknuts (14), washers (13), and bolts (8). Remove upper bracket (5). Discard locknuts.

TA50096

11-20. CARGO COMPARTMENT HEATER CONTROL REPLACEMENT (M1008 AND M1008A1) (Con't).

5. Remove 2 locknuts (9), washers (10), and bolts (11). Remove lower bracket (12). Discard locknuts.

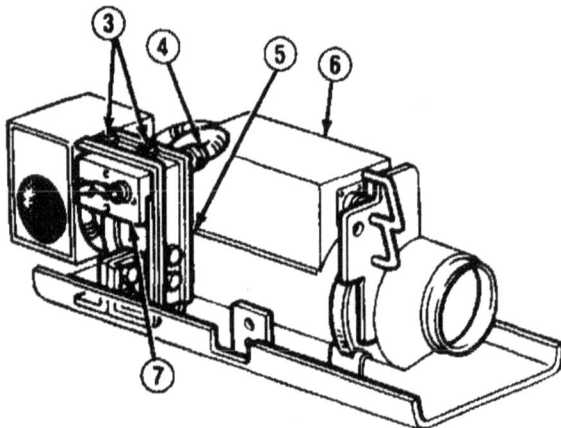

M1008

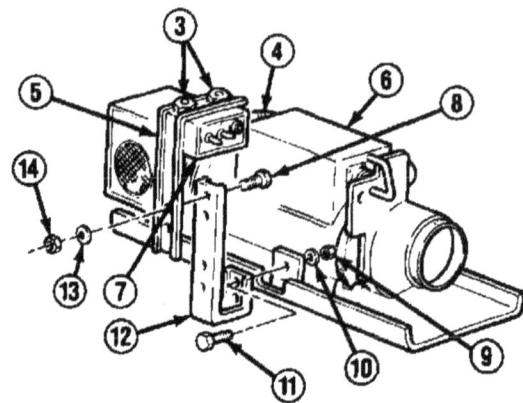

M1008A1

| b. | INSTALLATION |

NOTE

• If installing iead (4), perform steps 2-4 as required.

• If installing control box (7), perform steps 3 and 4.

1. Install lower bracket (12) on cargo compartment heater (6) bracket with 2 bolts (11), washers (10), and new locknuts (9). Install upper bracket (5) on lower bracket with 2 bolts (8), washers (13), and new locknuts (14).

2. Connect iead (4) to cargo compartment heater (6). install 2 clamps on lead. Install clamps on cargo compartment heater with 2 washers and screws.

3. Install control box (7) on upper bracket (5) with 2 nuts (3). Connect lead (4) to control box. Connect control box plug to heater wiring harness.

4. Install heater shieid (1) over cargo compartment heater (6) and lock 2 catches (2) in place.

FOLLOW-ON TASKS:

• Connect both battery negative cables. (See paragraph 4-38)
• Check operation of cargo compartment heater. (See TM 9-2320-289-10)

TA50097

11-21. CARGO COMPARTMENT HEATER AND FUEL FILTER MAINTENANCE (M1008 AND M1008A1).

| This task covers: | a. Removal | c. Assembly |
| | b. Disassembly | d. Installation |

INITIAL SETUP:

Equipment Condition
- Heater shield, control box, and lead removed. (See paragraph 11-20)
- Communications rack mounting hardware and ground strap removed (M1008A1 only). (See paragraph 4-48)

Personnel Required
- MOS 63B (2)

Materials/Parts
- Seven locknuts
- One gasket
- Two cotter pins
- RTV sealant (Item 41, Appendix C)

General Safety Instructions
- DO NOT perform this procedure near fire, flames, or sparks.

| a. REMOVAL |

WARNING

Diesel fuel is flammable. DO NOT perform this procedure near fire, flames, or sparks. A fire extinguisher must be on hand in work area. Failure to follow this warning may result in serious injury or death.

NOTE

Use suitable container to catch fuel from disconnected fuel line.

1. Close fuel shutoff valve (2). Loosen fitting (1) and disconnect fuel line.

2. Loosen clamp (4), disconnect air duct hose (3) from ventilator (6), and move air duct hose out of the way.

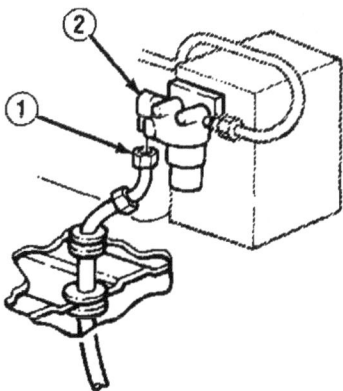

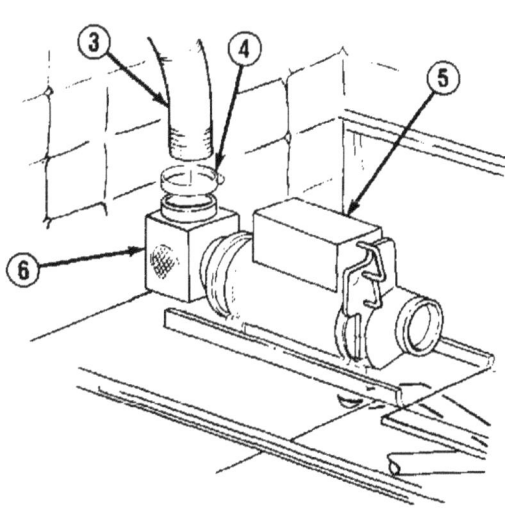

TA50098

11-21. CARGO COMPARTMENT HEATER AND FUEL FILTER MAINTENANCE (M1008 AND M1008A1) (Con't).

3. Loosen clamp (8) and disconnect exhaust pipe (7) from adapter (9).

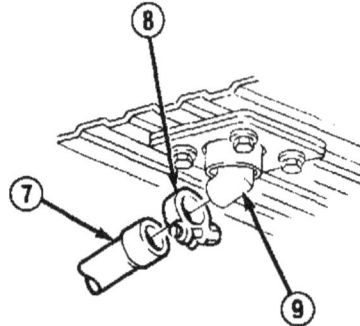

NOTE

*   **Assistance is required to perform steps 4 and 5.**

*   **Step 4 only applies to M1008A1.**

4. Tilt communications rack (11) forward and support.

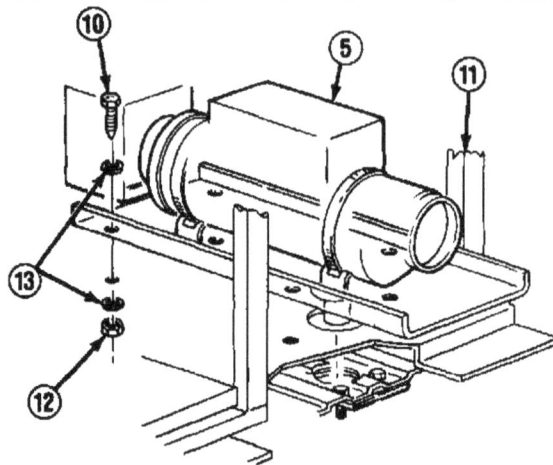

M1008A1

5. Remove cotter pin from adapter (9) and disconnect adapter from heater (5) if damaged. Discard cotter pin.

6. Remove 4 locknuts (12), 8 washers (13), and 4 screws (10). Remove heater (5) assembly. Discard locknuts.

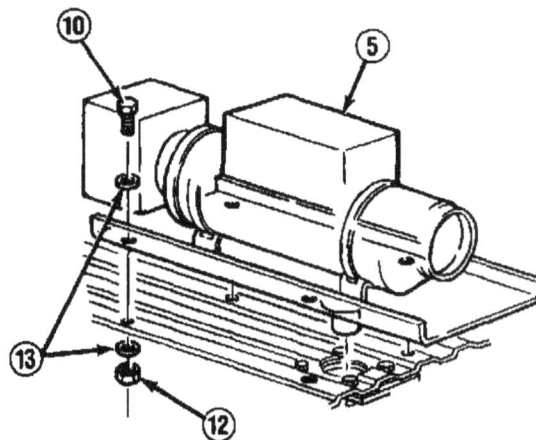

M1008

TA50099

11-21. CARGO COMPARTMENT HEATER AND FUEL FILTER MAINTENANCE (M1008 AND M1008A1) (Con't).

| b. | DISASSEMBLY |

NOTE

- If removing control lever (28) assembly, perform step 1.

- If removing outlet adapter (22), perform steps 1 and 2.

- If removing fuel filter (35), perform step 3.

- If removing ventilator (6), perform steps 1, 3, and 5.

- Clean old sealant from all pipe threads.

1. Loosen setscrew (31) and disconnect control lever (28) from. rod (32). Remove cotter pin (14), washer (15), and spring (16). Remove rod from ventilator (6). Discard cotter pin.

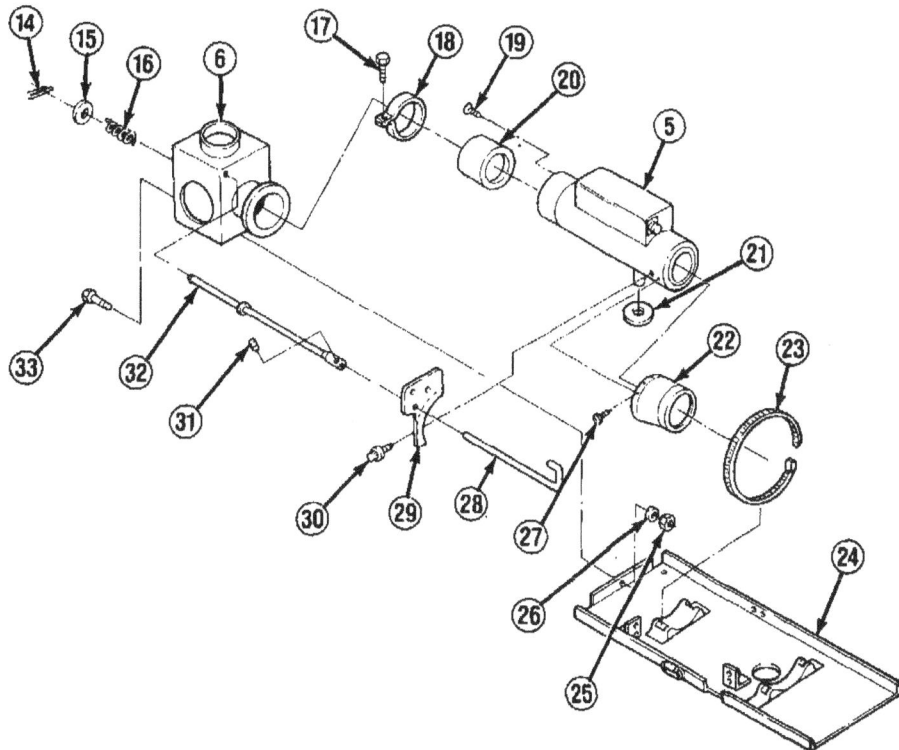

TA50100

11-21. CARGO COMPARTMENT HEATER AND FUEL FILTER MAINTENANCE (M1008 AND M1008A1) (Con't).

2.   Remove 2 screws (30) and bracket (29). Remove 4 screws (27) and outlet adapter (22).

3.   Loosen fitting (41) and disconnect fuel pipe (38) from adapter (42). Remove 2 locknuts (39), 4 washers (40), and 2 screws (43). Remove fuel filter (35) assembly and spacer (36). Remove fuel shutoff valve (2), elbow (34), and adapter. Discard locknuts.

4.   Loosen fitting (37) and disconnect fuel pipe (38) from heater (5).

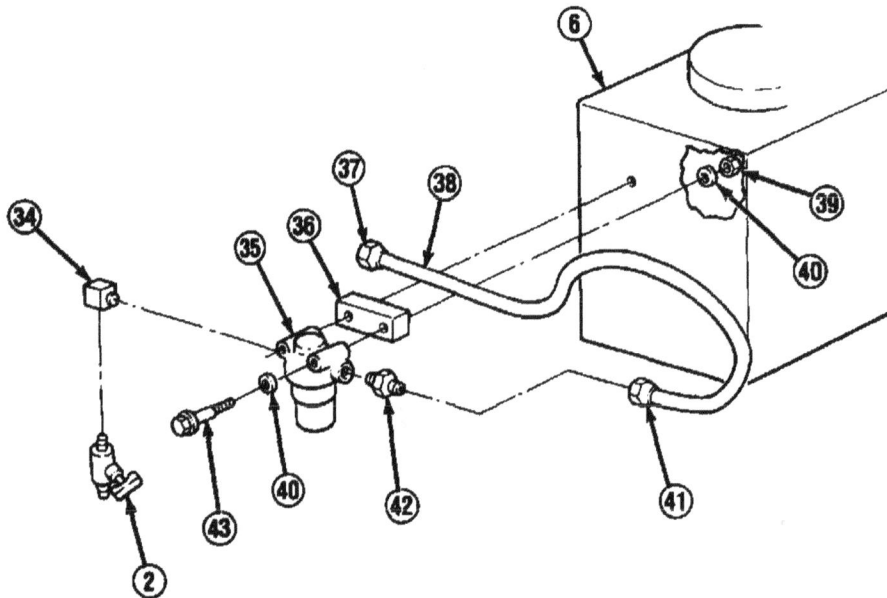

5.   Remove locknut (25), washer (26), and screw (33). Remove bolt (17) and clamp (18). Remove ventilator (6) from heater (5). Remove 3 screws (19) and inlet adapter (20) if damaged. Discard locknut.

6.   Unscrew 2 clamps (23) and open completely. Remove heater (5) and gasket (21) from mounting plate (24). Remove clamps if damaged. Discard gasket.

TA50101

11-21. CARGO COMPARTMENT HEATER AND FUEL FILTER MAINTENANCE (M1008 AND M1008A1) (Con't).

| c. | **ASSEMBLY** |

NOTE

- **If installing**   outlet adapter (22), perform steps 5 and 6.
- **If installing**   ventilator (6), perform steps 2, 4, and 6.
- **If installing**   fuel filter (35), perform step 4.
- **If installing**   control lever (28) assembly, perform step 6.
- **Apply pipe sealant to all pipe threads before installation.**

1.   Install 2 clamps (23) on mounting plate and position heater on mounting plate.   (24) if removed. Install new gasket (21) on heater (5) Tighten clamps around heater.

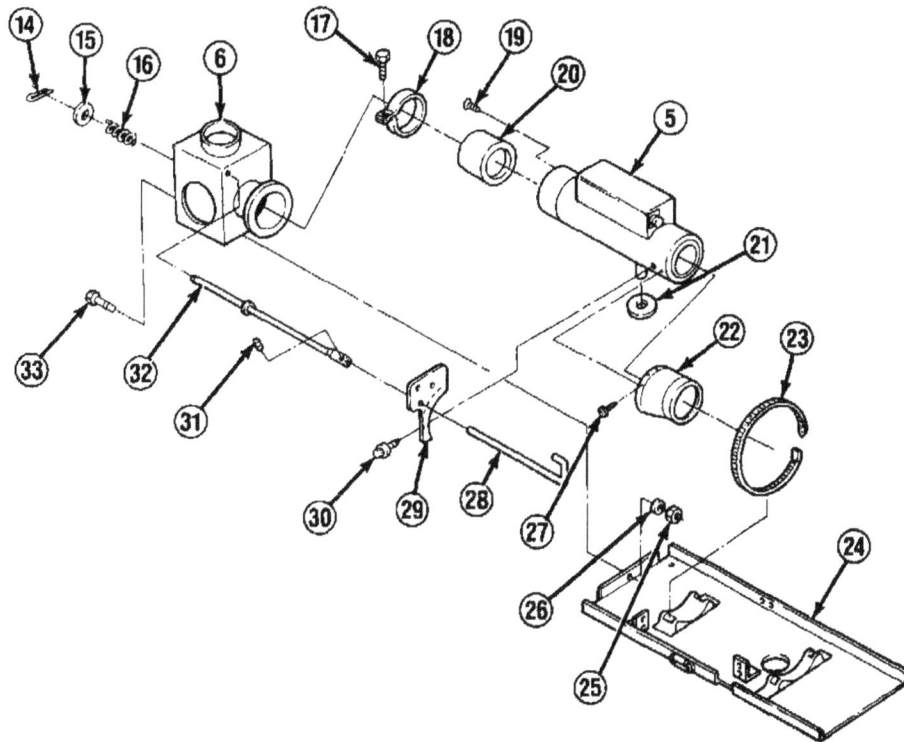

TA50102

11-21. CARGO COMPARTMENT HEATER AND FUEL FILTER MAINTENANCE (M1008 AND M1008A1) (Con't).

2. Install inlet adapter (20) on heater (5) with 3 screws (19) if removed. Install ventilator (6) on heater with clamp (18) and bolt (17). Install screw (33), washer (26), and new locknut (25).

3. Connect fuel pipe (38) to heater (5) and tighten fitting (37).

4. Install adapter (42), elbow (34), and fuel shutoff valve (2). Install spacer (36) and fuel filter (35) assembly with 2 screws (43), 4 washers (40), and 2 new locknuts (39). Connect fuel pipe (38) to adapter and tighten fitting (41).

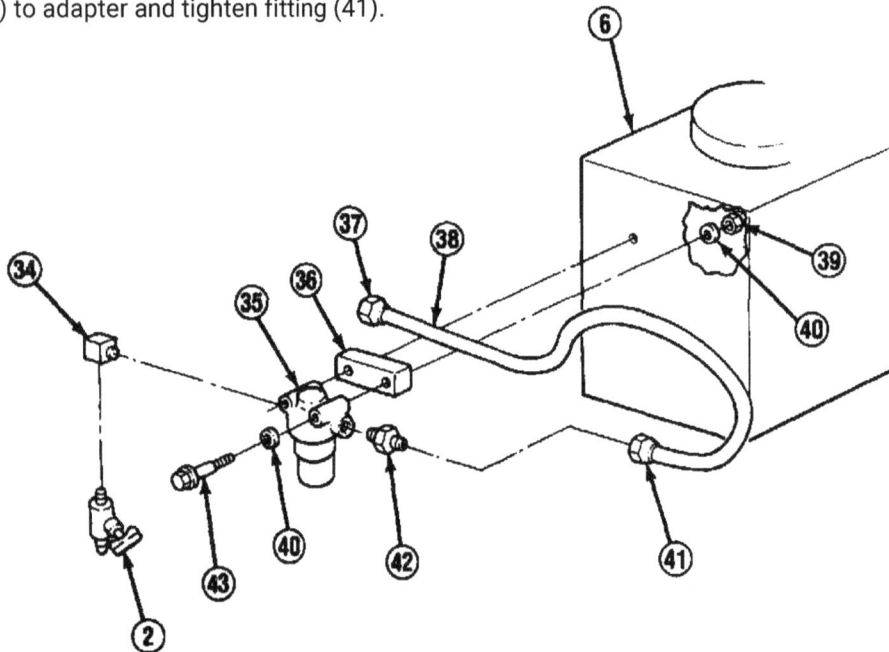

5. Install outlet adapter (22) with 4 screws (27), Install bracket (29) with 2 screws (30).

6. Install rod (32) in ventilator (6) with spring (16), washer (15), and new cotter pin (14). Connect control lever (28) to rod and tighten setscrew (31).

| d. | INSTALLATION |

1. If removed, install adapter (9) to heater (5) with new cotter pin.

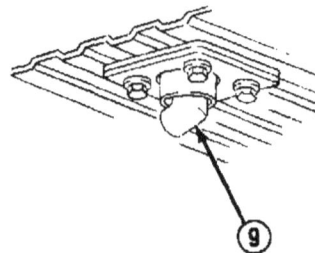

TA50103

11-21. CARGO COMPARTMENT HEATER AND FUEL FILTER MAINTENANCE (M1008 AND M1008A1) (Con't).

NOTE

Assistance is required to perform steps 2 and 3.

2. Install heater (5) assembly with 4 screws (10), 8 washers (13), and 4 new locknuts (12).

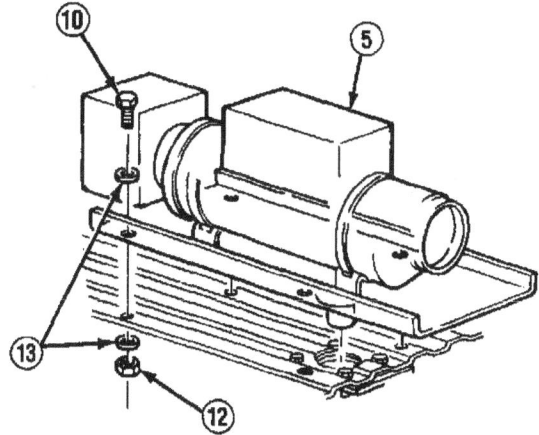

CAUTION

When lowering communications rack (11), ensure that heater exhaust adapter goes through hole in cargo bed. Failure to do this may result in damage t o heater exhaust adapter.

NOTE

Step 3 only applies   to M1008A1.

3. Lower communications rack (11) to cargo bed and aline mounting holes.

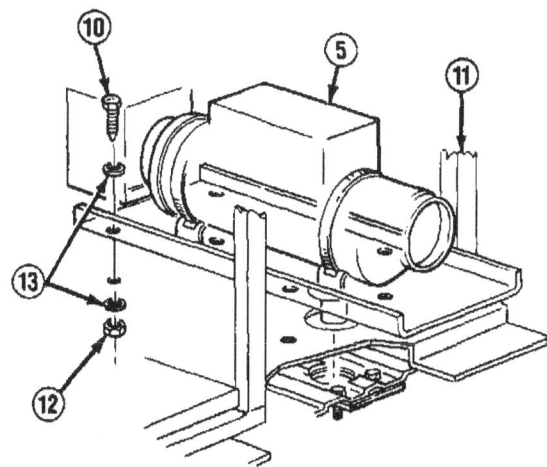

M1008A1

TA50104

11-21. CARGO COMPARTMENT HEATER AND FUEL FILTER MAINTENANCE (M1008 AND M1008A1) (Con't).

4. Connect exhaust pipe (7) to adapter (9) and tighten clamp (8).

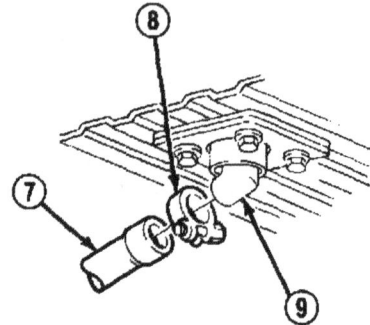

5. Connect air duct hose (3) to ventilator (6) and tighten clamp (4).

6. Connect fuel line to fuel shutoff valve (2) and tighten fitting (1).

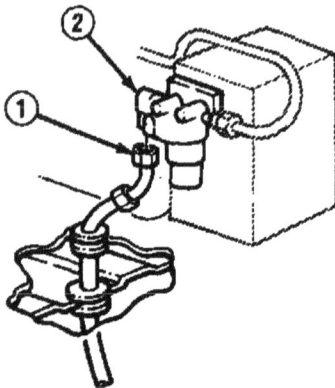

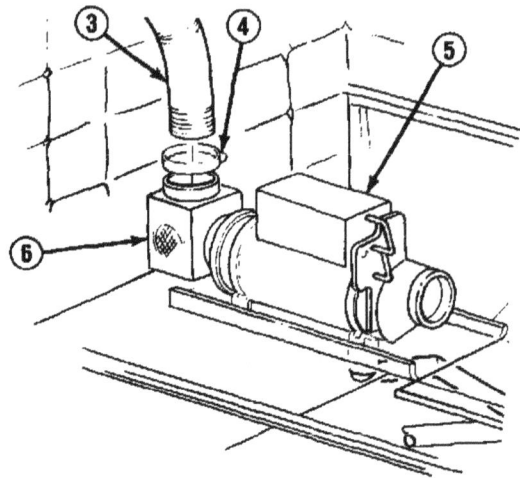

FOLLOW-ON TASKS:

*   Install communications rack mounting hardware and ground strap if removed. (See paragraph 4-48)
*   Install heater control box, lead, and shield. (See paragraph 11-20)
*   Bleed heater. (See paragraph 11-22)

TA50105

11-22. CARGO COMPARTMENT HEATER FUEL LINES REPLACEMENT (M1008 AND M1008A1).

This task covers:	a. Removal	c. Heater Bleeding
	b. Installation	

INITIAL SETUP:

Materials/Parts

- Four lockwashers
- RTV sealant (Item 41, Appendix C)
- plastic tube (Item 49, Appendix C)

General Safety Instructions

- DO NOT perform this procedure near fire, flames, or sparks.

---

a.	REMOVAL

WARNING

Diesel fuel is flammable, DO NOT perform this procedure near fire, flames, or sparks. A fire extinguisher must be on hand in work area. Failure to follow this warning may result in serious injury or death.

NOTE

• Clean old pipe sealant from all pipe threads.

• Use suitable container to catch fuel when disconnecting fuel lines.

1. Loosen fitting (21) and disconnect fuel pipe (12) from fuel hose assembly (24).

2. Loosen fitting (14) and disconnect fuel pipe (12) from tee (13). Remove bolt (17) and clamp (16) from coolant heater fuel line (15) and fuel pipe.

3. Remove bolt (19) and clamp (18) from frame (2). Remove nut (20) as required. Remove fuel pipe (12).

4. Remove 2 nuts (6), lockwashers (7), and screw (11) from clamp (23), clamp (8), and clamp (10). Separate wiring harness (22), fuel hose assembly (24), and brake line (9) from frame (2). Remove clamp (8). Discard lockwashers.

5. Remove 2 nuts (5), lockwashers (4), screws (25), and clamps (3). Loosen fitting (26) and disconnect fuel hose assembly (24) from fuel hose assembly (27). Remove fuel hose assembly (24). Discard lockwashers.

11-22. CARGO COMPARTMENT HEATER FUEL LINES REPLACEMENT (M1008 AND M1008A1) (Con't).

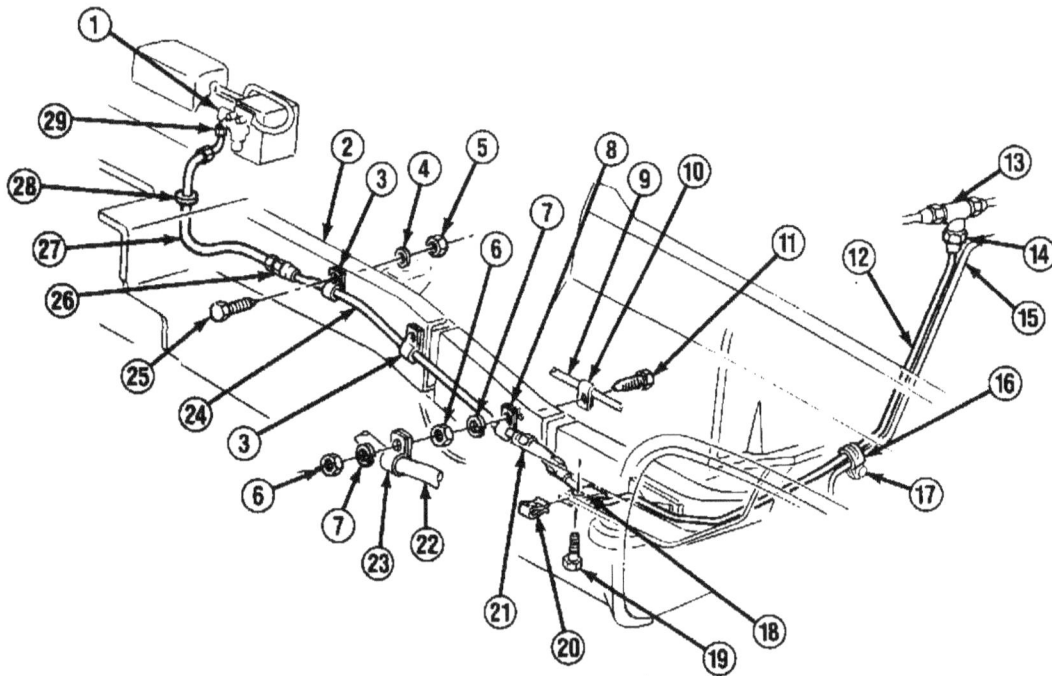

6. Remove grommet (28) from cargo bed. For M1008A1, also remove grommet (30) from communications rack.   Loosen fitting (29) an d disconnect fuel hose assembly (27) from fuel shutoff valve (1). Carefully pull fuel hose assembly through hole and remove.

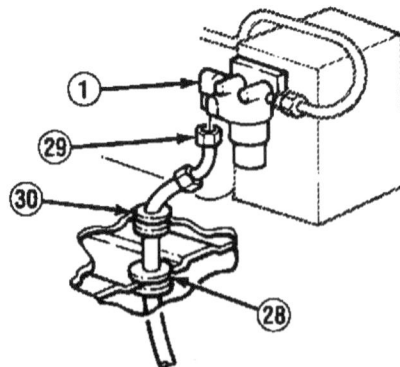

TA50106

11-22. CARGO COMPARTMENT HEATER FUEL LINES REPLACEMENT (M1008 AND M1008A1) (Con't).

| b. | INSTALLATION |

NOTE

Apply pipe sealant to all pipe threads before installation.

1. Connect fuel hose assembly (27) to fuel shutoff valve (1), but DO NOT tighten fitting (29). Feed fuel hose assembly through cargo bed and install grommet (28). For M1008A1, also install grommet (30) on fuel hose assembly and communications rack.

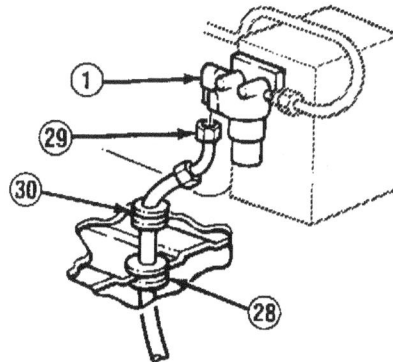

2. Position fuel hose assembly (24) along frame (2). Connect fuel hose assembly (27) to fuel hose assembly (24) and tighten fitting (26). Install 2 clamps (3) on fuel hose assembly (24) and install on frame with 2 screws (25), new lockwashers (4), and nuts (5).

3. Install clamp (8) on fuel hose assembly (24). Position brake line (9), fuel hose assembly, and wiring harness (22). Install screw (11) through clamp (10) and clamp (8). Install new lockwasher (7) and nut (6). Install clamp (23) with new lockwasher and nut.

4. Route fuel pipe (12) along bulkhead. Connect fuel pipe (12) to fuel hose assembly (24) and tighten fitting (21). Connect fuel pipe (12) to tee (13) and tighten fitting (14).

5. Install nut (20) if removed. Install clamp (18) on fuel pipe (12). Install clamp on frame (2) with bolt (19).

6. Install clamp (16) on fuel pipe (12) and coolant heater fuel line (15). Install clamp with bolt (17).

TA50107

11-22. CARGO COMPARTMENT HEATER FUEL LINES REPLACEMENT (M1008 AND M1008A1) (Con't).

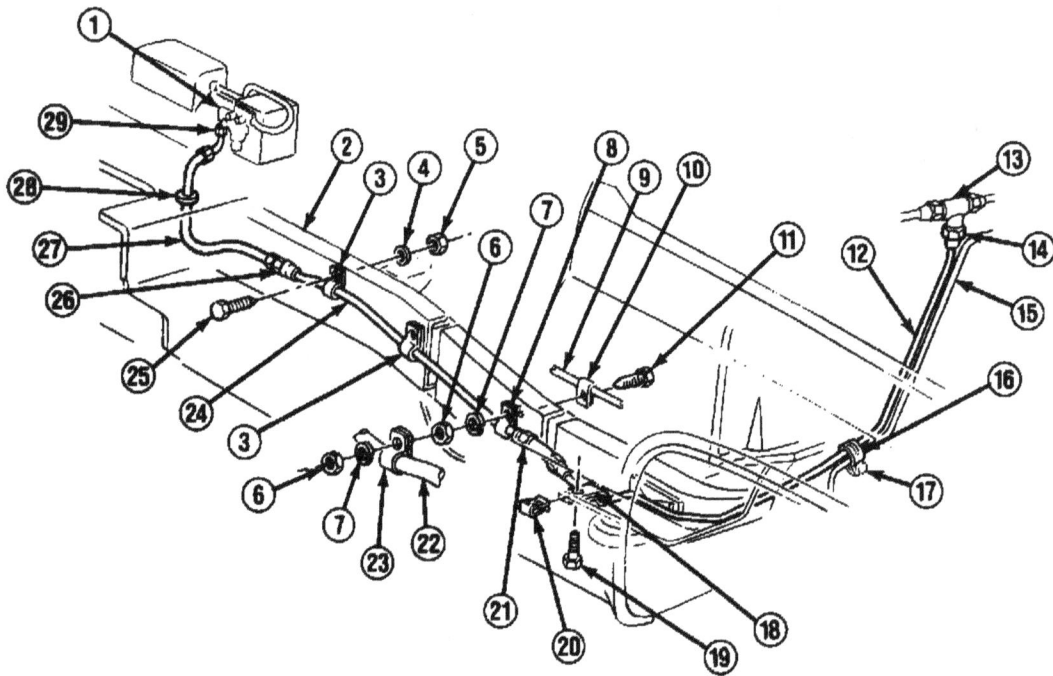

| c. | HEATER BLEEDING |

WARNING

Diesel fuel is flammable. DO NOT perform this procedure near fire, flames, or sparks. A fire extinguisher must be on hand in work area. Failure to follow this warning may result in serious injury or death.

NOTE

Use suitable container to catch fuel from disconnected fuel lines.

1. Connect both battery negative cables. (See paragraph 4-38)

TA50108

11-22. CARGO COMPARTMENT HEATER FUEL LINES REPLACEMENT (M1008 AND M1008A1) (Con't).

2.   Open 2 catches and remove heater shield, (See paragraph 11-20, REMOVAL, step 1) Loosen 2 screws (33) and remove cover (31). Open fuel shutoff valve (1). Disconnect lead from heater.

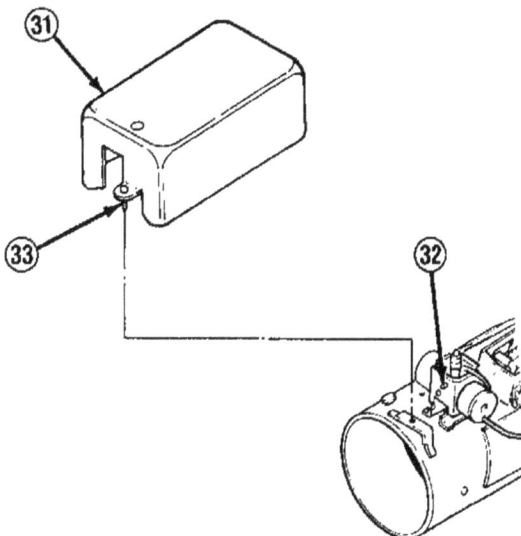

3.   Move fitting (29) clear of fuel shutoff valve (1). Hold cargo compartment heater control in "START" position. Continue operation until a clean steady flow of fuel is obtained, then shut off cargo compartment heater. Connect fitting to fuel shutoff valve.

4.   Connect lead to heater.

5.   Connect plastic tube to bleed port (32), then open bleed port. Hold cargo compartment heater control in "START" position. Continue operation until a clean, steady flow of fuel is obtained, then shut off cargo compartment heater. Close bleed port and remove plastic tube.

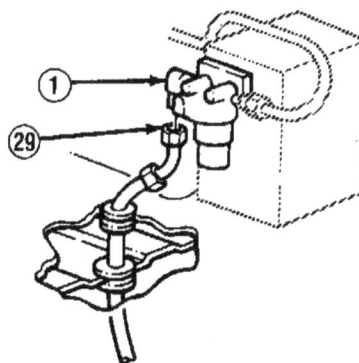

6.   Position cover (31) and tighten 2 screws (33). Install heater shield over heater and lock 2 catches in place. (See paragraph 11-20, INSTALLATION, step 4)

TA50109

11-23. CARGO COMPARTMENT HEATER WIRING HARNESS REPLACEMENT (M1008 AND M1008A1).

| This task covers: | a. Removal | b. Installation |

INITIAL SETUP:

Equipment Condition
• Rear battery box removed.
  (See paragraph 11-6)

Materials/Parts
• Three lockwashers
• Eleven straps

a. REMOVAL

NOTE

• **If removing wiring harness (1) from M1008, perform steps 1-4.**

• **If removing wiring harness from M1008A1, perform steps 5-7.**

• **Tag all leads and connectors for installation.**

1. Loosen 2 nuts (6) and remove positive accessory wiring terminal board cover (5). Remove nut and lockwasher from positive accessory wiring terminal board stud, and disconnect wiring harness (1) lead. Repeat for negative accessory wiring terminal board (7). Discard lockwashers.

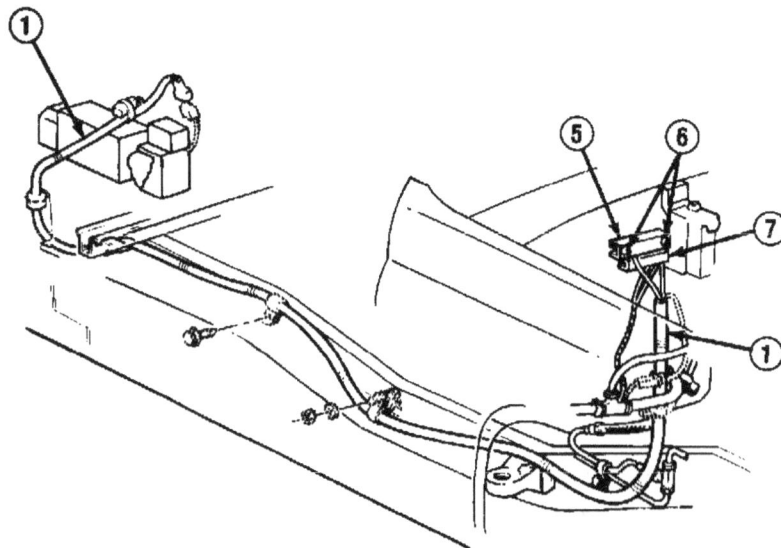

M1008

TA50110

11-23. CARGO COMPARTMENT HEATER WIRING HARNESS REPLACEMENT (M1008 AND M1008A1) (Con't).

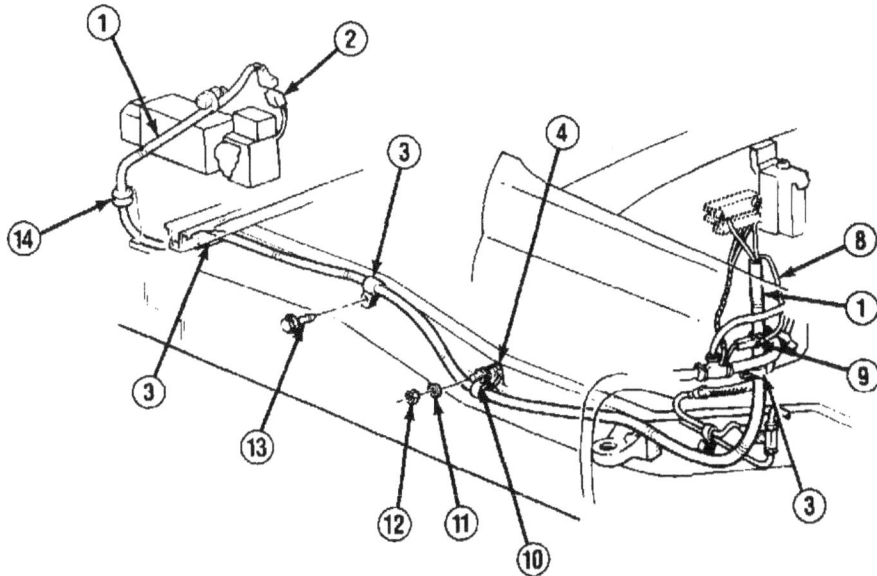

M1008

2. Disconnect wiring harness lead (8) from cab heater wiring harness connector (9).

3. Remove 3 screws (13) and clamps (3). Remove nut (12), lockwasher (11), and clamp (10) from heater fuel line clamp (4). Discard lockwasher.

4. Disconnect wiring harness (1) from heater control box plug (2). Remove grommet (14) from wiring harness and cargo bed. Carefully remove wiring harness through hole in cargo body.

5. Disconnect wiring harness (16) from cab heater wiring harness connector (19).

6. Remove 11 straps (20) from wiring harness (16) and radio feed cable (17). Discard straps.

7. Disconnect wiring harness (16) from junction box (18) and heater control box plug (15). Remove grommet (21) from wiring harness and cargo bed. Carefully remove wiring harness through hole in cargo body.

TA50111

11-23. CARGO COMPARTMENT HEATER WIRING HARNESS REPLACEMENT (M1008 AND M1008A1) (Con't).

| b. | INSTALLATION |

NOTE

- If installing   wiring harness (1) on M1008A1, perform steps 1-3.

- If installing   wiring harness (1) on MI 008, perform steps 4-7.

- It may be necessary to attach a guide wire to wiring harness to assist in installation.

1. Install wiring harness (16) through hole in cargo bed. Connect wiring harness to junction box (18) and heater control box plug (15). Install grommet (21) on wiring harness at hole in cargo body.

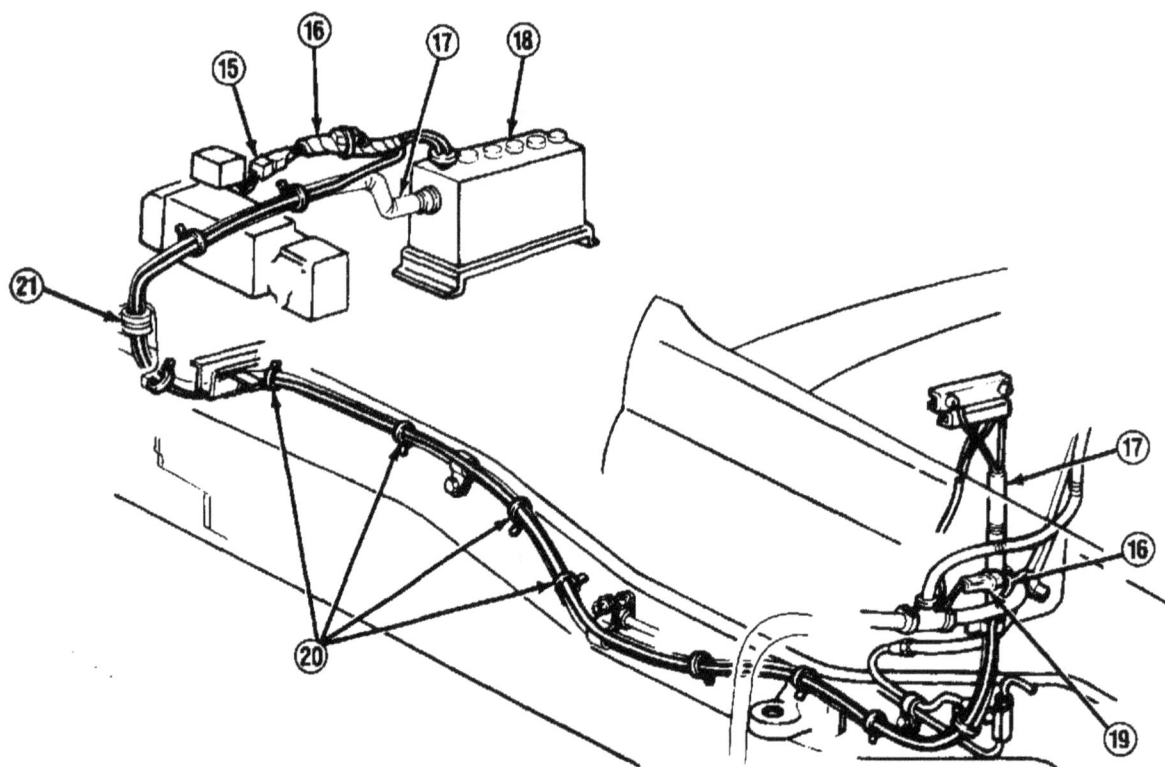

M1008A1

2. Install wiring harness (16) along radio feed cable (17) with 11 new straps (20).

3. Connect wiring harness (16) to cab heater wiring harness connector (19).

TA50112

11-23. CARGO COMPARTMENT HEATER WIRING HARNESS REPLACEMENT (M1008 AND M1008A1) (Con't).

4.　Install wiring harness (1) through hole in cargo bed. Connect wiring harness to heater control box plug (2). Install grommet (14) on wiring harness at hole in cargo bed.

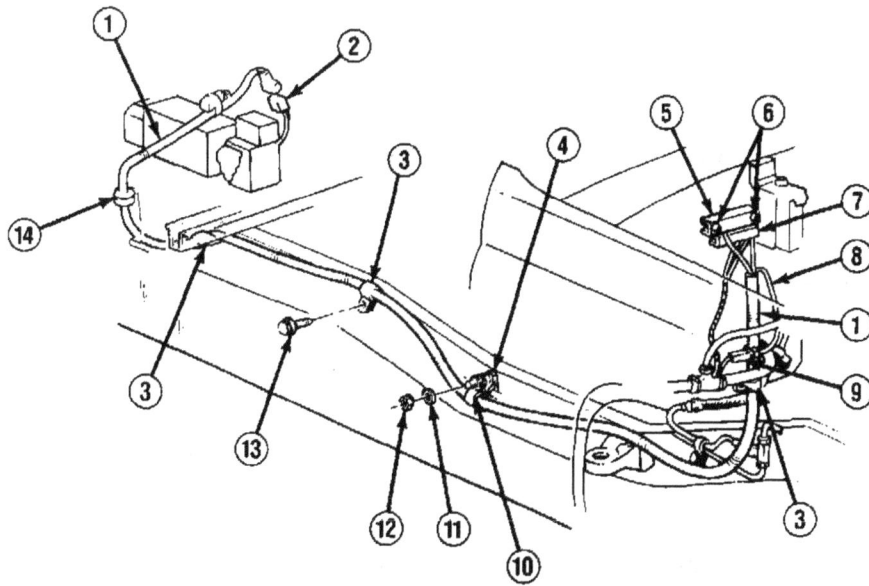

M1008

5.　Install clamp (10) on wiring harness (1). Install clamp on heater fuel line clamp (4) with new lockwasher (11) and nut (12). Install 3 clamps (3) on wiring harness. Install clamps on frame with 3 screws (13).

6.　Connect wiring harness lead (8) to cab heater wiring harness connector (9).

7.　Connect wiring harness (1) lead to positive accessory wiring terminal board stud and install new lockwasher and nut. Install positive accessory wiring terminal board cover (5) and tighten 2 nuts (6). Repeat for negative accessory wiring terminal board (7).

FOLLOW-ON TASKS:

* Install rear battery box. (See paragraph 11-6)
* Check operation of cargo compartment heater. (See TM 9-2320-289-10)

TA50113

11-24. CARGO COMPARTMENT HEATER EXHAUST PIPE AND VENTILATOR REPLACEMENT (M1008 AND M1008A1).

This task covers: a. Removal   b. Installation

INITIAL SETUP:

Materlals/Parts

- One cotter pin
- One exhaust pipe gasket
- One lockwasher
- One vent door gasket
- RTV sealant (Item 41, Appendix C)

Personnel Required

Ž MOS 63B (2)

General Safety Instructions

- Before attempting to service exhaust system, allow exhaust system to cool.

| a. | **REMOVAL** |

WARNING

Before attempting to service any part of exhaust system, allow exhaust system to cool. Failure to follow this warning will result in serious burns.

NOTE

- **If removing** exhaust components, perform steps 1-3.

- **If removing** strainer element, perform step 4.

- **If removing** ventilator, perform steps 4 and 5.

1. Remove bolt (4) and lockwasher (3) from side panel (2), and disconnect exhaust pipe (1). Discard lock-washer.

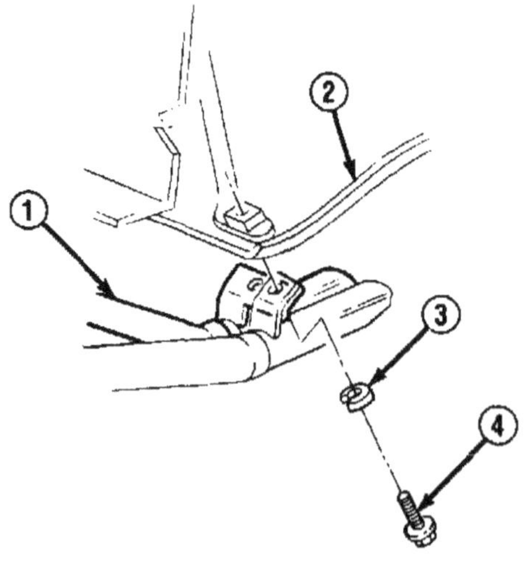

TA50114

11-24. CARGO COMPARTMENT HEATER EXHAUST PIPE AND VENTILATOR REPLACEMENT (M1008 AND M1008A1) (Con't).

2. Remove clamp (5) and disconnect exhaust pipe (1) from adapter (6).

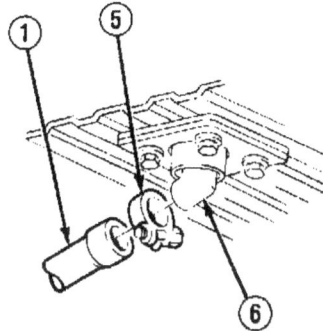

3. Remove 4 bolts (10), retainer (9), gasket (8) , and gasket (7) if damaged. Discard gasket (8).

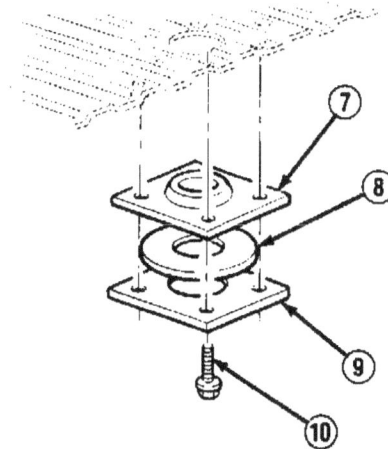

4. At upper right side of cargo compartment cover insulation, remove 4 screws (11), access door (12), strainer element (13), and gasket (14) from access cover (16). Clean strainer element. Discard strainer element if damaged. Discard gasket.

5. Remove 8 nuts (20), bolts (19), and ventilator (18) from enclosure (17). Remove 2 bolts (15) and access cover (16) from rear door assembly panel (21). Clean old sealant from all components.

| b. | INSTALLATION |

NOTE

- If installing   ventilator (18), perform steps 1 and 2.

- If installing   strainer element (13), perform step 2.

- If installing   exhaust components, perform steps 3-5.

1. Apply sealant to access cover (16) and install on rear door assembly panel (21) with 2 bolts (15). Apply sealant to ventilator (18) and install on enclosure (17) with 8 bolts (19) and nuts (20).

TA50115

11-24. CARGO COMPARTMENT HEATER EXHAUST PIPE AND VENTILATOR REPLACEMENT (MI 008 AND M1008A1) (Con't).

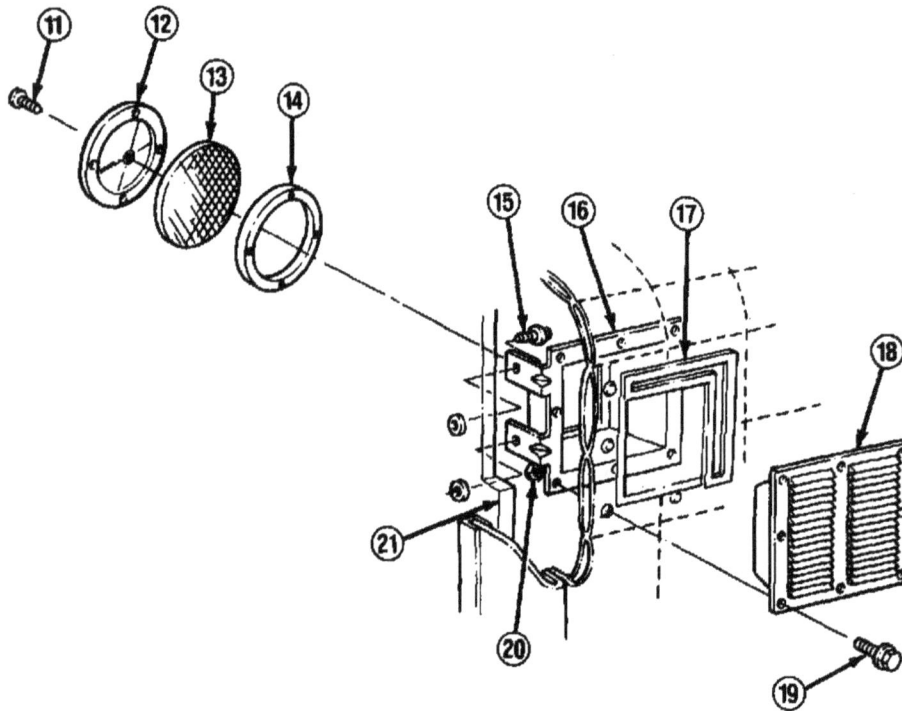

2.   Install new gasket (14), strainer element (13), and access door (12) on access cover (16) with 4 screws (11).

3.   Install gasket (7), new gasket (8), and retainer (9) with 4 bolts (10) if removed.

4.   Install clamp (5) on exhaust pipe (1). Connect exhaust pipe to adapter (6) and tighten clamp.

5.   Install exhaust pipe (1) on side panel (2) with new lockwasher (3) and bolt (4) .

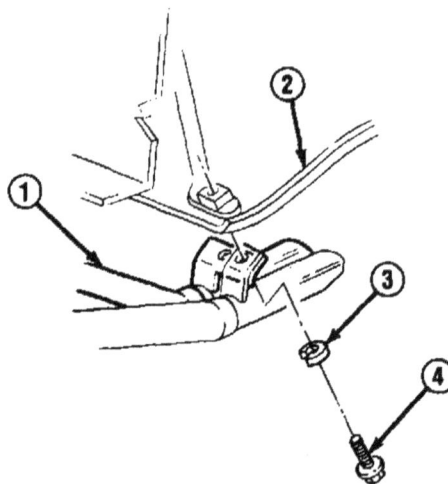

TA50116

11-25. CARGO COMPARTMENT HEATER AIR INLET REPLACEMENT (M1008 AND M1008A1).

| This task covers: | a. Removal | b. Installation |

INITIAL SETUP:

Materials/Parts
• RTV sealant (Item 41, Appendix C)

Personnel Required
• MOS 63B (2)

---

a.   REMOVAL

NOTE

• If removing air duct hose (3), perform steps 1 and 2.

• If removing ventilator   (8), perform step 3.

1.   Loosen clamp (5) and disconnect air duct hose (3) from ventilator (6). Unbuckle strap (4).

2.   Loosen clamp (2). Disconnect   air duct hose (3) from air inlet adapter assembly (1).

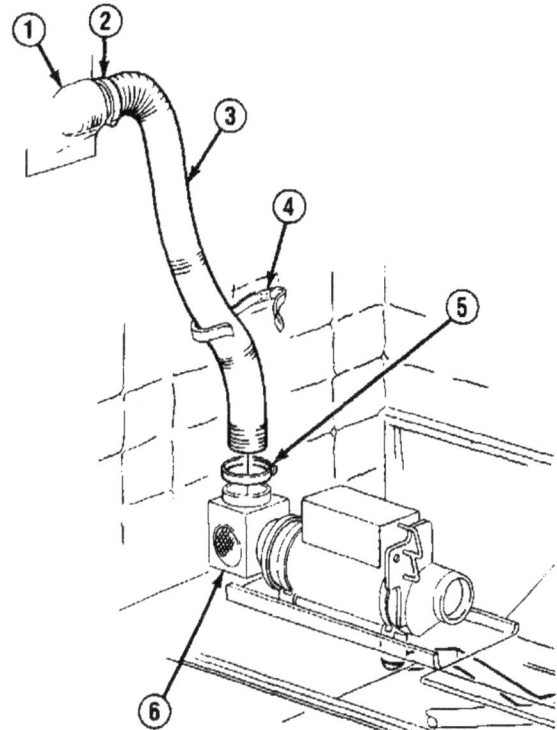

3.   Remove 4 nuts (7), bolts (9),   and ventilator (8) from air inlet adapter assembly (1). Clean old sealant from all components.

TA50117

11-25. CARGO COMPARTMENT HEATER AIR INLET REPLACEMENT (M1008 AND M1008A1) (Con't).

| b. | INSTALLATION |

NOTE

- **If installing ventilator (8), perform step 1.**

- **If installing air duct hose (3), perform steps 2 and 3.**

1. Apply sealant to ventilator (8) and install air inlet adapter (1) assembly with 4 bolts (9) and nuts (7).

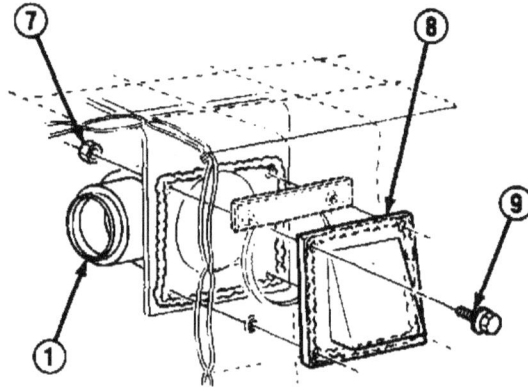

2. Connect air duct hose (3) to air inlet adapter assembly (1) and tighten clamp (2).

3. Connect air duct hose (3) to ventilator (6) and tighten clamp (5), Buckle strap (4) around air duct hose.

TA50118

Section V. CARGO COMPARTMENT ENCLOSURE KIT MAINTENANCE

11-26. CARGO COMPARTMENT ENCLOSURE KIT MAINTENANCE INDEX.

11-27. CARGO COVER INSULATOR REPLACEMENT (M1008 AND M1008A1).

This task covers:	a. Removal	b. Installation

INITIAL SETUP:

Material/Parts
- RTV sealant (Item 41, Appendix C)

Personnel Required
- MOS 63B (3)

a.	REMOVAL

1. Remove 4 screws (13) from each radio antenna bracket (14). Remove radio antenna bracket.

2. Remove 4 nuts (4), bolts (6), and air circulation ventilator (5). Clean off old sealant material.

3. Remove 8 nuts (1), bolts (3), and air circulation ventilator (2). Clean off old sealant material.

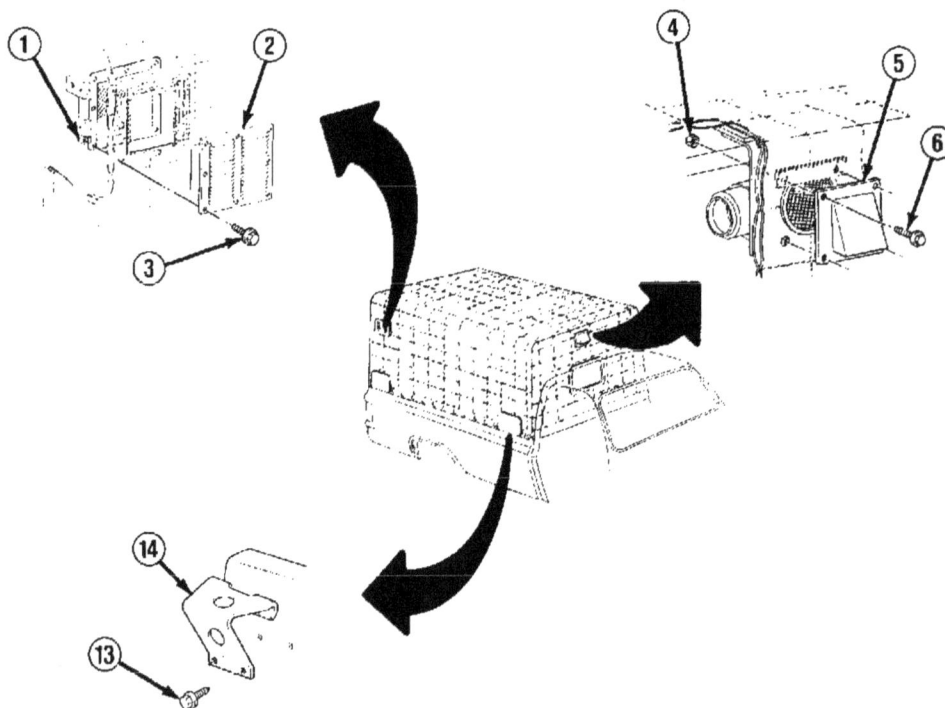

TA50119

11-27. CARGO COVER INSULATOR REPLACEMENT (M1008 AND M1008A1) (Con't).

4.   Remove 8 nuts (16), screws (18), and washers (17) holding cover insulator (15) to top and bottom of rear door opening panels.

5.   Remove 12 screws (20) securing cover insulator (15) to each side of rear door opening panels. Remove tube anchor nuts (19) only if damaged.

6.   Remove 32 screws (21) and washers (22) holding cover insulator (15) to each side of truck cargo box. Remove tube anchor nuts (23) only if damaged.

7.   Fold cover insulator (15) forward over front roof bow.

8.   On inside of cargo compartment, remove cover insulator (15) from turnbuttons on front rail assembly.

9.   On inside of cargo compartment, disconnect retaining strap at air inlet duct.

10.   Remove cover insulator (15) from truck.

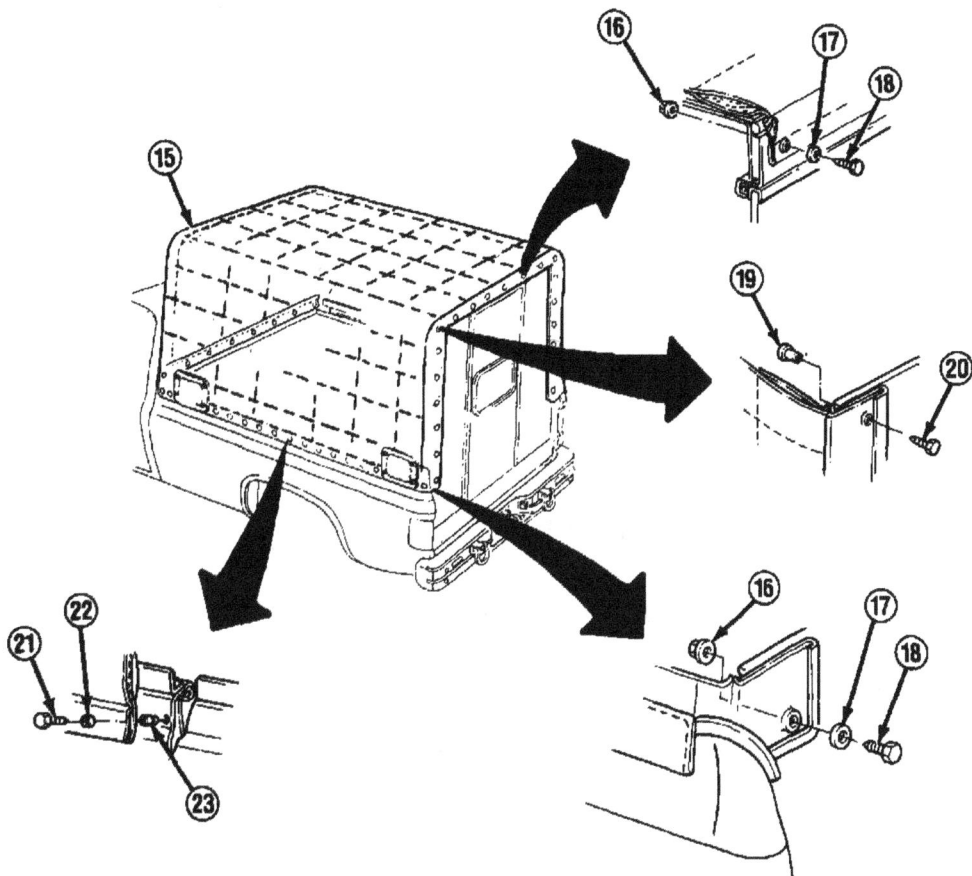

TA50120

11-27. CARGO COVER INSULATOR REPLACEMENT (M1008 AND M1008A1) (Con't).

11. Remove 18 screws (7) and nuts (12) from cargo cover insulator window assembly.

12. Remove retainer (8) and plastic window (9).

13. Remove gasket (10) and retainer (11) from opening.

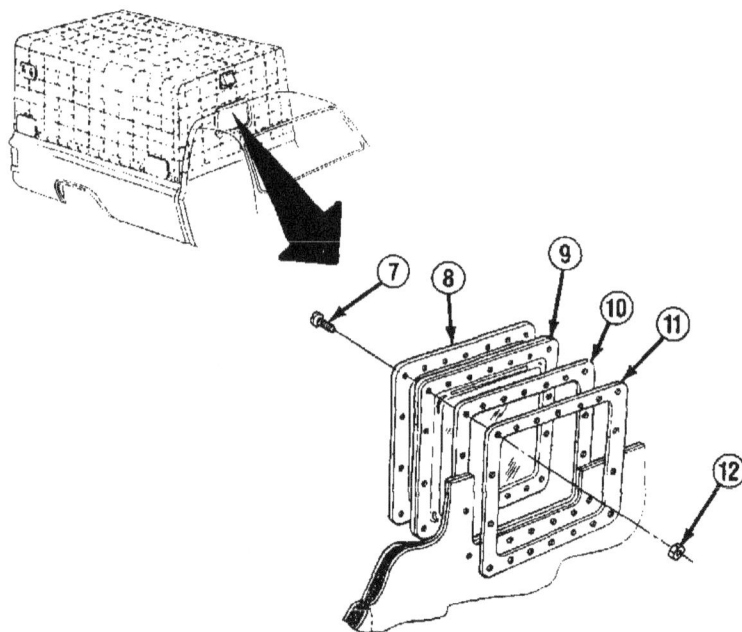

b.	INSTALLATION

1. Remove protective paper from plastic window (9).

2. Apply RTV sealant to mating surfaces. Install retainer (11) and gasket (10) to plastic window (9).

3. Install retainer (11), gasket (10), and plastic window (9) to opening in cargo cover insulator.

4. Apply RTV sealant to mating surfaces. Install retainer (8) and secure through all layers with 18 screws (7) and nuts (12).

5. Place folded cover insulator (15) over front roof bow.

6. If installing new cover insulator (15), remove window protective paper.

7. Spread cover insulator (15) over roof, alining front hole with air inlet adapter and right rear hole with air exhaust adapter.

8. On inside of cargo compartment, install cover insulator (15) to turnbuttons at front rail assembly.

TA50121

11-27. CARGO COVER INSULATOR REPLACEMENT (M1008 AND M1008A1) (Con't).

9. If removed, install tube anchor nuts (23). Aline grommets on both sides of cover insulator (15) with tube anchor nuts, Partially install 32 washers (22) and screws (21).

10. On inside of cargo compartment, install retaining strap around air inlet duct.

11. Aline grommets on back of cover insulator (15) with rear door opening panels.

12. Partially install 8 screws (18), washers (17), and nuts (16) at top and bottom of rear door opening panels.

13. If removed, install tube anchor nuts (19). Partially install 12 screws (20) down sides of rear door opening panels.

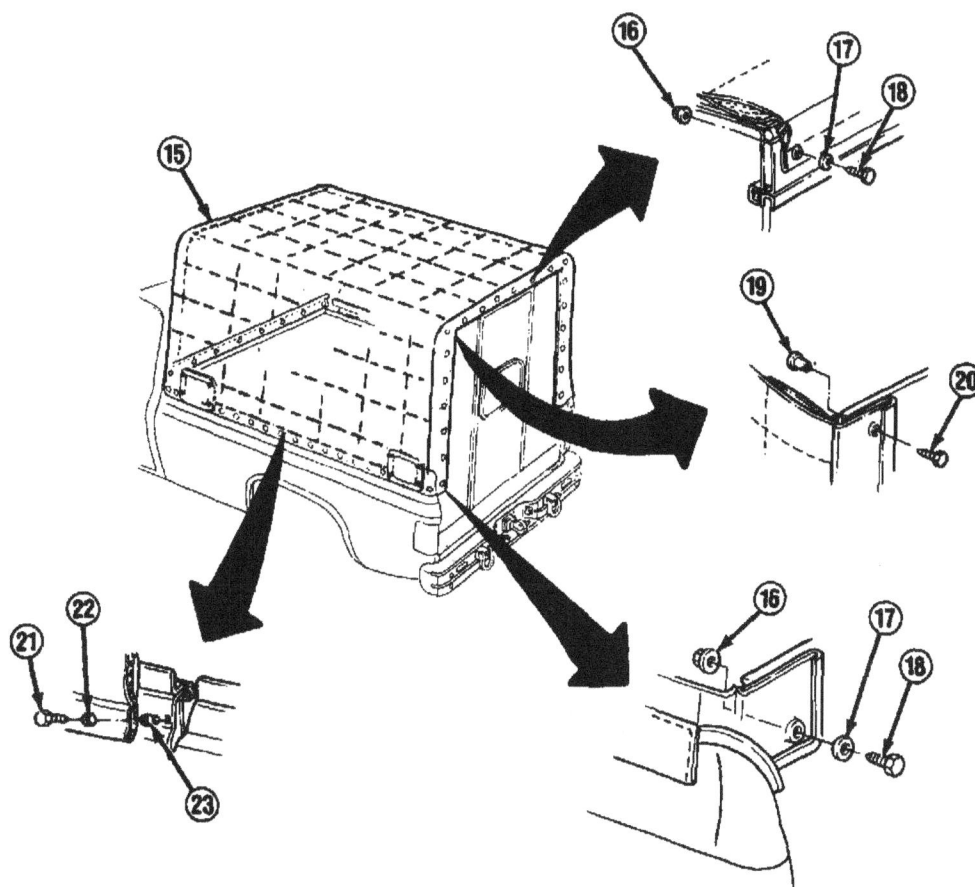

TA50122

11-27. CARGO COVER INSULATOR REPLACEMENT (M1008 AND M1008A1) (Con't).

14.   Apply RTV sealant to mating surfaces. Install air circulation ventilator (2) with 8 bolts (3) and nuts (1).

15.   Apply RTV sealant to mating surfaces. Install air circulation ventilator (5) with 4 bolts (6) and nuts (4).

CAUTION

DO NOT overtighten screws in tube anchor nuts or tube anchor nuts will break.

16.   Tighten all screws.

17.   Install each radio antenna bracket (14) with 4 screws (13).

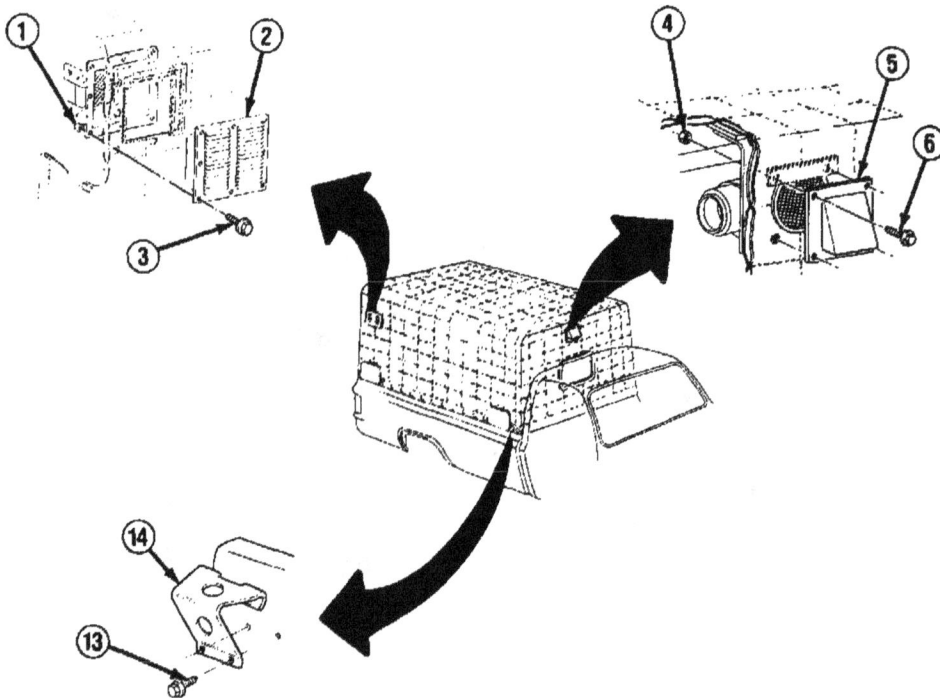

TA50123

11-28. FLOOR PANEL INSULATORS REPLACEMENT (M1008 AND M1008A1).

This task covers:	a. Removal	b. Installation

INITIAL SETUP:

Materials/Parts
- Seven locknuts

Personnel Required
- MOS 63B (2)

---

a.	**REMOVAL**

NOTE

- There will be no front insulator (18) or front outer insulator (5) If truck is equipped with communications rack.

- If removing   front insulator (18), perform step 1.

- If removing   front outer insulator (5), perform step 2.

- If removing   center insulator (16), perform steps 3-6.

- If removing   rear outer insulators (10), perform steps 3 and 7.

1.   Remove 3 locknuts   (17), 6 washers (2), 3 bolts (1), and front insulator (18) from truck.
Discard locknuts.

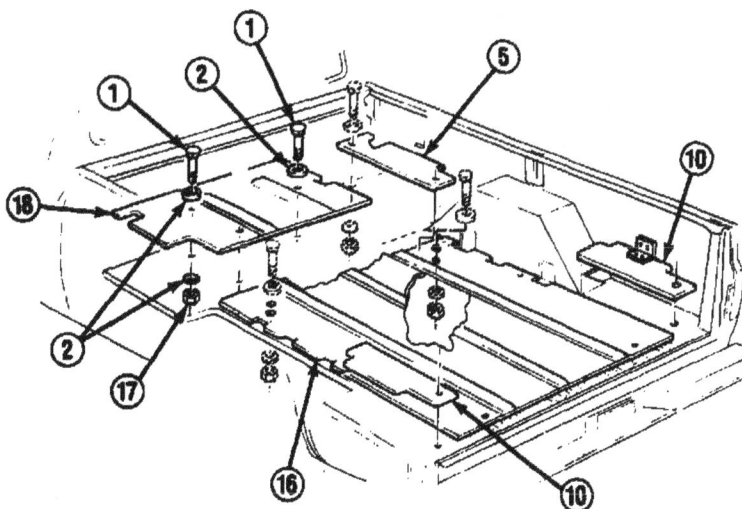

TA50124

11-28. FLOOR PANEL INSULATORS REPLACEMENT (M1008 AND M1008A1) (Con't).

2. Remove 2 locknuts (15), 4 washers (4), 2 bolts (3), and front outer insulator (5) from truck. Discard locknuts.

3. Remove rear door frame molding. (See paragraph 11-35)

4. Remove 2 locknuts (14), 4 washers (13), and 2 bolts (6) holding center insulator (16) to cargo box floor. Discard locknuts.

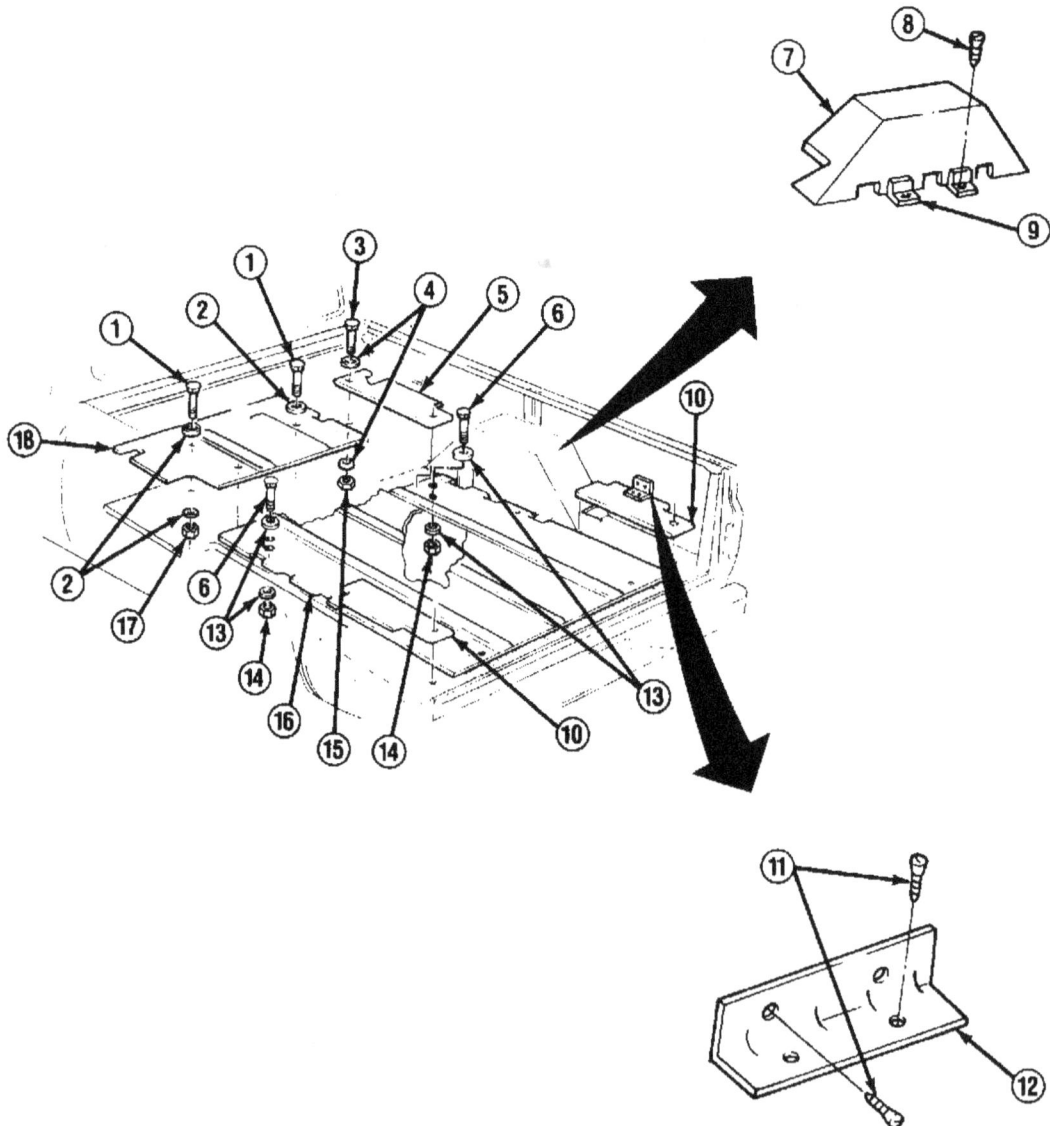

TA50125

11-28. FLOOR PANEL INSULATORS REPLACEMENT (M1008 AND M1008A1) (Con't).

5. Remove 16 screws (8) and 4 brackets (9) from 2 wheel house insulators (7).

6. Remove center insulator (16) from truck.

7. Remove 8 screws (11) and 2 brackets (12) holding 2 rear outer insulators (10) to rear side insulators. Remove rear outer insulators.

| b. | INSTALLATION |

NOTE

Ž If installing   rear outer insulators (10), perform steps 1, 2, and 5.

• If installing   center insulator (16), perform steps 3-5.

• If installing   front insulator (18), perform step 6.

• If installing   front outer insulator (5), perform step 7.

1. Place 2 rear outer insulators (10) in rear of cargo bed.

2. Install 2 brackets (12) to 2 rear outer insulators (10) and rear side insulators with 8 screws (11).

3. Place center insulator (16) in line with 2 mounting holes in floor and install 2 bolts (6), 4 washers (13), and 2 new locknuts (14).

4. Install 4 brackets (9) to 2 wheel house insulators (7) and center insulator (16) with 16 screws (8).

5. Install rear door frame molding. (See paragraph 11-35)

NOTE

There will be no front insulator (18) or front outer insulator (5) if truck is equipped with communications rack.

6. Install front insulator (18) with 3 bolts (1), 6 washers (2), and 3 new locknuts (17).

7. Install front outer insulator (5) with 2 bolts (3), 4 washers (4), and 2 new locknuts (15).

11-29. FRONT, SIDE, AND WHEEL HOUSE INSULATORS REPLACEMENT (M1008 AND M1008A1).

This task covers:	a. Remova l	b. Installation

INITIAL SETUP:

Equipment Condition
- Troop seat assembly removed. (See TM 9-2320-289-10)
- Communications rack removed (M1008A1 only). (See paragraph 4-48)

Materials/Parts
- One locknut (M1008)

---

a. REMOVAL

NOTE

- If removing wheel house insulator (21), perform steps 1-3.
- If removing front side insulators (12), perform steps 1, 4, and 6.
- If removing rear side insulators (13), perform steps 1, 2, 7, and 8.
- If removing front insulator (23), perform steps 5, 9, and 10.

1. Remove 4 screws (18) securing 2 brackets (10) to front side insulator (12).

2. Remove 4 screws (18) securing 2 brackets (20) to rear side insulator (13).

3. Remove 8 screws (18), 2 brackets (22), and wheel house insulator (21).

4. Remove cable attached to dummy receptacle connector (11) at right sidewall if present.

5. Remove 8 screws (18) securing 4 brackets (10) at front insulator (23).

6. Remove 4 screws (18) at 2 brackets (10) and remove front side insulator (12).

7. Remove 2 screws (14), bolts (16), bolts (17), and rear angle bracket (15).

8. Remove 4 screws (18), bracket (19), and rear side insulator (13).

9. Remove 2 bolts (7), washers (6), and wiring harness (5) from front insulator (23). Remove screw (8) and locknut (9) from ground wire (3) (M1008), or remove nut (2), ground strap (1), and ground wire (3) from stud (4) (M1008A1). Discard locknut.

10. Remove front insulator (23) from truck.

11-29. FRONT, SIDE, AND WHEEL HOUSE INSULATORS REPLACEMENT (M1008 AND M1008A1) (Con't).

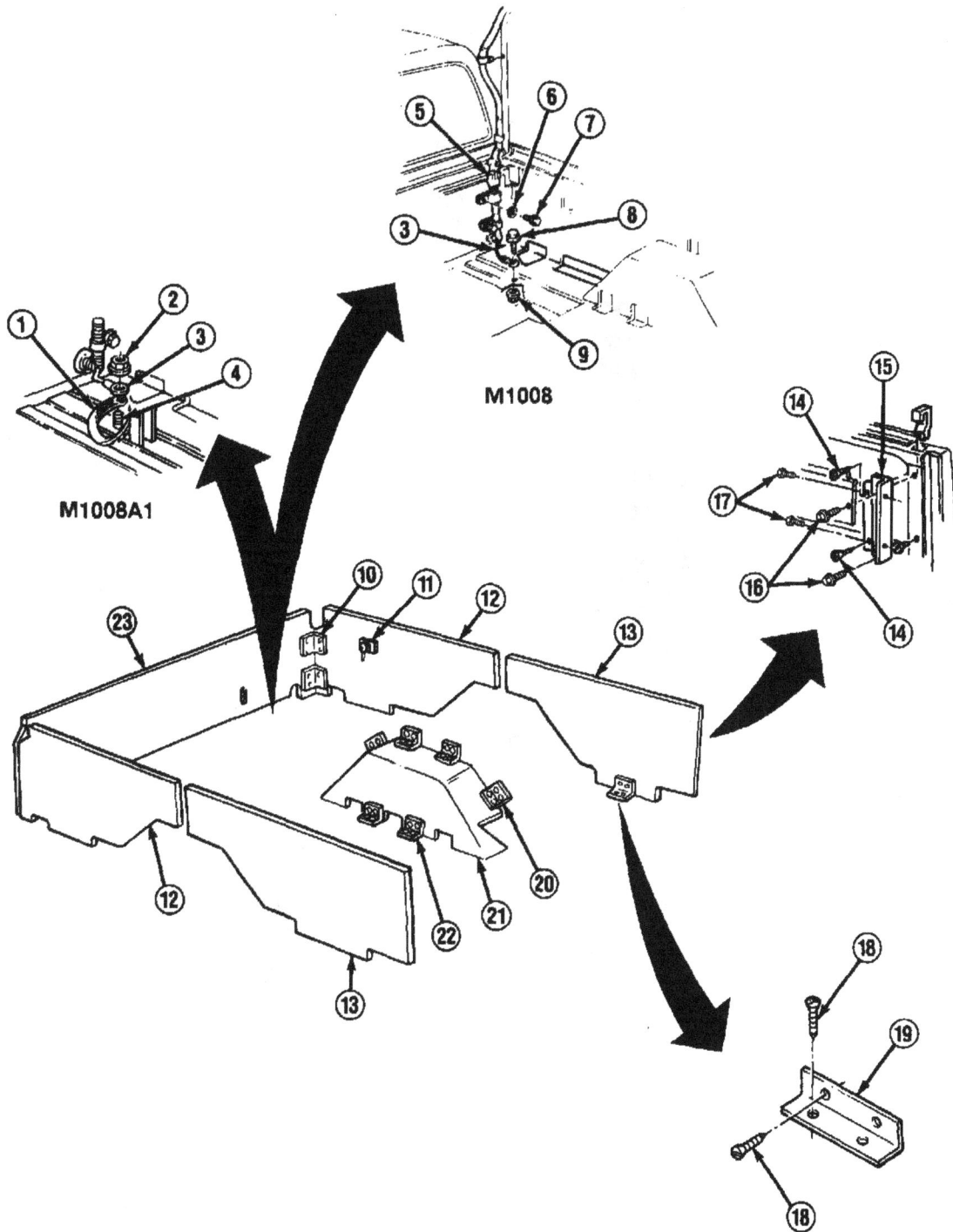

M1008

M1008A1

TA50126

11-29. FRONT, SIDE, AND WHEEL HOUSE INSULATORS REPLACEMENT (M1008 AND M1008A1) (Con't).

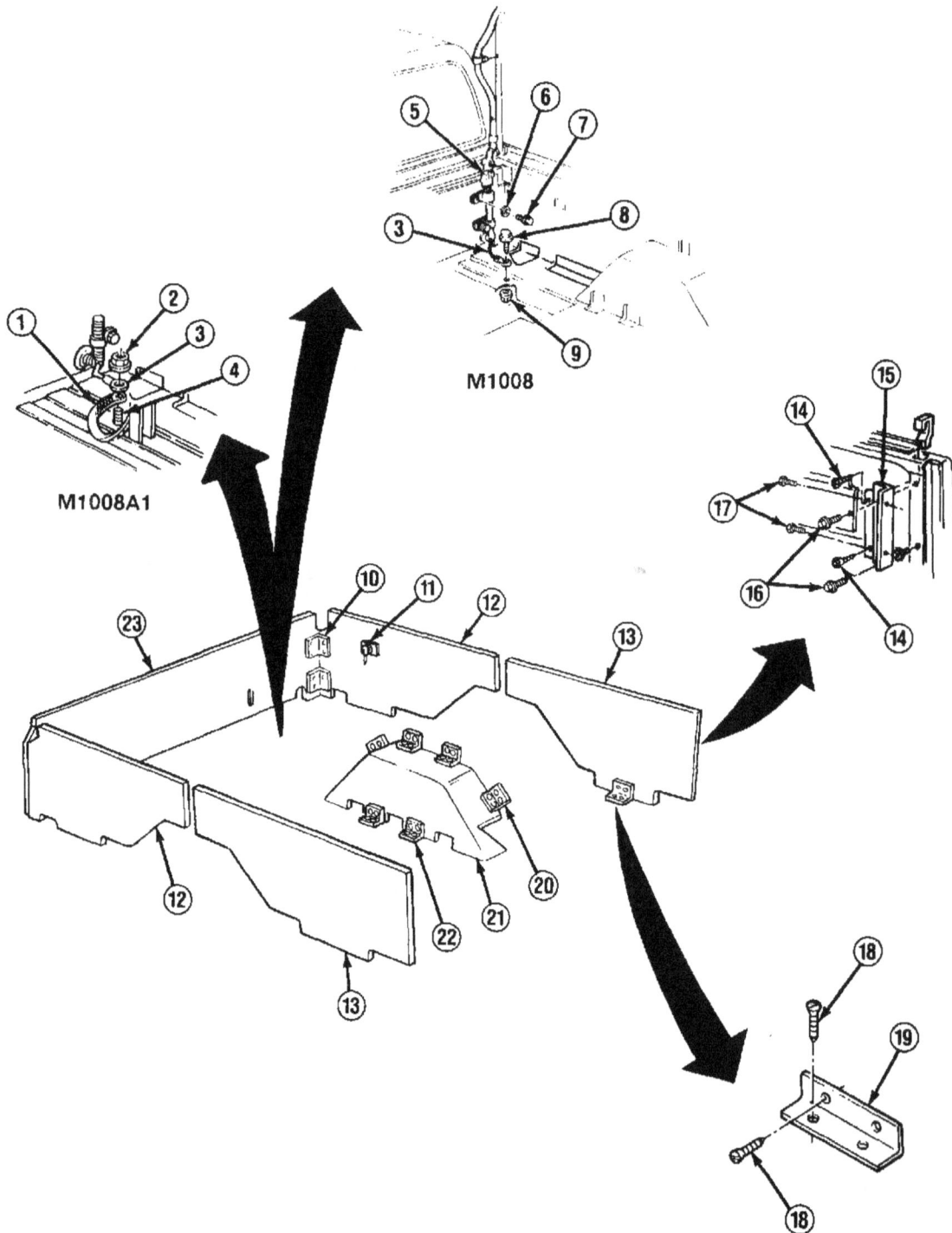

M1008

M1008A1

TA50127

11-29. FRONT, SIDE, AND WHEEL HOUSE INSULATORS REPLACEMENT (M1008 AND M1008A1) (Con't).

| b. | INSTALLATION |

NOTE

- If installing front insulator (23), perform steps 1, 2, and 5.

- If installing front side insulators (12), perform steps 3, 4, 6, and 11,

Ž If installing rear side insulators (13), perform steps 7-9, and 12,

- If Installing wheel house Insulators (21), perform steps 10-13.

1. Install front insulator (23) flush with front of cargo box.

2. Install ground wire (3) with screw (8) and new locknut (9) (M1008) or install ground wire (3) and ground strap (1) on stud (4) with nut (2) (M1008A1). Install wiring harness (5) to front insulator (23) with 2 bolts (7) and washers (6).

3. Install front side insulator (12) flush with side of cargo bed.

4. Install 2 brackets (10) to front side insulator (12) with 4 screws (18).

5. Install 8 screws (18) on 4 brackets (10) at front insulator (23),

6. Connect cable at dummy receptacle connector (11) if removed.

7. Install rear side insulator (13) flush with side of cargo bed.

8. Install bracket (19) to floor and to rear side insulator (13) with 4 screws (18).

9. Install rear angle bracket (15) with 2 screws (14) to rear side insulator (13), 2 bolts (16) into rear endgate post, and 2 bolts (17) into rear door side panel.

10. Install wheel house insulator (21) over wheel house flush with side and floor panels.

11. Install 2 brackets (20) to front side insulator 12) with 4 screws (18).

12. Install 2 brackets (20) to rear side insulator (13) with 4 screws (18).

13. Install 2 brackets (22) to floor with 8 screws (18).

FOLLOW-ON TASKS:

- Install troop seat assembly. (See TM 9-2320-289-10)
- Install communications rack if removed. (See paragraph 4-48)

11-30. ROOF COVER AND ENDGATE CURTAIN REPLACEMENT (M1009).

This task covers: a. Remova l   b. Installation

INITIAL SETUP:

Materials/Parts   *Personnel Required*

* Sealing compound, corrosion-resistant   * MOS 63B (2)
   (Item 42, Appendix C)

| a. | REMOVAL |

NOTE

* **If removing roof cover (6), perform steps 1-8.**

* **If removing endgate curtain (9), perform steps 2, 9, and 10.**

1.   Remove 4 screws (14) and radio antenna bracket (13) if present.

2.   Remove window flap (7) from 4 turnbuttons (8).

3.   Remove roof cover (6) from 4 turnbuttons (12).

4.   Remove 6 screws (15) and washers (16) on each side of truck.

5.   Pull roof cover (6) forward over cab of truck and place upside down.

6.   Remove 14 screws (2), washers (1), 2 side retainers (5), and 2 top retainers (3). Set screws aside for later use.

7.   Remove roof cover (6) from truck.

8.   Clean off corrosion-resistant sealing compound from cab roof.

9.   Remove endgate curtain (9) from 14 turnbuttons (10) and remove endgate curtain.

10.   Open endgate and inspect each side lip of endgate for tightness of 8 locknuts (11).

| b. | INSTALLATION |

NOTE

* **If installing endgate curtain (9), perform steps 1 and 2.**

* **If installing roof cover (6), perform steps 4-11.**

1.   Replace all broken turnbuttons (8 and 10) and tighten 8 locknuts (11).

2.   Replace any loose or damaged expansion shields (4) by applying corrosion-resistant sealing compound to holes and installing new expansion shields.

3.   Close endgate and install endgate curtain (9) to 14 turnbuttons (10).

11-30. ROOF COVER AND ENDGATE CURTAIN REPLACEMENT (M1009) (Con't).

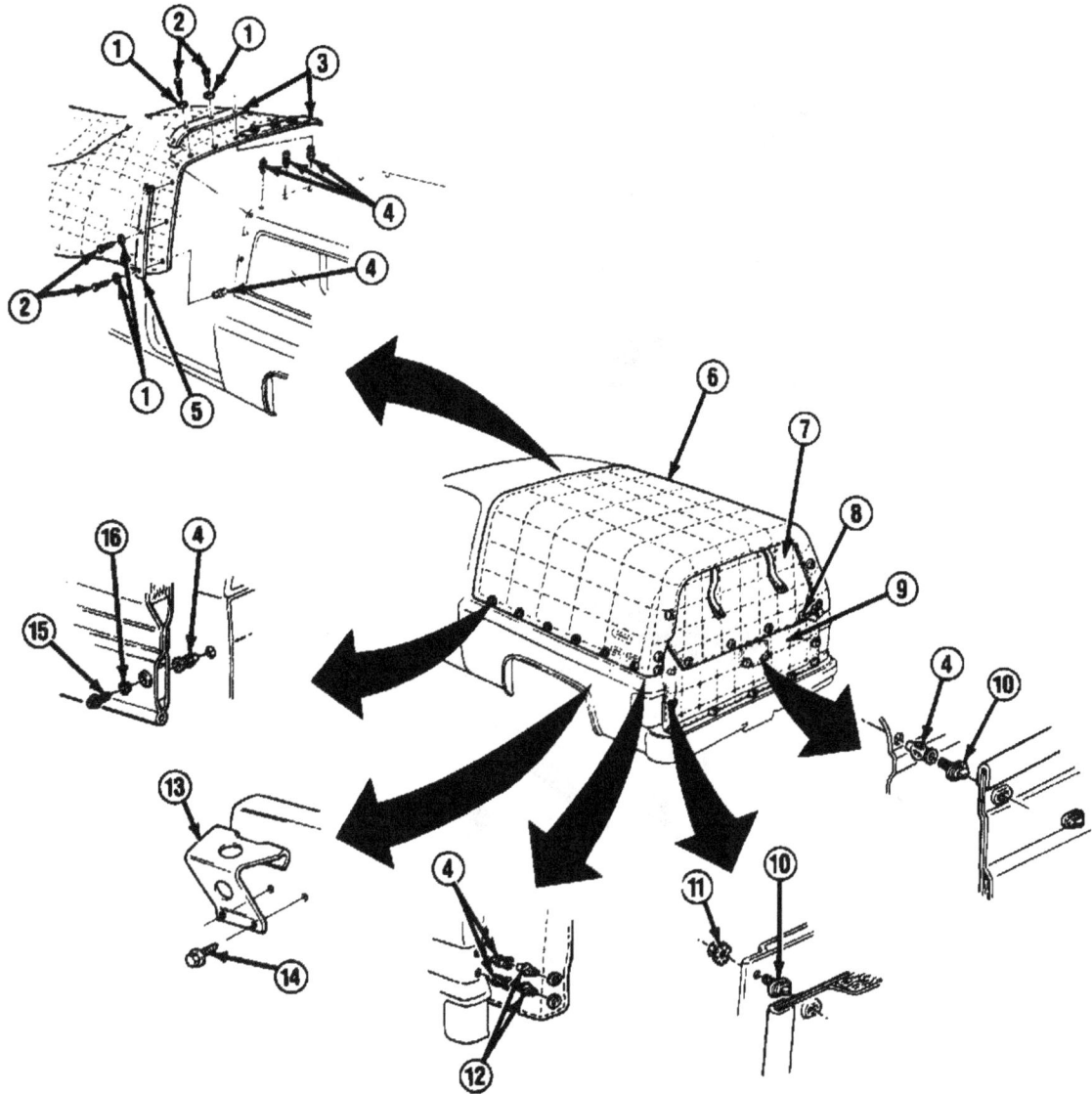

TA50128

11-30. ROOF COVER AND ENDGATE CURTAIN REPLACEMENT (M1009) (Con't).

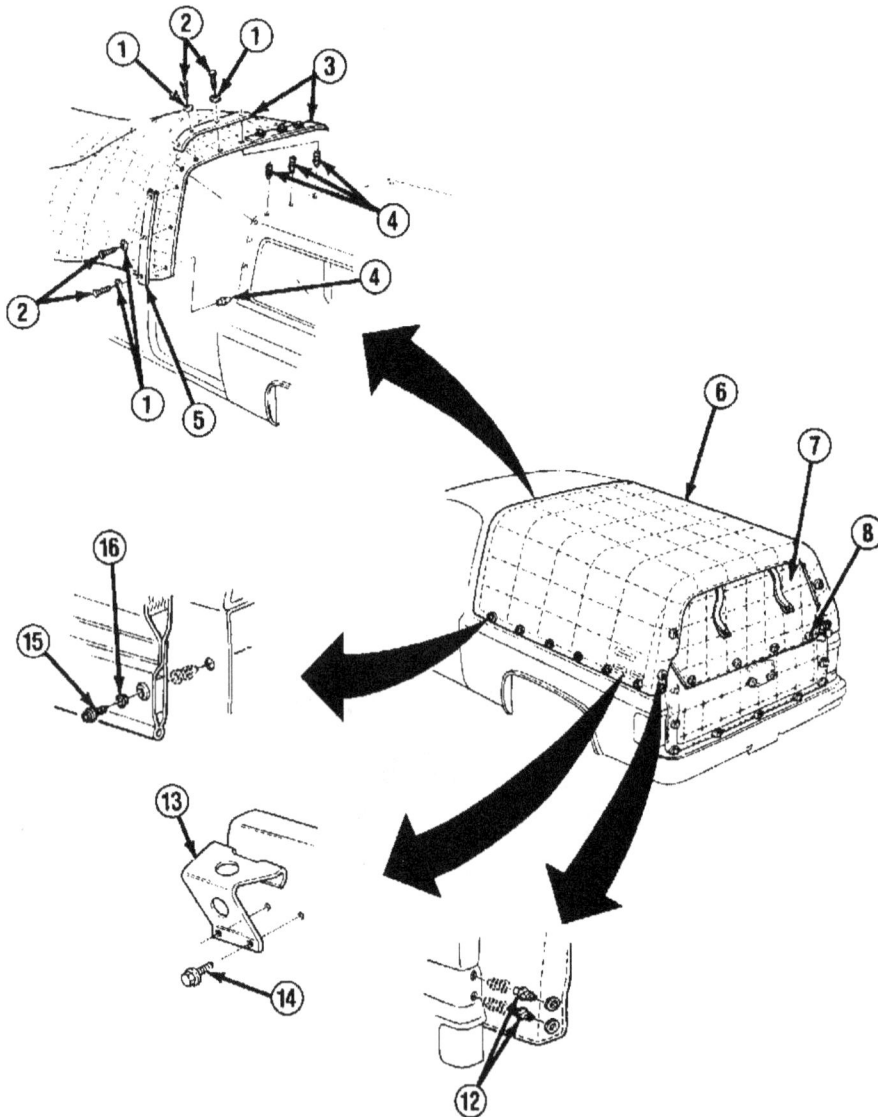

TA50129

11-30. ROOF COVER AND ENDGATE CURTAIN REPLACEMENT (M1009) (Con't).

4. Place roof cover (6), with lettering facing up, over cab and hood, with front fold over edge of removable cargo cover and centered right-to-left. Line up grommets in roof cover (6) with existing expansion shield (4) holes.

CAUTION

DO NOT overtighten   screws (2) in expansion shields (4) or expansion shields will break.

5. Install 2 top retainers (3) and 2 side retainers (5) with 14 washers (1) and screws (2).

6. Spread roof cover (6) over rear of truck and smooth it out.

7. Install bottom edges of roof cover (6) with 12 washers (16) and screws (15).

8. Install roof cover (6) to rear sides of truck with 4 turnbuttons (12).

9. Install window flap (7) to 4 turnbuttons (8).

10. Seal front edge of roof cover (6) with corrosion-resistant sealing compound. Seal top only. Stop at left and right side drip rails.

11. Install radio antenna bracket (13) through holes in roof cover (6) with 4 screws (14) if removed.

11-31. SIDE, WHEEL HOUSE, AND FLOOR INSULATORS REPLACEMENT (M1009).

This task covers:	a. Remova l	b. Installation

INITIAL SETUP:

Equipment *Condition*
- Rear seat removed. (See paragraph 10-23)

Materials/Parts
- Ten locknuts
- RTV sealant (Item 41, Appendix C)

Personnel Required
- *MOS 63B (2)*

---

a. REMOVAL

NOTE

- **Spare tire and spare tire carrier must be removed to perform this task.**

- **If removing wheel house insulators (1), perform step 1.**

- **If removing molding (13) and rear floor insulators (12), perform steps 2 and 3.**

- **If removing side insulators (6), perform steps 1 and   4.**

- **If removing front and floor insulators (17 and 22), perform steps 2 and 6 through 8.**

1. Remove 40 screws (2) and 10 brackets (3) from 2 wheel house insulators (1)   and remove wheel house insulators from wheel housings.

2. Remove 6 screws (14) and molding (13).

3. Remove 8 screws (4), 2 brackets (5), and 2 rear floor insulators (12).

4. Remove 6 bolts (8), 12 washers (7), and 6 locknuts (11) at 6 brackets (10).   Remove 2 side insulators (6). Discard locknuts.

5. Remove 12 screws (9) at 6 brackets (10) and remove brackets if damaged.

NOTE

If wheel house insulators (1) have not been removed, perform step 6.

6. Remove 16 screws (2) and 4 brackets (3) securing 2 wheel house insulators (1) to floor insulator (22).

7. Remove 4 locknuts (16), 8 washers (15), and 4 bolts (23). Remove 4 screws (18) at front edge of floor insulator (22) and remove floor insulator. Discard locknuts.

8. Remove 2 nuts (19), washers (20), bolts (21), and front insulator (17).

11-31. SIDE, WHEEL HOUSE, AND FLOOR INSULATORS REPLACEMENT (M1009) (Con't).

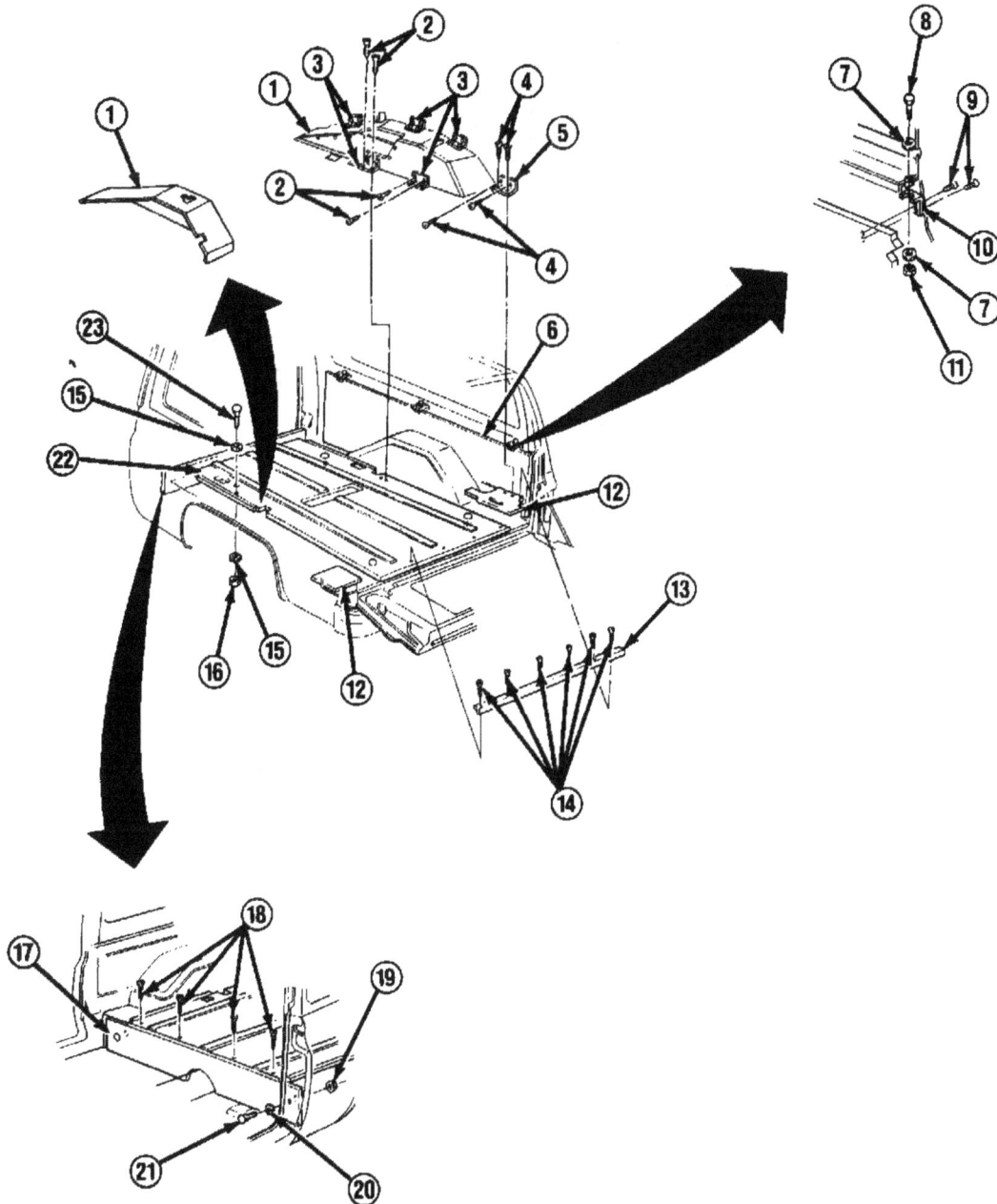

TA50130

11-31. SIDE, WHEEL HOUSE, AND FLOOR INSULATORS REPLACEMENT (M1009) (Con't).

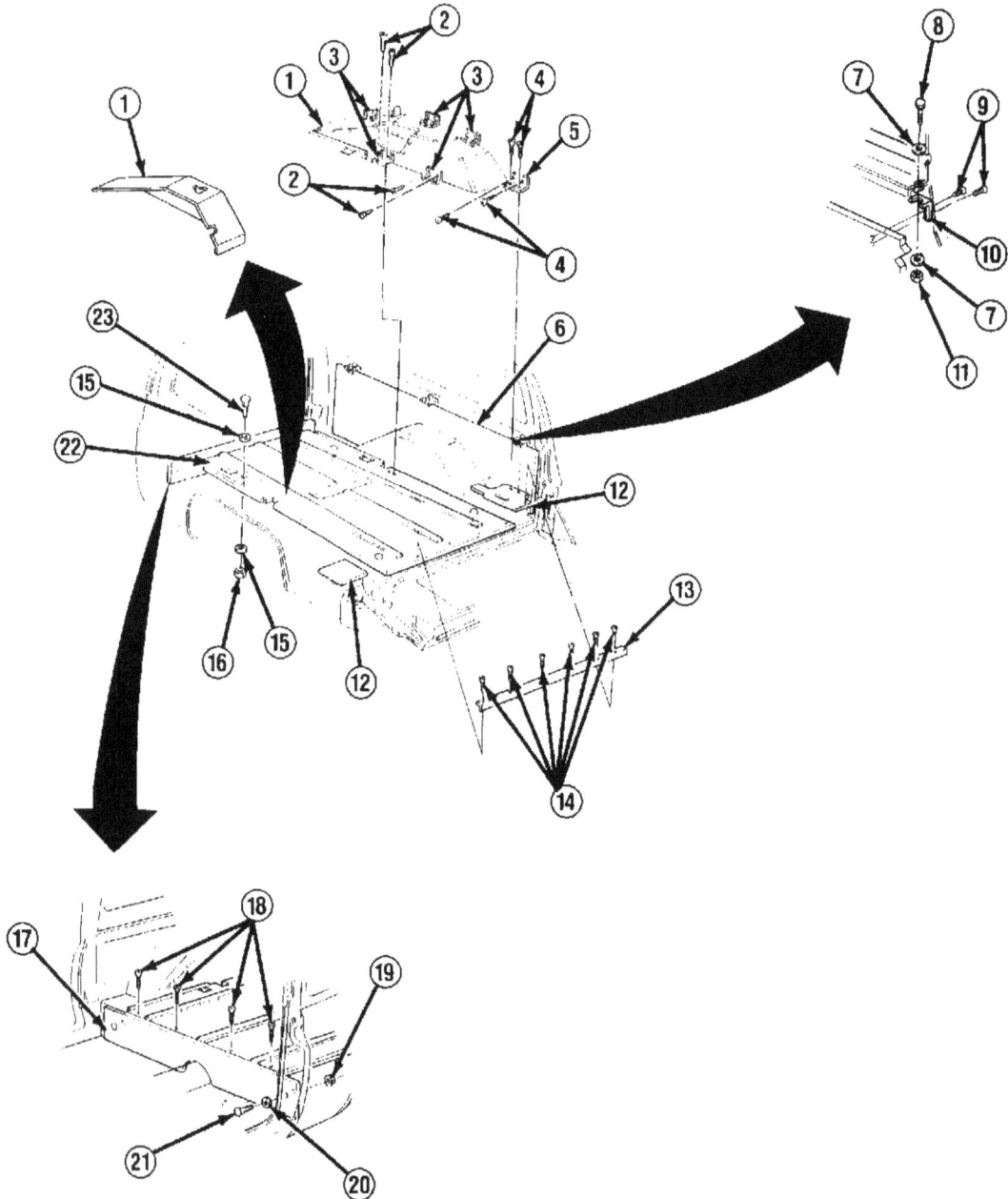

TA50131

11-31. SIDE, WHEEL HOUSE, AND FLOOR INSULATORS REPLACEMENT (M1009) (Con't).

| b. | INSTALLATION |

NOTE

- If installing   front and floor insulators (17 and 22), perform steps 1-4, and 9.

- If installing   side and rear floor insulators (6 and 12) and molding (13),   .   .
  perform steps 5-9.

- If installing wheel house Insulators (1), perform steps 10 and 11.

1. Apply RTV sealant to 2 bolts (21), Install f rent insulator (17) with bolts, washers (20), and nuts (19).

NOTE

Open and close endgate before securing floor insulator (22) to check clearance at endgate.

2. Place floor insulator (22) in cargo compartment, alining holes in floor insulator with holes in floor of truck.

3. Apply RTV sealant to 4 bolts (23), Install 4 bolts, 8 washers (15), and 4 new locknuts (16).

4. Install 4 screws (18) at front edge of floor insulator (22).

5. Install 6 brackets (10) to 2 side insulators (6) with 12 screws (9) if removed.

6. Install 2 side insulators (6) with 6 bolts (8), 12 washers (7), and 6 new locknuts (11).

7. Install 2 brackets (5) to 2 rear floor insulators (12) with 4 screws (4).

8. Install 2 brackets (5) to 2 side insulators (6) with 4 screws (4).

9. Install molding (13) with 6 screws (14).

10. Position 2 wheel house insulators (1) over wheel housings.

11. Install 10 brackets (3) with 40 screws (2).

12. Install spare tire carrier and spare tire.

FOLLOW-ON TASKS:

- Install rear seat. (See paragraph 10-23)

11-32. ROOF PANELS AND SUPPORTS REPLACEMENT (M1008 AND M1008A1).

This task covers: a. Removal b. Installation

INITIAL SETUP:

Equipment Condition

- Both battery negative cables disconnected. (See paragraph 4-38)
- Cargo cover insulator removed (if removing roof panels). (See paragraph 11 -27)

Personnel Required

- MOS 63B (2)

Materials/Parts

- Two locknuts

| a. | REMOVAL |

NOTE

- **If removing supports (12 and 15), perform steps 1-5.**

- **If removing roof panels (8), perform steps 1-9.**

- **If removing roof bow support, perform steps 10-13.**

- **Perform step 11 only if replacing right roof bow support.**

1. Disconnect domelight wiring harness connector (16) at ceiling.

2. Remove domelight wiring harness clips (14) from front support (15).

3. Remove 4 nuts (17) and roof support bracket (18) with attached domelight.

4. Remove 2 nuts (7) and disengage slot in front support (15) from air inlet adapter assembly (6). Remove front support and air inlet assembly.

5. Disengage rear support (12) from panel assembly (10) and remove rear support.

6. Remove 6 nuts (11) at panel assembly (10).

7. At front of roof bow (1), remove 2 nuts (5), retaining straps (4), and bolts (2).

8. Remove roof support bracket (3), 2 roof support brackets (13), and 3 roof support brackets (9) .

9. Remove 2 roof panels (8).

11-32. ROOF PANELS AND SUPPORTS REPLACEMENT (M1008 AND M1008A1) (Con't).

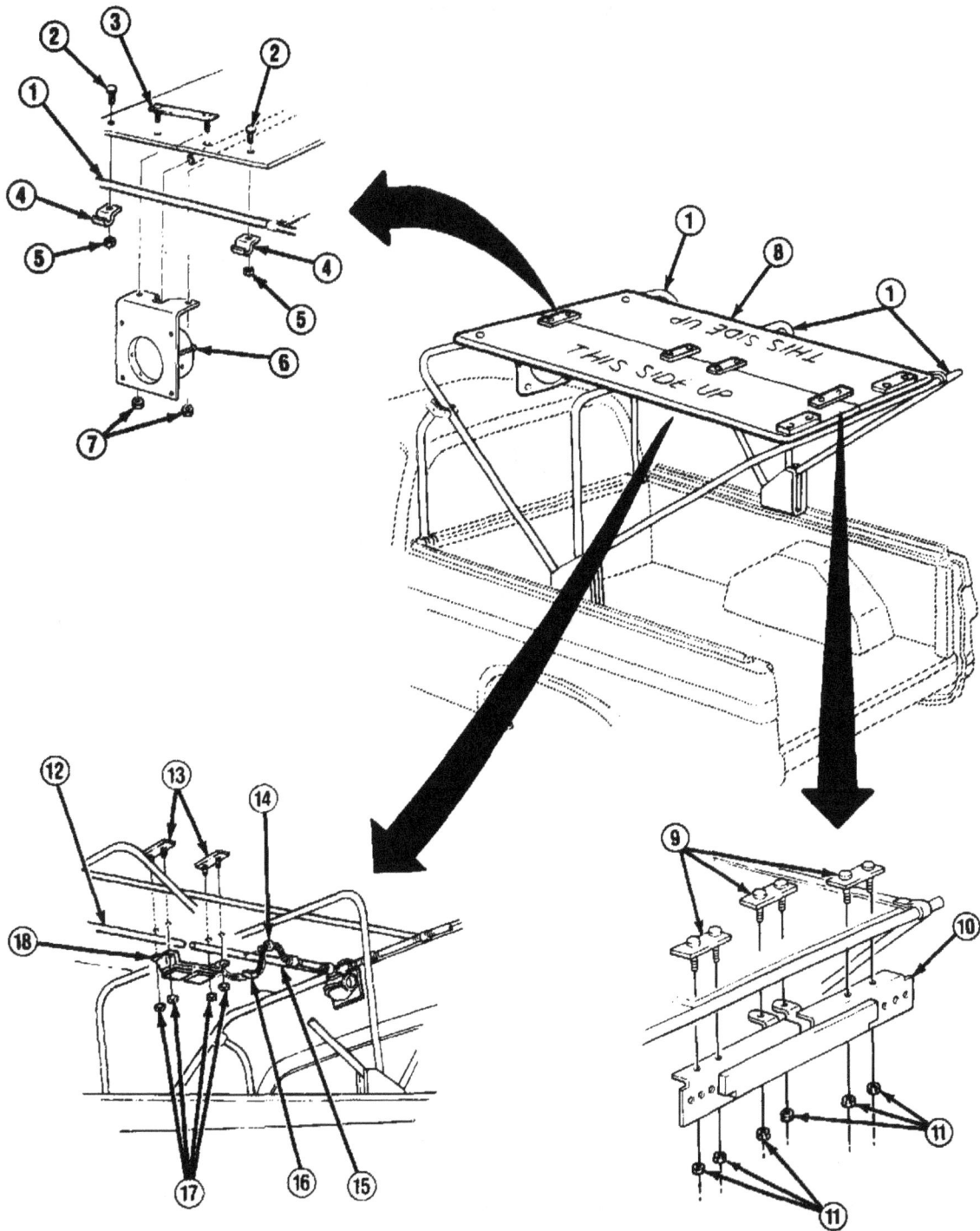

TA50132

11-32. ROOF PANELS AND SUPPORTS REPLACEMENT (M1008 AND M1008A1) (Con't).

10. Remove wiring harness (24) and clips (23) from right roof bow support (22).

11. Remove pin (26) from roof bow support (22) and remove roof bow support from front rail assembly (25).

12. Remove screw (27), locknut (29), pin (26), and clamp (28). Discard locknut.

13. Remove 2 screws (19), nuts (21), bracket (20), and roof bow support (22) from roof bow (1).

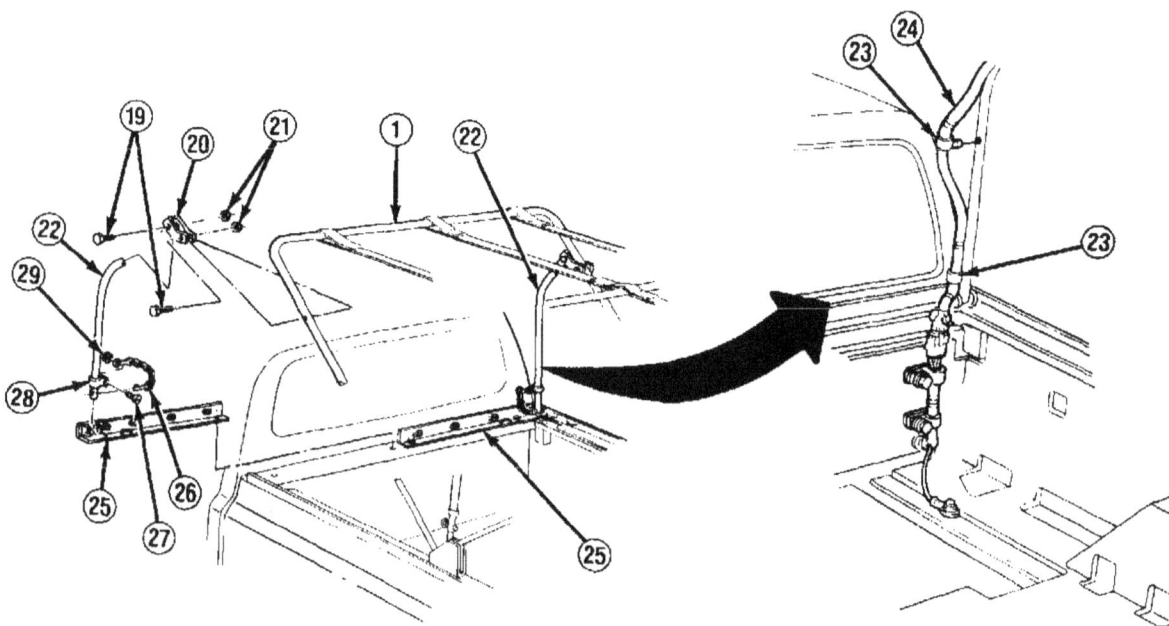

b.	INSTALLATION

NOTE

- **If installing roof bow supports (22), perform steps 1-4.**

- **If installing roof panels (8), perform steps 5-14.**

Ž **If installing supports, perform steps 10-14.**

1. Install clamp (28) to roof bow support (22). Install pin (26) to clamp with screw (27) and new locknut (29).

TA50133

11-32. ROOF PANELS AND SUPPORTS REPLACEMENT (M1008 AND M1008A1) (Con't).

2. Install bracket (20) to roof bow support (22) and to roof bow (1) with 2 screws (19) and nuts (21).

3. Install roof bow support (22) to front rail assembly (25) and secure with pin (26).

4. At right roof bow support (22) install wiring harness (24) and clips (23).

NOTE

When installing roof panels (8), place the words "THIS SIDE UP" (if present) to the outside.

5. Place 2 roof panels (8) on top of 3 roof bows (1) and center panels.

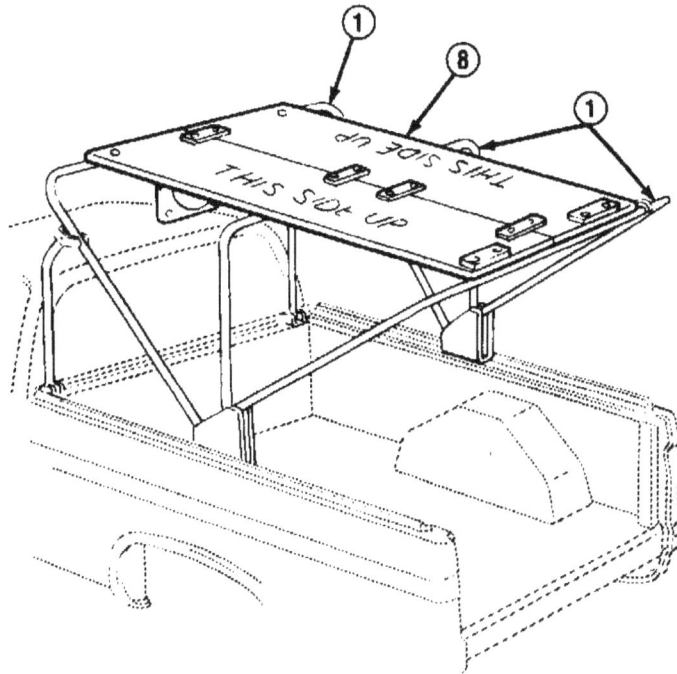

TA50134

11-32. ROOF PANELS AND SUPPORTS REPLACEMENT (M1008 AND M1008A1) (Con't).

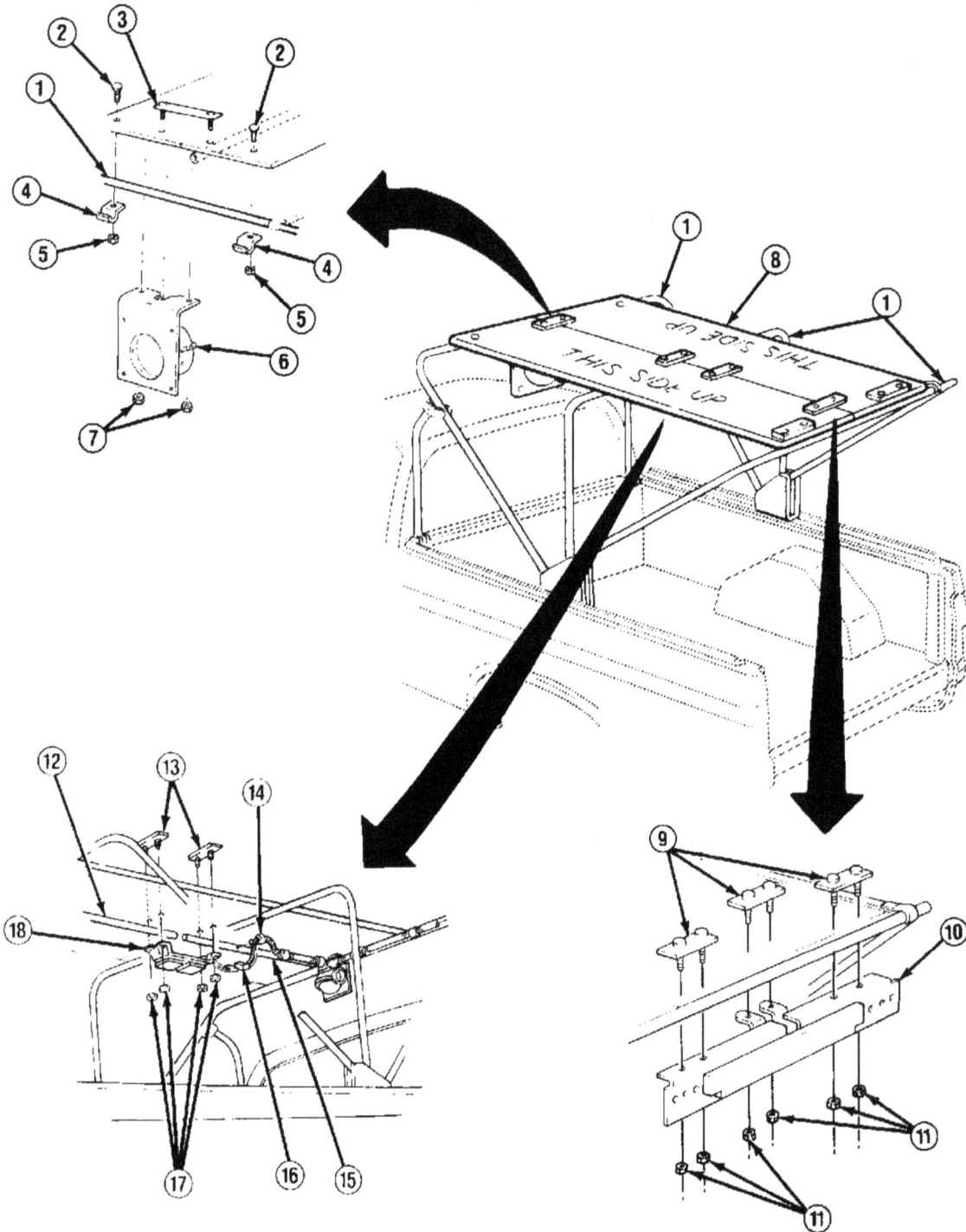

TA50135

11-32. ROOF PANELS AND SUPPORTS REPLACEMENT (M1008 AND M1008A1) (Con't).

6. Install 3 roof support brackets (9) to panel assembly (10) with 6 nuts (11).

7. Place roof support bracket (3) through 2 roof panels (8) and air inlet adapter assembly (6). Loosely install 2 nuts (7) but DO NOT tighten.

8. Place 2 roof support brackets (13) through 2 roof panels (8). DO NOT install 4 nuts (17).

9. At front edge of 2 roof panels (8), install 2 bolts (12), retaining straps (4), and nuts (5).

10. Install slotted end of rear support (2) into   panel assembly (10). Raise forward end of rear support to center bow support (1).

11. Install slotted end of front support (15) to air   inlet adapter assembly (6). Raise rear end of front support to center bow support (1).

12. Install roof support bracket (18) with attached domelight with 4 nuts (17).

13. Tighten 2 nuts (7) at air inlet adapter assembly (6).

14. Install domelight wiring harness clips (14) to front support (15) and connect domelight wiring harness connector (16) at ceiling.

FOLLOW-ON TASKS:

- Install cargo cover insulator. (See paragraph 11-27)
- Connect both battery negative cables. (See paragraph 4-38)

11-33. DOMELIGHT AND WIRING HARNESS REPLACEMENT (M1008 AND M1008A1).

This task covers:	a. Remova l	b. Installation

INITIAL SETUP:

Equipment Condition
* Both battery negative cables disconnected.
  (See paragraph 4-38)

Materials/Parts
* One locknut (M1008)

---

a.	**REMOVAL**

NOTE

* **If removing domelight, perform steps 1-5.**

* **If removing 2 bulbs (25), 2 lenses (26   and 29), or cover plate (28), perform steps 4 and 5.**

* **If removing wiring harness (12) and   electrical lead (3), perform steps 6-14.**

1. Disconnect electrical lead (3) from connector (22) at ceiling.

2. Remove 4 nuts (23) and   roof support bracket (30) from front and rear roof supports (1).

3. Remove 4 screws   (2) and roof support bracket   (30) from base assembly (24).

4. Remove 6 screws   (27) and cover plate   (28).

5. Remove blue   lens (29) and clear lens (26) from   cover plate (28) and 2 bulbs (25) from base assembly (24).

NOTE

Tag wires for installation.

6. Disconnect purple wire (18) from "DOME" and orange wire (16) from "T-LPS" positions on fuse box (17) under dash.

7. Remove grommet (15) at bulkhead and carefully pull wiring harness (12) through bulkhead. Discard grommet if damaged.

8. Remove 5 screws (14), clamps (13), and wiring harness (12) from under hood and along frame.

9. Disconnect wiring harness (12) from electrical lead (3) at connector at front of cargo box.

10. Remove 2 screws (6), washers (5), and clamps (20), and remove wiring harness (12) from front of cargo box.

11. Remove screw (7)   and locknut (8) from ground wire (10) (M1008), or nut (9) from stud (11), and remove ground wire (10) and communications rack ground strap (M1008A1). Discard locknut.

11-33. DOMELIGHT AND WIRING HARNESS REPLACEMENT (M1008 AND M1008A1) (Con't).

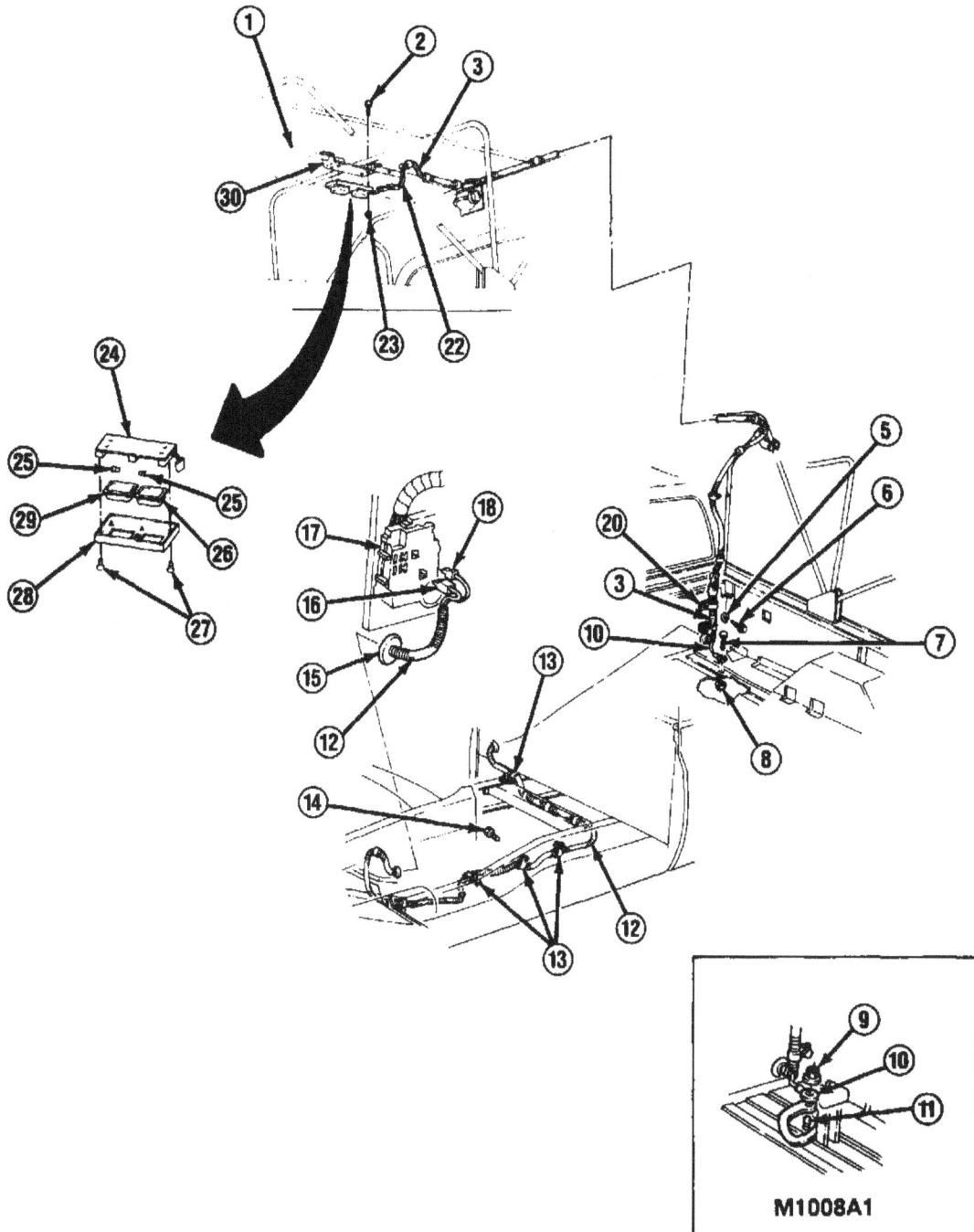

M1008A1

TA50136

11-33. DOMELIGHT AND WIRING HARNESS REPLACEMENT (M1008 AND M1008A1) (Con't).

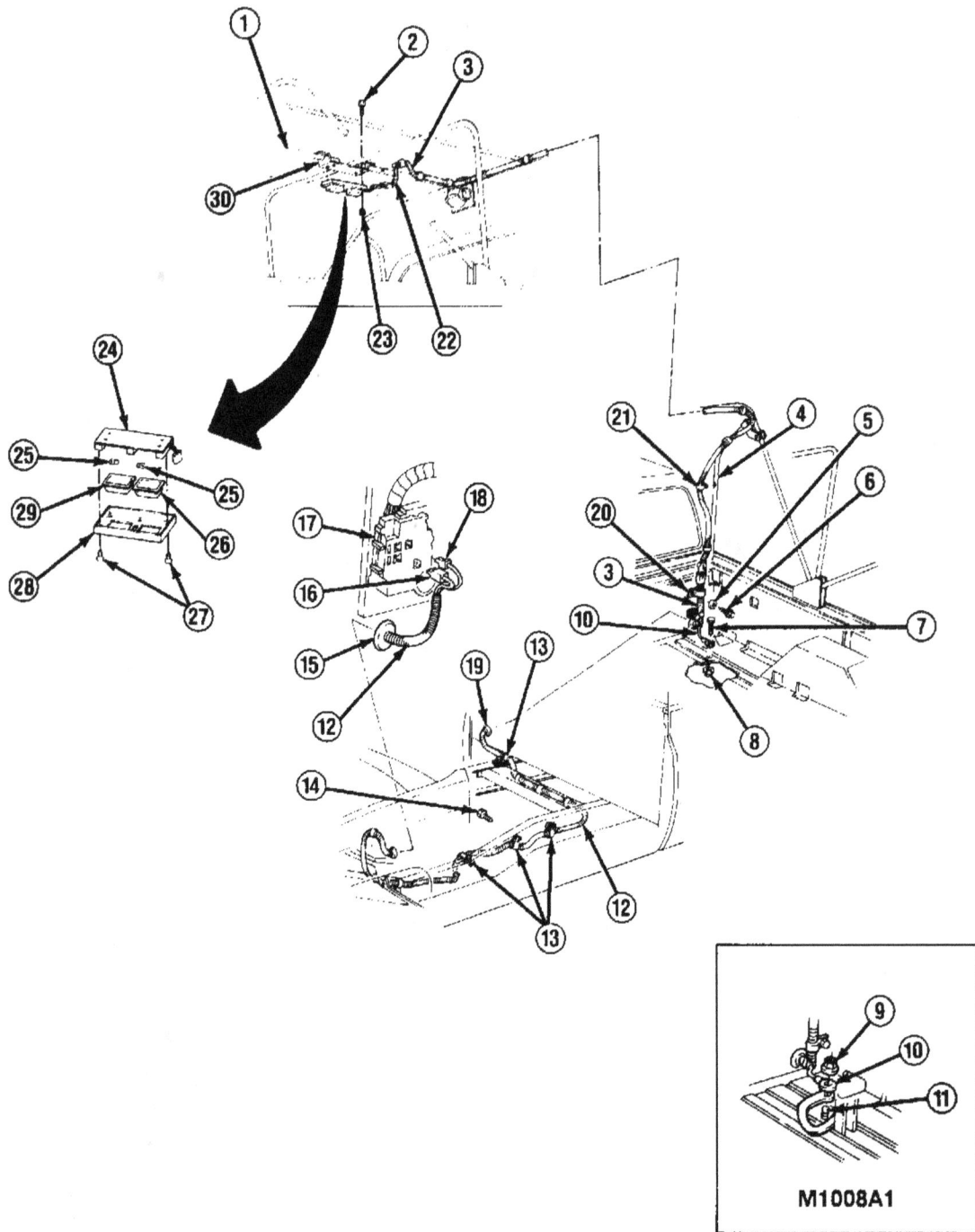

TA50137

11-33. DOMELIGHT AND WIRING HARNESS REPLACEMENT (M1008 AND M1008A1) (Con't).

12. Remove grommet (19) and carefully pull wiring harness (12) into cargo box and remove. DO NOT discard grommet.

13. Remove electrical lead (3) from clips (21) at right bow roof support (4), right side of front roof bow, and front section of roof support (1).

14. Disconnect electrical lead (3) from domelight at connector (22) and remove electrical lead.

b. INSTALLATION

NOTE

- **If installing domelight, perform steps 1-4 and 6.**

- **If installing wiring harness (12) and electrical iead (3), perform steps 5-13.**

1. Install 2 bulbs (25) into base assembly (24).

2. Install clear lens (26) and blue lens (29) into cover plate (28) with clear iens to the front. Install cover plate to base assembly (24) with 6 screws (27).

3. Install base assembly (24) to roof support bracket (30) with 4 screws (2).

4. Install roof support bracket (30) to 4 studs from roof supports (1) with 4 nuts (23).

5. Install electrical iead (3) to clips (21) at front section of roof support (1), right side of front roof bow, and right bow roof support (4).

6. Connect electrical lead (3) to domelight at connector (22).

7. Connect electrical iead (3) to wiring harness (12).

8. Carefully push wiring harness (12) through hole in cargo box front. install grommet (19).

9. Install ground wire (10) to cargo bed using boit (7) and new locknut (8) (M1008), or install ground wire (10) with communications rack ground strap to stud (11) with nut (9) (M1008A1).

10. Install wiring harness (12) to front of cargo box with 2 clamps (20), washers (5), and screws (6).

11. Install wiring harness (12) along frame and under hood with 5 clamps (13) and screws (14).

12. Carefully push wiring harness (12) through hole in left front of bulkhead and install grommet (15).

13. Connect purple wire (18) to "DOME" and orange wire (16) to "T-LPS" positions on fuse box (17) under dash.

FOLLOW-ON TASKS:

• Connect both battery negative cables. (See paragraph 4-38)
Ž Check operation of domelight.

11-34. REAR DOOR ASSEMBLY MAINTENANCE (M1008 AND M1008A1).

This task covers: a. Remova l c. Assembly
b. Disassembly d. Installation

INITIAL SETUP:

Materials/Parts

* RTV sealant (Item 41, Appendix C)

Personnel Required

* MOS 63B (2)

| a. | **REMOVAL** |

NOTE

If removing check strap (5), perform step 1.

1. Remove 4 nuts (4), screws (1), and washers (2) securing check strap (5) to rear door assembly (6) and rear side panel. Remove check strap from rear door assembly and door holder (3) from loop in check strap.

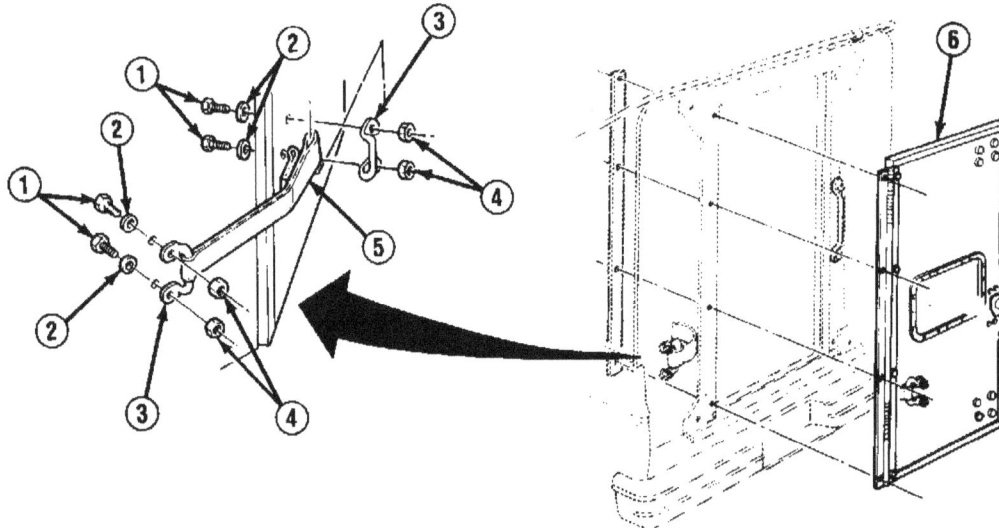

TA501i38

11-34. REAR DOOR ASSEMBLY MAINTENANCE (M1008 AND M1008A1) (Con't).

NOTE

Use an assistant to support rear door assembly (6) before performing step 3.

2. Remove 4 nuts (11), 4 screws (14), and 8 washers (9) holding rear door assembly (6) to hinge (10). Remove rear door assembly.

3. Remove 4 nuts (13), 4 screws (7), and 8 washers (8) holding hinge (10) to door opening panel assembly. Remove hinge and molding (12).

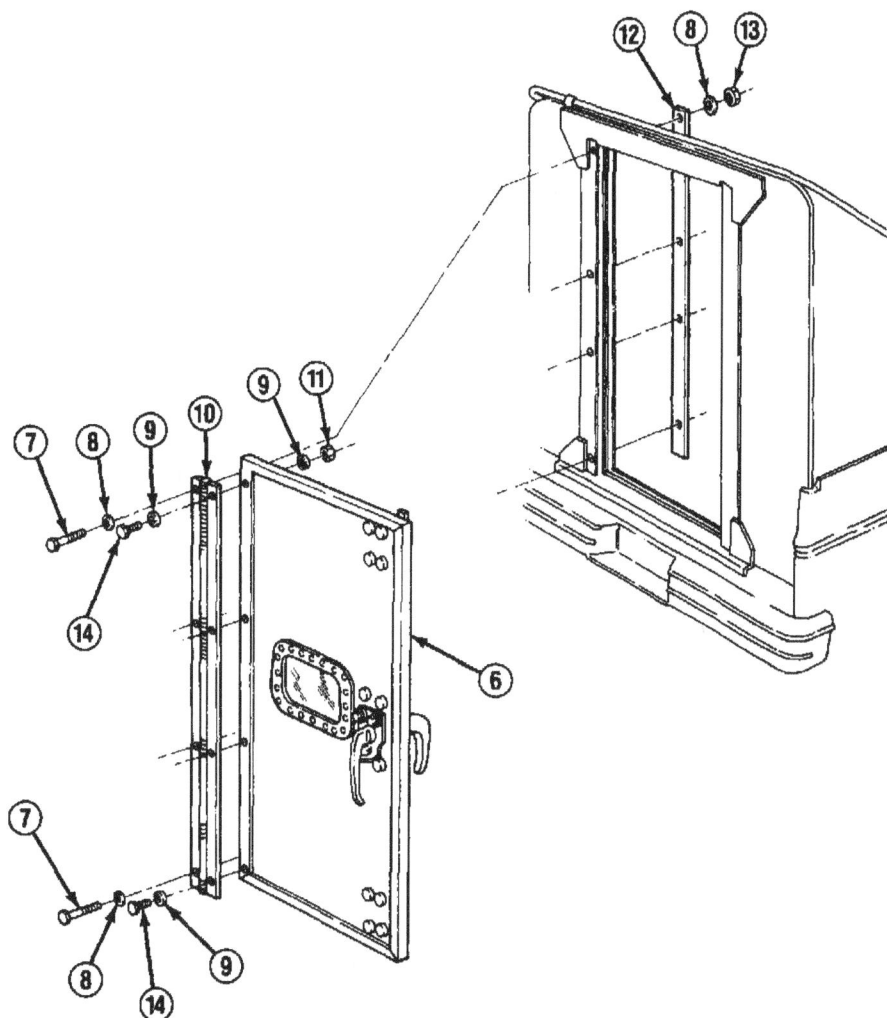

TA50139

11-34. REAR DOOR ASSEMBLY MAINTENANCE (M1008 AND M1008A1) (Con't).

| b. | DISASSEMBLY |

NOTE

- Latch assembly (19), handle assemblies (21 and 24), and window assembly (26, 27, 28, and 29) can be replaced without removing door assembly (6) from truck.

- If disassembling handle assemblies (21 and 24), perform steps 1 and 2.

- If disassembling latch assembly (19), perform steps 1 and 3 through 5.

- If disassembling door frames (15), perform step 6.

- If disassembling window assembly (26, 27, 28, and 29), perform steps 7 and 8.

1. Loosen setscrew and remove inner handle assembly (21).

2. Remove 3 screws (25) and outer handle assembly (24). Remove 3 nuts (22) from rear door assembly (6) by tapping them out if damaged.

3. Remove 8 screws (18) and 2 latch brackets (17).

4. Remove 4 screws (20) and latch assembly (19).

5. Remove 12 nuts (23) from rear door assembly (6) by tapping nuts out if damaged.

6. Remove 14 screws (16) and 4 door frames (15).

7. At window assembly, remove 18 screws (26), retainer (27), and gasket (28). Discard gasket only if worn.

8. Remove plastic window (29) from opening, Scrape off old RTV sealant from wood.

| c. | ASSEMBLY |

NOTE

If assembling window assembly (26, 27, 28 and 29), perform steps 1 and 2.

If assembling door frames (15), perform step 3.

If assembling latch assembly (19), perform steps 4-6.

If assembling handle assemblies (21 and 24), perform steps 7 and 8.

1. Apply RTV sealant to wood at window opening.

2. Install plastic window (29), gasket (28), and retainer (27) with 18 screws (26).

NOTE

1 door frame (15) is installed with 4 hinge screws.

3. Install 4 door frames (15) to rear door assembly (6) with 14 screws (16).

11-34. REAR DOOR ASSEMBLY MAINTENANCE (M1008 AND M1008A1) (Con't).

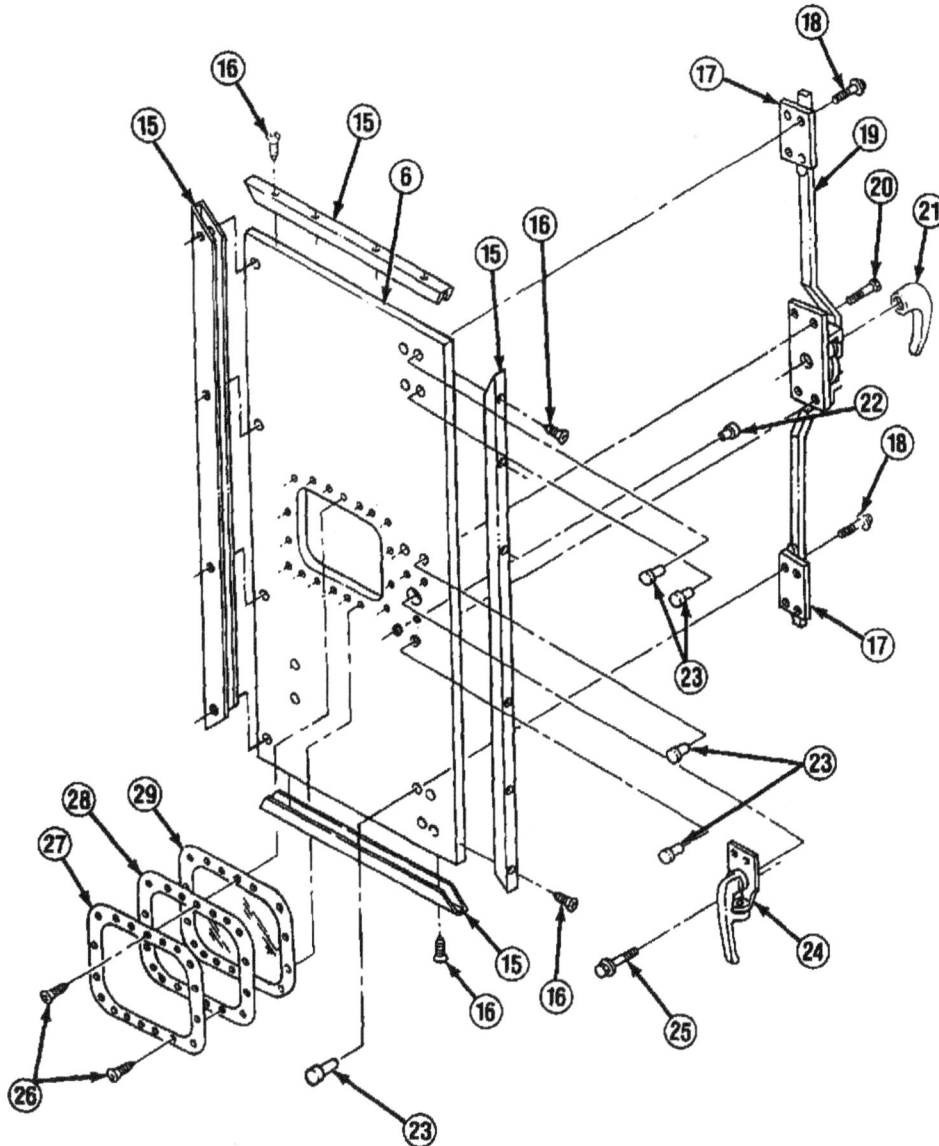

4. Install 12 nuts (23) and 3 nuts (22) into holes in rear door assembly (6) if removed.

5. Install 4 screws (20).

6. Install 2 latch brackets (17) with 8 screws (18).

7. Install outer handle assembly (24) with 3 screws (25).

8. Install inner handle assembly (21) and tighten setscrew.

TA50140

11-34. REAR DOOR ASSEMBLY MAINTENANCE (M1008 AND M1008A1) (Con't).

| d. INSTALLATION |

NOTE

- If installing hinge (10), molding (12), and rear door assembly (6), perform steps 1-3.

- If installing check strap (5), perform steps 4 and 5.

1. Install hinge (10) and molding (12) to door opening panel with 4 screws (7), 8 washers (8), and 4 nuts (13).

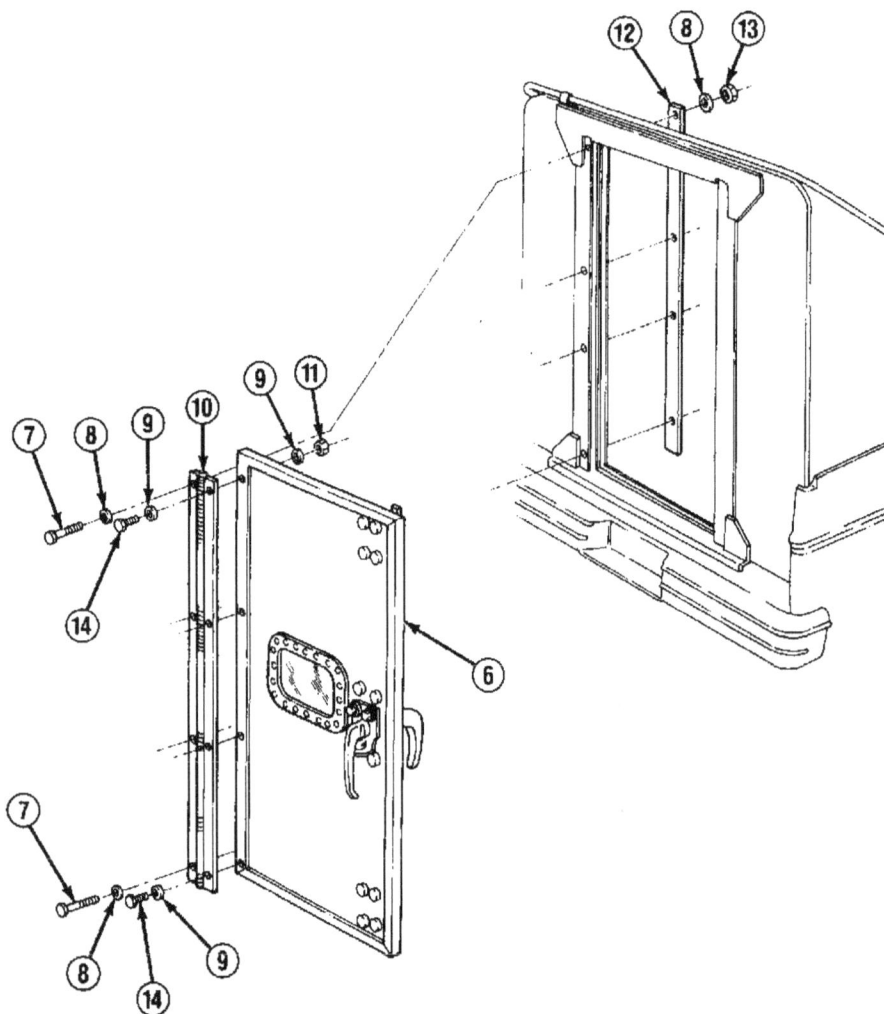

TA50141

11-34. REAR DOOR ASSEMBLY MAINTENANCE (M1008 AND M1008A1) (Con't).

NOTE

Use an assistant to support rear door assembly (6) while performing step 2.

2. Install rear door assembly (6) to hinge (10) with 4 screws (14), 8 washers (9), and 4 nuts (11).

3. Check operation of rear door assembly (6). If binding occurs, loosen nuts (11), adjust rear door assembly, and tighten nuts.

4. Install door holder (3) in loop at end of check strap (5).

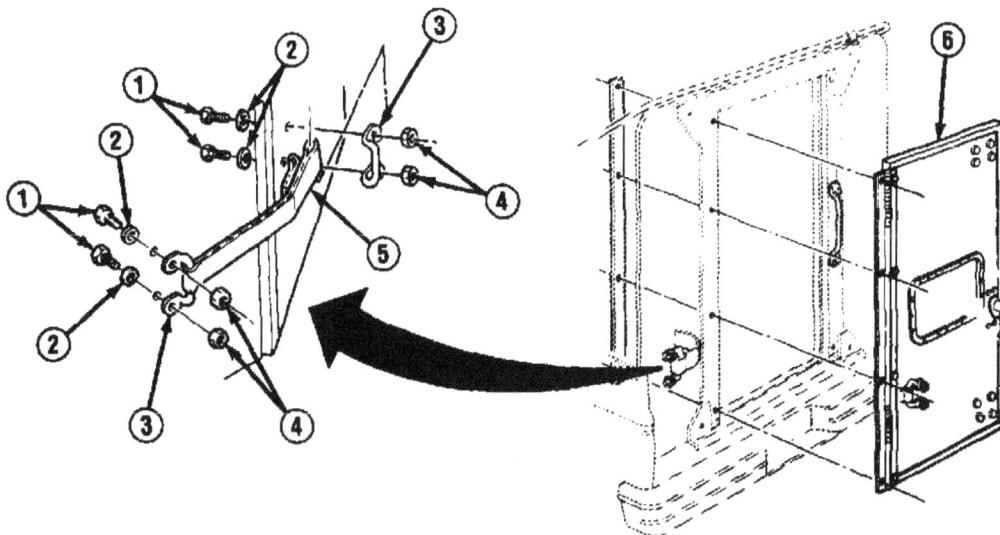

5. Install check strap (5) to rear door assembly (6) and rear side panel with 4 screws (1), washers (2), and nuts (4).

11-35. REAR DOOR FRAME AND PANEL ASSEMBLY REPLACEMENT (M1008 AND M1008A1).

This task covers:

a. Removal

b. Installation

INITIAL SETUP:

Equipment Condition

◄Cargo cover insulator removed.
(See paragraph 11-27)
◄Rear door assembly and hinge removed.
(See paragraph 11-34)

Personnel Required

◄MOS 63B (2)

| a. | **REMOVAL** |

NOTE

◄If removing   door frame assembly (7), perform steps 1-4.

◄If removing   left or right side panel assembly (6), perform steps 1-7.

◄If removing   molding (29), perform steps 4, 6, and 8.

◄If removing   molding, perform steps 1-7 and 9.

1.   Remove 2 nuts (16),   4 washers (10), 2 screws (11), and handle (12).

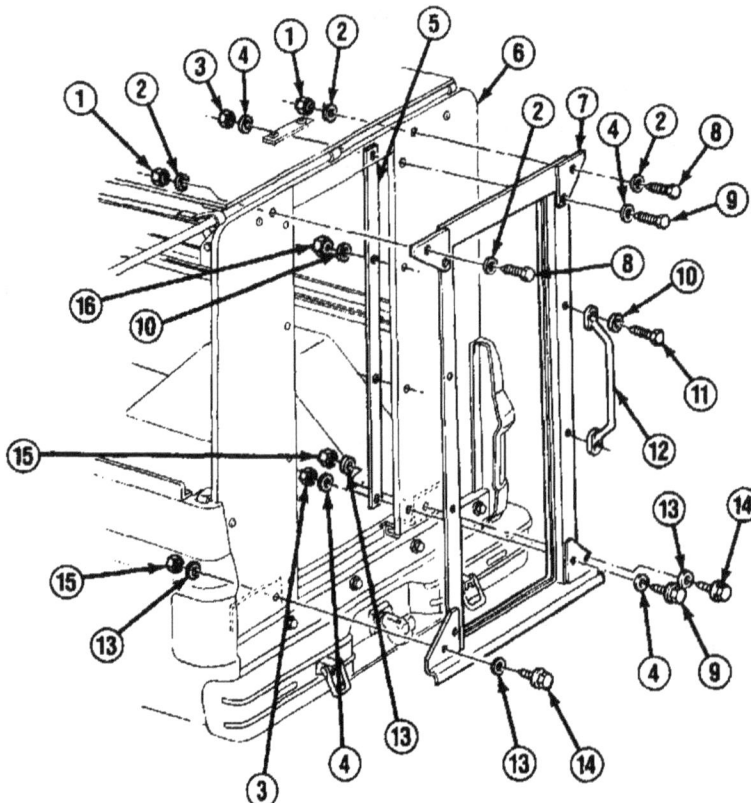

TA50143

11-35. REAR DOOR FRAME AND PANEL ASSEMBLY REPLACEMENT (M1008 AND M1008A1) (Con't).

2. Remove 2 nuts (1), 4 washers (2), and 2 screws (8) at top of door frame assembly (7).

3. Remove 2 nuts (3), 4 washers (4), 2 screws (9), and molding (5).

4. Remove 2 nuts (15), 4 washers (13), and 2 screws (14). Remove door frame assembly (7) by moving bottom rearward and downward.

NOTE

Left and right side panel assemblies (6) are removed the same way.

5. Remove 2 bolts (21) from 2 nuts (25) in right side panel assembly (6). Remove 2 nuts from right side panel assembly if damaged. Remove 2 bolts (19) from inside right side panel and remove air vent (20).

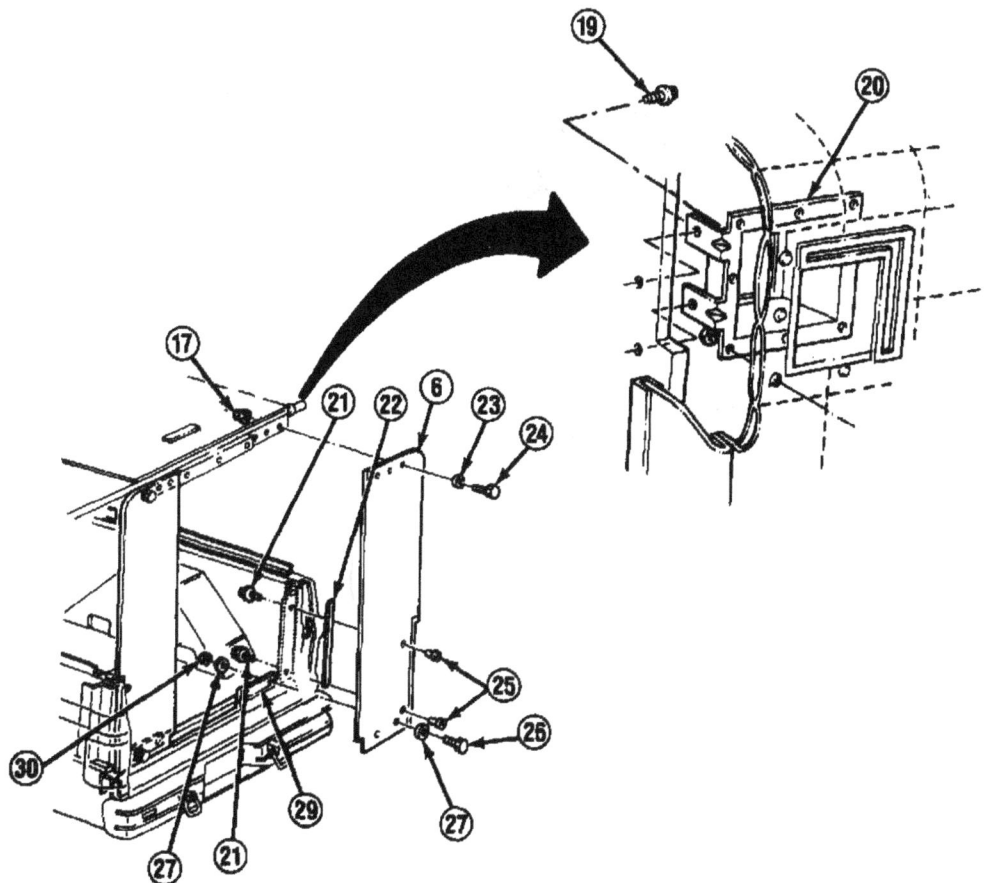

6. Remove nut (30), 2 washers (27), and screw (26) at bottom of right side panel assembly (6).

7. Remove extended nut (17), washer (23), and screw (24) at top of right side panel assembly (6). Remove right side panel assembly and rubber strip (22).

TA50144

11-35. REAR DOOR FRAME AND PANEL ASSEMBLY REPLACEMENT (M1008 AND M1008A1) (Con't).

8.   Remove 3 screws (32) from center of molding (29). Remove 4 nuts   (34), 8 washers (33), 4 bolts (31),   and molding.

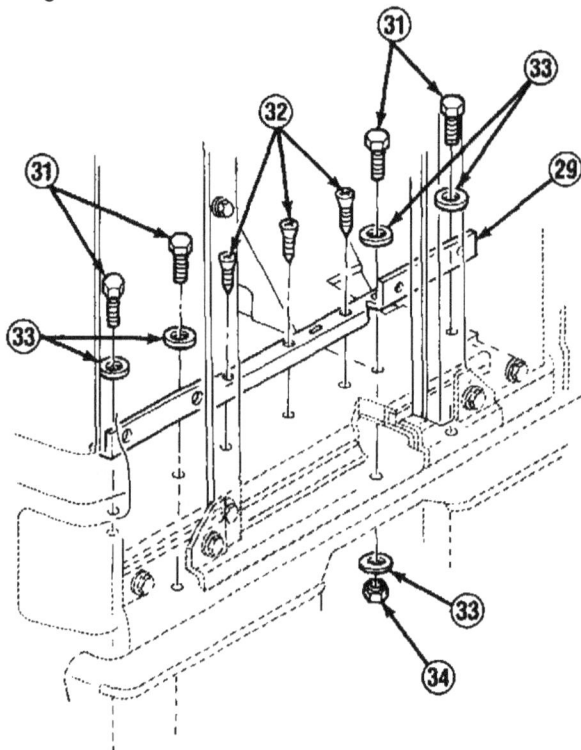

9.   Remove 5 bolts (38) and molding (36). Remove 2 gaskets (37) from molding. Replace gaskets if damaged. Remove 5 expansion shields (35) if damaged.

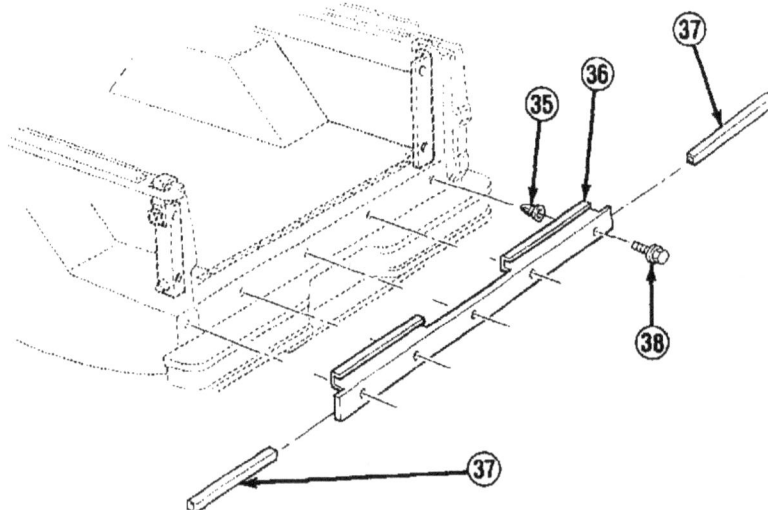

TA50145

11-35. REAR DOOR FRAME AND PANEL ASSEMBLY REPLACEMENT (M1008 AND M1008A1) (Con't).

| b. | INSTALLATION |

NOTE

◀f installing molding (36), perform steps 1 and 2.

◀f Installing molding (29), perform steps 3 and 4.

◀f installing left or right side panel assembly (6), perform steps 1-10.

◀f installing door frame assembly, perform steps 11-16.

1. Install 5 expansion shields (35) if removed.

2. Install 2 gaskets (37) into molding (36). Install molding with 5 bolts (38).

3. Install molding (29) to cargo floor with 4 bolts (31), 8 washers (33), and 4 nuts (34).

4. Install 3 screws (32) through center of molding (29).

NOTE

Left and right side panel assemblies (6) are installed the same way. Use an assistant to support side panel assemblies during installation.

5. Install 2 nuts (25) into right side panel assembly (6) if removed.

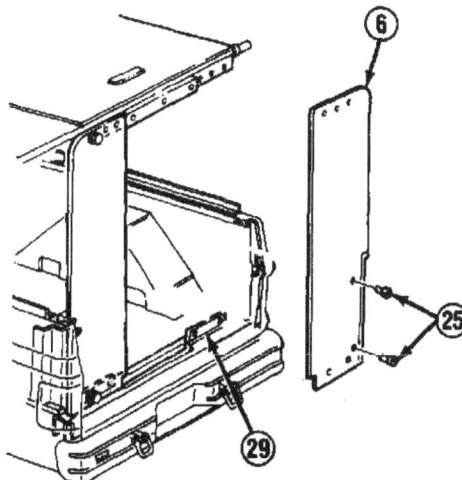

TA50146

11-35. REAR DOOR FRAME AND PANEL ASSEMBLY REPLACEMENT (M1008 AND M1008A1) (Con't).

6. Position rubber strip (22) at angle bracket (28). Install right side panel assembly (6) with 2 bolts (21) into 2 nuts (25).   DO NOT   fully tighten bolts. Install air vent (20) on right side panel assembly with 2 bolts (19),

7. Install screw (26), 2 washers (27), and nut (30) through bottom of right side panel assembly (6) into molding (29).

8. Install screw (24), washer (23), and extended nut (17) through top of   right side panel assembly (6) into panel assembly (18). DO NOT fully tighten extended nut.

9. Tighten 2 bolts (21) and extended nut (17).

NOTE

Use an   assistant to support   door frame assembly (7) during installation.

10. Install door frame assembly (7) with 2 screws (8), 4 washers (2), and 2 nuts (1). DO NOT fully tighten nuts.

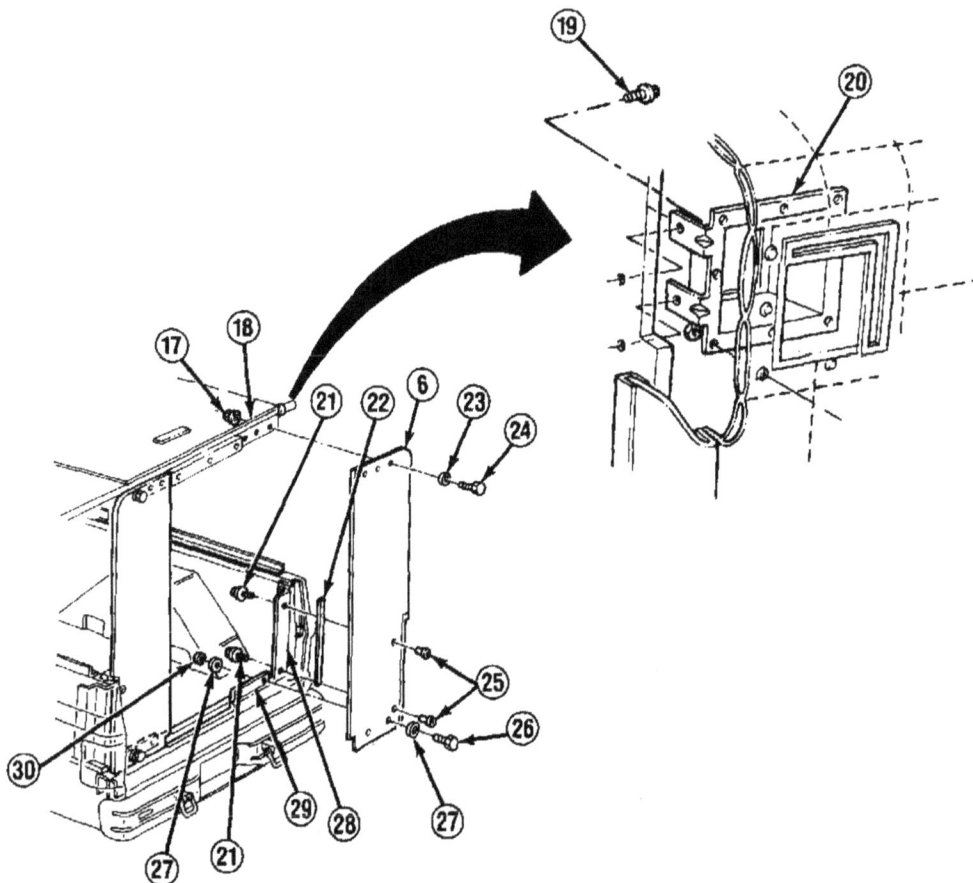

TA50147

11-35. REAR DOOR FRAME AND PANEL ASSEMBLY REPLACEMENT (M1008 AND M1008A1) (Con't).

11. Along bottom of door frame assembly (7), install 2 screws (14), 4 washers (13), and 2 nuts (15). DO NOT fully tighten nuts.

12. Install molding (5) on inside of right side panel assembly (6), and install 2 screws (9), 4 washers (4), and 2 nuts (3) through mounting holes. DO NOT fully tighten nuts.

13. Install handle (12) with 2 screws (11), 4 washers (10), and 2 nuts (16). Tighten nuts (1, 3, 15, and 16).

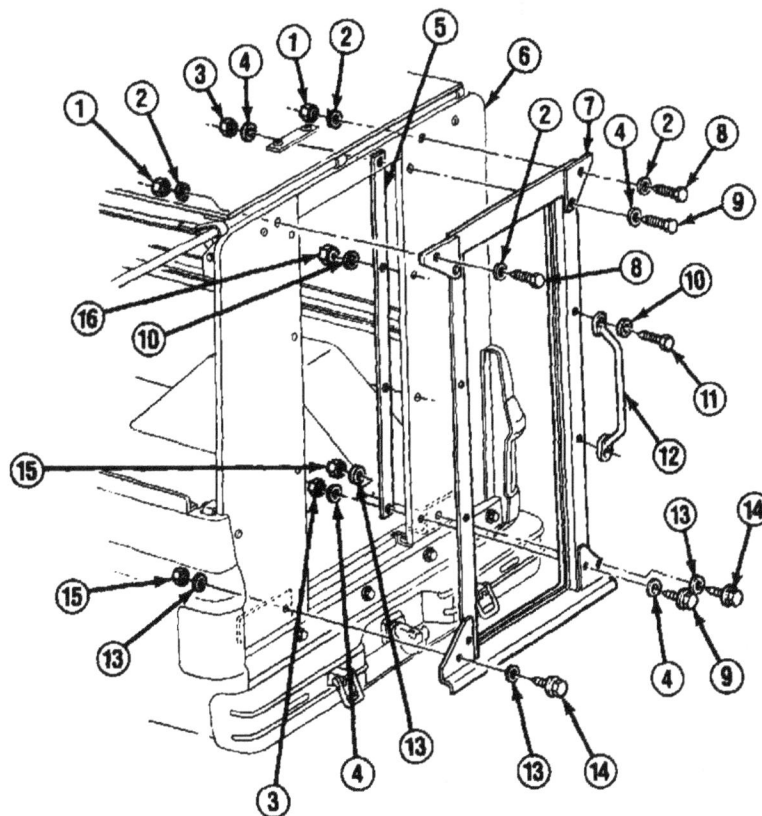

FOLLOW-ON TASKS:

- Install hinge and rear door assembly. (See paragraph 11-34)
- Install cargo cover insulator. (See paragraph 11-27)

TA50148

CHAPTER 12
PREPARATION FOR STORAGE OR SHIPMENT

12-1. OVERVIEW.

a. This chapter describes preparation of CUCV Series trucks for shipment within the continental United States and for limited storage.

b. This information is covered in the following sections:

    (1) Section I.   General Preparation of Truck for Shipment
    (2) Section II.   Loading and Movement
    (3) Section III.   Limited Storage

Section I. GENERAL PREPARATION OF TRUCK   FOR SHIPMENT

___

12-2.   GENERAL.

___

a. This section provides instructions on preserving and otherwise protecting CUCV Series trucks in preparation for shipment.

b. Protection for trucks and accompanying equipment must be sufficient to protect the materiel against deterioration and physical damage.

___

12-3.   CLEANING.

___

WARNING

___

Dry cleaning solvent P-D-680 is toxic and flammable. Always wear protective goggles and gloves and use only in a well-ventilated area. Avoid contact with skin, eyes, and clothes and DO NOT breathe vapors, DO NOT use near open flame or excessive heat. The solvent's flash point is 100°F-138°F (38°C-59°C). If you become dizzy while using cleaning solvent, immediately get fresh air and medical help. If solvent contacts eyes, immediately wash your eyes with water and get medical aid.

CAUTION

___

• **Do not use liquids under pressure for cleaning interior of truck.**

• **Prior to application of preservatives, surfaces must be cleaned to ensure removal of corrosion, soil, grease, or other acid and alkali residues.**

a. Interior of Truck.   Remove all dirt and other foreign matter from all painted metal surfaces of the truck by scrubbing with cloths soaked in dry cleaning solvent (Item 15, Appendix C). DO NOT apply solvent to electrical equipment, vinyl, or rubber parts of any nature. Notify your supervisor for cleaning of electrical equipment. Use warm water and mild soap for cleaning vinyl. Dry vinyl thoroughly. Apply preservative compound (Item 38, Appendix C) to vinyl and rubber.

b. Exterior of Truck.   Clean exterior surfaces of the truck to ensure removal of all dirt and foreign matter. After cleaning, immediately dry parts to remove excess cleaning solutions or residual moisture. Let parts air dry or wipe with clean, dry, lint-free cloths. (See MIL P-116).

12-4. LUBRICATION.

WARNING

Dry cleaning solvent P-D-680 is toxic and flammable, Always wear protective goggles and gloves and use only in a well-ventilated area. Avoid contact with skin, eyes, and clothes and DO NOT breathe vapors, DO NOT use near open flame or excessive heat. The solvent's flash point is 100°F-138°F (38°C-59°C). If you become dizzy while using cleaning solvent, immediately get fresh air and medical help. If solvent contacts eyes, immediately wash your eyes with water and get medical aid.

After cleaning has been accomplished, wipe all grease fittings clean with dry cleaning solvent (Item 15, Appendix C) and lubricate the truck in accordance with LO 9-2320-289-12. Remove excess grease after lubrication and before processing.

12-5. PRESERVATION.

a. All critical unpainted metal surfaces must be protected during shipment. Use procedures and materials listed in paragraphs (1) and (2) below. If the preservatives listed are not available, oil or grease specified in LO 9-2320-289-12 may be used for this purpose.

(1) **Battery Leads.**   Disconnect both batteries. (See paragraph 4-38). Each battery lead terminal, including the jumper lead ends, must be cleaned, coated with grease (Item 26, Appendix C) and wrapped with tape (Item 48, Appendix C).

(2) **Miscellaneous Preservation.**   Coat all unpainted, exposed, machined metal surfaces on the exterior of the truck with corrosion preventive compound (Item 13, Appendix C).

12-6. PACKAGING.

a. **Lenses.**   Cover all truck lamp lenses with grease proof barrier material (Item 5, Appendix C) and secure with tape (Item 48, Appendix C).

b. **Electrical Openings.**   Cover all electrical receptacles with tape (Item 48, Appendix C) or with plastic caps which will afford the same degree of protection.

12-7. PACKING.

a. Pack all Basis Issue Items (BII) and Additional Authorization List (AAL) items to prevent mechanical damage.

b. For shipment, disconnect both battery negative cables (see paragraph 4-38) and wrap with tape (Item 48, Appendix C).

12-8. MARKING.

Provide any necessary identification and precautionary markings in accordance with instructions in MIL-STD-129.

12-9. SHIPMENT OF ARMY DOCUMENTS.

Prepare all army shipping documents accompanying truck in accordance with DA Pam 738-750.

Section II. LOADING AND MOVEMENT

12-10. LOADING AND MOVEMENT.

For transportability guidance for the logistical handling and movement of the CUCV Series trucks, refer to TM 55-2320-289-14.

Section III. LIMITED STORAGE

12-11. GENERAL.

Commanders are responsible for ensuring that all trucks issued or assigned to their command are maintained in a serviceable condition and properly cared for, and that personnel under their command comply with technical instructions. Lack of time, lack of trained personnel, or lack of proper tools may result in a unit being incapable of performing maintenance for which it is responsible. In such cases, unit commanders may, with the approval of major commanders, place a truck that is beyond the maintenance capability of the unit in administrative storage or return it to supply agencies.

12-12. LIMITED STORAGE INSTRUCTIONS.

a. Time Limitations. Administrative storage is restricted to a period of 90 days and must not be extended unless the truck is reprocessed in accordance with subparagraph b. below.

b. Storage Procedure. Perform disassembly only as required to clean and preserve exposed surfaces. Except as otherwise noted, and to the maximum extent consistent with safe storage, place the truck in administrative storage in as nearly a completely assembled condition as practicable. Install and adjust equipment so that the truck may be placed in service and operated with minimum delay.

(1) The truck should be stored on level ground in the most favorable location available, preferably one which affords protection from exposure to the elements and from pilferage.

(2) Perform semiannual preventive maintenance checks and services (PMCS) on trucks intended for administrative storage. This maintenance consists of inspecting, cleaning, servicing, preserving, lubricating, adjusting, and replacing minor repair parts as required.

(3) Remove both batteries   and place in covered storage, maintaining a charged condition.

(4) Provide access to the   truck to permit inspection, servicing, and subsequent removal from storage.

c. Inspection in Storage.

(1) Visual inspection of trucks in administrative storage must be conducted at least once a month, and immediately following hard rain, heavy snowstorm, windstorm, or other severe weather conditions. Perform disassembly as required to fully ascertain the extent of any deterioration or damage found. A record of these inspections must be maintained for each truck in administrative storage, attached to the truck in such a manner as to protect the record from the elements.

(2) When rust or deterioration is found on a critical/machined surface, reprocessing for administrative storage must be immediately accomplished. Repair damage caused to the truck by severe weather conditions. Deterioration or damage to on-equipment materiel (OEM) must be repaired as necessary. Painted surfaces showing evidence of deterioration must be thoroughly cleaned, dried, and repainted, using paint of the same quality and color as the original paint.

APPENDIX A
REFERENCES

A-1. SCOPE.

This appendix lists all forms, field manuals, technical manuals, and other publications required for use with this manual.

A-2. INDEXES.

The following indexes should be frequently consulted for latest changes to, or revisions of, references given in this appendix and for new publications or instructions relating to materiel covered in this manual.

a. Military Publications:

Consolidated Index of Army Publications and Blank Forms ...	DA Pam 25-30
Equipment Improvement Report and Maintenance Digest	TB 43-0001-39
The Standard Army Publications System Users Index	DA Pam 310-10

b. General References:

Catalog of Abbreviations and Brevity Codes	AR 310-50
Dictionary of United States Army Terms	AR 310-25
Military Symbols	FM 101-5-1

A-3. SUPPLY CATALOGS.

The following Department of the Army Supply Catalogs pertain to this manual:

Shop Equipment, Automotive Maintenance and Repair: Organizational Maintenance: Common No. 1, Less Power (NSN 4910-00-754 -0654)	SC 4910-95-CL-A74
Shop Equipment, Automotive Maintenance and Repair: Organizational Maintenance: Common No. 2, Less Power (NSN 4910-00-754-0650)	SC 4910-95-CL-A72
Tool Kit, General Mechanic's: Automotive (NSN 5180-00-177-7033)	SC 4910-95-CL-N26

A-4. FORMS.

Refer to DA Pam 310-1, *Consolidated Index of Army Publications and Blank Forms,* for a current and complete list of blank forms. Refer to DA Pam 738-750, *The Army Maintenance*

Management System (TAMMS), for instructions on the use of maintenance forms pertaining to this materiel.

DA Form 285	US Army Accident Investigation Report
DA Form 348	Equipment Operator's Qualification Record (Except Aircraft)
DA Form 2028	Recommended Changes to Publications and Blank Forms
DA Form 2401	Organization Control Record for Equipment
DA Form 2402 . . . . Exchange Tag	
DA Form 2404	Equipment Inspection and Maintenance Worksheet
DA Form 2405	Maintenance Request Register
DA Form 2406	Materiel Condition Status Report
DA Form 2407	Maintenance Request
DA Form 2407-1	Maintenance Request – Continuation Sheet
DA Form 2408	Equipment Log Assembly (Records)
DA Form 2408-9	Equipment Control Record
DA Form 2409	Equipment Maintenance Log (Consolidated)
DD Form 314	Preventive Maintenance Schedule and Record
DD Form 518	Accident Identification Card
DD Form 1397	Processing and Reprocessing Record for Shipment, Storage, and Issue of Vehicles and Spare Engines
Standard Form 46	US Government Motor Vehicle Operator's Identification Card
Standard Form 91	Operator Report on Motor Vehicle Accidents
Standard Form 368	Quality Deficiency Report

A-5. OTHER PUBLICATIONS.

The following publications contain information pertinent to the major item materiel and associated equipment.

a. **Truck:**

Lubrication Order for Truck, ¾ and 1¼ Ton, 4x4, CUCV Series	LO 9-2320-289-12
Operator's Manual for Truck, ¾ and 1¼ Ton, 4X4, CUCV Series	TM 9-2320-289-10
Unit Maintenance Repair Parts and Special Tools List for Truck, ¾ and 1¼ Ton, 4X4, CUCV Series	TM 9-2320-289-20P
Warranty Procedures for Truck, ¾ and 1¼ Ton, 4X4, CUCV Series	TB 9-2300-295-15/24

b. **Camouflage :**

Camouflage, ...	FM 5-20
Camouflage Materials, ...	TM 5-200
Color, Marking, and Camouflage Painting of Military Vehicles, Construction Equipment, and Materials Handling Equipment, ...	TB 43-0209

c. **Decontamination:**

NBC Decontamination	FM 3-5

Chemical, Toxicological, and Missile Fuel Handlers
    Protective Clothing . . . .   TM 10-277
Operator's and Organizational Maintenance Manual
    (Including Repair Parts and Special Tools List) for
    Decontamination Apparatus, Portable, DS2,
    1½ Quart, ABC-M11 (NSN 4230-00-720-1618) . . . .   TM 3-4230-204-12&P

d. **General:**

Accident Reporting and Records. . . . .   AR 385-40
Army Motor Transport Units and Operations . . . .   FM 55-30
Basic Cold Weather Manual . . . .   FM 31-70
Chemical Agent Resistant Aliphatic Polyurethane Coating MIL-C-46168C
Cooling Systems: Tactical Vehicles . . . .   TM 750-254

Corrosion Prevention and Control: Including Rustproofing
    for Tactical Vehicles and Trailers.. . . . .   TB 43-0213
First Aid for Soldiers . . . .   FM 21-11
Functional Grouping Codes: Combat, Tactical, and Support
    Vehicles and Special Purpose Equipment . . . .   TB 750-93-1
General Fabric Repair . . . .   FM 10-16
Manual for the Wheeled Vehicle Driver . . . .   FM 21-305
Mountain Operations . . . .   FM 90-6
Northern Operations . . . .   FM 31-71
Operation and Maintenance of Ordnance Materiel
    in Cold Weather (0°F to -65°F). . . . .   FM 9-207
Painting instructions for Field Use. . . . .   TM 43-0139
Painting Procedures and Marking for Vehicles, Construction
    Equipment and Material Handling Equipment . . . .   MIL-STD-I 93
Petroleum Supply Point Equipment and Operations . . . .   FM 10-69
Prevention of Motor Vehicle Accidents . . . .   AR 385-55
Principles of Automotive Vehicles. . . . .   TM 9-8000
Procedures for Destruction of Tank-Automotive Equipment
    to Prevent Enemy Use . . . .   TM 750-244-6
Treatment and Painting of Materiel MIL-T-704J

e. **Maintenance and Repair:**

Chemical Agent Alarm Maintenance . . . .   TM 3-6665-225-12
Description, Use, Bonding Techniques
    and Properties of Adhesives . . . .   TB ORD 1032
Inspection, Care, and Maintenance of Antifriction Bearings . . .   TM 9-214
Mandatory Brake Hose Inspection and
    Replacement - Tactical Vehicles . . . .   TB 9-2300-405-14
Materials Used for Cleaning, Preserving, Abrading and
    Cementing Ordnance Materiel and Related Materials
    Including Chemicals . . . .   TM 9-247

Operator's and Organizational Maintenance Manual:
    Alarm, Chemical Agent, Automatic , ...   TM 3-6665-261-14

Operator's, Organizational, Direct Support and
General Support Maintenance Manual Including
Repair Parts List for Balancer, Vehicle Wheel
(Model M-76) . . . .   TM 9-4910-743-14&P
Operator's and Organizational Maintenance Manual Including
Repair Parts and Special Tools List for Simplified Test
Equipment for Internal Combustion Engines (STE/ICE) . . . . ,   TM 9-4910-571-12&P
Operator's Manual for Welding Theory and Application , , , . . .   TM 9-237
Operator's, Organizational, Direct Support and General
Support Maintenance Manual for Lead-Acid
Storage Batteries . . . .   TM 9-6140-200-14
Organizational Care, Maintenance & Repair of Pneumatic Tires,
Inner Tubes and Radial Tires... . . . .   TM 9-2610-200-24

Safety Inspection and Testing of Lifting Devices . . . .   TB 43-0142
Standards and Criteria for Technical Inspection
and Classification of Tires. . . . .   TM 9-2610-201-14
Use of Antifreeze Solutions and Cleaning Compounds
in Engine Cooling Systems . . . .   TB 750-651

f.   **Shipment and Limited Storage:**

Marking for Shipment and Storage MIL-STD-129
Methods of Preservation... . . . .   MIL-P-116
Packaging of Materiel . . . .   AR 700-15
Packaging of Materiel: Preservation   . . . .   TM 38-230-1
and TM 38-230-2

Preparation for Shipment and Limited Storage
of Wheeled Vehicles MIL-V-62038
Preparation for Shipment and Storage of Basic Issue Items
for Military Vehicles, Carriages and Equipment MIL-B-12841

Railcar Loading Procedures ... .   TM 55-601
Security of Tactical Wheeled Vehicles . . . .   TB 9-2300-422-20
Softwood Lumber MM-L-751
Standards for Overseas Shipment or Domestic Issue of
Special Purpose Vehicles, Combat, Tactical, Construction,
and Selected Industrial and Troop Support US Army
Tank-Automotive Readiness Command Managed Items . . . . .   TB 9-2300-281-35

APPENDIX B
MAINTENANCE ALLOCATION CHART

Section I. INTRODUCTION

B-1. GENERAL.

a. This section provides a general explanation of all maintenance and repair functions authorized at the various maintenance levels.

b. The Maintenance Allocation Chart (MAC) in Section II designates overall authority and responsibility for the performance of maintenance functions on the identified end item or component. The application of the maintenance functions to the end item or component will be consistent with the capacities and capabilities of the designated maintenance levels.

c. Section III lists the tools and test equipment (both special tools and common tool sets) required for each maintenance function as referenced from Section II.

d. Section IV contains supplemental instructions and explanatory notes for a particular maintenance function.

B-2. MAINTENANCE FUNCTIONS.

Maintenance functions will be limited to and defined as follows:

a. **Inspect.** To determine the serviceability of an item by comparing its physical, mechanical, and/or electrical characteristics with established standards through examination (e.g., by sight, sound, or feel).

b. **Test.** To verify serviceability by measuring the mechanical, pneumatic, hydraulic, or electrical characteristics of an item and comparing those characteristics with prescribed standards.

c. **Service.** Operations required periodically to keep an item in proper operating condition, i.e., to clean. (includes decontaminate, when required), to preserve, to drain, to paint, or to replenish fuel, lubricants, chemical fluids, or gases.

d. **Adjust.** To maintain or regulate, within prescribed limits, by bringing into proper or exact position, or by setting the operating characteristics to specified parameters.

e. **Aline.** To adjust specified variable elements of an item to bring about optimum or desired performance.

f. **Calibrate.** To determine and cause corrections to be made or to be adjusted on instruments or test, measuring, and diagnostic equipments used in precision measurement. Consists of comparisons of two instruments, one of which is a certified standard of known accuracy, to detect and adjust any discrepancy in the accuracy of the instrument being compared.

g. **Remove/Install.** To remove and install the same item when required to perform service or other maintenance functions. Install may be the act of emplacing, seating, or fixing into position a spare, repair part, or module (component or assembly) in a manner to allow the proper functioning of an equipment or system.

h. **Replace.** To remove an unserviceable item and install a serviceable counterpart in its place. "Replace" is authorized by the MAC and is shown as the third position code of the SMR code,

i. **Repair.** The application of maintenance services, including fault location/trouble-shooting, removal/installation, and disassembly/assemble procedures, and maintenance actions to identify troubles and restore serviceability to an item by correcting specific damage, fault, malfunction, or failure in a part, subassembly, module (component or assembly), end item, or system.

j. **Overhaul.** That maintenance effort (service/action) prescribed to restore an item to a completely serviceable/operational condition as required by maintenance standards in appropriate technical publications (i.e., DMWR). Overhaul is normally the highest degree of maintenance performed by the Army. Overhaul does not normally return an item to like new condition.

k. **Rebuild.** Consists of those services/actions necessary for the restoration o f unserviceable equipment to a like new condition in accordance with original manufacturing standards. Rebuild is the highest degree of materiel maintenance applied to Army equipment. The rebuild operation includes the act of returning to zero those age measurements (hours/miles, etc.) considered in classifying Army equipment/components.

B-3. EXPLANATION OF COLUMNS IN THE MAC, SECTION II.

a. **Column 1, Group Number.** Column 1 lists functional group code numbers, the purpose of which is to identify maintenance significant components, assemblies, subassemblies, and modules with the next higher assembly. End item group number shall be "00."

b. **Column 2, Component/Assembly.** Column 2 contains the names of components, assemblies, subassemblies, and modules for which maintenance is authorized.

c. **Column 3, Maintenance Function.** Column 3 lists the functions to be performed on the item listed in Column 2. (For a detailed explanation of these functions, see paragraph B-2.)

d. **Column 4, Maintenance Level.** Column 4 specifies, by the listing of a *work time* figure in the appropriate subcolumn(s), the level of maintenance authorized to perform the function listed in Column 3. This figure represents the active time required to perform that maintenance function at the indicated level of maintenance. If the number or complexity of the tasks within the listed maintenance function vary at different maintenance levels, appropriate work time figures will be shown for each level. The work time figure represents the average time required to restore an item (assembly, subassembly, component, module, end item, or system) to a serviceable condition under typical field operating conditions. This time includes preparation time (including any necessary disassembly/assembly time), troubleshooting/fault location time, and quality assurance/quality control time in addition to the time required to perform the specific tasks identified for the maintenance functions authorized in the Maintenance Allocation Chart. The symbol designations for the various maintenance levels are as follows:

C	*Unit (Operator or Crew)*
O	*Unit Organizational Maintenance*
F	*Intermediate Direct Support Maintenance*
H	*Intermediate General Support* Maintenance
D	*Depot Maintenance*

e. **Column 5, Tools and Equipment.** Column 5 specifies, by code, those common tool sets (not individual tools) and special tools, TMDE, and support equipment required to perform the designated function.

f. **Column 6, Remarks.** This column shall, when applicable, contain a letter code, in alphabetic order, which shall be keyed to the remarks contained in Section IV.

B-4. EXPLANATION OF COLUMNS IN TOOL AND TEST EQUIPMENT REQUIREMENTS, SECTION III.

a. **Column 1, Tool or Test Equipment Reference Code.** The tool and test equipment reference code correlates with a code used in the MAC, Section II, Column 5.

b. **Column 2 , Maintenance Level.** The lowest level of maintenance authorized to use the tool or test equipment.

c. **Column 3, Nomenclature.** Name or identification of the tool or test equipment.

d. **Column 4 , National/NATO Stock Number.** The National or NATO Stock Number of the tool or test equipment.

e. **Column 5 , Tool Number.** The manufacturer's part number.

B-5. EXPLANATION OF COLUMNS IN REMARKS, SECTION IV.

a. **Column 1, Reference Code.** The code recorded in Column 6, Section II.

b. **Column 2, Remarks.** This column lists information pertinent to the maintenance function being performed as indicated in the MAC, Section II.

Section II.   MAINTENANCE ALLOCATION CHART

(1) Group Number	(2) Component/Assembly	(3) Maintenance Function	(4) Maintenance Level					(5) Tools and Equipment	(6) Remarks
			Unit		Inter-mediate		Depot		
			C	O	F	H	D		
01	ENGINE								
0100	ENGINE, DIESEL	INSPECT	0.1	0.5					
		TEST			1.5			1,2,6	
		SERVICE		0.4				1,2,4	A
		REPLACE			4.0			1,2,4,6	
		REPAIR		0.3	1.0	16.0		1,2,4,6, 9,10	
		OVERHAUL					30.0		B
	ENGINE MOUNTS	INSPECT		0.3					
		REPLACE			1.5			1,4	
0101	CYLINDER HEAD, DIESEL	INSPECT		0.1	0.2				
		REPLACE			3.2			1,2,4,6	
		REPAIR				5.0		1,4	
	PLUGS (CYL. & CASE)	INSPECT		0.1	0.1				
		REPLACE				0.4		1,4,6	
	COVER, TMG GEAR	INSPECT		0.1					
		REPLACE			0.5			1,2,4,6	
		REPAIR			1.0			1,2,10	
0102	PULLEY, CONE CSHAFT	INSPECT	0.1						
		REPLACE		0.5				1,2	
	DAMPER ASSY, TORSIONAL	INSPECT		0.1					
		REPLACE			0.5			1,2,6	
	CRANKSHAFT, ENG	INSPECT				1.0			
		REPLACE				4.0		1,2,6,10	
		REPAIR				2.0		1,4	
	SEAL, CSHAFT REAR OIL	INSPECT			0.5				
		REPLACE			3.0			1,2,6,10	
0103	FLYWHEEL, ENG	INSPECT			0.5				
		REPLACE			3.0			1,2,6	

Section II. MAINTENANCE ALLOCATION CHART - Continued

(1) Group Number	(2) Component/Assembly	(3) Maintenance Function	(4) Maintenance Level					(5) Tools and Equipment	(6) Remarks
			Unit		Inter-mediate		Depot		
			C	O	F	H	D		
0104	PISTON, CONNROD								
	(CONNROD. PSTN)	INSPECT REPLACE				0.5 4.0		1,2,4,6	A
	(PSTN, INTERNAL COMBUSTION)	INSPECT REPLACE				0.5 2.0		1,4,6	A
0105	CAMSHAFT, VALVES. TIMING SYSTEM								
	(CMSHFT, ENG)	INSPECT REPLACE				0.5 3.0		1,2,6,10	
	(COVER, VALVE)	INSPECT REPLACE	0.1	0.1	1.2			1,4	
	(ROCKER ARM)	INSPECT REPLACE			0.5 1.0			1,2,6	
	(VALVE, EXH & INL)	INSPECT REPLACE REPAIR			0.5 1.0 0.8			1,2,6 1,6	
	(SPROCKET, CSHAFT)	REPLACE			0.6			1,4,6	
	(GEAR, F/INJ PMP DR)	INSPECT REPLACE			0.2 0.8			1,4,6	
	(CHAIN, CMSHFT TMG)	INSPECT REPLACE			0.5 1.0			1,4,6	
0106	ENGINE LUBRICATION SYSTEM								
	TUBE ASSY & SEAL. OIL LVL INDICATOR	INSPECT REPLACE	0.1	0.3				1,2	

Section II.   MAINTENANCE ALLOCATION CHART - Continued

(1)	(2)	(3)	(4) Maintenance Level					(5)	(6)
			Unit		Inter-mediate		Depot		
Group Number	Component/Assembly	Maintenance Function	C	O	F	H	D	Tools and Equipment	Remarks
0106 (Cont'd)	FILTER ASSY. OIL	INSPECT REPLACE	0.1	0.2				1,2	A
	PAN ASSY. ENG OIL	INSPECT REPLACE		0.1 0.4				1,2,4	
	PUMP & SCREEN ASSY. OIL	INSPECT REPLACE REPAIR			0.2 1.0 0.6			1,4,6 1,6	
	LINES, OIL COOLER	INSPECT REPLACE	0.1		0.5			1,2,4	
	VALVE, DEPRESSION REGULATOR	INSPECT REPLACE	0.1		0.5			1,2	
0108	MANIFOLDS, INTK & EXH								
	(MANIFOLD, INTK)	INSPECT REPLACE		0.1	1.0			1,4,6	
	(MANIFOLD ASSY. EXH)	INSPECT REPLACE		0.1 1.0				1,4,6	
03	**FUEL SYSTEM**								
0301	NOZZLE, F/INJ	INSPECT TEST REPLACE		0.1	0.3 0.5			1,2,9	
0302	PUMPS, FUEL SPLY								
	(GEAR, F/INJ PMP)	INSPECT REPLACE			0.3 0.8			1,2,6	
	(VALVE, TRANS VAC)	INSPECT ADJUST REPLACE	0.1	0.1 0.3				1,4,9 1,2	

Section II. MAINTENANCE ALLOCATION CHART - Continued

(1) Group Number	(2) Component/Assembly	(3) Maintenance Function	(4) Maintenance Level Unit C	O	Inter-mediate F	H	Depot D	(5) Tools and Equipment	(6) Remarks
0302 (Cont'd)	(PMP ASSY, F/INJ)	INSPECT		0.1	0.1				
		TEST			1.0				
		ADJUST			1.0				
		REPLACE			1.0			1,2,9	
		REPAIR			1.5	4.5		1,6,10	
		OVERHAUL					2.0		B
	(FUEL PMP, ENG)	INSPECT	0.1						
		REPLACE		0.5				1,2	
	LINES & FITTINGS								
	(PMP-TO-FLTR)	INSPECT	0.1						
		REPLACE		1.0				1,2,9	
	(VALVE, VAC-TO-PMP)	INSPECT	0.1						
		REPLACE		0.2				1	
	(F/INJ PMP-TO-NOZ)	INSPECT	0.1						
		REPLACE			1.0			1,6,9	
0304	AIR CLEANER ASSY	INSPECT	0.1						
		SERVICE	0.2						
		REPLACE	0.4	0.5				1,2	
0306	TANKS & LINES								
	(TANK ASSY, FUEL)	INSPECT	0.1						
		REPLACE		1.0				1,2,4,8	
	(LINES & FTGS)	INSPECT		0.2					
		REPLACE		1.0				1,2	
0309	FILTER ASSY, FUEL	INSPECT	0.1						
		SERVICE		0.2					
		REPLACE		0.5				1,2	

Section II.   MAINTENANCE ALLOCATION CHART - Continued

(1)	(2)	(3)	(4) Maintenance Level					(5)	(6)
			Unit		Inter-mediate		Depot		
Group Number	Component/Assembly	Maintenance Function	C	O	F	H	D	Tools and Equipment	Remarks
0311	ENGINE STARTING AIDS								
	(PLUG ASSY, GLOW)	INSPECT REPLACE		0.2 0.4				1,2	
	(SENSOR, GLOW PLUG)	INSPECT REPLACE		0.1 0.3				1,4	
0312	ACCELERATOR LINKAGE	INSPECT REPLACE		0.1 1.2				1,2,4	
	SOLENOID ASSY	INSPECT ADJUST REPLACE		0.2 0.1 0.5				1,4 1,2,4	
04	EXHAUST SYSTEM								
0401	MUFFLERS, PIPES, BRKTS	INSPECT REPLACE	0.1	1.0				1,2,4	
05	COOLING SYSTEM								
0501	RESERVOIR, COOL	INSPECT REPLACE	0.1	0.5				1,2	
	RADIATOR ASSY	INSPECT TEST SERVICE REPLACE REPAIR	0.1	0.1 0.5 1.5	1.3			1,2 1,2,6 1,2,6	
	PROBE ASSY, LOW COOLANT	INSPECT REPLACE		0.1 0.4				1,2	
0502	SHROUD, FAN RDTR	INSPECT REPLACE	0.1	1.0				1,2	

Section II. MAINTENANCE ALLOCATION CHART - Continued

(1) Group Number	(2) Component/Assembly	(3) Maintenance Function	(4) Maintenance Level					(5) Tools and Equipment	(6) Remarks
			Unit		Inter-mediate		Depot		
			C	O	F	H	D		
0503	THERMOSTAT, HSG, LINES								
	(HOSES)	INSPECT REPLACE	0.1	0.5				1,2	
	(WATER OUTLET, ENG CROSSOVER)	INSPECT REPLACE	0.1	0.5				1,2	
0504	PUMP ASSY, WATER	INSPECT REPLACE		0.1	1.3			1,2,6	
0505	FAN ASSY								
	PULLEY ASSY	INSPECT REPLACE	0.1	0.5				1,2,8	
	IMPELLER FAN, AXIAL	INSPECT REPLACE	0.1	0.4				1,2	
	CLUTCH, HUB FAN	INSPECT REPLACE		0.1 0.5				1,2	
06	ELECTRICAL SYSTEM								
0601	ALTERNATOR AND GENERATOR	INSPECT TEST REPLACE REPAIR		0.1 0.4 0.8	0.8			1,4 1,2,4 1,2,4,6	
	BRACKETS, MTG	INSPECT REPLACE	0.1	0.5				1,2	
	BELT, ALTNTR & GEN	INSPECT ADJUST REPLACE	0.1	0.2 0.4				1,4 1,4	

Section II. MAINTENANCE ALLOCATION CHART - Continued

(1) Group Number	(2) Component/Assembly	(3) Maintenance Function	(4) Maintenance Level					(5) Tools and Equipment	(6) Remarks
			Unit		Intermediate		Depot		
			C	O	F	H	D		
0601 Cont'd)	PULLEY, ALTNTR (M1010)	INSPECT REPLACE	0.1	0.5				1,4	
0602	REGULATOR, VOLTAGE (M1010)	INSPECT REPLACE		0.1	0.5			1,2,4	
	RELAY, ELECTRO-MAGNETIC	INSPECT REPLACE		0.1	0.5			1,2,4	
0603	STARTER, ENG ELEC	INSPECT TEST REPLACE REPAIR		0.1 0.2 1.0	4.0			2 1,2 1,2,4,6	
0607	WIRING HARNESS, INSTR	INSPECT TEST REPLACE REPAIR		0.2	0.4 2.0 1.0			2 1,2 1,4,6	
	CLUSTER ASSY, INSTR	INSPECT REPLACE		0.1 1.0				1,2,4	
	LAMPS, INSTR PANEL	INSPECT REPLACE	0.1	0.3				1,2	
	INDICATOR ASSY, GLOW PLUG	INSPECT REPLACE	0.1	0.4				1,2	
	HOUSING ASSY, DOOR AJAR (M1010)	INSPECT REPLACE	0.1	0.4				1,2	
	SWITCH ASSY, GPFU (M1010)	INSPECT REPLACE	0.1	0.5				1,2	
0608	BOARD, VEH ACCESS WRG	INSPECT REPLACE		0.1 0.5				1,2	
	CABLE ASSY, POS & NEG FEED (M1008A1)	INSPECT REPLACE	0.1	1.0				1,2	

Section II. MAINTENANCE ALLOCATION CHART - Continued

(1) Group Number	(2) Component/Assembly	(3) Maintenance Function	(4) Maintenance Level Unit C	O	Inter-mediate F	H	Depot D	(5) Tools and Equipmen	(6) Remarks
0608 (Cont'd)	RESISTOR (BTRY BSTR)	INSPECT		0.1					
		REPLACE		0.7				1,2	
	WIRE ASSY (BTRY BSTR)	INSPECT	0.1						
		TEST		0.1				2	
		REPLACE		0.5				1,2	
	RELAY, GLOW PLUG	INSPECT		0.1					
		TEST		0.3					
		REPLACE		0.5				1,2	
	SWITCH ASSY, BLACKOUT	INSPECT		0.1					
		REPLACE		0.5				1,2	
	SWITCH ASSY, HEADLAMP	INSPECT		0.1					
		REPLACE		0.4				1,2	
		REPAIR		0.2				1,2	
	SWITCH, DIMMER	INSPECT		0.1					
		REPLACE			0.5			1,2	
	SWITCH, IGNITION	INSPECT		0.1					
		REPLACE			1.0			1,2,8	
	SWITCH ASSY, TRANS DOWNSHIFT	INSPECT		0.1					
		REPLACE			0.5			1,2,4	
	FUSES (PANEL)	INSPECT		0.1					
		REPLACE		0.2				1,2	
0609	LAMP ASSY, BLACKOUT	INSPECT	0.1						
		REPLACE		0.3				1,2	
		REPAIR		0.1				1,2	
	BULBS, MKR LAMPS, & TAILLAMPS	INSPECT	0.1						
		REPLACE		0.2				1,2	
	LAMP ASSY, PARK	INSPECT	0.1						
		REPLACE		0.4				1,2,8	

Section II. MAINTENANCE ALLOCATION CHART - Continued

(1) Group Number	(2) Component/Assembly	(3) Maintenance Function	(4) Maintenance Level					(5) Tools and Equipment	(6) Remarks
			Unit		Inter- mediate		Depot		
			C	O	F	H	D		
0609 (Cont'd)	LAMP ASSY, HEADLAMP	INSPECT REPLACE REPAIR	0.1	0.4 0.5				1,2 1,2	
	LENS ASSY, TAILLAMP	INSPECT REPLACE	0.1	0.2				1,2,8	
	LAMP ASSY, TAIL (M1010 & M1031)	INSPECT REPLACE REPAIR	0.1	0.3 0.2				1,2,4 1,2	
	LAMP ASSY, REAR FENDER (M1028A2 & M1028A3)	INSPECT REPLACE REPAIR	0.1	0.3 0.2				1,2,4 1,2	
0610	SWITCH, ENG THERMOSTAT	TEST REPLACE		0.3 0.5				1,2	
	SWITCH ASSY, COLD ADVANCE	TEST REPLACE		0.3 0.5				1,2	
	SWITCH, ENG OIL PRESS	TEST REPLACE		0.3 0.5				1,8	
0611	HORN ASSY, ELEC	REPLACE		0.3				1,2	
	RELAY, HORN	REPLACE		0.2				1	
0612	BATTERY, STOR	INSPECT TEST SERVICE REPLACE	0.1	0.1 0.3	0.2 0.2			2 1,2 1,2	
	CABLE ASSY, BTRY POS	INSPECT REPLACE REPAIR	0.1	0.3 0.4				1,2 1,2	
	CABLE ASSY, BTRY NEG	INSPECT REPLACE REPAIR	0.1	0.3 0.4				1,2 1,2	

Section II.   MAINTENANCE ALLOCATION CHART - Continued

(1) Group Number	(2) Component/Assembly	(3) Maintenance Function	(4) Maintenance Level					(5) Tools and Equipment	(6) Remarks
			Unit		Inter-mediate		Depot		
			C	O	F	H	D		
0612 (Cont'd)	CONNECTOR ASSY, BTRY BSTR	INSPECT	0.1						
		REPLACE		0.5				1,2	
		REPAIR		0.5				1,2	
0613	HARNESS WIRING, FWD LAMP	INSPECT		0.1					
		TEST		0.2				2	
		REPLACE			3.0			1,2	
		REPAIR			4.0			1,2	
	WIRING ASSY, BRAKE INDICATOR	INSPECT		0.1					
		TEST		0.1				2	
		REPLACE			0.2			1,2	
	HARNESS ASSY, BODY WRG	INSPECT		0.1					
		TEST		0.2				2	
		REPLACE			2.0			1,2,8	
		REPAIR			4.0			1,2	
	HARNESS ASSY, FUEL SENDING (M1009)	INSPECT		0.1					
		TEST		0.1				2	
		REPLACE			1.0			1,2,4	
	HARNESS ASSY, REAR LAMP	INSPECT		0.2					
		TEST		0.2				2	
		REPLACE		1.5				1,2	
		REPAIR		1.0				1,2	
	HARNESS ASSY, TRLR WRG	INSPECT		0.1					
		TEST		0.2				2	
		REPLACE		1.0				1,2,4	
		REPAIR		1.5				1,2	
	HARNESS ASSY, INSTR PANEL EXT (M1010)	INSPECT		0.2					
		TEST		0.2				2	
		REPLACE			3.0			1,2,4	
		REPAIR			2.0			1,2	
	HARNESS ASSY, ENG WRG	INSPECT		0.1					
		TEST			0.5			2	
		REPLACE			2.0			1,2,4	
		REPAIR			1.0			1,6	

Section II.   MAINTENANCE ALLOCATION CHART - Continued

(1) Group Number	(2) Component/Assembly	(3) Maintenance Function	(4) Maintenance Level					(5) Tools and Equipment	(6) Remarks
			Unit		Inter-mediate		Depot		
			C	O	F	H	D		
0613 (Cont'd)	HARNESS ASSY, TERMINAL BOARD	INSPECT REPLACE REPAIR		0.1 1.0 0.5				1,2 1,2	
	HARNESS, GLOW PLUG	INSPECT TEST REPLACE REPAIR		0.1 0.1	0.5 0.4			2 1,2 1,6	
	HARNESS ASSY, DIAGNOSTIC	INSPECT TEST REPLACE		0.2 0.3	1.0			2 1,2,4	
	HARNESS ASSY, REAR FENDER LIGHTS (M1028A2 & M1028A3)	INSPECT TEST REPLACE		0.2 0.3	0.5			2 1,2,4	
	HARNESS ASSY, DOOR ALM (M1010)	INSPECT TEST REPLACE		0.1 0.2	1.0			2 1,2,4	
07	**TRANSMISSION**								
0705	SHIFT LINKAGE	INSPECT ADJUST REPLACE		0.1	0.2 0.5			1,2,4 1,2,4,6	
	INDICATOR ASSY, TRANS	INSPECT ADJUST REPLACE REPAIR		0.1 0.2 0.5 0.2				1,2 1,2 1,2	
	MODULATOR UNIT, TRANS	INSPECT REPLACE		0.1	0.3			1,2	
0710	MOUNT, TRANS UPR	INSPECT REPLACE		0.1	0.3			1,2	
	MOUNT, TRANS LWR	INSPECT REPLACE		0.1	0.3			1,2	

Section II. MAINTENANCE ALLOCATION CHART - Continued

(1) Group Number	(2) Component/Assembly	(3) Maintenance Function	(4) Maintenance Level					(5) Tools and Equipment	(6) Remarks
			Unit		Inter-mediate		Depot		
			C	O	F	H	D		
0710 (Cont'd)	TRANSMISSION, HYDR	INSPECT		0.1					
		TEST		0.3				1,2	
		SERVICE		1.1				1,2	
		REPLACE			2.0			1,2,6	A
		REPAIR				4.5		1,2,6,10	
		OVERHAUL					10.0		B
	CONVERTER, TRQ	INSPECT			1.0				
		REPLACE			3.0			1,2,6	
	PAN, TRANS FL	INSPECT		0.1					
		REPLACE		0.7				1,2,4	
	TUBE, TRANS FILL	INSPECT		0.1					
		REPLACE			0.3			1,2	
	CLUTCH ASSY, FWD	REPLACE				0.8		1,2,6,10	
		REPAIR				0.6		1,2,6,10	
	CLUTCH ASSY, DIR	REPLACE				0.8		1,2,4,6	
		REPAIR				0.5		1,2,4,10	
	BAND ASSY, FRONT	ADJUST				0.5		1,2,10	
		REPLACE				0.8		1,2,4,6,10	
	BAND ASSY, REAR	ADJUST				0.5		1,2,10	
		REPLACE				0.8		1,2,4,6,10	
	SUPPORT & GEAR ASSY	REPLACE				0.8		1,2,6,10	
		REPAIR				0.7		1,2,6,10	
0714	GOVERNOR ASSY	INSPECT			0.5				
		REPLACE			1.0			1,2	
	VALVE ASSY, CONTROL	REPLACE				0.7		1,2	
		REPAIR				0.3		1,6	
	COVER, REAR SERVO	INSPECT				0.5			
		REPLACE				1.0		1,2,6	

Section II. MAINTENANCE ALLOCATION CHART - Continued

(1) Group Number	(2) Component/Assembly	(3) Maintenance Function	(4) Maintenance Level					(5) Tools and Equipment	(6) Remarks
			Unit		Inter-mediate		Depot		
			C	O	F	H	D		
0721	FILTER ASSY, TRANS	SERVICE		0.5				1,2,6	
		REPLACE		0.5				1,2,6	
	PUMP ASSY	REPLACE				0.7		1,2,8	
		REPAIR				1.0		1,2,6,8	
	PIPE ASSY, TRANS FL COOLER	INSPECT		0.1					
		REPLACE			0.5			1,2	A
08	**TRANSFER AND DRIVE ASSEMBLY**								
0801	TRANSFER CASES	INSPECT		0.1					
		SERVICE		0.2				1	
		REPLACE			1.3			1,2,4,6	A
		REPAIR				4.0		1,2,4,6	
		OVERHAUL					2.8		B
	CASE ASSY, REAR HSG (MODEL 208)	INSPECT			0.1				
		REPLACE				0.7		1,2,4	
		REPAIR				0.3		1,2,4,10	
	PUMP HOUSING ASSY (MODEL 208)	REPLACE			0.3			1,2	
		REPAIR			0.2			1,2,4	
	HOUSING, MN SFT BSHG (MODEL 208)	REPLACE			0.7			1,2,4	
		REPAIR			0.3			1,2,4	
	FORK ASSY SHIFTER (MODEL 208)	REPLACE				0.7		1,2,4	
		REPAIR				0.3		1,2,4	
	SHAFT & SELECTOR ASSY (MODEL 208)	REPLACE				0.7		1,2,4	
		REPAIR				0.3		1,2,4	
	YOKE (MODEL 208)	REPLACE			0.3			1,2,4	
		REPAIR			0.2			1,2,4	

Section II. MAINTENANCE ALLOCATION CHART - Continued

(1) Group Number	(2) Component/Assembly	(3) Maintenance Function	(4) Maintenance Level Unit C	Unit O	Inter-mediate F	Inter-mediate H	Depot D	(5) Tools and Equipment	(6) Remarks
0801 (Cont'd)	CASE ASSY, FRONT HSG (MODEL 208)	INSPECT				0.1			
		REPLACE				1.0		1,2,4	
		REPAIR				0.8		1,2,4,10	
	FORK SHIFT ASSY, RNG (MODEL 208)	REPLACE				0.7		1,2,4	
		REPAIR				0.3		1,2,4	
	GEAR ASSY, PLANETARY (MODEL 208)	REPLACE				1.0		1,2,4	
		REPAIR				1.0		1,2,4	
	RETAINER ASSY, FRONT (MODEL 205)	REPLACE			0.3			1,2,4	
		REPAIR			0.2			1,2,4	
	EXTENSION & BUSHING ASSY, REAR (MODEL 205)	REPLACE			0.5			1,2,4	
		REPAIR			0.3			1,2,4	
	PLUG, DRAIN FILL	INSPECT		0.1					
		REPLACE		0.1				1,2,4	
0803	LEVER & LINKAGE (MODEL 208)	INSPECT		0.1					
		ADJUST		0.5				1,2,4	
		REPLACE		0.7				1,2,4	
	LEVER & LINKAGE (MODEL 205)	INSPECT		0.1					
		ADJUST		0.5				1,2,4	
		REPLACE		0.7				1,2,4	
09	PROPELLER SHAFTS								
0900	SHAFT ASSY, FRONT	INSPECT		0.1					
		SERVICE		0.1				4	
		REPLACE		0.6				1,2	
		REPAIR		0.8	1.0			1,2	
	BALL KIT, UNIV CV	INSPECT		0.1					
		SERVICE		0.1				4	
		REPLACE			0.4			1,2,6,9	

Section II.   MAINTENANCE ALLOCATION CHART - Continued

(1) Group Number	(2) Component/Assembly	(3) Maintenance Function	(4) Maintenance Level					(5) Tools and Equipment	(6) Remarks
			Unit		Inter-mediate		Depot		
			C	O	F	H	D		
0900 (Cont'd)	REPAIR KIT, UNIV JOINT	INSPECT SERVICE REPLACE		0.1 0.1 0.4				1,4 1,2,4	
	SHAFT ASSY, REAR	INSPECT REPLACE REPAIR		0.1 0.4 0.5				1,2 1,2,4	
10	FRONT AXLE								
1000	AXLE ASSEMBLIES	INSPECT SERVICE REPLACE REPAIR OVERHAUL		0.1 0.1	1.7	4.0	2.6	1,6 1,2,4,6 1,2,4,6, 9,10	B
	COVER, GEAR CARR	INSPECT REPLACE		0.1	0.6				
	CAP, VENT ASSY	INSPECT REPLACE		0.1 0.5					
	SPINDLES	REPLACE		1.0					
	SHAFTS	INSPECT REPLACE		0.1	1.0				
1002	CASE ASSY, DIFF	INSPECT REPLACE REPAIR				0.1 1.4 1.0		1,2,4,6, 9,10 1,2,4,6, 9,10	
	GEAR ASSY, DIFF	INSPECT REPLACE				0.1 1.5		1,2,4,6,9	
	FLANGE & YOKE ASSY, UNIV	INSPECT REPLACE REPAIR		0.1	0.7 0.4			1,2,4,6 2,4	

Section II. MAINTENANCE ALLOCATION CHART - Continued

(1) Group Number	(2) Component/Assembly	(3) Maintenance Function	(4) Maintenance Level Unit C	Unit O	Inter-mediate F	Inter-mediate H	Depot D	(5) Tools and Equipment	(6) Remarks
7004	REPAIR KIT, KINGPIN (ALL EXCEPT M1009)	INSPECT REPLACE REPAIR		0.1	2.0 1.0			1,2,4,6,8,9 4,6,8,9	
	REPAIR KIT, STRG KNUCKLE (M1009)	INSPECT REPLACE REPAIR		0.1	2.0 1.0			1,2,4,6,9 4,6,9	
	KNUCKLE ASSY, STRG	INSPECT REPLACE REPAIR		0.1	1.5 1.0			1,2,4,6,9 4,6,9	
11	REAR AXLE								
1100	AXLE ASSEMBLIES	INSPECT SERVICE REPLACE REPAIR OVERHAUL		0.1 0.1	1.5	4.0	2.0	1,6 1,2,4,6 1,2,4,6, 9,10	B
	CAP, VENT ASSY	INSPECT REPLACE		0.1 0.5				1,2	
	SHAFT, AXLE (ALL EXCEPT M1009)	INSPECT REPLACE		0.1 0.5				1,2	
	SHAFT, AXLE (M1009)	INSPECT REPLACE			0.1 1.0			1,2,4	
1101	ELDED ASSY, DIFF CARR (ALL EXCEPT M1009)	INSPECT REPLACE REPAIR			0.1	2.5 0.5		1,2,4,6, 9,10 1,2	
	WELDED ASSY, DIFF CARR (M1009)	INSPECT REPLACE			0.1	2.5		1,2,4,6, 9,10	
	COVER, GEAR CARR	INSPECT REPLACE		0.1	0.3				

Section II. MAINTENANCE ALLOCATION CHART - Continued

(1) Group Number	(2) Component/Assembly	(3) Maintenance Function	(4) Maintenance Level					(5) Tools and Equipment	(6) Remarks
			Unit		Inter-mediate		Depot		
			C	O	F	H	D		
1102	FLANGE & DEFLECTOR ASSY (ALL EXCEPT M1009)	INSPECT REPLACE REPAIR		0.1	0.5 0.2			1,2,6,9 2,6,9	
	FLANGE & DEFLECTOR ASSY (M1009)	INSPECT REPLACE		0.1	0.5			1,2,6,9	
	DIFF UNIT, SPIDER (ALL EXCEPT M1009)	REPLACE REPAIR				1.2 0.5		1,2,4,6,9 1,4,6,9	
	CASE ASSY, DIFF (M1009)	REPLACE REPAIR				1.5 0.8		1,2,4,6,9 1,4,6,9	
12	BRAKES								
1201	PARKING BRAKE, CABLE & BRKTS	INSPECT TEST SERVICE ADJUST REPLACE REPAIR	0.1 0.1	0.2 0.2 0.5 0.3				4 1,2 1,2 1,2	
1202	DISC BRAKE SHOE SETS	INSPECT REPLACE		0.1 1.0				1,2,4	
	SHOE KIT, REAR BK (ALL EXCEPT M1009)	REPLACE REPAIR		1.0	1.0			1,2,4 1,2,4	
	SHOE KIT, REAR BK (M1009)	REPLACE		0.8				1,2,4	
1204	CYLINDER ASSY, MA	INSPECT SERVICE REPLACE REPAIR	0.1	0.3 1.0 0.2				1,2,4 1,4	
	BOOSTER ASSY, HYDR	INSPECT REPLACE	0.1	1.4				1,2,4	

Section II. MAINTENANCE ALLOCATION CHART - Continued

(1) Group Number	(2) Component/Assembly	(3) Maintenance Function	(4) Maintenance Level					(5) Tools and Equipment	(6) Remarks
			Unit		Inter-mediate		Depot		
			C	O	F	H	D		
1204 (Cont'd)	LINES & FITTINGS	INSPECT REPLACE	0.1	0.1 0.5				1,2,4	
	VALVE, BK COMB	INSPECT REPLACE		0.1 1.0				1,2,4	
	VALVE, PROPORTIONING (ALL EXCEPT M1009)	INSPECT ADJUST REPLACE		0.1 0.2 1.0				1,4 1,2,4	
	CALIPER ASSY	INSPECT REPLACE REPAIR		0.1 0.5	0.3			1,2 1,4	
	CYLINDER ASSY, WHL	INSPECT REPLACE		0.1 1.5				1,2,4	
1206	PEDAL ASSY, BK	INSPECT REPLACE	0.1	0.5				1,2,4	
13	**WHEELS & TIRES**								
1311	WHEEL ASSEMBLIES	INSPECT REPLACE	0.1	0.4				1,2,4	
	LOCKING HUB, FRONT	INSPECT REPLACE	0.1	0.4				2,4	
	HUB & ROTOR ASSY, FRONT (ALL EXCEPT M1009)	INSPECT REPLACE REPAIR		0.1 0.7	0.2			4,6,8 4,6	
	HUB & DISC ASSY (M1009)	INSPECT REPLACE REPAIR		0.1 0.7	0.2			4,6,8 4,6	
	BEARINGS & SEALS	INSPECT SERVICE ADJUST REPLACE		0.1 1.2 0.2 1.0				2,4,8 2,4,8 2,4,8	

Section II.   MAINTENANCE ALLOCATION CHART - Continued

(1)	(2)	(3)	(4) Maintenance Level					(5)	(6)
			Unit		Inter-mediate		Depot		
Group Number	Component/Assembly	Maintenance Function	C	O	F	H	D	Tools and Equipment	Remarks
1311 (Cont'd)	DRUM, REAR BK	INSPECT REPLACE REPAIR		0.1 0.7	0.2			1,2,6,8 6	
1313	TIRES, PNEU	INSPECT SERVICE REPLACE REPAIR	0.1 0.2	0.3 0.3				1,2,4 2	
14	**STEERING**								
1401	COLUMN ASSY, STRG	INSPECT ADJUST REPLACE REPAIR	0.1	0.1	0.5 1.6	1.5		1,2,6 1,2,6 1,2,6,8	
	SHAFT WITH COUPLING STEERING	INSPECT REPLACE REPAIR	0.1	0.3	1.5			1,2,4 1,2,4	
	STEERING WHEEL	INSPECT REPLACE REPAIR	0.1	0.3 0.4				1,2,4 1,2,4	
	LEVER ASSY, SIG	INSPECT REPLACE	0.1	0.5				1,2	
	ARM, PITMAN	INSPECT REPLACE		0.1 0.7				1,2,8	
	STEERING DAMPER, SHOCK ABSORBER	INSPECT REPLACE		0.1 0.5				1,2	
	SOCKET, CONNROD	INSPECT SERVICE REPLACE		0.1 0.2 0.7				1,2 1,2	
	TIE-ROD END, STRG (ALL EXCEPT M1009)	INSPECT SERVICE REPLACE REPAIR		0.1 0.2 0.5 0.1				1,2 1,2	

Section II. MAINTENANCE ALLOCATION CHART - Continued

(1) Group Number	(2) Component/Assembly	(3) Maintenance Function	(4) Maintenance Level					(5) Tools and Equipment	(6) Remarks
			Unit		Inter-mediate		Depot		
			C	O	F	H	D		
1401 (Cont'd)	TIE-ROD END, STRG (M1009)	INSPECT SERVICE REPLACE		0.1 0.2 0.7				1,2	
1407	GEAR ASSY, PWR STRG	INSPECT REPLACE REPAIR		0.1 1.0		1.8		1,2,8 1,2,10	
1410	PULLEY, PWR BSTR PMP	INSPECT REPLACE	0.1	0.5				1,2,8	
	BELT, PWR BSTR PMP	INSPECT ADJUST REPLACE	0.1	0.1 0.4				1,4 1,4	
	PUMP ASSY, HYDR	INSPECT SERVICE REPLACE	0.1	0.1 0.6				1,2,4,8	
1411	LINES & HOSES	INSPECT REPLACE	0.2	0.7				1,2,4,8	
15	FRAME, TOWING ATTACHMENTS AND DRAWBAR								
1501	BUMPER, FRONT	INSPECT REPLACE	0.1	1.0				1,2	
	BUMPER, REAR	INSPECT REPLACE	0.1	1.0				1,2	
	FRAME ASSY , STRL	INSPECT REPLACE REPAIR		0.2	0.5	20.0 7.5		1,2,4,6 1,2,4,6	
	SIDEMEMBERS	REPLACE REPAIR				20.0 8.0		1,2,4,6 1,2,4,6	

Section II. MAINTENANCE ALLOCATION CHART - Continued

(1) Group Number	(2) Component/Assembly	(3) Maintenance Function	(4) Maintenance Level Unit C	O	Inter-mediate F	H	Depot D	(5) Tools and Equipment	(6) Remarks
1501 (Cont'd)	CROSSMEMBERS	REPLACE REPAIR				2.0 8.0		1,2,4,6 1,2,4,6	
1503	CLEVISES, PTL ASSY & BRKTS	INSPECT SERVICE REPLACE REPAIR	0.1	0.2 0.8 0.5				1,2 1,2,4 1,2	
1504	CARRIER, SPARE WHEEL	INSPECT REPLACE	0.1	0.5				1,2	
16	**SPRINGS AND SHOCK ABSORBERS**								
1601	SPRING ASSY, FRONT	INSPECT REPLACE		0.1	1.0			1,2,4,6	A
	BUMPER ASSY, FRONT	INSPECT REPLACE		0.1 0.5				1,2	
	SPRING ASSY, REAR (ALL EXCEPT M1028, M1028A1, M1028A2, & M1028A3)	INSPECT REPLACE		0.1	0.8			1,2,4,6	A
	SPRING ASSY, REAR (M1028, M1028A1, M1028A2, & M1028A3)	INSPECT REPLACE REPAIR		0.1	0.8 1.5			1,2,4,6 1,2,4,6	A A
	SHACKLE, LEAF SPRING	INSPECT REPLACE		0.1	0.5			1,4,6	
1604	SHOCK ABSORBERS	INSPECT REPLACE		0.1 0.4				1,2,4	
1605	SHAFT, FRONT STAB	INSPECT REPLACE REPAIR		0.1 0.7	0.4			1,2,4 1,2,4,6	A
	SHAFT, REAR STAB (M1028A2 & M1028A3)	INSPECT REPLACE		0.1 0.7				1,2,4	A A

Section II. MAINTENANCE ALLOCATION CHART - Continued

(1) Group Number	(2) Component/Assembly	(3) Maintenance Function	(4) Maintenance Level					(5) Tools and Equipment	(6) Remarks
			Unit		Inter-mediate		Depot		
			C	O	F	H	D		
18	BODY, CAB, HOOD, AND HULL								
1801	GUARD, RDTR GRL	INSPECT REPLACE	0.1	0.5				1,2	
	GRILLE ASSY, RDTR	INSPECT REPLACE	0.1	0.7				1,2	
	SUPPORT ASSY, RDTR	INSPECT REPLACE		0.1	1.0			1,2,4	
	COWL, TOP VENT PNL	INSPECT REPLACE	0.1	0.5				1,2	
	CABLE ASSY, HOOD LCH	INSPECT REPLACE		0.1 0.6				1,2	
	HOOD, ENG COMPT	INSPECT REPLACE	0.1	1.0				1,2	
	LATCH, HOOD	INSPECT SERVICE REPLACE	0.1 0.1	0.5				1,2 1,2	
	LATCH ASSY, HOOD SEC	INSPECT SERVICE REPLACE	0.1 0.1	0.5				1,2	
	INSTRUMENT PANEL TRIM	INSPECT REPLACE	0.1	0.5				1,2	
	CONTROL ASSY, VENT	INSPECT REPLACE		0.1	0.5			1,2	
	PANEL, INSTR	REPLACE REPAIR			1.5 1.0			1,2,4,6,8 1,2,4,6	

Section II.   MAINTENANCE ALLOCATION CHART - Continued

(1) Group Number	(2) Component/Assembly	(3) Maintenance Function	(4) Maintenance Level					(5) Tools and Equipment	(6) Remarks
			Unit		Inter- mediate		Depot		
			C	O	F	H	D		
1801 (Cont'd)	HANDLE ASSY, SIDE DOOR	INSPECT REPLACE	0.1	0.6				1,2,8	
	DOOR ASSY, CAB	INSPECT ALINE REPLACE		0.1 0.5 1.5				1,2,8 1,2,8	
	HINGE ASSY, DOOR	INSPECT SERVICE REPLACE		0.1 0.2 0.7				1,2,4	
	PANEL, INSIDE DOOR	INSPECT REPLACE	0.1	0.5				1,2,8	
	REGULATOR ASSY, DOOR WINDOW	INSPECT REPLACE		0.1 0.7				1,2,8	
	VENT ASSY, AIR	INSPECT REPLACE	0.1	0.7				1,2,8	
	CHANNEL, LIFT	INSPECT REPLACE		0.1 0.7				1,2,4	
	LOCK ASSY, DOOR	INSPECT REPLACE		0.1 0.7				1,2,4	
	CONTROL ASSY, FRONT DOOR	INSPECT REPLACE		0.1 0.5				1,2,4	
	BODY MOUNTS	INSPECT REPLACE		0.2 0.1	1.0			1,2,4	
	BODY UNIT ASSY, PU BOX	INSPECT REPLACE REPAIR	0.1	1.0 0.1	4.0			1,2,4 1,2,4,6,8	
	PANEL, WHL HSG (ALL EXCEPT M1009)	INSPECT REPLACE		0.1	0.6			1,2,4,5	

Section II. MAINTENANCE ALLOCATION CHART - Continued

(1) Group Number	(2) Component/Assembly	(3) Maintenance Function	(4) Maintenance Level					(5) Tools and Equipment	(6) Remarks
			Unit		Inter- mediate		Depot		
			C	O	F	H	D		
1801 (Cont'd)	PANEL, WHL HSG (M1009)	INSPECT REPLACE		0.1 0.5				 1,2,4	
	ENDGATE (ALL EXCEPT M1010)	INSPECT REPLACE REPAIR	0.1	 1.0 1.0				 1,2,4 1,2,4	
	REGULATOR, WINDOW ENDGATE (M1009)	INSPECT REPLACE		0.1 1.0				 1,2,4	
	LOCK UNIT, ENDGATE (M1009)	INSPECT REPLACE	0.1	 0.7				 1,2,4	
	LATCH ASSY, ENDGATE (M1009)	INSPECT SERVICE REPLACE	0.1 0.1	 0.5				 1,2	
	HANDLE ASSY, ENDGATE (M1009)	INSPECT REPLACE	0.1	 0.5				 1,2	
	TOP ASSY, REMOVABLE (M1009)	INSPECT REPLACE REPAIR	0.1		 1.0 1.0			 1,2,4 1,2,4	 B
1802	GLASS, SIDE DOORS	INSPECT REPLACE	0.1	 1.0				 1,2,8	
	GLASS, WSHLD & BACK WINDOW	INSPECT REPLACE	0.1		 1.5			 1,2,9	
	GLASS, SIDE WINDOW (M1009)	INSPECT REPLACE	0.1		 0.8			 1,2,9	
	GLASS, ENDGATE WINDOW (M1009)	INSPECT REPLACE	0.1	 0.5				 1,2	
	FRONT FENDER ASSY	INSPECT REPLACE REPAIR	0.1	 1.0	 1.0			 1,2,6 1,2	

Section II.   MAINTENANCE ALLOCATION CHART - Continued

(1) Group Number	(2) Component/Assembly	(3) Maintenance Function	(4) Maintenance Level Unit C	Unit O	Inter-mediate F	H	Depot D	(5) Tools and Equipment	(6) Remarks
1802 (Cont'd)	REAR FENDER ASSY (M1028A2 & M1028A3)	INSPECT REPLACE REPAIR	0.1	1.0	1.0			1,2,6 1,2	C
1805	MAT & INSULATOR FLOOR	INSPECT REPLACE	0.1		1.0			1,2,4	
1806	PAD ASSY, INSTR PANEL UPR TRIM	INSPECT REPLACE	0.1	1.0				1,2,4	
	BELT ASSY, SEAT	INSPECT REPLACE	0.1	0.5				1,2	
	SEATS	INSPECT REPLACE REPAIR	0.1	0.5 0.4	1.0			1,2,4 1,2,4	
	ADJUSTER ASSY, FRONT SEAT	INSPECT REPLACE REPAIR		0.1 0.7 1.0				1,2 1,2	
1808	RACK ASSY, COMMS ELEC	INSPECT REPLACE REPAIR	0.1	0.5 1.0				1,2 1,2,4	
	BRACKET, CHEM AGT	INSPECT REPLACE	0.1	0.3	0.4			1,2,5	
1812	AMBULANCE BODY	INSPECT REPLACE	0.2		8.0			1,2,4,6	
	BODYSIDE	INSPECT REPAIR	0.2		4.0			1,2,4	
	ROOF ASSY	INSPECT REPAIR	0.2		4.0			1,2,4	
	REAR FRAME ASSY	INSPECT REPAIR	0.2		4.0			1,2,4	

Section II. MAINTENANCE ALLOCATION CHART - Continued

(1) Group Number	(2) Component/Assembly	(3) Maintenance Function	(4) Maintenance Level					(5) Tools and Equipment	(6) Remarks
			Unit		Inter-mediate		Depot		
			C	O	F	H	D		
1812 (Cont'd)	FRONT FRAME ASSY	INSPECT REPAIR	0.2		4.0			1,2,4	
	LIGHT ASSY, FLOOD (M1010)	INSPECT REPLACE REPAIR	0.1	0.2 0.2				1,2 1,2	
	LIGHT ASSY, FLUOR (M1010)	INSPECT REPLACE REPAIR	0.1	0.3 0.2				1,2,4 1,2	
	LIGHT ASSY, BLACKOUT (M1010)	INSPECT REPLACE REPAIR	0.1	0.2 0.1				1,2 1,2	
	SWITCH ASSY, BLACKOUT (M1010)	INSPECT REPLACE REPAIR		0.1 0.3 0.2				1,2 1,2	
	DOOR ASSY, REAR (M1010)	INSPECT REPLACE REPAIR	0.1	1.5 1.0	1.0			1,2,4 1,2,4	
	LADDER, BOARDING (M1010)	INSPECT REPLACE REPAIR	0.1	0.3 0.5				1,2 1,2	
	STOWAGE BOX (M1010)	INSPECT REPLACE REPAIR	0.1	0.5 0.5				1,2,4 1,2,4	
	HARNESS, ACCESS	INSPECT TEST REPLACE	0.1	0.3	0.7			2 1,2,4	
	PANEL RELAY, PWR SPLY (M1010)	INSPECT REPLACE REPAIR		0.1	0.5 0.4			1,2,4 1,2,4	
	SEAT ASSY, ATT'S (M1010)	INSPECT REPLACE REPAIR	0.1	0.1 0.5				1,2 1,2	

Section II. MAINTENANCE ALLOCATION CHART - Continued

(1) Group Number	(2) Component/Assembly	(3) Maintenance Function	(4) Maintenance Level					(5) Tools and Equipment	(6) Remarks
			Unit		Inter-mediate		Depot		
			C	O	F	H	D		
1812 (Cont'd)	ITTER ASSY, UP R M1010)	INSPECT REPLACE REPAIR	0.1	0.1	0.2			1.2 1.2	
	ALF PARTITION (M1010	INSPECT REPAIR	0.1		0.5			1,2,4	
	IGHT ASSY, INTERIOR OCUS (M1010)	INSPECT REPLACE REPAIR	0.1	0.5 0.3				1.2 1.2	
	ATCH ASSY, DOOR M1010)	INSPECT REPLACE REPAIR	0.1	0.6 0.4				1.2 1.2	
	ULLMAN COLLAR M1010)	INSPECT REPLACE	0.1		1.5			1,2,4	
22	BODY, CHASSIS, AND ACCESSORY TEMS								
2201	ACKAGE, CARGO COV M1008 & M1008A1)	INSPECT REPLACE REPAIR	0.1	1.5 0.7				1.2 1.2	
	OP ASSY, CANVAS	INSPECT REPLACE REPAIR		0.1 0.2 0.5	1.0			1.2 1,2,6	
2202	LADE ASSY, WIPER	INSPECT REPLACE REPAIR	0.1	0.2 0.1				1.2 1.2	
	INK ASSY, WIPER	INSPECT REPLACE REPAIR		0.1 0.5 0.4				1.2 1.2	

Section II. MAINTENANCE ALLOCATION CHART - Continued

(1) Group Number	(2) Component/Assembly	(3) Maintenance	(4) Maintenance Level				(5) Equipment	(6) Remarks
			Unit	Inter- mediate		Depot		
			O	F	H	D		
2202 (Cont'd)	MOTOR, WSHLD WIPER	INSPECT REPLACE REPAIR	0.1	0.5 1.0			1,2,4 1,2,4	
	MIRROR ASSY, RV	INSPECT REPLACE	0.1	0.2			1,2,8	
	MIRROR ASSY, OUT RV	INSPECT REPLACE REPAIR	0.1	0.2 0.2			1,2,8 1,2,8	
	MOUNTS, ANTENNA	INSPECT REPLACE	0.1	0.6			1,2,4	
	BRACKET ASSY, RADIO MTG (M1009 & M1010)	INSPECT REPLACE	0.1	0.7	1.0		1,2,5	
2207	HEATER ASSY	INSPECT REPLACE REPAIR		0.1 1.0 0.4			1,2,4 1,2,4	
	CASE, HTR	INSPECT REPLACE REPAIR		0.1 0.2 0.2			1,2,4 1,2,4	
	BLOWER ASSY	REPLACE REPAIR		0.5 0.3			2,4 1,2,4	
	CONTROL ASSY	INSPECT REPLACE REPAIR	0.1	0.4 0.2			1,2,4 1,2,4	
	HOSES, HTR	INSPECT REPLACE	0.1	0.5			1,2	
	HEATER ASSY (M1010 PATIENT)	INSPECT REPLACE REPAIR	0.1	0.1 0.5 2.5			1,2,4 1,2,4	

Section II.   MAINTENANCE ALLOCATION CHART - Continued

(1) Group Number	(2) Component/Assembly	(3) Maintenance Function	(4) Maintenance Level					(5) Tools and Equipment	(6) Remarks
			Unit		Inter-mediate		Depot		
			C	O	F	H	D		
2207 (Cont'd)	FILTER ASSY (M1010 PATIENT)	INSPECT		0.1					
		SERVICE		0.2					
		REPLACE		0.3				1,2	
		REPAIR		0.2				1,2	
	CONTROL ASSY (M1010 PATIENT)	INSPECT	0.1						
		REPLACE		0.5				2,4	
		REPAIR			0.6			1,2,4	
	LINES & FITTINGS (M1010 PATIENT)	INSPECT	0.1						
		REPLACE		1.0	1.0			1,2,4	
	PUMP, FUEL ELEC (M1010 PATIENT)	INSPECT	0.1						
		TEST		0.2				1,2,4	
		REPLACE		0.5				1,2,4	
33	SPECIAL PURPOSE KITS								
3303	PUMP, FUEL, HTR	INSPECT	0.1						
		TEST		0.2					
		REPLACE		0.4				1,2	
	LINES, FUEL, HTR	INSPECT	0.1						
		REPLACE		0.5				1,2	
	HEATER COOLANT/ PERSONNEL (ENG COMPARTMENT)	INSPECT	0.1						
		TEST		0.5					
		REPLACE		1.0				1,2,4	
		REPAIR			2.5			1,2,4	
	WIRING, ELEC	INSPECT	0.1						
		TEST		0.2				1,2	
		REPLACE		0.5				1,2	
		REPAIR		0.2				1,2,4	
	BATTERY BOXES	INSPECT	0.1						
		REPLACE		4.0				1,2	

Section II.   MAINTENANCE ALLOCATION CHART - Continued

(1) Group Number	Component/Assembly	(3) Maintenance Function	(4) Maintenance Level					(5) Tools and Equipment	(6) Remarks
			Unit		Inter-mediate		Depot		
			C	O	F	H	D		
3303 (Cont'd)	DOMELIGHT	INSPECT	0.1						
		REPLACE		0.2				1,2	
		REPAIR		0.2				1,2	
	COVER, GRILLE RDTR	INSPECT	0.1						
		REPLACE		0.2				1,2	
		REPAIR			0.5			1,2,6	
	INSULATOR, HOOD ENG	INSPECT	0.1						
		REPLACE		0.2				1,2	
		REPAIR			0.5			1,2,6	
	INSULATOR, DOOR	INSPECT	0.1						
		REPLACE		0.5				1,2,6	
		REPAIR		1.0				1,2,6	
	INSULATOR, CARGO BOX	INSPECT	0.1	0.1					
		REPLACE		2.0				1,2	
		REPAIR			1.0			1,2,6	
	INSULATOR, FLOOR	INSPECT	0.1						
		REPLACE		1.0				1,2	
	WINTERIZATION HOSES & TUBES, ENG COMPT	INSPECT	0.1						
		REPLACE		1.0				1,2	
	CONTROL ASSY, HTR	INSPECT	0.1						
		TEST		0.3				1,2	
		REPLACE		0.5				1,2	
		REPAIR		1.5				1,2	
	PERSONNEL HEATER (CARGO AREA)	INSPECT	0.1						
		TEST		0.5					
		REPLACE		1.7				1,2,4	
		REPAIR			2.5			1,2,4,6	
	FILTER, FUEL, HTR	INSPECT		0.1					
		SERVICE		0.2				1,2	
		REPLACE		0.4				1,2	
		REPAIR		0.2				1,2	

Section II. IMAINTENANCE ALLOCATION CHART - Continued

(1) Group Number	(2) Component/Assembly	(3) Maintenance Function	(4) Maintenance Level					(5) Tools and Equipment	(6) Remarks
			Unit		Inter-mediate		Depot		
			C	O	F	H	D		
3307	SEAT ASSY, TROOP	INSPECT	0.1						
		REPLACE		1.0				1,2,4	
		REPAIR		1.0				1,2,4	
39	SEARCHLIGHT AND ELECTRICAL ILLUMI-NATING EQUIPMENT								
3901	SPOTLIGHT ASSY (M1010)	INSPECT	0.1						
		REPLACE		0.3				1,2	
		REPAIR		0.5				1,2	
47	GAGES, NONELEC-TRICAL								
4701	SPEEDOMETER ASSY	INSPECT		0.1					
		REPLACE		0.8				1,2,4	
	CABLE ASSY, SPDOM	REPLACE		0.5				1,2	
	GEAR, SPDOM	REPLACE			0.5			1,2,4	
52	AIR CONDITIONER								
5200	AIR CONDITIONER (M1010)	INSPECT	0.1	0.1					
		TEST			0.4				
		SERVICE			1.4			1,2,4	
		REPLACE			0.7			1,2,4	
		REPAIR			6.0			1,2,4,6	
	BOX ASSY, AIR OUT	REPLACE			1.5			1,2,4,6	
		REPAIR			0.6			1,2,4,6	
	PANEL ASSY, CONTROL	INSPECT	0.1						
		REPLACE		1.2				1,2,4	
		REPAIR		0.6				1,2,4	

Section II.   MAINTENANCE ALLOCATION CHART - Continued

(1) Group Number	(2) Component/Assembly	(3) Maintenance Function	(4) Maintenance Level					(5) Tools and Equipment	(6) Remarks
			Unit		Inter-mediate		Depot		
			C	O	F	H	D		
5200 (Cont'd)	FILTER, FRESH AIR	INSPECT		0.1					
		SERVICE		0.2				1,2	
		REPLACE		0.5				1,2	
	CASE ASSY, MAIN	INSPECT		0.1	0.1				
		REPLACE		1.5				1,2	
		REPAIR		0.5				1,2	
	COMPRESSOR ASSY, RFGT	INSPECT		0.1					
		TEST			0.4			1,2,6	
		SERVICE			1.4			1,2,6	
		REPLACE			1.0			1,2,9	
		REPAIR			2.0			1,2,4.10	A
	BRACKETS, MTG, COMPRESSOR	INSPECT	0.1						
		REPLACE		0.5				1,2	
	BELT, COMPRESSOR	INSPECT	0.1						
		ADJUST		0.2				1,2	
		REPLACE		0.3				1,2	
	LINES, RFGT	INSPECT	0.1	0.1					
		REPLACE			1.0			1,2,4	
	COVER ASSY	INSPECT	0.1						
		REPLACE		0.5				1,2	
		REPAIR		0.5				1,2	
	COIL, CONDENSER	INSPECT		0.1	0.1				
		REPLACE			1.0			1,2	
	COIL ASSY, EVAP	INSPECT			0.1				
		REPLACE			0.7			1,2,4	
		REPAIR			4.0			1,2,4	
	BLOWER ASSY, EVAP	INSPECT		0.1					
		REPLACE		0.5				1,2	
		REPAIR		0.3				1,2	

Section II. MAINTENANCE ALLOCATION CHART - Continued

(1) Group Number	(2) Component/Assembly	(3) Maintenance Function	(4) Maintenance Level					(5) Tools and Equipment	(6) Remarks
			Unit		Inter-me diate		Depot		
			C	O	F	H	D		
91	CBR EQUIPMENT								
9111	GAS-PARTICULATE FILTER **UNIT** (GPFU) SYSTEM (M1010)	INSPECT TEST SERVICE REPLACE REPAIR	0.1	0.3 0.2	0.3 1.0 2.0				

Section III. TOOL AND TEST EQUIPMENT REQUIREMENTS

(1) Tool or Test Equipment Reference Code	(2) Maintenance Level	(3) Nomenclature	(4) National/NATO Stock Number	(5) Tool Number
1	O	Tool Kit, General Mechanic's Automotive	5180-00-177-7033	
2	O	Shop Equipment, Automotive Maintenance and Repair, Unit Maintenance, Common No. 1	4910-00-754-0654	
3	O	Shop Equipment, Automotive Maintenance and Repair, Unit Maintenance, Common No. 1, Less Power	4910-00-754-0653	
4	O	Shop Equipment, Automotive Maintenance and Repair, Unit Maintenance, Common No. 2, Less Power	4910-00-754-0650	
5	O	Tool Kit, Welder's	5180-00-754-0661	
6	F, H	Shop Equipment, Automotive Maintenance and Repair, Field Maintenance	4910-00-754-0705	
7	F, H	Shop Equipment, Automotive Maintenance and Repair, Field Maintenance, Supplement	4910-00-754-0706	
		SPECIAL TOOL SET – UNIT MAINTENANCE		
8	O	TOOL KIT	5180-01-156-0466	J-33119
		Consisting of:		
		COMBINATION VALVE DEPRESSOR	4910-01-268-0255	J-23709
		HANDLE, DRIVER	5120-00-677-2259	J-8092
		INSERTER, BEARING, ANNULAR	5120-01-169-4878	J-23445-A
		WRENCH, NUT (Wheel Bearing)	5120-01-170-0628	J-26878-A
		WRENCH, OPEN END	5120-01-170-5473	J-33124
		WRENCH, NUT (Wheel Bearing)	5120-01-170-6664	J-34616
		BIT SET, SCREWDRIVER (Torx)	5120-01-178-6342	J-29843
		REMOVER, WHEEL BEARING (Outer)	5120-01-179-1034	J-24426
		PULLER, MECHANICAL (Pitman Arm)	5120-01-179-1318	J-6632-01
		INSTALLER, AXLE SEAL	4910-01-179-2516	J-29713
		INSTALLER, PULLEY, STEERING	4910-01-179-2517	J-25033-B
		REMOVER, CLIP, RETAINING	4910-01-179-2518	J-24595-B

Section III. TOOL AND TEST EQUIPMENT REQUIREMENTS - Continued

(1) Tool or Test Equipment Reference Code	(2) Maintenance Level	(3) Nomenclature	(4) National/NATO Stock Number	(5) Tool Number
8 (Cont'd)	O	REMOVER/INSTALLER, FUEL	4910-01-179-6340	J-24187
		SOCKET, OIL SWITCH	4910-01-179-6341	J-21757-03
		WRENCH, WHEEL BEARING	5120-01-180-0558	J-2222-C
		REMOVER, PULLEY, WATER	4910-01-181-1959	J-25034-B
		WRENCH, HUB NUT (Wheel Bearing)	5120-01-219-6753	J-6893-D
		BLOCK, VALVE GAGE	4820-01-179-4869	J-33043
	SPECIAL TOOL SET – DIRECT SUPPORT/INTERMEDIATE MAINTENANCE			
9	F	TOOL KIT	5180-01-155-3937	J-33120
		Consisting of:		
		CROWFOOT ATTACHMENT (Injection Line)	5120-00-189-7898	J-29698-A
		CROWFOOT ATTACHMENT (Fuel Line)	5120-00-224-7288	J-28402
		WRENCH, NUT (Differential)	5120-01-170-0627	J-24429
		INSERTER, BEARING, ANNULAR	5120-01-170-3279	J-23690
		ADAPTER, SOCKET WRENCH	5120-01-171-5233	J-29873
		REMOVER, ACCUMULATOR	4910-01-178-8864	J-26889
		GAGE ASSY, TIMING	4910-01-178-9788	J-29601
		PACKER, SEAL (Rear Main)	5120-01-179-1033	J-33154
		ADAPTER SET, BALL JOINT	4910-01-179-2515	J-23454-D
		COVER, MANIFOLD	4910-01-179-4870	J-29664-1
		REMOVER/INSTALLER (CV Joint)	4910-01-179-6339	J-23996
		LOCK PLATE COMPRESSION	4910-01-180-6155	J-23653-A
		INSTALLING TOOL (Weatherstrip)	5120-01-180-8592	J-26471
		SLEEVE, BALL STUD ADJUSTER	4910-01-181-1958	J-23447
		REMOVER, LOWER BALL JOINT	4910-01-182-2704	J-33122
		ADAPTER, SOCKET WRENCH	5120-01-183-8576	J-26871-A
		ADAPTER COMPRESSION	4910-01-238-2551	J-26999-30
		AXLE SPREADER		D-167
		ADAPTER SET USED WITH DD-914-P AND D-914-8		DD-914-95

Section III. TOOL AND TEST EQUIPMENT REQUIREMENTS - Continued

(1) Tool or Test Equipment Reference Code	(2) Maintenance Level	(3) Nomenclature	(4) National/NATO Stock Number	(5) Tool Number
		SPECIAL TOOL SET – GENERAL SUPPORT MAINTENANCE		
10	H	TOOL KIT	5180-01-155-3938	J-33121
		Consisting of:		
		WRENCH, SPANNER	5120-01-082-6436	J-7624
		INSTALLATION TOOL	5120-01-082-6448	J-7728
		REMOVER, BEARING, ANNULAR	5120-01-169-4876	J-29168
		INSERTER, BEARING, ANNULAR	5120-01-169-4877	J-21465-1
		INSERTER, BEARING, ANNULAR	5120-01-170-3278	J-29167
		CROWFOOT ATTACHMENT	5120-01-170-4436	J-33125
		COMPRESSOR, CLUTCH	5120-01-170-6703	J-34502
		PROTECTOR, SEAL	4910-01-178-0360	J-21409
		PROTECTOR, INNER SEAL	4910-01-178-0713	J-21363
		GAGE, PIN SELECTOR	4910-01-178-0722	J-21370
		CLUTCH REBUILDER, MO	4910-01-178-0724	J-23327
		PROTECTOR, INNER SEAL	4910-01-178-6551	J-21362
		HOLDING UNIT, GEAR	4910-01-178-8865	J-21795-02
		GAGE, PINION SETTING	4910-01-178-8866	J-21777-500
		PUNCH, HAND TOOL	5120-01-179-1032	J-21552
		SEAL INSTALLER, BEARING	4910-01-179-5530	J-29162
		INSTALLER, HUB & DRIVE	4910-01-179-6338	J-9480-B
		PULLER, DRIVE SPROCKET	4910-01-179-6364	J-26941
		WASHER, SHOULDERED	5310-01-179-9486	J-8107-2
		REMOVER, BUSHING	5120-01-180-7928	J-26252
		REMOVER, SPROCKET SUPPORT	4910-01-181-0183	J-29369-1
		GAGE, BEARING PRELOAD	4910-01-183-0044	J-22779
		PULLER, BEARING, CAM	5120-01-206-3818	J-35178

Section IV. REMARKS

(1) Reference Code	(2) Remarks
A	In this category, the needed tool to perform the required maintenance function was not listed in one of the tool sets shown in Section III of this MAC. If this tool is not available at the maintenance level that is performing the maintenance function on the component, the tool can be found in the *GSA Catalogue*. These tools consist of: PLIERS, SLIP JOINT . . . . 5120-00-223-7396 SOCKET . . . . 5130-00-227-6683 SOCKET . . . . 5120-00-235-5898 COMPRESSOR, PISTON RING . . . . 5120-00-250-6055 GAGE . . . . 5210-00-274-2857 PLIERS, SLIP JOINT . . . . 5120-00-278-0350 SOCKET, CROWFOOT . . . . 5120-00-317-8076 WRENCH, ADJUSTER . . . . 5120-00-449-8084 WRENCH, TORQUE . . . . 5120-00-541-3001 PLIERS, HOG RING . . . . 5120-00-595-9547 TOOL KIT, CANVAS REPAIR . . . . 5180-00-754-0731 REMOVAL TOOL, OIL FILTER . . . . 5120-00-865-0933 MALLET, WOOD 5120-00-926-7116
B	In this category, no specific times can be established. Time required for repair/overhaul will depend on the extent of the repair required for the damaged components.
C	If body side panel is also damaged and must be replaced, side panel must be cut using modification template to accept fender flares.

APPENDIX C
EXPENDABLE/DURABLE SUPPLIES AND MATERIALS LIST

Section I. INTRODUCTION

C-1. SCOPE.

This appendix lists expendable/durable supplies and materials you will need to maintain the CUCV Series trucks. This listing is for informational purposes only and is not authority to requisition the listed items. These items are authorized to you by CTA 50-970, *Expendable/Durable Items (Except Medical, Class V, Repair Parts, and Heraldic Items),* or CTA 8-100, *Army Medica l Department Expendable/Durable Items.*

C-2. EXPLANATION OF COLUMNS.

a. **Column (1) - Item Number.** This number is assigned to the entry in the listing and is referenced in the *Initial Setup* of applicable tasks under the heading of *Materials/Parts.*

b. **Column (2) - Level.** This column identifies the lowest level of maintenance that requires the listed item.

       C - Operator/Crew
       O - Unit Maintenance

c. **Column (3) - National Stock Number.** This is the National Stock Number assigned to the item; use it to request or requisition the item.

d. **Column (4) - Description** . Indicates the Federal item name and, if required, a description to identify the item. The last line for each item indicates the Federal Supply Code for Manufacturer (FSCM) in parentheses, followed by the part number, if applicable.

e. **Column (5) - Unit of Measure (U/M).** Indicates the measure used in performing the actual maintenance function. This measure is expressed by an alphabetical abbreviation (e.g., ea, in, pr, gal). If the unit of measure differs from the unit of issue, requisition the lowest unit of issue that will satisfy your requirements.

Section II. EXPENDABLE/DURABLE SUPPLIES AND MATERIALS LIST

(1) Item Number	(2) Level	(3) National Stock Number	(4) Description	(5) U/M
1.	O	5935-00-322-8959	ADAPTER: Connector (19207) 11677570	ea
2.	O	8040-00-262-9028	ADHESIVE: General Purpose, Type 1 (19203) 829899	pt
2.1.	O	8040-00-024-6991	ADHESIVE: (Interior Rearview Mirror) (11862) 1052369	ea
3.	C		ANTIFREEZE: Arctic (81349) MIL-A-11755	
		6850-00-174-1806	55 Gallon Drum	gal
4.	C		ANTIFREEZE: Ethylene Glycol, Inhibited, Heavy-duty, Single Package (81349) MIL-A-46153	
		6850-00-181-7929	1 Gallon Can	gal
		6850-00-181-7933	5 Gallon Can	gal
		6850-00-181-7940	55 Gallon Drum	gal
5.	O		BARRIER MATERIAL: Greaseproof (81349) MIL-B-121	
		8135-00-171-0930	100 Yard Roll	yd
6.	C		BRAKE FLUID: Silicone, Automotive, All Weather, Operational and Preservative (81349) MIL-B-46176	
		9150-01-102-9455	1 Gallon Can	gal
		9150-01-123-3152	5 Gallon Can	gal
		9150-01-072-8379	55 Gallon Drum	gal
7.	O	2590-00-398-6527	CABLE: 20 Feet, without Connectors (19207) 11682337-1	ea
8.	O	6150-01-022-6004	CABLE: with End Connectors (19207) 11682336-1	ea
9.	O		CHALK, MARKING: (81348) SS-C-255	
		7510-00-223-6701	1 Gross	gr
10.	C		CLEANING COMPOUND: Windshield Washer (81348) O-C-1901	
		6850-00-926-2275	1 Pint Bottle	pt
11.	O		COATING: Aliphatic Polyurethane, Chemical Agent Resistant, Forest Green (81349) MIL-C-46168C	
		8010-00-111-7937	1 Gallon Can	gal
		8010-00-111-8010	5 Gallon Can	gal

Section II. EXPENDABLE/DURABLE SUPPLIES AND
MATERIALS LIST - Continued

(1) Item Number	(2) Level	(3) National Stock Number	(4) Description	(5) U/M
12.	O	2510-00-567-0128	CONNECTOR, PLUG: (19207) 11682338	ea
13.	O		CORROSION PREVENTIVE COMPOUND: (81349) MIL-C-11796	
		8030-00-231-2354	5 Pound Carton	lb
14.	C		DETERGENT; General Purpose, Liquid (81349) MIL-D-16791	
		7930-00-282-9699	1 Gallon Can	gal
15.	C		DRY CLEANING SOLVENT: Type II (81348) P-D-680	
		6850-00-110-4498	1 Pint Can	pt
		6850-00-274-5421	5 Gallon Can	gal
		6850-00-285-8011	55 Gallon Drum	gal
16.	C		FUEL OIL DIESEL: Arctic, DF-A (81348) VV-F-800	
		9140-00-286-5282	5 Gallon Can	gal
		9140-00-286-5284	55 Gallon Drum	gal
17.	C		FUEL OIL DIESEL: Arctic, DF-2 (81348) VV-F-800	
		9140-00-286-5295	5 Gallon Can	gal
		9140-00-286-5296	55 Gallon Drum	gal
18.	C		FUEL OIL DIESEL: Winter, DF-1 (81348) VV-F-800	
		9140-00-286-5287	5 Gallon Can	gal
		9140-00-286-5288	55 Gallon Drum	gal
19.	O	5920-01-123-5212	FUSE: 5 amp (11862) 12004005	ea
20.	O	5920-01-123-5211	FUSE: 10 amp (11862) 12004007	ea
21.	O	5920-01-149-6952	FUSE: 15 amp (11862) 12004008	ea
22.	O	5920-01-085-0825	FUSE: 20 amp (11862) 12004009	ea

Section II. EXPENDABLE/DURABLE SUPPLIES AND MATERIALS LIST - Continued

(1) Item Number	(2) Level	(3) National Stock Number	(4) Description	(5) U/M
23.	O	5920-01-149-6953	FUSE: 25 amp (11862) 12004010	ea
24.	O	5920-01-188-6294	FUSE: 30 amp (11862) 12004011	ea
25.	O	5210-01-222-8068	GAGE: Plastic Adjustment (11862) 14061396	ea
26.	C		GREASE: Automotive and Artillery (81349) MIL-G-10924	
		9150-00-935-1017	14 Ounce Cartridge	oz
		9150-00-190-0904	1-3/4 Pound Can	lb
		9150-00-190-0905	6-1/2 Pound Can	lb
27.	O		GREASE: Molybdenum, Disulfide (81348) MIL-G-21164	
		9150-00-935-4018	6 Ounce Tube	oz
28.	C		HYDRAULIC FLUID: Transmission (24617) Dexron®II	
		9150-00-698-2382	1 Quart Can	qt
		9150-00-657-4959	5 Gallon Can	gal
29.	C		INHIBITOR: Corrosion, Liquid Cooling System (81349) MIL-A-53009	
		6850-00-160-3868	1 Quart Can	qt
30.	O		LOCTITE: (24617) 9985283	
31.	C		LUBRICATING OIL: Gear, Multipurpose, GO 75W (81349) MIL-L-2105	
		9150-01-035-5390	1 Quart Can	qt
		9150-01-035-5391	5 Gallon Can	gal
32.	C		LUBRICATING OIL: Gear, Multipurpose, GO 80/90 (81349) MIL-L-2105	
		9150-01-035-5392	1 Quart Can	qt
		9150-01-035-5393	5 Gallon Can	gal
33.	C		LUBRICATING OIL: General Purpose, Preservative, PL-S (81348) VVL800	
		9150-00-231-6689	1 Quart Can	qt

Section II. EXPENDABLE/DURABLE SUPPLIES AND MATERIALS LIST - Continued

(1) Item Number	(2) Level	(3) National Stock Number	(4) Description	(5) U/M
34.	C		LUBRICATING OIL: Internal Combustion Engine, Arctic, OEA (81349) MIL-L-46167	
		9150-00-402-4478	1 Quart Can	qt
		9150-00-402-2372	5 Gallon Can	gal
		9150-00-491-7197	55 Gallon Drum	gal
35.	C		LUBRICATING OIL: Internal Combustion Engine, Tactical Service, OE/HDO 10 (81349) MIL-L-2104	
		9150-00-189-6727	1 Quart Can	qt
		9150-00-186-6668	5 Gallon Can	gal
		9150-00-191-2772	55 Gallon Drum	gal
36.	C		LUBRICATING OIL: Internal Combustion Engine, Tactical Service, OE/HDO 15W/40 (81349) MIL-L-2104	
		9150-01-152-4117	1 Quart Can	qt
		9150-01-152-4118	5 Gallon Can	gal
		9150-01-152-4119	55 Gallon Drum	gal
37.	C		LUBRICATING OIL: Internal Combustion Engine, Tactical Service, OE/HDO 30 (81349) MIL-L-2104	
		9150-00-186-6681	1 Quart Can	qt
		9150-00-188-9858	5 Gallon Can	gal
		9150-00-189-6729	55 Gallon Drum	gal
38.	O		PRESERVATIVE COMPOUND: (331 50) X975	
		8030-01-220-1442	4 Ounce with Spray	oz
		8030-01-220-1441	8 Ounce with Spray	oz
		8030-01-220-1440	32 Ounce Bottle	oz
39.	O		PRIMER: Epoxy Coating (81349) MIL-P-521928	
		8010-00-264-8866	Kit	ea
40.	C		RAG: Wiping, Cotton and Cotton-Synthetic (58536) A-A-531	
		7920-00-205-1711	50 Pound Bale	lb
41.	O		SEALANT: Silicone, RTV (1 1862) 1052734	
		8030-01-159-4844	8-1/2 Ounce Tube	oz

Section II. EXPENDABLE/DURABLE SUPPLIES AND
MATERIALS LIST - Continued

(1) Item Number	(2) Level	(3) National Stock Number	(4) Description	(5) U/M
42.	O		SEALING COMPOUND: Corrosion-resistant, Type II (81349) MIL-S-81733	
		8030-00-009-5023	Kit	ea
43.	O		SEALING COMPOUND: Pipe. Anaerobic, with Teflon (05972) 592-31	
		8030-01-054-0740	50 Milliliter Tube	ml
44.	O		STRAP: Tie-down (06383) MS 3367-1-9	
		5975-00-074-2072	Box of 100	ea
45.	O	9905-00-537-8954	TAG: Marker, 50 Each (81349) MIL-T-12755	ea
46.	O		TAPE: Antiseize, 1/2 inch width (81349) MIL-T-27730A	
		8030-00-889-3535	260 Inch Roll	in
47.	O		TAPE: Duct, 2 inch width (07124) C-519	
		5640-00-103-2254	60 Yard Roll	yd
48.	O		TAPE: Pressure Sensitive Adhesive, Masking, Flat. 2 inch width (81349) MIL-T-2397	
		7510-00-473-9513	60 Yard Roll	yd
48.1.	O		TAPE: Pressure Sensitive Adhesive, Red. Flat. 1/2 inch width (52170) 650	
		7510-00-550-7126	72 Yard Roll	yd
49.	O	4720-00-964-1433	TUBE: Plastic Drain (81346) D1248-60TTYPE1 CLASSAGRADE4	ft
50.	O		TWINE: Fibrous, Cotton (String), 16-Ply (81348) T-T-871	
		4020-00-291-5901	375 Yard Spool	yd

APPENDIX D
ILLUSTRATED LIST OF MANUFACTURED ITEMS

Section I. INTRODUCTION

D-1.   SCOPE.

a. This appendix includes complete instructions for making items authorized to be manufactured or fabricated at unit maintenance.

b. A part number index in alphanumeric order is provided for cross-referencing the part number of the item to be manufactured to the figure which covers fabrication criteria. Items requiring complicated manufacturing instructions will be illustrated with dimensions and locations of holes to be drilled. Items requiring simple manufacturing instructions will not be illustrated.

c. All bulk materials needed for manufacture of an item are listed by National Stock Number, part number, or specification number in the manufacturing instructions.

d. All dimensions given in Section II, *Illustrated Manufacturing Instructions,* are in inches, except as noted.

Table D-1. Manufactured Items Part Number Cross-reference

PART NUMBER	FIGURE NUMBER	PART NUMBER	FIGURE NUMBER	PART NUMBER	FIGURE NUMBER
FLW-12	D-14	14063352	D-55	14076222	D-33
MS18029-13L-3	D-12	14063353	D-56	14076229	D-36
MS18029-13L-5	D-12	14063370	D-27	14076232	D-34
MS27212-4-3	D-13	14063373	D-27	14076271	D-37
MS27212-4-5	D-13	14066305	D-2	14076272	D-38
XX123	D-21	14072337	D-15	14076273	D-39
10012288	D-27	14072430	D-10	14076274	D-39
14027542	D-24	14074444	D-27	14076275	D-40
14033823	D-11	14074446	D-27	14076276	D-40
14040775	D-19	14074447	D-27	14076277	D-41
14041258	D-7	14074449	D-27	14076278	D-41
14063341	D-44	14074453	D-27	14076279	D-42
14063342	D-52	14075856	D-27	14076280	D-42
14063343	D-45	14075862	D-54	14076281	D-43
14063344	D-46	14075863	D-54	14076802	D-54
14063345	D-53	14075864	D-54	14076803	D-54
14063346	D-47	14075883	D-29	14076864	D-31
14063347	D-48	14075884	D-29	14076871	D-32
14063348	D-49	14076201	D-35	14076872	D-32
14063350	D-50	14076209	D-30	1488565	D-20
14063351	D-51	14076212	D-31	15590415	D-22

Table D-1. Manufactured Items Part Number Cross-reference (Continued)

PART NUMBER	FIGURE NUMBER	PART NUMBER	FIGURE NUMBER	PART NUMBER	FIGURE NUMBER
337714	D-26	3782732	D-26	9439048	D-17
15593599	D-28	474935	D-19	9439059	D-4
15599916	D-34	482995	D-27	9439068	D-4
15599235	D-34.1	487425	D-27	9439088	D-18
326560	D-35.1	6263870	D-3	9439091	D-18
329198	D-25	6263871	D-3	9439092	D-9
350371	D-20	8919163	D-16	9439117	D-5
365953	D-23	9438227	D-8	9439120	D-5
365953-1	D-23	9438999	D-6	9439128	D-5
3773684	D-19	9439004	D-6	9439363	D-1
3782730	D-25	9439010	D-6		

Section II. ILLUSTRATED MANUFACTURING INSTRUCTIONS

1. Fabricate from rubber hose, ¼ in. inside diameter, stock size 25 ft. long, NSN 4720-01-163-7833.

2. Cut to 3 in. long for Part Number 9439363.

Figure D-1. Nonmetallic Hose.

---

1. Fabricate from NSN 4720-01-184-0433, Part Number 14066306, FSCM 11862.

2. Cut to 7.01 in. long for Part Number 14066305.

Figure D-2. Fuel Drainback Hose.

---

1. Fabricate from fuel tank insulator, stock size 7 in. x 22 in., NSN 2590-01-155-7711.

2. Cut to 19.24 in. long for Part Number 6263870.

3. Cut to 15.75 in. long for Part Number 6263871.

Figure D-3. Fuel Tank Insulators.

---

1. Fabricate from rubber hose, 5/16 in. inside diameter, stock size 25 ft, long, NSN 4720-01-156-0547.

2. Cut to 7.48 in. long for Part Number 9439068.

3. Cut to 3.94 in. long for Part Number 9439059.

Figure D-4. Fuel Tank Drain Hose.

---

1. Fabricate from rubber hose, 3/8 in. inside diameter, stock size 25 ft. long, NSN 4720-01-156-0548.

2. Cut to 8.27 in. long for Part Number 9439128.

3. Cut to 3.94 in. long for Part Number 9439117.

4. Cut to 5.12 in. long for Part Number 9439120.

Figure D-5. Fuel Feed Hose.

Section II.   ILLUSTRATED MANUFACTURING INSTRUCTIONS
Continued

1.   Fabricate from rubber hose, ¼ in.   inside diameter, stock size 25 ft. long,
     NSN 4720-01-156-0549.

2.   Cut to 7.48 in. long for Part Number 9439010.

3.   Cut to 3.94 in. long for Part Number 9438999.

4.   Cut to 5.12 in. long for Part Number 9439004.

Figure D-6. Fuel Return Hose.

_____

1.   Fabricate from rubber hose, 5/8 in.   inside diameter, stock size 25 ft. long,
     NSN 4720-01-182-3457.

2.   Cut to 6.50 in. long for Part   Number 14041258.

Figure D-7.   Fuel Tank Fill Vent   Hose.

_____

1.   Fabricate from rubber hose, ¼ in.   inside diameter, stock size 25 ft. long,
     NSN 4720-01-155-7784.

2.   Cut to 9.84 in. long for Part Number 9438227.

Figure D-8. Fuel Return Hose.

_____

1.   Fabricate from rubber hose, 5/16 in.   inside diameter, stock size 25 ft. long,
     NSN 4720-01-156-0547.

2.   Cut to 25.59 in. long for Part Number 9439092.

Figure D-9. Fuel Filter Drain Hose.

_____

1.   Fabricate from rubber hose, 3/8 in.   inside diameter, stock size 24 ft. long,
     NSN 4720-01-159-5796.

2.   Cut to 59.00 in. long for Part Number 9439068.

Figure D-10. Coolant Reservoir Hose.

_____

Section II. ILLUSTRATED MANUFACTURING INSTRUCTIONS - Continued

1. Fabricate from heater hose, 5/8 in. inside diameter, stock size 25 ft. long, NSN 4720-00-432-1179.

2. Cut to 4.25 in. long for Part Number 14033823.

Figure D-11. Thermostat Bypass Hose.

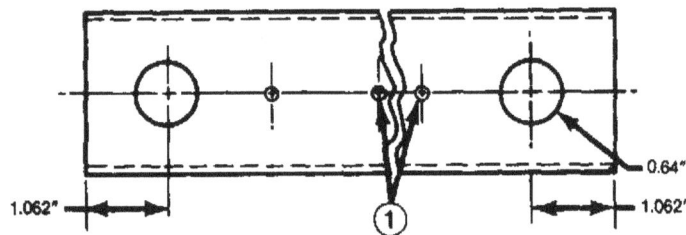

1. Fabricate from cover, stock size 12.041 in. long, NSN 5490-00-984-9088.

2. Count off 3 dimplings (1) from end of stock for Part Number MS18029-13L-3. Using dimpling as a center point, drill 0.64 in. diameter hole through first and third dimpling. Cut stock 1.062 in. from center of each hole, Total length will be 6.664 in.

3. Count off 5 dimplings (1) from end of stock for Part Number MS18029-13L-5. Using dimpling as a center point, drill 0.64 in. diameter hole through first and fifth dimpling. Cut stock 1.062 in. from center of each hole, Total length will be 9.664 in.

Figure D-12. Cover.

Section II. ILLUSTRATED MANUFACTURING INSTRUCTIONS - Continued

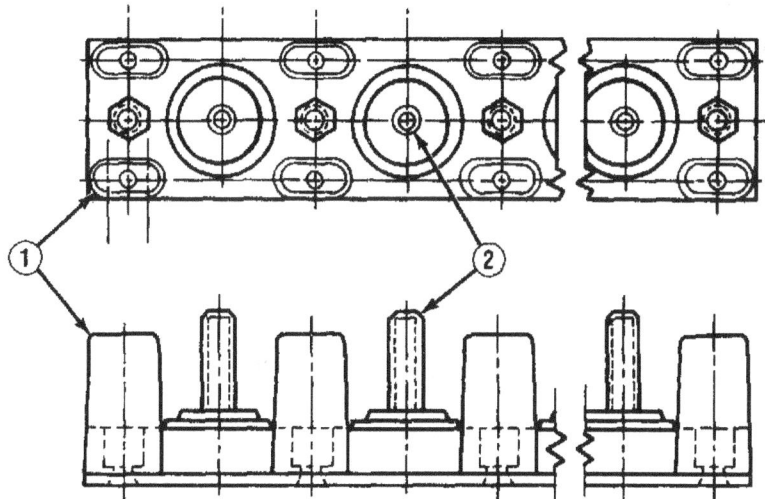

1. Fabricate from board, stock size 12.041 in. long, NSN 5940-00-753-7753.

2. Count off 4 pairs of flanges (1) from end of stock for Part Numbe   r
    MS27212-4-3. There will be a total of 3 studs (2) between these flanges. Cut
    stock 5.124 in. from outside of first pair of flanges to outside of fourth pair of
    flanges.

3. Count off 6 pairs of flanges (1) from end of stock for Part Numbe   r
    MS27212-4-5. There will be a total of 5 studs (2) between these flanges. Cut
    stock 8.124 in. from outside of first pair of flanges to outside of sixth pair of
    flanges.

Figure D-13. Accessory Wiring Terminal Board.

1. Fabricate from fuse link conductor, 3.0 mm diameter   ,   12 gage ,
    NSN 5920-01-219-0793.

2. Cut to 10 in. long for Part Number FLW-12.

Figure D-14. Fuse Link Wire.

TA49688

Section II. ILLUSTRATED MANUFACTURING INSTRUCTIONS - Continued

1. Fabricate from NSN 6150-01-159-6901, Part Number 14072336, FSCM 11862.

2. Cut 3.625 in. from 1 end for Part Number 14072337.

Figure D-15. Connector Link.

1. Fabricate from conduit, ½ in. inside diameter, stock size 15 ft. long, NSN 5975-01-160-8458.

2. Cut to 6.00 in. long for Part Number 8919163.

Figure D-16. Battery Booster Cable Conduit.

1. Fabricate from rubber hose, 5/16 in.   inside diameter, stock size 25 ft. long, NSN 4720-01-156-0547.

2. Cut to 1.77 in.   long for Part Number 9439048.

Figure D-17. Transfer Case Vent Hose.

1. Fabricate from rubber hose, 5/16 in. inside diameter, stock size 25 ft. long, NSN 4720-01-156-0547.

2. Cut to 20.67 in. long for Part Number 9439088.

3. Cut to 23.62 in. long for Part Number 9439091.

Figure D-18. Front Axle Vent Hose.

1$_0$ Fabricate from rubber hose, 5/16 in. inside diameter, stock size 25 ft. long, NSN 4720-01-148-2768.

2. Cut to 14.38 in. long for Part Number 14040775.

3. Cut to 24.00 in. long for Part Number 474935.

Figure D-19. Rear Axle Vent Hose.

Section II. ILLUSTRATED MANUFACTURING INSTRUCTIONS - Continued

1. Fabricate from rubber hose, 3/8 in. inside diameter, stock size 10 ft. long, NSN 4720-01-154-1241.

2. Cut to 1.75 in. long for Part Number 350371.

3. Cut to 20.50 in. long for Part Number 1488565.

4. Cut to 13.00 in. long for Part Number 3773684.

Figure D-20. Power Steering Hose.

1. Fabricate from chain, NSN 4010-00-129-3221.

2. Cut to 5.00 in. long for Part Number XX123.

Figure D-21. Pintle Chain.

1. Fabricate from front door trim panel seal, stock size 46.50 in. x 0.36 in. x 0.50 in., NSN 5330-01-096-7698.

2. Cut as required to fit for Part Number 15590415.

Figure D-22. Front Door Trim Panel Seal.

1. Fabricate from filler, stock size 0.047 in. x 100 ft. long, NSN 5330-00-753-8036.

2. Cut to 25.62 in. long for Part Number 365953.

3. Cut to 25.10 in. long for Part Number 365953-1.

Figure D-23. Glass Channel Filler.

1. Fabricate from filler, stock size 0.047 in. x 100 ft. long, NSN 5330-00-753-8036.

2. Cut to 60.00 in. long for Part Number 14027542.

Figure D-24. Endgate Sash Filler.

Section II. ILLUSTRATED MANUFACTURING   INSTRUCTIONS -
Continued

1. Fabricate from vacuum hose, 7/32 in. inside diameter, stock size 25 ft. long, NSN 4720-01-096-7718.

2. Cut to 46.00 in. long for Part Number 3782730.

3. Cut to 7.00 in. long for Part Number 329198.

Figure D-25. Pump Assembly Hose.

1. Fabricate from rubber hose, 5/32 in. inside diameter, stock size 25 ft. long, NSN 4720-00-230-6523.

2. Cut to 16.00 in. long for Part Number 337714.

3. Cut to 36.00 in. long for Part Number 3782732.

Figure D-26. Nozzle Assembly Hose.

1. Fabricate from heater hose, 5/8 in. inside diameter, stock size 25 ft. long, NSN 4720-00-432-1179.

2. Cut to 48,00 in. long for Part Number 487425.

3. Cut to 42.00 in. long for Part Number 482995.

4. Cut to 44.75 in. long for Part Number 10012288.

5. Cut to 43.00 in. long for Part Number 14063370.

6. Cut to 23.00 in. long for Part Number 14063373.

7. Cut to 24.00 in. long for Part Number 14065856.

8. Cut to 28.75 in. long for Part Number 14074444.

9. Cut to 3.00 in. long for Part Number 14074446.

10. Cut to 2.50 in. long for Part Number 14074447.

11. Cut to 21.50 in. long for Part Number 14074449.

12. Cut to 11.00 in. long for Part Number 14074453.

Figure D-27. Heater Hose.

Section II.   ILLUSTRATED MANUFACTURING INSTRUCTIONS - Continued

1.   Fabricate from insulator, NSN 2510-01-162-7224.

2.   Cut as required to fit for Part Number 15593599.

Figure D-28. Hood Insulator.

---

1.   Fabricate from metal strip, NSN 9510-00-516-5737.

2.   Cut to 24.20 in, long for Part Number 14075883.

2.   Cut to 29.62 in. long for Part Number 14075884.

Figure D-29. Retainer.

---

1.   Fabricate from softwood plywood, 1 in. thick, NSN 5530-00-129-7889.

2.   Using Figure FO-1, cut to dimensions shown and drill holes as indicated for Part Number 14076209.

3.   Remove all burrs.

4.   Treat and seal wood per MIL-T-704J, paragraph 3.2.4. Prime with epoxy primer coating (Item 39, Appendix C), per MIL-STD-I 93. Finish paint lusterless forest green (Item 11, Appendix C) on both sides.

Figure D-30. Rear Door.

---

1.   Fabricate from Part Number NSN 5330-01-163-5850, 14076235, FSCM 11862.

2.   Using 2 x stock material, cut to 30.60 in. long for Part Number 14076864.

3.   Using 4 x stock material, cut to 56.38 in. long for Part Number 14076212.

Figure D-31. Gasket.

Section II. ILLUSTRATED MANUFACTURING   INSTRUCTIONS-
Continued

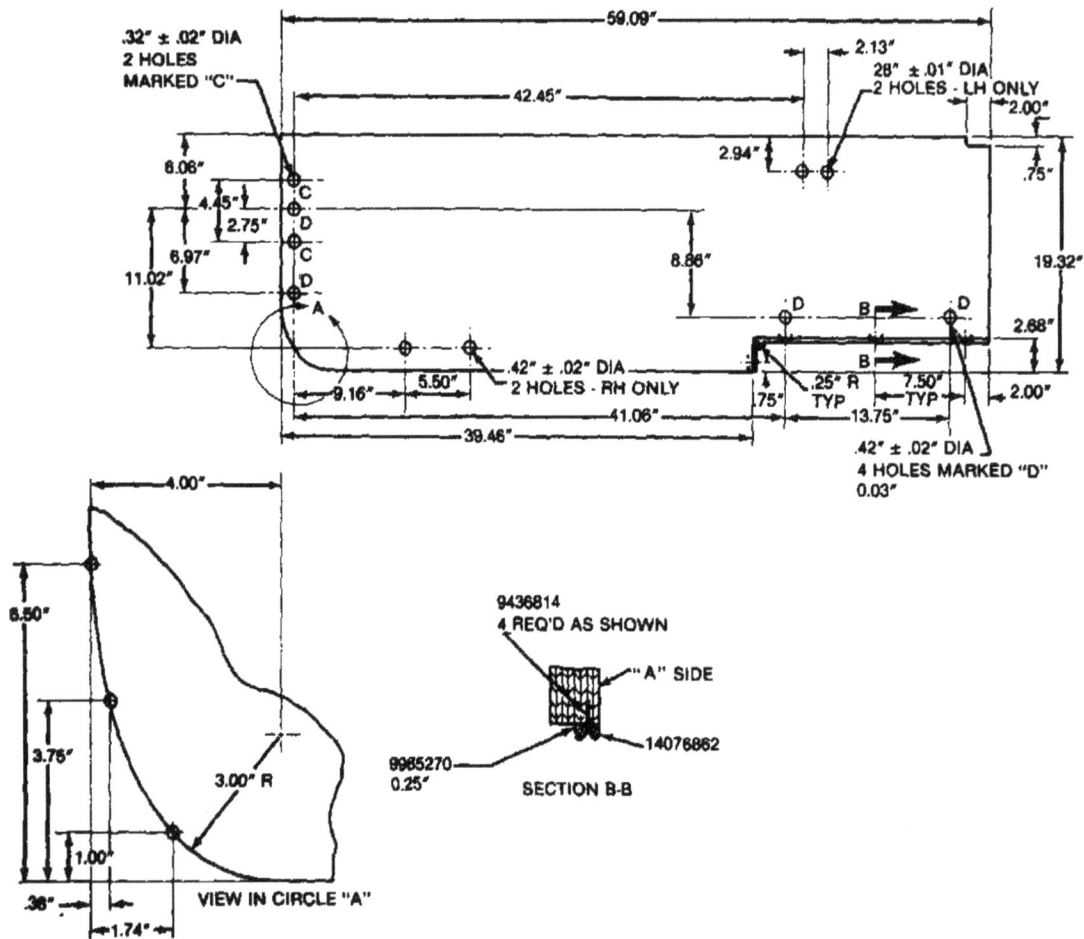

1.   Fabricate from softwood plywood, 1 in. thick, NSN 5530-00-129-7889.

2.   Cut to dimensions shown for Part Numbers 14076871 and 14076872.

NOTE

Part Number 14076871 is the left half (LH) panel and 14076872 is the right half (RH) panel. Only drill holes indicated for part to be fabricated.

3.   Drill holes as indicated.

4.   Remove all burrs.

5.   Treat and seal wood per MIL-T-704J, paragraph 3.2.4. Prime with epoxy primer coating (Item 39, Appendix C), per MIL-STD-193. Finish paint lusterless forest green (Item 11, Appendix C) on both sides.

Figure D-32. Panel Assembly.

TA49689

Section II. ILLUSTRATED MANUFACTURING INSTRUCTIONS - Continued

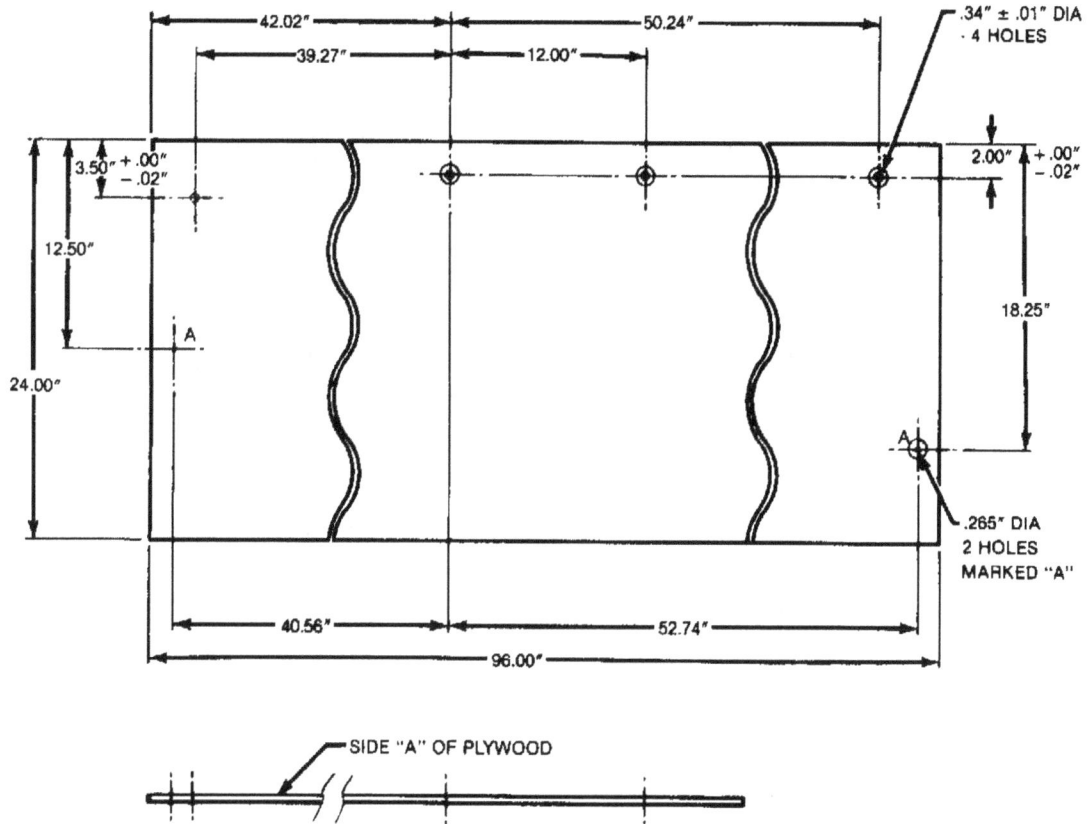

1. Fabricate from softwood plywood, ¼ in. thick, NSN 5530-00-129-7721.

2. Cut to 24.00 in. x 96.00 in. and drill holes as indicated for Part Number 14076222.

3. Remove all burrs.

4. Treat and seal wood per MIL-T-704J, paragraph 3.2.4. Prime with epoxy primer coating (Item 39, Appendix C), per MIL-STD-193. Finish paint lusterless forest green (Item 11, Appendix C) on both sides.

Figure D-33. Roof Panel.

TA49690

Section II. ILLUSTRATED MANUFACTURING INSTRUCTIONS - Continued

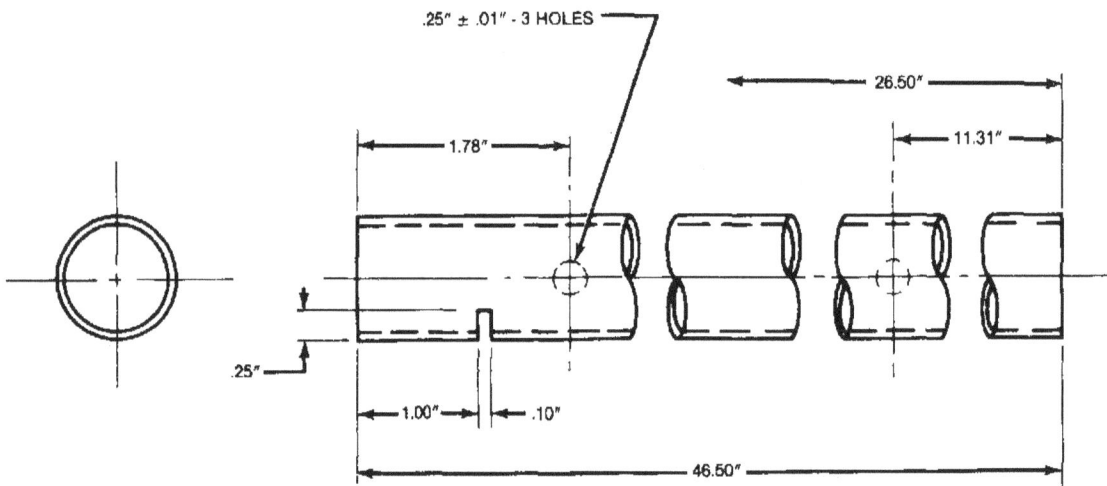

1.   Fabricate from metallic tube, 1 in. outside diameter, NSN 4720-00-288-7928.

2.   Cut to dimensions shown and drill holes as indicated for Part Number 14076232.

3.   Cut to 46.50 in. long for Part Number 15599916.

4.   Remove all burrs.

Figure D-34. Support.

1.   Fabricate from steel tubing, ¼ in. outside diameter, stock size 25 ft. long, NSN 4720-01-161-0138.

2.   Cut to 49.11 in. long for Part Number 15599235.

3.   Use old pipe as a guide and bend steel tubing to same shape.

Figure D-34.1. Transmission Vacuum Modulator Pipe.

TA49691

Section II. ILLUSTRATED MANUFACTURING INSTRUCTIONS - Continued

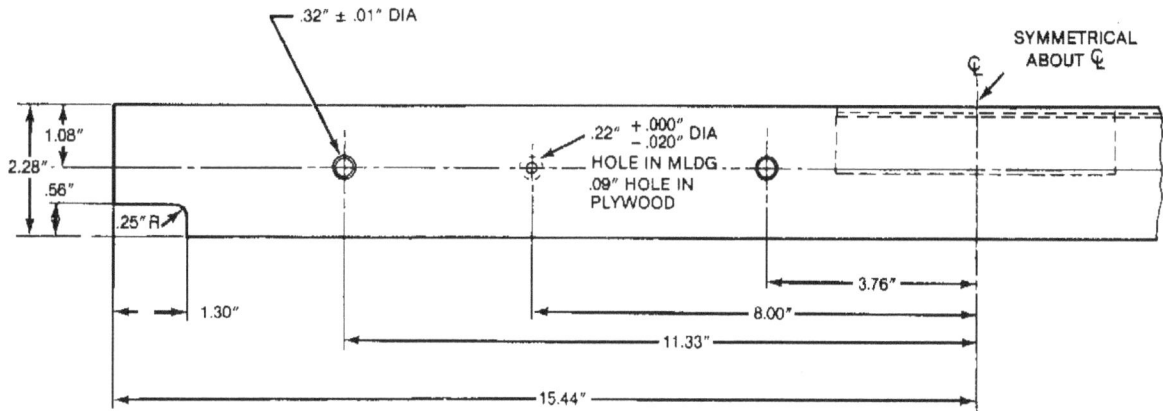

1. Fabricate from softwood plywood, 1 in. thick, NSN 5530-00-129-7889.

2. Cut to dimensions shown and drill holes as indicated for Part Number 14076201.

3. Remove all burrs.

4. Treat and seal wood per MIL-T-704J, paragraph 3.2.4. Prime with epoxy primer coating (Item 39, Appendix C), per MIL-STD-193. Finish paint lusterless forest green (Item 11, Appendix C) on both sides.

Figure D-35. Rear Door Panel.

---

1. Fabricate from rubber hose, 7/32 in. inside diameter, stock size 25 ft. long, NSN 4720-01-192-3519.

2. Cut to 1.30 in. long for Part Number 326560.

Figure D-35.1. Transmission Vacuum Modulator Hose.

TA49692

Section II. ILLUSTRATED MANUFACTURING INSTRUCTIONS - Continued

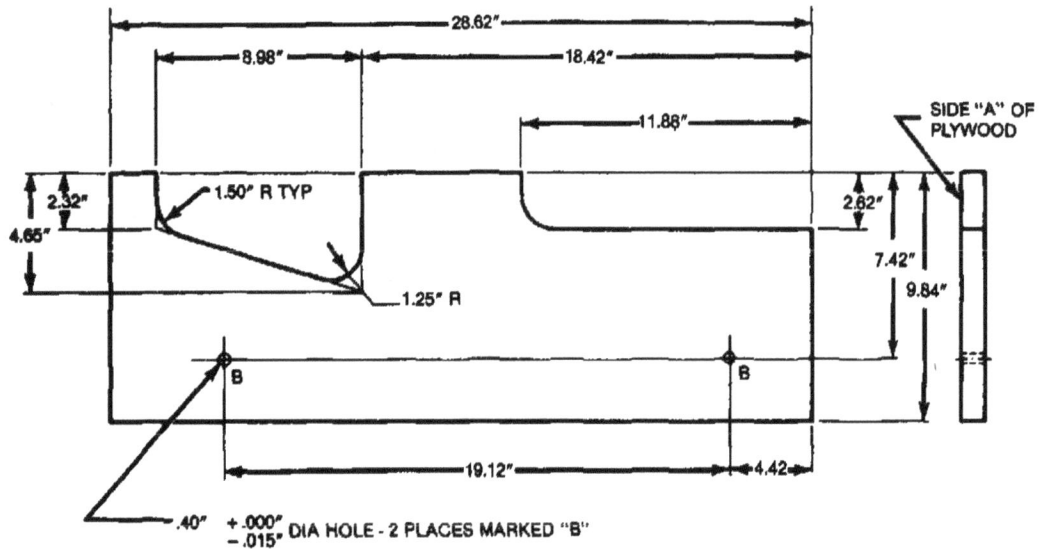

1. Fabricate from softwood plywood, 1 in. thick, NSN 5530-00-129-7889.

2. Cut to dimensions shown and drill holes as indicated for Part Number 14076229.

3. Remove all burrs.

4. Treat and seal wood per MIL-T-704J, paragraph 3.2.4. Prime with epoxy primer coating (Item 39, Appendix C), per MIL-STD-193. Finish paint lusterless forest green (Item 11, Appendix C) on both sides.

Figure D-36. Insulator.

TA49693

Section II. ILLUSTRATED MANUFACTURING INSTRUCTIONS - Continued

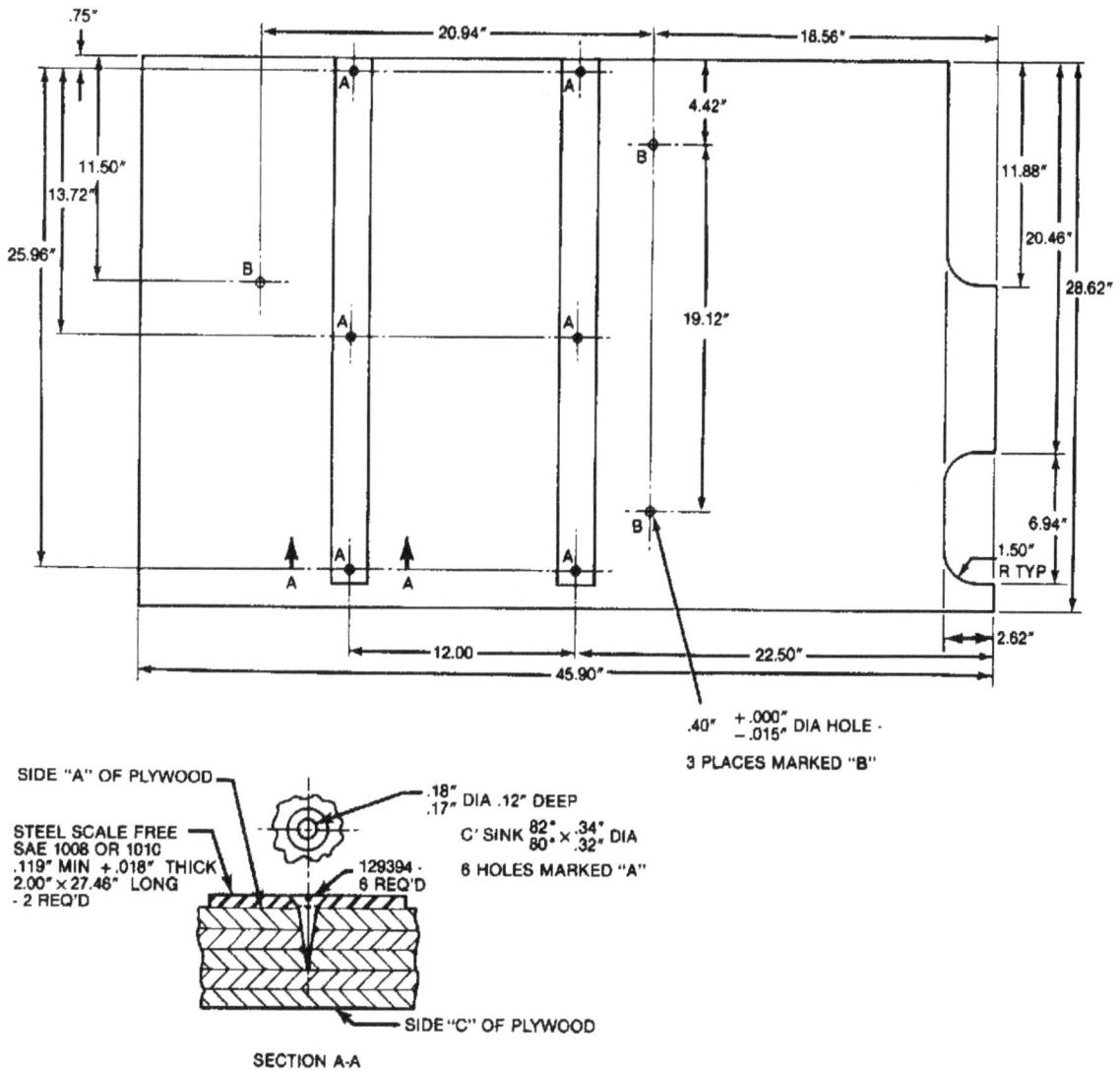

.40″ +.000″/−.015″ DIA HOLE ·
3 PLACES MARKED "B"

SIDE "A" OF PLYWOOD

STEEL SCALE FREE
SAE 1008 OR 1010
.119″ MIN +.018″ THICK
2.00″ × 27.46″ LONG
- 2 REQ'D

.18″/.17″ DIA .12″ DEEP

C' SINK 82°/80° × .34″/.32″ DIA

6 HOLES MARKED "A"

129394 ·
6 REQ'D

SIDE "C" OF PLYWOOD

SECTION A-A

1. Fabricate from softwood plywood, 1 in. thick, NSN 5530-00-129-7889.

2. Cut to dimensions shown and drill holes as indicated for Part Number 14076271.

3. Remove all burrs.

TA49694

Section II. ILLUSTRATED MANUFACTURING   INSTRUCTIONS - Continued

4. Treat and seal wood per MIL-T-704J, paragraph 3.2.4. Prime with epoxy primer coating (Item 39, Appendix C), per MIL-STD-193. Finish paint lusterless forest green (Item 11, Appendix C) on both sides.

Figure D-37. Insulator.

---

1. Fabricate from softwood plywood, 1 in. thick, NSN 5530-00-129-7889.

2. Using Figure FO-2, cut to dimensions shown and drill holes as indicated for Part Number 14076272.

3. Remove all burrs.

4. Treat and seal wood per MIL-T-704J, paragraph 3.2.4. Prime with epoxy primer coating (Item 39, Appendix C), per MIL-STD-193. Finish paint lusterless forest green (Item 11, Appendix C) on both sides.

Figure D-38. Insulator.

---

1. Fabricate from softwood plywood, ½ in. thick, NSN 5530-00-129-7777.

NOTE

Part Number 14076273 is the opposite part to 14076274, so all dimensions will be identical.

2. Using Figure FO-3, cut to dimensions shown and drill holes as indicated for Part Numbers 14076273 and 14076274.

3. Remove all burrs.

4. Treat and seal wood per MIL-T-704J, paragraph 3.2.4. Prime with epoxy primer coating (Item 39, Appendix C), per MIL-STD-193. Finish paint lusterless forest green (Item 11, Appendix C) on both sides.

Figure D-39. Insulator.

Section II. ILLUSTRATED MANUFACTURING INSTRUCTIONS - Continued

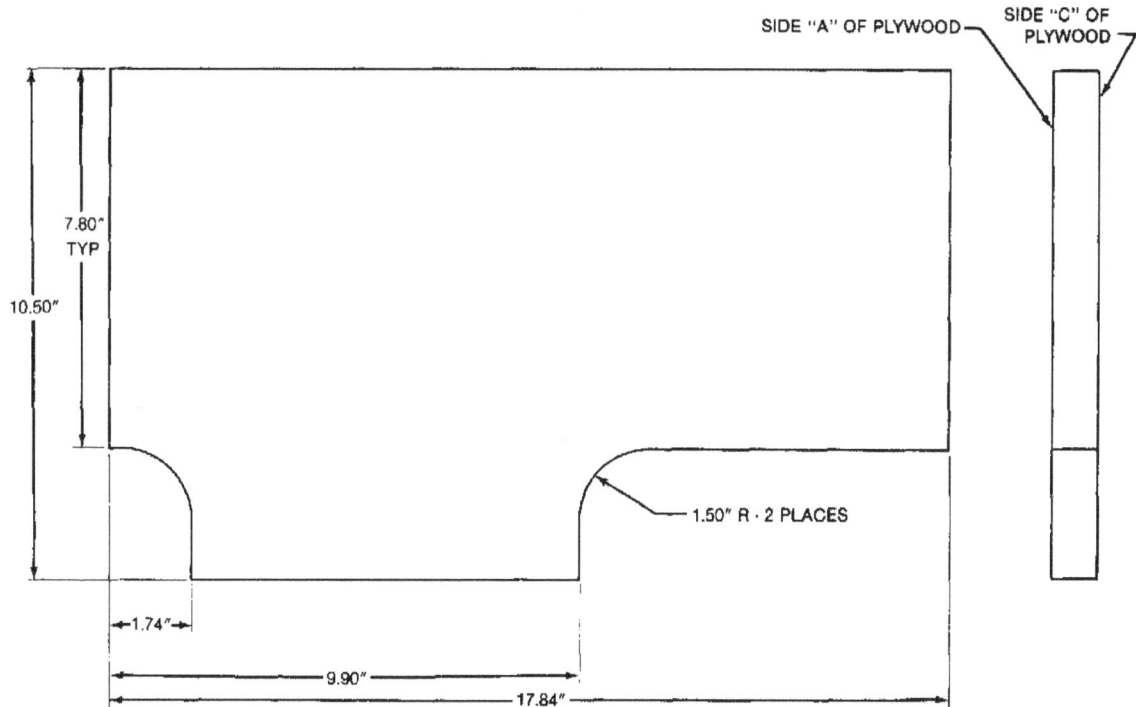

1. Fabricate from softwood plywood, 1 in. thick, NSN 5530-00-129-7889.

NOTE

Part Number 14076275 is the opposite part to 14076276, so all dimensions will be identical.

2. Cut to dimensions shown for Part Numbers 14076275 and 14076276.

3. Remove all burrs.

4. Treat and seal wood per MIL-T-704J, paragraph 3.2.4. Prime with epoxy primer coating (Item 39, Appendix C), per MIL-STD-193. Finish paint lusterless forest green (Item 11, Appendix C) on both sides.

Figure D-40. Insulator.

TA49695

Section II. ILLUSTRATED MANUFACTURING   INSTRUCTIONS -
Continued

1.   Fabricate from softwood plywood, ½ in. thick,   NSN 5530-00-129-7777.

NOTE

Except where noted, 14076277 is the opposite part to 14076278, so all dimensions will be identical.

2.   Using Figure FO-4, cut to dimensions shown for Part Numbers 14076277 and 14076278.

3.   Remove all burrs.

4.   Treat and seal wood per MIL-T-704J, paragraph 3.2.4. Prime with epoxy primer coating (Item 39, Appendix C), per MIL-STD-193. Finish paint lusterless forest green (Item 11,   Appendix C) on both   sides.

Figure D-41.   Insulator.

_____

1.   Fabricate from softwood plywood, ½ in. thick, NSN 5530-00-129-7777.

NOTE

Part Number 14076279 is the opposite part to 14076280, so all dimensions will be identical.

2.   Using Figure FO-5, cut to dimensions shown for Part Numbers 14076279 and 14076280.

3.   Remove all burrs.

4.   Treat and seal wood per MIL-T-704J, paragraph 3.2.4. Prime with epoxy primer coating (Item 39, Appendix C), per MIL-STD-193. Finish paint lusterless forest green (Item 11, Appendix C) on both sides.

Figure D-42. Insulator.

_____

Section II. ILLUSTRATED MANUFACTURING INSTRUCTIONS - Continued

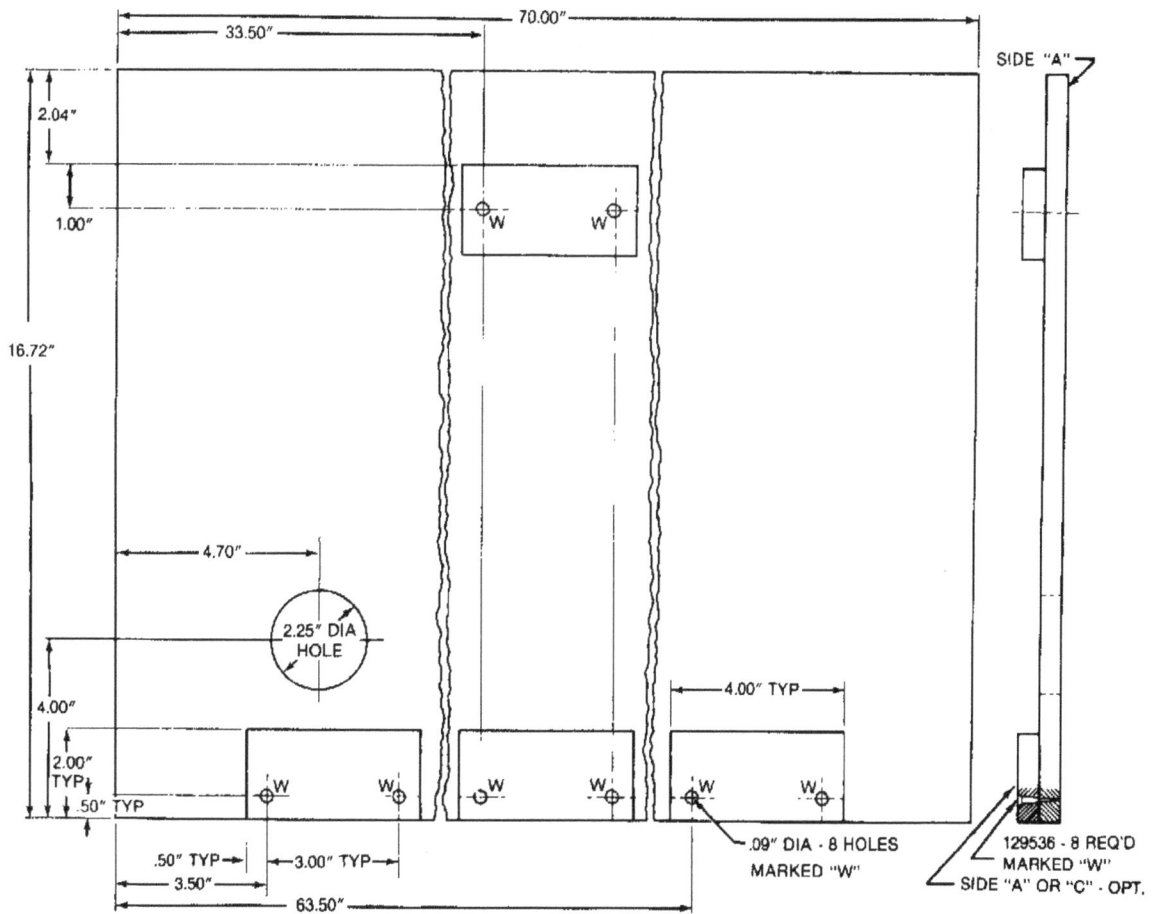

1. Fabricate from softwood plywood, ½ in. thick, NSN 5530-00-129-7777.

2. Cut to dimensions shown and drill holes as indicated for Part Number 14076281.

3. Remove ail burrs.

4. Treat and seal wood per MIL-T-704J, paragraph 3.2.4. Prime with epoxy primer coating (Item 39, Appendix C), per MIL-STD-193. Finish paint lusterless forest green (Item 11, Appendix C) on both sides.

Figure D-43. Insulator.

TA49696

Section II. ILLUSTRATED MANUFACTURING INSTRUCTIONS - Continued

1. Fabricate from softwood plywood, 1 in. thick, NSN 5530-00-129-7889.

2. Using Figure FO-6, cut to dimensions shown and drill holes as indicated   for Part Number 14063341.

3. Remove all burrs.

4. Treat and seal wood per MIL-T-704J, paragraph 3.2.4. Prime with epoxy primer coating (Item 39, Appendix C), per MIL-STD-193. Finish paint lusterless forest green (Item 11, Appendix C) on both sides.

Figure D-44. Insulation Assembly.

---

1. Fabricate from softwood plywood, ½ in. thick, NSN 5530-00-129-7777.

2. Using Figure FO-7, cut to dimensions shown and drill holes as indicated for Part Number 14063343.

3. Remove all burrs.

4. Treat and seal wood per MIL-T-704J, paragraph 3.2.4. Prime with epoxy primer coating (Item 39, Appendix C), per MIL-STD-193. Finish paint lusterless forest green (Item 11, Appendix C) on both sides.

Figure D-45. Right Half Panel Insulator.

---

1. Fabricate from softwood plywood, ½ in. thick, NSN 5530-00-129-7777.

2. Using Figure FO-8, cut to dimensions shown and drill holes as indicated for Part Number 14063344.

3. Remove all burrs.

4. Treat and seal wood per MIL-T-704J, paragraph 3.2.4. Prime with epoxy primer coating (Item 39, Appendix C), per MIL-STD-193. Finish paint lusterless forest green (Item 11, Appendix C) on both sides.

Figure D-46. Left Half Panel Insulator.

Section II. ILLUSTRATED MANUFACTURING INSTRUCTIONS - Continued

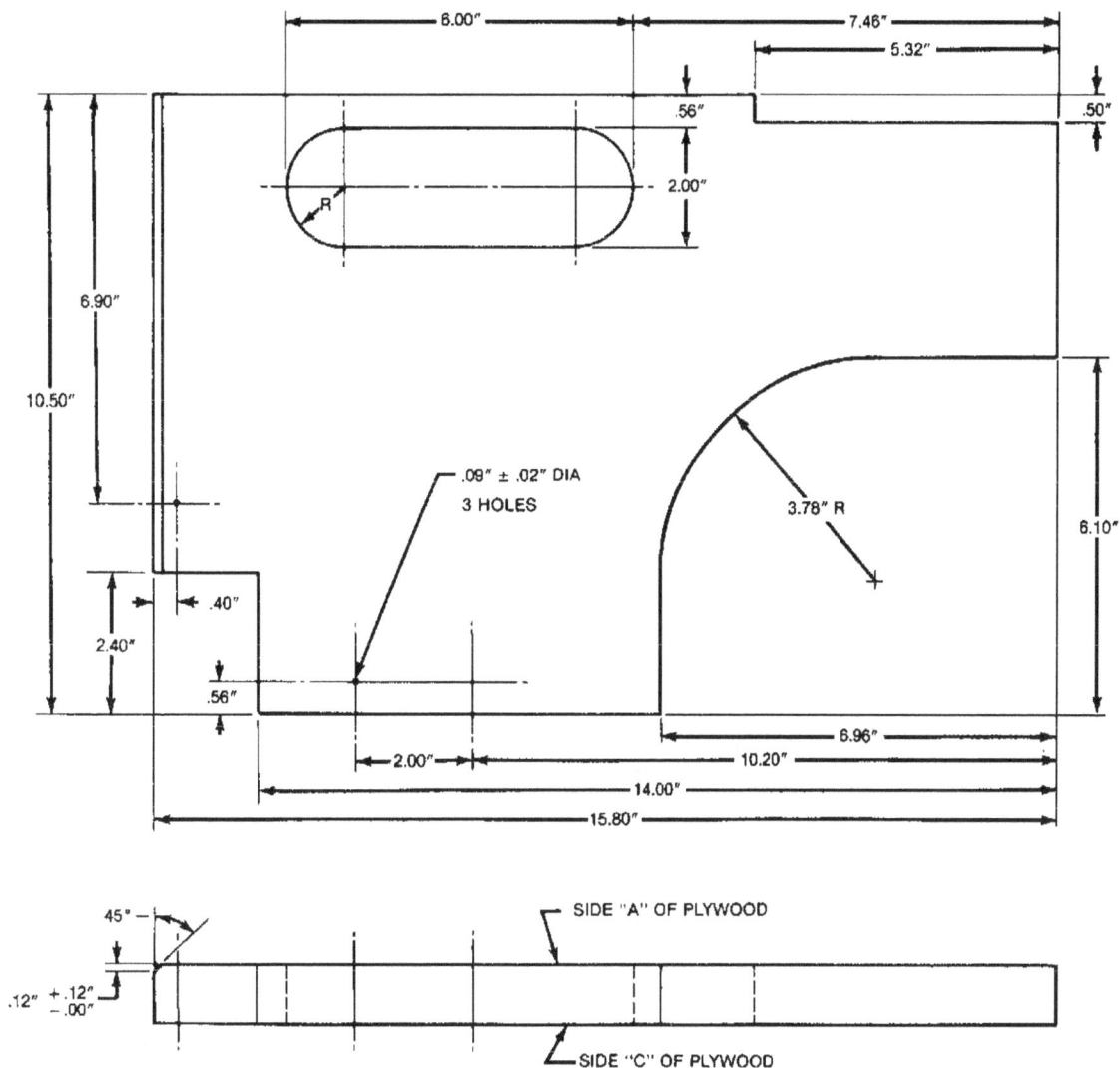

1. Fabricate from softwood plywood, 1 in. thick, NSN 5530-00-129-7889.

2. Cut to dimensions shown and drill holes as indicated for Part Number 14063346.

3. Remove all burrs.

4. Treat and seal wood per MIL-T-704J, paragraph 3.2,4. Prime with epoxy primer coating (Item 39, Appendix C), per MIL-STD-193. Finish paint lusterless forest green (Item 11, Appendix C) on both sides.

Figure D-47. Panel Insulator.

TA49697

Section II. ILLUSTRATED MANUFACTURING INSTRUCTIONS - Continued

1. Fabricate from softwood plywood, ½ in. thick, NSN 5530-00-129-7777.

2. Using Figure FO-9, cut to dimensions shown and drill holes as indicated for Part Number 14063347.

3. Remove all burrs.

4. Treat and seal wood per MIL-T-704J, paragraph 3.2.4. Prime with epoxy primer coating (Item 39, Appendix C), per MIL-STD-193. Finish paint lusterless forest green (Item 11, Appendix C) on both sides.

Figure D-48. Insulation.

1. Fabricate from softwood plywood, ½ in. thick, NSN 5530-00-129-7777.

2. Using Figure FO-10, cut to dimensions shown and drill holes as indicated for Part Number 14063348.

3. Remove all burrs.

4. Treat and seal wood per MIL-T-704J, paragraph 3.2.4. Prime with epoxy primer coating (Item 39, Appendix C), per MIL-STD-193. Finish paint lusterless forest green (Item 11, Appendix C) on both sides.

Figure D-49. Insulation.

1. Fabricate from structural angle steel, 1 in. x 1 in., NSN 9520-00-855-7037.

2. Cut to 56.00 in. long for Part Number 14063350.

3. Remove all burrs.

Figure D-50. Molding.

Section II. ILLUSTRATED MANUFACTURING INSTRUCTIONS - Continued

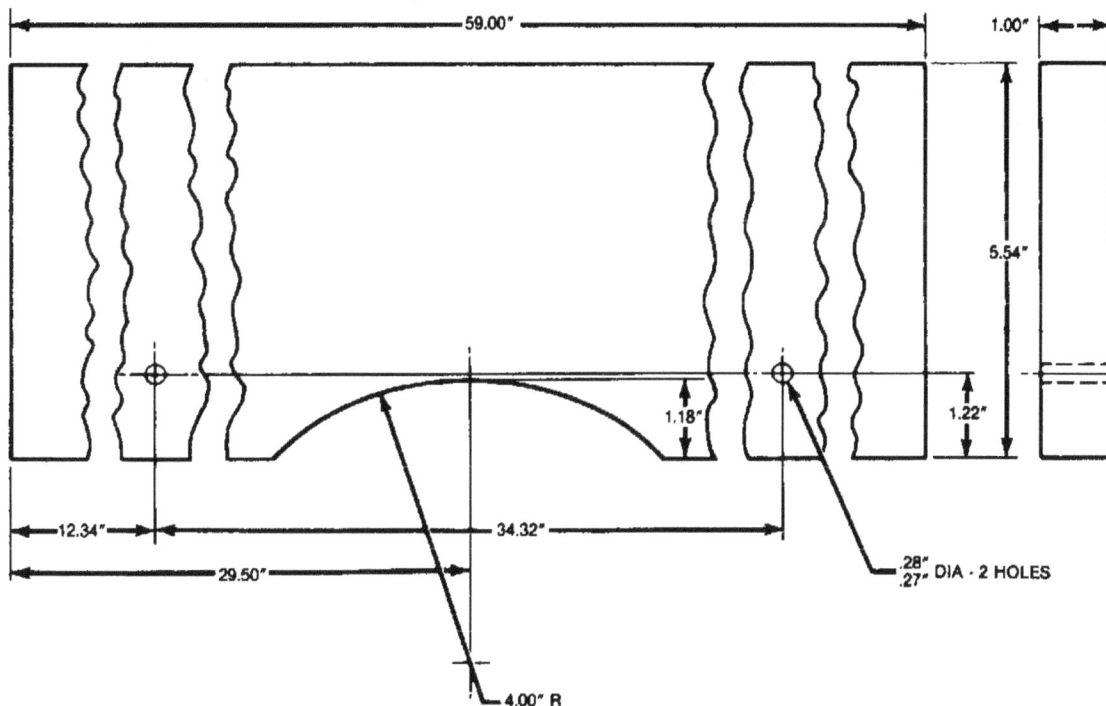

1. Fabricate from softwood plywood, 1 in. thick, NSN 5530-00-129-7889.

2. Cut to dimensions shown and drill holes as indicated for Part Number 14063351.

3. Remove all burrs.

4. Treat and seal wood per MIL-T-704J, paragraph 3.2.4. Prime with epoxy primer coating (Item 39, Appendix C), per MIL-STD-193. Finish paint lusterless forest green (Item 11, Appendix C) on both sides.

Figure D-51. Floor Insulator.

TA49698

Section II. ILLUSTRATED MANUFACTURING INSTRUCTIONS -
Continued

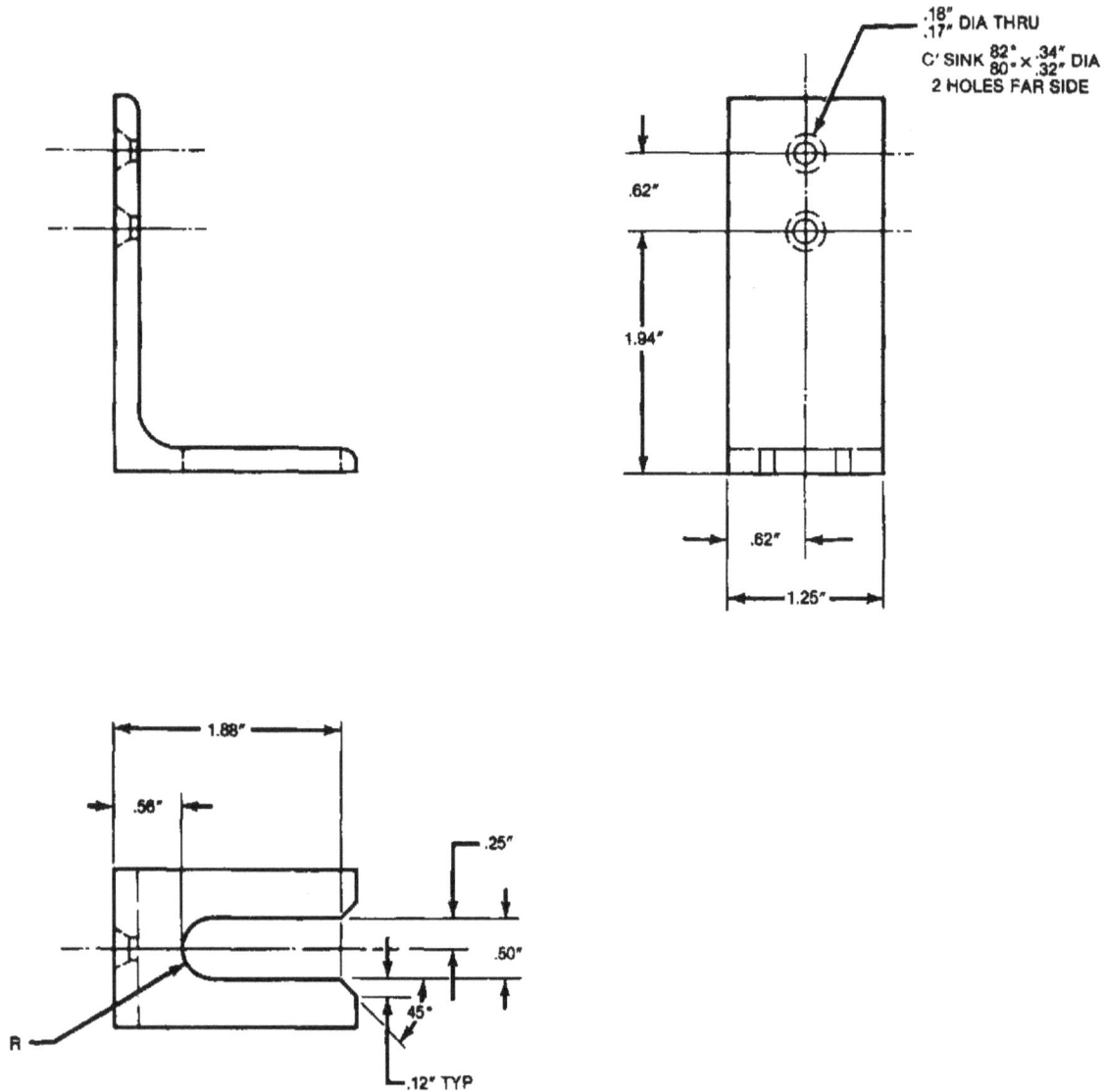

.18" / .17" DIA THRU

C' SINK 82° / 80° x .34" / .32" DIA
2 HOLES FAR SIDE

.62"

1.94"

.62"

1.25"

1.88"

.56"

.25"

.50"

45°

.12" TYP

R

1. Fabricate from structural angle steel, 3 in. x 3 in., NSN 9520-01-023-9271.

2. Cut to dimensions shown and drill holes as indicated for Part Number 14063342.

3. Remove all burrs.

Figure D-52. Bracket.

TA49699

Section II. ILLUSTRATED MANUFACTURING INSTRUCTIONS - Continued

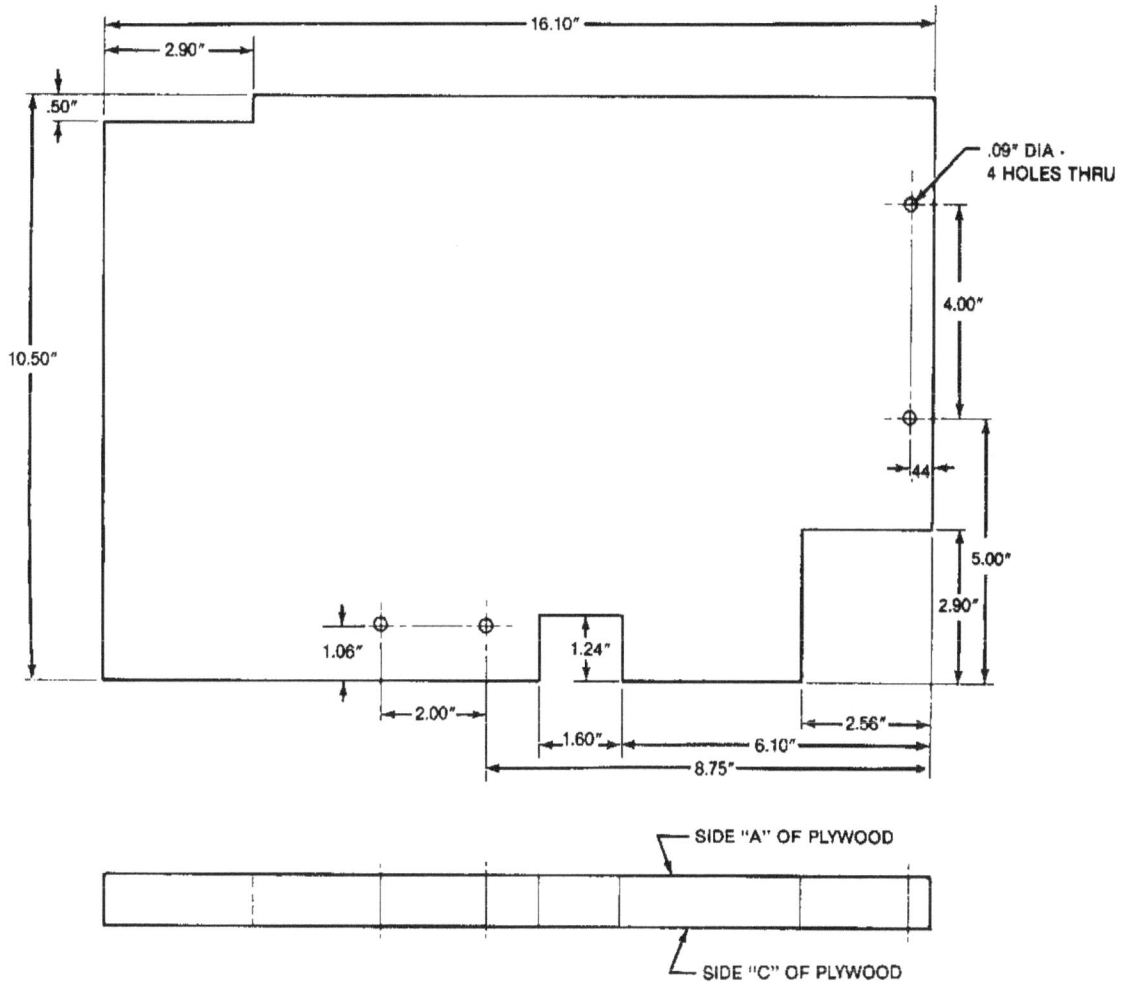

1. Fabricate from softwood plywood, 1 in. thick, NSN 5530-00-129-7889.

2. Cut to dimensions shown and drill holes as indicated for Part Number 14063345.

3. Remove all burrs.

4. Treat and seal wood per MIL-T-704J, paragraph 3.2.4. Prime with epoxy primer coating (Item 39, Appendix C), per MIL-STD-193. Finish paint lusterless forest green (Item 11, Appendix C) on both sides.

Figure D-53. Insulator.

TA49700

Section II. ILLUSTRATED MANUFACTURING INSTRUCTIONS - Continued

1. Fabricate from NSN 2510-01-158-9337, Part Number 462233, FSCM 11862.

2. Cut to fit for Part Numbers 14075862, 14075863, 14075864, 14076802, and 14076803.

Figure D-54. Floor Insulator.

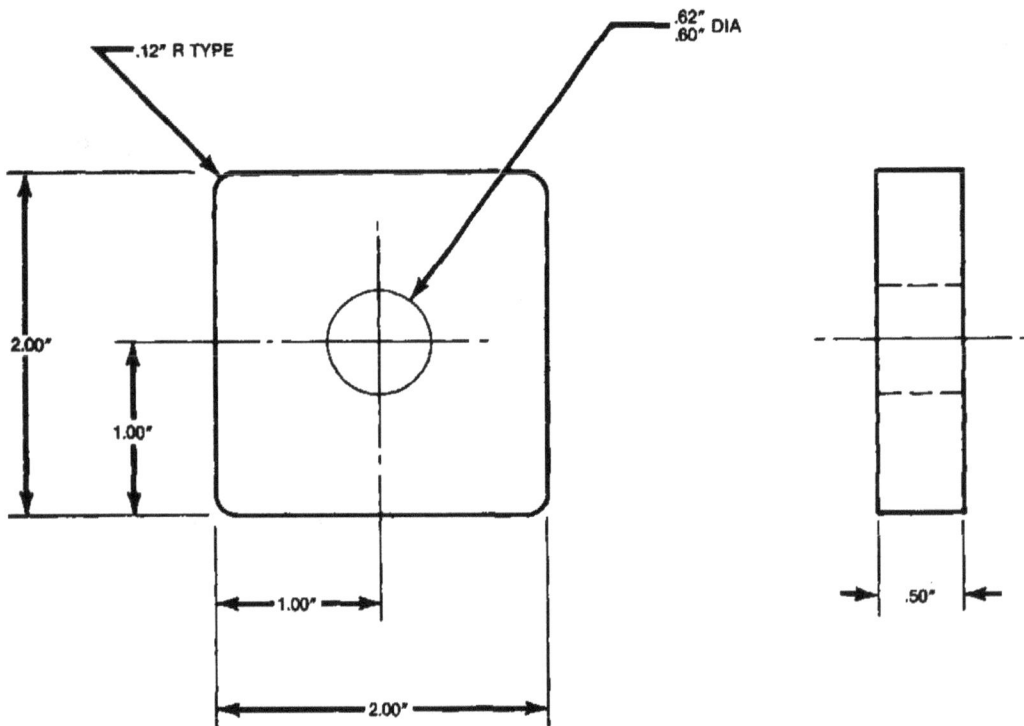

1. Fabricate from metal bar, ½ in. thick,   NSN 9510-00-063-4670.

2. Cut to dimensions shown and drill hole   as indicated for Part Number 14063352.

3. Remove all burrs.

Figure D-55. Spacer.

TA49701

Section II. ILLUSTRATED MANUFACTURING INSTRUCTIONS - Continued

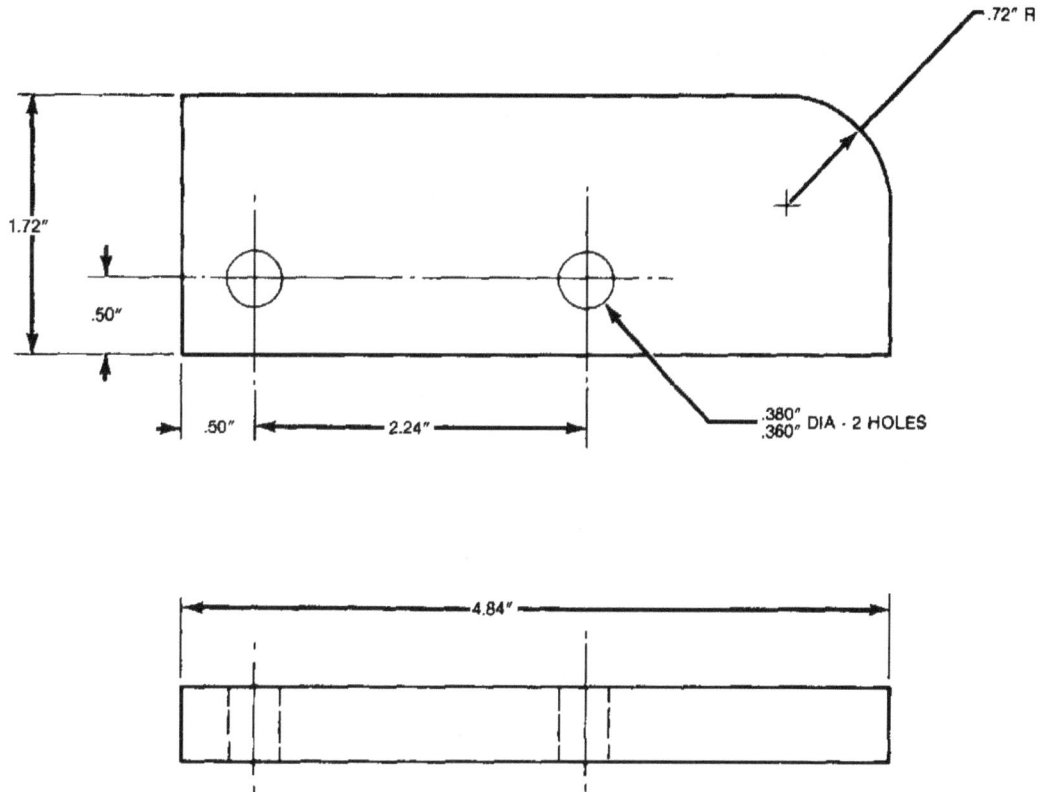

1. Fabricate from metal bar, ½ in. thick, NSN 9510-00-063-4670.

2. Cut to dimensions shown and drill holes as indicated for Part Number 14063353.

3. Remove all burrs.

Figure D-56. Spacer.

TA49702

APPENDIX E
TORQUE LIMITS

E-1.   SCOPE.

This appendix lists standard torque values, as shown in Table E-1, and provides general information for applying torque.   Special torque values and sequences are indicated in the maintenance procedures for applicable components.

E-2.   GENERAL.

a. Always use the torque values listed below when the maintenance procedure does not give a specific torque value.

b. Unless otherwise specified, standard torque tolerance shall be ± 10%.

c. Torque values listed are based on clean and dry threads. Reduce torque by 10% when engine oil is used as a lubricant.

Table E-1. Standard Torque Specifications

NUT OR BOLT SIZE (inch)	TORQUE				NUT OR BOLT SIZE (millimeter)	TORQUE			
	GRADE 5		GRADE S			GRADE 9.8		GRADE 10.9	
FINE & COARSE THREADS	lb.-ft.	N•m	lb.-ft.	N•m		lb.-ft.	N•m	lb.-ft.	N-m
1/4	6	6	10	14	6	10	14	12	16
5/16	15	20	21	29	8	20	27	23	31
3/8	26	35	37	50	10	40	54	48	65
7/16	43	58	60	81	12	70	95	80	109
1/2	65	88	90	122	14	113	153	132	179
9/16	90	122	130	176	16	176	239	207	261
5/8	130	176	178	241	20	343	465	399	541
3/4	185	251	260	353					
7/8	300	408	420	570					
1	440	597	635	861					

E-3. DRIVEBELT TENSION SPECIFICATIONS.

NOTE

- Using belt tensioning gage,   adjust belt tension as listed below.

- If belt has been replaced, refer to new belt specification, run engine for 15 minutes, and adjust to old belt specifications.

Table E-2. Drivebelt Tension Specifications

TENSION REQUIREMENT	ALTERNATOR	POWER STEERING PUMP	AIR CONDITIONER COMPRESSOR
NEW BELT: Before Operating Engine	146 lb. 650 N	146 lb. 650 N	169 lb. 750 N
OLD BELT: After Operating Engine	67 lb. 300 N	67 lb. 300 N	67 lb. 300 N

APPENDIX F
WIRING DIAGRAMS AND SCHEMATICS

F-1. SCOPE.

This appendix contains wiring diagrams and schematics of each CUCV Series electrical circuit. This appendix should be used when performing the *Electrical Troubleshooting* procedures in Table 2-4.

F-2. WIRING DIAGRAMS AND SCHEMATICS INDEX.

F-2. WIRING DIAGRAMS AND SCHEMATICS INDEX (Con't).

F-1. Starting Circuits (All Except M1010).

TA49741

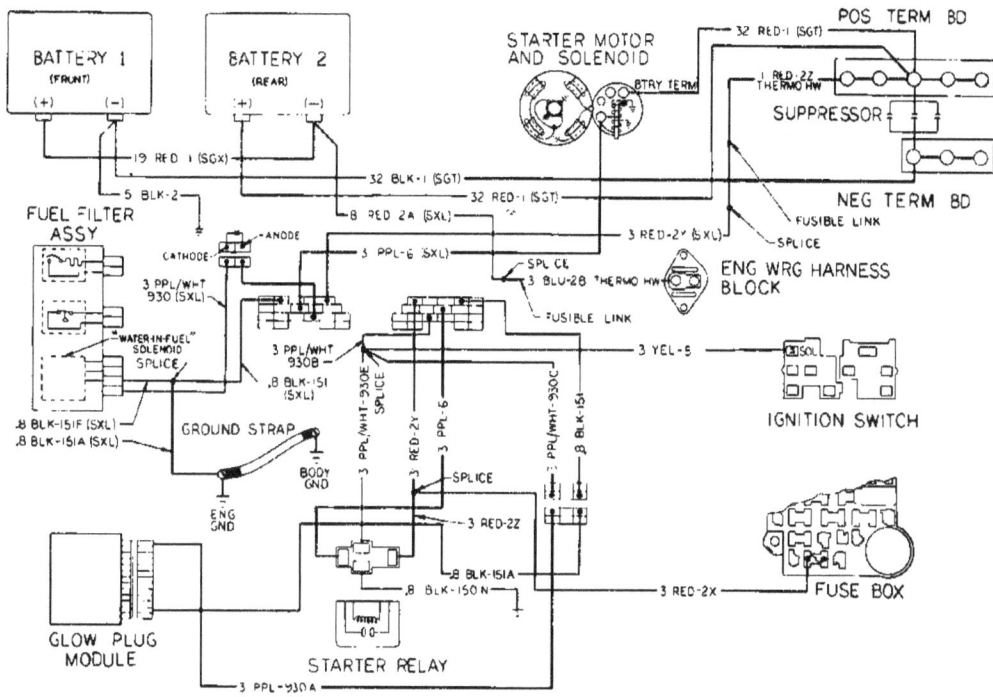

F-2. Starting Circuits (M1010).

TA49742

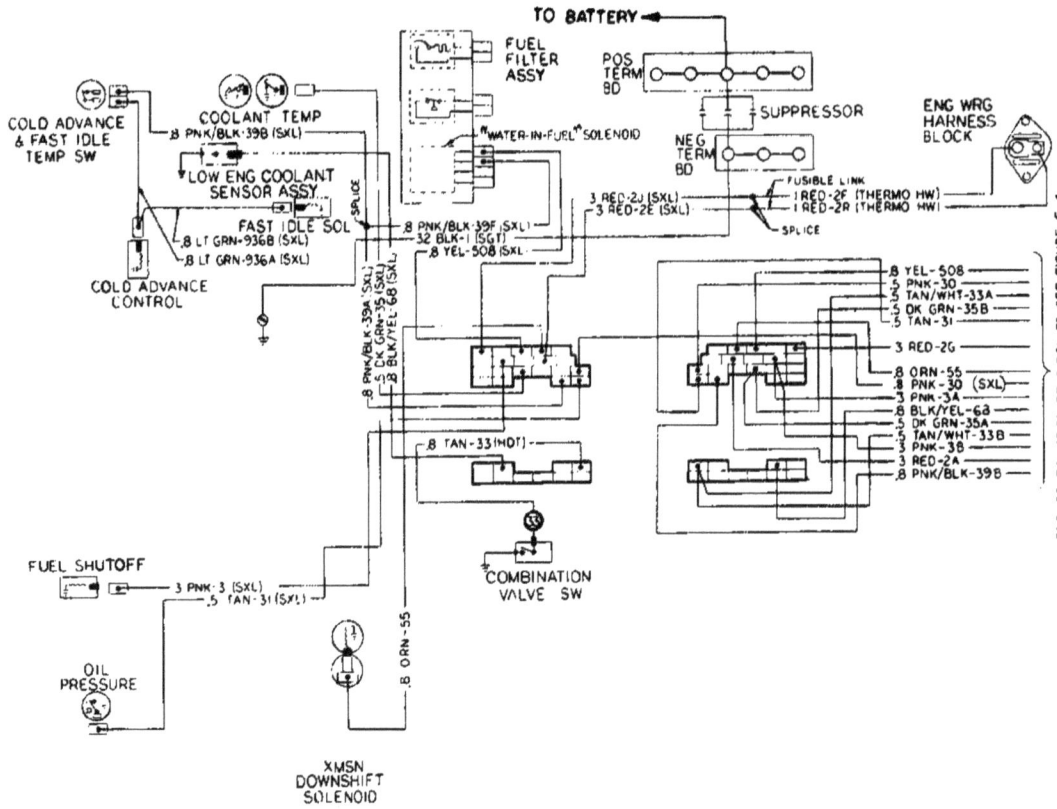

F-3. Engine Compartment Ignition Circuits (All Except M1010).

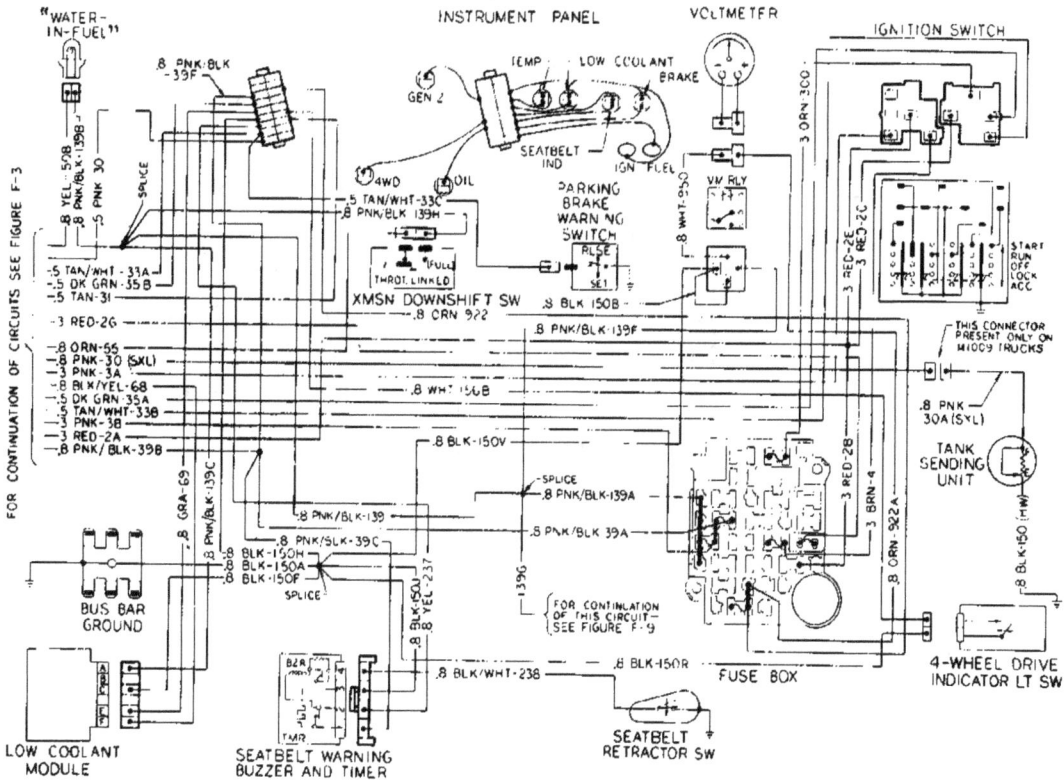

F-4. Cab Ignition Circuits (All Except M1010).

TA49744

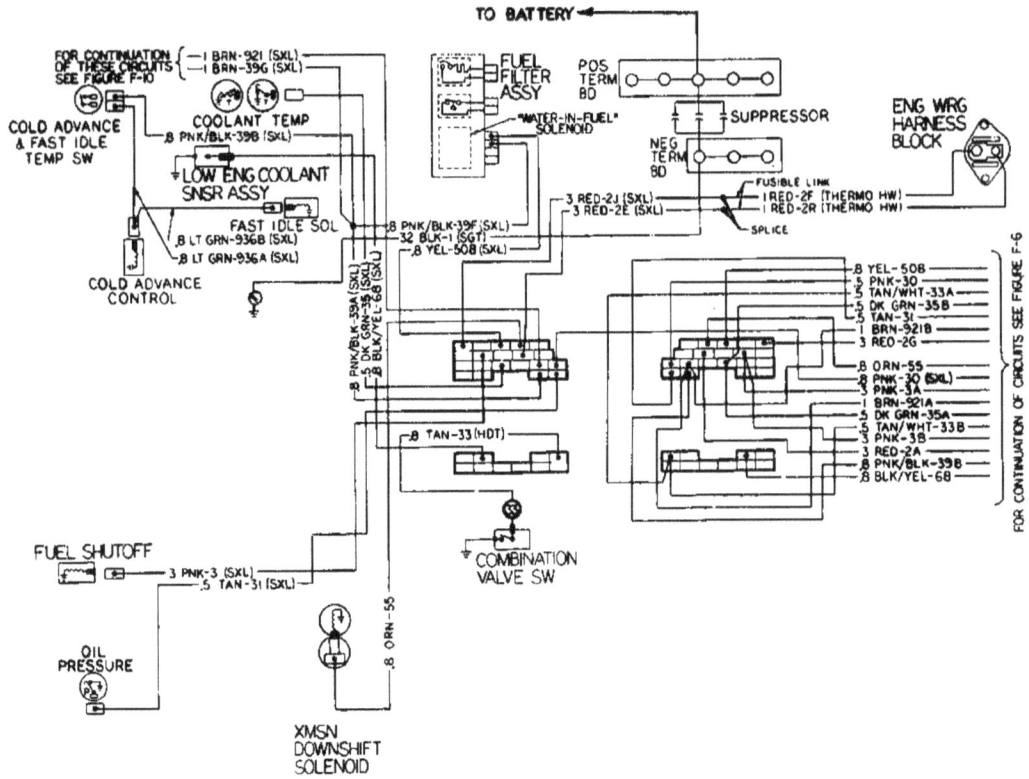

F-5. Engine Compartment Ignition Circuits (M1010).

TA49745

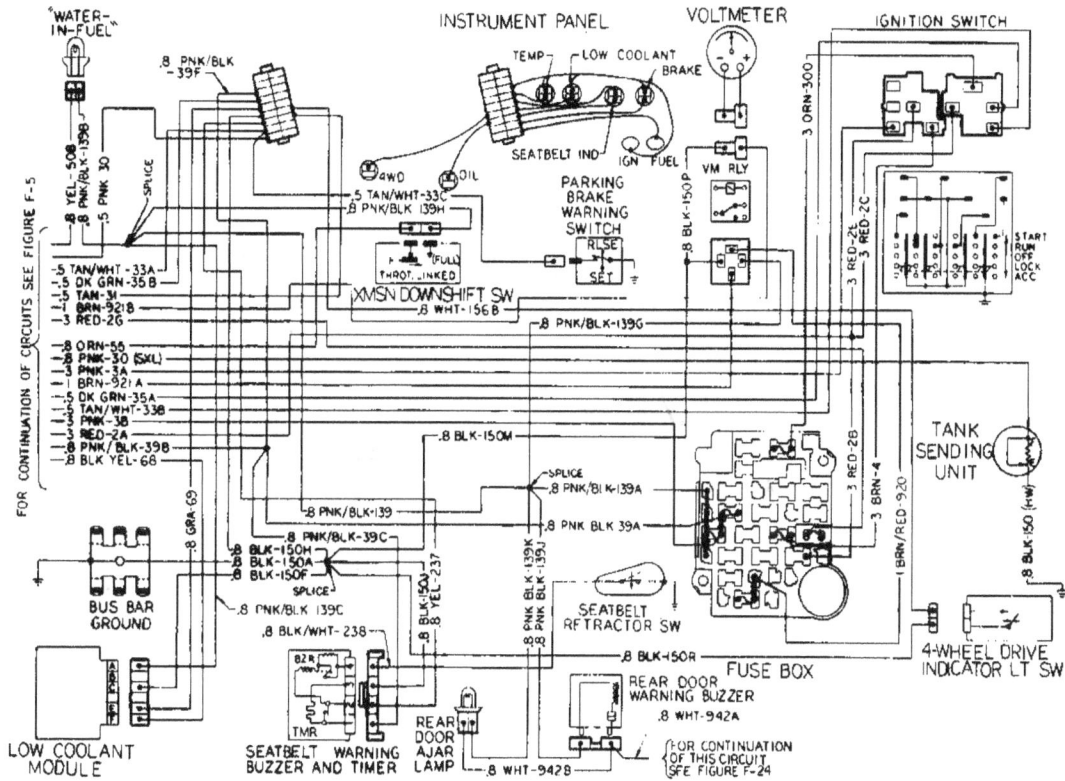

F-6. Cab Ignition Circuits (M1010).

TA49746

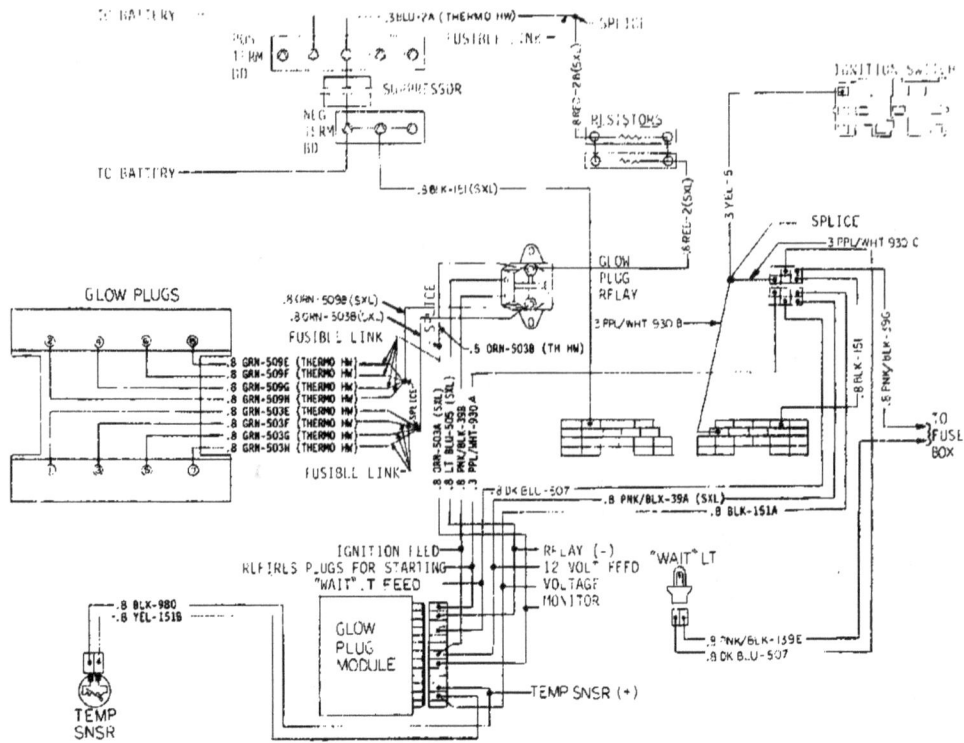

F-7. Glow Plug Circuits (All Except M1010).

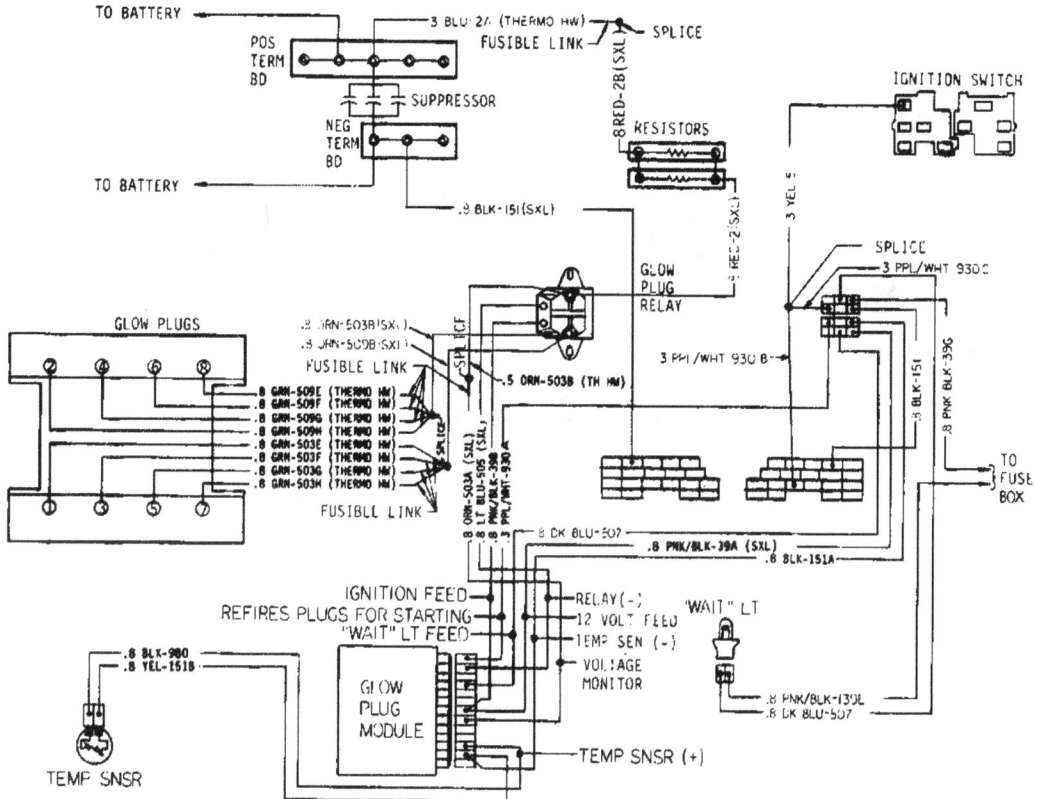

F-8. Glow Plug Circuits (M1010).

TA701845

F-9. Charging Circuits (All Except M1010).

TA49749

F-10. Charging Circuits (M1010).

F-11. Diagnostic Circuits (All Except M1010).

TA49751

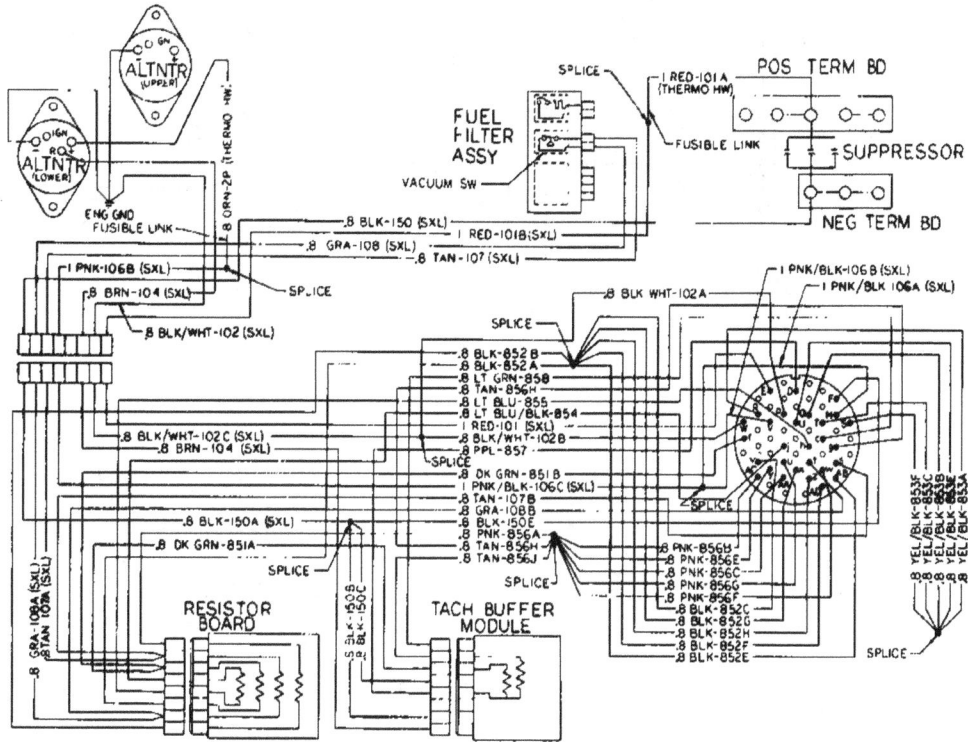

F-12. Diagnostic Circuits (M1010).

F-13. Service Lighting Circuits – Front (All Except M1010).

TA49753

F-14. Service Lighting Circuits – Rear (All Except M1010 and M1031).

F-14.1. Service Lighting Circuit – Rear (M1028A2).

F-15. Service Lighting Circuits – Rear (M1031).

F-16. Service Lighting Circuits - Front (M1010).

DIR SIG & HAZARD FLASHER SW

FLOODLIGHT LMP

MARKER LT RIGHT

.8 WHT-17A
.8 YEL-18
.8 BRN-27
.5 LT BLU-14A

STOPLIGHT SW
RIGHT REAR LT
LEFT REAR LT
SIGNAL FLASHER
HAZARD FLASHER
RIGHT FRONT LT
LEFT FRONT LT

HAZ SW   SIG SW

.8 DK GRN-19
.8 PPL-16
.5 DK BLU-15A

.8 TAN-12

DIMMER SW

HI   LO

TAIL STOP & DIR LT

B/U LT

.8 DK GRN-19C
.8 DK GRN-19B
.8 BRN-9B
.8 DK GRN-19A
.8 DK GRN-9
.8 LT GRN-24
.8 BLK-150D
.8 BLK-150E

1 YEL-10

LIGHT SW

1 LT GRN-11A
3 ORN/BLK-912A

X DOME LT
1 BAT FEED
2 PANEL LT
3 TAIL LT
4 TAIL LT
5 TAIL LT
6 FEED FUSED
H HEAD LT

2 PNK-945

.8 LT GRN-24

BACK-UP LT SW

SPLICE

SPLICE

3 ORN/BLK-912B
.8 WHT-156A
.8 BRN-9A

.8 WHT/BLK-913
.8 DK BLU-75F
1 DK GRN-44
.8 ORN-40C

SPOTLIGHT & FLOODLIGHT RLY

.8 PNK-340
.8 DK BLU-75E
2 DK BLU-341E

.8 ORN-140

.8 BLK 150R

BRAKE SW

.8 BRN-9B
.8 DK GRN-19E
.8 BRN-9
.8 YEL-18A
.8 LT GRN-24B

.8 BLK-150A

SPOTLIGHT

2 DK BLU-341C
SPLICE

FLOODLIGHT SWITCHES

2 DK BLU-341A
2 DK BLU-341B

.8 DK GRN-19A
.8 LT GRN-24A
.8 YEL-18A

.8 BRN-9A
.8 YEL-18C
.8 YEL-18
.8 YEL-18
.8 LT GRN-24
.8 BLK-150C
.8 BLK-150B (HDT)

B/U LT

TAIL STOP & DIR LT

MARKER LT LEFT

FOR CONTINUATION OF CIRCUITS SEE FIGURE F-16

.8 BRN-9
.8 DK GRN-19
.8 YEL-18
.8 LT GRN-24

2 PNK-945

2 PNK-945
2 PNK-947

2 PNK-945
2 PNK/BLK 947

2 PNK-947

2 PNK-945

FLOODLIGHT LMP

FOR CONTINUATION OF CIRCUITS—SEE FIGURE F-16

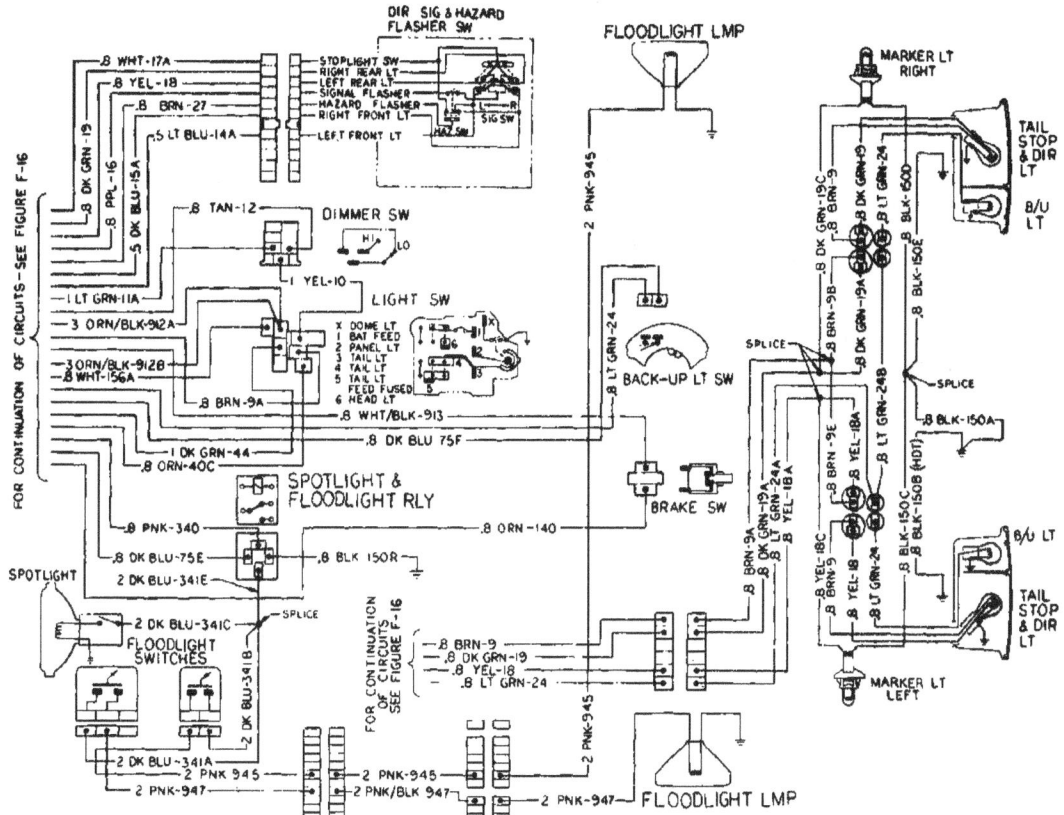

F-17. Service Lighting Circuits – Rear (M1010).

TA49767

F-19

TM 9-2320-289-20

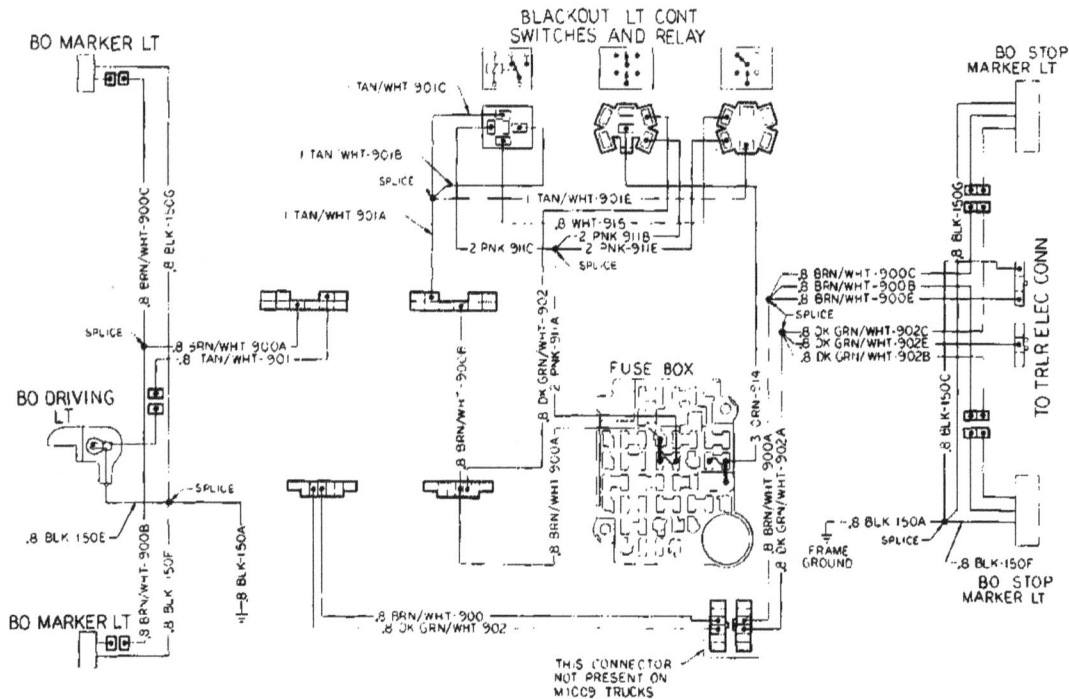

F-18. Blackout Lighting Circuits (All Except M1010).

F-19. Blackout Lighting Circuits (M1010).

TA49759

F-20. Wipers, Washer, Horn, and Heater Circuits (All Except M1010).

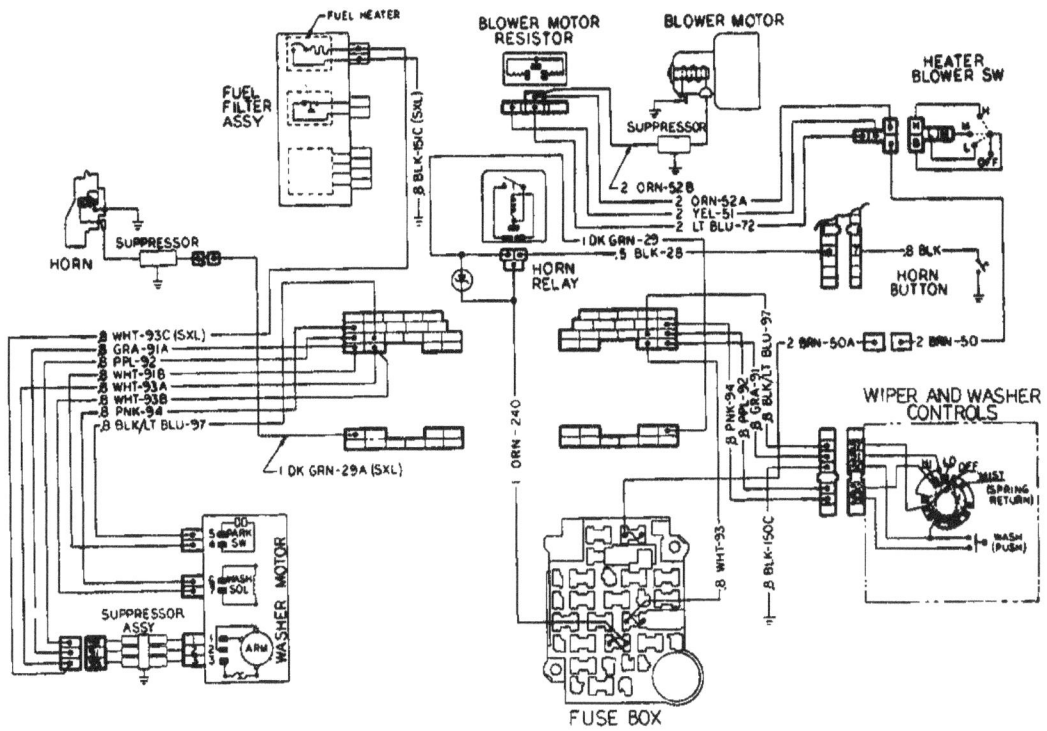

F-21. Wipers, Washer, Horn, and Heater Circuits (M1010).

COMBUSTION HEATER

FUEL CONT VALVE

OVHT SW

M

FLAME SW

(IN COLD OR START POSN)

IGNITER

IGN CONT

BLEND AIR BLOWER

HEATER CONTROL BOX

BLEND AIR DR BLO OFF SW

HTR CONT SW

IND LMP

28V, 200A SERVICE

ST

OFF

RUN

HEAT SW

CATHODE

ANODE

CB

2 GRA-980A

20A FUSE

FRESH AIR DR

OFF SW

2 LT BLU/RED-944A

2 LT BLU/RED-944A

CUTOUT SW

2 LT BLU-944

AUX HTR FUEL PUMP

2 GRA-980B

2 LT BLU-944

2 LT BLU-944

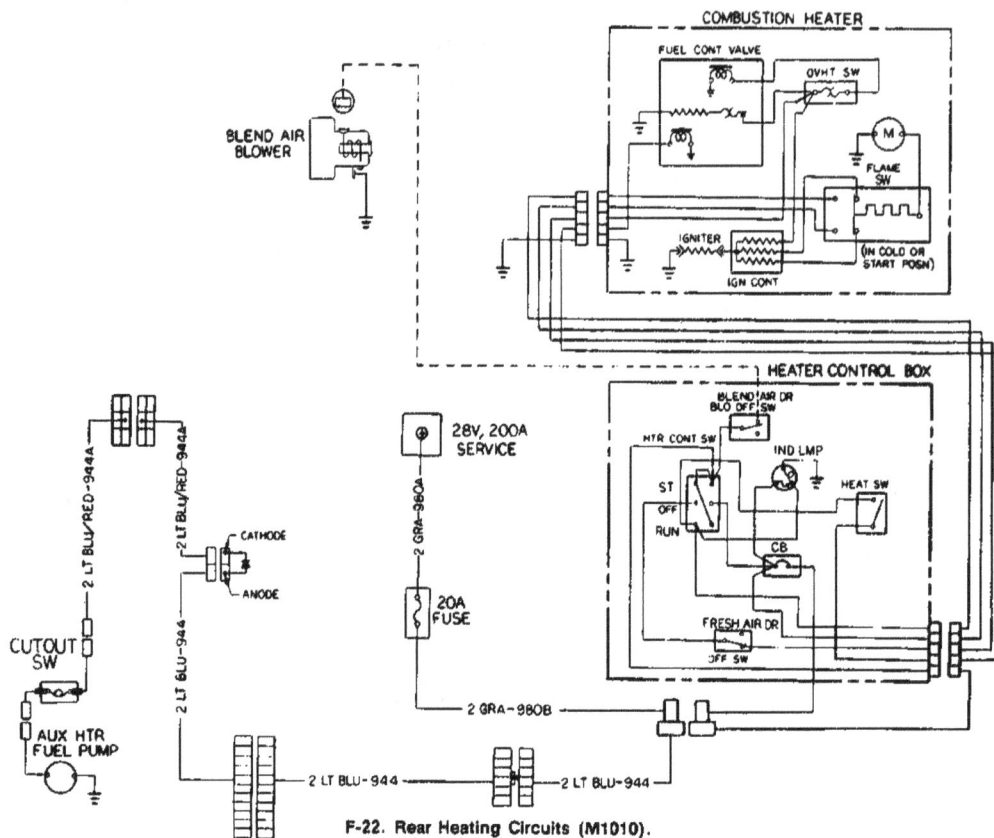

F-22. Rear Heating Circuits (M1010).

F-23. Gas-Particulate Filter Unit (GPFU) Heater Circuits (M1010).

TA49763

F-24. Interior Lighting Circuits (M1010).

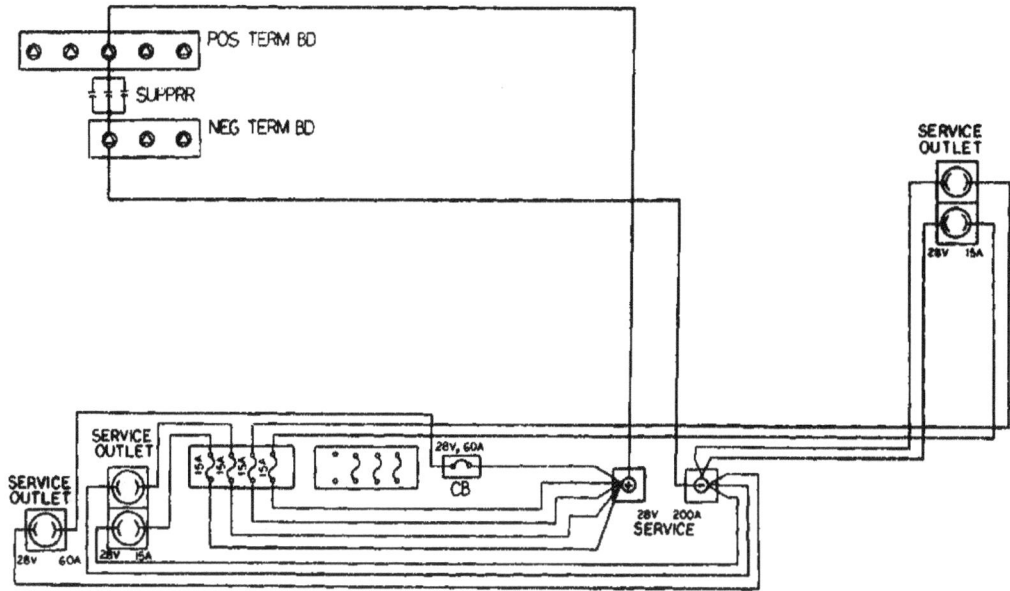

F-25. Service Outlet Circuits (M1010).

TA49765

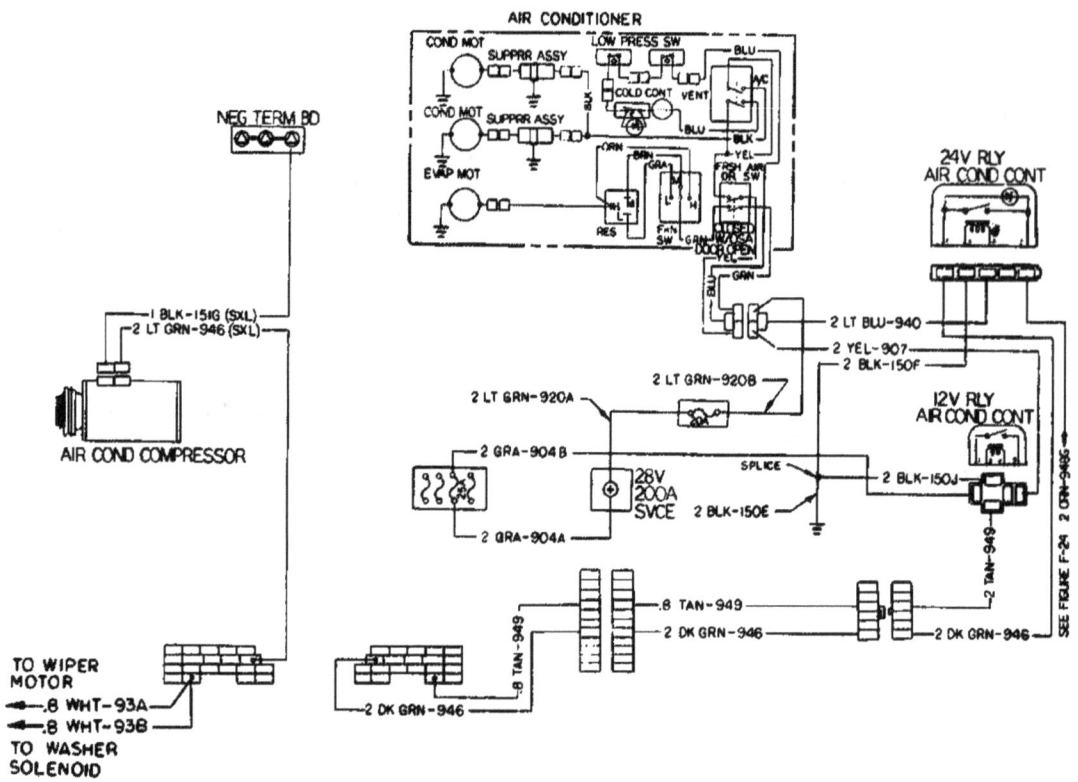

F-28. Air Conditioner Circuits (M1010).

TA49786

3 BLK-150A — 2 WHT-B
2 RED-C — 3 GRN-D
3 YEL-E

1 BLK-30A
1 DK BLU-87

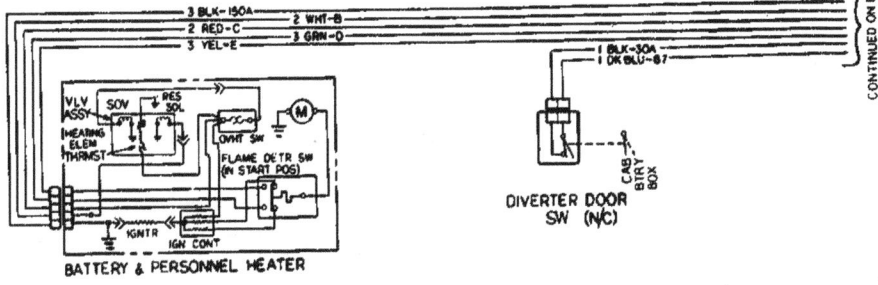

CONTINUED ON FIGURE F-29

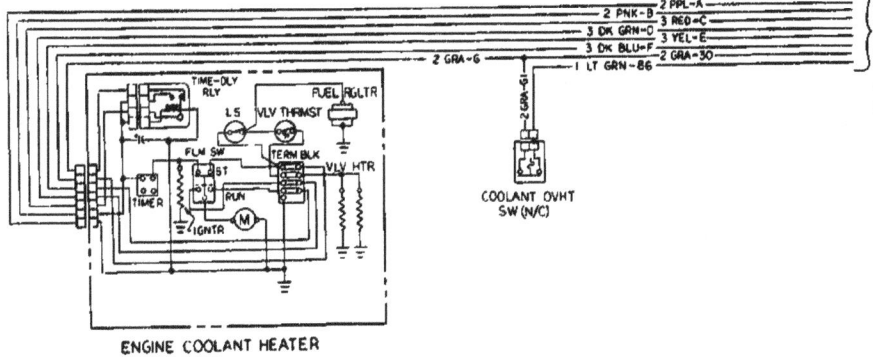

VLV ASSY
SOV
RES SOL
HEATING ELEM THRMST
FLAME DETR SW (IN START POS)
OVHT SW
M
IGNTR
IGN CONT

BATTERY & PERSONNEL HEATER

DIVERTER DOOR SW (N/C)
CAB BTRY BOX

2 PNK-B — 2 PPL-A
3 DK GRN-D — 3 RED-C
3 DK BLU-F — 3 YEL-E
2 GRA-6 — 2 GRA-30
1 LT GRN-86

2 GRA-61

CONTINUED ON FIGURE F-28

TIME-DLY RLY
FUEL RGLTR
LS
VLV THRMST
FLM SW
TERM BLK
START
RUN
VLV HTR
TIMER
IGNTR
M

ENGINE COOLANT HEATER

COOLANT OVHT SW (N/C)

F-27. Winterization Kit Cab Heater and Winterization Kit Engine Heater Circuits.

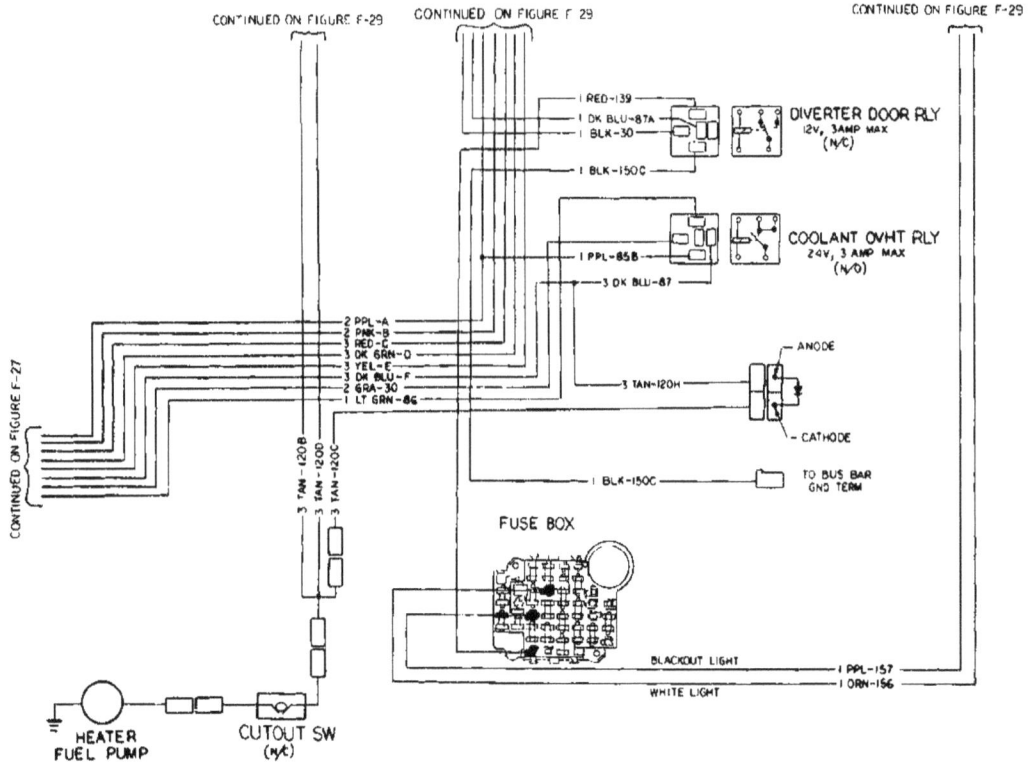

F-28. Winterization Kit Cab Heater and Winterization Kit Engine Heater Fuse Block and Relay Circuits.

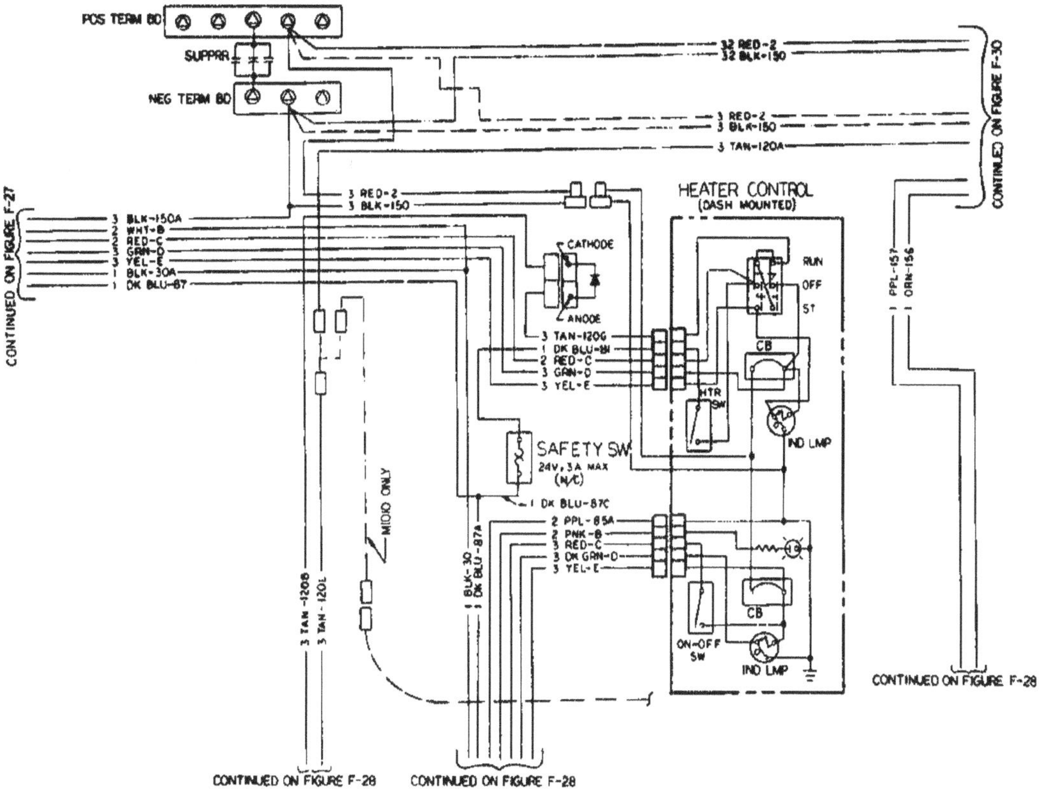

F-29. Winterization Kit Cab Heater and Winterization Kit Engine Heater Control Box Circuits.

TA49769

TM 9-2320-289-20

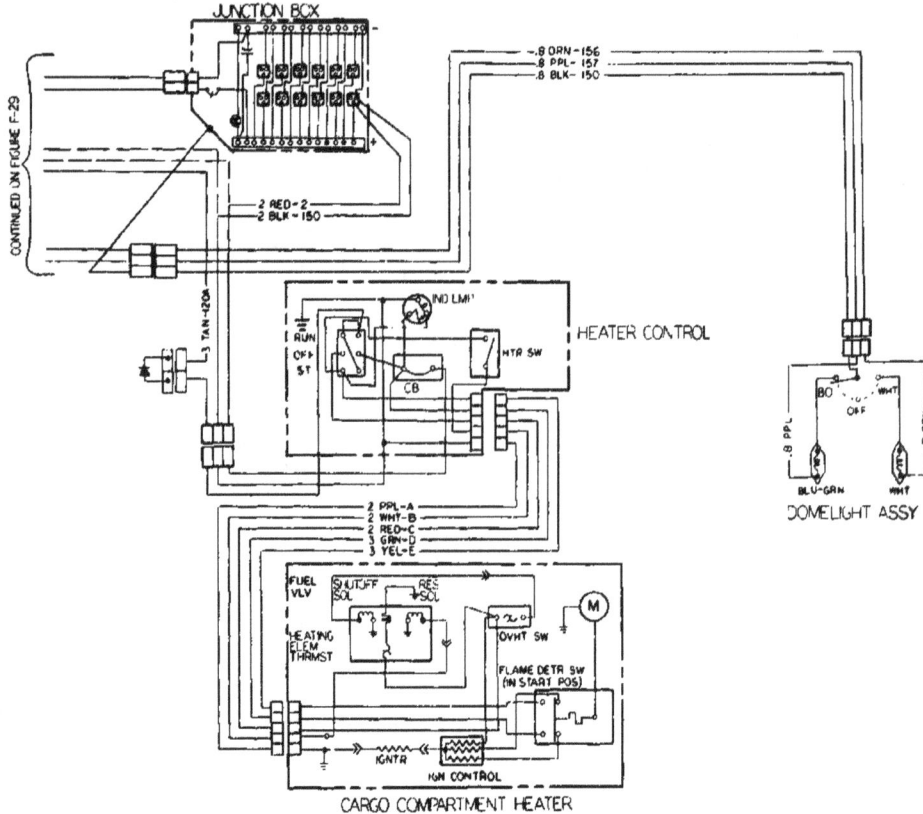

F-30. Winterization Kit Cargo Compartment Heater Circuits (M1008 and M1008A1).

TA49770

GLOSSARY

Section I. ABBREVIATIONS

a/c	Air Conditioner
air cond	Air Conditioner
altnr	Alternator
amp	Ampere
AR	Army Regulation
assy	Assembly
bd	Board
blk	Block
blo	Blower
bo	Blackout
btry	Battery
b/u	Back-up
C	Centigrade or Celsius
c	Operator/CrewLevel Maintenance
cb	Circuit Breaker
CDRV	Crankcase Depression Regulator Valve
₵	Centerline
cm	Centimeter
cond	Condenser
cont	Control
DA	Department of the Army
DD	Department of Defense
dir	Directional
dly	Delay
EIR	Equipment Improvement Recommendation
eng	Engine
F	Fahrenheit
F	Intermediate Direct Support Level Maintenance
f/inj	Fuel Injector
flm	Flame
FM	Field Manual
fr	Front
ft	Foot
gal	Gallon
GAWR	Gross Axle Weight Rating
gen	Generator
gnd	Ground
gr	Gross
GVWR	Gross Vehicle Weight Rating
"H"	High (on transfer case control lever indicator)
H	Intermediate General Support Level Maintenance
htr	Heater

I.D. . . . . Inside Diameter
in. . . . . Ignition
igntr . . . . .Ignitor
in . . . . Inch
km . . . . Kilometer
kPa . . . . Kilopascal
l . . . . Liter
L . . . . Left
"L" . . . . Low (on transfer case control lever indicator)
lb . . . .Pound
lmp . . . . Lamp
LO . . . . Lubrication Order
lt . . . . Light
m . . . . Meter
MAC . . . . Maintenance Allocation Chart
mar . . . . Marker
ml . . . . Milliliter
mm . . . . Millimeter
MOB . . . . Military Occupational Specialty
mot . . . . .Motor
"N" . . . . Neutral (on transmission and transfer case control lever indicators)
N . . . . Newton
NATO . . . . North Atlantic Treaty Organization
NBC . . . . Nuclear, Biological, or Chemical
n/c . . . . Normally Closed
neg . . . . Negative
N•m. . . . . • . . . .Newton-meter
no . . . . Normally Open
NSN . . . . National Stock Number
O . . . . Unit Level Maintenance
ovht . . . . .Overheat
02 . . . . Ounce
"P" . . . . Park (on transmission control lever indicator)
PMCS . . . . Preventive Maintenance Checks and Services
pos . . . . pos . . . . Positive
p r e s s . . . . Pressure
prkg . . . . .Parking
psi . . . . Pounds per Square inch
pt . . . . Pint
PRO . . . .Power Take-off
qt. . . . . Quart
R . . . . Radius
" R " . . . . Reverse (on transmission control lever indicator)
R . . . . Right
red . . . . Resistor
rgltr . . . . Regulator
rlse . . . . Release
rly . . . . rly . . . . Relay
RPSTL . . . . Repair Parts and Special Tools List
SAC . . . . Society of Automotive Engineers

sdr .... Sender
sig.. .... Signal
SMR .... Source, Maintenance, and Recoverability
snsr .... Sensor
sov .... Shutoff Valve
STE/ICE .... SimplifiedTestEquipment/Internal Combustion Engine
supprr.. .... Suppressor
svce.. .... Service
sw .... Switch
TB .... Technical Bulletin
T/C .... Transfer Case
temp .... Temperature
term .... Terminal
therm .... Thermometer
thrmst .... Thermostat
TM .... Technical Manual
tmr .... Timer
trans .... Transmission
trlr .... Trailer
TYP .... Typical Dimension
U/M .... Unit of Measure
v .... volt
vlv .... Valve
vm .... Voltmeter
vs .... Voltmeter Switch
wrg .... Wiring
xfr .... Transfer
xmsn .... Transmission

Section II. Definition OF UNUSUAL TERMS

Throughout this manual all assemblies, subassemblies, components, component parts, kits, and bulk items are referred to by their official nomenclature as found in the *Repair Parts* and *Special Tools List (RPSTL)* manual (TM 9-2320-289-20P).

INDEX

INDEX

INDEX

INDEX

INDEX

INDEX

INDEX

INDEX

INDEX

INDEX

INDEX

INDEX

INDEX

INDEX

INDEX

H

INDEX

INDEX

INDEX

INDEX

INDEX

M

INDEX

N

O

P

INDEX

INDEX

INDEX

INDEX

INDEX

☆ U.S. GOVERNMENT PRINTING OFFICE: 1996 746-014/20131

PIN: 053627-004

INDEX

INDEX

INDEX

INDEX

INDEX

INDEX

INDEX

INDEX

INDEX

INDEX

✦U.S. GOVERNMENT PRINTING OFFICE 1993-746-017/80065

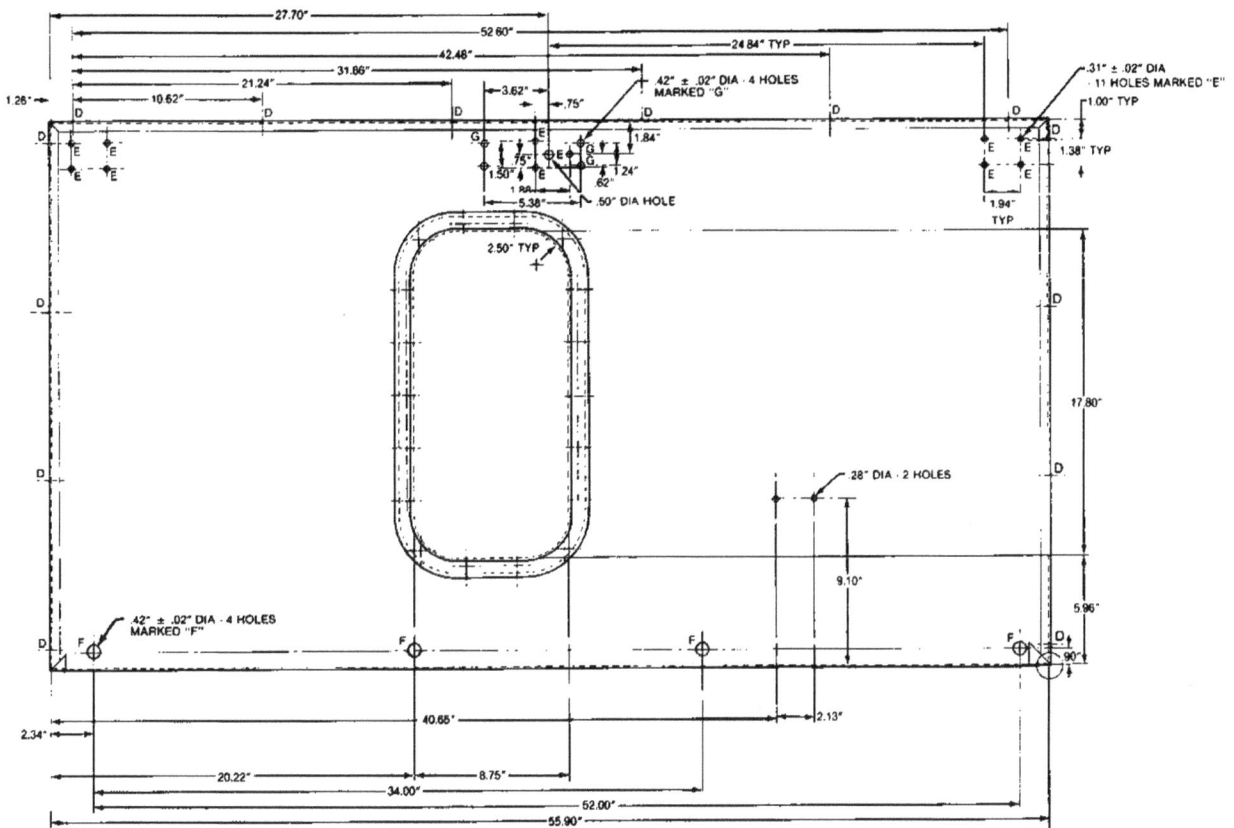

FO-1. Rear Door.

TA49607

FP-1/(FP-2 blank)

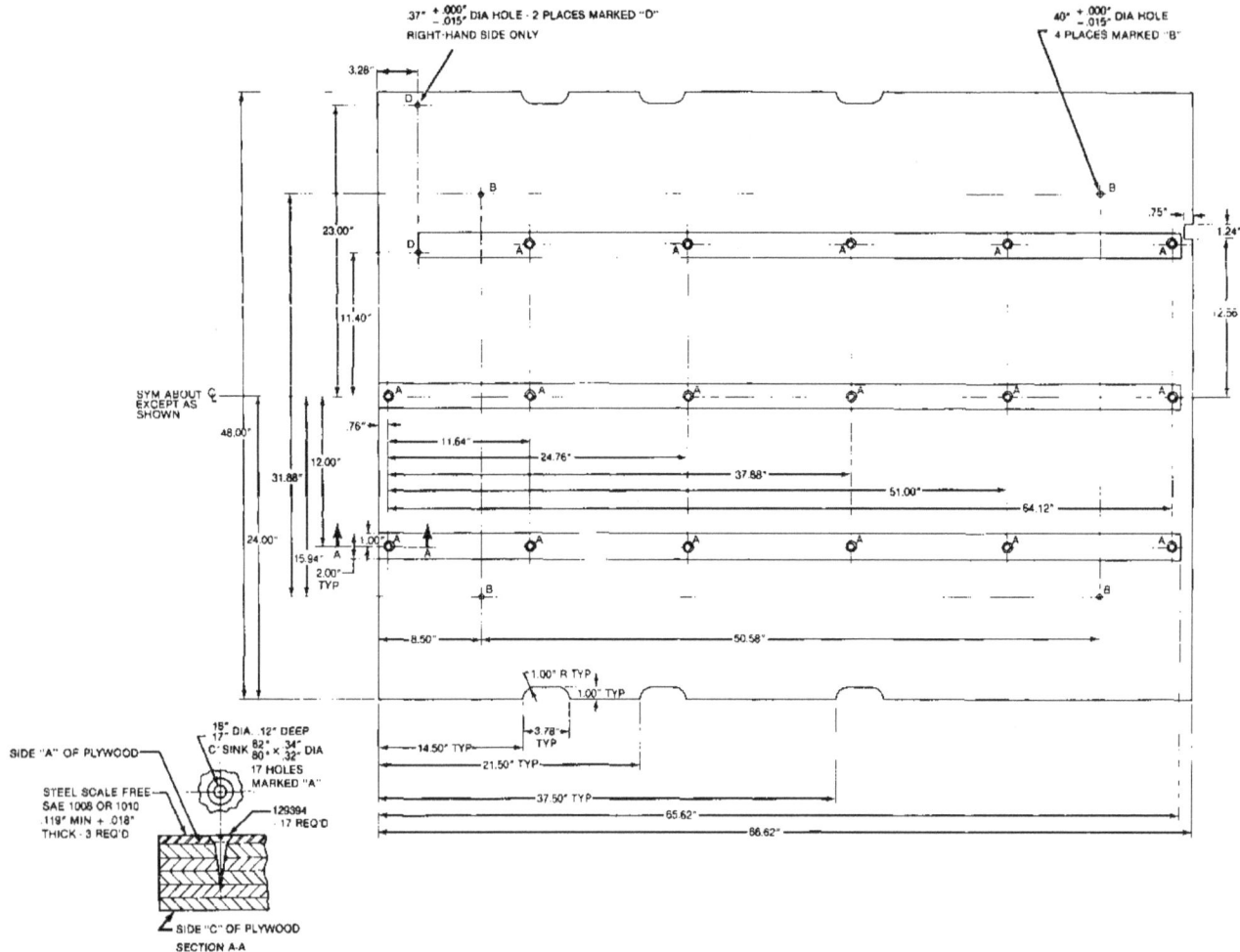

.37" +.000"/-.015" DIA HOLE - 2 PLACES MARKED "D"
RIGHT-HAND SIDE ONLY

.40" +.000"/-.015" DIA HOLE
4 PLACES MARKED "B"

3.28"

.75"

1.24"

2.56

23.00"

11.40"

SYM ABOUT ℄
EXCEPT AS
SHOWN

48.00"

31.88"

12.00"

24.00"

15.94"

1.00"

2.00"
TYP

.76"

11.64"

24.76"

37.88"

51.00"

64.12"

8.50"

50.58"

1.00" R TYP

1.00" TYP

14.50" TYP

3.78"
TYP

21.50" TYP

37.50" TYP

65.62"

86.62"

SIDE "A" OF PLYWOOD

.15"/.17" DIA, .12" DEEP
C'SINK .82"/.80" X .34"/.32" DIA
17 HOLES
MARKED "A"

STEEL SCALE FREE
SAE 1008 OR 1010
.119" MIN + .018"
THICK - 3 REQ'D

129394
17 REQ'D

SIDE "C" OF PLYWOOD
SECTION A-A

FO-2. Insulator.

TA49608

FP-3/(FP-4 blank)

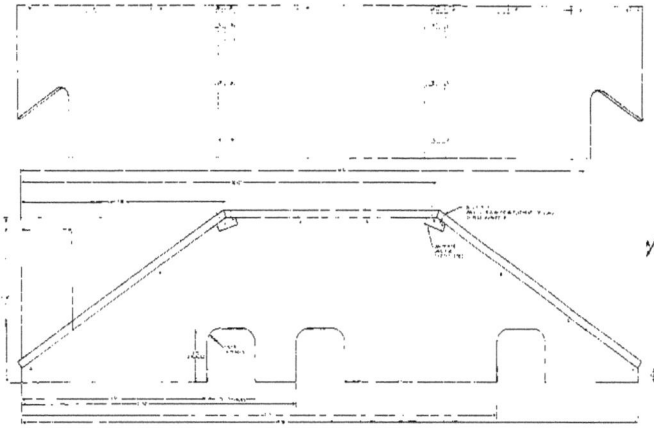

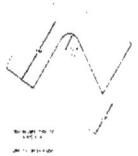

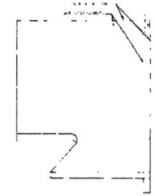

FO-1. Insulator

FO-1. (FO-1, blank)

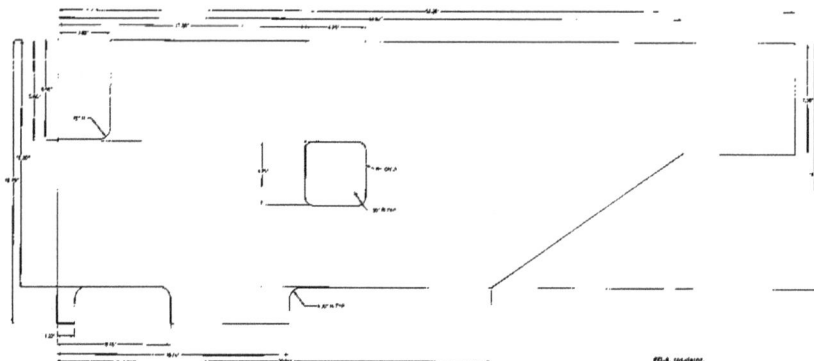

FIG-6. Insulator.

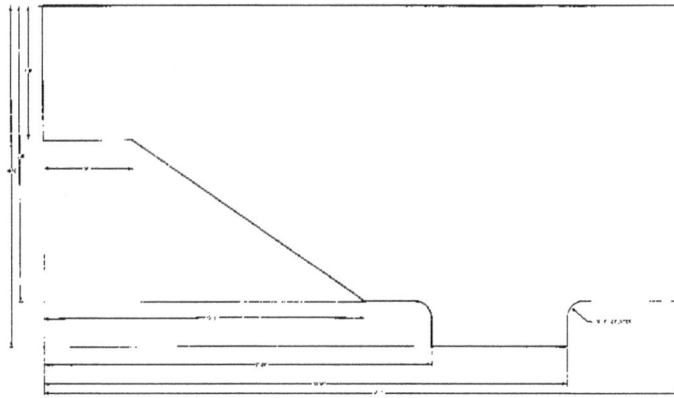

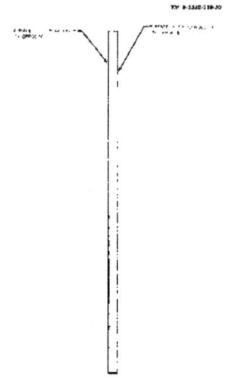

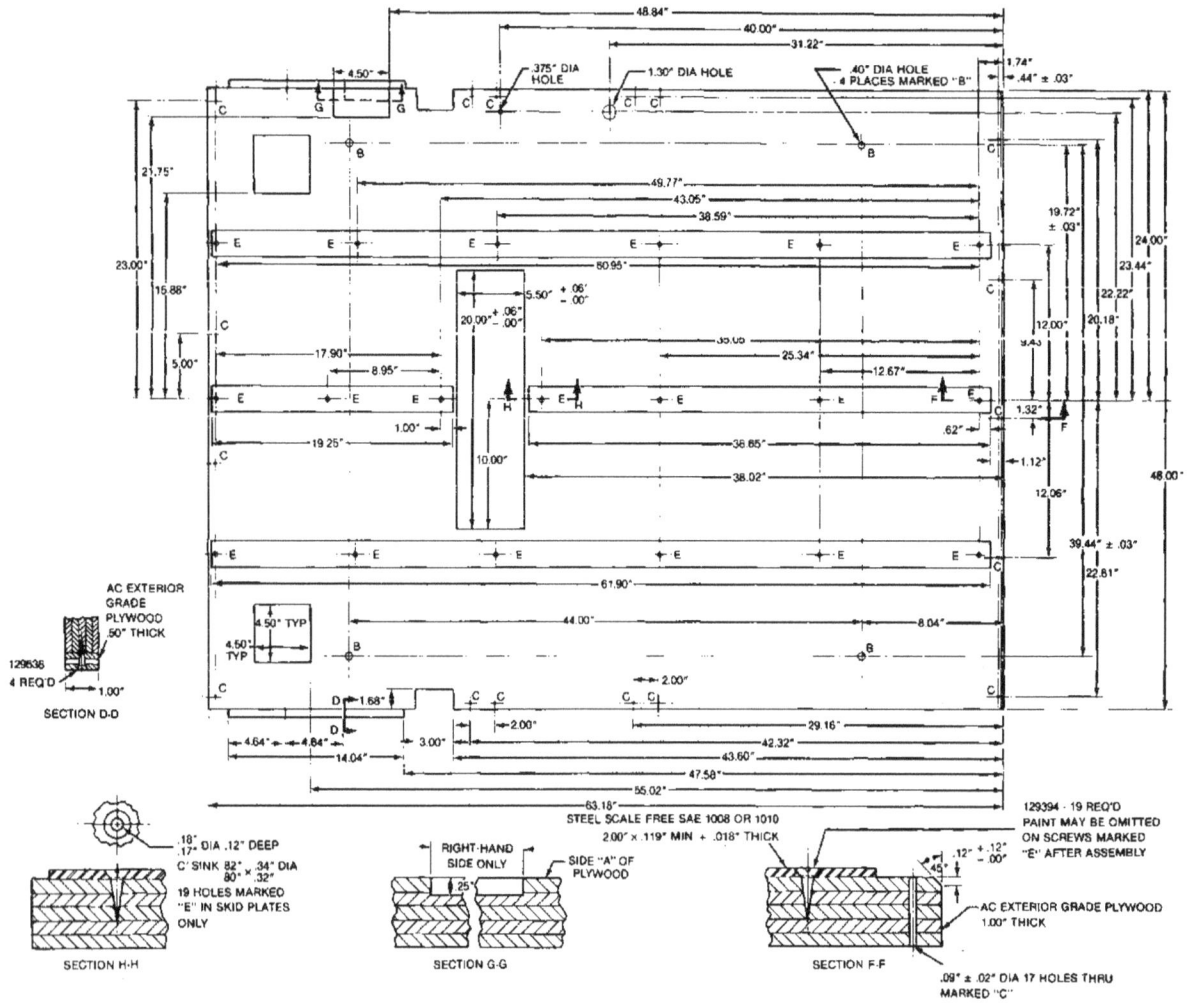

FO-6. Insulator Assembly.

TA49612I

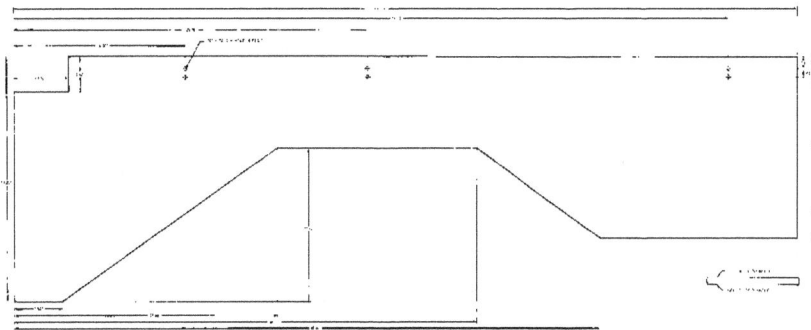

FIG-4 Right Half Panel Insulator

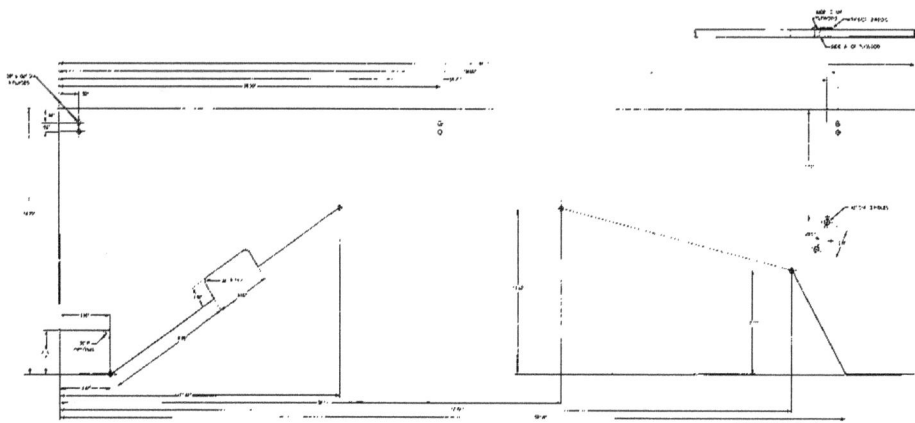

FO-8. Left Hall Panel Insulation.

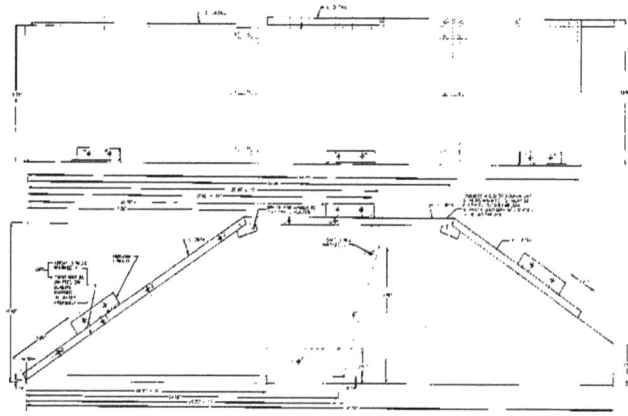

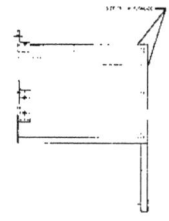

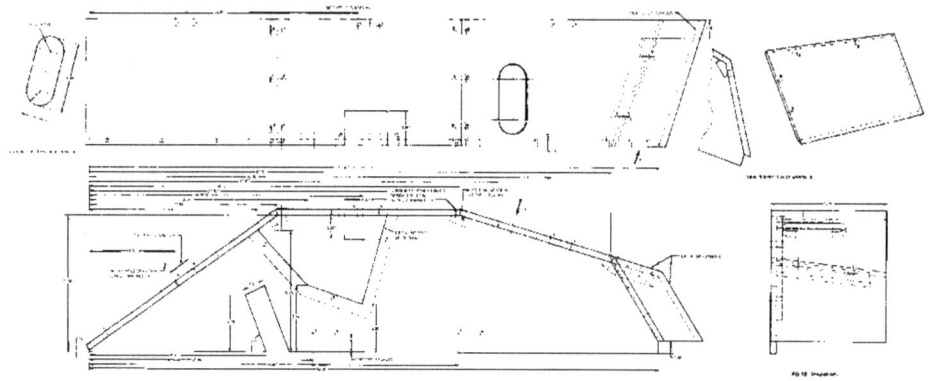

THE METRIC SYSTEM AND EQUIVALENTS

LINEAR MEASURE

1 Centimeter = 10 Millimeters = 0.01 Meters = 0.3937 Inches
1 Meter = 100 Centimeters = 1000 Millimeters = 39.37 Inches
1 Kilometer = 1000 Meters = 0.621 Miles

WEIGHTS

1 Gram = 0.001 Kilograms = 1000 Milligrams = 0.035 Ounces
1 Kilogram = 1000 Grams = 2.2 Lb.
1 Metric Ton = 1000 Kilograms = 1 Megagram = 1.1 Short Tons

LIQUID MEASURE

1 Milliliter = 0.001 Liters = 0.0338 Fluid Ounces
1 Liter = 1000 Milliliters = 33.82 Fluid Ounces

SQUARE MEASURE

1 Sq. Centimeter = 100 Sq. Millimeters = 0.155 Sq. Inches
1 Sq. Meter = 10,000 Sq. Centimeters = 10.76 Sq. Feet
1 Sq. Kilometer = 1,000,000 Sq. Meters = 0.386 Sq. Miles

CUBIC MEASURE

1 Cu. Centimeter = 1000 Cu. Millimeters = 0.06 Cu. Inches
1 Cu. Meter = 1,000,000 Cu. Centimeters = 35.31 Cu. Feet

TEMPERATURE

$\frac{5}{9}(°F - 32) = °C$
212° Fahrenheit is equivalent to 100° Celsius
90° Fahrenheit is equivalent to 32.2° Celsius
32° Fahrenheit is equivalent to 0° Celsius
$\frac{9}{5} °C + 32 = °F$

APPROXIMATE CONVERSION FACTORS

TO CHANGE	TO	MULTIPLY BY
Inches	Centimeters	2.540
Feet	Meters	0.305
Yards	Meters	0.914
Miles	Kilometers	1.609
Square Inches	Square Centimeters	6.451
Square Feet	Square Meters	0.093
Square Yards	Square Meters	0.836
Square Miles	Square Kilometers	2.590
Acres	Square Hectometers	0.405
Cubic Feet	Cubic Meters	0.028
Cubic Yards	Cubic Meters	0.765
Fluid Ounces	Milliliters	29.573
Pints	Liters	0.473
Quarts	Liters	0.946
Gallons	Liters	3.785
Ounces	Grams	28.349
Pounds	Kilograms	0.454
Short Tons	Metric Tons	0.907
Pound-Feet	Newton-Meters	1.356
Pounds per Square Inch	Kilopascals	6.895
Miles per Gallon	Kilometers per Liter	0.425
Miles per Hour	Kilometers per Hour	1.609

TO CHANGE	TO	MULTIPLY BY
Centimeters	Inches	0.394
Meters	Feet	3.280
Meters	Yards	1.094
Kilometers	Miles	0.621
Square Centimeters	Square Inches	0.155
Square Meters	Square Feet	10.764
Square Meters	Square Yards	1.196
Square Kilometers	Square Miles	0.386
Square Hectometers	Acres	2.471
Cubic Meters	Cubic Feet	35.315
Cubic Meters	Cubic Yards	1.308
Milliliters	Fluid Ounces	0.034
Liters	Pints	2.113
Liters	Quarts	1.057
Liters	Gallons	0.264
Grams	Ounces	0.035
Kilograms	Pounds	2.205
Metric Tons	Short Tons	1.102
Newton-Meters	Pound-Feet	0.738
Kilopascals	Pounds per Square Inch	0.145
Kilometers per Liter	Miles per Gallon	2.354
Kilometers per Hour	Miles per Hour	0.621

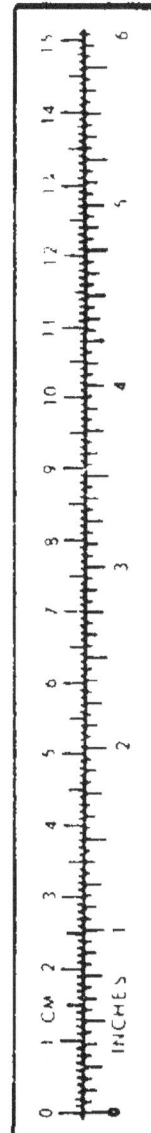

TA089991